## School Book Pages

### Finding Percent of a Whole Number

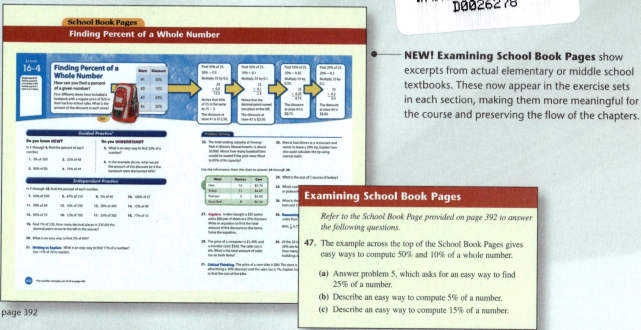

page 392

page 392

**NEW! Examining School Book Pages** show excerpts from actual elementary or middle school textbooks. These now appear in the exercise sets in each section, making them more meaningful for the course and preserving the flow of the chapters.

### Examining School Book Pages

*Refer to the School Book Page provided on page 392 to answer the following questions.*

**47.** The example across the top of the School Book Pages gives easy ways to compute 50% and 10% of a whole number.

**(a)** Answer problem 5, which asks for an easy way to find 25% of a number.

**(b)** Describe an easy way to compute 5% of a number.

**(c)** Describe an easy way to compute 15% of a number.

page 393

page 393

### Responding to Students

**31.** When asked to illustrate the concept of $\frac{2}{3}$ with a colored-region diagram, Shanti drew the figure shown. How would you respond to Shanti?

**32.** Like most fifth graders, Dana likes pizza. When given the choice of $\frac{1}{4}$ or $\frac{1}{6}$ of a pizza, Dana says, "Since 6 is bigger than 4 and I'm really hungry, I'd rather have $\frac{1}{6}$ of the pizza." Write a dialogue, including useful diagrams, to clear up Dana's misconception about fractions.

page 289

page 289

**Responding to Students** exercises give insight into the mathematical questions and procedures that children will come up with on their own, and offer ways to respond to them.

### From State Student Assessments

**41.** (Minnesota, Grade 5)

Which figure shows $\frac{3}{5}$ shaded?

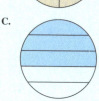

A.     B.

C.     D.

**42.** (Delaware, Grade 5)

John split a cake into four pieces. The pieces are *not* all the same shape. Do you believe the four pieces are the same size? Please explain.

page 330

page 330

**From State Student Assessments** problems provide examples of problems from the high-stakes standardized exams now used in many states. These problems make you aware of the types of knowledge that your future students will be asked to master.

# Mathematical Reasoning
## for Elementary Teachers

**6TH EDITION**

### Calvin T. Long
*Washington State University*

### Duane W. DeTemple
*Washington State University*

### Richard S. Millman
*Georgia Institute of Technology*

**Addison Wesley**

Boston   Columbus   Indianapolis   New York   San Francisco   Upper Saddle River
Amsterdam   Cape Town   Dubai   London   Madrid   Milan   Munich   Paris   Montréal   Toronto
Delhi   Mexico City   São Paulo   Sydney   Hong Kong   Seoul   Singapore   Taipei   Tokyo

Editor in Chief: Anne Kelly
Acquisitions Editor: Marnie Greenhut
Senior Content Editor: Elizabeth Bernardi
Editorial Assistant: Elle Driska
Senior Managing Editor: Karen Wernholm
Senior Production Project Manager: Tracy Patruno
Design Manager: Andrea Nix
Senior Designer: Barbara T. Atkinson
Digital Assets Manager: Marianne Groth
Production Coordinator: Kerri McQueen
Senior Media Producer: Christine Stavrou

Software Development: Bob Carroll and Marty Wright
Executive Marketing Manager: Roxanne McCarley
Marketing Assistant: Kendra Bassi
Senior Author Support/Technology Specialist: Joe Vetere
Rights and Permissions Advisor: Michael Joyce
Image Manager: Rachel Youdelman
Senior Manufacturing Buyer: Carol Melville
Senior Media Buyer: Ginny Michaud
Production Coordination, Illustrations, and Composition: Aptara®, Inc.
Interior Design: Harpie, LLC, Leslie Haimes
Cover Image: Marco Lens/Shutterstock

Credits appear on pages C1–C2, which constitutes a continuation of the copyright page.

Many of the designations used by manufacturers and sellers to distinguish their products are claimed as trademarks. Where those designations appear in this book, and Pearson was aware of a trademark claim, the designations have been printed in initial caps or all caps.

**Library of Congress Cataloging-in-Publication Data**

Long, Calvin T.
  Mathematical reasoning for elementary teachers / Calvin T. Long, Duane
W. DeTemple, Richard S. Milman. — 6th ed.
    p. cm.
  ISBN 0-321-69312-4
  1. Mathematics—Study and teaching (Elementary) I. DeTemple, Duane W.
II. Milman, Richard S. III. Title.
  QA135.6.L66 2012
  510—dc22
                                        2010016529

1 2 3 4 5 6 7 8 9 10—DOW—14 13 12 11 10

**Addison-Wesley**
is an imprint of

www.pearsonhighered.com

ISBN 10: 0-321-69312-4
ISBN 13: 978-0-321-69312-9

To the memory of my good wife and constant helpmate, Jean.     C.T.L.

To my wife, Janet, and my daughters, Jill and Rachel.     D.W.D.

To Sandy, for her loving support.     R.S.M.

# Contents

**Preface** ............................................................................ xiii

**Chapter 1**  **Thinking Critically** ...................................................... 1

1.1  **An Introduction to Problem Solving** ............................ 3

1.2  **Pólya's Problem-Solving Principles** ............................... 8
*Guess and Check • Make an Orderly List • Draw a Diagram*

1.3  **More Problem-Solving Strategies** ............................... 18
*Look for a Pattern • Make a Table • Use a Variable • Consider Special Cases • Pascal's Triangle*

1.4  **Algebra as a Problem-Solving Strategy** ...................... 29
*Use a Variable • Use Two Variables*

1.5  **Additional Problem-Solving Strategies** ...................... 39
*Working Backward • Eliminate Possibilities • The Pigeonhole Principle*

1.6  **Reasoning Mathematically** ...................................... 47
*Inductive Reasoning • Representational Reasoning • Mathematical Statements • Deductive Reasoning*

**Chapter 1**    **Summary** .................................................. 59

**Chapter 1**    **Review Exercises** ...................................... 62

**Chapter 1**    **Test** ........................................................ 65

**Chapter 2**  **Sets and Whole Numbers** ........................................ 67

2.1  **Sets and Operations on Sets** ................................... 69
*Venn Diagrams • Relationships and Operations on Sets • Using Sets for Problem Solving*

2.2  **Sets, Counting, and the Whole Numbers** .................... 79
*One-to-One Correspondence and Equivalent Sets • The Whole Numbers • Physical and Pictorial Representations for Whole Numbers • Ordering the Whole Numbers • Problem Solving with Whole Numbers and Venn Diagrams*

2.3  **Addition and Subtraction of Whole Numbers** .............. 89
*The Set Model of Whole-Number Addition • The Measurement (Number-Line) Model of Addition • Properties of Whole-Number Addition • Subtraction of Whole Numbers • Take-Away Model • Missing-Addend Model • Comparison Model • Number-Line Model*

2.4  **Multiplication and Division of Whole Numbers** ........... 100
*Multiplication of Whole Numbers • Multiplication as Repeated Addition • The Array Model for Multiplication • The Rectangular Area Model for Multiplication • The Skip-Count Model for Multiplication • The Multiplication Tree Model • The Cartesian Product Model of Multiplication • Properties of Whole-Number Multiplication • Division of*

*Whole Numbers • The Repeated-Subtraction Model of Division • The Partition Model of Division • The Missing-Factor Model of Division • Division by Zero Is Undefined • Division with Remainders • Why Does Quotient with Remainder (the Division Algorithm) Work? • Exponents and the Power Operation*

**Chapter 2**    **Summary** ................................................. 118

**Chapter 2**    **Review Exercises** ...................................... 122

**Chapter 2**    **Test** .................................................. 123

**Chapter 3    Numeration and Computation** ........................... 125

**3.1 Numeration Systems Past and Present** ..................... 127
*The Egyptian System • The Roman System • The Babylonian System • The Mayan System • The Indo-Arabic System • Physical Models for Positional Systems*

**3.2 Nondecimal Positional Systems** ........................... 138
*Base-Five Notation*

**3.3 Algorithms for Adding and Subtracting Whole Numbers** ............................................. 143
*The Addition Algorithm • The Subtraction Algorithm • Algorithms in Other Bases*

**3.4 Algorithms for Multiplication and Division of Whole Numbers** .................................................... 156
*Multiplication Algorithms • Multiplication in Other Bases • Division Algorithms*

**3.5 Mental Arithmetic and Estimation** ......................... 169
*The One-Digit Facts • Easy Combinations • Adjustment • Working from Left to Right • Estimation • Front-End Method • Rounding • Approximating by Rounding*

**Chapter 3**    **Summary** ................................................. 179

**Chapter 3**    **Review Exercises** ...................................... 182

**Chapter 3**    **Test** .................................................. 183

**Chapter 4    Number Theory** ....................................... 185

**4.1 Divisibility of Natural Numbers** ........................... 187
*Divides, Divisors, Factors, Multiples • Prime and Composite Numbers • The Divisors of a Natural Number • Two Questions About Primes • There Are Infinitely Many Primes • Determining Whether a Given Natural Number Is a Prime*

**4.2 Tests for Divisibility** ................................... 201
*Divisibility of Sums and Differences • Divisibility by 2, 5, and 10 • Divisibility by 4, 8, and Other Powers of 2 • Divisibility by 3 and 9 • Divisibility by 11 • Combining Divisibility Tests • A Unified Test for Divisibility by 7, 11, and 13 • Summary of Useful Divisibility Tests*

**4.3 Greatest Common Divisors and Least Common Multiples** ............................................ 209
*GCD Method 1: Greatest Common Divisors by Intersection of Sets • GCD Method 2: Greatest Common Divisor from Prime Factorizations •*

*GCD Method 3: Greatest Common Divisor from the Euclidean Algorithm • The Least Common Multiple • LCM Method 1: Least Common Multiples by Intersection of Sets • LCM Method 2: Least Common Multiples from Prime Factorizations • LCM Method 3: Least Common Multiples by Using the Euclidean Algorithm • An Application of the LCM • Using Technology to Find the GCD and LCM*

**Chapter 4  Summary** ..................................... 222

**Chapter 4  Review Exercises** ....................................... 224

**Chapter 4  Test** ........................................... 225

## Chapter 5  Integers ................................................. 227

**5.1  Representations of Integers** .................................. 229
*Absolute Value of an Integer • Criteria for the Representation of the Integers • Representing Integers with Colored Counters • The Addition-by-0 Property with Colored Counters • Negatives with Colored Counters • Mail-Time Representations of Integers • Number-Line Representations of Integers*

**5.2  Addition and Subtraction of Integers** ........................ 240
*Addition of Integers • Addition of Integers by Using Sets of Colored Counters • Addition of Integers by Using Mail-Time Stories • Addition of Integers by Using a Number Line • Ordering the Set of Integers • Subtraction of Integers by Using Sets of Colored Counters • The Equivalence of Subtraction and Adding the Opposite • Subtraction of Integers by Using Mail-Time Stories • Subtraction of Integers by Using the Number Line • Adding and Subtracting Integers with a Calculator*

**5.3  Multiplication and Division of Integers** ..................... 257
*Multiplication of Integers • Multiplication of Integers by Using Colored Counters • Multiplication of Integers by Using Mail-Time Stories • Multiplication of Integers by Using a Number Line • Division of Integers • Division with Remainders in the Integers*

**Chapter 5  Summary** ............................................. 269

**Chapter 5  Review Exercises** ...................................... 271

**Chapter 5  Test** ........................................... 272

## Chapter 6  Fractions and Rational Numbers ................... 273

**6.1  The Basic Concepts of Fractions and Rational Numbers** ............................................ 275
*Models for Fractions • Colored Regions • The Set Model • Fraction Strips • Fraction Circles • The Number-Line Model • Equivalent Fractions • Fractions in Simplest Form • Common Denominators • Rational Numbers • Ordering Fractions and Rational Numbers*

**6.2  Addition and Subtraction of Fractions** ..................... 292
*Addition of Fractions • Proper Fractions and Mixed Numbers • Subtraction of Fractions*

**6.3  Multiplication and Division of Fractions** .................... 301
*Multiplication of a Fraction by an Integer • Multiplication of an Integer by a Fraction • Multiplication of a Fraction by a Fraction • Division of Fractions • Algorithms for Calculating the Division of*

*Fractions • Reciprocals as Multiplicative Inverses in the Rational Numbers*

6.4 **The Rational Number System** .................................. 318

*Properties of Addition and Subtraction • Properties of Multiplication and Division • Properties of the Order Relation • The Density Property of Rational Numbers • Computations with Rational Numbers • Estimations • Mental Arithmetic*

**Chapter 6**    **Summary** ............................................. 331

**Chapter 6**    **Review Exercises** ................................... 334

**Chapter 6**    **Test** .................................................. 335

**Chapter 7**    **Decimals, Real Numbers, and Proportional Reasoning** ......................................... 337

7.1 **Decimals and Real Numbers** ............................... 339

*Representations of Decimals • Multiplying and Dividing Decimals by Powers of 10 • Terminating Decimals as Fractions • Repeating Decimals and Rational Numbers • Ordering Decimals • The Set of Real Numbers • Irrationality of $\sqrt{2}$ • Real Numbers and the Number Line*

7.2 **Computations with Decimals** .............................. 357

*Rounding Decimals • Adding and Subtracting Decimals • Multiplying Decimals • Dividing Decimals*

7.3 **Proportional Reasoning** ................................... 367

*Ratio • Proportion • Applications of Proportional Reasoning*

7.4 **Percent** ................................................... 381

*Percent • Solving the Three Basic Types of Percent Problems • Percentage Increase and Decrease • Compound Interest • The Mathematics of Growth*

**Chapter 7**    **Summary** ............................................. 394

**Chapter 7**    **Review Exercises** ................................... 397

**Chapter 7**    **Test** .................................................. 398

**Chapter 8**    **Algebraic Reasoning, Graphing, and Connections with Geometry** ................................. 399

8.1 **Algebraic Expressions, Functions, and Equations** .......... 402

*Variables • Algebraic Expressions • Equations and Their Solution • Defining Functions • Describing and Visualizing Functions*

8.2 **Graphing Points, Lines, and Elementary Functions** ......... 417

*The Cartesian Coordinate Plane • The Distance Formula • Slope • Equations of Lines • Nonlinear Functions (Quadratics and Exponentials)*

8.3 **Connections Between Algebra and Geometry** ............... 433

*Using Cartesian Coordinates to Do Geometric Problems • Parallel and Perpendicular Lines • Using Rigid Motions • Circles*

**Chapter 8**    **Summary** ............................................. 443

**Chapter 8**    **Review Exercises** ................................... 446

**Chapter 8**    **Test** .................................................. 447

**Chapter 9**  **Geometric Figures** ................................................. 449

9.1  **Figures in the Plane** ............................................. 455

*Points and Lines • Line Segments and the Distance Between Points • Rays, Angles, and Angle Measure • Pairs of Angles and the Corresponding-Angles Theorem • The Measure of Angles in Triangles • Directed Angles*

9.2  **Curves and Polygons in the Plane** ........................... 470

*Curves and Regions • Convex Curves and Figures • Polygonal Curves and Polygons • Triangles • Quadrilaterals • Regular Polygons*

9.3  **Figures in Space** ................................................. 490

*Planes and Lines in Space • Curves, Surfaces, and Solids • Polyhedra • Regular Polyhedra • Euler's Formula for Polyhedra • Cones and Cylinders*

9.4  **Networks** ......................................................... 504

*The Königsberg Bridge Problem • Counting Vertices, Edges, and Regions in Planar Networks • Connecting Euler's Formulas for Planar Networks and for Polyhedra*

**Chapter 9**  **Summary** .................................................. 515

**Chapter 9**  **Review Exercises** ....................................... 519

**Chapter 9**  **Test** ........................................................ 521


**Chapter 10**  **Measurement: Length, Area, and Volume** ........... 523

10.1  **The Measurement Process** .................................... 526

*The U.S. Customary, or "English," System of Measures • Metric Units: The International System • Length • Area • Volume and Capacity • Weight and Mass • Temperature • Unit Analysis*

10.2  **Area and Perimeter** ............................................ 542

*Measurements in Nonstandard Units • The Congruence and Addition Properties of Area • Areas of Polygons • Length of a Curve • The Area of a Circle*

10.3  **The Pythagorean Theorem** .................................... 564

*Proving the Pythagorean Theorem • Applications of the Pythagorean Theorem • The Converse of the Pythagorean Theorem*

10.4  **Volume** ........................................................... 572

*Volumes of Right Prisms and Right Cylinders • Volumes of Oblique Prisms and Cylinders • Volumes of Pyramids and Cones • Volume of a Sphere*

10.5  **Surface Area** ..................................................... 580

*Surface Area of Right Prisms and Cylinders • Surface Area of Pyramids • Surface Area of Right Circular Cones • Surface Area of a Sphere • Comparing Measurements of Similar Figures*

**Chapter 10**  **Summary** .................................................. 591

**Chapter 10**  **Review Exercises** ....................................... 594

**Chapter 10**  **Test** ...................................................... 596

**Chapter 11** | **Transformations, Symmetries, and Tilings** ......... 599

**11.1**   **Rigid Motions and Similarity Transformations** .......... 601
*The Four Basic Rigid Motions • Translations • Rotations • Reflections • Glide–Reflections • The Net Outcome of Two Successive Reflections • The Net Outcome of Three Successive Reflections • Classification of General Rigid Motions • Dilations and Similarity Motions*

**11.2**   **Patterns and Symmetries** .................................... 624
*What Is Symmetry? • Reflection Symmetry • Rotation Symmetry • Point Symmetry • Periodic Patterns: Figures with Translation Symmetries • Border Patterns and Their Classification • Wallpaper Patterns*

**11.3**   **Tilings and Escher-like Designs** ............................ 637
*Tiles and Tilings • Regular Tilings of the Plane • Semiregular Tilings of the Plane • Tilings with Irregular Polygons • Escher-like Tilings*

**Chapter 11**   **Summary** ............................................... 650

**Chapter 11**   **Review Exercises** ...................................... 653

**Chapter 11**   **Test** .................................................... 654

**Chapter 12** | **Congruence, Constructions, and Similarity** ......... 657

**12.1**   **Congruent Triangles** ......................................... 659
*Congruent Line Segments and Their Construction • Corresponding Parts and the Congruence of Triangles • The Side–Side–Side (SSS) Property • The Triangle Inequality • The Side–Angle–Side (SAS) Property • The Angle–Side–Angle (ASA) Property • The Angle–Angle–Side (AAS) Property • Are There SSA and AAA Congruence Properties?*

**12.2**   **Constructing Geometric Figures** ........................... 676
*Constructing Parallel and Perpendicular Lines • Constructing the Midpoint and Perpendicular Bisector of a Line Segment • Constructing the Angle Bisector • Constructing Regular Polygons • Mira™ and Paper-Folding Constructions • Constructions with Geometry Software*

**12.3**   **Similar Triangles** ............................................ 692
*The Angle–Angle–Angle (AAA) and Angle–Angle (AA) Similarity Properties • The Side–Side–Side (SSS) Similarity Property • The Side–Angle–Side (SAS) Similarity Property • Geometric Problem Solving with Similar Triangles*

**Chapter 12**   **Summary** ............................................... 705

**Chapter 12**   **Review Exercises** ...................................... 707

**Chapter 12**   **Test** .................................................... 709

**Chapter 13** | **Statistics: The Interpretation of Data** ................. 711

**13.1**   **Organizing and Representing Data** ......................... 713
*Dot Plots • Stem-and-Leaf Plots • Histograms • Line Graphs • Bar Graphs • Pie Charts • Pictographs • Choosing Good Visualizations*

**13.2**   **Measuring the Center and Variation of Data** .............. 731
*Measures of Central Tendency • The Mean • The Median • The Mode • Measures of Variability • Box Plots • The Standard Deviation*

**13.3** **Statistical Inference** ............................................ **749**

*Populations and Samples • Population Means and Standard Deviations • Estimating Population Means and Standard Deviations • Distributions • z Scores and Percentiles*

**Chapter 13** **Summary** ................................................... **760**

**Chapter 13** **Review Exercises** ....................................... **762**

**Chapter 13** **Test** ........................................................ **765**

**Chapter 14** **Probability** ...................................................... **767**

**14.1** **Experimental Probability** ................................. **769**

*Connections with Statistics • Additional Examples of Computing Experimental Probabilities • Events and the Sample Space • Independent Events • Experimental Probability and Geometry • Simulation*

**14.2** **Principles of Counting** ...................................... **780**

*Counting and the Word Or • Counting and the Word And • Complementary Events and Counting*

**14.3** **Permutations and Combinations** ........................ **791**

*Factorials • Formulas for Permutations and Combinations • Problem Solving with Combinations and Permutations*

**14.4** **Theoretical Probability** ..................................... **801**

*Conditional Probability • Probability Trees • Computing Probability by Using Permutations and Combinations • Complementary Events • Properties of Probability • Odds • Expected Value • Geometric Probability*

**Chapter 14** **Summary** ................................................... **820**

**Chapter 14** **Review Exercises** ....................................... **823**

**Chapter 14** **Test** ........................................................ **825**

**Appendix A** **Manipulatives in the Mathematics Classroom** .... **827**

**Appendix B** **Getting the Most Out of Your Calculator** ............. **830**

**Appendix C** **A Brief Guide to *The Geometer's Sketchpad*** ............. **840**

**Appendix D** **Resources** ................................................... **851**

**Answers to Selected Problems** ..................................... **A-1**

**Credits** ................................................................ **C-1**

**Mathematical Lexicon** ............................................... **ML-1**

**Index** .................................................................. **I-1**

 # Preface

## To the Future Teacher

You may be wondering what to expect from a college course in mathematics for prospective elementary or middle school teachers. Will this course simply repeat arithmetic and other material that you already know, or will the subject matter be new and interesting? In this preface, we will give a positive answer to that question and at the same time provide a useful orientation to the text.

This book is designed to help you, as a future teacher, add to the depth of your knowledge about the mathematics of elementary and middle school. Most institutions structure their teacher education curriculum to include a sequence of mathematics content courses that typically serves as a prerequisite for the methods course, which deals with, among other ideas, how school children learn mathematics as they grow and develop.

The book focuses on the content needed for future teachers and does so with an eye toward giving you a deep background into why things work (and why some things don't). Emphasis is placed on the **mathematical knowledge needed for teaching,** a topic very much a part of research in mathematics education today and which is emphasized at the end of each chapter. This depth, called **conceptual understanding,** is a very important part of being a teacher. To decide whether the methods or ideas of your students are right or wrong and be able to explain to the students why is one of the most important aspects of teaching. In addition, the depth of your basic skills will be increased during this course as you participate in solving problems and performing operations in a number of different ways.

### Problem Solving and Mathematical Reasoning

Problem solving (or, said another way, "mathematical reasoning") is stressed throughout the text and is a theme of this book. This emphasis begins in Chapter 1 on problem solving and continues not only in the discussion of the various topics, but, perhaps even more importantly, in virtually all sections of the problem sets. In fact, the text is replete with activities, investigations, and a host of problems with results and answers that are attractive, surprising, and unexpected, yet are designed to engage you in thoughtfully doing mathematics.

At first, problem solving may seem daunting, but don't be afraid to try and perhaps fail; then try again. As you gain experience and begin to acquire an arsenal of strategies, you will become increasingly successful and will even begin to find the challenge of solving a problem stimulating and enjoyable. Quite often, with much surprise, this has been the experience of students in our classes as they successfully match wits with problems and gain insights and confidence that together lead to even more success.

You should not expect to see instantly into the heart of a problem or to know immediately how it can be solved. The text contains many problems that check your understanding of basic concepts and build basic skills, but you will also continually encounter problems requiring multiple steps and reflection. These problems are not unreasonably hard. (Indeed, many would be suitable with only minor modifications for use in classes you will subsequently teach.) However, they do require thought. Expect to try a variety of approaches, be willing to discuss possibilities with your classmates, and form a study group to engage in cooperative problem solving. This is the way mathematics is done, even by professionals, and as you gain experience, you will increasingly feel the real pleasure of success and the beginning development of a mathematical habit of your mind. Also, you will greatly improve your thinking and problem-solving skills if you take the time to write carefully worded solutions that explain your method and reasoning. Similarly, it will help you engage in mathematical conversations with your instructor and with other students. Research shows that mechanical skills learned by rote without understanding are soon forgotten and guarantee failure, both for you now and for your students later. By contrast, the ability to think creatively makes it more likely that the task can be successfully completed. *Conceptual understanding of the material is the key to your success and the future success of your students.*

## How to Read This Book

*Learning mathematics is not a spectator sport.*

No mathematics textbook can be read passively. To understand the concepts and to benefit from the examples, you must be an active participant in a conversation with the text. Often, this means that you need to check a calculation, make a drawing, take a measurement, construct a model, or use a calculator or computer. If you first attempt to answer questions raised in the examples on your own, the solutions written in the text will be more meaningful and useful than they would be without your personal involvement.

Many of the problems, including all the chapter review problems and chapter test problems, are fully or partially answered in the back of the book. These answers give you an additional source of worked examples. But again, you will benefit most fully by attempting to solve the problems on your own (or in a study group) before you check your reasoning by looking up the answer provided in the text.

# Guiding Philosophy and Approach

The content and processes of mathematics are presented in an appealing and logically sound way with these four major goals in mind:

- to develop positive attitudes toward mathematics and the teaching of mathematics,
- to develop mathematical knowledge and skills, with particular emphasis on problem solving and mathematical reasoning,
- to develop a conceptual understanding of the mathematics of elementary school, and
- to develop excellent teachers of mathematics.

In short, this text follows the approach contained in *The Mathematical Education of Teachers* published by the Conference Board of the Mathematical Sciences in 2001. The goals of the book are to implement the recommendations of the National Council of Teachers of Mathematics (NCTM) *Principles and Standards for School Mathematics* (the *Principles and Standards*) published in the year 2000. The *Principles and Standards* are to "ensure quality, indicate goals, and promote positive changes in mathematics education in grades preK–12." We also cite and follow the *Principles and Standards* throughout the text. The NCTM *Curricular Focal Points for Pre-kindergarten through Grade 8* (published in March 2006) has reemphasized these goals and given them coherence through the grade levels.

Aside from mastering content and skills, teachers often pattern their own teaching after the ways they have been taught. This text models effective teaching by emphasizing

- activities
- manipulatives
- investigations
- written projects
- discussion questions
- appropriate use of technology

and above all else,

- problem solving, mathematical reasoning, and conceptual understanding.

## New in This Edition

**Algebra and Problem Solving** Section 1.4 and Chapter 8 show how the use of a variable can play a powerful and clarifying role in word, pattern, and geometric problems. The idea of the use of algebra in problem solving has been expanded in two ways. First, Section 1.4, Algebra as a Problem-Solving

Strategy, which was a new approach in the previous edition, has had a number of problems added to it that form a platform for the material of Chapter 8. Second, Chapter 8 has been restructured so that the material is now separated into three sections; the first continues to be about algebraic expressions, functions, and equations; the second section now emphasizes points, lines, and the functions that appear in elementary or middle school; and the third shows the strong connections between algebra and geometry. Furthermore, there is a significant increase in the number of problems in the chapter and, in particular, in those which mix algebra and geometry. Because algebra itself is now being introduced in the early grades, the study by future teachers of algebraic ideas (and the relationship of algebra to geometry) is more important than ever.

**MHM** **Mathematical Habit of the Mind**   The idea of a mathematical habit of the mind is a recommendation of the important document *The Mathematical Education of Teachers,* which is a part of our guiding philosophy. There is a belief that teachers who can help their students think more mathematically will be able to understand the concepts they themselves teach in more depth. We have adopted the **MHM** icon to mean "explore," "explain," or "expand." One example is "Amanda's Telephone Number E-mail" (Example 1.14, page 35), in which thinking with algebra easily solves a "mystery" (how something works). The problems and discussions in the text that are indicated with the icon are mathematical situations where we ask students to think more deeply about mathematics. In this edition, whenever the icon appears, we explain, either in the text or in the solutions to the problems, why we believe that the statement or problem in question shows a mathematical habit of the mind.

**Sequencing of Geometry Chapters**   The geometry chapters are now together, one after the other. The purpose of this rearrangement from the previous editions is to emphasize the coherence of the geometry section (Chapters 9 through 12 in this edition) and to allow the prospective teacher to get a better view of the breadth of the geometry that is covered in elementary and middle school. The geometry sections also provide a background for geometric probability, which is discussed in Chapter 14. Since Chapter 8 now includes material on coordinate geometry, the chapters on statistics and probability have been repositioned at the end of the text.

**Volume and Surface Area of Solids**   In most texts for future teachers, these two topics have been included together in one section. Based on student and instructor feedback, in this edition we have separated the topics of volume and surface area into two separate sections. Because students often find surface area more difficult than volume, we have covered volume first, in Section 10.4. Then, Section 10.5 deals with surface area, but because one of the difficulties in understanding the two topics is the difference between them, the problems at the end of the section include both surface area and volume. Both topics are discussed conceptually, as is typical of our approach.

**Statistics**   In this chapter, the view of statistics as a science and as a background for decision making is the focus of the chapter. Recognizing that many students did not have any statistics when they were in elementary or middle school, the chapter emphasizes the variety of statistical representations and interpretations. Here we are motivated by the well thought out and influential recent publication *Guidelines for Assessment and Instruction in Statistics Education (GAISE) Report: A Pre-K–12 Curriculum Framework (2007),* which advocates statistical literacy. To show that statistics really is a part of the elementary school curriculum, eight SSA problems are now included in each of Sections 13.1 and 13.2. The authors would also like to thank Dr. William Rayens, professor of statistics at the University of Kentucky, for his valuable review of the chapter on statistics in the last edition.

**Activity Manual References**   References to the Activity Manual are found throughout the Annotated Instructor's Edition. The blue margin annotations indicate which activity from the manual would be useful when teaching specific content, making it much easier to integrate activities into the course.

**Responding to Students Problems (RTS)**   Throughout the problem sets, there are many new problems that give examples of the ways in which children try to use mathematical techniques. A really important part of being an excellent teacher is to be able to analyze what the children are doing and then give them help at a conceptual level or show them why their method works. The RTS problems show that future teachers will need a thorough understanding of mathematical content in order to answer students' questions. We want to thank Jean Anderson, who has 25 years of experience teaching in elementary and middle school in DeKalb, Georgia, and both Shea Dickerson and Angela Gonzales, fourth-grade teachers in Lexington, Kentucky, for their contributions to the RTS problems and for increasing the authors' understanding of how children invent new strategies and the ways that they may misunderstand mathematics.

**Expanded State Student Assessment Problems (SSA)** A significant number of SSA problems have been added so that, except in Chapter 1, almost every section has three or more such problems. Solving SSA problems will show you why the material of nearly all sections is needed in elementary or middle school. Furthermore, to learn mathematics conceptually is to be able to respond to open-ended questions, which are becoming more and more a part of SSA problems and are included in a number of sections.

**Examining School Book Pages Problems (SBP)** These problems are content questions for future teachers that use interesting real elementary and middle school textbooks as the basis of the question. Rather than simply insert school book pages without any real context, these problems use the pages to focus students on the relevant mathematical content of the page. School Book Pages and corresponding questions are at the end of nearly every exercise set.

**The Chapter in Relation to Future Teachers** Rather than providing an overview at the end of each chapter, this new sixth edition gives a description of the chapter from the point of view of what future teachers will need to teach your students. Such an approach is sometimes described as "mathematical knowledge for teaching" and is an important area of research whose results will reach deeply into students' future classrooms.

## Overview of Content

- **Problem Solving** We begin the text with an extensive introduction to problem solving in Chapter 1. This theme continues throughout the text in special problem-solving examples and is featured in the problems grouped under the headings "Thinking Critically," "Teaching Concepts," "Thinking Cooperatively," "Making Connections," "Communicating," "Using a Calculator," and "Using a Computer." New in this sixth edition is the use of the recently added Section 1.4, "Algebra as a Problem-Solving Strategy," as a platform for the expanded Chapter 8, which applies algebra to geometry.

- **Number Systems** Chapters 2, 3, 5, 6, and 7 focus on the various number systems and make use of discussion, pictorial and graphical representations, and manipulatives to promote an understanding of the systems, their properties, and the various modes of computation. There is plenty of opportunity for drill and practice, as well as for individual and cooperative problem solving, reasoning, and communication.

- **Number Theory** Chapter 4 contains much material that is new, interesting, and relevant to students' careers as future teachers. Notions of divisibility, divisors, multiples, greatest common divisors, and least common multiples are developed first via informative diagrams and then through the use of manipulatives, sets, prime-factor representations, and the Euclidean algorithm.

- **Algebraic Reasoning and Representation** Although algebraic notions are used earlier in the text, Chapter 8 gives a careful and readable discussion of algebraic ideas needed in elementary and middle school. Included in the discussion are variables; algebraic expressions and equations; linear, quadratic, and exponential functions; simple graphing in the Cartesian plane; and especially the intimate relationship between algebra and geometry, in the last section of the chapter. All of these concepts are increasingly appearing in texts for elementary and middle school students. Schoolteachers must therefore be conversant with algebraic and geometric ideas to be comfortable teaching from current texts. Chapter 8, however, is not meant as a comprehensive review of algebra: Its focus is on the algebra that is a part of the elementary and middle school curriculum.

- **Geometry** The creative and inductive nature of geometric discovery is emphasized in Chapters 9, 10, 11, and 12. These chapters will help students view geometry in an exciting new way that is much less formal than they have seen before. The text's approach to geometry is constructive and visual. Students are often asked to draw, cut, fold, paste, count, and so on, making geometry an experimental science. While the traditional construction and measurement tools continue to have a place, the visual and dynamic scope of geometry is enhanced with computer geometry software, such as *The Geometer's Sketchpad*. Problem solving and applications permeate the geometry chapters, and sections on tiling and symmetry provide an opportunity to highlight the aesthetic and artistic aspects of geometry. Examples are taken from culturally diverse sources.

- **Statistics** Chapter 13, on statistics, is designed to give students an appreciation of the basic measures and graphical representations of data. The informed citizen needs to be aware of the power of statistics as a way of predicting and describing, as well as of the way statistics can mislead. This section has been modified in this edition to include "Responding to Students" problems, because statistics has become a part of the K–5 curriculum. In addition, students will generate their own data sets. There is also a discussion of the standardized normal distribution, as well as of $z$ scores and percentiles.

- **Probability** In Chapter 14, we first study experimental probability—probability based on experience and repeated trials. This study prepares the way for the subsequent examination of the elements of the theoretical probability of an event, based on counting and other a priori considerations. The great surprise for students is how closely the results agree, particularly when the number of trials is large. Of course, it is necessary to consider various methods of counting in order to compute theoretical probabilities. At the same time, counting is an important topic in its own right, and we have made it accessible through the use of tree diagrams, Venn diagrams, and careful explanation of the use of the words *or* and *and*. Probability is also now introduced in elementary schools.

- **The "Mathematical Lexicon"** Many of the words, prefixes, and suffixes forming the vocabulary of mathematics are derived from words and word roots from Latin, Greek, and other languages. The lexicon serves as an aid to learning and understanding the language of mathematics.

## Topics of Special Interest

The text includes several topics that many students will find especially interesting. These topics provide stimulating opportunities to hone such mathematical reasoning skills as problem solving, pattern recognition, algebraic representation, and calculator and computer usage. The following topics are threaded into several chapters and problem sets:

- **The Fibonacci Numbers and the Golden Ratio.** The Fibonacci numbers (1, 1, 2, 3, 5, 8, . . .) and the Golden Ratio have surprised and fascinated people over the ages and continue to serve as an unlimited source for mathematical and pedagogical examples. It is not always obvious that there is a connection to the Fibonacci numbers. Much of the charm of such exercises consists in the surprise of discovery in unexpected places.

- **Pascal's Triangle.** This well-known triangular pattern that has roots in ancient China has unexpected applications to counting the number of paths through a square lattice and to combinatorics, and to is replete with patterns awaiting discovery.

- **Triangular Numbers.** The numbers in the third column of Pascal's triangle (1, 3, 6, 10, 15, 21, . . .) appear in almost countless unexpected contexts.

- **Magic Squares and Other Magic Patterns.** These topics provide interesting practice in basic number patterns and number facts.

## Features for the Future Classroom

A teacher of mathematics should be aware of the historical development of mathematics, have some knowledge of the principal contributors to mathematics, and realize that mathematics continues to be a lively area of research. The text contains a number of features that future teachers will find to be valuable in the classroom:

- **Hands On activities** at the beginning of each chapter serve as an introduction to the material to be covered in the chapter. These activities offer games and puzzles that can be adapted for future elementary classrooms.

- **Pólya Principles** have been used in an increasing number of examples, with solutions written so as to highlight his four-step approach to problem solving—an approach that will be quite useful.

- **Into the Classroom** provides insights into teaching the topics of this text to elementary and middle school children. These tips often come from elementary or middle school teachers.

- **Examining School Book Pages** contains content problems derived from actual elementary or middle school textbooks and shows how topics from the text are made meaningful to schoolchildren. These pages also show that the materials in this text are central to the elementary or middle school curriculum. The pages appear as the last problems within a problem set.

- **Cooperative Investigations** are activities within the body of the chapters that use small groups to explore the concepts under discussion. Other activities can be found in MyMathLab (see Media Supplements) and in the Activities Manual by Dolan et al. (see Student Supplements).

- **Highlights from History** illustrate the contributions individuals have made to mathematics and provide a cultural, historical, and personal perspective on the development of mathematical concepts and thought.

- **Did You Know?** provides examples of recent advancements in mathematics, often demonstrating the important role the subject has in today's world and in our personal lives. This feature also highlights excerpts from mathematical literature that have relevance to the classroom teacher.

## Chapter Elements

Except for Chapter 1, each chapter is consistently and meaningfully structured according to the following pattern:

- **Chapter Opener.** A class activity called "Hands On" introduces the chapter topic. The Hands On activities are followed by a "Key Ideas" feature that reveals the interconnections among the various parts of mathematics previously discussed and between mathematics and the real world.

- **Examples** are often presented in a *problem-solving mode,* asking students to independently obtain a solution that can be compared with the solution presented in the text. Solutions are frequently structured in the Pólya four-step format.

- **Figures and Tables.** A large number of figures and tables reinforce the concepts, problems, and solutions.

- **Think Clouds.** These notes serve as quick reminders and clarify key points in discussions.

 - **Mathematical Habit of Mind.** This feature presents thought-provoking insights on thinking mathematically, with an explanation of why there is a mathematical habit of mind either in the text or in the answer.

- **From the NCTM Principles and Standards.** Extensive excerpts from the *NCTM Principles and Standards* help you understand the relevance of topics and what students will be expected to teach.

- **Cooperative Investigations** provide activities, open-ended problems, and opportunities for *cooperative learning.*

- **Problem Sets** are organized according to the following categories:
  - **<u>Understanding Concepts</u>** problems provide drills and reinforce basic concepts.
  - **<u>Teaching Concepts</u>** problems pose questions that cause you to carefully consider how you might go about clarifying subtle and often misunderstood points for your students in classes you will soon teach. The act of answering these questions often forces one to think more deeply about them and come to a better understanding of the subtleties involved. The number of such problems has increased in this edition.
  -  **<u>Responding to Students</u>** exercises give the opportunity for future teachers to see what mathematical questions and procedures children will come up with on their own and ways to respond to them.
  - **<u>Thinking Critically</u>** problems offer problem-solving practice related to the section topic. Many of these problems can be used as classroom activities or with small groups.

- **Thinking Cooperatively** problems provide cooperative problem-solving experiences specifically for small groups.
- **Making Connections** problems apply the section concepts to solving real-life problems and to other parts of mathematics.
- **Communicating** exercises offer opportunities to write about mathematics and to investigate mathematics as a language.
- **Using a Calculator** problems are best solved with a calculator. These problems are highlighted by an icon, .
- **Using a Computer** problems give you the opportunity to use various types of software. Again, a suitable icon, , indicates when the use of a computer would be helpful or desirable.
-  **From State Student Assessments** problems provide examples of problems from the exams now in use in many states to assess student progress. These problems help make you aware of the types of knowledge that your future students will be asked to master. The number of such exercises has increased significantly in this edition.
- **Examining School Book Pages** problems contain content questions for future teachers based on problems found in real elementary and middle school textbooks. School Book Pages and corresponding questions are at the end of nearly every exercise set and provide a context for the content.

- **Chapter in Relation to Future Teachers** is a brief essay that discusses the importance of the material just covered in the context of future teaching and helps place the chapter in relation to the remainder of the book.

- **End-of-Chapter Material** Each chapter closes with the following features:
  -  **Chapter Summary** has been restructured into a table format, with more complete information in order to make it more helpful for reviewing the chapter. The summary will include *Key Concepts, Vocabulary,* and *Notation,* and may also include *Theorems, Properties, Formulas, Procedures,* and *Strategy.*
  - **Chapter Review Problems**
  - **Chapter Tests** All chapter tests have been reorganized to more accurately reflect what students might expect on an actual test in class. We have continued the practice of changing the order so that the problems are not sequenced as they occur in the text. This approach creates a more realistic experience for promoting learning and better performance on exams.

# Note for the Instructor

The principal goals of this text are to impart mathematical reasoning skills, a deep conceptual understanding, and a positive attitude to those who aspire to be elementary or middle school teachers. To help meet these goals, we have made a concerted effort to involve students in mathematical learning experiences that are intrinsically interesting, relevant for teaching, often surprising, and even aesthetically pleasing. With enhanced skill at mathematical reasoning and a positive attitude toward mathematics come confidence and an increased willingness to learn the mathematical content, skills, and effective teaching techniques necessary to become a fine teacher of mathematics.

In our own classes, we have found it extremely profitable to spend considerable time on Chapter 1. This effort has gone a long way toward changing student attitudes and promoting their ability to reason mathematically. A course that begins and continues with an extensive study of the number systems and algorithms of arithmetic is not attractive or interesting to students who feel that they already know these things and have found them dull. By contrast, the material in Chapter 1 and the many problems in the problem sets are new, stimulating, and not what students have previously experienced. We have found that, aside from enhancing interest, the extensive time spent on Chapter 1 develops attitudes, mathematical habits of the mind, and skills that make it possible to deal much more quickly with the usual material on number systems, algorithms, and all the subsequent ideas that are important to the teaching of mathematics in elementary schools. Note, however, that some instructors prefer to intersperse topics from Chapter 1 throughout their courses as they cover subsequent chapters. Another approach is to begin with Chapters 2 and 3, and then present Chapter 1.

We have also found that it is helpful to answer the frequently asked question, "Why are we here?" by going beyond the discussions of conceptual understanding and showing the kinds of questions that children may ask. This approach by the third author to the issue of future teachers' attitude in a mathematics content course, which has been quite successful at the University of Kentucky, consists of spending only one hour watching children solve math problems in which they either show that they understand the material deeply and well or are confused. We have had success with the CD *IMAP: Integrating Mathematics and Pedagogy to Illustrate Children's Reasoning,* by Randy Philipp and Candace Cabral (2005), Pearson, Merrill Prentice Hall. One hour spent early in the course with a few well-chosen video clips is a tremendous help in answering the "why" question of this paragraph.

## Prerequisite Mathematical Background

This text is for use in mathematics content courses for prospective elementary and middle school teachers. We assume that the students enrolled in these courses have completed two years of high school algebra and one year of high school geometry. We do not assume that the students will be highly proficient in algebra and geometry, but rather that they have a basic knowledge of those subjects and reasonable arithmetic skills. Typically, students bring widely varying backgrounds to these courses, and this text is written to accommodate that diversity.

## Course Flexibility

The text contains ample material for either two or three semester-length courses. At Washington State University, elementary education majors are required to take two three-semester hour courses, with the option for an elective third course that is particularly suited to the needs of upper elementary and middle school teachers. Our text is used in all three courses. The following suggestions are for single semester-length courses, but instructors should have little difficulty selecting material that fits the coverage needed for courses in a quarter system:

- A first course, *Problem Solving and Numbers Systems,* covers Chapters 1 through 7. Our own first course devotes at least five weeks to Chapter 1. The problem-solving skills and enthusiasm developed in this chapter make it possible to move through most of the topics in Chapters 2 through 7 more quickly than usual. However, as noted earlier, some instructors prefer to intersperse topics from Chapter 1 among topics covered later in their courses. There is considerable latitude in which topics an instructor might choose to give a lighter or heavier emphasis.

- A second course, *Algebra, Basic Geometry, Statistics, and Probability,* covers Chapters 8 through 14, with the optional inclusion of computer geometry software. (Appendix C gives a brief introduction to *"The Geometer's Sketchpad."*)

- An alternative second course, *Informal Geometry,* covers Chapters 9 through 12, with the optional inclusion of computer geometry software.

  Once the basic notions and symbolism of geometry have been covered in Sections 9.1 and 9.2, the remaining chapters in geometry can be taken up in any order. Section 9.3, on figures in space, should be covered before the instructor takes up surface area and volume in Sections 10.4 and 10.5.

- Many universities use the text for a three-course sequence: "Problem Solving and Number Systems" (Chapters 1–7), "Algebra and Geometry" (Chapters 8–12), and "Probability and Statistics" (Chapters 13 and 14).

# Acknowledgments

We would like to thank the following individuals who reviewed either the current or previous editions of our text:

Khadija Ahmed
*Monroe County Community College*

Richard Anderson-Sprecher
*University of Wyoming*

James E. Arnold
*University of Wisconsin–Milwaukee*

Bill Aslan
*Texas A & M University–Commerce*

Scott Barnett
*Henry Ford Community College*

James K. Bidwell
*Central Michigan University*

Martin V. Bonsangue
*California State University–Fullerton*

James R. Boone
*Texas A & M University*

Peter Braunfeld
*University of Illinois–Urbana*

Tricia Muldoon Brown*
*University of Kentucky*

Jane Buerger
*Concordia College*

Louis J. Chatterly
*Brigham Young University*

Phyllis Chinn
*Humboldt State University*

Lynn Cleary
*San Juan College*

Max Coleman
*Sam Houston State University*

Dr. Cherlyn Converse
*California State University–Fullerton*

Dana S. Craig
*University of Central Oklahoma*

Lynn D. Darragh
*San Juan College*

Allen Davis
*Eastern Illinois University*

Gary A. Deatsman
*West Chester University*

Sheila Doran
*Xavier University*

Arlene Dowshen
*Widener University*

Stephen Drake
*Northwestern Michigan College*

Joseph C. Ferrar
*Ohio State University*

Marjorie A. Fitting
*San Jose State University*

Gina Foletta
*Northern Kentucky University*

Grace Peterson Foster
*Beaufort County Community College*

Sonja L. Goerdt*
*St. Cloud State University*

Tamela D. Hanebrink*
*Southeast Missouri State University*

Lisa Hansen*
*Western New England College*

Ward Heilman
*Bridgewater State College*

Fay Jester
*Pennsylvania State University*

Wilburn C. Jones
*Western Kentucky University*

Carol Juncker
*Delgado Community College*

Eric B. Kahn*
*Bloomsburg University*

Jane Keiser
*Miami University*

Greg Klein
*Texas A & M University*

Mark Klespis
*Sam Houston State University*

Randa Kress
*Idaho State University*

Martha Ann Larkin
*Southern Utah University*

Verne Leininger*
*Bridgewater College*

Charlotte K. Lewis
*University of New Orleans*

Jim Loats
*Metropolitan State College of Denver*

Catherine Louchart
*Northern Arizona University*

Carol Lucas
*University of Central Oklahoma*

Jennifer Luebeck
*Sheridan College*

Dr. Dixie Metheny
*Montana State University*

David Anthony Milazzo*
*Niagara County Community College*

Eldon L. Miller
*University of Mississippi*

Carla Moldavan
*Berry College*

Marlene M. Naquin*
*University of Southern Mississippi–Gulf Coast*

Beth Noblitt
*Northern Kentucky University*

F. A. Norman
*University of North Carolina–Charlotte*

Jon Odell
*Richland Community College*

Bonnie Oppenheimer
*Mississippi University for Women*

Anthony Piccolino
*Montclair State College*

Buddy Pierce
*Southeastern Oklahoma University*

Jane Pinnow
*University of Wisconsin–Parkside*

Robert Powers
*University of Northern Colorado*

Tamela D. Randolph
*Southeast Missouri State University*

Craig Roberts
*Southeast Missouri State University*

Michael Roitman
*Kansas State University*

Jane M. Rood
*Eastern Illinois University*

Lisa M. Scheuerman
*Eastern Illinois University*

Darcy Schroeder*
*Arizona State University*

Julie Sliva
*San Jose State University*

Carol J. Steiner
*Kent State University*

Richard H. Stout
*Gordon College*

Elizabeth Turner Smith
*University of Louisiana–Monroe*

Christine Wetzel-Ulrich
*North Hampton Community College*

Kimberly Vincent
*Washington State University*

*Denotes reviewers of the sixth edition.*

# Supplements

## Student Supplements

### Mathematics Activities for Elementary Teachers, Sixth Edition

ISBN-10: 0-321-71539-X / ISBN-13: 978-0-321-71539-5

- By Dan Dolan, Jim Williamson, and Mari Muri.
- Provides hands-on, manipulative-based activities keyed to the text that involve future elementary school teachers discovering concepts, solving problems, and exploring mathematical ideas.
- **New!** Colorful, perforated paper manipulatives in a convenient storage pack.
- Activities can be adapted for use with elementary students at a later time.

### Student's Solutions Manual

ISBN-10: 0-321-69386-8 / ISBN-13: 978-0-321-69386-0

- Provides detailed, worked-out solutions to all exercises that are answered at the back of the student text.

### Video Resources on DVD

ISBN-10: 0-321-71650-7 / ISBN-13: 978-0-321-71650-7

- Complete set of digitized videos reviewing chapter content for student use at home or on campus.
- Affordable, portable, and ideal for distance learning and supplemental instruction.

### E-Manipulatives CD

ISBN-10: 0-321-64080-2 / ISBN-13: 978-0-321-64080-2

- Twenty-one Flash-based manipulatives investigate, explore, and practice new concepts and solve specific problems that will help students develop a conceptual understanding of key ideas.
- Helps explore the way elementary students would use manipulatives in the classroom.

### Connecting Mathematics for Elementary Teachers

ISBN-10: 0-321-54266-5 / ISBN-13: 978-0-321-54266-3

- By David Feikes, Keith Schwingendorf, and Jeff Gregg.
- Provides general descriptions of children's learning and shows how children approach mathematics differently than adults.

### When Will I Ever Teach This?

ISBN-10: 0-321-23717-X / ISBN-13: 978-0-321-23717-0

- By Sharon E. Taylor and Susie Lanier.
- Allows students to see when and where a topic occurs in the curriculum and also to see how it is presented in a text.

## Instructor Supplements

### Annotated Instructor's Edition

ISBN-10: 0-321-69354-X / ISBN-13: 978-0-321-69354-9

- All answers included, with answers to most exercises on the page where they occur. Longer answers are in the back of the book.

### Instructor's Solutions Manual

ISBN-10: 0-321-69355-8 / ISBN-13: 978-0-321-69355-6

- Provides complete solutions to all problems in the text.

### NEW! Insider's Guide

ISBN-10: 0-321-69385-X / ISBN-13: 978-0-321-69385-3

- Provides suggestions, teaching tips, project ideas, sample syllabi, and other useful information.
- A great resource for new professors, adjuncts, and veteran professors looking for new ideas.
- Also available for download from Pearson Education's online catalog at www.pearsonhighered.com or within MyMathLab.

### ONLINE SUPPLEMENTS

*Available for download from Pearson Education's online catalog at www.pearsonhighered.com or within MyMathLab.*

### Instructor's Testing Manual

- Contains prepared tests with answer keys for each chapter.

### Instructor's Guide to Mathematics Activities for Elementary Teachers, Sixth Edition

- Contains answers for all activities, as well as additional teaching suggestions for some activities.

### Instructor's Guide to Connecting Mathematics for Elementary Teachers

- Contains correlations to all of Pearson's math for elementary teachers textbooks as well as tips and teaching suggestions on how to incorporate the book into your course and syllabus.

### PowerPoint Lecture Presentation

- Fully editable lecture slides include definitions, key concepts, and examples for every section of the text.

### TestGen®

- Enables instructors to build, edit, print, and administer a test, using a computerized bank of questions developed to cover all the objectives of the text.
- Algorithmically based, allowing instructors to create multiple, but equivalent, versions of the same question or test with the click of a button.
- Tests can be printed or administered online.

# Media Supplements

## MyMathLab® Online Course (access code required)

MyMathLab® is a series of text-specific, easily customizable online courses for Pearson Education's textbooks in mathematics and statistics. MyMathLab gives you the tools you need to deliver all or a portion of your course online, whether your students are in a lab or working from home.

- MyMathLab provides a rich and flexible set of course materials, featuring free-response exercises that are algorithmically generated for unlimited practice and mastery.
- Students can also use online tools, such as video lectures, animations, and a multimedia textbook, to independently improve their understanding and performance.
- Instructors can use MyMathLab's homework and test managers to select and assign online exercises correlated directly with the textbook, as well as media related to that textbook, and they can also create and assign their own online exercises and import TestGen® tests for added flexibility.
- MyMathLab's online grade book—designed specifically for mathematics and statistics— automatically tracks students' homework and test results and gives the instructor control over how to calculate final grades. You can also add offline (paper-and-pencil) grades to the grade book.
- MyMathLab also includes access to the **Pearson Tutor Center** (www.pearsontutorservices. com). The Tutor Center is staffed by qualified mathematics instructors who provide textbook-specific tutoring for students via toll-free phone, fax, e-mail, and interactive Web sessions. MyMathLab is available to qualified adopters. For more information, visit our website at www.mymathlab.com or contact your Pearson representative.

### *New to the MyMathLab course:*

- A new type of problem using *Integrated Mathematics and Pedagogy* (IMAP) videos to test students' understanding of concepts and content in the context of children's reasoning processes.
- A correlation of IMAP videos with the text, along with guidelines on when and how this material might be used in the course.
- Emanipulatives and IMAP videos integrated into the multimedia textbook.
- The Image Library contains all art from the text, for instructors to use in their own presentations and handouts.

## MathXL® Online Course (access code required)

MathXL® is a powerful online homework, tutorial, and assessment system that accompanies Pearson Education's textbooks in mathematics or statistics. With MathXL, instructors can

- Create, edit, and assign online homework and tests using algorithmically generated exercises correlated to the textbook at the objective level.
- Create and assign their own online exercises and import TestGen tests for added flexibility.
- Maintain records of all students work tracked in MathXL's online grade book.

With MathXL, students can

- Take chapter tests in MathXL and receive personalized study plans or personalized homework assignments based on their test results.
- Use the study plan or the homework to link directly to tutorial exercises for the objectives they need to study.
- Access supplemental animations and video clips directly from selected exercises.

MathXL is available to qualified adopters. For more information, visit our website at www.mathxl.com, or contact your Pearson representative.

# About the Authors

**Calvin Long** received his B.S. in mathematics from the University of Idaho. Following M.S. and Ph.D. degrees in mathematics from the University of Oregon, he worked briefly as an analyst for the National Security Agency and then joined the faculty at Washington State University. His teaching ran the gamut from elementary algebra through graduate courses and included frequently teaching the content courses for prospective elementary school teachers.

His other professional activities include serving on numerous committees of the National Council of Teachers of Mathematics and the Mathematical Association of America, and holding various leadership positions in those organizations. Professor Long has also been heavily engaged in directing and instructing in-service workshops and institutes for teachers at all levels, has given over one hundred presentations at national and regional meetings of NCTM and its affiliated groups, and has presented invited lectures on mathematics education abroad.

Professor Long has coauthored two books and is the sole author of a text in number theory. In addition, he has authored over 90 articles on mathematics and mathematics education and also served as a frequent reviewer for a variety of mathematics journals, including *The Arithmetic Teacher* and *The Mathematics Teacher*. In 1986 he received the Faculty Excellence Award in Teaching from Washington State University, and in 1991 he received a Certificate for Meritorious Service to the Mathematical Association of America.

Aside from carrying out his professional activities, Cal enjoys listening to, singing, and directing classical music; reading; fly fishing; camping; and backpacking.

**Duane DeTemple** received his B.S. with majors in applied science and mathematics from Portland State College. Following his Ph.D. in mathematics from Stanford University, he was a faculty member at Washington State University, where he is now a professor emeritus of mathematics. He has been extensively involved with teacher preparation and professional development at both the elementary and secondary levels. Professor DeTemple has been a frequent consultant to projects sponsored by the Washington State Office of the Superintendent of Public Instruction, the Higher Education Coordinating Board, and other boards and agencies.

Dr. DeTemple has coauthored three other books and over 90 articles on mathematics or mathematics materials for the classroom. He is a member of the Washington State University President's Teaching Academy and, in 2007, was the recipient of the WSU Sahlin Faculty Excellence Award for Instruction and the Distinguished Teaching Award of the Pacific Northwest Section of the Mathematical Association of America.

In addition to teaching and researching mathematics, Duane enjoys reading, listening to and playing music, hiking, biking, canoeing, traveling, and playing tennis.

**Richard Millman** received a B.S. from the Massachusetts Institute of Technology and a Ph.D. from Cornell University in mathematics. He is a professor of mathematics and director of the Center for Education Integrating Science, Mathematics, and Computing at the Georgia Institute of Technology, and he was formerly the Outreach Professor of Mathematics at the University of Kentucky, which supports preservice and in-service teacher training for PreK–12 mathematics teachers.

Dr. Millman has coauthored four books in mathematics, coedited three others, and received ten peer-reviewed grants. He has published over 50 articles about mathematics or mathematics education and has taught a wide variety of mathematics and mathematics education courses throughout the undergraduate and graduate curriculum, including those for preservice teachers. He received, with a former student, an Excel Prize for Expository Writing for an article in *The Mathematics Teacher* and was a Member-at-Large of the Council of the American Mathematical Society. He was principal investigator and project director for ALGEBRA CUBED, a grant from the National Science Foundation to improve algebra education in rural Kentucky. He is now the principal investigator of another NSF grant, SLIDER, in which students use a curriculum based on engineering design in the context of building robots to learn eighth-grade physical science and math.

Rich enjoys traveling, writing about mathematics, losing golf balls, listening to music, and going to plays and movies. He also loves and is enormously proud of his grandchildren, with whom he enjoys discussing the conceptual basis of mathematics, among other topics.

# Thinking Critically

**1.1** An Introduction to Problem Solving

**1.2** Pólya's Problem-Solving Principles

**1.3** More Problem-Solving Strategies

**1.4** Algebra as a Problem-Solving Strategy

**1.5** Additional Problem-Solving Strategies

**1.6** Reasoning Mathematically

# Hands On
## The Gold Coin Game

### Material Needed

15 markers (preferably circular, and yellow if possible) for each pair of students.

### Directions

This is a two-person game. Each pair of players is given 15 gold coins (markers) on the desktop. Taking alternate turns, each player removes one, two, or three coins from the desktop. The player who takes the last coin wins the game. Play several games, with each player alternately playing first. Try to devise a winning strategy, first individually as you play and then thinking jointly about how either the first or second player can play so as to force a win.

### Questions to Consider

1. To discover a winning strategy, it might be helpful to begin with fewer coins. Start with just 7 coins, and see if it is possible for one player or the other to play in such a way as to guarantee a win. Try this several times, and do not move on to question 2 until the answer is clear from what happened with 7 coins.
2. This time, start with 11 coins on the desktop. Is it now possible for one player or the other to force a win? Play several games until both you and your partner agree that there is a winning strategy, and then see how the player using that strategy should play.
3. Extend the strategy you developed in step 2 to the original set of 15 coins.
4. Would the strategy work if you began with 51 markers? Explain carefully and clearly.

### Variation

Devise a similar game in which the player taking the last coin *loses* the game, and explain how one player or the other can force a win for your new game.

---

**CHAPTER PREVIEW**   This first chapter is dedicated to how one goes about solving a mathematical problem and how one learns to reason mathematically. Each problem to be solved needs some thought. In order to help the reader answer the questions, we present a large number of strategies for problem solving. The key question then is "Which of the strategies should I use?" The answer is to do many problems for practice and you will ultimately instinctively go to the appropriate strategy for answering the problem. Of course, there may be many different ways to attack a problem, so it is important to try a number of strategies until you find one that works.

Why should a text devoted to future teachers focus on problem solving and mathematical reasoning? One of the most prominent features of current efforts to reform and revitalize mathematics instruction in American schools has been the recommendation that such instruction should stress problem solving and quantitative reasoning. That this emphasis continues is borne out by the fact that it appears as the first of the process standards in the National Council of Teachers of Mathematics' (NCTM's) *Principles and Standards for School Mathematics*, published in 2000. (See the Problem-Solving Standard on the next page.) Children need to learn to *think* about quantitative situations in insightful and imaginative ways—just memorizing seemingly arbitrary rules for computation is unproductive.

Of course, if children are to learn problem solving, their teachers must themselves be good teachers of problem solving. Thus, the purpose of this chapter, and indeed of this entire book, is to help you to think more critically, analytically, and thoughtfully, in order to be more comfortable with mathematical reasoning and discourse and to bring those mathematical habits of the mind to your classroom.

MHM

**KEY IDEAS**
- Using the four problem-solving principles of George Pólya
- Having a variety of problem-solving strategies available to you (there are 12 that are highlighted in this chapter, with more to come later)
- The idea of algebra as a problem-solving strategy
- The use of the Pigeonhole Principle

- The need to look for patterns: using inductive reasoning to form a conjecture
- Deductive reasoning
- The rule of indirect reasoning

## Problem Solving Standard

Instructional programs from prekindergarten through grade 12 should enable all students to—

- *build new mathematical knowledge through problem solving;*
- *solve problems that arise in mathematics and in other contexts;*
- *apply and adapt a variety of appropriate strategies to solve problems;*
- *monitor and reflect on the process of mathematical problem solving.*

Problem solving is the cornerstone of school mathematics. Without the ability to solve problems, the usefulness and power of mathematical ideas, knowledge, and skills are severely limited. Students who can efficiently and accurately multiply but who cannot identify situations that call for multiplication are not well prepared. Students who can both develop *and* carry out a plan to solve a mathematical problem are exhibiting knowledge that is much deeper and more useful than simply carrying out a computation. Unless students can solve problems, the facts, concepts, and procedures they know are of little use. The goal of school mathematics should be for all students to become increasingly able and willing to engage with and solve problems.

Problem solving is also important because it can serve as a vehicle for learning new mathematical ideas and skills (Schroeder and Lester 1989). A problem-centered approach to teaching mathematics uses interesting and well-selected problems to launch mathematical lessons and engage students. In this way, new ideas, techniques, and mathematical relationships emerge and become the focus of discussion. Good problems can inspire the exploration of important mathematical ideas, nurture persistence, and reinforce the need to understand and use various strategies, mathematical properties, and relationships.

SOURCE: *Principles and Standards for School Mathematics by NCTM, page 182. Copyright © 2000 by the National Council of Teachers of Mathematics. Reproduced with permission of the National Council of Teachers of Mathematics via Copyright Clearance Center. NCTM does not endorse the content or validity of these alignments.*

## 1.1

# An Introduction to Problem Solving

When the children arrived in Frank Capek's fifth-grade class one day, this "special" problem was on the blackboard:

> *Old MacDonald had a total of 37 chickens and pigs on his farm. All together, they had 98 feet. How many chickens were there and how many pigs?*

After organizing the children into problem-solving teams, Mr. Capek asked them to solve the problem. "Special" problems were always fun and the children got right to work. Let's listen in on the group with Mary, Joe, Carlos, and Sue:

> *"I'll bet there were 20 chickens and 17 pigs," said Mary.*
>
> *"Let's see," said Joe. "If you're right there are 2 × 20, or 40, chicken feet and 4 × 17, or 68, pig feet. This gives 108 feet. That's too many feet."*
>
> *"Let's try 30 chickens and 7 pigs," said Sue. "That should give us fewer feet."*
>
> *"Hey," said Carlos. "With Mary's guess we got 108 feet, and Sue's guess gives us 88 feet. Since 108 is 10 too much and 88 is 10 too few, I'll bet we should guess 25 chickens—just halfway between Mary's and Sue's guesses!"*

These children are using a **Guess and Check** strategy. If their guess gives an answer that is too large or too small, they adjust the guess to get a smaller or larger answer as needed. This can be a very effective strategy. By the way, is Carlos's guess right?

Let's look in on another group:

*"Let's make a table,"* said Nandita. *"We've had good luck that way before."*

*"Right, Nani,"* responded Ann. *"Let's see. If we start with 20 chickens and 17 pigs, we have 2 × 20, or 40, chicken feet and 4 × 17, or 68, pig feet. If we have 21 chickens, . . . ."*

> This is a powerful refinement of guess and check.

| Chickens | Pigs | Chicken Feet | Pig Feet | Total |
|----------|------|--------------|----------|-------|
| 20 | 17 | 40 | 68 | 108 |
| 21 | 16 | 42 | 64 | 106 |
| 22 | 15 | 44 | 60 | 104 |
| . | . | . | . | . |
| . | . | . | . | . |
| . | . | . | . | . |

*Making a table to look for a pattern* is often an excellent strategy. Do you think that the group with Nandita and Ann will soon find a solution? How many more rows of the table will they have to fill in? Can you think of a shortcut?

*Mike said, "Let's draw a picture. We can draw 37 circles for heads and put two lines under each circle to represent feet. Then we can add two extra feet under enough circles to make 98. That should do it."*

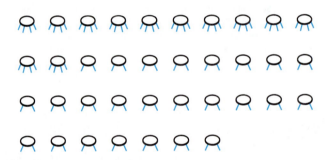

Drawing a picture is often a good strategy. Does it work in this case?

*"Oh! The problem is easy,"* said Jennifer. *"If we have all the pigs stand on their hind legs, then there are 2 × 37, or 74, feet touching the ground. That means that the pigs must be holding 24 front feet up in the air. This means that there must be 12 pigs and 25 chickens!"*

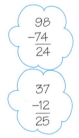

It helps if you can be ingenious like Jennifer, but it is not essential, and children *can* be taught strategies like the following:

Guess and check

Make a table

Look for a pattern

Draw a picture

These and other useful strategies will be discussed later (see page 30 and Sections 1.4 and 1.5), but for now let's try some problems on our own.

**EXAMPLE 1.1 Guessing Toni's Number**

Toni is thinking of a number. If you double the number and add 11, the result is 39. What number is Toni thinking of?

**Solution 1**

Guessing and checking

Guess 10.  $2 \cdot 10 + 11 = 20 + 11 = 31.$  This is too small.
Guess 20.  $2 \cdot 20 + 11 = 40 + 11 = 51.$  This is too large.
Guess 15.  $2 \cdot 15 + 11 = 30 + 11 = 41.$  This is a bit large.
Guess 14.  $2 \cdot 14 + 11 = 28 + 11 = 39.$  This checks!
Toni's number must be 14.

**Solution 2**

Making a table and looking for a pattern

| Trial Number | Result Using Toni's Rule | |
|---|---|---|
| 5 | $2 \cdot 5 + 11 = 21$ | |
| 6 | $2 \cdot 6 + 11 = 23$ | 2 larger |
| 7 | $2 \cdot 7 + 11 = 25$ | 2 larger |
| 8 | $2 \cdot 8 + 11 = 27$ | 2 larger |
| . | . | . |
| . | . | . |
| . | . | . |

We need to get to 39, and we jump by 2 each time we take a step of 1. Therefore, we need to take

$$\frac{39 - 27}{2} = \frac{12}{2} = 6$$

more steps; we should guess $8 + 6 = 14$ as Toni's number, as before.

**EXAMPLE 1.2 Guessing and Checking**

(a) Place the digits 1, 2, 3, 4, and 5 in these circles so that the sums across and vertically are the same. Is there more than one solution?

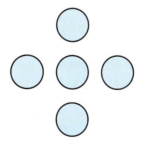

(b) Can part (a) be accomplished if 2 is placed in the center? Why or why not?

**Solution**

(a) Using the guess and check strategy, suppose we put the 3 in the center circle. Since the sums across and down must be the same, we must pair the remaining numbers so that they have equal sums. But this is easy, because $1 + 5 = 2 + 4$. Thus, one solution to the problem is as shown here:

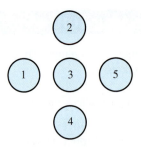

Checking further, we find other solutions, such as these:

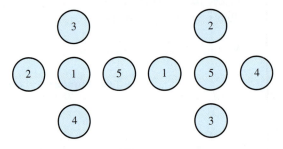

(b) What about putting 2 in the center? The remaining digits are 1, 3, 4, and 5, and these cannot be grouped into two pairs with equal sums, since one sum is necessarily odd and the other even. Therefore, there is no solution with 2 in the center circle.

## Problem Set 1.1

Exercises numbered in red are answered in the back of the text.

## Understanding Concepts

1. Levinson's Hardware has a number of bikes and trikes for sale. There are 27 seats and 60 wheels, all told. Determine how many bikes and how many trikes there are.

| Bikes | Trikes | Bikes Wheels | Trike Wheels | Total |
|-------|--------|--------------|--------------|-------|
| 17 | 10 | 34 | 30 | 64 |
| 18 | 9 | 36 | 27 | 63 |
| . | . | . | . | . |
| . | . | . | . | . |
| . | . | . | . | . |

(a) Use the guess and check strategy to find a solution.

(b) Complete the table to find a solution.

(c) Find a solution by completing this diagram.

(d) Would Jennifer's method work for this problem? Explain briefly.

2. (a) Mr. Akika has 32 18-cent and 29-cent stamps, all told. The stamps are worth $8.07. How many of each kind of stamp does he have?

(b) Summarize your solution method in one or two *carefully* written sentences.

3. Make up a problem similar to problems 1 and 2.

4. (a) Place the digits 4, 6, 7, 8, and 9 in the circles to make the sums horizontally and vertically equal 19.

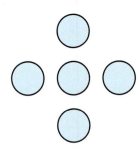

(b) Is there more than one answer to part (a)? Explain briefly. Digits should be used once and only once.

5. Xin has nine coins with a total value of 48 cents. What coins does Xin have?

6. Who am I? If you multiply me by 5 and subtract 8, the result is 52.

**7.** Who am I? If you multiply me by 15 and add 28, the result is 103.

**8.** Make up a problem like problems 5 and 6.

**9. (a)** Using each of 1, 2, 3, 4, 5, and 6 once and only once, fill in the circles so that the sums of the numbers on each of the three sides of the triangle are equal.

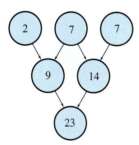

  **(b)** Does part (a) have more than one solution?

  **(c)** Write up a brief, but careful, description of the thought process you used in solving this problem.

**10.** In this diagram, the sum of any two horizontally adjacent numbers is the number immediately below and between them:

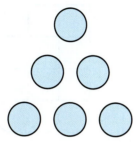

Using the same rule of formation, complete these arrays:

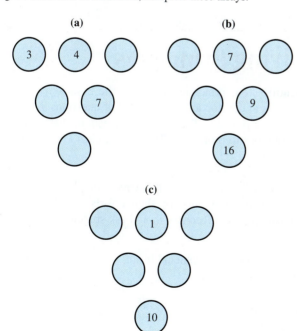

  **(d)** Is there more than one solution to part (a)? part (b)? part (c)?

**11.** Study the sample diagram. Note that

$$2 + 8 = 10,$$
$$5 + 3 = 8,$$
$$2 + 5 = 7, \text{ and}$$
$$3 + 8 = 11.$$

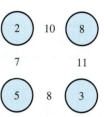

If possible, complete each of these diagrams so that the same pattern holds:

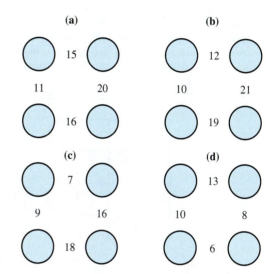

**12.** Study this sequence of numbers: 3, 4, 7, 11, 18, 29, 47, 76. Note that $3 + 4 = 7, 4 + 7 = 11, 7 + 11 = 18$, and so on. Use the same rule to complete these sequences:

  **(a)** 1, 2, 3, _____, _____, _____, _____

  **(b)** 2, _____, 8, _____, _____, _____, _____

  **(c)** 3, _____, _____, 13, _____, _____, _____

  **(d)** 2, _____, _____, _____, _____, 26

  **(e)** 2, _____, _____, _____, _____, 11

**13. (a)** Use each of the numbers 2, 3, 4, 5, and 6 once and only once to fill in the circles so that the sum of the numbers in the three horizontal circles equals the sum of the numbers in the three vertical circles.

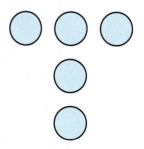

  **(b)** Can you find more than one solution?

(c) Can you have a solution with 3 in the middle of the top row? Explain in two *carefully* written sentences.

14. (a) In the following magic square, compute the sums of the numbers in each row, column, and diagonal of the square and write your answers in the appropriate circles:

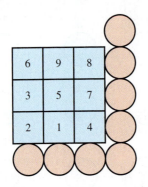

(b) Interchange the 2 and 8 and the 4 and 6 in the array in part (a) to create the magic *subtraction* square shown next. For each row, column, and diagonal, add the two end entries and subtract the middle entry from this sum.

15. (a) Write the digits 0, 1, 2, 3, 4, 5, 6, 7, and 8 in the small squares to create another magic square. (*Hint:* Relate this to problem 14. Also, you may want to write these digits on nine small squares of paper that you can move around easily to check various possibilities.)

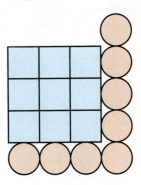

(b) Make a magic subtraction square using the numbers 0, 1, 2, 3, 4, 5, 6, 7, and 8. Digits should be used once and only once.

16. Make up a guess and check problem of your own and solve it.

## 1.2

# Pólya's Problem-Solving Principles

### Strategies

- Guess and check.
- Make an orderly list.
- Draw a diagram.

In *How to Solve It,** George Pólya identifies four principles that form the basis for any serious attempt at problem solving. He then proceeds to develop an extensive list of questions that teachers should ask students who need help in solving a problem. These are also questions that students can and should ask themselves as they seek solutions to problems. (The NCTM cites Pólya's insightful approach, as can be seen on page 9.)

**Pólya's First Principle: Understand the Problem**   This principle seems too obvious to be mentioned. However, students are often stymied by their efforts to solve a problem because they don't understand it fully or even in part. Teachers should ask students such questions as the following:

- Do you understand all the words used in stating the problem? If not, look them up in the index, in a dictionary, or wherever they can be found.
- What are you asked to find or show?
- Can you restate the problem in your own words?
- Is there yet another way to state the problem?
- What does *(key word)* really mean and what is its definition?

---

*George Pólya, *How to Solve It* (Princeton, NJ: Princeton University Press, 1988).

- Can you work out some numerical examples that would help make the problem clear?
- Can you think of a picture or diagram that might help you understand the problem?
- Is there enough information to enable you to find a solution?
- Is there extraneous information and does that matter?
- What do you really need to know to find a solution?

## Highlight from History
### George Pólya (1887–1985)

How does one most efficiently proceed to solve a problem? Can the art of problem solving be taught, or is it a talent possessed by only a select few? Over the years, many have thought about these questions, but none so effectively and definitively as the late George Pólya, and he maintained that the skill of problem solving can be taught.

Pólya was born in Hungary in 1887 and received his Ph.D. in mathematics from the University of Budapest. He taught for many years at the Swiss Federal Institute of Technology in Zurich and would no doubt have continued to do so but for the advent of Nazism in Germany. Deeply concerned by this threat to civiliza-

tion, Pólya moved to the United States in 1940 and taught briefly at Brown University and then, for the remainder of his life, at Stanford University. He was

extraordinarily capable both as a mathematician and as a teacher. He also maintained a lifelong interest in studying the thought processes that are productive in both learning and doing mathematics. Indeed, among the numerous books that he wrote, he seemed most proud of *How to Solve It* (1945), which has sold over a million copies and has been translated into at least 21 languages. This book, along with his two two-volume treatises *Mathematics and Plausible Reasoning* (1954) and *Mathematical Discovery* (1962), form the definitive basis for much of the current thinking in mathematics education and are as timely and important today as when they were written.

**Pólya's Second Principle: Devise a Plan**   Devising a plan for solving a problem once it is fully understood may still require substantial effort. But don't be afraid to make a start—you may be on the right track. There are often many reasonable ways to try to solve a problem, and the

## Apply and Adapt a Variety of Appropriate Strategies to Solve Problems

Of the many descriptions of problem-solving strategies, some of the best known can be found in the work of Pólya (1957). Frequently cited strategies include using diagrams, looking for patterns, listing all possibilities, trying special values or cases, working backward, guessing and checking, creating an equivalent problem, and creating a simpler problem. An obvious question is, How should these strategies be taught? Should they receive explicit attention, and how should they be integrated with the mathematics curriculum? As with any other component of the mathematical tool kit, strategies must receive instructional attention if students are expected to learn them. In the lower grades, teachers can help children express, categorize, and compare their strategies. Opportunities to use strategies must be embedded naturally in the curriculum across the content areas. By the time students reach the middle grades, they should be skilled at recognizing when various strategies are appropriate to use and should be capable of deciding when and how to use them.

SOURCE: *Principles and Standards for School Mathematics* by NCTM, pp 53–54. Copyright © 2000 by the National Council of Teachers of Mathematics. Reproduced with permission of the National Council of Teachers of Mathematics via Copyright Clearance Center. NCTM does not endorse the content or validity of these alignments.

successful idea may emerge only gradually after several unsuccessful trials. A partial list of strategies include the following:

- use algebra
- guess and check
- make an orderly list or table
- think of the problem as partially solved
- eliminate possibilities
- solve an equivalent problem
- use symmetry
- consider special cases (experiment)
- use direct reasoning
- solve an equation
- use the pigeonhole principle
- look for a pattern
- draw a picture
- think of a similar problem already solved
- solve a simpler problem (experiment)
- use a model
- work backward
- use a formula
- be ingenious!

Skill at choosing an appropriate strategy is best learned by solving many problems. As you gain experience, you will find choosing a strategy increasingly easy—and the satisfaction of making the right choice and having it work is considerable! Again, teachers can turn the preceding list of strategies into appropriate questions to ask students in helping them learn the art of problem solving.

### Pólya's Third Principle: Carry Out the Plan   

Carrying out the plan is usually easier than devising the plan. In general, all you need is care and patience, given that you have the necessary skills. If a plan does not work immediately, be persistent. If it still doesn't work, discard it and try a new strategy. Don't be discouraged; this is the way mathematics is done, even by professionals.

### Pólya's Fourth Principle: Look Back   

Much can be gained by looking back at a completed solution to analyze your thinking and ascertain just what the key was to solving the problem. This is how we gain "mathematical power," the ability to come up with good ideas for solving problems never encountered before. In working on a problem, something may be lurking in the back of your mind from a previous effort that says, "I'll bet if . . . ," and the plan does indeed work! This notion of looking back is a part of a "mathematical habit of the mind," as the student will see what else may have happened while solving the problem. (See p. 000 of the preface.)

Questions to ask yourself in looking back after you have successfully solved a problem include the following:

- What was the key factor that allowed me to devise an effective plan for solving this problem?
- Can I think of a simpler strategy for solving the problem?
- Can I think of a more effective or powerful strategy for solving the problem?
- Can I think of *any* alternative strategy for solving the problem?
- Can I think of any other problem or class of problems for which this plan of attack would be effective?

Looking back is an often overlooked, but extremely important, step in developing problem-solving skills.

Let's now look at some examples of problems and some strategies for solving them.

## Guess and Check

> **PROBLEM-SOLVING STRATEGY 1   Guess and Check**
>
> Make a guess and check to see if it satisfies the demands of the problem. If it doesn't, alter the guess appropriately and check again. When the guess finally checks, a solution has been found.

Students often feel that it is not "proper" to solve a problem by guessing. But guessing is like experimenting, giving us insight into what the next guess should be. A process of guessing, checking, altering the guess if it does not check, guessing again in light of the preceding check, and so on is a legitimate and effective strategy. When a guess finally checks, there can be no doubt that a solution has been found. If we can be sure that there is only one solution, then *the* solution has been found. Moreover, the process is often quite efficient and may be the only approach available.

**EXAMPLE 1.3** **Using Guess and Check**

In the first diagram, the numbers in the big circles are found by adding the numbers in the two adjacent smaller circles as shown. Complete the second diagram so that the same pattern holds.

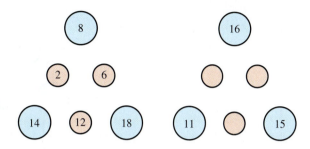

**Solution**

**Understand the Problem**

Considering the example, it is pretty clear that we must find three numbers—$a$, $b$, and $c$—such that

$$a + b = 16,$$
$$a + c = 11, \quad \text{and}$$
$$b + c = 15.$$

How should we proceed?*

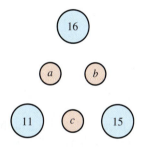

**Devise a Plan**

Let's try the *guess and check* strategy. It worked on several problems somewhat like this one in the last problem set. Also, even if the strategy fails, it may at least suggest an approach that will work.

**Carry Out the Plan**

We start by guessing a value for $a$. Suppose we guess that $a$ is 10. Then, since $a + b$ must be 16, $b$ must be 6. Similarly, since $b + c$ must be 15, $c$ must be 9. But then $a + c$ is 19, instead of 11 as it is supposed to be. This does not check, so we guess again.

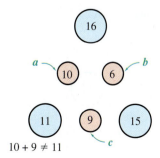

$$10 + 9 \neq 11$$

---

*Students who know algebra could solve this system of simultaneous equations, but elementary school students don't know algebra.

Since 19 is too large, we try again with a smaller guess for *a*. Guess that *a* is 5. Then, *b* is 11 and *c* is 4. But then *a* + *c* is 9, which is too small, but by just a little bit. We should guess that *a* is just a bit larger than 5.

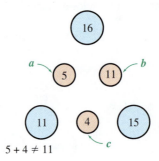

Guess that *a* = 6. This implies that *b* is 10 and *c* is 5. Now *a* + *c* is 11 as desired, and we have the solution.

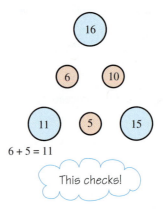

### Look Back

Guess and check worked fine. Our first choice of 10 for *a* was too large, so we chose a smaller value. Our second choice of 5 was too small, but quite close. Choosing *a* = 6, which is between 10 and 5, but quite near 5, we obtained a solution that checked. Each check led us closer to the solution. Surely, this approach would work equally well on other similar problems.

But wait. Have we fully understood this problem? Might there be an easier solution?

Look back at the initial example and at the completed solution to the problem. Do you see any special relationship between the numbers in the large circles and those in the small circles?

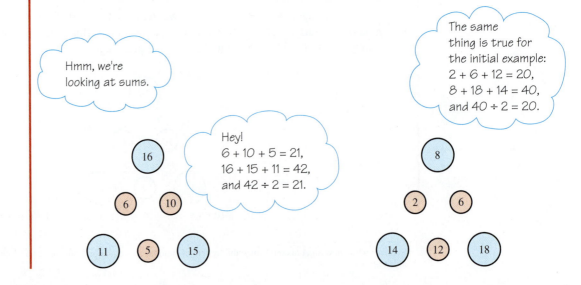

That's interesting; the sum of the numbers in the small circles in each case is just half the sum of the numbers in the large circles. Could we use this strategy to find another solution method?

Sure! Since $16 + 15 + 11 = 42$ and $a + b + c$ is half as much, $a + b + c = 21$. But $a + b = 16$, so $c$ must equal 5; that is,

$$c = 21 - 16 = 5,$$
$$b = 21 - 11 = 10, \quad \text{and}$$
$$a = 21 - 15 = 6.$$

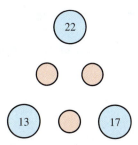

This is much easier than our first solution and, for that matter, the algebraic solution. Quickly now, does it work on this diagram? Try it.

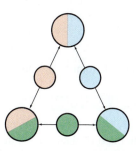

But there's one more thing: Do you understand *why* the sum of the number's in the little circles equals half the sum of the numbers in the big circles? This diagram might help:

## Make an Orderly List

> **PROBLEM-SOLVING STRATEGY 2    Make an Orderly List**
>
> For problems that require a consideration of many possibilities, make an orderly list or a table to ensure that no possibilities are missed.

Sometimes a problem is sufficiently involved that the task of sorting out all the possibilities seems quite forbidding. Often, these problems can be solved by making a carefully structured list so that you can be sure that all of the data and all of the cases have been considered, as in the next example.

**EXAMPLE 1.4**   Making an Orderly List

How many different total scores could you make if you hit the dartboard shown with three darts?

**Solution**

It's often helpful to restate the problem in a different way.

**Understand the Problem**

Three darts hit the dartboard and each scores a 1, 5, or 10. The total score is the sum of the scores for the three darts. There could be three 1s, two 1s and a 5, one 5 and two 10s, and so on. The fact that we are told to find the total score when throwing three darts at a dartboard is just a way of asking what sums can be made by using three numbers, each of which is either 1, 5, or 10.

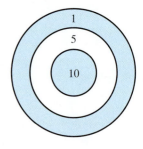

**Devise a Plan**

If we just write down sums hit or miss, we will almost surely overlook some of the possibilities. Using an orderly scheme instead, we can make sure that we obtain all possible scores. Let's make such a list. We first list the score if we have three 1s, then if we have two 1s and one 5, then two 1s and no 5s, and so on. In this way, we can be sure that no score is missed.

**Carry Out the Plan**

| Number of 1s | Number of 5s | Number of 10s | Total Score |
|:---:|:---:|:---:|:---:|
| 3 | 0 | 0 | 3 |
| 2 | 1 | 0 | 7 |
| 2 | 0 | 1 | 12 |
| 1 | 2 | 0 | 11 |
| 1 | 1 | 1 | 16 |
| 1 | 0 | 2 | 21 |
| 0 | 3 | 0 | 15 |
| 0 | 2 | 1 | 20 |
| 0 | 1 | 2 | 25 |
| 0 | 0 | 3 | 30 |

The possible total scores are listed. There are ten different total scores.

**Look Back**

Here, the key to the solution was in being systematic. We were careful first to obtain all possible scores with three 1s, then two 1s, then no 1s. With two 1s, there could be either a 5 or a 10, as shown. For one 1, the only possibilities are two 5s and no 10s, one 5 and one 10, or no 5s and two 10s. Constructing the table in this orderly way makes it clear that we have not missed any possibilities.

## Draw a Diagram

> **PROBLEM-SOLVING STRATEGY 3**   Draw a Diagram
>
> Draw a diagram or picture that represents the data of the problem as accurately as possible.

The aphorism "A picture is worth a thousand words" is certainly applicable to solving many problems. Language used to describe situations and state problems often can be clarified by drawing a suitable diagram, and unforeseen relationships and properties often become clear. As with the problem of the pigs and chickens on Old MacDonald's farm, even problems that do not appear to have pictorial relationships can sometimes be solved with this technique. Would you immediately draw a picture in attempting to solve the problem in the next example? Some would and some wouldn't, but it's surely the most efficient approach.

**EXAMPLE 1.5** **Using a Diagram**

In a stock car race, the first five finishers in some order were a Ford, a Pontiac, a Chevrolet, a Buick, and a Dodge.

**(a)** The Ford finished 7 seconds before the Chevrolet.
**(b)** The Pontiac finished 6 seconds after the Buick.
**(c)** The Dodge finished 8 seconds after the Buick.
**(d)** The Chevrolet finished 2 seconds before the Pontiac.

In what order did the cars finish the race?

**Solution**     **Understand the Problem**

We are told how each of the cars finished the race relative to one other car. The question is, "Can we use just this information to determine the order in which the five cars finished the race?"

**Devise a Plan**

Imagine the cars in a line as they race toward the finish. If they do not pass one another, this is the order in which they will finish the race. We can draw a line to represent the track at the finish of the race and place the cars on it according to the conditions of the problem. We mark the line off in time intervals of one second. Then, using the first letter of each car's name to represent the car, we see if we can line up $B$, $C$, $D$, $F$, and $P$ according to the given information.

**Carry Out the Plan**

In the following line with equally spaced points that represent 1-second time intervals, pick some point and label it $C$ to represent the Chevrolet's finishing position:

Then $F$ is 7 seconds ahead of $C$ by condition (a), as shown. Conditions (b) and (c) cannot yet be used, since they do not relate to the position of either $C$ or $F$. However, (d) allows us to place $P$ 2 seconds behind (to the left of) $C$, as follows:

Since (b) relates the finishing position of $B$ to $P$, we place $B$ 6 seconds ahead of $P$:

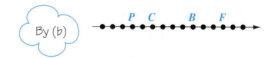

Similarly, (c) relates the finishing positions of $D$ and $B$ and allows us to place $D$ 8 seconds behind (to the left of) $B$. Since this accounts for all the cars, a glance at the following diagram reveals the order in which the cars finished the race:

Note that we repeatedly drew the line for pedagogical purposes in order to show the placement of the cars as each new condition was used. Ordinarily, all the work would be done on a single line, because it is not necessary to show what happens at each stage as we did here.

**Look Back**

Like the problem of the pigs and chickens on Old MacDonald's farm, this problem may not immediately suggest drawing a picture. However, having seen pictures used to solve these problems will help you to see how pictures can be used to solve other, even vaguely related, problems.

## Problem Set 1.2

Exercises numbered in red are answered in the back of the text.

### Understanding Concepts

1. Deirdre is thinking of a number. If you multiply it by 5 and add 13, you get 48. Could Deirdre's number be 10? Why or why not?

2. Lisa is thinking of a number. If you multiply it by 7 and subtract 4, you get 17. What is the number?

3. Vicky is thinking of a number. Twice the number increased by 1 is 5 less than 3 times the number. What is the number? (*Hint:* For each guess, compute two numbers and compare.)

4. In Mrs. Garcia's class, they sometimes play a game called **Guess My Rule.** The student who is It makes up a rule for changing one number into another. The other students then call out numbers, and the person who is It tells what number the rule gives back. The first person in the class to guess the rule then becomes It and gets to make up a new rule.

(a) For Juan's rule, the results were

| Numbers chosen | 2 | 5 | 4 | 0 | 8 |
|---|---|---|---|---|---|
| Numbers Juan gave back | 7 | 22 | 17 | −3 | 37 |

Could Juan's rule have been "Multiply the chosen number by 5 and subtract 3"? Could it have been "Reduce the chosen number by 1, multiply the result by 5, and then add 2"? Are these rules really different? Discuss briefly.

(b) For Mary's rule, the results were

| Numbers chosen | 3 | 7 | 1 | 0 | 9 |
|---|---|---|---|---|---|
| Numbers Mary gave back | 10 | 50 | 2 | 1 | 82 |

What is Mary's rule?

(c) For Peter's rule, the results were

| Numbers chosen | 0 | 1 | 2 | 3 | 4 |
|---|---|---|---|---|---|
| Numbers Peter gave back | 7 | 10 | 13 | 16 | 19 |

Observe that the students began to choose the numbers in order, starting with 0. Why is that a good idea? What is Peter's rule?

5. As in Example 1.3, the numbers in the big circles are the sums of the numbers in the two small adjacent circles. Place numbers in the empty circles in each of these arrays so that the same scheme holds.

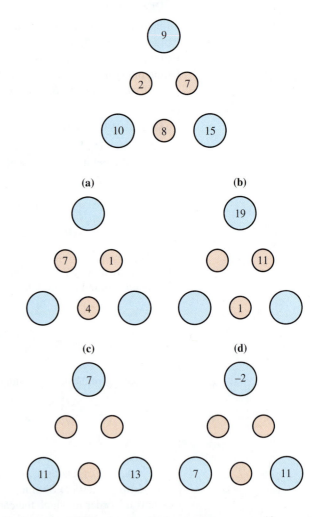

6. How many different amounts of money can you pay if you use four coins including only nickels, dimes, and quarters?

7. How many different ways can you make change for a 50-cent coin by using quarters, nickels, dimes, and pennies?

8. List the three-digit numbers that use each of the digits 2, 5, and 8 once and only once.

9. List the three-digit numbers that use each of 0, 3, and 5 once and only once.

10. When Anita made a purchase, she gave the clerk a dollar and received 21 cents in change. Complete this table to show what Anita's change could have been:

| Number of Dimes | Number of Nickels | Number of Pennies |
|:---:|:---:|:---:|
| 2 | 0 | 1 |

11. Julie has 25 pearls. She put them in three velvet bags, with an odd number of pearls in each bag. What are the possibilities?

12. A rectangle has an area of 120 cm². Its length and width are whole numbers.
    (a) What are the possibilities for the two numbers?
    (b) Which possibility gives the smallest perimeter?

13. The product of two whole numbers is 96 and their sum is less than 30. What are the possibilities for the two numbers?

14. Peter and Jill each worked a different number of days, but earned the same amount of money. Use these clues to determine how many days each worked:

    Peter earned $20 a day.
    Jill earned $30 a day.
    Peter worked 5 more days than Jill.

15. Bob can cut through a log in 1 minute. How long will it take Bob to cut a 20-foot log into 2-foot sections? (*Hint:* Draw a diagram.)

16. How many posts does it take to support a straight fence 200 feet long if a post is placed every 20 feet?

17. How many posts does it take to support a fence around a square field measuring 200 feet on a side if posts are placed every 20 feet?

18. Albright, Badgett, Chalmers, Dawkins, and Ertl all entered the primary to seek election to the city council. Albright received 2000 more votes than Badgett and 4000 fewer than Chalmers. Ertl received 2000 votes fewer than Dawkins and 5000 votes more than Badgett. In what order did each person finish in the balloting?

19. Nine square tiles are laid out on a table so that they make a solid pattern. Each tile must touch at least one other tile along an entire edge. The squares all have sides of length 1.

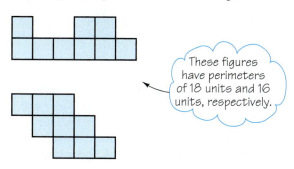

These figures have perimeters of 18 units and 16 units, respectively.

(a) What are the possible perimeters of the figures that can be formed? (The perimeter is the distance around the figure.)
(b) Which figure has the least perimeter?

20. For each of the strategies that follow, write a word problem that would use the method. Show the solution you have in mind.
    (a) Guess and Check
    (b) Make an orderly list
    (c) Draw a diagram

## Teaching Concepts

21. Read one of the following from NCTM's *Principles and Standards for School Mathematics*:
    (a) Problem Solving Standard for Grades Pre-K–2, pages 116–121
    (b) Problem Solving Standard for Grades 3–5, pages 182–187
    (c) Problem Solving Standard for Grades 6–8, pages 256–261

    Write a critique of the standard you read, emphasizing your own reaction. How do the recommendations compare with your own school experience?

## Thinking Cooperatively

22. There is a 2-mile-long traffic jam on the highway. How many cars are in the traffic jam? (*Hint:* This problem is purposefully vague and quite open ended. It has been used successfully with fourth-grade students in Germany.) Discuss in your groups what information is needed to come up with a solution.

## From State Student Assessments

23. (Kentucky, Grade 5) Note this is an open response question.
    Once a week, the students at Park City School get to choose the main dish and side items they will have for lunch. The choices they have this week are shown below.

| Choice of 1 Main Dish | Choice of 2 Side Items |
|:---:|:---:|
| tacos | corn |
| hamburgers | piece of fruit |
| | French fries |

(a) Based on the choices above, what are ALL of the different combinations of one main dish and two side items that are possible? Show your work in an organized list, chart, or table.
(b) Next week, in addition to the choices of one main dish and two side items, the students will have the choice of one dessert—either cake OR ice cream. How many different combinations of one main dish, two side items,

and one dessert will there be? Explain or show how you got your answer.

24. (Washington State, Grade 4)

Four students create their own Good Fitness Games. The students run their fastest and do as many sit-ups and pull-ups as they can. Their results follow. The students want to pick an overall winner. They decide that all the events are equally important. Tell who you think the overall winner is. Explain your thinking using words, numbers, or pictures.

| | 50-Meter Dash | Sit-Ups | 600-Meter Run | Pull-Ups |
|---|---|---|---|---|
| **Sarah** | 10 seconds | 42 | 3 minutes, 15 seconds | 4 |
| **Jan** | 7 seconds | 37 | 3 minutes, 50 seconds | 2 |
| **Angel** | 8 seconds | 38 | 3 minutes, 20 seconds | 6 |
| **Mike** | 9 seconds | 27 | 3 minutes, 30 seconds | 8 |

## 1.3 More Problem-Solving Strategies

### Strategies

- Look for a pattern.
- Make a table.
- Consider special cases.

### Look for a Pattern

> **PROBLEM-SOLVING STRATEGY 4  Look for a Pattern**
>
> Consider an ordered sequence of particular examples of the general situation described in the problem. Then carefully scrutinize these results, looking for a pattern that may be the key to the problem.

It is no overstatement to assert that this strategy is the most important of all problem-solving strategies. In fact, mathematics is often characterized as the study of patterns, and patterns occur in some form in almost all problem-solving situations. Think about the problems we have already considered, and you will see patterns everywhere—numerical patterns, geometrical patterns, counting patterns, listing patterns, rhetorical patterns—patterns of all kinds.

Some problems, like those in the next examples, are plainly pattern problems, but looking for a pattern is rarely a bad way to start solving a problem.

### EXAMPLE 1.6 Looking for Patterns in Numerical Sequences

For each of the following numerical sequences, fill in the next three blanks:

(a) 1, 4, 7, 10, 13, _____, _____, _____
(b) 19, 20, 22, 25, 29, _____, _____, _____
(c) 1, 1, 2, 3, 5, _____, _____, _____
(d) 1, 4, 9, 16, 25, _____, _____, _____

**Solution**

**Understand the Problem**

In each case, we are asked to discover a reasonable pattern suggested by the first five numbers and then to continue the pattern for three more terms.

**Devise a Plan**

Questions we might ask ourselves and answer in search of a pattern include the following: Are the numbers growing steadily larger? steadily smaller? How is each number related to its predecessor? Is it perhaps the case that a particular term depends on its two predecessors? on its three predecessors? Perhaps each term depends in a special way on the number of the term in the sequence; can we notice any such dependence? Are the numbers in the sequence somehow special numbers that

## Highlight from History
### Fibonacci

The most talented mathematician of the Middle Ages was Leonardo of Pisa (ca. 1170–1250), the son of a Pisan merchant named Bonaccio. The Latin *Leonardo Filius Bonaccio* (Leonardo, son of Bonaccio) was soon contracted to Leonardo, Fibonacci. This was further shortened simply to Fibonacci, which is still popularly used today. The young Fibonacci was brought up in Bougie—still an active port in modern Algeria—where his father served for many years as customs manager. It was here and on numerous

trips throughout the Mediterranean region with his father that Fibonacci became acquainted with the Indo–Arabic numerals and the algorithms for computing with them that we still use today. Fibonacci did outstanding original work in geometry and number theory and is best known today for the remarkable sequence

1, 1, 2, 3, 5, 8, 13, 21, 34, 55, 89, . . . ,

which bears his name. However, his most important contribution to Western civilization remains his popularization of the

Indo–Arabic numeration system in his book *Liber Abaci*, written in 1202. This book so effectively illustrated the vast superiority of that system over the other systems then in use that it soon was widely adopted not only in commerce but also in serious mathematical studies. Its use so simplified computational procedures that its effect on the rapid growth of mathematics during the Renaissance and beyond can only be characterized as profound.

we recognize? This is rather like playing *Guess My Rule*. Let's see how successful we can be.* This example also introduces the Fibonacci numbers, which will be used throughout the book.

**Carry Out the Plan**

In each of (a), (b), (c), and (d), the numbers grow steadily larger. How is each term related to the preceding term or terms in each case? Are the terms related to their numbered place in the sequence? Do they have a special form we can recognize?

(a) For the sequence in part (a), each number listed is 3 greater than its predecessor. If this pattern continues, the next three numbers will be 16, 19, and 22.

(b) Here the numbers increase by 1, by 2, by 3, and by 4. If we continue this scheme, the next three numbers will be 5 more, 6 more, and 7 more than their predecessors. This would give 34, 40, and 47.

(c) If we use the ideas of (a) and (b) for this sequence, we should check how much greater each entry is than its predecessor. The numbers that must be added are *0, 1, 1,* and *2*; that is, *0 + 1 = 1, 1 + 1 = 2, 1 + 2 = 3,* and *2 + 3 = 5*. This just amounts to adding any two consecutive terms of the sequence to obtain the next term. Continuing this scheme, we obtain 8, 13, and 21.

The sequence 1, 1, 2, 3, 5, 8, 13, 21, . . . , where we start with 1 and 1 and add any two consecutive terms to obtain the next, is called the **Fibonacci sequence,** and the numbers are called the **Fibonacci numbers.** We denote the Fibonacci numbers by $F_1 = 1, F_2 = 1, F_3 = 2, F_4 = 3, \ldots, F_n = $ the $n$th Fibonacci number, and so on. In particular, observe that

$$F_3 = 2 = 1 + 1 = F_2 + F_1,$$
$$F_4 = 3 = 2 + 1 = F_3 + F_2,$$
$$F_5 = 5 = 3 + 2 = F_4 + F_3,$$

and so on. In general, any particular entry in the sequence is the sum of its two predecessors. The Fibonacci numbers first appeared in A.D. 1202 in the book *Liber Abaci* by Leonardo of Pisa (Fibonacci), the leading mathematician of the thirteenth century.

(d) Here, 4 is 3 larger than 1, 9 is 5 larger than 4, 16 is 7 larger than 9, and 25 is 9 larger than 16. The terms seem to be increasing by the next largest <u>odd</u> number each time. Thus, the

---

*Actually, there is a touchy point here. To be strictly accurate, any three numbers you choose in each case can be considered correct. There are actually infinitely many different rules that will give you any first five numbers followed by any three other numbers. What we seek here are relatively simple rules that apply to the given numbers and tell how to obtain the next three in each case.

next three numbers should probably be $25 + 11 = 36, 36 + 13 = 49$, and $49 + 15 = 64$. Alternatively, in this case we may recognize that the numbers 1, 4, 9, 16, and 25 are special numbers. Thus, $1 = 1^2, 4 = 2^2, 9 = 3^2, 16 = 4^2$, and $25 = 5^2$. The sequence appears to be just the sequence of <u>square numbers</u>. The sixth, seventh, and eighth terms are just $6^2 = 36, 7^2 = 49$, and $8^2 = 64$, as before.

### Look Back

In all four sequences, we checked to see how much larger each number was than its predecessor. In each case, we were able to discover a pattern that allowed us to write the next three terms of the sequence. In part (d), we also noted that the first term was $1^2$, the second term was $2^2$, the third term was $3^2$, and so on. Thus, it was reasonable to guess that each term was the square of the number of its position in the sequence. This allowed us to write the next few terms with the same result as before.

We have already seen in earlier examples how making a table is often an excellent strategy, particularly when combined with the strategy of looking for a pattern. Like drawing a picture or making a diagram, making a table often reveals unexpected patterns and relationships that help to solve a problem.

## Make a Table

> **PROBLEM-SOLVING STRATEGY 5**   Make a Table
>
> Make a table reflecting the data in the problem. If done in an orderly way, such a table may reveal patterns and relationships that suggest how the problem can be solved.

### EXAMPLE 1.7   Applying Make a Table

(a) Draw the next two diagrams to continue this sequence of dots:

• •• ••• •••• _____, _____,

(b) How many dots are in each figure?

_____, _____, _____, _____, _____, _____

(c) How many dots would be in the one-hundredth figure?

(d) How many dots would be in the one-millionth figure?

**Solution**

### Understand the Problem

What is given?

In part (a), we are given an ordered sequence of arrays of dots. We are asked to recognize how the arrays are being formed and to continue the pattern for two more diagrams. In part (b), we are asked to record the number of dots in each array in part (a). In parts (c) and (d), we are asked to determine specific numerical terms in the sequence of part (b).

### Devise a Plan

In part (a), we are asked to continue the pattern of a sequence of arrays of dots. As with numerical sequences, our strategy will be to see how each array relates to its predecessor or predecessors, hoping to discern a pattern that we can extend two more times.

In part (b), we will simply count and record the numbers of dots in the successive arrays in part (a).

In parts (c) and (d), we will study the numerical sequence of part (b) just as we did in Example 1.6, hoping to discern a pattern and understand it sufficiently well that we can determine its one-hundredth and one-millionth terms.

### Carry Out the Plan

In part (a), we observe that the arrays of dots are similar, but that each array has one more two-dot column than its predecessor. Thus, the next two arrays are

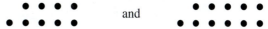

and

For part (b), we count the dots in each array of part (a) to obtain

$$1, 3, 5, 7, 9, 11, \ldots.$$

These are just the odd numbers, and we could write out the first one million odd numbers and so answer parts (c) and (d). But surely there's an easier way.

Let's review how the successive terms were obtained. A table may help.

Reviewing this table carefully, we finally experience an Aha! moment:

| Number of Entry | Entry |
|---|---|
| 1 | $1 = 1$ |
| 2 | $3 = 1 + 2$ |
| 3 | $5 = 1 + 2 + 2 = 1 + 2 \times 2$ |
| 4 | $7 = 1 + 2 + 2 + 2 = 1 + 3 \times 2$ |
| 5 | $9 = 1 + 2 + 2 + 2 + 2 = 1 + 4 \times 2$ |

The *second* term is $1 + 1 \times 2$.    $2 - 1$

The *third* term is $1 + 2 \times 2$.    $3 - 1$

The *fourth* term is $1 + 3 \times 2$.    $4 - 1$

The number of 2s added is one less than the number of the term. Therefore, the one-hundredth term is

$$1 + 99 \times 2 = 199 \qquad 100 - 1$$

and the one-millionth term is

$$1 + (1{,}000{,}000 - 1) \times 2 = 1 + 999{,}999 \times 2 = 1{,}999{,}999.$$

### Look Back

The basic observation was that each diagram could be obtained by adding a column of two dots to its predecessor. Hence, the successive terms in the numerical sequence were obtained by adding 2 to each entry to get the next entry. Using this notion, we examined the successive terms and discovered that any entry could be found by subtracting 1 from the number of the entry, doubling the result, and adding 1. But this last sentence is rather cumbersome, and we have already seen that using *symbols* can make it easier to write mathematical statements. If we use $n$ for the number of the term, the sentence in question can be translated into this mathematical sentence:

$$q_n = (n - 1) \times 2 + 1 = 2n - 2 + 1 = 2n - 1.^*$$

$2n - 1$ is the $n$th odd number.

---

*Symbols like this are often called *variables,* and the formula $q_n = 2n - 1$ is an example of a function. These notions are of considerable importance in mathematics and will be discussed in Chapter 8.

Here $q_n$, read "$q$ sub $n$," is the formula that gives the $n$th entry in the sequence of part (b). All we have to do is replace $n$ by 1, 2, 100, and so on, to find the first entry, the second entry, the one-hundredth entry, and so on. Thus,

$$q_1 = 2 \times 1 - 1 = 1,$$

$$q_2 = 2 \times 2 - 1 = 3,$$

$$q_{100} = 2 \times 100 - 1 = 199,$$

and so on.

## Use a Variable

In the preceding example, and even earlier, we saw how using symbols or **variables** often makes it easier to express mathematical ideas and so to solve problems.

The equation $q_n = 2n - 1$ should remind you of your algebra courses in middle or high school. This equation assigns, to each stage $n$ in the process, a number given by $q_n = 2n - 1$, in other words, the $n$th odd number. If we prefer, we can go in the other direction; that is, if we are given an odd number $q_n$, we can tell what the stage (the value for $n$) is for the odd number.

Sometimes we want to use a variable in representing the general term in a sequence. Thus, as we saw in Example 1.7, $2n - 1$ is the $n$th odd number. In the expression $2n - 1$, $n$ is the variable and it can be replaced by any natural number. For example, if we want to know which odd number 85 is, we need to determine $n$ such that

$$2n - 1 = 85.$$

This implies that $2n = 86$, so $n = 43$. Hence, 85 is the 43rd odd number.*

## Consider Special Cases

> **PROBLEM-SOLVING STRATEGY 6**   **Consider Special Cases**
>
> In trying to solve a complex problem, consider a sequence of special cases. This will often show how to proceed naturally from case to case until one arrives at the case in question. Alternatively, the special cases may reveal a pattern that makes it possible to solve the problem.

## Pascal's Triangle

One of the most interesting and useful patterns in all of mathematics is the numerical array called "Pascal's triangle."

Consider the problem of finding how many different paths there are from $A$ to $P$ on the grid shown in Figure 1.1 if you can only move *down* along edges in the grid. If we start to trace out paths without care, our chances of finding all possibilities are not good.

**FIGURE 1.1**
A path from $A$ to $P$

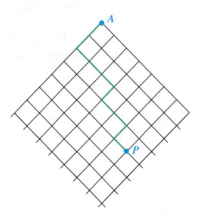

---

*These notions will be discussed in greater detail in the next section and in Chapter 8.

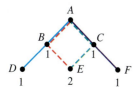

**FIGURE 1.2**

Solving an easier similar
problem

A strategy that is often helpful is to **solve an easier, similar problem** (special cases). It would certainly be easier if *P* were not so far down in the grid. Consider the easier, similar problem of finding the number of paths from *A* to *E* in Figure 1.2. This process begins our **experimenting** with this problem.

Or consider solving a similar *set* of easier problems all at once. How many different paths are there from *A* to each of *B*, *C*, *D*, *E*, and *F*? (Note that this is an example of considering a series of special cases.) Clearly, there is only one way to go from *A* to each of *B* and *C*, and we indicate this fact by the 1s under *B* and *C* in Figure 1.2. Also, the only route to *D* is through *B*, so there is only one path from *A* to *D*, as indicated. For the same reason, there is one path from *A* to *F*. By contrast, there are two ways to go from *A* to *E*—one route through *B* and one through *C*. We indicate this fact by placing a 2 under *E* on the diagram. This approach certainly doesn't solve the original problem, but it gives us a start and even suggests how we might proceed. Consider the diagram in Figure 1.3.

**FIGURE 1.3**

The number of paths from
*A* to *P*

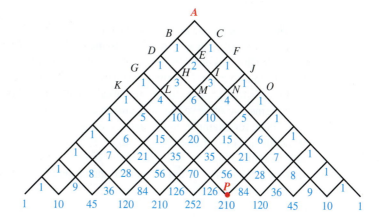

Having determined the number of paths from *A* to each of *B*, *C*, *D*, *E*, and *F*, could we perhaps determine the number of paths to *G*, *H*, *I*, and *J* and then continue on down the grid to eventually solve the original problem?

1. Always moving downward, we see that the only way to get to *G* from *A* is via *D*. But there is only one path to *D* and only one path from *D* to *G*. Thus, there is only one path from *A* to *G*, and we enter a 1 under *G* on the diagram, as shown.

2. The only way to get to *H* from *A* is via *D* or *E*. Since there is only one path from *A* to *D* and one from *D* to *H*, there is only one path from *A* to *H* via *D*. However, since there are two paths from *A* to *E* and one path from *E* to *H*, there are two paths from *A* to *H* via *E*. The number of paths from *A* to *H* is the number via *D* plus the number via *E*—that is, 1 + 2 = 3 paths—and we enter 3 under *H* on the diagram as shown.

3. The arguments for *I* and *J* are the same as for *H* and *G*, so we enter 3 and 1 under *I* and *J*, respectively, on the diagram.

4. The first three steps reveal a very nice pattern that enables us to solve the original problem with ease. There can be only one path to any edge vertex on the grid, since we have to go straight down the edge to get to such a vertex. For any interior point on the grid, however, we can always reach that point by paths through the points immediately above and to the left and right of such a point. Since there is only one path from each of these points to the point in question, the total number of paths to this point is the *sum* of the number of paths to these preceding two points. Thus, we easily generate the number of paths from *A* to any given point in the grid by simple addition. In particular, there are 210 different paths from *A* to *P*, as we initially set out to determine.

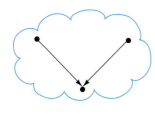

Without the grid and with an additional 1 at the top to complete a triangle, the number array in Figure 1.4 is called **Pascal's triangle** and comes up frequently in mathematics and this text. It also provides elementary school students with ways to experiment with numbers.

**FIGURE 1.4**
Pascal's triangle

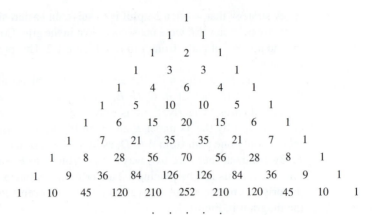

```
                              1
                           1     1
                        1     2     1
                     1     3     3     1
                  1     4     6     4     1
               1     5    10    10     5     1
            1     6    15    20    15     6     1
         1     7    21    35    35    21     7     1
      1     8    28    56    70    56    28     8     1
   1     9    36    84   126   126    84    36     9     1
1    10    45   120   210   252   210   120    45    10     1
              .     .     .     .     .
```

The array is named after the French mathematician Blaise Pascal (1623–1662), who showed that these numbers play an important role in the theory of probability. However, the triangle was certainly known in China as early as the twelfth century. An interesting and clear depiction of the famous triangle from a fourteenth-century manuscript is shown in Figure 1.5.

Pascal's triangle is rich with remarkable patterns and is also extremely useful. Before discussing the patterns, we observe that it is customary to call the single 1 at the top of the triangle the zeroth row (since, for example, in the path-counting problem just discussed, this 1 would represent a path of length 0). For consistency, we will also call the initial 1 in any row the zeroth element in the row, and the initial diagonal of 1s the zeroth diagonal. (See Figure 1.6.) Thus, 1 is the zeroth element in the fourth row, 4 is the first element, 6 the second element, and so on.

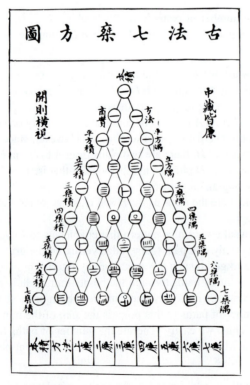

**FIGURE 1.5**
Pascal's triangle from Chu Shih-Chieh's *Ssu Yuan Yii Chien*, A.D. 1303

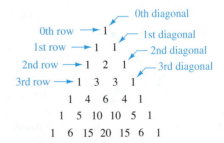

**FIGURE 1.6**
Numbered rows and diagonals in Pascal's triangle

**EXAMPLE 1.8** **Finding a Pattern in the Row Sums of Pascal's Triangle**

*Consider special cases.* *Look for a pattern.*

(a) Compute the sum of the elements in each of rows zero through four of Pascal's triangle.
(b) Look for a pattern in the results of part (a) and guess a general rule.
(c) Use Figure 1.4 to check your guess for rows five through eight.
(d) Give a convincing argument that your guess in part (b) is correct.

**Solution**

### Understand the Problem

In part (a), we must add the elements in the indicated rows. In part (b), we are asked to discover a pattern in the numbers generated in part (a). In part (c), we must compute the sums for four more rows and see if the results obtained continue the pattern guessed in part (b). In part (d), we are asked to argue convincingly that our guess in part (b) is correct.

### Devise a Plan

Part (a) is certainly straightforward: We must compute the desired sums. To find the pattern requested in part (b), we should ask the question "Have we ever seen a similar problem before?" The answer, of course, is a resounding "yes": All the problems in this section, but particularly Example 1.6, have involved looking for patterns. Surely, the techniques that succeeded earlier should be tried here. Appropriate questions to ask and answer include the following: "How are the successive numbers related to their predecessors?" "Are the numbers special numbers that we can easily recognize?" "Can we relate the successive numbers to their numbered locations in the sequence of numbers being generated?" Answering these questions should help us make the desired guess. As you start to ask the questions of yourselves or other students, you are developing a mathematical habit of the mind (MHM).

**MHM**

For part (c), we will compute the sums of the elements in rows five through eight to see if these numbers agree with our guess in part (b). If they *don't* agree, we will go back and modify our guess. If they *do* agree, we will proceed to part (d) and try to make a convincing argument that our guess is correct. About all we have to go on is the fact that the initial and terminal elements in each row are 1s and that the sum of any two consecutive elements in a row is the element between these two elements but in the next row down.

### Carry Out the Plan

(a) $1 = 1$
$1 + 1 = 2$
$1 + 2 + 1 = 4$
$1 + 3 + 3 + 1 = 8$
$1 + 4 + 6 + 4 + 1 = 16$

(b) It appears that each number in part (a) is just twice its predecessor. The numbers are

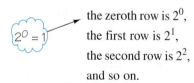

$$1, \quad 2 \cdot 1 = 2^1, \quad 2 \cdot 2 = 2^2, \quad 2 \cdot 2^2 = 2^3, \quad 2 \cdot 2^3 = 2^4.$$

It appears that the sum of the elements in

$2^0 = 1$ → the zeroth row is $2^0$,
the first row is $2^1$,
the second row is $2^2$,
and so on.

Our guess is that the sum of the elements in the *n*th row is $2^n$.

(c) Computing these sums for the next four rows, we have

| | |
|---|---|
| fifth row | $1 + 5 + 10 + 10 + 5 + 1 = \ 32 = 2^5$ |
| sixth row | $1 + 6 + 15 + 20 + 15 + 6 + 1 = \ 64 = 2^6$ |

seventh row          $1 + 7 + 21 + 35 + 35 + 21 + 7 + 1 = 128 = 2^7$

eighth row      $1 + 8 + 28 + 56 + 70 + 56 + 28 + 8 + 1 = 256 = 2^8$

Since these results do not contradict our guess, we proceed to try to make a convincing argument that our guess is correct.

**(d)** What happens as we go from one row to the next? How is the next row obtained? Consider the third and fourth rows, shown in the diagram that follows. The arrows show how the fourth row is obtained from the third, and we see that each of 1, 3, 3, and 1 in the third row appears *twice* in the sum of the elements in the fourth row. Since this argument would hold for any two consecutive rows, the sum of the numbers in any row is just twice the sum of the numbers in the preceding row. Hence, from above, the sum of the numbers in the ninth row must be $2 \times 2^8 = 2^9$, in the tenth row it must be $2 \cdot 2^9 = 2^{10}$, and so on. Thus, the result is true in general, as claimed.

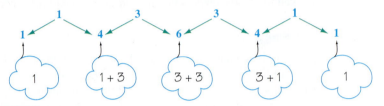

**Look Back**

Several aspects of our solution merit special comment. Beginning with the strategies of considering special cases and looking for a pattern, we were led to guess that the sum of the elements in the $n$th row of the triangle is $2^n$. In an attempt to argue that this guess was correct, we considered the special case of obtaining the fourth row from the third. This showed that the sum of the elements in the fourth row was twice the sum of the elements in the third row. *Since the argument did not depend on the actual numbers that appeared in the third and fourth rows, but only on the general rule of formation of the triangle,* it would hold for any two consecutive rows and so actually proves that our conjecture is correct. This type of argument is called **arguing from a special case** and is an important problem-solving strategy.

## Problem Set 1.3

Exercises numbered in red are answered in the back of the text.

### Understanding Concepts

**1.** Look for a pattern and fill in the next three blanks with the most likely choices for each sequence:

  **(a)** 2, 5, 8, 11, _____ _____ _____

  **(b)** $-5, -3, -1, 1,$ _____ _____ _____

  **(c)** 1, 1, 3, 3, 6, 6, 10, _____ _____ _____

  **(d)** 1, 3, 4, 7, 11, _____ _____ _____

  **(e)** 2, 6, 18, 54, _____ _____ _____

**2. (a)** Fill in the blanks to continue this dot sequence in the most likely way:

$\bullet, \ \bullet \ \bullet, \ \bullet \ \bullet \ \bullet, \ \bullet \ \bullet \ \bullet \ \bullet, \ \underline{\quad}, \ \underline{\quad}$

  **(b)** What number sequence corresponds to the sequence of dot patterns of part (a)?

  **(c)** What is the tenth term in the sequence of part (b)? the one-hundredth term?

  **(d)** Which term in the sequence is 101? (*Hint:* How many 3s must be added to 2 to get 101?)

**3.** Sequences like $2, 5, 8, \ldots$, where each term is greater (or less) than its predecessor by a constant amount, are called **arithmetic** (a-rith-met′-ic) **progressions.** Find the number of terms in each of these arithmetic progressions:

  **(a)** $5, 7, 9, \ldots, 35$

  **(b)** $-4, 1, 6, \ldots, 46$

  **(c)** $3, 7, 11, \ldots, 67$

**4.** Consider the sequence $8, 5, 2, -1, \ldots, -52$.

  **(a)** Is the sequence an arithmetic progression? Why or why not?

  **(b)** How many terms are there in the sequence?

**5. (a)** Fill in the blanks to continue this sequence of equations:

$$1 = 1$$
$$1 + 2 + 1 = 4$$
$$1 + 2 + 3 + 2 + 1 = 9$$
$$1 + 2 + 3 + 4 + 3 + 2 + 1 = 16$$
$$\underline{\hspace{3cm}} = \underline{\hspace{2cm}}$$
$$\underline{\hspace{3cm}} = \underline{\hspace{2cm}}$$

**(b)** Compute this sum:

$$1 + 2 + 3 + \cdots + 99 + 100 + 99$$
$$+ \cdots + 3 + 2 + 1 = \underline{\hspace{2cm}}$$

**(c)** Fill in the blank to complete this equation:

$$1 + 2 + 3 + \cdots + (n - 1)$$
$$+ n + (n - 1) + \cdots + 3$$
$$+ 2 + 1 = \underline{\hspace{2cm}}$$

**6. (a)** Fill in the blanks to continue this sequence of equations:

$$1 = 0 + 1$$
$$1 + 3 + 1 = 1 + 4$$
$$1 + 3 + 5 + 3 + 1 = 4 + 9$$
$$\underline{\hspace{2cm}} = \underline{\hspace{2cm}}$$
$$\underline{\hspace{2cm}} = \underline{\hspace{2cm}}$$

**(b)** What expression, suggested by part (a), should be placed in the blank to complete this equation?

$$1 + 3 + 5 + \cdots + (2n - 3) + (2n - 1)$$
$$+ (2n - 3) + \cdots + 5 + 3 + 1 = \underline{\hspace{2cm}}$$

(*Hint:* The number preceding $n$ is $n - 1$.)

**7.** Writers of standardized tests often pose questions like "What is the next term in the sequence $2, 4, 8, \ldots$?"

**(a)** How would you answer this question?

**(b)** Evaluate the expressions $2^n$, $n^2 - n + 2$, and $n^3 - 5n^2 + 10n - 4$ in the following chart by replacing $n$ successively by 1, 2, 3, and 4:

| $n$ | **1** | **2** | **3** | **4** |
|---|---|---|---|---|
| $2^n$ | | | | |
| $n^2 - n + 2$ | | | | |
| $n^3 - 5n^2 + 10n - 4$ | | | | |

**(c)** In light of the results in (b), what criticism would you make of the test writer who would write a test question like that above? Compare the wording above with that in problem 1 of this problem set.

**8.** Here is the start of a 100 chart:

| 1 | 2 | 3 | 4 | 5 | 6 | 7 | 8 | 9 | 10 |
|---|---|---|---|---|---|---|---|---|---|
| 11 | 12 | 13 | 14 | 15 | 16 | 17 | 18 | 19 | 20 |
| 21 | 22 | 23 | 24 | 25 | 26 | 27 | 28 | 29 | 30 |

Shown next are parts of the chart. Without extending the chart, determine which numbers should go in the lavender squares.

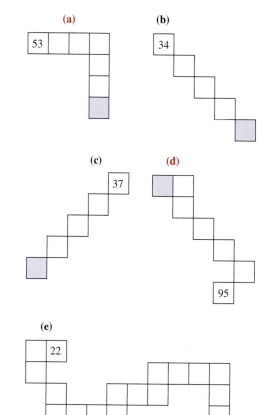

**9.** Five blue (B) and five red (R) discs are lined up in the arrangement B B B B B R R R R R:

Switching just two adjacent discs at a time, what is the least number of moves you can make to achieve the arrangement B R B R B R B R B R shown here?

(*Hint:* How many moves are required to rearrange B B R R to B R B R? B B B R R R to B B R B R R? and so on.)

**10 (a)** Complete the next two of this sequence of equations:

$$1 = 1$$
$$1 - 4 = -3$$
$$1 - 4 + 9 = 6$$
$$1 - 4 + 9 - 16 = -10$$
$$\underline{\hspace{2cm}} = \underline{\hspace{2cm}}$$
$$\underline{\hspace{2cm}} = \underline{\hspace{2cm}}$$

**(b)** Write the seventh and eighth equations in the sequence of equations of part (a).

**(c)** Write general equations suggested by parts (a) and (b) for even $n$ and for odd $n$, where $n$ is the number of the equation.

**11. (a)** How many rectangles are there in each of these figures? (*Note:* Rectangles may measure 1 by 1, 1 by 2, 1 by 3, and so on.)

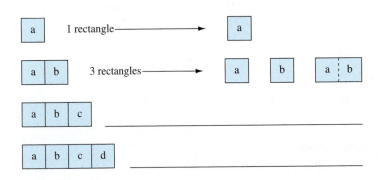

**(b)** How many rectangles are in this figure? _____

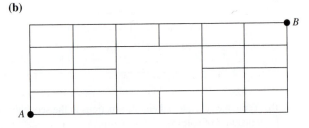

**(c)** How many rectangles are in a $1 \times n$ strip like that in part (b)?

**(d)** Argue carefully and lucidly that your guess in part (c) is correct. (*Hint:* How many of each type of rectangle begin with each small square?)

---

**12.** If one must always move downward along the lines of the grid shown, how many different paths are there from point $A$ to each of these points?

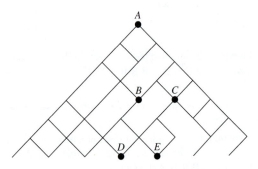

**13.** If one must always move upward or to the right on each of the grids shown, how many paths are there from $A$ to $B$?

**(a)**

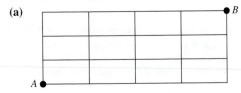

**(b)**

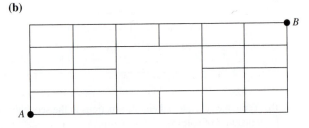

**14.** If one must follow along the paths of the following diagram in the direction of the arrows, how many paths are there from $C$ to $E$?

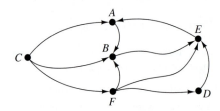

**15.** How many chords are determined by joining dots on a circle if there are

**(a)** 4 dots?     **(b)** 10 dots?

**(c)** 100 dots?     **(d)** $n$ dots?

**(e)** Argue that your solution to part (d) is correct.

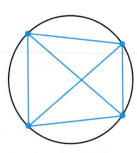

**16. (a)** How many games are played in a round-robin tournament with 10 teams if every team plays every other team once?

**(b)** How many games are played if there are 11 teams?

**(c)** Is this problem related to problem 15 of this problem set? If so, how?

**17.** Here is an addition table:

| + | 0 | 1 | 2 | 3 | 4 | 5 | 6 | 7 | 8 | 9 |
|---|---|---|---|---|---|---|---|---|---|---|
| 0 | 0 | 1 | 2 | 3 | 4 | 5 | 6 | 7 | 8 | 9 |
| 1 | 1 | 2 | 3 | 4 | 5 | 6 | 7 | 8 | 9 | 10 |
| 2 | 2 | 3 | 4 | 5 | 6 | 7 | 8 | 9 | 10 | 11 |
| 3 | 3 | 4 | 5 | 6 | 7 | 8 | 9 | 10 | 11 | 12 |
| 4 | 4 | 5 | 6 | 7 | 8 | 9 | 10 | 11 | 12 | 13 |
| 5 | 5 | 6 | 7 | 8 | 9 | 10 | 11 | 12 | 13 | 14 |
| 6 | 6 | 7 | 8 | 9 | 10 | 11 | 12 | 13 | 14 | 15 |
| 7 | 7 | 8 | 9 | 10 | 11 | 12 | 13 | 14 | 15 | 16 |
| 8 | 8 | 9 | 10 | 11 | 12 | 13 | 14 | 15 | 16 | 17 |
| 9 | 9 | 10 | 11 | 12 | 13 | 14 | 15 | 16 | 17 | 18 |

**(a)** Find the sum of the entries in these squares of entries from the addition table:

| 2 | 3 |
|---|---|
| 3 | 4 |

| 5 | 6 |
|---|---|
| 6 | 7 |

| 11 | 12 |
|----|----|
| 12 | 13 |

| 15 | 16 |
|----|----|
| 16 | 17 |

Look for a pattern and write a clear and simple rule for finding such sums almost at a glance.

**(b)** Find the sum of the entries in these squares of entries from the table:

| 4 | 5 | 6 |
|---|---|---|
| 5 | 6 | 7 |
| 6 | 7 | 8 |

| 10 | 11 | 12 |
|----|----|----|
| 11 | 12 | 13 |
| 12 | 13 | 14 |

| 14 | 15 | 16 |
|----|----|----|
| 15 | 16 | 17 |
| 16 | 17 | 18 |

**(c)** Write a clear and simple rule for computing these sums.

**(d)** Write a clear and simple rule for computing the sum of the
**MHM** entries in any square of entries from the addition table.

**18.** Write a problem whose solution involves
  **(a)** looking for a pattern.
  **(b)** making up a table.

**19. (a)** Compute the square root of the product of the six elements surrounding an element in Pascal's triangle. In  particular, do this for the six entries surrounding each of 4, 15, and 35.

  **(b)** Does the limited amount of data from part (a) suggest a general conjecture? What appears to be true in general?

**20.** (Read carefully before responding) How much dirt is there in a hole 10 meters long, 5 meters wide, and 3 meters deep?

**21.** (Read carefully before responding) If pencils are 5 cents each, how many are there in a dozen?

**22.** (Read carefully before responding) Joni has two U.S. coins in her pocket. One of the coins is not a quarter. If the total value of the coins is 26 cents, what are the two coins?

## From State Student Assessments

**23.** (Washington State, Grade 4)
Look at the following list of numbers. Describe two different patterns you see in these numbers.

$$9 \quad 18 \quad 27 \quad 36 \quad 45 \quad 54 \quad 63 \quad 72 \quad 81 \quad 90$$

**24.** (Michigan, Grade 4)
Justin created the following number pattern:

$$0, 1, 4, 13, 40, \underline{\quad\quad}.$$

What is the rule to find the next number in the pattern?
  A. Add 1 to the last number.
  B. Add 9 to the last number.
  C. Triple the last number and add 1.
  D. Double the last number and add 3.

## 1.4

# Algebra as a Problem-Solving Strategy

**Strategies**
- Use a variable.
- Use two variables.

## Use a Variable

In Example 1.7, we saw a use of the language of algebra when we wrote the solution of the example as $q_n = 2n - 1$. But algebra is more—much more—than just a language. Algebra can also solve problems that look very hard or appear to be a mathematical trick. In fact, we believe in **algebra as a great explainer** in much of mathematics at all levels because it clarifies so much. Algebra is now appearing informally in elementary school and is used by students in grade 7 or even earlier.

In this section, we shall explore the algebra-based problem-solving strategy "Use a variable," in which we first use a variable name for what we are looking at and then do some algebra to solve the problem. Using symbols or **variables** often makes it easier to express mathematical ideas and so to solve problems with the algebra that you already know from school. In Chapter 8, we'll describe, in detail, algebra as it is needed for teaching in elementary or middle school but because the use of algebra is so pervasive and so much a part of problem solving, we introduce algebra as the great facilitator early and continue it as a thread in the book.

> **DEFINITION** *Variable*
> A **variable** is a symbol (usually a letter) that can represent any of the numbers in some set of numbers.

### EXAMPLE 1.9 Using A Variable—Gauss' Insight

Carl Gauss (1777–1855) is generally acknowledged as one of the greatest mathematicians of all time. When Gauss was just 10 years old, the teacher instructed the students in his class to add all the numbers from 1 to 100, expecting this to take a long time. To the teacher's surprise, young Gauss completed the task very quickly.

**Solution**

Gauss' strategy was to use a variable, and his insight was that numbers can be added in any order! If

$$s = 1 + 2 + 3 + \cdots + 100,$$

then, also,

$$s = 100 + 99 + 98 + \cdots + 1.$$

> $1 + 100 = 101$
> $2 + 99 = 101$
> $3 + 98 = 101$
> $\vdots$
> $100 + 1 = 101$

Therefore, adding these two expressions for $s$, we obtain

$$2s = 101 + 101 + 101 + \cdots + 101,$$

$$2s = 100 \times 101,$$

> a sum with 100 terms

and

$$s = \frac{100 \times 101}{2} = 5050.$$

The key in this example is to define a variable in such a way that we can finish the problem by using an algebraic insight (like Gauss') or by recognizing the equation as one that we already know how to solve.

## Highlight from History

### Carl Friedrich Gauss (1777–1855)

Carl Friedrich Gauss was born of poor parents in Braunschweig, Germany, in 1777 and was both a child prodigy (see "Example 1.9, Using a Variable—Gauss' Insight") and an incredibly productive mathematician. Gauss contributed an enormous amount of new mathematics that not only solved a number of already existing problems, but also opened many fresh paths of research into a variety of aspects of both applied and theoretical mathematics. He did seminal work in number theory (about how fast the number of primes grows), statistics (method of least squares, the Gaussian, or bell, curve),

and non-Euclidean geometry, all before he was 17. He also produced groundbreaking research in establishing complex numbers, proved (when he was 20) that every polynomial of degree $n$ can be solved and has $n$ roots (called the "fundamental theorem of algebra") and gave three other proofs of this theorem later in his life, and made substantive contributions to astronomy and physics, the geometry of curved surfaces, and the theory of functions. At the age of 63, he decided to learn Russian and spoke and read it well, although not fluently. His depth and reach across mathematics is truly amazing.

> **PROBLEM-SOLVING STRATEGY 7   Use a Variable**
>
> Often, a problem requires that a number be determined. Represent the number by a variable, and use the conditions of the problem to set up an equation that can be solved to ascertain the desired number.

## EXAMPLE 1.10  Using a Variable to Determine a General Formula

Look at these corresponding geometrical and numerical sequences:

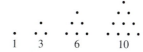

For fairly obvious reasons, the numbers 1, 3, 6, and 10 are called **triangular numbers.** (The diagram with a single dot is considered a *degenerate triangle*.) The numbers 1, 3, 6, and 10 are the first four triangular numbers. Find a formula for the *n*th triangular number.

**Solution**

### Understand the Problem

Having just gone through a similar problem in Example 1.7, we understand that we are to find a formula for $t_n$, the *n*th triangular number.

### Devise a Plan

The geometrical and numerical sequences in the statement of the problem suggest that we look for a pattern. How is each diagram related to its predecessor? How is each triangular number related to its predecessor? We'll try to guess patterns.

### Carry Out the Plan

We add a diagonal of two dots to the first diagram to obtain the second, a diagonal of three dots to the second diagram to obtain the third, and so on. Thus, the next two diagrams should be as shown here (we can think of this process as experimenting):

Numerically, we add 2 to the first triangular number to obtain the second, 3 to the second triangular number to obtain the third, and so on. To make this rule even more clear, we can construct the following table:

| Number of Entry | Entry |
|:---:|:---|
| 1 | $t_1 = 1$ |
| 2 | $t_2 = 1 + 2 = 3$ |
| 3 | $t_3 = 1 + 2 + 3 = 6$ |
| 4 | $t_4 = 1 + 2 + 3 + 4 = 10$ |
| 5 | $t_5 = 1 + 2 + 3 + 4 + 5 = 15$ |

Indeed, it appears that

$$t_n = 1 + 2 + 3 + \cdots + n.$$

Then, using Gauss' insight, we obtain

$$t_n = n + (n - 1) + (n - 2) + \cdots + 1.$$

So,

$$2t_n = (n + 1) + (n + 1) + (n + 1) + \cdots + (n + 1)$$
$$= n(n + 1)$$

and

$$t_n = \frac{n(n + 1)}{2},$$

as required.

$$1 + n = n + 1$$
$$2 + (n - 1) = n + 1$$
$$3 + (n - 2) = n + 1$$
$$\vdots$$
$$n + 1 = n + 1$$

*A sum with n terms*

### Look Back

Looking back, we note that the key to our solution lay in considering the sequence of special cases $t_1, t_2, t_3, t_4$, and $t_5$ and in looking for a pattern. This approach is an example of Problem-Solving Strategy 6, considering special cases or experimenting.

It is helpful to view algebraic thinking for problem solving as a circle of connected ideas, beginning and ending with the pattern or problem that is being investigated. The essential steps are shown in Figure 1.7 and are developed in more detail throughout the remainder of this section. The figure gives an overview of MHM.

**FIGURE 1.7**
The steps in algebraic reasoning

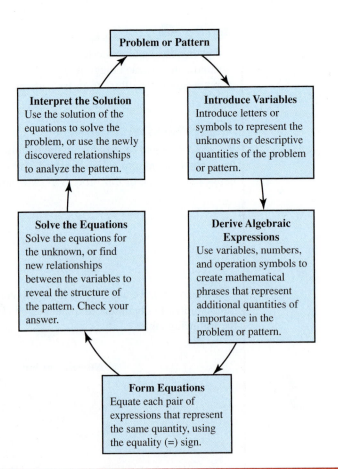

**Problem or Pattern**

**Interpret the Solution**
Use the solution of the equations to solve the problem, or use the newly discovered relationships to analyze the pattern.

**Introduce Variables**
Introduce letters or symbols to represent the unknowns or descriptive quantities of the problem or pattern.

**Solve the Equations**
Solve the equations for the unknown, or find new relationships between the variables to reveal the structure of the pattern. Check your answer.

**Derive Algebraic Expressions**
Use variables, numbers, and operation symbols to create mathematical phrases that represent additional quantities of importance in the problem or pattern.

**Form Equations**
Equate each pair of expressions that represent the same quantity, using the equality (=) sign.

**EXAMPLE 1.11  Forming, Checking, and Evaluating Algebraic Expressions**

Toothpicks can be used to form "cross" patterns, such as the three shown that follow. Additional crosses are formed by following the same pattern of construction. What is the number of squares in the $n$th cross? How many toothpicks are required to construct the $n$th cross?

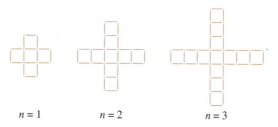

$n = 1$          $n = 2$          $n = 3$

**Solution**

**Understand the Problem**

We seek two expressions that each involve the variable $n$. One is to give the number of squares in the $n$th cross, and the other expression must give the number of toothpicks required to form the pattern. We see that $n$ also gives the number of squares in each of the four "arms" of the cross.

**Devise a Plan**

Each new pattern is created by adding a new square to each of the four arms of the preceding pattern. That is, the number of squares is increased by four in each new pattern. This strategy suggests that we look for an expression of the form $a + 4n$, where we will need to determine the value of the constant $a$. Similarly, adding one square to an arm of the cross requires three additional toothpicks, so adding a square to each of the four arms requires 12 additional toothpicks. This pattern suggests that we look for an expression of the form $b + 12n$ to give the number of toothpicks in the $n$th cross, where the constant $b$ will need to be determined.

**Carry Out the Plan**

In the first cross pattern, $n = 1$. Evaluating $a + 4n$ at $n = 1$ gives $a + 4$, and since there are 5 squares in the pattern, we get the equation $a + 4 = 5$. That is, $a = 1$ and the number of squares in the $n$th cross is given by $1 + 4n$. The constant $b$ in the expression $b + 12n$ can be determined similarly: There are 16 toothpicks in the $n = 1$ pattern, so we must have $b + 12 = 16$. That is, $b = 4$ and the number of toothpicks in the $n$th pattern is given by the expression $4 + 12n$.

**Look Back**

The plan that has been followed will apply to any sequence in which each new term is a fixed number larger than the preceding term. That is, we have an arithmetic sequence. For example, to find an expression that gives the $n$th term of the sequence $3, 9, 15, 21, \ldots$, we would look for an expression of the form $c + 6n$, since 6 is the common difference of the sequence. Choosing $n = 1$, we note that the constant $c$ must satisfy the condition $c + 6 = 3$. That is, $c = 3 - 6 = -3$. Thus, the $n$th term is given by the expression $6n - 3$.

**EXAMPLE 1.12  Setting Up and Solving an Equation: Can I Get a C?**

Larry has exam scores of 59, 77, 48, and 67. What score does he need on the next exam to bring his average for all five of the exams to 70?

**Solution**

Let the variable $s$ denote Larry's minimum needed score on the fifth exam. The domain of $s$ is the set of numbers between 0 and 100. Using the variable $s$, we find that the expression giving Larry's average over all five tests is the sum of his scores divided by 5, or

$$\frac{59 + 77 + 48 + 67 + s}{5}.$$

Since Larry is looking for the lowest score *s* that will give him a 70 average, we form the equation

$$\frac{59 + 77 + 48 + 67 + s}{5} = 70.$$

To solve this equation, we multiply each side of the equation by 5 and add the sum of the first four test scores to get

$$251 + s = 350.$$

Finally, we subtract 251 from both sides of the equation to solve for *s*:

$$s = 350 - 251 = 99.$$

Larry must hope for a 99 or 100 on the last test. It is easy to check that our solution is correct by taking the average of 59, 77, 48, 67, and 99.

This section concludes with two more examples that illustrate the steps in algebraic reasoning shown in Figure 1.7.

## EXAMPLE 1.13  Solving a Rate Problem: Tom and Huck Whitewash a Fence

Two years ago, it took Tom 8 hours to whitewash a fence. Last year, Huck took just 6 hours to whitewash the fence. This year, Tom and Huck have decided to work together so that they'll have time left in the afternoon to angle for catfish. How long will the job take the two boys?

**Solution**  Let $T$ denote the time, in hours, that Tom and Huck together need to whitewash the fence. That is, $T$ is the unknown. Since Tom can whitewash the fence in 8 hours, he can whitewash $\frac{1}{8}$ of the fence per hour.

In $T$ hours, Tom will have whitewashed $\frac{T}{8}$ of the fence. Similarly, Huck whitewashes $\frac{1}{6}$ of the fence per hour, and he therefore can whitewash $\frac{T}{6}$ of the fence in $T$ hours. Working together, the boys will whitewash the entire fence when

$$\frac{T}{8} + \frac{T}{6} = 1.$$

Multiplying both sides by 48 gives the equivalent equation

$$6T + 8T = 48.$$

That is, $14T = 48$, so $T = \frac{48}{14} = 3\frac{3}{7}$. Thus, working together, Tom and Huck can whitewash the fence in just less than three and a half hours and will enjoy an afternoon of fishing.

Many people who don't take time to think in depth about the Tom and Huck problem will answer 7 hours (because the average of 6 and 8 is 7). The "check your answer" part of our "Steps in Algebraic Reasoning" (Figure 1.7) shows that 7 hours can't be correct. After all, for Tom and Huck to take 7 hours means that it would take them longer together then it would if Huck did it himself!

## Use Two Variables

There are many math tricks, puzzles, and jokes that circulate around the Internet. They often look quite mysterious and give the impression of magic. In fact, many can be understood with Pólya's problem-solving principles, and a number involve the use of algebra. Looking at math problems through the lens of algebra (**"algebra as the great explainer"**) can take the mystery away from a number of processes and provides a conceptual explanation. The next example is an actual e-mail that we received from our friend Amanda, who found the math trick amazing.

MHM    **EXAMPLE 1.14** **Using Variables (Amanda's Telephone Number E-Mail)**

"Here is the math trick so unbelievable that it will stump you.

Grab a calculator. (You won't be able to do this one in your head.)
Key in the first three digits of your phone number (not the area code).
Multiply by 80.
Add 1.
Multiply by 250.
Add the last four digits of your phone number.
Add the last four digits of your phone number again.
Subtract 250.
Divide the number by 2.

Do you recognize the number? Does it always turn out to be your number?"

**Solution**    **Understand the Problem**

To make sure that we understand what's going on, the first step is to see if the procedure works with our own phone number. Let's first try Amanda's phone number of 257-6821.

Step 6 has some ambiguity because the instruction "add the last four digits" could mean that we should add 6, 8, 2, and 1 or add the number 6821. If you try the first way, you'll see that the process fails, so we took the second interpretation.

The process does work for Amanda's number, because 2,576,821 of step 9 is $257 (10,000) + 6821$. (See Table 1.1.) Thus, expressed as a phone number, 2,576,821 is 257-6821. Since there is nothing special about the number used, it may well be that the "math trick" always works. However, we can't try all the phone numbers, so just guessing and checking is not feasible. We should go to the next Pólya principle to see if Amanda's trick always works—that is, to see if we always get the original phone number back.

| **TABLE 1.1** | **VERIFICATION OF AMANDA'S MATH TRICK BY USING HER PHONE NUMBER, 257-6821** |
|---|---|
| **Step** | **Result** |
| 2. Start with 257 | 257 |
| 3/4. Multiply by 80, add 1 | $80(257) + 1 = 20,561$ |
| 5. Multiply by 250 | $(250)(20,561) = 5,140,250$ |
| 6/7. Add 6821 twice | 5,153,892 |
| 8. Subtract 250 | 5,153,642 |
| 9. Divide by 2 | 2,576,821 |

**Devise a Plan**

The question "Does it always work?" in the problem gives a direction for our plan. Example 1.13 is solved by looking at all possibilities at once by letting the time needed to whitewash the fence be the variable $T$. Let's see whether that approach will work for Amanda's problem. The first step in planning is to decide what variable to use for which quantity. It is tempting to let $x$ be a phone number. If you try this approach, however, you will see that we can't do steps 2 or 3 in terms of $x$ because we must have only the first three digits of the seven-digit phone number. Looking at the procedure again, we see that, although there are seven digits, only the first three and the last four are used, none of them individually. Our plan, then, is to name the first three digits with the variable $y$ and the last four with the variable $z$ and go through the Pólya principles by using algebra.

### Carry Out the Plan

Let the telephone number be given and let $y$ be the first three digits of the number and $z$ the last four. (Thus, in the case of Amanda's number, 257-6821, $y = 257$ and $z = 6821$.) We will now follow steps 2 through 9 exactly as in Table 1.1 and see what happens.

What is the final answer after all nine steps? The result at step 9 is $10,000y + z$. (See Table 1.2.) However, $10,000y$ takes the three-digit number $y$ (257 in our example) and adds four zeros (to get 2,570,000). Thus, the first three digits of the seven-digit number $10,000y + z$ are the digits of the number $y$.

What are the last four digits of $10,000y + z$? They are exactly the digits of $z$ (for example, $2,570,000 + 6821 = 2,576,821$). The "math trick" works because $10,000y + z$ is a way to express in algebra the phone number (without area code) $y$-$z$. (That's $y$ hyphen $z$, not subtraction.) Note that we didn't need a calculator to do the problem!

| TABLE 1.2 | VERIFICATION OF AMANDA'S MATH TRICK BY USING THE PHONE NUMBER WHOSE FIRST THREE DIGITS ARE $y$ AND LAST FOUR ARE $z$ |
|---|---|
| **Step** | **Results** |
| 2. Start with $y$ | $y$ |
| 3/4. Multiply by 80, add 1 | $80y + 1$ |
| 5. Multiply by 250 | $250(80y + 1) = 20,000y + 250$ |
| 6/7. Add $z$ twice | $20,000y + 250 + 2z$ |
| 8. Subtract 250 | $20,000y + 2z$ |
| 9. Divide by 2 | $(20,000y + 2z)/2 = 10,000y + z$ |

### Look Back

In the explanation of Amanda's phone number problem, we used "algebra as the great explainer" because we were trying to show that something involving numbers was <u>always</u> correct. At first, we thought of solving the problem by using only one variable, but we recognized that there were really two different numbers involved; that is, a phone number is made up of two parts (plus an area code), and we needed different names for the two of them. We then went through some algebraic steps and finished the problem. Since we proved the result for all seven-digit numbers, not just some specific ones, we have given a carefully reasoned argument which shows that the result is always true. This approach is also an example of the "Proof and Reasoning Standard" of the NCTM.

## Problem Set 1.4

Exercises numbered in red are answered in the back of the text.

### Understanding Concepts

1. **(a)** Draw three diagrams to continue this dot sequence:

   ∙ ∙, ∙ ∙ ∙, ∙ ∙ ∙ ∙,

   **(b)** What number sequence corresponds to the pattern of part (a)?

   **(c)** What is the tenth term in the sequence of part (b)? the one-hundredth term?

   **(d)** Which even number is $2n$?

   **(e)** What term in the sequence is 2402?

2. Example 1.1 (Guessing Toni's Number, in Section 1.1) was solved by using guess and check. Do the example again, applying algebra this time. (*Suggestion:* Use a variable.)

3. Jackson is thinking of a number, which, if you triple it and subtract 13, ends with a result of 2. What number is Jackson thinking of? (*Suggestion:* Use a variable.)

4. Maria picks an integer, divides it by 2, and then adds 12 to what she has. When she tells you that she now has 10, can you tell her what integer she started with? (*Suggestion:* Use a variable.)

5. The first three trains in a sequence of trapezoid trains are shown below. Verify that the number $t$ of toothpicks required to form a train with $c$ trapezoidal cars is given by the formula $t = 1 + 4c$.

**6.** A rectangular table seats 6 people: 1 person on each end and 2 on each of the longer sides. Thus, two tables placed end to end seat 10 people.

   **(a)** How many people can be seated if $n$ tables are placed in a line end to end?

   **(b)** How many tables, set end to end, are required to seat 24 people?

**7.** (Handshake Problem) There are $n$ people in a room, and each of them will shake hands with every other person once and only once. The general question of how many handshakes take place is best done through the insights gained by experimenting (Problem-Solving Strategy 6).

   **(a)** If there are 3 people in the room, how many handshakes are there?

   **(b)** If there are 6 people, how many handshakes are made?

   **(c)** If there are 200 people, how many handshakes are there?

   **(d)** If there are $n$ people, how many handshakes are there?

Imagination can generate many variants of the Handshake Problem. This exercise gives rise to a number of other problems through the use of the Mathematical Habit of the Mind.

**8.** (Feuding Handshake Problem) There are 100 people in a
MHM room, half of whom don't speak to the other half. Assume that if they won't speak to each other, they won't shake hands. How many handshakes are there if everyone shakes hands only once (if they shake at all)?

**9.** (Marital Handshake Problem) There are 100 people consisting
MHM of 50 married couples in a room. Assuming that no husband or wife shakes the other's hand but everyone else shakes hands exactly once, how many handshakes are there?

**10.** (Your Handshake Problem) Make up a handshake problem
MHM similar to problems 7, 8, and 9.

**11.** Old MacDonald has 100 chickens and goats altogether in the barnyard. In all, there are 286 feet. How many chickens and how many goats are in the barnyard? (*Suggestion:* Use Problem-Solving Strategy 7.)

**12.** Consider the following sequence of equations:

$$1 = 1$$
$$3 + 5 = 8$$
$$7 + 9 + 11 = 27$$
$$13 + 15 + 17 + 19 = 64$$
$$\underline{\quad} + \underline{\quad} + \underline{\quad} + \underline{\quad} + \underline{\quad} = \underline{\quad}$$

   **(a)** Fill in the blanks to continue the sequence of equations.

   **(b)** Guess a formula for the number on the right of the $n$th equation.

   **(c)** Check that the expression $n^2 - n + 1$ generates the first number in the sum on the left of each equation and that $n^2 + n - 1$ generates the last number in the sum.

   **(d)** Use the result of part (c) to prove that your guess to part (b) is correct. (*Hint:* How many terms are in the sum on the left of the $n$th equation?)

**13.** We have already considered the triangular numbers,

and the square numbers,

   **(a)** Draw the next two figures to continue this sequence of dot patterns:

   **(b)** List the sequence of numbers that corresponds to the sequence of part (a). These are called **pentagonal numbers.**

   **(c)** Complete this list of equations suggested by parts (a) and (b):

$$1 = 1$$
$$1 + 4 = 5$$
$$1 + 4 + 7 = 12$$
$$1 + 4 + 7 + 10 = 22$$
$$\underline{\qquad\qquad} = \underline{\qquad}$$
$$\underline{\qquad\qquad} = \underline{\qquad}$$

Observe that each pentagonal number is the sum of an arithmetic progression.

   **(d)** Compute the 10th term in the arithmetic progression $1, 4, 7, 10, \ldots$.

   **(e)** Compute the 10th pentagonal number.

   **(f)** Determine the $n$th term in the arithmetic progression $1, 4, 7, 10, \ldots$.

   **(g)** Compute the $n$th pentagonal number, $p_n$.

**14.** **(a)** The **hexagonal numbers** are associated with this sequence of dot patterns:

   Complete the next two diagrams in the sequence.

   **(b)** Write the first five hexagonal numbers.

   **(c)** What is the tenth hexagonal number?

   **(d)** Compute a formula for $h_n$, the $n$th hexagonal number.

**15.** Example 1.3 of Section 1.2 was solved by using guess and check. Do the example again but this time with algebra. (Use three variables.)

**16.** The following figure shows an addition pyramid, in which each number is the sum of the two numbers immediately below it:

For each of the following incomplete addition pyramids, show that the values in each square can be determined by forming and solving an equation in the unknown variable shown:

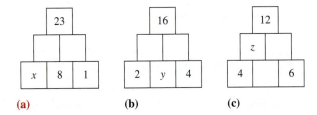

**(a)**          **(b)**          **(c)**

17. In the circle patterns shown, each number in a large circle is the sum of the numbers in the two adjacent small circles. The pattern on the left is complete, but the pattern on the right needs to be completed. Do so by letting $x$ denote the value in one of the small circles. Now obtain expressions and equations that let you solve for $x$, and determine the values in all three small circles.

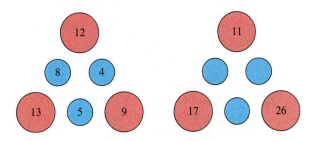

18. Find the numbers to place in each of the five small circles shown so that each number given in a large circle is the sum of the numbers in the two adjacent small circles. Do so by letting one of the values in a small circle be denoted by an unknown and then obtaining and solving an equation for the unknown.

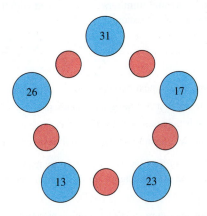

19. Use algebra to solve the following problems from Problem Set 1.1:
    (a) Problem 11a.
    (b) Problem 11d.

20. Find a formula for the (positive) difference of the squares of
    **MHM** consecutive integers by doing parts (a) and (b).

(a) By way of an experiment, fill in the following table of integers:

| $n$ | 1 | 2 | 3 | 4 | 5 | 6 |
|---|---|---|---|---|---|---|
| $n^2$ | 1 | 4 | | | | |
| $(n + 1)^2$ | 4 | 9 | | | | |
| difference | 3 | 5 | | | | |

Do you see a pattern?

(b) Using algebra, write a formula for the difference of the squares of consecutive numbers (larger minus smaller), and give a reason that it works.

## Thinking Critically

21. Consider each of the following addition problems in which the digits are reversed:

    $23 + 32$    $42 + 24$    $17 + 71$    $51 + 15$    $67 + 76$

    (a) What do the answers of all of these have in common?
    (b) Using algebra, show that if $a$ and $b$ are digits, then the sum of the numbers represented by $ab$ and $ba$ is always divisible by 11. (*Hint:* Since $a$ is the first digit and $b$ is the second, $ab$ represents the number $10a + b$. What number does $ba$ represent and what is the sum of $ab$ and $ba$?)

22. Consider each of the following subtraction problems in which the digits are reversed:

    $32 - 23$    $42 - 24$    $71 - 17$    $51 - 15$    $76 - 67$

    (a) What do the answers of all of these computations have in common?
    (b) Using algebra, show that if $a$ and $b$ are digits, then the difference of the numbers represented by $ab$ and $ba$ is always divisible by 9. (*Hint:* Since $a$ is the first digit and $b$ is the second, $ab$ represents the number $10a + b$. What number does $ba$ represent and what is the difference of $ab$ and $ba$?)

23. Dana received grades of 78, 86, and 94 on the first three exams. For an A, the average on four exams must be at least 90. What can Dana do to get an A?

24. A rectangle is 3 times as long as it is wide and has the same perimeter as a square whose area is 4 square feet larger than that of the rectangle. What are the dimensions of both the rectangle and the square?

25. In Section 1.1, Mr. Capek's fifth-grade class found multiple methods of solving "Old MacDonald's problem." How would you solve it by using algebra?

26. How would you generalize the formula of problem 20?
    **MHM** (a) If $x$ and $y$ differ by 2, show that the difference of their squares is twice their sum.
    (b) To formulate a generalization of part (a), what condition on the difference of $x$ and $y$ would you suggest? Write a problem that generalizes (a) and prove your result by using algebra.

**27.** Algebra can be used to prove results, as we will see in Chapter 4. Although the intent of this text is not to emphasize formal proofs, we do want to show the power of algebra. Here's a beginning problem: Show that the square of an even integer is a multiple of 4. (*Hint:* Start with the definition! We know that if $x$ is an even number, then there is another integer $n$ with $x = 2n$. What is $x^2$?)

## From State Student Assessments

**28.** (Illinois, Grade 5)

$$\text{🍎} + \text{♦} = 10$$
$$\text{♦} - \text{🍎} = 2$$

Each ♦ has the same value.
Each 🍎 has the same value.
What is the value of the ♦ ?

**29.** (Kentucky, Grade 5)
José had 64 baseball cards. He gave 12 cards to his sister. Then he divided the remaining cards equally among his FOUR friends. How many cards did each of his friends get?

**(a)** 13 cards

**(b)** 16 cards

**(c)** 17 cards

**(d)** 18 cards

**30.** (Kentucky, Grade 8).
(*Note:* This is the exact problem from the Kentucky, Grade 8, exam. There is no test booklet contained in this text.)

For this open-response question, use the grid provided in this test booklet to create any required charts or graphs.

Two small children were playing a game. The goal of the game was to be the first one to reach the door. The children started the game by standing 20 feet away from the door, and then they each took a turn to do the following:

- Child A moved **one-half** the distance between herself and the door on each move.

- Child B moved **1 foot** toward the door on each move.

  **(a)** How far was each child from the door after the **first** move?

  **(b)** After **four** moves, which child was closer to the door? Show your work.

  **(c)** Child A claimed that the game was unfair because she would never reach the door. Explain why her statement is correct or incorrect.

# 1.5

# Additional Problem-Solving Strategies

## Strategies

- Work backward.
- Eliminate possibilities.
- Use the Pigeonhole Principle.

## Working Backward

> **PROBLEM-SOLVING STRATEGY 8   Work Backward**
>
> Start from the desired result and work backward step-by-step until the initial conditions of the problem are achieved.

Many problems require that a sequence of events occur that results in a desired final outcome. These problems at first seem obscure and intractable, and you may be tempted to try a guess and check approach. However, it is often easier to work backward from the end result to see how the process would have to start to achieve the desired end. To make this idea more clear, consider the next example.

## EXAMPLE 1.15   Working Backward—The Gold Coin Game

This is a two-person game. Place 15 golden coins (markers) on a desktop. The players play in turn and, on each play, can remove one, two, or three coins from the desktop. The player who takes the last coin wins the game. Can one player or the other devise a strategy that guarantees a win? (*Note:* This is the problem of the Hands On activity presented at the beginning of the chapter, where you were expected to arrive at the solution by repeatedly trying simpler cases. We think that you will find the approach here much more effective and insightful.)

**Solution**    **Understand the Problem**

The assertion that the game is played with gold coins is just so much window dressing. What is important is that the players start with 15 objects; that they can remove 1, 2, or 3 objects on each play; and that the player who takes the last object wins the game. The question is, How can one play in such a way that he or she is sure of winning?

### Devise a Plan

Since it is not clear how to begin to play or how to continue as the play proceeds, we turn the problem around to see how the game must end. We then work backward step-by-step to see how we can guarantee that the game ends as we desire.

### Carry Out the Plan

We carry out the plan by presenting an imaginary dialogue that you could have with yourself to arrive finally at the solution to the problem. This dialog (or conversation with a friend) is a sign of the MHM.

Q. What must be the case just before the last person wins the game?
A. There must be 1, 2, or 3 markers on the desk.
Q. So how can I avoid leaving this arrangement for my opponent?
A. Clearly, I must leave at least 4 markers on the desk in my next-to-last move. Indeed, if I leave precisely 4 markers, my opponent must take 1, 2, or 3, leaving me with 3, 2, or 1. I can remove all of these on my last play to win the game.
Q. So how can I be sure to leave precisely 4 markers on my next-to-last play?
A. If I leave 5, 6, or 7 markers on my previous play, my opponent can leave *me* with 4 markers and he or she can then win. Thus, I must be sure to leave my opponent 8 markers on the previous play.
Q. All right. So how can I be sure to leave 8 markers on the previous play?
A. Well, I can't leave 9, 10, or 11 markers on the previous play, or my opponent can take 1, 2, or 3 markers as necessary and so leave me with 8 markers. But then, as just seen, my opponent can be sure to win the game. Therefore, at this point, I must leave 12 markers on the desk.
Q. Can I be sure of doing this?
A. Only if I play first and remove 3 markers the first time. Otherwise, I have to be lucky and hope that my opponent will make a mistake and still allow me to leave 12, 8, or 4 markers at the end of one of my plays. The following strategy outlines the play if I get to play first:

- I take 3 markers, leaving 12.
- My opponent takes 1, 2, or 3 markers, leaving 11, 10, or 9.
- I take 3, 2, or 1 marker as needed to make sure that I leave 8.
- My opponent takes 1, 2, or 3 markers, leaving 7, 6, or 5.
- I take 3, 2, or 1 marker as needed to ensure that 4 markers are left on the desk.
- My opponent takes 1, 2, or 3 markers, leaving 3, 2, or 1.
- I take the remaining markers and win the game!

### Look Back

In looking back, it is important to ask such questions as these:

- What was the key feature that led me to eventually solve this problem?
- Could I use this strategy to solve variations of the problem? For example, suppose the game started with 21 coins or 37 coins or, in general, with $n$ coins.
- Suppose that each player could take up to 5 coins at a time. How would that affect the strategy?
- Could I use the successful strategy I just employed to solve other similar (or not so similar) problems?
- Could I devise other problems for which this strategy would lead to a solution?

Working backward is a must in many problem-solving situations, particularly with a problem like this one. The desired strategy to win the game described is not at all clear. Here the strategy of working backward is somewhat similar to considering special cases and looking for a pattern. It is as if we started with just a few markers so that the strategy was more apparent and gradually increased the number of markers until we reached the given number of 15. Working backward is a powerful strategy that ought to be in every problem solver's repertoire.

## Eliminate Possibilities

One way of determining what must happen in a given situation is to determine what the possibilities are and then to eliminate them one by one. If you can eliminate all but one possibility in this way, then that possibility must prevail. Suppose that either John, Jim, or Yuri is singing in the shower. Suppose also that you are able to recognize both John's voice and Yuri's voice, but that you do not recognize the voice of the person singing in the shower. Then the person in the shower must be Jim. This is another important problem-solving strategy that should not be overlooked.

> **PROBLEM-SOLVING STRATEGY 9** Eliminate Possibilities
>
> Suppose you are guaranteed that a problem has a solution. Use the data of the problem to decide which outcomes are impossible. Then at least one of the possibilities not ruled out must prevail. If all but one possibility can be ruled out, then it must prevail.

Of course, if you use this strategy on a problem and *all* possibilities can be correctly ruled out, the problem has no solution. Don't be misled. It is certainly possible to have problems with no solution! Consider the problem of finding a number such that 3 more than twice the number is 15 and 6 more than 4 times the number is 34. This problem has no solution, since the first condition is satisfied only by 6 and the second is satisfied only by 7. Yet $6 \neq 7$.

However, if we know that a problem has a solution, it is sometimes easier to determine what can't be true than what must be true. In this approach to problem solving, one eliminates possibilities until the only possibility left must yield the desired solution.

Consider the next example.

## EXAMPLE 1.16 Eliminating Possibilities

Beth, Jane, and Mitzi play on the basketball team. Their positions are forward, center, and guard. Given the following information, determine who plays each position:

(a) Beth and the guard bought a milk shake for Mitzi.
(b) Beth is not a forward.

**Solution**

### Understand the Problem

Given the clues (a) and (b), we are to determine which girl plays each position.

### Devise a Plan

The problem is confusing. Perhaps, if we make a table of possibilities, we can use the clues to eliminate some of them and so arrive at a conclusion.

### Carry Out the Plan

The table showing all possibilities is as follows:

|         | Beth | Jane | Mitzi |
|---------|------|------|-------|
| forward |      |      |       |
| center  |      |      |       |
| guard   |      |      |       |

Using the clues in the order given, we see from (a) that neither Beth nor Mitzi is the guard, and we put Xs in the table to indicate this. But then it is clear that Jane is the guard, and we put an O in the appropriate cell to indicate this as well. The table now looks like this:

|          | Beth | Jane | Mitzi |
|----------|------|------|-------|
| forward  |      |      |       |
| center   |      |      |       |
| guard    | X    | O    | X     |

But if Jane is the guard, she is not the center or forward, so we also X out these cells:

|          | Beth | Jane | Mitzi |
|----------|------|------|-------|
| forward  |      | X    |       |
| center   |      | X    |       |
| guard    | X    | O    | X     |

This appears to be all the information we can get from condition (a), so we turn to condition (b), which tells us that Beth is not the forward. After we X out this cell, it becomes clear that Beth is the center. So we place an O in the Beth–center cell and an X in the Mitzi–center cell. This leaves the forward position as the only possibility for Mitzi, so we place an O in the Mitzi–forward cell. The completed table is as shown here:

|          | Beth | Jane | Mitzi |
|----------|------|------|-------|
| forward  | X    | X    | O     |
| center   | O    | X    | X     |
| guard    | X    | O    | X     |

We conclude that Mitzi plays forward, Beth plays center, and Jane plays guard. Note that, in order to make the step-by-step process of eliminating possibilities clearer, we repeatedly redrew the table as the solution progressed. However, all the work could have been done in a single table and normally would have been.

**Look Back**

In this problem, we were confronted with data not easily analyzed. To bring order into this chaos, it seemed reasonable to make a table allowing for all possibilities and then to use the given statements to decide which possibilities could be ruled out. In this way, we were able to delete possibilities systematically until the only remaining possibilities completed the solution.

Eliminating possibilities is often a successful approach to solving a problem.

## The Pigeonhole Principle

If 101 guests are staying at a hotel with 100 rooms, can we make any conclusion about how many people there are in a room? It is likely that a number of the rooms are empty, since some of the guests probably include married couples, families with children, and friends staying together to save money. But suppose most of the hotel's guests desire single rooms. How many such persons could the hotel accommodate? If there were just one person per room, all 100 rooms would be occupied, with one person left over. Thus, if *all* 101 guests are to be accommodated, there must be at least two persons in one of the rooms. To summarize,

> *If 101 guests are staying in a hotel with 100 guest rooms, then at least one of the rooms must be occupied by at least two guests.*

This reasoning is essentially trivial, but it is also surprisingly powerful. Indeed, it is so often useful that it is called **the Pigeonhole Principle,** which is stated next.

---

**PROBLEM-SOLVING STRATEGY 10** The Pigeonhole Principle

If $m$ pigeons are placed into $n$ pigeonholes and $m > n$, then there must be at least two pigeons in one pigeonhole.

---

For example, if we place three pigeons into two pigeonholes, then there must be at least two pigeons in one pigeonhole. To make this quite clear, consider all possibilities as shown here:

| Pigeonhole Number 1 | Pigeonhole Number 2 |
|---|---|
| 3 pigeons | 0 pigeons |
| 2 pigeons | 1 pigeon |
| 1 pigeon | 2 pigeons |
| 0 pigeons | 3 pigeons |

In every case, there are at least two pigeons in one of the pigeonholes.

A second useful way to understand this reasoning is to try to avoid the conclusion by spreading out the pigeons as much as possible. Suppose we start by placing one pigeon into each pigeonhole as indicated in the table that follows. Then we have one more pigeon to put into a pigeonhole, and it must go in either hole number one or hole number two. In either case, one of the holes must contain a second pigeon and the conclusion follows.

| Pigeonhole Number 1 | Pigeonhole Number 2 |
|---|---|
| 1 | 1 |

**EXAMPLE 1.17** Using the Pigeonhole Principle

A student working in a tight space can barely reach a box containing 12 rock CDs and 12 classical CDs. Her position is such that she cannot see into the box. How many CDs must she select to be sure that she has at least 2 of the same type of CDs?

**Solution**

**Understand the Problem**

The box contains 12 rock CDs and 12 classical CDs. The student is in a tight spot and can barely reach the box into which she cannot see. In one attempt, she wants to select enough to be sure that she has at least two CDs of the same type. We must determine how many CDs she must select to ensure the desired result.

**Devise a Plan**

Let's consider possibilities. To make sure that we don't miss one, we make an orderly list.

**Carry Out the Plan**

If the student chooses two CDs, she must have one of the following:

| | | |
|---|---|---|
| Two rock CDs | and | zero classical CDs |
| One rock CD | and | one classical CD |
| Zero rock CDs | and | two classical CDs |

Two CDs are *not* enough; she might get one of each kind. But if she selects a third CD, she will end up with a third rock CD, a second rock CD, a second classical CD, or a third classical CD. In any case, she will have two CDs of the same type and the condition of the problem will be satisfied. Therefore, she needs to select only three CDs from the box.

**Look Back**

We certainly solved the problem by considering possibilities. But might there be an easier solution? Choosing CDs of two kinds is much like putting pigeons into two pigeonholes. Thus, if we select three CDs, then, by the Pigeonhole Principle, at least two must be the same kind, and we have the same result as before. Also, be sure to read the "Into the Classroom" feature shown next.

## Into the Classroom

### Make Use of Incorrect Responses

**MHM** Observe that the number 12 in the statement of the preceding problem is misleading (only two CDs of each kind in the box are really needed), and this causes many students to respond that the answer is 13. Often, students make incorrect responses that serve as good springboards to useful classroom discussions. Rather than just saying that the response of 13 *is* incorrect, a good teacher may say something like "Well, Pete, that's not quite right, but could you think of a question related to this problem for which 13 *is* the correct answer?" This response not only corrects Pete but also gives him an immediate opportunity to redeem himself in the eyes of the class. The ensuing discussion will both inform Pete and enhance the understanding of the entire class. Other questions that might be discussed are as follows: "What questions might be asked for which 14 is the correct answer?" "How many CDs must the student select to be sure that she has 12 rock CDs?" Also, one might repeat the problem with 12 rock CDs, 12 classical CDs, and 12 country and western CDs and ask similar questions. The possibilities are almost limitless. The idea of using a student's incorrect response is a wonderful way to explore the concepts that you are talking about. It is also a process that is an MHM.

## Problem Set 1.5

Exercises numbered in red are answered in the back of the text.

### Understanding Concepts

1. Play this game with a partner. The first player marks down 1, 2, 3, or 4 tallies on a sheet of paper. The second player then adds to this by marking down 1, 2, 3, or 4 more tallies. The first player to exceed a total of 30 loses the game. Can one player or the other devise a surefire winning strategy? Explain carefully.

2. Consider this mathematical machine:

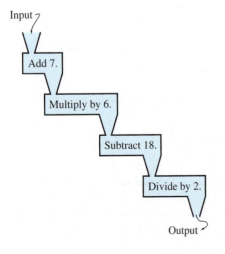

Input
Add 7.
Multiply by 6.
Subtract 18.
Divide by 2.
Output

(a) What number would you have to use as input if you wanted 39 as the output?

(b) What would you have to input to obtain an output of 48?

(c) Describe a different strategy for attacking this problem than the one you used for parts (a) and (b).

(d) How would you solve parts (a) and (b) by the "use a variable" problem-solving strategy?

3. Josh wanted to buy a bicycle but didn't have enough money. After Josh told his troubles to Sam Slick, Sam said, "I can fix that. See that fence? Each time you jump that fence, I'll double your money. There's one small thing though: You must give me $32 each time for the privilege of jumping." Josh agreed, jumped the fence, received his payment from Sam Slick, and paid Sam $32. Repeating the routine twice more, Josh was distressed to find that, on the last jump, after Sam had made his payment to Josh, Josh had only $32 with which to pay Sam and so had nothing left. Sam, of course, went merrily on his way, leaving Josh wishing that he had known a little more about mathematics.

(a) How much money did Josh have before he made his deal with Sam?

(b) Suppose the problem is the same, but this time Josh jumps the fence 5 times before running out of money. How much money did Josh start with this time?

**4.** Liping is thinking of a number. If you multiply her number by 71, add 29, and divide by 2, you obtain 263.

   **(a)** What is Liping's number? Solve this problem by working backward.

   **(b)** Solve the problem by the "use a variable" problem-solving strategy.

**5.** A stack of 10 cards numbered $0, 1, 2, \ldots, 9$ in some order lies face up on a desk. Form a new stack as follows: Place the top card face up in your hand, place the second card face up **under** the first card, place the third card face up **on top** of the new stack, place the fourth card face up **on the bottom** of the new stack, and so on. What should be the arrangement of the original stack so that the cards in the new stack are numbered in increasing order from the top down.

**6.** Moe, Joe, and Hiram are brothers. One day, in some haste, they left home with each one wearing the hat and coat of one of the others. Joe was wearing Moe's coat and Hiram's hat. Whose hat and coat was each one wearing?

**7.** Lisa Kosh-Granger likes to play number games with the students in her class, since it improves their skill at both mental arithmetic and critical thinking. Solve each of these number riddles she gave to her class:

   **(a)** I'm thinking of a number.

   > The number is odd.
   > It is more than 1 but less than 100.
   > It is greater than 20.
   > It is less than $5 \cdot 7$.
   > The sum of its digits is 7.
   > It is evenly divisible by 5.

   What is the number? Was all the information needed?

   **(b)** I'm thinking of a number.

   > The number is not even.
   > The sum of its digits is divisible by 2.
   > The number is a multiple of 11.
   > It is greater than $4 \cdot 5$.
   > It is a multiple of 3.
   > It is less than $7 \cdot 8 + 23$.

   What is the number? Is more than one answer possible?

   **(c)** I am thinking of a number.

   > The number is even.
   > It is not divisible by 3.
   > It is not divisible by 4.
   > It is not greater than $9^2$.
   > It is not less than $8^2$.

   What is the number? Is more than one answer possible?

**8.** Saturday afternoon, Aaron, Boyd, Carol, and Donna stopped by the soda fountain for treats. Altogether, they ordered a chocolate malt, a strawberry milk shake, a banana split, and a double-dip walnut ice cream cone. Given the following information, who had which treat?

   **(a)** Both boys dislike chocolate.

   **(b)** Boyd is allergic to nuts.

   **(c)** Carol bought a malt and a milk shake for Donna and herself.

   **(d)** Donna shared her treat with Boyd.

**9.** Four married couples belong to a bridge club. The wives' names are Kitty, Sarah, Josie, and Anne. Their husbands' names (in some order) are David, Will, Gus, and Floyd.

   > Will is Josie's brother.
   > Josie and Floyd dated some, but then Floyd met his present wife.
   > Kitty is married to Gus.
   > Anne has two brothers.
   > Anne's husband is an only child.

   Use this table to sort out who is married to whom:

   |       | Kitty | Sarah | Josie | Anne |
   |-------|-------|-------|-------|------|
   | David |       |       |       |      |
   | Will  |       |       |       |      |
   | Floyd |       |       |       |      |
   | Gus   |       |       |       |      |

**10.** **(a)** Jorge chose one of the numbers $1, 2, 3, \ldots, 1024$ and challenged Sherrie to determine the number by asking no more than ten questions to which Jorge would respond truthfully either "yes" or "no." Determine the number he chose if the questions and answers are as follows:

   | *Questions* | *Answers* |
   |-------------|-----------|
   | Is the number greater than 512? | no |
   | Is the number greater than 256? | no |
   | Is the number greater than 128? | yes |
   | Is the number greater than 192? | yes |
   | Is the number greater than 224? | no |
   | Is the number greater than 208? | no |
   | Is the number greater than 200? | yes |
   | Is the number greater than 204? | no |
   | Is the number greater than 202? | no |
   | Is the number 202? | no |

   **(b)** In part (a), Sherrie was able to dispose of 1023 possibilities by asking just ten questions. How many questions would Sherrie have to ask to determine Jorge's number if it is one of $1, 2, 3, \ldots, 8192$? if it is one of $1, 2, 3, \ldots, 8000$? Explain briefly but clearly. (*Hint:* Determine the differences between 512, 256, 128, 192, and so on.)

   **(c)** How many possibilities might be disposed of with 20 questions?

**11.** If it takes 867 digits to number the pages of a book starting with page 1, how many pages are in the book?

**12.** **(a)** How many students must be in a room to be sure that at least two are of the same sex?

   **(b)** How many students must be in a room to be sure that at least six are boys or at least six are girls?

**13.** **(a)** How many people must be in a room to be sure that at least two people in the room have the same birthday (not birth date)? Assume that there are 365 days in a year.

   **(b)** How many people must be in a room to be sure that at least three have the same birthday?

14. Show that, in any collection of 11 natural numbers, there must be at least 2 whose difference is evenly divisible by 10. (*Helpful question:* When is the difference of 2 natural numbers divisible by 10?)

15. **(a)** In any collection of seven natural numbers, show that there must be two whose sum or difference is divisible by 10. (*Hint:* Try a number of particular cases. Try to choose numbers that show that the conclusion is false. What must be the case if the sum of two natural numbers is divisible by 10?)

    **(b)** Find six numbers for which the conclusion of part (a) is false.

16. Show that, if five points are chosen in or on the boundary of a square with a diagonal of length $\sqrt{2}$ inches, at least two of them must be no more than $\dfrac{\sqrt{2}}{2}$ inches apart. (*Hint:* Consider the figure shown and use the Pigeonhole Principle.)

17. Show that if five points are chosen in or on the boundary of an equilateral triangle with sides 1 meter long, at least two of them must be no more than $\frac{1}{2}$ meter apart.

18. Think of 10 cups, with 1 marble in the first cup, 2 marbles in the second cup, 3 marbles in the third cup, and so on. Show that, if the cups are arranged in a circle in any order whatsoever, then some three adjacent cups in the circle must contain a total of at least 17 marbles.

19. A fruit grower packs apples in boxes. Each box contains at least 240 apples and at most 250 apples. How many boxes must be selected to be certain that at least three boxes contain the same number of apples?

20. Show that, at a party of 20 people, there are at least 2 people with the same number of friends at the party. Assume that the friendship is mutual. (*Hint:* Consider the following three cases: (i) Everyone has at least one friend at the party; (ii) precisely one person has no friends at the party; (iii) at least two people have no friends at the party.)

21. Argue convincingly that at least two people in New York have precisely the same number of hairs on their heads. (*Hint:* You may need to determine a reasonable figure for the number of hairs on a human head.)

## Teaching Concepts

22. Read one of the following from NCTM's *Principles and Standards for School Mathematics:*

    **(a)** Reasoning and Proof Standard for Grades Pre-K–2, pages 122–126

    **(b)** Reasoning and Proof Standard for Grades 3–5, pages 188–192

    **(c)** Reasoning and Proof Standard for Grades 6–8, pages 262–267

    Write a critique of the standard you read, emphasizing your own reaction. How do the recommendations compare with your own school experience?

## From State Student Assessments

23. (Washington State, Grade 4)
    Dan baked some cookies. Sam took half of the cookies. Then Sue took half of the remaining cookies. Later, Lisa took half of the cookies that were left. When Dan came home, he saw only three cookies. Tell how you could figure out how many cookies Dan baked altogether. Explain your thinking using words, numbers, or pictures.

24. (Washington State, Grade 4)
    Emily, Mei, and Andrew go to the same camp. They each like different games. Use the information in the figure shown to find out which game Mei likes best. Their favorites are tug-of-war, rope skipping, and relay race.

    Emily's favorite game does *not* use a rope.
    Andrew does *not* like tug-of-war.

    Which is Mei's favorite game?

    A. Tug-of-war

    B. Relay race

    C. Rope skipping

**Figure for Problem 24**

Tug-of-war

Rope skipping

Relay race

# 1.6

# Reasoning Mathematically

In this concluding section on critical thinking, we will extend our strategies of problem solving. In particular, we will discuss the following topics, each of which will be helpful in the chapters to come:

- inductive reasoning,
- representational reasoning,
- mathematical statements,
- deductive reasoning.

Reading the NCTM *Reasoning and Proof Standard* (p. 47) gives us an overview of the major role that mathematical reasoning plays in K–12 education. The content of that standard, in particular, is central to the MHM. This was said somewhat differently when we were discussing Amanda's Telephone Number E-Mail (Example 1.14). The point in either case is that if we are mathematically curious enough to want to know <u>why</u>, <u>how</u>, or <u>how general</u> a statement can be made, then we are under the umbrella of the MHM.

## Inductive Reasoning

We use **inductive reasoning** to draw a general conclusion based on information obtained from specific examples. For example, think about the bears you've seen, maybe in zoos, in pictures in magazines, or perhaps even in the wild. On the basis of these experiences, you would likely draw the conclusion that bears are brown or black, or even white if you've seen a polar bear. Here's a mathematical example: Consider the square numbers 4, 9, 16, 25, and 36. Notice that they are either multiples of 4 or one more than a multiple of 4. We can check that this property of squares is also true for other squares—say, 49, 64, 81, and 100. Even $1^2 = 1$ passes our check, since 1 is one more than 4 times 0. Thus, inductive reasoning leads us to the generalization that the square of any whole number is either a multiple of 4 or one more than a multiple of 4.

> **DESCRIPTION**    *Inductive Reasoning*
> **Inductive reasoning** is drawing a conclusion based on evidence obtained from specific examples. The conclusion drawn is called a **generalization.**

Inductive reasoning is a powerful way to create and organize information. However, it only suggests what *seems* to be true, since we have not yet checked that the property holds for *all* examples. For example, there is a rare type of bear in southeastern Alaska called the blue bear. Although it is a genetic variant of the black bear, its fur is dark blue. Thus, the existence of the blue bear tells us that the statement "all bears are black, brown, or white" is false. Such an example, one that disproves a statement, is called a **counterexample.** It is interesting to notice that a proof of a generalization requires us to demonstrate that a certain property holds for every possible case, but a generalization can be proved to be false by finding just *one* counterexample.

**EXAMPLE 1.18  Using Inductive Reasoning in Mathematics**

Examine the generalizations that follow. Test the validity of each generalization with additional evidence. If you believe that the generalization is valid, try to offer additional reasons that this is so. If you believe that the generalization may be false, search for a counterexample.

**(a)** Consider three consecutive integers, such as 8, 9, and 10. Exactly one of these three numbers is a multiple of 3. Similarly, each of the consecutive triples 33, 34, and 35 and 121, 122, and 123 includes precisely one multiple of 3. Thus, in any string of three consecutive integers, it is probably true that exactly one is a multiple of 3.

**(b)** Place $n$ points on a circle. Next, join each pair of these points with a line segment (that is, with a chord of the circle) such that no more than two chords intersect at a single point. As shown in the following diagrams, the number of regions in the circle doubles with each additional point placed on the circle, giving the sequence 1, 2, 4, and 8:

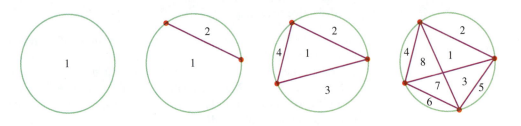

In conclusion, it is probably true that there are $2^{n-1}$ regions created by drawing chords between $n$ points on a circle.

**(c)** $3 \times 439 = 1317$, and the sum of the digits of the product is $1 + 3 + 1 + 7 = 12$, a multiple of 3. Similarly, $3 \times 2687 = 8061$, and the sum of digits of this product is $8 + 0 + 6 + 1 = 15$, again a multiple of 3. Thus, it is probably true that the sum of the digits of any whole-number multiple of 3 is also a multiple of 3.

**Solution**

**(a)** Additional examples support the general conclusion. If the whole numbers are written in the form **0** 1 2 **3** 4 5 **6** 7 8 **9** 10 11 **12** 13 . . . , with the multiples of 3 shown in bold, we see that any three numbers in succession include exactly one of the bold numbers. Thus, the assertion *appears* to be true.

**(b)** Let's draw a sketch of the next two cases, with $n = 5$ and 6 points on the circle:

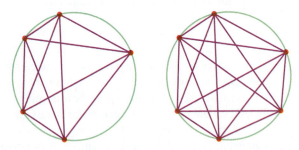

When $n = 5$ points are placed on the circle, we see that there are $16 = 2^{5-1}$ regions, which supports the generalization. However, the doubling pattern breaks down with $n = 6$ points on the circle, since we do not get 32 regions as we had expected. How many regions do the chords joining 6 points on a circle create?

**(c)** Additional examples all exhibit the same property. In Chapter 4, we will prove that the sum of the digits of any whole number divisible by 3 is also divisible by 3.

## Reasoning and Proof Standard

Instructional programs from prekindergarten through grade 12 should enable all students to—

- *recognize reasoning and proof as fundamental aspects of mathematics;*
- *make and investigate mathematical conjectures;*
- *develop and evaluate mathematical arguments and proofs;*
- *select and use various types of reasoning and methods of proof.*

During grades 3–5, students should be involved in an important transition in their mathematical reasoning. Many students begin this grade band believing that something is true because it has occurred before, because they have seen several examples of it, or because their experience to date seems to confirm it. During these grades, formulating conjectures and assessing them on the basis of evidence should become the norm. Students should learn that several examples are not sufficient to establish the truth of a conjecture and that counterexamples can be used to disprove a conjecture. They should learn that by considering a range of examples, they can reason about the general properties and relationships they find.

Mathematical reasoning develops in classrooms where students are encouraged to put forth their own ideas for examination. Teachers and students should be open to questions, reactions, and elaborations from others in the classroom. Students need to explain and justify their thinking and learn how to detect fallacies and critique others' thinking. They need to have ample opportunity to apply their reasoning skills and justify their thinking in mathematics discussions. They will need time, many varied and rich experiences, and guidance to develop the ability to construct valid arguments and to evaluate the arguments of others. There is clear evidence that in classrooms where reasoning is emphasized, students do engage in reasoning and, in the process, learn what constitutes acceptable mathematical explanation (Lampert 1990; Yackel and Cobb 1994, 1996).

SOURCE: *Principles and Standards for School Mathematics by NCTM, pp. 56 & 188. Copyright © 2000 by the National Council of Teachers of Mathematics. Reproduced with permission of the National Council of Teachers of Mathematics via Copyright Clearance Center. NCTM does not endorse the content or validity of these alignments.*

---

**PROBLEM-SOLVING STRATEGY 11    Use Inductive Reasoning**

- Observe a property that holds in several examples.
- Check that the property holds in other examples. In particular, attempt to find an example in which the property does not hold (i.e., try to find a counterexample).
- If the property holds in every example, state a generalization that the property is probably true in general.

---

A generalization that seems to be true, but has yet to be proved, is called a **conjecture.** Once a conjecture is given a proof, it is called a **theorem.** The logical thought process that brings us to a conjecture or, even better, the proof of a theorem is a gem of MHM.

## Representational Reasoning

In mathematics, a *representation* is an object that captures the essential information needed for understanding and communicating mathematical properties and relationships. Often, the representation conveys information visually, as in a diagram, a graph, a map, or a table. At other times, the representation is symbolic, such as a letter denoting a variable or an algebraic expression or equation. The representation can also be a physical object, such as a paper model of a cube or an arrangement of pebbles to represent a whole number. The excerpt on the next page from the NCTM *Principles and Standards for School Mathematics* points out that a representation can even be simply a mental image.

## Representation Standard for Grades 3-5

Instructional programs from prekindergarten through grade 12 should enable all students to—

- *create and use representations to organize, record, and communicate mathematical ideas;*
- *select, apply, and translate among mathematical representations to solve problems;*
- *use representations to model and interpret physical, social, and mathematical phenomena.*

In grades 3–5, students need to develop and use a variety of representations of mathematical ideas to model problem situations, to investigate mathematical relationships, and to justify or disprove conjectures. They should use informal representations, such as drawings, to highlight various features of problems; they should use physical models to represent and understand ideas such as multiplication and place value. They should also learn to use equations, charts, and graphs to model and solve problems. These representations serve as tools for thinking about and solving problems. They also help students communicate their thinking to others. Students in these grades will use both external models—ones that they can build, change, and inspect—as well as mental images.

SOURCE: *Principles and Standards for School Mathematics by NCTM, page 206. Copyright © 2000 by the National Council of Teachers of Mathematics. Reproduced with permission of the National Council of Teachers of Mathematics via Copyright Clearance Center. NCTM does not endorse the content or validity of these alignments.*

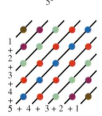

**FIGURE 1.8**

Any square number is a pyramidal sum

Here is an example to illustrate how a representation can reveal and explain a property. Consider the "pyramidal sums" shown in this list:

$$1 = 1$$
$$1 + 2 + 1 = 4$$
$$1 + 2 + 3 + 2 + 1 = 9$$
$$1 + 2 + 3 + 4 + 3 + 2 + 1 = 16$$

Using inductive reasoning, we would likely draw the conclusion that the $n$th pyramidal sum is the square number $n^2$. That is,

$$1 + 2 + 3 + \cdots + (n - 1) + n + (n - 1) + \cdots + 3 + 2 + 1 = n^2.$$

To see why this is so, recall that any square number can be represented as a square pattern of dots. For example, $5^2$ is represented by the $5 \times 5$ array shown in Figure 1.8. If we sum the numbers of dots along each diagonal of the square, as seen at the right of the figure, we see very clearly why $1 + 2 + 3 + 4 + 5 + 4 + 3 + 2 + 1$ is equal to the square number $5^2$. In our "mind's eye," where we can create a mental image of the most general case, we see why any pyramidal sum is a square number. Here, MHM comes from the inspiration of looking at the figure in a different way (in this case, sideways).

In the next example, we use dot drawings with colored pencils on squared paper in order to make some more discoveries about number patterns through the use of representations.

**EXAMPLE 1.19   Using Dot Representations to Discover Number Patterns**

Recall that the triangular and square numbers can be represented with dot patterns as shown here:

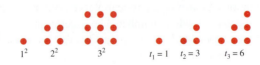

**(a)** Draw dot figures to show that $t_3 + t_3 = 3 \cdot 4$ and $t_4 + t_4 = 4 \cdot 5$. By inductive reasoning, why can you conclude that $t_n = \dfrac{n(n+1)}{2}$?

**(b)** Draw dot figures to show that $t_3 + t_4 = 4^2$ and $t_4 + t_5 = 5^2$. What generalization can you make?

**(c)** Draw dot figures to show that $7^2 = 1 + 8t_3$ and $9^2 = 1 + 8t_4$. (*Hint:* The 1 is the center dot in your square.) By inductive reasoning, what do you think is the value of $1 + 8t_{50}$? of $1 + 8t_n$?

**Solution**

**(a)** We generalize that two dot patterns, each representing $t_n$, can form an $n$-by-$(n+1)$ rectangle. Therefore,

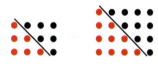

$$t_n + t_n = n(n+1), \quad \text{or} \quad t_n = \frac{n(n+1)}{2}.$$

**(b)** The patterns shown suggest that the patterns representing $t_{n-1}$ and $t_n$ can be arranged to form an $n$-by-$n$ square. We conclude that $t_{n-1} + t_n = n^2$.

**(c)** Eight triangular dot patterns together with a single dot can be arranged to form a square with an odd number of dots in each row. Inductive reasoning suggests that $1 + 8t_{50} = 101^2 = 10{,}201$ and, in general, that $1 + 8t_n = (2n + 1)^2$.

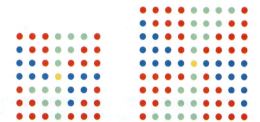

## Mathematical Statements

In mathematics, a **statement** is a declarative sentence that is either true or false, but not both. Thus, "$2 + 3 = 5$" is a true statement, and "pigs can fly" is a false statement. "Shut the door" is not a statement, since it is not a declarative sentence. The sentence "This sentence is a false statement" is declarative, but not a mathematical statement, since it is neither true nor false. (If it is true, then it is false, and if it is false, then it is true—so it is neither true nor false!)

Two statements—say, $p$ and $q$—are often combined to form another statement by using **and** and **or** operations.

- **And:** "$p$ and $q$" is true when statement $p$ and statement $q$ are both true, and false when either or both of $p$ and $q$ are false.
- **Or:** "$p$ or $q$" is true when either statement $p$ or statement $q$ (or even both) is true, and false only when both $p$ and $q$ are false.

This description can also be given a representation known as a **truth table,** as shown in Figure 1.9.

**FIGURE 1.9**
The truth table for "*p* and
*q*" and "*p* or *q*"

| *p* | *q* | *p* and *q* | *p* or *q* |
|-----|-----|-------------|------------|
| T   | T   | T           | T          |
| T   | F   | F           | T          |
| F   | T   | F           | T          |
| F   | F   | F           | F          |

Yet another way to combine two statements is to form a **conditional statement,** or **"if . . . then"** statement.

- **If . . . then:** "If *p* then *q*" is true when the truth of statement *p* guarantees the truth of statement *q*.

For example, you have probably encountered the conditional statement "If a whole number has 0 as its last digit, then it is divisible by 10." Often, "if *p* then *q*" is read as "*p* implies *q*" and is written $p \rightarrow q$. The truth table for $p \rightarrow q$ is shown in Figure 1.10.

**FIGURE 1.10**
The truth table for $p \rightarrow q$,
which shows that $p \rightarrow q$ is
false when, and only
when, *p* is true and *q* is
false

| *p* | *q* | $p \rightarrow q$ |
|-----|-----|-------------------|
| T   | T   | T                 |
| T   | F   | F                 |
| F   | T   | T                 |
| F   | F   | T                 |

The big surprise in Figure 1.10 is that $p \rightarrow q$ is true when *p* is false, independently of whether *q* is true or false. Thus, "If the moon is made of green cheese, then pigs can fly" is a true conditional statement! Fortunately, the moon is not made of green cheese, so we don't need to be on the lookout for flying pigs.

Many theorems of mathematics have the "if *p* then *q*" form.

**EXAMPLE 1.20 Proving an "If . . . Then" Statement**

Prove the following theorem:

*If* n *is any whole number, then* n$^2$ *is either a multiple of 4 or 1 larger than a multiple of 4.*

**Solution**

**Understand the Problem**

We must show that *any* whole number *n*, when squared, has one of two forms: Either it is a multiple of 4, so that $n^2 = 4j$ for some whole number *j*, or else $n^2 = 4k + 1$ for some whole number *k*. Earlier, we used inductive reasoning that supported the truth of the theorem.

**Devise a Plan**

The whole numbers are 0, 1, 2, 3, 4, 5, 6, . . . , alternating between even and odd. Their squares are 0, 1, 4, 9, 16, 25, 36, . . . , alternating between multiples of 4 and numbers that are 1 larger than a multiple of 4. These two mathematical facts suggest that we consider two cases: when *n* is even and when *n* is odd. We also know that when *n* is even, it can be written as $n = 2r$ for some whole number *r*, and when *n* is odd, it can be written as $n = 2s + 1$ for some whole number *s*. Thus, we need to consider the two cases $(2r)^2$ and $(2s + 1)^2$ and use algebra.

**Carry Out the Plan**

If $n = 2r$, it follows that $n^2 = (2r)^2 = 4r^2$. That is, $n^2 = 4j$, where $j = r^2$. Similarly, when $n = 2s + 1$, we have $n^2 = (2s + 1)^2 = 4s^2 + 4s + 1 = 4(s^2 + s) + 1$. That is, $n^2 = 4k + 1$ for $k = s^2 + s$.

$(2s + 1)^2 = (2s + 1)(2s + 1)$

$= 4s^2 + 2s + 2s + 1$

$= 4s^2 + 4s + 1$

**Look Back**

Let's take a closer look at the squares of the odd numbers—that is, the numbers 1, 9, 25, 49, 81, . . . . These numbers are not only one larger than a multiple of 4; they're even one more than a multiple of 8. This was actually shown earlier in Example 1.19 (c): Using dot pattern representations, we discovered that $(2n + 1)^2 = 8t_n + 1$, where $t_n$ is the $n$th triangular number. We can also use dot pattern representations to visualize why the square of an even number is four times another square. The following figure shows that $10^2 = 4 \times 5^2$:

This proof involves algebra, once again showing how algebra can be used to explain many things.

## Deductive Reasoning

Suppose that we have a collection of true statements. If we can argue on the basis of these statements that another statement must also be true, then we are using **deductive reasoning.** Example 1.20 is an example of deductive reasoning, since we showed that if a number is a square whole number, then it is either a multiple of 4 or one larger than a multiple of 4.

The list of true statements we begin with are known as the **premises,** or **hypotheses,** of the argument. The new true statement that we obtain is called the **conclusion** of the argument.

Here is another example of deductive reasoning:

| | | |
|---|---|---|
| **Hypothesis:** | *Statement 1.* | If you wish to become a successful elementary school teacher, then you must become proficient in mathematical reasoning. |
| | *Statement 2.* | You wish to become a successful elementary school teacher. |
| **Conclusion:** | *Statement 3.* | You must become proficient in mathematical reasoning. |

In symbols, if we let $p$ denote the statement "You wish to become a successful elementary school teacher" and $q$ denote the statement "You need to become proficient in mathematical reasoning," then we have reached the conclusion by using the **rule of direct reasoning.**

### RULE OF DIRECT REASONING

Hypotheses: $\begin{cases} \text{If } p \text{ then } q \\ p \text{ is true} \end{cases}$

Conclusion:    Therefore, $q$ is true

The rule of direct reasoning may seem straightforward, but it is sometimes used incorrectly. Here is an example of invalid reasoning called the "fallacy of the converse."

If I am a good person, then nothing bad will happen to me.
Nothing bad has happened to me.                                    } INVALID REASONING
Therefore, I am a good person.

This argument is invalid, since even if $p \rightarrow q$ is true and $q$ is true, nothing can be said about whether $p$ is true or not. This concept is clearly shown in the truth table of Figure 1.10.

On the other hand, the truth table does show that if $p \rightarrow q$ is true and $q$ is *false*, then $p$ is also necessarily false. Thus, we have the very useful **rule of indirect reasoning.**

---

**RULE OF INDIRECT REASONING**

Hypotheses:      $\begin{cases} \text{If } p \text{ then } q \\ q \text{ is false} \end{cases}$

Conclusion:      Therefore, $p$ is false

---

The rule of indirect reasoning is often used to give a **proof by contradiction.** That is, if we take a statement $p$ and derive a false statement $q$ from it, then we know that $p$ is false. The checkerboard tiling problem presented in Example 1.21 is a classic example of indirect reasoning and proof by contradiction. In Chapter 4, we will use this method to show that the $\sqrt{2}$ is not a rational number.

## EXAMPLE 1.21 Tiling a Checkerboard with Dominos

It is easy to cover the 64 squares of an 8-by-8 checkerboard with 32 dominos, where each domino covers two adjacent squares, one red and one black, of the checkerboard. But what if two diagonally opposite squares are removed? Can the 62 remaining squares be covered with 31 dominos?

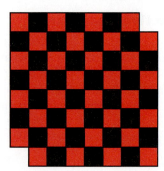

**Solution**   If you believed that the modified board could be tiled, you would search for an arrangement of 31 dominos that covers all 62 squares. After a few unsuccessful trials, you might begin to have doubts. Let's use indirect reasoning, or reasoning by contradiction, and assume (though you haven't found it) that there is an arrangement of 31 dominos that covers the modified board. Notice that each domino, whether vertical or horizontal, covers one red and one black square, so that an equal number of red and black squares must be covered. However, the two squares we've removed have the same color (black in the diagram). This means that we have left behind 30 squares of one color and 32 squares of the other color. This situation contradicts our observation that any arrangement of the dominos covers an equal number of squares of the two colors. Thus, the assumption that a domino tiling exists leads to a falsehood, so our assumption must also be false. That is, there is no tiling of the modified checkerboard with dominos.

The rule of indirect reasoning is also misused with some frequency. Here is an example of what is called the "fallacy of the inverse":

If I am wealthy, then I am happy.
I am not wealthy. $\Bigg\}$ INVALID REASONING
Therefore, I am not happy.

An examination of the truth table in Figure 1.10 shows that, if $p \rightarrow q$ is true and $p$ is false, $q$ can be either true or false.

Deductive reasoning provides another important strategy for problem solving.

---

**PROBLEM-SOLVING STRATEGY 12    Use Deductive Reasoning**

- To show that a statement $q$ is true, look for a statement $p$ such that $p \rightarrow q$ is true. If $p$ is true, you can deduce that $q$ is also true by direct reasoning.
- To show that a statement $p$ is false, show that $p \rightarrow q$, where $q$ is false. That is, show that assuming $p$ leads to a contradiction. Then $p$ is false by indirect reasoning.

---

In this section, we have highlighted inductive, representational, and deductive reasoning. These modes of mathematical thought will be used throughout the remainder of this book and will be supplemented with some additional methods, such as proportional reasoning in Chapter 7, algebraic reasoning in Chapter 8, statistical reasoning in Chapter 13, and geometrical reasoning in Chapters 9–12.

## Problem Set 1.6

Exercises numbered in red are answered in the back of the text.

### Understanding Concepts

 **1. (a)** Compute the products $9 \times 9, 79 \times 9, 679 \times 9$, and $5679 \times 9$.

**(b)** Use inductive reasoning (don't calculate yet) to describe in words what you expect are the values of these products: $45679 \times 9, 345679 \times 9, 2345679 \times 9$, and $12345679 \times 9$.

**(c)** Use a calculator to see if your inductive reasoning was correct in part (b).

**2. (a)** Compute the value of these expressions: $1 \times 9 + 2, 12 \times 9 + 3$, and $123 \times 9 + 4$.

**(b)** Use inductive reasoning (don't calculate yet) to describe in words what you expect are the values of these expressions: $1234 \times 9 + 5, 12345 \times 9 + 6, 123456 \times 9 + 7, 1234567 \times 9 + 8, 12345678 \times 9 + 9$, and $123456789 \times 9 + 10$.

**(c)** Use a calculator to check that your inductive reasoning was correct in part (b).

**3. (a)** Compute the value of these expressions: $1 \times 8 + 1, 12 \times 8 + 2$, and $123 \times 8 + 3$.

**(b)** Use inductive reasoning (don't calculate yet) to describe in words what you expect are the values of these expressions: $1234 \times 8 + 4, 12345 \times 8 + 5, 123456 \times 8 + 6, 1234567 \times 8 + 7, 12345678 \times 8 + 8$, and $123456789 \times 8 + 9$.

**(c)** Use a calculator to check that your inductive reasoning was correct in part (b).

**4.** Consider a three-digit number $abc$, where the digit $a$, in the hundreds position, is larger than the units digit $c$. Now reverse the order of the digits to get the number $cba$. Subtract your

two three-digit numbers, and let the difference be *def*. Finally, reverse the digits of *def* to form the number *fed*, and add this number to *def*. Altogether, you should do the following addition and subtraction steps with your beginning number *abc*:

$$\begin{array}{r} abc \\ - \ cba \\ \hline def \end{array} \qquad \begin{array}{r} def \\ + \ fed \\ \hline ???? \end{array}$$

Choose several examples of three-digit numbers *abc*, and carry out the subtraction and addition steps. Use inductive reasoning to make a generalization about this process.

5. **(a)** Compute these products:

$1 \times 1089 =$ _____
$2 \times 1089 =$ _____
$3 \times 1089 =$ _____
$4 \times 1089 =$ _____
$5 \times 1089 =$ _____
$6 \times 1089 =$ _____
$7 \times 1089 =$ _____
$8 \times 1089 =$ _____
$9 \times 1089 =$ _____

**(b)** Did you have to compute all the products in part (a) to be pretty sure that you knew what all the answers would be? Explain briefly.

**(c)** Do you see any other interesting patterns in part (a)? Explain briefly.

6. **(a)** Use inductive reasoning on the function $f(x) = x^6 - 14x^4 + 49x^2 - 36$ to see what the value of $f(x)$ might be for all $x$. Start with $x = -1, 1, -2, 2, -3$, and 3, and substitute into the equation. What might you conclude from these substitutions?

**(b)** Is the guess that you would make from inductive reasoning using just the values for $x$ above correct? Why?

7. At the beginning of this section, we gave an argument using dot representations of a square to show that any square number is a pyramidal sum (Figure 1.8). Give an algebraic proof of this fact by using Gauss' insight. (This is another example of the power of algebra as a great explainer.)

8. Use a ruler to draw two line segments and label three points on each line as follows:

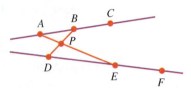

The segments $\overline{AE}$ and $\overline{BD}$ (shown in red) intersect to define point $P$. In the same way, draw the segments $\overline{AF}$ and $\overline{CD}$ to define the intersection point $Q$. Finally, draw the segments $\overline{BF}$ and $\overline{CE}$ to define the intersection point $R$. What seems to be special about the relative positions of the three points $P$, $Q$, and $R$? Use inductive reasoning to make a generalization, and test your conclusion by drawing a new pair of lines and points.

9. The given figure suggests that the number of pieces into which a pie is divided is doubled with each additional cut across the pie. Do you believe this is a valid generalization, or can you find a counterexample?

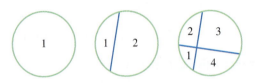

10. Suppose that logs are stacked on level ground. All of the logs in the bottom row must be side by side, and any log in an upper row must touch two lower logs. The ways to stack $n$ circular logs are as follows for $n = 1, 2, 3$, and 4 logs, showing that the respective numbers of stacking arrangements are 1, 1, 2, and 3:

**(a)** Do the Fibonacci numbers $F_1 = 1, F_2 = 1, F_3 = 2, F_4 = 3, F_5 = 5, F_6 = 8, \ldots$, first encountered in Example 1.6 (c), correctly count the number of ways to stack $n$ logs? Investigate this generalization by drawing arrangements of 5 and 6 logs.

**(b)** Use inductive reasoning to investigate the number of ways to stack logs at most two layers high, where, as before, the bottom row of logs must be side by side and logs in the second row must rest on two logs of the bottom row.

11. Suppose a flagpole is erected on one of $n$ blocks, with all of the blocks to the right (if any) used to attach guy wires and an equal number of blocks to the left of the pole also used as points of attachment of guy wires. Any block can be used to attach at most one guy wire. Here are the three permissible arrangements of a flagpole and guy wires on a row of four blocks:

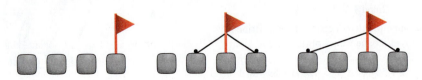

Use inductive reasoning to discover the number of arrangements of a flagpole and guy wires on a row of $n$ blocks.

**12.** Consider the three triangles of pennies shown, each pointing upward. It is easy to see that the triangle of 3 pennies on the left can be inverted (i.e., made to point downward) by moving one penny.

(a) What is the smallest number of pennies that must be moved in order to invert the 6-penny triangle?

(b) Show that the 10-penny triangle can be inverted by moving just 3 pennies.

(c) What do you think is the minimum number of pennies that must be moved to invert the 15-penny triangle? Experiment to see if you are justified in drawing this conclusion.

**13. (a)** The fifth pentagonal number $P_5$ is the sum of the arithmetic progression 1, 4, 7, 10, 13. (See problem 13, Problem Set 1.4.) Why does the dot pattern representation displayed here show that $P_5 = 1 + 4 + 7 + 10 + 13$? Give your answer in words and in a diagram drawn on triangular dot paper.

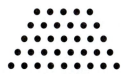

(b) Extend your dot representation of part (a) to show that $P_6$ is 51.

(c) Color a triangular dot pattern to show that $P_5 = 5 + 3t_4$, where $t_4 = 10$ is the fourth triangular number.

(d) Use triangular dot paper to show that $P_6 = 6 + 3t_5$.

(e) By inductive reasoning, and recalling that $t_{n-1} = \frac{1}{2}(n-1)n$, obtain a formula for the $n$th pentagonal number $P_n = 1 + 4 + 7 + \cdots + (3n - 2)$.

**14.** Consider the trapezoidal numbers $1 + 1 + 1, 1 + 2 + 2 + 2 + 1, 1 + 2 + 3 + 3 + 3 + 2 + 1,\ldots$, where the $n$th trapezoidal number is $1 + 2 + \cdots + n + n + n + \cdots + 2 + 1$.

(a) Create a dot pattern representation of the trapezoidal numbers.

(b) Notice that $1 + 1 + 1 = 1 \times 3, 1 + 2 + 2 + 2 + 1 = 2 \times 4$, and $1 + 2 + 3 + 3 + 3 + 2 + 1 = 3 \times 5$. Show how the dots in a representation of a trapezoidal number can be rearranged into a rectangle with two more columns than rows.

(c) Using inductive reasoning, show what general formula gives the $n$th trapezoidal number.

**15.** A log in the woods is just long enough to have space for seven frogs on top. Suppose there are three green frogs on the left and three red frogs on the right, with one empty space between. The frogs wish to change ends of the log, so that the three green frogs are on the right and the three red frogs are on the left. A frog can either move into an empty adjacent space or hop over one adjacent frog to an empty space on the opposite side of the frog being jumped over.

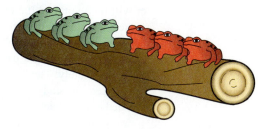

(a) Represent the frog problem with a physical model made from colored counters and a row of squares drawn on paper, as shown here:

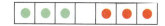

Use your model to show that the frogs can exchange ends of the log in 15 moves. This exercise may take several trials to find an efficient order in which to move the frogs. (*Suggestion:* Work in pairs, with one partner moving the counters and the other partner counting the number of moves.)

(b) On a three-space log that has space for one frog of each color and a single space between, the frogs can trade ends in three moves. What is the minimum number of moves to trade ends on a five-space log, where two green frogs start on the left and two red frogs start on the right?

(c) Examine your answers for the minimum number of moves to have $n = 1, 2$, or 3 green frogs trade ends with the same number of red frogs on the other end of the log and with just one extra space between them. What conjecture can you make for the case of $n$ frogs of each color separated by one extra space? (*Hint:* There is a connection between the frog-jumping problem and the trapezoidal numbers of problem 14.)

**16.** Each of the numbers $2^5 - 2 = 32 - 2 = 30$, $3^5 - 3 = 243 - 3 = 240$, and $4^5 - 4 = 1024 - 4 = 1020$ is a multiple of 30.

(a) Use a calculator to calculate additional values of $n^5 - n$. Do these examples continue to suggest that every number of the form $n^5 - n$ is a multiple of 30?

(b) It can be shown that $n^5 - n = n(n^4 - 1) = n(n^2 - 1)(n^2 + 1) = n(n - 1)(n + 1)(n^2 + 1)$.

Explain why this factorization lets you deduce that $n^5 - n$ is divisible by 3. This is an example of algebra as an explanation in a proof.

**(c)** Suppose that $d$ is the units (i.e., the rightmost) digit of the whole number $n$. What is the units digit of $n^5$? Use a calculator to compute the fifth powers of the digits 0, 1, 2, 3, 4, 5, 6, 7, 8, and 9, and then explain how to deduce that $n^5 - n$ is divisible by 10.

**17.** Use deductive reasoning to show that if $n$ is a multiple of 3, then $n^2$ is a multiple of 9. (*Note:* A multiple of $k$ is a number of the form $ks$, where $s$ is a whole number.)

**18.** Use indirect reasoning to show that if $n^2$ is odd, then $n$ is also odd. (This problem shows the value of algebra in a proof.)

## The Chapter in Relation to Future Teachers

What is problem solving really about? Problem solving concerns itself with techniques to help analyze a situation, give insights, and, in many cases, suggest a course of action or even provide a solution regardless of whether the problem is one of mathematics or life. Your personal and work worlds are full of situations that need carefully thought through solutions, and our main point is that clear, analytical thinking aided by various techniques such as the ones in this chapter will help you and the children you will teach arrive at good solutions. Problem solving permeates the educational process, and encouraging it in your students will help prepare them for their future.

Is problem solving a part of the mathematical education of elementary and middle school students? Absolutely! The State Student Assessment questions are ample evidence of the clear need for your students to study problem-solving techniques, and ten State Student Assessment questions are included in this chapter.

More importantly, problem solving runs throughout mathematics. Every homework exercise, test, or in-class assignment is a form of problem solving. Insights are obtained by looking for solutions by means of different problem-solving strategies, whether those strategies lead to a solution to the original problem or not. Mathematics is learned through the process of solving problems, not by obtaining a correct answer alone.

How can you learn to teach problem solving? During your next course in mathematics for teachers, a "methods" course, you will spend quite a bit of time answering that question. What follows are some bits of advice that come from this content course. Another fine source is the NCTM standards on problem solving on p. 3.

- Set out now to develop a store of interesting and challenging problems appropriate to the skill levels of the students in your class. This process should continue over your professional lifetime. A good start is to keep your present textbook and to use many of the problems you find here as is or modified to be more accessible to your students.
- Really listen to your students. They often have good ideas. They also frequently find it difficult to express their ideas clearly. Listening carefully and helping your students to communicate clearly are important traits.
- Don't be afraid of problems you don't already know how to solve. Say, "Well, I don't know. Let's work together and see what we can come up with." Indeed, many students will be excited and motivated by the prospect of "working with my teacher" to solve a problem. They also learn not to be afraid to tackle the unknown, to make mistakes, and yet to persevere until a solution is finally achieved. Working together to argue about and ask about mathematics is very much a part of MHM.
- Don't be too quick to help your students or to simply tell them how to solve a problem.
- Develop a long list of leading questions you can ask of your students and that they can ask themselves, to help clarify their thinking and eventually arrive at a solution.

# Chapter 1 Summary

| Section 1.1   An Introduction to Problem Solving | Page Reference |
|---|---|
| **CONCEPTS** | |
| • **General introduction:** a classroom discussion. | 3 |
| **STRATEGIES** | |
| • **Guess and check strategy:** Make a guess and check it to see if it satisfies the demands of the problem. If it doesn't, alter the guess appropriately and check again. When the guess finally checks, a solution has been found. | 4, 10 |
| • **Make a table:** Make a table reflecting the data in the problem. If done in an orderly way, such a table may reveal patterns and relationships that suggest how the problem can be solved. | 4, 10 |
| • **Look for a pattern:** Consider an ordered sequence of particular examples of the general situation described in the problem. Then carefully scrutinize results, looking for a pattern that may be the key to the problem. | 4, 10 |
| • **Draw a picture:** Draw a picture that represents the data of the problem as accurately as possible. | 4, 10 |

| Section 1.2   Pólya's Problem-Solving Principles | Page Reference |
|---|---|
| **CONCEPTS** | |
| • **Understand the problem:** Make sure that the words, conditions, and what is to be found are completely understood. | 8 |
| • **Devise a plan:** Carefully consider the problem and think of a possible approach to finding a solution. | 9 |
| • **Carry out your plan:** If it doesn't work out, try again. If it still doesn't solve the problem, modify the plan and try yet again. | 10 |
| • **Look back:** It is important to reexamine your thinking to see what led you to the solution. This is how you gain "mathematical power." | 10 |
| • **Problem-solving strategy of "Guess and Check":** Guessing is a good way to start to gain understanding of a problem, but guessing gives a solution or solutions only if the guess checks. | 10 |
| • **Problem-solving strategy of "make an orderly list":** This strategy helps avoid the omission of other possibilities. | 13 |
| • **Problem-solving strategy of "draw a diagram":** A diagram often clarifies a problem. | 14 |
| **STRATEGIES** | |
| • **Pólya's principles:** The four principles that form the basis for any serious attempt at problem solving—understand the problem, devise a plan, carry out the plan, and look back. | 8 |
| • **Problem solving strategies** | |
| • **Make an orderly list:** For problems that require a consideration of many possibilities, make an orderly list or a table to ensure that no possibilities are missed. | 13 |
| • **Draw a diagram:** Draw a diagram or picture that represents the data of the problem as accurately as possible. | 14 |
| • **Guess my rule:** Game where one student makes up a rule for changing one number into another. The other students then call out numbers and the person who made up the rule tells what numbers the rule gives back. The first person in the class to guess the rule then gets to be the person to make up a new rule. | 16 |

| Section 1.3   More Problem-Solving Strategies | Page Reference |
|---|---|

**CONCEPTS**

- **Look for a pattern:** Patterns often suggest what the answer to a problem should be. — 18

- **Make a table:** A table helps you search for patterns and eliminate possibilities that do not meet all of the criteria required of a solution. — 20

- **Consider special cases (experiment):** What is true in the general case must also be true in a special case. What is true in a special case *suggests* what is true in the general case. — 22

- **Solve an easier, similar problem:** Solving an easier, but similar, problem often suggests how to solve the problem at hand. — 22

- **Argue from special cases:** An argument made from a special case or similar problem, but depending on general principles (not properties applying only to the special case), often serves to provide a path to prove the general case. — 22

**DEFINITIONS**

- **Fibonacci number, $F_n$:** Any number in the Fibonacci sequence. — 19

- **Fibonacci sequence:** The sequence 1, 1, 2, 3, 5, 8, 13, 21, . . . , where it starts with 1 and 1 and add any two consecutive terms to obtain the next. — 19

- **Pascal's triangle:** A triangular array of numbers in which each number is the sum of the two directly above it. Its patterns are useful in probability and in binomial expansions, as well as other areas of math. — 23, 24

**STRATEGIES**

- **Look for a pattern:** Consider an ordered sequence of particular examples of the general situation described in the problem. Then carefully scrutinize results, looking for a pattern that may be the key to the problem. — 18

- **Make a table:** Make a table reflecting the data in the problem. If done in an orderly way, such a table may reveal patterns and relationships that suggest how the problem can be solved. — 20

- **Experiment:** The strategy of considering easier similar problems (special cases) in order to solve a given problem or describe a given pattern. — 23

- **Consider special cases:** Consider a sequence of special cases when trying to solve a complex problem. This will often show how to proceed naturally from case to case until one arrives at the case in question. Alternatively, the special cases may reveal a pattern that makes it possible to solve the problem. — 22

| Section 1.4   Algebra as a Problem-Solving Strategy | Page Reference |
|---|---|

**CONCEPTS**

- **Use a variable:** A symbol (or more than one) can often be used to represent and determine a number that is the answer to a problem. Variables represent quantities that are unknown or can change. — 29, 34

- **Algebra as a great explainer:** Algebra is a unifying concept. — 29

- **Algebraic expressions:** An algebraic expression is a mathematical expression involving variables, numbers, and operation symbols. — 32

- **Algebraic reasoning:** Algebraic reasoning is used to solve problems and understand patterns by following these steps: introduce variables, derive algebraic expressions, form equations, solve equations, and interpret the solution of the equations in the context of the original problem or pattern. — 32

| | |
|---|---|
| • **Equation:** Setting two algebraic expressions that represent the same quantity equal to one another creates an equation. | 32 |
| • **Triangular numbers, $t_n$:** $t_n$ is the total number of dots in a triangle of $n$ rows whose first row has 1 dot, second has 2 dots, third has 3, etc. until the last row, which has $n$ dots. | 31 |

## FORMULA

| | |
|---|---|
| • **Gauss' insight:** $2t_n = n(n + 1)$ where the sum of the first $n$ integers is $t_n$. | 30, 32 |

## STRATEGIES

| | |
|---|---|
| • **Use a variable or variables:** Use a variable, or variables, when a problem requires a number be determined. Represent the number by variable, and use the conditions of the problem to set up an equation that can be solved to ascertain the desired number. | 22, 29, 30 |
| • **Algebra as a great explainer:** Algebra can solve problems that appear to be quite hard or mathematical tricks. It is used in many levels of mathematics because it clarifies so much. | 29 |
| • **Algebraic reasoning:** A cyclical method used in investigating a problem. The cycle involves introducing variables, deriving algebraic expressions, forming equations, solving equations, and interpreting the solution to discover a pattern. | 32 |

| **Section 1.5    Additional Problem-Solving Strategies** | **Page Reference** |
|---|---|

## CONCEPTS

| | |
|---|---|
| • **Work backward:** If you can't see how to start a solution, perhaps you can start from the desired conclusion and work backward to the beginning of the problem. | 39, 40 |
| • **Eliminate possibilities:** If all possibilities but one can be ruled out, that possibility must be checked. If it works, then it is the answer. | 41 |
| • **Use the pigeonhole principle:** If you have items to consider that can be placed in different categories, but you have more items than categories, then at least two items must be in some one category. This fact may lead to a solution to your problem. | 42, 43 |

## STRATEGIES

| | |
|---|---|
| • **Work backward:** Start from the desired result and work backward step-by-step until the initial conditions of the problem are achieved. | 39 |
| • **Eliminate possibilities:** Suppose you are guaranteed that a problem has a solution. Use the data of the problem to decide which outcomes are impossible. Then at least one of the possibilities not ruled out must prevail. If all but one possibility can be ruled out, then it must prevail. | 41 |
| • **Pigeonhole principle:** If $m$ pigeons are placed into $n$ pigeonholes and $m > n$, then there must be at least two pigeons in one pigeonhole. | 42, 43 |

| **Section 1.6    Reasoning Mathematically** | **Page Reference** |
|---|---|

## CONCEPTS

| | |
|---|---|
| • **Inductive reasoning:** This type of reasoning entails drawing a general conclusion on the basis of a consideration of special cases. It does not necessarily yield truth, but suggests what may be true. It gives rise to conjectures. | 47, 49 |
| • **Representational reasoning:** Various physical, pictorial, or even mental representations often make a problem clearer and make it possible to find a solution. | 49 |
| • **Mathematical statements:** These are declarative statements that are either true or false. | 51 |
| • **If . . . then:** A statement of the form "if $p$ is true, then $q$ is true." | 52 |

| | |
|---|---|
| • **Deductive reasoning:** This type of reasoning entails drawing necessary conclusions from given information to arrive at a proof or a solution to a problem. | 53 |
| • **Rule of direct reasoning:** If $p$ implies $q$, then $q$ can be shown to be true by showing that $p$ is true. | 53 |
| • **Rule of indirect reasoning:** If $p$ implies $q$ and $q$ is false, then $p$ is false. This is the basis for proof by contradiction. | 54 |

**DEFINITIONS**

| | |
|---|---|
| • A **counterexample** is an example that disproves a statement. | 47 |
| • A **conjecture** is a generalization that seems to be true, but has yet to be proved. | 49 |
| • A **theorem** is a conjecture that is given a proof. | 49 |
| • A **statement** is a declarative sentence that is either true or false, but not both. | 51 |
| • A **conditional statement,** or "*if . . . then*" *statement*, is a way to combine two statements. "If $p$ then $q$" is true when the truth of statement $p$ guarantees the truth of statement $q$. | 52 |
| • A **premise,** or **hypothesis,** is a list of true statements that we know at the beginning of an argument. | 53 |
| • The **conclusion** is the new true statement that we obtain for the argument. | 53 |

**STRATEGIES**

| | |
|---|---|
| • **Inductive reasoning:** First, observe a property that holds in several examples. Next, check that the property holds in other examples. In particular, attempt to find an example in which the property does not hold. Then, if the property holds in every example, state a generalization that the property is probably true in general (but there is no guarantee that it is true yet.) | 47, 49 |
| • **Proof by contradiction:** If we take a statement $p$ and derive a false statement from it, then we know $p$ is false. | 54 |
| • **Rule of indirect reasoning:** If a truth table shows $p \rightarrow q$ and $q$ is false, then $p$ is also necessarily false. | 54 |
| • **Rule of deductive reasoning:** If there is a collection of true statements, we can argue on the basis of these statements that another statement must also be true. | 53 |

## Chapter Review Exercises

### Sections 1.1 and 1.2

1. Standard Lumber has 8-foot and 10-foot two-by-fours. If Mr. Zimmermann bought 90 two-by-fours with a total length of 844 feet, how many were 8 feet long? Do the problem twice, using different strategies.

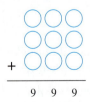

2. **(a)** Using each of 1, 2, 3, 4, 5, 6, 7, 8, and 9 once and only once, fill in the circles in this diagram so that the sum of the three-digit numbers formed is 999:

**(b)** Is there more than one solution to this problem? Explain briefly.

**(c)** Is there a solution to this problem with the digit 1 not in the hundreds column? Explain briefly.

**3.** Bill's purchases at the store cost \$4.79. In how many ways can Bill receive change if he pays with a 5-dollar bill?

**4.** How many three-letter code words can be made by using the letters $a$, $e$, $i$, $o$, and $u$ at most once each time?

**5.** A flower bed measuring 8 feet by 10 feet is bordered by a concrete walk 2 feet wide. What is the area of the concrete walk?

**6.** Karen is thinking of a number. If you double it and subtract 7, you obtain 11. What is Karen's number?

**7. (a)** Chanty is It in a game of *Guess My Rule*. If you give her a number, she uses her rule to determine another number. The numbers the other students gave Chanty and her responses are as shown. Can you guess her rule?

| Student Input | Chanty's Responses |
|:---:|:---:|
| 2 | 8 |
| 7 | 33 |
| 4 | 18 |
| 0 | −2 |
| 3 | 13 |
| ⋮ | ⋮ |

**(b)** Can you suggest a better strategy for the students to use in attempting to determine Chanty's rule? Explain briefly.

## Section 1.3

**8.** Study this sequence: 2, 6, 18, 54, 162, . . . . Each number is obtained by multiplying the preceding number by 3. The sequences in (a) through (e) are formed in the same way, but with a different multiplier. Complete each sequence.

**(a)** 3, 6, 12, _____, _____, _____

**(b)** 4, _____, 16, _____, _____, _____

**(c)** 1, _____, _____, 216, _____, _____

**(d)** 2, _____, _____, _____, 1250, _____

**(e)** 7, _____, _____, _____, _____, 7

**9.** Because of the high cost of living, Kimberly, Terry, and Otis each hold down two jobs, but no two have the same occupation. The occupations are doctor, engineer, teacher, lawyer, writer, and painter. Given the following information, determine the occupations of each individual:

**(a)** The doctor had lunch with the teacher.

**(b)** The teacher went fishing with Kimberly, who is not the writer.

**(c)** The painter is related to the engineer.

**(d)** The doctor hired the painter to do a job.

**(e)** Terry lives next door to the writer.

**(f)** Otis beat Terry and the painter at tennis.

**(g)** Otis is not the doctor.

**10. (a)** Write down the next three rows to continue this sequence of equations.

$$2 = 1^3 + 1$$
$$4 + 6 = 2^3 + 2$$
$$8 + 10 + 12 = 3^3 + 3$$
$$\underline{\hspace{2cm}} = \underline{\hspace{1cm}}$$
$$\underline{\hspace{2cm}} = \underline{\hspace{1cm}}$$
$$\underline{\hspace{2cm}} = \underline{\hspace{1cm}}$$

**(b)** Write down the 10th row in the sequence in part (a).

**11. (a)** How many terms are in the arithmetic progression 7, 10, 13, 16, . . . , 79?

**(b)** Compute the sum of the terms in part (a).

**12. (a)** A **geometric progression** is a sequence of numbers wherein each term is a constant multiple of the preceding term. Thus, 3, 6, 12, 24, . . . , 3072 is a geometric progression since each term is twice its predecessor.
Analyzing these terms, we have

$$3 = 3,$$
$$6 = 2^1 \cdot 3,$$
$$12 = 2 \cdot 6 \ = 2(2^1 \cdot 3) = 2^2 \cdot 3,$$
$$24 = 2 \cdot 12 = 2(2^2 \cdot 3) = 2^3 \cdot 3,$$
$$\vdots$$

Which term in the sequence is 3072?

**(b)** Let $S = 3 + 6 + 12 + 24 + \cdots + 1536 + 3072$ denote the sum of the progression. Compute $S$.

**(c)** Note that $2S = 6 + 12 + 24 + \cdots + 3072 + 6144$.

**(d)** Note that $2S - S = S$, and use (b) and (c) to compute $S$ a second time.

**13.** Compute the sum of the geometric progression whose terms are 5, 15, 45, . . . , 295245.

**14.** Consider a circle divided by $n$ chords in such a way that every chord intersects every other chord interior to the circle and no three chords intersect in a common point. Complete the table that follows and answer these questions:

**(a)** Into how many regions is the circle divided by the chords?
**(b)** How many points of intersection are there?
**(c)** Into how many segments do the chords divide one another?

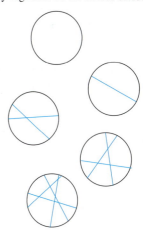

| Number of Chords | Number of Regions | Number of Intersections | Number of Segments |
|---|---|---|---|
| 0 | 1 | 0 | 0 |
| 1 | 2 | 0 | 1 |
| 2 | 4 | 1 | 4 |
| 3 | | | |
| 4 | | | |
| 5 | | | |
| 6 | | | |
| ⋮ | | | |
| $n$ | | | |

**15.** Recall Pascal's triangle:

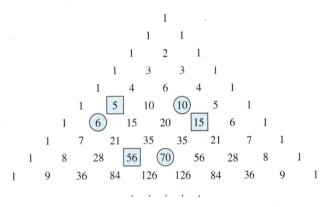

Consider the pattern of entries in the diagram enclosed in circles and squares. Compute the product of the circled entries in Pascal's triangle and the product of the squared entries for several placements of this pattern in the triangle. Does your work suggest a plausible conjecture? Explain briefly. Find other hexagonal patterns of entries with the observed property.

**16.** Compute the following sums associated with Pascal's triangle:

(a) $1 + 1 \cdot 2$

(b) $1 + 2 \cdot 2 + 1 \cdot 2^2$

(c) $1 + 3 \cdot 2 + 3 \cdot 2^2 + 1 \cdot 2^3$

(d) What do these sums suggest? Explain briefly.

(e) Compute the sums

$$1 + 1 \cdot 3,$$
$$1 + 2 \cdot 3 + 1 \cdot 3^2, \text{ and}$$
$$1 + 3 \cdot 3 + 3 \cdot 3^2 + 1 \cdot 3^3.$$

(f) What do (a), (b), (c), (d), and (e) together suggest? What might you do to check your guess further? Explain briefly.

## Section 1.4

**17.** Bernie weighs 90 pounds plus half his own weight. How much does Bernie weigh?

**18.** A "hex-square train" is made with toothpicks, alternating between hexagonal and square "cars" in the train. For example, following are three-car and four-car hex-square trains:

(a) Evidently, 14 toothpicks are required to form a three-car train. Give a formula for the number of toothpicks required to form an $n$-car train. (*Suggestion:* Take separate cases for trains with an odd or an even number of cars.)

(b) A certain hex-square train requires 102 toothpicks. How many hexagons and how many squares are in the train?

**19.** The sum of two real numbers is 7 and their difference is 9. Use the Problem-Solving Strategy to solve for the numbers.

(a) Guess and Check.

(b) Use a Variable.

## Section 1.5

**20.** How many cards must be drawn from a standard deck of 52 playing cards to be sure that

(a) at least two are of the same suit?

(b) at least three are of the same suit?

(c) at least two are aces?

**21.** How many books must you choose from among a collection of 7 mathematics books, 18 books of short stories, 12 chemistry books, and 11 physics books to be certain that you have at least 5 books of the same type?

## Section 1.6

**22.** (a) Compute these products:

$$67 \times 67 = \underline{\hspace{2cm}}$$
$$667 \times 667 = \underline{\hspace{2cm}}$$
$$6667 \times 6667 = \underline{\hspace{2cm}}$$

(b) Guess the result of multiplying 6,666,667 by itself. Are you sure your guess is correct? Explain in one *carefully* written sentence.

**23.** (a) Compute these products:

$$1 \times 142{,}857 = \underline{\hspace{2cm}}$$
$$2 \times 142{,}857 = \underline{\hspace{2cm}}$$
$$3 \times 142{,}857 = \underline{\hspace{2cm}}$$
$$4 \times 142{,}857 = \underline{\hspace{2cm}}$$
$$5 \times 142{,}857 = \underline{\hspace{2cm}}$$

(b) Predict the product of 6 and 142,857. Now calculate the product and see if your prediction was correct.

(c) Predict the result of multiplying 7 times 142,857, and then compute this product.

(d) What does part (c) suggest about apparent patterns? Explain.

**24.** Draw three line segments $l$, $m$, and $n$ from a common point $O$, and draw two triangles $\Delta ABC$ and $\Delta A'B'C'$ with corresponding vertices on $l$, $m$, and $n$, respectively, as shown. Let $P$, $Q$, and $R$ be the points where the lines $\overline{AB}$ and $\overline{A'B'}$, $\overline{AC}$ and $\overline{A'C'}$, and $\overline{BC}$ and $\overline{B'C'}$, respectively, intersect. What seems to be true about $P$, $Q$, and $R$?

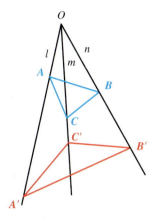

**25.** In Example 1.19, we used representations to show that the square of an odd number is one more than a multiple of 8. Use the fact from Example 1.19 that, if $n$ is odd, then $n = 2s + 1$ for some whole number $s$ and $n^2 = 4(s^2 + s) + 1$. Note that $s^2 + s = s(s + 1) = 2\dfrac{s(s + 1)}{2}$. Argue that $\dfrac{s(s + 1)}{2}$ is a whole number and hence that $n^2 = 8q + 1$ for some whole number $q$. That is, again, $n^2$ is one more than a multiple of 8.

**26.** In this section, we saw that the sum of the digits of a multiple of 3 is also a multiple of 3. Is the same thing true of multiples of 6? Why or why not?

## Chapter Test

**1.** If five pigeons are placed into two pigeonholes, what is the least possible number of pigeons in the pigeonhole with the greatest number of pigeons?

**2.** Perform these multiplications as quickly as possible:

$$2345679 \times 9 = \underline{\hspace{1cm}}$$
$$1345679 \times 9 = \underline{\hspace{1cm}}$$
$$1245679 \times 9 = \underline{\hspace{1cm}}$$
$$1235679 \times 9 = \underline{\hspace{1cm}}$$
$$1234679 \times 9 = \underline{\hspace{1cm}}$$
$$1234579 \times 9 = \underline{\hspace{1cm}}$$
$$1234569 \times 9 = \underline{\hspace{1cm}}$$
$$1234568 \times 9 = \underline{\hspace{1cm}}$$

**3.** Consider the arithmetic progression whose first four terms are 1, 3, 5, and 7.

(a) Determine the 100th term in this progression.

(b) Determine the sum of the first 100 terms in this progression.

**4.** (a) Write the next two lines in this sequence of equations:

$$2 = 2 = 0^2 + 2 \cdot 1^2$$
$$2 + 5 + 2 = 9 = 1^2 + 2 \cdot 2^2$$
$$2 + 5 + 8 + 5 + 2 = 22 = 2^2 + 2 \cdot 3^2$$
$$\underline{\hspace{3cm}} = \underline{\hspace{1.5cm}}$$
$$\underline{\hspace{3cm}} = \underline{\hspace{1.5cm}}$$

(b) Write the 10th line in the sequence of part (a).

**5.** A frog is in a well 12 feet deep. Each day he climbs up 3 feet, and each night he slips back 2 feet. How many days will it take the frog to get out of the well?

**6.** Determine the sum of the elements in the first 10 rows in Pascal's triangle—i.e., rows 0 through 9.

**7.** While three watchmen were guarding an orchard, a thief slipped in and stole some apples. On his way out, he met the three watchmen, one after another, and to each in turn he gave half the apples he had and two besides. In this way, he managed to escape with one apple. How many had he stolen originally?

**8.** Consider the following equations:

$$1 = 0 + 1 = 1 - 0;$$
$$2 + 3 + 4 = 1 + 8 = 9 - 0;$$
$$5 + 6 + 7 + 8 + 9 = 8 + 27 = 36 - 1;$$
$$10 + 11 + 12 + 13 + 14 + 15 + 16 =$$
$$27 + 64 = 100 - 9.$$

(a) Continue this sequence for two more equations.

(b) What is the 10th row in the sequence?

(c) What is the $n$th row in the sequence?

**9.** (a) Make a magic square using each of the numbers 2, 7, 12, 27, 32, 37, 52, 57, and 62 once, and only once.

(b) Make a magic subtraction square using each of the numbers in part (a) once, and only once.

**10.** Note that

$$S_1 = \frac{1}{1 \cdot 2} = \frac{1}{2},$$

$$S_2 = \frac{1}{1 \cdot 2} + \frac{1}{2 \cdot 3} = \frac{2}{3},$$

$$S_3 = \frac{1}{1 \cdot 2} + \frac{1}{2 \cdot 3} + \frac{1}{3 \cdot 4} = \frac{3}{4},$$

Use inductive reasoning to show that

$$S_n = \frac{1}{1 \cdot 2} + \frac{1}{2 \cdot 3} + \cdots + \frac{1}{n(n + 1)} = \frac{n}{n + 1}.$$

# Sets and Whole Numbers

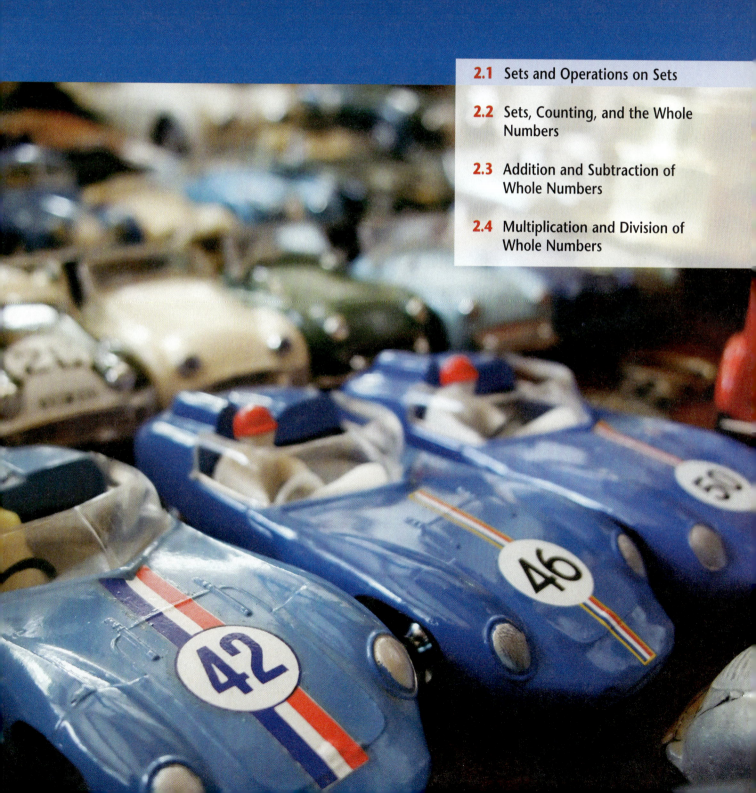

**2.1** Sets and Operations on Sets

**2.2** Sets, Counting, and the Whole Numbers

**2.3** Addition and Subtraction of Whole Numbers

**2.4** Multiplication and Division of Whole Numbers

## Hands On
### Counting Cars and Trains

### Materials Needed

A set of Cuisenaire® rods (or colored number strips) for each cooperative group of three or four students. The rods, which have lengths from 1 to 10 centimeters, are color coded as follows:

1   White
2   Red
3   Light Green
4   Purple
5   Yellow
6   Dark Green
7   Black
8   Brown
9   Blue
10  Orange

### Directions

Form a train by placing one or more rods end to end; each rod in a train is a car. For example, in the figure to the right there are four ways to form trains that have the same overall length as the light-green (LG) rod.

The order in which the cars appear is taken into account, so we consider the red–white and white–red trains as two different trains. (Imagine that the engine is the rightmost car and the caboose is the leftmost car.)

### Questions to Consider

1. How many trains can you form that have the same length as the purple rod?
2. How many trains can you form that have the same length as the yellow rod?
3. What pattern do you observe in the number of trains of length 3, 4, and 5? On the basis of the pattern, predict the number of trains of length 8.
4. How many trains can be formed of length $n$, where $n$ is any whole number and you use cars of lengths l up to $n$? Can you justify your conjecture? Can you give more than one justification?
5. A train made up of only red and white cars is called an RW-train. Answer questions 1 through 4 for RW-trains.
6. Call a train with no white cars a $\overline{W}$-train. Answer questions 1 through 4 for $\overline{W}$-trains.

 **MHM**   In the Hands On activity above, you will start by trying a few examples (in parts 1, 2, and 3) and then decide (in part 4) whether a pattern emerges to solve the general case. You will see that experimenting with $n = 3, 4, 5,$ and $8$ gives insights into the solution of part 4 for any train of length $n$. In your Mathematical Habit of the Mind, do other questions occur to you? Parts 5 and 6 are two examples of MHM questions. What about others?

**CHAPTER PREVIEW**   The notion of a **set** (a collection of objects) is introduced in Chapter 2 as the primary way of describing **whole numbers** such as 0, 1, 2, 3, . . . . We will see that operations on sets form the basis of fundamental arithmetic operations on whole numbers, such as addition, subtraction, multiplication, and division. Because each child learns differently, we give a number of models of addition, subtraction, multiplication, and division of whole numbers and look at their properties through these models.

**KEY IDEAS**
- Sets and operations on sets, such as union and intersection
- The relationship between sets and whole numbers
- Modeling whole-number addition through the use of sets or through measurement on the number line
- Subtraction and its models
- Various models of multiplication and division of whole numbers
- Properties of whole-number multiplication and division

The transition from gathering food to producing food occurred some 10,000 years ago, marking the change from the Paleolithic to the Mesolithic age. Agriculture required farmers to stay in one place for long periods, so people designed and constructed permanent dwellings. This change gave rise to problems dealing with quantity and form: laying out fields, tending flocks, measuring the amount of grain that should be stored over the winter, and knowing whether excess grain could be traded to neighboring villages. Thus, the two important branches of mathematics—number and geometry—have origins concurrent with the dawn of civilization.

Until about 600 B.C., mathematics was pursued primarily for its practical, decorative, and religious values. Problems in land apportionment, interest payments, and tax rates required solution for the development of commerce. Many problems of a mathematical nature were solved during the construction of irrigation canals, temples, and pyramids. Interest in astronomy grew out of the need for calendars that were sufficiently accurate to forecast flood and growing seasons. Number systems

A portion of the Rhind papyrus that discusses the measurement of the area of a triangle and the slopes of pyramids. The papyrus, which contains 85 mathematical problems, was copied c. 1575 B.C. by the scribe Ahmes from a work written almost three centuries earlier.

and notations were developed, and even some empirically derived formulas from algebra and geometry were known. However, little use was made of symbol-

The Incas recorded and communicated quantitative data with quipus. A quipu is an assemblage of cords, with numerical values determined by the colors of the cords, the way the cords are spaced and interconnected, and the types and placement of knots tied in the cords. The quipu shown is in the Museo Nacional de Antropologia y Arqueologia, Lima, Peru.

ism, scant attention was given to abstraction and general methods, and nowhere was the notion of proof or even informal justification to be found. In fact, it required thousands of years of mathematical thought for the concept of zero to emerge and its importance to be recognized.

**2.1**

# Sets and Operations on Sets

The notion of a set originated with the German mathematician Georg Cantor (1845–1918) in the last half of the nineteenth century. Sets have now become indispensable to nearly every branch of mathematics. Sets make it possible to organize, classify, describe, and communicate. For example, each number system—the whole numbers, the integers, the rational numbers, and the real numbers—is best viewed as a set together with a list of the operations on the numbers and the properties that these operations obey.

Intuitively, a set is a collection of objects. An object that belongs to the collection is called an **element** or **member** of the set. Words like *collection, family,* and *class* are frequently used interchangeably with "set." In fact, a set of dishes, a collection of stamps, and the class of 2008 at your high school are all examples of sets.

Cantor requires that a set be *well defined.* This means two things. First, there is a **universe** of objects that are allowed into consideration. Second, there are only two choices for each object. Any object in the universe either is an element of the set or is not an element of the set. For example, "the first few presidents of the United States" is not a well-defined set, since "few" is a matter of varying opinion. By contrast, "the first three presidents of the United States" does provide an adequate verbal description of a set, with the understanding that the universe is all people who have ever lived.

There are three ways to define a set:

**Word Description:**    The set of the first three presidents of the United States
**Listing in Braces:**    {George Washington, Thomas Jefferson, John Adams}
**Set-Builder Notation:**    $\{x \mid x$ is one of the first three presidents of the United States$\}$

The last expression is read "the set of all $x$ such that $x$ is one of the first three presidents of the United States." More generally, set-builder notation, $\{x \mid x \ldots\}$, is read "the set of all $x$ such that $x$ is . . ."

The order in which elements in a set are listed is arbitrary, so listing Jefferson, the third president, before Adams is permissible. However, each element should be listed just once. The letter $x$ used in set-builder notation can be replaced with any convenient letter. The letter $x$ is a variable representing any member of the universe, and the set contains exactly those members of the universe which meet the defining criteria listed to the right of the vertical bar. In some books, a colon replaces the vertical bar.

Capital letters $A$, $B$, $C$, . . . are generally used to denote sets. Membership is symbolized by $\in$, so that if $P$ designates the preceding set of three U.S. presidents, then John Adams $\in P$, where $\in$ is read "is a member of" or "is an element of." The symbol $\notin$ is read "is not a member of," so James Monroe $\notin P$. It is useful to choose letters that suggest the set being designated.

One of the very useful notions in this chapter is that of the positive integers, or natural numbers. We formalize the concept with a definition using set notation.

**DEFINITION**    *Natural Numbers*
A **natural number,** or **counting number,** is a member of the set $N = \{1, 2, 3, \ldots\}$,

where the ellipsis ". . ." indicates "and so on."

**EXAMPLE  2.1  Describing Sets**

Each set that follows is taken from the universe $N$ of the natural numbers and is described either in words, by listing the set in braces, or with set-builder notation. Provide the two remaining types of description for each set.

(a) The set of natural numbers greater than 12 and less than 17.
(b) $\{x \mid x = 2n$ and $n = 1, 2, 3, 4, 5\}$
(c) $\{3, 6, 9, 12, \ldots\}$
(d) The set of the first 10 odd natural numbers.
(e) $\{1, 3, 5, 7, \ldots\}$
(f) $\{x \mid x = n^2$ and $n \in N\}$

**Solution**

(a) $\{13, 14, 15, 16\}$; listing
$\{n \mid n \in N$ and $12 < n < 17\}$; set builder
(b) $\{2, 4, 6, 8, 10\}$; listing
The set of the first five even natural numbers; word description.
(c) The set of all natural numbers that are multiples of 3; word description
$\{x \mid x = 3n$ and $n \in N\}$; set builder
(d) $\{1, 3, 5, 7, 9, 11, 13, 15, 17, 19\}$
$\{x \mid x = 2n - 1$ and $n = 1, 2, \ldots, 10\}$; set builder
(e) The set of the odd natural numbers; word description
$\{x \mid x = 2n - 1$ and $n \in N\}$; set builder
(f) $\{1, 4, 9, 16, 25, \ldots\}$; listing
The set of the squares of the natural numbers; word description.

## Venn Diagrams

Sets can be represented pictorially by **Venn diagrams,** named for the English logician John Venn (1834–1923). The universal set, which we denote by $U$, is usually represented by a rectangle. Any set within the universe is represented by a closed loop lying within the rectangle. The region inside the loop is associated with the elements in the set. An example is given in Figure 2.1, which shows the Venn diagram for the set of vowels $V = \{a, e, i, o, u\}$ in the universe $U = \{a, b, c, \ldots, z\}$.

> A Venn diagram is an example of how a representation can aid the teaching and understanding of a concept. The Representation Standard is discussed in detail in the NCTM's *Principles and Standards for School Mathematics.*

**FIGURE 2.1**

The Venn diagram showing the set of vowels in the universe of the 26-letter alphabet

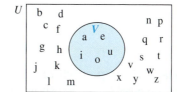

Coloring, shading, or cross-hatching are also useful devices to distinguish the sets in a Venn diagram. For example, set $A$ is blue in Figure 2.2, and the set of elements of the universe that do not belong to $A$ is colored red.

**FIGURE 2.2**

The Venn diagram of set $A$ (shown in blue), its complement $\overline{A}$ (shown in red), and the universal set $U$ (the region within the rectangle)

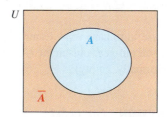

The elements in the universe that are not in set $A$ form a set called the **complement** of $A$, which is written $\overline{A}$.

> **DEFINITION**    *The Complement of a Set A*
>
> The **complement of set $A$,** written $\overline{A}$, is the set of elements in the universal set $U$ that are not elements of $A$. That is,
>
> $$\overline{A} = \{x \mid x \in U \text{ and } x \notin A\}.$$

### EXAMPLE  2.2  Finding Set Complements

Let $U = N = \{1, 2, 3, \ldots\}$ be the set of natural numbers. For the following sets $E$ and $F$, find the complementary sets $\overline{E}$ and $\overline{F}$:

(a) $E = \{2, 4, 6, \ldots\}$
(b) $F = \{n \mid n > 10\}$

**Solution**

(a) $\overline{E} = \{1, 3, 5, \ldots\}$. That is, the complement of the set $E$ of even natural numbers is the set $\overline{E}$ of odd natural numbers.
(b) $\overline{F} = \{1, 2, 3, 4, 5, 6, 7, 8, 9, 10\}$.

## Relationships and Operations on Sets

Consider several sets, labeled $A, B, C, D, \ldots$, whose members all belong to the same universal set $U$. It is useful to understand how sets may be related to one another and how two or more sets can be used to define new sets.

> **DEFINITION**    *Subset*
>
> The set $A$ is a **subset** of $B$, written $A \subseteq B$, if, and only if, every element of $A$ is also an element of $B$.

If *A* is a subset of *B*, then every element of *A* also belongs to *B*. In this case, it is useful in the Venn diagram to place the loop representing set *A* within the loop representing set *B*, as shown in Figure 2.3.

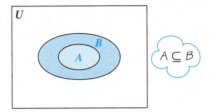

**DEFINITION** *Equal Sets and Proper Subset*

If two sets *A* and *B* have precisely the same elements, then they are **equal** and we write $A = B$. If $A \subseteq B$, but $A \neq B$, we say that *A* is a **proper subset** of *B* and write $A \subset B$.

If $A \subset B$, there must be some element of *B* that is not also an element of *A*; that is, there is some *x* for which $x \in B$ and $x \notin A$. The set of all women senators is a proper subset of the set of all senators.

It is useful to have some terminology and notation for a set with no elements in it. For example, the set of all ten-year-olds in the United States who vote in presidential elections is the empty set (or, more informally, empty).

**DEFINITION** *Empty Set*

A set that has no elements in it is called the **empty set** and is written $\varnothing$, similar to (but not the same as) the Greek letter phi.

**DEFINITION** *Intersection of Sets*

The **intersection** of two sets *A* and *B*, written $A \cap B$, is the set of elements common to both *A* and *B*. That is,

$$A \cap B = \{x \mid x \in A \text{ and } x \in B\}.$$

For example, $\{a, b, c, d\} \cap \{a, d, e, f\} = \{a, d\}$. The symbol $\cap$ is a special mathematical symbol called a **cap.** (See Figure 2.4a.)

**DEFINITION** *Disjoint*

Two sets *C* and *D* are **disjoint** if *C* and *D* have no elements in common. That is, "*C* and *D* are disjoint" means that $C \cap D = \varnothing$. (See Figure 2.4b.)

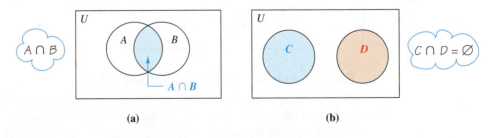

(a)                    (b)

**DEFINITION** *Union of Sets*

The **union** of sets *A* and *B*, written $A \cup B$, is the set of all elements that are in *A* or *B*. That is,

$$A \cup B = \{x \mid x \in A \text{ or } x \in B\}.$$

For example, if $A = \{a, e, i, o, u\}$ and $B = \{a, b, c, d, e\}$, then $A \cup B = \{a, b, c, d, e, i, o, u\}$. Elements such as "a" and "e" that belong to both $A$ and $B$ are listed just once in $A \cup B$. The word *or* in the definition of union is used in the inclusive sense of "and/or." The symbol for union is the **cup,** $\cup$. The cup symbol must be carefully distinguished from the letter $U$ used to denote the universal set. (See Figure 2.5.)

**FIGURE 2.5**
The shaded region corresponds to the union, $A \cup B$, of sets $A$ and $B$.

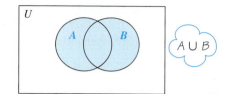

---

**EXAMPLE 2.3** **Performing Operations on Sets**

Let $U = \{p, q, r, s, t, u, v, w, x, y\}$ be the universe, and let $A = \{p, q, r\}$, $B = \{q, r, s, t, u\}$, and $C = \{r, u, w, y\}$. Locate all ten elements of $U$ in a three-loop Venn diagram, and then find the following sets:

(a) $A \cup C$     (b) $A \cap C$     (c) $A \cup B$     (d) $A \cap B$
(e) $\overline{B}$        (f) $\overline{C}$        (g) $A \cup \overline{B}$     (h) $A \cap \overline{C}$

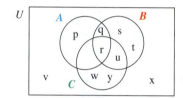

**Solution**

(a) $A \cup C = \{p, q, r, u, w, y\}$        (b) $A \cap C = \{r\}$
(c) $A \cup B = \{p, q, r, s, t, u\}$        (d) $A \cap B = \{q, r\}$
(e) $\quad \overline{B} = \{p, v, w, x, y\}$          (f) $\quad \overline{C} = \{p, q, s, t, v, x\}$
(g) $A \cup \overline{B} = \{p, q, r, v, w, x, y\}$     (h) $A \cap \overline{C} = \{p, q\}$

---

## Using Sets for Problem Solving

The notions of sets and their operations are often used to understand a problem and communicate its solution. Moreover, Venn diagrams provide a visual representation that is useful for understanding and communication.

---

**EXAMPLE 2.4** **Using Sets to Solve a Problem in Color Graphics**

The cathode-ray tube (CRT) on a color monitor uses three types of phosphors, each of which, when excited by an electron beam, produces one of three colors—red, blue, or green. By exciting different combinations of phosphors, a wider range of colors is possible. Use a Venn diagram to show what combinations are possible.

**Solution** Introduce three loops in a Venn diagram—one for each of the component colors. As shown here, eight colors can be achieved. Most computers also allow the intensity of each color to be specified. In this way, many more colors can be obtained.

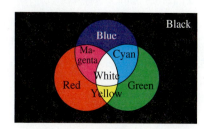

Notice that if red and green are excited, including blue will produce white. Similarly, if red is excited, including both green and blue will again produce white. In symbols, this relationship becomes

$$(R \cap G) \cap B = R \cap (G \cap B).$$

Since the result is independent of where the parentheses are placed, this equation illustrates what is called the **associative property** of the intersection operation. Because the order in which the intersections are performed has no effect on the outcome, we do not need parentheses, and it is meaningful to write $R \cap G \cap B$. Similarly, union is associative, and it is meaningful to write $R \cup G \cup B$, without parentheses.

## Into the Classroom

### Sets Education for Elementary School Children

Sets provide a basis for defining the whole numbers. The operations and properties of the system of whole numbers can be defined and understood through their connection with corresponding operations and properties of sets. However, it is not appropriate to use *abstract* notions of set theory to teach young children. Instead, the teacher should use activities with physical collections of objects to give concrete, hands-on experiences with the idea of sets and associated number concepts. It is critically important to use an approach that has meaning in the child's world. Colored  chips, attribute pieces, tiles, beans, and so on all become useful concrete embodiments of elements that may be organized and classified into sets—sets that can be seen, touched, and manipulated. The older child can later move successfully to pictorial representation. Later still, the student will become comfortable dealing with abstract models, represented entirely in words and symbols.

The associative property is just one example of a number of useful properties that hold for set operations and relations. The properties listed in the theorem that follows can be proved by reasoning directly from the definitions given earlier. They can also be justified by considering appropriately shaded Venn diagrams.

**THEOREM** *Properties of Set Operations and Relations*

**1.** Transitivity of inclusion

$$\text{If } A \subseteq B \text{ and } B \subseteq C, \text{ then } A \subseteq C$$

**2.** Commutativity of union and intersection

$$A \cup B = B \cup A$$
$$A \cap B = B \cap A$$

**3.** Associativity of union and intersection

$$A \cup (B \cup C) = (A \cup B) \cup C$$
$$A \cap (B \cap C) = (A \cap B) \cap C$$

**4.** Properties of the empty set

$$A \cup \varnothing = \varnothing \cup A = A$$
$$A \cap \varnothing = \varnothing \cap A = \varnothing$$

**5.** Distributive property of union and intersection

$$A \cap (B \cup C) = (A \cap B) \cup (A \cap C)$$
$$A \cup (B \cap C) = (A \cup B) \cap (A \cup C)$$

**EXAMPLE 2.5 Verifying Properties with Venn Diagrams**

(a) Verify the distributive property $A \cap (B \cup C) = (A \cap B) \cup (A \cap C)$ (first part of number 5 in preceding theorem).

(b) Show that $A \cup B \cap C$ is not meaningful without parentheses.

**Solution**

(a) To shade the region corresponding to $A \cap (B \cup C)$, we intersect the $A$ loop with the loop formed by the overlapping circles of $B \cup C$:

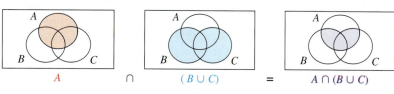

$$A \qquad \cap \qquad (B \cup C) \qquad = \qquad A \cap (B \cup C)$$

The shaded regions are the same.

Next, we combine the two almond-shaped regions $A \cap B$ and $A \cap C$ to form $(A \cap B) \cup (A \cap C)$:

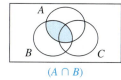 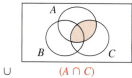 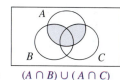

$$(A \cap B) \qquad \cup \qquad (A \cap C) \qquad = \qquad (A \cap B) \cup (A \cap C)$$

The shaded regions at the right agree, which verifies that intersection distributes over union; that is,

$$A \cap (B \cup C) = (A \cap B) \cup (A \cap C).$$

(b) The request in Example 2.5(b) means that, without specifying the order of the operations $\cap$ and $\cup$, the symbol $A \cup B \cap C$ makes no sense. If the union is taken first, we have the expression $(A \cup B) \cap C$, corresponding to the region shaded on the left in the following figure. If the intersection is taken first, we have the expression $A \cup (B \cap C)$, corresponding to the region shaded in the Venn diagram on the right. The shaded regions are different, so in general $(A \cup B) \cap C \neq A \cup (B \cap C)$.

The shaded regions are different.

$$(A \cup B) \cap C \qquad\qquad\qquad\qquad A \cup (B \cap C)$$

We can also consider the particular case $A = \{a\}, B = \{a, b\}, C = \{b, c\}$, for which $(A \cup B) \cap C = \{b\}$ and $A \cup (B \cap C) = \{a, b\}$. We see that $(A \cup B) \cap C \neq A \cup (B \cap C)$, since $\{b\} \neq \{a, b\}$. An example which shows that a statement is false is called a **counterexample.** Examples may shed some light as to why a statement *might* be true. A proof would show that it is always true. A counterexample shows that a statement is false.

Venn diagrams are part of the mathematics of elementary school, as we see from the State Student Assessment problems in this section and the next. More generally, sets appear in such diverse areas as digital photography, visual arts, and color graphics (Example 2.4). In art, the nineteenth-century technique of oil painting called pointillism consists of constructing the painting through the use of points of different colors; that is, objects, which are really subsets of the painting, can be identified as a collection of points, all of the same color. Seurat's painting *Sunday Afternoon on the Island of La Grande Jatte* is a beautiful example of this technique.

## Problem Set 2.1

Exercises numbered in red are answered in the back of the text.

## Understanding Concepts

Problem numbers in color indicate that the answer to that problem can be found at the back of the book.

1. Write the following sets by listing their elements:

   (a) The set of states in the United States that border Nevada

   (b) The set of states in the United States whose names begin with the letter *M*

   (c) The set of states in the United States whose names contain the letter *Z*

2. Write the following sets:

   (a) The set of letters used in the sentence "List the elements in a set only once."

   (b) The set of letters that are needed to spell these words: *team, meat, mate,* and *tame*

3. Let $U = \{1, 2, 3, \ldots, 20\}$. Write the following sets by listing the elements in braces:

   (a) $\{x \in U \mid 6 < x \le 13\}$

   (b) $\{x \in U \mid x \text{ is odd and } 9 \le x \le 13\}$

   (c) $\{x \in U \mid x \text{ is divisible by } 4\}$

   (d) $\{x \in U \mid x = 2n \text{ for some } n \in N\}$

   (e) $\{x \in U \mid x = 2n + 1 \text{ for some } n \in N\}$

   (f) $\{x \in U \mid x = n^2 \text{ for some } n \in N\}$

4. Write these sets in set-builder notation, where $U = \{1, 2, \ldots, 20\}$.

   (a) $\{11, 12, 13, 14\}$     (b) $\{6, 8, 10, 12, 16\}$

   (c) $\{4, 8, 12, 16, 20\}$   (d) $\{2, 5, 10, 17\}$

5. Use set-builder notation to write the following subsets of the natural numbers:

   (a) The even natural numbers larger than 12

   (b) The squares of the odd numbers larger than or equal to 25

   (c) The natural numbers divisible by 3

6. Decide whether the following statements asserting set relationships are *true* or *false*:

   (a) $\{s, c, r, a, m, b, l, e, d\} = \{a, b, c, d, e, l, m, r, s\}$

   (b) $\{6\} \subseteq \{6, 7, 8\}$

   (c) $\{6, 7, 23\} = \{7, 23, 6\}$

   (d) $\{7\} \subset \{6, 7, 23\}$

   (e) $\{6, 7, 23\} \subset \{7, 23, 6\}$

   (f) $\{6\} \subseteq \{7\}$

7. Let $U = \{a, b, c, d, e, f, g, h\}$, $A = \{a, b, c, d, e\}$, $B = \{a, b, c\}$, and $C = \{a, b, h\}$. Locate all eight elements of $U$ in a three-loop Venn diagram, and then list the elements in the following sets:

   (a) $B \cup C$     (b) $A \cap B$     (c) $B \cap C$

   (d) $A \cup B$     (e) $\overline{A}$     (f) $A \cap C$

   (g) $A \cup (B \cap C)$

8. Let $L = \{6, 12, 18, 24, \ldots\}$ be the set of multiples of 6, and let $M = \{45, 90, 135, \ldots\}$ be the set of multiples of 45.

   (a) Find four more elements of set $M$.

   (b) Describe $L \cap M$.

   (c) What is the smallest element in $L \cap M$?

9. Let $G = \{n \mid n \text{ divides } 90\}$ and $D = \{n \mid n \text{ divides } 144\}$. In listed form, $G = \{1, 2, 3, 5, 6, 9, 10, 15, 18, 30, 45, 90\}$.

   (a) Find the listed form of the set $D$.

   (b) Find $G \cap D$.

   (c) Which element of $G \cap D$ is largest?

10. Draw and shade Venn diagrams that correspond to the following sets:

    (a) $A \cap B \cap C$          (b) $A \cup (B \cap \overline{C})$

    (c) $(A \cap B) \cup C$        (d) $\overline{A} \cup (B \cap C)$

    (e) $A \cup B \cup C$          (f) $\overline{A} \cap B \cap C$

11. For each part, draw a Venn diagram whose loops for sets $A$, $B$, and $C$ show that the conditions listed must hold.

    (a) $A \subseteq C, B \subseteq C, A \cap B = \varnothing$

    (b) $C \subseteq (A \cap B)$

    (c) $(A \cap B) \subseteq C$

12. If $A \cup B = A \cup C$, is it necessarily true that $B = C$? Give a proof, or provide a counterexample.

13. Let $U$ be the set of natural numbers 1 through 20, let $A$ be the set of even numbers in $U$, and let $B$ be the set of numbers in $U$ that are divisible by 3.

    (a) Find $\overline{A \cap B}, \overline{A} \cup \overline{B}, \overline{A \cup B},$ and $\overline{A} \cap \overline{B}$.

    (b) What two pairs of the four sets of part (a) are equal?

14. The 12 shapes in the Venn diagram shown are described by the following attributes:

    Shape:  circle, hexagon, or triangle
    Size:   small or large
    Color:  red or blue

    Let $C$, $H$, and $T$ denote the respective sets of circular, hexagonal, and triangular shapes. Similarly, let $S$, $L$, $R$, and $B$ denote the sets of small, large, red, and blue shapes, respectively. The set $A$ contains the shapes that are small and not a triangle, so $A = S \cap \overline{T}$.

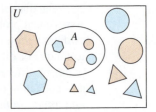

Describe which shapes are found in these sets:

**(a)** $R \cap C$   **(b)** $L \cap H$   **(c)** $T \cup H$

**(d)** $L \cap T$   **(e)** $B \cap \overline{C}$   **(f)** $H \cap S \cap R$

**15.** Let $C$, $H$, $T$, $S$, $L$, $R$, and $B$ denote the sets of attribute shapes described in problem 14. The set of small hexagons can be written $S \cap H$ in symbolic form. Express the following sets in symbolic form:

**(a)** The large triangles

**(b)** The blue polygonal (i.e., noncircular) shapes

**(c)** The small or triangular shapes

**(d)** The shapes that either are blue circles or are red

## Teaching Concepts

**16.** A large group activity can effectively teach set concepts to children. For example, let the classroom be the universe of the students. Use lengths of rope (about 30 feet, adjusting for the size of the class) to form Venn diagram loops on the floor. Place signs in the loops to identify the sets being considered. Once the signs are placed, have the children stand in the appropriate loop or in overlapping regions of two or more loops, depending on the defining property of the set. For example, if loop $A$ corresponds to the girls in the class, then the girls should stand inside the loop and the boys should stand outside the loop. Now create other interesting classroom Venn diagram activities.

**(a)** Define sets $B$ and $C$ for which $B$ is a subset of $C$.

**(b)** Define sets $D$ and $E$ that are disjoint.

**(c)** Define sets $F$, $G$, and $H$ in a way that you believe there is a good likelihood that students will be found in all eight regions of the classroom Venn diagram.

## Responding to Students

**17.** A student is told that $A \cup B$ is the set of all elements that belong to $A$ or to $B$. However, when asked to find the union of $A = \{a, b, c, d\}$, and $B = \{c, d, e, f, g, h\}$, the student says that the answer is $\{a, b, e, f, g, h\}$. How is the word *or* in the definition of set union being misunderstood? Give the student an everyday example where *or* is used in the mathematical sense.

**18.** Students are told that the set of natural numbers ($N$) is a subset of the set of whole numbers ($W$). Have students represent this relationship with a Venn diagram and then explain it in words and symbols. Would your students think that $0 \in N$? Zero will be continue to be a source of confusion as children begin to develop mathematical number sense.

## Thinking Critically

**19.** Circular loops in a Venn diagram divide the universe $U$ into distinct regions.

| No sets | 1 set | 2 sets |
|---------|-------|--------|
| 1 region | 2 regions | 4 regions |

**(a)** Draw a diagram with three circles that gives the largest number of regions.

**(b)** How many regions do the four circles define in this figure?

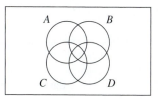

**(c)** Verify that the four-circle diagram is missing a region corresponding to $A \cap \overline{B} \cap \overline{C} \cap D$. What other set has no corresponding region?

**(d)** Will this Venn diagram allow for all possible combinations of four sets? Explain briefly, but carefully.

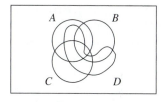

**20.** The English mathematician Augustus DeMorgan (1806–1871) showed that

$$\overline{A \cap B} = \overline{A} \cup \overline{B} \quad \text{and} \quad \overline{A \cup B} = \overline{A} \cap \overline{B}.$$

These identities are now called DeMorgan's laws.

**(a)** Use a sequence of Venn diagrams to explain, in words and pictures, how to shade the regions corresponding to $\overline{A \cap B}$ and $\overline{A} \cup \overline{B}$. The final shaded regions obtained should be identical, justifying DeMorgan's first law.

**(b)** Carefully explain how to justify DeMorgan's second law by shading Venn diagrams.

**21.** Each of the objects depicted in problem 14 is described by its attributes: shape (three choices), size (two choices), and color (two choices). The number of pieces in a full set of shapes can be varied by changing the number of attributes and the number of possible choices of an attribute. How many pieces are contained in the following attribute sets?

**(a)** Shape: circle, hexagon, equilateral triangle, isosceles right triangle, rectangle, square
Size: large, small
Color: red, blue

**(b)** Use the attributes in part **(a)**, but also include this attribute: Thickness: thick, thin

## Thinking Cooperatively

**22.** Attribute cards can be made by drawing different shapes on cards, varying the figure shown, the color used, and so on. Here are some examples of a few attribute cards:

**(a)** Conjecture how many cards make a full deck. Explain how you got your answer.

**(b)** Form groups of three to five students. Each group is to design and make a set of attribute cards, drawing simple figures on small rectangles of card stock with colored pens.

**(c)** Exchange decks of attribute cards among the cooperative groups. Shuffle each deck and turn over just a few of the cards. Can each group predict the number of cards in the complete deck? Carefully explain the reasoning used.

## Making Connections

**23.** If a penny (P) and a nickel (N) are flipped, the possible outcomes can be listed by forming all of the subsets that could represent heads. There are four possible outcomes: $\varnothing$, {P}, {N}, and {P, N}. For example, $\varnothing$ is the outcome for which both coins land on tails.

**(a)** List the possible outcomes if a penny, nickel, and dime (D) are flipped. How many outcomes (i.e., subsets of {P, N, D}) did you find?

**(b)** List the subsets of {P, N, D, Q}, where Q represents a quarter. How many subsets did you find?

**(c)** How many of the subsets {P, N, D, Q} contain Q? How many do not contain Q?

**(d)** Use inductive reasoning to describe the number of subsets of a set with *n* elements.

**24. The ABO System of Blood Typing.** Until the beginning of the twentieth century, it was assumed that all human blood was identical. About 1900, however, the Austrian-American pathologist Karl Landsteiner discovered that blood could be classified into four groups according to the presence of proteins called antigens. This discovery made it possible to transfuse blood safely. A person with the antigens A, B, or both A and B has the respective blood type A, B, or AB. If neither antigen is present, the type is O. Draw and label a Venn diagram that illustrates the ABO system.

**25. The Rh System of Blood Typing.** In 1940, Karl Landsteiner (see problem 24) and the American pathologist Alexander Wiener discovered another protein that coats the red blood cells of some persons. Since the initial research was on rhesus monkeys, a person with the protein is classified as Rh positive (Rh+) and a person whose blood cells lack the protein is Rh negative (Rh−). Draw and label a Venn diagram illustrating the classification of blood into the eight major types: A+, A−, B+, B−, AB+, AB−, O+, and O−.

## Communicating

**26.** The word *set* has been given precise mathematical meaning. The same word is also used as part of our ordinary language. For example, you may own a set of golf clubs. Make a list of other examples in which *set*—or *family, aggregate, class,* or *collection*—is used, and discuss to what extent the usage corresponds to the mathematical concept of *set.*

**27.** Many of the terms introduced in this section also have meaning in nonmathematical contexts. For example,

*complement, union,* and *intersection* are used in ordinary speech. Other terms, such as *transitive, commutative, associative,* and *distributive,* are rare in everyday usage, but there are closely related words that are quite common, such as *transit, commute, associate,* and *distribute.* Discuss the differences and similarities in the meanings of the words, and word roots, of the terms introduced in this section.

## From State Student Assessments

**28.** (Washington State, Grade 4)
Ms. Yonan took a survey in her class to see how many students like hamburgers, pizza, or hot dogs. The results of the survey are shown in the chart.

| **Number of Students Who Like:** | | |
|---|---|---|
| **Only 1 of These Foods** | **Only 2 of These Foods** | **All 3 of These Foods** |
| 14 | 10 | 4 |

Look at the following three Venn diagrams. Choose the diagram that best represents the results of this survey.

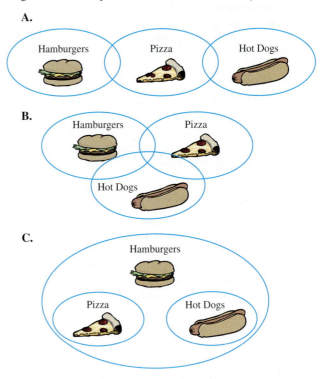

**29.** (Delaware, Grade 5)
Look at the Venn diagram below.

• Add the following numbers to your Venn diagram: 20, 24, 30, 36.

• Explain why you put each number where you did.

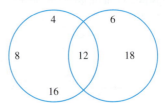

**30.** (Texas, Grade 6)

Look at set $V$ and set $W$ shown below.

Set $V = \{1, 3, 5, 7, 9, 11, \ldots\}$

Set $W = \{3, 6, 9, 12, 15, 18, \ldots\}$

Which of the following numbers could belong to both set $V$ and set $W$?

**F.** 35      **G.** 25      **H.** 21      **J.** 31

**31.** (Virginia, Grade 8)

Sarah is filling numbers in the Venn diagram. No number is to be entered more than once.

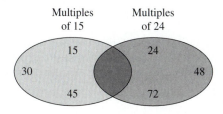

Multiples of 15        Multiples of 24

15        24

30        48

45        72

What is the least number that can be appropriately placed in the shaded (overlapped) area of the diagram?

**A.** 360

**B.** 240

**C.** 120

**D.** 60

**32.** (New York, Grade 7—this is an open response item)

Carlotta asks 30 campers which outdoor activity they enjoy. Of these campers, 13 enjoy swimming, 17 enjoy baseball, and 8 enjoy both swimming and baseball.

**(a)** Draw a Venn diagram using the information above.

**(b)** How many campers did **not** select any outdoor activity?

## 2.2

# Sets, Counting, and the Whole Numbers

If you attend a student raffle, you might hear the following announcement when the entry forms are drawn:

> *The student with ticket 50768-973 has just won second prize—four tickets to the big game this Saturday.*

> There are three types of numbers.

This sentence contains three numbers, each of a different type, and each serving a different purpose.

First, the number of the ticket identifies the ticket. Such a number is called a **nominal number** or an **identification.** A nominal number is a sequence of digits used as a name or label. Telephone numbers, social security numbers, account numbers with stores and banks, serial numbers, and driver's license numbers are just a few examples of the use of numbers for identification and naming. The role such numbers play in contemporary society has expanded rapidly with the advent of computers.

The next type of number used by the raffle announcer is one that represents a place in a sequence. The words *first, second, third, fourth,* and so on are used to describe the relative positions of the objects. A number that describes where an object is in an ordered sequence is called an **ordinal number.** Thus, ordinal numbers communicate location in an ordered collection. "First class," "second rate," "third base," "fifth page," "sixth volume," and "21st century" are all familiar examples of ordinal numbers.

The final use of a number by the raffle announcer is to tell how many tickets had been won. That is, the prize is a set of tickets, and *four* tells us *how many* tickets are in the set. More specifically, the **cardinal number** of a set is the number of objects in the set. Thus, a cardinal number, or **cardinality,** helps communicate the basic notion of "how many."

Notice that numbers, of whatever type, can be expressed verbally (in a language) or symbolically (in a numeration system). For example, the number of moons of Mars is "two" in English, "zwei" in German, and "dos" in Spanish. Symbolically, we could write 2 in the Indo-Arabic (or Hindu-Arabic*) system or II in Roman numerals. Numeration, as a system of symbolic representation of numbers, is closely related to algorithms for computation. Numeration systems, both historic and contemporary, are described in Chapter 3.

---

*"Indo" refers to India, the region of origination of the symbols. "Hindu" refers to the predominant religion of India.

In the remainder of this section, we explore the notion of "how many" (cardinal numbers) more fully. Of special importance is the set of whole numbers, which can be viewed as the set of cardinal numbers of finite sets.

## One-to-One Correspondence and Equivalent Sets

Suppose, when you come to your classroom, each student is seated at his or her desk. You would immediately know, *without counting*, that the number of children and the number of occupied desks are the same. This example illustrates the concept of a **one-to-one correspondence** between sets, in which each element of one set is paired with exactly one element of the second set and each element of either set belongs to exactly one of the pairs.

> **DEFINITION**    *One-to-One Correspondence*
> A **one-to-one correspondence** between sets $A$ and $B$ is an assignment, for each element of $A$, of exactly one element of $B$ in such a way that all elements of $B$ are used. It can also be thought of as a pairing of elements between $A$ and $B$ such that each element of $A$ is matched with one and only one element of $B$ and every element of $B$ has an element of $A$ assigned to it.

Figure 2.6 illustrates a one-to-one correspondence between the sets of board members and offices of the Math Club.

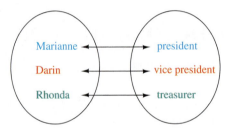

**FIGURE 2.6**
A one-to-one correspondence between the sets of board members {Marianne, Darin, Rhonda} and offices {president, vice president, treasurer} of the Math Club

Because there is a one-to-one correspondence between the sets $\{m, d, r\}$ and $\{p, v, t\}$ (abbreviating the names of the elements of each set), we say that they are **equivalent sets** and write $\{m, d, r\} \sim \{p, v, t\}$. By contrast, the set $\{m, d, r\}$ is neither equal nor equivalent to $\{m, d\}$.

More generally, we have the following definition:

> **DEFINITION**    *Equivalent, or Matching, Sets*
> Sets $A$ and $B$ are **equivalent** if there is a one-to-one correspondence between $A$ and $B$. When $A$ and $B$ are equivalent, we write $A \sim B$. We also say that equivalent sets **match**. If $A$ and $B$ are not equivalent, we write $A \nsim B$.

It is easy to see that equal sets match. To see why, suppose that $A = B$. Then, since each $x$ in $A$ is also in $B$, the natural matching $x \leftrightarrow x$ is a one-to-one correspondence between $A$ and $B$. Thus, $A \sim B$. Conversely, there is no reason to believe that equivalent sets must be equal. For example, $\{\square, \bigstar\}$ is equivalent to $\{1, 2\}$, but $\{\square, \bigstar\} \neq \{1, 2\}$.

## EXAMPLE 2.6    Investigating Sets for Equivalence

Let $A = \{x \mid x \text{ is a moon of Mars}\}$
$B = \{x \mid x \text{ is a former U.S. president whose last name is Adams}\}$
$C = \{x \mid x \text{ is one of the Brontë sisters of nineteenth-century literary fame}\}$
$D = \{x \mid x \text{ is a satellite of the fourth-closest planet to the sun}\}$

Which of these relationships, $=$, $\neq$, $\sim$, and $\nsim$, holds between distinct pairs of the four sets?

**Solution**

It is useful to write the sets in listed form:

$A = D = \{\text{Deimos, Phobos}\}$, $B = \{\text{John Adams, John Quincy Adams}\}$, and
$C = \{\text{Anne, Charlotte, Emily}\}$.

Therefore, looking at the foursets, we see that

$$A \neq B, A \neq C, A = D, B \neq C, B \neq D, C \neq D,$$
$$A \sim B, A \not\sim C, A \sim D, B \not\sim C, B \sim D, \text{ and } C \not\sim D.$$

## The Whole Numbers

The sets $\{a, b, c\}$, $\{\square, \bigcirc, \triangle\}$, $\{\text{Mercury, Venus, Earth}\}$, and $\{\text{Larry, Moe, Curly}\}$ are distinct, but they do share the property of "threeness." The English word *three* and the Indo-Arabic numeral 3 are used to identify this common property of all sets that are equivalent to $\{1, 2, 3\}$. In a similar way, we use the word *two*, and the symbol 2, to convey the idea that all of the sets that are equivalent to the set $\{1, 2\}$ have the same cardinality.

Some sets are quite large, and it is difficult to know how large $n$ must be for the set to be equivalent to the set $\{1, 2, 3, \ldots, n\}$. For example, the set of people alive in the world in the year 2009 would require $n$ to be around $6.804 \times 10^9$ (i.e., $n$ is about 6.804 billion). Even so, this is an example of a finite set. In general, a set is said to be **finite** if it either is the empty set or is equivalent to a set $\{1, 2, 3, \ldots, n\}$ for some natural number $n$. Sets that are not finite are called **infinite.** For example, the set $N$ of all of the natural numbers is an infinite set. It is usually easy to know whether a set is finite or infinite, but not always. In Chapter 4, we'll see Euclid's clever proof that the set of prime numbers $\{2, 3, 5, 7, 11, 13, 17, 19, 23, 29, 31, \ldots\}$ is an infinite set.

The whole numbers, as defined shortly, allow us to classify any finite set according to how many elements the set contains. It is useful to adopt the symbol $n(A)$ to represent the cardinality of the finite set $A$. If $A$ is not the empty set, then $n(A)$ is a counting number. The cardinality of the empty set, however, requires a new name and symbol: We let **zero** designate the cardinality of the empty set and write $0 = n(\emptyset)$.

> Use $n(A)$ to denote the number of elements in set $A$.

A common error is made by omitting the $n(\ )$ symbol: Be sure *not* to write "$A = 4$" when your intention is to state that $n(A) = 4$.

---

> **DEFINITION** *The Whole Numbers*
>
> The **whole numbers** are the cardinal numbers of finite sets—that is, the numbers of elements in finite sets. If $A \sim \{1, 2, 3, \ldots, m\}$, then $n(A) = m$ and $n(\emptyset) = 0$, where $n(A)$ denotes the cardinality of set $A$. The set of whole numbers is written $W = \{0, 1, 2, 3, \ldots\}$.

---

## EXAMPLE 2.7 Determining Whole Numbers

For each set, find the whole number that gives the number of elements in the set:

**(a)** $M = \{x \mid x \text{ is a month of the year}\}$
**(b)** $A = \{a, b, c, \ldots, z\}$
**(c)** $B = \{n \in N \mid n \text{ is a square number smaller than 200}\}$
**(d)** $Z = \{n \in N \mid n \text{ is a square number between 70 and 80}\}$
**(e)** $S = \{0\}$

**Solution**

**(a)** $n(M) = 12$, since $M \sim \{1, 2, 3, \ldots, 12\}$, and this amounts to counting the elements in $M$.
**(b)** $n(A) = 26$
**(c)** $n(B) = 14$, since $14^2 = 196 \in B$ but $15^2 = 225 \notin B$. Note that we don't have to write out all of the members of $B$ to solve this problem. Still, it is easy to do:
$B = \{1, 4, 9, 16, 25, 36, 49, 64, 81, 100, 121, 144, 169, 196, \}$, and $B$ contains 14 elements.
**(d)** $n(Z) = 0$, since $8^2 = 64 < 70$ but $9^2 = 81 > 80$. Therefore, there are no square numbers between 70 and 80 and $Z = \emptyset$.
**(e)** $n(S) = 1$, since the set $\{0\}$ contains one element. This shows that zero is *not* the same as "nothing"!

## Physical and Pictorial Representations for Whole Numbers

Here are just a few physical and pictorial representations useful for explaining whole- and natural-number concepts to your elementary school students. In the next chapter, additional representations are introduced that help illustrate connections to numeration and algorithms for the operations of arithmetic.

**Tiles**    Tiles are congruent squares, each about 2 centimeters ($\frac{3}{4}$ inch) on a side. They should be sufficiently thick to be easily picked up and moved about. Colored plastic tiles are available from suppliers, but tiles are easily handmade from vinyl tile or cardboard. Of course, beans, circular discs, and other objects can be used as well. However, square tiles can be arranged into rectangular patterns, and such patterns reveal many of the fundamental properties of the whole numbers. (See Figure 2.7.)

**FIGURE 2.7**
Some representations of "six" with square tiles

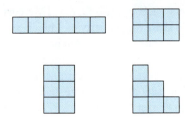

**Cubes**    Cubes are much like tiles, but they can form both three-dimensional and two-dimensional patterns. Several attractive versions are commercially available. Unifix™ Cubes can be snapped together to form linear groupings. MathLink® Cubes permit planar and spatial patterns, as we see in Figure 2.8.

**FIGURE 2.8**
Some representations of "12" with cubes

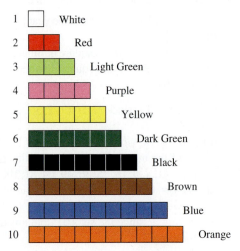

**Number Strips and Rods**    Colored strips of cardboard or heavy paper, divided into squares, can be used to demonstrate and reinforce whole-number properties and operations. The squares should be ruled off, and colors can be used to visually identify the number of squares in a strip, as indicated in Figure 2.9. These number strips are nearly interchangeable with Cuisenaire® rods, which have been used effectively for many years. The colors shown in the figure correspond to those of Cuisenaire® rods. Whole numbers larger than 10 are illustrated by placing strips, or rods, end to end to form a "train."

**FIGURE 2.9**
Number strips for the natural numbers 1 through 10

| 1 | White |
|---|-------|
| 2 | Red |
| 3 | Light Green |
| 4 | Purple |
| 5 | Yellow |
| 6 | Dark Green |
| 7 | Black |
| 8 | Brown |
| 9 | Blue |
| 10 | Orange |

**Number Line**   The number line is a pictorial model in which two distinct points on a line are labeled 0 and 1 and then the remaining whole numbers are marked off in succession with the same spacing. (See Figure 2.10.) Any whole number is interpreted as a distance from 0, which can be shown by an arrow. The number-line model is particularly important because it can also be used to visualize the number systems that are developed later in this book.

> The number line begins at 0, not at 1.

**FIGURE 2.10**
Illustrating "two" and "five" on the number-line model of the whole numbers

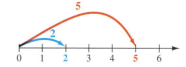

The number line will also help us represent operations involving whole numbers and the ordering of the whole numbers.

## Ordering the Whole Numbers

We often wish to relate the number of elements in two given sets. For example, if each child in the class is given one cupcake, and there are some cupcakes left over, we would know that there are more cupcakes than children. Notice that children have been matched to a *proper* subset of the set of cupcakes.

The order of the whole numbers can be defined in the following way:

> **DEFINITION**   *Ordering the Whole Numbers*
>
> Let $a = n(A)$ and $b = n(B)$ be whole numbers, where $A$ and $B$ are finite sets. If $A$ matches a *proper* subset of $B$, we say that ***a* is less than *b*** and write $a < b$.

The expression $b > a$ is read "$b$ is greater than $a$" and is equivalent to $a < b$. Also, $a \leq b$ means "$a$ is less than or equal to $b$." The use of rods or the number line shows that $a < b$ if, and only if, $a + c = b$ for some $c > 0$.

**EXAMPLE  2.8   Showing the Order of Whole Numbers**

Use **(a)** sets, **(b)** tiles, **(c)** rods, and **(d)** the number line to show that $4 < 7$.

**Solution**

**(a)** The diagram which follows shows that a set with 4 elements matches a proper subset of a set with 7 elements. Therefore, $4 < 7$. Note that 3 elements of the second set have no matches.

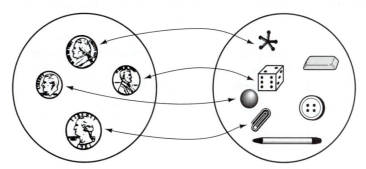

**(b)** By setting tiles side by side, it is seen that the 4 colored tiles match a proper subset of the 7 uncolored tiles. Here, 3 uncolored tiles are left unmatched.

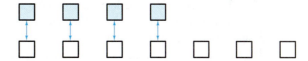

**(c)** With rods, the order of whole numbers is interpreted by comparing the lengths of the rods:

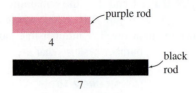

**(d)** On the number line, $4 < 7$ because 4 is to the left of 7.

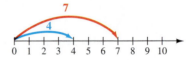

## Problem Solving with Whole Numbers and Venn Diagrams

Venn diagrams and the associated concept of a whole number can often be used as a practical problem-solving tool, as we illustrate in the next example. These problems appear often in the State Student Assessments. (See problem 37 in Problem Set 2.2.)

**EXAMPLE 2.9  Solving a Classification Problem**

In a recent survey, the 60 students living in Harris Hall were asked about their enrollments in science, engineering, and humanities classes. The results were as follows:

24 are taking a science class.
22 are taking an engineering class.
17 are taking a humanities class.
5 are taking both science and engineering classes.
4 are taking both science and humanities classes.
3 are taking both engineering and humanities classes.
2 are taking classes in all three areas.

How many students are not taking classes in any of the three areas? How many students are taking a class in just one area? Using a Venn diagram, indicate the number of students in each region of the diagram.

**Solution**    Let $S$, $E$, and $H$ denote the set of students in science, engineering, and humanities classes, respectively. Since $n(S \cap E \cap H) = 2$, begin by placing the 2 in the region of the Venn diagram corresponding to the subset $S \cap E \cap H$. Then, by comparing $n(S \cap E \cap H) = 2$ and $n(E \cap H) = 3$, we conclude that there is one student who is taking both engineering and humanities, but not a science class. This conclusion allows us to fill in the 1 in the Venn diagram. Analogous reasoning leads to the entries within the loops of the following Venn diagram:

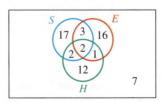

The values within the loops account for 53 of the 60 students, so it follows that 7 students are not taking classes in any of the three areas. Also, since $17 + 16 + 12 = 45$, we conclude that 45 students are taking a class in just one area.

## Problem Set 2.2

Exercises numbered in red are answered in the back of the text.

### Understanding Concepts

**1.** Classify by type—cardinal, ordinal, or nominal—the numbers that appear in these sentences:

   **(a)** On June 13, Chang was promoted to first vice president.

   **(b)** In the fourth week of class, Alonzo received a 93 on the second exam.

**2.** For each pair of sets, decide whether the sets are equivalent to one another:

   **(a)** $\{1, 2, 3, 4, 5\}$ and $\{x \mid x$ is a letter in the phrase "PANAMA BANANA MAN"$\}$

   **(b)** $\{a, b, c\}$ and $\{w, x, y, z\}$

   **(c)** $\{o, n, e\}$ and $\{t, w, o\}$

   **(d)** $\{0\}$ and $\varnothing$

**3.** Let $A$, $B$, and $C$ be finite sets, with $A \subset B \subseteq C$ and $n(B) = 5$.

   **(a)** What are the possible values of $n(A)$?

   **(b)** What are the possible values of $n(C)$?

**4.** Use counting to determine the whole number that corresponds to the cardinality of these sets:

   **(a)** $A = \{x \mid x \in N$ and $20 < x \leq 27\}$

   **(b)** $B = \{x \mid x \in N$ and $x + 1 = x\}$

   **(c)** $C = \{x \mid x \in N$ and $(x - 1)(x - 9) = 0\}$

   **(d)** $D = \{x \mid x \in N, 1 \leq x \leq 100$, and $x$ is divisible by both 5 and 8$\}$

**5.** Let
$A = \{n \mid n$ is a cube of a natural number and $1 \leq n \leq 100\}$;
$B = \{s \mid s$ is a state in the United States that borders Mexico$\}$.
Is $A \sim B$?

**6.** Let $N = \{1, 2, 3, 4, \ldots\}$ be the set of natural numbers and $S = \{1, 4, 9, 16, \ldots\}$ be the set of squares of the natural numbers. Then $N \sim S$, since we have the one-to-one correspondence $1 \leftrightarrow 1, 2 \leftrightarrow 4, 3 \leftrightarrow 9, 4 \leftrightarrow 16, \ldots n \leftrightarrow n^2$. (This example is interesting, since it shows that an infinite set can be equivalent to a proper subset of itself.) Show that each of the following pairs of sets are equivalent by carefully describing a one-to-one correspondence between the sets:

   **(a)** The whole numbers and natural numbers:
$W = \{0, 1, 2, 3, \ldots\}$ and $N = \{1, 2, 3, 4, \ldots\}$

   **(b)** The sets of odd and even natural numbers:
$D = \{1, 3, 5, 7, \ldots\}$ and $E = \{2, 4, 6, 8, \ldots\}$

   **(c)** The set of natural numbers and the set of powers of 10:
$N = \{1, 2, 3, 4, \ldots\}$ and $\{10, 100, 1000, \ldots\}$

**7.** Decide which of the following sets are finite:

   **(a)** $\{$grains of sand on all the world's beaches$\}$

   **(b)** $\{$whole numbers divisible by the number 46,182,970,138$\}$

   **(c)** $\{$points on a line segment that is 1 inch long$\}$

**8.** The figure that follows shows two line segments, $L_1$ and $L_2$. The rays through point $P$ give, geometrically, a one-to-one correspondence between the points on $L_1$ and the points on $L_2$—for example, $Q_1 \leftrightarrow Q_2$.

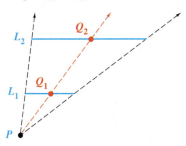

Use similar geometric diagrams to show that the figures that follow are equivalent sets of points. Describe all possible locations of point $P$.

   **(a)** Two concentric circles

   **(b)** A circle and an inscribed square

   **(c)** A triangle and its circumscribing circle

   **(d)** A semicircle and its diameter

**9.** Decide whether the statements that follow are true or false. If false, give a counterexample; that is, give an example of two finite sets $A$ and $B$ that satisfy the hypothesis (the "if part"), but not the conclusion, of the statement.

   **(a)** If $A \subseteq B$, then $n(A) \leq n(B)$.

   **(b)** If $n(A) < n(B)$, then $A \subset B$.

   **(c)** If $n(A \cup B) = n(A)$, then $B \subseteq A$.

   **(d)** If $n(A \cap B) = n(A)$, then $A \subseteq B$.

**10.** Let $A$ and $B$ be finite sets.

   **(a)** Explain why $n(A \cap B) \leq n(A)$.

   **(b)** Explain why $n(A) \leq n(A \cup B)$.

   **(c)** Suppose $n(A \cap B) = n(A \cup B)$. What more can be said about $A$ and $B$?

11. A survey of 700 households revealed that 300 had only a TV, 100 had only a computer, and 100 had neither a TV nor a computer. How many households have both a TV and a computer? Use a two-loop Venn diagram to find your answer.

12. Let $U = \{1, 2, 3, \ldots, 1000\}$. Also, let $F$ be the subset of numbers in $U$ that are multiples of 5, and let $S$ be the subset of numbers in $U$ that are multiples of 6. Since $1000 \div 5 = 200$, it follows that $n(F) = n(\{5 \cdot 1, 5 \cdot 2, \ldots, 5 \cdot 200\}) = 200$.

    (a) Find $n(S)$ by using a method similar to the one which showed that $n(F) = 200$.

    (b) Find $n(F \cap S)$.

    (c) Label the number of elements in each region of a two-loop Venn diagram with universe $U$ and subsets $F$ and $S$.

13. Finish labeling the number of elements in the regions in the Venn diagram shown, where the subsets $A$, $B$, and $C$ of the universe $U$ satisfy the conditions listed.

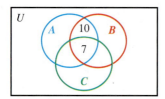

$n(U) = 100$

$n(A) = 40$

$n(B) = 50$

$n(C) = 30$

$n(A \cap B) = 17$

$n(B \cap C) = 12$

$n(A \cap C) = 15$

$n(A \cap B \cap C) = 7$

14. A poll of students showed that 55 percent liked basketball, 40 percent liked soccer, 55 percent liked football, 25 percent liked both basketball and soccer, 20 percent liked both soccer and football, 20 percent liked both basketball and football, and 10 percent liked all three sports. Use a Venn diagram to answer these questions: What percentage of students likes only one sport? What percentage does not like any of the three sports?

15. Number tiles can be arranged to form patterns that relate to properties of numbers.

    (a) Arrange number tiles to show why $1, 4, 9, 16, 25, \ldots$ are called the "square" numbers.

    (b) Arrange number tiles to show why $1, 3, 6, 10, 15, \ldots$ are called "triangular" numbers.

16. In a college mathematics class, all the students are also taking anthropology, history, or psychology, and some of the students are taking two, or even all three, of these courses. If (i) 40 students are taking anthropology, (ii) 11 students are taking history, (iii) 12 students are taking psychology, (iv) 3 students are taking all three courses, (v) 6 students are taking anthropology and history, and (vi) 6 students are taking psychology and anthropology,

(a) how many students are taking only anthropology?

(b) how many students are taking anthropology or history?

(c) how many students are taking history and anthropology, but not psychology?

## Teaching Concepts

17. Describe how you might teach a very young child the idea of color and the words such as *blue* or *red* that describe particular colors. Do you see any similarities in teaching the idea of color and the idea of number, including such words as *two* or *five*?

18. Suggest a method to convey the notion of zero to a young child.

19. Imagine yourself teaching a third grader the transitive property of "less than," whereby $a < b$ and $b < c$ allow you to conclude that $a < c$. (A proof is outlined in problem 25.) Write an imagined dialogue with the student, using number strips (or Cuisinaire rods) as a manipulative.

20. Which of the numbers that follow is a square number (meaning the square of an integer)? Use a diagram to support your answer.

$$\boxed{200 \quad 300 \quad 400 \quad 500 \quad 600}$$

## Responding to Students

21. Zack has trouble working a problem from the Fayette County (Kentucky) Public Schools Grade 4 Learning Check. He is not sure of where 27 or 14 should go. First do the Learning Check yourself, and then explain to Zack where 27 and 14 go and why. (This problem was given in October 2005 as a Mathematics Open-Response Question.)

    The diagram that follows shows how Zack is grouping some numbers:

    - One circle has multiples of 3.
    - The other circle has multiples of 4.
    - The shaded space is for numbers that are multiples of both 3 and 4.
    - Numbers that are not a multiple of 3 or 4 go in the space outside the circles.

    Zack has already placed the numbers 1, 5, 8, 12, and 30 in the correct spaces in the diagram.

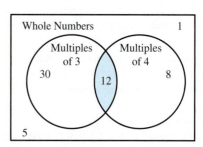

    (a) Make a copy of the diagram on your paper. Write each of the following numbers in the correct space in your diagram:

    $$24, 16, 27, 14, 32$$

**(b)** Identify one more number *less than 40* that goes in *each* of the four spaces in the diagram. Be sure to tell in which space in the diagram each number belongs. Explain how you know that the numbers you used are placed correctly.

**22.** Richard is working with square numbers and is confused. He says that $0^2$ equals 0 and $2^2$ equals 4, so $5^2 = 10$.

**(a)** What does Richard think that the rule is?

**(b)** Using centimeter grid paper, show Richard what the representations of the first five square numbers are.

## Thinking Critically

**23. (a)** How many ways can three balls of different colors—yellow, red, and green—be put in a ball can?

**(b)** How many different one-to-one correspondences are there between the two sets $\{1, 2, 3\}$ and $\{y, r, g\}$?

**(c)** Explain why a dozen dyed eggs, all of different colors, can be placed in a carton in $12 \times 11 \times 10 \times 9 \times 8 \times 7 \times 6 \times 5 \times 4 \times 3 \times 2 \times 1$ ways. (*Suggestion:* How many ways can you put the first egg into the carton? How many ways can you put the second egg into the carton? . . . How many ways are left to put the last egg into the carton?)

**(d)** How many different one-to-one correspondences are there between the two sets $\{1, 2, 3, \ldots, 12\}$ and $\{a, b, c, d, e, f, g, h, i, j, k, l\}$?

**24.** Consider a three-element set $C = \{a, b, c\}$. This set has one subset with no elements—namely, $\varnothing$; three subsets with one element—$\{a\}$, $\{b\}$, and $\{c\}$; three subsets with two elements—$\{a, b\}$, $\{b, c\}$, and $\{a, c\}$; and one subset with three elements—$\{a, b, c\}$. This fills in row $n = 3$ of the table below, where the entry in row $n$ and column $r$ gives the number of ways to choose different subsets of $r$ elements from a set of $n$ elements.

**(a)** Find all of the subsets of each of the four sets $\varnothing$, $A = \{a\}$, $B = \{a, b\}$, and $D = \{a, b, c, d\}$, and fill in the table through row $n = 4$.

**(b)** What pattern of numbers do you see in the table? Use the pattern to fill in the next two rows.

**25.** Use the ideas of sets and the definition of the order relation for the whole numbers to justify the transitive property of "less than." That is, if $k$, $l$, and $m$ are whole numbers satisfying $k < l$ and $l < m$, then $k < m$. (*Suggestion:* Consider sets satisfying $K \subset L \subset M$.)

**26.** Evelyn's Electronics Emporium hired Sloppy Survey Services (SSS) to poll 100 households at random. Evelyn's report from SSS contained the following data on ownership of a TV, VCR, or stereo:

| | |
|---|---|
| TV only | 8 |
| TV and VCR (at least) | 70 |
| TV, VCR, and stereo | 65 |
| Stereo only | 3 |
| Stereo and TV (at least) | 74 |
| No TV, VCR, or stereo | 4 |

Evelyn, who assumes that anyone with a VCR also has a TV, is wondering if she should believe the figures. Should she?

**27.** At a school with 100 students, 35 students were taking Arabic, 32 Bulgarian, and 30 Chinese. Twenty students take only Arabic, 20 take only Bulgarian, and 14 take only Chinese. In addition, 7 students are taking both Arabic and Bulgarian, some of whom also take Chinese. How many students are taking all three languages? None of these three languages?

**28.** A political polling organization sent out a questionnaire that asked the following question: "Which taxes—income, sales, or excise—would you be willing to have raised?" Sixty voters' opinions were tallied by the office clerk:

| Tax | Number Willing to Raise the Tax |
|---|---|
| Income | 20 |
| Sales | 28 |
| Excise | 29 |
| Income and sales | 7 |
| Income and excise | 8 |
| Sales and excise | 10 |
| Unwilling to raise any tax | 5 |

The clerk neglected to count how many, if any, of the 60 voters are willing to raise all three of the taxes. Can you help the pollsters? Explain how.

**29.** There are 40 students in the Travel Club. They discovered that 17 members have visited Mexico, 28 have visited Canada, 10 have been to England, 12 have visited both Mexico and Canada, 3 have been only to England, and 4 have been only to Mexico. Some club members have not been to any of the three foreign countries, and, curiously, an equal number have been to all three countries.

| | $r = 0$ | $r = 1$ | $r = 2$ | $r = 3$ | $r = 4$ | $r = 5$ | $r = 6$ |
|---|---|---|---|---|---|---|---|
| $n = 0$ | | | | | | | |
| $n = 1$ | | | | | | | |
| $n = 2$ | | | | | | | |
| $n = 3$ | 1 | 3 | 3 | 1 | | | |
| $n = 4$ | | | | | | | |
| $n = 5$ | | | | | | | |
| $n = 6$ | | | | | | | |

(a) How many students have been to all three countries?

(b) How many students have been only to Canada?

30. Letitia, Brianne, and Jake met at the mall on December 31. Letitia said that she intends to come to the mall every third day throughout the next year. Brianne said that she intends to be there every fourth day, and Jake said he would be there every fifth day. Letitia said that she knew she would be at the mall a total of 121 days, since $365 \div 3$ is 121 with a remainder of 2. Brianne said that she'd be at the mall 91 days, since $365 \div 4$ is 91 with a remainder of 1. Moreover, Brianne said that of those 91 days, she would expect to see Letitia 30 times, since they will both be coming every 12 days and $365 \div 12$ is 30 with a remainder of 5.

(a) How many days will all three friends meet at the mall in the next year?

(b) Use reasoning similar to that of Letitia and Brianne to construct a three-loop Venn diagram that shows the number of times the three friends go to the mall in all of the possible combinations.

(c) How many days in the year will Jake be at the mall by himself?

(d) How many days in the year will none of the three be at the mall?

## Making Connections

31. In the late 20th century, modern society entered what some observers have called "the information age." People are now accustomed to being identified by number as often as by name. Make a list of your own identification numbers—social security, credit card, telephone, and so on. It may be helpful to look through your wallet!

32. Blood tests of 100 people showed that 45 had the A antigen and 14 had the B antigen. (See problem 24 of Section 2.1.) Another 45 had neither antigen and so are of type O. How many people are of type AB, having both the A and B antigens? Draw and label a Venn diagram that shows the number of people with blood types A, B, AB, and O.

## Communicating

33. The English words for the whole numbers are *zero, one, two, three,* and so on. Make similar lists in Spanish, French, and other languages. For example, your list in German would begin *null, eins, zwei, drei,* . . . . Do you notice any common roots of the words?

## From State Student Assessments

34. (Washington State, Grade 4)
What numbers do $W$, $X$, and $Y$ probably represent on the number line?

A. $W = 100, X = 200, Y = 500$

B. $W = 150, X = 300, Y = 400$

C. $W = 150, X = 300, Y = 525$

35. (Massachusetts, Grade 3)
Seth read 5 chapter books and 9 picture books. Anna read 16 chapter books.

Which number sentence correctly compares the total number of books Seth read with the number of books Anna read?

A. $5 + 9 < 16$      B. $5 + 9 > 16$

C. $16 = 5 + 9$      D. $9 = 16 - 5$

36. (Massachusetts, Grade 4)
Max and Sam wrote a number sentence to show that Max is older than Sam. In their number sentence,

- $M$ represents Max's age in years, and
- $S$ represents Sam's age in years.

Which number sentence shows that Max is older than Sam?

A. $M < S$          B. $M > S$

C. $M = S$          D. $M + S = 10$

37. (Kentucky, Grade 8)

*Use the Venn diagram below to answer this question.*

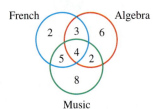

At Kentucky Middle School, students may take up to three electives. The Venn diagram shows the numbers of students in Mrs. Lawton's homeroom class who are taking the electives of music, French, and/or algebra. What is the *total* number of students who are taking *both* French and algebra?

A. 22              B. 7

C. 4               D. 3

38. (Texas, Grade 7)
The numbers in Set $N$ are multiples of 4.

| | | |
|---|---|---|
| 8 | 64 | 32 |
| 48 | | |
| 60 | 16 | |

$N = $

The numbers in Set $P$ are multiples of 3.

| | | |
|---|---|---|
| 33 | 42 | 51 |
| 21 | | |

$P = $

Which number could be a member of both Set $N$ and Set $P$?

A. 27

B. 20

C. 36

## 2.3

# Addition and Subtraction of Whole Numbers

In this section, we introduce the operations of addition and subtraction on the set of whole numbers $W = \{0, 1, 2, 3, \ldots\}$. In each operation, two whole numbers are combined to form another whole number. Because *two* whole numbers are added to form the sum, addition is called a **binary operation.** Similarly, subtraction is defined on a pair of numbers, so subtraction is also a binary operation.

The definitions of addition and subtraction are accompanied by a variety of conceptual models that give the operations both intuitive and practical meaning. It is vitally important that children be able to interpret and express, in a variety of ways, operations and their properties through manipulatives and visualization so that they will have a conceptual understanding of arithmetic. Activities with these representations prepare them to understand computation and build confidence in their ability to select the appropriate operations for problem solving.

## The Set Model of Whole-Number Addition

The whole numbers answer the basic question "How many?" For example, if Alok collects baseball cards and $A$ is the set of cards in his collection, then $a = n(A)$ is the number of cards he owns. Suppose his friend Barbara has a collection of different baseball cards, forming a set $B$ with $b = n(B)$ cards. If Alok and Barbara decide to combine their collections, the new collection would be the set $A \cup B$ and would contain $n(A \cup B)$ cards. The **addition, or sum,** of $a$ and $b$ can be defined as the number of cards in the combined collection. That is, the sum of two whole numbers $a$ and $b$ is given by $a + b = n(A \cup B)$, where $A$ and $B$ are disjoint sets, $a = n(A)$, and $b = n(B)$.

Addition answers the question "How many elements are in the union of two disjoint sets?" Figure 2.11 illustrates how the set model is used to show that $3 + 5 = 8$. First, disjoint sets $A$ and $B$ are found, with $n(A) = 3$ and $n(B) = 5$. Since $n(A \cup B) = 8$, we have shown that $3 + 5 = 8$. By using physical objects such as beans to form the sets, there is no question about disjointness.

**FIGURE 2.11**
Showing $3 + 5 = 8$ with the set model of addition

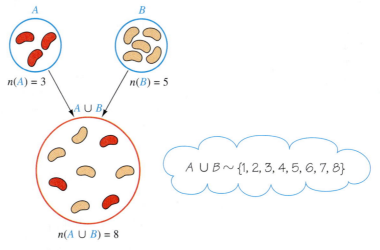

Here is the general definition:

**DEFINITION** *The Addition of Whole Numbers*
Let $a$ and $b$ be any two whole numbers. If $A$ and $B$ are any two disjoint sets for which $a = n(A)$ and $b = n(B)$, then the **sum of $a$ and $b$,** written $a + b$, is given by

$$a + b = n(A \cup B).$$

The expression $a + b$ is read "$a$ plus $b$," where $a$ and $b$ are called the **addends** or **summands.**

## EXAMPLE 2.10  Using the Set Model of Addition

The University Math Club membership includes 14 women and 11 men. The club members major in math, in physics, or in both of these areas.

**(a)** How many students belong to the Math Club?

**(b)** If 21 club members major at least in math, and 6 at least in physics, how many have double majors in both?

**Solution**

**(a)** If $C$ denotes the set of members of the club, then $C = M \cup W$, where $M$ and $W$ denote the sets of men and women members, respectively. Since $M$ and $W$ are disjoint sets, the number of club members is

$$n(C) = n(M \cup W) = n(M) + n(W) = 11 + 14 = 25.$$

**(b)** Let $A$ denote the set of club members with a math major and $B$ the set of club members with a physics major. Since $n(A) + n(B) = 21 + 6 = 27$ is 2 more than the 25 members of the club, 2 club members belong to both sets $A$ and $B$. That is, $n(A \cap B) = 2$ club members have a double major. Notice that the equation $n(A \cup B) = n(A) + n(B) - n(A \cap B)$ is valid in this case. (See problem 28 of the problem set for Section 2.3).

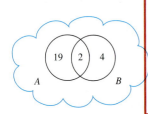

The set model of addition can be illustrated with manipulatives such as the tiles, cubes, strips, and rods described in the previous section. Many addition facts and patterns become evident when they are discovered and visualized by means of concrete representations. An example is the triangular numbers $t_1 = 1, t_2 = 3, t_3 = 6, \ldots$ introduced in Chapter 1. Recall that $t_n$ denotes the $n$th triangular number, where the name refers to the triangular pattern that can be formed with $t_n$ objects. By using number-tile patterns, as shown in Figure 2.12, we see that the sum of any two successive triangular numbers forms a square number. Indeed, we have the general formula

$$t_{n-1} + t_n = n^2, \qquad n = 2, 3, \ldots.$$

**FIGURE 2.12**

The sum of two successive triangular numbers is a square number

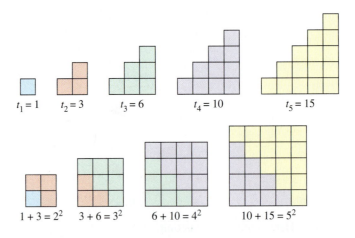

$t_1 = 1$    $t_2 = 3$    $t_3 = 6$    $t_4 = 10$    $t_5 = 15$

$1 + 3 = 2^2$    $3 + 6 = 3^2$    $6 + 10 = 4^2$    $10 + 15 = 5^2$

## The Measurement (Number-Line) Model of Addition

On the number line, whole numbers are geometrically interpreted as distances. Addition can be visualized as combining two distances to get a total distance. If we wish to add 3 and 5, we can draw 3 as usual, starting at 0. The number 5 can be thought of, in this case, as starting at any point and going five whole numbers to the right. Combining the two distances 3 and 5 can be represented by starting the arrow for 5 at 3 and counting 5 to the right for its finish, as shown in Figure 2.13. It is important to notice that the two distances are not overlapping and the tail of the arrow representing 5 is placed at the head of the arrow representing 3. The result of the addition is 8, which is indicated on the number line by circling the 8.

**FIGURE 2.13**
Illustrating 3 + 5 on the number line

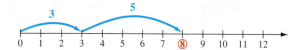

## Properties of Whole-Number Addition

Using models or going back to definitions for addition is not a good way, of course, to actually do computation. In the next few pages, we give some properties of whole-number addition and subtraction that we already use automatically to help simplify the way in which we add and subtract. Proceeding in this manner gives a conceptual background for why the procedures that we have been accustomed to actually work.

The sum of any two whole numbers is also a whole number, so we say that the set of whole numbers has the **closure property** under addition. This property is so obvious for addition that it may seem unnecessary to mention it. However, the set of whole numbers is not closed under subtraction or division. For example, is $3 - 5$ a whole number? Even under addition, many subsets of whole numbers do not have the closure property. For example, if $D = \{1, 3, 5, \ldots\}$ denotes the subset of the odd whole numbers, then $D$ does *not* have the closure property under addition. (For instance, the sum of 1 and 3 is even and hence is not in $D$.) By contrast, the set of even whole numbers, $E = \{0, 2, 4, 6, \ldots\}$, *is* closed under addition; this is so because the sum of any two even whole numbers is also an even whole number.

Some other important properties of whole-number addition correspond to properties of operations on finite sets. For example, the **commutative property** of union, $A \cup B = B \cup A$, proves that $a + b = b + a$ for all whole numbers $a$ and $b$. Similarly, the **associative property** $A \cup (B \cup C) = (A \cup B) \cup C$ tells us that $a + (b + c) = (a + b) + c$. Since $A \cup \varnothing = \varnothing \cup A = A$, we obtain the additive-identity property of zero, $a + 0 = 0 + a = a$. Zero is said to be the **additive identity** because of this property.

The properties in the next theorem can all be proven from the definition of whole-number addition and what we already know about operations on sets. We will, however, use reasoning through models, instead of formal, mathematical proof, to demonstrate the theorem.

| **THEOREM** | *Properties of Whole-Number Addition* |
|---|---|
| **Closure Property** | If $a$ and $b$ are any two whole numbers, then $a + b$ is a unique whole number. |
| **Commutative Property** | If $a$ and $b$ are any two whole numbers, then $a + b = b + a$. |
| **Associative Property** | If $a$, $b$, and $c$ are any three whole numbers, then $a + (b + c) = (a + b) + c$. |
| **Additive-Identity Property of Zero** | If $a$ is any whole number, then $a + 0 = 0 + a = a$. |

The last three of these properties can be described informally as "order of addition doesn't matter," "grouping of addition doesn't matter," and "adding zero doesn't matter," respectively. (See problem 27 of the Problem Set for Section 2.4 for similar statements about multiplication.)

The properties of whole-number addition can also be illustrated with physical and pictorial models of the whole numbers. Figure 2.14 shows how the associative property can be depicted with number strips.

The addition properties are very useful when we add several whole numbers, since we are permitted to rearrange the order of the addends and the order in which pairs of addends are summed.

**FIGURE 2.14**
Illustrating the associative property $(3 + 5) + 2 = 3 + (5 + 2)$ with number strips or Cuisenaire® rods

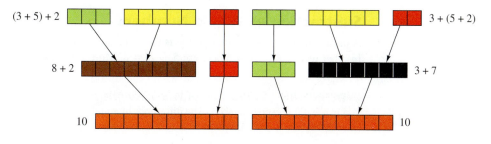

**EXAMPLE 2.11    Using the Properties of Whole-Number Addition**

(a) Which property justifies each of the following statements?
(i)   $8 + 3 = 3 + 8$
(ii)  $(7 + 5) + 8 = 7 + (5 + 8)$
(iii) A million plus a quintillion is not infinite.
(b) Justify each equality:

$$
\begin{aligned}
(20 + 2) + (30 + 8) &= 20 + [2 + (30 + 8)] & \text{(i)} \\
&= 20 + [(30 + 8) + 2] & \text{(ii)} \\
&= 20 + [30 + (8 + 2)] & \text{(iii)} \\
&= (20 + 30) + (8 + 2) & \text{(iv)}
\end{aligned}
$$

**Solution**

(a) (i) Commutative property, (ii) associative property, (iii) the sum is a whole number by the closure property and is therefore a finite value.
(b) (i) associative property, (ii) commutative property, (iii) associative property, (iv) associative property.

The number line is a very useful way for children to discover the properties of arithmetic.

**EXAMPLE 2.12    Illustrating Properties of Arithmetic on the Number Line via the Measurement Model**

What properties of whole-number addition are shown on the following number lines?

(a)
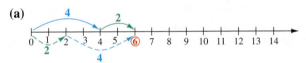

(b)
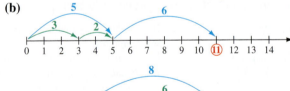

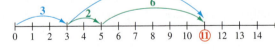

(c)
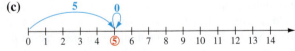

**Solution**

(a) The commutative property: $4 + 2 = 2 + 4$.
(b) The associative property: $(3 + 2) + 6 = 3 + (2 + 6)$.
(c) The additive-identity property: $5 + 0 = 5$.

## Subtraction of Whole Numbers

A usual way to introduce subtraction is to define subtraction in terms of the related addition problem. In other words, $8 - 3 = 5$ because $5 + 3 = 8$. More formally, we have the following definition:

**DEFINITION    Subtraction of Whole Numbers**

Let $a$ and $b$ be whole numbers. The **difference of $a$ and $b$,** written $a - b$, is the unique whole number $c$ such that $a = b + c$. That is, $a - b = c$ if, and only if, there is a whole number $c$ such that $a = b + c$.

Let's look for a minute at the definition of subtraction but use the letter $x$ to be the difference of $a$ and $b$. This notation would mean that $x = a - b$ when $x$ is a whole number such that $a = b + x$. As an example, subtracting 5 from 8 is the same as solving $8 = 5 + x$. For $x$ viewed this way, algebra becomes a way of describing subtraction. The last two sentences give an example of what's called "prealgebra" and is now a part of mathematics in grades 3–5.

The expression $a - b$ is read "$a$ minus $b$," where $a$ is the **minuend** and $b$ is the **subtrahend.**

## Into the Classroom

### Using Addition Properties to Learn Addition Facts

As children learn addition, the properties of whole-number addition should become a habit of thought from the very beginning. Indeed, the properties are useful even for learning and recalling the sums of one-digit numbers, as found in the addition table shown. The commutative property $a + b = b + a$ means that the entries above the diagonal repeat the entries below the diagonal. Also, the first column of addition with 0 is easy by the additive-identity property. The next four columns, giving addition with 1, 2, 3, and 4, can be learned by "counting on." For example, $8 + 3$ is viewed as "8 plus 1 makes 9, plus 1 more makes 10, plus 1 more makes 11." The diagonal entries $1 + 1 = 2, 2 + 2 = 4, \ldots$ are the "doubles," which are readily learned by knowing how to count by twos: 2, 4, $\ldots$, 18. The remaining entries in the table can be obtained by combining "doubles" and "counting on." For example, $6 + 8$ is viewed as $6 + (6 + 2)$, which is $(6 + 6) + 2$; knowing that 6 doubled is 12 and counting on 2 gives the answer of 14.

Other effective strategies include the following:

*Making tens:*    For example, $8 + 6 = (8 + 2) + 4 = 10 + 4 = 14$.
*Counting back:*    For example, 9 is 1 less than 10, so $6 + 9$ is 1 less than $6 + 10 = 16$, giving 15. In symbols, this amounts to

$$6 + 9 = (6 + 10) - 1 = 16 - 1 = 15.$$

> Look for patterns. They also help you learn the facts!

| + | 0 | 1 | 2 | 3 | 4 | 5 | 6 | 7 | 8 | 9 |
|---|---|---|---|---|---|---|---|---|---|---|
| 0 | 0 | 1 | 2 | 3 | 4 | 5 | 6 | 7 | 8 | 9 |
| 1 | 1 | 2 | 3 | 4 | 5 | 6 | 7 | 8 | 9 | 10 |
| 2 | 2 | 3 | 4 | 5 | 6 | 7 | 8 | 9 | 10 | 11 |
| 3 | 3 | 4 | 5 | 6 | 7 | 8 | 9 | 10 | 11 | 12 |
| 4 | 4 | 5 | 6 | 7 | 8 | 9 | 10 | 11 | 12 | 13 |
| 5 | 5 | 6 | 7 | 8 | 9 | 10 | 11 | 12 | 13 | 14 |
| 6 | 6 | 7 | 8 | 9 | 10 | 11 | 12 | 13 | 14 | 15 |
| 7 | 7 | 8 | 9 | 10 | 11 | 12 | 13 | 14 | 15 | 16 |
| 8 | 8 | 9 | 10 | 11 | 12 | 13 | 14 | 15 | 16 | 17 |
| 9 | 9 | 10 | 11 | 12 | 13 | 14 | 15 | 16 | 17 | 18 |

$$a - b = c$$

$c$ is the difference of $a$ and $b$
$b$ is the subtrahend
$a$ is the minuend

This definition relates subtraction to addition and is the definition most easily extended to the integers, rational numbers, and real numbers.

Since $8 = 5 + 3$, the definition tells us that $8 - 5 = 3$. However, the practical value of subtraction is not revealed in the definition. To understand the nature and value of subtraction as it is often introduced to children, we will introduce four conceptual models: **take away, missing addend, comparison,** and **number line** (or **measurement**). The following four problems respectively illustrate each of the four conceptual models:

**Take away:**
Eroll has $8 and spends $5 for a ticket to the movies. How much money does Eroll have left?

**Missing addend:**
Alice has read 5 chapters of her book. If there are 8 chapters in all, how many more chapters must she read to finish the book?

**Comparison:**
Georgia has 8 mice and Tonya has 5 mice. How many more mice does Georgia have than Tonya?

**Number line (measurement):**
Mike hiked up the mountain trail 8 miles. Five of these miles were hiked after lunch. How many miles did Mike hike before lunch?

In all four problems, the answer is 3, because we know the addition fact $8 = 5 + 3$. For example, Eroll's $8, when written as $5 + $3, shows that a $5 movie ticket and the $3 still in his pocket account for all of the $8 he had originally. The cashier at the box office "took away" 5 of Eroll's 8 dollars, leaving him with $3. Thus, the problem is an example of the **take-away model** of subtraction. Alice, having read 5 chapters, wants to know how many more chapters she must read; the emphasis now is on what number is to be added to 5 to get 8, so the second problem illustrates the **missing-addend model** of subtraction. Similarly, the remaining problems illustrate the **comparison model** and the **number-line** (or **measurement**) **model** of subtraction.

The four basic conceptual models of the subtraction $8 - 5$ are visualized as follows:

## Take-Away Model

1. Start with 8 objects.
2. Take away 5 objects.
3. How many objects are left?

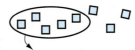

## Missing-Addend Model

1. Start with 5 objects.
2. How many more objects are needed to give a total of 8 objects?

## Comparison Model

1. Start with two collections, with 8 objects in one collection and 5 in the other.

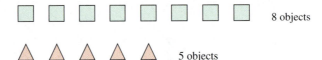

8 objects

5 objects

2. How many more objects are in the larger collection?

## Number-Line Model

1. Move forward (to the right) 8 units.

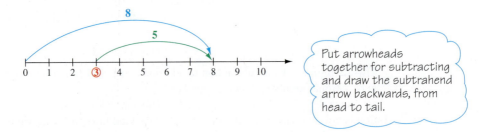

Put arrowheads together for subtracting and draw the subtrahend arrow backwards, from head to tail.

2. Remove a jump to the right of 5 units.
3. What is the distance from 0?

Notice that the head of the arrow representing 5 is positioned at the head of the arrow representing 8 and is drawn backwards, since it is subtracted. The result of the subtraction, 3, is shown by circling the 3.

It is important to notice that the whole numbers 8 and 5 are each represented by a right-pointing arrow. Since the outcome of the subtraction $8 - 5$ is 3, the arrow from 0 to 3 on the number line is also right pointing.

More generally, any whole number is represented on a number line as a right-pointing arrow. In Chapter 5, the whole numbers are enlarged to include the positive and negative integers. There, right-pointing arrows represent the positive integers (natural numbers) and left-pointing arrows represent the negative integers.

---

**EXAMPLE 2.13  Identifying Conceptual Models of Subtraction**

In each case, identify the conceptual model of subtraction that best fits the problem:

**(a)** Mary got 43 pieces of candy trick-or-treating on Halloween. Karen got 36 pieces. How many more pieces of candy does Mary have than Karen?

**(b)** Mary gave 20 pieces of her 43 pieces of candy to her sick brother, Jon. How many pieces of candy does Mary have left?

**(c)** Karen's older brother, Ken, collected 53 pieces of candy. How many more pieces of candy would Karen need to have as many as Ken?

**(d)** Ken left home and walked 10 blocks east along Grand Avenue, trick-or-treating. The last 4 blocks were after crossing Main Street. How far is Main Street from Ken's house?

**Solution**

**(a)** Comparison model
**(b)** Take-away model
**(c)** Missing-addend model
**(d)** Number-line model

---

The set of whole numbers is not closed under subtraction. For example, $2 - 5$ is undefined, since there is no whole number $n$ that satisfies $2 = 5 + n$. Similar reasoning shows that subtraction is not commutative, so the order in which $a$ and $b$ are taken is important. Neither is subtraction associative, which means that parentheses must be placed with care in expressions involving subtractions. For example,

$$5 - (3 - 1) = 5 - 2 = 3, \quad \text{but} \quad (5 - 3) - 1 = 2 - 1 = 1.$$

## Cooperative Investigation

### Diffy

The process in this activity is sometimes called "Diffy." The name comes from the process of taking successive differences of whole numbers, and the activity provides an interesting setting for practicing skills in subtraction. Work in pairs to check each other's calculations.

### Directions

**Step 1.** Make an array of circles as shown, and choose four whole numbers to place in the top four circles.

**Step 2.** In the first three circles of the second row, write the differences of the numbers above and to the right and left of the circle in question, always being careful to subtract the smaller of these two numbers from the larger. In the fourth circle of the second row, place the difference of the numbers in the first and fourth circles in the preceding row, again subtracting the smaller number from the larger.

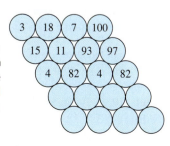

**Step 3.** Repeat step 2 to fill in successive rows of circles in the diagram. You may stop if you obtain a row of zeros.

**Step 4.** Replace the four numbers in the top row, and then repeat steps 1, 2, and 3 several times, each time replacing the four numbers in the top row with different numbers.

### Questions

1. Do you think the process will always stop?
2. Can you find four numbers such that the process terminates at the first step? the second step? the third step? Try several sets of starting numbers.
3. On the basis of your work so far, what do you guess is the largest number of steps needed for the process to stop?
4. Can you find four starting numbers such that the process requires eight steps to reach termination?
5. Try Diffy with the starting numbers 17, 32, 58, and 107.

## Problem Set 2.3

Exercises numbered in red are answered in the back of the text.

### Understanding Concepts

1. Let $A = \{$apple, berry, peach$\}$, $B = \{$lemon, lime$\}$, and $C = \{$lemon, berry, prune$\}$.

    (a) Find (i) $n(A \cup B)$, (ii) $n(A \cup C)$, and (iii) $n(B \cup C)$.

    (b) In which case is the number of elements in the union *not* the sum of the number of elements in the individual sets?

2. Let $n(A) = 4$ and $n(A \cup B) = 8$.

    (a) What are the possible values of $n(B)$?

    (b) If $A \cap B = \varnothing$, what is the only possible value of $n(B)$?

3. Draw number strips (or rods) to illustrate

    (a) $4 + 6 = 10$;

    (b) $2 + 8 = 8 + 2$; and

    (c) $3 + (2 + 5) = (3 + 2) + 5$.

4. Illustrate each of the given additions with a number-line diagram. Circle the value on the number line that corresponds to the sum.

    (a) $3 + 5$      (b) $5 + 3$

    (c) $4 + 2$      (d) $0 + 6$

    (e) $3 + (5 + 7)$      (f) $(3 + 5) + 7$

5. Make up a word problem that uses the set model of addition to illustrate $30 + 28$.

6. Make up a word problem that uses the measurement model of addition to illustrate $18 + 25$.

7. Which of the given sets of whole numbers is closed under addition? If the set is not closed, give an example of two elements from the set whose sum is not in the set.

    (a) $\{10, 15, 20, 25, 30, 35, 40, \ldots\}$

    (b) $\{1, 2, 3, \ldots, 1000\}$

    (c) $\{0\}$

    (d) $\{1, 5, 6, 11, 17, 28, \ldots\}$

    (e) $\{n \in N \mid n \geq 19\}$

    (f) $\{0, 3, 6, 9, 12, 15, 18, \ldots\}$

8. What properties of addition are used in these equalities?

    (a) $14 + 18 = 18 + 14$

    (b) $12,345,678 + 97,865,342$ is a whole number.

    (c) $18 + 0 = 18$

    (d) $(17 + 14) + 13 = 30 + 14$

    (e) $(12 + 15) + (5 + 38) = 50 + 20$

9. An easy way to add $1 + 2 + 3 + 4 + 5 + 6 + 7 + 8 + 9 + 10$ is to write the sum as $(1 + 10) + (2 + 9) + (3 + 8) + (4 + 7) + (5 + 6) = 11 + 11 + 11 + 11 + 11 = 55$.

    (a) Compute $1 + 2 + 3 + \cdots + 20$. Describe your procedure.

    (b) What properties of addition are you using to justify why your procedure works?

10. Illustrate each of the given subtractions with a number-line diagram. Remember to put the heads of the minuend and subtrahend arrows together.

    (a) $7 - 3$      (b) $7 - 4$

    (c) $7 - 7$      (d) $7 - 0$

11. If $5 + 9 = 14$, then $9 + 5 = 14$, $14 - 9 = 5$, and $14 - 5 = 9$. Many elementary texts call such a group of four basic facts a "fact family."

    (a) What is the fact family that contains $5 + 7 = 12$?

    (b) What is the fact family that contains $12 - 4 = 8$?

12. (a) Draw four number-line diagrams to illustrate each of the number facts in the fact family (see problem 11) $5 + 9 = 14$, $9 + 5 = 14$, $14 - 9 = 5$, and $14 - 5 = 9$.

    (b) Repeat part (a), but for the fact family that contains $11 - 4 = 7$.

**13.** For each of the following problems, which subtraction model—take away, missing addend, comparison, or measurement—corresponds best to that problem?

(a) Ivan solved 18 problems and Andreas solved 13 problems. How many more problems has Ivan solved than Andreas?

(b) On Malea's 12-mile hike to Mirror Lake, she came to a sign that said she had 5 miles left to reach the lake. How far has Malea walked so far?

(c) Jake has saved $45 toward the $60 CD player he wants to buy. How much money does he have to add to his savings to purchase the player?

(d) Joshua has a book of 10 pizza coupons. If he used 3 coupons to buy pizza for Friday's party, how many coupons does he have left?

**14.** For each of the following four conceptual models for subtraction, write a word problem that corresponds well to that problem.

(a) Take away

(b) Missing addend

(c) Comparison

(d) Measurement (number line)

**15.** Jeff must read the last chapter of his book. It begins on the top of page 241 and ends at the bottom of page 257. How many pages must he read?

**16.** Notice that $(6 + (8 - 5)) - 2 = 7$, but a different placement of parentheses on the left side would give the statement $(6 + 8) - (5 - 2) = 11$. Place parentheses to turn these equalities into *true* statements:

(a) $8 - 5 - 2 - 1 = 2$

(b) $8 - 5 - 2 - 1 = 4$

(c) $8 - 5 - 2 - 1 = 0$

(d) $8 + 5 - 2 + 1 = 12$

(e) $8 + 5 - 2 + 1 = 10$

**17.** Each circled number is the sum of the adjacent row, column, or diagonal of the numbers in the square array:

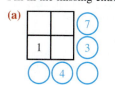

Fill in the missing entries in these patterns:

(a)  (b)

**18.** The first figure shown illustrates that the numbers 1, 2, 3, 4, 5, 6 can be placed around a triangle in such a way that the three numbers along any side sum to 9, which is shown circled. Arrange the numbers 1, 2, 3, 4, 5, 6 to give the sums circled in the next three figures.

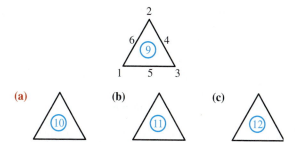

## Teaching Concepts

**19.** Suppose that Andrea told you that "Blake and I started out with the same number of marbles, but I gave him one of mine. Now Blake has one more marble than me." Why is Andrea's reasoning incorrect? How can you address her misunderstanding?

**20.** The addition operation can be represented with beans and loops of string, as illustrated in Figure 2.11. In words and pictures, describe how you would use this representation to illustrate the properties of whole-number addition to a youngster. For example, your figure illustrating the associative property will be something like the number-strip diagram in Figure 2.14.

**21.** Invent ways to use a double-six set of dominoes to teach children basic addition facts and addition properties. Notice that a blank half of the domino can represent zero.

**22.** How would you show that, for any whole number $a$, $a + 0 = a$ if

(a) you were starting from our definition of addition and the audience is your university class?

(b) you were talking to your class of fourth graders?

**23.** How would you explain to a student that filling in the boxes in (a) and (b) are related?

(a) $\Box - 3 = 26$    (b) $\Box = 29 - 3$

## Responding to Students

**24.** Jane and Angel are twin sisters in the second grade who share a room and have a pet mouse collection of 8 mice. Angel says she adores 6 of them, but Jane says that that is impossible, since she loves 7 and there aren't 13 mice. Is Jane right? How would you explain to the sisters the conceptual reason for your answer?

**25.** In an attempt to do a three-digit subtraction, Yuan writes

$$
\begin{array}{r}
706 \\
- 327 \\
\hline
421
\end{array}
$$

(a) Identify what she is doing incorrectly.

(b) How will you help correct her error?

**26.** Phillip was asked to subtract 279 from 386 and writes

$$
\begin{array}{r}
77 \\
386 \\
- \ 279 \\
\hline
102
\end{array}
$$

Identify what Phillip is doing incorrectly.

**27.** Carmen has moved to the United States from Europe and has learned an algorithm for subtraction. She uses it to find $52 - 17$ as follows:

$52 + 10 = 62$,   so   $52 + 10 = 50 + 12$;

$-(17 + 10) = -27$,   so   $-(17 + 10) = -(20 + 7)$

So her answer is $30 + 5 = 35$.

   **(a)** What properties does Carmen's algorithm use? Is her method correct?

   **(b)** Now solve another subtraction problem, $71 - 38$, with Carmen's algorithm. Use the traditional algorithm to check your work.

## Thinking Critically

**28.** If $A = \{a, b, c, d\}$ and $B = \{c, d, e, f, g\}$, then $n(A \cup B) = n(\{a, b, c, d, e, f, g\}) = 7, n(A) = 4, n(B) = 5$, and $n(A \cap B) = n(\{c, d\}) = 2$. Since $7 = 4 + 5 - 2$, this suggests that

$$n(A \cup B) = n(A) + n(B) - n(A \cap B).$$

Use Venn diagrams to justify this formula for arbitrary finite sets $A$ and $B$.

**29.** Since $12 \times 16 = 192$ and $5 \times 40 = 200$, it follows that among the first 200 natural numbers $\{1, 2, \ldots, 200\}$ there are 16 that are multiples of 12 and 40 that are multiples of 5. Just 3, namely, 60, 120, and 180, are multiples of *both* 5 and 12. Use the formula of problem 28 to find how many natural numbers in the set $\{1, 2, \ldots, 200\}$ are divisible by *either* 12 or 5 or both.

**30. Adams's Magic Hexagon.** In 1957, Clifford W. Adams discovered a magic hexagon in which the sum of the numbers in any "row" is 38. Fill in the empty cells of the partially completed hexagon shown, using the whole numbers $6, 7, \ldots, 15$, to re-create Adams's discovery. When completed, each cell will contain one of the numbers $1, 2, \ldots, 19$.

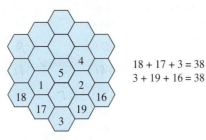

$18 + 17 + 3 = 38$
$3 + 19 + 16 = 38$

**31. A Magic Hexagram.** The numbers $1, 2, \ldots, 12$ can be entered into the 12 regions of the diagram that follows so that each of the six rows of five triangles (shown by

the arrows) contains numbers that sum to the magic constant 33. The first six numbers have been put into place, so you are challenged to enter the last six numbers, 7 through 12, to finish this magic hexagram discovered in 1991 by the mathematicians Brian Bolt, Roger Eggleton, and Joe Gilks.

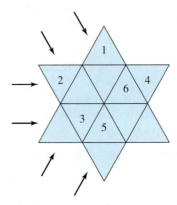

**32.** There is a nonempty subset of the whole numbers that is closed under subtraction. Find this subset.

**33.** The set $C$ contains 2 and 3 and is closed under addition.

   **(a)** What whole numbers must be in $C$?

   **(b)** What whole numbers may not be in $C$?

   **(c)** Are there any whole numbers definitely not in $C$?

   **(d)** How would your answers to (a), (b), and (c) change if 2 and 4 instead of 2 and 3 were contained in $C$?

**34.** The triangular numbers $t_1 = 1, t_2 = 3, t_3 = 6, \ldots$ are shown in Figure 2.12.

   **(a)** Complete the following table of the first 15 triangular numbers:

| $n$ | 1 | 2 | 3 | 4 | 5 | 6 | 7 | 8 | 9 | 10 | 11 | 12 | 13 | 14 | 15 |
|-----|---|---|---|---|---|---|---|---|---|----|----|----|----|----|----|
| $t_n$ | 1 | 3 | 6 | 10 | | | | | | | | | | | |

   **(b)** The first 10 natural numbers can be expressed as sums of triangular numbers. For example, $1 = 1, 2 = 1 + 1$, $3 = 3, 4 = 1 + 3, 5 = 1 + 1 + 3, 6 = 6, 7 = 1 + 6$, $8 = 1 + 1 + 6, 9 = 3 + 6$, and $10 = 10$. Show that the natural numbers 11 through 25 can be written as a sum of triangular numbers. Use as few triangular numbers as possible each time.

   **(c)** Choose 5 more numbers at random (don't look at your table!) between 26 and 120, and write each of them as a sum of as few triangular numbers as possible. What is the largest number of triangular numbers needed?

   **(d)** On July 10, 1796, the 19-year-old Carl Friedrich Gauss wrote in his notebook, "EUREKA! NUM $= \triangle + \triangle + \triangle$." What theorem do you think Gauss had proved?

**35. Fibonacci Sums.** Recall the Fibonacci numbers $1, 1, 2, 3, 5, 8, 13, 21, 34, 55, 89, 144, \ldots$. Sameer claims that any natural number can be written as a sum of two or more distinct Fibonacci numbers. For example, $29 = 21 + 5 + 3$ and $55 = 34 + 21$. Do you think Sameer might be right? Investigate this possibility yourself, and offer your opinion to support or refute Sameer's contention.

## Thinking Cooperatively

**36.** The table shown represents a partially complete scrambled addition table. The row and column headings are not set up in numerical order, and many entries are blank. See if your cooperative team can complete the table.

| + | 5 | | | | 2 | | | 3 | |
|---|---|---|---|---|---|---|---|---|---|
| 3 | | | | | | | | | |
| | | | | 18 | | | | | |
| | | | 12 | | | | | | |
| | | 5 | | | 6 | | | | |
| | | | | | | 0 | | | |
| | | 8 | | | | | | 14 | |
| 5 | | | | | | | | | |
| | | | | | | | | | |
| | | | | | 3 | | | | |
| 8 | | | | | | 16 | | | |

**37.** Have your cooperative team make up its own incomplete scrambled addition-table puzzle, similar to the one in problem 36. It may be helpful to use two colors, to separate the entries that are given from the entries that are determined by what is given. Trade puzzles among groups and see which presents the most challenge.

**38.** Three numbers (not necessarily all different) are determined by rolling three dice. By using either two or three of these numbers (not just one), together with parentheses and $+$ and $-$ symbols, the objective of the game is to form expressions equalling the seven numbers 0, 1, 2, 3, 4, 5, and 6 on a hex board as shown. The team filling in all seven positions on the board first is the winning team. If no team fills in all seven positions, the dice are rolled again. For example, a roll of 3, 3, and 4 would allow you to fill in 0 (as $3 - 3$), 1 (as $4 - 3$), 2 (as $(3 + 3) - 4$), 4 (as $(3 - 3) + 4$ or $(3 + 4) - 3$, for example), and 6 (as $3 + 3$). Your team would hope to fill in the 3 and 5 on the next roll of the dice. Play the game in class, and practice with these questions:

**(a)** Show that you should be able to win the game with the roll 1, 4, 5.

**(b)** Can you win the game with a single roll of 2, 3, 5?

**(c)** Can you win the game with a single roll of 2, 4, 6?

**39.** In the Hands-On activity at the beginning of the chapter,
**MHM** Counting Cars and Trains (page 68), write two additional questions that could be asked and then give solutions to them.

## Making Connections

**40.** Addition and subtraction problems arise frequently in everyday life. Consider such activities as scheduling time, making budgets, sewing clothes, making home repairs, planning finances, modifying recipes, and making purchases. Make a list of five addition and five subtraction problems you have encountered at home or in your work. Which conceptual model of addition or subtraction corresponds best to each problem?

## From State Student Assessments

**41.** (Massachusetts, Grade 4)
Corey worked these problems.

$$2 + 8 = 10 \qquad 6 + 6 = 12 \qquad 10 + 4 = 14$$
$$12 + 2 = 14 \qquad 8 + 4 = 12 \qquad 2 + 6 = 8$$

When Corey finished, he said, "I think that the sum of ANY two even numbers is always an even number." Maya looked at Corey's work. She thought a bit and said, "I think that the sum of any two ODD numbers is always an odd number."

**(a)** Is Corey correct? Explain the reasons for your answer by using pictures, numbers, or words.

**(b)** Is Maya correct? Explain the reasons for your answer by using pictures, numbers, or words.

**42.** (Massachusetts, Grade 4)
Which of the following problems CANNOT be solved using the number sentence below?

$$15 - 8 = \square$$

**A.** Siu Ping had 15 trading cards. She gave 8 to Jim. How many does she have now?

**B.** Siu Ping needs 15 more trading cards than Jim has. Jim has 8. How many does Siu Ping need?

**C.** Siu Ping has 15 trading cards. Jim has 8. How many more does Siu Ping have than Jim?

**D.** Siu Ping needs 15 trading cards. She has 8. How many more does she need?

**43.** (Texas, Grade 7)
Which situation is best represented by the equation $x - 4 = 16$?

**A.** Miranda picked 16 apples and ate $\frac{1}{4}$ of them. What is $x$, the number of apples she had left?

**B.** Felipe ran for 16 minutes and walked for 4 minutes. What is $x$, the difference between the time he spent running and the time he spent walking?

**C.** Jordan spent $4 of his allowance and had $16 left. What is $x$, the total amount of Jordan's allowance?

**D.** Cecilia has hit 4 of the last 16 balls pitched. What is $x$, the total number of balls pitched?

**44.** (Georgia, Grade 3).
When you subtract one of these numbers from 900, the answer is greater than 400. Which number is it?

**A.** 712     **B.** 667

**C.** 579     **D.** 459

**45.** (Georgia, Grade 3).

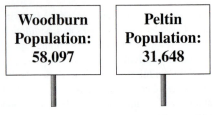

How much *greater* is the population of Woodburn than Peltin?

**A.** 26,449    **B.** 27,651

**C.** 87,745    **D.** 90,645

**46.** (Georgia, Grade 3)

Jaleesa was born in 1962. When she was 20 years old, she went to college. Five years later she started her own business. How many can you find out what year Jaleesa started her business?

**A.** $1962 - 20 - 5$

**B.** $1962 + 20 + 5$

**C.** $1962 + 20 - 5$

**D.** $1962 - 20 + 5$

# 2.4

# Multiplication and Division of Whole Numbers

## Multiplication of Whole Numbers

There are six conceptual models for the multiplication of two numbers: **multiplication as repeated addition,** the **array model for multiplication,** the **rectangular area model for multiplication,** the **skip-count model for multiplication,** the **multiplication tree model,** and the **Cartesian product model.** Each of these models provides a useful conceptual and visual representation of the multiplication operation. For a given context in a problem, it is frequently clear which model provides the most natural representation, but often there are several models that are each a reasonable choice. We will discuss now what they are ad the properties that they have.

## Multiplication as Repeated Addition

Misha has an after-school job at a local bike factory. Each day, he has a 3-mile round-trip walk to the factory. At his job, he assembles 4 hubs and wheels. How many hubs and wheels does he assemble in 5 afternoons? How many miles does he walk to and from his job each week?

These two problems can be answered by repeated addition. Misha assembles

$$4 + 4 + 4 + 4 + 4 = 20$$    *Sum of 5 fours, written 5 · 4*

hubs and wheels. Repeated addition is illustrated by the set diagram shown in Figure 2.15.

**FIGURE 2.15**

A set model shows that 5 times 4 is 20, since $4 + 4 + 4 + 4 + 4 = 20$ by repeated addition

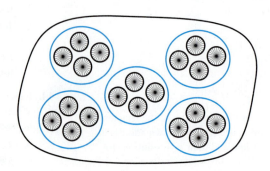

Misha walks

$$3 + 3 + 3 + 3 + 3 = 15$$

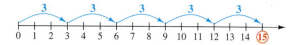

Sum of 5 threes, written $5 \cdot 3$

miles each week. This is illustrated by the number-line model shown in Figure 2.16. It is also called **skip counting.**

**FIGURE 2.16**
Number-line model to
show that 5 times 3 is 15

If Misha worked only one day in the week, he would assemble $1 \cdot 4 = 4$ wheels. If he were sick all week and missed work entirely, he would not assemble any wheels; therefore $0 \cdot 4 = 0$.

Since multiplication is defined for all pairs of whole numbers, and the outcome is also a whole number, we see that multiplication is a binary operation that is closed on the set of whole numbers.

---

**DEFINITION**  *Multiplication of Whole Numbers as Repeated Addition*

Let $a$ and $b$ be any two whole numbers. Then the **product** of $a$ and $b$, written $a \cdot b$, is defined by

$$a \cdot b = \underbrace{b + b + \cdots + b}_{a \text{ addends}} \text{ when } a \neq 0$$

and by

$$0 \cdot b = 0.$$

---

The dot symbol for multiplication is often replaced by a cross, $\times$ (not to be mistaken for the letter $x$), or by a star, $*$ (asterisk), the symbol computers use most often. Sometimes no symbol at all is used, or parentheses are placed around the factors. Thus, the expressions

$$a \cdot b, \quad a \times b, \quad a * b, \quad ab, \quad \text{and} \quad (a)(b)$$

all denote the multiplication of $a$ and $b$. Each whole number, $a$ and $b$, is a **factor** of the product $a \cdot b$, and often $a \cdot b$ is read "$a$ times $b$."

## The Array Model for Multiplication

Suppose Lida, as part of her biology research, planted 5 rows of bean seeds and each row contained 8 seeds. How many seeds did she plant in her rectangular plot?

The 40 seeds Lida planted form a 5-by-8 rectangular array, as shown in Figure 2.17. In the array model, the numbers of rows and columns in the rectangular array easily identify the factors in the multiplication. Also, the result of the product is found by counting the number of individual objects in the array.

**FIGURE 2.17**
Array model showing that
$5 \cdot 8 = 40$

5 rows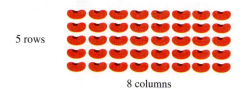

8 columns

## The Rectangular Area Model for Multiplication

Janet wants to order square ceramic tiles to cover the floor of her 4-foot-by-6-foot hallway. If the tiles are each 1 square foot, how many will she need to order? The rectangular area model, as shown in Figure 2.18, shows that 24 tiles are required.

**FIGURE 2.18**
Rectangular area model
showing that 4 × 6 = 24

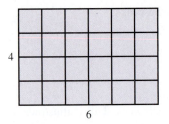

In this model, the dimensions of the rectangle correspond to the factors and the area of the rectangle corresponds to the value of the product. In later chapters, we will show that the rectangular area model for multiplication is especially important because it extends from whole-number multiplication to the multiplication of rational numbers, integers, and even real numbers. For example, if Janet's floor measured $4\frac{1}{2}$ by 6 feet, the array would show that Janet needs $4\frac{1}{2} \times 6 = 27$ tiles, with some of the tiles needing to be cut.

## The Skip-Count Model for Multiplication

In the early primary grades, examples similar to Figure 2.16 are a popular way to introduce multiplication. One other way of interpreting 5 times 3 is to start with 0 and skip to 3 as our first position, then skip 3 more to 6 as our second position (or, said another way, skip from 3 to 6 and count to 2). We then skip from 6 to 9 (count of 3), 9 to 12 (count of 4), and, finally, 12 to 15 (count of 5). We have skipped by 3 five times to get 15. This method for $a \cdot b$ is called "skip counting" because we skip by the number $b$ exactly $a$ times.

## The Multiplication Tree Model

Melissa has a box of 4 flags, colored red, yellow, green, and blue. How many ways can she display 2 of the flags on a flagpole? It is useful to think of the two decisions Melissa must make. First, she must select the upper flag, and next, she must choose the lower flag from those remaining in the box. There are 4 choices for the upper flag, and for *each* of these choices there are 3 choices for the lower flag. The multiplication tree shown in Figure 2.19 represents the product 4 × 3.

**FIGURE 2.19**

A multiplication tree
showing that 4 × 3 = 12

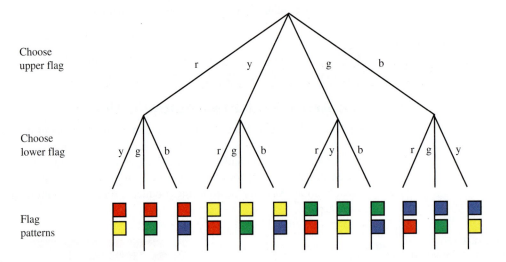

Choose
upper flag

Choose
lower flag

Flag
patterns

The multiplication tree in Figure 2.19 looks more like a tree if you turn it upside down. Multiplication trees can also grow from the right or the left.

## The Cartesian Product Model of Multiplication

At Jackson's Ice Cream Shop, a customer can order either a sugar or a waffle cone and one of four flavors of ice cream: vanilla, chocolate, mint, and raspberry. Any ice cream cone order can be written as an **ordered pair (a, b),** where the first component $a$ of the ordered pair indicates the type of cone and the second component $b$ of the ordered pair indicates the flavor. For example, if $C = \{s, w\}$ and

$F = \{v, c, m, r\}$ are the respective sets of cone types and flavors, then an order for raspberry ice cream in a waffle cone corresponds to the ordered pair (w, r). The total set of ice cream orders can be pictured in a rectangular array much like the figures used to model multiplication as a rectangular array:

|  |  | Flavor | | | |
|---|---|---|---|---|---|
|  |  | **v** | **c** | **m** | **r** |
| **Type of Cone** | **s** | (s, v) | (s, c) | (s, m) | (s, r) |
|  | **w** | (w, v) | (w, c) | (w, m) | (w, r) |

The set of ordered pairs shown in the table is called the **Cartesian product** of $C$ and $F$, written $C \times F$, where the cross symbol $\times$ should not be confused with the letter $x$. The name "Cartesian" honors the French mathematician and philosopher René Descartes (1596–1650). Here is the general definition of the Cartesian product of two sets:

> **DEFINITION**  *Cartesian Product of Sets*
> The **Cartesian product** of sets $A$ and $B$, written $A \times B$, is the set of all ordered pairs whose first component is an element of set $A$ and whose second component is an element of set $B$. That is,
>
> $$A \times B = \{(a, b) \mid a \in A \text{ and } b \in B\}.$$

At Jackson's, there are $n(C) = 2$ ways to choose the type of cone and $n(F) = 4$ ways to choose the flavor of ice cream. This gives $n(C \times F) = 2 \cdot 4 = 8$ ways to order an ice cream cone. More generally, the Cartesian product of sets gives us an alternative way to define the multiplication of whole numbers:

> **ALTERNATIVE DEFINITION**  *Multiplication of Whole Numbers via the Cartesian Product*
> Let $a$ and $b$ be whole numbers, and suppose that $A$ and $B$ are any sets for which $a = n(A)$ and $b = n(B)$. Then $a \cdot b = n(A \times B)$.

Since $\varnothing \times B = \varnothing$ (there are no ordered pairs in $\varnothing \times B$, since no first component can be chosen from $\varnothing$) and $0 = n(\varnothing)$, this definition of multiplication is consistent with the earlier definition of multiplication by 0—that is, $0 \cdot b = b \cdot 0 = 0$.

## EXAMPLE 2.14  Using the Cartesian Product Model of Multiplication

To get to work, Juan either walks, rides the bus, or takes a cab from his house to downtown. From downtown, he either continues on the bus the rest of the way to work or catches the train to his place of business. How many ways can Juan get to work?

**Solution**

If $A = \{w, b, c\}$ is the set of possibilities for the first leg of his trip and $B = \{b, t\}$ is the next set of choices, then Juan has, altogether,

$$3 \cdot 2 = n(A \times B) = n(\{(w, b), (w, t), (b, b), (b, t), (c, b), (c, t)\}) = 6$$

ways to commute to work. We notice that it doesn't matter whether or not $A$ and $B$ have an element in common.

## Properties of Whole-Number Multiplication

It follows from the definition that the set of whole numbers is **closed under multiplication:** The product of any two whole numbers is a unique whole number. We also observed earlier that $0 \cdot b = 0$ and $1 \cdot b = b$ for all whole numbers $b$.

By rotating a rectangular array through $90°$, we interchange the number of rows and the number of columns in the array, but we do not change the total number of objects in the array. Thus, $a \cdot b = b \cdot a$, which demonstrates the **commutative property of multiplication.** An example is shown in Figure 2.20.

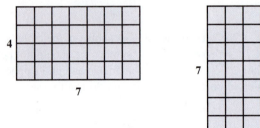

Since, as we already have seen, $1 \cdot b = b$ for any whole number $b$, it follows by the commutative property that $1 \cdot b = b \cdot 1 = b$. This makes 1 a **multiplicative identity.**

The reason that $a \cdot (b \cdot c) = (a \cdot b) \cdot c$ (the **associative property**) is that both sides of this equation can be represented as the volume of a box (rectangular prism) whose sides are $a$, $b$, and $c$. Only the length, width, and height are interchanged. (See Figure 2.21 for the case in which $a = 4, b = 3,$ and $c = 5$.) This means that an expression such as $4 \cdot 3 \cdot 5$ is meaningful without parentheses: The product is the same for both ways parentheses can be placed.

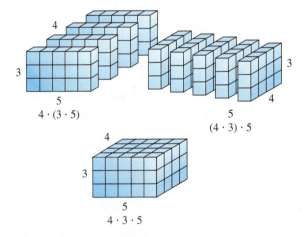

There is one more important property, the **distributive property,** that relates multiplication and addition. This property is the basis for the multiplication algorithm discussed in the next chapter. The distributive property can be nicely visualized by the rectangular area model. Figure 2.22 illustrates that $4 \cdot (6 + 3) = (4 \cdot 6) + (4 \cdot 3)$; that is, the factor 4 *distributes* itself over each term in the sum $6 + 3$.

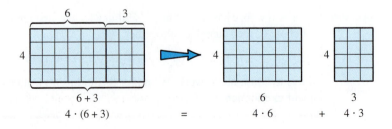

Shown next is a summary of the properties of multiplication on the whole numbers. Each property can be proved from the definition of multiplication of whole numbers.

---

**THEOREM** *Properties of Whole-Number Multiplication*

| | |
|---|---|
| **Closure Property** | If $a$ and $b$ are any two whole numbers, then $a \cdot b$ is a unique whole number. |
| **Commutative Property** | If $a$ and $b$ are any two whole numbers, then $a \cdot b = b \cdot a$. |
| **Associative Property** | If $a$, $b$, and $c$ are any three whole numbers, then $a \cdot (b \cdot c) = (a \cdot b) \cdot c$. |
| **Multiplicative Identity Property of One** | The number 1 is the unique whole number for which $b \cdot 1 = 1 \cdot b = b$ holds for all whole numbers $b$. |
| **Multiplication-by-Zero Property** | For all whole numbers $b$, $0 \cdot b = b \cdot 0 = 0$. |
| **Distributive Property of Multiplication over Addition** | If $a$, $b$, and $c$ are any three whole numbers, then $a \cdot (b + c) = (a \cdot b) + (a \cdot c)$ and $(a + b) \cdot c = (a \cdot c) + (b \cdot c)$. |

---

**EXAMPLE 2.15 Multiplying Two Binomial Expressions**

(a) Use the properties of multiplication to justify the formula $(a + b)(c + d) = ac + ad + bc + bd$. Each of the factors $(a + b)$ and $(c + d)$ are called **binomials,** since each factor has two terms.
(b) Visualize $(2 + 4)(5 + 3)$ with an area model drawn on squared paper.
(c) Illustrate the expansion $(a + b)(c + d) = ac + ad + bc + bd$ with the area model of multiplication.
(d) Visualize $16 \cdot 28 = (10 + 6) \cdot (20 + 8) = 200 + 80 + 120 + 48$ with an area diagram.
(e) Show that $(x + 7) \cdot (2x + 5) = 2x^2 + 5x + 14x + 35$ with an area diagram.

**Solution**

(a) $(a + b)(c + d) = (a + b)c + (a + b)d$   Distributive property

$\qquad\qquad\quad = ac + bc + ad + bd$   Distributive property

$\qquad\qquad\quad = ac + ad + bc + bd$   Commutative property of addition

(b)

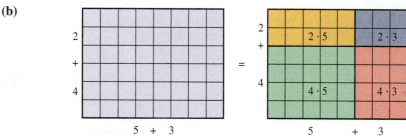

(c)   (d)   (e)

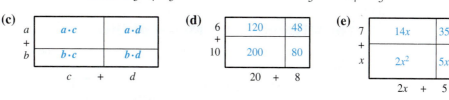

## Division of Whole Numbers

There are three conceptual models for the division $a \div b$ of a whole number $a$ by a nonzero whole number $b$: the **repeated-subtraction** model, the **partition** model, and the **missing-factor** model. We will now discuss what these models are and the properties they have.

## The Repeated-Subtraction Model of Division

Ms. Rislov has 28 students in her class whom she wishes to divide into cooperative learning groups of 4 students per group. If each group requires a set of Cuisenaire® rods, how many sets of rods must Ms. Rislov have available? The answer, 7, is pictured in Figure 2.23 and is obtained by counting how many times groups of 4 can be formed, starting with 28. Thus, $28 \div 4 = 7$. The repeated-subtraction model can be realized easily with physical objects; the process is called **division by grouping.** Since groups of 4 are being "measured out" of the class of 28, repeated subtraction is also called **measurement division.**

**FIGURE 2.23**

Division as repeated subtraction: $28 \div 4 = 7$ because seven 4s can be subtracted from 28

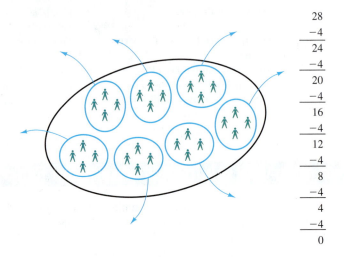

$$
\begin{array}{r}
28 \\
-4 \\
\hline
24 \\
-4 \\
\hline
20 \\
-4 \\
\hline
16 \\
-4 \\
\hline
12 \\
-4 \\
\hline
8 \\
-4 \\
\hline
4 \\
-4 \\
\hline
0
\end{array}
$$

## The Partition Model of Division

When Ms. Rislov checked her supply cupboard, she discovered she had only 4 sets of Cuisenaire® rods to use with the 28 students in her class. How many students must she assign to each set of rods? The answer, 7 students in each group, is depicted in Figure 2.24. The partition model is also realized easily with physical objects, in which case the process is called **division by sharing** or **partitive division.**

**FIGURE 2.24**

Division as a partition: $28 \div 4 = 7$ because when 28 objects are partitioned into 4 equal-sized sections, there are 7 objects in each partition

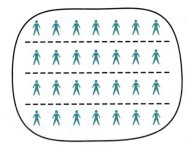

## The Missing-Factor Model of Division

In the repeated-subtraction model, $28 \div 4 = 7$ because, when grouped by 4s, seven groups will be formed. That is, $28 = 4 + 4 + 4 + 4 + 4 + 4 + 4 = 7 \cdot 4$. However, in the partition model, $28 \div 4 = 7$ because $28 = 7 + 7 + 7 + 7 = 4 \cdot 7$. In both cases, the division $28 \div 4$ can be viewed as finding the factor $c$ for which $28 = 4 \cdot c$ or $28 = c \cdot 4$. The missing-factor model is usually the concept adopted to define division formally:

**DEFINITION** *Division in Whole Numbers*

Let $a$ and $b$ be whole numbers with $b \neq 0$. Then $a \div b = c$ if, and only if, $a = b \cdot c$ for a unique whole number $c$.

When we defined subtraction in the last section, we interpreted it in terms of algebra. What would an algebraic equation look like to describe division in whole numbers? By analogy, it would be as follows: Let $a$ and $b$ be whole numbers with $b \neq 0$. Then $b$ divides $a$ if, and only if, there is a unique whole number $x$ for which $a = bx$. As an illustration, we can solve the equation $3 = 2x$ for $x$, but we won't get a whole number for an answer. That means that 2 does not divide 3. Said another way, the integers are not closed under division. Chapter 4, "Number Theory," will go into depth about this subtle difference between multiplication and division.

The symbol $a \div b$ is read "$a$ divided by $b$," where $a$ is the **dividend** and $b$ is the **divisor**. If $a \div b = c$, then we say that $b$ **divides** $a$ or $b$ is a **divisor** of $a$, and $c$ is called the **quotient:**

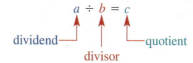

Division is also symbolized by $a/b$ or $\dfrac{a}{b}$; the slash notation is used by most computers.

Any multiplication fact with nonzero factors is related to three other equivalent facts that form a **fact family.** For example,

$$3 \cdot 5 = 15, \qquad 15 \div 3 = 5,$$
$$5 \cdot 3 = 15, \quad \text{and} \quad 15 \div 5 = 3$$

form a fact family. Note that a fact family can be represented with the rectangular array model, as shown in Figure 2.25 with arrays of colored discs.

**FIGURE 2.25**
Rectangular arrays, formed with colored discs, illustrate the fact family $3 \cdot 5 = 15$, $15 \div 3 = 5$, $5 \cdot 3 = 15$, and $15 \div 5 = 3$

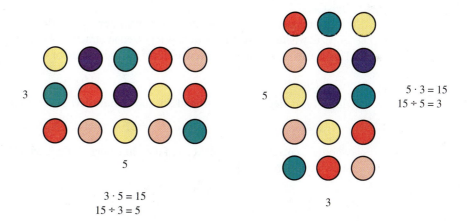

$$3 \cdot 5 = 15$$
$$15 \div 3 = 5$$

$$5 \cdot 3 = 15$$
$$15 \div 5 = 3$$

---

**EXAMPLE 2.16  Computing Quotients with Manipulatives**

Suppose you have 78 number tiles. Describe how to illustrate $78 \div 13$ with the tiles, using each of the three basic conceptual models for division.

**Solution**

(a) **Repeated subtraction.** Remove groups of 13 tiles each. Since 6 groups are formed, $78 \div 13 = 6$.

(b) **Partition.** Partition the tiles into 13 equal-sized parts. Since each part contains exactly 6 tiles, $78 \div 13 = 6$.

(c) **Missing factor.** Use the 78 tiles to form a rectangle with 13 rows. Since it turns out there are 6 columns in the rectangle, $78 \div 13 = 6$.

## Division by Zero Is Undefined

The definition of division tells us that $12 \div 3 = 4$, since 4 is the unique whole number for which $12 = 3 \times 4$. Division *into zero* is also defined. For example, $c = 0$ is the unique whole number for which $0 = 5 \times c$, so $0 \div 5 = 0$. However, division *by zero* (or "$a \div 0$") is not defined for any whole number $a$. The reason for this can best be explained by taking the cases $a \neq 0$ and $a = 0$ separately.

**Case 1: $a \neq 0$.** In this case, "$a \div 0$" would be equivalent to finding the missing factor $c$ that makes $a = c \cdot 0$. But $c \cdot 0 = 0$ for all whole numbers $c$, so there is no solution when $a \neq 0$. Thus, $a \div 0$ is undefined for $a \neq 0$.

**Case 2: $a = 0$.** In this case, "$0 \div 0$" is equivalent to finding a *unique* whole number $c$ for which $0 = 0 \cdot c$. But that equation is satisfied by every choice for the factor $c$. Since no *unique* factor $c$ exists, the division of 0 by 0 is also undefined.

In the division $a \div b$, there is no restriction on the dividend $a$. For all $b \neq 0$, we have $0 \div b = 0$, since $0 = b \cdot 0$.

The multiplicative identity 1 has two simple, but useful, relationships to division:

$$\frac{b}{b} = 1 \qquad \text{for all } b, \qquad \text{where } b \neq 0;$$

$$\frac{a}{1} = a \qquad \text{for all } a.$$

## Division with Remainders

Consider the division problem $27 \div 6$. There is no whole number $c$ that satisfies $27 = c \cdot 6$, so $27 \div 6$ is not defined in the whole numbers. That is, the set of whole numbers is *not closed* under division.

By allowing the possibility of a **remainder,** we can extend the division operation. Consider $27 \div 6$, where division is viewed as repeated subtraction. Four groups of 6 can be removed from 27. This leaves 3, which are too few to form another group of 6. Thus, we can write

$$27 = 4 \cdot 6 + 3.$$

Here, 4 is called the **quotient** and 3 is the **remainder.** This information is also written

$$27 \div 6 = 4\,R\,3,$$

where R separates the quotient from the remainder. A representation of division with a remainder is shown in Figure 2.26.

**FIGURE 2.26**
Representing division with a remainder: $27 \div 6 = 4\,R\,3$

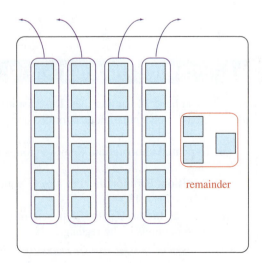

remainder

In general, we have the following result:

---

**THEOREM** *The Division Algorithm*

Let $a$ and $b$ be whole numbers with $b \neq 0$. Then there is a unique whole number $q$ called the **quotient** and a unique whole number $r$ called the **remainder** such that

$$a = q \cdot b + r, \qquad 0 \leq r < b.$$

---

It is common to write

$$a \div b = q \, \text{R} \, r$$

if $a = q \cdot b + r, 0 \leq r < b$. The quotient $q$ is the largest whole number of groups of $b$ objects that can be formed from $a$ objects, and the remainder $r$ is the number of objects that are left over. The remainder is 0 if, and only if, $b$ divides $a$ according to the definition of division in whole numbers. This important case is explored fully in Chapter 4.

## Why Does Quotient with Remainder (the Division Algorithm) Work?

When we were in elementary school, we were all taught how to find the quotient and remainder but not why it works. In the example we discussed in the previous section, with $a = 27$ and $b = 6$, the quotient $q$ is 4 and the remainder is $r = 3$.

Conceptually, by using the repeated subtraction of $b$, we have a process that gives the quotient and remainder of $a$ by $b$. Here's how the process works in the case of the example we just did in which $b < a$, where $a = 27$ and $b = 6$. Starting with $a$ and subtracting $b$, there are only two possibilities (Figure 2.27).

**FIGURE 2.27**
Algorithm for division as repeated subtraction

$$\text{(if 21 is larger than } b) \rightarrow \text{subtract } b \text{ again}$$
$$27 \rightarrow 27 - 6 = 21 \Big\langle$$
$$\text{(if 21 is less than } b) \rightarrow \text{finished}$$

The subtraction process is repeated until we get to the finished stage. For our example, the picture of the algorithm (process) is shown in Figure 2.28

**FIGURE 2.28**
Example of division algorithm as repeated subtraction

$$a = 27 \xrightarrow{-6} 27 - 6 = 21 \xrightarrow{-6} 15 \xrightarrow{-6} 9 \xrightarrow{-6} 3 \rightarrow \text{finished}$$

The algorithm stopped because, after subtracting $b$ enough times (4 in this example), we ended with an integer, $r = 3$, so that $0 \leq r < b = 6$. How many times did we subtract $b$ from $a$? We did it $q = 4$ times. Thus, $a - qb = r$, which is the same as $a = qb + r$. From this one example, and others from Problem Set 2.4, it becomes clear that this "repeated-subtraction" process will always stop. Therefore, the division algorithm works.

---

**EXAMPLE 2.17** **Using the Division Algorithm to Solve the Marching-Band Problem**

Mr. Garza was happy to see that so many students in the school band had turned out for the parade. He had them form into rows of 6, but it turned out that just 1 tuba player was in the back row. To his dismay, when he re-formed the band into rows of 5, there was still a lone tuba player in the back row. In desperation, Mr. Garza had the band reassemble into rows of 7. To his relief, every row was filled! What is the smallest size possible for the parade band?

**Solution**    If we let $n$ denote the number of students marching in the band, then we know that when $n$ is divided by 6 the remainder is 1. Thus, $n = 6q + 1$ for some whole number $q = 0, 1, 2, \ldots$. This means that $n$ is somewhere in the list of numbers that are 1 larger than a multiple of 6:

$$1, 7, 13, 19, 25, 31, 37, 43, 49, 55, 61, 67, 73, 79, 85, 91, 97, 103, \ldots$$

Similarly, $n \div 5$ has a remainder of 1, so $n$ is also a number in this list:

$$1, 6, 11, 16, 21, 26, 31, 36, 41, 46, 51, 56, 61, 66, 71, 76, 81, 86, 91, 96, 101, \ldots$$

Finally, 7 is a divisor of $n$, so $n$ is one of these numbers:

$$7, 14, 21, 28, 35, 42, 49, 56, 63, 70, 77, 84, 91, 98, 105, \ldots$$

Comparing the three lists, we find that 91 is the smallest number common to all three lists, so it is possible that there are 91 band members. Mr. Garza has arranged them in 13 rows, since $91 \div 7 = 13$.

**FROM** *The NCTM Principles and Standards*

## Understanding Meanings of Operations and How They Relate to One Another

In grades 3–5, students should focus on the meanings of, and relationship between, multiplication and division. It is important that students understand what each number in a multiplication or division expression represents. For example, in multiplication, unlike addition, the factors in the problem can refer to different units. If students are solving the problem $29 \times 4$ to find out how many legs there are on 29 cats, 29 is the number of cats (or number of groups), 4 is the number of legs on each cat (or number of items in each group), and 116 is the total number of legs on all the cats. Modeling multiplication problems with pictures, diagrams, or concrete materials helps students learn what the factors and their product represent in various contexts.

Students should consider and discuss different types of problems that can be solved using multiplication and division. For example, if there are 112 people traveling by bus and each bus can hold 28 people, how many buses are needed? In this case, $112 \div 28$ indicates the number of groups (buses), where the total number of people (112) and the size of each group (28 people in each bus) are known. In a different problem, students might know the number of groups and need to find how many items are in each group. If 112 people divide themselves evenly among four buses, how many people are on each bus? In this case, $112 \div 4$ indicates the number of people on each bus, where the total number of people and the number of groups (buses) are known. Students need to recognize both types of problems as division situations, should be able to model and solve each type of problem, and should know the units of the result: is it 28 buses or 28 people per bus? Students in these grades will also encounter situations where the result of division includes a remainder. They should learn the meaning of a remainder by modeling division problems and exploring the size of remainders given a particular divisor. For example, when dividing groups of counters into sets of 4, what remainders could there be for groups of different sizes?

SOURCE: *Principles and Standards for School Mathematics by NCTM, page 151. Copyright © 2000 by the National Council of Teachers of Mathematics. Reproduced with permission of the National Council of Teachers of Mathematics via Copyright Clearance Center. NCTM does not endorse the content or validity of these alignments.*

## Exponents and the Power Operation

Instead of writing $3 \cdot 3 \cdot 3 \cdot 3 \cdot 3$, we can follow a notation introduced by René Descartes and write $3^5$. This operation is called "taking 3 to the fifth power." The general definition is described as follows:

**DEFINITION** *The Power Operation for Whole Numbers*

Let $a$ and $m$ be whole numbers, where $m \neq 0$. Then **$a$ to the $m$th power,** written $a^m$, is defined by

$$a^1 = a, \quad \text{if } m = 1,$$

and

$$a^m = \overbrace{a \cdot a \cdot \ldots \cdot a}^{m \text{ times}}, \quad \text{if } m > 1.$$

The number $a$ is called the **base,** $m$ is called the **exponent** or **power,** and $a^m$ is called an **exponential expression.** Special cases include squares and cubes. For example, $7^2$ is read "7 squared," and $10^3$ is read "10 cubed." On most computers, $7^2$ and $10^3$ would be typed in as $7\char`^2$ and $10\char`^3$, where the circumflex $\char`^$ separates the base from the exponent. Calculators often have a $\boxed{\char`^}$ or $\boxed{y^x}$ key to compute powers. For example, $3\ \boxed{y^x}\ 2\ \boxed{=}$ will give the answer 9.

## EXAMPLE 2.18 Working with Exponents

Compute the following products and powers, expressing your answers in the form of a single exponential expression $a^m$:

(a) $7^4 \cdot 7^2$        (b) $6^3 \cdot 6^5$        (c) $2^3 \cdot 5^3$
(d) $3^2 \cdot 5^2 \cdot 4^2$        (e) $(3^2)^5$        (f) $(4^2)^3$

**Solution**

(a) $7^4 \cdot 7^2 = (7 \cdot 7 \cdot 7 \cdot 7) \cdot (7 \cdot 7) = 7 \cdot 7 \cdot 7 \cdot 7 \cdot 7 \cdot 7 = 7^6$
(b) $6^3 \cdot 6^5 = (6 \cdot 6 \cdot 6) \cdot (6 \cdot 6 \cdot 6 \cdot 6 \cdot 6)$
$\qquad = 6 \cdot 6 \cdot 6 \cdot 6 \cdot 6 \cdot 6 \cdot 6 \cdot 6 = 6^8$
(c) $2^3 \cdot 5^3 = (2 \cdot 2 \cdot 2) \cdot (5 \cdot 5 \cdot 5) = (2 \cdot 5) \cdot (2 \cdot 5) \cdot (2 \cdot 5)$
$\qquad = (2 \cdot 5)^3 = 10^3$
(d) $3^2 \cdot 5^2 \cdot 4^2 = (3 \cdot 3) \cdot (5 \cdot 5) \cdot (4 \cdot 4) = (3 \cdot 5 \cdot 4) \cdot (3 \cdot 5 \cdot 4)$
$\qquad = (3 \cdot 5 \cdot 4)^2 = 60^2$
(e) $(3^2)^5 = (3)^2 \cdot (3)^2 \cdot (3)^2 \cdot (3)^2 \cdot (3)^2$
$\qquad = (3 \cdot 3) \cdot (3 \cdot 3) \cdot (3 \cdot 3) \cdot (3 \cdot 3) \cdot (3 \cdot 3)$
$\qquad = 3 \cdot 3 \cdot 3 \cdot 3 \cdot 3 \cdot 3 \cdot 3 \cdot 3 \cdot 3 \cdot 3 = 3^{10}$
(f) $(4^2)^3 = (4^2) \cdot (4^2) \cdot (4^2) = (4 \cdot 4) \cdot (4 \cdot 4) \cdot (4 \cdot 4)$
$\qquad = 4 \cdot 4 \cdot 4 \cdot 4 \cdot 4 \cdot 4 = 4^6$

Example 2.18 reveals that the multiplication of exponentials follows useful patterns that can be used to shorten calculations. For example, $7^4 \cdot 7^2 = 7^{4+2}$ and $6^3 \cdot 6^5 = 6^{3+5}$ are two examples of the general rule $a^m \cdot a^n = a^{m+n}$ for multiplying exponentials with the same base. Similarly, $2^3 \cdot 5^3 = (2 \cdot 5)^3$ is a case of $a^n \cdot b^n = (a \cdot b)^n$, and $(3^2)^5 = 3^{2 \cdot 5}$ is an example of $(a^m)^n = a^{m \cdot n}$.

---

**THEOREM**  *Multiplication Rules of Exponentials*

Let $a$, $b$, $m$, and $n$ be whole numbers, where $m \neq 0$ and $n \neq 0$. Then

(i)  $a^m \cdot a^n = a^{m+n}$;
(ii)  $a^m \cdot b^m = (a \cdot b)^m$;
(iii)  $(a^m)^n = a^{m \cdot n}$.

---

**Proof of (i):** $a^m \cdot a^n = a^{m+n}$

$$a^m \cdot a^n = \underbrace{a \cdot a \cdot \cdots \cdot a}_{m \text{ factors}} \cdot \underbrace{a \cdot a \cdot \cdots \cdot a}_{n \text{ factors}}$$
$$= \underbrace{a \cdot a \cdot \cdots \cdot a}_{m + n \text{ factors}}$$
$$= a^{m+n}$$

The proofs of (ii) and (iii) are similar.

If the formula $a^m \cdot a^n = a^{m+n}$ were extended to allow $m = 0$, it would state that $a^0 \cdot a^n = a^{0+n} = a^n$. This suggests that it is reasonable to define $a^0 = 1$ when $a \neq 0$.

> **DEFINITION** *Zero as an Exponent*
> Let $a$ be any whole number, $a \neq 0$. Then $a^0$ is defined to be 1, or $a^0 = 1$.

Another way to see that $a^0 = 1$ makes sense is to look at various powers of $a$. Although we have not yet formally defined $a$ to a negative power, we know from our previous experience that $a^{-n} = 1/a^n$. Thus, we can look at a sequence for $a = 2$ and guess what the question mark denotes:

$$2^4 = 16, 2^3 = 8, 2^2 = 4, 2^1 = 2, 2^0 = ?, 2^{-1} = \tfrac{1}{2}, 2^{-2} = \tfrac{1}{4}, 2^{-3} = \tfrac{1}{8}, 2^{-4} = \tfrac{1}{16}.$$

Isn't it natural to think that $2^0 = 1$ or, for that matter, that $a^0 = 1$, for any positive integer?

To see why $0^0$ is *not* defined, notice that there are two conflicting patterns:

$$3^0 = 1, 2^0 = 1, 1^0 = 1, 0^0 = ?$$
$$0^3 = 0, 0^2 = 0, 0^1 = 0, 0^0 = ?$$

The multiplication formula $a^m \cdot a^n = a^{m+n}$ can also be converted to a corresponding division fact. For example,

$$a^{5-3} \cdot a^3 = a^{(5-3)+3} = a^5$$

so

$$a^5/a^3 = a^{5-3}.$$

In general, we have the following theorem:

> **THEOREM** *Rules for Division of Exponentials*
> Let $a$, $b$, $m$, and $n$ be whole numbers, where $m \geq n > 0$, $b \neq 0$, and $a \div b$ is defined. Then
>
> $$\textbf{(i)} \ b^m/b^n = b^{m-n}$$
>
> and
>
> $$\textbf{(ii)} \ (a^m/b^m) = (a/b)^m.$$

## EXAMPLE 2.19 Working with Exponents

Rewrite these expressions in exponential form $a^m$:

**(a)** $5^{12} \cdot 5^8$     **(b)** $7^{14}/7^5$     **(c)** $3^2 \cdot 3^5 \cdot 3^8$

**(d)** $8^7/4^7$     **(e)** $2^{5-5}$     **(f)** $(3^5)^2/3^4$

**Solution**

**(a)** $5^{12+8} = 5^{20}$     **(b)** $7^{14-5} = 7^9$

**(c)** $3^{2+5+8} = 3^{15}$     **(d)** $(8/4)^7 = 2^7$

**(e)** $2^0 = 1$     **(f)** $3^{5 \cdot 2 - 4} = 3^6$

## Problem Set 2.4

Exercises numbered in red are answered in the back of the text.

## Understanding Concepts

**1.** What multiplication fact is illustrated in each of the diagrams shown? Name the multiplication model that is illustrated.

**(a)**

**(b)**

**(c)**

**(d)**

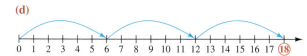

**(e)**

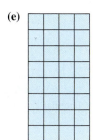

**(f)**

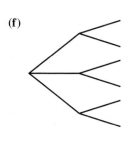

4. The Cartesian product of finite and nonempty sets can be illustrated by the intersections of a crossing-line pattern, as follows:

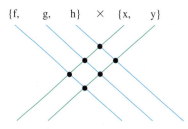

$$\{f, \quad g, \quad h\} \quad \times \quad \{x, \quad y\}$$

**(a)** Explain why the number of intersection points in the crossing-line pattern for $A \times B$ is $a \cdot b$, where $a = n(A)$ and $b = n(B)$.

**(b)** Draw the crossing-line pattern for $\{\square, \triangle\} \times \{\heartsuit, \diamondsuit, \clubsuit, \spadesuit\}$.

2. Discuss which model of multiplication—set model (repeated addition), number-line (measurement), array, rectangular area, multiplication tree, or Cartesian product—best fits the following problems:

**(a)** A set of dominoes came in a box containing 11 stacks of 5 dominoes each. How many dominoes are in the set?

**(b)** Marja has 3 skirts that she can "mix or match" with 6 blouses. How many outfits does she have to wear?

**(c)** Harold hiked 10 miles each day until he crossed the mountains after 5 days. How many miles was his hike?

**(d)** Ace Widget Company makes 35 widgets a day. How many widgets are made in a 5-day workweek?

**(e)** Janet's sunroom is 9 by 18 feet. How many 1-square-foot tiles does she need to cover the floor?

**(f)** Domingo rolls a die and flips a coin. How many outcomes are there?

 3. Multiplication as repeated addition can be illustrated on most calculators. For example, $4 \cdot 7$ is computed by $7 \boxplus 7 \boxplus 7 \boxplus 7 \boxminus$. Each press of the $\boxplus$ key completes any pending addition and sets up the next one, so the intermediate products $2 \cdot 7 = 14$ and $3 \cdot 7 = 21$ are displayed along the way. Many calculators have a "constant" feature, which enables the user to avoid having to reenter the same addend over and over. For example, $\boxplus 734 \boxminus \boxminus \boxminus$, or $734 \boxplus \boxplus \boxplus$ may compute $3 \cdot 734$; it all depends on how your particular calculator operates.

**(a)** Explain carefully how repeated addition is best accomplished on your calculator.

**(b)** Use repeated addition on your calculator to compute the given products. Check your result by using the $\boxtimes$ key.

  **(i)** $4 \cdot 9$       **(ii)** $7 \times 536$

  **(iii)** $6 \times 47{,}819$   **(iv)** $56{,}108 \times 6$ (What property may help?)

5. Which of the given sets of whole numbers are closed under multiplication? Explain your reasoning.

  **(a)** $\{1, 2\}$     **(b)** $\{0, 1\}$     **(c)** $\{0, 2, 4\}$

  **(d)** $\{0, 2, 4, \ldots\}$ (the even whole numbers)

  **(e)** $\{1, 3, 5, \ldots\}$ (the odd whole numbers)

  **(f)** $\{1, 2, 2^2, 2^3\}$

  **(g)** $\{1, 2, 2^2, 2^3, \ldots\}$

  **(h)** $\{1, 7, 7^2, 7^3, \ldots\}$

6. Which of the given subsets of the whole numbers $W = \{0, 1, 2, \ldots\}$ are closed under multiplication? Explain carefully.

  **(a)** $\{0, 1, 2, 3, 4, 6, 7, \ldots\}$ (i.e., the whole numbers except for 5)

  **(b)** $\{0, 1, 2, 3, 4, 5, 7, 8, \ldots\}$

  **(c)** $\{0, 1, 4, 5, 6, \ldots\}$

7. What properties of whole-number multiplication justify these equalities?

  **(a)** $4 \cdot 9 = 9 \cdot 4$

  **(b)** $4 \cdot (6 + 2) = 4 \cdot 6 + 4 \cdot 2$

  **(c)** $0 \cdot 439 = 0$

  **(d)** $7 \cdot 3 + 7 \cdot 8 = 7 \cdot (3 + 8)$

  **(e)** $5 \cdot (9 \cdot 11) = (5 \cdot 9) \cdot 11$

  **(f)** $1 \cdot 12 = 12$

8. What property of multiplication is illustrated in the accompanying diagrams?

**Diagrams for Problem 8**

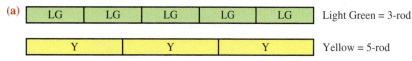

**(b)**

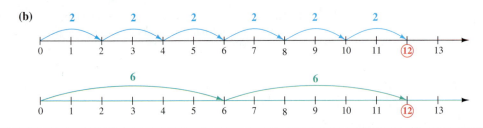

---

9. Use the rectangular area model to illustrate each of the given statements. Make drawings similar to Figure 2.22.

   (a) $(2 + 5) \cdot 3 = 2 \cdot 3 + 5 \cdot 3$

   (b) $3 \cdot (2 + 5 + 1) = 3 \cdot 2 + 3 \cdot 5 + 3 \cdot 1$

   (c) $(3 + 2) \cdot (4 + 3) = 3 \cdot 4 + 3 \cdot 3 + 2 \cdot 4 + 2 \cdot 3$

10. The FOIL method is a useful way to recall how to expand the product of two binomials $(a + b) \times (c + d)$: Multiply the First terms, the Outer terms, the Inner terms, and the Last terms of the binomials, and sum the four products to obtain the formula $(a + b) \times (c + d) = ac + ad + bc + bd$. Carefully explain how the rectangular area diagram shown justifies the FOIL method. The important point of this problem is for you to understand the reason FOIL actually works, rather than being able to "just use it." Again, it is the conceptual understanding that is crucial for teaching.

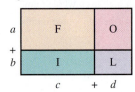

11. Use the following figure to show that the product of trinomials, $(a + b + c) \cdot (d + e + f)$, can be written as a sum of nine products:

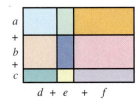

12. Modify Figure 2.21 to show how the associative property $3 \cdot (2 \cdot 4)$ can be illustrated with arrays of cubes in three-dimensional space.

13. What properties of multiplication make it easy to compute these values mentally?

   (a) $7 \cdot 19 + 3 \cdot 19$

   (b) $24 \cdot 17 + 24 \cdot 3$

   (c) $36 \cdot 15 - 12 \cdot 45$

14. What division facts are illustrated in the accompanying diagrams?

   (a)                    (b)

  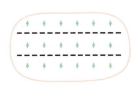

15. A 2-by-3 rectangular array is associated with the fact family $2 \cdot 3 = 6, 3 \cdot 2 = 6, 6 \div 2 = 3$, and $6 \div 3 = 2$. What fact family is associated with each of these rectangular arrays?

   (a) 4 by 8          (b) 6 by 5

16. Discuss which of three conceptual models of division— repeated-subtraction, partition, and missing-factor—best corresponds to the problems that follow. More than one model may fit.

   (a) Preston owes $3200 on his car. If his payments are $200 a month, how many months will Preston make car payments?

   (b) An estate of $76,000 is to be split among four heirs. How much can each heir expect to inherit?

   (c) Anita was given a grant of $375 to cover expenses on her trip. She expects that it will cost her $75 a day. How many days can she plan to be gone?

17. In the Division Algorithm, use the method of repeated subtraction to solve the given division problems. Include a diagram that shows the algorithm with arrows, similar to the example of Figure 2.28.

   (a) The remainder of 19 on division by 5

   (b) The remainder of 18 on division by 9

   (c) The remainder of 25 on division by 8

   (d) The remainder of 14 on division by 7

   (e) The remainder of 7 on division by 14

   (f) What is the quotient in each of these cases?

18. In the Division Algorithm, why is there no alternative in Figure 2.27 that gives what to do if one of the stages comes up with a negative remainder?

19. Use repeated subtraction on your calculator to compute the given division problems, where remainders are possible. Be sure to take advantage of the "constant" feature of your calculator.

   (a) $78 \div 13$          (b) $832 \div 52$

   (c) $96 \div 14$          (d) $548,245 \div 45,687$

20. Solve for the unknown whole number in the following expressions:

   (a) $y \div 5 = 5 \,\mathrm{R}\, 4$          (b) $20 \div x = 3 \,\mathrm{R}\, 2$

21. Rewrite each of the following in the form of a single exponential:

   (a) $3^{20} \cdot 3^{15}$          (b) $4^8 \cdot 7^8$

   (c) $(3^2)^5$          (d) $x^7 \cdot x^9$

   (e) $y^3 \cdot z^3$          (f) $(t^3)^4$

22. Write each of the following as $2^m$ for some whole number $m$:

   (a) 8          (b) $4 \cdot 8$

   (c) 1024          (d) $8^4$

**23.** Find the exponents that make the following equations true:

(a) $3^m = 81$          (b) $3^n = 531,441$

(c) $4^p = 1,048,576$    (d) $2^q = 1,048,576$

## Teaching Concepts

**24.** Large-group kinesthetic activities are often an effective way to deepen one's understanding of basic concepts. For example, have the children hold hands in groups of three and count the number of groups to illustrate the concept of division by 3 with the repeated-subtraction (grouping) model of division. Carefully describe analogous large-group activities that illustrate

(a) multiplication as repeated addition;

(b) multiplication as an array;

(c) partitive division;

(d) missing-factor division.

**25.** When the class was asked to pose a meaningful problem that corresponded to the division $14 \div 3$, Peter's problem was answered by 4, Tina's by 5, and Andrea's by 4 with a remainder of 2. Carefully explain how all three children may be correct by posing three problems of your own that give their answers.

**26.** Discuss how division can be modeled with number strips. Write a brief essay that includes several examples, each illustrated with carefully drawn figures.

**27.** The theorem that describes the property of whole numbers in addition in Section 2.3, page 91, is followed by an informal way to describe three of the four properties for addition. What would be your description of the middle four properties of whole-number multiplication in the theorem on page 105 of this section?

## Responding to Students

**28.** A student is given two problems and asked to fill in the blanks. He responds to them as given in the second column:

Problem   $7 \times 7 =$ ___   Student Response   $7 \times 7 = 49$

Problem   ___ $\div 7 = 7$   Student Response   $1 \div 7 = 7$

What is this student doing incorrectly?

**29.** Your student, Shannon, bought 18 nuts and 18 bolts. The bolts were 86 cents each and the nuts were 14 cents each. She figured out the cost in her head and handed the clerk $18. She asked you why the clerk did it the way that he did (which follows). How would you respond to her?

$$\begin{array}{r} \overset{4}{86} \\ \times 18 \\ \hline 688 \\ 86 \\ \hline 1548 \end{array} \qquad \begin{array}{r} \overset{3}{14} \\ \times 18 \\ \hline 112 \\ 14 \\ \hline 252 \end{array} \qquad \begin{array}{r} \overset{1\ 1}{15.48} \\ +\ 2.52 \\ \hline 18.00 \end{array}$$

**30.** Nelson baked 36 cupcakes. In each pan, he baked 6 cupcakes. Students were asked to write an equation that tells how to find $p$, the number of *pans* of cupcakes he baked. One student

answered that it was $36 - 6 = p$. What error did this student make and what would you suggest?

**31.** Emily is having trouble multiplying two-digit numbers. She is a wonderful art student, so you are trying to teach her a visual method for multiplication. How would you help her by drawing a rectangular area model for $32 \times 23$ after you've shown the partial products as follows?

$$\begin{array}{r} 32 \\ \times 23 \\ \hline 6 \\ 90 \\ 40 \\ 600 \\ \hline 736 \end{array}$$

## Thinking Critically

**32.** The binary operation $\star$ is defined for the set of shapes $\{\bigcirc, \square, \triangle\}$ according to the table that follows. For example, $\triangle \star \square = \bigcirc$.

| $\star$ | $\bigcirc$ | $\square$ | $\triangle$ |
|---|---|---|---|
| $\bigcirc$ | $\bigcirc$ | $\square$ | $\triangle$ |
| $\square$ | $\square$ | $\triangle$ | $\bigcirc$ |
| $\triangle$ | $\triangle$ | $\bigcirc$ | $\square$ |

Is the operation closed? commutative? associative? Is there an identity shape?

**33.** (a) Verify that the three numbers in every row, column, and diagonal in the following square have the same product, making the square a *magic multiplication square*:

| 8 | 256 | 2 |
|---|---|---|
| 4 | 16 | 64 |
| 128 | 1 | 32 |

(b) Write each number in the magic multiplication square as a power of 2, and then explain how the multiplication square can be obtained from a related magic addition square.

(c) Create a magic multiplication square with the numbers 1, 3, 9, 27, 81, 243, 729, 2187, and 6561.

**34.** (a) The Math Club wants to gross $500 on its raffle. Raffle tickets are $2 each and 185 tickets have been sold so far. The answer is 65. What is the question?

(b) A total of 67 eggs was collected from the henhouse and placed in standard egg cartons. If the answer is 5, what is the question? If the answer is 7, what is the question?

**35.** There are 318 folding chairs being set up in rows in an auditorium, with 14 chairs being put in each row, starting at the front of the auditorium.

**(a)** If the answer is 22, what is the question?

**(b)** If the answer is 10, what is the question?

**36.** A certain whole number less than 100 leaves the remainders 1, 2, 3, and 4 when divided, respectively, by 2, 3, 4, and 5. What is the whole number?

## Thinking Cooperatively

**37.** Each team is given a game sheet as shown. The teacher rolls three dice (or a die 3 times) to determine three numbers $x$, $y$, and $z$. Each team uses whole-number operations, including raising a number to a power, involving all three numbers exactly once, to obtain expressions equal to as many of the numbers $0, 1, 2, \ldots, 18$ as possible. The team filling all regions of the game sheet first is the winner. If no team has won at the end of the first roll, the numbers $x$, $y$, and $z$ are replaced by rolling the dice again. Each team now fills in remaining empty positions on the game sheet, using the new set of three numbers. The dice are rolled again until there is a winning team. Suppose the dice turn up the numbers 2, 3, 3. Show that at least 14 of the regions on the board can be filled.

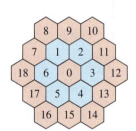

## Using a Calculator

**38.** Let $T_n$ denote the sum of the first $n$ triangular numbers, so that

$$T_n = 1 + 3 + 6 + 10 + \cdots + t_n,$$

where

$$t_n = 1 + 2 + 3 + \cdots + n.$$

Now observe that

$$T_1 = 1 = 1 \cdot 2 \cdot \tfrac{3}{6};$$
$$T_2 = 1 + 3 = 4 = 2 \cdot 3 \cdot \tfrac{4}{6};$$
$$T_3 = 1 + 3 + 6 = 10 = 3 \cdot 4 \cdot \tfrac{5}{6}.$$

**(a)** See if the pattern continues to hold for $T_4, T_5, \ldots, T_{12}$.

**(b)** What is $T_{100}$?

**39.** The eighth triangular number is $t_8 = (8 \cdot 9)/2 = 36$, which is also a square number, since $6^2 = 36$. Verify that the triangular numbers $t_{49}, t_{288}$, and $t_{1681}$ are also square numbers. Recall that $t_n = n(n + 1)/2$.

## From State Student Assessments

**40.** (Texas, Grade 5)
Ricky is trying to decide which outfit to wear to a party. His choices are shown in the diagram.

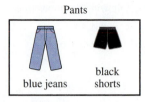
Pants — blue jeans, black shorts

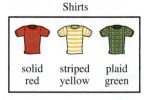
Shirts — solid red, striped yellow, plaid green

Shoes — tennis shoes, sandals

How many possible different outfits can Ricky create if he chooses 1 pair of pants, 1 shirt, and 1 pair of shoes?

**A.** 7 **B.** 8 **C.** 10 **D.** 12

**41.** (Illinois, Grade 5)
Which expression fits the diagram below?

**A.** $4 \times (3 \times 3)$ **B.** $3 \times (4 \times 4)$ **C.** $3 + (3 \times 4)$

**D.** $3 + (3 + 4)$ **E.** $3 \times (3 + 4)$

**42.** (Michigan, Grade 4)
Robert is cutting oranges for his soccer teammates. He will cut each orange into 4 pieces. Each player will get 2 pieces. There are 20 players on the team. How many oranges does Robert need to cut?

**A.** 5 **B.** 8 **C.** 10 **D.** 12

**43.** (Massachusetts, Grade 4)
Was this problem given on Valentine's Day?

Which of the following is a model of $4 \times 3$?

**A.**

**B.**

**C.**

**D.**

**44.** (Virginia, Grade 4)
Which is true?

**A.** $18 + 9 = 18 \times 9$ **B.** $9 + 18 = 18 + 9$

**C.** $9 \div 18 = 18 \div 9$ **D.** $9 - 18 = 18 - 9$

See "Examining School Book Pages" on page 118 for questions related to the pages shown below.

## School Book Pages

## The Distributive Property

### Lesson 2-4

**Understand It!**
You can use the Distributive Property to compute some products mentally.

## The Distributive Property

**How can you use the Distributive Property to evaluate expressions?**

The **Distributive Property** states that multiplying a sum (or difference) by a number gives the same result as multiplying each number in the sum (or difference) by the number and adding (or subtracting) the products.

**Distributive Property**

$$a(b+c) = a(b) + a(c) \qquad a(b-c) = a(b) - a(c)$$

### Guided Practice*

**Do you know HOW?**

In **1** through **4**, find each missing number.

1. $8(7 + 23) = 8(7) + 8(\ \ )$
2. $4(28) = 4(20) + 4(\ \ )$
3. $8(57) - 8(7) = 8(\ \ )$
4. $5(26 - 3) = 5(\ \ ) - 5(3)$

**Do you UNDERSTAND?**

5. Why is it easier to evaluate $7 \times 60$ than to evaluate $7 \times 55 + 7 \times 5$?

6. Tony read 22 pages in the morning and 28 pages in the afternoon for 5 days. Lois read 47 pages each day for 5 days. Explain how to use the Distributive Property to find how many pages each of them read.

### Independent Practice

**Leveled Practice** In **7** through **16**, use the Distributive Property to find each missing number.

7. $6(32) = 6(\ \ ) + 6(2)$
8. $20(5) - 20(2) = 20(\ \ )$
9. $3(28) + (3)2 = (30)$
10. $9(23) = 9(\ \ ) + 9(3)$
11. $6(46) - 6(6) = 6(\ \ )$
12. $4(33) = 4(30) + 4(\ \ )$
13. $30(22 - 10) = 30(22) - 30(\ \ )$
14. $8(99) = 8(100) - 8(\ \ )$
15. $20(33 - 5) = 20(\ \ )$
    $= 20(\ \ ) + 20(8)$
16. $5(42) + 5(5) = 5(\ \ )$
    $= 5(\ \ ) + 5(7)$

DIGITAL Animated Glossary www.pearsonsuccessnet.com

40

*For another example, see Set D on page 57.

---

Use the Distributive Property to break apart a number to find the product for $5 \times 27$.

$5 \times 27$ → Break 27 apart.
$5(20 + 7)$ → $27 = 20 + 7$ → Multiply each addend.
$5(20) + 5(7)$
$100 + 35$ → Add.
$135$
$5 \times 27 = 135$

Use the Distributive Property to join numbers together to find $8(32) - 8(2)$.

$8(32) - 8(2)$
$8(32 - 2)$ → Join factors.
$8(30)$ → Subtract.
$240$ → Multiply.
$8(32) - 8(2) = 240$

### Independent Practice

Use the Distributive Property and mental math to evaluate.

**Tip** When doing mental math, choose to join or break apart based on which is easier.

17. $7(29)$
18. $6(21) + 6(31)$
19. $5(22) + 5(8)$
20. $8(47)$
21. $6(41) + 6(9)$
22. $30(3) + 30(5)$
23. $3(21) - 3(11)$
24. $5(25 - 3)$

**Problem Solving**

25. **Writing to Explain** The 6th graders ordered lunch from the Big Group Menu. They ordered 22 organic chilis and 8 veggie plates. Their order can be expressed as $6(22) + 6(8)$. Explain what mental math steps you would use to find the total cost of the order.

**Data**

| Big Group Menu | |
| --- | --- |
| Organic Chili | $6.00 |
| Chicken Tacos | $4.00 |
| Fruit Salad | $5.00 |
| Organic Salad | $5.00 |
| Veggie Plate | $6.00 |

26. Using the Big Group Menu, write and solve a problem where you can use the Distributive Property.

27. **Writing to Explain** Jamal said that 9.45 is greater than 9.8 because 45 is greater than 8. Is he correct? Explain.

28. Hiroko put money in a savings account each week. After 9 weeks, there was $49.50 in the account. If Hiroko put the same amount in each week, how much did she save each week?

49.50
? Amount saved each week

29. **Think About the Process** Which choice shows a problem with common factors that could be used for mental math?

A $3(45) + 3(5)$
B $4(18) - 7(8)$
C $2(22) + 3(33)$
D $8(39) + 4(40)$

41

Lesson 2-4

## Examining School Book Pages

*Refer to the School Book Pages provided on page 117 to answer the following questions.*

45. Design a Big Group Menu which has prices that include decimals (but are not integers). Then construct two problems that are similar to problem 26 of the School Book Page, one of which can be used for mental math via the distributive property and the other of which could not be solved without paper and pencil.

46. (a) Read carefully and solve problem 29 of this problem set.
    (b) Reread problem 29, to see if more than one of these problems could be done in your head, thanks to the distributive law.
    (c) Do you think a sixth grader would be able to find a second problem that could be done in his or her head?

## The Chapter in Relation to Future Teachers

The simplest mathematical idea of all is counting, but what must a future teacher know in order to help children learn counting and the operations of the basic arithmetic of whole numbers? In Chapter 2, sets were introduced and were used in counting, addition, subtraction, multiplication, and division. A variety of models to perform these operations was discussed. The background of this chapter will help you respond to questions from students and work with them to understand the concepts of whole-number arithmetic. The combination of conceptual understanding and procedural fluency in students is the goal toward which elementary school teachers strive.

## Chapter 2 Summary

| Section 2.1   Sets and Operations on Sets | Page Reference |
|---|---|
| **CONCEPTS** | |
| • **Set:** A set is a collection of objects from a specified universe. A set can be described verbally, by a list, or with set-builder notation. | 69, 70 |
| • **Venn diagram:** Sets can be visualized with Venn diagrams, in which the universe is a rectangle and closed loops inside the universe correspond to sets. Elements of a set are associated with points within the loop corresponding to that set. | 71 |
| • **Set operations and relations.** Sets are combined and related in the following ways: set complement ($\overline{A}$), subset ($A \subseteq B$), proper subset ($A \subset B$), intersection ($A \cap B$), and union ($A \cup B$). | 71, 72, 73 |
| **DEFINITIONS** | |
| • A **universe** ($U$) consists of the objects allowed into consideration for a set. | 69 |
| • An **element,** or member, is an object that belongs to the collection, or set. | 69 |
| • A **natural number,** or **counting number,** is a member of the set $N = \{1, 2, 3, \ldots\}$, where the ellipsis "$\ldots$" indicates "and so on." | 70 |
| • The **complement of set,** written ($\overline{A}$), is the set of elements in the universal set $U$ that are not elements of $A$. | 71 |
| • The set $A$ is a **subset** of $B$, written $A \subseteq B$, if, and only if, every element of $A$ is also an element of $B$. | 71 |
| • A set $A$ is an **equal set** of a set $B$, written $A = B$, if, and only if, $A$ and $B$ have precisely the same elements. | 72 |
| • A **proper subset,** $A \subset B$, is when $A \subseteq B$, but there must be some element of $B$ that is not also an element of $A$, $A \neq B$. | 72 |
| • An **empty set** is a set that has no elements in it and is written $\varnothing$. | 72 |

| | |
|---|---|
| • The **intersection** of two sets $A$ and $B$, written $A \cap B$, is the set of elements common to both $A$ and $B$. | 72 |
| • **Disjoint** sets are two sets that have no elements in common, written $A \cap B = \varnothing$. | 72 |
| • The **union** of sets $A$ and $B$, written $A \cup B$, is the set of all elements that are in $A$ or $B$. | 72 |
| • A **counterexample** is an example which shows that a statement is false. | 75 |

**PROPERTIES**

| | |
|---|---|
| • **Transitive property of set inclusion:** If $A \subseteq B$ and $B \subseteq C$, then $A \subseteq C$ | 74 |
| • **Commutative property of union and intersection:** $A \cup B = B \cup A$ <br> $\qquad\qquad A \cap B = B \cap A$ | 74 |
| • **Associative property of union and intersection:** $A \cup (B \cup C) = (A \cup B) \cup C$ <br> $\qquad\qquad A \cap (B \cap C) = (A \cap B) \cap C$ | 74 |
| • **Distributive property of union and intersection:** $A \cap (B \cup C) = (A \cap B) \cup (A \cap C)$ <br> $\qquad\qquad A \cup (B \cap C) = (A \cup B) \cap (A \cup C)$ | 74 |

**NOTATION**

| | |
|---|---|
| • A set as a list in braces: $\{a, b, \ldots\}$ | 70 |
| • Set-builder notation: $\{x \mid x \text{ is } (condition)\}$ | 70 |

| Section 2.2   Sets, Counting, and the Whole Numbers | Page Reference |
|---|---|

**CONCEPTS**

| | |
|---|---|
| • **Types of number:** Nominal numbers name objects (e.g., an ID number), ordinal numbers indicate position (e.g., 5th place), and cardinal numbers indicate the number of elements in a set (e.g., there are 9 justices of the U.S. Supreme Court). | 79 |
| • **Equivalence of sets:** Two sets are equivalent if, and only if, there is a one-to-one correspondence (or matching) of the elements of the two sets. | 80 |
| • **Whole numbers:** The whole numbers are the cardinal numbers of finite sets, with zero being the cardinal number of the empty set. Whole numbers can be represented and visualized by a variety of manipulatives and diagrams, including **tiles, cubes, number strips, rods,** and the **number line.** | 81, 82, 83 |
| • **Order of the whole numbers:** The whole numbers are ordered, so that $m$ is less than $n$ if a set with $m$ elements is a proper subset of a set with $n$ elements. | 83 |

**DEFINITIONS**

| | |
|---|---|
| • A **nominal number,** or **identification,** is a sequence of digits used as a name or label. | 79 |
| • An **ordinal number** describes location in an ordered sequence with the words *first, second, third, fourth,* and so on, communicating the basic notion of "where." | 79 |
| • A **cardinal number** of a set is the number of objects in the set, communicating the basic notion of "how many." | 79 |
| • **One-to-one correspondence** between sets is the concept that each element of one set is paired with exactly one element of another set, and each element of either set belongs to exactly one of the pairs. | 80 |
| • Sets $A$ and $B$ are **equivalent,** or **matching,** if there is a one-to-one correspondence between $A$ and $B$, written $A \sim B$. | 80 |
| • A **finite** set is a set that is either the empty set or a set equivalent to $\{1, 2, 3, \ldots, n\}$, for some natural number $n$. | 81 |

| | |
|---|---|
| • An **infinite** set is a set that is not finite. One way to think of an infinite set is that, if you were to list all members of the set, the list would go on forever. | 81 |
| • **Whole numbers** are the cardinal numbers of finite sets, which means they are the numbers of elements in finite sets. | 81 |
| • **Less than,** $a < b$: A way to relate the number of elements in two given sets, $A$ and $B$ where $n(A) = a$ and $n(B) = b$. There are less elements in set $A$ than there are in set $B$, or $A$ is a proper subset of $B$. | 83 |
| • **Greater than,** $a > b$: A way to relate the number of elements in two given sets, $A$ and $B$ where $n(A) = a$ and $n(B) = b$. There are more elements in set $A$ than there are in set $B$, or $B$ is a proper subset of $A$. | 83 |

**NOTATION**

| | |
|---|---|
| • **Zero, $0 = n(\varnothing)$:** Zero designates the cardinality of the empty set. | 81 |

| **Section 2.3   Addition and Subtraction of Whole Numbers** | **Page Reference** |
|---|---|

**CONCEPTS**

| | |
|---|---|
| • **Addition of whole numbers:** Addition of whole numbers is defined by $a + b = n(A \cup B)$, where $a = n(A)$, $b = n(B)$, and $A$ and $B$ are disjoint finite sets. Addition can be visualized on the number line with the **measurement model** or using the **set model.** | 89, 90, 91 |
| • **Closure property:** The sum of two whole numbers is a whole number. | 91 |
| • **Commutative property:** For all whole numbers $a$ and $b$, $a + b = b + a$. | 91 |
| • **Associative property:** For all whole numbers $a$, $b$, and $c$, $a + (b + c) = (a + b) + c$. | 91 |
| • **Zero property of addition:** Zero is an additive identity, so $a + 0 = 0 + a = a$ for all whole numbers $a$. | 91 |
| • **Conceptual models of subtraction:** These models include the **take-away model,** the **missing-addend model,** the **comparison model,** and the **number-line (or measurement) model.** | 93, 94, 95 |

**DEFINITIONS**

| | |
|---|---|
| • A **binary operation** is an operation in which two whole numbers are combined to form another whole number. | 89 |
| • The **addition,** or **sum,** of $a$ and $b$ is the total number of the combined collection, written $a + b.$ | 89 |
| • The **addends,** or **summands,** of the expression $a + b$ are $a$ and $b$. | 89 |
| • The **difference,** written $a - b,$ is the unique whole number $c$ such that $a = b + c$. | 92 |
| • In the expression $a - b$, the **minuend** is $a$. | 93 |
| • In the expression $a - b$, the **subtrahend** is $b$. | 93 |

**PROPERTIES**

| | |
|---|---|
| • **Properties of addition** | |
| • **Closure property:** If $a$ and $b$ are any two whole numbers, then $a + b$ is a unique whole number. | 91 |
| • **Commutative property:** If $a$ and $b$ are any two whole numbers, then $a + b = b + a$. | 91 |
| • **Associative property:** If $a$, $b$, and $c$ are any three whole numbers, then $a + (b + c) = (a + b) + c$. | 91 |
| • **Additive-identity property of zero:** If $a$ is any whole number, then $a + 0 = 0 + a = a$. | 91 |

| Section 2.4 Multiplication and Division of Whole Numbers | Page Reference |
|---|---|

**CONCEPTS**

- **Multiplication:** Multiplication is defined as a repeated addition, so that $a \cdot b = b + b + \cdots + b$, where there are $a$ addends.  | 100

- **Conceptual models of multiplication:** These models include the **array model,** the rectangular area model, the **multiplication tree model,** the **skip-count model,** and the **Cartesian product** $[a \cdot b = n(A \times B)]$. Here, $A \times B$ denotes the Cartesian product of sets $A$ and $B$. | 100, 101, 102, 103

- **Properties of multiplication:** For all whole numbers $a$, $b$, and $c$, $a \cdot b$ is a whole number (the closure property), $a \cdot b = b \cdot a$ (the commutative property), $a \cdot (b \cdot c) = (a \cdot b) \cdot c$ (the associative property), $a \cdot (b + c) = a \cdot b + a \cdot c$ (the distributive property), $1 \cdot a = a \cdot 1 = a$ (one is a multiplicative identity), and $0 \cdot a = a \cdot 0 = 0$ (multiplication-by-zero property) | 104, 105

- **Division:** $a \div b, b \neq 0$, is defined if, and only if, there is a unique whole number $c$ such that $a = b \cdot c$. | 105, 106

- **Conceptual models of division:** These models include the **repeated-subtraction (grouping) model,** the **partition (sharing) model,** and the **missing-factor model,** where the missing factor $c$ in the multiplication equation $a = b \cdot c$ is calculated. | 106

**DEFINITIONS**

- **Multiplication (product), $a \cdot b$:** The operation of adding $a$ to itself $b$ times; also denoted $a \times b$, $a*b$, $ab$ and $(a)(b)$ | 101

- A **factor** is each whole number $a$ and $b$ of the product $a \cdot b$. | 101

- **Repeated addition model:** A way to represent the multiplication operation; Where $a$ and $b$ are any two whole numbers, $a$ multiplied by $b$, written $a \cdot b$, is defined by $a \cdot b = b + b + \cdots + b$ with $a$ addends, when $a$ is not zero and by $0 \cdot b = 0$. | 100

- **Ordered pair $(a, b)$** is the representation of the first component, $a$, from one set and a second component, $b$, from another set. It also indicates the Cartesian coordinates of a point. | 102

- The **Cartesian product** of sets $A$ and $B$, written $A \times B$, is the set of all ordered pairs whose first component is an element of set $A$ and whose second component is an element of set $B$. | 103

- **Division,** written $a \div b$, or $a/b$: Let $a$ and $b$ be whole numbers with $b \neq 0$. Then $a \div b = c$ if, and only if, $a = b \cdot c$ for a unique whole number $c$. | 105, 106

- In the expression $a \div b$, $a$ is the **dividend.** | 107

- In the expression $a \div b$, $b$ is the **divisor.** | 107

- For any positive whole number $a$ (the base) and any whole number $m$ (the **exponent,** or **power**), $a$ **to the $m$th power,** $a^m$, is defined by $a^m = a \cdot a \cdots a$, where there are $m$ factors of $a$. Also, $a^0 = 1$. | 110, 111, 112

**THEOREM**

- **The division algorithm:** Let $a$ and $b$ be whole numbers with $b \neq 0$. Then there is a unique whole number $q$ called the **quotient** and a unique whole number $r$ called the **remainder** such that $a = q \cdot b + r, 0 \leq r < b$. It is common to write $a \div b = q$ R $r$ if $a = q \cdot b + r, 0 \leq r < b$. | 109, 110

## PROPERTIES

- **Properties of multiplication**
  - **Closure property:** If $a \cdot b$ are any two whole numbers, then $a \cdot b$ is a unique whole number. — 104, 105
  - **Commutative property:** If $a$ and $b$ are any two whole numbers, then $a \cdot b = b \cdot a$. — 104, 105
  - **Associative property:** If $a$, $b$, and $c$ are any three whole numbers, then $a \bullet (b \bullet c) = (a \bullet b) \bullet c$. — 104, 105
  - **Multiplicative identity:** The number 1 is the unique whole number for which $b \bullet 1 = 1 \bullet b = b$ holds for all whole numbers $b$. — 105
  - **Multiplication-by-zero property:** For all whole numbers $b$, $0 \bullet b = b \bullet 0 = 0$. — 105
  - **Distributive property of multiplication over addition:** If $a$, $b$, and $c$ are any three whole numbers, then $a \bullet (b + c) = (a \bullet b) + (a \bullet c)$ and $(a + b) \bullet c = (a \bullet c) + (b \bullet c)$. — 104, 105

## FORMULA

- **Multiplication—division fact family:** The set of four equivalent facts that may be assumed when one of the four facts is given. In the family, there are two multiplication statements, for example $a \bullet b = c$ and $b \bullet a = c$ (provided that neither $a$ nor $b$ is zero) and two division statements, for example $c \div a = b$ and $c \div b = a$ (provided that neither $a$ or nor $b$ is zero.) — 107

- **Multiplication rules of exponentials:** Let $a$, $b$, $m$, and $n$ be whole numbers, where $m \neq 0$ and $n \neq 0$. Then (i) $a^m \bullet a^n = a^{m+n}$ (ii) $a^m \bullet b^m = (a \bullet b)^m$ (iii) $(a^m)^n = a^{m \bullet n}$. — 111

## NOTATION

- **Exponential expression:** $a^m$, where $a$ is the base and $m$ is the exponent. — 111

# Chapter Review Exercises

## Section 2.1

1. Let $U = \{n \mid n$ is a whole number and $2 \leq n \leq 25\}$,

   $S = \{n \mid n \in U$ and $n$ is a square number$\}$, and
   $P = \{n \mid n \in U$ and $n$ is a prime number$\}$ ($n > 1$ is *prime* when it is divisible by just two different whole numbers: itself and 1).
   Let $T = \{n \mid n \in U$ and $n$ is a power of $2\}$.

   (a) Write $S$, $P$, and $T$ in listed form.

   (b) Find the following sets: $\overline{P}$, $S \cap T$, $S \cup T$, and $S \cap \overline{T}$.

2. Draw a Venn diagram of the sets $S$, $P$, and $T$ in problem 1.

3. Replace each box $\square$ with one of the symbols $\cap$, $\cup$, $\subset$, $\subseteq$, or $=$ to give a correct statement for general sets $A$, $B$, and $C$.

   (a) $A \square A \cup B$

   (b) If $A \subseteq B$ and $A$ is not equal to $B$, then $A \square B$.

   (c) $A \square (B \cup C) = (A \cap B) \cup (A \cap C)$

   (d) $A \square \varnothing = A$

## Section 2.2

4. Let $S = \{s, e, t\}$ and $T = \{t, h, e, o, r, y\}$. Find $n(S)$, $n(T)$, $n(S \cup T)$, $n(S \cap T)$, $n(S \cap \overline{T})$, and $n(T \cap \overline{S})$.

5. Show that the set of square natural numbers less than 101 is in one-to-one correspondence with the set $\{a, b, c, d, e, f, g, h, i, j\}$.

6. Show that the set of cubes, $\{1, 8, 27, \ldots\}$, is equivalent to the set of natural numbers.

7. Label the number of elements in each region of a two-loop Venn diagram for which $n(U) = 20$, $n(A) = 7$, $n(B) = 9$, and $n(A \cup B) = 11$.

## Section 2.3

8. Explain how to illustrate $5 + 2$ with

   (a) the set model of addition;

   (b) the number-line (measurement) model of addition.

9. What properties of whole-number addition are illustrated on the following number lines?

   (a)

   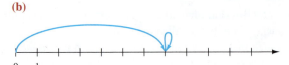

   (b)

   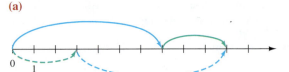

**10.** Draw figures that illustrate $6 - 4$,

    **(a)** using sets.

    **(b)** using the number line.

## Section 2.4

**11.** Draw representations of the product $4 \times 2$, using the given representation:

    **(a)** A set diagram

    **(b)** An array of discrete objects

    **(c)** A rectangular area

    **(d)** A multiplication tree

    **(e)** A number-line diagram

**12.** Let $A = \{p, q, r, s\}$ and $B = \{x, y\}$.

    **(a)** Find $A \times B$.

    **(b)** What product is modeled with $A \times B$?

**13.** Whiffle balls 2 inches in diameter are packed individually in cubical boxes, and then the boxes are packed in cartons of 3 dozen balls. What are the dimensions of a suitable rectangular carton?

**14.** A drill sergeant lines up 92 soldiers in rows of 12, except for a partial row in the back. How many rows are formed? How many soldiers are in the back row?

**15.** Draw figures that illustrate the division problem $15 \div 3$, using these models:

    **(a)** Repeated subtraction (grouping objects in a set)

    **(b)** Partition (sharing objects)

    **(c)** Missing factor (rectangular array)

## Chapter Test

**1.** What operation on whole numbers is being illustrated in the following diagrams?

    **(a)**

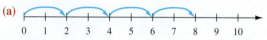

    **(b)**

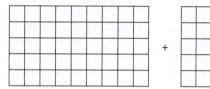

    **(c)**

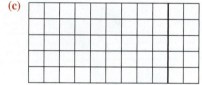

    **(d)**

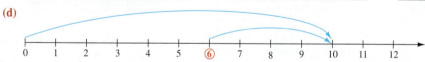

**2.** The following sentence contains three types of numbers: "On the *15th* of April, Joe Taxpayer sent in form *1040* and a money order for *$253*."

Name and describe the three kinds of numbers.

**3.** Let $S = \{1, 2, 4, 8, 16, \ldots\}$ denote the set of powers of 2.

    **(a)** Is $S$ closed under multiplication?

    **(b)** Is $S$ closed under addition?

Explain why you answered as you did.

**4.** Explain why $5 < 8$, using the definition of whole-number inequality given in terms of sets.

**5.** Let "&" denote the binary operation on the set $W$ of whole numbers defined by

$$a \,\&\, b = a + b + ab.$$

    **(a)** Is $W$ closed under &?

    **(b)** Is & commutative?

    **(c)** Is & associative?

    **(d)** Is there an identity element for & in $W$?

**6.** Discuss which conceptual model of subtraction you feel best corresponds to each of the following problems:

    **(a)** On Monday, Roberto hiked 11 miles to the lake. On Friday at noon, he had hiked 6 miles back down the trail. How much farther does Roberto have to hike to get back to the trailhead?

    **(b)** Kerri has 56 customers on her paper route, but her manager left her only 48 papers. How many extra papers should she have brought over before starting her delivery?

**(c)** All but 7 of the 3 dozen picnic plates were used. How many people came to the picnic?

**7.** What property of whole numbers justifies the following equalities?

**(a)** $4 + (6 + 2) = (4 + 6) + 2$

**(b)** $8 \cdot (4 + x) = 8 \cdot 4 + 8x$

**(c)** $3 + 0 = 0 + 3 = 3$

**(d)** $2 \cdot (8 \cdot 5) = (2 \cdot 8) \cdot 5$

**8.** Shade regions in Venn diagrams that correspond to the following sets:

**(a)** $A \cap (B \cup C)$

**(b)** $A \cup B$

**(c)** $(A \cap \overline{B}) \cup (B \cap \overline{A})$

**9.** Show how to illustrate the following properties of whole-number multiplication with the rectangular array model:

**(a)** $2 \cdot (4 + 3) = 2 \cdot 4 + 2 \cdot 3$

**(b)** $2 \cdot 5 = 5 \cdot 2$

**10.** Let $n(A \times B) = 21$. What are all of the possible values of $n(A)$?

**11.** Let $A = \{w, h, o, l, e\}$, $B = \{n, u, m, b, e, r\}$, and $C = \{z, e, r, o\}$. Find

**(a)** $n(A \cup B)$

**(b)** $n(B \cap \overline{C})$

**(c)** $n(A \cap C)$

**(d)** $n(A \times C)$

**12.** Let $A$ and $B$ be two sets in the universe $U = \{a, b, c, \ldots, z\}$. If $n(A) = 12$, $n(B) = 14$, and $n(A \cup B) = 21$, find $n(A \cap B)$ and $n(\overline{A \cap B})$.

**13.** Suppose $A \cap B = A$. What can you say about $A \cap \overline{B}$?

**14.** Althea made 5 gallons of root beer and wishes to bottle it in 10-ounce bottles.

**(a)** How many bottles does she need? Remember that a quart contains 32 ounces.

**(b)** Discuss which model of division—grouping or sharing—corresponds best to your answer for part **(a)**.

# Numeration and Computation

**3.1** Numeration Systems Past and Present

**3.2** Nondecimal Positional Systems

**3.3** Algorithms for Addition and Subtraction of Whole Numbers

**3.4** Algorithms for Multiplication and Division of Whole Numbers

**3.5** Mental Arithmetic and Estimation

## Hands On

## Numbers from Rectangles

### Material Needed

1. One rectangle of each of these shapes for each student:

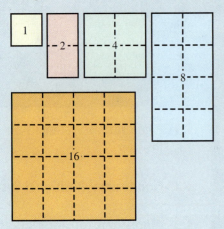

2. One record sheet like this for each student:

| | 16 | 8 | 4 | 2 | 1 |
|---|---|---|---|---|---|
| 0 | 0 | 0 | 0 | 0 | 0 |
| 1 | 0 | 0 | 0 | 0 | 1 |
| 18 | 1 | 0 | 0 | 1 | 0 |
| 19 | 1 | 0 | 0 | 1 | 1 |

| | 16 | 8 | 4 | 2 | 1 |
|---|---|---|---|---|---|
| 20 | 1 | 0 | 1 | 0 | 0 |
| 21 | | | | | |
| 38 | | | | | |
| 39 | | | | | |

### Directions

**Step 1.** Use the rectangles to determine whether or not there are representations of each of the numbers 0, 1, 2, . . . , 39 as a sum of the numbers 1, 2, 4, 8, or 16, with each of the latter group of numbers used at most once.

**Step 2.** For each representation determined in Step 1, record the numbers (rectangles) used by placing a 0 or a 1 in the appropriate columns of the record sheet. The rows for 0, 1, 18, 19, and 20 have been done for you.

(a) Do all the numbers from 0 through 39 have such a representation?

(b) What additional numbers could be represented if you had a 32 rectangle?

(c) Describe any interesting patterns you see on your record sheet.

---

**CHAPTER PREVIEW**

In Chapter 3, we will consider how numbers have been represented historically—especially in the modern **decimal (base-ten)** system. The symbols for writing numbers are called **numerals,** and the methods for calculating are called **algorithms.** Taken together, any particular system of numerals and algorithms is called a **numeration system.** We will give algorithms for addition, subtraction, multiplication, and division of whole numbers and will show some physical representations of these systems. Such representations depend crucially on the notion of **exchange** (what you may have called "borrowing" or "carrying" when you were in school) in the representation of a whole number. Because of the need for procedural fluency, the chapter finishes with methods of estimating answers and a discussion of some practices associated with mental arithmetic.

**KEY IDEAS**

- Numeration systems in the past and present, in both base ten and other bases, including the Egyptian, Roman, Babylonian, Mayan, and Indo-Arabic (**decimal**) systems
- Representation of numeration systems by physical objects such as units, strips, and mats or sticks in bundles
- The use of **exchanging** to simplify the tasks of addition, subtraction, multiplication, and division of whole numbers
- Methods (**algorithms**) for addition, subtraction, multiplication, and division of whole numbers
- Ways in which to make careful **estimations** of a final answer as a check
- Ways in which we might do mental arithmetic faster.

# 3.1

# Numeration Systems Past and Present

To appreciate the power of the Indo-Arabic (or Hindu-Arabic) numeration system, or decimal system, as we now call it, it is important to know something about numeration systems of the past. Just as the idea of number historically arose from the need to determine "how many," the demands of commerce in an increasingly sophisticated society stimulated the development of convenient symbolism for writing numbers and methods for calculating.

The earliest means of recording numbers consisted of creating a set of tallies—marks on stone, stones in a bag, notches in a stick—one for one, for each item being counted. Indeed, the original meaning of the word *tally* was "a stick with notches cut into it to record debts owed or paid." Often such a stick was split in half, with one half going to the debtor and the other half to the creditor. It is still common practice today to keep count by making tallies, or marks, with the minor, but useful, refinement of marking off the tallies in groups of five. Thus,

is much easier to read as 23 than is

But such systems for recording numbers were much too simplistic for large numbers and for calculating.

Of the various systems used in the past, we consider only four here: the Egyptian, the Roman, the Babylonian, and the Mayan systems.

## The Egyptian System

As early as 3400 B.C., the Egyptians developed a system for recording numbers on stone tablets using **hieroglyphics** (Table 3.1). This system was based on the number 10, as is our modern system, and probably for the same reason. That is, we humans come with a built-in "digital" calculator, as it were, with 10 convenient "keys" (fingers).

| TABLE 3.1 | EGYPTIAN SYMBOLS FOR POWERS OF 10 | | | | | | |
|---|---|---|---|---|---|---|---|
| **Power of 10** | $10^0 = 1$ | $10^1 = 10$ | $10^2 = 100$ | $10^3 = 1000$ | $10^4 = 10{,}000$ | $10^5 = 100{,}000$ | $10^6 = 1{,}000{,}000$ |
| **Egyptian Symbol Description** | a staff | a yoke | a scroll | a lotus flower | a pointing finger | a fish | an amazed person |

The Egyptians had symbols for the first few powers of 10 and then combined symbols additively to represent other numbers. (See Table 3.1.) The system was cumbersome, not only because it required numerous symbols to represent even relatively small numbers, but also because computation was awkward. Thus, 336 would be written as

and 125 was written as

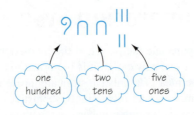

Then 336 + 125 was found by combining all the symbols to obtain

and then replacing 10 of the symbols for 1 by one symbol for 10 to finally obtain

representing 461. You can easily imagine how cumbersome multiplication (as repeated addition) and division (as repeated subtraction) was in this system.

## The Roman System

The **Roman system of numeration** is already somewhat familiar from its current usage on the faces of analog watches and clocks, on cornerstones, and on the façades of buildings to record when they were built. Originally, like the Egyptian system, the Roman system was completely additive, with the familiar symbols shown in Table 3.2.

| TABLE 3.2 | ROMAN NUMERALS AND THEIR MODERN EQUIVALENTS | | | | | | |
|---|---|---|---|---|---|---|---|
| **Roman Symbol** | I | V | X | L | C | D | M |
| **Modern Equivalent** | 1 | 5 | 10 | 50 | 100 | 500 | 1000 |

With these symbols, 1959 originally was written as

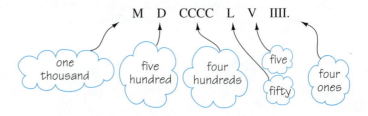

Later, a subtractive principle was introduced to shorten the notation: If a single symbol for a lesser number was written to the left of a symbol for a greater number, then the lesser number was to be *subtracted* from the greater number. The common representations of this principle were as shown here:

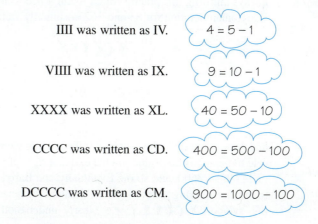

IIII was written as IV.    $4 = 5 - 1$

VIIII was written as IX.    $9 = 10 - 1$

XXXX was written as XL.    $40 = 50 - 10$

CCCC was written as CD.    $400 = 500 - 100$

DCCCC was written as CM.    $900 = 1000 - 100$

With this subtractive principle, 1959 could be written more succinctly as

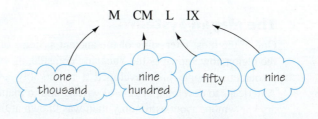

M  CM  L  IX

one thousand    nine hundred    fifty    nine

As with the Egyptian system, arithmetic* calculations using Roman numerals were quite cumbersome. For this reason, much of the commercial calculation of the time was performed on devices such as abacuses, counting boards, sand trays, and the like.

## The Babylonian System

Developed about the same time as the Egyptian system, and much earlier than the Roman system, the **Babylonian system** was more sophisticated than either in that it introduced the notion of **place value,** in which the position of a symbol in a numeral determined the value of the numeral. In particular, this made it possible to write numerals for even very large numbers by using very few symbols. Indeed, the system utilized only two symbols, ▼ for 1 and ❮ for 10, and combined these additively to form the "digits" 1 through 59. Thus,

$$❮❮▼ \quad \text{and} \quad ❮❮❮▼▼▼▼$$

represented 21 and 34, respectively. Beyond 59, the system was positional to base 60 (a sexagesimal system), where the positions from right to left represented multiples of successive powers of 60 and the multipliers (digits) were the composite symbols for 1 through 59. Thus,

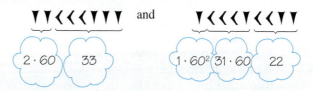

▼▼❮❮❮▼▼▼  and  ▼❮❮❮❮▼❮❮❮▼▼

$2 \cdot 60$   33      $1 \cdot 60^2$  $31 \cdot 60$  22

represented $2 \cdot 60^1 + 33 = 153$ and $1 \cdot 60^2 + 31 \cdot 60^1 + 22 = 5482$, respectively.

---

*When used as a noun, "arithmetic" is pronounced ə-rith′mə-tik. When used as an adjective, it is pronounced ar′ith-met′ik.

A difficulty with the Babylonian system was the lack of a symbol for zero. In writing numerals, scribes simply left a space if a certain position value was not to be used, and, since spacing was not always uniform, this practice often made it necessary to infer values from context. For example, the Babylonian notation for 83 and 3623 originally were, respectively,

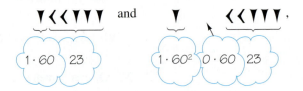

and these could easily be confused if the spacing were not clear. Indeed, there was no way even to indicate missing position values on the extreme right of a numeral, so ▼ could represent 1 or $1 \cdot 60^1 = 60$ or $1 \cdot 60^2 = 3600$, and so on. Eventually, the Babylonians employed the symbol ♠ as a placeholder to indicate missing position values, though they never developed the notion of zero as a number. With this symbol, ▼❬❬▼▼▼ was clearly understood as $1 \cdot 60 + 23 = 83$ and ▼♠❬❬▼▼▼ was unmistakably

$$1 \cdot 60^2 + 23 = 3623.$$

## The Mayan System

One of the most interesting of the ancient systems of numeration was developed by the Mayans in the region now known as the Yucatán Peninsula, in southeastern Mexico. As early as A.D. 200, these resourceful people had developed a remarkably advanced society. They were the first Native Americans to develop a system of writing and to manufacture paper and books. Their learned scholars knew more about astronomy than was known at that time anywhere else in the world. Their calendar was very accurate, with a 365-day year and a leap year every fourth year. In short, many scholars believe that the Mayans developed the most sophisticated society ever attained by early residents of the Western Hemisphere.

Like their other achievements, the **Mayan system of numeration** was unusually advanced. Actually, there were *two* systems. Both systems were positional systems like the Babylonian system and our present base-ten, or decimal, system, and both contained a symbol for zero. One system was a base-twenty, or vigesimal, system based on powers of 20 and utilizing rather involved hieroglyphics for the numerals 1 through 19. Since the vigesimal system has not survived in written form, we describe the second system, which was a modification of the first, devised to facilitate computations related to the calendar. It has the advantage that $18 \cdot 20 = 360$ is much closer to the length of a year than is $20 \cdot 20 = 400$.* Thus, the positions were for 1, 20, $18 \cdot 20$, $18 \cdot 20^2$, $18 \cdot 20^3$, and so on, rather than $20^2, 20^3, 20^4, \ldots$ as with the first system. Also, the second system used a simple set of symbols for the numerals 0 through 19, as shown in Table 3.3.

---

*The Mayan calendar was composed of 18 months of 20 days each, with 5 additional days not associated with any month and with the provision for a leap year.

**TABLE 3.3    MAYAN NUMERALS FOR 0 THROUGH 19**

| Mayan Symbol | Modern Equivalent | Mayan Symbol | Modern Equivalent |
|---|---|---|---|
| | 0 | | 10 |
| | 1 | | 11 |
| | 2 | | 12 |
| | 3 | | 13 |
| | 4 | | 14 |
| | 5 | | 15 |
| | 6 | | 16 |
| | 7 | | 17 |
| | 8 | | 18 |
| | 9 | | 19 |

The Mayans wrote their numerals in a vertical style with the unit's position on the bottom. For example, the number 43,487 would appear as

$$6 \cdot 18 \cdot 20^2 = 43,200$$
$$0 \cdot 18 \cdot 20 = 0$$
$$14 \cdot 20 = 280$$
$$7 \cdot 1 = \underline{\phantom{00}7}$$
$$43,487$$

All that is needed to convert a Mayan numeral to modern notation is a knowledge of the digits and the value of the position each digit occupies, as shown in Table 3.4.

**TABLE 3.4    POSITION VALUES IN THE MAYAN SYSTEM**

| Position Level | Position Value |
|---|---|
| · | · |
| · | · |
| · | · |
| fifth | $18 \cdot 20^3 = 144,000$ |
| fourth | $18 \cdot 20^2 = 7,200$ |
| third | $18 \cdot 20 = 360$ |
| second | 20 |
| first | 1 |

## EXAMPLE 3.1    Using Mayan Notation to Write a Number

Write 27,408 in Mayan notation.

**Solution**    We will not need the fifth, or any higher, position, since $18 \cdot 20^3 = 144{,}000$ is already greater than 27,408. How many 7200s, 360s, 20s, and 1s are needed? This question can be answered by repeated subtraction, or, more simply, by division. From the arithmetic

$$
\begin{array}{r} 3 \\ 7200\overline{)27{,}408} \\ 21{,}600 \\ \hline 5\ 808 \end{array}
\qquad
\begin{array}{r} 16 \\ 360\overline{)5808} \\ 360 \\ \hline 2208 \\ 2160 \\ \hline 48 \end{array}
\qquad
\begin{array}{r} 2 \\ 20\overline{)48} \\ 40 \\ \hline 8 \end{array}
\qquad
\begin{array}{r} 8 \\ 1\overline{)8} \\ 8 \\ \hline 0 \end{array}
$$

it follows that we need three 7200s, sixteen 360s, two 20s, and eight 1s. Thus, in Mayan notation, 27,408 appears as

$$3 \cdot 7200 = 21{,}600$$
$$16 \cdot 360 = 5760$$
$$2 \cdot 20 = 40$$
$$8 \cdot 1 = \underline{\quad 8}$$
$$27{,}408$$

The ingenuity of this system, particularly since it involves the 18s, is easy to overlook. It turns out that such a positional system *will not work* unless the value of each position is a number that evenly divides the value of the next-higher position. This fact is not at all obvious!

### The Indo-Arabic System

Today, the most universally used system of numeration is the **Indo-Arabic,** or **decimal, system.** The system was named jointly for the East Indian scholars who invented it at least as early as 800 B.C. and for the Arabs who transmitted it to the Western world. Like the Mayan system, it is a positional system. Since its *base* is 10, it requires special symbols for the numbers 0 through 9. Over the years, various notational choices have been made, as shown in Table 3.5.

**TABLE 3.5    SYMBOLS FOR ZERO THROUGH NINE, ANCIENT AND MODERN**

The common symbols 0, 1, 2, 3, 4, 5, 6, 7, 8, and 9 are called **digits,** as are our fingers and toes, and it is easy to imagine the historical significance of this terminology. With these 10 symbols and the idea of positional notation, all that is needed to write the numeral for any whole number is the value of each digit and the value of the position the digit occupies in the numeral. In the decimal system, the positional values, as shown in Table 3.6, are well known.

| TABLE 3.6 | POSITIONAL VALUES IN BASE TEN | | | | | |
|---|---|---|---|---|---|---|
| Position Names ... | Hundred Thousands | Ten Thousands | Thousands | Hundreds | Tens | Units |
| Decimal Form ... | 100,000 | 10,000 | 1000 | 100 | 10 | 1 |
| Powers of 10 ... | $10^5$ | $10^4$ | $10^3$ | $10^2$ | $10^1$ | $10^0$ |

As our number words suggest, the symbol 2572 means 2 thousands plus 5 hundreds plus 7 tens plus 2 ones. In so-called **expanded notation,** we write

*2000 + 500 + 70 + 2*

$$2572 = 2\cdot 1000 + 5\cdot 100 + 7\cdot 10 + 2\cdot 1$$
$$= 2\cdot 10^3 + 5\cdot 10^2 + 7\cdot 10^1 + 2\cdot 10^0.$$

The amount each digit contributes to the number is the value of the digit times the value of the position the digit occupies in the representation.

## Physical Models for Positional Systems

**The Classroom Abacus**   The Indo-Arabic scheme for representing numbers derived historically from the use of counting boards and abacuses of various types to facilitate computations in commercial transactions. Such devices are still useful today in helping children to understand the basic concepts. One device, commercially available for classroom use, is shown in Figure 3.1.

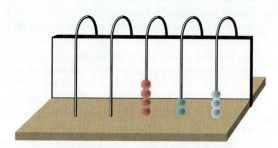

**FIGURE 3.1**

A classroom demonstration abacus

The device consists of a series of wire loops fixed into a wooden base and with a vertical shield affixed to the center of the base under the wire loops so that the back is hidden from the students. On each wire loop are beads that can be moved from behind the shield to the front and vice versa.

To demonstrate counting and positional notation, one begins by moving beads from behind the shield to the front on the wire to the students' right (the instructor's left), counting 1, 2, 3, and so on as the beads are moved to the front of the shield. Once 10 beads on the first wire are counted, all 10 are moved back behind the shield, and the fact that 10 beads on this wire have all been counted once is recorded by moving a single bead to the front of the shield on the second wire. The count 11, 12, 13, and so on then continues with a single bead on the first wire again moved forward with each count. When the count reaches 20, 10 beads on the first wire will have been counted a second time, and this is recorded by moving a second bead forward on the second wire and moving the beads on the first wire to the back again. Then the count continues. When the count reaches, for example, 34, the children will see the arrangement of beads illustrated schematically in Figure 3.2, with three beads showing on the second wire and four beads showing on the first wire. A natural way to record the result is to write 34—that is, 3 tens and 4 ones. Note that we never leave ten beads up on any wire.

**FIGURE 3.2**
Thirty-four on the classroom abacus

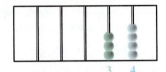

What happens if we count to 100—that is, if we count 10 beads on the first wire 10 times? Since we move one bead on the second wire forward each time we count 10 beads on the first wire, we will have 10 beads showing on the second wire. But we record this on the abacus by moving one bead forward on the third wire and moving all beads on the second wire back behind the shield. Thus, each bead showing on the first wire counts for 1, each bead showing on the second wire counts for 10, each bead showing on the third wire counts for 100, and so on. If we count, for example, to 423, the arrangement of beads is as illustrated earlier in Figure 3.1, and the count is naturally recorded as 423.

Approached in this way, the notion of place value becomes much more concrete. One can actually experience the fact that each bead on the second wire counts for 10, each bead on the third wire counts for 100, and so on—particularly if one is allowed to handle the device and move the beads while counting. One can also see that the counting process on the abacus can proceed as far as desired, though more and more wire loops would have to be added to the device. It follows that any whole number can be represented in one, and only one, way in our modern system by using only the digits 0, 1, 2, 3, 4, 5, 6, 7, 8, and 9.

Other physical devices can also be used to illustrate positional notation, and many are even more concrete than the historical abacus just mimicked.

## Into the Classroom

### Mary Cavanaugh Discusses the Use of Manipulatives

Teaching for meaning in mathematics is a major focus of math educators. The work of Piaget and others suggests that students begin their exploration of mathematical concepts through hands-on experiences with manipulatives. Manipulatives appeal to several senses and are used to physically involve students in a learning situation. Students manipulate the objects with actions such as forming, ordering, comparing, tracing, joining, or separating groups. By these actions they gain an understanding of the meanings of number and various operations in mathematics.

Research points to multidigit numeration as the pivotal concept that students must learn with the help of manipulatives before they can succeed in learning computational algorithms. A comfortable progression through representing numbers, trading, and computing with manipulatives is developmentally appropriate for providing a solid foundation for understanding arithmetic concepts. Premature introduction of paper-and-pencil procedures pushes students into memorizing a complex sequence of mathematical acts before the acts have meaning.

Manipulating objects allows students to develop internal images of number and the relative magnitude of number that can be recalled when needed. Pictures of concrete materials that follow manipulative experiences form a connection between the internal images, the pictures, and abstract symbols. The guidance of teachers is needed to help bridge the gap between what is learned from manipulatives and what is written using mathematical symbols.

A research recommendation, easily realized with manipulatives, is that teachers can and should expect students to enjoy the learning of mathematics. Concrete materials appeal to a variety of senses and motivate students. The frequent use of manipulatives in the classroom helps make the expectation of enjoyment evident.

SOURCE: *From Scott Foresman* Exploring Mathematics, Grades 1-7, *by L. Carey Bolster, et al. Copyright ©1994 Pearson Education, Inc. Reprinted with permission.*

**Sticks in Bundles** One simple idea for introducing positional notation is to use bundles of small sticks, which can be purchased inexpensively at almost any craft store. Single sticks are 1s. Ten sticks can be bound together in a bundle to represent 10. Ten bundles can be banded together to represent 100, and so on. Thus, 34 would be represented as shown in Figure 3.3.

### Unifix™ Cubes

Here, single cubes represent 1s. Ten cubes snapped together to form a stick represent 10. Ten sticks bound together represent 100, and so on. Again, 34 would be represented as shown in Figure 3.4.

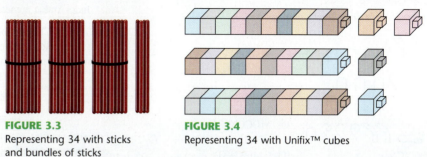

**FIGURE 3.3**
Representing 34 with sticks and bundles of sticks

**FIGURE 3.4**
Representing 34 with Unifix™ cubes

### Units, Strips, and Mats

Pieces for this concrete realization of the decimal system are easily cut from graph paper with reasonably large squares. A unit is a single square, a strip is a block of 10 squares, and a mat is a square 10 units on a side, as illustrated in Figure 3.5. To make the units, strips, and mats more substantial and hence easier to manipulate, the graph paper can be pasted to a substantial tagboard or copied on reasonably heavy stock. Using units, strips, and mats, we would represent 254 as shown in Figure 3.6.

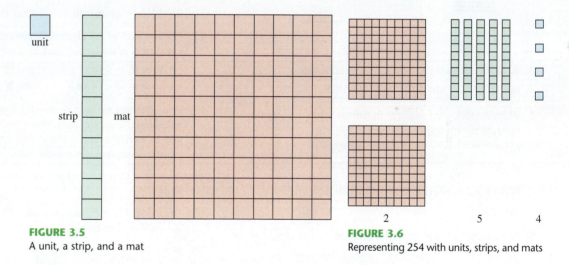

**FIGURE 3.5**
A unit, a strip, and a mat

**FIGURE 3.6**
Representing 254 with units, strips, and mats

### Base-10 Blocks

These commercially prepared materials include single cubes that represent 1s, sticks called "longs" made up of 10 cubes that represent 10, "flats" made up of 10 longs that represent 100, and "blocks" made up of 10 flats that represent 1000, as shown in Figure 3.7.

**FIGURE 3.7**
Base-10 blocks for 1, 10, 100, and 1000

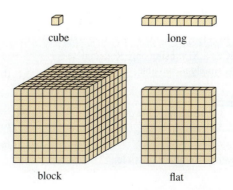

## Problem Set 3.1

Exercises numbered in red are answered in the back of the text.

### Understanding Concepts

**1.** Write the Indo-Arabic equivalent of each of the following:

**(a)**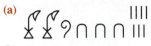

**(b)** ΘΘΘ∩∩∩ ΘΘ ∩∩∩ |||

**(c)**

**(d)** MDCCXXIX

**(e)** DCXCVII

**(f)** CMLXXXIV

**(g)** ▼▲

**(h)** ▼▲▲

**(i)** ▼▼▲<<<<▼▼

**(j)** ▼▼<<<▼▼

**(k)**

**(l)**

**2.** Write the following numbers in Egyptian notation:

**(a)** 11    **(b)** 597    **(c)** 1949

**3.** Write the following numbers in Roman notation, using the subtraction principle as appropriate:

**(a)** 9    **(b)** 974

**(c)** 1996    **(d)** 2009

**4.** Write these numbers in Babylonian notation:

**(a)** 251    **(b)** 3022    **(c)** 18,741

**5.** Write these numbers in Mayan notation:

**(a)** 12    **(b)** 584    **(c)** 12,473

**6.** Add ΘΘΘ ∩∩∩∩ ∩∩∩∩ ||| and ΘΘ ∩∩∩∩ ∩∩∩∩ |||,

using only Egyptian notation. Write your answer as simply as possible.

**7.** Add MDCCCXVI and MCCCLXIV, using only Roman notation. Write your answer as simply as possible.

**8.** Add ⎯•⎯ and ⎯•⎯ , using only Mayan

notation. Write your answer as simply as possible.

**9. (a)** Write 2002, 2003, and 2004 in Roman numerals.

  **(b)** To date, what year has had the Roman numeral with the most symbols? Give your answer in both Roman and Indo-Arabic numerals.

**10.** The ancient Chinese rod system of numeration was a base-ten positional system like our modern system, but with two possible arrangements for the digits 1 through 9:

1  2  3  4  5  6  7  8  9
| || ||| |||| ||||| T TT TTT TTTT
一 二 三 亖 亖 ⊥ ⊥ ⊥ ⊥

For easy reading, the vertical arrangement was used in the columns corresponding to the even powers of 10 and the horizontal arrangement for the columns corresponding to the odd powers of 10. A blank space was used for the digit 0. Thus, 12,462 would appear as | 二 |||| ⊥ ||. Write the modern equivalent of the following numbers:

**(a)** 三 T 亖 ||||

**(b)** 二 T 亖 |||

**(c)** ⊥  三 TT

**(d)** ||| ⊥  亖 T

**11.** Write each of the following numbers, using the Chinese rod system of notation:

**(a)** 2763    **(b)** 38,407    **(c)** 804    **(d)** 7561

**12.** Perform each of the given computations, using the Chinese rod system of notation. Check by using modern notation.

**(a)** ||| ⊥ |||| + || 亖 |

**(b)** 三 TT 亖 T + |||| ⊥ ||

**(c)** ⊥ || 二 |||| − T 二 ||

**(d)** TT 亖 |||| − || 亖 |||

**13.** Draw a sketch to illustrate how the number 452 is represented with units, strips, and mats. (See Figures 3.5 and 3.6.) Use dots to represent units, vertical line segments to represent strips, and squares to represent mats.

**14.** Draw a sketch to illustrate the number 234, using base-ten blocks.

**15.** Draw a sketch of the exposed side of a classroom abacus to illustrate the number 2475.

**16.** Write 24,872 and 3071 in expanded notation.

**17.** Suppose you have 3 mats, 24 strips, and 13 units, for a total count of 553. Briefly describe the exchanges you would make to keep the same total count but have the smallest possible number of manipulative pieces.

**18.** Suppose you have 2 mats, 7 strips, and 6 units in one hand and 4 mats, 5 strips, and 9 units in the other.

  **(a)** Put all these pieces together and describe the exchanges required to keep the same total count but with the smallest possible number of manipulative pieces.

  **(b)** Explain briefly, but clearly, what kind of mathematics the manipulation in part (a) represents.

**19.** Suppose you have 3 mats and 6 units on your desk and want to remove a count represented by 3 strips and 8 units.

  **(a)** Describe briefly, but clearly, the exchange that must take place to accomplish the desired task.

**(b)** After removing the 3 strips and 8 units, what manipulative pieces are left on your desk?

**(c)** What kind of mathematics does the manipulation in part (a) represent?

## Teaching Concepts

**20.** Recall that units, strips, and mats are typically made from graph paper (see Figure 3.5). How would you augment this simple set of manipulatives to make one representing the number 1000 for a lesson you might teach to a class of third graders?

**21.** Triana has 12 dollars and 33 dimes in her piggy bank, while Leona has 9 dollars and 11 dimes.

**(a)** If the girls pool their money, how many dollars and dimes will they have? Note that this question can be answered without adding; one can simply count on, instead.

**(b)** If the girls buy their mother a bottle of perfume for $25, how much money will they have left over?

**(c)** Describe any exchanges you made in determining the answer to part (b).

**22.** Jon works at odd jobs for Mr. Taylor. On four successive Saturdays, he worked 6 hours and 35 minutes, 4 hours and 15 minutes, 7 hours and 30 minutes, and 5 hours and 20 minutes, respectively. All told, how many 8-hour days, how many hours, and how many minutes was this amount of time equivalent to? (Make sure that the number of hours in your answer is less than 8 and that the number of minutes is less than 60.)

**23.** Make up a problem along the lines of problem 22 but using hours, days, and weeks.

**24.** **(a)** How does a problem like problem 21 help students to understand positional notation?

**(b)** Would understanding the notion of exchanging help students who are studying calculation with fractions to deal with a problem like this?

$$2\frac{3}{7}$$
$$+ 2\frac{5}{7}$$

Explain.

## Responding to Students

**25.** How does a problem like problem 22 help students to understand positional notation? Explain.

**26.** Tom and Marsha are playing a game with 10-sided dice. The object of the game is to make the largest 5-digit number possible when 5 dice are rolled. The numbers rolled are 8, 0, 9, 0, and 2. Tom is losing most rounds. What can you do to help him win?

## From State Student Assessments

**27.** (Illinois, Grade 3)
Find the missing number that makes the sentence true.
500 + ____ + 9 = 569
○ 50          ○ 69
○ 60          ○ 90

**28.** (Connecticut, Grade 4)
What number is shown by the blocks in this picture?

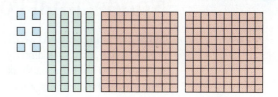

642          264
426          246

**29.** (Connecticut, Grade 4)
Which means the same as 385?
300 + 80 + 5
30 + 800 + 5
300 + 80 + 50
3 + 8 + 5

**30.** (Connecticut, Grade 4)
Which means the same as 2 tens and 18 ones?
28
38
318
2018

**31.** (Texas, Grade 5)
The table below shows the area, in square kilometers, of four lakes.

Area of Four Lakes

| Lake | Area (km²) |
|------|-----------|
| H | 59,600 |
| M | 57,800 |
| S | 82,100 |
| O | 18,960 |
| E | ? |

Lake E has a greater area than Lake O but a smaller area than Lake M. Which could be the area of Lake E?

**A.** 76,760 km²

**B.** 57,800 km²

**C.** 25,700 km²

**D.** 18,960 km²

**32.** (Texas, Grade 4)
In 2004 there were four million, three hundred thirty-one thousand, seven hundred fifty-one students in Texas public schools. How is this number written in standard form?

**A.** 400,331,751

**B.** 4,331,751

**C.** 4,000,331,751

**D.** 4,300,751

## 3.2

# Nondecimal Positional Systems

In the preceding section, we discussed several numeration systems, including the decimal system in common use today. As already mentioned, the decimal system is a positional system based on the number 10. This is probably so because we have ten fingers and, historically, as now, people often counted on their fingers. One very useful application of bases other than base ten is as a way to deepen our understanding of number systems, arithmetic in general, and our own decimal system. Although bases other than base ten were in the K–5 curriculum in the past, they are not present currently. However, nondecimal positional systems are studied in the "math methods" course that is a part of an elementary education degree and may return to elementary school in the future. Other bases are used in the world. For example, computers and calculators depend on base 2 in order to operate. We will discuss addition and subtraction in base five in the next section and multiplication in base six in the one following that.

### Base-Five Notation

For our purposes, perhaps the quickest route to understanding **base-five notation** is to consider again the abacus of Figure 3.1. This time, however, we allow only 5 beads to be moved forward on each wire. As before, we start with the wire to the students' right (our left) and move 1 bead forward each time as we count 1, 2, 3, and so on. When we reach 5, we have counted the first wire once, and we record this on the abacus by moving 1 bead forward on the second wire while moving all 5 beads on the first wire to the back. We continue to count, and when the count reaches 10, we will have counted all the beads on the first wire a second time. We move a second bead forward on the second wire and again move all the beads on the first wire to the back. Thus, each bead on the second wire counts for 5; that is, the second wire is the "fives" wire. When the count reaches 19, the abacus will appear as in Figure 3.8, and

$$19 = 3 \cdot 5 + 4.$$

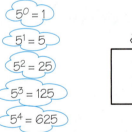
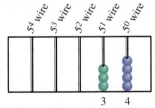

If we continue the count to 25, all the beads on the first wire will have been counted five times. This means that we have moved all 5 beads to the front on the *second* wire. We record that fact on the abacus by returning these beads to the back of the abacus and moving 1 bead forward on the *third* wire. Thus, the third wire becomes the $25 = 5^2$ wire. The count can be continued in this way, and it is apparent that any whole number will eventually be counted and can be recorded on the abacus with only 0, 1, 2, 3, or 4 beads per wire showing at the front; that is, we need only the digits 0, 1, 2, 3, and 4 in base five. For example, if we continue the counting process up to 113, the abacus will have 3 beads on the units wire, 2 on the fives wire, and 4 on the twenty-fives wire—that is,

$$113 = 4 \cdot 5^2 + 2 \cdot 5 + 3.$$

Just as we shorten $4 \cdot 10^2 + 2 \cdot 10 + 3$ to 423, someone working in base five also shortens $4 \cdot 5^2 + 2 \cdot 5 + 3$ to 423. Thus, the three-digit sequence 423 can represent many different numbers, depending on which base is chosen. To the average person, who doesn't even think about it, it means "four hundred twenty-three." To our base-five friend, it could mean *flug globs zeit-tab*—that is, $4 \cdot 5^2 + 2 \cdot 5 + 3$. Note that our base-five friend certainly would *not* say "one hundred thirteen," since that is decimal, or base-ten, language. To avoid confusion in talking about base-five numeration, we agree that we will *not* say "four hundred twenty-three" when we read 423 as a base-five numeral. Instead, we will say "four two three, base five" and will write $423_{\text{five}}$, where the subscript "five" indicates the base.

In base six, we understand that

$$423_{\text{six}} = 4 \cdot 6^2 + 2 \cdot 6 + 3,$$

and we read the numeral as "four two three, base six." Doing that arithmetic makes it clear that $423_{\text{six}} = 159_{\text{ten}}$. As an additional example, $423_{\text{twelve}}$ should be read "four two three, base twelve," and in expanded form we have

$$423_{\text{twelve}} = 4 \cdot 12^2 + 2 \cdot 12 + 3 = 603_{\text{ten}}.$$

Unless expressly stated to the contrary, a numeral written *without* a subscript should be read as a base-ten numeral.

Observe that, in base five, we need the digits 0, 1, 2, 3, and 4, and we need to know the values of the positions in base five. In base six, the digits are 0, 1, 2, 3, 4, and 5, and we need to know the positional values in base six. In base twelve, we use the digits 0, 1, 2, 3, 4, 5, 6, 7, 8, 9, T, and E, where T and E are, respectively, the digits for 10 and 11. For these three bases, the positional values are given in Table 3.7.

**TABLE 3.7  DIGITS AND POSITIONAL VALUES IN BASES FIVE, SIX, AND TWELVE**

| | | | **DECIMAL VALUES OF POSITIONS** | | | | |
|---|---|---|---|---|---|---|---|
| **Base b** | **Digits used** | $\cdots$ | $b^4$ | $b^3$ | $b^2$ | $b^1$ | **units ($b^0 = 1$)** |
| **Five** | 0, 1, 2, 3, 4 | $\cdots$ | $5^4 = 625$ | $5^3 = 125$ | $5^2 = 25$ | $5^1 = 5$ | $5^0 = 1$ |
| **Six** | 0, 1, 2, 3, 4, 5 | $\cdots$ | $6^4 = 1296$ | $6^3 = 216$ | $6^2 = 36$ | $6^1 = 6$ | $6^0 = 1$ |
| **Twelve** | 0, 1, 2, 3, 4, 5, 6, 7, 8, 9, T, E | $\cdots$ | $12^4 = 20{,}736$ | $12^3 = 1728$ | $12^2 = 144$ | $12^1 = 12$ | $12^0 = 1$ |

## EXAMPLE 3.2 Converting from Base-Five to Base-Ten Notation

Write the base-ten representation of $3214_{\text{five}}$.

**Solution** We use the place values of Table 3.7 along with the digit values. Thus,

$$
\begin{aligned}
3214_{\text{five}} &= 3 \cdot 5^3 + 2 \cdot 5^2 + 1 \cdot 5^1 + 4 \cdot 5^0 \\
&= 3 \cdot 125 + 2 \cdot 25 + 1 \cdot 5 + 4 \cdot 1 \\
&= 375 + 50 + 5 + 4 \\
&= 434.
\end{aligned}
$$

Therefore, "three two one four, base five" is four hundred thirty-four.

## EXAMPLE 3.3 Converting from Base-Ten to Base-Five Notation

Write the base-five representation of 97.

**Solution** Recall that 97 without a subscript has its usual meaning as a base-ten numeral.

We begin with the notion of grouping. Suppose that we have 97 beans and want to put them into groups of single beans (units), groups of 5 beans (fives), groups of five groups of 5 beans each (twenty-fives), and so on. The problem is to complete the grouping by using the least possible number of groups. This means that we must use as many of the larger groups as possible. Diagrammatically, we have

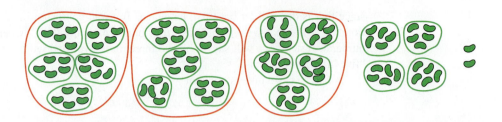

so $97_{\text{ten}} = 342_{\text{five}}$. Arithmetically, this corresponds to determining how many of each position value in base five are required to represent 97. The answer can be determined by successive divisions. Referring to Table 3.7 for position values, we see that 125 is too big. Thus, we begin with 25 and divide successive remainders by successively lower position values:

$$
\begin{array}{lll}
\quad\;3 & \quad\;4 & \quad\;2 \\
25\overline{)97} & 5\overline{)22} & 1\overline{)2} \\
\quad\;75 & \quad\;20 & \quad\;2 \\
\overline{\quad22} & \overline{\quad\;2} & \overline{\quad0}
\end{array}
$$

These divisions reveal that we need three 25s, four 5s, and two 1s, or, in tabular form,

| 25s | 5s | 1s |
|-----|----|----|
| 3   | 4  | 2  |

Thus,

$$97_{\text{ten}} = 342_{\text{five}}.$$

As a check, we note that

$$
\begin{aligned}
342_{\text{five}} &= 3 \cdot 25 + 4 \cdot 5 + 2 \\
&= 75 + 20 + 2 \\
&= 97_{\text{ten}}.
\end{aligned}
$$

## Problem Set 3.2

Exercises numbered in red are answered in the back of the text.

### Understanding Concepts

1. In a long column, write the base-five numerals for the numbers from 0 through 25.

2. Briefly describe the pattern or patterns you observe in the list of numerals in problem 1.

3. Here are the base-six representations of the numbers from 0 through 35, arranged in a rectangular array:

| 0  | 1  | 2  | 3  | 4  | 5  |
|----|----|----|----|----|----|
| 10 | 11 | 12 | 13 | 14 | 15 |
| 20 | 21 | 22 | 23 | 24 | 25 |
| 30 | 31 | 32 | 33 | 34 | 35 |
| 40 | 41 | 42 | 43 | 44 | 45 |
| 50 | 51 | 52 | 53 | 54 | 55 |

Briefly describe any patterns you observe in this array.

4. What would be the entries in the next two rows of the table in problem 3?

5. Write the base-ten representations of each of the following:
   (a) $413_{\text{five}}$  (b) $2004_{\text{five}}$  (c) $10_{\text{five}}$
   (d) $100_{\text{five}}$  (e) $1000_{\text{five}}$  (f) $2134_{\text{five}}$

6. The abacus of Figure 3.8 has "five" playing the role of "ten." Thus, 42 would be represented on the abacus as shown here. Moreover, it would be recorded as 132 and read as "one three two" and *not* as "one hundred thirty-two." What numbers would be represented if the beads on the abacus described are as shown in the following diagrams?

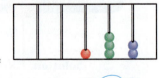

   (a)

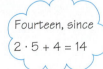

   Fourteen, since $2 \cdot 5 + 4 = 14$

**(b)**

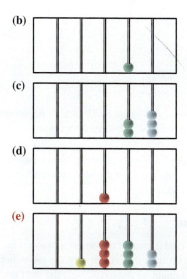

**(c)**

**(d)**

**(e)**

7. The number represented in the diagram of problem 6b would be recorded as 10 ("one zero"). How would the numbers for parts (a), (c), (d), and (e) naturally be recorded?

8. Suppose the abacus of problem 6 is configured as shown here:

   **(a)** What number does this arrangement represent?

   **(b)** How would this number naturally be recorded?

   **(c)** Suppose the number shown in part (a) is increased by 7. Draw a diagram to show how the abacus will then be configured.

9. Write the base-ten representations of each of the following numbers that are in base six:

   **(a)** $413_{six}$    **(b)** $2004_{six}$    **(c)** $10_{six}$

   **(d)** $100_{six}$    **(e)** $1000_{six}$    **(f)** $2134_{six}$

10. Write the base-ten representation of each of the given numbers. Remember that in base twelve the symbols for the digits 10 and 11 are T and E, respectively.

    **(a)** $413_{twelve}$    **(b)** $2004_{twelve}$    **(c)** $10_{twelve}$

    **(d)** $100_{twelve}$    **(e)** $1000_{twelve}$    **(f)** $2TE4_{twelve}$

11. Determine the base-five representation for each of the given numbers. Remember that a numeral with no subscript is understood to be in base ten.

    **(a)** 362    **(b)** 27    **(c)** 5    **(d)** 25

12. Determine the base-six representation for each of the following numbers which are in base ten:

    **(a)** 342    **(b)** 21    **(c)** 6    **(d)** 216

13. Determine the base-twelve representation for each of the following numbers:

    **(a)** 2743    **(b)** 563    **(c)** 144    **(d)** 1584

14. Base two is a very useful base. Since it requires only two digits—0 and 1—it is the system on which all calculators and computers are based.

    **(a)** Make a table of position values for base two up as far as $2^{10} = 1024$.

    **(b)** Write each of these numbers in base-ten notation:

    **(i)** $1101_{two}$    **(ii)** $111_{two}$    **(iii)** $1000_{two}$

    **(iv)** $10101_{two}$

    **(c)** Write each of these numbers in base-two notation:

    **(i)** 24    **(ii)** 18    **(iii)** 2

    **(iv)** 8

    **(d)** Write the numbers from 0 to 31 in base-two notation in a vertical column, and write a short paragraph discussing any pattern you observe.

    **(e)** In three or four sentences, compare part (d) of this problem with the Hands On activity at the beginning of the chapter.

15. **(a)** How can you use the five-bead classroom abacus to convince your students that every whole number can be represented *uniquely* (i.e., in one, and only one, way) in base-five notation?

    **(b)** How would you modify the drawing in Figure 3.8 to illustrate the base-five representation of $3241_{five}$?

## Teaching Concepts

16. Explain how you would respond to one of your students who claims that the base-five representation of $188_{ten}$ is $723_{five}$. Note that $7 \cdot 5^2 + 2 \cdot 5 + 3 = 188_{ten}$.

17. **(a)** In trying to help your students to better understand positional notation, you might ask them what sort of number system people who counted on both their fingers and toes might have invented.

    **(b)** If your students had trouble answering the question in part (a), what might you do to help?

## Thinking Critically

18. Here's an interesting trick. Consider these pictures of cards you might make for use in your class:

| 1 3 5 7 9 11 | 2 3 6 7 10 11 | 4 5 6 7 12 13 |
|---|---|---|
| 13 15 17 19 21 | 14 15 18 19 22 | 14 15 20 21 22 |
| 23 25 27 29 31 | 23 26 27 30 31 | 23 28 29 30 31 |

| 8 9 10 11 12 13 | 16 17 18 19 20 21 |
|---|---|
| 14 15 24 25 26 | 22 23 24 25 26 |
| 27 28 29 30 31 | 27 28 29 30 31 |

    **(a)** Record the first number of each card that has the day of the month on which you were born.

    **(b)** Add the numbers in part (a).

    **(c)** Surprised? Our experience is that elementary school students are, too, and that they immediately want to know how the "trick" works. See if you can discover the secret by carefully comparing the cards with your answer to problem 14, part (d).

19. **(a)** Add $11,111,111_{two}$ and $1_{two}$ in base two.

    **(b)** What are the base-two numerals for $2^n$ and $2^n - 1$? Explain briefly, describing a pattern.

**20.** Recall that the rows of Pascal's triangle (see Section 1.3) are numbered 0, 1, 2, 3, . . . . Thus, row five is 1, 5, 10, 10, 5, 1, which has four odd entries. Also, the base-two representation of 5 is $101_{two}$, with two 1s and $2^2 = 4$. Remarkably, if $f$ is the number of 1s in the base-two representation of $n$, then $2^f$ gives the number of odd entries in the $n$th row of Pascal's triangle. Verify that this is true for the following rows of Pascal's triangle:

(a) row $n = 7$, whose entries are 1, 7, 21, 35, 35, 21, 7, 1

(b) row $n = 8$, whose entries are 1, 8, 28, 56, 70, 56, 28, 8, 1

(c) row $n = 11$, whose entries are 1, 11, 55, 165, 330, 462, 462, 330, 165, 55, 11, 1

**21.** The two one-digit sequences of 0s and 1s are 0 and 1. The four two-digit sequences of 0s and 1s are 00, 10, 01, and 11.

(a) Write down all of the three-digit sequences of 0s and 1s. Can you think of an easy way to do this? Explain.

(b) Write down all of the four-digit sequences of 0s and 1s. Can you think of an easy way to do this? Explain.

(c) How many five-digit sequences of 0s and 1s are there?

(d) How many $n$-digit sequences of 0s and 1s are there? Explain why this is so.

**22.** (a) Think of each three-digit sequence of 0s and 1s in problem 21a as a base-two numeral. What are the base-ten equivalents of these numerals?

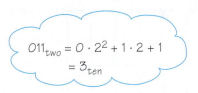

$$011_{two} = 0 \cdot 2^2 + 1 \cdot 2 + 1$$
$$= 3_{ten}$$

(b) Think of each four-digit sequence of 0s and 1s in problem 21b as a base-two numeral. What are the base-ten equivalents of these numerals?

(c) Think of each $n$-digit sequence of 0s and 1s as a base-two numeral. What do you think are the base-ten equivalents of these numerals? Explain.

### Using a Calculator

**23.** (a) Lyudmila discovered a method to convert a numeral in any base to its equivalent in base ten with the use of her calculator. For example, to convert $423_{five}$, she used the entry string

$$4 \,\boxed{\times}\, 5 \,\boxed{+}\, 2 \,\boxed{=}\, \boxed{\times}\, 5 \,\boxed{+}\, 3 \,\boxed{=}$$

to obtain the correct result of 113. Similarly, to convert $4075_{eight}$, she used the string

$$4 \,\boxed{\times}\, 8 \,\boxed{+}\, 0 \,\boxed{=}\, \boxed{\times}\, 8 \,\boxed{+}\, 7 \,\boxed{=}$$
$$\boxed{\times}\, 8 \,\boxed{+}\, 5 \,\boxed{=}$$

to obtain the correct result of 2109. Lyudmila isn't quite sure why her procedure works. Write an imaginary dialogue with her to help her understand why the method is valid.

(b) Would this method succeed on an ordinary four-function calculator?

## Cooperative Investigation
### A Remarkable Base-Three Trick

Practice performing this trick with a partner until you both can do it with ease.

Mathematical magic certainly has a place in the classroom. Students find it interesting, fun, and highly motivational. Consider the following problem: You are given 12 coins that appear identical, but one of the coins is false and is either too heavy or too light—you don't know which. You have a balance scale and are to find the false coin and to determine whether it is heavy or light in just three weighings. This is a difficult problem that is usually solved by considering a whole series of cases. However, if you know base-three arithmetic, you can determine the false coin so quickly right in front of your class that you appear to be a real wizard! Here's how it can be done:

1. Number the coins from 1 through 12.
2. With your back turned, ask your students (partner) to agree on the number of the coin they (he or she) wants to be false and to decide whether the coin is to be heavy or light.
3. Indicate that you are going to make three weighings, and ask the students (your partner) what the movement of the *left-hand* pan on each weighing will be. If the left-hand pan goes up, record a 2. If it balances, record a 1. If it goes down, record a 0. Now use the results of these weighings to form a three-digit base-three numeral. The first weighing determines the *nines* digit, the second weighing determines the *threes* digit, and the third weighing determines the *units* digit. If the base-ten number determined in this way is less than 13, it names the false coin. If the number is more than 13, then 26 minus the number generated names the false coin. You can tell, by knowing which is the false coin, whether it is heavy or light by noting how the left-hand pan moved on a weighing involving the false coin.

I            II            III

Note the addition in base-three notation,

$$\begin{array}{r} 201 \\ +021 \\ \hline 222 \end{array}$$

and $222_{three} = 26_{ten}$

For example, suppose the students (your partner) choose(s) coin 7 as the false coin and decide(s) that it should be heavy. Then, on the three weighings, the left-hand pan goes down, goes up, and balances, and we generate $021_{three} = 7$, the number of the false coin. Moreover, since coin 7 was in the left-hand pan, which went down on the first weighing, coin 7 must be heavy. On the other hand, suppose that coin 7 is light. Then, on the three weighings, the left-hand pan goes up, goes down, and balances, and we generate $201_{three} = 19$. But then $26 - 19 = 7$, so coin 7 is the false coin and must be light, since the left-hand pan went up on the first weighing.

Our experience is that children like the trick very much and are strongly motivated to learn base-three notation in order to pull the trick on their friends and parents. Note that, to do the trick well, students must be able to perform mental calculations quickly—itself a worthy goal.

## 3.3

# Algorithms for Adding and Subtracting Whole Numbers

In this section, we will discuss <u>how</u> we add and subtract integers and <u>why</u> the methods actually work. The customary approaches are called the **addition algorithm** and the **subtraction algorithm.** The problems include other methods such as the **scratch method** for addition. (See problem 24.) During your teaching career, you will find that children have a marvelous sense of invention. When a child comes up with a different way to add or subtract numbers, you, as a teacher, must decide whether the child has found a correct way to do the problem. If the child makes a mistake, you will need to correct that child's approach. The point here is, of course, that teachers must have a conceptual understanding of the material in order to be able to help their students, regardless of whether the child is correct or incorrect. You will practice helping students with their approaches in the "Responding to Students" problems throughout the text.

The first step in the construction of algorithms is to understand **positional notation.** We have seen in Section 3.1 that, for a positional system with, for example, base ten, the two-digit number 35 means 3 tens plus 5. In addition, there are many physical models for positional systems. We will first discuss making exchanges in base ten and then develop the addition and subtraction algorithms in a conceptual manner. **Place value,** or positional notation, is the foundation on which the operations of arithmetic are built. (See the NCTM's view of place value on p. 144.)

## Place-Value Concepts and Calculators

Place-value concepts can be developed and reinforced using calculators. For example, students can observe values displayed on a calculator and focus on which digits are changing. If students add 1 repeatedly on a calculator, they can observe that the units digit changes every time, but the tens digit changes less frequently. Through classroom conversations about such activities and patterns, teachers can help focus students' attention on important place-value ideas.

· · · · ·

Students also develop understanding of place value through the strategies they invent to compute. . . . Thus, it is not necessary to wait for students to fully develop place-value understandings before giving them opportunities to solve problems with two- and three-digit numbers. When such problems arise in interesting contexts, students can often invent ways to solve them that incorporate and deepen their understanding of place value, especially when students have opportunities to discuss and explain their invented strategies and approaches.

· · · · ·

As students encounter problem situations in which computations are more cumbersome or tedious, they should be encouraged to use calculators to aid in problem solving. In this way, even students who are slow to gain fluency with computation skills will not be deprived of worthwhile opportunities to solve complex mathematics problems and to develop and deepen their understanding of other aspects of number.

SOURCE: *Principles and Standards for School Mathematics by NCTM, pp. 81, 82, 86, 87. Copyright © 2000 by the National Council of Teachers of Mathematics. Reproduced with permission of the National Council of Teachers of Mathematics via Copyright Clearance Center. NCTM does not endorse the content or validity of these alignments.*

## The Addition Algorithm

Consider the following addition:

$$
\begin{array}{r}
\overset{1}{\phantom{+}28} \\
+45 \\
\hline
73
\end{array}
$$

This process depends entirely on our positional system of notation. But why does it work that way? Why "carry the 1"? Why add by columns? To many people, these procedures remain a great mystery—you add this way because you were told to—and it's simply done by rote with no understanding.

As noted earlier, children learn abstract notions by first experiencing them concretely with devices they can actually see, touch, and manipulate. Thus, one should introduce the **addition algorithm** with manipulatives like base-ten blocks; sticks and bundles of sticks; units, strips, and mats; and abacuses—or, better yet, by using a number of these devices. For illustrative purposes here, we use units, strips, and mats.

After cutting out their strips and mats, students will be aware that there are 10 units on a strip and 10 strips, or 100 units, on a mat, and they will be aware that, in manipulating their materials, they can make these exchanges back and forth as needed.

### EXAMPLE 3.4 Making Exchanges with Units, Strips, and Mats

Suppose a number is represented by 15 units, 11 strips, and 2 mats. What exchanges must be made in order to represent the same number but with the smallest number of manipulative pieces?

**Solution**  **Understand the Problem**

We are given the mats, strips, and units indicated in the statement of the problem and are asked to make exchanges that reduce the number of loose pieces of apparatus while keeping the same number of units in all.

### Devise a Plan

Since we know that 10 units form a strip and 10 strips form a mat, we can reduce the number of loose pieces by making these exchanges.

### Carry Out the Plan

If we actually had in hand the pieces described, we would physically make the desired exchanges. Here in the text, we illustrate the exchanges pictorially.

We reduce the number of pieces by replacing 10 units by 1 strip and 10 strips by 1 mat. This gives 3 mats, 2 strips, and 5 units, for 325 units as shown.

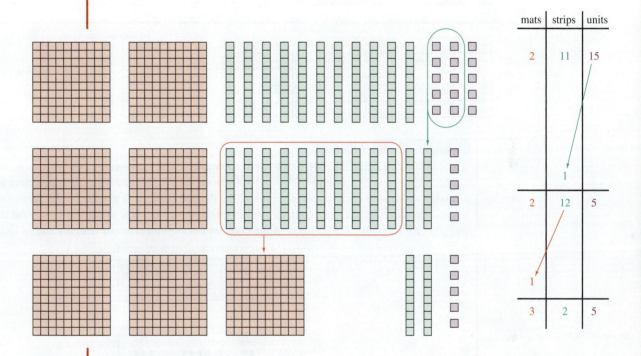

### Look Back

No more combining can take place, because it takes 10 units to make a strip and 10 strips to make a mat. Thus, we finish with 3 mats, 2 strips, and 5 units, for a total of 325 units. Moreover, we have not changed the total number of units, since

$$2 \cdot 100 + 11 \cdot 10 + 15 = 200 + 110 + 15 = 325.$$

## EXAMPLE 3.5 Developing the Addition Algorithm

Find the sum of 135 and 243.

**Solution**

### With Units, Strips, and Mats

One hundred thirty-five is represented by 1 mat, 3 strips, and 5 units, and 243 is represented by 2 mats, 4 strips, and 3 units, as shown. All told, this gives a total of 3 mats, 7 strips, and 8 units. Therefore, since no exchanges are possible, the sum is 378. Note how this illustrates the column-by-column addition algorithm typically used in pencil-and-paper calculation.

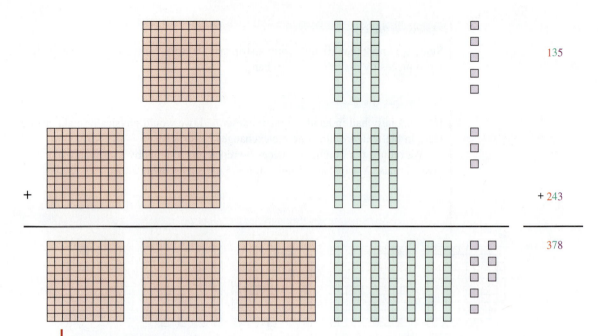

### With Place-Value Cards

A somewhat more abstract approach to this problem is to use **place-value cards**—that is, cards marked off in squares labeled 1s, 10s, and 100s from right to left and with the appropriate number of markers placed in each square to represent the desired number. A marker on the second square is worth 10 markers on the first square, a marker on the third square is worth 10 markers on the second square, and so on. The addition of the two numbers in this example is illustrated as follows:

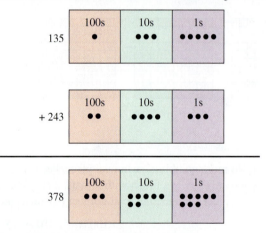

### With Place-Value Diagrams and Instructional Algorithms

An even more abstract approach that leads finally to the usual algorithm is provided by **place-value diagrams** and **instructional algorithms**. The instructional algorithm is also called the **partial-sum algorithm**. The final algorithm is also known as the **traditional**, or **final**, **algorithm**. Here they are, applied to this example:

| Place-Value Diagram | | | Instructional Algorithm | Final Algorithm |
|---|---|---|---|---|
| 100s | 10s | 1s | | |
| 1 | 3 | 5 | 135 | 135 |
| + 2 | 4 | 3 | + 243 | + 243 |
| 3 | 7 | 8 | 8 ← 5 + 3 | 378 |
| | | | 70 ← 30 + 40 | *Compress the result to a single line.* |
| | | | 300 ← 100 + 200 | |
| | | | 378 | |

Notice how the degree of abstraction steadily increases as we move through the various solutions. If the elementary school teacher goes directly to the final algorithm, many students will be lost along the way. The approach from the concrete gradually moving toward the abstract is more likely to impart the desired understanding.

**EXAMPLE 3.6   Adding with Exchanging**

Find the sum of 357 and 274.

**Solution**   **With Units, Strips, and Mats**

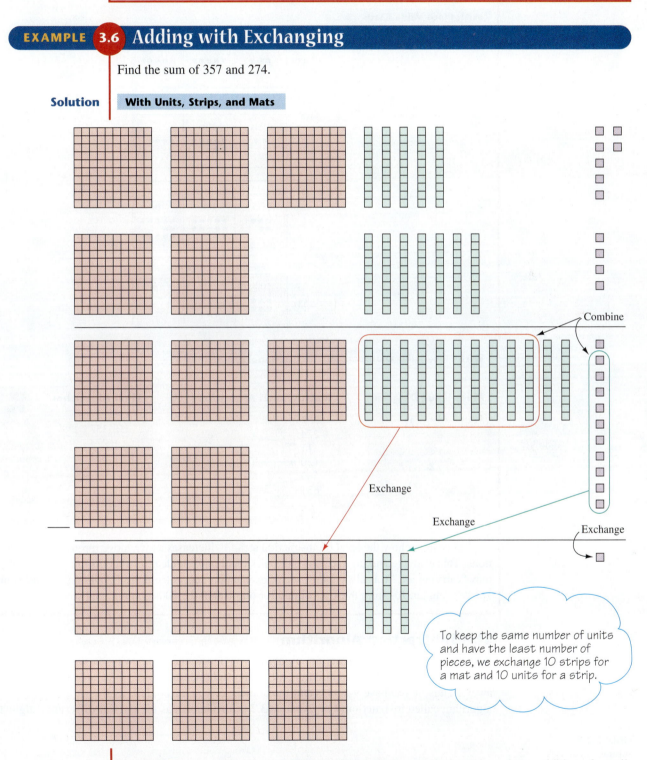

Combine

Exchange

Exchange

Exchange

To keep the same number of units and have the least number of pieces, we exchange 10 strips for a mat and 10 units for a strip.

Note how the preceding diagram illustrates not only the usual column-by-column addition of pencil-and-paper arithmetic but also "carrying," or, more appropriately stated, "exchanging." The 1 "carried" from the first column to the second indicates the exchange of 10 units for one 10 (represented by 1 strip), and the 1 carried from the second column to the third indicates the exchange of ten 10s (that is, 10 strips) for 100 (represented by 1 mat). Many teachers try to avoid the traditional word *carry,* since it encourages students to perform the algorithms by rote, with no understanding of what they are actually doing. Words like *exchange, trade,* and *regroup* are much more descriptive and actually describe what is being done.

**With Place-Value Cards**

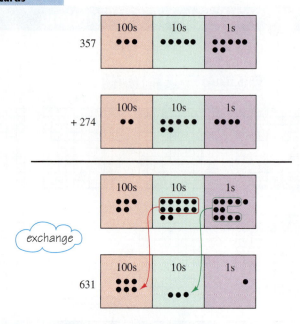

**With Place-Value Diagrams and Instructional Algorithms**

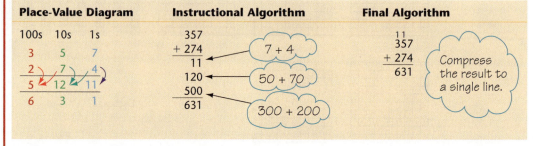

Notice again how the level of abstraction steadily increases as we move through these solutions. This example and the various solutions should make it clear to students that at no point are they "carrying a 1." It is always the case of exchanging ten 1s from the 1s column for one 10 in the 10s column, ten 10s from the 10s column for one 100 in the 100s column, and so on.

## The Subtraction Algorithm

We can illustrate the **subtraction algorithm** in much the same way as we did the addition algorithm. For primary school children, the idea of subtraction is often understood in terms of "take away." Thus, if you have 9 apples and I take away 5, you have 4 left, as shown in Figure 3.9. The algorithm called **instructional** in Example 3.7 is also known as the **partial-difference algorithm.**

**FIGURE 3.9**
Subtraction as "take away"

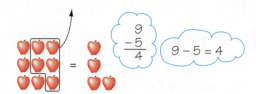

**EXAMPLE 3.7** **Subtracting Without Exchanging**

Subtract 243 from 375.

Solution

**With Units, Strips, and Mats**

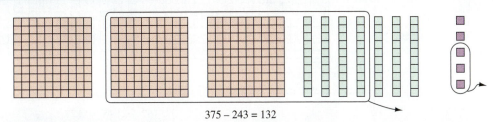

375 − 243 = 132

**With Place-Value Cards**

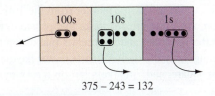

375 − 243 = 132

**With Place-Value Diagrams and Instructional Algorithms**

| Place-Value Diagram | Instructional Algorithm | Final Algorithm |
|---|---|---|
| 100s  10s  1s | 375 | 375 |
| 3  7  5 | − 243 | − 243 |
| − 2  4  3 | 2    ⟵  5 − 3 | 132 |
| 1  3  2 | 30  ⟵  70 − 40 | Compress the result to a single line. |
|  | 100 ⟵ 300 − 200 |  |
|  | 132 |  |

**EXAMPLE 3.8** **Subtracting with Exchanging**

Subtract 185 from 362.

Solution

**With Units, Strips, and Mats**

We start with 3 mats, 6 strips, and 2 units:

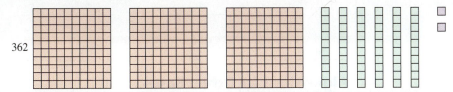

362

We want to take away 1 mat, 8 strips, and 5 units. Since we cannot pick up 5 units from our present arrangement, we exchange a strip for 10 units to obtain 3 mats, 5 strips, and 12 units:

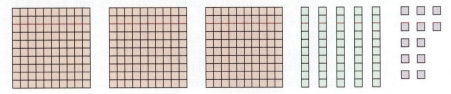

We can now take away 5 units, but we still cannot pick up 8 strips. Therefore, we exchange a mat for 10 strips to obtain 2 mats, 15 strips, and 12 units. Finally, we are able to take away 1 mat, 8 strips, and 5 units (i.e., 185 units), as shown here:

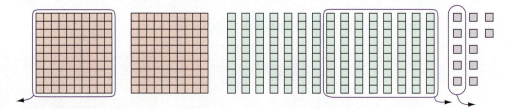

This leaves 1 mat, 7 strips, and 7 units. So

$$362 - 185 = 177.$$

**With Place-Value Cards**

We must take away 1 marker from the 100s square, 8 markers from the 10s square, and 5 markers from the 1s square. To make this possible, we trade 1 marker from the 10s square for 10 markers on the 1s square and we trade 1 marker on the 100s square for 10 markers on the 10s square. Now, taking away the desired markers, we have 1 marker left on the 100s square, 7 markers left on the 10s square, and 7 markers left on the 1s square, for 177:

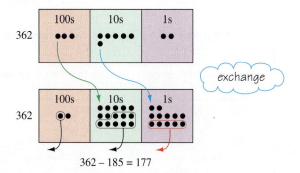

$$362 - 185 = 177$$

**With Place-Value Diagrams and Instructional Algorithms**

| Place-Value Diagram | Instructional Algorithm | Final Algorithm |
|---|---|---|
| 100s  10s  1s | | |
| 3   6   2 | 3   6   2 | |
| − 1   8   5 | − 1   8   5 | |
| 3   5   12 | 3   5   (12) | 2¹5 |
| − 1   8   5 | − 1   8   5 | 3 6¹2 |
| 2   15   12 | 2   (15)   (12) | −1 8 5 |
| − 1   8   5 | − 1   8   5 | 1 7 7 |
| 1   7   7 | 1   7   7 | |

*exchange*

## Algorithms in Other Bases

The algorithms for addition and subtraction are just as valid in base five, or any other base, as they are in base ten, and notations can be developed with manipulatives just as for base ten. Our approach, therefore, is to consider other bases right along with base ten. By studying bases together this way, you gain a greater understanding of the whole idea of positional notation and the related algorithms. In base five, for example, the place-value cards would have a units or 1s square; a 5s square; a $5^2$, or 25s, square; and so on. With sticks, we could use loose sticks, bundles of 5 sticks, bundles of 5 bundles of sticks, and so on. With units, strips, and mats, we would have units, strips with 5 units each, and mats with 5 strips per mat.

**Adding in Base Five**   The next example shows how the addition algorithm works in base five. Let's see how the process works with place-value cards.

**EXAMPLE 3.9**   **Adding in Base Five**

Compute the sum of $143_{five}$ and $234_{five}$ in base-five notation.

**Solution**   **With Place-Value Cards**

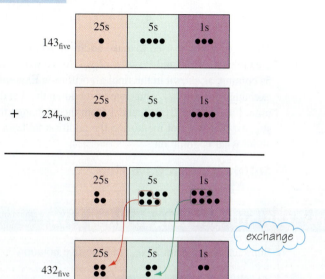

**With Place-Value Diagrams and Instructional Algorithms**

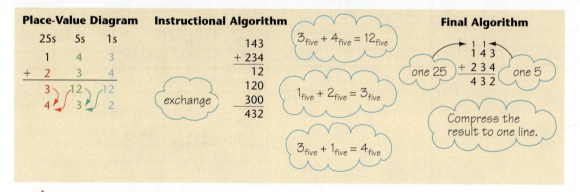

So the sum is $432_{five}$.

To check the addition, we convert everything to base ten, in which we feel comfortable:

$$143_{five} = 1 \cdot 25 + 4 \cdot 5 + 3 \cdot 1 = 48_{ten}$$
$$234_{five} = 2 \cdot 25 + 3 \cdot 5 + 4 \cdot 1 = 69_{ten}$$
$$432_{five} = 4 \cdot 25 + 3 \cdot 5 + 2 \cdot 1 = 117_{ten}$$

The result is confirmed, since $48_{ten} + 69_{ten} = 117_{ten}$.

The difficulty in doing base-five arithmetic is unfamiliarity with the meaning of the symbols—we do not recognize at a glance, for example, that $8_{ten} = 13_{five}$, since $13_{five}$ is 1 five and 3 ones. By contrast, thinking of units, strips with 5 units per strip, and so on, we do not find it hard to think of 1 strip and 3 units as 8. In fact, doing arithmetic in another base gives good practice in mental arithmetic, which is a desirable end in itself. Of course, elementary school children memorize the addition and multiplication tables in base ten so that the needed symbols are readily recalled, and we could do the same thing here. The addition table in base five, for example, is as follows:

| + | 0 | 1 | 2 | 3 | 4 |
|---|---|---|---|---|---|
| **0** | 0 | 1 | 2 | 3 | 4 |
| **1** | 1 | 2 | 3 | 4 | 10 |
| **2** | 2 | 3 | 4 | 10 | 11 |
| **3** | 3 | 4 | 10 | 11 | 12 |
| **4** | 4 | 10 | 11 | 12 | 13 |

These numerals are in base five.

This table could be used to make addition in base five easier and more immediate. For example, from the table, we see that $3 + 4 = 12_{\text{five}}$. So we write down the 2 and exchange the five 1s for a 5 in the 5s column, as shown in the final algorithm in Example 3.9. Next, $4 + 3 = 12_{\text{five}}$, and the 1 from the exchange gives $13_{\text{five}}$. Thus, we write down the 3 and exchange the five 5s for one 25 in the next column. Finally, $1 + 2 = 3$, and 1 from the exchange makes 4, so we obtain $432_{\text{five}}$ as before. Still, we suggest that you not memorize the addition table in base five; it is far better just to think carefully about what is going on.

### Subtracting in Base Five

**EXAMPLE 3.10  Subtracting in Base Five**

Subtract $143_{\text{five}}$ from $234_{\text{five}}$ in base-five notation.

**Solution**

**With Place-Value Cards**

There is no problem in taking away 3 markers from the 1s square, but we cannot remove 4 markers from the 5s square without exchanging 1 marker on the 25s square for 5 markers on the 5s square. Taking away the desired markers, we are left with zero 25s, four 5s, and one 1, for $41_{\text{five}}$:

**With Place-Value Diagrams and Instructional Algorithms**

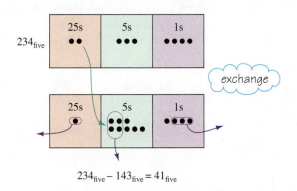

So the answer is $41_{five}$.

As a check, we already know that $243_{five} = 69_{ten}$ and $143_{five} = 48_{ten}$. Since $69 - 48 = 21$ and $41_{five} = 4 \cdot 5 + 1 \cdot 1 = 21$, the calculation checks.

## Problem Set 3.3

Exercises numbered in red are answered in the back of the text.

### Understanding Concepts

1. Sketch the solution to $36 + 75$, using

   (a) mats, strips, and units. Draw a square for a mat, a vertical line segment for a strip, and a dot for a unit.

   (b) place-value cards marked 1s, 10s, and 100s from right to left.

2. Use the instructional algorithm for addition to perform the following additions:

   (a) $23 + 44$    (b) $57 + 84$    (c) $324 + 78$

3. Sketch the solution to $275 - 136$, using

   (a) mats, strips, and units.

   (b) place-value cards marked 1s, 10s, and 100s from right to left.

4. Use the instructional algorithm for subtraction to perform these subtractions:

   (a) $78 - 35$    (b) $75 - 38$    (c) $414 - 175$

5. The calculation of the difference $523 - 247$ might look like this:

$$\begin{array}{r} {}^{4}\phantom{0}{}^{1}1 \\ \cancel{5}\cancel{2}{}^{1}3 \\ -2\,4\,7 \\ \hline 2\,7\,6 \end{array}$$

   Carefully discuss the exchanges indicated. How would you explain these to a third grader?

6. The calculation of the difference $30{,}007 - 1098$ might look like this:

$$\begin{array}{r} {}^{2}\phantom{0}{}^{9}\phantom{0}{}^{9}\phantom{0}{}^{9} \\ \cancel{3}{}^{1}\cancel{0}{}^{1}\cancel{0}{}^{1}\cancel{0}{}^{1}7 \\ -\,1\,0\,9\,8 \\ \hline 2\,8{,}9\,0\,9 \end{array}$$

   Carefully discuss the exchanges indicated.

7. Perform these additions and subtractions, being careful not to leave more than 59 seconds or 59 minutes in your answers:

   (a)   3 hours, 24 minutes, 54 seconds
       $+2$ hours, 47 minutes, 38 seconds

   (b)   7 hours, 56 minutes, 29 seconds
       $+3$ hours, 27 minutes, 52 seconds

   (c)   5 hours, 24 minutes, 54 seconds
       $-2$ hours, 47 minutes, 38 seconds

   (d)   7 hours, 46 minutes, 29 seconds
       $-3$ hours, 27 minutes, 52 seconds

8. The column-by-column addition of the numbers 36 and 52 is shown next. State the property of the whole numbers that jus-

tifies each of these steps. We begin with expanded notation as a justification of the first line:

$$\begin{aligned} 36 + 52 &= (3 \cdot 10 + 6) + (5 \cdot 10 + 2) \quad \text{expanded notation} \\ &= 3 \cdot 10 + [6 + (5 \cdot 10 + 2)] \quad \textbf{(a)} \underline{\hspace{2cm}} \\ &= 3 \cdot 10 + [(6 + 5 \cdot 10) + 2] \quad \textbf{(b)} \underline{\hspace{2cm}} \\ &= 3 \cdot 10 + [(5 \cdot 10 + 6) + 2] \quad \textbf{(c)} \underline{\hspace{2cm}} \\ &= 3 \cdot 10 + [5 \cdot 10 + (6 + 2)] \quad \textbf{(d)} \underline{\hspace{2cm}} \\ &= (3 \cdot 10 + 5 \cdot 10) + (6 + 2) \quad \textbf{(e)} \underline{\hspace{2cm}} \\ &= (3 + 5) \cdot 10 + (6 + 2) \quad \textbf{(f)} \underline{\hspace{2cm}} \\ &= 8 \cdot 10 + 8 \quad \text{addition facts} \\ &= 88 \quad \text{expanded notation} \end{aligned}$$

9. (a) In a single column, write the base-four representations of the numbers from 0 to 15 inclusive.

   (b) Briefly discuss any pattern you noticed in part (a).

10. Complete the addition table shown for base four arithmetic by placing the sum $a + b$ at the intersection of the $a$th row and the $b$th column. The subscript "four" may be omitted here.

| + | 0 | 1 | 2 | 3 |
|---|---|---|---|---|
| 0 |   |   |   |   |
| 1 |   |   |   |   |
| 2 |   |   |   |   |
| 3 |   |   |   |   |

11. Complete the given computations in base-four notation. The numerals are written in base four, and the subscript indicating base four may be omitted from your work. Check your work by converting to base-ten notation.

   (a) $\begin{array}{r} 231 \\ +\ 121 \\ \hline \end{array}$    (b) $\begin{array}{r} 303 \\ +\ 33 \\ \hline \end{array}$    (c) $\begin{array}{r} 1223 \\ +\ 231 \\ \hline \end{array}$

   (d) $\begin{array}{r} 333 \\ +\ 101 \\ \hline \end{array}$    (e) $\begin{array}{r} 32 \\ +13 \\ \hline \end{array}$    (f) $\begin{array}{r} 302 \\ -\ 103 \\ \hline \end{array}$

   (g) $\begin{array}{r} 212 \\ -\ 33 \\ \hline \end{array}$    (h) $\begin{array}{r} 3102 \\ -1033 \\ \hline \end{array}$

### Teaching Concepts

12. The hand calculation of the sum of 279 and 84 involves two exchanges and might appear as follows:

$$\begin{array}{r} {}^{1}\,{}^{1}\phantom{0} \\ 279 \\ 84 \\ \hline 363 \end{array}$$

Carefully describe each of the exchanges. How would you explain these to a third grader?

**13.** While Sylvia was trying to balance her checkbook, her calculator battery went dead. When she added up the outstanding checks by hand, her work looked like this:

```
 1 1
2109
 308
  19
 207
 129
 208
 219
 307
  29
 108
  17
 209
 118
————
3987
```

> Note the exchange from the units column to the hundreds column.

**(a)** Is the addition correct?

**(b)** Discuss each of the exchanges shown.

**(c)** Would you have proceeded as Sylvia did?

**(d)** How else might the addition been carried out?

**(e)** What would you say to a student of yours who did the computation as Sylvia did?

**14.** In a long-distance relay race of 50 miles, the four runners on one team had the following times: 1 hour, 2 minutes, 23 seconds; 51 minutes, 31 seconds; 1 hour, 47 seconds; and 48 minutes, 27 seconds. What was the total time for the team? Comment on the exchanges involved in solving this problem. (*Note:* The final answer should be stated with the least possible number of minutes and seconds.)

**15.** Read the Number and Operations Standard for Grades Pre-K–2, pages 78–88 in NCTM's *Principles and Standards for School Mathematics,* and write a critique of the standard, emphasizing your own reaction to the recommendations. How do the recommendations compare with your own school experience?

## Responding to Students

**16.** How would you respond to one of your students who subtracted 229 from 2003 as

```
   1 9 9
2̶0̶0̶¹3
−  2 2 9
————————
  1 7 7 4
```

saying that he or she had exchanged one of the 200 tens for 10 units?

**17.** Examine the given student responses to the same addition problem below. What possible reason(s) can you give for their errors? How would you help each student correct the work?

```
 426
+397
————
```

**(a)** Thomas, who sometimes isn't careful with routine single-digit arithmetic, writes the solution as

```
 426
+397
————
 818
```

**(b)** Annabelle wrote down

```
 426
+397
————
 713
```

**(c)** Xiao gives the solution as

```
 426
+397
————
 803
```

**18.** Examine the given responses of fourth-grade students to the subtraction problem. Generally, subtraction errors are more common than addition errors.

```
 722
−558
```

What errors is each student making, and why is the student making them? What steps would you take to help the students correct their mistakes?

**(a)** Richard writes the solution as

```
  1112
 7̶2̶2̶
−5 5 8
————————
 2 6 4
```

**(b)** Jeff's computation is

```
 81111
 7̶2̶2̶
−5 5 8
————————
  363
```

**(c)** Sandy used the following steps:

```
    10
     ↓
  8 1 12
 7̶2̶2̶
−5 5 8
————————
 3 5 4
```

**19.** When asked to take the number 29,457,300 and add 1 million more, fourth graders Drew and Alonzo gave the following responses:

**(a)** 210,457,300 (Drew).

**(b)** 39,457,300 (Alonzo).

What error did each of the boys make, and why do you think he made it? How would you help him correct his work?

## Thinking Critically

**20.** On his way to school, Peter dropped his arithmetic paper in a puddle of water, blotting out some of his work. What digits should go under the blots in these problems? (The base is ten.)

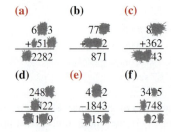

**(a)**
```
6■3
+■51■
———————
■2282
```

**(b)**
```
77■
+■2
————
871
```

**(c)**
```
8■
+362
————
■43
```

**(d)**
```
248■
−■22
————
■1■9
```

**(e)**
```
4■2
−1843
—————
■15■
```

**(f)**
```
34■5
−■748
—————
■2■
```

**21.** Find the missing digits in each of these base-ten addition problems:

(a)
```
    _437
    2_1
  + 347_
   6_94
```

(b)
```
    _721
    901_
  + 71_3
   _0_26
```

(c)
```
    38_1
    24_3
  + 512_
   __5_9
```

(d)
```
    5_4
    612_
  + 8_1
   76_6
```

**22.** Fill in the missing digits in each of these base-ten subtraction problems:

(a)
```
    _3_
  - 2_1
   594
```

(b)
```
    3__4
  - _346
   175_
```

(c)
```
    7_4_
  - _5_4
   808
```

(d)
```
    63__4
  - 2_12_
   _6209
```

**23.** The given additions and subtractions are written in different bases. Determine the base used in each case. (*Hint:* There may be more than one correct answer.)

(a)
```
    231
  + 414
   1200
```

(b)
```
    231
  + 414
   1045
```

(c)
```
    231
  + 414
   645
```

(d)
```
    344
  + 143
   1042
```

(e)
```
    523
  - 254
   236
```

(f)
```
    523
  - 254
   247
```

(g)
```
    523
  - 254
   28E
```

(h)
```
    1020
  - 203
   312
```

**24.** There is a rather interesting addition algorithm called the **scratch method** that proceeds as follows: Consider the sum

```
   2 834
   8̶7̶6̶
   4 835
   2̶ 743
  10,988
```

Begin by adding from the top down in the units column. When you add a digit that makes your sum 10 or more, scratch out the digit as shown and make a mental note of the units digit of your present sum. Start with the digit noted and continue adding and scratching until you have completed the units column, writing down the units digit of the last sum as the units digit of the answer, as shown. Now count the number of scratches in the units column and, starting with this number, add on down the tens column, repeating the scratch process as you go. Continue the entire process until all the columns have been added. This gives the desired answer. Explain why the algorithm works.

## Thinking Cooperatively

For each of the next three problems, work with a partner. For each problem, make sure that the answers you give are agreed upon by your partner.

**25.** Give each pair of students a set of the 10 digits, each printed on a square of heavy paper.

(a) Have the students choose and place the digits on the desktop to form the greatest four-digit number that is a multiple of 6.

(b) Can any odd number be a multiple of 6? Why or why not?

(c) Have the students choose and place the digits on the desktop to form the least six-digit number for which the sum of the digits is at least 20.

(d) Have the students choose and place the digits on the desktop to form the greatest six-digit number for which the sum of the digits is less than 20.

**26.** Form two four-digit numbers using each of 1, 2, 3, 4, 5, 6, 7, and 8 once, and only once, so that

(a) the sum of the two numbers is as large as possible.

(b) the sum of the two numbers is as small as possible.

(c) You can do better than guess and check on parts (a) and (b). Explain your solution strategy briefly.

(d) Is there only one answer to each of parts (a) and (b)? Explain in two sentences.

**27.** (a) Form two four-digit numbers using each of the digits 1, 2, 3, 4, 5, 6, 7, and 8 precisely once so that

   (i) the difference of the two numbers is a natural number that is as small as possible.

   (ii) the difference of the two numbers is as large as possible.

(b) Briefly explain the strategy you used in solving this problem.

(c) Is there more than one solution to parts (a) and (b)? Why or why not?

## Making Connections

**28.** Julien spent 1 hour and 45 minutes mowing the lawn and 2 hours and 35 minutes trimming the hedge and some shrubs. How long did he work altogether?

**29.** (a) Mr. Kobayashi has four pieces of oak flooring left over from a job he just completed. If they are 3′ 8″, 4′ 2″, 6′ 10″, and 5′ 11″ long, what total length of flooring does he have left over? Make sure that the number of inches in your answer is less than 12.

(b) If Mr. Kobayashi uses 9′ 10″ of the flooring left over in part (a) to make a picture frame, how much flooring does he have left over then?

**30.** After her dad gave her an allowance of 10 dollars, Ellie had 25 dollars and 25 cents. After buying a stuffed kangaroo for 14 dollars and 53 cents, including tax, how much money did Ellie have left?

**31.** It was 25 minutes after 5 in the morning when Ari began his paper route. If it took him an hour and three-quarters to deliver the papers, at what time did he finish?

## From State Student Assessments

**32.** (Texas, Grade 5)
The table below shows the start and end times of a movie at a theater.

MOVIE TIMES

| Start | End |
| --- | --- |
| 12:30 P.M. | 2:45 P.M. |
| 3:00 P.M. | 5:15 P.M. |
| 6:45 P.M. | 9:00 P.M. |
| 9:20 P.M. | 11:35 P.M. |

According to the information in the table, which of the following statements is true?

**F.** The end time is exactly 2 hours 45 minutes after the start time.

**G.** The end time is exactly 2 hours 15 minutes after the start time.

**H.** The end time is exactly 2 hours 30 minutes after the start time.

**J.** The end time is exactly 3 hours 45 minutes after the start time.

**33.** (Georgia, Grade 4)
If you change the digit 6 to a 9 in the number 56,907, what will be the difference?

**A.** Three hundred            **B.** Nine hundred

**C.** One thousand            **D.** Three thousand

**34.** (Georgia, Grade 4)
Fay picked apples in the orchard. She picked 45 apples on Monday, 57 on Tuesday, and 39 on Wednesday. How many apples did she pick in all?

**A.** 84     **B.** 92     **C.** 102     **D.** 141

**35.** (Texas, Grade 4)
A hiker is climbing a mountain that is 6238 feet high. She stops to rest at 4887 feet. How many more feet must she climb to reach the top?

**F.** 2351 feet     **G.** 1451 feet     **H.** 1361 feet

**I.** 1351 feet     **J.** Not here

**36.** (California, Grade 4)

Solve: $619{,}581 - 23{,}183 = ?$

Solve: $6747 + 321{,}105 = ?$

## Examining School Book Pages

*Refer to the School Book Pages provided on page 157 to answer the following questions.*

**37.** On the sample page, *regroup* was used in the "one-way" box on p. 43, instead of *borrow*. Why is it better to use words like *regroup*, *exchange*, and *trade* rather than *borrow*?

**38.** In the "Subtracting across Zero" example, the authors have given two ways to solve the problem. Do you think that that is a good approach? Justify your answer.

## 3.4 Algorithms for Multiplication and Division of Whole Numbers

In most ancient numeration systems, multiplication and division were quite complicated. The decimal system makes these processes much easier, but many people still find them confusing. At least part of the difficulty has been that the ideas are often presented as a collection of rules to be learned by rote, with little or no effort made to impart understanding. In this section, we will see the conceptual basis of a number of different algorithms for multiplication and division; that is, you will now see why they work!

### Multiplication Algorithms

Multiplication is repeated addition. Thus, $2 \cdot 9$ means $9 + 9$, $3 \cdot 9$ means $9 + 9 + 9$, and so on. But repeated addition is slow and tedious, and easier algorithms exist. As with addition and subtraction, these algorithms should be introduced by starting with concrete approaches and gradually becoming more and more abstract. The development should proceed through units, strips, and mats; place-value cards; classroom abacuses; and so on. Let's consider the product $9 \cdot 3$.

*See "Examining School Book Pages" on page 156 for questions related to the pages shown below.*

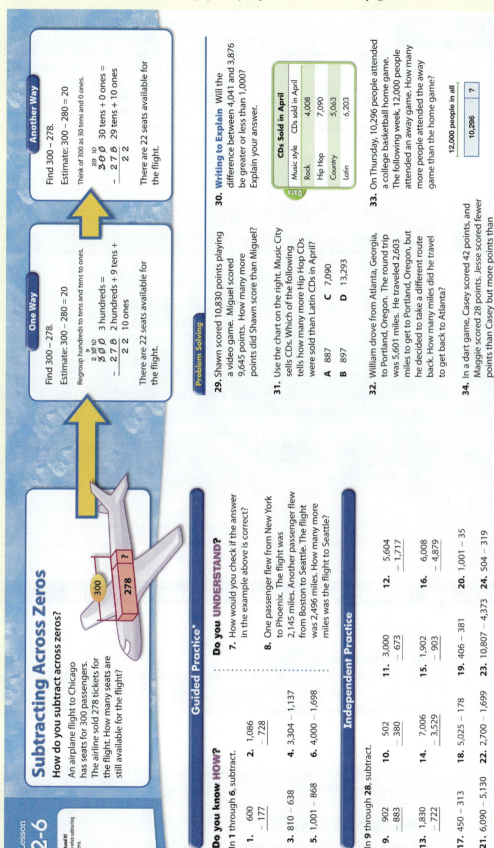

Lesson
**2-6**

**Understand It!**
Regroup when subtracting across zeros.

## Subtracting Across Zeros

### How do you subtract across zeros?

An airplane flight to Chicago has seats for 300 passengers. The airline sold 278 tickets for the flight. How many seats are still available for the flight?

**One Way**

Find 300 − 278.

Estimate: 300 − 280 = 20

Regroup hundreds to tens and tens to ones.

$$\begin{array}{r} \overset{2}{\cancel{3}}\,\overset{9}{\cancel{0}}\,\overset{10}{0} \\ -\;2\;7\;8 \\ \hline 2\;2 \end{array}$$

3 hundreds =
2 hundreds + 9 tens +
10 ones

There are 22 seats available for the flight.

**Another Way**

Find 300 − 278.

Estimate: 300 − 280 = 20

Think of 300 as 30 tens and 0 ones.

$$\begin{array}{r} \overset{29}{\cancel{3}\cancel{0}}\,\overset{10}{0} \\ -\;2\;7\;8 \\ \hline 2\;2 \end{array}$$

30 tens + 0 ones =
29 tens + 10 ones

There are 22 seats available for the flight.

### Guided Practice*

**Do you know HOW?**

In **1** through **6**, subtract.

1.  600
    − 177

2.  1,086
    −  728

3.  810 − 638

4.  3,304 − 1,137

5.  1,001 − 868

6.  4,000 − 1,698

**Do you UNDERSTAND?**

7. How would you check if the answer in the example above is correct?

8. One passenger flew from New York to Phoenix. The flight was 2,145 miles. Another passenger flew from Boston to Seattle. The flight was 2,496 miles. How many more miles was the flight to Seattle?

### Independent Practice

In **9** through **28**, subtract.

9.   902
     − 883

10.  502
     − 380

11.  3,000
     −  673

12.  5,604
     − 1,717

13.  1,830
     −  722

14.  7,006
     − 3,529

15.  1,902
     −  903

16.  6,008
     − 4,879

17. 450 − 313

18. 5,025 − 178

19. 406 − 381

20. 1,001 − 35

21. 6,090 − 5,130

22. 2,700 − 1,699

23. 10,807 − 4,373

24. 504 − 319

25. 3,000 − 1,047

26. 5,001 − 368

27. 700 − 520

28. 900 − 406

*For another example, see Set E on page 51.

### Problem Solving

29. Shawn scored 10,830 points playing a video game. Miguel scored 9,645 points. How many more points did Shawn score than Miguel?

30. **Writing to Explain** Will the difference between 4,041 and 3,876 be greater or less than 1,000? Explain your answer.

31. Use the chart on the right. Music City sells CDs. Which of the following tells how many more Hip Hop CDs were sold than Latin CDs in April?

    A  887      C  7,090
    B  897      D  13,293

**Data**

| CDs Sold in April | |
| --- | --- |
| Music style | CDs sold in April |
| Rock | 4,008 |
| Hip Hop | 7,090 |
| Country | 5,063 |
| Latin | 6,203 |

32. William drove from Atlanta, Georgia, to Portland, Oregon. The round trip was 5,601 miles. He traveled 2,603 miles to get to Portland, Oregon, but he decided to take a different route back. How many miles did he travel to get back to Atlanta?

33. On Thursday, 10,296 people attended a college basketball home game. The following week, 12,000 people attended an away game. How many more people attended the away game than the home game?

12,000 people in all

| 10,296 | ? |
| --- | --- |

34. In a dart game, Casey scored 42 points, and Maggie scored 28 points. Jesse scored fewer points than Casey but more points than Maggie. Which is a possible score for Jesse?

    A  50 points      C  34 points
    B  46 points      D  26 points

Lesson 2-6

42    43

**FROM** *The NCTM Principles and Standards*

Research suggests that by solving problems that require calculation, students develop methods for computing and also learn more about operations and properties (McClain, Cobb, and Bowers 1998; Schifter 1999). As students develop methods to solve multidigit computation problems, they should be encouraged to record and share their methods. As they do so, they can learn from one another, analyze the efficiency and generalizability of various approaches, and try one another's methods. In the past, common school practice has been to present a single algorithm for each operation. However, more than one efficient and accurate computational algorithm exists for each arithmetic operation. In addition, if given the opportunity, students naturally invent methods to compute that make sense to them (Fuson forthcoming; Madell 1985). The following episode, drawn from unpublished classroom observation notes, illustrates how one teacher helped students analyze and compare their computational procedures for division:

*Students in Ms. Sparks' fifth-grade class were sharing their solutions to a homework problem, 728 ÷ 34. Ms. Sparks asked several students to put their work on the board to be discussed. She deliberately chose students who had approached the problem in several different ways. As the students put their work on the board, Ms. Sparks circulated among the other students, checking their homework.*

*Henry had written his solution:*

$$34 \times 10 = 340$$
$$34 \times 20 = 680$$

$$\begin{array}{r} 680 \\ + 34 \\ \hline 714 \end{array} \qquad \begin{array}{r} 728 \\ - 714 \\ \hline 14 \end{array}$$

*Henry explained to the class, "Twenty 34s plus one more is 21. I knew I was pretty close. I didn't think I could add any more 34s, so I subtracted 714 from 728 and got 14. Then I had 21 remainder 14."*

## EXAMPLE 3.11 Developing the Multiplication Algorithm

Compute the product of 9 and 3.

**Solution**

### Using Units, Strips, and Mats

Since $9 \cdot 3 = 3 + 3 + 3 + 3 + 3 + 3 + 3 + 3 + 3$, we can illustrate this as shown with 9 rows of 3 units each. Simplifying the original array by appropriately exchanging units for strips, we eventually have 2 strips and 7 units, which is recorded as 27. Of course, elementary school children should actually handle the materials, making the necessary exchanges of units for strips.

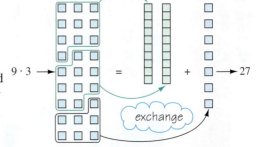

### Using Place-Value Cards

With place-value cards, students should start with 9 rows of 3 markers each on the 1s square of their place-value cards, as shown here. They should then exchange 10 markers on the 1s square for 1 marker on the 10s square as many times as possible and record the fact that this gives 2 tens plus 7 units, or 27.

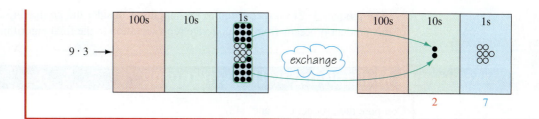

Using manipulatives as illustrated, children can experience, learn, and actually *understand* all the one-digit multiplication facts. It should not be the case that $9 \cdot 3 = 27$ is a string of meaningless symbols memorized by rote. This basic fact must be understood conceptually.

Once the one-digit facts are thoroughly understood *and memorized,* as they must be, one can move on to more complicated problems. Consider, for example, $3 \cdot 213$. This multiplication could be illustrated with units, strips, and mats, but, for brevity, we will go directly to place-value cards, expanded notation, and, finally, to an algorithm, as illustrated in Example 3.12. Again, we make use of the understanding that $3 \cdot 213 = 213 + 213 + 213$. For multiplication, the **instructional algorithm** is also known as the **partial-products algorithm.**

Multiplication can be done in a number of ways. The key to establishing methods to actually perform a multiplication is to have a deep understanding of positional systems and notation. Using this knowledge and the distributive law for whole numbers leads to a number of different algorithms. We will illustrate **expanded notation,** the instructional (or partial-products) algorithm, and the final algorithm. There are a number of other algorithms for multiplication, three of which are included in problems 17, 23, and 24 (the lattice algorithm, Egyptian algorithm, and Russian peasant algorithm, respectively). The lattice algorithm is a method that is also taught at a number of schools in the United States.

In addition to the algorithms that are presented in this text, students will invent their own ways of multiplying or doing other operations. Their ideas should be encouraged, as we see from the quote from NCTM on the previous page.

---

**EXAMPLE 3.12** **Computing a Product with a Multidigit Number**

Compute the product of 3 and 213.

**Solution** **Using Place-Value Cards, Expanded Notation, and Algorithms**

Place-value cards

|  | 100s | 10s | 1s |
|---|---|---|---|
| $3 \cdot 213$ | •• ••<br>•• | •<br>•<br>• | •••<br>•••<br>••• |
|  | 6 | 3 | 9 |

Expanded notation

$3 \cdot (200 + 10 + 3)$    *expanded notation*
$= 600 + 30 + 9$    *distributive property*
$= 639$    *expanded notation*

Instructional algorithm

$$
\begin{array}{r}
213 \\
\times\ 3 \\
\hline
9 \\
30 \\
600 \\
\hline
639
\end{array}
$$

$3 \times 3$
$3 \times 10$
$3 \times 200$

Final algorithm

$$
\begin{array}{r}
213 \\
\times\ 3 \\
\hline
639
\end{array}
$$

*Compress the computation.*

The product $3 \cdot 213$ did not require exchanging. Consider the product $4 \cdot 243$. The presentation of this product proceeds from the concrete representation to the final algorithm.

## EXAMPLE 3.13 Multiplying with Exchanging

Compute the product of 4 and 243.

**Solution**

**Using Place-Value Cards, Expanded Notation, and Algorithms**

Place-value cards

$4 \cdot 243$      972

Instructional algorithm

Expanded notation

$$4(200 + 40 + 3)$$

*distributive property*

$$= 800 + 160 + 12$$

$$= 972$$

$$\begin{array}{r} 243 \\ \times\ 4 \\ \hline 12 \\ 160 \\ 800 \\ \hline 972 \end{array}$$

$4 \times 3$
$4 \times 40$
$4 \times 200$

Final algorithm

$$\begin{array}{r} \overset{1\ 1}{243} \\ \times\ \ 4 \\ \hline 972 \end{array}$$

*Compress the computation and place the exchanges above the 4 and 2.*

The preceding development represents many lessons. However, the various demonstrations should be clearly tied together, and enough time should be spent to ensure that each level of the chain of reasoning is understood before proceeding to the next.

Finally, consider the product $15 \cdot 324$. Unquestionably, the most efficient algorithm is that provided by the calculator. The pencil-and-paper algorithm, however, is not difficult, as the series of calculations in Example 3.14 shows.

## EXAMPLE 3.14 Multiplying Multidigit Numbers

Compute the product of 15 and 324.

**Solution**

**Using Expanded Notation, an Instructional Algorithm, and the Final Algorithm**

Expanded notation

$$15 \cdot 324 = (10 + 5) \cdot 324$$

*distributive property*

$$= 10 \cdot 324 + 5 \cdot 324$$

*expanded notation*

$$= 10(300 + 20 + 4) + 5(300 + 20 + 4)$$

*distributive property*

$$= 3000 + 200 + 40 + 1500 + 100 + 20$$

$$= 4860$$

Instructional algorithm

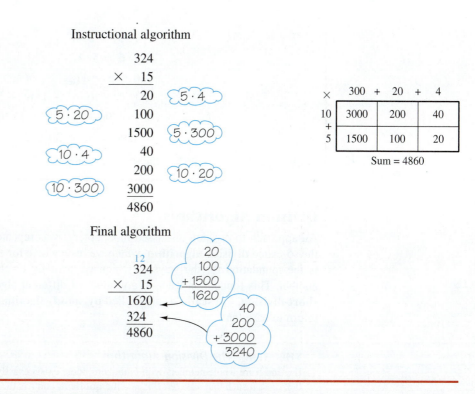

$$
\begin{array}{r}
324 \\
\times \quad 15 \\
\hline
20 \\
100 \\
1500 \\
40 \\
200 \\
3000 \\
\hline
4860
\end{array}
$$

$5 \cdot 4$

$5 \cdot 20$

$5 \cdot 300$

$10 \cdot 4$

$10 \cdot 20$

$10 \cdot 300$

| $\times$ | 300 | + | 20 | + | 4 |
|---|---|---|---|---|---|
| 10 | 3000 | | 200 | | 40 |
| + | | | | | |
| 5 | 1500 | | 100 | | 20 |

Sum = 4860

Final algorithm

$$
\begin{array}{r}
\overset{12}{324} \\
\times \quad 15 \\
\hline
1620 \\
324 \\
\hline
4860
\end{array}
$$

$$
\begin{array}{r}
20 \\
100 \\
+ 1500 \\
\hline
1620
\end{array}
$$

$$
\begin{array}{r}
40 \\
200 \\
+ 3000 \\
\hline
3240
\end{array}
$$

## Multiplication in Other Bases

As with the algorithms for addition and subtraction, the multiplication algorithm depends on the idea of positional notation, but is independent of the base. The arithmetic is more awkward for bases other than ten, since we do not think in other bases as we do in base ten, but the ideas are the same. However, working in other bases not only enhances our understanding of base ten but also provides an interesting activity that helps to improve mental arithmetic skills. Let's consider an example.

**EXAMPLE 3.15** **Multiplication in Base Six**

Compute the product $324_{\text{six}} \cdot 15_{\text{six}}$ in base six.

**Solution** We use the base-six positional values from Table 3.7 and the instructional algorithm of Example 3.14. To simplify notation, we will write all *numerals* in base-six notation so that the subscripts will be omitted. Finally, the numeral *words* will have their usual base-ten meaning. The work proceeds as follows, with descriptive comments in the think cloud:

$$
\begin{array}{r}
324 \\
\times \quad 15 \\
\hline
32 \\
140 \\
2300 \\
40 \\
200 \\
3000 \\
\hline
10152
\end{array}
$$

Think

$5 \times 4 = \text{twenty} = 3 \text{ sixes} + 2 \text{ units} = 3 \cdot 6^1 + 2 \cdot 6^0 = 32_{\text{six}}$

$5 \times 20 = 5 \times 2 \text{ sixes} = 10 \text{ sixes} = (1 \cdot 6 + 4) \cdot 6^1 = 1 \cdot 6^2 + 4 \cdot 6^1 + 0 \cdot 6^0 = 140_{\text{six}}$

$5 \times 300 = 5 \times 3 \text{ thirty-sixes} = 15 \text{ thirty-sixes} = (2 \cdot 6 + 3) \cdot 6^2 = 2 \cdot 6^3 + 3 \cdot 6^2 + 0 \cdot 6^1 + 0 \cdot 6^0 = 2300_{\text{six}}$

$10 \times 4 = 1 \text{ six} \times 4 = 4 \cdot 6^1 + 0 \cdot 6^0 = 40_{\text{six}}$

$10 \times 20 = 1 \text{ six} \times 2 \text{ sixes} = 2 \cdot 6^2 + 0 \cdot 6^1 + 0 \cdot 6^0 = 200_{\text{six}}$

$10 \times 300 = 1 \text{ six} \times 3 \text{ thirty-sixes} = 3 \cdot 6^3 + 0 \cdot 6^2 + 0 \cdot 6^1 + 0 \cdot 6^0 = 3000_{\text{six}}$

To check, we convert all numerals to base ten:

$$
\begin{aligned}
324_{\text{six}} &= 3 \cdot 6^2 + 2 \cdot 6^1 + 4 \cdot 6^0 \\
&= 3 \cdot 36 + 2 \cdot 6 + 4 \cdot 1 \\
&= 108 + 12 + 4 = 124_{\text{ten}}
\end{aligned}
$$

$$15_{six} = 1 \cdot 6^1 + 5 \cdot 6^0$$
$$= 1 \cdot 6 + 5 \cdot 1$$
$$= 6 + 5 = 11_{ten}$$
$$10{,}152_{six} = 1 \cdot 6^4 + 0 \cdot 6^3 + 1 \cdot 6^2 + 5 \cdot 6^1 + 2 \cdot 6^0$$
$$= 1 \cdot 1296 + 0 \cdot 216 + 1 \cdot 36 + 5 \cdot 6 + 2 \cdot 1$$
$$= 1296 + 36 + 30 + 2 = 1364_{ten}$$

Since $11_{ten} \cdot 124_{ten} = 1364_{ten}$, the check is complete.

## Division Algorithms

An approach to division discussed in Chapter 2 was repeated subtraction. This ultimately led to the so-called **division algorithm,** which we restate here for easy reference: The division algorithm is the foundation for the ways in which we actually do the division of one whole number by another. This foundation leads to a number of different algorithms, including the **long-division, short-division,** and **scaffold** (also called **pyramid**) algorithms, which are discussed next. We now return to base ten.

> **THEOREM** *The Division Algorithm*
> If $a$ and $b$ are whole numbers with $b$ not zero, there exists exactly one pair of whole numbers $q$ and $r$ with $0 \leq r < b$ such that $a = bq + r$. $q$ is the **quotient,** and $r$ is the **remainder,** of $a$ divided by $b$.

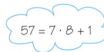

**The Long-Division Algorithm**   Suppose we want to divide 941 by 7. Doing this by repeated subtraction will take a long time, even with a calculator. But suppose we subtract several 7s at a time and keep track of the number we subtract each time. Indeed, since it is so easy to multiply a number by 10, 100, 1000, and so on, let's subtract hundreds of 7s, tens of 7s, and so on. The work might be organized like this:

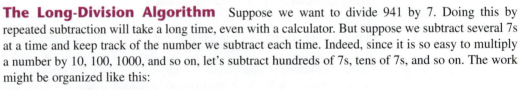

$$
\begin{array}{r}
7\overline{)941} \\
\underline{700} \quad \text{Subtract} \quad 100 \quad \text{7s} \\
241 \\
\underline{70} \quad \text{Subtract} \quad 10 \quad \text{7s} \\
171 \\
\underline{70} \quad \text{Subtract} \quad 10 \quad \text{7s} \\
101 \\
\underline{70} \quad \text{Subtract} \quad 10 \quad \text{7s} \\
31 \\
\underline{28} \quad \text{Subtract} \quad \underline{\phantom{0}4} \quad \text{7s} \\
3 \qquad\qquad 134 \quad \text{number of 7s subtracted}
\end{array}
$$

Since $3 < 7$, the process stops and we see that 941 divided by 7 gives a quotient of 134 and a remainder of 3. As a check, we note that $941 = 7 \cdot 134 + 3$. The preceding work could have been shortened if we had subtracted the three tens of 7s all at once and then the four 7s all at once, like this:

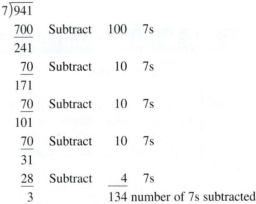

$$
\begin{array}{r}
7\overline{)941} \\
\underline{700} \quad 100 \quad \text{7s} \\
241 \\
\underline{210} \quad 30 \quad \text{7s} \\
31 \\
\underline{28} \quad \underline{\phantom{0}4} \quad \text{7s} \\
3 \qquad 134
\end{array}
$$

A slightly different form of this algorithm, which we call the **scaffold algorithm,** is obtained by writing the 100, 30, and 4 above the division symbol. This algorithm is also known as the **pyramid algorithm** and appears as follows:

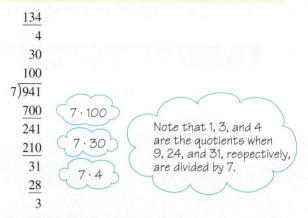

$$
\begin{array}{r}
134 \\
\underline{\phantom{0}4} \\
30 \\
100 \\
7\overline{)941} \\
\underline{700} \quad 7 \cdot 100 \\
241 \\
\underline{210} \quad 7 \cdot 30 \\
31 \\
\underline{28} \quad 7 \cdot 4 \\
3
\end{array}
$$

Note that 1, 3, and 4 are the quotients when 9, 24, and 31, respectively, are divided by 7.

Many teachers prefer the scaffold algorithm as the final algorithm for division, since it fully displays the mathematics being done. Others still cling to the following form, which is easily obtained from the scaffold algorithm, even though it seriously masks the mathematics and forces many students to rely on rote memorization rather than understanding:

$$
\begin{array}{r}
1 \;\; 3 \, 4 \\
7\overline{)9{}^{2}4{}^{3}1} \\
\underline{7} \\
24 \\
\underline{21} \\
31 \\
\underline{28} \\
3
\end{array}
$$

Look at how compressed the notation is in this long-division algorithm or in the final algorithm compared with the scaffold algorithm. It may be that the notation is simplified, but the concepts can be obscured in the long-division or final algorithm.

A further example with a larger divisor may be helpful.

**EXAMPLE 3.16  Using the Long-Division Algorithm**

Divide 28,762 by 307.

**Solution**

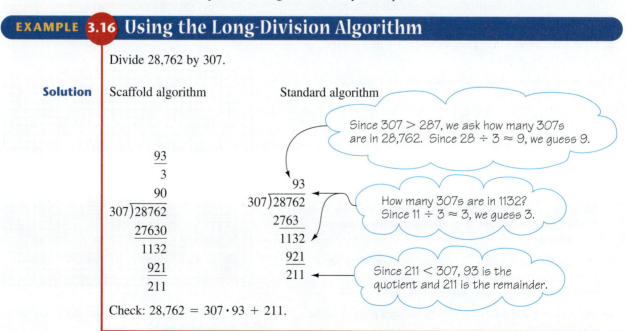

Scaffold algorithm

$$
\begin{array}{r}
93 \\
\underline{\phantom{0}3} \\
90 \\
307\overline{)28762} \\
\underline{27630} \\
1132 \\
\underline{921} \\
211
\end{array}
$$

Standard algorithm

$$
\begin{array}{r}
93 \\
307\overline{)28762} \\
\underline{2763} \\
1132 \\
\underline{921} \\
211
\end{array}
$$

Since 307 > 287, we ask how many 307s are in 28,762. Since 28 ÷ 3 ≈ 9, we guess 9.

How many 307s are in 1132? Since 11 ÷ 3 ≈ 3, we guess 3.

Since 211 < 307, 93 is the quotient and 211 is the remainder.

Check: $28{,}762 = 307 \cdot 93 + 211$.

**The Short-Division Algorithm**  A division algorithm that is quite useful, even in this calculator age, is the **short-division** algorithm. This is a much simplified version of the long-division algorithm and is quite useful and quick when the divisor is a single digit. It can be developed from the scaffold method as we did a moment ago. Also, it follows directly from the long-division algorithm if that is already known.

---

**EXAMPLE 3.17  Using the Short-Division Algorithm**

Divide 2834 by 3 and check your answer.

**Solution**  Consider the following divisions, which show how the short-division algorithm comes from the long-division algorithm:

$$
\begin{array}{r}
944 \\
3\overline{)2834} \\
27 \\
\hline
13 \\
12 \\
\hline
14 \\
12 \\
\hline
2
\end{array}
$$

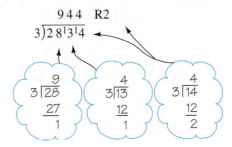

---

## Problem Set 3.4

Exercises numbered in red are answered in the back of the text.

### Understanding Concepts

*(Note: Problems 1 through 11 are all base-ten problems.)*

1. **(a)** Make a suitable drawing of units and strips to illustrate the product $4 \cdot 8 = 32$.

   **(b)** Make a suitable sketch of place-value cards to illustrate the product $4 \cdot 8 = 32$.

2. Make a suitable sketch of place-value cards to illustrate the product $3 \cdot 254 = 762$.

3. **(a)** In the product shown, what does the red 2 actually represent?

   $$
   \begin{array}{r}
   \overset{2}{274} \\
   \times\ 34 \\
   \hline
   1096 \\
   8220 \\
   \hline
   9316
   \end{array}
   $$

   **(b)** In the product shown in part (a), when multiplying $4 \cdot 7$, one "exchanges" a 2. What is actually being exchanged?

4. The diagram shown in the next column illustrates the product $27 \cdot 32$. Discuss how this product is related to finding the product by the instructional algorithm for multiplication.

5. Justify each step in this calculation by stating a property of the whole numbers:

$$
\begin{array}{ll}
17 \cdot 4 = (10 + 7) \cdot 4 & \text{expanded notation} \\
= 10 \cdot 4 + 7 \cdot 4 & \text{(a) _____} \\
= 10 \cdot 4 + 28 & \text{one-digit multiplication fact} \\
= 10 \cdot 4 + (2 \cdot 10 + 8) & \text{expanded notation} \\
= 4 \cdot 10 + (2 \cdot 10 + 8) & \text{(b) _____} \\
= (4 \cdot 10 + 2 \cdot 10) + 8 & \text{(c) _____} \\
= (4 + 2) \cdot 10 + 8 & \text{(d) _____} \\
= 6 \cdot 10 + 8 & \text{one-digit addition fact} \\
= 68 & \text{expanded notation}
\end{array}
$$

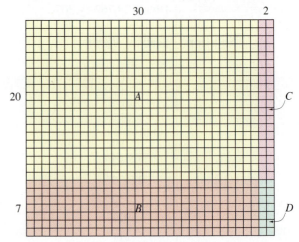

6. Draw a sequence of sketches of units, strips, and mats to illustrate dividing 429 by 3.

**7.** What calculation does this sequence of sketches illustrate? Explain briefly.

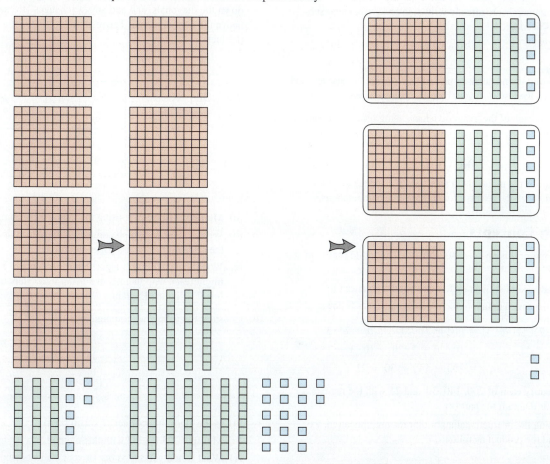

**8.** Multiply 352 by 27, using the instructional algorithm for multiplication.

**9.** Find the quotient $q$ and a remainder $r$ when $a$ is divided by $b$, and write the result in the form $a = bq + r$ of the division algorithm for each of these choices of $a$ and $b$:

(a) $a = 27, b = 4$

(b) $a = 354, b = 29$

(c) $a = 871, b = 17$

**10.** Perform each of the given divisions by the scaffold method. In each case, check your results by using the equation of the division algorithm.

(a) $351\overline{)7425}$     (b) $23\overline{)6814}$     (c) $213\overline{)3175}$

**11.** Use short division to find the quotient and remainder for each division given. Check each result.

(a) $5\overline{)873}$     (b) $7\overline{)2432}$     (c) $8\overline{)10,095}$

*(Note: Problems 12 through 15 are in bases other than ten.)*

**12.** Construct base-five addition and multiplication tables.

**13.** What is being illustrated by the given sequence of sketches of place-value cards? Explain briefly.

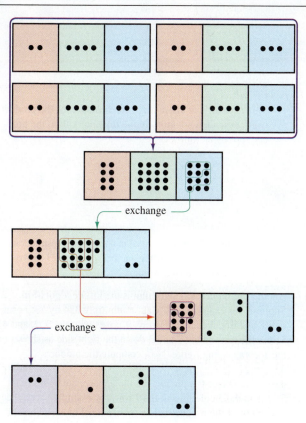

**14.** Carry out the multiplications shown, using base-five notation. All the numerals are already written in base five, so no subscript is needed.

(a)   23
    $\times$ 3

(b)   432
    $\times$ 41

(c)   2013
    $\times$ 23

(d) Convert the numerals in parts (a), (b), and (c) to base ten, and check the results of your base-five computations.

**15.** Carry out each of the given divisions, using base-five notation. All numerals are already in base five, so the subscripts are omitted.

(a) 4)231

(b) 32)2342

(c) 213)34,122

(d) Convert the numerals in parts (a), (b), and (c) to base ten, and check the results of your base-five computations.

## Teaching Concepts

**16.** Problem 4 of this problem set shows a diagram to represent the product $27 \cdot 32$.

(a) Draw a similar diagram to represent the product $17 \cdot 23$.

(b) In expanded notation, the product appears as follows:

$$(10 + 7) \cdot (20 + 3) = (10 + 7) \cdot 20 + (10 + 7) \cdot 3$$
$$= 10 \cdot 20 + 7 \cdot 20 + 10 \cdot 3 + 7 \cdot 3$$
$$= 200 + 140 + 30 + 21$$

Identify each of 200, 140, 30, and 21 with the regions in your diagram for part (a).

(c) Using the instructional algorithm for multiplication, we find the product as follows:

```
   23
   17
   21
  140
   30
  200
  391
```

This is clearly an alternative representation of the product, using expanded notation. In the final algorithm, the product appears as follows:

```
    2
   23
   17
  161
   23
  391
```

Explain the 2 that is exchanged in terms of the instructional algorithm, and show how the numbers 161 and 23 derive from the instructional algorithm.

**17.** Another multiplication algorithm is the **lattice algorithm.** Suppose, for example, you want to multiply 324 by 73. Form a two-by-three rectangular array of boxes with the 3, 2, and 4 across the top and the 7 and 3 down the right side as shown in the accompanying figure. Now compute the products $3 \cdot 7 = 21, 2 \cdot 7 = 14, 4 \cdot 7 = 28, 3 \cdot 3 = 9, 2 \cdot 3 = 6$, and $4 \cdot 3 = 12$. Place the products in the appropriate boxes (e.g., $3 \cdot 7$ is in the 3 column and the 7 row, for example), with the units digit of the product below the diagonal in each box and

the tens digit (if there is one) above the diagonal. Now add down the diagonals, and add any "exchanges" to the sum above the next diagonal. The result of 23,652 is the desired product.

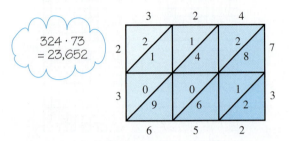

(a) Multiply 374 by 215, using the lattice algorithm.

(b) Write a short paragraph comparing the lattice algorithm with the standard pencil-and-paper algorithm.

(c) Would presenting this algorithm to students in a class you might teach help them gain a better understanding of positional notation? Explain.

**18.** Consider the following computation:

```
    374
 ×   23
    748
   1122
   8602
```

(a) Is the algorithm correct? Explain briefly.

(b) Multiply 285 by 362 with this method.

(c) What would you say to one of your students who multiplied multidigit numbers in the manner shown here? Would you insist that there is really just one correct way to perform the pencil-and-paper calculation? Explain.

## Responding to Students

**19.** Look at "from The NCTM Principles and Standards" on page 158 of this section. How would you respond to Henry if you were Ms. Sparks?

**20.** Hector, a fourth-grade student, has not had previous instruction in two-digit–by–two-digit multiplication and attempted a two-digit multiplication problem as follows:

```
     39
 ×   42
 15,276
```

What algorithm was he trying to use, but did so incorrectly?

**21.** What division errors by the fourth graders do you see in each problem?

(a)
```
    220
 3)862
```

(b)
```
      2
 3)862
  -6↓↓
   262
```

(c)
```
   28R2
 3)806
  -6 ↓
    26
   -24
     2
```

**22.** Why might a third- or fourth-grade student struggle with the following division problem? Find the number for the blank if
___ ÷ 3 = 8.

## Thinking Critically

**23.** The *Egyptian algorithm* for multiplication was one of the interesting subjects explained in the Rhind papyrus mentioned in Chapters 1 and 2. We will explain the algorithm with an example. Suppose we want to compute 19 times 35. Successively doubling 35, we obtain this list:

$$\to \quad 1 \cdot 35 = \quad 35$$
$$\to \quad 2 \cdot 35 = \quad 70$$
$$4 \cdot 35 = 140$$
$$8 \cdot 35 = 280$$
$$\to 16 \cdot 35 = 560$$

$19 = 1 + 2 + 16$

Adding the results in the indicated rows gives us 665 as the desired product.

**(a)** After carefully considering the preceding computation, write a short paragraph explaining how and why the process always works.

**(b)** This scheme is also known as the *duplation algorithm*. Use duplation to find the product of 24 and 71.

**24.** The *Russian peasant algorithm* for multiplication is similar to the duplation algorithm described in problem 23. To find the product of 34 and 54, for example, successively divide the 34 by 2 (ignoring remainders if they occur) and successively multiply 54 by 2. This gives the following lists:

| 34 | 54 |
|----|-----|
| 17 | 108 |
| 8 | 216 |
| 4 | 432 |
| 2 | 864 |
| 1 | 1728 |
| | 1836 |

Now cross out the even numbers in the left-hand column and the companion numbers in the right-hand column. Add the remaining numbers in the right-hand column to obtain the desired product. To see why the process works, consider the products $34 \cdot 54 = 1836$ and $17 \cdot 108 = 1836$. Also, consider $8 \cdot 216, 4 \cdot 432,$ and $2 \cdot 864$.

**(a)** Why are $34 \cdot 54$ and $17 \cdot 108$ the same?

**(b)** Why are $17 \cdot 108$ and $8 \cdot 216$ different? How much do they differ?

**(c)** Why are $8 \cdot 216, 4 \cdot 432, 2 \cdot 864,$ and $1 \cdot 1728$ all the same?

**(d)** Write a short paragraph explaining why the Russian peasant algorithm works.

**(e)** Use the Russian peasant algorithm to compute $29 \cdot 81$ and $11 \cdot 243$.

## Thinking Cooperatively

Divide into small groups to work each of the next four problems. In each case, discuss possible strategies among the members of your group and develop an answer agreed upon by the entire group.

**25.** Use each of 1, 3, 5, 7, and 9 once, and only once, in the boxes to obtain the largest possible product in each case:

**(a)**

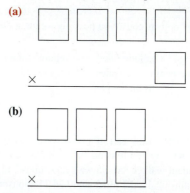

**(b)**

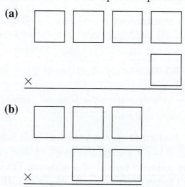

**26.** Use each of 1, 3, 5, 7, and 9 once, and only once, in the boxes to obtain the smallest possible product in each case:

**(a)**

**(b)**

**27.** A druggist has a balance scale to weigh objects. She also has two 1-gram weights, two 3-gram weights, two 9-gram weights, and two 27-gram weights. She places an object to be weighed in one pan and her weights in the other.

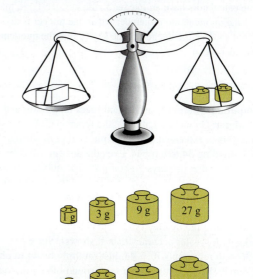

**(a)** What weights can she weigh in this way?

**(b)** What mathematics would this activity be illustrating if you did it in one of your classes?

28. Suppose that you had only one of each type of weight and that you could put weights in both scales, some along with the object being weighed.

    (a) What weights of objects could you possibly weigh in this way?

    (b) Could you "weigh" a balloon filled with helium that was tied to one of the pans of the scales and that exerted an upward pull of 11 grams on the pan?

## Making Connections

29. Alicia, Arturo, and Adam took part in a walk for a charity. Each had sponsors who agreed to contribute 5 dollars for each mile their student walked. Alicia walked 4 miles and had 6 sponsors. Arturo walked 7 miles and had 11 sponsors. Adam walked 8 miles and had 7 sponsors. In all, how much money was contributed to the charity on the students' behalf?

30. On Monday, Melody practiced her piano lesson for 48 minutes. On each of Tuesday and Wednesday, she practiced for a full hour. On Thursday, she practiced for only 35 minutes.

    (a) All told, how many minutes had she practiced before her piano lesson on Friday?

    (b) Express the time Melody practiced in hours and minutes, using as fcw minutes as possible.

31. The students in the third-grade class at Franklin Grade School wanted to earn $165 to buy a wheelchair for one of their classmates who had been seriously injured in an accident. The students planned to sell boxes of cookies at $2.25 per box. How many boxes would they need to sell? (*Suggestion:* Express the amounts of money in pennies.)

## Using a Calculator

32. **Computing Quotients on a Calculator with Integer Divide.** Some calculators have an integer divide key, $\boxed{\text{INT} \div}$, that gives the quotient and remainder when one integer is divided by another. Use the integer divide key to find the quotient and remainder when

    (a) 723 is divided by 37.

    (b) 34,723 is divided by 508.

33. **Computing Quotients and Remainders on a Standard Calculator.** On most calculators, the remainder of a division of integers is expressed as the decimal part of the display. Thus, dividing 34,678 by 44 gives the answer 788.13636 on a calculator that displays eight digits. The quotient is the integer part of the displayed answer, and the decimal part of the display is R ÷ 44, where R is the remainder. To compute the remainder, subtract the quotient, 788, leaving 0.1363636 in the display (since the calculator actually works with greater accuracy than it shows). Since 0.1363636 represents R ÷ 44, just multiply by 44 to obtain the remainder. Actually, because of round-off error, your calculator may give 5.9999997, which you should interpret as 6, since R is a whole number. To check, note that 34,678 = 788 · 44 + 6. Note also that other calculators may well give something different from 5.9999997, depending on their built-in accuracy, but it will be a number quite close to 6 and should be so interpreted. Without resorting to the integer divide key, use your calculator to compute the quotient and remainder when

    (a) 276,523 is divided by 511.

    (b) 347,285 is divided by 87.

    (c) 374,821 is divided by 357.

## From State Student Assessments

34. (Washington State, Grade 4)
    When Lori tries multiplying with her calculator, she gets the following results:

    $$8 \times 3 = 34 \qquad 4 \times 2 = 18$$
    $$9 \times 5 = 55 \qquad 8 \times 4 = 42$$

    Lori knows her multiplication facts and knows that something is wrong with her calculator. She wants to multiply $9 \times 6$. Explain what is wrong with Lori's calculator and tell what she needs to do to get the correct answer. Use words, numbers, or pictures.

35. (Connecticut, Grade 4)
    Which number fact goes with this picture?

    | ☺ | ☺ | ☺ |
    |---|---|---|
    | ☺ | ☺ | ☺ |
    | ☺ | ☺ | ☺ |
    | ☺ | ☺ | ☺ |
    | ☺ | ☺ | ☺ |

    $$5 + 3 =$$
    $$5 \div 3 =$$
    $$5 \times 3 =$$
    $$5 - 3 =$$

36. (Texas, Grade 4)
    Which number sentence should **NOT** have a 6 in the box?

    **A.** $18 \div \square = 3$      **B.** $28 \div 4 = \square$

    **C.** $30 \div \square = 5$      **D.** $36 \div 6 = \square$

37. (Kentucky, Grade 5)
    Grandpa gave his collection of 584 pennies to his 8 grandchildren. If each grandchild received the same number of pennies, how many pennies did each child get?

    Which computation can be used to solve the preceding problem?

    **A.** $584 \times 8$      **B.** $584 \div 8$

    **C.** $584 + 8$      **D.** $584 - 8$

*Refer to the School Book Pages provided on page 170 to answer the following questions.*

## Examining School Book Pages

**38.** Write a paragraph describing the **Understand It!** statement on p. 82 of the School Book Page, emphasizing what you believe is the key point of that statement.

**39.** Problem 31 on p. 83 of the School Book Page is an example of prealgebra.

**(a)** What is the correct answer to the problem as stated?

**(b)** What is another correct answer that could be added to the list?

**(c)** If you were to give this question to your fourth-grade class, would you prefer a multiple-choice or an open-response answer?

**40.** Problem 29 on p. 83 of the School Book Page is different from the other problems on the page. Why do you think that the authors might have included this problem?

## Calvin and Hobbes                          by Bill Watterson

## 3.5

# Mental Arithmetic and Estimation

We start with mental arithmetic by looking at techniques such as easy combinations, making adjustments, and working from left to right.

### The One-Digit Facts

It is essential that the basic addition and multiplication facts be memorized, since all other numerical calculations and estimations depend on that foundation. At the same time, this should not be rote memorization of symbols. Using a variety of concrete objects, students should actually *experience* the fact that $8 + 7 = 15$, that $9 \cdot 7 = 63$, and so on. Moreover, rather than having children simply memorize the addition and multiplication tables, the tables should be learned by the frequent and long-term use of manipulatives, games, puzzles, oral activities, and appropriate problem-solving activities. In the same way, children learn the basic properties of the whole numbers, which, in turn, can be used to recall some momentarily forgotten arithmetic fact. For example, $7 + 8$ can be recalled as $7 + 7 + 1$, $6 \cdot 9$ can be recalled as $5 \cdot 9 + 9$ or as $6 \cdot 10 - 6$, and so on. In the same way, the properties of whole numbers, along with the **one-digit facts,** form the basis for mental calculation.

### Easy Combinations

There are several strategies for mental calculation. One is to always look for **easy combinations,** especially regrouping to find multiples of 10. The next example shows how this works.

# Special Quotients

*See "Examining School Book Pages" on page 169 for questions related to the pages shown below.*

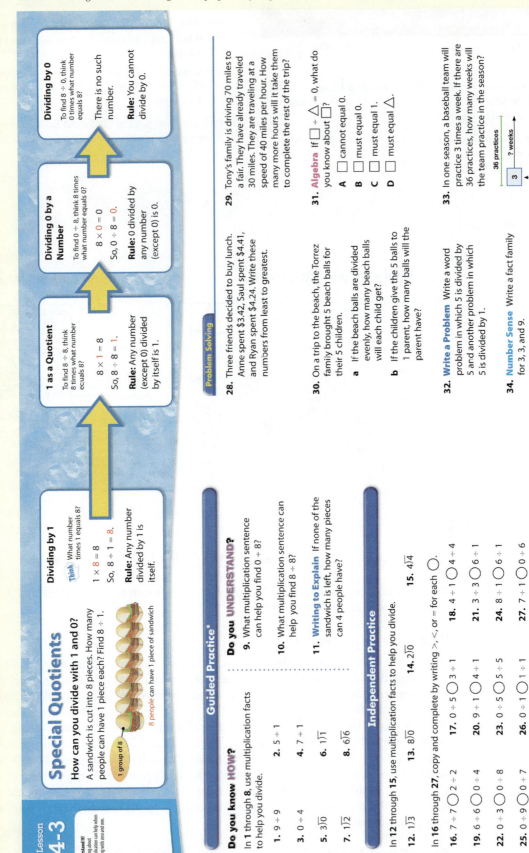

**Lesson 4-3**

**Understand It!**
Thinking about multiplication can help when dividing with zero and one.

## Special Quotients

### How can you divide with 1 and 0?

A sandwich is cut into 8 pieces. How many people can have 1 piece each? Find 8 ÷ 1.

8 people can have 1 piece of sandwich

1 group of 8

### Dividing by 1

**Think** What number times 1 equals 8?

$1 × 8 = 8$

So, $8 ÷ 1 = 8$.

**Rule:** Any number divided by 1 is itself.

### 1 as a Quotient

To find 8 ÷ 8, think 8 times what number equals 8?

$8 × 1 = 8$

So, $8 ÷ 8 = 1$.

**Rule:** Any number (except 0) divided by itself is 1.

### Dividing 0 by a Number

To find 0 ÷ 8, think 8 times what number equals 0?

$8 × 0 = 0$

So, $0 ÷ 8 = 0$.

**Rule:** 0 divided by any number (except 0) is 0.

### Dividing by 0

To find 8 ÷ 0, think 0 times what number equals 8?

There is no such number.

**Rule:** You cannot divide by 0.

---

## Guided Practice*

### Do you know HOW?

In **1** through **8**, use multiplication facts to help you divide.

**1.** 9 ÷ 9     **2.** 5 ÷ 1

**3.** 0 ÷ 4     **4.** 7 ÷ 1

**5.** $3\overline{)0}$     **6.** $1\overline{)1}$

**7.** $1\overline{)2}$     **8.** $6\overline{)6}$

### Do you UNDERSTAND?

**9.** What multiplication sentence can help you find 0 ÷ 8?

**10.** What multiplication sentence can help you find 8 ÷ 8?

**11.** **Writing to Explain** If none of the sandwich is left, how many pieces can 4 people have?

## Independent Practice

In **12** through **15**, use multiplication facts to help you divide.

**12.** $1\overline{)3}$    **13.** $8\overline{)0}$    **14.** $2\overline{)0}$    **15.** $4\overline{)4}$

In **16** through **27**, copy and complete by writing >, <, or = for each ◯.

**16.** 7 ÷ 7 ◯ 2 ÷ 2    **17.** 0 ÷ 5 ◯ 3 ÷ 1    **18.** 4 ÷ 1 ◯ 4 ÷ 4

**19.** 6 ÷ 6 ◯ 0 ÷ 4    **20.** 9 ÷ 1 ◯ 4 ÷ 1    **21.** 3 ÷ 3 ◯ 6 ÷ 1

**22.** 0 ÷ 3 ◯ 0 ÷ 8    **23.** 0 ÷ 5 ◯ 5 ÷ 5    **24.** 8 ÷ 1 ◯ 6 ÷ 1

**25.** 0 ÷ 9 ◯ 0 ÷ 7    **26.** 0 ÷ 1 ◯ 1 ÷ 1    **27.** 7 ÷ 1 ◯ 0 ÷ 6

*For another example, see Set C on page 93.

**82**

---

### Problem Solving

**28.** Three friends decided to buy lunch. Anne spent $3.42, Saul spent $4.41, and Ryan spent $4.24. Write these numbers from least to greatest.

**29.** Tony's family is driving 70 miles to a fair. They have already traveled 30 miles. They are traveling at a speed of 40 miles per hour. How many more hours will it take them to complete the rest of the trip?

**30.** On a trip to the beach, the Torrez family brought 5 beach balls for their 5 children.

  **a** If the beach balls are divided evenly, how many beach balls will each child get?

  **b** If the children give the 5 balls to 1 parent, how many balls will the parent have?

**31.** **Algebra** If □ ÷ △ = 0, what do you know about □?

  **A** □ cannot equal 0.

  **B** □ must equal 0.

  **C** □ must equal 1.

  **D** △ must equal 0.

**32.** **Write a Problem** Write a word problem in which 5 is divided by 5 and another problem in which 5 is divided by 1.

**33.** In one season, a baseball team will practice 3 times a week. If there are 36 practices, how many weeks will the team practice in the season?

36 practices

? weeks

3 ← Practices in one week

**34.** **Number Sense** Write a fact family for 3, 3, and 9.

Lesson 4-3    **83**

---

**EXAMPLE 3.18 Using Easy Combinations**

Use mental processes to perform these calculations:

(a) $35 + 7 + 15$      (b) $8 + 3 + 4 + 6 + 7 + 12 + 4 + 3 + 6 + 3$

(c) $25 \cdot 8$      (d) $4 \cdot 99$      (e) $57 - 25$      (f) $47 \cdot 5$

**Solution**

(a) Using the commutative and associative properties, we have

$$35 + 7 + 15 = 35 + 5 + 10 + 7 = 40 + 10 + 7 = 50 + 7 = 57.$$

Think    $35, 40, 50, 57$    The answer is 57.

(b) Note numbers that add to 10 or multiples of 10:

$$8 + 3 + 4 + 6 + 7 + 12 + 4 + 3 + 6 + 3 = 56$$

Think    $20, 30, 40, 50, 53, 56$    The answer is 56.

(c) $25 \cdot 8 = 25 \cdot 4 \cdot 2 = 100 \cdot 2 = 200$

Think    $25, 100, 200$    The answer is 200.

(d) $4 \cdot 99 = 4(100 - 1) = 400 - 4 = 396$

Think    $400 - 4 = 396$

(e) $57 - 25 = 50 - 25 + 7 = 25 + 7 = 32$

Think    $50 = 2 \cdot 25$, so $50 - 25$ plus 7 gives 32.

Think    Two quarters are worth 50¢.

(f) $47 \cdot 5 = 47 \cdot 10 \div 2 = 470 \div 2 = 235$

Think    $47, 470, 235$

## Adjustment

In parts (d) and (e) of Example 3.18, we made use of the fact that 99 and 57 are close to 100 and 50, respectively. This is an example of adjustment. **Adjustment** simply means that, at the beginning of a calculation, we modify numbers to minimize the mental effort required by adding zero. In Example 3.19a, the key is that $3 - 3 = 0$.

## EXAMPLE 3.19 Using Adjustment in Mental Calculation

Use mental processes to perform these calculations:

**(a)** $57 + 84$      **(b)** $83 - 48$      **(c)** $286 + 347$
**(d)** $493 \cdot 7$      **(e)** $2646 \div 9$      **(f)** $639 \div 7$

**Solution**

**(a)** $57 + 84 = (57 + 3) + (84 - 3)$
$= 60 + 81 = 60 + 80 + 1$
$= 140 + 1 = 141$

Think    $57 + 84$,   $60 + 81$,   $140$,   $141$

**(b)** $83 - 48 = (83 + 2) - (48 + 2) = 85 - 50 = 35$

Think    $83 - 48$,   $85 - 50$,   $35$

**(c)** $286 + 347 = (286 + 14) + (347 - 14)$
$= 300 + 300 + 47 - 14$
$= 600 + 33 = 633$

Think    $300$,   $647 - 14$,   $633$

**(d)** $493 \cdot 7 = (500 - 7) \cdot 7 = 3500 - 49 = 3451$

Think    $(500 - 7) \cdot 7$,   $3500 - 49$,   $3451$

**(e)** $2646 \div 9 = (2700 - 54) \div 9 = 300 - 6 = 294$

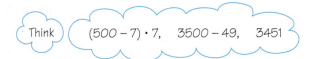

Think    $\div 9$,   $2700 - 54$,   $300 - 6$,   $294$

**(f)** $639 \div 7 = (630 + 7 + 2) \div 7 = 90 + 1 \, \text{R} \, 2 = 91 \, \text{R} \, 2$

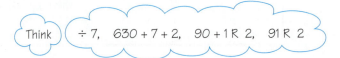

Think    $\div 7$,   $630 + 7 + 2$,   $90 + 1 \, \text{R} \, 2$,   $91 \, \text{R} \, 2$

## Working from Left to Right

Because it tends to reduce the amount one has to remember, many expert mental calculators **work from left to right,** rather than the other way around as in most of our standard algorithms.

**EXAMPLE  3.20  Working from Left to Right**

Use mental processes to perform these calculations:

(a) $352 + 647$    (b) $739 - 224$    (c) $4 \cdot 235$

**Solution**

(a) $352 + 647 = (300 + 50 + 2) + (600 + 40 + 7)$
$\qquad\qquad\quad = (300 + 600) + (50 + 40) + (2 + 7)$
$\qquad\qquad\quad = 900 + 90 + 9 = 999$

> Think  *900, 990, 999*

(b) $739 - 224 = (700 + 30 + 9) - (200 + 20 + 4)$
$\qquad\qquad\quad = (700 - 200) + (30 - 20) + (9 - 4)$
$\qquad\qquad\quad = 500 + 10 + 5 = 515$

> Think  *500, 510, 515*

(c) $4 \cdot 235 = 4(200 + 30 + 5)$
$\qquad\quad = 800 + 120 + 20$
$\qquad\quad = 920 + 20$
$\qquad\quad = 940$

> Think  *800, 120, 920, 940*

Left-to-right methods often combine nicely with an understanding of positional notation to simplify mental calculation. For example, since $4200 = 42 \cdot 100$, we might compute the sum

$$
\begin{array}{r}
3700 \\
900 \\
2800 \\
+\ 5600 \\
\end{array}
$$

by thinking of

$$
\begin{array}{r}
37 \\
9 \\
28 \\
+\ 56 \\
\end{array}
$$

Then, working from left to right, we think

> *30, 50, 100, 107, 116, 124, 130 times 100. The answer is 13,000.*

## Estimation

The ever-increasing use of calculators and computers makes it essential that students develop skill at **computational estimation** (or **estimation,** for short.) On the one hand, if you are asked to multiply .983 by 1.17, you will need a calculator, of course. On the other hand, since both numbers are about 1, you should expect the answer to be close to 1. If the number on the calculator comes out to be 234.5623 for the product, then, clearly, you have entered at least one of the two numbers incorrectly. Your skill at estimation enables you to recognize, without much work, that you couldn't possibly have the correct answer.

The goal of estimation is to be able to see, without doing much computation yourself, how large an answer should be or what it should be close to. In order to have that ability, comfort with doing simple arithmetic should be of second nature. For example, the *NCTM Principles and Standards* says that students should ". . . compute fluently and makes reasonable estimates." (For more details, see the NCTM's view of estimation on this page.)

## Estimation

Estimation serves as an important companion to computation. It provides a tool for judging the reasonableness of calculator, mental, and paper-and-pencil computations. However, being able to compute exact answers does not automatically lead to an ability to estimate or judge the reasonableness of answers, as Reys and Yang (1998) found in their work with sixth and eighth graders. Students in grades 3–5 will need to be encouraged to routinely reflect on the size of an anticipated solution. Will $7 \times 18$ be smaller or larger than 100? If 3/8 of a cup of sugar is needed for a recipe and the recipe is doubled, will more or less than one cup of sugar be needed? Instructional attention and frequent modeling by the teacher can help students develop a range of computational estimation strategies including flexible rounding, the use of benchmarks, and front-end strategies. Students should be encouraged to frequently explain their thinking as they estimate. As with exact computation, sharing estimation strategies allows students to access others' thinking and provides many opportunities for rich class discussions.

SOURCE: *Principles and Standards for School Mathematics* by NCTM, *pages 155–156. Copyright © 2000 by the National Council of Teachers of Mathematics. Reproduced with permission of the National Council of Teachers of Mathematics via Copyright Clearance Center. NCTM does not endorse the content or validity of these alignments.*

## Front-End Method

Another method, which is even easier than the previous one, also starts on the left, but then almost ignores the other digits. This approach, called **front-end estimation,** adds the numbers under the assumption that all their digits except the first on the left are zero and then makes some changes on the basis of the second digit. Here's an example:

### EXAMPLE 3.21    Front-End Addition and Subtraction

Use front-end estimation to give an approximate answer to each of the following problems:

**(a)** $352 + 647$         **(b)** $739 - 224$

**Solution**

**(a)** By ignoring the second and third digits, we first think of $300 + 600 = 900$. However (and this is the "make some changes" part), considering that there are 5 tens in the first number and 4 tens in the second, we estimate that we need to adjust our original estimation of 900 by adding 9 tens, or about 100. Thus, we have the better estimate of 1000 for an answer.

**(b)** Here we think of the answer as being close to $700 - 200 = 500$. When we look at the second digits, there are 3 tens from which we could subtract 2 tens, so no adjustment is needed.

Note that, on the one hand, the answers to Examples 3.20 and 3.21 are close, but not the same. That shouldn't be surprising, since we are only estimating, not trying to find the exact answer. On the other hand, the two examples should end up with numbers that are close.

## Rounding

Often, we are *not* interested in exact values. This is certainly true when we are *estimating* the results of numerical calculations, and it is frequently the case that exact values are actually unobtainable. What does it mean, for example, to say that the population of California in 2000 was 28,874,293? Even if this is supposed to be the actual count on a given day, it is almost surely in error because of the sheer difficulty in conducting a census. What does "population" mean? At first, it seems obvious, but does the term include transients, those who have a home in California and in other states, or those who are homeless? How does one keep track of births and deaths during the year? Just defining the term *population* is difficult. In gross terms, it is probably accurate to say that the population of California was approximately 29,000,000, or 29 million people. To obtain this figure, we **round** to the nearest million. This is accomplished by considering the digit in the hundred thousands position. If this digit is 5 or more, we increase the digit in the millions position by 1 and replace all the digits to the right of this position by 0s. If the hundred thousands digit is 4 or less, we leave the millions digit unchanged and replace all the digits to its right by 0s.

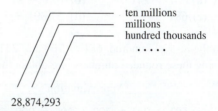

28,874,293

> ### Rounding by Using the 5-Up Rule
> **(i)** Determine to which position you are rounding.
> **(ii)** If the digit to the right of this position is 5 or more, add 1 to the digit in the position to which you are rounding. Otherwise, leave the digit unchanged.
> **(iii)** Replace with 0s all digits to the right of the position to which you are rounding.

**EXAMPLE 3.22  Using the 5-Up Rule to Round Whole Numbers**

Round 27,250 to the position indicated.

**(a)** The nearest ten thousand.       **(b)** The nearest thousand.
**(c)** The nearest hundred.            **(d)** The nearest ten.

**Solution**

**(a)** The digit in the ten thousands position is 2. Since the digit to its right is 7 and $7 > 5$, we add 1 to 2 and replace all digits to the right of the rounded digit with 0s. This gives 30,000.

**(b)** This time 7 is the critical digit, and 2 is the digit to its right. Thus, to the nearest thousand, 27,250 is rounded to 27,000.

**(c)** Here, 2 is the digit in the hundreds position, and 5 is to its right. Thus, 27,250 is rounded to 27,300 to the nearest hundred.

**(d)** This time 5 is the critical digit, and 0 is the digit on its right. Thus, no change need be made, because 27,250 is already rounded to the nearest ten.

## Approximating by Rounding

Rounding is often used in finding estimates. The advantage of **approximating by rounding** is that it gives a single estimate that is reasonably close to the desired answer. The idea is to round the numbers involved in a calculation to the position of the leftmost one or two digits and to use these rounded numbers in making the estimate. For example, consider the sum $467 + 221$. Rounding to the nearest hundred, we have

$$467 \approx 500 \quad \text{and} \quad 221 \approx 200,$$

where we use the symbol $\approx$ to mean "is approximated by." Thus, we obtain the approximation

$$467 + 221 \approx 500 + 200 = 700.$$

The actual answer is 688, so the approximation is reasonably good. Rounding to the nearest ten usually gives an even closer approximation if it is needed. Thus,

$$467 \approx 470, \qquad 221 \approx 220,$$

and $470 + 220$ give the very close approximation 690.

---

**EXAMPLE 3.23** **Approximating by Rounding**

Round to the leftmost digit to find approximate answers to each of these calculations. Also, compute the exact answer in each case.

(a) $681 + 241$      (b) $681 - 241$
(c) $681 \cdot 241$      (d) $57,801 \div 336$

**Solution**

To the nearest hundred, $681 \approx 700$ and $241 \approx 200$. Also, $57,801 \approx 60,000$ and $336 \approx 300$. Using these rounded numbers, we obtain the approximations shown.

Approximation             Exact Answer

(a) $681 + 241 \approx 700 + 200 = 900$      $681 + 241 = 922$
(b) $681 - 241 \approx 700 - 200 = 500$      $681 - 241 = 440$
(c) $681 \cdot 241 \approx 700 \cdot 200 = 140,000$      $681 \cdot 241 = 164,121$
(d) $57,801 \div 336 \approx 60,000 \div 300 = 200$      $57,801 \div 336 = 172 \,\mathrm{R}\, 9$

Here, the quotient is approximately 200.

Note that we round first and then perform the computation to obtain an estimate. Students will mistakenly add first and then round off, defeating the purpose of the method.

---

## Problem Set 3.5

Exercises numbered in red are answered in the back of the text.

### Understanding Concepts

1. Calculate the given expression mentally, using easy combinations. Write a sequence of numbers indicating intermediate steps in your thought process. The first one is done for you.

(a) $7 + 11 + 5 + 3 + 9 + 16 + 4 + 3$

Think   10, 30, 50, 55, 58

(b) $6 + 9 + 17 + 5 + 8 + 12 + 3 + 6$
(c) $27 + 42 + 23$      (d) $47 - 23$
(e) $48 \cdot 5$           (f) $21,600 \div 50$

2. Calculate mentally, using adjustment. Write down a sequence of numbers indicating intermediate steps in your thought process. The first one is done for you.

(a) $78 + 64$

Think   80 + 62,   140, 142

(b) $294 + 177$    (c) $306 - 168$    (d) $294 - 102$
(e) $479 + 97$     (f) $3493 \div 7$     (g) $412 \cdot 7$

3. Perform the given calculations mentally from left to right. Write down a sequence of numbers indicating intermediate steps in your thought process.

(a) $425 + 362$    (b) $363 + 274$    (c) $572 - 251$
(d) $764 - 282$    (e) $3 \cdot 342$
(f) $47 + 32 + 71 + 9 + 26 + 32$

**4.** Using the technique of front end estimation, find an approximate value for each of the following:

(a) $425 + 362$      (b) $363 + 274$

(c) $572 - 251$      (d) $764 - 282$

(e) Are you surprised that the answers to this question are not the same as those of number 3?

**5.** Round 631,575 to the

(a) nearest ten thousand.

(b) nearest thousand.

(c) nearest hundred.

**6.** Round each of these numbers to the position indicated:

(a) 947 to the nearest hundred.

(b) 850 to the nearest hundred.

(c) 27,462,312 to the nearest million.

(d) 2461 to the nearest thousand.

**7.** Rounding to the leftmost digit, calculate approximate values for each of these sums and differences:

(a) $478 + 631$    (b) $782 + 346$    (c) $678 - 431$

(d) $257 \cdot 364$    (e) $7403 \cdot 28$    (f) $28{,}329 \div 43$

(g) $71{,}908 \div 824$

**8.** Rounding to the nearest thousand and using mental arithmetic, estimate each of these sums and differences:

(a) 
```
   17,281
    6 564
   12,147
    2 481
 + 13,671
```

(b) 
```
   2734
   3541
   2284
   3478
 + 7124
```

(c) 
```
   28,341
      942
    2 431
    4 716
 + 12,824
```

(d) 
```
    4270
 -  1324
```

(e) 
```
   21,243
 -  7 824
```

(f) 
```
   37,481
 - 16,249
```

 (g) Use your calculator to compute the exact value of the answers to parts (a) through (f).

**9.** Using rounding to the leftmost digit, estimate these products:

(a) $2748 \cdot 31$    (b) $4781 \cdot 342$    (c) $23{,}247 \cdot 357$

 (d) Use your calculator to determine the exact values of the products in parts (a) through (c).

**10.** Use rounding to the leftmost digit to estimate the quotient in each of the following divisions:

(a) $29{,}342 \div 42$    (b) $7431 \div 37$    (c) $79{,}287 \div 429$

(d) Use your calculator to determine the exact (in the case of nonrepeating decimals) values of the quotients in parts (a) through (c).

## Teaching Concepts

**11.** (a) Would rounding to the leftmost digit give a very good estimate of this sum? Why or why not?

```
   1478
   2395
   1492
 + 5481
```

(b) What would you suggest that your students do to obtain a more accurate estimate?

(c) Compute the accurate answer to the addition in part (a).

**12.** How would you respond to one of your students who rounded 27,445 to the nearest thousand as follows: 27,445; 27,450; 27,500; 28,000?

**13.** Read the Number and Operations Standard for Grades 3–5, pages 148–156, from NCTM's *Principles and Standards for School Mathematics,* and write a short critique of the standard discussed there, emphasizing your own reaction. How do these recommendations compare with your own school experience?

**14.** When asked to round 1268 to the nearest ten, Raphael replied that it was 1278. What was the fifth grader thinking?

**15.** When asked to round 8452 to the nearest one hundred, Sally says that the answer is 8000. How would you respond?

**16.** Elementary school students will be asked to round 217 to the nearest ten. Some will write

```
200   300
  ↖   ↗
    217
```

and try to decide whether the answer should be 200 or 300. How would you help them move to a correct approach?

## Responding to Students

**17.** Jean is solving her problems by using rounding. Here is how she solved two problems:

(a) 
```
   449
 + 333
```
782 She says that it rounds to 800.

(b) 
```
   881
 + 449
```
1330 She says that it rounds to 1300.

Is she following rounding procedures for addition? Does rounding work for her? What would you suggest?

**18.** Richard asks his teacher, Ms. Rocchio, why he got an answer different from hers when it came to rounding 845. He rounded 845 to 850 and then rounded 850 to 900. Her answer was 800. Was Richard or Ms. R. correct and why?

## Thinking Critically

**19.** Theresa and Fontaine each used their calculators to compute $357 + 492$. Fontaine's answer was 749 and Theresa's was 849. Who was most likely correct? In two brief sentences, tell how estimation can help you decide whose answer was probably correct.

20. (a) Use rounding to estimate the results of each of the following calculations:

    (i) $\dfrac{452 + 371}{281}$

    (ii) $\dfrac{3 \cdot 271 + 465}{74 + 9}$

    (iii) $\dfrac{845 \cdot 215}{416}$

    (b) Use your calculator to determine the exact answer to each of parts (i) through (iii).

21. Sometimes the last digits of numbers can help you decide whether calculator computations are correct.

    (a) Given that one of 27,453; 27,587; and 27,451 is the correct result of multiplying 283 by 97, which answer is correct?

    (b) In two brief sentences, tell how a consideration of last digits helped you answer part (a).

22. Since 25,781; 24,323; 26,012; and 25,243 are all about the same size, about how large is their sum? Explain briefly.

## Making Connections

23. Utah, Colorado, New Mexico, and Arizona are the only four states in the United States that meet at a common corner. The areas of the four states are, respectively, 82,168 square miles, 103,730 square miles, 121,365 square miles, and 113,642 square miles.

    (a) Mentally estimate the combined area of the four states, writing down a sequence of numerals to indicate your thought process.

    (b) Compute the actual sum of the areas in part (a).

24. At the time it was published, an atlas gave the population of Colorado as 3,849,400.

    (a) Approximately how many people per square mile lived in Colorado at that time? Write down a sequence of numerals to indicate your thought process.

    (b) Determine the answer to part (a) correct to the nearest unit.

25. The same atlas that provided the data in problem 24 gave the area and population of Delaware as 1955 square miles and 731,900 people. About how many times as many people per square mile lived in Delaware as in Colorado at the time the atlas was published? Write down a sequence of numerals to indicate your thought process.

26. While grocery shopping with $40, you buy the following items at the prices listed:

| | |
|---|---|
| 2 gallons of milk | $2.29 a gallon |
| 1 dozen eggs | $1.63 per dozen |
| 2 rolls of paper towels | $1.21 per roll |
| 1 5-pound pork roast | $1.98 per pound |
| 2 boxes of breakfast cereal | $3.19 each |
| 1 azalea | $9.95 each |

    (a) About how much will all of this cost?

    (b) If you don't buy the azalea, about how much change should you receive?

## From State Student Assessments

27. (Connecticut, Grade 4)
    Joe needs to subtract 319 from 799. Which of the following would be BEST for Joe to use to ESTIMATE the difference?

    $$700 - 300$$
    $$700 - 400$$
    $$800 - 300$$
    $$800 - 400$$

28. (Washington State, Grade 4)
    Solve $52 \times 40$.

    **A.** 2800  **B.** 2080  **C.** 280  **D.** 208

29. (Washington State, Grade 4)
    Estimate the answer. Show how you found your estimate.

    $$9\overline{)820}$$

30. (Washington State, Grade 4)
    Solve the problem.

    $$\begin{array}{r} 254 \\ + \ 67 \\ \hline \end{array}$$

    **A.** 211  **B.** 221  **C.** 311  **D.** 321

31. (Georgia, grade 3)
    Which strategy correctly demonstrates $4 \times 38$ using mental math?
    **A.** $4(2 \times 19)$
    **B.** $2 \times 2 \times 38$
    **C.** $2 \times 2 \times 2 \times 19$
    **D.** $(4 \times 30) + (4 \times 8)$

32. (Virginia, Grade 4)
    Which product is between 550 and 600?
    **A.** $52 \times 12$  **B.** $45 \times 12$
    **C.** $56 \times 12$  **D.** $48 \times 12$

## The Chapter in Relation to Future Teachers

Numerals, or symbols for writing numbers, and algorithms (methods for calculating), together called a numeration system, are the basis of Chapter 3. Success in learning math requires, first, that your students have a deep understanding of the concept of positional notation for numbers. A deep understanding of positional notation means realizing that 423 (base ten) is really 4 times $10^2$ + 2 times 10 + 3 ones, and that is the foundational idea which allows children to learn the basic arithmetic operations. Being able to introduce, understand, and use algorithms is what teachers can bring to their students to make mathematics easier and more useful.

Knowledge of the historical background of mathematics is quite helpful in understanding the concepts discussed in any mathematics course. For numeration, a historical approach is especially popular, and we have introduced the reader to the use of the Egyptian, Roman, Babylonian, Mayan, and Indo-Arabic (decimal) systems.

## Chapter 3 Summary

| Section 3.1   Numeration Systems Past and Present | Page Reference |
|---|---|
| **CONCEPTS** | |
| • **Egyptian system:** An additive system using hieroglyphic symbols which was developed for recording numbers on stone tablets as early as 3400 B.C. | 127 |
| • **Roman system:** An additive system using letters or Roman numerals to represent numbers. They are somewhat familiar from their current usage on the faces of analog watches and clocks. | 128 |
| • **Babylonian system:** A base-sixty positional system with just two symbols combined additively to represent the digits 1 through 59. Although a symbol to represent zero was not present originally, the system eventually acquired such a symbol as a placeholder, but not as a number. It introduced the notion of place value. | 129 |
| • **Mayan system:** A positional system to base twenty for the first two positions, while, from the third position on, the positions are $18 \cdot 20, 18 \cdot 20^2, \ldots$ The digits are a rather simple set of well-chosen symbols. | 130, 131 |
| • **Indo-Arabic, or decimal, system:** Also known as the Hindu-Arabic system, this is our present positional base-ten system. | 132 |
| • **Digits and expanded notation:** For example, in base ten, the 10 digits are $0, 1, 2, 3, \ldots, 9$, and $4073 = 4 \cdot 10^3 + 0 \cdot 10^2 + 7 \cdot 10^1 + 3 \cdot 10^0$ is in expanded form. | 133 |
| • **Physical models for positional systems:** Abacus; sticks in a bundle; Unifix™ cubes; units, strips, mats; and base-ten blocks. | 133, 135 |
| **DEFINITIONS** | |
| • **Numerals** are the symbols for writing numbers. | 126 |
| • **Algorithms** are methods for calculating. | 126 |
| • A **numeration system** is any particular system of numerals and algorithms. | 126 |
| • **Place,** or **positional, value** is the notion that the position of a symbol in a numeral determines the value of the numeral. | 129 |
| **FORMULA** | |
| • The **decimal (base 10) system:** The Indo-Arabic system, is a positional numeration system based on the number 10 and is the modern system of numeration. | 126, 132 |
| • **Roman system of numeration:** Consisted of a few letters and made use of a subtractive principle but calculations were cumbersome. | 128 |
| • **Mayan system of numeration:** Consisted of two positional systems, one that used involved hieroglyphics and was based on the number 20, and another that was devised to facilitate computations related to the Mayan calendar. | 130 |

| NOTATION | |
|---|---|
| • **Expanded notation:** The amount each digit contributes to the number is the value of the digit times the value of the position the digit occupies in the representation. For example, $2572 = 2 \cdot 1000 + 5 \cdot 100 + 7 \cdot 10 + 2 \cdot 1$. | 133 |

| Section 3.2   Nondecimal Positional Systems | Page Reference |
|---|---|
| **CONCEPTS** | |
| • **Positional systems:** Notational systems like our present Indo-Arabic system but with bases other than just ten. | 138 |
| • **Converting from base ten to another base:** The method for converting from base-ten notation to notation in another base. | 139, 140 |
| • **Converting from other bases to base ten:** The method for converting from notation in some other base to base-ten notation. | 139 |
| **NOTATION** | |
| • **Base-five notation** is a positional numeration system whose base is the number 5. | 138 |

| Section 3.3   Algorithms for Adding and Subtracting Whole Numbers | Page Reference |
|---|---|
| **CONCEPTS** | |
| • **Use of manipulative devices:** Units, strips, and mats; place-value cards; place-value diagrams as models. | 148, 149, 150 |
| • **Understanding of positional notation and place value:** Knowing that a number is given in terms of the sum of each of its decimal digits times a power of its base. | 143 |
| • **Instructional algorithms:** Greatly expanded algorithms that enhance student conceptual understanding of standard algorithms. | 143, 146, 148 |
| • **Exchanging:** Ten units can be exchanged for 1 ten, 10 tens can be exchanged for 1 hundred, and so on. | 126 |
| • **Algorithms for addition and subtraction in other bases:** Similar to corresponding base-ten algorithms. | 150 |
| **FORMULA** | |
| • **Exchange** is used to simplify the tasks of addition, subtraction, multiplication, and division. It clarifies the idea of "carrying a 1". For example, in the addition algorithm and using base 10, one can exchange 10 units for 1 strip or 10 strips for 1 mat. | 126 |
| **NOTATION** | |
| • **Positional notation** is the notion that the position of a symbol in a numeral determines the value of the numeral. This is the foundation on which the operations of arithmetic are built. | 143 |
| **PROCEDURE** | |
| • **Algorithms for addition and subtraction** involve column-by-column addition or subtraction of integers in order to simplify the tasks of a complex addition or subtraction problem. There are many different correct procedures. Exchanging is used in both addition and subtraction. | 143, 144, 148, 149 |
| • **Partial sum or instructional algorithm** uses simple, one-digit subtraction of numbers with corresponding place values to help complete subtractions of numbers with two or more digits. | 146, 148 |

- **Traditional, or final, algorithm** shows addition or subtraction in the usual, familiar column-by-column algorithm.    146

- **Partial-difference algorithm** uses the idea of "taking away" to help clarify the subtraction operation.    148

- **Addition and subtraction in nondecimal bases** follows the approach of base-ten algorithms.    150, 151, 152

| **Section 3.4   Algorithms for Multiplication and Division of Whole Numbers** | **Page Reference** |
|---|---|

**CONCEPTS**

- **Multiplication:** Various algorithms for multiplying in base-ten notation.    156

- **Multiplication in nondecimal bases:** Similar to base-ten multiplication algorithms.    160, 161

- **Division:** Various algorithms, including long division, for dividing in base-ten notation.    162, 163

- **Short-division algorithm:** A neat algorithm for dividing by a single digit.    164

**DEFINITION AND THEOREM**

- **The division algorithm:** If $a$ and $b$ are whole numbers with $b \neq 0$, there exists exactly one pair of whole numbers $q$ and $r$ with $0 \leq r < b$ such that $a = bq + r$. $q$ is the **quotient** and $r$ is the **remainder,** of $a$ divided by $b$.    162

**PROCEDURES**

- **Expanded notation:** The amount each digit contributes to the number is the value of the digit times the value of the position the digit occupies in the representation. For example, in base 10, $2572 = 2 \cdot 1000 + 5 \cdot 100 + 7 \cdot 10 + 2 \cdot 1$    159

- **Partial-products, or instructional, algorithm** uses a step-by-step process of the multiplication of one-digit numbers in order to solve the multiplication of numbers with two or more digits through the use of place value.    159

- **Multiply with exchanging** uses the idea of trading ten items of a certain place value with one in the next highest place value in order to complete the multiplication.    160

- **Multiplication in nondecimal bases** follows the approach of base-ten algorithms.    161

- **Scaffold or pyramid algorithm** is another version of the long-division algorithm where the quotient is placed above the division symbol.    163

- **Short-division algorithm** is a compressed version of the long-division algorithm, eliminating the process of writing down subtraction operations.    164

- **Lattice algorithm** is another method for solving complex multiplication problems using a rectangular array of boxes to organize simple multiplication operations.    166

- **Egyptian algorithm** is another method for solving complex multiplication problems involving the breakdown of one of the factors and the doubling of the other. It is also known as the duplation algorithm.    167

- **Russian peasant algorithm** is another method for solving complex multiplication problems which involves successively dividing one of the factors by two, then crossing out even quotients and adding odd quotients.    167

| **Section 3.5   Mental Arithmetic and Estimation** | **Page Reference** |
|---|---|

**CONCEPTS**

- **Easy combinations:** In doing a calculation, combine numbers that add to 10 or to a multiple of 10.    169

| | |
|---|---|
| • **Adjustment:** Change numbers to 10 or multiples of 10, with subsequent adjustment to allow for those changes by adding zero in a clever way. | 171 |
| • **Work from left to right:** This approach is often easier than working from right to left. | 172 |
| • **Estimate:** If an exact answer is not required, do mental arithmetic with rounded numbers. | 173 |
| • **Rounding:** The 5-up rule, rounding to the leftmost digit. | 175 |

| **PROCEDURES** | |
|---|---|
| • **Adjustment:** Modify numbers by adding zero at the beginning of a calculation to minimize the mental effort required. | 171 |
| • **Working from left to right:** Work from left to right to reduce the amount one has to remember. | 172 |
| • **Front-end method of estimation:** Add the numbers under the assumption that all their digits except the first on the left are zero and then make some changes on the basis of the second digit. | 173, 174 |
| • **Obtaining approximate answers by rounding:** Consider the place you want to round. If the digit to its right is 5 or more, then increase the original digit by 1 and replace all the digits to its right with zeros. If its its 4 or less, the digit remains unchanged and replace the digits to its right with zeros. You then carry out your operation with the rounded numbers. | 175, 176 |

| **STRATEGIES** | |
|---|---|
| • **Easy Combinations:** Look for easy combinations, especially regrouping to find multiples of 10, when doing mental calculation. | 169 |
| • **Estimation, or computational estimation:** Estimate what you think the answer of the problem is likely to be near to determine if your computation has had any errors. | 173 |

| **BASIC** | |
|---|---|
| • **One-digit facts** are those basic addition and multiplication facts upon which all other numerical calculations and estimations depend. | 169 |

## Chapter Review Exercises

### Section 3.1

1. Write the Indo-Arabic equivalent of each of these numbers:
   (a)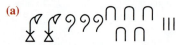
   (b)
   (c) MCMXCVIII

2. Write 234,572 in Mayan notation.

3. Suppose you have 5 mats, 27 strips, and 32 units, for a total count of 802. Briefly describe the exchanges that must be made to represent this number with the smallest possible number of manipulative pieces. How many mats, strips, and units result?

### Section 3.2

4. Find the base-ten equivalent of each of the following numbers:
   (a) $101101_{two}$  (b) $346_{seven}$  (c) $2T9_{twelve}$

5. Write $287_{ten}$ as a numeral in each base indicated:
   (a) Base five  (b) Base two  (c) Base seven

### Section 3.3

6. Sketch the solution to $47 + 25$, using mats, strips, and units. Draw a square for each mat, a vertical line segment for each strip, and a dot for each unit.

7. Use the instructional algorithm for addition to perform the following additions:
   (a) $42 + 54$  (b) $47 + 35$  (c) $59 + 63$

8. Use sketches of place-value cards to illustrate each of these subtractions:
   (a) $487 - 275$  (b) $547 - 152$

9. Perform the given calculations in base-five notation. Assume that the numerals are already written in base five.

(a)
$$\begin{array}{r} 2433 \\ + 141 \\ \hline \end{array}$$

(b)
$$\begin{array}{r} 2433 \\ - 141 \\ \hline \end{array}$$

(c)
$$\begin{array}{r} 243 \\ \times 42 \\ \hline \end{array}$$

## Section 3.4

10. Perform these multiplications, using the instructional algorithm for multiplication:

(a) $4 \times 357$     (b) $27 \times 642$

11. Use the scaffold method to perform each of these divisions:

(a) $7\overline{)895}$     (b) $347\overline{)27,483}$

12. Use the short-division algorithm to perform each of these divisions:

(a) $5\overline{)27,436}$     (b) $8\overline{)39,584}$

13. Carry out each of the given multiplications in base five. Assume that the numerals are already written in base five.

(a) $23 \cdot 42$     (b) $2413 \cdot 332$

14. Use the Russian peasant method to compute the product $42 \cdot 35$.

## Section 3.5

15. Round 274,535

(a) to the nearest one hundred thousand.

(b) to the nearest ten thousand.

(c) to the nearest thousand.

16. Rounding to the leftmost digit, compute approximations to the answers to each of these expressions:

(a) $657 + 439$     (b) $657 - 439$

(c) $657 \cdot 439$     (d) $1657 \div 23$

## Chapter Test

1. Make a schematic drawing, using mats, strips, and units to illustrate the addition of 74 and 48. Draw squares for mats, straight-line segments for strips, and dots for units.

2. Round 3,376,500 to the

(a) nearest million.

(b) nearest one hundred thousand.

(c) nearest ten thousand.

(d) nearest one thousand.

3. Place the digits 1, 3, 5, 7, and 9 in the proper boxes to achieve the maximum product:

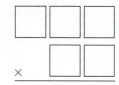

4.  (a) Compute the integers nearest to each of

$$f_1 = \frac{1 + \sqrt{2}}{\sqrt{8}}, \quad f_2 = \frac{(1 + \sqrt{2})^2}{\sqrt{8}},$$

and

$$f_3 = \frac{(1 + \sqrt{2})^3}{\sqrt{8}}, \text{ and } f_4 = \frac{(1 + \sqrt{2})^4}{\sqrt{8}}.$$

(b) Guess the most likely choices of nearest integers for $f_5$ and $f_6$.

(c) Guess what rule (other than that of part (a)) might be used to obtain the successive values of $f_n$.

5. Write the base-ten equivalents of each of the following numbers:

(a) $21022_{\text{three}}$     (b) $317_{\text{eight}}$     (c) $4213_{\text{five}}$

6. Fill in the missing digits in this addition problem:

$$\begin{array}{r} 2\_37 \\ + \_22\_ \\ \hline \_00\_1 \end{array}$$

7. Fill in the missing digits in this subtraction problem:

$$\begin{array}{r} \_23\_ \\ - \ 35\_2 \\ \hline 4\_94 \end{array}$$

8. Round each number to the leftmost digit to estimate the sum

$$378 + 64 + 291 + 39 + 3871.$$

9.  (a) Compute the following pairs of quantities:

| | | |
|---|---|---|
| $1^3$ | and | $1^2$; |
| $1^3 + 2^3$ | and | $(1 + 2)^2$; |
| $1^3 + 2^3 + 3^3$ | and | $(1 + 2 + 3)^2$; |
| $1^3 + 2^3 + 3^3 + 4^3$ | and | $(1 + 2 + 3 + 4)^2$. |

(b) Compute the square roots of the answers to the computations of part (a).

(c) Guess a formula for $1^3 + 2^3 + \cdots + n^3$ and for $(1 + 2 + 3 + \cdots + n)^2$.

10. Write 39,485 in Mayan notation.

11. Compute the sum of this arithmetic progression:

$$3 + 8 + 13 + \cdots + 123$$

12. Place the digits 0, 2, 4, 6, and 8 in the proper boxes to obtain the least product, assuming that 0 cannot be placed in either of the left-hand boxes:

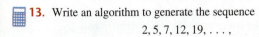

**13.** Write an algorithm to generate the sequence
$$2, 5, 7, 12, 19, \ldots ,$$
where we start with 2 and 5 and add each two consecutive terms to obtain the next term.

**14.** Perform each of the given calculations entirely in base five. The numerals are already written in base five.

(a)
$$\begin{array}{r} 242 \\ + \ 43 \\ \hline \end{array}$$

(b)
$$\begin{array}{r} 242 \\ - \ 43 \\ \hline \end{array}$$

(c)
$$\begin{array}{r} 242 \\ \times \ 43 \\ \hline \end{array}$$

**15.** Compute the sum of this geometric progression:
$$3 + 15 + 75 + \cdots + 1{,}171{,}875$$

**16.** Write $281_{\text{ten}}$ as a numeral in each of these bases:

(a) Base five

(b) Base two

(c) Base twelve

# Number Theory

**4.1** Divisibility of Natural Numbers

**4.2** Tests for Divisibility

**4.3** Greatest Common Divisors and Least Common Multiples

## Hands On

## Primes and Composites via Rectangular Arrays

### Materials Needed

1. Twenty-five small cubes or number tiles for each student or small group of students.
2. One record sheet like this for each student:

| Values of $n$ | Dimensions of Rectangles | Number of Rectangles | Factors of $n$ |
|---|---|---|---|
| 1 | | | |
| 2 | | | |
| 3 | | | |
| *4 | $1 \times 4$, $2 \times 2$, $4 \times 1$ | 3 | 1, 2, 4 |
| 5 | | | |
| 6 | | | |
| 7 | | | |
| 8 | | | |
| 9 | | | |
| 10 | | | |
| 11 | | | |
| 12 | | | |
| 19 | | | |
| 20 | | | |
| 21 | | | |
| 22 | | | |
| 23 | | | |
| 24 | | | |
| 25 | | | |

### Directions

1. For each value of $n$, make up all possible rectangular arrays of $n$ tiles. Then, on your record sheet, record the dimensions of each rectangle and the number of rectangles. For $n = 4$, we have the rectangles shown here, and we fill in the fourth row of the record sheet as shown.

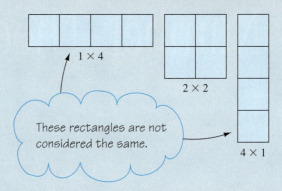

These rectangles are not considered the same.

2. In Chapter 2, we used diagrams like this to illustrate the product $3 \cdot 5 = 15$:

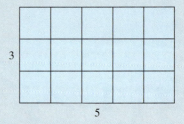

We call 3 and 5 *factors* of 15. Label the last column of your record sheet "Factors of $n$," and list the factors in increasing order for each value of $n$. The row for $n = 4$ is done for you.

3. Natural numbers that have exactly two factors are called *prime numbers*. Place a P along the left side of your record sheet next to each prime number.

4. Numbers with more than two factors are called *composite numbers*. Place a C along the left-hand side of your record sheet next to each composite number.

5. Is 1 a prime or composite number or neither? Why?

6. Put an asterisk just to the left of each $n$ that has an odd number of factors. Do these numbers seem to share some other property? State a guess (conjecture) about natural numbers with an odd number of factors.

7. Carefully considering all the data on your record sheet, see if you can guess a number that has just seven factors. Check to see that your guess is correct.

**CHAPTER PREVIEW** The whole numbers $W = \{0, 1, 2, \ldots\}$ were introduced in Chapter 2, where we examined the basic operations of addition and multiplication together with their respective inverse operations of subtraction and division. Then, in Chapter 3, we examined how a whole number can be represented symbolically within a numeration system, and we used the place-value numeration system to devise algorithms to calculate sums, differences, products, and quotients of whole numbers. In this chapter, we examine additional properties of the whole numbers that revolve around two interrelated themes: the divisibility of one natural number by another and the representation of a given natural number as a product of other natural numbers. In particular, you will discover how to answer the two questions in the accompanying excerpt from the NCTM *Principles & Standards* shown above.

The study of the properties of the whole numbers is known as **number theory.**

**KEY IDEAS**

- Divisors, factors, and multiples of whole numbers
- The classification of a natural number $n \geq 2$ as a prime or composite number
- The representation of a composite number as a product of prime numbers
- How to test a natural number for primality and divisibility
- Given two (or more) natural numbers, how to find the largest natural number that divides each of the given numbers, a number called the **greatest common divisor.**
- Given two (or more) natural numbers, how to find the smallest natural number that can be divided by each of the given numbers, a number called the **least common multiple.**

**FROM The NCTM Principles and Standards**

Understanding of number develops in prekindergarten through grade 2 as children count and learn to recognize "how many" in sets of objects. A key idea is that a number can be decomposed and thought about in many ways. For instance, 24 is 2 tens and 4 ones and also 2 sets of twelve. Making a transition from viewing "ten" as simply the accumulation of 10 ones to seeing it both as 10 ones *and* as 1 ten is an important first step for students toward understanding the structure of the base-ten number system (Cobb and Wheatley 1988). Throughout the elementary grades, students can learn about classes of numbers and their characteristics, such as which numbers are odd, even, prime, composite, or square.

Throughout their study of numbers, students in grades 3–5 should identify classes of numbers and examine their properties. For example, integers that are divisible by 2 are called *even numbers* and numbers that are produced by multiplying a number by itself are called *square numbers*. Students should recognize that different types of numbers have particular characteristics; for example, square numbers have an odd number of factors and prime numbers have only two factors.

Students can also work with whole numbers in their study of number theory. Tasks, such as the following, involving factors, multiples, prime numbers, and divisibility, can afford opportunities for problem solving and reasoning.

**1.** Explain why the sum of the digits of any multiple of 3 is itself divisible by 3.
**2.** A number of the form *abcabc* always has several prime-number factors. Which prime numbers are always factors of a number of this form? Why?

SOURCE: Principles and Standards for School Mathematics by NCTM, pages 33, 151, and 217. Copyright © 2000 by the National Council of Teachers of Mathematics. Reproduced with permission of the National Council of Teachers of Mathematics via Copyright Clearance Center. NCTM does not endorse the content or validity of these alignments.

## 4.1

# Divisibility of Natural Numbers

### Divides, Divisors, Factors, Multiples

In Chapter 3, we considered the division algorithm. If $a$ and $b$ are whole numbers with $b$ not zero, then, when we divide $a$ by $b$, we obtain a unique quotient $q$ and remainder $r$ such that $a = bq + r$ and $0 \leq r < b$. Thus, the division

$$\begin{array}{r} 4 \ \text{R} \ 2 \\ 3\overline{)14} \end{array}$$

is equivalent to the equation

$$14 = 3 \cdot 4 + 2.$$

Of special interest in this chapter is the case when the remainder $r$ is zero. Then $a = bq$, and we say that **$b$ divides $a$ evenly** or, more simply, **$b$ divides $a$.** This relationship is expressed in other terminology as indicated here:

> **DEFINITION**    *Divides, Factor, Divisor, Multiple*
>
> If $a$ and $b$ are whole numbers with $b \neq 0$ and there is a whole number $q$ such that $a = bq$, we say that $b$ **divides** $a$. We also say that $b$ is a **factor** of $a$ or a **divisor** of $a$ and that $a$ is a **multiple** of $b$. If $b$ divides $a$ and $b$ is less than $a$, it is called a **proper divisor** of $a$.

> The words **factor** and **divisor** have the same meaning.

A useful model for the ideas "$b$ divides $a$" and "$a$ is a multiple of $b$" has already been provided by the array models for multiplication of natural numbers in Chapter 2. Thus, the 5-by-7 rectangular array in Figure 4.1 illustrates the fact that 5 and 7 are both divisors of 35 and that 35 is a multiple of 5 and also of 7.

**FIGURE 4.1**
Array model showing that 5 and 7 are factors of 35 and that 35 is a multiple of both 5 and 7

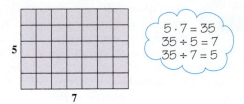

$$5 \cdot 7 = 35$$
$$35 \div 5 = 7$$
$$35 \div 7 = 5$$

The whole numbers that are divisible by 2, or, equivalently, that are multiples of 2, are known as the **even** whole numbers. Divisibility allows us to make the following precise definition:

> **DEFINITION**    *Even and Odd Whole Numbers*
>
> A whole number $a$ is **even** precisely when it is divisible by 2. A whole number that is not even is called an **odd** whole number.

It is useful to examine carefully the implications of this definition, to deeply understand both what it means and what it doesn't mean. As with all definitions, preservice teachers need to know the exact definition and model this precision when working with their future students. For example, as has occurred in the elementary school classroom, how would you respond to a child who argues that 6 is even because it is divisible by 2 but is also odd because it is divisible by 3? (see problem 19).

In the following example, the precise definitions just given are combined to provide a very useful representation of the even and odd whole numbers:

---

**EXAMPLE 4.1    Representing Even and Odd Whole Numbers**

**(a)** Explain why a whole number $a$ is even if, and only if, there is a whole number $k$ such that

$$a = 2k.$$

**(b)** Explain why a whole number $b$ is odd if, and only if, there is a whole number $j$ such that

$$b = 2j + 1.$$

**Solution**

**(a)** By definition, $a$ is even if, and only if, $a$ is divisible by 2. By the definition of divisibility by 2, this is the case precisely when there is a whole number $k$ for which $a = 2k$.

**(b)** The whole number $b$ is odd precisely when 2 is *not* a divisor of $b$. Therefore, $b$ is odd if, and only if, it leaves a nonzero remainder $r$ when divided by 2. That is, $b = 2j + r$, where $j$ is some whole number and $0 < r < 2$. Evidently, $r = 1$ and we see that $b$ is odd if, and only if, there is a representation of the form $b = 2j + 1$.

**MHM**   Example 4.1 points to a useful algebraic Mathematical Habit of the Mind: To prove that a given integer is even or odd, investigate whether it can be written in the form $2k$ for some whole number $k$, or be written as $2j + 1$ for some whole number $j$. In the opposite direction, if you are investigating a property involving a general even or odd number, it is often helpful to know that it can be written as either $2k$ or $2j + 1$.

**EXAMPLE 4.2   The Divisors, or Factors, of 6**

List all the factors of 6.

**Solution**   We must find all the whole numbers $b$ for which there is another whole number $q$ for which $6 = bq$. This is equivalent to finding all rectangular arrays with area 6 and sides of length $b$ and $q$.

By trial and error, we find that there are only four such rectangles, as shown next, and accordingly, the desired factors of 6 are 1, 2, 3, and 6. We say that 1, 2, 3, and 6 are factors, or divisors, of 6 and that 6 is a multiple of each of 1, 2, 3, and 6. It is also correct to say that 1 divides 6, 2 divides 6, 3 divides 6, and 6 divides 6. The proper divisors of 6 are 1, 2, and 3.

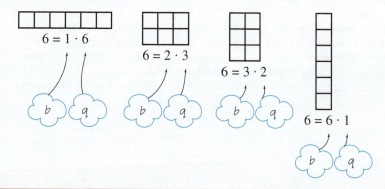

## Prime and Composite Numbers

Since $1 \cdot a = a$, 1 and $a$ are *always* factors of $a$ for every natural number $a$. For this reason, 1 and $a$ are often called trivial factors of $a$, and $1 \cdot a$ and $a \cdot 1$ are trivial factorings. Some numbers, such as 2, 3, 5, and 7, have only trivial factorings. Other numbers, such as 6, have nontrivial factorings. The number 1 stands alone, since it has only one factor: 1 itself. All this is summarized in the following definition:

> **DEFINITION   *Primes, Composite Numbers, and Units***
> A natural number that possesses exactly two different factors—itself and 1—is called a **prime number.** A natural number that possesses more than two different factors is called a **composite number.** The number 1 is called a **unit;** it is neither prime nor composite.

The primes are sometimes called the building blocks of the natural numbers, since every natural number other than 1 is either a prime or a product of primes. For example, consider the number 180. This number is composite, since, for example, we can write $180 = 10 \cdot 18$. Moreover, 10 and 18 are both composite, since $10 = 2 \cdot 5$ and $18 = 2 \cdot 9$. Now, 2 and 5 are both primes and cannot be factored further. But $9 = 3 \cdot 3$, and 3 is a prime. We simply continue to factor a composite number into smaller and smaller factors and stop when we can proceed no further—that is, when the factors are all primes. In the case of the number 180, we see that

$$180 = 10 \cdot 18$$
$$= 2 \cdot 5 \cdot 2 \cdot 9$$
$$= 2 \cdot 5 \cdot 2 \cdot 3 \cdot 3,$$

and this is a product of primes.

## Highlight from History
### Sophie Germain (1776–1831)

Sophie Germain grew up in a time of social, political, and economic upheaval in France. To shield Germain from the violence in the streets of Paris during the time of the fall of the Bastille, her wealthy parents confined their 13-year-old daughter to the family's library. There, she chanced upon J. E. Montucla's *History of Mathematics,* which recounts the legend of Archimedes' death. The story tells how a Carthaginian soldier, heedless of orders to spare the renowned mathematician, killed the unsuspecting Archimedes, who remained absorbed in a geometry problem. Germain wished to explore for herself a subject of such compelling interest.

Germain's family initially resisted her determination to study mathematics, but

eventually they gave her the freedom to follow her intellectual instincts. Since women were not permitted to enroll in the École Polytechnique, which opened in Paris in 1794, she resorted to collect-

ing lecture notes from various professors at the university. Her lack of a formal mathematical education was compensated for by her courage to overcome strenuous challenges.

Germain's early research was in number theory. She corresponded regularly with the great Carl Friedrich Gauss, who gave her work high praise. At the turn of the century, her attention turned increasingly to the mathematical theory of vibrating elastic surfaces. Her prizewinning paper on vibrating elastic plates in 1816 placed her in the ranks of the most celebrated mathematicians of the time. Gauss recommended that she be awarded an honorary doctorate from the University of Göttingen, but unfortunately Sophie Germain's death came before the awarding of the degree.

A convenient way of organizing this work is to develop a **factor tree,** as shown in Figure 4.2, to keep track of each step in the process. But there are other ways to factor 180, as these factor trees show:

$$180 = 10 \cdot 18$$
$$10 = 2 \cdot 5$$
$$18 = 2 \cdot 9$$
$$9 = 3 \cdot 3$$

$$180 = 2 \cdot 5 \cdot 2 \cdot 3 \cdot 3$$

**FIGURE 4.2**
A factor tree for 180

$$180 = 2 \cdot 2 \cdot 5 \cdot 3 \cdot 3 \qquad 180 = 3 \cdot 2 \cdot 2 \cdot 3 \cdot 5$$

Another method for finding the prime factors of a number is to use prime divisors and short division until you arrive at a quotient that is a prime. For 180, we have these three sequences of divisions, each read from the bottom upward:

$$180 = 2 \cdot 2 \cdot 3 \cdot 3 \cdot 5 \qquad 180 = 5 \cdot 2 \cdot 2 \cdot 3 \cdot 3 \qquad 180 = 3 \cdot 3 \cdot 2 \cdot 2 \cdot 5$$

This procedure is sometimes called **stacked short division.**

Both the factor tree and the stacked short-division method leave a written record of the calculations, which can often be done by mental arithmetic.

The most important thing about all the factorings shown for the number 180 is that, no matter what method is used and no matter how it is carried out, the *same prime factors always result*. That this is always the case is stated here without proof:

> **THEOREM**  *Simple-Product Form of the Fundamental Theorem of Arithmetic*
> Every natural number greater than 1 is a prime or can be expressed as a product of primes in one, and only one, way, apart from the order of the prime factors.

The preceding theorem is the reason that we do not think of 1 as either a prime or a composite number. If 1 were considered a prime, the theorem would not be true. For example, we could multiply 180 by any number of factors of 1, and the prime factorization of 180 would not be unique.

$$180 = 2 \cdot 2 \cdot 3 \cdot 3 \cdot 5$$
$$= 1 \cdot 2 \cdot 2 \cdot 3 \cdot 3 \cdot 5$$
$$= 1 \cdot 1 \cdot 2 \cdot 2 \cdot 3 \cdot 3 \cdot 5$$
$$= \cdots$$

**EXAMPLE 4.3**  **The Prime Factors of 600**

Represent 600 as a product of prime factors.

**Solution**  Using a factor tree:

```
                600
               /   \
             30     20
            / \     / \
          15   2   2   10
         / \           / \
        3   5         2   5
```

Using stacked short division:

```
         5
      5)25
      2)50
      2)100
      3)300
      2)600
```

$$600 = 2 \cdot 2 \cdot 2 \cdot 3 \cdot 5 \cdot 5$$

In Example 4.3, we can also write 600 as a product of primes by collecting like primes together and writing their products as powers; that is, we write $600 = 2^3 \cdot 3^1 \cdot 5^2$. Since this could be done for any natural number, it is useful to give an alternative version of the **fundamental theorem of arithmetic.**

> **THEOREM**  *Prime-Power Form of the Fundamental Theorem of Arithmetic*
> Every natural number $n$ greater than 1 is a power of a prime or can be expressed as a product of powers of different primes in one, and only one, way, apart from order. This representation is called the **prime-power representation of $n$.**

**EXAMPLE 4.4**  **The Prime-Power Representation of 675**

Determine the prime-power representation of 675.

**Solution**

```
         3
      3)9
      3)27
      5)135
      5)675
```

Using the stacked short-division method, we see that $675 = 3^3 \cdot 5^2$.

## The Divisors of a Natural Number

The prime-power representation of a number makes it easy to determine the divisors of the number. As an example, from Example 4.4 we know that $675 = 3^3 \cdot 5^2$. If $r$ is a divisor of say, 675, with a quotient $s$, then

$$rs = 675 = 3^3 \cdot 5^2.$$

Since $3^0 = 1, 3^1 = 3, 3^2 = 9,$ and $3^3 = 27$ are the only powers of 3 that divide 675, they are also the only powers of 3 that divide $r$. Similarly, $5^0 = 1, 5^1 = 5,$ and $5^2 = 25$ are the only powers of 5 that divide $r$. Altogether, we conclude that any divisor $r$ of 675 is the product of one of the four numbers $1, 3^3, 3^2,$ and $3^3$ multiplied by one of the three numbers $5^0, 5^1,$ and $5^2$. Moreover, any of these products is a divisor of 675. For example, the product $3^2 \cdot 5^1 = 45 = d$ is a divisor of 675, with the quotient $3^1 \cdot 5^1 = 15 = q$. All of the divisors of 675 can be written down in the following list of $4 \cdot 3 = 12$ numbers:

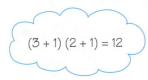

$(3 + 1)(2 + 1) = 12$

| | | |
|---|---|---|
| $1 = 3^0 \cdot 5^0$ | $5 = 3^0 \cdot 5^1$ | $25 = 3^0 \cdot 5^2$ |
| $3 = 3^1 \cdot 5^0$ | $15 = 3^1 \cdot 5^1$ | $75 = 3^1 \cdot 5^2$ |
| $9 = 3^2 \cdot 5^0$ | $45 = 3^2 \cdot 5^1$ | $225 = 3^2 \cdot 5^2$ |
| $27 = 3^3 \cdot 5^0$ | $135 = 3^3 \cdot 5^1$ | $675 = 3^3 \cdot 5^2$ |

The argument just given extends to the case where there are more than two prime factors. For example, since $140 = 2^2 \cdot 5^1 \cdot 7^1$, it follows that the divisors of 140 are all numbers that can be written in the form $2^a \cdot 5^b \cdot 7^c$, where $0 \le a \le 2, 0 \le b \le 1,$ and $0 \le c \le 1$. Altogether, there are $3 \cdot 2 \cdot 2 = 12$ different divisors of 140.

The general case is described in this theorem:

**THEOREM**    *The Divisors of a Natural Number*

Let $n$ be a natural number whose prime-power factorization has the form $n = p^a q^b \cdots v^c$, where the primes $p, q, \ldots, v$ are raised to the respective powers $a, b, \ldots, c$. Then a number $r$ is a divisor of $n$ if, and only if, $r$ has a prime factorization of the form $r = p^j q^k \cdots v^l$, where $0 \le j \le a, 0 \le k \le b, \ldots, 0 \le l \le c$. The number of divisors of $n$ is given by $N = (a + 1)(b + 1) \cdots (c + 1)$.

---

**EXAMPLE  4.5**   **The Divisors of 600**

List all the divisors of 600.

**Solution**

Since $600 = 2^3 \cdot 3^1 \cdot 5^2$, the divisors must be all the numbers of the form $2^r \cdot 3^s \cdot 5^t$ with $0 \le r \le 3,$ $0 \le s \le 1,$ and $0 \le t \le 2$. We make a systematic list of the divisors as follows:

| | | |
|---|---|---|
| $1 = 2^0 \cdot 3^0 \cdot 5^0$ | $5 = 2^0 \cdot 3^0 \cdot 5^1$ | $25 = 2^0 \cdot 3^0 \cdot 5^2$ |
| $2 = 2^1 \cdot 3^0 \cdot 5^0$ | $10 = 2^1 \cdot 3^0 \cdot 5^1$ | $50 = 2^1 \cdot 3^0 \cdot 5^2$ |
| $4 = 2^2 \cdot 3^0 \cdot 5^0$ | $20 = 2^2 \cdot 3^0 \cdot 5^1$ | $100 = 2^2 \cdot 3^0 \cdot 5^2$ |
| $8 = 2^3 \cdot 3^0 \cdot 5^0$ | $40 = 2^3 \cdot 3^0 \cdot 5^1$ | $200 = 2^3 \cdot 3^0 \cdot 5^2$ |
| $3 = 2^0 \cdot 3^1 \cdot 5^0$ | $15 = 2^0 \cdot 3^1 \cdot 5^1$ | $75 = 2^0 \cdot 3^1 \cdot 5^2$ |
| $6 = 2^1 \cdot 3^1 \cdot 5^0$ | $30 = 2^1 \cdot 3^1 \cdot 5^1$ | $150 = 2^1 \cdot 3^1 \cdot 5^2$ |
| $12 = 2^2 \cdot 3^1 \cdot 5^0$ | $60 = 2^2 \cdot 3^1 \cdot 5^1$ | $300 = 2^2 \cdot 3^1 \cdot 5^2$ |
| $24 = 2^3 \cdot 3^1 \cdot 5^0$ | $120 = 2^3 \cdot 3^1 \cdot 5^1$ | $600 = 2^3 \cdot 3^1 \cdot 5^2$ |

Note that the four choices for $r$, the two choices for $s$, and the three choices for $t$ show that there are $4 \cdot 2 \cdot 3 = 24$ divisors of 600.

## Two Questions About Primes

Since we have just seen how important the primes are as "building blocks" for the natural numbers, it is reasonable to ask the following two questions:

- How many primes are there?
- How does one determine whether a given natural number is a prime?

We answer these questions in the order asked.

## There Are Infinitely Many Primes

The answer to the first question is that there are infinitely many primes, a result shown by the Greek mathematician Euclid in ancient times. To see this, we describe a step-by-step process that determines at least one new prime at each step. Since the process can be continued without end, it follows that the set of primes is infinite. The argument of Euclid follows in the next paragraph.

Since 1 is the only natural number less than 2, the only factors of 2 are 1 and 2 itself. Thus, 2 is a prime. Consider $3 = 2 + 1$. Since 2 does not divide 3, the only divisors of 3 are 1 and 3. So 3 is also a prime. Now consider $7 = 2 \cdot 3 + 1$. Recalling the division algorithm, we find that if you divide 7 by either 2 or 3, there is a remainder of 1. Thus, 2 does not divide 7 and 3 does not divide 7. But, by the fundamental theorem of arithmetic, 7 must have a prime divisor. Therefore, 7 has a prime factor different from both 2 and 3. In fact, 7 is itself a prime. Similarly, $43 = 2 \cdot 3 \cdot 7 + 1$ leaves a remainder of 1 when divided by 2, 3, or 7. Thus, 43 is divisible by a prime different from 2, 3, and 7. In fact, 43 is also a prime. We next consider $1807 = 2 \cdot 3 \cdot 7 \cdot 43 + 1$. As before, 1807 is not divisible by any of 2, 3, 7, or 43 (since all leave a remainder of 1), so there must exist a prime other than these primes. In this case, $1807 = 13 \cdot 139$, where both 13 and 139 are primes. In any event, if we multiply all the known primes together and add 1, we obtain a number that must be divisible by at least one new prime. Since this process can be continued *ad infinitum,* it follows that there is no end to the list of primes; that is, there are infinitely many primes, as shown by the Greek mathematician Euclid over 2000 years ago.

> **THEOREM**   *The Number of Primes*
> There are infinitely many primes.

## Determining Whether a Given Natural Number is a Prime

We now answer the second question posed about primes: How can one determine whether a given natural number $n$ is prime? Let's first assume that $n$ is composite. That is, assume that $n$ can be written as the product $n = ab$, where each factor $a$ and $b$ is larger than 1. Then, assuming that $a$ is the smaller factor, so that $1 < a \le b$, we have $a^2 = a \cdot a \le a \cdot b = n$. Thus, by taking square roots, $1 < a \le \sqrt{n}$. If $p$ is a prime divisor of $a$, including the possibility that $p = a$, then $p$ also divides $n$. Since $p \le a \le \sqrt{n}$, we have this theorem:

> **THEOREM**   *Prime Divisors of n*
> If $n$ is composite, then there is a prime $p$ such that $p$ divides $n$ and $p \le \sqrt{n}$ (i.e., $p^2 \le n$).

As with any theorem, it is important how it can be used effectively as a tool for applications. Here is how the theorem can be interpreted to form a test for primality.

> **TEST FOR PRIMALITY**
> Let $n$ be any natural number, with $n > 1$. Compute $\sqrt{n}$ and make a list of the prime numbers 2, 3, 5, . . . , $p$ for which $p \le \sqrt{n}$. If none of the primes in list divide $n$, then $n$ is a prime number.

To use this test, we still need to know all the primes less than or equal to $\sqrt{n}$. Remarkably, a systematic method for determining all the primes up to a given limit was devised by the Greek mathematician Eratosthenes (276–195 B.C.). Aptly called the **sieve of Eratosthenes,** the method depends only on counting. Suppose we want to determine all the primes up to 100. Since 1 is neither prime nor composite, we write down all the whole numbers from 2 to 100. Note that 2 is a prime, since its only possible factors are itself and 1. However, every second number after 2 is a multiple of 2 and therefore is composite. Thus, we delete, or "sieve out," these numbers from our list. The next number not deleted is 3. It must be a prime, since it is not a multiple of 2, the only smaller prime. We now "sieve out" all multiples of 3 after 3 itself; that is, we strike from the list every third number after 3, whether it has been struck out before or not. The next number not already deleted, namely 5, must also be a prime, since it is not a multiple of 2 or 3, the only primes smaller than 5. Thus, 5 is a prime, and every fifth number after 5 must be deleted since it is a multiple of 5. In the same way, we determine that 7 is a prime and delete every seventh number after 7. The next number not deleted is 11, but $11 > \sqrt{100} = 10$, so we see that 2, 3, 5 and 7 are a listing of all of the prime numbers that are less than 10. Since we have deleted all the numbers up to 100 that have one or more of these primes as a divisor, the numbers that remain must all be prime. Thus, the circled numbers in Figure 4.3 are a complete list of all prime numbers through 100.

**FIGURE 4.3**
The sieve of Eratosthenes for $n = 100$

| | | | | | | | | | |
|---|---|---|---|---|---|---|---|---|---|
| | 2 | 3 | ~~4~~ | 5 | ~~6~~ | 7 | ~~8~~ | ~~9~~ | ~~10~~ |
| 11 | ~~12~~ | 13 | ~~14~~ | ~~15~~ | ~~16~~ | 17 | ~~18~~ | 19 | ~~20~~ |
| ~~21~~ | ~~22~~ | 23 | ~~24~~ | ~~25~~ | ~~26~~ | ~~27~~ | ~~28~~ | 29 | ~~30~~ |
| 31 | ~~32~~ | ~~33~~ | ~~34~~ | ~~35~~ | ~~36~~ | 37 | ~~38~~ | ~~39~~ | ~~40~~ |
| 41 | ~~42~~ | 43 | ~~44~~ | ~~45~~ | ~~46~~ | 47 | ~~48~~ | ~~49~~ | ~~50~~ |
| ~~51~~ | ~~52~~ | 53 | ~~54~~ | ~~55~~ | ~~56~~ | ~~57~~ | ~~58~~ | 59 | ~~60~~ |
| 61 | ~~62~~ | ~~63~~ | ~~64~~ | ~~65~~ | ~~66~~ | 67 | ~~68~~ | ~~69~~ | ~~70~~ |
| 71 | ~~72~~ | 73 | ~~74~~ | ~~75~~ | ~~76~~ | ~~77~~ | ~~78~~ | 79 | ~~80~~ |
| ~~81~~ | ~~82~~ | 83 | ~~84~~ | ~~85~~ | ~~86~~ | ~~87~~ | ~~88~~ | 89 | ~~90~~ |
| ~~91~~ | ~~92~~ | ~~93~~ | ~~94~~ | ~~95~~ | ~~96~~ | 97 | ~~98~~ | ~~99~~ | ~~100~~ |

## EXAMPLE 4.6 Determining the Primality of 439

Show that 439 is a prime.

**Solution**

### Understand the Problem

We must show that 439 has no factors other than itself and 1.

### Devise a Plan

By the test for primality, 439 is prime if it is not divisible by any prime. In that case, there must be no prime divisor $p$ such that $p \leq \sqrt{439}$.

### Carry Out the Plan

First, compute the square root: $\sqrt{439} \doteq 21$. From the sieve of Eratosthenes, we see that 2, 3, 5, 7, 11, 13, 17, and 19 are all of the prime numbers through 21. Putting 439 in the memory of our calculator and using [MR] repeatedly, we easily complete the desired divisions and determine that none of these primes divides 439. Thus, 439 is a prime by the test for primality.

### Look Back

There was no need to check for divisibility by all of the prime numbers through 439. We only had to check that the eight prime numbers 2, 3, 5, . . . , 19 were not divisors of 439.

### Did You Know?

The largest prime known at this writing is $2^{43112609} - 1$, discovered on August 23, 2008. It is a huge number with 12,978,189 digits in its decimal representation. Normally, determining the primality of such a large number would be beyond the power of even the largest and fastest computers. However, the special form of this number, $2^p - 1$, where $p$ is prime, makes it especially susceptible to attack by a relatively fast algorithm. Numbers of the form $2^p - 1$ are called Mersenne numbers, after the French monk Father Marin Mersenne, who discovered the first few primes of this form early in the 17th century. Checking such numbers for primality has now become a test of the speed of new computers and a pastime for computer buffs who are willing to let their personal computers work at the task for countless hours. If you want to keep up with the latest on these large primes, you can check the World Wide Web at www.mersenne.org/prime.htm.

---

**EXAMPLE 4.7    Determining a Prime Factor of $2 \cdot 3 \cdot 5 \cdot 7 \cdot 11 \cdot 13 + 1$**

Determine a prime factor of $2 \cdot 3 \cdot 5 \cdot 7 \cdot 11 \cdot 13 + 1 = 30,031$.

**Solution**

**Understand the Problem**

Our task is clear enough. We must find a prime number that divides 30,031.

**Devise a Plan**

By now, we are beginning to gain more mathematical power as we remember past solutions. Indeed, the proof that there are infinitely many primes comes to mind, as well as the need to check only for prime factors no larger than the square root of the number being examined. Let's combine these two approaches to solve the problem.

**Carry Out the Plan**

By the division algorithm, we immediately see that dividing $2 \cdot 3 \cdot 5 \cdot 7 \cdot 11 \cdot 13 + 1 = 30,031$ by 2, 3, 5, 7, 11, or 13 leaves a remainder of 1. Since $\sqrt{30,031} \doteq 173.3$, we also know that we must check only for prime factors of 30,031 that are no larger than 173. We can begin by using the list of primes given by the sieve of Eratosthenes shown in Figure 4.3. Placing the number 30,031 in the memory of our calculator, and using the $\boxed{\text{MR}}$ memory recall button, we can check if any of the primes 17, 19, 23, 29, 31, . . . divide 30,031. Fairly quickly, we discover that 59 is a divisor, with a quotient of 509. We have now determined that 59 is a prime divisor of 30,031.

**Look Back**

It is natural to ask if the quotient 509 is prime. Since $\sqrt{509} \doteq 22.6$, and we already know that none of the primes 2, 3, 5, . . . , 19 divide 509, we conclude that 509 must be prime. That is, we have determined that $59 \cdot 509$ is the prime factorization of 30,031.

---

## Problem Set 4.1

Exercises numbered in red are answered in the back of the text.

### Understanding Concepts

1. Draw array diagrams to show that

   (a) 4 is a factor of 36.    (b) 6 is a factor of 36.

2. Draw array diagrams to illustrate all the factorings of 35, taking order into account; that is, think of $1 \cdot 35$ as different from $35 \cdot 1$.

3. (a) List the first 10 positive multiples of 8, starting with $1 \cdot 8 = 8$.

   (b) List the first 10 positive multiples of 6, starting with $1 \cdot 6 = 6$.

   (c) Use parts (a) and (b) to determine the least natural number that is a multiple of both 8 and 6.

4. Use the representations shown in Example 4.1 to show why the sum of the squares of two consecutive whole numbers is 1 larger than a multiple of 4.

**5.** Complete this table of all factors of 18 and their corresponding quotients:

| Factors of 18 | 1 | 2 | | | |
|---|---|---|---|---|---|
| Corresponding quotients | 18 | 9 | | | |

**6.** Construct factor trees for each of these numbers:

    **(a)** 72    **(b)** 126    **(c)** 264    **(d)** 550

**7.** Use stacked short division to find all the prime factors of each of these numbers:

    **(a)** 700    **(b)** 198    **(c)** 450    **(d)** 528

**8. (a)** List all the divisors (factors) of 48.

    **(b)** List all the divisors (factors) of 54.

    **(c)** Use parts (a) and (b) to find the largest common divisor of 48 and 54.

**9. (a)** Determine the prime-power representations of both 136 and 102.

    **(b)** Determine the set of all divisors (factors) of 136.

    **(c)** Determine the set of all divisors of 102.

    **(d)** Determine the greatest divisor of both 136 and 102.

**10.** Determine the prime-power representation of each of these numbers:

    **(a)** 48    **(b)** 108    **(c)** 2250    **(d)** 24,750

**11.** Let $a = 2^3 \cdot 3^1 \cdot 7^2$.

    **(a)** Is $2^2 \cdot 7^1 = 28$ a factor of $a$? Why or why not?

    **(b)** Is $2^1 \cdot 3^2 \cdot 7^1 = 126$ a factor of $a$? Why or why not?

    **(c)** One factor of $a$ is $b = 2^2 \cdot 3^1$. What is the quotient when $a$ is divided by $b$?

    **(d)** How many different factors does $a$ possess?

    **(e)** Make an orderly list of all of the factors of $a$.

**12.** To determine whether 599 is a prime, which primes must you check as possible divisors?

**13.** Use your calculator and the information from the sieve of Eratosthenes in Figure 4.3 to determine whether 1139 is prime. If it is not prime, give its prime factors.

**14.** Add five more rows to Figure 4.3, and use the sieve of Eratosthenes to determine all of the prime numbers between 100 and 150. [*Suggestion:* First sieve out every other number beginning with 100, then every third number beginning with 102, and so on.]

## Teaching Concepts

**15. (a)** If $n$ is composite, is it true that all prime factors of $n$ must not exceed $\sqrt{n}$?

    **(b)** How would you convince your class that it is sometimes the case that one or more prime factors of a composite number $n$ are greater than $\sqrt{n}$ even though it is always the case that at least one prime factor of $n$ must be less than $\sqrt{n}$?

**16. (a)** If $n$, $b$, and $c$ are natural numbers and $n$ divides $bc$, is it necessarily the case that $n$ divides $b$ or $n$ divides $c$? Justify your answer.

**(b)** How would you explain to your class that your answer to part (a) is correct? Would it be useful to discuss the role of counterexamples here?

**17.** Which of the following are true and which are false? Justify your answer in each case.

    **(a)** $n$ divides 0 for every natural number $n$.

    **(b)** 0 divides $n$ for every natural number $n$.

    **(c)** 1 divides $n$ for every natural number $n$.

    **(d)** $n$ divides $n$ for every natural number $n$.

    **(e)** 0 divides 0.

    **(f)** How would you explain to your class that your answers to parts (a) through (e) are correct?

## Responding to Students

**18.** Emma has checked that 90 is divisible by the primes 2, 3, and 5 and therefore thinks that the prime factorization of 90 is $2 \cdot 3 \cdot 5$. What is Emma forgetting?

**19.** Respond to the child who claims that 6 is both even and odd since it is divisible by both 2 and the odd number 3.

**20.** A fourth grader claims that "zero is nothing, so zero is neither even nor odd." What's your response?

## Thinking Critically

**21. (a)** Any whole number $n$ divisible by 2 has the representation $n = 2k$ for some whole number $k$. How can a number $n$ divisible by 3 be represented?

    **(b)** Use part (a) to prove that the sum of any three consecutive whole numbers is divisible by 3.

    **(c)** Is the sum of the squares of any three consecutive whole numbers ever divisible by 3?

**22. (a)** Which of the primes less than 100 shown in the sieve of Eratosthenes (Figure 4.3) are adjacent to (i.e., 1 more or 1 less than) a multiple of 6?

    **(b)** What is the first prime that is not adjacent to a multiple of 6?

    **(c)** Show that every prime larger than 3 is necessarily adjacent to a multiple of 6. (*Hint:* By the division algorithm, every natural number $n$ must leave a remainder $r$ when divided by 6, with $0 \leq r < 6$ (i.e., every natural number can be written in the form $n = 6q + r$, where $0 \leq r < 6$). What are the possibilities for $r$ when $n$ is a prime?)

    **(d)** Note that part (c) does *not* say that every multiple of 6 is adjacent to a prime. Find the first multiple of 6 that is not adjacent to a prime. (*Suggestion:* Extend the sieve of Eratosthenes up to 130, and recall that the multiples of 6 can be generated by using the built-in constant function on your calculator.)

**23. (a)** List all the distinct factors of $9 = 3^2$.

    **(b)** Find three natural numbers (other than 9) that have precisely three distinct factors.

    **(c)** Find three natural numbers that have precisely four distinct factors.

**24.** The numbers 6 and 28 are said to be **perfect** numbers, since each is equal to the sum of its proper divisors. Indeed, $6 = 1 + 2 + 3$ and $28 = 1 + 2 + 4 + 7 + 14$.

   **(a)** Determine the prime-power representation of 496.

   **(b)** Show that 496 is a perfect number.

   **(c)** Determine the prime-power representation of 8128.

   **(d)** Show that 8128 is a perfect number.

   **(e)** Write 31 and 127 in the form $2^n - 1$.

   **(f)** Recalling that 6 and 28 are perfect numbers and considering the results of parts (a), (b), (c), and (d), make a conjecture about the prime-power representation of an even perfect number.

   **(g)** Given that 8191 is a prime number, determine the prime factorization of 33,550,336 and show that the number you obtain is perfect. Does this result strengthen your confidence in your conjecture in part (f)?

**25.** A number is said to be **deficient** if the sum of its proper divisors is less than the number. Similarly, a number is said to be **abundant** if the sum of its proper divisors is greater than the number. Thus, 14 is deficient, since $1 + 2 + 7 < 14$, and 12 is abundant, since $1 + 2 + 3 + 4 + 6 > 12$. Classify each of the following as deficient or abundant:

   **(a)** 10     **(b)** 18     **(c)** 20     **(d)** 16     **(e)** 468

   **(f)** $2^n$, where $n$ is a natural number

   **(g)** $p$, where $p$ is a prime

**26.** A pair of natural numbers $m$ and $n$ are called **amicable** if the sum of the proper divisors of $m$ equals $n$ and the sum of the proper divisors of $n$ equals $m$. Show that 220 and 284 are an amicable pair.

**27.** A prime number $p$ such that $2p + 1$ is also prime is called a **Germain prime,** after the eminent 19th-century German mathematician Sophie Germain (see the Highlight from History in this section.) Which of 11, 13, 97, 241, and 359 are Germain primes?

**28.** If $p$ is a prime, $b$ and $c$ are natural numbers, and $p$ divides $bc$, `MHM` is it necessarily the case that $p$ divides $b$ or $p$ divides $c$? Justify your answer.

**29.** Assume that $p$ and $q$ are different prime numbers and that $n$ `MHM` is a natural number. Argue briefly that if $p$ divides $n$ and $q$ divides $n$, then $pq$ divides $n$. The results of problems 28 and 29 are very useful when one is working with primes and divisors.

**30.** Draw a square measuring 10 centimeters on a side. Draw vertical and horizontal line segments dividing the square into rectangles of areas 12, 18, 28, and 42 square centimeters, respectively. Where should $A$, $B$, $C$, and $D$ be located?

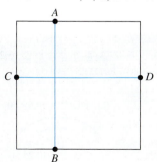

**31.** Consider the set of positive even whole numbers, $E = \{2, 4, 6, 8, \ldots\}$.

   **(a)** Why do you think 2, 6, and 10 are the first three "prime" numbers in the number system $E$? Give a careful definition, and then identify the first 10 "primes" in $E$. (*Hint:* Notice that $4 = 2 \times 2$ and $8 = 2 \times 4$.)

   **(b)** Describe the "primes" in $E$ in general. Do they have a simple representation?

   **(c)** Is there a "fundamental theorem of arithmetic" for $E$? Discuss the ways in which it agrees with and differs from the corresponding theorem for the whole numbers.

**32.** **(a)** If a prime number $p$ divides a natural number $n$, why is $p$ not a divisor of $n + 1$?

   **(b)** Explain why the product of adjacent natural numbers $n(n + 1)$ for any $n > 1$ has at least two different primes in its prime factorization.

   **(c)** By part (b) with $n = 2$, it follows that $2 \cdot 3 = 6$ has at least two different prime factors. Explain why $6 \cdot 7 = 42$ has at least three different prime factors. Indeed, 42 has the three prime factors 2, 3, and 7.

   **(d)** Explain why $42 \cdot 43 = 1806$ has at least four different prime factors. Check your answer by giving the prime factorization of 1806.

   **(e)** What is the least number of different prime factors of $1806 \cdot 1807 = 3{,}263{,}442$? You don't need to calculate them, although it happens that 13 and 139 are two of the prime factors.

   **(f)** Give a new argument proving that there are infinitely many primes.

**33.** **(a)** What pairs of prime numbers sum to 313?

   **(b)** What triples of prime numbers sum to 100?

**34.** **(a)** The following rectangle has been partially covered with 1-by-2 dominoes:

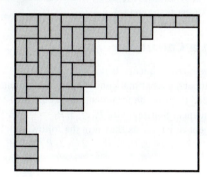

   Without actually completing the tiling, describe how to determine the total number of dominoes that are needed to tile the rectangle.

   **(b)** The two types of triominoes, each made from three unit squares, are shown here:

   Can triominoes, of either or both types, be used to tile the square shown in part (a)? Explain carefully.

## Thinking Cooperatively

**35.** First, complete the following activity as a class: If there are *n* students in the class, write large numerals 1 through *n* on 3 × 5 cards and neatly arrange them in order from left to right along the chalk tray, with the numerals facing the board. Now have the students form a line at the left of the board. The first student walks along the board and turns each card around, so the numbers 1, 2, 3, . . . now show. The second student then turns every second card around, so the odd-numbered cards remain face outward and the evens now face the board. The third student turns each third card the opposite way, and so on until the last student in line turns around just the *n*th-and-last card. Now break into small groups of three or four students to consider these questions:

(a) What are the numbers facing outward from the board?

(b) Explain why this has happened. (*Suggestion:* Make a table that shows the sequence of events.)

**36.** Work with members of your cooperative group to complete this activity. The Fibonacci numbers 1, 1, 2, 3, 5, 8, 13, . . . were defined in Section 1.4, Example 1.6.

(a) Extend the following table so that it shows the first 30 Fibonacci numbers:

| $n$ | 1 | 2 | 3 | 4 | 5 | 6 | 7 | 8 | 9 | 10 | . . . |
|-----|---|---|---|---|---|---|---|---|---|----|-------|
| $F_n$ | 1 | 1 | 2 | 3 | 5 | 8 | 13 | 21 | 34 | 55 | . . . |

(b) Which Fibonacci numbers $F_m$ are divisible by $F_3 = 2$? Carefully describe the pattern you discover.

(c) Which Fibonacci numbers $F_m$ are divisible by $F_4 = 3$? by $F_5 = 5$? Describe the patterns you discover.

(d) If *r* is a natural number, conjecture which Fibonacci numbers are divisible by $F_r$ on the basis of your observations in parts (b) and (c).

## Using a Calculator

**37.** The Perrin sequence is defined similarly to the Fibonacci numbers, except that consecutive pairs of numbers are added to form the term that *follows* the next term in the sequence. Starting with $P_0 = 3, P_1 = 0$, and $P_2 = 2$, the sequence begins as shown in the following table, where $P_3 = 3 + 0 = 3, P_4 = 0 + 2 = 2, P_5 = 2 + 3 = 5$, and so on:

| $n$ | 0 | 1 | 2 | 3 | 4 | 5 | 6 | 7 | 8 | 9 | 10 | 11 | 12 |
|-----|---|---|---|---|---|---|---|---|---|---|----|----|----|
| $P_n$ | 3 | 0 | 2 | 3 | 2 | 5 | 5 | 7 | 10 | 12 | 17 | 22 | 29 |

(a) Extend the table to show the Perrin numbers $P_n$ for $n \leq 32$. Work with your group to check for accuracy.

(b) As a group, formulate a conjecture about when *n* divides $P_n$.

**38.** Use a calculator to determine the prime-power representation of each of these numbers:

(a) 548  (b) 936  (c) 274  (d) 45,864

(e) Use the results of parts (a), (b), (c), and (d) to determine which, if any, of the numbers you found divide(s) another of the numbers you found.

**39.** Determine the prime-power representation of each of these integers:

(a) 894,348  (b) 245,025  (c) 1,265,625

(d) Which of the numbers in parts (a), (b), and (c) are squares?

(e) What can you say about the prime-power representation of a square? Explain briefly.

(f) Guess how you might know from a glance at its prime-power representation that 93,576,664 is the cube of a natural number. Explain.

## From State Student Assessments

**40.** (Texas, Grade 6)

What is the prime factorization of 220?

A. $2 \cdot 5 \cdot 11$  B. $2^2 \cdot 5 \cdot 5$

C. $2^2 \cdot 5 \cdot 11$  D. $2 \cdot 55$

**41.** (Massachussetts, Grade 5)

What is the total number of factors of 12?

A. 4  B. 6

C. 8  D. 12

**42.** (Massachussetts, Grade 8)

Which of the following is the prime factorization of 72?

A. $2^3 \cdot 3^2$  B. $2^4 \cdot 3^3$

C. $8 \cdot 3^2$  D. $2^3 \cdot 9$

**43.** (Kentucky, Grade 5)

Mrs. Radford was showing her students how to find all the factors of a composite number by making RAINBOW PATTERNS. She used the numbers 48 and 50 to demonstrate the RAINBOW PATTERN. She then chose a pair of factors from each number to make FACTOR TREES.

• She used RAINBOW PATTERNS to find all the factors.

Rainbow Pattern for 48

1  2  3  4  6  8  12  16  24  48

This RAINBOW PATTERN shows that $6 \times 8 = 48, 4 \times 12 = 48$, $3 \times 16 = 48, 2 \times 24 = 48$, and $1 \times 48 = 48$.

Rainbow Pattern for 50

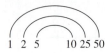

1  2  5  10  25  50

## School Book Pages

# Prime Factorization

Lesson
**5-2**

**Understand It!**
Every whole number greater than 1 is either a prime number or a composite number.

## Prime Factorization

**How can you write the prime factorization of a number?**

Whole numbers greater than 1 are either prime or composite numbers.

A prime number has exactly two factors, 1 and itself. The numbers 2, 3, and 5 are prime numbers.

| Model | Dimension | Factors |
|---|---|---|
| | $1 \times 2$ | 1, 2 |
| | $1 \times 3$ | 1, 3 |
| | $1 \times 4$ | 1, 4 |
| | $2 \times 2$ | 2 |
| | $1 \times 5$ | 1, 5 |

A composite number has more than two factors and can be written as the product of its prime factors. This is called its prime factorization.

4 is a composite number. The factors of 4 are 1, 2, and 4. 2 is its only prime factor. The prime factorization of 4 is $2 \times 2$, or $2^2$.

To find the prime factorization of 60, write its factors, beginning with the smallest prime factor.

$60 = 2 \times 30$ ← 2 is a factor of 60.
$= 2 \times 2 \times 15$ ← 2 is a factor again.
$= 2 \times 2 \times 3 \times 5$ ← 3 and 5 are factors.
$= 2^2 \times 3 \times 5$ ← Use exponents.

**Another Example** **How can you use a factor tree to find the prime factorization of a number?**

### One Way

To find the prime factorization of 72, begin with the smallest prime factor. Write factors until all the factors are prime numbers.

72
2 × 36
2 × 2 × 18
2 × 2 × 2 × 9
2 × 2 × 2 × 3 × 3

$72 = 2 \times 2 \times 2 \times 3 \times 3$
$72 = 2^3 \times 3^2$

### Another Way

To find the prime factorization of 72, begin with any two factors of 72. Write factors until all the factors are prime numbers.

72
6 × 12
2 × 3 · 3 × 4
2 × 3 × 3 × 2 × 2

**Arrange prime factors in order.**

$72 = 2 \times 2 \times 2 \times 3 \times 3$
$72 = 2^3 \times 3^2$

There is only one prime factorization for any number.

## Guided Practice*

### Do you know HOW?

In **1** through **8**, write the prime factorization of each number. If it is prime, write *prime*.

1. 18  2. 23  3. 32  4. 45
5. 89  6. 169  7. 216  8. 243

### Do you UNDERSTAND?

9. How do the two factor trees above show that there is only one prime factorization for 72?

10. Is 1 prime or composite?

124

*For another example, see Set B on page 140.

## Independent Practice

In **11** through **25**, write the prime factorization of each number. If it is prime, write *prime*.

**Tip** *Choose easy factors. For example, for 1,300, start with $1,300 = 13 \times 100$.*

11. 26    12. 47    13. 68    14. 125    15. 490
16. 750   17. 210   18. 2,100  19. 120    20. 65
21. 300   22. 27    23. 38    24. 99     25. 57

27. Which is a prime number?
A 33    B 35    C 37    D 39

### Problem Solving

26. **Geometry** A triangle has 63° and 30° angles. What is the measure of the third angle? Is it acute, right, or obtuse?

28. **Writing to Explain** Raul makes a conjecture that every odd number greater than 3 can be expressed as the sum of two primes. Use the number 11 to explain that Raul is wrong.

A famous unsolved problem referred to as *Goldbach's conjecture* states that every even number greater than 2 can be written as the sum of two prime numbers. For example, $4 = 2 + 2$, $6 = 3 + 3$, $8 = 3 + 5$, and so on. Computers have shown that Goldbach's conjecture is true for all even numbers up to 100,000,000,000!

In **29** through **33**, use *Goldbach's conjecture*. Show that each number can be written as the sum of two primes.

29. 18   30. 30   31. 32   32. 46   33. 66

Animated Glossary
www.pearsonsuccessnet.com

**DIGITAL**

Lesson 5-2

125

• She used FACTORS TREES to find all the PRIME factors.

Family Tree for 48

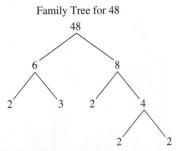

This FACTOR TREE shows that 2 and 3 are prime factors of 48 and that $2 \times 3 \times 2 \times 2 \times 2 = 48$.

Family Tree for 50

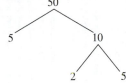

(a) Choose a COMPOSITE number between 51 and 100.

(b) Make a RAINBOW PATTERN that shows ALL the factors of the number you chose.

(c) Pick ONE PAIR of factors of the number you chose in part (a). Make a FACTOR TREE that shows all the prime factors of your chosen number.

**44.** (California, Grade 5)

Determine the prime factors of all numbers through 50, and write the numbers as the product of their prime factors by using exponents to show multiples of a factor (e.g., $24 = 2 \times 2 \times 2 \times 3 = 2^3 \times 3$)

## Examining School Book Pages

*Refer to the School Book Pages provided on page 199 to answer the following questions.*

**45.** The factor trees shown on p. 124 of the School Book Pages are somewhat different from the ones used in this section. Describe the difference and discuss which form you prefer. By looking very carefully, you should be able to discover an error in the tree at the right of the page.

**46.** The Goldbach conjecture is described on p. 125 of the School Book Pages.

(a) Verify the Goldbach conjecture for 100 by finding all pairs of primes that sum to 100.

(b) Although there is just one way to express the smaller even numbers as a sum of two primes, there are often many ways to express even a little larger even numbers as a sum of two primes. For example, $16 = 3 + 13 = 5 + 11$ and $18 = 5 + 13 = 7 + 11$. Can every even number larger than 12 be expressed in more than one way as a sum of two primes?

(c) Suppose that Raul, learning that his conjecture in problem 28 is incorrect, revises the conjecture to claim that every odd number larger than 5 is the sum of three prime numbers. Show that Raul is correct if it assumed that Goldbach's conjecture is correct.

(d) Just after problem 28 it is stated that Goldbach's conjecture is true for all even numbers up to $10^{14}$. Do an Internet search to see if the conjecture has been shown to be true for any higher even numbers.

## Cooperative Investigation

## Representing Integers as Sums

### Materials Needed

One copy of the sheet outlined next for each student.

### Directions

Divide the class into groups of three or four students each and have them carry out the directions on the handout.

### Investigation 1. Representing Natural Numbers as a Sum of Consecutive Integers

Some numbers can be written as a sum of two or more consecutive positive integers. For example, $3 = 1 + 2$ and $15 = 4 + 5 + 6$ (alternatively, $15 = 1 + 2 + 3 + 4 + 5$). By contrast, 2 cannot be written as the sum of two or more consecutive integers. Fill in the rest of this table, and then conjecture what pattern is revealed in your table.

| n | | n | n | n |
|---|---|---|---|---|
| 1 | X | 11 | 21 | 31 |
| 2 | X | 12 | 22 | 32 |
| 3 | 1 + 2 | 13 | 23 | 33 |
| 4 | | 14 | 24 | 34 |
| 5 | | 15 | 25 | 35 |
| 6 | | 16 | 26 | 36 |
| 7 | | 17 | 27 | 37 |
| 8 | | 18 | 28 | 38 |
| 9 | | 19 | 29 | 39 |
| 10 | | 20 | 30 | 40 |

### Investigation 2. Representing Numbers with Sums of Consecutive Evens or Odds

Some numbers can be written as a sum of two or more consecutive even or consecutive odd positive integers. For example, $6 = 2 + 4$, and $45 = 5 + 7 + 9 + 11 + 13$ (alternatively, $45 = 13 + 15 + 17$). On the other hand, 2 cannot be written as the sum of two or more consecutive integers that are all even or all odd. Fill in this table and then conjecture what pattern is revealed in your table:

| n | | n | n | n |
|---|---|---|---|---|
| 1 | X | 11 | 21 | 31 |
| 2 | X | 12 | 22 | 32 |
| 3 | | 13 | 23 | 33 |
| 4 | | 14 | 24 | 34 |
| 5 | | 15 | 25 | 35 |
| 6 | 2 + 4 | 16 | 26 | 36 |
| 7 | | 17 | 27 | 37 |
| 8 | | 18 | 28 | 38 |
| 9 | | 19 | 29 | 39 |
| 10 | | 20 | 30 | 40 |

## 4.2

# Tests for Divisibility

It is usually difficult to determine the divisors of a given natural number. However, the divisibility tests described in this section can often identify at least some of the smaller divisors. Children typically enjoy using divisibility tests, since they are carried out quickly and usually involve only mental arithmetic. The tests are also a topic that encourages students to think mathematically as they answer the question "Why does this test work?" The rationale behind nearly every test presented in this section can be explained by understanding how divisibility relates to sums and differences.

## Divisibility of Sums and Differences

It is clear that 3 divides both 66 and 18. Indeed, $66 = 3 \cdot 22$ and $18 = 3 \cdot 6$. Since multiplication distributes over addition and subtraction, we have

$$84 = 66 + 18 = 3 \cdot 22 + 3 \cdot 6 = 3(22 + 6) = 3 \cdot 28$$

and

$$48 = 66 - 18 = 3 \cdot 22 - 3 \cdot 6 = 3(22 - 6) = 3 \cdot 16.$$

That is, since 3 divides both 66 and 18, then it also divides their sum and difference.

More generally, we have the following useful theorem:

> **THEOREM** *Divisibility of Sums and Differences*
>
> Let $d$, $a$, and $b$ be natural numbers. Then if $d$ divides both $a$ and $b$, it also divides both their sum, $a + b$, and their difference, $a - b$.

> **PROOF** Since $d$ divides $a$ and $b$, it follows that $a = dj$ and $b = dk$ for some natural numbers $j$ and $k$. By the distributive property of multiplication over addition, we then have $a + b = dj + dk = d(j + k)$. That is, $a + b = dq$, where $q = j + k$. Therefore, $d$ divides the sum $a + b$. Similarly, using the distributive property of multiplication over subtraction gives $a - b = dj - dk = d(j - k) = dr$, where $r = j - k$. This shows that if $d$ divides $a$ and $b$, then $d$ divides their difference, $a - b$.

## Divisibility by 2, 5, and 10

Is 9276 divisible by 2? You may already know that it is, because the units digit 6 is an even number. But why does this simple test work, and how would you explain it to a youngster? The key idea is to write $9276 = 9270 + 6$ in the form

$$9276 = 927 \cdot 10 + 6.$$

Since 2 divides 10 and 6, 2 also divides $927 \cdot 10$ and 6. Then, by the divisibility-of-sums-and-differences theorem, it follows that 2 divides 9276.

The analysis can be generalized to any natural number $n$. Dividing $n$ by 10, we see that

$$n = q \cdot 10 + r,$$

where $r$ is the units digit of $n$. Using the divisibility-of-sums-and-differences theorem, together with the fact that 10 is divisible by 2, we see that $n$ is divisible by 2 precisely when $r$ is divisible by 2—that is, when the units digit $r$ is 0, 2, 4, 6, or 8.

Similarly, since 10 is divisible by 5, it follows that $n$ is divisible by 5 exactly when $r$ is also divisible by 5—that is, when the units digit is 0 or 5. Finally, $n$ is divisible by 10 only when the units digit is 0. Thus, we have proved the following theorem:

> **THEOREM** *Tests for Divisibility by 2, 5, and 10*
>
> Let $n$ be a natural number. Then $n$ is
>
> - divisible by 2 exactly when its base-ten units digit is 0, 2, 4, 6, or 8;
> - divisible by 5 exactly when its base-ten units digit is 0 or 5;
> - divisible by 10 exactly when its base-ten units digit is 0.

## Divisibility by 4, 8, and Other Powers of 2

Our successful justification of the divisibility tests for 2, 5, and 10 suggests that we reexamine our reasoning to see if it can be modified to derive other divisibility tests. Since our initial idea was to divide a given natural number $n$ by 10, let's investigate what divisibility tests we can obtain by dividing $n$ by 100.

Dividing a natural number $n$ by 100, we can write $n$ in the form

$$n = q \cdot 100 + r, \quad 0 \leq r \leq 99,$$

where the remainder $r$ is the number formed from the last two digits of $n$. Of course, 2, 5, and 10 are divisors of 100, but there are several new divisors as well, such as 4, 20, 25, and 50. Arguing just as before, we conclude that $n$ is divisible by 4, or 20, or 25, or 50 precisely when the number $r$ formed from the last two digits of $n$ is divisible, respectively, by 4, or 20, or 25, or 50. For example, the number 9276 is divisible by 4, since $76 = 4 \cdot 19$. However, 9276 is not divisible by 20, 25, or 50, since 76 is not divisible by any of these numbers.

If $n$ is divided by 1000, we obtain

$$n = q \cdot 1000 + r, \quad 0 \leq r \leq 999,$$

where $r$ is the number formed by the last three digits of $n$. As before, if $d$ is any divisor of 1000, then it is also a divisor of $n$ exactly when $d$ is a divisor of $r$. Since $1000 = 2 \cdot 2 \cdot 2 \cdot 5 \cdot 5 \cdot 5$, among the choices for $d$ are 8, 125, and 500. For example, $n = 4{,}357{,}832$ is divisible by 8 (since $832 = 8 \cdot 104$), but it is not divisible by either 125 or 500, since neither 125 nor 500 divides $r = 832$.

Divisibility tests for any power $2^m$ can be obtained by division by $10^m$, showing us that a natural number $n$ is divisible by $2^m$ if, and only if, the number $r$ formed by the last $m$ digits of the base-ten representation of $n$ is divisible by $2^m$. Since divisibility by 4 and 8 are the most useful cases, we state the following theorem:

**THEOREM**    *Tests for Divisibility by 4 and 8*

Let $n$ be a natural number. Then $n$ is divisible by 4 exactly when the number represented by its last two base-ten digits is divisible by 4. Similarly, $n$ is divisible by 8 exactly when the number represented by its last three base-ten digits is divisible by 8.

**EXAMPLE 4.8**    **Using the Divisibility Tests for 2, 4, 5, 8, and 10**

Decide whether each of the following statements is true or false, giving a reason for each answer:

**(a)** 2 divides 54,628.
**(b)** 4 divides 54,628.
**(c)** Since both 2 and 4 are divisors of 54,628, 8 is also a divisor, because $2 \cdot 4 = 8$.
**(d)** 5 divides $2439 + 8206$.

**Solution**

**(a)** True, since 2 divides the units digits 8.
**(b)** True, since 4 divides 28.
**(c)** False, since $628 = 8 \cdot 78 + 4$ shows that 8 does not divide 628 and therefore 8 does not divide 54,628. Note that if a number is divisible by 4, then $4 = 2 \cdot 2$ appears in the prime factorization of the number and therefore the number is also divisible by 2. However, we have no reason to know if $2 \cdot 2 \cdot 2$ appears in the prime factorization of 54,628 so we do not know if that number is divisible by 8.
**(d)** True. Since $9 + 6 = 15$, the last digit of the sum is a 5. Note that a sum may be divisible by 5 even though neither addend is divisible by 5.

## Divisibility by 3 and 9

The tests for **divisibility by 3 and 9** depend on the simple observation that every power of 10 is 1 larger than an obvious multiple of 3 and 9:

$$10 = 9 + 1, \ 100 = 99 + 1, \ 1000 = 999 + 1, \ 10{,}000 = 9999 + 1, \ldots$$

Let's use this observation to test whether $n = 27{,}435$ is divisible by 3 or 9. Using expanded notation, we have

$$n = 27{,}435 = 2 \cdot 10{,}000 + 7 \cdot 1{,}000 + 4 \cdot 100 + 3 \cdot 10 + 5$$

$$= 2 \cdot (9999 + 1) + 7 \cdot (999 + 1) + 4 \cdot (99 + 1) + 3 \cdot (9 + 1) + 5$$

$$= \underbrace{(2 \cdot 9999 + 7 \cdot 999 + 4 \cdot 99 + 3 \cdot 9)}_{\substack{\text{a number divisible} \\ \text{by 3 and by 9}}} + \underbrace{(2 + 7 + 4 + 3 + 5)}_{\substack{\text{the sum of the} \\ \text{digits of } n}}$$

By the divisibility-of-sums-and-differences theorem, the preceding equation shows that $n$ is divisible by 3 or 9 precisely when the sum $s$ of its digits is also divisible by 3 or 9. For example, the sum of the digits of $n = 832,452$ is $8 + 3 + 2 + 4 + 5 + 2 = 24$. Since 24 is divisible by 3 but is not divisible by 9, it follows that 832,452 is divisible by 3 but is not divisible by 9.

The same procedure can be applied to any natural number $n$; therefore, we have the following theorem:

> **THEOREM** *Tests for Divisibility by 3 and 9*
> A natural number $n$ is divisible by 3 if, and only if, the sum of its digits is divisible by 3. Similarly, $n$ is divisible by 9 if, and only if, the sum of its digits is divisible by 9.

## Divisibility by 11

To devise a test for divisibility by 11, we will take advantage of the fact that the powers of 10 alternate between being 1 more and 1 less than a multiple of 11, as follows:

$$10 = 11 - 1, 10^2 = 99 + 1 = 11 \cdot 9 + 1, 10^3 = 1001 - 1 = 11 \cdot 91 - 1,$$
$$10^4 = 9999 + 1 = 11 \cdot 909 + 1, 10^5 = 100,001 - 1 = 11 \cdot 9091 - 1,$$
$$10^6 = 999,999 + 1 = 11 \cdot 90909 + 1, \ldots$$

To test whether $n = 8,571,937$ is divisible by 11, the preceding formulas show that

$$8,571,937 = 8(10^6) + 5(10^5) + 7(10^4) + 1(10^3) + 9(10^2) + 3(10) + 7$$
$$= 8(11 \cdot 90909 + 1) + 5(11 \cdot 9091 - 1) + 7(11 \cdot 909 + 1)$$
$$+ 1(11 \cdot 91 - 1) + 9(11 \cdot 9 + 1) + 3(11 - 1) + 7$$
$$= 11 \cdot (\text{some integer}) + 8 - 5 + 7 - 1 + 9 - 3 + 7.$$

By the divisibility-of-sums-and-differences theorem, $n = 8,571,937$ is divisible by 11 exactly when $8 - 5 + 7 - 1 + 9 - 3 + 7 = (8 + 7 + 9 + 7) - (5 + 1 + 3) = 22$ is divisible by 11. Since $22 = 2 \cdot 11$, it follows that 8,571,937 is also divisible by 11.

The same analysis can be applied to the base-ten representation of any natural number; thus, we have the following theorem:

> **THEOREM** *A Divisibility Test for 11*
> A natural number $n$ is divisible by 11 exactly when the sums of digits in the even and odd positions of $n$ have a difference that is divisible by 11.

**EXAMPLE 4.9** **Testing for Divisibility by 11**

Show that $n = 8,193,246,781,053,476,109$ is divisible by 11 and that $m = 76,124,738,465,372,103$ is not divisible by 11.

**Solution**  First consider $n$. Using mental arithmetic, we find that

$$8 + 9 + 2 + 6 + 8 + 0 + 3 + 7 + 1 + 9 = 53$$

and

$$1 + 3 + 4 + 7 + 1 + 5 + 4 + 6 + 0 = 31.$$

Since $53 - 31 = 22$ and 11 divides 22, it follows that 11 divides $n$. In fact,

$$8,193,246,781,053,476,109 \div 11 = 744,840,616,459,406,919.$$

Now consider $m = 76,124,738,465,372,103$. Using mental arithmetic, we find that

$$7 + 1 + 4 + 3 + 4 + 5 + 7 + 1 + 3 = 35$$

and

$$6 + 2 + 7 + 8 + 6 + 3 + 2 + 0 = 34.$$

Since $35 - 34 = 1$ and 11 does not divide 1, it follows that 11 does not divide $m$. Here,

$$76,124,738,465,372,103 \div 11 = 6,920,430,769,579,282 \text{ R } 1.$$

## Combining Divisibility Tests

Consider the natural number $n = 6735$. Since the last digit is 5, it follows that $n$ is divisible by 5. Moreover, the sum of the digits of $6735, 6 + 7 + 3 + 5 = 21$, is divisible by 3, so $n$ is also divisible by 3. Thus, the prime factorization of $n$ includes at least one factor of 3 and one factor of 5, so their product $3 \cdot 5 = 15$ is also a divisor of $n$.

It may seem at first that if we know that a number $n$ has two divisors $a$ and $b$, then their product $a \cdot b$ must also be a divisor of $n$. However, this may not be the case if $a$ and $b$ share a common prime divisor. As an example of this situation, consider $m = 5396$. The last digit of $m$ is even, so $m$ is divisible by 2. Also, 4 divides the number 96 formed from the last two digits, so $m$ is also divisible by 4. It is tempting to claim that $m$ is therefore divisible by $2 \cdot 4 = 8$, but this is not so, since $5396 = 8 \cdot 674 + 4$. We can be assured that the product of two divisors $a$ and $b$ is also a divisor only when $a$ and $b$ have no common prime divisor. In the example, the two divisors 2 and 4 of $m$ have the common prime divisor 2, and we know for sure only that there are two occurrences of the prime number 2 in the prime factorization of $m$.

The following theorem summarizes what can be said about the possibility of multiplying two divisors to get a third divisor:

> **THEOREM**  *Divisibility by Products*
>
> Let $a$ and $b$ be divisors of a natural number $n$. If $a$ and $b$ have no common divisor other than 1, then their product $ab$ is also a divisor of $n$.

**EXAMPLE 4.10  Combining Divisibility Tests**

Decide whether each statement is true or false without actually dividing. Give a reason for each answer.

(a) 45 divides 43,695.    (b) 33 divides 632,481.    (c) 6 divides 876,324.
(d) 4 divides 876,324.    (e) 24 divides 876,324.    (f) 88 divides 845,240.

**Solution**

(a) True. 5 is a divisor, since the last digit is 5, and 9 is a divisor, since the sum of the digits of $43,695, 4 + 3 + 6 + 9 + 5 = 27$, is divisible by 9. Since 5 and 9 have no common factor other than 1, $5 \cdot 9 = 45$ divides 43,695.

(b) False. If 33 were a divisor, then 11 would also be a divisor. However, the difference $(6 + 2 + 8) - (3 + 4 + 1) = 8$ is not divisible by 11.

(c) True. 2 is a divisor since the last digit 4 is even, and 3 is also a divisor, since the sum of the digits of $876,324, 8 + 7 + 6 + 3 + 2 + 4 = 30$, is divisible by 3. Since 2 and 3 have no common divisor other than 1, $2 \cdot 3 = 6$ divides 876,324.

(d) True. 4 divides the number 24 formed by the last two digits.

(e) False (even though 4 and 6 are divisors). If 24 were a divisor, then 8 would also be a divisor. However, the number 324 formed from the last three digits of 876,324 is not divisible by 8.

(f) True. 8 is a divisor of 240, so 8 divides 845,240. The difference $(8 + 5 + 4) - (4 + 2 + 0) = 17 - 6 = 11$ is divisible by 11, so 845,240 is divisible by 11. Since 8 and 11 have no common factor other than 1, we conclude that 845,240 is divisible by $8 \cdot 11 = 88$.

## Highlight from History

### Srinivasa Ramanujan (1887–1920)

Perhaps the most exotic and mysterious of all mathematicians was Srinivasa Ramanujan, born to a high-caste family of modest means in Kumbakonam in southern India in 1887. Largely self-taught, Ramanujan wrote a letter in 1913 to the eminent English mathematician G. H. Hardy at Cambridge University in which he included a list of formulas he had discovered. Of the formulas, Hardy wrote, "[such formulas] defeated me completely . . . a single look at them is enough to show that they were written by a mathematician of the highest class. They must be true because, if they were not true, no one would have had the imagination to invent them. Finally (you must remember that I knew nothing about Ramanujan and had to think of every possibility), the writer must be completely honest, because great mathematicians are commoner than thieves and humbugs of such incredible skill."

In any event, Hardy arranged for Ramanujan to come to England in 1914, and the two collaborated intensively for the next three years, with Ramanujan using his unorthodox methods and fantastic intuition to come up with deep and totally unexpected results that Hardy, with his considerable intellectual power and formal training, then proved. Ramanujan fell ill in 1917 and returned to India, where he died in 1920.

The English mathematician J. E. Littlewood once remarked that every positive integer was one of Ramanujan's friends. Once, during Ramanujan's illness, Hardy visited him in the hospital in Putney. Trying to find a way to begin the conversation, Hardy remarked that he had come to the hospital in cab number 1729 and that he could not imagine a more uninteresting number, to which Ramanujan replied, "No, it is a very interesting number; it is the smallest number that can be written as the sum of two cubes in two different ways!"*

*$1729 = 9^3 + 10^3 = 1^3 + 12^3$

## A Unified Test for Divisibility by 7, 11, and 13

Serendipitously, the product of the three primes 7, 11, and 13 is 1001, just one more than $10^3$. It can also be shown that $10^6$ is just one less than a multiple of $7 \cdot 11 \cdot 13$. This alternating pattern continues, so that $10^9$, $10^{12}$, . . . are successfully one more, then one less, . . . than a multiple of $7 \cdot 11 \cdot 13$. Thus, by grouping the digits by threes, starting at the right, we have a way to simultaneously test a number for divisibility by 7, 11, and 13. As an example, consider 1,486,024,085. Grouping digits by threes gives

$$1{,}486{,}024{,}085 = 1(10^9) + 486(10^6) + 24(10^3) + 85$$
$$= (\text{some multiple of } 7 \cdot 11 \cdot 13) - 1 + 486 - 24 + 85.$$

Since $-1 + 486 - 24 + 85 = 546 = 6 \cdot 7 \cdot 13$, it follows that 1,486,024,085 is divisible by 7 and 13 but is not divisible by 11.

**EXAMPLE 4.11  Divisibility by 7, 11, and 13**

Test whether $n = 8{,}346{,}261{,}059{,}482{,}647$ is divisible by 7, 11, or 13.

**Solution**  Breaking $n$ up into three-digit numbers and computing the respective sums of the numbers in even positions and odd positions, we have

|       |     |       |
|-------|-----|-------|
| 008   | and | 346   |
| 261   |     | 059   |
| 482   |     | 647   |
| 751   |     | 1052  |

The test number is $1052 - 751 = 301$. Since $7 \cdot 43 = 301$, 7 divides 301 and hence 7 divides $n$. However,

$$301 = 11 \cdot 27 + 4 \quad \text{and} \quad 301 = 13 \cdot 23 + 2.$$

Thus, 11 does not divide 301, and 13 does not divide 301, so neither 11 nor 13 divides $n$.

## Summary of Useful Divisibility Tests

Divisibility tests can be derived for many other natural numbers, but the tests of most value are collected in Table 4.1.

| TABLE 4.1 | TESTS FOR DIVISIBILITY BY 2, 3, 4, 5, 6, 8, 9, 10, AND 11 |
|---|---|
| **Divisor** | **Test** |
| 2 | Last digit must be 0, 2, 4, 6, or 8 |
| 3 | Sum of digits must be divisible by 3 |
| 4 | Last two digits must form a number divisible by 4 |
| 5 | Last digit must be 0 or 5 |
| 6 | Number must be divisible by 2 and 3 |
| 8 | Last three digits must form a number divisible by 8 |
| 9 | Sum of digits must be divisible by 9 |
| 10 | Last digit must be 0 |
| 11 | The difference of the sums of the digits in even and odd position must be divisible by 11 |

The table does not include the unified test for 7, 11, and 13. Problem 17 describes another test for 7, with its derivation outlined in problem 18.

## Problem Set 4.2

Exercises numbered in red are answered in the back of the text.

### Understanding Concepts

**1.** Test each number for divisibility by each of 2, 3, and 5. Do the work mentally.

(a) 1554    (b) 1999    (c) 805    (d) 2450

**2.** Use the results of problem 1 to decide which, if any, of the numbers in problem 1 are divisible by

(a) 6.    (b) 10.    (c) 15.    (d) 30.

**3.** (a) Verify that $10^6 - 1$ is divisible by $7 \cdot 11 \cdot 13$.

(b) Verify that $10^9 + 1$ is divisible by $7 \cdot 11 \cdot 13$.

**4.** Test each of these numbers for divisibility by 7, 11, and 13:

(a) 253,799    (b) 834,197    (c) 1,960,511

**5.** Use the results of problem 4 to decide which of the numbers in problem 4 are divisible by

(a) 77.    (b) 91.    (c) 143.    (d) 1001.

**6.** Is 1,927,643,001,548 divisible by 11? Explain briefly.

**7.** (a) At a glance, determine the digit $d$ so that $87,543,24d$ is divisible by 4. Is there more than one answer? Explain.

(b) Can you choose the digit $d$ so that $87,543,24d$ is divisible by 8 and not 16? Explain.

**8.** Determine the digit $d$ so that $6,34d,217$ is divisible by 11.

**9.** (a) Fill in the missing units digit so that $897,650,243,28\_$ is divisible by 6. Can this be done in more than one way?

(b) Fill in the missing digit so that the number in part (a) is divisible by 11.

**10.** A palindrome is a number that reads the same forward and backward, such as 2,743,472.

(a) Give a clear, but brief, argument showing that every palindrome with an even number of digits is divisible by 11.

(b) Is it possible for a palindrome with an odd number of digits to be divisible by 11? Explain.

### Teaching Concepts

**11.** The following number-rod diagram illustrates why 3 is a divisor of 9:

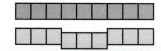

(a) Use a number-rod diagram to show that 6 is divisible by 3.

(b) Use a number-rod diagram to show that, since 3 divides 9 and 6, 3 must also divide the sum $9 + 6$.

(c) Use number-rod diagrams to show that 2 is a divisor of 6 and 10.

(d) Use the diagrams in part (c) to explain why 2 is a divisor of $16 = 10 + 6$ and $4 = 10 - 6$.

## Responding to Students

**12.** A student claims that 157,163 is divisible by 3 since the last digit in the number is 3. Explain how you would correct the student's thinking.

**13.** A student claims that, to multiply a two-digit number by 11, all you have to do is write a three-digit number whose first and last digits are the first and last digits of the two-digit number and whose middle digit is the sum of the digits of the two-digit number (e.g., $32 \cdot 11 = 352$).

   **(a)** Is this ever true?

   **(b)** Is this always true?

   **(c)** If a three-digit number is such that the middle digit is the sum of its first and last digits, is the number divisible by 11?

   **(d)** How would you discuss (a), (b), and (c) with a class of fourth graders?

**14.** Tia claims that 24 divides 420 since 6 and 4 both divide 420. Explain how you would correct Tia's thinking.

**15.** Max claims that 15 does not divide $177 + 48$ since 15 does not divide 177 and 15 does not divide 48.

   **(a)** Is Max correct?

   **(b)** How would you respond to Max?

## Thinking Critically

**16.** Prime numbers do not appear with any obvious regularity. For example, it seems possible to find quite long strings of consecutive composite numbers, such as the string of seven consecutive composite numbers 90, 91, 92, 93, 94, 95, and 96. An important Mathematical Habit of the Mind is to be alert to asking such questions as "Is it always the case that . . .?" "What if . . .?" "Is there a . . .?" and so on. Looking over the list of prime numbers suggests that we ask this question:

   *Is there a limit on the length of a string of consecutive composite numbers?* To help you answer this question, it is useful to look at products of successive natural numbers known as *factorials*, where $n!$ (read as "$n$ factorial") is

defined by the product of the first $n$ natural numbers. That is, $n! = n \cdot (n - 1) \cdot (n - 2) \cdots \cdot 3 \cdot 2 \cdot 1$. As an example, $11! = 11 \cdot 10 \cdot 9 \cdot 8 \cdot 7 \cdot 6 \cdot 5 \cdot 4 \cdot 3 \cdot 2 \cdot 1$.

   **(a)** It is clear that $11!$ is divisible by the ten divisors 2, 3, . . . , 11. Why are these ten numbers also divisors of the ten consecutive natural numbers $11! + 2, 11! + 3, . . . , 11! + 11$?

   **(b)** Part (a) has shown that $11! + 2, 11! + 3, . . . , 11! + 11$ are ten consecutive composite natural numbers. Describe how to create a list of 100 consecutive composite natural numbers.

   **(c)** Explain why there are arbitrarily long strings of consecutive composite natural numbers.

**17.** Here is another test for divisibility of a number $n$ by 7:

   **A Divisibility-by-7 Test.** Let $r$ be the last digit of $n$, and let $q$ be the number obtained from $n$ by dropping its last digit (i.e., $n = 10q + r$). Then $n$ is divisible by 7 if, and only if, the number $m = q - 2r$ is divisible by 7.

   For example, $n = 40,061$ is divisible by 7 if, and only if, $4006 - 2 = 4004$ is divisible by 7; 4004 is divisible by 7 if, and only if, $400 - 8 = 392$ is divisible by 7; and finally, 392 is divisible by 7 if, and only if, $39 - 4 = 35$ is divisible by 7. Since $35 = 7 \cdot 5$, it follows that 40,061 is divisible by 7.

   Use the test to check each of the following numbers for divisibility by 7, without actually doing the division:

   **(a)** 686         **(b)** 2951         **(c)** 18,487

**18.** The divisibility test for 7 given in problem 17 makes the following claim: $n = 10q + r$ is divisible by 7 if, and only if, $m = q - 2r$ is divisible by 7.

   Use *algebraic reasoning* to prove this claim, following these two steps:

   **(a)** Assume that $10q + r$ is divisible by 7, so that $10q + r = 7k$ for some natural number $k$. Now show that $10m$ is divisible by 7, where $m = q - 2r$. Why do you then know that $m$ is divisible by 7?

   **(b)** Assume that $m = q - 2r$ is divisible by 7. Then show by algebraic reasoning that $n = 10q + r$ is divisible by 7.

**19.** Show that every number whose decimal representation has the form $abc,abc$ is divisible by 7, 11, and 13.

## Thinking Cooperatively

**20.** The digits of $n = 354,278$ sum to $3 + 5 + 4 + 2 + 7 + 8 = 29$, which leaves a remainder of 2 when divided by 9. Does $n$ also leave a remainder of 2 when divided by 9? In a team of three to four, first discuss, and then write a report answering, the following question: *Can remainders also be determined from a divisibility test?*

**21.** The first 30 Fibonacci numbers are displayed in the following table:

| $n$ | 1 | 2 | 3 | 4 | 5 | 6 | 7 | 8 | 9 | 10 |
|-----|---|---|---|---|---|---|---|---|---|----|
| $F_n$ | 1 | 1 | 2 | 3 | 5 | 8 | 13 | 21 | 34 | 55 |

| $n$ | 11 | 12 | 13 | 14 | 15 | 16 | 17 | 18 | 19 | 20 |
|-----|----|----|----|----|----|----|----|----|----|----|
| $F_n$ | 89 | 144 | 233 | 377 | 610 | 987 | 1597 | 2584 | 4181 | 6765 |

| $n$ | 21 | 22 | 23 | 24 | 25 | 26 | 27 | 28 | 29 | 30 |
|-----|----|----|----|----|----|----|----|----|----|----|
| $F_n$ | 10,946 | 17,711 | 28,657 | 46,368 | 75,025 | 121,393 | 196,418 | 317,811 | 514,229 | 832,040 |

Do the following in cooperation with three or four other students, and in each case come to a consensus on the conjectures you make:

**(a)** In problem 36 of Problem Set 4.1, you were asked to conjecture which Fibonacci numbers were divisible by 2, by 3, and by 5. If you did not do that problem, do it now.

**(b)** List the first three Fibonacci numbers that are divisible by 4.

**(c)** On the basis of the limited data of part (b), guess what must be true of $n$ if 4 divides $F_n$.

**(d)** Use the results of part (a) to guess what must be true of $n$ if 6 divides $F_n$.

**(e)** Note that 7 divides $F_8$, 7 divides $F_{16}$, and 7 divides $F_{24}$. Conjecture what must be true about $n$ if 7 divides $F_n$.

**(f)** What do the results of parts (a) through (e) suggest about the divisibility of Fibonacci numbers by natural numbers?

## Making Connections

**22.** A common error in banking is to interchange, or transpose, some of the digits in a number involved in a transaction. For example, a teller may pay out $43.34 on a check actually written for $34.43 and hence be short by $8.91 at the end of the day. Show that such a mistake always causes the teller's balance sheet to show an error, in terms of pennies—here 891—that is divisible by 9. (*Hint:* Recall that, in the proof of the divisibility test for 9, we showed that every number differs from the sum of its digits by a multiple of 9.)

**23.** If a teller's record of the day's work is out of balance by an amount, in pennies, that is a multiple of 9, is it necessarily the case that he or she has made a transposition error in the course of the day's work? Explain.

## From State Student Assessments

**24.** (Massachussetts, Grade 6)
The clues below describe a three-digit number.

> The hundreds digit is 4. The ones digit is 3. The three-digit number is divisible by 3.

Which of the following could be the tens digit of the number?

**A.** 2      **B.** 3      **C.** 6      **D.** 9

**25.** (Massachussetts, Grade 4)
Classes that visit the Life Science Museum are divided into groups of 4 students for each tour guide. Which of the following classes would **not** be able to form groups of 4 students with none left over?

**A.** A class of 36 students      **B.** A class of 40 students

**C.** A class of 46 students      **D.** A class of 52 students

## 4.3

# Greatest Common Divisors and Least Common Multiples

An architect is designing an elegant display room for an art museum. One wall is to be covered with large square marble tiles. To obtain the desired visual effect, the architect wants to use the largest tiles possible. If the wall is 12 feet high and 42 feet long, how large can the tiles be?

If the tiles measure 4 feet on a side, the possible height of the wall must be a multiple of 4 (that is, 4 must be a divisor of 12). Indeed, the length of the side of a tile must be a divisor of both the height and length of the wall (that is, a common divisor of both 12 and 42). Since the sets of divisors of 12 and 42 are $D_{12} = \{1, 2, 3, 4, 6, 12\}$ and $D_{42} = \{1, 2, 3, 6, 7, 14, 21, 42\}$, respectively, the tile size must be chosen from the set $D_{12} \cap D_{42} = \{1, 2, 3, 6\}$, the set of common divisors of both 12 and 42. Thus, if the tiles are to be as large as possible, they must measure 6 feet on a side, since 6 is the largest of the common divisors of 12 and 42.

Considerations like those in the previous paragraph lead to the notion of the greatest common divisor of two natural numbers, defined formally as follows:

> Elementary school textbooks most often use **GCF**. Calculators and spreadsheets most often use **GCD** (or gcd).

> **DEFINITION** *Greatest Common Divisor*
>
> Let $a$ and $b$ be whole numbers not both 0. The greatest natural number $d$ that divides both $a$ and $b$ is called their **greatest common divisor,** and we write $d = \text{GCD}(a, b)$.

Since divisors are also called **factors,** the greatest common divisor is often called the **greatest common factor,** and $\text{GCD}(a, b)$, is often written as **GCF$(a, b)$.** For example, $\text{GCD}(12, 42) = 6$, which can also be written as $\text{GCF}(12, 42) = 6$.

MHM    It is important here, as with every new definition, to examine its wording and meaning with the utmost care. For example, we should ask, "Why is the GCD not defined when both $a$ and $b$ are 0?" The answer should be clear: *Every* natural number $d$, no matter how large, divides 0, so there is no *largest* common divisor. We should also ask, "How do we know that there *exists* at least one common divisor of any two whole numbers?" The answer is easy: 1 is a divisor of *every* whole number, so 1 is always a common divisor of any set of whole numbers. Finally, "Why does there exist a *largest* natural number that divides both $a$ and $b$?" Here's the answer: The largest divisor of $a$ is $a$ itself, and the largest divisor of $b$ is $b$; therefore, the largest divisor of both $a$ and $b$ is no larger than the smaller of $a$ and $b$.

The concept of the greatest common divisor has many applications, but one of the most important is its connection to expressing fractions in simplest form. For example, the fraction $\frac{12}{42}$ can be simplified by dividing its numerator and denominator by 6, the GCD of 12 and 42, to obtain the simplest form $\frac{2}{7}$. It is therefore important to be able to compute the greatest common divisor; fortunately, there are several useful methods that can be employed.

### GCD Method 1: Greatest Common Divisors by Intersection of Sets

This method works well when the numbers involved are small and all of the divisors of both numbers are easily written down. By way of explanation, it is probably best to present an example.

**EXAMPLE 4.12    Finding the Greatest Common Divisor by Intersection of Sets**

Find the greatest common divisor of 18 and 45.

**Solution**    Let $D_{18}$ and $D_{45}$ denote the sets of divisors of 18 and 45, respectively. Since

$$D_{18} = \{1, 2, 3, 6, 9, 18\} \quad \text{and} \quad D_{45} = \{1, 3, 5, 9, 15, 45\},$$

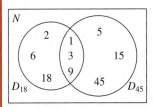

$D_{18} \cap D_{45} = \{1, 3, 9\}$ is the set of common divisors of 18 and 45. Thus, $\text{GCD}(18, 45) = 9$.

The sets of divisors can be visualized with a Venn diagram with loops representing the two sets of divisors $D_{18}$ and $D_{45}$ in the universe $N$ of the natural numbers. The common divisors are those natural numbers in the overlapped region representing the intersection of sets, and the largest number in the intersection is the greatest common divisor.

### GCD Method 2: Greatest Common Divisor from Prime Factorizations

The greatest common divisor can also be found by using prime factorizations. For example, to find $\text{GCD}(270, 630)$, first determine the prime factorizations $270 = 2 \cdot 3 \cdot 3 \cdot 3 \cdot 5$ and $630 = 2 \cdot 3 \cdot 3 \cdot 5 \cdot 7$ and then write the factorizations, aligning each repeated factor vertically. The GCD is then the product of the prime factors that appear in both factorizations. That is,

$$270 = 2 \cdot 3 \cdot 3 \cdot 3 \cdot 5$$
$$630 = 2 \cdot 3 \cdot 3 \quad \cdot \quad 5 \cdot 7$$
$$\text{GCD}(270, 630) = 2 \cdot 3 \cdot 3 \quad \cdot \quad 5$$

so $\text{GCD}(270, 630) = 2 \cdot 3 \cdot 3 \cdot 5 = 90$.

It is even easier to use prime-power factorizations, where the GCD is the product of primes that appear in each factorization raised to the smaller exponent. To help compare the two factorizations, it is helpful to allow 0 as an exponent so that both factorizations have the same sequence of primes. For example, since $5^0 = 1$ and $7^0 = 1$, it follows that $168 = 2^3 \cdot 3^1 \cdot 5^0 \cdot 7^1$ and $90 = 2^1 \cdot 3^2 \cdot 5^1 \cdot 7^0$. Therefore, choosing the smaller exponents in the factorizations, we find that $\text{GCD}(168, 90) = 2^1 \cdot 3^1 \cdot 5^0 \cdot 7^0 = 6$.

The method works in general and is described by the following theorem:

---

**THEOREM** *Greatest Common Divisor from Prime Factorizations*

Let $a$ and $b$ be natural numbers. Then the GCD($a$, $b$) is the product of the prime powers in the prime-power factorizations of $a$ and $b$ that have the smaller exponents (including zero).

---

**EXAMPLE 4.13** **Finding the Greatest Common Divisor by Using Prime-Power Representations**

Compute the greatest common divisor of 504 and 3675.

**Solution**  We first find the prime-power representation of each number:

$$
\begin{array}{r}
3 \\
3\overline{)9} \\
7\overline{)63} \\
2\overline{)126} \\
2\overline{)252} \\
2\overline{)504}
\end{array}
\qquad\qquad
\begin{array}{r}
3 \\
7\overline{)21} \\
7\overline{)147} \\
5\overline{)735} \\
5\overline{)3675}
\end{array}
$$

$$504 = 2^3 \cdot 3^2 \cdot 5^0 \cdot 7^1 \qquad\qquad 3675 = 2^0 \cdot 3^1 \cdot 5^2 \cdot 7^2$$

Choosing the smaller of the exponents on each prime that appears in both factorizations, we see that

$$\text{GCD}(504, 3675) = 2^0 \cdot 3^1 \cdot 5^0 \cdot 7^1 = 21.$$

As a check, we note that $504 \div 21 = 24$, that $3675 \div 21 = 175$, and that 24 and 175 have no common factor other than 1.

---

## GCD Method 3: Greatest Common Divisor from the Euclidean Algorithm

This method for finding greatest common divisors is found in Book IV of Euclid's *Elements,* written in about 300 B.C. It has the distinct advantage of working unfailingly no matter how large the two numbers are or how complicated the arithmetic is. It all depends on the division algorithm.

Dividing $a$ by $b$, we obtain a quotient $q$ and a remainder $r$ such that

$$a = bq + r, \qquad 0 \le r < b.$$

But then

$$r = a - bq.$$

Therefore, by the divisibility-of-sums-and-differences theorem (page 202), $d$ divides $a$ and $d$ divides $b$ if, and only if, $d$ divides $b$ and $d$ divides $r$. Thus, $a$ and $b$ have the same set of divisors as $b$ and $r$ and, hence, the same greatest common divisor.

---

**THEOREM** *The GCD and the Division Algorithm*

Let $a$ and $b$ be any two natural numbers with $a \ge b$, and let $q$ and $r$ be, respectively, the quotient and remainder determined by the division algorithm. That is,

$$a = bq + r, \qquad 0 \le r < b.$$

Then, GCD($a$, $b$) = GCD($b$, $r$).

---

**MHM**  A useful Mathematical Habit of the Mind to develop is to ask yourself how a theorem or a formula can become the basis of a computational procedure to carry out a calculation. Such a step-by-step process is known as an **algorithm.** For example, in Chapter 3 we developed algorithms based on whole-number properties and base-ten representations that allow us to calculate sums, differences, products, and divisions.

Let's now examine how the theorem we have just proved allows us to devise an algorithm that will calculate the GCD($a$, $b$) of two given natural numbers $a$ and $b$, where we assume that $a \geq b$. We first notice that we can replace the given numbers $a$ and $b$ with a smaller pair of numbers $b$ and $r$ that have the same greatest common divisor. This a good first step, but we can use the same idea again as a second step, replacing $b$ and $r$ by the smaller pair of numbers $r$ and $s$, where $s$ is the remainder obtained when $b$ is divided by $r$. We can continue to take further steps following the same procedure, discarding quotients and obtaining a decreasing list of remainders. Eventually, we must reach a remainder of 0, with some number $z$ being the last positive remainder. But by the theorem, the GCD of each pair of retained remainders is unchanged, so we have

$$\text{GCD}(a, b) = \text{GCD}(b, r) = \text{GCD}(r, s) = \cdots = \text{GCD}(z, 0) = z.$$

The procedure we have just described is called the **Euclidean algorithm** for calculating the greatest common divisor. To see it in action, suppose we wish to calculate the greatest common divisor of 3144 and 1539. Then we carry out the following sequence of divisions with remainder, discarding quotients as we go:

| Division with Remainder | GCD Equality Shown |
|---|---|
| 2 R 66<br>1539$\overline{)3144}$ | GCD(3144, 1539) = GCD(1539, 66) |
| 23 R 21<br>66$\overline{)1539}$ | GCD(1539, 66) = GCD(66, 21) |
| 3 R 3<br>21$\overline{)66}$ | GCD(66, 21) = GCD(21, 3) |
| 7 R 0<br>3$\overline{)21}$ | GCD(21, 3) = GCD(3, 0) = 3 |

Since the last nonzero remainder is 3, it follows that GCD(3144, 1539) = 3.

> **THEOREM** *The Euclidean Algorithm*
> Let $a$ and $b$ be any two natural numbers, with $a \geq b$. Divide $a$ by $b$ to get a remainder $r$. If $r = 0$, then $b = \text{GCD}(a, b)$, but if $r > 0$, divide $b$ by $r$ to get a remainder $s$. If $s = 0$, then $r = \text{GCD}(a, b)$, but if $s > 0$, divide $r$ by $s$ to get a remainder $t$. Continue the division-with-remainder process until a remainder of 0 results. Then the last nonzero remainder is $\text{GCD}(a, b)$.

## EXAMPLE 4.14 Using the Euclidean Algorithm

Compute GCD(18,411, 1649), using the Euclidean algorithm.

**Solution**  Using the Euclidean algorithm, we have

$$\begin{array}{ccc} 11\text{ R }272 & 6\text{ R }17 & 16\text{ R }0 \\ 1649\overline{)18,411} & 272\overline{)1649} & 17\overline{)272} \end{array}$$

so that 17 is the last positive remainder. Therefore, GCD(18,411, 1649) = 17.

## The Least Common Multiple

In 14th-century France, the style of choral motet writing called *Ars Nova* was such that, while the tenor line was written in a repeated pattern of a fixed number of measures (an isorhythmic pattern), the other three parts were written in an isorhythmic pattern with a different number of measures. The motet could end only when *all* of the parts simultaneously came to the end of their respective pattern. It is then natural to ask, "How many measures must be sung to reach the first place at which the motet can be ended?"

Let's consider an example in which the tenor isorhythmic pattern is 8 measures long. The tenor, if singing alone, could end at 8, 16, 24, 32, 40, 48, 56, 64, . . . measures—that is, after any multiple of 8 measures. However, if the other parts have an isorhythmic pattern that is 6 measures long, these patterns must end after a multiple of 6 measures, namely, after 6, 12, 18, 24, 30, 36, 42, 48, 54, 60, . . . measures. Both patterns end simultaneously at any *common* multiple of 6 and 8—that is, after 24, 48, 72, . . . measures. We see that the motet must be at least 24 measures long, since 24 is the smallest multiple of both 6 and 8. In mathematical terminology, we say that 24 is the **least common multiple** of 6 and 8.

In general, we have the following definition:

> **DEFINITION**   *Least Common Multiple*
>
> Let $a$ and $b$ be natural numbers. The least natural number $m$ that is a multiple of both $a$ and $b$ is called their **least common multiple,** and we write $m = \text{LCM}(a, b)$.

The least common multiple is especially important for computing with fractions, since the least common multiple is used to find the least common denominator. There are several methods available to determine an LCM.

## LCM Method 1: Least Common Multiples by Intersection of Sets

The following method is simple and works particularly well if the two numbers are not large: Let $a$ and $b$ be any two natural numbers. The sets of natural-number multiples of $a$ and $b$ are

$$M_a = \{a, 2a, 3a, \ldots\} \qquad \text{and} \qquad M_b = \{b, 2b, 3b, \ldots\}.$$

Therefore, $M_a \cap M_b$ is the set of all natural-number common multiples of $a$ and $b$, and the least number in this set is the least common multiple of $a$ and $b$. Since $ab$ is clearly a common multiple of both $a$ and $b$, one need not extend the sets beyond this product. Indeed, it is always the case that $\text{LCM}(a, b) \leq ab$.

**EXAMPLE 4.15  Finding a Least Common Multiple by Set Intersection**

Find the least common multiple of 9 and 15.

**Solution**   Since $9 \cdot 15 = 135$, we consider the sets

$$M_9 = \{9, 18, 27, 36, 45, 54, 63, 72, 81, 90, 99, 108, 117, 126, 135, \ldots\};$$
$$M_{15} = \{15, 30, 45, 60, 75, 90, 105, 120, 135, \ldots\};$$
$$M_9 \cap M_{15} = \{45, 90, 135, \ldots\}.$$

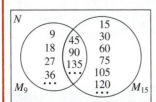

Since $M_9 \cap M_{15}$ is the set of all natural-number common multiples of 9 and 15, the least element of this set is $\text{LCM}(9, 15)$. Therefore, $\text{LCM}(9, 15) = 45$. Notice that $\text{GCD}(9, 15) = 3$, so $\text{GCD}(9, 15) \cdot \text{LCM}(9, 15) = 3 \cdot 45 = 135 = 9 \cdot 15$.

The set intersection method of finding the LCM can also be illustrated by a Venn diagram, as shown at the left. The numbers in the overlapped loops are the common multiples, and the smallest of these is the least common multiple.

## LCM Method 2: Least Common Multiples from Prime Factorizations

The least common multiple can be found by using prime factorizations, a method similar to the procedure used earlier to find the GCD. For example, to find $\text{LCM}(270, 630) = \text{LCM}(2 \cdot 3 \cdot 3 \cdot 3 \cdot 5, 2 \cdot 3 \cdot 3 \cdot 5 \cdot 7)$, write the factorizations aligned vertically to show the prime factors that are repeated. The LCM is then the product of the factors that appear in at least one of the factorizations. That is,

$$270 = 2 \cdot 3 \cdot 3 \cdot 3 \cdot 5$$
$$630 = 2 \cdot 3 \cdot 3 \, \cdot \quad 5 \cdot 7$$
$$\text{LCM}(270, 630) = 2 \cdot 3 \cdot 3 \cdot 3 \cdot 5 \cdot 7,$$

so $2 \cdot 3 \cdot 3 \cdot 3 \cdot 5 \cdot 7 = 1890$ is the least common multiple.

Prime-power expansions can also be used, but this time the prime powers with the larger exponents are multiplied to find the LCM. Again, it is helpful to allow the exponent zero so that the same sequence of primes appears in both factorizations. For example, since $168 = 2^3 \cdot 3^1 \cdot 5^0 \cdot 7^1$ and $90 = 2^1 \cdot 3^2 \cdot 5^1 \cdot 7^0$, then $\text{LCM}(168, 90) = 2^3 \cdot 3^2 \cdot 5^1 \cdot 7^1$ is found by choosing the larger exponents in the factorizations.

> **THEOREM**   *Least Common Multiple from Prime-Power Factorizations*
> Let $m$ and $n$ be natural numbers. Then the $\text{LCM}(m, n)$ is the product of the prime powers in the prime-power factorizations of $m$ and $n$ that have the larger exponents.

**EXAMPLE 4.16   Finding LCMs and GCDs by Using Prime-Power Representations**

**Solution**

$5^0 = 1$
$2^0 = 1$

Compute the least common multiple and greatest common divisor of $m = 2268 = 2^2 \cdot 3^4 \cdot 7^1$ and $n = 77{,}175 = 3^2 \cdot 5^2 \cdot 7^3$.

Both the least common multiple and the greatest common divisor will be of the form $2^a \cdot 3^b \cdot 5^c \cdot 7^d$. For the greatest common divisor, we choose the *smaller* of the two exponents with which each prime appears in $m$ and $n$, and for the least common multiple, we choose the *larger* of each pair of exponents. Thus, since

$$m = 2^2 \cdot 3^4 \cdot 5^0 \cdot 7^1 \qquad \text{and} \qquad n = 2^0 \cdot 3^2 \cdot 5^2 \cdot 7^3,$$

we have

$$\text{GCD}(m, n) = 2^0 \cdot 3^2 \cdot 5^0 \cdot 7^1 = 63$$

and

$$\text{LCM}(m, n) = 2^2 \cdot 3^4 \cdot 5^2 \cdot 7^3 = 2{,}778{,}300.$$

Since both the smaller and larger exponents on each prime were used in finding $\text{GCD}(m, n)$ and $\text{LCM}(m, n)$, it follows that

$$mn = \text{GCD}(m, n) \cdot \text{LCM}(m, n).$$

Thus,

$$mn = 2268 \cdot 77{,}175 = 175{,}032{,}900$$

and

$$\text{GCD}(m, n) \cdot \text{LCM}(m, n) = 63 \cdot 2{,}778{,}300 = 175{,}032{,}900.$$

The last part of the solution in Example 4.16, showing that $mn = \text{GCD}(m, n) \cdot \text{LCM}(m, n)$, can be repeated in general, so we have the following important theorem:

> **THEOREM**   $mn = GCD(m, n) \cdot LCM(m, n)$
> If $m$ and $n$ are any two natural numbers, then $mn = \text{GCD}(m, n) \cdot \text{LCM}(m, n)$.

## LCM Method 3: Least Common Multiples by Using the Euclidean Algorithm

As noted in the previous theorem, if $m$ and $n$ are natural numbers, then $GCD(m, n) \cdot LCM(m, n) = mn$. Thus,

$$LCM(m, n) = \frac{mn}{GCD(m, n)},$$

and we have already learned that $GCD(m, n)$ can always be found by means of the Euclidean algorithm.

---

**EXAMPLE 4.17** **Finding a Least Common Multiple by the Euclidean Algorithm**

Find the least common multiple of 2268 and 77,175 by using the Euclidean algorithm.

**Solution** These are the same two numbers treated in Example 4.16. However, here our procedure is totally different, since we no longer need to know the prime factorizations of the given numbers. Using the Euclidean algorithm, we have these divisions:

$$2268 \overline{)77{,}175} \quad 34 \text{ R } 63 \qquad 63 \overline{)2268} \quad 36 \text{ R } 0$$

Since the last nonzero remainder is 63, $GCD(2268, 77{,}175) = 63$ and

$$LCM(2268, 77{,}175) = \frac{2268 \cdot 77{,}175}{63}$$
$$= 2{,}778{,}300,$$

as before.

---

## An Application of the LCM

**EXAMPLE 4.18** **Using the LCM to Investigate the "Calendar Round"**

The ancient Mayan culture* of Central America adopted and refined a calendar first devised by the Zapotecs, an ancient indigenous culture centered at Monte Albán in southern Mexico. The Calendar Round, represented by the wheel calendar shown in the accompanying photo, is based on a combination of two cycles: the Tzlok'in ("count of days") 260-day cycle and the Haab', a cycle consisting of 18 months of 20 days each plus a period of 5 "nameless days." The Calendar Round was the period required for the Tzlok'in and Haab' cycles to end together. What is the length of the Calendar Round period, as measured in both days and Haab' "years"?

**Solution** The Haab' is a period of $18 \times 20 + 5 = 365$ days. Thus, the Calendar Round has a duration of LCM(260, 365). Using the prime factorizations $260 = 2^2 \cdot 5 \cdot 13$ and $365 = 5^1 \cdot 73^1$, we see that the Calendar Round is $2^2 \cdot 5^1 \cdot 13^1 \cdot 73^1 = 18{,}980$ days long. Since $365 = 5 \cdot 73$ is one Haab', the Calendar Round is $2^2 \cdot 13^1 = 52$ Haab's, or about 52 years in duration. The Mayans were well aware that a true solar year was about a quarter of a day longer than a Haab'.

---

*The Mayan calendric systems are very interesting mathematically, and more information about them is easily available on the Internet. Of considerable current interest is the Long Count Calendar, which began (in its Gregorian calendar equivalent) on September 6, 3114 B.C., and will complete its first cycle on December 21, 2012. It's amazing that the Mayans could pinpoint a winter solstice so far into the future.

## Using Technology to Find the GCD and LCM

Scientific calculators, graphing calculators, spreadsheets, and other computational machines and programs usually have built-in functions that compute greatest common divisors and least common multiples. However, even the simpler types of calculators frequently found in elementary and middle school classrooms are still very helpful. For example, many calculators have an integer divide button $\boxed{\text{Int} \div}$ that gives the result of a division of natural numbers as a quotient and a remainder rather than as a decimal. This makes it very convenient to carry out the Euclidean algorithm. As an example, here are the keystrokes for computing the GCD of 308 and 252.

| Key In | 308 | $\boxed{\text{Int} \div}$ | 252 | $\boxed{=}$ |
|--------|-----|------|-----|-----|
| Display | 308 | 308 | 252 | 1 R 56 |

| Key In | 252 | $\boxed{\text{Int} \div}$ | 56 | $\boxed{=}$ |
|--------|-----|------|-----|-----|
| Display | 252 | 252 | 56 | 4 R 28 |

| Key In | 56 | $\boxed{\text{Int} \div}$ | 28 | $\boxed{=}$ |
|--------|-----|------|-----|-----|
| Display | 56 | 56 | 28 | 2 R 0 |

Since 28 was the last nonzero remainder, we have GCD(308, 252) = 28. It is then easy to calculate that LCM(308, 252) — 2772 with these keystrokes:

| Key In | 308 | $\boxed{\times}$ | 252 | $\boxed{\div}$ | 28 | $\boxed{=}$ |
|--------|-----|-----|-----|-----|-----|-----|
| Display | 308 | 308 | 252 | 77616 | 28 | 2772 |

For a calculator without the integer-divide feature, you'll need to work a bit harder to determine the needed remainders. (See problem 29.)

## Problem Set 4.3

Exercises numbered in red are answered in the back of the text.

### Understanding Concepts

1. Find the greatest common divisor of each of these pairs of numbers by the method of intersection of sets of divisors:

   (a) 24 and 27

   (b) 14 and 22

   (c) 48 and 72

2. Find the least common multiple of each of these pairs of numbers by the method of intersection of sets of multiples:

   (a) 24 and 27

   (b) 14 and 22

   (c) 48 and 72

3. Use the results of problems 1 and 2 to show that

   (a) $24 \cdot 27 = \text{GCD}(24, 27) \cdot \text{LCM}(24, 27)$.

   (b) $14 \cdot 22 = \text{GCD}(14, 22) \cdot \text{LCM}(14, 22)$.

   (c) $48 \cdot 72 = \text{GCD}(48, 72) \cdot \text{LCM}(48, 72)$.

4. Use the method based on prime-power representations to find the greatest common divisor and least common multiple of each of these pairs of numbers:

   (a) $r = 2^2 \cdot 3^1 \cdot 5^3$ and $s = 2^1 \cdot 3^3 \cdot 5^2$

   (b) $u = 5^1 \cdot 7^2 \cdot 11^1$ and $v = 2^2 \cdot 5^3 \cdot 7^1$

   (c) $w = 2^2 \cdot 3^3 \cdot 5^2$ and $x = 2^1 \cdot 5^3 \cdot 7^2$

5. Use the Euclidean algorithm to find each of the following:

   (a) GCD(3500, 550) and LCM(3500, 550)

   (b) GCD(3915, 825) and LCM(3915, 825)

   (c) GCD(624, 1044) and LCM(624, 1044)

6. Use the definition of GCD and LCM, not a calculation, to find

   (a) GCD(40, 40).

   (b) GCD(19, 190).

   (c) GCD(59, 0).

   (d) LCM(25, 25).

   (e) LCM(13, 130).

   (f) LCM(47, 1).

**7.** Write a statement that generalizes each part of problem 6. As an example, for part (a), your statement would be "If *n* is any natural number, then GCD(*n*, *n*) = *n*."

## Teaching Concepts

**8.** Cuisenaire® rods are colored rods 1 centimeter square and of lengths 1 cm, 2 cm, 3 cm, . . . , 10 cm, as shown here:

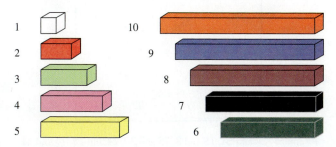

We say that a smaller rod *measures* a longer rod if a number of the smaller rods placed end to end are the same length as the given rod.

**(a)** Which rods will measure the 9-rod?

**(b)** Which rods will measure the 6-rod?

**(c)** What is the greatest common divisor of 9 and 6?

**(d)** Place the 10-rod and the 8-rod end to end to form an "18-train" as in the "Counting Cars and Trains" Hands On activity of Chapter 2. Which rods or trains will measure the 18-train?

**(e)** Place the 7-rod and the 5-rod end to end to form a 12-train. Which rods or trains will measure the 12-train?

**(f)** What is the greatest common divisor of 12 and 18?

**(g)** Describe how you might use Cuisenaire® rods to demonstrate the notion of greatest common divisor to children.

**9.** Cuisenaire® rods are described in the preceding problem.

**(a)** What is the shortest train or length that can be measured by both 4-rods and 6-rods?

**(b)** What is the least common multiple of 4 and 6?

**(c)** What is the shortest train or length that can be measured by both 6-rods and-9 rods?

**(d)** What is the least common multiple of 6 and 9?

**(e)** Briefly describe how you could use Cuisenaire® rods to demonstrate the notion of the least common multiple to children.

**10. (a)** Indicate how you could use a number line to illustrate the notion of the greatest common divisor to children.

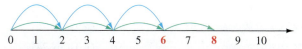

**(b)** Indicate how you could use a number line to illustrate the notion of the least common multiple to children.

## Responding to Students

**11.** How would you respond to a student who claims that GCD(0, *n*) = *n* for every whole number *n*?

**12.** Since *n* divides 0 for every natural number *n*, how would you respond to a student who claims that LCM(0, *n*) = 0 for every natural number *n*?

**13.** How would you respond to Tawana, who claims that *mn* is the least common multiple of *m* and *n* in every case?

**14.** Paulita says, "Why do we have to learn about greatest common divisors, anyway? It seems like a waste of time to me." How would you respond to Paulita?

**15.** Gerald says, "I can see that greatest common divisors can be useful, but how about least common multiples? They seem like just a lot of busywork to me." How would you respond to Gerald?

## Thinking Critically

**16.** The following figure shows that a 5″-by-5″ square tile can be used to cover a floor that measures 60″ by 105″:

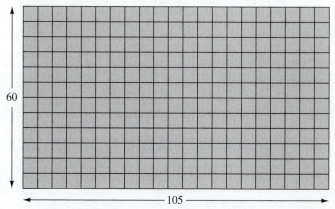

**(a)** List all of the sizes of squares tiles that can be used to tile the floor. What is the largest size of square tile that can be used?

**(b)** How many square tiles of the largest size are used to cover the floor?

**(c)** Suppose you wish to tile a hallway measuring 48″ wide by 216″ long. What is the largest size of square tile that can be used, and how many tiles of this size are required?

**(d)** Generalize your results: What is the largest size of square tile that can be used to cover an *m* × *n* rectangle, and how many tiles of that size are required?

**17.** The following figure shows that an 8″-by-12″ rectangular brick can tile a 48″-by-48″ square.

**(a)** Is there a smaller sized square that can be tiled with 8″-by-12″ bricks, all placed horizontally? Explain why or why not.

**(b)** What is the smallest square that can be tiled with horizontal 9″-by-12″ bricks? Explain your reasoning.

(c) More generally, what is the smallest square that can be tiled with *m*-by-*n* rectangular bricks, with all bricks having the same orientation?

(d) How many bricks are required to tile the smallest square with bricks of size *m* by *n*? Obtain a simple formula involving both the GCD and LCM of *m* and *n*, and check your answer against your answers to parts (a) and (b).

18. The notions of the greatest common divisor and the least

**MHM** common multiple extend naturally to more than two numbers. Moreover, the prime-power method extends naturally to finding $\text{GCD}(a, b, c)$ and $\text{LCM}(a, b, c)$.

(a) If $a = 2^2 \cdot 3^1 \cdot 5^2$, $b = 2^1 \cdot 3^3 \cdot 5^1$, and $c = 3^2 \cdot 5^3 \cdot 7^1$, compute $\text{GCD}(a, b, c)$ and $\text{LCM}(a, b, c)$.

(b) Is it necessarily true that $\text{GCD}(a, b, c) \cdot \text{LCM}(a, b, c) = abc$?

(c) Find numbers *r*, *s*, and *t* such that $\text{GCD}(r, s, t) \cdot \text{LCM}(r, s, t) = rst$.

19. Use the method of intersection of sets to compute the following:

(a) $\text{GCD}(18, 24, 12)$ and $\text{LCM}(18, 24, 12)$

(b) $\text{GCD}(8, 20, 14)$ and $\text{LCM}(8, 20, 14)$

(c) Is it true that $\text{GCD}(8, 20, 14) \cdot \text{LCM}(8, 20, 14) = 8 \cdot 20 \cdot 14$?

20. (a) Compute $\text{GCD}(6, 35, 143)$ and $\text{LCM}(6, 35, 143)$.

(b) Is it true that $\text{GCD}(6, 35, 143) \cdot \text{LCM}(6, 35, 143) = 6 \cdot 35 \cdot 143$?

(c) Guess under what conditions $\text{GCD}(a, b, c) \cdot \text{LCM}(a, b, c) = abc$.

21. The LCM method demonstrated in the table that follows is popular in Asian countries. The idea is quite simple: Factor out any prime divisor of one or more terms, and replace each term containing the prime factor by its quotient. Continue until the last row contains only distinct prime numbers and 1s. Then multiply the extracted primes and the primes in the last row to obtain the prime-power form of the LCM. The method works equally well with any number of terms, so we compute $\text{LCM}(75, 24, 30, 42)$.

| 2 | 75 | 24 | 30 | 42 |
|---|----|----|----|----|
| 3 | 75 | 12 | 15 | 21 |
| 2 | 25 | 4 | 5 | 7 |
| 5 | 25 | 2 | 5 | 7 |
| | 5 | 2 | 1 | 7 |

Thus, $\text{LCM}(75, 24, 30, 42) = 2 \cdot 3 \cdot 2 \cdot 5 \cdot 5 \cdot 2 \cdot 7 = 2^3 \cdot 3^1 \cdot 5^2 \cdot 7^1$.

Use this method to find these LCMs in prime-power form:

(a) $\text{LCM}(48, 25, 35)$

(b) $\text{LCM}(40, 28, 12, 63)$

(c) $\text{LCM}(250, 28, 44, 110)$

## Thinking Cooperatively

22. **Euclid's Game** is a two-player game that starts with two natural numbers written on the game board. Taking alternate turns, each player chooses any two different numbers on the board

whose difference does not yet appear. The result of the subtraction is written on the board. The first player unable to make a move loses the game. For example, if the two starting numbers are 76 and 52 (shown circled), then, after five plays the board may look as shown. Play Euclid's Game several times with your partner. You may choose the starting pair of numbers from this list or make up your own:

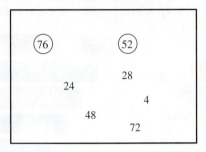

17 and 51, 28 and 24, 15 and 8, 75 and 39, 24 and 18, 70 and 21.

Now respond to these questions, working with your game partner:

(a) Is it possible to determine all of the numbers that will appear on the board ahead of time? If so, describe how this can be done.

(b) Given the starting numbers 52 and 76, should you choose to play first or second?

(c) Given the two starting numbers *m* and *n*, how should you determine to play first or second?

[*Note:* Euclid's Game can be played online by going to the site http://www.cut-the-knot.org.]

23. Work through this problem as a group project. You will particularly want to consult with the members of your group as you respond to parts (e), (f), (g), and (h). Recall that the Fibonacci numbers up to $F_{30}$ are displayed in problem 21 of Problem Set 4.2.

(a) In problem 36 of Problem Set 4.1, you should have guessed that for $m > 2$, $F_m$ divides $F_n$ if, and only if, *m* divides *n*. Compute each of these quotients: $F_{12} \div F_6$, $F_{18} \div F_9$, and $F_{30} \div F_{15}$.

(b) If *n* is composite, must $F_n$ be composite? Explain briefly.

(c) If *n* is a prime, must $F_n$ be a prime? Explain briefly.

(d) Complete the following list:

$\text{GCD}(F_6, F_9) = \text{GCD}(8, 34) = 2 = F_3 \quad \text{GCD}(6, 9) = 3$

$\text{GCD}(F_{14}, F_{21}) = \text{GCD}(377, 10{,}946)$

$\qquad\qquad\qquad = 13 = F_7 \qquad\qquad \text{GCD}(14, 21) = 7$

$\text{GCD}(F_{10}, F_{15}) = \qquad\qquad\qquad\qquad \text{GCD}(10, 15) =$

$\text{GCD}(F_{20}, F_{30}) = \qquad\qquad\qquad\qquad \text{GCD}(20, 30) =$

$\text{GCD}(F_{16}, F_{24}) = \qquad\qquad\qquad\qquad \text{GCD}(16, 24) =$

$\text{GCD}(F_{12}, F_{18}) = \qquad\qquad\qquad\qquad \text{GCD}(12, 18) =$

(e) On the basis of the calculations in part (d), make a conjecture about $\text{GCD}(F_m, F_n)$.

(f) Test your conjecture by computing $\text{GCD}(F_{24}, F_{28})$.

(g) Does the result of part (f) prove that your conjecture in part (e) is correct?

**(h)** If GCD($F_{16}, F_{20}$) were to equal 4, what could you conclude about your conjecture in part (e)?

**(i)** Actually compute the value of GCD($F_{16}, F_{20}$).

## Making Connections

**24.** Fractions will not be discussed in this text until Chapter 6. However, in elementary school you should have learned that a fraction $\frac{a}{b}$ can be written in simplest terms (i.e., as $\frac{c}{d}$, where $c$ and $d$ have no common factor other than 1) by dividing both $a$ and $b$ by GCD($a, b$). For example, $\frac{16}{20} = \frac{4}{5}$, since GCD(16, 20) = 4, $16 \div 4 = 4$, and $20 \div 4 = 5$. Compute the following:

**(a)** GCD(6, 8)　　　　**(b)** GCD(18, 24)

**(c)** GCD(132, 209)　　**(d)** GCD(315, 375)

Find a fraction in simplest terms that is equivalent to each of these:

**(e)** $\frac{6}{8}$　　　　　　**(f)** $\frac{18}{24}$

**(g)** $\frac{132}{209}$　　　　**(h)** $\frac{315}{375}$

**25.** The front wheel of a tricycle has a circumference of 54 inches, and the back wheels have a circumference of 36 inches.

If points $P$ and $Q$ are both touching the sidewalk when Marja starts to ride, how far will she have ridden when $P$ and $Q$ first touch the sidewalk at the same time again?

**26.** Sarah Speed and Hi Velocity are racing cars around a track. If Sarah can make a complete circuit in 72 seconds and Hi completes a circuit in 68 seconds,

**(a)** how many seconds will it take for Hi to first pass Sarah at the starting line?

**(b)** how many laps will Sarah have made when Hi has completed one more lap than she has?

**27.** In a machine, a gear with 45 teeth is engaged with a gear with 96 teeth, with teeth $A$ and $B$ on the small and large gears, respectively, in contact as shown. How many more revolutions will the small gear have to make before $A$ and $B$ are again in the same position?

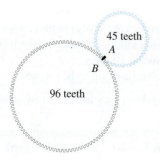

**28.** **Cicadas and Prime Numbers.** There are two common types of periodical cicadas. The most prevalent is the 17-year cicada (genus *Magicicada*), for which a brood of nymphs emerges from the ground to breed and lay eggs after a 17-year underground wait. The 13-year cicada (also of genus *Magicicada*) has a similar life cycle, but with a 13-year interval between one emergence and the next. Studies show that having a prime-number interval, such as 13 or 17, offers evolutionary advantages to each species. In particular, there is less interference between the two species when they live in the same region.

**(a)** If broods of 13- and 17-year species happened to emerge in the same year, how many years will pass before this interference is repeated?

**(b)** Suppose, hypothetically, that there exist 12- and 18-year species of cicadas. If both species happened to emerge the same year, in how many years will they interfere with one another again?

**(c)** Answer part (b) again, but for hypothetical 9- and 15-year species.

## Using a Calculator

**29. (a)** Devise a sequence of keystrokes to carry out division with remainder for a simple calculator that has only the decimal-divide key $\boxed{\div}$. Illustrate your method by finding both the quotient 2 and remainder 21 when 117 is divided by 48. Look for a way to use the memory to avoid reentering the divisor.

**(b)** With your simple calculator, practice using the procedure devised to answer part (a) to show that $48 \div 21 = 2$ R 6 and $21 \div 6 = 3$ R 3. By mental arithmetic, $6 \div 3 = 2$ R 0; what does this tell you about GCD(117, 48)? Why is that so?

**30.** Compute the following GCD and LCM by implementing the Euclidean algorithm on a calculator:

**(a)** GCD(6600, 10500)　　**(b)** LCM(6600, 10500)

**31.** Compute the following with a calculator:

**(a)** GCD(42957, 35217)　　**(b)** LCM(42957, 35217)

## From State Student Assessments

**32.** (Texas, Grade 4)
Which is the least common multiple of 12 and 15?

　**A.** 45　　**B.** 48　　**C.** 60　　**D.** 72

**33.** (Arizona, Grade 7}
What is the greatest common factor (GCF) of the following numbers? 12, 15, 18, 36

　**A.** 3　　**B.** 6　　**C.** 18　　**D.** 36

**34.** (Arizona, Grade 6)
What is the least common multiple (LCM) of 4 and 14?

　**A.** 2　　**B.** 14　　**C.** 28　　**D.** 56

**35.** (Oregon State, Grade 7)
The 10th-grade class at Forest Grove High School could be divided into equal-sized groups of 6, 12, or 17 students for photos. What is the least number of students in the 10th-grade class?

　**A.** 102　　**B.** 204　　**C.** 306　　**D.** 404

**36.** (Massachussetts, Grade 6)

This is an open-response question.

- BE SURE TO ANSWER AND LABEL ALL PARTS OF THE QUESTION.
- Show all your work (diagrams, tables, or computations) in your Student Answer Booklet.
- If you do the work in your head, explain in writing how you did the work.

A local bakery celebrated its one-year anniversary on Saturday. On that day, every 4th customer received a free cookie. Every 6th customer received a free muffin.

**(a)** Did the 30th customer receive a free cookie, a free muffin, both, or neither? Show or explain how you got your answer.

**(b)** Casey was the first customer to receive both a free cookie and a free muffin. What number customer was Casey? Show or explain how you got your answer.

**(c)** Tom entered the bakery after Casey. He received a free cookie only. What number customer could Tom have been? Show or explain how you got your answer.

**(d)** On that day, the bakery gave away a total of 29 free cookies. What was the total number of free muffins the bakery gave away on that day? Show or explain how you got your answer.

**37.** (Texas, Grade 6)

Mrs. Sandoval has 60 folders, 45 pairs of scissors, and 30 rulers. What is the greatest common factor Mrs. Sandoval can use to divide the school supplies in equal groups?

**A.** 3      **B.** 5      **C.** 10      **D.** 15

**38.** (Texas, Grade 7)

Mrs. Blackburn wrote the following riddle on the board for her mathematics class:

> We are two-digit numbers. Our greatest common factor is 16. Our difference is 48. Our sum is 112.

What are the two numbers of the riddle?

**A.** 16 and 48, because their greatest common factor is 16

**B.** 32 and 80, because their difference is 48 and their greatest common factor is 16

**C.** 16 and 64, because their difference is 48 and their greatest common factor is 16

**D.** 48 and 96, because their difference is 48

## Examining School Book Pages

*Refer to the School Book Pages provided on page 221 to answer the following questions.*

**39.** **(a)** Could the problem about fish filets and buns be solved without the picture of the packages shown on the left-hand page?

**(b)** The solution given in Step 2 states that Loren must buy 24 fish filets and 24 buns. What's a more practical answer to the problem when Loren goes to the store?

**40.** **(a)** Solve problem 28, using the method demonstrated at the top of the page.

**(b)** Solve problem 28 again, but this time assuming that cashews come in 18-oz cans and that you want to buy equal amounts of pecans, almonds, peanuts, and cashews. [Suggestion: Look for a way to simplify your work!]

## The Chapter in Relation to Future Teachers

In this chapter, we have introduced the basic number-theoretic notions of divisibility, factoring, factors and multiples, primes and composite numbers, least common multiples, and greatest common divisors. These ideas not only are useful in other parts of mathematics and in disciplines like computer science but also provide interesting and stimulating motivational material for the elementary mathematics classroom. Increasingly, number-theoretic notions are appearing in elementary school texts, and these ideas must be thoroughly understood by teachers.

Understandably, most current research in mathematics is far too technical to describe to younger students, but number theory is an exception, since many of its results and unsolved problems are quite easily explained to students in the upper elementary or middle school years. For example, it is not too difficult to find triples of natural numbers $(a, b, c)$ for which $a^2 + b^2 = c^2$. For example, $(3, 4, 5)$ is such a triple, corresponding to a right triangle with sides of length 3, 4, and 5. Indeed, even the ancient Greek mathematicians knew that infinitely many such so-called **Pythagorean triples** exist. But what if the Pythagorean relation is modified just a little, so that the goal is to find triples of natural numbers for which $a^n + b^n = c^n$ for other values of $n$? It wasn't until 1993, after hundreds of years of effort, that the mathematician Andrew Wiles proved that no triples exist for $n > 2$.

Here are some other questions that are easy to ask but have yet to be answered:

- **Twin-Prime Conjecture** If both $p$ and $p + 2$ are prime, they are called twin primes. *Are there infinitely many twin primes?*
- **Germain Primes** If both $p$ and $2p + 1$ are prime, then $p$ is a *Germain prime*, named for the mathematician Sophie Germain. (See problem 27 from Problem Set 4.1.) *Are there infinitely many*

SOURCE: From Envision Math Student Edition Grade 5. Copyright © 2011 Pearson Education, Inc. or its affiliates. Used by permission. All rights reserved.

# Common Multiples and Least Common Multiple

---

**Lesson 10-2**

**Understand It!**
Making a list of multiples for two numbers is helpful when trying to determine the least common multiple.

## Common Multiples and Least Common Multiple

### How do you find the least common multiple?

Loren is buying fish fillets and buns for the soccer team dinner. What is the smallest number of fish fillets and buns she can buy to have the same number of each?

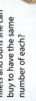

**Step 1**

Find the common multiples of 6 and 8.

Remember that a multiple of a number is a product of a given whole number and another whole number.

A **common multiple** is a number that is a multiple of two or more numbers.

List the multiples of 6 and 8.

6: 6, 12, 18, 24, 30, 36, 42, 48, 54, …

8: 8, 16, 24, 32, 40, 48, 56, …

Two common multiples of 6 and 8 are 24 and 48.

**Step 2**

Find the least common multiple of 6 and 8.

A **least common multiple (LCM)** is the least number that is a multiple of both numbers.

Both 24 and 48 are common multiples of 6 and 8. So, the LCM of 6 and 8 is 24. Loren will need to buy 24 fish fillets and 24 buns.

---

### Guided Practice*

**Do you know HOW?**

In **1** through **6**, find the LCM of each pair of numbers.

**1.** 2 and 4

**2.** 3 and 4

2: 2, 4, 6, 8, …          3: 3, 6, 9, 12, 15, …

4: 4, 8, 12, 16, …        4: 4, 8, 12, 16, …

**3.** 3 and 7

**4.** 8 and 15

**5.** 12 and 18

**6.** 6 and 18

**Do you UNDERSTAND?**

**7.** In the example above, why is 24 the LCM of 6 and 8?

**8.** How many packages of each does Loren need to buy to have 24 fish fillets and 24 buns?

---

### Independent Practice

**Leveled Practice** In **9** through **27**, find the LCM of each pair of numbers.

**9.** 2 and 4

2: 2, 4, …

4: 4, 8, …

**10.** 2 and 3

2: 2, 4, 6, 8, …

3: 3, 6, 9, 12, …

**11.** 5 and 6

5: 5, 10, 15, 20, 25, 30, 35, 40, …

6: 6, 12, 18, 24, 30, 36, 42, …

**12.** 3 and 5

**13.** 6 and 8

**14.** 4 and 5

**15.** 3 and 10

**16.** 4 and 9

**17.** 8 and 20

**18.** 6 and 9

**19.** 10 and 12

**20.** 8 and 12

**21.** 4 and 6

**22.** 8 and 16

**23.** 12 and 16

**24.** 8 and 9

**25.** 4 and 12

**26.** 5 and 10

**27.** 14 and 21

*For another example, see Set B on page 274.

---

### Problem Solving

**28.** Pecans are sold in 6-oz cans, almonds in 9-oz cans, and peanuts in 12-oz cans. What is the least number of ounces you can buy to have equal amounts of pecans, almonds, and peanuts?

**29.** **Writing to Explain** Can you always find the LCM for two numbers by multiplying them together? Why or why not?

**30.** **Number Sense** The batting averages of three players are 0.261, 0.267, 0.264. Write the averages in order from least to greatest. Use <.

**31.** A cell phone call costs $0.07 per minute for the first 25 minutes and $0.10 per minute for each additional minute. How much would a 47-minute call cost?

**32.** **a** Peter is distributing pamphlets about dog care and samples of dog biscuits. The dog biscuits come in packages of 12 and the pamphlets are in packages of 20. What is the smallest number of samples and pamphlets he needs to distribute without having any left over?

**b** How many packages of dog biscuits and pamphlets will Peter need?

**33.** Katie bought dinner at 5 different restaurants. Each dinner cost between $12 and $24. What is a reasonable total cost for all 5 dinners?

**A** less than $60

**B** more than $150

**C** between $24 and $60

**D** between $60 and $120

**34.** Julie drank $1\frac{2}{3}$ cups of cranberry juice. Her brother said she drank $\frac{5}{3}$ cups of juice. Is her brother correct? Explain your answer.

**35.** A factory whistle blows every 30 minutes. The clock tower chimes every 15 minutes. If they both sounded at 1:00 P.M., at what time will you hear them both at the same time again?

*Germain primes?* The largest known Germain prime is currently $p = 183{,}027 \cdot 2^{265440} - 1$, discovered in 2010. This Germain prime has 79,911 digits.

- **Goldbach Conjecture** *Is every even number that is larger than 4 the sum of two prime numbers?* It was shown in 2009 that every even natural number up to $16 \times 10^{17}$ is the sum of two primes!
- **Odd Perfect Numbers** The ancient Greeks called a number *perfect* if it equals the sum of its proper divisors. For example, $6 = 1 + 2 + 3$, $28 = 1 + 2 + 4 + 7 + 14$, and $496 = 1 + 2 + 4 + 8 + 16 + 31 + 62 + 124 + 248$ are the first three perfect numbers. Currently, there are 47 known perfect numbers, and all are even. *Are there any odd perfect numbers?* (If one exists, then it is larger than $10^{300}$.)

## Chapter 4 Summary

In what follows, unless expressly stated to the contrary, all symbols represent whole numbers.

| Section 4.1   Divisibility of Natural Numbers | Page Reference |
|---|---|

**CONCEPTS**

| | |
|---|---|
| • **Divisibility and factorization:** Given a natural number, $n$, the determination of the divisors of $n$ and its representation as a product of natural numbers. | 194 |
| • **Determination of primality:** A test to classify a given natural number as a prime number, a composite number, or the unit number 1. | 194 |

**DEFINITIONS**

| | |
|---|---|
| • $b$ **divides** $a$ when they are two whole numbers and $b \neq 0$, and there is a whole number $q$ such that $a = bq$. | 188 |
| • When $a = bq$, $b$ is a **factor,** or **divisor,** of $a$. | 188 |
| • A **proper divisor** is when $b$ divides $a$ and $b$ is less than $a$ when $a = bq$. | 188 |
| • When $a = bq$, $a$ is a **multiple** of $b$. | 188 |
| • Whole numbers are **even** when they are divisible by 2. A whole number that is not even is called an **odd** whole number. | 188 |
| • A **prime number** is a natural number that possesses exactly two different factors, itself and 1. | 189 |
| • A **composite number** is a natural number that possesses more than 2 different factors. | 189 |
| • The number 1 is a **unit;** it is neither prime nor composite. | 189 |

**THEOREMS**

| | |
|---|---|
| • **Fundamental theorem of arithmetic:** Every natural number greater than 1 is a prime or can be expressed as a product of primes in one, and only one, way, apart from the order of the prime factors. | 191 |
| • **Prime-power representation of $n$:** Every natural number greater than 1 is a power of a prime or can be expressed as a product of powers of different primes in one, and only one, way, apart from order. | 191 |
| • **Prime power representation of divisors of $n$:** Any divisor of $n$ is a product of prime powers of the form $p^j$, $0 \leq j < k$, where $p^k$ is a term in the prime power representation of $n$. | 192 |
| • **Infinitude of primes:** There are infinitely many prime numbers. | 193 |
| • **Primality test:** If a natural number $n \geq 2$ has no prime divisor $p$ for $2 \leq p \leq \sqrt{n}$, then $n$ is a prime number. | 193 |

## PROCEDURE

| | |
|---|---|
| • **Factor tree:** A method of factoring composite numbers into smaller and smaller ones until only primes remain. | 191 |
| • **Stacked short division:** A method of factoring composite into prime numbers using prime divisors and short division. | 191 |
| • **Sieve of Eratosthenes:** A systematic counting method for determining a table of all of the primes up to a given limit derived by the Greek mathematician Eratosthenes. | 194 |

## Section 4.2   Tests for Divisibility | Page Reference

### CONCEPTS

| | |
|---|---|
| • **Divisibility test:** A method to quickly determine, often with mental arithmetic, whether a natural number is divisible by a specified number. | 201 |

### THEOREMS

| | |
|---|---|
| • **Divisibility by 2, 5, and 10:** Let $n$ be a natural number. Then $n$ is | |
|   • divisible by 2 exactly when its base-ten units digit is 0, 2, 4, 6, 8. | 202 |
|   • divisible by 5 exactly when its base-ten units digit is 0 or 5. | 202 |
|   • divisible by 10 exactly when its base-ten units digit is 0. | 202 |
| • **Divisibility of sums and differences:** If $n$ divides both $a$ and $b$, then $n$ also divides their sum $a + b$ and their difference $a - b$. | 202 |
| • **Divisibility by 4, 8, and other powers of 2:** Let $n$ be a natural number. Then $n$ is divisible by 4 exactly when the number represented by its last two base-ten digits is divisible by 4. Similarly, $n$ is divisible by 8 exactly when the number represented by its last three base-ten digits is divisible by 8. | 203 |
| • **Divisibility by 3 and 9:** A natural number $n$ is divisible by 3 if, and only if, the sum of its digits is divisible by 3. Similarly, $n$ is divisible by 9 if, and only if, the sum of its digits is divisible by 9. | 204 |
| • **Divisibility by 11:** A natural number $n$ is divisible by 11 exactly when the sums of digits in the even and odd positions of $n$ have a difference that is divisible by 11. | 204 |
| • **Divisibility by products:** Let $a$ and $b$ be divisors of a natural number $n$. If $a$ and $b$ have no common divisor other than 1, then their product $ab$ is also a divisor of $n$. | 205 |
| • **Simultaneous test for divisibility by 7, 11 and 13:** Let $n$ be a natural number. Break $n$ into three-digit numbers and compute the respective sums of the numbers in even positions and odd positions. Find the difference of the two sums; if that number is divisible by 7, 11, or 13, respectively, then $n$ will be a respective multiple of those numbers. | 206 |

## Section 4.3   Greatest Common Divisors and Least Common Multiples | Page Reference

### DEFINITIONS

| | |
|---|---|
| • The **greatest common divisor, GCD($a$, $b$),** is the greatest natural number $d$ that divides both $a$ and $b$. | 209 |
| • The **greatest common factor, GCF($a$, $b$),** is an alternative description of the greatest common divisor, with GCD($a$, $b$) = GCF($a$, $b$). | 209 |
| • The **least common multiple, LCM($a$, $b$),** is the least natural number $m$ that is a multiple of both $a$ and $b$. | 213 |

**THEOREMS**

- **GCD and the division algorithm:** Let $a \div b = q \, \mathrm{R} \, r$. Then $\mathrm{GCD}(a, b) = \mathrm{GCD}(b, r)$.     211

- **The Euclidean algorithm:** Let $a$ and $b$ be any two natural numbers, with $a \geq b$. Divide $a$ by $b$ to get a remainder $r$. If $r = 0$, the $b = \mathrm{GCD}(a, b)$, but if $r > 0$, divide $b$ by $r$ to get a remainder $s$. If $s = 0$, then $r = \mathrm{GCD}(a, b)$, but if $s > 0$, divide $r$ by $s$ to get a remainder $t$. Continue the division with remainder process until a remainder of 0 results. Then the last nonzero remainder is $\mathrm{GCD}(a, b)$.     212

- **Product of the GCD and LCM:** For any two natural numbers, $\mathrm{GCD}(a, b) \cdot \mathrm{LCM}(a, b) = ab$.     215

**PROCEDURES**

- **GCD by set intersection:** $\mathrm{GCD}(a, b)$ is the largest member of the intersection of the sets of divisors of $a$ and $b$.     210

- **GCD from prime power representations:** $\mathrm{GCD}(a, b)$ is the product of the prime powers of the form $p^s, 0 \leq s$, where $s$ is the smaller power of the prime $p$ in the prime power representations of $a$ and $b$.     211

- **GCD by the Euclidean algorithm:** Given $a$ and $b$, repeatedly use division with remainder, discarding quotients, to calculate     212

$$a \div b = q \, \mathrm{R} \, r, b \div r = q' \, \mathrm{R} \, s, \ldots, x \div y = q''' \, \mathrm{R} \, z, y \div 3 = q'''' \, \mathrm{R} \, 0$$

  Then the last nonzero remainder, $z$, is the greatest common divisor:

$$\mathrm{GCD}(a, b) = z$$

- **LCM by set intersection:** $\mathrm{LCM}(a, b)$ is the least member of the intersection of the sets of multiples of $a$ and $b$.     213

- **LCM from prime power representations:** $\mathrm{LCM}(a, b)$ is the product of the prime powers of the form $p^t$, where $t$ is the larger power of the prime $p$ in the prime power representations of $a$ and $b$.     213

- **LCM by the Euclidean algorithm:** First use the Euclidean Algorithm to find the greatest common divisor $\mathrm{GCD}(a, b)$ of $a$ and $b$, and then calculate the least common multiple using the formula     215

$$\mathrm{LCM}(a, b) = \frac{ab}{\mathrm{GCD}(a, b)}$$

## Chapter Review Exercises

### Section 4.1

1. Draw rectangular diagrams to illustrate the factorings of 15, taking order into account; that is, think, for example, of $1 \cdot 15$ as different from $15 \cdot 1$.

2. Construct a factor tree for 96.

3. (a) Determine the set $D_{60}$ of all divisors of 60.

   (b) Determine the set $D_{72}$ of all divisors of 72.

   (c) Use $D_{60} \cap D_{72}$ to determine $\mathrm{GCD}(60, 72)$.

4. (a) Determine the prime-power representation of 1200.

   (b) Determine the prime-power representation of 2940.

   (c) Use parts (a) and (b) to determine $\mathrm{GCD}(1200, 2940)$ and $\mathrm{LCM}(1200, 2940)$.

5. Use information from the sieve of Eratosthenes in Figure 4.3 to determine whether 847 is prime or composite.

6. (a) Determine a composite natural number $n$ with a prime factor greater than $\sqrt{n}$.

   (b) Does the $n$ in part (a) have a prime divisor less than $\sqrt{n}$? If so, what is it?

7. Determine natural numbers $r$, $s$, and $m$ such that $r$ divides $m$ and $s$ divides $m$, but $rs$ does not divide $m$.

8. Use the number $n = 3 \cdot 5 \cdot 7 + 11 \cdot 13 \cdot 17$ to determine a prime different from 3, 5, 7, 11, 13, or 17.

## Section 4.2

9. Using mental methods, test each number for divisibility by 2, 3, 5, and 11:
   - (a) 9310
   - (b) 2079
   - (c) 5635
   - (d) 5665

10. Test each number for divisibility by 7, 11, and 13:
    - (a) 10,197
    - (b) 9373
    - (c) 36,751

11. Use the results of problem 9 to decide which of these are *true*:
    - (a) 15 divides 9310.
    - (b) 33 divides 2079.
    - (c) 55 divides 5635.
    - (d) 55 divides 5665.

12. Let $m = 3^4 \cdot 7^2$.
    - (a) How many divisors does $m$ have?
    - (b) List all the divisors of $m$.

13. Determine $d$ so that $2,765,301,2d3$ is divisible by 11.

14. (a) Determine the least natural number divisible by both $q$ and $m$ if $q = 2^3 \cdot 3^5 \cdot 7^2 \cdot 11^1$ and $m = 2^1 \cdot 7^3 \cdot 11^3 \cdot 13^1$.
    - (b) Determine the largest number less than the $q$ of part (a) that divides $q$.

## Section 4.3

15. (a) Find the greatest common divisor of 63 and 91 by the method of intersection of sets of divisors.
    - (b) Find the least common multiple of 63 and 91 by the method of intersection of sets of multiples.
    - (c) Demonstrate that $\text{GCD}(63, 91) \cdot \text{LCM}(63, 91) = 63 \cdot 91$.

16. If $r = 2^1 \cdot 3^2 \cdot 5^1 \cdot 11^3$, $s = 2^2 \cdot 5^2 \cdot 11^2$, and $t = 2^3 \cdot 3^1 \cdot 7^1 \cdot 11^3$, determine each of the following:
    - (a) $\text{GCD}(r, s, t)$
    - (b) $\text{LCM}(r, s, t)$

17. Determine each of the following, using the Euclidean algorithm:
    - (a) $\text{GCD}(119790, 12100)$
    - (b) $\text{LCM}(119790, 12100)$

18. Seventeen-year locusts and 13-year locusts both emerged in 1971. When will these insects' descendants next emerge in the same year?

## Chapter Test

1. Using mental methods, test each of these numbers for divisibility by 2, 3, 9, 11, and 13:
   - (a) 62,418
   - (b) 222,789

2. Let $m = 2^3 \cdot 5^2 \cdot 7^1 \cdot 11^4$ and $n = 2^2 \cdot 7^2 \cdot 11^3$.
   - (a) Does $r$ divide $m$ if $r = 2^2 \cdot 5^1 \cdot 7^2 \cdot 11^3$? Why or why not?
   - (b) How many divisors does $m$ have?
   - (c) Determine $\text{GCD}(m, n)$.
   - (d) Determine $\text{LCM}(m, n)$.

3. How many different factors does each of these numbers have?
   - (a) $2310 = 2^1 \cdot 3^1 \cdot 5^1 \cdot 7^1 \cdot 11^1$
   - (b) $5,336,100 = 2^2 \cdot 3^2 \cdot 5^2 \cdot 7^2 \cdot 11^2$

4. If $a = 2^1 \cdot 3^3 \cdot 5^2$ and $b = 2^3 \cdot 3^2 \cdot 5^1 \cdot 7^1$, compute each of the following:
   - (a) $\text{GCD}(a, b)$
   - (b) $\text{LCM}(a, b)$
   - (c) $\text{GCD}(a, b) \cdot \text{LCM}(a, b)$
   - (d) $a \cdot b$

5. Determine the prime-power representation of each of these numbers.
   - (a) 1400
   - (b) 5445
   - (c) 4554

6. Indicate whether each of these is *always true* (T) or *not always true* (F).
   - (a) If $a$ divides $c$ and $b$ divides $c$, then $ab$ divides $c$.
   - (b) If $r$ divides $s$ and $s$ divides $t$, then $r$ divides $t$.
   - (c) If $a$ divides $b$ and $a$ divides $c$, then $a$ divides $(b + c)$.
   - (d) If $a$ does not divide $b$ and $a$ does not divide $c$, then $a$ does not divide $(b + c)$.

7. Determine whether 281 is prime.

8. Use the Euclidean algorithm to determine $\text{GCD}(154, 553)$ and $\text{LCM}(154, 553)$.

9. Use the Euclidean algorithm to determine each of the following:
   - (a) $\text{GCD}(13,534, 997,476)$
   - (b) $\text{LCM}(13,534, 997,476)$

10. (a) Make a factor tree for 8532.
    - (b) Write the prime-power representation of 8532.
    - (c) Name the largest natural number smaller than 8532 that divides 8532.
    - (d) Name the smallest number larger than 8532 that is divisible by 8532.

# Integers

**5.1** Representations of Integers

**5.2** Addition and Subtraction of Integers

**5.3** Multiplication and Division of Integers

## Hands On

### The Debit/Credit Game

**Materials needed**

1. Red and black markers and a pair of dice.
2. Scoring sheets as shown in the following sample, three or four for each student:

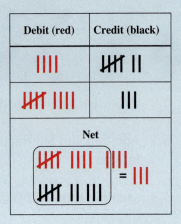

| Debit (red) | Credit (black) |
|:-:|:-:|
| IIII | ⊮ II |
| ⊮ IIII | III |

Net

⊮ IIII IIII = III
⊮ II IIII

**Directions**

Each student chooses an opponent. Play several games with the following rules:

1. Take turns rolling the dice, entering your score with tally marks as shown in the sample. You may enter your score in any of the four boxes. If it is recorded as a credit, use the black marker; if it is recorded as a debit, use the red marker.
2. The game ends when each player has made four rolls and has recorded two credits and two debits on the score sheet. Use a loop as shown in the sample to cancel a red debit tally and a black credit tally in pairs, leaving the net value shown by the tally marks that have not been canceled.
3. The winner is the player with the highest net worth.

**Question**

What strategy will help you win the game?

---

**CHAPTER PREVIEW**  A new system of numbers called the **integers** is defined and investigated in this chapter. The set of integers, denoted by $I$, includes the set of whole numbers $W = \{0, 1, 2, 3, \ldots\}$ together with the **negative integers,** denoted by $-1, -2, -3, \ldots$. Altogether, the set of integers is written

$$I = \{\ldots, -3, -2, -1, 0, 1, 2, 3, \ldots\}.$$

Note that $N \subset W \subset I$:

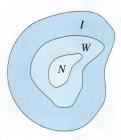

Here, the set of natural numbers $N = \{1, 2, 3, \ldots\}$ is now known as the set of **positive integers.** As the notation suggests, each positive integer $n$ is associated with a corresponding negative integer, denoted by $-n$, that is called its **opposite.** The association can also be reversed, so that, for example, the opposite of $-4$, denoted by $-(-4)$, is the positive integer 4. The most important property of the integers is that the sum of an integer $n$ and its opposite $-n$, is 0; that is, $n + (-n) = 0$. Another way to describe this property is that every integer $n$ has an **additive inverse** $-n$. Since $0 + 0 = 0$, the additive inverse of 0 is itself; that is, $-0 = 0$.

The following excerpt from the NCTM *Principles & Standards* gives a brief description of what is expected of elementary and middle school students with regard to the integers:

Middle-grades students should also work with integers. In lower grades, students may have connected negative integers in appropriate ways to informal knowledge derived from everyday experiences, such as below-zero winter temperatures or lost yards of football plays. In the middle grades, students should extend these initial understandings of integers. Positive and negative integers should be seen as useful for noting relative changes or values. Students can also appreciate the utility of negative integers when they work with equations whose solution requires them, such as 2x + 7 = 1.

SOURCE: *Principles and Standards for School Mathematics by NCTM, pages 217–218. Copyright © 2000 by the National Council of Teachers of Mathematics. Reproduced with permission of the National Council of Teachers of Mathematics via Copyright Clearance Center. NCTM does not endorse the content or validity of these alignments.*

**KEY IDEAS**

- Additive inverses (opposites)
- Absolute value
- Representations of the integers with colored counters, mail-time situations, number line
- Using representations to understand the arithmetic operations of addition, subtraction, multiplication, and division in the system of integers
- Why subtracting is equivalent to adding the opposite
- Why the multiplication of two negative integers is a positive integer
- Applications of the integers to real-life problems

## 5.1

# Representations of Integers

The integers are an extension of the system of whole numbers, obtained by starting with the whole numbers $W = \{0, 1, 2, 3, \ldots\}$ and then creating additional numbers denoted by $-1, -2, -3, \ldots$ to form the set of integers $I = \{\ldots, -3, -2, -1, 0, 1, 2, 3, \ldots\}$. As the following definition indicates, the integers $I$ have the additive-inverse property, a property that does not hold for the whole numbers:

---

**DEFINITION** *The Integers*

The integers $I = \{\ldots, -3, -2, -1, 0, 1, 2, 3, \ldots\}$ consist of

- the natural numbers $\{1, 2, 3, \ldots\}$, now called the **positive integers,**
- the **negative integers** $\{\ldots, -3, -2, -1\}$, and
- the number 0, which is neither negative nor positive.

Moreover,

- 0 is the **additive identity** in $I$, with $0 + n = n + 0 = n$ for all integers $n$, and
- $-n$ is the **additive inverse** of the positive integer $n$, having the property that

$$n + (-n) = (-n) + n = 0.$$

---

Notice that if we were to start with a negative integer, $-n$, then the same formula $n + (-n) = (-n) + n = 0$ shows that $n$ is the additive inverse of $-n$. For example, the additive inverse of $-3$ is 3, so we have $-(-3) = 3$. More generally, we see that *every* integer, whether positive, negative or zero, can be paired with its additive inverse, $-n$. The additive inverse, $-n$, is also called the **negative** of $n$ or the **opposite** of $n$. It is important to observe how parentheses are used, and expressions such as "$--3$" and "$3 + -3 = 0$" are incorrect. Instead, we write $-(-3) = 3$ and $3 + (-3) = 0$. Even 0 has an opposite, namely, itself, since $0 + 0 = 0$; that is, $-0 = 0$.

> On a calculator, the opposite of a number is obtained by pressing the negation, or change sign, key, which is often labeled $+/-$ or $(-)$.
> Taking the opposite is not the same as subtracting, for which the subtraction key $-$ is used.

More generally, we see that the integers have the following property:

> **PROPERTY** *The Additive-Inverse Property of a Number System*
> A number system has the **additive-inverse property** if, and only if, for every number $n$ in the system, there is a number $m$ in the system for which $n + m = m + n = 0$.

To see that the whole numbers do not have the additive inverse property, it is enough to check that the whole number 1 does not have an additive inverse. Indeed, $1 + m \geq 1 + 0 - 1 \neq 0$ for all whole numbers $m$, since $m \geq 0$.

## Absolute Value of an Integer

Given an integer $n$, either $n$ or its opposite, $-n$, is a nonnegative integer known as the absolute value of $n$, written as $|n|$. The absolute value is also called the magnitude of an integer.

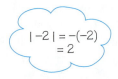

> **DEFINITION** *Absolute Value of an Integer*
> If $n$ is an integer, then its **absolute value,** or **magnitude,** is the nonnegative integer $|n|$ given by
> $$|n| = \begin{cases} n \text{ if } n \text{ is positive or 0} \\ -n \text{ if } n \text{ is negative.} \end{cases}$$

## EXAMPLE 5.1 Determining Absolute Values

Determine the absolute values of these integers.

   **(a)** $-71$      **(b)** 29      **(c)** 0      **(d)** $-852$

**Solution**

**(a)** Since $-71$ is negative, $|-71| = -(-71) = 71$.
**(b)** Since 29 is positive, $|29| = 29$.
**(c)** $|0| = 0$.
**(d)** Since $-852$ is negative, $|-852| = -(-852) = 852$.

## Criteria for the Representation of the Integers

Any representation of the integers $I = \{\ldots, -2, -1, 0, 1, 2, 3, \ldots\}$, whether by means of a manipulative, as a visualization, or as a conceptual model, must first make the following fundamental ideas abundantly clear:

- how each integer is represented, including the possibility than an integer can be represented in multiple ways;
- how the representation of any nonzero number describes both the magnitude (or *absolute value*) and the *sign*—positive or negative—of the number;

- how 0, the unique integer with a zero magnitude, is represented;
- why the addition-by-zero property holds, so that $n + 0 = 0 + n = n$ for all integers; and finally,
- how every integer $n$ is paired with its *opposite* (also known as its *negative* or its *additive inverse*), $-n$, so that $n + (-n) = 0$.

Three models for the integers will now be introduced: colored counters, mail-time stories, and the number line. Yet a fourth model is described by the balloon model found in the Cooperative Investigations of Sections 5.2 and 5.3. Throughout this chapter, we will rely on these models to understand the fundamental properties of the integers and their arithmetic.

## Representing Integers with Colored Counters

In the colored-counter model, an integer is represented by a set of colored counters—red and black discs, or sometimes red and yellow, are often used. Some examples are shown in Figure 5.1.

**FIGURE 5.1**
Colored-counter representations of positive 5 and negative 2

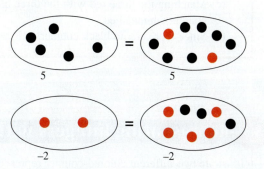

It is important to understand that a pair of oppositely colored counters, one red and one black, neutralize one another. For this reason, the colored-counter model is sometimes called a "charge" model, in which a black counter is a "unit positive charge" that is annihilated by a "unit negative charge" red counter. Since oppositely colored counters neutralize one another, any colored-counter representation of an integer can be altered either by deleting or by adding pairs of oppositely colored counters. For example, starting with the 5B loop with five black counters that represents 5, we can add two oppositely colored BR pairs to the loop to give the equivalent 7B2R representation of 5 shown in Figure 5.1. In the other direction, starting with a 3B5R loop as shown at the bottom right of Figure 5.1, we can remove three BR pairs of counters from the loop, to leave the equivalent, but simpler, representation 2R. Thus, both of the bottom loops represent negative 2, which is written $-2$.

In general, a loop of colored counters *represents a positive integer* if there are more black counters than red, and the number of unpaired black counters is the absolute value of the positive integer. The positive integers are identified as the natural numbers. Similarly, if more red than black counters are in the loop, the number represented is a negative integer whose absolute value is the excess number of red counters.

Of special importance are loops that have an equal number of red and black counters, since these each represent 0. Three equivalent representations of 0 are shown in Figure 5.2.

**FIGURE 5.2**
Three colored-counter representations of 0

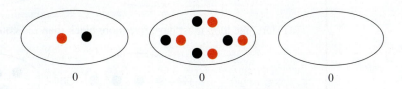

Since there is neither an excess of black nor an excess of red counters, 0 is neither positive nor negative, and it has an absolute value of 0.

EXAMPLE 5.2 **Interpreting Sets of Colored Counters as Integers**

Determine the integer represented by each of these loops of colored counters:

(a) 　　　　(b)

(c) 　　　　(d)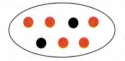

Solution

(a) Matching the two red counters with two of the black counters, we get 3B, representing the integer 3.

(b) Matching the red counter with a black counter, we get 2B, representing the integer 2.

(c) Matching the three red with the three black counters, we get 0; we have no red or black counters unmatched.

(d) Since there are no black counters, 3R represents the negative integer −3.

EXAMPLE 5.3 **Representing Integers with Sets of Colored Counters**

Illustrate two different colored-counter representations for each of these integers:

(a) 2　　　　(b) −3　　　　(c) 0　　　　(d) 5

Solution

(a) Here, the loops must have two more black counters than red counters. Two possibilities are

 and

(b) Here, the loop must have three fewer black counters than red counters. Possibilities include

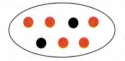 and

(c) Here, the loop must contain the same number of red and black counters or no counters at all. Possibilities include

 and

(d) Here, the loop must have five more black than red counters. Possibilities include

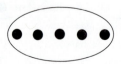 and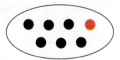

### The Addition-by-0 Property with Colored Counters

Viewing addition as "putting together," the colored-counter model interprets addition straightforwardly: Simply combine the counters in the loops to get a loop that represents the sum. This idea will be explored in detail in the next section, but the case of addition by 0 deserves special attention. Two examples are shown in Figure 5.3, where we see that $3 + 0 = 3$ and $0 + (-2) = -2$.

**FIGURE 5.3**

Illustrating the addition-by-0 property with colored counters

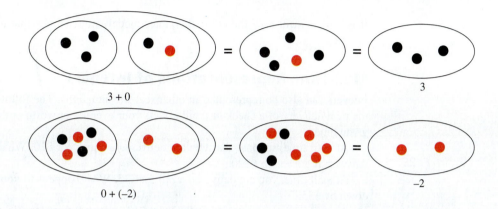

More generally, we see that the addition-by-0 property holds for the integers. That is, for every integer $n$—positive, zero, or negative—we have

$$n + 0 = 0 + n = n.$$

### Negatives with Colored Counters

Suppose that the color of each counter which represents an integer $n$ is reversed, so that red becomes black and black becomes red. The integer represented by the loop with reversed colors is the negative of the integer $n$, written as $-n$. For example, if 5 is represented by 5B, then its opposite is the integer $-5$ represented by 5R. Similarly, if $-3$ is represented by 3R, then its opposite is the integer 3 represented by 3B. Since reversing colors twice returns each counter to its original color, we have this result:

> **THEOREM**  *The Opposite of the Opposite of an Integer*
> For every integer $n$, $-(-n) = n$.

**EXAMPLE 5.4  Determining Negatives**

Determine the negative of each of these integers:

    **(a)** 4      **(b)** $-2$      **(c)** 0      **(d)** $-320$

**Solution**

    **(a)** The negative of 4 is $-4$.
    **(b)** The negative of $-2$ is $-(-2) = 2$.
    **(c)** The negative of 0 is $-0 = 0$, since 0 is neither positive nor negative.
    **(d)** The negative of $-320$ is $-(-320) = 320$.

> *Note that the negative of a negative integer is positive.*

Because addition is modeled by combining colored counters, it becomes clear that, when an integer $n$ is added to its opposite, $-n$, every counter of one color is matched to a counter of the opposite color. That is, the result is 0. The case $5 + (-5) = 0$ is shown in Figure 5.4.

**FIGURE 5.4**
Illustrating that 5 + (−5) =
0 with colored counters

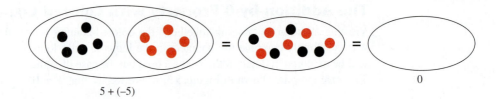

5 + (−5)

0

It is now evident how the colored-counter model demonstrates that every integer has an additive inverse.

## Mail-Time Representations of Integers

Integers can also be represented in other real-life situations. The following examples illustrate how the mail delivery of a check or a bill affects your overall net worth or the value of your assets at any given time:

At mail time, suppose that you are delivered a check for $20. What happens to your net worth? Answer: It goes up by $20.

At mail time, you are delivered a bill for $35. What happens to your net worth? Answer: It goes down by $35.

At mail time, you received a check for $10 and a bill for $10. What happens to your net worth? Answer: It stays the same.

These examples can be easily generalized. A positive integer $n$ is represented by a check for $n$ dollars, a negative integer, $−m$, is represented by a bill for $m$ dollars, and 0 is represented by either no checks or bills or by a check and a bill, each for the same amount. The absolute value is the number of dollars shown on the amount payable or amount due.

---

**EXAMPLE 5.5** **Interpreting Mail-Time Situations**

(a) At mail time, you are delivered a check for $27. What happens to your net worth?
(b) At mail time, you are delivered a bill for $36. Are you richer or poorer? By how much?

**Solution**

(a) Your net worth goes up $27.
(b) Poorer. Your net worth goes down by $36.

---

**EXAMPLE 5.6** **Describing Mail-Time Situations for Given Integers**

Describe a mail-time question corresponding to each of these integers:

(a) −42          (b) 75          (c) 0

**Solution**

(a) At mail time, the letter carrier brought you a bill for $42. Are you richer or poorer, and by how much?
(b) At mail time, you were delivered a check for $75. What happens to your net worth?
(c) Quite to your surprise, at mail time the mail carrier skipped your house, so you received no checks and no bills. Are you richer or poorer, and by how much?

## Number-Line Representations of Integers

We have already used a number line to illustrate whole numbers, and it can be used equally effectively to represent integers. Choose an arbitrary point to denote 0 on the number line. Then successively measure out unit distances on each side of 0, and label successive points to the right of 0 with successive positive integers and points to the left with successive negative integers, as shown in Figure 5.5. The arrow at the right end of the number line indicates how the integers are ordered. For example, $-4 < -2$, since $-4$ is to the left of $-2$. In some elementary texts, arrows are placed at both ends of the number line, though the left arrow is later dropped when the number line becomes identified as the $x$-axis.

**FIGURE 5.5**

Representing integers on a number line

The number-line representation of the integers corresponds nicely to marking thermometers with degrees above 0 and degrees below 0, and with the practice in most parts of the world (with the notable exceptions of North America and Russia) of numbering floors above ground and below ground in a skyscraper. It also corresponds to the countdown of the seconds to liftoff and beyond in a space shuttle launch. The count 9, 8, 7, 6, 5, 4, 3, 2, 1, liftoff!, 1, 2, 3, . . . is not really counting backward and then forward, but forward all the time. The count is actually

| | |
|---|---|
| 9 seconds before liftoff | $-9$ |
| 8 seconds before liftoff | $-8$ |
| $\cdot$ | $\cdot$ |
| $\cdot$ | $\cdot$ |
| $\cdot$ | $\cdot$ |
| 1 second before liftoff | $-1$ |
| Liftoff! | 0 |
| 1 second after liftoff | 1 |
| 2 seconds after liftoff | 2 |

and so on. This example is familiar to children and helps to make positive and negative numbers real and understandable.

Integers are also represented by curved arrows. For example, *an arrow from any point to a point 5 units to the right represents 5,* and *an arrow from any point to a point 5 units to the left represents* $-5,$ as illustrated in Figure 5.6. The figure also shows that 0 is the arrow whose head and tail coincide.

**FIGURE 5.6**

Using arrows to represent integers

It is important to understand that each integer is represented in two ways: either as a *position* along the number line or as an *arrow* that describes a "jump" along the number line. A point on the line that is $n$ units to the right of 0 represents the positive integer $n$, and its opposite, $-n$, is the point on the opposite side of 0 that is equally far from 0. Alternatively, the arrow representing a positive integer $n$ is a right-pointing arrow $n$ units long, and its opposite, $-n$, is the left-pointing arrow of the same length. The 0 arrow is like a jump straight up, which makes no net forward or backward motion along the number line.

Unlike points on the number line, which remain in a fixed position, arrows are free to translate from side to side. It is this freedom to translate arrows that allows them to be combined to define new arrows. Therefore, arrows are used to illustrate how integers are added and subtracted, as will be shown in detail in the next section. For now, it is enough to notice that combining an arrow representing $n$ with the 0 arrow does not change the length or direction of the $n$ arrow. That is, $n + 0 = 0 + n = n$. Also, if jumps of equal length, but opposite direction, are combined, there is no net motion along the number line, so $n + (-n) = 0$. These fundamental ideas are shown in Figure 5.7.

**FIGURE 5.7**
Using the number-line
model to show that
$9 + 0 = 9$ and
$6 + (-6) = 0$

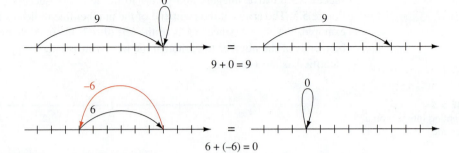

$9 + 0 = 9$

$6 + (-6) = 0$

On the number line, the absolute value is the length of the jump given by the arrow that represents the integer in question. Or, if integers are viewed as points along the number line, then the absolute value is the distance from the point in question to 0, as shown in Figure 5.8.

**FIGURE 5.8**
The absolute value of
both 5 and −5 is 5.

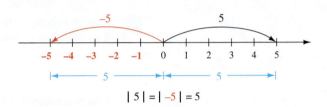

$|5| = |-5| = 5$

---

**EXAMPLE 5.7 Determining Absolute Values with the Number-Line Model**

Determine the absolute values of these integers:

(a) −11    (b) 13    (c) 0    (d) −9

**Solution**    We plot the numbers on the number line and determine the distance of the points from 0.

(a) $|-11| = 11 = -(-11)$ since $-11$ is 11 units from 0.
(b) $|13| = 13$ since 13 is 13 units from 0.
(c) $|0| = 0$ since 0 is 0 units from 0.
(d) $|-9| = 9 = -(-9)$ since $-9$ is 9 units from 0.

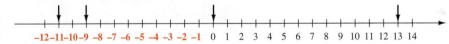

---

## Problem Set 5.1

Exercises numbered in red are answered in the back of the text.

### Understanding Concepts

1. Draw two colored-counter diagrams to represent each of these integers:

   (a) 5B          (b) 2R
   (c) 0           (d) −3          (e) 3

2. Draw a colored-counter diagram with the least number of counters to represent each of the following:

   (a) 3           (b) −4
   (c) 0           (d) 2

3. (a) Describe a mail-time situation that illustrates 14.

   (b) Describe a mail-time situation that illustrates −27.

4. (a) At mail time, you receive a check for $25 and an envelope with neither a bill nor a check. What addition-by-0 fact has been illustrated?

   (b) At mail time, you receive a postcard from your friend and a bill for $32. What addition fact is illustrated?

   (c) What is illustrated if your mailbox has a bill for $10 and a check for $10?

5. At mail time, you are delivered a check for $48 and a bill for $31.

**(a)** Are you richer or poorer, and by how much?

**(b)** What integer addition does this situation illustrate?

**6. (a)** At mail time, you are delivered a check for $27 and a bill for $42. What integer does this situation illustrate?

**(b)** Describe a different mail-time situation that illustrates the same integer as in part (a).

**7. (a)** Draw a number line and plot the points representing these integers:

**(i)** 0      **(ii)** 4      **(iii)** −4      **(iv)** 8

**(v)** (4 + 8)/2

**(b)** Where is (4 + 8)/2 relative to 4 and 8?

**8.** What integers are represented by the curved arrow on each of these number-line diagrams?

**(a)**

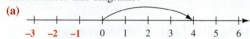

**(b)**

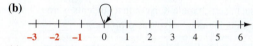

**(c)**

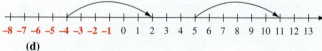

**(d)**

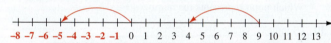

**9.** Draw number-line arrow diagrams to represent each of these integers:

**(a)** 7      **(b)** 0      **(c)** −9      **(d)** 9

**10. (a)** Find the absolute values of these quantities:

**(i)** 34      **(ii)** 4 − 4

**(iii)** −76      **(iv)** 17 − 5

**(b)** How far is it between 5 and 17 on the number line?

**11.** For what values of $x$ are these equations true?

**(a)** $|x| = 13$      **(b)** $|x| + 1 = 2$      **(c)** $|x| + 5 = 0$

**12.** Determine all pairs $(x, y)$ of integer values of $x$ and $y$ for which $|x| + |y| = 2$.

## Teaching Concepts

**13. (a)** How would you use colored counters to help students understand that $-(-4) = 4$?

**(b)** How would you use colored counters to help students understand that $-(-n) = n$ for every integer $n$ (positive, negative, or 0)?

**14.** The definition of absolute value is often confusing to students. On the one hand, they understand that the absolute value of a number is always positive. On the other hand, the definition states that $|n| = -n$ sometimes. How would you explain this seeming contradiction?

## Responding to Students

**15.** Althea claims that $-0 = 0$. How would you respond to Althea? Is she correct?

**16.** Lili doesn't think she has any need for negative integers and she can get along fine without them. What questions might you ask to get her to rethink her opinion?

## Thinking Critically

**17. (a)** What colored counters would have to be added to this set in order to represent −3?

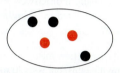

**(b)** Could the question in part (a) be answered in more than one way?

**(c)** How many different representations of −3 can be made with 20 or fewer counters?

**18.** If all the counters are used each time, list all the integers that can be represented with

**(a)** 12 counters.      **(b)** 11 counters.

**19. (a)** If all the counters are used each time, describe the set of integers that can be represented with $n$ counters.

**(b)** How many different integers are representable by using $n$ counters as in part (a)?

**20.** If some or all of the counters are used each time, describe the set of integers that can be represented

**(a)** with 12 counters.

**(b)** with 11 counters.

**(c)** with $n$ counters.

## Thinking Cooperatively

Do the next three problems with a group of two or three other students. At each step, discuss your solution with the other members of your group and determine a consensus answer for the group.

**21.** Imagine that a football field is an integer number line, with the 0 at midfield, and to score a touchdown you need to reach the goal line at 50 yards. The opposing team's goal line is at −50, so your "own territory" of the field is between the −50 and 0 yard lines.

**(a)** Starting at midfield, suppose your first two plays go for 15 yards and 12 yards. How deep into your opposition's territory are you from midfield? Answer in words and a number-line diagram.

**(b)** On the third play, a pass of 20 yards is intercepted and run back 72 yards. How far away from your goal line was the interception made? Where does the opposing team now have the ball? How far away from their goal line are they? Answer in words and a number-line diagram.

**(c)** In your group, make up your own football number-line problem. Now trade problems with other groups, and answer another group's problem.

**(d)** In your group, draw an arrow diagram on a football field number line showing −50 to 50. Now trade diagrams between groups, and invent a football story that matches the diagram.

22. **(a)** What integers are represented by these arrays of counters?

**(b)** Considering the pattern of answers to part (a), what integer would be represented by a similar array with $n$ rows and $n$ columns?

23. **(a)** How many black and how many red counters are there in a triangular array like this, but with 20 rows?

You should not actually need to make a diagram with 20 rows in order to answer this question.

**(b)** Write a brief explanation of your solution to part (a).

**(c)** Repeat part (a), but with a triangular array with 21 rows.

**(d)** What integers are represented by the triangular arrays in parts (a) and (c)?

**(e)** Make a table of integers represented by triangular arrays like those in parts (a) and (c), but with $n$ rows for $n = 1, 2, 3, 4, 5, 6, 7,$ and 8.

**(f)** Carefully considering the table of part (e), conjecture what integer is represented in a triangular array like those in parts (a) and (c), but with $n$ rows, where $n$ is any natural number. (*Suggestion:* Consider $n$ odd and $n$ even separately.)

## Making Connections

24. A delivery truck leaves the warehouse on Xavier at East 2nd street and drives east on Xavier to pick up a package at East 9th Street. The truck then heads west on Xavier to deliver the package at West 5th Street, first crossing East 1st, then Main Street, and then West 1st Street.

**(a)** Draw a number-line–and–arrow diagram that shows the truck's journey.

**(b)** Use absolute values to compute the total distance traveled from the warehouse to West 5th Street.

**(c)** Suppose the truck now drives east three blocks to a gas station on Xavier. What is the cross street of the gas station, and how many blocks is it from the warehouse?

25. The highest point on the North American continent is the summit of Mount McKinley, at 20,320 feet above sea level. The lowest point is Badwater Basin in Death Valley and is 282 feet below sea level.

**(a)** What is the difference in elevation between these two extreme elevations in North America?

**(b)** The diameter of Earth is about 8000 miles and a mile is 5280 feet. What percent of Earth's diameter is your answer to part (a)?

26. In Europe, the floor of a building at ground level is called the ground floor. What in America is called the second floor is called the first floor in Europe, and so on.

**(a)** If an elevator in a tall building in Paris, France, starts on the fifth basement level below ground, B5, and goes up 27 floors, on which numbered floor does it stop?

**(b)** What would the answer to part (a) be if the building were located in New York?

27. If an elevator starts on basement level B3 and goes down to B6, how far down has it gone?

28. The Wildcats made a first down on their own 33-yard line. On the next three plays, they lost 9 yards on a fumble, lost 6 yards when their quarterback was sacked, and completed a 29-yard pass play. Where was the line of scrimmage for the next play?

## From State Student Assessments

29. (Massachusetts, Grade 8. Note that students were *not* allowed to use calculators to solve this problem.)

*Use the number line below to answer the question.*

Which point represents the number $(-2)^4$?

30. (Kentucky, Grade 5)
Corina was investigating information about the natural wonders of the world. She found that Mt. Everest is the highest mountain in the world. It is 29,028 feet ABOVE sea level. She found that the Marianas Trench in the Pacific Ocean is the lowest point on Earth. It is 35,840 feet BELOW sea level.

**(a)** If Corina could throw a rock from the top of Mt. Everest to the bottom of the Marianas Trench, how many feet would it fall?

**(b)** Draw a diagram and explain your answer to part (a).

## Examining School Book Pages

*Refer to the School Book Pages provided on page 239 to answer the following questions.*

31. **(a)** The table started here lists one of the pairs of words found on the School Book Pages that refer to negative and positive integers:

| Negative | Positive |
|---|---|
| loss | gain |

List the other word pairs from the School Book Pages to continue the table.

**(b)** Add other pairs of words to form an even more complete table.

32. The School Book Page says that $-5$ is read "negative five." Would it also be correct to say "minus five"? Explain your reasoning carefully.

*See "Examining School Book Pages" on page 238 for questions related to the pages shown below.*

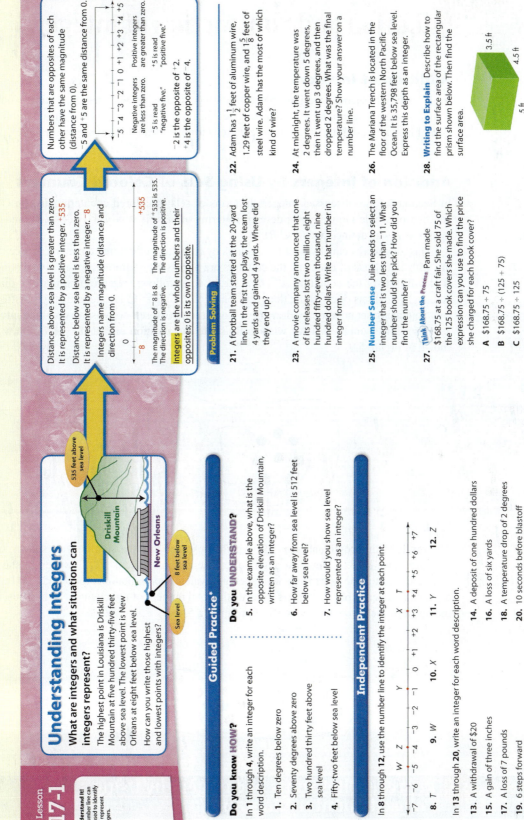

## 5.2 Addition and Subtraction of Integers

### Addition of Integers

In the previous section, we introduced the integers together with representations such as colored counters, mail-time stories, and number lines. In this section, we consider the addition and subtraction of integers, using the same representations to give meaning to these operations.

### Addition of Integers by Using Sets of Colored Counters

In Section 5.1, we discussed integers in terms of sets of colored counters. Also, in Chapter 2, the addition of whole numbers was defined in terms of sets. If $a = n(A)$, $b = n(B)$, and $A \cap B = \varnothing$, then $a + b$ was defined as $n(A \cup B)$.

This idea works equally well for integers by using sets of colored counters. Notice that, in working with actual sets of counters, the counters are necessarily different, so any two distinct sets $A$ and $B$ clearly satisfy the condition $A \cap B = \varnothing$. In what follows, we presume that the diagrams show actual physical sets of counters; thus, the condition $A \cap B = \varnothing$ is automatically satisfied. Moreover, we avoid using set notation by drawing a loop around two sets we wish to combine into a single set. Suppose, for example, that we wish to illustrate the addition of 8 and −3. We draw the diagram shown in Figure 5.9.

**FIGURE 5.9**
Diagram of colored counters illustrating
$8 + (-3) = 5$

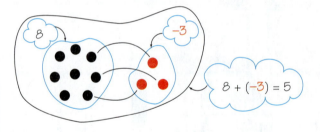

The result of this combination is 5B, which illustrates that the sum is 5, as shown. Of course, in Figure 5.9, we used the simplest possible representation of 8 and −3. However, as shown in Figure 5.10, the result is the same if we use other, equivalent representations for 8 and −3. In both figures, the total number of black counters exceeds the total number of red counters by 5. Thus, in each case, the result of the combined set is 5B, representing 5.

**FIGURE 5.10**
Another representation of
$8 + (-3) = 5$, using sets
of colored counters

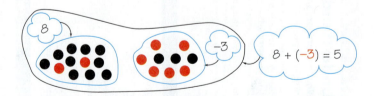

**EXAMPLE 5.8** **Representing Sums of Integers by Using Colored-Counter Diagrams**

Draw appropriate diagrams of colored counters to illustrate each of these sums:

    **(a)** $(-3) + 5$     **(b)** $(-2) + (-4)$     **(c)** $5 + (-7)$     **(d)** $4 + (-4)$

**Solution**

**(a)** Using the simplest representations of −3 and 5, we draw this diagram:

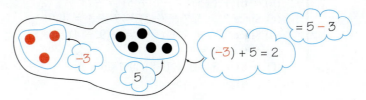

Since the combined set has a score of 2B, this diagram represents 2. Thus, $(-3) + 5 = 2$, and we note that $2 = 5 - 3$ as well. Hence, $(-3) + 5 = 5 - 3 = 2$.

**(b)** This sum can be represented as follows:

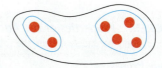

Since the combined set has a score of 6R, the diagram illustrates the sum

$$(-2) + (-4) = -6,$$

and we note that $-6 = -(2 + 4)$. Thus,

$$(-2) + (-4) = -(2 + 4) = -6.$$

**(c)** $5 + (-7) = -2 = -(7 - 5)$.

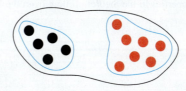

**(d)** $4 + (-4) = 0 = 4 - 4$.

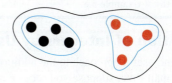

The results of Example 5.8 are entirely typical, and motivate this definition.

---

**DEFINITION** *Addition of Integers*

Let $m$ and $n$ be positive integers so that $-m$ and $-n$ are negative. Then the following are true:

- $(-m) + (-n) = -(m + n)$.
- If $m > n$, then $m + (-n) = m - n$.
- If $m < n$, then $m + (-n) = -(n - m)$.
- $n + (-n) = (-n) + n = 0$.

---

**EXAMPLE 5.9 Adding Integers**

Compute these sums:

**(a)** $7 + 11$      **(b)** $(-6) + (-5)$      **(c)** $7 + (-3)$

**(d)** $4 + (-9)$      **(e)** $6 + (-6)$      **(f)** $(-8) + 3$

**Solution**

(a) $7 + 11 = 18$
(b) $(-6) + (-5) = -(6 + 5) = -11$
(c) Since $7 > 3$, $7 + (-3) = 7 - 3 = 4$.
(d) Since $4 < 9$, $4 + (-9) = -(9 - 4) = -5$.
(e) $6 + (-6) = 0$
(f) $(-8) + 3 = 3 + (-8)$, and since $8 > 3$, $3 + (-8) = -(8 - 3) = -5$. Therefore, $(-8) + 3 = -5$.

The first four properties listed in the theorem that follows are the same as for the whole numbers. However, the "existence of negatives" property is true of the integers, but not of the whole numbers.

---

**THEOREM**    *Properties of the Addition of Integers*

Let $m$, $n$, and $r$ be integers. Then the following hold:

| | |
|---|---|
| **Closure Property** | $m + n$ is an integer. |
| **Commutative Property** | $m + n = n + m$. |
| **Associative Property** | $m + (n + r) = (m + n) + r$. |
| **Additive-Identity Property of 0** | $0 + m = m + 0 = m$. |
| **Existence of Negatives** | $(-m) + m = m + (-m) = 0$. |

---

**PROOF**    Since we have defined integers in terms of unions of sets of colored counters, the first four properties in the theorem follow from the fact that, for any sets $M$, $N$, and $R$,

$$M \cup N \text{ is a set,}$$
$$M \cup N = N \cup M,$$
$$M \cup (N \cup R) = (M \cup N) \cup R, \text{ and}$$
$$\varnothing \cup M = M \cup \varnothing = M.$$

The existence of the negative, or additive inverse, of $m$ for every integer $m$ follows as a generalization of part (d) of Example 5.8.

---

> Bringing something *to* you is adding.

## Addition of Integers by Using Mail-Time Stories

A second useful approach to the addition of integers is by means of mail-time stories.

At mail time, suppose you receive a check for $13 and another check for $6. Are you richer or poorer, and by how much? Answer: Richer by $19. This story illustrates that $13 + 6 = 19$.

**EXAMPLE 5.10    Adding Integers by Using Mail-Time Stories**

Write the addition equation illustrated by each of these stories:

(a) At mail time, you receive a bill for $3 and a check for $5. Are you richer or poorer, and by how much?
(b) At mail time, you receive a bill for $2 and another bill for $4. Are you richer or poorer, and by how much?
(c) At mail time, you receive a check for $5 and a bill for $7. Are you richer or poorer, and by how much?
(d) At mail time, you receive a check for $4 and a bill for $4. Are you richer or poorer, and by how much?

**Solution**

(a) Receiving a bill for $3 and a check for $5 makes you $2 richer. The story illustrates that $(-3) + 5 = 2$.
(b) Receiving a bill for $2 and another bill for $4 makes you $6 poorer. The story illustrates that $(-2) + (-4) = -6$.

**(c)** Receiving a check for \$5 makes you richer by \$5, but receiving a bill for \$7 makes you \$7 poorer. The net effect is that you are \$2 poorer. The story illustrates that $5 + (-7) = -2$.

**(d)** Receiving a \$4 check and a \$4 bill exactly balances out, and you are neither richer nor poorer. The story illustrates that $4 + (-4) = 0$.

Note that these results are exactly the results of Example 5.8. Moreover, the arguments hold in general, and we are again led to the theorem immediately preceding Example 5.9.

## Addition of Integers by Using a Number Line

Suppose we want to illustrate $5 + 4$ on a number line. This addition can be thought of as starting at 0 and counting 5 units to the right (in the positive direction on the number line) and then "counting on" 4 more units to the right. Figure 5.11 shows that this is the same as counting 9 units to the right from 0 straight away. Thus, $5 + 4 = 9$.

**FIGURE 5.11**
Illustrating $5 + 4 = 9$ on a number line

Since 4 is represented by moving 4 units to the right, it follows that $-4$ is represented by moving 4 units to the left. Thus, the addition $5 + (-4)$ is depicted on the number line as in Figure 5.12.

**FIGURE 5.12**
Illustrating $5 + (-4) = 1$ on a number line

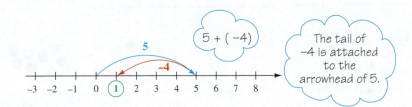

We count 5 units to the right from 0 and then "move" 4 units to the left in the direction of the $-4$ arrow. As seen on the diagram, this justifies $5 + (-4) = 1$.

**EXAMPLE 5.11** **Adding Integers on a Number Line**

What addition fact is illustrated by each of these diagrams?

Remember that $a + b$ is represented by a jump of $a$ units followed by a jump of $b$ units, where the tail of the $a$ arrow is at 0 and the tail of the $b$ arrow is at the head of the $a$ arrow.

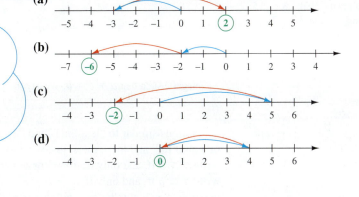

**Solution** | Since counting in the direction indicated by an arrow means adding, these diagrams represent the following sums:

**(a)** $-3 + 5 = 2$    **(b)** $(-2) + (-4) = -6$    **(c)** $5 + (-7) = -2$    **(d)** $4 + (-4) = 0$

Note that the results are again precisely the same as in Example 5.8.

**EXAMPLE 5.12 Drawing a Number-Line Diagram for a Given Sum**

Draw a number-line diagram to illustrate $(-7) + 4$.

**Solution** | Since $-7$ is indicated by counting 7 units to the left from 0 (in the direction indicated by the negation sign on the $-7$), and adding 4 is indicated by counting on to the right (in the positive direction, since 4 is a positive integer), we have this diagram:

Thus, $(-7) + 4 = -3 = -(7 - 4)$.

## Ordering the Set of Integers

The set with three black counters shown in Figure 5.13 contains fewer counters than the set with seven black counters. Accordingly, we say that *3 is less than 7* and write $3 < 7$. We also observe that $3 + 4 = 7$ and say that 7 is 4 more than 3.

**FIGURE 5.13**
Comparing 3 and 7;
$3 < 7$

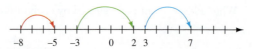

This idea is also easily illustrated on a number line, as shown in Figure 5.14. In particular, we note again that $3 + 4 = 7$, which implies that *3 is to the left of 7* on a number line. With that idea in mind, we extend the notion of "less than" to the set of all integers. In particular, if $a$ is to the left of $b$ on a number line, then there is a positive integer $c$ such that $a + c = b$, so $a < b$. That is, $a < b$ precisely when there is a right-pointing arrow extending from $a$ to $b$. Figure 5.14 shows that $-8 < -5, -3 < 2$, and $3 < 7$.

**FIGURE 5.14**
Number-line diagram
showing that $-8 < -5$,
$-3 < 2$, and $3 < 7$

> **DEFINITION**  *Less Than and Greater Than for the Set of Integers*
>
> Let $a$ and $b$ be integers. We say that **$a$ is less than $b$** and write $a < b$ if, and only if, there is a positive integer $c$ such that $a + c = b$. We say that **$b$ is greater than $a$** and write $b > a$ if, and only if, $a < b$.

Notions similar to "less than" and "greater than" are **"less than or equal to"** and **"greater than or equal to,"** and these mean just what they say. That is, we say that $a$ is less than or equal to $b$ and write $a \leq b$ if, and only if, $a < b$ or $a = b$. Similarly, we say that $a$ is greater than or equal to $b$ and write $a \geq b$ if, and only if, $a > b$ or $a = b$. Moreover, it is important to note that if $a$ and $b$ are any two points on a number line, either $a$ is to the left of $b$, $a = b$, or $a$ is to the right of $b$. Thus, the integers satisfy the so-called **law of trichotomy**.

## Into the Classroom

### Nancy Rolsen on Comparing and Ordering Integers

Students seem to gain a better understanding of positive and negative numbers through active participation. When comparing and ordering integers, I give each student a large index card with an integer written on it and have them form a human number line by standing in the order of their integers. I put masking tape on the floor to make a number line and we mark off the integers in equal intervals. At the beginning of the unit I use the number line for comparing and ordering integers. Later I have students show addition of integers on this number line.

SOURCE: Scott Foresman–Addison Wesley Middle School Math, *Course 2*, p. 428, by Randall I. Charles et al. Copyright © 2002 Pearson Education, Inc. Reprinted with permission.

---

**THEOREM**   *The Law of Trichotomy*

If $a$ and $b$ are any two integers, then precisely one of these three possibilities must hold:

$$a < b \quad \text{or} \quad a = b \quad \text{or} \quad a > b$$

Since the law of trichotomy holds for the integers, they are said to be *ordered*—that is, they can be lined up on a number line in order of increasing size.

## EXAMPLE 5.13 Ordering Pairs of Integers

Place a less-than sign or a greater-than sign in the circle as appropriate:

(a) $17 \bigcirc 121$      (b) $2 \bigcirc -7$      (c) $-7 \bigcirc -27$      (d) $0 \bigcirc -6$

**Solution**

(a) $17 < 121$, since $17 + 104 = 121$.
(b) $2 > -7$, since $-7 + 9 = 2$.
(c) $-7 > -27$, since $-27 + 20 = -7$.
(d) $0 > -6$, since $-6 + 6 = 0$.

> 104, 9, 20, and 6 are all positive.

## EXAMPLE 5.14 Ordering a Set of Integers

Plot each of these integers on a number line, and then list them in increasing order: $-5, -9, 7, 0, 12$, and $-8$.

**Solution**

Reading from left to right, we see that

$$-9 < -8 < -5 < 0 < 7 < 12.$$

## EXAMPLE 5.15 Illustrating Properties of Inequalities with Number-Line Diagrams

Let $a$, $b$, and $n$ be integers for which $a < b$. Use number-line diagrams to show that

(a) $a + n < b + n$.
(b) $-b < -a$.

**Solution**

**(a)** Let $c$ be the right-pointing arrow from $a$ to $b$. Adding $n$ to both $a$ and $b$ moves the corresponding points in the same direction and by the same distance along the number line. That is, $a$ is moved to the point $a + n$, and $b$ is moved to the point $b + n$. Therefore, the same right-pointing arrow $c$ extends from $a + n$ to $b + n$, and we see from the number-line diagram that $a + n < b + n$.

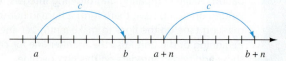

**(b)** Taking the opposite is the same as reflecting to the corresponding point opposite 0. The diagram that follows shows that $-b$ is to the left of $-a$, so $-b < -a$. More precisely, the diagram shows that if $a + c = b$, then $(-b) + c = -a$.

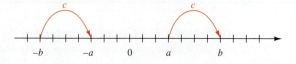

## Subtraction of Integers by Using Sets of Colored Counters

As with the subtraction of whole numbers, one approach to the subtraction of integers is the notion of "take away." Consider the subtraction

$$7 - (-3).$$

Modeling 7 with counters, we must "take away" a representation of $-3$. Since any representation of $-3$ must have at least three red counters, we must use a representation of 7 with at least three red counters. The simplest representation of this subtraction is shown in Figure 5.15.

**FIGURE 5.15**
Colored-counter representation of $7 - (-3) = 10$

Thus, $7 - (-3) = 10$. Also, the result does not change if we use another representation of 7 with at least three red counters, since equivalent representations are obtained by adding (or deleting) the same number of counters of each color from a given representation. A second representation of $7 - (-3) = 10$ is shown in Figure 5.16.

**FIGURE 5.16**
A second colored-counter representation of $7 - (-3) = 10$

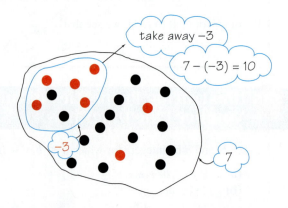

**EXAMPLE 5.16** **Subtracting by Using Colored Counters**

Write out the subtraction equations illustrated by these diagrams:

**(a)**
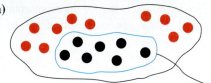

**(b)**
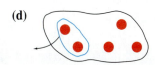

**(c)**

**(d)**

**Solution**  (a) Since the large loop contains ten red counters and seven black counters, it represents $-3$. The small loop contains seven black counters and thus represents 7. If we remove the small loop of counters as indicated, we are left with ten red counters, representing $-10$. Thus, this diagram illustrates the subtraction $(-3) - 7 = -10$.
(b) This diagram represents the subtraction $(-3) - (-1) = -2$.
(c) This diagram represents the subtraction $(-3) - 1 = -4$.
(d) This diagram represents the subtraction $(-5) - (-2) = -3$.

**EXAMPLE 5.17** **Drawing Diagrams for Given Subtraction Problems**

Draw a diagram of colored counters to illustrate each of these subtractions, and determine the result in each case:

**(a)** $7 - 3$        **(b)** $(-7) - (-3)$        **(c)** $7 - (-3)$        **(d)** $(-7) - 3$

**Solution**  (a) Many different diagrams could be drawn, but the simplest is shown here:

(b) As in part (a), we can use a diagram with counters of only one color:

(c) This subtraction is illustrated in Figures 5.15 and 5.16.
(d) Here, in order to remove three black counters (that is, subtract 3), the representation for $-7$ must have at least three black counters. The simplest diagram is the following:

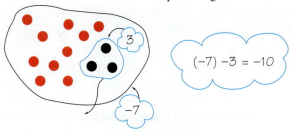

Subtraction with the colored-counter model is viewed as taking away. For example, in Figure 5.17, the black outer loop represents 5 as 9B4R (nine black and four red counters). If the four red counters are removed, we are left with the nine black counters, so $5 - (-4) = 9$. Suppose we invert this process, which can be likened to watching a movie shown in reverse. We would then start with the nine black counters and add the four red counters to give the representation 9B4R of 5. That is, the inverse of the subtraction $5 - (-4) = 9$ is the equivalent addition $9 + (-4) = 5$.

**FIGURE 5.17**
Diagram illustrating both
$5 - (-4) = 9$ and
$5 = (-4) + 9$

$5 - (-4) = 9$

$5 = (-4) + 9$

More generally, any subtraction $a - b = c$ is equivalent to the addition $a = b + c$. This relationship allows us to define subtraction precisely as the inverse of addition:

---

**DEFINITION**   *Subtraction of Integers*
If $a$, $b$, and $c$ are integers, then

$$a - b = c$$

if, and only if, $a = b + c$.

---

This was also the definition of subtraction of whole numbers. Thus, as before, we have a family of equivalent facts; that is,

$$a - b = c, \quad a = b + c, \quad a = c + b, \quad \text{and} \quad a - c = b$$

all express the same relationship among the integers $a$, $b$, and $c$. If we know that any one of these equations is true, then all are true.

## The Equivalence of Subtraction and Adding the Opposite

We have just seen that the subtraction $5 - 2$ is illustrated with colored counters by beginning with a set of 5 black counters and then removing 2 of them. Since 3 black counters remain, we have $5 - 2 = 3$. However, there is another way to delete 2 of the black counters: Simply annihilate them by adding 2 red counters. Thus, we have $5 + (-2) = 3$. As shown in Figure 5.18, there are two ways to accomplish the same purpose: Either remove counters to show that $5 - 2 = 3$ or add opposite counters to show that $5 + (-2) = 3$.

**FIGURE 5.18**
Subtracting by adding the negative

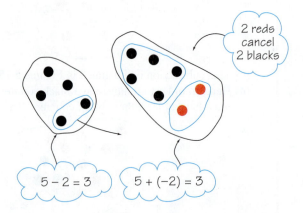

2 reds
cancel
2 blacks

$5 - 2 = 3$       $5 + (-2) = 3$

Since the effect of adding the negative of 2 to 5 is the same as subtracting 2 from 5, we have

$$5 - 2 = 5 + (-2).$$

Moreover, since the opposite of an integer represented by a set of counters is always represented by the set with all the colors reversed, this proposition is true in general and can be expressed as a theorem:

> To subtract, add the negative.

**THEOREM**   *Subtracting by Adding the Opposite*

Let $a$ and $b$ be any integers. Then

$$a - b = a + (-b).$$

Finally, since, as we have already seen, the set of integers is closed under addition, an immediate consequence of this theorem is that, unlike the set of whole numbers, *the set of integers is closed under subtraction.*

**THEOREM**   *Closure Property for the Subtraction of Integers*

The set of integers is closed under subtraction.

**EXAMPLE 5.18** **Subtracting by Adding the Opposite**

Perform each of these subtractions as additions:

   **(a)** $7 - 3$     **(b)** $(-7) - (-3)$     **(c)** $7 - (-3)$     **(d)** $(-7) - 3$

**Solution**   We make use of the theorem stating that $a - b = a + (-b)$ for any integers $a$ and $b$.

   **(a)** $7 - 3 = 7 + (-3) = 4$
   **(b)** $(-7) - (-3) = (-7) + 3 = -4$
   **(c)** $7 - (-3) = 7 + 3 = 10$
   **(d)** $(-7) - 3 = -7 + (-3) = -10$

## Subtraction of Integers by Using Mail-Time Stories

For this model of subtraction to work, we must imagine a situation where checks and bills are immediately credited or debited to your account as soon as they are delivered, whether they are really intended for you or not. If an error has been made by the mail carrier, he or she must return and reclaim delivered mail and take it to the intended recipient. Thus,

   bringing a check adds a positive number,
   bringing a bill adds a negative number,
   taking away a check subtracts a positive number, and
   taking away a bill subtracts a negative number.

**EXAMPLE 5.19** **Subtraction Facts from Mail-Time Stories**

Indicate the subtraction facts that are illustrated by each of the following mail-time stories:

   **(a)** The mail carrier brings you a check for $7 and takes away a check for $3. Are you richer or poorer, and by how much?
   **(b)** The mail carrier brings you a bill for $7 and takes away a bill for $3. Are you richer or poorer, and by how much?
   **(c)** The mail carrier brings you a check for $7 and takes away a bill for $3. Are you richer or poorer, and by how much?
   **(d)** The mail carrier brings you a bill for $7 and takes away a check for $3. Are you richer or poorer, and by how much?

**Solution**   (a) You are $4 richer. This illustrates the subtraction fact $7 - 3 = 4$.
(b) You are $4 poorer. This illustrates the subtraction fact $(-7) - (-3) = -4$.
(c) You are $10 richer. This illustrates the subtraction fact $7 - (-3) = 10$.
(d) You are $10 poorer. This illustrates the subtraction fact $(-7) - 3 = -10$.

Note that these are precisely the same subtractions that were illustrated in Example 5.17 with diagrams of colored counters and in Example 5.18 by adding negatives.

## Subtraction of Integers by Using the Number Line

The addition $5 + 3 = 8$ is illustrated on a number line in Figure 5.19.

**FIGURE 5.19**
The sum $5 + 3 = 8$ on the number line

Now consider the subtraction

$$5 - 3.$$

In this instance, we start at 0 and count five units to the right as before, and now we must *remove* three units, as represented by the right-pointing arrow of length 3. Figure 5.20 shows that the result is then 2, as we already know from the subtraction of whole numbers. In particular, this diagram accurately models the missing-addend approach to subtraction. Here, the dashed red arrow (for 2) shows what must be added to 3 to obtain 5. (Recall that arrows representing positive integers point right, and those representing negative integers point left.) Also, it might be helpful, when modeling subtraction by using arrows on a number line, to draw the arrow representing the subtrahend by starting with the head of this arrow at the head of the arrow representing the minuend and drawing from the arrowhead of the subtrahend backward toward the tail the necessary number of units. For example, $5 - 3 = 2$ since we also see that $2 + 3 = 5$.

**FIGURE 5.20**
The subtraction $5 - 3 = 2$ on the number line

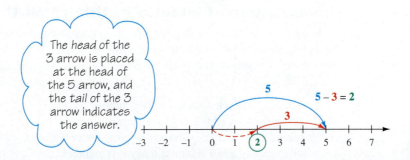

The head of the 3 arrow is placed at the head of the 5 arrow, and the tail of the 3 arrow indicates the answer.

---

**EXAMPLE 5.20  Drawing Diagrams to Illustrate Subtraction on the Number Line**

Illustrate each of these subtractions on a number line, and give the result in each case:

(a) $7 - 3$          (b) $(-7) - (-3)$          (c) $7 - (-3)$          (d) $(-7) - 3$

**Solution**   (a)

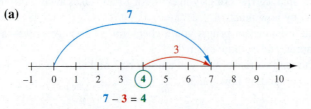

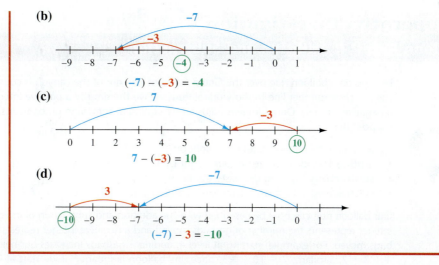

(b)

$(-7) - (-3) = -4$

(c)

$7 - (-3) = 10$

(d)

$(-7) - 3 = -10$

> This is a subtraction diagram.

The number line is particularly useful in demonstrating the result

$$a - b = a + (-b)$$

noted earlier. For example, let's compare the subtraction diagram for $(-7) - 3 = -10$ shown in the solution of Example 5.20 with the addition diagram for $(-7) + (-3) = -10$ shown in Figure 5.21. It is clear that subtracting a "jump" is equivalent to adding a jump in the opposite direction. However, addition and subtraction diagrams are not identical: Arrowheads are placed together for subtraction, but the tail of an arrow is placed at the head of an arrow in an addition diagram.

$$(-7) - 3 = (-7) + (-3)$$

**FIGURE 5.21**
The sum $(-7) + (-3) = -10$
on the number line

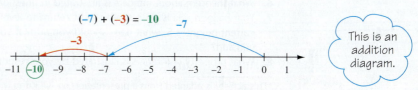

$(-7) + (-3) = -10$

> This is an addition diagram.

## Adding and Subtracting Integers with a Calculator

Integers can also be added and subtracted on a calculator, but care must be taken, since integers are both positive and negative. It's important to distinguish the subtraction key $\boxed{-}$ from the change sign ("take the opposite") key $\boxed{+/-}$ or $\boxed{(-)}$.

Thus, $27 + (-83)$ can be found by keying the string

$$27 \boxed{+} \boxed{(-)} 83 \boxed{=} \quad \text{or} \quad 27 \boxed{+} 83 \boxed{+/-} \boxed{=}$$

into your calculator, and the result is $-56$. Similarly, entering the string

$$\boxed{(-)} 71 \boxed{-} \boxed{(-)} 93 \boxed{=} \quad \text{or} \quad 71 \boxed{+/-} \boxed{-} 93 \boxed{+/-} \boxed{=}$$

performs the subtraction

$$(-71) - (-93) = 22.$$

## EXAMPLE 5.21 Adding and Subtracting Integers with a Calculator

Perform these computations by using the $\boxed{(-)}$ or $\boxed{+/-}$ key:

**(a)** $(-27) + (-95)$        **(b)** $(-27) - (-95)$        **(c)** $3250 + (-4729)$

**Solution** | In each case, we indicate the key string entered into the calculator and the resulting answer:

**(a)** $\boxed{(-)} 27 \boxed{+} \boxed{(-)} 95 \boxed{=}$, $-122$, or $27 \boxed{+/-} \boxed{+} 95 \boxed{+/-} \boxed{=}$

**(b)** $\boxed{(-)} 27 \boxed{-} \boxed{(-)} 95 \boxed{=}$, $68$, or $27 \boxed{+/-} \boxed{-} 95 \boxed{+/-} \boxed{=}$

**(c)** $3250 \boxed{+} \boxed{(-)} 4729 \boxed{=}$, $-1479$, or $3250 \boxed{+} 4729 \boxed{+/-} \boxed{=}$

## Cooperative Investigation
## Balloon Rides* I: Addition and Subtraction

Let's go on a balloon ride over the Grand Canyon! The rim of the canyon is considered level 0, and we use a vertical number line to show our altitude above the rim (by a positive integer) or below the rim (by a negative integer). Our altitude is adjusted by adding or removing gasbags or sandbags. Indeed, let's suppose that

- **adding** 1 gasbag increases our height by 1;
- **adding** 1 sandbag decreases our height by 1;
- **subtracting** 1 gasbag decreases our height by 1;
- **subtracting** 1 sandbag increases our height by 1.

Our balloon ride can now be described with the addition and subtraction of integers, where a positive integer represents the number of gasbags moved and a negative integer represents the number of sandbags moved. For example, starting at level 4, adding 3 gasbags increases our height to level 7. That is, $4 + 3 = 7$. Similarly, $7 - 10 = -3$, since, in "balloon language," if we start at level 7 and remove 10 gasbags, we lower our altitude by 10 units to end up at level $-3$, 3 units below the canyon rim.

### Problems and Questions for Small Groups

1. Translate $4 + (-9) = -5$ into balloon language.
2. Translate the balloon language statement "Starting at $-3$, we added 7 sandbags to reach level $-10$."
3. Translate $8 - 3 = 5$ into balloon language.
4. Translate "Starting at $-5$, we removed 8 sandbags to get to level 3" into an integer equation.
5. Give two ways, each described in both balloon language and an integer equation, to start at level 3 and go to level 11. You are allowed to move bags of only one type.
6. What theorem about integers is illustrated in question 5?
7. Your balloon ride is over, so you must return to level 0 to land safely on the canyon rim. If your current height is 5, what bags should you add? If your current height were $-7$, what bags should you add?
8. What property of integers is illustrated by your response to question 7?

*This activity is adapted from a presentation by Bill Kring.

---

## Problem Set 5.2

Exercises numbered in red are answered in the back of the text.

### Understanding Concepts

1. Draw diagrams of colored counters to illustrate these computations, and state the answer in each case:

   (a) $8 + (-3)$　　(b) $(-8) + 3$　　(c) $(-8) - (-3)$
   (d) $8 - (-3)$　　(e) $9 + 4$　　(f) $9 + (-4)$
   (g) $(-9) + 4$　　(h) $(-9) - (-4)$

2. Describe mail-time situations that illustrate each computation, and state the answer in each case:

   (a) $(-27) + (-13)$　　(b) $(-27) - 13$
   (c) $27 + 13$　　(d) $27 - 13$
   (e) $(-41) + 13$　　(f) $(-41) - 13$
   (g) $(-13) + 41$　　(h) $13 - 41$

3. Draw number-line diagrams that illustrate each computation, and state the answer in each case:

   (a) $8 + (-3)$　　(b) $8 - (-3)$
   (c) $(-8) + 3$　　(d) $(-8) - (-3)$

   (e) $4 + (-7)$　　(f) $4 - (-7)$
   (g) $(-4) + 7$　　(h) $(-4) - (-7)$

4. Write each of these subtractions as an addition:

   (a) $13 - 7$　　(b) $13 - (-7)$
   (c) $(-13) - 7$　　(d) $(-13) - (-7)$
   (e) $3 - 8$　　(f) $8 - (-3)$
   (g) $(-8) - 13$　　(h) $(-8) - (-13)$

5. Perform each of these computations:

   (a) $27 - (-13)$　　(b) $12 + (-24)$
   (c) $(-13) - 14$　　(d) $-81 + 54$
   (e) $(-81) - 54$　　(f) $(-81) - (-54)$
   (g) $(-81) + (-54)$　　(h) $27 + (-13)$
   (i) $(-27) - 13$

6. Use mental arithmetic to estimate the given sums and differences. Indicate the reasoning you have used to make your estimates.

   (a) $(-356) + 148$　　(b) $728 + (-273)$
   (c) $298 - (-454)$　　(d) $-827 - 370$

**7.** By 2 P.M., the temperature in Cutbank, Montana, had risen 31° from a nighttime low of 41° below 0.

   **(a)** What was the temperature at 2 P.M.?

   **(b)** What computation does part (a) illustrate?

**8. (a)** If the high temperature on a given day was 2° above 0 and the morning's low was 27° below zero, how much did the temperature rise during the day?

   **(b)** What computation does part (a) illustrate?

**9. (a)** If the high temperature for a certain day was 8° above 0 and that night's low temperature was 27° below 0, how much did the temperature fall?

   **(b)** What computation does part (a) illustrate?

**10.** During the day, Sam's Soda Shop took in $314. That same day, Sam paid a total of $208 in bills.

   **(a)** Was Sam's net worth more or less at the end of the day? by how much?

   **(b)** What computation does part (a) illustrate?

**11.** During the day, Sam's Soda Shop took in $284. Also, Sam received a check in the mail for $191 as a refund for several bills that he had inadvertently paid twice.

   **(a)** Was Sam's net worth more or less at the end of the day? by how much?

   **(b)** What computation does part (a) illustrate?

   **(c)** If you think of the $191 check as removing or taking away the bills previously paid, what computation does this represent? Explain.

**12.** Place a less-than sign or a greater-than sign in each circle to make a *true* statement.

   **(a)** $-117 \bigcirc -24$     **(b)** $0 \bigcirc -4$     **(c)** $18 \bigcirc 12$

   **(d)** $18 \bigcirc -12$     **(e)** $-5 \bigcirc 1$     **(f)** $-5 \bigcirc -9$

**13.** List these numbers in increasing order from least to greatest: $-5, 27, 5, -2, 0, 3, -17$.

## Teaching Concepts

**14.** In this chapter, the integers are represented in several ways: by colored counters, mail-time stories, and a number line. Why is it important to have a variety of models of the integers in the classroom?

**15.** Maximus Planudes (c. A.D. 1255–1305) helped introduce Indo-Arabic numerals and arithmetic calculation into Europe. In *The Great Calculation According to the Indians,* he states, "It is not possible to take a greater from a lesser number, for it is not possible to take away what is not there." The question still arises even today. Design a poster for the upper elementary school classroom that shows how integers—both positive and negative—are used today.

## Responding to Students

**16.** Keyshawn drew the following diagram to illustrate the subtraction of −3 from 7, arguing that you have to count from 7

on the number line 3 steps in the opposite direction from that indicated by −3:

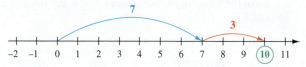

How would you respond to Keyshawn? Compare Keyshawn's response with the solutions to part (c) of both Example 5.19 and Example 5.20.

**17.** Melanie says that adding the opposite, $-n$, of a number $n$ to $m + n$ just exactly nullifies the effect of adding $n$ to $m$. Is Melanie right? How would you respond to her?

**18.** Julliene answered "No" to the question "Is the inequality $10 \geq 7$ a correct assertion?" She maintained that the inequality should be $10 > 7$. Is Julliene correct? How would you respond to her?

**19.** Armand said that to represent subtracting −3 from 7 by using colored counters, you could add three black counters to seven black counters.

   **(a)** Is Armand correct?

   **(b)** Determine the difference $7 - (-3)$.

   **(c)** How would you respond to Armand?

## Thinking Critically

**20.** Which of the following are *true?*

   **(a)** $3 < 12$     **(b)** $-3 < -12$

   **(c)** $-3 < 12$     **(d)** $3 < -12$

**21.** If $a < b$, is $a \leq b$ true? Explain.

**22.** If $a \geq b$, is $a > b$ true? Explain.

**23.** Is $2 \geq 2$ true? Explain.

**24.** For which integers $x$ is it true that $|x| < 7$?

**25.** For which integers $x$ is it true that $|x| > 99$?

**26. (a)** Compute each of these absolute values:

   **(i)** $|5 - 11|$     **(ii)** $|(-4) - (-10)|$

   **(iii)** $|8 - (-7)|$     **(iv)** $|(-9) - 2|$

   **(b)** Draw a number line, and determine the distance between the points on, the number line for each of these pairs of integers.

   **(i)** 5 and 11     **(ii)** −4 and −10

   **(iii)** 8 and −7     **(iv)** −9 and 2

   **(c)** Since parts (a) and (b) are completely representative of the corresponding general cases, state a general theorem summarizing these results.

**27. (a)** Compute each of these pairs of expressions:

   **(i)** $|7 + 2|$          and $|7| + |2|$

   **(ii)** $|(-8) + 5|$     and $|-8| + |5|$

   **(iii)** $|7 + (-6)|$     and $|7| + |-6|$

   **(iv)** $|(-9) + (-5)|$     and $|-9| + |-5|$

   **(v)** $|6 + 0|$          and $|6| + |0|$

   **(vi)** $|0 + (-7)|$     and $|0| + |-7|$

**(b)** Since the results of part (a) are completely typical, place one of the signs $>$, $<$, $\geq$, and $\leq$ in the circle to make the following a *true* statement: For any integers $a$ and $b$,

$$|a + b| \bigcirc |a| + |b|.$$

**28. (a)** Make a magic square using the integers $-4, -3, -2, -1, 0, 1, 2, 3,$ and $4$.

**(b)** Complete the magic square using the integers $-7, -6, \ldots, 0, 1, \ldots, 8$. What is the magic sum?

|    | -6 | 8  | 1  |
|----|----|----|----|
| 4  |    |    | -2 |
| -7 |    | 2  |    |
|    | 3  |    |    |

**29.** In each of the following diagrams, determine numbers to place in the red circles so that the sum of the numbers in each pair of adjacent red circles is the number in the corresponding large blue circle:

**(a)**

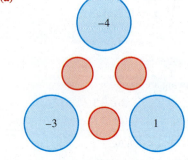

**(b)**

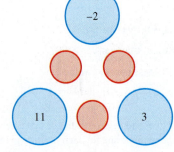

**30. (a)** Perform these pairs of computations:

**(i)** $7 - (-3)$ and $(-3) - 7$

**(ii)** $(-2) - (-5)$ and $(-5) - (-2)$

**(b)** Does the commutative law for subtraction hold for the set of integers? Explain briefly.

**31.** Does the associative law for subtraction hold for the set of integers (i.e., is $a - (b - c) = (a - b) - c$ true for all integers $a$, $b$, and $c$)? If so, explain why. If not, give a counterexample.

## Thinking Cooperatively

Do the next five problems in a group with two or three other students. At each step, discuss your solution with the other

members of your group and determine a consensus answer for your group.

**32.** Recall that the $n$th triangular number is given by $t_n = n(n + 1)/2$, so that $t_1 = 1, t_2 = 3, t_3 = 6, t_4 = 10, t_5 = 15, t_6 = 21, \ldots$. The first four *alternating sums* are $1 = 1, 1 - 3 = -2, 1 - 3 + 6 = 4$, and $1 - 3 + 6 - 10 = -6$.

**(a)** Compute the next four alternating sums.

**(b)** Describe the pattern of alternating sums of the form $1 - 3 + 6 - 10 + \cdots + t_{2n-1}$ that contain the first $2n - 1$ triangular numbers.

**(c)** Describe the pattern of alternating sums of the form $1 - 3 + 6 - 10 + \cdots + t_{2n-1} - t_{2n}$ that contain the first $2n$ triangular numbers. (*Suggestion*: How are these values related to the triangular numbers?)

**33.** Recall that the Fibonacci numbers are $F_1 = 1, F_2 = 1, F_3 = 2, F_4 = 3, F_5 = 5, \ldots$, where each new term in the sequence is obtained from the recursive formula $F_{n+2} = F_{n+1} + F_n, n = 1, 2, 3, \ldots$

**(a)** Use the recursive formula to explain why it is reasonable to let $F_0 = 0$.

**(b)** Extend the Fibonacci numbers to define $F_{-1}, F_{-2}, F_{-3}$, and $F_{-4}$.

**(c)** Describe carefully how $F_{-n}$ is related to $F_n$.

**(d)** Repeat parts (a), (b), and (c), but for the Lucas sequence $L_1 = 1, L_2 = 3, L_3 = 4, L_4 = 7, L_5 = 11, \ldots$, where $L_{n+2} = L_{n+1} + L_n$.

**34.** Investigate the following sums of sequences of sums of Fibonacci numbers:

**(a)** Find $F_1, F_1 + F_3, F_1 + F_3 + F_5, F_1 + F_3 + F_5 + F_7, \ldots$. In particular, give a formula involving the Fibonacci numbers for the sum $F_1 + F_3 + F_5 + \cdots + F_{2n-1}$.

**(b)** Find $F_2, F_2 + F_4, F_2 + F_4 + F_6, F_2 + F_4 + F_6 + F_8, \ldots$. Give a formula for the general case $F_2 + F_4 + F_6 + \cdots + F_{2n}$.

**(c)** Find $F_1, F_1 + F_2, F_1 + F_2 + F_3, F_1 + F_2 + F_3 + F_4, \ldots$. Give a formula for the general case $F_1 + F_2 + F_3 + \cdots + F_n$.

**35.** Repeat problem 34, but for the corresponding alternating sums:

**(a)** Find $F_1, F_1 - F_3, F_1 - F_3 + F_5, F_1 - F_3 + F_5 - F_7, \ldots$. In particular, give a formula involving the Fibonacci numbers for the sum $F_1 - F_3 + F_5 + \cdots + (-1)^{n+1}F_{2n-1}$.

**(b)** Find $F_2, F_2 - F_4, F_2 - F_4 + F_6, F_2 - F_4 + F_6 - F_8, \ldots$. Give a formula for the general case $F_2 - F_4 + F_6 + \cdots + (-1)^{n+1}F_{2n}$.

**(c)** Find $F_1, F_1 - F_2, F_1 - F_2 + F_3, F_1 - F_2 + F_3 - F_4, \ldots$. Give a formula for the general case $F_1 - F_2 + F_3 + \cdots + (-1)^{n+1}F_n$.

## Making Connections

**36.** One day Anne had the flu. At 8 A.M. her temperature was $101°$. By noon her temperature had increased by $3°$, and then it fell $5°$ by 6 in the evening.

**(a)** Write a single addition equation to determine Anne's temperature at noon.

**(b)** Write a single equation using both addition and subtraction to determine Anne's temperature at 6 P.M.

**37.** Vicky was 12 years old on her birthday today.

**(a)** How old was Vicky on her birthday 7 years ago?

**(b)** How old will Vicky be on her birthday 7 years from now?

**(c)** Write addition equations that answer both parts (a) and (b) of this problem.

**38.** Greg's bank balance was $4500. During the month, he wrote checks for $510, $87, $212, and $725. He also made deposits of $600 and $350. What was his balance at the end of the month?

**39.** A ball is thrown upward from the top of a building 144 feet high. Let $h$ denote the height of the ball above the top of the building $t$ seconds after it was thrown. It can be shown that $h = -16t^2 + 96t$ feet.

**(a)** Complete this table of values of $h$:

| $t$ | 0 | 1 | 2 | 3 | 4 | 5 | 6 | 7 |
|---|---|---|---|---|---|---|---|---|
| $h$ | 0 | 80 | | | | | | |

**(b)** Give a carefully worded plausibility argument (not a proof) that the greatest value of $h$ in the table is the greatest height the ball reaches.

**(c)** Carefully interpret (explain) the meaning of the value of $h$ when $t = 7$.

**40.** The velocity, in feet per second, of the ball in problem 39 is given by the equation $v = -32t + 96$.

**(a)** Complete the table of values of $v$ in the table shown.

**(b)** Carefully interpret (explain) the value of $v$ when $t = 0$.

**(c)** Interpret the value of $v$ when $t = 3$.

| $t$ | 0 | 1 | 2 | 3 | 4 | 5 | 6 | 7 |
|---|---|---|---|---|---|---|---|---|
| $r$ | 96 | 64 | | | | | | |

**(d)** Carefully interpret the meaning of the values of $v$ for $t = 4, 5, 6,$ and 7.

**(e)** Compare the values of $v$ for $t = 0$ and 6, 1 and 5, and 2 and 4. What do these values tell you about the motion of the ball?

### ▦ Using a Calculator

**41.** When we write $a - b + c - d$, it is understood that we mean $(((a - b) + c) - d)$. The operations are performed from left to right, as on a calculator with algebraic logic.

**(a)** Compute $1 - 2 + 3 - \cdots + 99$.

**(b)** Could you think of an easy way to complete part (a) without a calculator?

**(c)** Compute $1 - 2 + 3 - \cdots + 99 - 100$.

**42.** Use your calculator to perform these calculations:

**(a)** $3742 + (-2167)$      **(b)** $(-2751) + (-3157)$

**(c)** $(-2167) - 3742$      **(d)** $(-3157) - (-2751)$

**(e)** $-(3571 - 5624)$      **(f)** $-[49{,}002 + (-37{,}621)]$

### From State Student Assessments

**43.** (California, Grade 4)
True or false?

**1.** $-9 > -10$

**2.** $-31 < -29$

**44.** (Massachusetts, Grade 6)
Corazón used the number-line model shown below to help her write a true number sentence.

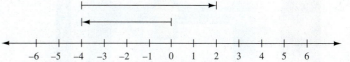

Which of the following could be Corazón's number sentence?

**A.** $-4 + 2 = 6$      **B.** $-4 + 6 = 2$

**C.** $2 + 6 = -4$      **D.** $2 + -4 = 6$

**45.** (Massachusetts, Grade 7)
At 7:00 A.M., the temperature was $-6°F$. The temperature was $8°F$ higher at noon. Which of the following expressions can be used to calculate the temperature at noon?

**A.** $-6 + 8$      **B.** $-6 - 8$

**C.** $8 + 6$      **D.** $8 - (-6)$

### Examining School Book Pages

*Refer to the School Book Pages provided on page 256 to answer the following questions.*

**46.** On the School Book Pages that follow, subtraction is defined in this way:

Rule: Subtracting an integer is the same as adding its opposite. Discuss how this definition differs from the definition of integers in this text. In particular, do the conceptual models of subtraction—take away, missing addend, comparison—correspond to "adding its opposite"?

**47. (a)** How would the subtraction $4 - 3$ be illustrated with the method shown in Step 2 at the top of page 235 of the School Book Pages?

**(b)** On p. 231 of the School Book Pages, the following diagram is used to illustrate the addition $4 + (-3)$ (except for the use of straight arrows, the diagram matches those shown in this text for the addition operation):

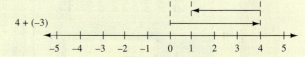

$4 + (-3)$

Compare your subtraction diagram from part (a) for $4 - 3$ with the preceding addition diagram for $4 + (-3)$.

**(c)** Use the diagram advocated in this text, but with straight horizontal arrows, to illustrate the subtraction $4 - 3$.

# School Book Pages

## Subtracting Integers

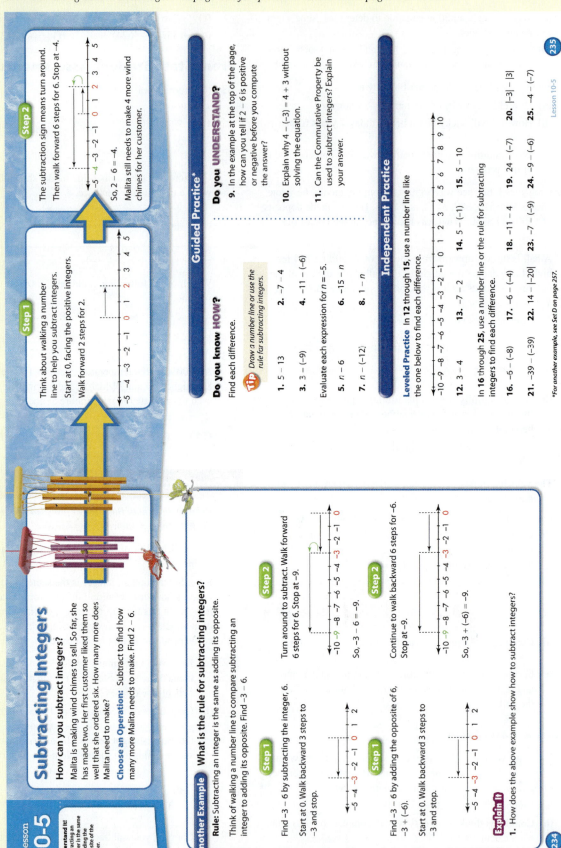

### Lesson 10-5

**Understand It!**
Subtracting an integer is the same as adding the opposite of the integer.

## Subtracting Integers

**How can you subtract integers?**

Malita is making wind chimes to sell. So far, she has made two. Her first customer liked them so well that she ordered six. How many more does Malita need to make?

**Choose an Operation:** Subtract to find how many more Malita needs to make. Find $2 - 6$.

**Step 1**

Think about walking a number line to help you subtract integers.

Start at 0, facing the positive integers.

Walk forward 2 steps for 2.

**Step 2**

The subtraction sign means turn around. Then walk forward 6 steps for 6. Stop at −4.

So, $2 - 6 = -4$.

Malita still needs to make 4 more wind chimes for her customer.

### Another Example  What is the rule for subtracting integers?

**Rule:** Subtracting an integer is the same as adding its opposite.

Think of walking a number line to compare subtracting an integer to adding its opposite. Find $-3 - 6$.

**Step 1**

Find $-3 - 6$ by subtracting the integer, 6.

Start at 0. Walk backward 3 steps to −3 and stop.

**Step 2**

Turn around to subtract. Walk forward 6 steps for 6. Stop at −9.

So, $-3 - 6 = -9$.

**Step 1**

Find $-3 - 6$ by adding the opposite of 6, $-3 + (-6)$.

Start at 0. Walk backward 3 steps to −3 and stop.

**Step 2**

Continue to walk backward 6 steps for −6. Stop at −9.

So, $-3 + (-6) = -9$.

**Explain It!**

1. How does the above example show how to subtract integers?

### Guided Practice*

**Do you know HOW?**

Find each difference.

**Tip** *Draw a number line or use the rule for subtracting integers.*

1. $5 - 13$
2. $-7 - 4$
3. $3 - (-9)$
4. $-11 - (-6)$

Evaluate each expression for $n = -5$.

5. $n - 6$
6. $-15 - n$
7. $n - (-12)$
8. $1 - n$

**Do you UNDERSTAND?**

9. In the example at the top of the page, how can you tell if $2 - 6$ is positive or negative before you compute the answer?

10. Explain why $4 - (-3) = 4 + 3$ without solving the equation.

11. Can the Commutative Property be used to subtract integers? Explain your answer.

### Independent Practice

**Leveled Practice** In **12** through **15**, use a number line like the one below to find each difference.

12. $3 - 4$
13. $-7 - 2$
14. $5 - (-1)$
15. $5 - 10$

In **16** through **25**, use a number line or the rule for subtracting integers to find each difference.

16. $-5 - (-8)$
17. $-6 - (-4)$
18. $-11 - 4$
19. $24 - (-7)$
20. $|-3| - |3|$
21. $-39 - (-39)$
22. $14 - |-20|$
23. $-7 - (-9)$
24. $-9 - (-6)$
25. $-4 - (-7)$

*For another example, see Set D on page 257.

Lesson 10-5   235

234

## 5.3

# Multiplication and Division of Integers

### Multiplication of Integers

Just as the set of integers is an extension of the set of whole numbers, multiplication and division in the set of integers are direct extensions of these operations for whole numbers. Recall that multiplication was defined in Chapter 2 as repeated addition. Thus, by definition,

$$4 \cdot 3 = 3 + 3 + 3 + 3 = 12.$$

In like manner, we have

$$4 \cdot (-3) = (-3) + (-3) + (-3) + (-3) = -12.$$

So far so good, but what meaning can be given to multiplication by a negative integer? For example, what is meant by $(-4) \cdot 3$ and by $(-4) \cdot (-3)$? Let's see what is suggested by representing the integers with colored counters.

### Multiplication of Integers by Using Colored Counters

As illustrated in Figure 5.22, we can start with an empty set of counters and then add four sets of either 3 black or 3 red counters to see that $4 \cdot 3 = 12$ and $4 \cdot (-3) = -12$.

**FIGURE 5.22**
Using colored counters to show that $4 \cdot 3 = 12$ and $4 \cdot (-3) = -12$

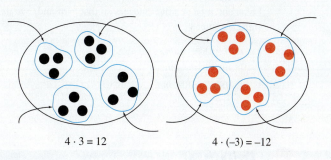

$$4 \cdot 3 = 12 \qquad\qquad 4 \cdot (-3) = -12$$

More generally, we see that

$$m \cdot n = mn \qquad \text{and} \qquad m \cdot (-n) = -mn.$$

> *Positive times positive gives positive.*

> *Positive times negative gives negative.*

Since multiplication by a positive integer is repeated addition, the most natural interpretation of multiplication by a negative integer is repeated subtraction. For example, let's start with zero represented by a loop with 12 black and 12 red counters, as shown in Figure 5.23. To determine the

**FIGURE 5.23**
Using colored counters to show that $(-4) \cdot 3 = -12$ and $(-4) \cdot (-3) = 12.$

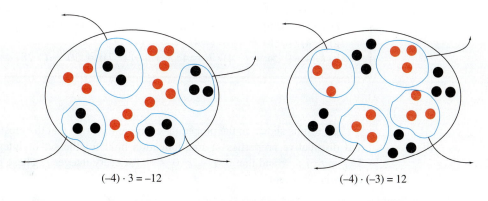

$$(-4) \cdot 3 = -12 \qquad\qquad (-4) \cdot (-3) = 12$$

product $(-4) \cdot 3$, we remove four sets that each contain 3 black counters, as shown at the left of the figure. Since we are left with 12 red counters, the colored-counters model tells us that $(-4) \cdot 3 = -12$. Similarly, as shown at the right of the figure, when four sets that each contain 3 red counters are removed, we are left with 12 black counters, corresponding to the equation $(-4) \cdot (-3) = 12$.

Figure 5.23 tells us, more generally, that

$$(-m) \cdot n = -m \quad \text{and} \quad (-m) \cdot (-n) = mn.$$

*negative times positive gives negative*

*negative times negative gives positive*

Collecting these results together, we have the following theorem:

---

**THEOREM** *The Rule of Signs for Multiplication of Integers*

Let $m$ and $n$ be positive integers so that $-m$ and $-n$ are negative integers. Then the following **rules of signs** are true:

- $m \cdot (-n) = -mn$;
- $(-m) \cdot n = -mn$;
- $(-m) \cdot (-n) = mn$.

---

**EXAMPLE 5.22 Multiplying Integers**

Compute these products:

(a) $(-7) \cdot (-8)$        (b) $(-8) \cdot (-7)$

(c) $3 \cdot (-7)$        (d) $(-7) \cdot 3$

(e) $[8 \cdot (-5)] \cdot 6$        (f) $8 \cdot [(-5) \cdot 6]$

(g) $(-4) \cdot [(-5) + 7]$        (h) $(-4) \cdot (-5) + (-4) \cdot 7$

**Solution**

(a) $(-7) \cdot (-8) = 7 \cdot 8 = 56$

(b) $(-8) \cdot (-7) = 8 \cdot 7 = 56$

(c) $3 \cdot (-7) = -(3 \cdot 7) = -21$

(d) $(-7) \cdot 3 = -(7 \cdot 3) = -21$

(e) $[8 \cdot (-5)] \cdot 6 = [-(8 \cdot 5)] \cdot 6 = (-40) \cdot 6 = -(40 \cdot 6) = -240$

(f) $8 \cdot [(-5) \cdot 6] = 8 \cdot [-(5 \cdot 6)] = 8 \cdot (-30) = -(8 \cdot 30) = -240$

(g) $(-4) \cdot [(-5) + 7] = (-4) \cdot 2 = -(4 \cdot 2) = -8$

(h) $(-4) \cdot (-5) + (-4) \cdot 7 = 4 \cdot 5 + [-(4 \cdot 7)] = 20 + (-28) = -8$

The results shown in the preceding example illustrate that the closure, commutative, associative, and distributive properties of multiplication hold for the set of integers. We have also seen that $1 \cdot r = r \cdot 1 = r$ and that $0 \cdot r = r \cdot 0 = 0$, for every integer $r$. These properties are collected in the following theorem.

**THEOREM** *Multiplication Properties of Integers*

Let $r$, $s$, and $t$ be any integers. Then

| | |
|---|---|
| **Closure Property** | $rs$ is an integer. |
| **Commutative Property** | $rs = sr$. |
| **Associative Property** | $r(st) = (rs)t$. |
| **Distributive Property** | $r(s + t) = rs + rt$. |
| **Multiplicative-Identity Property of 1** | $1 \cdot r = r \cdot 1 = r$. |
| **Multiplicative Property of 0** | $0 \cdot r = r \cdot 0 = 0$ |

## Multiplication of Integers by Using Mail-Time Stories

Recall that, in mail-time stories, the mail carrier bringing checks and bills corresponds to the addition of positive and negative numbers, respectively. Similarly, taking away checks and bills corresponds to subtracting positive and negative numbers, respectively.

Suppose the letter carrier brings five bills for $11 each. Are you richer or poorer, and by how much? Answer: Poorer by $55. Since this is repeated addition, it illustrates the product

$$5 \cdot (-11) = -55.$$

Suppose the mail carrier takes away four bills for $13 each. Are you richer or poorer, and by how much? Answer: Richer by $52. This illustrates the product

$$(-4) \cdot (-13) = 52,$$

since four bills for the same amount are *taken away*.

---

**EXAMPLE 5.23** **Writing Mail-Time Stories for Multiplication of Integers**

Write a mail-time story to illustrate each of these products:

(a) $(-4) \cdot 16$      (b) $(-4) \cdot (-16)$
(c) $4 \cdot (-16)$      (d) $4 \cdot 16$

**Solution**

(a) The letter carrier takes away four checks for $16 each. Are you richer or poorer, and by how much? Answer: $64 poorer; $(-4) \cdot 16 = -64$.
(b) The letter carrier takes away four bills for $16 each. Are you richer or poorer, and by how much? Answer: $64 richer; $(-4) \cdot (-16) = 64$.
(c) The letter carrier brings four bills for $16 each. Are you richer or poorer, and by how much? Answer: Poorer by $64; $4 \cdot (-16) = -64$.
(d) The letter carrier brings you four checks for $16 each. Are you richer or poorer, and by how much? Answer: Richer by $64; $4 \cdot 16 = 64$.

---

Mail-time stories are an especially effective way to interpret multiplication by a negative integer simply as repeated subtraction. For example, $(-3)5 = -15$, since subtracting 5 three times gives $-15$. Similarly, $(-3)(-5) = 15$, since subtracting $-5$ three times gives the positive integer 15.

## Multiplication of Integers by Using a Number Line

Think of

$3 \cdot 4$ as $4 + 4 + 4$,

$3 \cdot (-4)$ as $(-4) + (-4) + (-4)$,

$(-3) \cdot (4)$ as $-4 - 4 - 4$, and

$(-3) \cdot (-4)$ as $-(-4) - (-4) - (-4)$.

These multiplications can be illustrated on the number line as shown in Figure 5.24. Remember that jumps are added by tracing the jump arrow forward from tail to head and jumps are subtracted by tracing the jump arrow in reverse from head to tail.

**FIGURE 5.24**
Multiplication on the number line

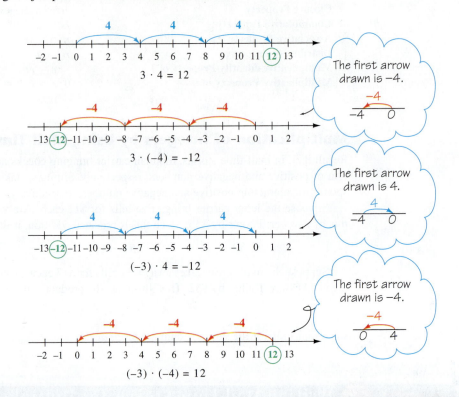

## EXAMPLE 5.24 Multiplying Integers by Using a Number Line

What products do these diagrams illustrate?

**(a)**

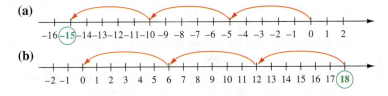

**(b)**

**Solution**

(a) Starting with the tail of the rightmost arrow at 0, we move in the direction of the arrows 5 units to the left, then 5 more units to the left, and finally 5 more units to the left. Thus, we are *adding* $-5$ to $-5$ to $-5$, and the result is $3 \cdot (-5) = -15$.

(b) Here, we start with the head of the leftmost arrow at 0 and move in the direction *opposite* to the direction of the arrows, 6 units to the right, 6 more units to the right, and finally 6 more units to the right. Since the arrows are directed from right to left, we are *subtracting* $-6$ and $-6$ and $-6$. The result is $(-3) \cdot (-6) = 18$.

## Division of Integers

In discussing division of natural numbers, we considered families of facts. Thus, the equations

$$12 = 3 \cdot 4 \qquad 12 \div 3 = 4$$
$$12 = 4 \cdot 3 \qquad 12 \div 4 = 3$$

all express the same relationship between the numbers 12, 3, and 4. Indeed, one definition of division of whole numbers was the following:

If $a$, $b$, and $c$ are whole numbers with $b \neq 0$, then $a \div b = c$ if, and only if, $a = bc$.

Thus, to find the quotient $143 \div 11$, we determine $c$ such that $143 = 11 \cdot c$. Since $11 \cdot 13 = 143$, it follows that $c = 13$, so $143 \div 11 = 13$.

Applying the same ideas to integers, we have the following fact families:

**(a)** $\quad 12 = (-3) \cdot (-4) \qquad\qquad 12 \div (-3) = -4$
$\qquad\quad 12 = (-4) \cdot (-3) \qquad\qquad 12 \div (-4) = -3$

**(b)** $\quad -12 = 3 \cdot (-4) \qquad\qquad (-12) \div 3 = -4$
$\qquad\quad -12 = (-4) \cdot 3 \qquad\qquad (-12) \div (-4) = 3$

These equations are typical and, as in the case of the natural numbers, lead to the following definition of division in the set of integers:

> **DEFINITION** *Division of Integers*
> If $a$, $b$, and $c$ are integers with $b \neq 0$, then $a \div b = c$ if, and only if, $a = b \cdot c$.

MHM

Division by 0 is not defined in the integers, for the same reasons that it was not defined in the whole numbers. Thus, in doing arithmetic in the integers, it continues to be important never to divide by 0. For example, suppose you want to find *all* integers $n$ for which $n^2 = -4n$. It is tempting to divide each side of the equation by $n$ and say that $n = -4$. But this assumes you are looking for a nonzero $n$, and the second solution, $n = 0$, will be overlooked.

**EXAMPLE 5.25** **Dividing Integers**

Perform the following divisions:

**(a)** $28 \div 4$      **(b)** $28 \div (-4)$      **(c)** $(-28) \div 4$      **(d)** $(-28) \div (-4)$

**Solution** The solutions depend entirely on the preceding definition:

**(a)** $28 \div 4 = 7$, since $28 = 4 \cdot 7$.
**(b)** $28 \div (-4) = -7$, since $28 = (-4) \cdot (-7)$.
**(c)** $(-28) \div 4 = -7$, since $-28 = 4 \cdot (-7)$.
**(d)** $(-28) \div (-4) = 7$, since $-28 = (-4) \cdot 7$.

Since these results are entirely typical, we state here the rule of signs for division of integers:

> **THEOREM** *Rule of Signs for Division of Integers*
> Let $m$ and $n$ be positive integers so that $-m$ and $-n$ are negative integers, and suppose that $n$ divides $m$. Then the following are true:
>
> • $\quad m \div (-n) = -(m \div n)$;
> • $\quad (-m) \div n = -(m \div n)$;
> • $\quad (-m) \div (-n) = m \div n$.

Thus, *given that n divides m,* it follows that

• a positive integer divided by a negative integer is a negative integer,
• a negative integer divided by a positive integer is a negative integer,
• a negative integer divided by a negative integer is a positive integer, and
• a positive integer divided by a positive integer is a positive integer.

**EXAMPLE 5.26** **Performing Division of Integers**

Compute each quotient if possible:

**(a)** $(-24) \div (-8)$  **(b)** $24 \div (-8)$  **(c)** $48 \div 12$
**(d)** $(-48) \div 12$  **(e)** $(-57) \div 19$  **(f)** $(-12) \div 0$
**(g)** $(-51) \div (-17)$  **(h)** $28 \div (9 - 5)$  **(i)** $(27 + 9) \div (-4)$

**Solution**    We use the preceding theorem and the definition of division of integers.

**(a)** $(-24) \div (-8) = 3$. Check: $-24 = (-8) \cdot 3$.
**(b)** $24 \div (-8) = -3$. Check: $24 = (-8) \cdot (-3)$.
**(c)** $48 \div 12 = 4$. Check: $48 = 12 \cdot 4$.
**(d)** $(-48) \div 12 = -4$. Check: $-48 = 12 \cdot (-4)$.
**(e)** $(-57) \div 19 = -3$. Check: $-57 = 19 \cdot (-3)$.
**(f)** $(-12) \div 0$ is not defined, since there is no number $c$ such that $-12 = 0 \cdot c$.
**(g)** $(-51) \div (-17) = 3$. Check: $-51 = (-17) \cdot 3$.
**(h)** $28 \div (9 - 5) = 28 \div 4 = 7$. Check: $28 = 4 \cdot 7$.
**(i)** $(27 + 9) \div (-4) = 36 \div (-4) = -9$. Check: $36 = (-4) \cdot (-9)$.

## Division with Remainders in the Integers

In Chapter 2, we saw that, under the assumption that remainders are permitted, the division algorithm allowed us to divide any whole number by a positive whole number. Let's see if the division algorithm can be extended to the integers. Consider, for example, dividing $-17$ by 5. The largest integer multiple of 5 that is less than or equal to $-17$ is $-20$, since $-20 = (-4) \cdot 5 \le -17 < (-3) \cdot 5 = -15$. Also, since $-17$ is 3 larger than $-20$, it follows that $-17 = (-4) \cdot 5 + 3$, where $0 \le 3 < 5$. That is, we can write

$$-17 \div 5 = -4 \, \text{R} \, 3.$$

This result can also be visualized on the number line. Figure 5.25 shows that $-17$ is positioned between the two adjacent multiples $-20$ and $-15$ of 5. Since it is 3 units larger than $(-4) \cdot 5$, so have $-17 = -4 \cdot 5 + 3$.

**FIGURE 5.25**
$-17 \div 5 = -4 \, \text{R} \, 3$, since
$-17 = (-4) \cdot 5 + 3$

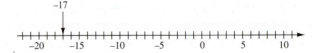

Similar reasoning applies in general: Given any integer $a$ and any positive integer $b$, let $q$ be the largest integer for which $q \cdot b \le a < (q + 1) \cdot b$. Setting $r = a - qb$, we obtain the following extension of the division algorithm to the integers:

> **THEOREM** *The Division Algorithm in the Integers*
> Let $a$ and $b$ be integers, with $b$ positive. Then there is a unique integer $q$, the quotient, and a unique non-negative integer $r$, the remainder, such that
>
> $$a = q \cdot b + r, \quad 0 \le r < b.$$

**EXAMPLE 5.27** **Using the Division Algorithm in the Integers**

Find the quotient and remainder for each of these divisions by 12:

**(a)** $41 \div 12$    **(b)** $-41 \div 12$    **(c)** $-11 \div 12$    **(d)** $-48 \div 12$

**Solution**   The integer multiples of 12 are $\{\ldots, -60, -48, -36, -24, -12, 0, 12, 24, 36, 48, \ldots\}$.

    **(a)** Since $36 \leq 41 < 48$ and $41 - 36 = 5$, we get $41 \div 12 = 3\,\mathrm{R}\,5$.
    **(b)** Since $-48 \leq -41 < -36$ and $-41 - (-48) = 7$, we get $-41 \div 12 = -4\,\mathrm{R}\,7$.
    **(c)** Since $-12 \leq -11 < 0$ and $-11 - (-12) = 1$, we get $-11 \div 12 = -1\,\mathrm{R}\,1$.
    **(d)** Since $-48 \leq -48 < -36$ and $-48 - (-48) = 0$, we get $-48 \div 12 = -4\,\mathrm{R}\,0$.

## Cooperative Investigation

## Balloon Rides* II: Multiplication and Division

Balloon Rides I of Section 5.2 explored the balloon model of integer addition and subtraction. In this activity, that model is extended to multiplication and division. Once again, the altitude of our balloon is controlled by adding or removing either gasbags or sandbags to or from the balloon. However, there is one important difference: We now assume that *we always start at level 0,* the height of the canyon rim. Given next are some integer multiplication and division examples to help you get started. You want to translate back and forth between "balloon language" and the corresponding equations in integers.

### Example 1

In balloon language, suppose that "three times, you add a pair of gasbags to your balloon, so, starting at level 0, you rise to level 6." This statement translates to the integer multiplication formula $3 \times 2 = 6$.

### Example 2

The equation $(-4) \times 3 = -12$ translates into balloon language as "four times, you remove a group of three gasbags, so, starting at level 0, the balloon sinks to level $-12$."

### Example 3

"To reach an altitude of $-15$ starting at level 0, what can we do with groups of gasbags, where there are 5 gasbags per group?" Since the removal of each group of 5 gasbags lowers the height by 5, we need to remove three groups. Therefore, $-15 \div 5 = -3$, or equivalently, $-15 = (-3) \times 5$.

### Example 4

Starting at level 0, how can we reach an altitude of $-15$ by using groups of sandbags, with 5 sandbags per group? This time, we must add three groups of sandbags. Therefore, $-15 \div (-5) = 3$, or equivalently, $-15 = 3 \times (-5)$.

### Problems and Questions for Small Groups

1.  Evaluate $4 \times (-2)$, using both balloon language and integer equations.
2.  Starting at level 0, suppose 6 pairs of sandbags are added. What is your new altitude? Give your answer both in balloon language and an integer equation.
3.  There are two balloons, both starting at level 0. Balloon A adds 3 pairs of gasbags, whereas balloon B removes 3 pairs of sandbags. What are the new heights of balloons A and B?
4.  Discuss what general property of integer multiplication is illustrated in question 3.
5.  Suppose both gasbags and sandbags come in groups of 4 bags. Starting at level 0, how can you reach a height of $-20$? Give more than one answer.
6.  Suppose that both gasbags and sandbags come either individually or bundled in groups of a single size. Starting at level $-8$, you can reach level 7 by removing three groups of the same type of bag. What type of bag has been removed, and how many bags have been bundled into each group?
7.  Using the balloon model, invent and solve your own algebra problem.

---

*This activity is adapted from a presentation by Bill Kring.

## Problem Set 5.3

Exercises numbered in red are answered in the back of the text.

## Understanding Concepts

1. Perform these multiplications:
   (a) $7 \cdot 11$
   (b) $7 \cdot (-11)$
   (c) $(-7) \cdot 11$
   (d) $(-7) \cdot (-11)$
   (e) $12 \cdot 9$
   (f) $12 \cdot (-9)$
   (g) $(-12) \cdot 9$
   (h) $(-12) \cdot (-9)$
   (i) $(-12) \cdot 0$

2. Perform these divisions:
   (a) $36 \div 9$
   (b) $(-36) \div 9$
   (c) $36 \div (-9)$
   (d) $(-36) \div (-9)$
   (e) $(-143) \div 11$
   (f) $165 \div (-11)$
   (g) $(-144) \div (-9)$
   (h) $275 \div 11$
   (i) $72 \div (21 - 19)$

3. Write another multiplication equation and two division equations that are equivalent to $(-11) \cdot (-25{,}753) = 283{,}283$.

4. Write two multiplication equations and another division equation that are equivalent to $(-1001) \div 11 = -91$.

5. What computations do these mail-time stories illustrate?
   (a) The mail carrier brings you six checks for $13 each. Are you richer or poorer? by how much?
   (b) The mail carrier brings you four bills for $23 each. Are you richer or poorer? by how much?
   (c) The mail carrier takes away three bills for $17 each. Are you richer or poorer? by how much?
   (d) The mail carrier takes away five checks for $20 each. Are you richer or poorer? by how much?

6. What computations do these number-line diagrams represent?
   (a)

   (b)
   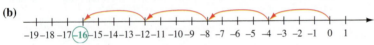
   (c)
   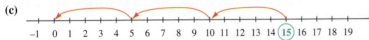

7. Draw a number-line diagram to illustrate $(-4) \cdot 3 = -12$.

8. Illustrate the following operations with colored-counter diagrams:
   (a) $2 \times (-3)$
   (b) $(-2) \times 3$
   (c) $(-2) \times (-3)$
   (d) $(-2) \times 3 + 2$

9. Use the division algorithm in the integers to compute the quotient and remainders of these division problems:
   (a) $-15 \div 4$
   (b) $-28 \div 10$
   (c) $-57 \div 19$

10. The following colored-counter diagram shows two representations of $-4$:

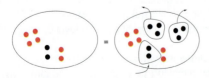

At the left is a loop containing 6 red and 2 black counters. At the right, beginning with a loop that represents zero with 6 red and 6 black counters, we see that removing two loops of 3 black counters and adding a loop with 2 black counters leaves us with the same representation of $-4$ as shown at the left.

(a) What division with remainder in the integers is illustrated by the diagram?

(b) Create a diagram with colored counters that illustrates the division algorithm in the integers for $-5 \div 4$.

11. Use mental arithmetic to give estimates of the given products and quotients. Indicate how you obtained each of your estimates.
    (a) $-21 \times 18$
    (b) $(-32) \times (-28) \times 31$
    (c) $254 \div (-49)$
    (d) $-6642 \div -223$

## Teaching Concepts

12. Make a report describing "bank" arithmetic, for which a positive integer is the amount of a deposit and a negative is the amount of a loan. For example, the expression "$30 + (-100)$" represents the change in your net assets in the bank when you make a $30 deposit and take out a loan for $100, and the expression "$(-3) \cdot (-50)$" is the change made by making three payments of $50 on your loans. Create a collection of expressions and problems involving all four operations: $+, \times, -, \div$. Be sure to include examples that show why "a negative of a negative is a positive" and "a negative times a negative is a positive."

**13. (a)** If we assume that the integers obey the distributive property as illustrated earlier in this section, then a proof of the rule of signs is available. Fill in the blanks to justify the steps of these proofs:

**(i)** $3 \cdot 0 = 0$ _____

$3 \cdot [5 + (-5)] = 0$      Definition of additive inverse

$3 \cdot 5 + 3 \cdot (-5) = 0$ _____

$3 \cdot (-5) = -(3 \cdot 5)$ _____

**(ii)** If $a$ and $b$ are any positive integers, then

$a \cdot 0 = 0$ _____

$a[b + (-b)] = 0$ _____

$ab + a(-b) = 0$ _____

$a \cdot (-b) = -(ab)$ _____

**(iii)** $0 \cdot 5 = 0$ _____

$[3 + (-3)] \cdot 5 = 0$      Definition of additive inverse

$3 \cdot 5 + (-3) \cdot 5 = 0$ _____

$(-3) \cdot 5 = -(3 \cdot 5)$ _____

**(iv)** If $a$ and $b$ are any positive integers, then

$0 \cdot b = 0$ _____

$[a + (-a)] \cdot b = 0$ _____

$ab + (-a)b = 0$ _____

$(-a)b = -(ab)$ _____

**(v)** $(-3) \cdot 0 = 0$ _____

$(-3) \cdot [5 + (-5)] = 0$ _____

$(-3) \cdot 5 + (-3) \cdot (-5) = 0$ _____

$-(3 \cdot 5) + (-3) \cdot (-5) = 0$      By part (iii)

$(-3) \cdot (-5) = 3 \cdot 5$ _____

**(vi)** $(-a) \cdot 0 = 0$ _____

$(-a) \cdot [b + (-b)] = 0$ _____

$(-a)b + (-a)(-b) = 0$ _____

$-(ab) + (-a)(-b) = 0$ _____

$(-a)(-b) = ab$ _____

**(b)** Would parts (ii), (iv), and (vi) be appropriate for an elementary school classroom? Why or why not?

**(c)** Might parts (i), (iii), and (v) be appropriate for an upper elementary or middle school classroom? Discuss.

## Responding to Students

**14.** Marni claims that $\sqrt{4} = -2$ because $(-2) \cdot (-2) = 4$. Daniel claims that Marni is wrong, since everyone knows that $\sqrt{4} = 2$. How would you settle the disagreement between Marni and Daniel?

**15.** Kris obtained the equation $n(n - 3) = n$ and claims that, after dividing each side by $n$, she gets the equation $n - 3 = 1$, which is solved by $n = 4$. Is Kris correct, or has she overlooked a possibility?

**16.** Vijay obtained the inequality $n^2 \leq 9$, where $n$ must be an integer. He claims that there are four possible values of $n$, namely, 0, 1, 2, and 3. Is Vijay correct, or has he overlooked other solutions?

## Thinking Critically

**17.** Let $n$ be any integer. What, if anything, can be said about the sign of each of the expressions that follow? Your answers may be "always positive," "always nonnegative," "can't tell," and so on.

**(a)** $n + 5$        **(b)** $n^2$        **(c)** $n^2 + 1$

**(d)** $n^3$        **(e)** $-n^4$

**18.** Let $a$ and $b$ be positive integers, with $a < b$. Prove that if $c$ is a negative integer, then $ac > bc$. (*Suggestion:* Try using specific numbers first.)

**19.** The equation $a(b - c) = ab - ac$ expresses the distributive law for multiplication over subtraction. Is it true for all integers $a$, $b$, and $c$? If so, explain why. If not, give a counterexample.

**20.** Decide whether the properties that follow are true or false in the integers, where $a$, $b$, and $c$ can be arbitrarily chosen integers. If the statement is true, give a proof, and if the statement is false, give a counterexample by choosing explicit values for $a$, $b$, and $c$.

(a) If $a < b$, then $a^2 < b^2$.

(b) If $a^2 < b^2$, then $a < b$.

(c) If $ac \leq bc$, then $a \leq b$.

(d) $(a - b)(a + b) = a^2 - b^2$.

**21.** Another way to discover the rule of signs for integer multiplication is to look at patterns. Here is an example: Starting with $4 \cdot 3 = 12, 4 \cdot 2 = 8, 4 \cdot 1 = 4$, and $4 \cdot 0 = 0$, and continuing to decrease each product by four, we see that the next terms in the pattern are $4 \cdot (-1) = -4, 4 \cdot (-2) = -8, 4 \cdot (-3) = -12$. That is, a positive integer $m$ times a negative integer, $-n$, is the negative integer given by $m \cdot (-n) = -mn$. Continue each of the following patterns, and then name the corresponding rule of signs that emerges from the pattern:

(a) $4 \cdot (-3) = -12, 3 \cdot (-3) = -9, 2 \cdot (-3) = -6,$
$1 \cdot (-3) = -3$

(b) $(-3) \cdot (-4) = 12, (-3) \cdot (-3) = 9, (-3) \cdot (-2) = 6,$
$(-3) \cdot (-1) = 3$

**22.** Complete each of the number patterns that follow so that the number in each blue circle is the sum of the two numbers in the adjacent red circles. Indicate whether the solution to each pattern is unique.

(a)

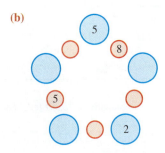

(b)

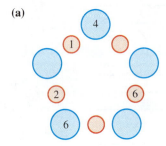

(c)

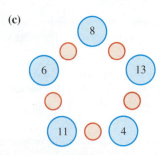

(d) In the general number pattern, suppose that $A, B, C, D,$ and $E$ are known integers and you wish to solve for the unknown integers $u, v, w, x, y,$ and $z$, where the following conditions hold:

$u + v = A, v + w = B, w + x = C,$
$x + y = D, y + u = E.$ (*)

**MHM**

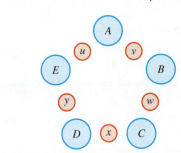

If the sum of the given numbers is even, say, $A + B + C + D + E = 2S$, show that there are integers $u, v, w, x, y,$ and $z$ that uniquely solve the problem. In particular, show that $u = S - B - D$, and then find similar equations for $v, w, x, y,$ and $z$. [A useful habit of mind when working with equations is to see what can be learned by combining equations, say, by addition or subtraction. *Suggestion*: Add all five equations in (*).]

**23.** Consider the following four-large-circle version of problem 22:

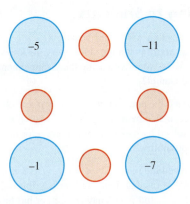

(a) Complete the following diagram so that the same relationships hold:

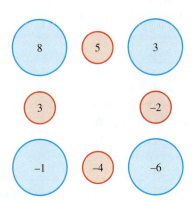

(b) Is a puzzle like this always solvable? Explain. (*Hint*: Let $x$, $y, z,$ and $w$ be the numbers in the small circles.)

(c) What must be the case to ensure that a puzzle with six large circles is solvable? Is the solution unique? Explain carefully.

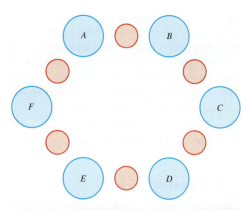

**24.** Use the numbers $-8, -6, -4, -2, 0, 2, 4, 6$, and $8$ to make a magic square. What should the sum in each row, column, and diagonal be? What should the middle number be?

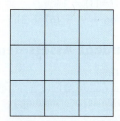

**25.** Use the numbers $-7, -6, -5, -1, 0, 1, 5, 6$, and $7$ to make a magic square.

**26. (a)** Using each of $-3, -1, 1$, and $3$ at most once, what sums can be found? For example, three such sums are

$$3 + (-1) = 2, (-3) + (-1) = -4, \text{ and } 1 = 1.$$

**(b)** What strategy did you use to solve part (a)? Explain.

## Thinking Cooperatively

Work with two or three other students to complete this problem.

**27. Exploring Clock Arithmetic.** In 12-hour clock arithmetic,

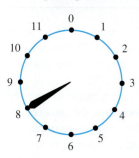

operations are first evaluated with integer arithmetic, but then the resulting sum, difference, product, or quotient is replaced with its remainder when the result is divided by 12. For example, in clock arithmetic, since $8 + 11 = 19$ and $19 \div 12 = 1 \, R \, 7$, we write $8 +_{12} 11 = 7$. Notice that starting at 0 (i.e., at 12 o'clock) and moving forward first by 8 hours and then by 11 hours, you arrive at 7 o'clock.

Similarly, $8 \times 11 = 88$ and $88 \div 12 = 7 \, R \, 4$, so $8 \times_{12} 11 = 4$, meaning that starting at 12 o'clock and moving clockwise 8 jumps of 11 hours each, the clock will then show 4 o'clock. Thus, in 12-hour clock arithmetic, there are just 12 numbers, namely, those in the set

$$I_{12} = \{0, 1, 2, 3, 4, 5, 6, 7, 8, 9, 10, 11\}.$$

In your group of three to four people, explore the properties of 12-hour clock arithmetic by responding to these tasks and questions:

**(a)** Create an addition $+_{12}$ table and a multiplication $\times_{12}$ table for 12-hour clock arithmetic.

**(b)** What properties hold for clock addition, $+_{12}$, in the set $I_{12}$?

**(c)** Does the number system $I_{12}$ have the additive-inverse property?

**(d)** What properties hold for clock multiplication, $\times_{12}$, in the set $I_{12}$?

**(e)** If $m, n \in I_{12}$ and $m \times_{12} n = 1$, does it necessarily follow that $m = n = 1$?

**(f)** If $m, n \in I_{12}$ and $m \times_{12} n = 0$, does it necessarily follow that either $m = 0$ or $n = 1$?

**28.** Investigate the expressions that follow, written in terms of the Fibonacci numbers $F_1 = 1, F_2 = 1, F_3 = 2, F_4 = 3, F_5 = 5, \ldots$ In particular, conjecture a general formula that evaluates each expression, and then test the formula on several examples.

**(a)** $F_{n+1}^2 - F_{n-1}^2, \quad n = 1, 2, 3, \ldots$

**(b)** $F_{n-1}F_{n+1} - F_n^2, \quad n = 1, 2, 3, \ldots$

**(c)** $F_{n+2}F_{n+1} - F_nF_{n-1}, \quad n = 1, 2, 3, \ldots$

## Making Connections

**29.** The members of the Pep Club tried to raise money by raffling off a pig, agreeing that if they actually lost money on the enterprise, they would share the loss equally.

**(a)** If they lost \$105 and there are 15 members in the club, how much did each club member have to pay?

**(b)** What arithmetic might be used to illustrate this story? Explain.

**30.** It cost \$39 each to buy sweatshirts for members of the Pep Club.

**(a)** If there are 15 members in the Pep Club, what was the total cost?

**(b)** What arithmetic might be used to illustrate this story? Explain.

**31.** It is common to report a golfer's score on a hole in relation to par. For example, one stroke over par is a bogey and two strokes over par is a double bogey. Scores one, two, or three strokes below par are respectively a birdie, an eagle, or the extremely rare albatross.

**(a)** Erratic Ernie scored an albatross, 2 eagles, 5 birdies, 7 pars, a bogey, and 2 double bogeys on a par-72 eighteen-hole course. What was Ernie's score for the round?

**(b)** In July 2009, PGA golfer Mark Calcavecchia started with 2 pars, but then shot a record 9 straight birdies on holes 3 through 11. He followed this feat with bogeys on the next two holes and finished the round with pars. What was his final score on the par-72 course?

**32.** The Diffy process described in the Cooperative Investigation in Section 2.3 employed whole numbers. Explain why the process is essentially unchanged if we start with all negative or a mixture of positive and negative integers.

**33. Diffy Revisited.** It's sometimes productive to investigate a problem in integers by paying attention only to the *parity* of the integers; that is, instead of exact values, keep track only of whether the integers are even or odd. For example, the Fibonacci sequence 1, 1, 2, 3, 5, 8, 13, 21, 34, . . . has the parity sequence *d, d, e, d, d, e, d, d, e, . . .* , where *d* denotes an odd number and $e$ denotes an even number, so we immediately see that every third Fibonacci number is even and the others are odd. In this exercise, you'll use parity considerations to examine Diffy (also known as the Four Number Game) in which a 4-tuple of numbers $(h, i, j, k)$ is converted to a sequence of new 4-tuples by the following rule taken at each step:

$$(h, i, j, k) \rightarrow (|h - i|, |i - j|, |j - k|, |k - h|).$$

As an example, if the initial 4-tuple is $(2, 3, 5, 7)$, then

$$(2, 3, 5, 7) \rightarrow (1, 2, 2, 5) \rightarrow (1, 0, 3, 4) \rightarrow (1, 3, 1, 3) \rightarrow$$
$$(2, 2, 2, 2) \rightarrow (0, 0, 0, 0),$$

so the game ends in five steps. Taking only parity into account, we see that this game has the form

$$(e, d, d, d) \rightarrow (d, e, e, d) \rightarrow (d, e, d, e) \rightarrow (d, d, d, d) \rightarrow$$
$$(e, e, e, e) \rightarrow (e, e, e, e).$$

(a) Show that any Diffy game comes to a 4-tuple of the form $(e, e, e, e)$ at least by the fourth step. (*Suggestion*: Since Diffy started on $(h, i, j, k)$ is equivalent to the game starting on the permutation $(i, j, k, h)$, any game must start with one of the parity patterns $(e, e, e, e)$, $(d, e, e, e)$, $(d, d, e, e)$, $(d, e, d, e)$, $(d, d, d, e)$, and $(d, d, d, d)$.)

(b) By part (a), after 4 steps of Diffy, each of the four numbers in the resulting 4-tuple is divisible by 2. What can you say about the numbers in the 4-tuple obtained after 8 steps? After 12 steps? After 16 steps? Test your reasoning by carrying out Diffy beginning with the 4-tuple $(81, 149, 274, 504)$.

(c) Give an argument that Diffy must always terminate by eventually reaching the 4-tuple $(0, 0, 0, 0)$.

(d) Show that the Three Number Game $(h, i, j) \rightarrow (|h - i|, |i - j|, |h - j|)$ need not terminate. (*Suggestion*: try a game starting with $(0, 0, 1)$.)

## Using a Calculator

34. Calculate each of these examples without using the $\boxed{M+}$, $\boxed{M-}$, or $\boxed{MR}$ key on your calculator:

(a) $31 - 47 + 88 + 16 - 5$

(b) $57 + 165 \div (-11) + 17$

(c) $(47 + 81 - 56 + 9) \div (67 - 31 - 9)$

## From State Student Assessments

35. (Massachusetts, Grade 8)
(Calculators are not allowed here because one can obtain the correct answer without understanding.)

Compute: $(-2)(-5)(-1) =$

---

## The Chapter in Relation to Future Teachers

History shows that the concept of a negative number is not a simple one. For example, the ancient Greek mathematician Diophantus recognized negative numbers as early as A.D. 275, but rejected them as absurd. Thus, he refused to accept $x = -4$ as a meaningful solution of the equation $4x + 20 = 4$.

Therefore, the classroom teacher is faced with a nontrivial task: How can negative integers be made meaningful and useful to young children? As shown throughout this chapter, the integers can be effectively represented by manipulatives and pictorial models, including colored counters and mail-time stories. In addition, the integers can be visualized as positions and movements on a number line, an approach that builds naturally on the whole-number line that is already familiar to students. Within the framework of each of these representations, the arithmetic operations are illustrated in a natural setting that will seem sensible in a child's world. Especially in our contemporary world, it is easy to find applications of the integers. In particular, the teacher will want to relate how integers are used to record yards lost and gained in football, a golf score relative to par, a temperature relative to zero, profits and losses, amounts saved and owed, and so on.

Finally, it is important to understand that the system of integers has important new properties not found in the whole-number system. The most important is that subtraction is now a closed operation, so an equation such as $x + 5 = 3$ is now solved by the negative integer $-2$. Of course, it is still the case that an equation such as $5x = 3$ has no solution $x$, even in the integers. In Chapter 6, the integers are extended to the still larger system of rational numbers, where there is a solution of $5x = 3$, namely, the fraction $x = \frac{3}{5}$.

# Chapter 5 Summary

In what follows, all symbols represent integers.

| Section 5.1   Representations of Integers | Page Reference |
|---|---|

**CONCEPTS**

- **Integers:** An extension of the whole number system to include both the negative integers and the whole numbers. — 229

- **Colored counters:** Each integer is represented by a loop containing counters of two colors, often red and black or yellow and black. If $n$ is positive, the loop contains $n$ more black than red counters. A negative integer, $-m$, is a loop with $m$ more red than black counters. A loop with equally many red and black counters represents 0. — 231

- **Mail time stories:** A positive integer $n$ is represented by a check in the amount of $n$ dollars, and a negative integer $-m$ is represented by a bill in the amount of $m$ dollars. — 234

- **Number line:** A positive integer $n$ is represented by a point $n$ units to the right of the point that represents 0, or alternatively as a right-pointing arrow of length $n$. A negative integer $-m$ is represented by a point $m$ units to the left of 0, or alternatively as a left-pointing arrow of length $m$. — 234

**DEFINITIONS**

- **Integers:** The set of numbers $I = \{\ldots, -3, -2, -1, 0, 1, 2, 3, \ldots\}$. — 228, 229

- **Positive integers:** The term given to the set of natural numbers $\{1, 2, 3, \ldots\}$ when considered as a subset of the integers. — 228

- **Negative integers,** or **opposites:** The numbers $-1, -2, -3, \ldots$ for which $n + (-n) = (-n) + n = 0$. — 229

- **Additive identity property of 0:** For all integers $n$, $n + 0 = 0 + n = n$ — 229

- **Additive inverse property of a number system:** A system of numbers for which every element $n$ has an additive inverse $m$, so that $n + m = m + n = 0$. The number $m$ is called the **additive inverse** of $n$, written as $m = -n$. — 230

- **Absolute value,** or **magnitude,** of an integer $n$ is the nonnegative integer $|n| = n$ if $n$ is nonnegative and $|n| = -n$ if $n$ is negative. — 230

**THEOREM**

- **Opposite of the opposite:** For all integers $n$, $-(-n) = n$. — 233

| Section 5.2   Addition and Subtraction of Integers | Page Reference |
|---|---|

**CONCEPTS**

- **Addition of integers:** The binary operation modeled by combining loops in the colored counter representation, placing several checks or bills in the mail box, or combining jumps on the number line. — 240, 242, 243

- **Subtraction of integers:** The binary operation modeled by removing one loop from another in the colored counted representation, removing checks or bills from a mail box, or removing one jump from another on the number line. — 246, 250

**DEFINITIONS**

- **Addition of integers:** If $m$ and $n$ are positive integers, then $(-m) + (-n) = -(m + n)$, $m + (-n) = m - n$ if $m > n$, $m + (-n) = -(n - m)$ if $m < n$, and $m + (-m) = 0$. — 241

| | |
|---|---|
| • The integer $a$ is **less than** $b$, $a < b$, if $a + c = b$ for some positive integer $c$, and $a$ is **greater than** $b$, $a < b$, if $b < a$. | 245 |
| • **Subtraction of integers:** For any integers $a$, $b$, and $c$, $a - b = c$ if, and only if, $a = b + c$. | 248 |

**THEOREMS**

| | |
|---|---|
| • **Properties of integer addition:** Given any integers $m$, $n$, and $r$, addition is closed ($m + n$ is an integer), commutative ($m + n = n + n$), associative ($m + (n + r) = (m + n) + r$), with 0 the additive identity ($m + 0 = 0 + m = m$), and $-m$ the additive inverse ($m + (-m) = (-m) + m = 0$). | 242 |
| • **Law of trichotomy:** Given any integers, $a$ and $b$, precisely one of the three possibilities $a < b$, $b > a$, or $a = b$ holds. | 245 |
| • **Subtraction by adding the opposite:** Let $a$ and $b$ be any integers. Then $a - b = a + (-b)$. | 249 |
| • **Closure of the integers under subtraction:** Let $a$ and $b$ be any integers. Then their difference $a - b$ is an integer. | 249 |

| Section 5.3  **Multiplication and Division of Integers** | **Page Reference** |
|---|---|

**CONCEPTS**

| | |
|---|---|
| • **Multiplication** by a positive integer is repeated addition, and multiplication by a negative integer is repeated subtraction. | 257 |
| • **Division** is the inverse of multiplication, so that $a \div b$ is the unique integer $c$ for which $a = b \cdot c$. | 260 |
| • **Division with remainder:** Given any integer $n$ and a positive integer $b$, there are unique integers $q$ and $r$ for which $n = qb + r, 0 \le r < b$. This can also be written $n \div b = q \text{ R } r$, where $q$ is the quotient and $r$ is the remainder. | 262 |

**DEFINITIONS**

| | |
|---|---|
| • **Multiplication of integers:** If $m$ and $n$ are integers, with $m$ positive, then $m \cdot n = n + n + \cdots + n$ and $(-m) \cdot n = -(n + n + \cdots + n)$. | 257 |
| • **Division of integers:** If $a$, $b$, and $c$ are integers, with $b \ne 0$, then $a \div b = c$ if and only if $a = b \cdot c$. | 261 |

**THEOREMS**

| | |
|---|---|
| • **The rule of signs for multiplication:** If $m$ and $n$ are positive integers, then $m \cdot (-n) = -mn$, $(-m) \cdot n = -mn$, and $(-m) \cdot (-n) = mn$. | 258 |
| • **Properties of integer multiplication:** Given any integers $m$, $n$, and $r$, multiplication is closed ($m \cdot n$ is an integer), commutative ($m \cdot n = n \cdot n$), associative ($m \cdot (n \cdot r) = (m \cdot n) \cdot r$), distributes over addition ($m \cdot (n + r) = m \cdot n + m \cdot r$), has the multiplicative identity 1 ($m \cdot 1 = 1 \cdot m = m$), and has the multiplication by 0 property ($m \cdot 0 = 0 \cdot m = 0$). | 259 |
| • **The rule of signs for division:** If $m$ and $n$ are positive integers, then $m \div (-n) = -(m \div n), (-m) \div n = -(m \div n)$, and $(-m) \div (-n) = m \div n$. | 261 |
| • **Division algorithm in the integers:** Let $a$ and $b$ be integers, with $b$ positive. Then there is a unique integer $q$, the quotient, and a unique nonnegative integer $r$, the remainder, such that $a = q \cdot b + r, 0 \le r < b$. | 262 |

## Chapter Review Exercises

### Section 5.1

**1.** You have 15 counters colored black on one side and red on the other.

   **(a)** If you drop them on your desktop and 7 come up black and 8 come up red, what integer is represented?

   **(b)** If you drop them on your desktop and twice as many come up black as red, what number is being represented?

   **(c)** What numbers are represented by all possible drops of the 15 counters?

**2.** **(a)** If the mail carrier brings you a check for $12, are you richer or poorer, and by how much? What integer does this situation illustrate?

   **(b)** If the mail carrier brings you a bill for $37, are you richer or poorer, and by how much? What integer does this situation illustrate?

**3.** **(a)** 12° above 0 illustrates what integer?

   **(b)** 24° below 0 illustrates what integer?

**4.** **(a)** List five different loops of colored counters that represent the integer −5.

   **(b)** List five different loops of colored counters that represent the integer 6.

**5.** **(a)** Give a mail-time story that illustrates −85.

   **(b)** Give a mail-time story that illustrates 47.

**6.** **(a)** What number must you add to 44 to obtain 0?

   **(b)** What number must you add to −61 to obtain 0?

### Section 5.2

**7.** What addition is represented by this diagram?

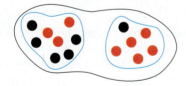

**8.** What subtraction is represented by this diagram?

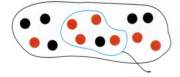

**9.** What additions and subtractions are represented by these mail-time stories?

   **(a)** At mail time, the letter carrier brings you a check for $45 and a bill for $68. Are you richer or poorer, and by how much?

   **(b)** At mail time, the letter carrier brings you a check for $45 and takes away a bill for $68 left previously. Are you richer or poorer, and by how much?

**10.** What additions and/or subtractions do these number-line diagrams represent?

   **(a)**

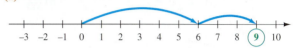

   **(b)**

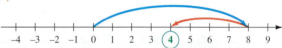

   **(c)**

   **(d)**

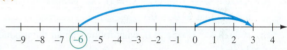

   **(e)**

   **(f)**

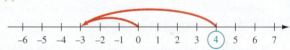

   **(g)**

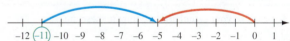

**11.** Perform these additions and subtractions:

   **(a)** $5 + (-7)$           **(b)** $(-27) - (-5)$

   **(c)** $(-27) + (-5)$      **(d)** $5 - (-7)$

   **(e)** $8 - (-12)$       **(f)** $8 - 12$

**12.** **(a)** If it is 15° below 0 and the temperature falls 12°, what temperature is it?

   **(b)** What arithmetic does this situation illustrate?

**13.** **(a)** Dina's bank account was overdrawn by $12. What was her balance after she deposited the $37 she earned working at a local pizza parlor?

   **(b)** What arithmetic does this situation illustrate?

**14.** **(a)** Plot these numbers on a number line: $-2, 7, 0, -5, -9$, and 2.

   **(b)** List the numbers in part (a) in increasing order.

   **(c)** Determine what integer must be added to each number in your list from part (b) to obtain the next.

## Section 5.3

**15.** What products do these number-line diagrams represent?

**(a)**

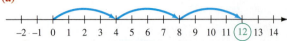

**(b)**

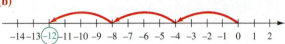

**(c)**

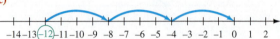

**(d)**

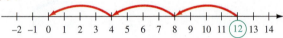

**16. (a)** Show that $3 \cdot 5 + 3 \cdot (-5) = 0$. (*Suggestion:* Begin with the fact that $3 \cdot 0 = 0$.)

**(b)** If $3 \cdot 5 + 3 \cdot (-5) = 0$, what follows about the product $3 \cdot (-5)$?

**(c)** Show that $-(3 \cdot 5) + (-3) \cdot (-5) = 0$. (*Suggestion:* Begin with the fact that $0 \cdot (-5) = 0$, and use the result of part (a).)

**(d)** If $-(3 \cdot 5) + (-3) \cdot (-5) = 0$, what follows about the product $(-3) \cdot (-5)$?

**17.** Perform each of these computations:

**(a)** $(-8) \cdot (-7)$      **(b)** $8 \cdot (-7)$

**(c)** $(-8) \cdot 7$      **(d)** $84 \div (-12)$

**(e)** $(-84) \div 7$      **(f)** $(-84) \div (-7)$

**18.** Write a mail-time story to illustrate each of these products:

**(a)** $7 \cdot (12)$     **(b)** $(-7) \cdot (13)$     **(c)** $(-7) \cdot (-13)$

**19.** Prove that if $d$ divides $n$, then $d$ divides $-n$, $-d$ divides $n$, and $-d$ divides $-n$.

**20.** If $a$ and $b$ are integers, the greatest common divisor (GCD) of $a$ and $b$ is the largest positive integer dividing both $a$ and $b$. Compute each of the following:

**(a)** GCD$(255, -39)$      **(b)** GCD$(-1001, 2651)$

**21.** Show that if $n$ is an integer not divisible by 2 or 3, then $n^2 - 1$ is divisible by 24. (*Hint:* By the division algorithm, $n$ must be of one of these forms: $6q, 6q + 1, 6q + 2, 6q + 3, 6q + 4$, and $6q + 5$.)

## Chapter Test

**1.** Mary Lou's checkbook balance was $129. What was it after she deposited $341 and then wrote checks for $13, $47, and $29? What arithmetic does this illustrate?

**2.** At mail time, if the mail carrier took away five bills for $27 each, are you richer or poorer, and by how much? What calculation does this illustrate?

**3. (a)** Use your calculator to compute these sums:

$$1 =$$
$$1 - 4 =$$
$$1 - 4 + 9 =$$
$$1 - 4 + 9 - 16 =$$
$$1 - 4 + 9 - 16 + 25 =$$

**(b)** Make a conjecture suggested by the pattern of part (a).

**4. (a)** What sums can be obtained by using only the numbers $-10$, $-5, -2, -1, 1, 2, 5$, and $10$, each at most once and without using any number with its double (i.e., you can't use 5 with 10, 1 with 2, $-1$ with $-2$, or $-5$ with $-10$)?

**(b)** Do the representations in part (a) appear to be unique?

**5.** Perform each of these computations:

**(a)** $(-7) + (-19)$      **(b)** $(-7) - (-19)$

**(c)** $7 - (-19)$      **(d)** $7 + (-19)$

**(e)** $(-6859) \div 19$      **(f)** $(-24) \cdot 17$

**(g)** $36 \cdot (-24)$      **(h)** $(-1155) \div (-11)$

**(i)** $0 \div (-27)$

**6.** Find *all* integers that solve the following equations:

**(a)** $|a + 2| = 5$

**(b)** $3m - 4 = 5m + 6$

**(c)** $n \div 5 = -4 \, \text{R} \, 1$

**(d)** $t(t^2 + 8) = 3t^3$

**7.** Write a mail-time story to illustrate the subtraction $7 - (-4) = 11$.

**8.** The Fibonacci sequence is formed by adding any two consecutive numbers in the sequence to obtain the next number. If the same rule is followed in each of these sequences, correctly fill in the blanks:

**(a)** $-5, -3,$ _____, _____, _____, _____

**(b)** $7,$ _____, $2,$ _____, _____, _____

**(c)** $6,$ _____, _____, _____, $-12,$ _____

**9.** Tammie, Jody, and Nora formed a small club. After a pizza party celebrating the first anniversary of the club's existence, they owed the local pizzeria $27. The bill was paid and shared equally by the three girls. Was each one richer or poorer, and by how much? What arithmetic does this illustrate?

**10.** Draw a number-line diagram to illustrate each of these calculations:

**(a)** $(-7) + 10$     **(b)** $10 - (-7)$     **(c)** $7 \cdot (-5)$

**11.** The least common multiple (LCM) of integers $a$ and $b$ is the least *positive* integer divisible by both $a$ and $b$. Compute LCM$(-240, 54)$.

# 6

# Fractions and Rational Numbers

**6.1** The Basic Concepts of Fractions and Rational Numbers

**6.2** Addition and Subtraction of Fractions

**6.3** Multiplication and Division of Fractions

**6.4** The Rational Number System

## Hands On
## Folded Fractions

### Materials Needed

Each student (or cooperating pair of students) should have about six paper squares (4- to 5-inch side length) and several colored pencils. Patty Paper (waxed paper that serves as meat-patty separators) works very well.

### Example: Folding Quarters

A unit of area is defined as the area of a square.

 = 1

Fold the unit square in half twice vertically and then unfold. Since the four rectangles are congruent (i.e., have the same shape and size), each rectangle represents the fraction $\frac{1}{4}$.

Coloring individual rectangles gives representations of the fractions $\frac{0}{4}, \frac{1}{4}, \frac{2}{4}, \frac{3}{4}$, and $\frac{4}{4}$. (Notice that we count regions, not folds or fold lines.)

$$\frac{0}{4} \qquad \frac{1}{4} \qquad \frac{2}{4} \qquad \frac{3}{4} \qquad \frac{4}{4}$$

Quarters can also be obtained by other folding procedures. For example, we can make a vertical half fold followed by a horizontal half fold to create four small squares within the unit square. This technique illustrates why $\frac{1}{2} \times \frac{1}{2} = \frac{1}{4}$.

If one colored fraction pattern can be rearranged and regrouped to cover the same region of the unit as another fraction pattern, we say that the two fractions are equivalent. For example, the following rearrangement and regrouping shows that $\frac{2}{4}$ is equivalent to $\frac{1}{2}$:

Therefore, we write $\frac{2}{4} = \frac{1}{2}$.

### Fraction Folding Activities and Problems

1. **Eighths.** Fold a square into quarters as in the example, and also fold along the two diagonals.
   **(a)** Identify these fractions:

   **(b)** How many *different* ways can two of the eight regions be colored to give a representation of $\frac{2}{8}$? Two colorings are considered identical if one pattern can be rotated to become identical to the second pattern.

2. **Sixths.** "Roll" the paper square into thirds, flatten, and then fold in half in the opposite direction to divide the square into six congruent rectangles. This procedure illustrates that $\frac{1}{2} \times \frac{1}{3} = \frac{1}{6}$.

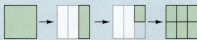

   How many *different* ways can you represent the fraction $\frac{3}{6}$? Remember that two patterns are different only if one cannot be rotated to become identical to another.

3. **Identifying fractions.** The leftmost shaded region shown in the figure is bounded by segments joining successive midpoints of the sides of the square. What is the area of the shaded region? The region can be divided into smaller regions that are easy to rearrange into a pattern which shows that $\frac{1}{2}$ of the square is shaded.

   Use similar multiple representations of the same amount of shaded region to identify the fractions represented by the following colored regions:
   **(a)** The shaded region obtained by joining the midpoints of the vertical edges of the square with the $\frac{1}{3}$ and $\frac{2}{3}$ points along the horizontal edges:

   **(b)** The shaded region obtained by joining the $\frac{1}{3}$ and $\frac{2}{3}$ points along the vertical and horizontal edges:

   **(c)** The shaded square whose corners are the intersections of the segments joining the corners of the unit square to the midpoint of an opposite side of the unit square (*Suggestion:* Rearrange the unshaded regions to create squares, each congruent to the shaded square.)

**CHAPTER PREVIEW**

The goal of this chapter is to introduce the rational numbers, focusing on the properties, computational procedures, and applications of this number system. A rational number is defined as a number that can be expressed in the form of a fraction $\frac{a}{b}$, where the numerator $a$ is any integer and the denominator $b$ is any nonzero integer. The set of all rational numbers is denoted by $Q$ Since any integer $n \in I$ is considered to be the rational number $\frac{n}{1} \in Q$, the rational number system is an extension of the system of integers, $I$.

**KEY IDEAS**

- Fraction basics: unit, denominator, numerator
- Fraction models: colored regions (area model), set model, fraction strips, fraction circles, number-line model
- Equivalence of fractions and the fundamental law of fractions
- Simplest form
- Common denominator, least common denominator
- Order relation on the fraction
- Arithmetic operations on fractions, and their illustration with fraction models
- Proper fractions and mixed numbers
- Reciprocals
- Algorithms for division, including the "invert-and-multiply" rule
- The meaning of a fraction as an operator
- Rational number system $Q$, where $N \subset W \subset I \subset Q$
- Properties of the rational number system
- Existence of multiplicative inverses of nonzero rational numbers
- Density property of the rational numbers
- Computations (exact, approximate, mental) with rational numbers
- Applications of rational numbers

**6.1**

# The Basic Concepts of Fractions and Rational Numbers

Fractions were first introduced in *measurement* problems, to express a quantity that is less than a whole unit. Indeed, the word *fraction* comes from the Latin word *fractio,* meaning "the act of breaking into pieces." Figure 6.1 shows a measuring cup and a ruler, two common items on which fractions appear.

**FIGURE 6.1**

Fractions are used on measuring cups and rulers to indicate subdivisions of the basic unit

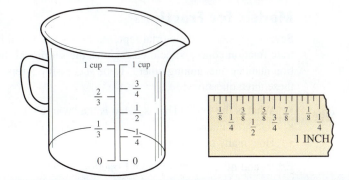

Fractions may be used to indicate capacity, length, weight, area, or indeed any quantity for which it is sensible to subdivide a fundamental unit of measure into some number of equal-sized parts. To interpret the meaning of any fraction $\frac{a}{b}$, we must

- agree on the **unit** (e.g., the unit is a cup, an inch, the area of the hexagon in a set of pattern blocks, a whole pizza, and so on);
- understand that the unit is **subdivided into $b$ parts of equal size;** and
- understand that we are considering $a$ **of the parts of the unit.**

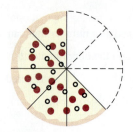

**FIGURE 6.2**
Choosing a whole pizza as the unit and subdividing it into 8 equal parts shows that $\frac{3}{8}$ of the pizza has been eaten and $\frac{5}{8}$ remains

The number $b$ is called the **denominator** of the fraction, a word derived from the Latin *denominare,* meaning "namer." The number $a$ is called the **numerator,** derived from the Latin *numeros,* meaning "number."

For example, suppose the unit is one pizza, as shown in Figure 6.2. The pizza has been divided into 8 parts, and 3 parts have been consumed. Using fractions, we can say that $\frac{3}{8}$ of the pizza was eaten and $\frac{5}{8}$ of the pizza remains.

The notion of a subdivided unit of measure motivates the following formal definition of a fraction:

> **DEFINITION** *Fractions*
>
> A **fraction** is an ordered pair of integers $a$ and $b$, $b \neq 0$, written $\frac{a}{b}$ or $a/b$. The integer $a$ is called the **numerator** of the fraction, and the integer $b$ is called the **denominator** of the fraction.

Notice that this definition permits the numerator or denominator to be a negative integer or zero. For example, $\frac{-3}{-8}, \frac{-4}{12}, \frac{31}{-4}$, and $\frac{0}{1}$ are all fractions according to the definition just given. Both negative and positive integers are allowed in order to ensure that additive inverses exist in the rational number system $Q$, as will be seen in Section 2 of this chapter.

Any integer $m$ is viewed as the fraction $\frac{m}{1}$. Usually, the denominator 1 is not written explicitly. For example, we write 3 instead of $\frac{3}{1}$.

## Models for Fractions

Several physical and pictorial representations are useful in the elementary school classroom to illustrate fraction concepts: colored regions, the set model, fraction strips, fraction circles, and the fraction number line, among others. To be successful, a representation of a fraction must clearly answer these three questions:

- What is the unit? (That is, what is the "whole"?)
- Into how many equal parts (the denominator) has the unit been subdivided?
- How many of these parts (the numerator) are under consideration?

Errors and misconceptions about fractions indicate that at least one of these three questions has not been properly answered or clearly considered. Perhaps the most frequently occurring error is the failure to identify the unit to which the fraction refers, since the notation $\frac{a}{b}$ makes the numerator and denominator explicit, but the unit is left implicit.

## Colored Regions

A shape is chosen to represent the unit and is then subdivided into subregions of equal size. A fraction is visualized by coloring some of the subregions. Three examples are shown in Figure 6.3. Colored-region models are sometimes called *area* models.

**FIGURE 6.3**
Some colored-region models for fractions

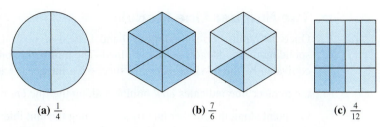

(a) $\frac{1}{4}$          (b) $\frac{7}{6}$          (c) $\frac{4}{12}$

## The Set Model

The unit is a finite set $U$ of objects, where we recall that $n(U)$ denotes the number of elements in $U$. Each subset $A$ of $U$ corresponds to the fraction $\frac{n(A)}{n(U)}$. For example, the set of 10 apples shown in Figure 6.4 contains a subset of 3 that are wormy. Therefore, we would say that $\frac{3}{10}$ of the apples are wormy. In Chapter 14, we will see that the set model of fractions is particularly useful in probability. An apple drawn at random from the 10 apples has a $\frac{3}{10}$ probability of being wormy. Sometimes, the set model is called the *discrete model*.

**FIGURE 6.4**
The set model depicts that $\frac{3}{10}$ of the apples are wormy

## Fraction Strips

Here the unit is defined by a rectangular strip. A fraction such as $\frac{3}{6}$ is modeled by shading 3 of 6 equally sized subrectangles of the rectangle. Sample fraction strips are shown in Figure 6.5. A set of fraction strips typically contains strips for the denominators 1, 2, 3, 4, 6, 8, and 12.

**FIGURE 6.5**
Examples of fractions modeled by fraction strips

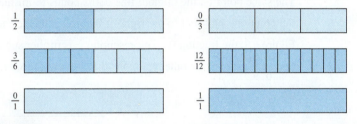

## Fraction Circles

The unit is a circular region, subdivided by uniformly spaced radial segments corresponding to the denominator. The number of shaded sectors indicates the numerator of the fraction. This visual model is particularly effective, since it is easily drawn and interpreted by children. Several fractions depicted with fraction circles are shown in Figure 6.6.

**FIGURE 6.6**
Fractions depicted with fraction circles

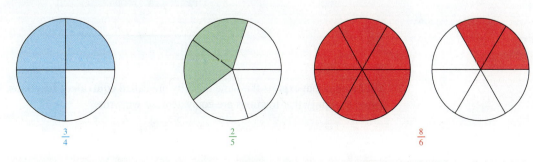

$\frac{3}{4}$          $\frac{2}{5}$          $\frac{8}{6}$

## The Number-Line Model

Once the points corresponding to 0 and 1 are assigned on a number line, all of the points corresponding to the integers are determined. The unit is the length of the line segment from 0 to 1 or, equivalently, the distance between successive integer points. As before, the arrow at the right of the number line indicates how numbers along the line are ordered. A fraction such as $\frac{5}{4}$ is assigned to a point along the number line by subdividing the unit interval into equal parts and then counting off 5 of these lengths to the right of 0. Typical fractions are shown in Figure 6.7. Notice that the same point on the fraction number line can be named by different fractions. For example, $\frac{1}{2}$ and $\frac{2}{4}$ both correspond to the same distance. The number-line model has the advantage of allowing negative fractions, such as $-\frac{3}{4}$, to be represented.

**FIGURE 6.7**
Fractions as points on the number-line model

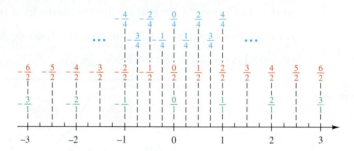

As with the number-line model for the whole numbers and the integers, fractions will also be represented as "jumps" along the number line, as shown by right-pointing or left-pointing arrows. Figure 6.8 shows several arrow representations of fractions.

**FIGURE 6.8**
Fractions as "jumps" along the number line

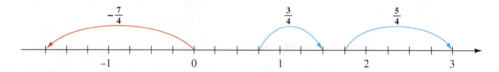

## Equivalent Fractions

The same point on the number line corresponds to infinitely many different fractions. For example, the point one-half unit to the right of 0 corresponds to the fractions $\frac{1}{2}, \frac{2}{4}, \frac{3}{6}$, and so on. Similarly, in Figure 6.9, the fraction strip representing $\frac{2}{3}$ is further subdivided by the vertical dashed lines to show that $\frac{4}{6}, \frac{6}{9}$, and $\frac{8}{12}$ are other fractions that express the *same* shaded portion of a whole strip.

**FIGURE 6.9**
The fraction-strip model showing that $\frac{2}{3}, \frac{4}{6}, \frac{6}{9}$, and $\frac{8}{12}$ are equivalent fractions

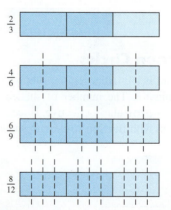

Fractions that express the same quantity are called **equivalent fractions.** The equality symbol, =, is used to signify that fractions are equivalent, so we write

$$\frac{2}{3} = \frac{4}{6} = \frac{6}{9} = \frac{8}{12}.$$

The number of additional dashed lines between each vertical pair of solid lines shown in Figure 6.9 can be increased arbitrarily; therefore,

$$\frac{2}{3} = \frac{2 \cdot n}{3 \cdot n}$$

for $n = 1, 2, \ldots$. In this way, beginning with one fraction $\frac{a}{b}$, we obtain an infinite list, $\frac{2a}{2b}, \frac{3a}{3b}, \frac{4a}{4b}, \ldots$, of equivalent fractions.

In sum, we have the following important property known as the **fundamental law of fractions.**

---

**PROPERTY**  *The Fundamental Law of Fractions*

Let $\frac{a}{b}$ be a fraction. Then

$$\frac{a}{b} = \frac{an}{bn}, \quad \text{for any integer } n \neq 0.$$

---

Equivalent fractions can also be obtained by dividing both the numerator and denominator by a common factor. For example, the numerator and denominator of $\frac{35}{21}$ are each divisible by 7, so, by the fundamental law,

$$\frac{35}{21} = \frac{5 \cdot 7}{3 \cdot 7} = \frac{5}{3}.$$

Now suppose we are given two fractions, say, $\frac{3}{12}$ and $\frac{2}{8}$, and we wish to know if they are equivalent. From the fundamental law of fractions, we know that

$$\frac{3}{12} = \frac{3 \cdot 8}{12 \cdot 8} = \frac{24}{96} \qquad \text{and} \qquad \frac{2}{8} = \frac{2 \cdot 12}{8 \cdot 12} = \frac{24}{96}.$$

Thus, $\frac{3}{12}$ and $\frac{2}{8}$ are equivalent fractions. More generally, two given fractions $\frac{a}{b}$ and $\frac{c}{d}$ are respectively equivalent to $\frac{ad}{bd}$ and $\frac{bc}{bd}$ if, and only if, the numerators are equal. This result, known as the **cross-product property,** is stated in the following theorem.

---

**THEOREM**  *The Cross-Product Property of Equivalent Fractions*

The fractions $\frac{a}{b}$ and $\frac{c}{d}$ are **equivalent** if, and only if, $ad = bc$. That is,

$$\frac{a}{b} = \frac{c}{d} \qquad \text{if, and only if,} \qquad ad = bc$$

---

MHM   The cross-product formula provides an easy check for the equivalence of two fractions. However, it should always be used with the understanding that it is checking that numerators agree when the two fractions are expressed with a *common* denominator.

---

**EXAMPLE  6.1  Examining Fraction Equivalence with Pizza Diagrams**

Enrique and Ana each ordered a large pizza. Enrique likes large pieces, so he requested that his pizza be cut into 8 pieces. Ana, however, requested that her pizza be cut into 12 pieces, since she likes smaller pieces. Enrique ate 6 pieces of his pizza, and Ana ate 9 pieces. Enrique claims that he ate less than Ana, since he ate 3 fewer pieces. Use words and diagrams (similar to Figure 6.2) to confirm or refute Enrique's claim.

**Solution**    The following pizza diagrams show that both Enrique and Ana have eaten $\frac{3}{4}$ of their pizzas and both have $\frac{1}{4}$ of their pizza remaining:

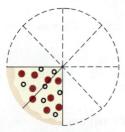

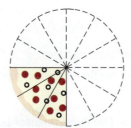

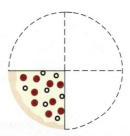

Enrique's pizza                    Ana's pizza        A pizza that is $\frac{3}{4}$ eaten, with $\frac{1}{4}$ remaining

This result can also be verified with the fundamental law of fractions: $\frac{6}{8} = \frac{2 \cdot 3}{2 \cdot 4} = \frac{3}{4}$ and $\frac{9}{12} = \frac{3 \cdot 3}{3 \cdot 4} = \frac{3}{4}$. Alternatively, $\frac{6}{8} = \frac{9}{12}$ can be checked by means of the cross-product property: $6 \cdot 12 = 8 \cdot 9$.

## Fractions in Simplest Form

Often, it is preferable to use the simplest equivalent form of a fraction instead of a more complicated fraction. For example, it may be best to use $\frac{2}{3}$ instead of $\frac{400}{600}$ and to use $\frac{-3}{4}$ instead of $\frac{75}{-100}$.

> **DEFINITION**    *Fractions in Simplest Form*
>
> A fraction $\frac{a}{b}$ is in **simplest form** if $a$ and $b$ have no common divisor larger than 1 and $b$ is positive.

A fraction in simplest form is also said to be in **lowest terms** or in **reduced form,** though the term *reduced* is best avoided because it mistakenly suggests that the fraction is smaller than an equivalent one that is not in simplest form.

There are several ways to determine the simplest form of a fraction $\frac{a}{b}$.

**Method 1.  Divide successively by common factors.** Suppose we want to write $\frac{560}{960}$ in simplest form. Using the fundamental law of fractions, we successively divide both numerator and denominator by common factors. Since 560 and 960 are both divisible by 10, it follows that

$$\frac{560}{960} = \frac{56 \cdot 10}{96 \cdot 10} = \frac{56}{96}.$$

But both 56 and 96 are even (that is, divisible by 2), so

$$\frac{56}{96} = \frac{28 \cdot 2}{48 \cdot 2} = \frac{28}{48}.$$

Again, 28 and 48 are easily seen to be divisible by 4, so

$$\frac{28}{48} = \frac{7 \cdot 4}{12 \cdot 4} = \frac{7}{12}.$$

Finally, since 7 and 12 have no common factor other than 1, $\dfrac{7}{12}$ is the simplest form of $\dfrac{560}{960}$. Indeed, one might quickly and efficiently carry out this simplification as follows to obtain the desired result.

$$\dfrac{\overset{\overset{\overset{7}{28}}{\cancel{560}}}{\underset{\underset{12}{48}}{\cancel{960}}}} \qquad \text{or} \qquad \dfrac{560}{960} = \dfrac{56}{96} = \dfrac{28}{48} = \dfrac{7}{12}.$$

**Method 2. Divide $a$ and $b$ by GCD $(a, b)$.** Using the ideas of Chapter 4, we determine that GCD(560, 960) = 80. Therefore, $\dfrac{560}{960} = \dfrac{560 \div 80}{960 \div 80} = \dfrac{7}{12}$.

**Method 3. Divide by the common factors in the prime-power representation of $a$ and $b$.** Using this method, we have

$$\dfrac{560}{960} = \dfrac{2^4 \cdot 5 \cdot 7}{2^6 \cdot 3 \cdot 5} = \dfrac{7}{2^2 \cdot 3} = \dfrac{7}{12}.$$

Some classroom calculators also have the capability of converting a fraction to simplest form.

---

**EXAMPLE 6.2** **Simplifying Fractions**

Find the simplest form of each fraction.

(a) $\dfrac{240}{72}$      (b) $\dfrac{-450}{1500}$      (c) $\dfrac{294}{-84}$

**Solution**

(a) By Method 1, $\dfrac{240}{72} = \dfrac{120}{36} = \dfrac{60}{18} = \dfrac{10}{3}$, where the successive common factors 2, 2, and 6 were divided into the numerator and denominator.

(b) We have $1500 = 3 \cdot 450 + 150$ and $450 = 3 \cdot 150 + 0$. The Euclidean algorithm then shows that GCD(450, 1500) = 150. Thus, by Method 2,

$$\dfrac{-450}{1500} = \dfrac{-450 \div 150}{1500 \div 150} = \dfrac{-3}{10}.$$

(c) Using Method 3 this time, we find that

$$\dfrac{294}{-84} = \dfrac{2 \cdot 3 \cdot 7^2}{(-2) \cdot 2 \cdot 3 \cdot 7} = \dfrac{7}{-2} = \dfrac{-7}{2}.$$

---

## Common Denominators

Fractions with the same denominator are said to have a **common denominator.** In working with fractions, it is often helpful to replace them with equivalent fractions that share a common denominator. For example, $\dfrac{5}{8}$ and $\dfrac{7}{10}$ can each be replaced by equivalent fractions with the common denominator $8 \cdot 10 = 80$, so

$$\dfrac{5}{8} = \dfrac{5 \cdot 10}{8 \cdot 10} = \dfrac{50}{80} \qquad \text{and} \qquad \dfrac{7}{10} = \dfrac{7 \cdot 8}{10 \cdot 8} = \dfrac{56}{80}.$$

In the same way, any two fractions $\dfrac{a}{b}$ and $\dfrac{c}{d}$ can be rewritten with the common denominator $b \cdot d$, since $\dfrac{a}{b} = \dfrac{a \cdot d}{b \cdot d}$ and $\dfrac{c}{d} = \dfrac{c \cdot b}{d \cdot b}$.

It is sometimes worthwhile to find the common positive denominator that is as small as possible. Assuming that $\dfrac{a}{b}$ and $\dfrac{c}{d}$ are in simplest form, we require a common denominator that is a multiple of both $b$ and $d$. The least such common multiple is called the **least common denominator** and is the least common multiple of $b$ and $d$. For the example $\dfrac{5}{8}$ and $\dfrac{7}{10}$, we would calculate LCM(8, 10) = 40, so 40 is the least common denominator. Therefore,

$$\frac{5}{8} = \frac{5 \cdot 5}{8 \cdot 5} = \frac{25}{40} \quad \text{and} \quad \frac{7}{10} = \frac{7 \cdot 4}{10 \cdot 4} = \frac{28}{40}.$$

The least common denominator can often be determined by mental arithmetic. Consider, for example, $\dfrac{5}{6}$ and $\dfrac{3}{8}$. With a little practice, it won't take long to notice that $4 \cdot 6 = 24$ and $3 \cdot 8 = 24$ and that 24 is the least common denominator. Thus, $\dfrac{5}{6} = \dfrac{20}{24}$ and $\dfrac{3}{8} = \dfrac{9}{24}$ when written with the least common denominator.

---

**EXAMPLE 6.3    Finding Common Denominators**

Find equivalent fractions with a common denominator.

**(a)** $\dfrac{5}{6}$ and $\dfrac{1}{4}$        **(b)** $\dfrac{9}{8}$ and $\dfrac{-12}{7}$

**(c)** $\dfrac{14}{-16}$ and $\dfrac{11}{12}$        **(d)** $\dfrac{3}{4}, \dfrac{5}{8}$, and $\dfrac{2}{3}$

**Solution**

**(a)** By mental arithmetic, the least common denominator of $\dfrac{5}{6}$ and $\dfrac{1}{4}$ is 12. Therefore, $\dfrac{5}{6} = \dfrac{10}{12}$ and $\dfrac{1}{4} = \dfrac{3}{12}$. This can be shown with fraction strips:

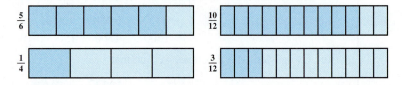

**(b)** Since 8 and 7 have no common factors other than 1, $8 \cdot 7 = 56$ is the least common denominator:

$$\frac{9}{8} = \frac{9 \cdot 7}{8 \cdot 7} = \frac{63}{56} \quad \text{and} \quad \frac{-12}{7} = \frac{-12 \cdot 8}{7 \cdot 8} = \frac{-96}{56}.$$

**(c)** First we simplify $\dfrac{14}{-16}$ to $\dfrac{-7}{8}$. Since 8 and 12 have 4 as their greatest common divisor, it follows that $\text{LCM}(8, 12) = \dfrac{8 \cdot 12}{\text{GCD}(8, 12)} = \dfrac{96}{4} = 24$. Thus,

$$\frac{14}{-16} = \frac{-7}{8} = \frac{-7 \cdot 3}{8 \cdot 3} = \frac{-21}{24} \quad \text{and} \quad \frac{11}{12} = \frac{11 \cdot 2}{12 \cdot 2} = \frac{22}{24}.$$

**(d)** With three fractions, it is still possible to use the product of all of the denominators as a common denominator. Since $4 \cdot 8 \cdot 3 = 96$, we have

$$\frac{3}{4} = \frac{3 \cdot 8 \cdot 3}{4 \cdot 8 \cdot 3} = \frac{72}{96}, \quad \frac{5}{8} = \frac{5 \cdot 4 \cdot 3}{8 \cdot 4 \cdot 3} = \frac{60}{96}, \quad \text{and} \quad \frac{2}{3} = \frac{2 \cdot 4 \cdot 8}{3 \cdot 4 \cdot 8} = \frac{64}{96}.$$

Alternatively, LCM(4, 8, 3) = 24, so

$$\frac{3}{4} = \frac{3 \cdot 6}{4 \cdot 6} = \frac{18}{24}, \quad \frac{5}{8} = \frac{5 \cdot 3}{8 \cdot 3} = \frac{15}{24}, \quad \text{and} \quad \frac{2}{3} = \frac{2 \cdot 8}{3 \cdot 8} = \frac{16}{24}.$$

These equations express the three fractions as equivalent fractions with the least common denominator.

## Rational Numbers

We have seen that different fractions can express the same number amount. Also, different fractions can correspond to the same point on a number line. For example, the fraction strips in Figure 6.9 each show that two-thirds of a whole strip has been shaded, but the fraction that represents this amount can be any one of the choices $\frac{2}{3}, \frac{4}{6}, \frac{6}{9}, \ldots$ Similarly, in Figure 6.7 the single point on the number line at a distance one-half unit to the left of the origin can be expressed by any of the equivalent fractions $\frac{-1}{2}, \frac{1}{-2}, \frac{-2}{4}, \frac{2}{-4}, \ldots$

Any number that can be represented by a fraction or any of its equivalent fractions is called a **rational number.** A rational number is therefore an infinite set of equivalent fractions. Any one of these equivalent fractions can be used to represent that rational number. Notice that it would be correct to say that $\frac{2}{3}$ and $\frac{10}{15}$ are different fractions, since their numerators and denominators are different. However, $\frac{2}{3}$ and $\frac{10}{15}$ are equivalent fractions; therefore, both $\frac{2}{3}$ and $\frac{10}{15}$ represent the *same* rational number.

---

**DEFINITION**   *Rational Numbers*

A **rational number** is a number that can be represented by a fraction $\frac{a}{b}$, where $a$ and $b$ are integers, $b \neq 0$. Two rational numbers are **equal** if, and only if, they can be represented by equivalent fractions.

---

The **set of rational numbers** is denoted by $Q$, where the letter $Q$ reminds us that a fraction is represented as a quotient. A rational number such as $\frac{3}{4}$ can also be represented by $\frac{6}{8}, \frac{30}{40}$, or any other fraction that is equivalent to $\frac{3}{4}$. Recall that any integer $n \in I$ is identified with the rational number $\frac{n}{1}$, so the integers $I$ are a proper subset of the rational numbers $Q$.

---

**EXAMPLE 6.4   Representing Rational Numbers**

How many different rational numbers are given in this list of five fractions?

$$\frac{2}{5}, \quad 3, \quad \frac{-4}{-10}, \quad \frac{39}{13}, \quad \text{and} \quad \frac{7}{4}$$

**Solution**   Since $\frac{2}{5} = \frac{-4}{-10}$ and $\frac{3}{1} = \frac{39}{13}$, there are three different rational numbers: $\frac{2}{5}$, 3, and $\frac{7}{4}$.

## Ordering Fractions and Rational Numbers

Given two fractions with a common positive denominator, the order of the fractions is immediately obvious from the numerator. For example, $\frac{3}{7} < \frac{4}{7}$. It is also obvious that two fractions with the same numerator and different positive denominators are easily put in order. For example, $\frac{5}{6} > \frac{5}{8}$, since sixths are larger than eighths and, consequently, 5 sixths is larger than 5 eighths.

More work is needed for fractions with different numerators and denominators. Sometimes a **transitive strategy** is effective, in which two fractions are individually compared with a benchmark. For example, to determine the larger of $\frac{3}{7}$ and $\frac{5}{9}$, we see that $\frac{3}{7} < \frac{1}{2}$ and $\frac{1}{2} < \frac{5}{9}$, so $\frac{3}{7} < \frac{5}{9}$, where $\frac{1}{2}$ is a benchmark. Another useful method of ordering is to use the **residual strategy,** in which "remainders" are compared. For example, $\frac{8}{9} < \frac{10}{11}$ because $\frac{8}{9}$ is $\frac{1}{9}$ short of being a unit but $\frac{10}{11}$ is only $\frac{1}{11}$ short of being a unit.

Manipulatives and pictorial representations of fractions also reveal the order relation. For example, the following excerpt from the NCTM Principles and Standards shows how parallel number lines help visualize the order relation:

**FROM *The NCTM Principles and Standards***

During grades 3–5, students should build their understanding of fractions as parts of a whole and as division. They will need to see and explore a variety of models of fractions, focusing primarily on familiar fractions such as halves, thirds, fourths, fifths, sixths, eighths, and tenths. By using an area model in which part of a region is shaded, students can see how fractions are related to a unit whole, compare fractional parts of a whole, and find equivalent fractions. They should develop strategies for ordering and comparing fractions, often using benchmarks such as 1/2 and 1. For example, fifth graders can compare fractions such as 2/5 and 5/8 by comparing each with 1/2—one is a little less than 1/2, and the other is a little more. By using parallel number lines, each showing a unit fraction and its multiples, students can see fractions as numbers, note their relationship to 1, and see relationships among fractions, including equivalence.

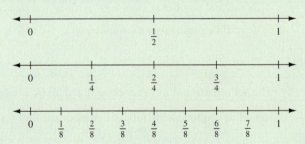

Source: *Principles and Standards for School Mathematics by NCTM, page 150. Copyright © 2000 by the National Council of Teachers of Mathematics. Reproduced with permission of the National Council of Teachers of Mathematics via Copyright Clearance Center. NCTM does not endorse the content or validity of these alignments.*

Fraction strips can also be effectively employed to understand the order of fractions. For example, by aligning the fraction strips for $\frac{3}{4}$ and $\frac{5}{6}$ vertically, as shown in Figure 6.10(a), it becomes geometrically apparent that $\frac{3}{4}$ represents a smaller shaded portion of a whole strip than $\frac{5}{6}$ does. The comparison can be made even clearer by replacing the strips $\frac{3}{4}$ and $\frac{5}{6}$ by the equivalent strips $\frac{9}{12}$ and $\frac{10}{12}$, as shown in Figure 6.10(b). Since $9 < 10$, it follows that $\frac{9}{12}$ is less than $\frac{10}{12}$ and therefore that $\frac{3}{4}$ is less than $\frac{5}{6}$.

**FIGURE 6.10**

Showing that $\frac{3}{4} < \frac{5}{6}$ and $\frac{9}{12} < \frac{10}{12}$ with fraction strips

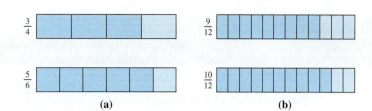

(a)          (b)

Although the transitive and residual strategies are often useful, it is sometimes best to compare fractions by taking the effort to first rewrite them with a common denominator. To be specific, suppose we wish to compare $\frac{a}{b}$ and $\frac{c}{d}$, assuming that both $b$ and $d$ are positive. Then, $\frac{a}{b} = \frac{ad}{bd}$ and $\frac{c}{d} = \frac{bc}{bd}$, we may now simply compare $ad$ and $bc$. Because this reasoning applies in general, we adopt this criterion as the definition of the order relation on the natural numbers.

> **DEFINITION**   *Order Relation on the Rational Numbers*
>
> Let two rational numbers be represented by the fractions $\frac{a}{b}$ and $\frac{c}{d}$, with $b$ and $d$ positive. Then $\frac{a}{b}$ is **less than** $\frac{c}{d}$, written $\frac{a}{b} < \frac{c}{d}$, if, and only if, $ad < bc$.

The corresponding relations "less than or equal to," $\leq$; "greater than," $>$; and "greater than or equal to," $\geq$, are defined similarly.

**EXAMPLE 6.5   Comparing Rational Numbers**

Replace the box by the proper relation $<$, $=$, or $>$. for each pair of rational numbers.

**(a)** $\frac{3}{4} \square \frac{2}{5}$

**(b)** $\frac{15}{29} \square \frac{6}{11}$

**(c)** $\frac{2106}{7047} \square \frac{234}{783}$

**(d)** $\frac{-10}{13} \square \frac{22}{-29}$

**Solution**

**(a)** Since $3 \cdot 5 = 15 > 8 = 2 \cdot 4$, we have $\frac{3}{4} > \frac{2}{5}$. Alternatively, $\frac{1}{2}$ can be used as a benchmark, with $\frac{3}{4} > \frac{1}{2}$ and $\frac{2}{5} < \frac{1}{2}$. Thus, $\frac{3}{4} > \frac{2}{5}$ by the transitive strategy.

**(b)** Since $15 \cdot 11 = 165 < 174 = 6 \cdot 29$, we have $\frac{15}{29} < \frac{6}{11}$. Alternatively, $\frac{1}{2}$ can be used as a benchmark for the residual strategy: $\frac{15}{29} = \frac{30}{58} > \frac{29}{58} = \frac{1}{2}$ shows that $\frac{15}{29}$ is $\frac{1}{58}$ larger than $\frac{1}{2}$. But $\frac{6}{11} = \frac{12}{22} > \frac{11}{22} = \frac{1}{2}$ shows that $\frac{6}{11}$ is $\frac{1}{22}$ larger than $\frac{1}{2}$. Since $\frac{1}{58} < \frac{1}{22}$, we have $\frac{15}{29} < \frac{6}{11}$.

**(c)** Using a calculator, we find that $2106 \cdot 783 = 1,648,998 = 7047 \cdot 234$. Thus, the two fractions are equivalent: $\frac{2106}{7047} = \frac{234}{783}$.

**(d)** First we write $\frac{22}{-29}$ as $\frac{-22}{29}$ so that its denominator is positive. Then, since $-10 \cdot 29 = -290 < -286 = -22 \cdot 13$, we conclude that $\frac{-10}{13} < \frac{22}{-29}$.

## Cooperative Investigation

## Exploring Fraction Concepts with Fraction Tiles

The basic concepts of fractions are best taught with a variety of manipulative materials that can be purchased from education supply houses or, alternatively, can be homemade from patterns printed and cut from card stock. The commercially made manipulatives are usually colored plastic, with the unit a square, a circle, a rectangle, or some other shape that can be subdivided in various ways to give denominators such as 2, 3, 4, 6, 8, and 12. Usually, the shapes are also available in translucent plastic for demonstrations on an overhead projector. In the following activity, you will make and then work with a set of *fraction tiles*:

### Materials

Each group of three or four students needs a set of fraction tiles, either a plastic set or a set cut from card stock using a pattern such as the one shown (at reduced scale) to the right. The pieces at the right are lettered A through G, but can also be described by their color.

### Directions

If a B tile is chosen as the unit, then the fraction 1/2 is represented by a D tile, which can be verified by comparing two D tiles and one B tile. Similarly, an A tile represents 2, and 2/3 is represented by two E tiles or by a C tile. Now use your fraction tile set to answer and discuss the questions that follow. Compare and discuss your answers within your group.

### Questions

1. If an A tile is the unit, find (one or more) tiles to represent $\frac{1}{3}, \frac{2}{3}, \frac{3}{3}, \frac{4}{3}, \frac{2}{6}$, and $\frac{5}{12}$.

2. If a C tile is $\frac{1}{6}$, what fractions are represented by each of the other tiles?

3. If a B tile represents $\frac{3}{2}$, represent these fractions with tiles: $\frac{1}{2}, \frac{1}{1}, \frac{1}{4}, \frac{3}{1}$, and $\frac{3}{4}$.

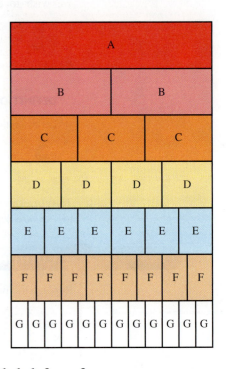

---

## Problem Set 6.1

Exercises numbered in red are answered in the back of the text.

## Understanding Concepts

1. What fraction is represented by the darker shaded portion of the following figures?

(a)

(b)

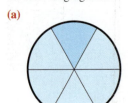

(c)

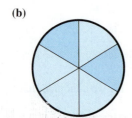

(d)

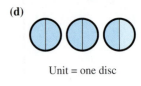

Unit = one disc

(e)

(f)

**2.** Subdivide and shade the unit octagons shown to represent the given fraction.

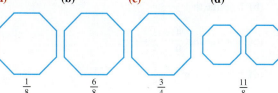

**(a)**  **(b)**  **(c)**  **(d)**

$\frac{1}{8}$  $\frac{6}{8}$  $\frac{3}{4}$  $\frac{11}{8}$

**3.** Consider the following set of objects:

What fraction of the objects in the set

**(a)** are green?

**(b)** are squares?

**(c)** are rectangles?

**(d)** are quadrilaterals (four-sided polygons)?

**(e)** have no line of symmetry?

**4.** Draw fraction circle diagrams to represent these fractions:

**(a)** $\frac{2}{3}$    **(b)** $\frac{1}{4}$    **(c)** $\frac{2}{8}$    **(d)** $\frac{7}{12}$

**5.** For each lettered point on the number lines shown, express its position by a corresponding fraction. Remember, it is the number of subintervals in a unit interval that determines the denominator, not the number of tick marks.

**(a)**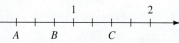

**(b)**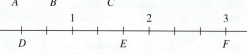

**(c)**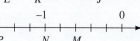

**(d)**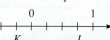

**(e)**

**6.** For each number-line diagram, list the fractions represented by the arrows:

**(a)**

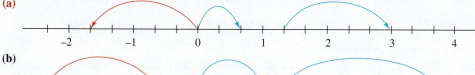

**(b)**

**7.** Find the missing numerator or denominator required to form a fraction that estimates the shaded area in each of these unit rectangles:

**(a)** $\frac{1}{?}$

**(b)** $\frac{?}{4}$

**(c)** $\frac{17}{?}$

**(d)** $\frac{?}{13}$

**8. (a)** The rectangle shown is $\frac{2}{3}$ of a unit. What is the unit?
(*Suggestion:* Divide the rectangle into two identical rectangles.)

**(b)** The rectangle shown is $\frac{5}{2}$ of a whole. What is the whole?
(*Suggestion:* Use the idea from part (a), but first decide the number of parts into which to subdivide the rectangle.)

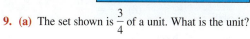

**9. (a)** The set shown is $\frac{3}{4}$ of a unit. What is the unit?

**(b)** The set shown is $\frac{5}{3}$ of a unit. What is the unit?

10. Depict the fraction $\frac{4}{6}$ with the following models:

    (a) Fraction-circle model     (b) Set model

    (c) Fraction-strip model     (d) Number-line model

11. Express the following quantities by a fraction placed in the blank space:

    (a) 20 minutes is _____ of an hour.

    (b) 30 seconds is _____ of a minute.

    (c) 5 days is _____ of a week.

    (d) 25 years is _____ of a century.

    (e) A quarter is _____ of a dollar.

    (f) 3 eggs is _____ of a dozen.

    (g) 2 feet is _____ of a yard.

    (h) 3 cups is _____ of a quart.

12. In Figure 6.9, fraction strips show that $\frac{2}{3}, \frac{4}{6}, \frac{6}{9},$ and $\frac{8}{12}$ are equivalent fractions. Use a similar drawing of fraction strips to show that $\frac{3}{4}, \frac{6}{8},$ and $\frac{9}{12}$ are equivalent fractions.

13. What equivalence of fractions is shown in these pairs of colored-region models?

    (a)           (b)           (c)

    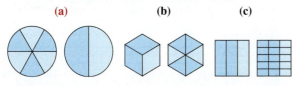

14. Find four different fractions equivalent to $\frac{4}{9}$.

15. Subdivide and shade the unit square on the right to illustrate that the given fractions are equivalent.

    (a)           (b)           (c)

    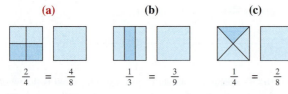

    $\frac{2}{4} = \frac{4}{8}$      $\frac{1}{3} = \frac{3}{9}$      $\frac{1}{4} = \frac{2}{8}$

16. Fill in the missing integer to make the fractions equivalent.

    (a) $\frac{4}{5} = \frac{}{30}$           (b) $\frac{6}{9} = \frac{2}{}$

    (c) $\frac{-7}{25} = \frac{}{500}$         (d) $\frac{18}{3} = \frac{-6}{}$

17. Determine whether each set of two fractions is equivalent by calculating equivalent fractions with a common denominator.

    (a) $\frac{18}{42}$ and $\frac{3}{7}$          (b) $\frac{18}{49}$ and $\frac{5}{14}$

    (c) $\frac{9}{25}$ and $\frac{140}{500}$        (d) $\frac{24}{144}$ and $\frac{32}{96}$

18. Determine which of these pairs of fractions are equivalent:

    (a) $\frac{78}{24}$ and $\frac{546}{168}$        (b) $\frac{243}{317}$ and $\frac{2673}{3487}$

    (c) $\frac{412}{-864}$ and $\frac{-308}{616}$

19. (a) Is it true that $\frac{4 \cdot 3}{9 \cdot 3} = \frac{12}{27}$?

    (b) Is it true that $\frac{4 \cdot 3}{9 \cdot 3} = \frac{4}{9}$?

    (c) Is it true that $\frac{4 + 3}{9 + 3} = \frac{7}{12}$?

    (d) Is it true that $\frac{4 + 3}{9 + 3} = \frac{4}{9}$?

20. Rewrite the following fractions in simplest form:

    (a) $\frac{84}{144}$    (b) $\frac{208}{272}$    (c) $\frac{-930}{1290}$    (d) $\frac{325}{231}$

21. Find the prime factorizations of the numerators and denominators of these fractions, and use them to express the fractions in simplest form:

    (a) $\frac{96}{288}$      (b) $\frac{247}{-75}$      (c) $\frac{2520}{378}$

22. For each of these sets of fractions, determine equivalent fractions with a common denominator:

    (a) $\frac{3}{11}$ and $\frac{2}{5}$        (b) $\frac{5}{12}$ and $\frac{2}{3}$

    (c) $\frac{4}{3}, \frac{5}{8},$ and $\frac{1}{6}$      (d) $\frac{1}{125}$ and $\frac{-3}{500}$

23. For each of these sets of fractions, determine equivalent fractions with the least common denominator.

    (a) $\frac{3}{8}$ and $\frac{5}{6}$        (b) $\frac{1}{7}, \frac{4}{5},$ and $\frac{2}{3}$

    (c) $\frac{17}{12}$ and $\frac{7}{32}$      (d) $\frac{17}{51}$ and $\frac{56}{42}$

24. Describe how to order each pair of fractions, using the idea of common denominators, common numerators, the transitive strategy, or the residual strategy.

    (a) $\frac{11}{7}, \frac{11}{9}$    (b) $\frac{3}{13}, \frac{4}{13}$    (c) $\frac{13}{18}, \frac{7}{12}$    (d) $\frac{9}{11}, \frac{8}{10}$

25. Order the rational numbers from least to greatest in each part.

    (a) $\frac{2}{3}, \frac{7}{12}$    (b) $\frac{2}{3}, \frac{5}{6}$    (c) $\frac{5}{6}, \frac{29}{36}$

    (d) $\frac{-5}{6}, \frac{-8}{9}$    (e) $\frac{2}{3}, \frac{5}{6}, \frac{29}{36}, \frac{8}{9}$

26. Find the numerator or denominator of these fractions to create a fraction that is close to $\frac{1}{2}$, but is slightly larger:

    (a) $\frac{}{20}$    (b) $\frac{7}{}$    (c) $\frac{}{17}$    (d) $\frac{30}{}$

27. Decide whether each statement is *true* or *false*. Explain your reasoning in a brief paragraph.

    (a) There are infinitely many ways to replace two fractions with two equivalent fractions that have a common denominator.

    (b) There is a unique least common denominator for a given pair of fractions.

**(c)** There is a least positive fraction.

**(d)** There are infinitely many fractions between 0 and 1.

**28.** How many different rational numbers are in this list?

$$\frac{27}{36}, 4, \frac{21}{28}, \frac{24}{6}, \frac{3}{4}, \frac{-8}{-2}$$

## Teaching Concepts

**29.** Number rods (or Cuisenaire® rods) can be used to illustrate the basic concepts of fractions. For example, suppose that the brown rod is the whole (that is, the unit). Then, since a train of two purple rods has the length of the brown rod, we see that the purple rod represents the fraction $\frac{1}{2}$:

**(a)** Which rod represents $\frac{1}{4}$? $\frac{3}{4}$?

**(b)** What fraction does a train made from the red and orange rods laid end to end represent?

**(c)** Using the discussion and questions in this problem as a model, write several more activities and accompanying questions that you feel would be effective in the elementary school classroom to teach basic fraction concepts with the use of number rods as a manipulative.

**30.** Go on a "fraction safari" to the grocery store (or in a magazine or newspaper). Find at least five fractions. For each fraction, describe the unit, the numerator, and the denominator. Summarize your discoveries in a poster suitable for an elementary school classroom.

## Responding to Students

**31.** When asked to illustrate the concept of $\frac{2}{3}$ with a colored-region diagram, Shanti drew the figure shown. How would you respond to Shanti?

**32.** Like most fifth graders, Dana likes pizza. When given the choice of $\frac{1}{4}$ or $\frac{1}{6}$ of a pizza, Dana says, "Since 6 is bigger than 4 and I'm really hungry, I'd rather have $\frac{1}{6}$ of the pizza." Write a

dialogue, including useful diagrams, to clear up Dana's misconception about fractions.

**33.** Nicole claims that $\frac{3}{4} < \frac{5}{8}$ because $3 < 5$ and $4 < 8$. Is Nicole correct, or how can you help her understanding?

**34.** Miley has been asked to compare 3/8 and 4/13. She says that if she had three 3/8, she would have 9/8, a bit more than 1, but if she had three 4/13, she would have 12/13, which is less than 1. Therefore, Miley claims that 3/8 > 4/13. Is Miley's reasoning valid?

## Thinking Critically

**35.** What fraction represents the part of the whole region that has been shaded? Draw additional lines to make your answer visually clear. For example, $\frac{2}{6}$ of the regular hexagon on the left is shaded, since the entire hexagon can be subdivided into six congruent regions, as shown on the right.

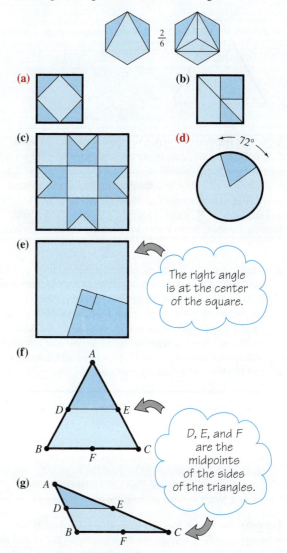

**36.** Start with a square piece of paper and join each corner to the midpoint of the opposite side, as shown in the left-hand figure. Shade the slanted square that is formed inside the original square. What fraction of the large square have you shaded? It will help to cut the triangular pieces as shown on the right and reattach them to form some new squares.

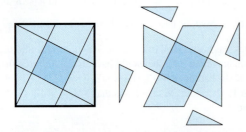

37. Start with an equilateral triangle cut from paper and join each corner to the one-third point of the opposite side, as shown in the left-hand figure. Shade the small equilateral triangle that is formed inside the large triangle. What fraction of the large triangle have you shaded? It will help to cut the six triangular pieces as shown on the right and reattach them to form some new equilateral triangles.

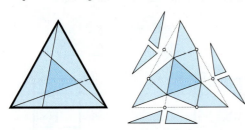

38. Solve this fraction problem from ancient India: "In what time will four fountains, being let loose together, fill a cistern, which they would severally [i.e., individually] fill in a day, in half a day, in a quarter and in a fifth part of a day?" (Reference: *History of Hindu Mathematics,* by B. Datta and A. N. Singh. Bombay, Calcutta, New Delhi, Madras, London, New York: Asia Publishing House, 1962, p. 234.)

39. (a) Andrei bought a length of rope at the hardware store. He used half of it to make a bow painter (a rope located at the front of the canoe) for his canoe and then used a third of the remaining piece to tie up a roll of carpet. He now has 20 feet of rope left. What was the length of rope Andrei purchased? Since it is often helpful to visualize a problem, obtain your answer pictorially by adding additional marks and labels to the following drawing:

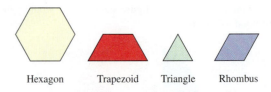

Used for painter

(b) Answer part (a) with a new diagram, but with these revised data: Andrei used one-third of the rope to make a leash for his dog and one-fourth of the remaining rope to tie up a bundle of stakes. This left 15 feet of the rope unused. What was the original length of the rope?

40. The following row of Pascal's triangle (see Chapter 1) has been separated by a vertical bar drawn between the 15 and the 20, with 3 entries of the row to the left of the bar and 4 entries to the right of the bar:

$$1 \quad 6 \quad 15 \quad | \quad 20 \quad 15 \quad 6 \quad 1$$

Notice that $\dfrac{15}{20} = \dfrac{3}{4}$. That is, the two fractions formed by the entries adjacent to the dividing bar and by the number of entries to the left and the right of the bar are equivalent fractions. Was this equivalence an accident, or is it a general property of Pascal's triangle? Investigate the property further by placing the dividing bar in new locations and examining other rows of Pascal's triangle.

41. Consider the fractions

$$r_1 = \frac{F_2}{F_1} = \frac{1}{1}, r_2 = \frac{F_4}{F_3} = \frac{3}{2}, r_3 = \frac{F_6}{F_5} = \frac{8}{5}, \ldots, r_m = \frac{F_{2n}}{F_{2n-1}}, \ldots$$

and

$$s_1 = \frac{F_3}{F_2} = \frac{2}{1}, s_2 = \frac{F_5}{F_4} = \frac{5}{3}, s_3 = \frac{F_7}{F_6} = \frac{13}{8}, \ldots, s_m = \frac{F_{2n+1}}{F_{2n}}, \ldots$$

formed from the Fibonacci numbers

$$F_1 = 1, F_2 = 1, F_3 = 2, F_4 = 3, F_5 = 5, F_6 = 8, F_7 = 13, F_8 = 21, \ldots.$$

Use the identity $F_{m+1}F_{m-1} = F_m^2 + (-1)^m$ to prove these inequalities:

(a) $r_n < r_{n+1}$ (*Suggestion:* Let $m = 2n$ in the identity to get the inequality $F_{2n+1}F_{2n-1} = F_{2n}^2 + (-1)^{2n} = F_{2n}^2 + 1 > F_{2n}^2$. Then add $F_{2n}F_{2n-1}$ to both sides of the inequality.)

(b) $s_{n+1} > s_n$

(c) $r_n < s_n$

(d) $r_m < s_n$ for all positive integers $m$ and $n$ (*Suggestion:* Given any $m$ and $n$, let $k$ be an integer larger than both $m$ and $n$, and then use parts (a), (b), and (c).)

## Thinking Cooperatively

The next two problems develop the concept of a fraction with the aid of pattern blocks, a popular and versatile manipulative that is used successfully in many elementary school classrooms. The following four shapes should be available to students working in groups of two or three:

Hexagon    Trapezoid    Triangle    Rhombus

42. Use your pattern blocks to answer these questions:

(a) Choose the hexagon as the unit. What fraction is each of the other three pattern blocks?

(b) Choose the trapezoid as the unit. What fraction is each of the other three pattern blocks?

(c) Choose the rhombus as the unit. What fraction is each of the other three pattern blocks?

43. (a) A hexagon and six triangles are used to form a six-pointed star. Choose the star as the unit. Next, form pattern-block

shapes corresponding to each of these fractions: $\frac{1}{6}, \frac{1}{4}, \frac{1}{3}, \frac{2}{3},$ and $\frac{3}{4}.$ Use as few pieces as you can for each shape.

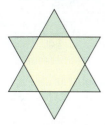

**(b)** Create a pattern-block shape that will be defined as the unit and for which you may form other pattern-block shapes corresponding to the fractions $\frac{1}{8}$ and $\frac{5}{8}.$

**44.** Working in pairs, shuffle an ordinary 52-card deck and deal 26 cards each to you and your partner. Let the number of red and black cards in your hand be denoted by $r$ and $b$, respectively. Similarly, let $R$ and $B$, respectively, denote the number of red and black cards in your partner's hand. Now form the fractions $r/b$ and $B/R$. Do you see any surprises? Can you explain what is happening? Work together with your partner to write a clear explanation.

## Making Connections

**45.** Francisco's pickup truck has a 24-gallon gas tank and an accurate fuel gauge. Estimate the number of gallons in the tank at these readings:

**(a)**          **(b)**          **(c)**

**46.** If 153 of the 307 graduating seniors go on to college, it is likely that a principal would claim that $\frac{1}{2}$ of the class is college bound.

Give simpler convenient fractions that approximately express the data in these situations:

**(a)** Estebán is on page 310 of a 498-page novel. He has read _____ of the book.

**(b)** Myra has saved $73 toward the purchase of a $215 plane ticket. She has saved _____ of the amount she needs.

**(c)** Nine students in Ms. Evaldo's class of 35 students did perfect work on the quiz. _____ of the class scored 100% on the quiz.

**(d)** The Math Club has sold 1623 of the 2400 raffle tickets. It has sold _____ of the available tickets.

**47.** **Fractions in Probability.** If a card is picked at random from an ordinary deck of 52 playing cards, there are 4 ways it can be an ace, since it could be the ace of hearts, diamonds, clubs, or spades. To measure the chances of drawing an ace, it is common to give the probability as the rational number $\frac{4}{52}.$

In general, if $n$ equally likely outcomes are possible and $m$ of these outcomes are successful for an event to occur, then the

probability of the event is $\frac{m}{n}.$ As another example, $\frac{5}{6}$ is the probability of rolling a single die and having more than one spot appear. Give fractions that express the probability of the following events:

**(a)** Getting a head in the flip of a fair coin

**(b)** Drawing a face card from a deck of cards

**(c)** Rolling an even number on a single die

**(d)** Drawing a green marble from a bag that contains 20 red, 30 blue, and 25 green marbles

**(e)** Drawing either a red or a blue marble from the bag of marbles described in part (d).

**48.** What fraction represents the probability that the spinner shown comes up (a) yellow? (b) red? (c) blue? (d) not blue?

## From State Student Assessments

**49.** (Minnesota, Grade 5)

Four children drew fraction pictures. Which drawing is $\frac{2}{3}$ shaded?

**A.** Aaron's    **B.** Betsy's    **C.** Carla's    **D.** Daisy's

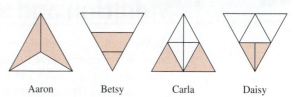

Aaron        Betsy        Carla        Daisy

**50.** (Kentucky, Grade 5)
Mrs. Washington asked her students what fractional part of these 12 circles is shaded.

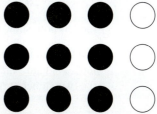

Odessa thinks the answer is $\frac{9}{12}.$ Bob thinks the answer is $\frac{3}{4}.$

**(a)** Who is correct—Odessa, Bob, or both?

**(b)** Write how you would explain your answer to part (a) to Odessa and Bob. Draw your own pictures to go with your explanation.

**51.** (Texas, Grade 4)
The two pans of brownies below show what was left after several students finished eating.

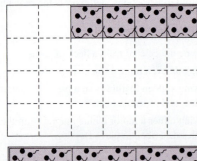

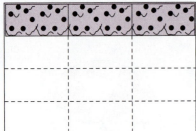

Which of the following compares the portion of brownies left in each pan?

A. $\dfrac{4}{24} < \dfrac{3}{12}$    B. $\dfrac{3}{24} > \dfrac{4}{24}$

C. $\dfrac{4}{20} > \dfrac{3}{9}$    D. $\dfrac{4}{12} < \dfrac{3}{12}$

**52.** (Oregon, Grade 5)
Jules's eyes are covered. If he were to throw a dart at this board, how likely is it that a dart that hits the board would land on a shaded box?

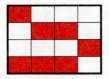

A. More than three-fourths the time
B. Less than half the time
C. About half the time
D. More than half the time

**53.** (Massachusetts, Grade 6)
Which point on the number line shown below appears to be located at $1\dfrac{3}{8}$?

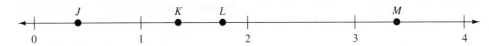

## 6.2

# Addition and Subtraction of Fractions

In this section, we consider the addition and subtraction of fractions. The geometric and physical models of fractions serve to motivate the definition of both operations. The primary goal here is to learn how manipulatives and visualizations are used to convey the meaning of these operations to children. Since rational numbers are represented with fractions, we are simultaneously defining sums and differences of rational numbers.

## Addition of Fractions

The sum of $\dfrac{3}{8}$ and $\dfrac{2}{8}$ is illustrated in two ways in Figure 6.11. The fraction circle and number-line models both show that $\dfrac{3}{8} + \dfrac{2}{8} = \dfrac{5}{8}$. The fraction circle visualization corresponds to the set model of addition, and the number-line visualization corresponds to the measurement model of addition. The models suggest that the sum of two fractions with a common denominator should be found by adding the two numerators. This suggestion motivates the following definition:

> **DEFINITION**  *Addition of Fractions*
>
> Let two fractions $\dfrac{a}{b}$ and $\dfrac{c}{b}$ have a common denominator. Then their **sum** is the fraction given by
>
> $$\frac{a}{b} + \frac{c}{b} = \frac{a+c}{b}.$$

**FIGURE 6.11**

Showing that $\frac{3}{8} + \frac{2}{8} = \frac{5}{8}$

with the fraction-circle and number-line models

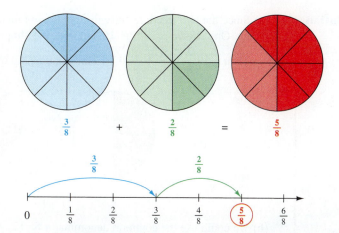

$$\frac{3}{8} \qquad + \qquad \frac{2}{8} \qquad = \qquad \frac{5}{8}$$

To add fractions with unlike denominators, we first rewrite the fractions with a common denominator. For example, to add $\frac{1}{4}$ and $\frac{2}{3}$, we rewrite them with 12 as a common denominator:

$$\frac{1}{4} = \frac{1 \cdot 3}{4 \cdot 3} = \frac{3}{12} \qquad \text{and} \qquad \frac{2}{3} = \frac{2 \cdot 4}{3 \cdot 4} = \frac{8}{12}.$$

According to the preceding definition, we then have

$$\frac{1}{4} + \frac{2}{3} = \frac{1 \cdot 3}{4 \cdot 3} + \frac{2 \cdot 4}{3 \cdot 4} = \frac{1 \cdot 3 + 2 \cdot 4}{4 \cdot 3} = \frac{3 + 8}{12} = \frac{11}{12}.$$

The procedure just followed can be modeled with fraction strips, as shown in Figure 6.12. It is important to see how the fraction strips are aligned.

**FIGURE 6.12**

The fraction-strip model showing that $\frac{1}{4} + \frac{2}{3} =$

$\frac{3}{12} + \frac{8}{12} = \frac{11}{12}$

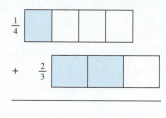

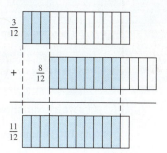

The same procedure can be followed to add any two fractions $\frac{a}{b}$ and $\frac{c}{d}$. We have

$$\frac{a}{b} + \frac{c}{d} = \frac{a \cdot d}{b \cdot d} + \frac{c \cdot b}{d \cdot b} = \frac{ad + bc}{bd}.$$

Rewrite the fractions with a common denominator.

Add the numerators, and retain the common denominator.

**EXAMPLE 6.6  Adding Fractions**

Show how to compute each of the sums of fractions that follow. Imagine that you are giving a careful explanation to a fifth grader, using an appropriate representation of fraction addition to illustrate how you obtain the answer.

**(a)** $\frac{1}{2} + \frac{3}{8}$ **(b)** $\frac{3}{8} + \frac{-7}{12}$ **(c)** $\left(\frac{3}{4} + \frac{5}{6}\right) + \frac{2}{3}$ **(d)** $\frac{3}{4} + \left(\frac{5}{6} + \frac{2}{3}\right)$

**Solution**

(a) Since the two fractions have different denominators, we first look for a common denominator. One choice is $2 \cdot 8 = 16$, but it's even simpler to use the least common denominator, 8. Then $\dfrac{1}{2} + \dfrac{3}{8} = \dfrac{4}{8} + \dfrac{3}{8} = \dfrac{7}{8}$. This relationship can also be shown with fraction circles:

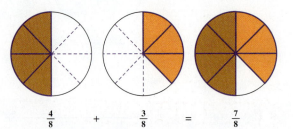

$$\frac{4}{8} \quad + \quad \frac{3}{8} \quad = \quad \frac{7}{8}$$

(b) We could use the common denominator $8 \cdot 12 = 96$, but since 4 is a common divisor of 8 and 12, we can also use the common denominator $96 \div 4 = 24$. This is the least common denominator, and we get $\dfrac{3}{8} + \dfrac{-7}{12} = \dfrac{9}{24} + \dfrac{-14}{24} = \dfrac{9 + (-14)}{24} = \dfrac{-5}{24}$. The following number-line diagram shows the same result:

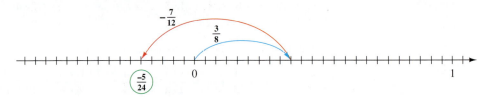

(c) The parentheses tell us first to compute

$$\frac{3}{4} + \frac{5}{6} = \frac{9}{12} + \frac{10}{12} = \frac{19}{12}.$$

Then we compute

$$\left(\frac{3}{4} + \frac{5}{6}\right) + \frac{2}{3} = \frac{19}{12} + \frac{2}{3} = \frac{19}{12} + \frac{8}{12} = \frac{19 + 8}{12} = \frac{27}{12},$$

which simplifies to $\dfrac{9}{4}$.

(d) The sum in parentheses is

$$\frac{5}{6} + \frac{2}{3} = \frac{5}{6} + \frac{4}{6} = \frac{9}{6} = \frac{3}{2}.$$

Then we have

$$\frac{3}{4} + \left(\frac{5}{6} + \frac{2}{3}\right) = \frac{3}{4} + \frac{3}{2} = \frac{3}{4} + \frac{6}{4} = \frac{9}{4}.$$

Parts (c) and (d) of Example 6.6 show that

$$\left(\frac{3}{4} + \frac{5}{6}\right) + \frac{2}{3} = \frac{3}{4} + \left(\frac{5}{6} + \frac{2}{3}\right),$$

since each side represents the fraction $\dfrac{9}{4}$. This result is a particular example of the associative property for the addition of fractions. The properties of addition and subtraction of fractions, and therefore of rational numbers, will be explored in Section 6.4.

## Proper Fractions and Mixed Numbers

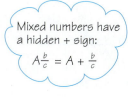

Mixed numbers have a hidden + sign:
$$A\frac{b}{c} = A + \frac{b}{c}$$

The sum of a natural number and a positive fraction is most often written as a **mixed number.** For example, $2 + \frac{3}{4}$ is written $2\frac{3}{4}$ and is read "two and three-quarters." It is important to realize that it is the addition symbol, $+$, that is suppressed, since the common notation $xy$ for multiplication might suggest, incorrectly, that $2\frac{3}{4}$ is $2 \cdot \frac{3}{4}$. Thus, $2\frac{3}{4} = 2 + \frac{3}{4}$, not $\frac{6}{4}$.

A mixed number can always be rewritten in the standard form $\frac{a}{b}$ of a fraction. For example,

$$2\frac{3}{4} = 2 + \frac{3}{4} = \frac{8}{4} + \frac{3}{4} = \frac{11}{4}.$$

Thus, $-2\frac{3}{4} = -\left(2\frac{3}{4}\right) = \frac{-11}{4}$.

Mixed numbers and their equivalent forms as a fraction can be visualized this way:

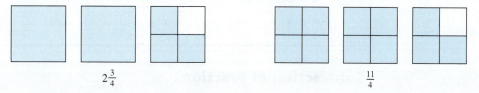

$$2\frac{3}{4} \qquad\qquad\qquad \frac{11}{4}$$

Since $A\frac{b}{c} = \frac{Ac}{c} + \frac{b}{c} = \frac{Ac + b}{c}$, it is an easy calculation to write a mixed number as a fraction:
$$A\frac{b}{c} = \frac{Ac + b}{c}.$$

A fraction $\frac{a}{b}$ for which $0 \le |a| < b$ is called a **proper fraction.** For example, $\frac{2}{3}$ is a proper fraction, but $\frac{3}{2}, \frac{-8}{5}$, and $\frac{6}{6}$ are not proper fractions. It is common, though not necessary, to rewrite fractions that are not proper as mixed numbers. For example, to express $\frac{439}{19}$ as a mixed number, we first use division with a remainder to find that $439 = 23 \cdot 19 + 2$. Then we have

$$\frac{439}{19} = \frac{23 \cdot 19 + 2}{19} = \frac{23}{1} + \frac{2}{19} = 23 + \frac{2}{19} = 23\frac{2}{19}.$$

In mixed-number form, it is obvious that $23\frac{2}{19}$ is just slightly larger than 23; this fact was not evident in the original fraction form $\frac{439}{19}$. Nevertheless, it is perfectly acceptable to express rational numbers as "improper" fractions. In general, the fractional form $\frac{a}{b}$ is the more convenient form for arithmetic and algebra, and the mixed-number form is easiest to understand for practical applications. For example, it would be more common to buy $2\frac{1}{4}$ yards of material than to request $\frac{9}{4}$ yards.

---

**EXAMPLE 6.7  Working with Mixed Numbers**

**(a)** Give an improper fraction for $3\frac{17}{120}$.  **(b)** Give a mixed number for $\frac{355}{113}$.

**(c)** Give a mixed number for $\frac{-15}{4}$.  **(d)** Compute $2\frac{3}{4} + 4\frac{2}{5}$.

**Solution**

**(a)** $3\dfrac{17}{120} = \dfrac{3}{1} + \dfrac{17}{120} = \dfrac{3 \cdot 120 + 1 \cdot 17}{120} = \dfrac{360 + 17}{120} = \dfrac{377}{120}$.

This rational number was given by Claudius Ptolemy around A.D. 150 to approximate $\pi$, the ratio of the circumference of a circle to its diameter.

It has better accuracy than $3\dfrac{1}{7}$, the value proposed by Archimedes in about 240 B.C.

**(b)** Using the division algorithm, we calculate that $355 = 3 \cdot 113 + 16$. Therefore,

$$\dfrac{355}{113} = \dfrac{3 \cdot 113 + 16}{113} = \dfrac{3}{1} + \dfrac{16}{113} = 3\dfrac{16}{113},$$

which corresponds to a point somewhat to the right of 3 on the number line. The value $\dfrac{355}{113}$ was used around A.D. 480 in China to approximate $\pi$; as a decimal number, it is correct to six places!

**(c)** $\dfrac{-15}{4} = \dfrac{-(3 \cdot 4 + 3)}{4} = -\left(3 + \dfrac{3}{4}\right) = -3\dfrac{3}{4}$.

**(d)** $2\dfrac{3}{4} + 4\dfrac{2}{5} = 2 + 4 + \dfrac{3}{4} + \dfrac{2}{5} = 6 + \dfrac{15}{20} + \dfrac{8}{20} = 6 + \dfrac{23}{20} = 7\dfrac{3}{20}$.

## Subtraction of Fractions

Figure 6.13 shows how the take-away, measurement, and missing-addend conceptual models of the subtraction operation can be illustrated with colored regions, the number line, and fraction strips. In each case, we see that $\dfrac{7}{6} - \dfrac{3}{6} = \dfrac{4}{6}$.

**FIGURE 6.13**
Models which show that
$\dfrac{7}{6} - \dfrac{3}{6} = \dfrac{4}{6}$

Take-away model:

Begin with $\dfrac{7}{6}$.

Remove $\dfrac{3}{6}$.

This leaves $\dfrac{4}{6}$.

Measurement model:

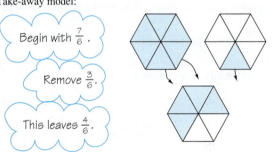

Heads of arrows are together for subtraction. The arrow for the number being subtracted is drawn in reverse from head to tail.

Missing-addend model:

Given: $\dfrac{7}{6}$

and $\dfrac{3}{6}$

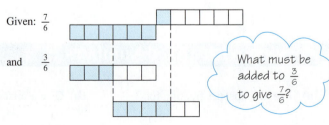

What must be added to $\dfrac{3}{6}$ to give $\dfrac{7}{6}$?

Since $\dfrac{3}{6} + \dfrac{4}{6} = \dfrac{7}{6}$, then $\dfrac{7}{6} - \dfrac{3}{6} = \dfrac{4}{6}$.

Subtraction of whole numbers and integers was defined on the basis of the missing-addend approach, which emphasizes that subtraction is the inverse operation to addition. Subtraction of fractions is defined in the same way:

> **DEFINITION** *Subtraction of Fractions*
>
> Let $\dfrac{a}{b}$ and $\dfrac{c}{d}$ be fractions. Then $\dfrac{a}{b} - \dfrac{c}{d} = \dfrac{e}{f}$ if, and only if, $\dfrac{a}{b} = \dfrac{c}{d} + \dfrac{e}{f}$.

For two fractions $\dfrac{a}{b}$ and $\dfrac{c}{b}$ with the same denominator, the formula $\dfrac{a}{b} - \dfrac{c}{b} = \dfrac{a - c}{b}$ follows easily from the definition. For fractions with unlike denominators, it is necessary first to find a common denominator.

**EXAMPLE 6.8  Subtracting Fractions**

Show, as you might to a student, the steps to compute these differences:

**(a)** $\dfrac{4}{5} - \dfrac{2}{3}$  **(b)** $\dfrac{103}{24} - \dfrac{-35}{16}$  **(c)** $4\dfrac{1}{4} - 2\dfrac{2}{3}$

**Solution**  **(a)** $\dfrac{4}{5} - \dfrac{2}{3} = \dfrac{4 \cdot 3}{5 \cdot 3} - \dfrac{5 \cdot 2}{5 \cdot 3} = \dfrac{12}{15} - \dfrac{10}{15} = \dfrac{12 - 10}{15} = \dfrac{2}{15}.$

The subtraction can also be shown with a number-line diagram. Since both fractions are positive, both arrows point to the right, and since this is a subtraction, the arrowheads are together.

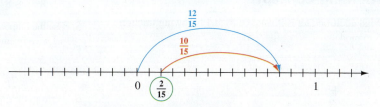

**(b)** Since LCM(24, 16) = 48, the least common denominator, 48, can be used to give

$$\frac{103}{24} - \frac{-35}{16} = \frac{206}{48} - \frac{-105}{48} = \frac{206 - (-105)}{48} = \frac{311}{48}.$$

**(c)** $4\dfrac{1}{4} - 2\dfrac{2}{3} = \dfrac{17}{4} - \dfrac{8}{3} = \dfrac{17 \cdot 3}{4 \cdot 3} - \dfrac{4 \cdot 8}{4 \cdot 3} = \dfrac{51}{12} - \dfrac{32}{12} = \dfrac{51 - 32}{12} = \dfrac{19}{12} = 1\dfrac{7}{12}.$

Alternatively, subtraction of mixed numbers can follow the familiar regrouping algorithm:

$$
\begin{array}{ccccc}
4\dfrac{1}{4} & & 4\dfrac{3}{12} & & 3\dfrac{15}{12} \\[2mm]
-2\dfrac{2}{3} & & -2\dfrac{8}{12} & & -2\dfrac{8}{12} \\[2mm]
\hline
& & & & 1\dfrac{7}{12}
\end{array}
$$

$$4\dfrac{3}{12} = 3 + \dfrac{12}{12} + \dfrac{3}{12} = 3\dfrac{15}{12}$$

This can also be visualized with the area model of fractions:

## Into the Classroom

### Charlotte Jenkins Discusses Addition and Subtraction of Fractions

I use paper plate activities to introduce adding and subtracting fractions with different denominators. To find $\frac{5}{8} + \frac{1}{4}$, I give each student two paper plates. I ask students to draw lines to divide one plate into fourths and the other into eighths. Then I have them cut the plates to join $\frac{1}{4}$ of one to $\frac{5}{8}$ of the other, and ask them to describe the result. To find $\frac{5}{8} - \frac{1}{4}$, I give each student one paper plate. I ask students to draw lines to divide the plate into eighths and shade five of the eighths. Then I have them cut $\frac{1}{4}$ of the area and describe the shaded amount that is left. I have students repeat the activities to find other sums and differences.

SOURCE: Scott Foresman–Addison Wesley Middle School Math Course 1 Teacher's Edition, p. 320, © 2002 Pearson Education, Inc. Reprinted with permission.

## Problem Set 6.2

Exercises numbered in red are answered in the back of the text.

### Understanding Concepts

1. **(a)** What addition fact is illustrated by the following fraction-strip model?

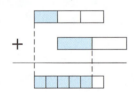

   **(b)** Illustrate $\frac{1}{6} + \frac{1}{4}$ with the fraction-strip model.

   **(c)** Illustrate $\frac{2}{3} + \frac{3}{4}$ with the fraction-strip model. (The sum will require two strips.)

2. Use fraction circles to illustrate these sums:

   **(a)** $\frac{2}{5} + \frac{6}{5}$    **(b)** $\frac{1}{4} + \frac{1}{2}$    **(c)** $\frac{2}{3} + \frac{1}{4}$

3. The points A, B, C, . . . , G, and H are equally spaced along the rational number line:

   **(a)** What rational number corresponds to point G?

   **(b)** What point corresponds to $\frac{1}{2}$?

   **(c)** Are there lettered points that correspond to $\frac{1}{4}$? to $\frac{1}{6}$?

   **(d)** Which lettered points are nearest to either side of $\frac{4}{7}$?

4. Represent each of these sums with a number-line diagram:

   **(a)** $\frac{1}{8} + \frac{3}{8}$    **(b)** $\frac{1}{4} + \frac{5}{4}$    **(c)** $\frac{2}{3} + \frac{1}{2}$

5. Use the number-line model to illustrate the given sums. Recall that negative fractions are represented by arrows that point to the left.

   **(a)** $\frac{3}{4} + \frac{-2}{4}$    **(b)** $\frac{-3}{4} + \frac{2}{4}$    **(c)** $\frac{-3}{4} + \frac{-1}{4}$

6. Perform the given additions. Express each answer in simplest form.

   **(a)** $\frac{2}{7} + \frac{3}{7}$    **(b)** $\frac{6}{5} + \frac{4}{5}$    **(c)** $\frac{3}{8} + \frac{11}{24}$

   **(d)** $\frac{6}{13} + \frac{2}{5}$    **(e)** $\frac{5}{12} + \frac{17}{20}$    **(f)** $\frac{6}{8} + \frac{-25}{100}$

   **(g)** $\frac{-57}{100} + \frac{13}{10}$    **(h)** $\frac{213}{450} + \frac{12}{50}$

7. Express these fractions as mixed numbers:

   **(a)** $\frac{9}{4}$    **(b)** $\frac{17}{3}$    **(c)** $\frac{111}{23}$    **(d)** $\frac{3571}{-100}$

8. Express these mixed numbers as fractions:

   **(a)** $2\frac{3}{8}$    **(b)** $15\frac{2}{3}$    **(c)** $111\frac{2}{5}$    **(d)** $-10\frac{7}{9}$

9. **(a)** What subtraction fact is illustrated by this fraction-strip model?

   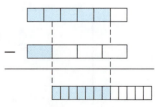

   **(b)** Use the fraction-strip model to illustrate $\frac{2}{3} - \frac{1}{4}$.

**10. (a)** What subtraction fact is illustrated by this colored-region model?

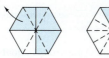

**(b)** Use a fraction circle model to illustrate $\frac{2}{3} - \frac{1}{4}$.

**11. (a)** What subtraction fact is illustrated by this number-line model?

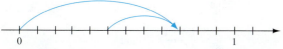

**(b)** Illustrate $\frac{2}{3} - \frac{1}{4}$ with the number-line model.

**12.** Compute these differences, expressing each answer in simplest form:

**(a)** $\frac{5}{8} - \frac{2}{8}$        **(b)** $\frac{3}{5} - \frac{2}{4}$        **(c)** $2\frac{2}{3} - 1\frac{1}{3}$

**(d)** $4\frac{1}{4} - 3\frac{1}{3}$        **(e)** $\frac{6}{8} - \frac{5}{12}$        **(f)** $\frac{1}{4} - \frac{14}{56}$

**(g)** $\frac{137}{214} - \frac{-1}{3}$        **(h)** $\frac{-23}{100} - \frac{198}{1000}$

**13.** Use mental arithmetic to estimate the following sums and differences to the nearest integer:

**(a)** $\frac{19}{22} + \frac{31}{15}$        **(b)** $1\frac{5}{11} + 4\frac{1}{2}$

**(c)** $7\frac{53}{97} - 2\frac{5}{9}$        **(d)** $6\frac{2}{3} + 8\frac{11}{32} - 2\frac{1}{29}$

**14.** An alternative, but equivalent, definition of rational number inequality is the following:

$$\frac{a}{b} < \frac{c}{d} \quad \text{if, and only if,} \quad \frac{c}{d} - \frac{a}{b} > 0.$$

Use the alternative definition to verify these inequalities.

**(a)** $\frac{2}{3} < \frac{3}{4}$        **(b)** $\frac{4}{5} < \frac{14}{17}$        **(c)** $\frac{19}{10} < \frac{99}{50}$

## Teaching Concepts

**15.** In the number-rod diagram shown, the brown rod has been adopted as the unit. Therefore, the red rod is $\frac{1}{4}$, the purple rod is $\frac{1}{2}$, and the dark-green rod is $\frac{3}{4}$. Since the train formed with the purple and dark-green rod has the length of the brown-plus-red train, we have $\frac{1}{2} + \frac{3}{4} = 1\frac{1}{4}$.

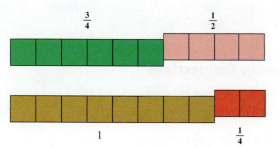

**(a)** Use number rods to create another illustration of the addition of fractions. Use both words and diagrams to describe your example clearly.

**(b)** Use number rods to create an illustration of the subtraction of fractions.

## Responding to Students

The "pizza stories" discussed in problems 16–18 suggest common misconceptions students have about fractions and their arithmetic. Use words and diagrams to formulate helpful responses for each of situation described.

**16.** The Estevez family ordered a large pepperoni pizza and a medium tomato-and-green-pepper pizza. Since $\frac{1}{3}$ of the pepperoni pizza was not eaten and $\frac{1}{2}$ of the other pizza remains, Paco claims that $\frac{1}{3} + \frac{1}{2} = \frac{5}{6}$ of a pizza remains. Is Paco correct?

**17.** After the pizza party, it was discovered that just 2 pieces of one of the pizzas were consumed, leaving 6 more slices. Dannea was told that she could have half of the leftover pizza, but to leave the rest for her brother. Dannea reasoned that the whole pizza was 8 slices, so that half of the pizza was 4 slices. Does her brother have a reason to complain when he discovered that Dannea left him just 2 slices? In particular, what principle of fractions has Dannea violated?

**18.** Katrina claims that since $\frac{2}{6}$ of one pizza and $\frac{3}{4}$ of a second pizza were not eaten, "$\frac{2}{6} + \frac{3}{4} = \frac{5}{10} = \frac{1}{2}$" of a pizza is left over for tomorrow's lunch. Respond to Katrina in a helpful way.

**19.** Melanie got 1 hit in 3 times at bat in the first baseball game, giving her a hitting average of $\frac{1}{3}$. In the second game, her average was $\frac{2}{5}$, since she had 2 hits in 5 times at bat. She then claims that her two-game average is $\frac{1}{3} + \frac{2}{5} = \frac{3}{8}$, because she had 3 hits in her 8 times at bat. Melanie's brother John objects, since he knows that $\frac{1}{3} + \frac{2}{5} = \frac{5}{15} + \frac{6}{15} = \frac{11}{15}$ and $\frac{11}{15} \neq \frac{3}{8}$. Who is right, Melanie or John?

## Thinking Critically

**20.** A worm is on page 1 of Volume 1 of a set of encyclopedias neatly arranged on a shelf. He (or she—how do you tell?) eats straight through to the last page of Volume 2. If the covers of each volume are $\frac{1}{8}''$ thick and the pages are a total of $\frac{3}{4}''$ thick in each of the volumes, how far does the worm travel?

**21.** When the sultan died, he left a stable with 17 horses. His will stipulated that half of his horses should go to his oldest son, one third to his middle son, and a ninth to his youngest son. The executor of the estate decided to make the distribution easier by contributing his own horse to the estate. With 18 horses now available, he gave 9 horses (a half) to the oldest son, 6 horses (a third) to the middle son, and 2 horses (a ninth) to the youngest son. This satisfied the terms of the will, and since only $9 + 6 + 2 = 17$ horses were given to the sons, the executor was able to retain his own horse. Explain what has happened.

22. Find the missing fractions in the following Magic Fraction Squares so that the entries in every row, column, and diagonal add to 1:

**(a)**

| $\frac{1}{2}$ | $\frac{1}{12}$ | |
|---|---|---|
| $\frac{1}{4}$ | | |
| | | |

**(b)**

| | | |
|---|---|---|
| | $\frac{1}{3}$ | $\frac{3}{5}$ |
| | | $\frac{2}{15}$ |

23. Start with any triangle, and let its area be the unit. Next, trisect each side of the triangle and join these points to the opposite vertices. This creates a dissection of the unit triangle, as illustrated in the accompanying figure. Amazingly, the areas of regions shown are precisely the fractions shown in the figure.

For example, the inner lavender hexagon has area $\frac{1}{10}$, and the area of each green triangle is $\frac{1}{21}$.

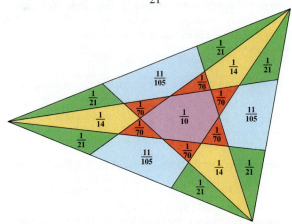

(a) Verify that the large triangle is a unit triangle by summing the areas of the regions within the triangle.

(b) What is the area of the three-pointed star composed of the hexagon, the six red triangles, and the three yellow quadrilaterals?

(c) What is the area of the triangle composed of the hexagon and the three red triangles on every other side of the hexagon? (*Note:* Your answer can also be proved with the method suggested in problem 37 of Problem Set 6.1.)

24. With the exception of $\frac{2}{3}$, which was given the hieroglyph ⌔, the ancient Egyptians attempted to express all fractions as a sum of different fractions, each with 1 as the numerator.

(a) Verify that $\frac{23}{25} = \frac{1}{2} + \frac{1}{3} + \frac{1}{15} + \frac{1}{50}$.

(b) Verify that $\frac{7}{29} = \frac{1}{6} + \frac{1}{24} + \frac{1}{58} + \frac{1}{87} + \frac{1}{232}$.

(c) Verify that $\frac{7}{29} = \frac{1}{5} + \frac{1}{29} + \frac{1}{145}$.

(d) If ⎮ represents $1\frac{1}{2}$, and ⬭ is interpreted as "one over," does the symbol ⌔ seem reasonable for $\frac{2}{3}$?

25. The Rhind (or Ahmes) papyrus of about 1650 B.C. opens with the words "Directions for Obtaining the Knowledge of All Dark Things." The papyrus solves 85 problems and includes a table expressing the fractions with numerator 2 and the odd denominators 5 through 101 as a sum of unit (numerator of 1) fractions. For example, the first two entries in the table are

$$\frac{2}{5} = \frac{1}{3} + \frac{1}{15} \quad \text{and} \quad \frac{2}{7} = \frac{1}{4} + \frac{1}{28}.$$

(a) Verify the next entry of the table: $\frac{2}{9} = \frac{1}{5} + \frac{1}{45}$.

(b) Verify the general formula

$$\frac{2}{2n-1} = \frac{1}{n} + \frac{1}{n(2n-1)}.$$

(c) Let $n = 51$ in the formula of part (b) to find the last entry in the table.

26. **Diffy with Fractions.** We previously played the Diffy game, described in Section 2.3, with whole numbers. Shown here are the beginning lines of Diffy when the entries are fractions. A new line is formed by subtracting the smaller fraction from the larger.

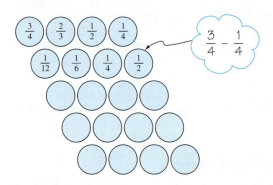

(a) Fill in additional lines of the Diffy array. Does it terminate?

(b) Try fraction Diffy with these fractions in your first row: $\frac{2}{7}, \frac{4}{5}, \frac{3}{2}$, and $\frac{5}{6}$.

(c) Suppose you know that Diffy with whole-number entries always terminates with 0, 0, 0, and 0. Does it necessarily follow that Diffy with fractions must terminate? Explain your reasoning carefully.

## Making Connections

27. A "2 by 4" piece of lumber is planed from a rough board to a final size of $1\frac{1}{2}''$ by $3\frac{1}{2}''$. Find the dimensions $x$ and $y$ of the shape created with two such boards.

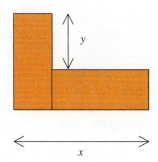

**28.** A wall in a house is made with sheets of $\frac{5}{8}$-inch drywall screwed to the short edges of the vertical 2-by-4 studs within the wall. (See problem 27). How thick is the resulting wall?

**29.** A $1\frac{1}{4}''$ drywall screw is countersunk (i.e., screwed until it is below the surface of the drywall) by $\frac{1}{16}''$ to fasten a $\frac{5}{8}''$ sheet of drywall to the ceiling joist.

   **(a)** How much of the screw extends into the joist?

   **(b)** How much of the screw is within the drywall?

**30.** A board $10\frac{1}{2}$ inches long is sawn off a board that is 2 feet long. If the width of the saw cut is $\frac{1}{16}''$, what is the length of the remaining piece?

**31.** A picture is printed on an $8\frac{1}{2}''$-by-11$''$ piece of photographic paper and placed symmetrically in a frame whose opening is 8$''$ by 10$''$. What are the dimensions of the strips on the sides of the picture that are hidden by the frame?

## Communicating

**32.** For each fraction operation that follows, make up a realistic word problem whose solution requires the computation shown. Try to create an interesting and original situation.

   **(a)** $\frac{19}{32} + \frac{1}{4}$      **(b)** $3\frac{1}{4} - 1\frac{1}{16}$

**33.** Respond to a student who asks, "Should fractions always be written in simplest form, or are there situations in which it would be better not to simplify?"

## From State Student Assessments

**34.** (Arizona Grade 5)
Which of the following lists the mixed numbers in order from **least to greatest**?

   **A.** $7\frac{1}{7}$   $4\frac{3}{7}$   $2\frac{4}{7}$   $1\frac{6}{7}$

   **B.** $5\frac{2}{7}$   $6\frac{1}{7}$   $6\frac{5}{7}$   $7\frac{3}{7}$

   **C.** $2\frac{3}{7}$   $2\frac{1}{7}$   $3\frac{4}{7}$   $4\frac{2}{7}$

   **D.** $6\frac{2}{7}$   $3\frac{3}{7}$   $3\frac{5}{7}$   $5\frac{4}{7}$

**35.** (Massachusetts, Grade 4)
What is the solution to the problem shown below?

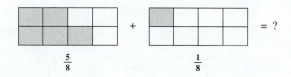

   **A.** $\frac{6}{8}$      **B.** $\frac{6}{10}$      **C.** $\frac{6}{16}$      **D.** $\frac{5}{64}$

**36.** (Massachusetts, Grade 6)
Henry had a piece of rope that was $23\frac{1}{2}$ inches long. Henry cut the rope into two pieces so that one piece was $8\frac{1}{4}$ inches long. What was the length of the other piece of rope?

   **A.** $15\frac{1}{4}$      **B.** $15\frac{1}{2}$      **C.** $31\frac{1}{3}$      **D.** $31\frac{3}{4}$

# 6.3

# Multiplication and Division of Fractions

As a pleasant surprise, multiplication and division of fractions are computationally easier than addition and subtraction. For example, we will discover that the product of $\frac{3}{4}$ and $\frac{2}{5}$ is computed simply by multiplying the respective numerators and denominators to get $\frac{6}{20}$. Division is only slightly trickier: To compute $\frac{2}{5} \div \frac{3}{4}$, we can use the "invert and multiply rule" to get the answer, $\frac{2}{5} \times \frac{4}{3} = \frac{8}{15}$. However, even though multiplication and division of fractions are easy computationally, these operations are quite difficult to understand conceptually. To successfully impart a deep understanding of the multiplication and division of fractions, teachers need to be able to answer these questions:

- *How* can multiplication be illustrated with manipulatives? with pictorial representations?
- *Why* is multiplication defined with such a simple formula?
- *How* is a fraction interpreted as a multiplicative operator?
- *In what way* can division still be viewed as repeated subtraction or as a missing factor?
- *What* justifies the "invert and multiply rule"?
- *What* real-life problems require the multiplication or division of fractions?

It is important to understand that the multiplication of fractions is a natural extension of the multiplication operation on the integers. It is helpful to take a stepwise approach in which first a fraction is multiplied by an integer and then an integer is multiplied by a fraction. These two preliminary steps prepare the student for the general definition of how two fractions are multiplied.

Similarly, we will make the division of fractions meaningful by continuing to view division as repeated subtraction (grouping), as a partition (sharing), and as a missing factor.

## Multiplication of a Fraction by an Integer

Suppose three family-sized pizzas were ordered for a party and a fourth of each pizza was not consumed by the partygoers. Viewing multiplication by a positive integer as repeated addition, we see clearly from the fraction circle diagram in Figure 6.14 that $3 \cdot \dfrac{1}{4} = \dfrac{1}{4} + \dfrac{1}{4} + \dfrac{1}{4} = \dfrac{3}{4}$ of a pizza is left over.

**FIGURE 6.14**

A fraction-circle diagram shows that $3 \cdot \dfrac{1}{4} = \dfrac{3}{4}$

---

**EXAMPLE  6.9   Multiplying a Fraction by an Integer**

(a) Use fraction strips to show that $3 \cdot \dfrac{3}{8} = \dfrac{9}{8}$.

(b) Use a number line to show that $4 \cdot \dfrac{2}{3} = \dfrac{8}{3}$.

(c) Use a number line to show that $-3 \cdot \dfrac{5}{6} = \dfrac{-15}{6}$.

**Solution**   (a) Three fraction strips, each representing $\dfrac{3}{8}$, are aligned to show that their combined shaded region represents $\dfrac{9}{8}$:

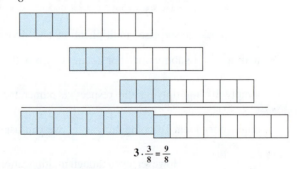

$$3 \cdot \tfrac{3}{8} = \tfrac{9}{8}$$

**(b)** Four jumps of length $\dfrac{2}{3}$ arrive at the point $\dfrac{8}{3}$:

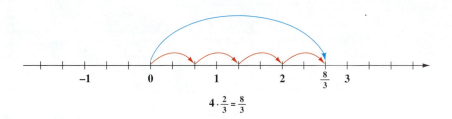

$$4 \cdot \frac{2}{3} = \frac{8}{3}$$

**(c)** The repeated subtraction of three jumps, each of length $\dfrac{5}{6}$, takes us to the point $\dfrac{-15}{6}$ on the number line:

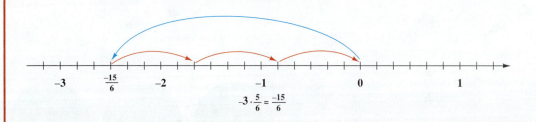

$$-3 \cdot \frac{5}{6} = \frac{-15}{6}$$

## Multiplication of an Integer by a Fraction

Imagine that we are taking a 5-mile hike and we meet someone on the trail who estimates that we have come two-thirds of the way to our destination. How many miles have we covered? This is an easy question to answer: One-third of the 5 mile trail is $\dfrac{5}{3}$ miles long, and we have covered twice this distance, so we have hiked $\dfrac{10}{3}$ miles so far.

We see that "two thirds of" gives meaning to $\dfrac{2}{3}$ as an **operator:** To take two-thirds of 5, first divide 5 into 3 equal parts and then take 2 of those parts. That is, $\dfrac{2}{3} \cdot 5 = 2 \cdot \dfrac{5}{3} = \dfrac{10}{3}$. Here are some other examples related to the hike:

- If the entire hike will take 6 hours, we had been hiking $\dfrac{2}{3} \cdot 6 = \dfrac{12}{3} = 4$ hours when we met the other hiker.

- If we brought 2 liters of water for the hike, we might estimate that we have used $\dfrac{2}{3} \cdot 2 = \dfrac{4}{3}$ liters of our water.

Additional examples of how a fraction is used as a multiplicative operator are shown in Figure 6.15. In each case, we multiply by a fraction $\dfrac{a}{b}$ by first making a partition into $b$ equal parts and then taking $a$ of those parts. That is, $\dfrac{a}{b} \cdot n = a \cdot \dfrac{n}{b} = \dfrac{an}{b}$.

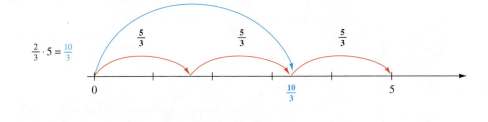

$$\frac{2}{3} \cdot 5 = \frac{10}{3}$$

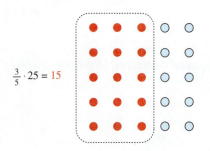

$$\frac{3}{5} \cdot 25 = 15$$

$$\frac{3}{4} \cdot 3 = \frac{9}{4}$$

## Multiplication of a Fraction by a Fraction

In earlier chapters, the rectangular area model provided a useful visualization of multiplication for the whole numbers and integers. This model works equally well to motivate the general definition of the multiplication of two fractions.

In Figure 6.16(a), there is a reminder of how the rectangular area model is used with the whole numbers: We simply create a shaded rectangle that is 2 units high and 3 units long and notice that 6 unit

**FIGURE 6.16**
Extending the area model
of multiplication to
fractions

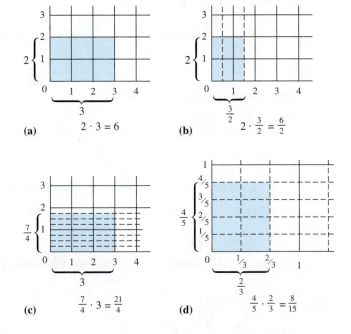

$$2 \cdot 3 = 6$$  **(a)**

$$2 \cdot \frac{3}{2} = \frac{6}{2}$$  **(b)**

$$\frac{7}{4} \cdot 3 = \frac{21}{4}$$  **(c)**

$$\frac{4}{5} \cdot \frac{2}{3} = \frac{8}{15}$$  **(d)**

squares fill the rectangle. That is, $2 \cdot 3 = 6$. In Figure 6.16(b), the rectangular area model reconfirms the result $2 \cdot \dfrac{3}{2} = \dfrac{2 \cdot 3}{2} = \dfrac{6}{2}$ for how to multiply a fraction by a whole number. Similarly, Figure 6.16(c) shows us that the product of the whole number 3 and the fraction $\dfrac{7}{4}$ is given by $\dfrac{7}{4} \cdot 3 = \dfrac{7 \cdot 3}{4} = \dfrac{21}{4}$.

Finally, in Figure 6.16(d), we see that the product of the fractions $\dfrac{4}{5}$ and $\dfrac{2}{3}$ is given by $\dfrac{4}{5} \cdot \dfrac{2}{3} = \dfrac{8}{15}$, since 8 rectangles are shaded and there are 15 congruent rectangles that fill a 1-by-1 unit square. We see that the product of the numerators, $4 \cdot 2 = 8$, gives us the number of small shaded rectangles and forms the numerator of the answer. The denominator of the answer is the product $5 \cdot 3 = 15$ of the denominators and counts the number of small rectangles in a unit square.

---

**DEFINITION**   *Multiplication of Fractions*

Let $\dfrac{a}{b}$ and $\dfrac{c}{d}$ be fractions. Then their **product** is given by

$$\frac{a}{b} \cdot \frac{c}{d} = \frac{ac}{bd}.$$

---

Often a product, say, $\dfrac{4}{5} \cdot \dfrac{2}{3}$, is read as four-fifths "of" two-thirds, which emphasizes how $\dfrac{4}{5}$ is an operator applied to the fraction $\dfrac{2}{3}$. The association between "of" and "times" is natural for multiplication by whole numbers and extends to multiplication of fractions. For example, "I'll buy three *of* the half-gallon-size bottles" is equivalent to buying $3 \cdot \dfrac{1}{2} = \dfrac{3}{2} = 1\dfrac{1}{2}$ gallons.

---

**EXAMPLE 6.10  Calculating Products of Fractions**

Use Figure 6.16 as a model to illustrate these two products:

    **(a)** $\dfrac{5}{8} \cdot \dfrac{2}{3}$      **(b)** $3\dfrac{1}{7} \cdot 5\dfrac{1}{4}$

**Solution**

**(a)** Let a rectangle denote a whole unit of area. Next, use vertical lines to divide the unit into 3 equal parts, so that shading the 2 leftmost rectangles light yellow represents $\dfrac{2}{3}$. Similarly, use horizontal lines to divide the unit rectangle into 8 equal parts, and shade the lower 5 rectangles blue to represent $\dfrac{5}{8}$ of the whole rectangle. The green part of the whole, shaded with both colors, then represents $\dfrac{5}{8}$ of the $\dfrac{2}{3}$ part of the whole. Observing that the whole rectangle has been divided into 24 small rectangles, and 10 of these are within the overlapped region that received both the yellow and blue

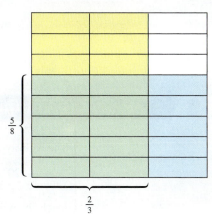

color, we now see that $\frac{5}{8} \cdot \frac{2}{3} = \frac{10}{24}$. We also see that the product of the numerators, $5 \cdot 2 = 10$, gives the number of small rectangles and is the numerator of our answer. Also, the product of the denominators, $8 \cdot 3 = 24$, gives the number of small rectangles in a unit rectangle and is the denominator of the fraction that represents the product.

**(b)** Equivalently, we want to model the product $\frac{22}{7} \cdot \frac{21}{4}$ by the rectangular area diagram. The doubly shaded, green region contains $22 \cdot 21$ small rectangles, where each unit square contains $4 \cdot 7 = 28$ small rectangles. Thus, $3\frac{1}{7} \cdot 5\frac{1}{4} = \frac{22 \cdot 21}{7 \cdot 4}$, which simplifies to $\frac{22 \cdot 21}{4 \cdot 7} = \frac{11 \cdot 3}{2 \cdot 1} = \frac{33}{2} = 16\frac{1}{2}$. This answer can also be seen in the figure by noticing that the green region contains 15 unit squares and 42 small rectangles. Since $42 = 28 + 14$, the small rectangles cover $1\frac{1}{2}$ unit squares. Altogether, we again arrive at the final answer of $16\frac{1}{2}$.

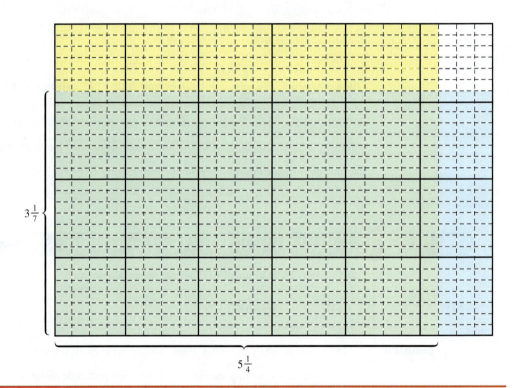

$3\frac{1}{7}$

$5\frac{1}{4}$

**EXAMPLE 6.11 Computing the Area and Cost of a Carpet**

The hallway in the Bateks' house is a rectangle 4 feet wide and 20 feet long; that is, it measures $\frac{4}{3}$ yards by $\frac{20}{3}$ yards. What is the area of the hallway in square yards? Mrs. Batek wants to know how much she will pay to buy carpet priced at \$18 per square yard to carpet the hall.

**Solution**    Since $\dfrac{4}{3} \cdot \dfrac{20}{3} = \dfrac{80}{9} = 8\dfrac{8}{9}$, the area is $8\dfrac{8}{9}$ square yards, or nearly 9 square yards. This can be seen in

the accompanying diagram, which shows the hallway divided into six full square yards, six $\dfrac{1}{3}$-square-

yard rectangular regions, and eight square regions that are each $\dfrac{1}{9}$ of a square yard. Thus, the total

area is $6 + \dfrac{6}{3} + \dfrac{8}{9} = 8\dfrac{8}{9}$ square yards. At \$18 per square yard, the cost of the carpet will be

$8\dfrac{8}{9} \cdot 18 = \dfrac{80}{9} \cdot 18 = 160$ dollars.

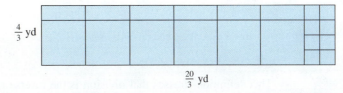

Multiplication of fractions can also be illustrated on the number line, as shown in the next example.

---

**EXAMPLE  6.12  Multiplying Fractions on the Number Line**

Illustrate why $\dfrac{2}{3} \cdot \dfrac{4}{5} = \dfrac{8}{15}$ with a number-line diagram.

**Solution**    It's helpful to view $\dfrac{2}{3}$ as a multiplicative operator. That is, first partition $\dfrac{4}{5}$ into three equal intervals,

each of length $\dfrac{4}{15}$. Since two jumps of length $\dfrac{4}{15}$ arrive at $\dfrac{8}{15}$, the diagram confirms that $\dfrac{2}{3} \cdot \dfrac{4}{5} = \dfrac{8}{15}$.

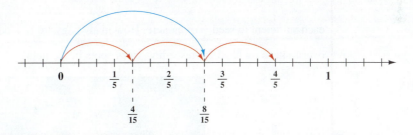

---

## Division of Fractions

To motivate the definition of division, consider the division problem $\dfrac{4}{3} \div \dfrac{1}{6}$. Viewing division as

repeated subtraction, we want to know this: "How many one-sixths are in $\dfrac{4}{3}$?" Since $\dfrac{4}{3} = \dfrac{8}{6} = 8 \cdot \dfrac{1}{6}$,

it follows that there are eight one-sixths in $\dfrac{4}{3}$. That is, $\dfrac{4}{3} \div \dfrac{1}{6} = 8$, since $\dfrac{4}{3} = 8 \cdot \dfrac{1}{6}$.

Let's try another example: Consider the division problem $\dfrac{7}{12} \div \dfrac{1}{6}$. That is, we want to determine

how many one-sixths are in $\dfrac{7}{12}$. Since $\dfrac{7}{12} = \dfrac{7}{2 \cdot 6} = \dfrac{7}{2} \cdot \dfrac{1}{6}$, there are $\dfrac{7}{2}$, or $3\dfrac{1}{2}$, one-sixths in $\dfrac{7}{12}$. That

is, $\dfrac{7}{12} \div \dfrac{1}{6} = \dfrac{7}{2}$, since $\dfrac{7}{12} = \dfrac{7}{2} \cdot \dfrac{1}{6}$.

In general, to find the fraction $\frac{m}{n}$ that solves the division $\frac{a}{b} \div \frac{c}{d} = \frac{m}{n}$, we are really looking for the missing factor $\frac{m}{n}$ in the multiplication formula $\frac{a}{b} = \frac{m}{n} \cdot \frac{c}{d}$. The missing-factor interpretation is used to define the division of fractions.

---

**DEFINITION** *Division of Fractions*

Let $\frac{a}{b}$ and $\frac{c}{d}$ be fractions, where $\frac{c}{d}$ is not zero. Then $\frac{a}{b} \div \frac{c}{d} = \frac{m}{n}$ if, and only if,

$$\frac{a}{b} = \frac{m}{n} \cdot \frac{c}{d}.$$

---

This definition stresses that division is the inverse operation of multiplication. However, other conceptual models of division—as a measurement (that is, as a repeated subtraction or grouping) and as a partition (or sharing)—continue to be important. Indeed, it is these models that are best represented with manipulatives and diagrams, enabling the teacher to convey a deep understanding of what division of fractions really means and how it is used to solve problems. In the next two examples, the solution to meaningful problems is obtained by reasoning directly from the concept of division either as a grouping or as a sharing. Notice that no formula or computational rule is required to obtain the answer. It is very important to keep the conceptual notion of division in mind and not rely simply on rules and formulas that have no intrinsic meaning.

**MHM**

## EXAMPLE 6.13 Seeding a Lawn: Division of Fractions by Grouping

The new city park will have a $2\frac{1}{2}$-acre grass playfield. Grass seed can be purchased in large bags, each sufficient to seed $\frac{3}{4}$ of an acre. How many bags are needed? Will there be some grass seed left over to keep on hand for reseeding worn spots in the field?

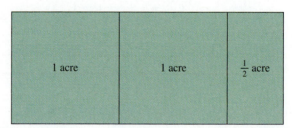

**Solution** The answer will be given by determining the number of $\frac{3}{4}$-acre regions in the $2\frac{1}{2}$-acre field. That is, we must compute the division $2\frac{1}{2} \div \frac{3}{4}$. In the diagram that follows, the field is grouped into four regions. Three of these regions each cover $\frac{3}{4}$ of an acre and therefore require a whole bag of seed. There is also a $\frac{1}{4}$-acre region that will use $\frac{1}{3}$ of a bag. Thus, a total of $2\frac{1}{2} \div \frac{3}{4} = 3\frac{1}{3}$ bags of seed are needed for the playfield. We conclude that four bags of seed should be ordered, which is enough for the initial seeding and leaves $\frac{2}{3}$ of a bag on hand for reseeding.

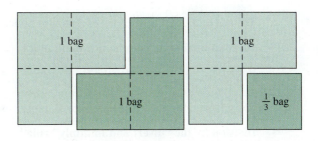

Example 6.14 uses the sharing, or partitive, model of division.

**EXAMPLE 6.14 Making Cookies: Division of Fractions by Sharing**

Jesse has enough flour to make $2\frac{1}{2}$ recipes of chocolate chip cookies and $1\frac{1}{3}$ cups of chocolate chips. How many cups of chocolate chips will be in each recipe?

**Solution**    The chocolate chips and recipes are shown on the following two fraction strips, where each brown rectangle represents a third of a cup of chocolate chips and each yellow rectangle represents a half recipe of cookies:

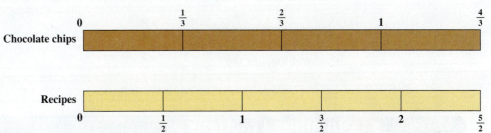

To compare the two figures, we subdivide each brown rectangle into 5 parts and each yellow rectangle into 4 parts:

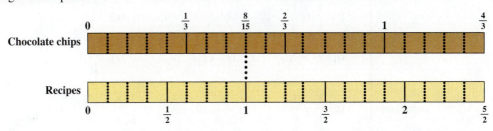

Since 15 small brown squares correspond to a cup of chocolate chips, each small brown square represents $\frac{1}{15}$ of a cup of chips. Therefore, $\frac{8}{15}$ of a cup of chips are seen to correspond to one recipe, and we conclude that $\frac{4}{3} \div \frac{5}{2} = \frac{8}{15}$.

## Algorithms for Calculating the Division of Fractions

There are three ways to simplify the calculation of a quotient of fractions:

- **Division by finding common numerators**

    In Example 6.14, it was shown that $\frac{4}{3} \div \frac{5}{2} = \frac{20}{15} \div \frac{20}{8} = \frac{8}{15}$.

To verify the formula $\dfrac{a}{b} \div \dfrac{a}{c} = \dfrac{c}{b}$, we just notice that $\dfrac{a}{b} = \dfrac{a}{c} \cdot \dfrac{c}{b}$.

- **Division by finding common denominators**

  Earlier, it was shown that $\dfrac{7}{12} \div \dfrac{1}{6} = \dfrac{7}{12} \div \dfrac{2}{12} = \dfrac{7}{2}$.

  To verify the formula $\dfrac{a}{b} \div \dfrac{c}{b} = \dfrac{a}{c}$, we simply observe that $\dfrac{a}{b} = \dfrac{c}{b} \cdot \dfrac{a}{c}$.

- **Division by the "invert and multiply" rule**

  In Example 6.13, it was shown that $\dfrac{5}{2} \div \dfrac{3}{4} = \dfrac{20}{6}$, since $\dfrac{20}{6} = \dfrac{10}{3} = 3\dfrac{1}{3}$.

  This calculation suggests that $\dfrac{a}{b} \div \dfrac{c}{d} = \dfrac{a}{b} \cdot \dfrac{d}{c}$, where the divisor $\dfrac{c}{d}$ is "inverted" and becomes a

  factor $\dfrac{d}{c}$ that is multiplied by $\dfrac{a}{b}$. This "invert and multiply" formula may be verified by observing

  that $\left( \dfrac{a}{b} \cdot \dfrac{d}{c} \right) \cdot \dfrac{c}{d} = \dfrac{adc}{bcd} = \dfrac{a}{b}$.

The following theorem summarizes these useful formulas for the division of fractions:

**THEOREM** *Formulas for the Division of Fractions*

**Common-numerator rule** $\dfrac{a}{b} \div \dfrac{a}{c} = \dfrac{c}{b}$

**Common-denominator rule** $\dfrac{a}{b} \div \dfrac{c}{b} = \dfrac{a}{c}$

**Invert-and-multiply rule** $\dfrac{a}{b} \div \dfrac{c}{d} = \dfrac{a}{b} \cdot \dfrac{d}{c}$

**EXAMPLE 6.15 Dividing Fractions**

Compute these division problems:

(a) $\dfrac{3}{4} \div \dfrac{1}{8}$  (b) $\dfrac{2}{5} \div \dfrac{2}{3}$  (c) $3 \div \dfrac{4}{3}$

(d) $39 \div 13$  (e) $13 \div 39$  (f) $4\dfrac{1}{6} \div 2\dfrac{1}{3}$

**Solution**

(a) $\dfrac{3}{4} \div \dfrac{1}{8} = \dfrac{6}{8} \div \dfrac{1}{8} = 6$, or $\dfrac{3}{4} \div \dfrac{1}{8} = \dfrac{3}{4} \cdot \dfrac{8}{1} = \dfrac{24}{4} = 6$.

(b) $\dfrac{2}{5} \div \dfrac{2}{3} = \dfrac{3}{5}$, or $\dfrac{2}{5} \div \dfrac{2}{3} = \dfrac{2}{5} \cdot \dfrac{3}{2} = \dfrac{2 \cdot 3}{5 \cdot 2} = \dfrac{3}{5}$.

(c) $3 \div \dfrac{4}{3} = \dfrac{3}{1} \cdot \dfrac{3}{4} = \dfrac{9}{4}$.  (d) $39 \div 13 = \dfrac{39}{1} \cdot \dfrac{1}{13} = \dfrac{39}{13} = 3$.

(e) $13 \div 39 = \dfrac{13}{1} \cdot \dfrac{1}{39} = \dfrac{13}{39} = \dfrac{1}{3}$.

(f) $4\dfrac{1}{6} \div 2\dfrac{1}{3} = \dfrac{25}{6} \div \dfrac{7}{3} = \dfrac{25}{6} \cdot \dfrac{3}{7} = \dfrac{25 \cdot 3}{6 \cdot 7} = \dfrac{25 \cdot 1}{2 \cdot 7} = \dfrac{25}{14}$.

## Reciprocals as Multiplicative Inverses in the Rational Numbers

The "invert and multiply" rule, though not the definition of division, has an important consequence: The division of any rational by a nonzero rational number has a unique quotient that is also a rational number. That is, the nonzero rational numbers are closed under division. This was not true of the system of integers. For example, $3 \div 8$ cannot be written as any integer. But when 3 and 8 are interpreted as the fractions $\frac{3}{1}$ and $\frac{8}{1}$, the we see that $3 \div 8 = \frac{3}{1} \div \frac{8}{1} = \frac{3}{8}$.

More precisely stated, the nonzero fraction $\frac{c}{d}$ is "inverted" by forming its **reciprocal.**

---

**DEFINITION** *Reciprocal of a Fraction*

The **reciprocal** of a nonzero fraction $\frac{c}{d}$ is the fraction $\frac{d}{c}$.

---

Since $\frac{c}{d} \cdot \frac{d}{c} = \frac{d}{c} \cdot \frac{c}{d} = 1$, and 1 is the multiplicative identity, we say that the reciprocal of a nonzero fraction is its **multiplicative inverse.** Multiplicative inverses are very useful for solving equations, as shown in the next two examples.

**EXAMPLE 6.16  Using the Reciprocal**

On a cruise to the Caribbean, $\frac{2}{3}$ of the women passengers on board are married to $\frac{5}{6}$ of the men passengers. There are also 9 more women than men on board. How many passengers are on the ship?

**Solution**

**Understand the Problem**

Information is given about the number of men and women passengers. We assume that each married woman is paired with one married man, her husband. Our goal is to determine the number of passengers on board.

**Devise a Plan**

Although we are asked only for the total number of passengers, it is probably helpful to determine both the number of women and the number of men. Summing these two numbers will give us our answer. Thus, we can introduce variables for the number of men and women, use the given information to form equations, and finally solve these equations to find our answer. Since the given information involves fractions, we expect that we need to be skillful working with the arithmetic of fractions.

**Carry Out the Plan**

Let the variables $m$ and $w$ represent the respective number of men and women passengers. The information given is equivalent to the equations $\frac{2}{3}w = \frac{5}{6}m$ and $w = m + 9$. The first equation can be solved for $w$ by multiplying both sides by the reciprocal of $\frac{2}{3}$, namely, $\frac{3}{2}$, so

$$w = \left(\frac{3}{2} \cdot \frac{2}{3}\right) \cdot w = \frac{3}{2} \cdot \left(\frac{2}{3} \cdot w\right) = \frac{3}{2} \cdot \left(\frac{5}{6} \cdot m\right) = \left(\frac{3}{2} \cdot \frac{5}{6}\right) \cdot m = \frac{5}{4} \cdot m.$$

Comparing this equation with $w = m + 9$, we obtain the new relation $\frac{5}{4}m = m + 9$. Subtracting $m$ from both sides gives $\frac{1}{4} \cdot m = 9$. To solve for $m$, we multiply this equation by the reciprocal of

$\frac{1}{4}$, which is 4, to get $m = 4 \cdot 9 = 36$. Therefore, there are 36 men, $36 + 9 = 45$ women, and $36 + 45 = 81$ passengers in all.

**MHM**

### Look Back

It is always a good idea to ask if a problem can be solved differently. The figure that follows shows clearly all of the information given in the problem: $\frac{2}{3}$ of the women are married to $\frac{5}{6}$ of the men, and there are 9 more women than men. The dotted lines have been added to divide each region into rectangles of equal size.

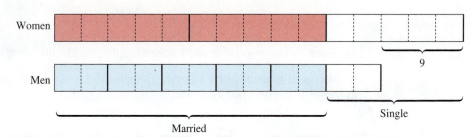

Evidently, 3 small rectangles represent 9 passengers, so each small rectangle represents 3 passengers. The diagram now makes it clear there are $3 \cdot 3 \cdot 5 = 45$ women, $3 \cdot 6 \cdot 2 = 36$ men, and 81 passengers in all.

In Example 6.17, the missing-factor model of division is used to solve a real-life problem. The reciprocal, being a multiplicative inverse, allows us to solve for the missing factor.

## EXAMPLE 6.17  Bottling Root Beer: Illustrating Division of Fractions with the Missing-Factor Model

Ari is making homemade root beer. The recipe he followed nearly fills a 5-gallon glass jug, and he estimates that it contains $4\frac{3}{4}$ gallons of root beer. He is now ready to bottle his root beer. How many $\frac{1}{2}$-gallon bottles can he fill?

**Solution**    Let $x$ denote the number of half-gallon bottles required, where $x$ will be allowed to be a fraction, since we expect that some bottle may be only partially filled. We must then solve the equation

$$x \cdot \frac{1}{2} = 4\frac{3}{4},$$

since this is the missing-factor problem that is equivalent to the division problem $4\frac{3}{4} \div \frac{1}{2}$.

Since

$$4\frac{3}{4} = \frac{19}{4} = \frac{19}{2} \cdot \frac{1}{2},$$

it follows that the missing factor is $x = \frac{19}{2} = 9\frac{1}{2}$.

The situation is shown in the accompanying figure. Ari will need 9 half-gallon bottles, and he will probably see if he can also find a quart bottle to use.

Since $4\frac{3}{4}$ gallons will fill $9\frac{1}{2}$ half-gallon bottles, $4\frac{3}{4} \div \frac{1}{2} = 9\frac{1}{2}$. That is, $\frac{19}{4} \div \frac{1}{2} = \frac{19}{2}$.

$4\frac{3}{4}$ gallons

Half-gallon bottles

## Did You Know?

### Division of Fractions: Contrasting Teachers from the United States and China

The difference between the mathematical knowledge of the U.S. teachers and that of the Chinese teachers became more striking with the topic of division by fractions. The first contrast was presented in calculation. The interview question of this chapter asked the teachers to calculate $1\frac{3}{4} \div \frac{1}{2}$. The process of calculation revealed features of teachers' procedural knowledge and of their understanding of mathematics, as well as of their attitude toward the discipline.

In the two previous chapters* all teachers presented a sound procedural knowledge. This time, only 43% of the U.S. teachers succeeded in calculation and none of them showed an understanding of the rationale of the algorithm. Most of these teachers struggled. Many tended to confound the division-by-fractions algorithm with those for addition and subtraction or for multiplication. These teachers' procedural knowledge was not only weak in division with fractions, but also in other operations with fractions. Reporting that they were uncomfortable doing calculation with mixed numbers or improper fractions, these teachers also had very limited knowledge about the basic features of fractions.

All of the Chinese teachers succeeded in their calculations and many of them showed enthusiasm in doing the problem. These teachers were not satisfied by just calculating and getting an answer. They enjoyed presenting various ways of doing it—using decimals, using whole numbers, applying the three basic laws, etc. They went back and forth across subsets of numbers and across different operations, added and took off parentheses, and changed the order of operations. They did this with remarkable confidence and amazingly flexible skills. In addition, many teachers made comments on various calculation methods and evaluated them. Their way of "doing mathematics" showed significant conceptual understanding.

*on subtraction with regrouping and multidigit multiplication

SOURCE: Knowing and Teaching Elementary Mathematics: Teachers' Understanding of Fundamental Mathematics in China and in the United States, by Liping Ma. Copyright © 1999 by Taylor & Francis Group LLC - BOOKS. Reproduced with permission of TAYLOR & FRANCIS GROUP LLC - Books via Copyright Clearance Center.

## Problem Set 6.3

Exercises numbered in red are answered in the back of the text.

### Understanding Concepts

**1. (a)** What fraction multiplication is illustrated with this fraction-circle diagram?

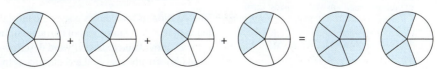

**(b)** Draw a fraction-circle diagram that illustrates $5 \cdot \dfrac{3}{4}$.

2. Draw number-line diagrams that illustrate these products:

(a) $4 \cdot \dfrac{3}{8}$    **(b)** $-4 \cdot \dfrac{3}{8}$    **(c)** $4 \cdot \left(\dfrac{-3}{8}\right)$    **(d)** $-4 \cdot \left(\dfrac{-3}{8}\right)$

3. **(a)** What fraction multiplication is illustrated by this number-line diagram?

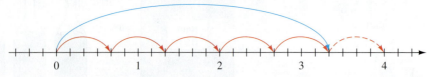

**(b)** Draw a number-line diagram to illustrate that $\dfrac{3}{4} \times 5 = \dfrac{15}{4} = 3\dfrac{3}{4}$.

4. What multiplication facts are illustrated by these rectangular area models?

(a)

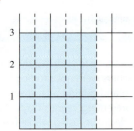

(b)

(c)

5. Illustrate these multiplications with the rectangular area model used in problem 5:

(a) $2 \times \dfrac{3}{5}$    **(b)** $\dfrac{3}{2} \times \dfrac{3}{4}$    **(c)** $1\dfrac{2}{3} \times 2\dfrac{1}{4}$

6. A rectangular plot of land is $2\dfrac{1}{4}$ miles wide and $3\dfrac{1}{2}$ miles long. What is the area of the plot, in square miles? Draw a sketch that verifies your answer.

7. Find the reciprocals of the following fractions:

(a) $\dfrac{3}{8}$    **(b)** $\dfrac{4}{3}$    **(c)** $2\dfrac{1}{4}$

(d) $\dfrac{1}{8}$    **(e)** $5$    **(f)** $1$

8. Compute each of these products, expressing each answer in lowest terms:

(a) $\dfrac{5}{4} \times \dfrac{12}{25}$    **(b)** $\dfrac{7}{8} \times \dfrac{2}{21}$

(c) $\dfrac{-3}{5} \times \dfrac{10}{21}$    **(d)** $\dfrac{4}{7} \times \dfrac{21}{16}$

9. Use the common-numerator and common-denominator rules to compute these divisions, expressing each answer in lowest terms:

(a) $\dfrac{5}{4} \div \dfrac{3}{4}$    **(b)** $\dfrac{7}{8} \div \dfrac{7}{11}$

(c) $\dfrac{2}{5} \div \dfrac{7}{5}$    **(d)** $\dfrac{4}{7} \div \dfrac{4}{21}$

10. Compute these divisions, expressing each answer in simplest form:

(a) $\dfrac{2}{5} \div \dfrac{3}{4}$    **(b)** $\dfrac{6}{11} \div \dfrac{4}{3}$    **(c)** $\dfrac{100}{33} \div \dfrac{10}{3}$

(d) $2\dfrac{3}{8} \div 5$    **(e)** $3 \div 5\dfrac{1}{4}$    **(f)** $\dfrac{21}{25} \div \dfrac{7}{25}$

11. Compute the fraction with the simplest form that is equivalent to the given expression.

(a) $\dfrac{2}{3} \cdot \left(\dfrac{3}{4} + \dfrac{9}{12}\right)$    **(b)** $\left(\dfrac{3}{5} - \dfrac{3}{10}\right) \div \dfrac{6}{5}$

(c) $\left(\dfrac{2}{5} \div \dfrac{4}{15}\right) \cdot \dfrac{2}{3}$

12. Set up and evaluate expressions to solve these map problems:

(a) Each inch on a map represents an actual distance of $2\dfrac{1}{2}$ miles. If the map shows Helmer as being $3\dfrac{3}{4}$ inches due east of Deary, how far apart are the two towns?

(b) A map shows that Spokane is 60 miles north of Colfax. A ruler shows that the towns are $3\dfrac{3}{4}$ inches apart on the map. How many miles are represented by each inch on the map?

13. Carefully describe each step in the arithmetic of fractions that is required to solve these equations:

(a) $\dfrac{2}{5}x - \dfrac{3}{4} = \dfrac{1}{2}$    **(b)** $\dfrac{2}{3}x + \dfrac{1}{4} = \dfrac{3}{2}x$

14. I am a fraction whose product with 7 is the same as my sum with 7. Who am I?

## Teaching Concepts

 The division of fractions is one of the most difficult concepts to teach in the elementary school curriculum. In each problem that follows, provide pictures and word descriptions that you believe would effectively convey the central ideas to a youngster. Some of the examples in the section can be used as models.

**15.** Sean has a job mowing grass for the city, using a riding mower. He can mow $\frac{5}{6}$ of an acre per hour. How long will he need to mow the 3-acre city park?

**16.** Angie, Bree, Corrine, Dot, and Elaine together picked $3\frac{3}{4}$ crates of strawberries. How many crates should each be allotted in order to distribute the berries evenly?

**17.** Gerry is making a pathway out of concrete stepping-stones. The path is 25 feet long, and each stone extends $1\frac{2}{3}$ of a foot along the path. By letting $x$ denote the number of stones, Gerry knows that he needs to solve the equation $x \cdot 1\frac{2}{3} = 25$, but he isn't sure how to solve for $x$. Provide a careful explanation.

## Responding to Students

**18.** Respond to Eva's statement:

> I know that multiplication by $\frac{3}{4}$ means splitting into 4 equal parts and then taking 3 of the parts. I also know that division is the inverse of multiplication, so division by $\frac{3}{4}$ means splitting into 3 equal parts and then taking 4 of the parts. So, instead of dividing by $\frac{3}{4}$, I might just as well multiply by $\frac{4}{3}$.

Children (and adults!) often have difficulties relating fractions and their arithmetic to practical situations. In problems 19–21, respond to the children, who have been asked to pose a multiplication problem that requires the answer to $\frac{1}{4}$ of $\frac{2}{3}$.

**19.** There is $\frac{2}{3}$ of a pizza left. Suzanne then ate $\frac{1}{4}$ of a pizza. How much pizza is left?

**20.** There is $\frac{2}{3}$ of a pizza left. Jamie ate $\frac{1}{4}$ of the remaining pieces. How many pieces of pizza now remain?

**21.** There is $\frac{2}{3}$ of a cake left. One-fourth of Miguel's class-mates want some of the cake. How much cake is each child given?

In problems 22 and 23, respond to the children, who have been asked to pose a problem that corresponds to the division of $1\frac{3}{4}$ by $\frac{1}{2}$.

**22.** There is $1\frac{3}{4}$ of a pizza left, and Kelly needs to share it equally with her brother. How much pizza does each child get?

**23.** There are $1\frac{3}{4}$ cups of chocolate chips in a bag. If a cookie recipe calls for a half-cup of chocolate chips, how many recipes can be made?

## Thinking Critically

**24.** Jason and Kathy are driving in separate cars from home to Grandma's house, each driving the same route that passes through Midville. They both travel at 50 miles per hour, and Kathy left 4 hours ahead of Jason. They have the following conversation on their cell phones:

Jason:  "Home is half as far away as Midville."
Kathy:  "Grandma's house is half as far away as Midville."

How far is Grandma's from home? (*Suggestion:* Draw a picture.)

**25.** A bag contains red, green, and blue marbles. One-fifth of the marbles are red, there are $\frac{1}{3}$ as many blue marbles as green marbles, and there are 10 fewer red marbles than green marbles. Determine the number of marbles in the bag in these two approaches.

(a) Use algebraic reasoning (i.e., introduce variables, form equations, and then solve the equations).

(b) Use the set model of fractions, labeling the following Venn diagram:

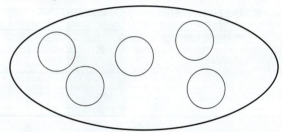

**26.** The positive rational numbers 3 and $1\frac{1}{2}$ are an interesting pair because their sum is equal to their product: $3 + \frac{3}{2} = \frac{6}{2} + \frac{3}{2} = \frac{9}{2}$ and $3 \cdot \frac{3}{2} = \frac{9}{2}$.

(a) Show that $3\frac{1}{2}$ and $1\frac{2}{5}$ have the same sum and product.

(b) Show that $2\frac{3}{5}$ and $1\frac{5}{8}$ have the same sum and product.

(c) If two positive rational numbers $\frac{a}{b}$ and $\frac{c}{d}$ have the same sum and product, what must be true of the sum of their reciprocals?

**27.** Three children had just cut their rectangular cake into three equal parts, as shown, to share, when a fourth friend joined them. Describe how to make one additional straight cut through the cake so that all four can share the cake equally.

**28. (a)** Verify that $\dfrac{21}{8} \div \dfrac{7}{4} = \dfrac{21 \div 7}{8 \div 4} = \dfrac{3}{2}$.

**(b)** Show that if $a \div c = m$ and $b \div d = n$, then
$$\frac{a}{b} \div \frac{c}{d} = \frac{a \div c}{b \div d} = \frac{m}{n}.$$

**29. Illustrating Fraction Division with the Rectangular Area Model.** The following sequence of diagrams illustrates why $\dfrac{3}{8} \div \dfrac{2}{5} = \dfrac{15}{16}$, since it shows that the number of two-fifths in three-eighths is $\dfrac{15}{16}$.

**A.** Shade $\dfrac{3}{8}$ of a unit rectangle, using vertical lines

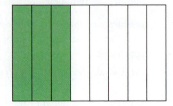

**B.** Use horizontal lines to create a rectangle of area $\dfrac{2}{5}$

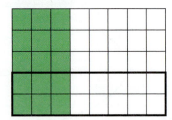

**C.** Move the shaded boxes into the $\dfrac{2}{5}$ rectangle

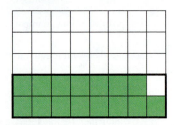

Make similar diagrams that illustrate each of these division problems:

**(a)** $\dfrac{2}{5} \div \dfrac{3}{4}$  **(b)** $\dfrac{3}{5} \div \dfrac{5}{6}$

**(c)** $\dfrac{7}{8} \div \dfrac{1}{3}$ [*Suggestion*: Make a row of rectangles, each of area $\dfrac{1}{3}$, to wholly or partially cover the shaded boxes.]

**30.** Solve this problem found in the Rhind papyrus: "A quantity and its $\dfrac{1}{7}$th added together become 19. What is the quantity?"

**31. Divvy.** The process called Divvy is like Diffy, except that the larger fraction is *divided* by the smaller. The first few rows of a sample Divvy are shown.

**(a)** Continue to fill in additional rows, using a calculator if you like.

**(b)** Try Divvy with $\dfrac{2}{7}, \dfrac{4}{5}, \dfrac{3}{2}$, and $\dfrac{5}{6}$ in the first row.

Don't let complicated fractions put you off! Things should get better if you persist.

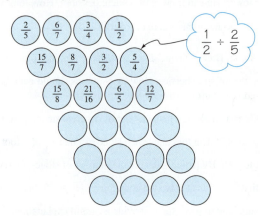

## Making Connections

**32.** At a certain university, a student's senior thesis is acceptable if at least $\dfrac{3}{4}$ of the student's committee votes in its favor. What is the smallest number of favorable votes needed to accept a thesis if the committee has 3 members? 4 members? 5 members? 6 members? 7 members? 8 members?

**33.** A sign on a rolled-up canvas says that the canvas contains 42 square yards. The width of the canvas, which is easily measured without unrolling, is 14 feet (or $4\dfrac{2}{3}$ yards). What is the length of the piece of canvas, in yards?

**34.** Tongue-and-groove decking boards are each $2\dfrac{1}{4}$ inches wide. How many boards must be placed side by side to build a deck 14 feet in width?

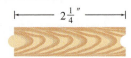

**35.** Six bows can be made from $1\dfrac{1}{2}$ yards of ribbon. How many bows can be made from $5\dfrac{3}{4}$ yards of ribbon?

**36.** Andre has 35 yards of material available to make aprons. Each apron requires $\dfrac{3}{4}$ yard. How many aprons can Andre make?

**37.** Gisela paid $28 for a skirt that was "$\dfrac{1}{3}$ off." What was the original price of the skirt?

**38.** A soup recipe calls for $2\dfrac{3}{4}$ cups of chicken broth and will make enough to serve 8 people. How much broth is required if the recipe is modified to serve 6 people?

**39.** The label on a large 4-liter bottle claims to be the equivalent of $5\dfrac{1}{3}$ small bottles. What is the size of a small bottle?

*See "Examining School Book Pages" on page 318 for questions related to the pages shown below.*

**Lesson 9-3**

**Understand It!**
A division expression containing fractions can be changed to an equivalent multiplication expression to solve.

## Dividing Fractions

**How can you find the quotient of two fractions?**

Andrew has $\frac{3}{4}$ of a gallon of lemonade. He wants to pour it into $\frac{1}{6}$-gallon containers. How many containers can he fill?

**Choose an Operation** Divide to find the number of containers.

**Step 1**

Find $\frac{3}{4} \div \frac{1}{6}$.

To divide by a fraction, rewrite the problem as a multiplication problem using the reciprocal of the divisor.

$\frac{6}{1}$ is the reciprocal of $\frac{1}{6}$.

$$\frac{3}{4} \div \frac{1}{6} = \frac{3}{4} \times \frac{6}{1}$$

**Step 2**

Look for common factors to simplify. Then multiply.

$$\frac{3}{\underset{2}{4}} \times \frac{\overset{3}{6}}{1} = \frac{9}{2}$$

$$\frac{9}{2} = 4\frac{1}{2}$$

Andrew can fill 4 containers, plus $\frac{1}{2}$ of an additional container.

### Guided Practice*

**Do you know HOW?**

In **1** through **4**, find each quotient. Simplify, if possible.

1. $\frac{3}{4} \div \frac{2}{3}$
2. $\frac{3}{12} \div \frac{1}{8}$
3. $\frac{1}{2} \div \frac{4}{5}$
4. $\frac{7}{10} \div \frac{2}{5}$

**Do you UNDERSTAND?**

5. In the example above, did it change the answer to simplify before multiplying?

6. In the example at the top, how many $\frac{1}{8}$-gallon containers could Andrew fill?

### Independent Practice

In **7** through **22**, find each quotient. Simplify, if possible.

7. $\frac{1}{2} \div \frac{1}{2}$
8. $\frac{1}{2} \div \frac{1}{4}$
9. $\frac{7}{8} \div \frac{1}{8}$
10. $\frac{2}{3} \div \frac{3}{4}$

11. $\frac{1}{9} \div \frac{1}{5}$
12. $\frac{2}{7} \div \frac{1}{2}$
13. $\frac{2}{9} \div \frac{4}{5}$
14. $\frac{1}{2} \div \frac{2}{4}$

15. $\frac{3}{8} \div \frac{1}{9}$
16. $\frac{2}{3} \div \frac{1}{4}$
17. $\frac{2}{5} \div \frac{1}{8}$
18. $\frac{5}{6} \div \frac{2}{3}$

19. $\frac{6}{7} \div \frac{1}{3}$
20. $\frac{7}{8} \div \frac{1}{2}$
21. $\frac{12}{14} \div \frac{14}{12}$
22. $\frac{5}{14} \div \frac{4}{7}$

In **23** through **26**, evaluate each expression for $x = \frac{5}{6}$.

23. $x \div \frac{3}{9}$
24. $\frac{10}{13} \div x$
25. $\frac{5}{8} \div x$
26. $x \div \frac{9}{10}$

### Problem Solving

27. Tomas tiled $\frac{1}{2}$ of his bathroom floor in blue. He tiled $\frac{2}{3}$ of the remaining bathroom floor in green. He used white tiles for the rest of the bathroom. How much of the bathroom had white tiles? Use the picture to help find your solution.

| $\frac{1}{2}$ | |
|---|---|
| $\frac{2}{3} \times \frac{1}{2}$ | ? |

28. Luis has an 8-cup bag of trail mix to share. If he gives 9 friends $\frac{2}{3}$ of a cup each, how much trail mix does he have left?

29. Which fraction has the greatest value?

A $\frac{7}{12}$  C $\frac{3}{4}$

B $\frac{2}{3}$  D $\frac{7}{9}$

30. **Algebra** Write an equation for each statement, then solve.

a One-half of a watermelon was shared among 4 people. How much watermelon did each person get?

b A recipe for cookies calls for $\frac{1}{4}$ cup of almonds. If Sara has $1\frac{1}{2}$ cups of almonds, how many recipes of cookies can she make?

c Reena runs a quarter of a mile and then walks one-eighth mile. If she continues this pattern 10 times, how far will she run?

31. **Make a Table** A restaurant sells 9 daily specials for every 6 full-price meals sold. At this rate, how many daily specials will have been sold when 30 full-price meals have been sold?

32. **Writing to Explain** Write an explanation to a friend telling him or her how to find $\frac{3}{4} \div \frac{2}{3}$.

33. Simplify the following expressions.

a $2 + (10 - \frac{6}{3})$

b $5(6 + 3)$

c $\frac{10}{(25 - 5)}$

206     *For another example, see Set B on page 218.

207     Lesson 9-3

## Communicating

**40.** For each fraction operation that follows, make up a realistic word problem whose solution requires the computation shown. Try to create an interesting and original situation.

(a) $\dfrac{4}{5} \times \dfrac{7}{8}$    (b) $\dfrac{9}{10} \div \dfrac{3}{5}$

## From State Student Assessments

**41.** (Kentucky, Grade 4)
**Mowing the Yard.** The green shaded area of the picture below shows what part of the yard Jessie mowed in 30 minutes.

She wonders about how long it takes her to mow the whole yard. Write a note to Jessie

**A.** telling her about how long it takes to mow her whole yard and

**B.** explaining to her how you found your answer. Be sure to include a drawing of the yard in your explanation.

**42.** (Delaware, Grade 5)
Four children want to share seven brownies. They can cut the brownies to make the shares even. How many brownies should each child get? Please explain with words and/or pictures how you got your answer.

**43.** (Massachusetts, Grade 7)
It took a ball 1 minute to roll 90 feet. What was this ball's average rate of speed, in feet per second?

**A.** $\dfrac{2}{3}$ feet per second    **B.** $1\dfrac{1}{2}$ feet per second

**C.** 2 feet per second    **D.** 3 feet per second

### Examining School Book Pages

*Refer to the School Book Pages provided on page 317 to answer the following questions.*

**44.** In Lesson 9-1 of enVisionMATH 6, the division problem $3 \div \dfrac{3}{4}$ is solved with the use of the following number-line diagram, which shows that $3 \div \dfrac{3}{4} = 4$, since there are 4 segments each of length $\dfrac{3}{4}$ in the segment of length 3.

Create a similar diagram for the lemonade problem in Lesson 9-3 to show that $\dfrac{3}{4} \div \dfrac{1}{6} = 4\dfrac{1}{2}$.

**45.** In Lesson 9-1 of enVisionMATH 6, the division problem $\dfrac{1}{2} \div 3$ is solved with this sequence of rectangular area diagrams:

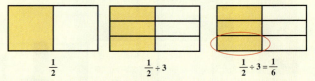

$\dfrac{1}{2}$            $\dfrac{1}{2} \div 3$            $\dfrac{1}{2} \div 3 = \dfrac{1}{6}$

Solve Problem 32 of Lesson 9-3 by creating a rectangular area diagram similar to the preceding one from Lesson 9-1. [*Suggestion*: Problem 29 may be helpful.]

## 6.4

# The Rational Number System

This section explores the properties of the rational numbers. Many properties will be familiar, since the integers have the same properties. However, we will also discover some important new properties of rational numbers that have no counterpart in the integers. This section also gives techniques for estimation and computation and presents additional examples of the application of rational numbers to the solution of practical problems.

## Properties of Addition and Subtraction

To add two rational numbers, we first represent the rational numbers by fractions with a common denominator and then add the two numerators. For example, to add $\dfrac{5}{6}$ and $\dfrac{3}{10}$, we could use the common denominator 30; thus,

$$\frac{5}{6} + \frac{3}{10} = \frac{25}{30} + \frac{9}{30} = \frac{34}{30}.$$

We could also have used the common denominator 60 to find that

$$\frac{5}{6} + \frac{3}{10} = \frac{50}{60} + \frac{18}{60} = \frac{68}{60}.$$

The two answers, namely, $\frac{34}{30}$ and $\frac{68}{60}$, are different fractions. However, they are equivalent fractions, and both represent the *same* rational number, $\frac{17}{15}$, when expressed by a fraction in simplest form. More generally, *any* two rational numbers have a unique rational number that is their sum. That is, the rational numbers are closed under addition.

It is also straightforward to check that addition in the rational numbers is commutative and associative. For example, $\frac{5}{6} + \frac{3}{10} = \frac{3}{10} + \frac{5}{6}$ and $\frac{3}{4} + \left(\frac{-1}{3} + \frac{2}{5}\right) = \left(\frac{3}{4} + \frac{-1}{3}\right) + \frac{2}{5}$. Similarly, 0 is the additive identity. For example, $\frac{7}{9} + 0 = \frac{7}{9}$, since $0 = \frac{0}{9}$.

The rational numbers share one more property with the integers, namely, the existence of **negatives,** or **additive inverses.** We have the following definition:

---

**DEFINITION** *Negative or Additive Inverse*

Let $\frac{a}{b}$ be a rational number. Its **negative, or additive inverse,** written $-\frac{a}{b}$, is the rational number $\frac{-a}{b}$.

---

For example, $-\frac{4}{7} = \frac{-4}{7}$. This is the additive inverse of $\frac{4}{7}$, since

$$\frac{4}{7} + \left(-\frac{4}{7}\right) = \frac{4}{7} + \frac{-4}{7} = \frac{4 + (-4)}{7} = \frac{0}{7} = 0.$$

As another example, $-\left(-\frac{3}{4}\right) = -\left(\frac{-3}{4}\right) = \frac{-(-3)}{4} = \frac{3}{4}$, which illustrates the general property $-\left(-\frac{a}{b}\right) = \frac{a}{b}$.

A negative is also called an **opposite.** This term describes how a rational number and its negative are positioned on the number line: $-\frac{a}{b}$ is on the opposite side of 0 from $\frac{a}{b}$.

The properties of addition on the rational numbers are listed in the following theorem:

---

**THEOREM** *Properties of Addition of Rational Numbers*

Let $\frac{a}{b}, \frac{c}{d}$, and $\frac{e}{f}$ be rational numbers. Then following properties hold:

| | |
|---|---|
| **Closure Property** | $\frac{a}{b} + \frac{c}{d}$ is a rational number. |
| **Commutative Property** | $\frac{a}{b} + \frac{c}{d} = \frac{c}{d} + \frac{a}{b}$ |
| **Associative Property** | $\left(\frac{a}{b} + \frac{c}{d}\right) + \frac{e}{f} = \frac{a}{b} + \left(\frac{c}{d} + \frac{e}{f}\right)$ |
| **Zero is an Additive Identity** | $\frac{a}{b} + 0 = \frac{a}{b}$ |
| **Existence of Additive Inverses** | $\frac{a}{b} + \left(-\frac{a}{b}\right) = 0$, where $-\frac{a}{b} = \frac{-a}{b}$ |

In the integers, we discovered that subtraction was equivalent to addition of the negative. The same result holds for the rational numbers. Since the rational numbers are closed under addition and every rational number has a negative, this means that the rational numbers are closed under subtraction.

> **THEOREM** *Formulas for Subtraction of Rational Numbers*
>
> Let $\dfrac{a}{b}$ and $\dfrac{c}{d}$ be rational numbers. Then $\dfrac{a}{b} - \dfrac{c}{d} = \dfrac{a}{b} + \left(-\dfrac{c}{d}\right) = \dfrac{ad - bc}{bd}$.

Subtraction is neither commutative nor associative, as examples such as $\dfrac{1}{2} - \dfrac{1}{4} \neq \dfrac{1}{4} - \dfrac{1}{2}$ and $1 - \left(\dfrac{1}{2} - \dfrac{1}{4}\right) \neq \left(1 - \dfrac{1}{2}\right) - \dfrac{1}{4}$ show. This means that subtraction requires that careful attention be given to the order of the terms and the placement of parentheses.

## EXAMPLE 6.18 Subtracting Rational Numbers

Compute the following differences:

(a) $\dfrac{3}{4} - \dfrac{7}{6}$     (b) $\dfrac{2}{3} - \dfrac{-9}{8}$     (c) $\left(-2\dfrac{1}{4}\right) - \left(4\dfrac{2}{3}\right)$

**Solution**

(a) $\dfrac{3}{4} - \dfrac{7}{6} = \dfrac{3 \cdot 6}{4 \cdot 6} - \dfrac{4 \cdot 7}{4 \cdot 6} = \dfrac{18 - 28}{24} = \dfrac{-10}{24} = \dfrac{-5}{12} = -\dfrac{5}{12}.$

(b) $\dfrac{2}{3} - \dfrac{-9}{8} = \dfrac{2}{3} + \dfrac{9}{8} = \dfrac{2 \cdot 8}{3 \cdot 8} + \dfrac{3 \cdot 9}{3 \cdot 8} = \dfrac{16}{24} + \dfrac{27}{24} = \dfrac{43}{24}.$

(c) $\left(-2\dfrac{1}{4}\right) - \left(4\dfrac{2}{3}\right) = (-2 - 4) - \left(\dfrac{1}{4} + \dfrac{2}{3}\right) = -6 - \left(\dfrac{3}{12} + \dfrac{8}{12}\right) = -6\dfrac{11}{12}.$

## Properties of Multiplication and Division

Multiplication of rational numbers includes all of the properties of multiplication on the integers. For example, let's investigate the distributive property of multiplication over addition by considering a specific case:

$$\dfrac{2}{5} \cdot \left(\dfrac{3}{4} + \dfrac{7}{8}\right) = \dfrac{2}{5} \cdot \left(\dfrac{6}{8} + \dfrac{7}{8}\right) = \dfrac{2}{5} \cdot \dfrac{13}{8} = \dfrac{26}{40}.$$     Add first; then multiply.

$$\dfrac{2}{5} \cdot \dfrac{3}{4} + \dfrac{2}{5} \cdot \dfrac{7}{8} = \dfrac{6}{20} + \dfrac{14}{40} = \dfrac{12}{40} + \dfrac{14}{40} = \dfrac{26}{40}.$$     Multiply first; then add.

These computations show that multiplication by $\dfrac{2}{5}$ distributes over the sum $\dfrac{3}{4} + \dfrac{7}{8}$. A similar calculation proves the general distributive property $\dfrac{a}{b} \cdot \left(\dfrac{c}{d} + \dfrac{e}{f}\right) = \dfrac{a}{b} \cdot \dfrac{c}{d} + \dfrac{a}{b} \cdot \dfrac{e}{f}$.

As we previewed in Section 6.3, there is one important new property of multiplication of rational numbers that is *not* true for the integers: the existence of multiplicative inverses. For example, the nonzero rational number $\dfrac{5}{8}$ has the multiplicative inverse $\dfrac{8}{5}$, since

$$\dfrac{5}{8} \cdot \dfrac{8}{5} = 1.$$

This property does not hold in the integers. For example, since there is no integer $m$ for which $2 \cdot m = 1$, the integer 2 does not have a multiplicative inverse in the set of integers.

---

**THEOREM**  *Properties of Multiplication of Rational Numbers*

Let $\dfrac{a}{b}, \dfrac{c}{d}$, and $\dfrac{e}{f}$ be rational numbers. Then the following properties hold:

**Closure Property**  $\dfrac{a}{b} \cdot \dfrac{c}{d}$ is a rational number.

**Commutative Property**  $\dfrac{a}{b} \cdot \dfrac{c}{d} = \dfrac{c}{d} \cdot \dfrac{a}{b}$

**Associative Property**  $\left(\dfrac{a}{b} \cdot \dfrac{c}{d}\right) \cdot \dfrac{e}{f} = \dfrac{a}{b} \cdot \left(\dfrac{c}{d} \cdot \dfrac{e}{f}\right)$

**Distributive Property of Multiplication over Addition and Subtraction**

$$\dfrac{a}{b} \cdot \left(\dfrac{c}{d} + \dfrac{e}{f}\right) = \dfrac{a}{b} \cdot \dfrac{c}{d} + \dfrac{a}{b} \cdot \dfrac{e}{f} \quad \text{and} \quad \dfrac{a}{b} \cdot \left(\dfrac{c}{d} - \dfrac{e}{f}\right) = \dfrac{a}{b} \cdot \dfrac{c}{d} - \dfrac{a}{b} \cdot \dfrac{e}{f}$$

**Multiplication by 0**  $0 \cdot \dfrac{a}{b} = 0$

**One is a Multiplicative Identity**  $1 \cdot \dfrac{a}{b} = \dfrac{a}{b}$

**Existence of Multiplicative Inverse**  If $\dfrac{a}{b} \neq 0$, then there is a unique rational number, namely, $\dfrac{b}{a}$, for which $\dfrac{a}{b} \cdot \dfrac{b}{a} = 1$.

$0 = \dfrac{0}{1}$

$1 = \dfrac{1}{1}$

---

**EXAMPLE 6.19  Solving an Equation with the Multiplicative Inverse**

Consuela paid \$36 for a pair of shoes at a "one-fourth off" sale. What was the price of the shoes before the sale?

**Solution**  Let $x$ be the original price of the shoes, in dollars. Consuela paid $\dfrac{3}{4}$ of this price, so $\dfrac{3}{4} \cdot x = 36$. To solve this equation for the unknown $x$, multiply both sides by $\dfrac{4}{3}$ to get

$$\dfrac{4}{3} \cdot \dfrac{3}{4} \cdot x = \dfrac{4}{3} \cdot 36.$$

But $\dfrac{4}{3} \cdot \dfrac{3}{4} = 1$ by the multiplicative inverse property, so

$$1 \cdot x = \dfrac{4 \cdot 36}{3} = 48.$$

Since 1 is a multiplicative identity, it follows that $1 \cdot x = x = 48$. Therefore, the original price of the pair of shoes was \$48.

---

In Section 6.3, we discovered that the fractions are closed under division, since any division $\dfrac{a}{b} \div \dfrac{c}{d}$ (where $c \neq 0$) is given by the fraction $\dfrac{a \cdot d}{b \cdot c}$. Thus, since the rational numbers are represented by fractions, the rational numbers are also closed under division. However, division in the rational numbers is neither commutative nor associative, which means that it is important to place terms in their proper order and to use parentheses to avoid ambiguities. For example, $\dfrac{1}{3} \div \dfrac{1}{2} = \dfrac{2}{3}$, but $\dfrac{1}{2} \div \dfrac{1}{3} = \dfrac{3}{2}$, which shows that division is not commutative. Also, since division is not associative, an expression such as 2/3/4 requires us to place parentheses to know if we wish to compute $(2/3)/4 = 2/12 = 1/6$ or $2/(3/4) = 8/3$.

## Properties of the Order Relation

The order relation has many useful properties that are not difficult to prove. The most useful are the **transitive property**, the **addition property**, the **multiplication property**, and the **trichotomy property**.

---

**THEOREM**   *Properties of the Order Relation on the Rational Numbers*

Let $\dfrac{a}{b}, \dfrac{c}{d}$, and $\dfrac{e}{f}$ be rational numbers.

**Transitive Property**

$$\text{If } \frac{a}{b} < \frac{c}{d} \text{ and } \frac{c}{d} < \frac{e}{f}, \text{ then } \frac{a}{b} < \frac{e}{f}.$$

**Addition Property**

$$\text{If } \frac{a}{b} < \frac{c}{d}, \text{ then } \frac{a}{b} + \frac{e}{f} < \frac{c}{d} + \frac{e}{f}.$$

**Multiplication Property**

$$\text{If } \frac{a}{b} < \frac{c}{d} \text{ and } \frac{e}{f} > 0, \text{ then } \frac{a}{b} \cdot \frac{e}{f} < \frac{c}{d} \cdot \frac{e}{f}.$$

$$\text{If } \frac{a}{b} < \frac{c}{d} \text{ and } \frac{e}{f} < 0, \text{ then } \frac{a}{b} \cdot \frac{e}{f} > \frac{c}{d} \cdot \frac{e}{f}.$$

**Trichotomy Property**   Exactly one of the following holds:

$$\frac{a}{b} < \frac{c}{d}, \frac{a}{b} = \frac{c}{d}, \text{ or } \frac{a}{b} > \frac{c}{d}.$$

---

## The Density Property of Rational Numbers

By the definition of inequality,

$$\frac{1}{2} < \frac{2}{3}.$$

Alternatively, using 6 as a common denominator yields

$$\frac{3}{6} < \frac{4}{6},$$

and with 12 as a common denominator, we have

$$\frac{6}{12} < \frac{8}{12}.$$

In the last form, we see that $\dfrac{7}{12}$ is a rational number that is between $\dfrac{6}{12}$ and $\dfrac{8}{12}$. That is,

$$\frac{1}{2} < \frac{7}{12} < \frac{2}{3},$$

as shown in Figure 6.17.

**FIGURE 6.17**

The rational number $\frac{7}{12}$ is

between $\frac{1}{2}$ and $\frac{2}{3}$.

The idea used to find a rational number that is between $\frac{1}{2}$ and $\frac{2}{3}$ can be extended to show that between *any* two rational numbers there is some other rational number. This interesting fact is called the **density property** of the rational numbers. The analogous property does not hold in the integers. For example, there is no integer between 1 and 2.

> **THEOREM**    *The Density Property of Rational Numbers*
>
> Let $\frac{a}{b}$ and $\frac{c}{d}$ be any two rational numbers, with $\frac{a}{b} < \frac{c}{d}$. Then there is a rational number $\frac{e}{f}$ between
>
> $\frac{a}{b}$ and $\frac{c}{d}$; that is, $\frac{a}{b} < \frac{e}{f} < \frac{c}{d}$.

**EXAMPLE 6.20**  **Finding Rational Numbers between Two Rational Numbers**

Find a rational number between the two given fractions.

**(a)** $\frac{2}{3}$ and $\frac{3}{4}$      **(b)** $\frac{5}{12}$ and $\frac{3}{8}$

**Solution**

**(a)** Using $2 \cdot 3 \cdot 4 = 24$ as a common denominator, we have $\frac{2}{3} = \frac{16}{24}$ and $\frac{3}{4} = \frac{18}{24}$. Since

$\frac{16}{24} < \frac{17}{24} < \frac{18}{24}$, it follows that $\frac{17}{24}$ is one answer.

**(b)** If we use 48 as a common denominator, we have $\frac{5}{12} = \frac{20}{48}$ and $\frac{3}{8} = \frac{18}{48}$. Thus, $\frac{19}{48}$ is one

answer. Alternatively, we could use 480 as a common denominator, writing $\frac{5}{12} = \frac{200}{480}$ and

$\frac{3}{8} = \frac{180}{480}$. This makes it clear that $\frac{181}{480}, \frac{182}{480}, \ldots, \frac{199}{480}$ are all rational numbers between $\frac{3}{8}$ and

$\frac{5}{12}$. Using a larger common denominator allows us to identify even more rational numbers

between the two given rationals.

## Computations with Rational Numbers

To work confidently with rational numbers, it is important to develop skills in estimation, rounding, mental arithmetic, efficient pencil-and-paper computation, and the use of the calculator.

## Estimations

In many applications, the exact fractional value can be rounded off to the nearest integer value; if more precision is required, values can be rounded to the nearest half, third, or quarter.

**EXAMPLE 6.21** **Using Rounding of Fractions to Convert a Brownie Recipe**

Krishna's recipe, shown in the box, makes two dozen brownies. He'll need five dozen for the Math Day picnic, so he wants to adjust the quantities of his recipe. How should this be done?

**Solution**

Since Krishna needs $2\frac{1}{2}$ times the number of brownies given by his recipe, he will multiply the quantities by $\frac{5}{2}$. For example, $\frac{5}{2} \times 4 = 10$, so he will use 10 squares of chocolate. Similarly, he will use $\frac{5}{2} \times 2 = 5$ cups of sugar, $2\frac{1}{2}$ teaspoons of vanilla, and $2\frac{1}{2}$ cups of flour. However, $\frac{5}{2} \times \frac{3}{4} = \frac{15}{8} = 1\frac{7}{8}$, so Krishna will use "just short" of 2 cups of butter. Similarly, $\frac{5}{2} \times \frac{5}{4} = \frac{25}{8} = 3\frac{1}{8}$, so Krishna will use about 3 cups of chopped walnuts. Finally, $\frac{5}{2} \times 3 = \frac{15}{2} = 7\frac{1}{2}$, so he will use either 7 or 8 eggs.

> **Brownie Recipe (2 dozen)**
> 4 squares chocolate
> $\frac{3}{4}$ cup butter
> 2 cups sugar
> 3 eggs
> 1 teaspoon vanilla
> 1 cup flour
> $1\frac{1}{4}$ cups chopped walnuts

## Mental Arithmetic

By taking advantage of the properties, formulas, and algorithms associated with the various operations, it is often possible to simplify the computational process. Some useful strategies are demonstrated in the next example.

**EXAMPLE 6.22** **Computational Strategies for Rational Number Arithmetic**

Perform these computations mentally:

(a) $53 - 29\frac{3}{5}$

(b) $\left(2\frac{1}{8} - 4\frac{2}{3}\right) + 7\frac{7}{8}$

(c) $\frac{7}{15} \times 90$

(d) $\frac{3}{8} \times 14 + \frac{3}{4} \times 25$

(e) $4\frac{1}{6} \times 18$

(f) $\frac{5}{8} \times \left(\frac{7}{10} \times \frac{24}{49}\right)$

**Solution**

(a) Adding $\frac{2}{5}$ to each term gives $53 - 29\frac{3}{5} = 53\frac{2}{5} - 30 = 23\frac{2}{5}$.

(b) $\left(2\frac{1}{8} - 4\frac{2}{3}\right) + 7\frac{7}{8} = \left(2 + 7 + \frac{1}{8} + \frac{7}{8}\right) - 4\frac{2}{3}$

$= 10 - 4\frac{2}{3} = 10\frac{1}{3} - 5 = 5\frac{1}{3}$.

(c) $\frac{7}{15} \times 90 = 7 \times \frac{90}{15} = 7 \times 6 = 42$.

(d) $\frac{3}{8} \times 14 + \frac{3}{4} \times 25 = \frac{3}{8} \times 14 + \frac{3}{8} \times 50$

$= \frac{3}{8} \times (14 + 50) = \frac{3}{8} \times 64$

$= 3 \times \frac{64}{8} = 3 \times 8 = 24$.

(e) $4\frac{1}{6} \times 18 = \left(4 + \frac{1}{6}\right) \times 18 = 4 \times 18 + \frac{1}{6} \times 18 = 72 + 3 = 75$.

(f) $\frac{5}{8} \times \left(\frac{7}{10} \times \frac{24}{49}\right) = \frac{5}{10} \times \frac{7}{49} \times \frac{24}{8} = \frac{1}{2} \times \frac{1}{7} \times 3 = \frac{3}{14}$.

**EXAMPLE 6.23** **Designing Wooden Stairs**

A deck is 4′ 2″ above the surface of a patio. How many steps and risers should there be in a stairway that connects the deck to the patio? The decking is $1\frac{1}{2}''$ thick, the stair treads are $1\frac{1}{8}''$ thick, and the steps should each rise the same distance, from one to the next. Calculate the vertical dimension of each riser.

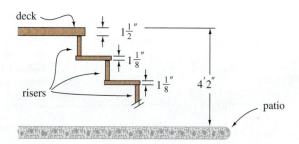

**Solution**  | **Understand the Problem**

We have been given some important dimensions, including the thickness of the treads and the deck. We have *not* been told what dimension to cut the risers. This, we see from the figure, depends on the number of steps we choose, with a lower rise corresponding to a greater number of steps. We must choose a number of steps that feels natural to walk on. We must also be sure that each step rises the same amount.

**Devise a Plan**

If we know what vertical rise from step to step is customary, we can first get a reasonable estimate of the number of steps to use. Once it is agreed what number of steps to incorporate into the design, we can calculate the height of each riser. The riser meeting the deck must be adjusted to account for the decking being thicker than the stair tread.

**Carry Out the Plan**

A brief survey of existing stairways shows that most steps rise 5″ to 7″ from one to the next. Since $4'\,2'' = 50''$, $\frac{50}{5} = 10$, and $\frac{50}{7} = 7\frac{1}{7}$, then 8, or perhaps 9, steps will work well, including the step onto the deck itself. Let's choose 8. Then $\frac{50''}{8} = 6\frac{2''}{8} = 6\frac{1''}{4}$; that is, each combination of riser plus tread is to be $6\frac{1''}{4}$. Since the treads are $1\frac{1}{8}''$ thick, the first seven risers require the boards to be cut $6\frac{1''}{4} - 1\frac{1''}{8} = 5\frac{1''}{8}$ wide. Since the decking is $1\frac{1}{2}''$ thick, the uppermost riser is $6\frac{1''}{4} - 1\frac{1''}{2} = 4\frac{3''}{4}$ wide.

**Look Back**

If we are concerned that the steps will take up too much room on the patio, we might use a steeper, 7-step design. Each riser plus tread would then rise $7\frac{1''}{7}$. Experienced carpenters would think of this value as a "hair" more than $7\frac{1''}{8}$ and cut the lower six risers from a board 8″ wide, for a total rise of $7\frac{1''}{8}$. The last riser is cut to make any final small adjustment.

## Problem Set 6.4

Exercises numbered in red are answered in the back of the text.

### Understanding Concepts

1. Explain what properties of addition of rational numbers can be used to make this sum very easy to compute:

$$\left(3\frac{1}{5} + 2\frac{2}{5}\right) + 8\frac{1}{5}$$

2. What properties can you use to make these computations easy?

   (a) $\dfrac{2}{5} + \left(\dfrac{3}{5} + \dfrac{2}{3}\right)$

   (b) $\dfrac{1}{4} + \left(\dfrac{2}{5} + \dfrac{3}{4}\right)$

   (c) $\dfrac{2}{3} \cdot \dfrac{1}{8} + \dfrac{2}{3} \cdot \dfrac{7}{8}$

   (d) $\dfrac{3}{4} \cdot \left(\dfrac{5}{9} \cdot \dfrac{4}{3}\right)$

3. Find the negatives (i.e., the additive inverses) of the given rational numbers. Show each number and its negative on the number line.

   (a) $\dfrac{4}{5}$     (b) $\dfrac{-3}{2}$     (c) $\dfrac{8}{-3}$     (d) $\dfrac{4}{2}$

4. Compute the given sums of rational numbers. Explain what properties of rational numbers you find useful. Express your answers in simplest form.

   (a) $\dfrac{1}{6} + \dfrac{2}{-3}$

   (b) $\dfrac{-4}{5} + \dfrac{3}{2}$

   (c) $\dfrac{9}{4} + \dfrac{-7}{8}$

   (d) $\dfrac{3}{4} + \dfrac{-5}{8} + \dfrac{7}{-12}$

5. Compute the given differences of rational numbers. Explain what properties you find useful. Express your answers in simplest form.

   (a) $\dfrac{2}{5} - \dfrac{3}{4}$

   (b) $\dfrac{-6}{7} - \dfrac{4}{7}$

   (c) $\dfrac{3}{8} - \dfrac{1}{12}$

   (d) $3\dfrac{2}{5} - \dfrac{7}{10}$

   (e) $2\dfrac{1}{3} - 5\dfrac{3}{4}$

   (f) $-4\dfrac{2}{3} - \dfrac{-19}{6}$

6. Calculate the given products of rational numbers. Explain what properties of rational numbers you find useful. Express your answers in simplest form.

   (a) $\dfrac{3}{5} \cdot \dfrac{7}{8} \cdot \left(\dfrac{5}{3}\right)$

   (b) $\dfrac{-2}{7} \cdot \dfrac{3}{4}$

   (c) $\dfrac{-4}{3} \cdot \dfrac{6}{-16}$

   (d) $3\dfrac{1}{8} \cdot 2\dfrac{1}{5} \cdot (40)$

   (e) $\dfrac{14}{15} \cdot \dfrac{60}{7}$

   (f) $\left(\dfrac{4}{11} \cdot \dfrac{22}{7}\right) \cdot \left(\dfrac{-3}{8}\right)$

7. Find the reciprocals (i.e., the multiplicative inverses) of the given rational numbers. Show each number and its reciprocal on the number line.

   (a) $\dfrac{3}{2}$     (b) $\dfrac{4}{-9}$     (c) $\dfrac{-4}{-11}$

   (d) $5$     (e) $-2$     (f) $2\dfrac{1}{2}$

8. Use the properties of the operations of rational number arithmetic to perform these calculations. Express your answers in simplest form.

   (a) $\dfrac{2}{3} \cdot \dfrac{4}{7} + \dfrac{2}{3} \cdot \dfrac{3}{7}$

   (b) $\dfrac{4}{5} \cdot \dfrac{2}{3} - \dfrac{3}{10} \cdot \dfrac{2}{3}$

   (c) $\dfrac{4}{7} \cdot \dfrac{3}{2} - \dfrac{4}{7} \cdot \dfrac{6}{4}$

   (d) $\left(\dfrac{4}{7} \cdot \dfrac{2}{5}\right) \div \dfrac{2}{7}$

9. Justify each step in the proof of the distributive property of multiplication over addition that follows. In this case, the two addends have a common denominator, but the operation is always possible for any rational addends by using a common denominator for the two fractions.

   $\dfrac{a}{b} \cdot \left(\dfrac{c}{d} + \dfrac{e}{d}\right) = \dfrac{a}{b} \cdot \dfrac{c + e}{d}$     (a) Why?

   $= \dfrac{a \cdot (c + e)}{b \cdot d}$     (b) Why?

   $= \dfrac{a \cdot c + a \cdot e}{b \cdot d}$     (c) Why?

   $= \dfrac{a \cdot c}{b \cdot d} + \dfrac{a \cdot e}{b \cdot d}$     (d) Why?

   $= \dfrac{a}{b} \cdot \dfrac{c}{d} + \dfrac{a}{b} \cdot \dfrac{e}{d}$     (e) Why?

10. If $\dfrac{a}{b} \cdot \dfrac{4}{7} = \dfrac{2}{3}$, what is $\dfrac{a}{b}$? Carefully explain how you obtain your answer. What properties do you use?

11. Solve each equation for the rational number $x$. Show your steps and explain what property justifies each step.

    (a) $4x + 3 = 0$

    (b) $x + \dfrac{3}{4} = \dfrac{7}{8}$

    (c) $\dfrac{2}{3}x + \dfrac{4}{5} = 0$

    (d) $3\left(x + \dfrac{1}{8}\right) = -\dfrac{2}{3}$

12. The Fahrenheit and Celsius temperature scales are related by the formula $F = \dfrac{9}{5}C + 32$. For example, a temperature of 20° Celsius corresponds to 68° Fahrenheit, since

    $$\dfrac{9}{5} \cdot 20 + 32 = 36 + 32 = 68.$$

**(a)** Explain what properties of rational number arithmetic permit you to deduce the equivalent formula $C = \dfrac{5}{9}(F - 32)$ relating the two temperature scales.

**(b)** Fill in the missing entries in this table:

| °C | −40° | | 0° | 10° | 20° | |
|---|---|---|---|---|---|---|
| °F | | −13° | | 68° | 104° | 212° |

**(c)** Electronic signboards frequently give the temperature in both Fahrenheit and Celsius degrees. What is the temperature if both readings are the same (i.e., F = C)? the negative of one another (i.e., F = −C)? Answer the latter question with an exact rational number and the approximate integer that would be seen on the signboard.

**13.** Arrange each group of rational numbers in increasing order. Show, at least approximately, the numbers on the number line.

**(a)** $\dfrac{4}{5}, -\dfrac{1}{5}, \dfrac{2}{5}$  **(b)** $\dfrac{-3}{7}, \dfrac{4}{7}, \dfrac{-5}{7}$

**(c)** $\dfrac{3}{8}, \dfrac{1}{2}, \dfrac{3}{4}$  **(d)** $\dfrac{-7}{12}, \dfrac{-2}{3}, \dfrac{3}{-4}$

**14.** Verify these inequalities:

**(a)** $\dfrac{-4}{5} < \dfrac{-3}{4}$  **(b)** $\dfrac{1}{10} > -\dfrac{1}{4}$  **(c)** $\dfrac{-19}{60} > \dfrac{-1}{3}$

**15.** The properties of the order relation can be used to solve inequalities. For example, if $-\dfrac{2}{3}x + \dfrac{1}{4} < -\dfrac{1}{2}$, then

$$-8x + 3 < -6 \quad \text{(multiply by 12)}$$
$$-8x < -9 \quad \text{(subtract 3 from both sides)}$$
$$8x > 9 \quad \text{(multiply by } -1\text{, which reverses the direction of inequality)}$$
$$x > \dfrac{9}{8} \quad \text{(divide both sides by 8)}$$

That is, all rational numbers $x$ greater than $\dfrac{9}{8}$, and only these, satisfy the given inequality. Solve the inequalities that follow. Show all your steps.

**(a)** $x + \dfrac{2}{3} > -\dfrac{1}{3}$  **(b)** $x - \left(-\dfrac{3}{4}\right) < \dfrac{1}{4}$

**(c)** $\dfrac{3}{4}x < -\dfrac{1}{2}$  **(d)** $-\dfrac{2}{5}x + \dfrac{1}{5} > -1$

**16.** Find a rational number that is between the two given rational numbers.

**(a)** $\dfrac{4}{9}$ and $\dfrac{6}{11}$  **(b)** $\dfrac{1}{9}$ and $\dfrac{1}{10}$

**(c)** $\dfrac{14}{23}$ and $\dfrac{7}{12}$  **(d)** $\dfrac{141}{568}$ and $\dfrac{183}{737}$

**17.** Find three rational numbers between $\dfrac{1}{4}$ and $\dfrac{2}{5}$.

**18.** In the "Hagar the Horrible" cartoon shown early in Section 6.1, Lucky Eddie is counting by eighths to 10 to begin the charge. Propose a method for Lucky Eddie to count with fractions that forever delays the charge. What property of rational numbers did you use?

**19.** For each given rational number, choose the best estimate from the list provided.

**(a)** $\dfrac{104}{391}$ is approximately $\dfrac{1}{3}, \dfrac{1}{4}$, or $\dfrac{1}{2}$.

**(b)** $\dfrac{217}{340}$ is approximately $\dfrac{1}{3}, \dfrac{1}{2}$, or $\dfrac{2}{3}$.

**(c)** $\dfrac{-193}{211}$ is approximately $-\dfrac{1}{2}, -1, 1$, or $\dfrac{1}{2}$.

**(d)** $\dfrac{453}{307}$ is approximately $\dfrac{3}{4}, 1, 1\dfrac{1}{3}$, or $1\dfrac{1}{2}$.

**20.** Use estimations to choose the best approximation of the following expressions:

**(a)** $3\dfrac{19}{40} + 5\dfrac{11}{19}$ is approximately $8, 8\dfrac{1}{2}, 9$, or $9\dfrac{1}{2}$.

**(b)** $2\dfrac{6}{19} + 5\dfrac{1}{3} - 4\dfrac{7}{20}$ is approximately $3, 3\dfrac{1}{3}, 3\dfrac{1}{4}$, or $4$.

**(c)** $17\dfrac{8}{9} \div 5\dfrac{10}{11}$ is approximately $2, 3, 3\dfrac{1}{2}$, or $4$.

**21.** First do the given calculations mentally. Then use words and equations to explain your strategy.

**(a)** $\dfrac{1}{2} + \dfrac{1}{4} + \dfrac{3}{4}$  **(b)** $\dfrac{5}{2} \cdot \left(\dfrac{2}{5} - \dfrac{2}{10}\right)$

**(c)** $\dfrac{3}{4} \cdot \dfrac{12}{15}$  **(d)** $\dfrac{2}{9} \div \dfrac{1}{3}$

**(e)** $2\dfrac{2}{3} \times 15$  **(f)** $3\dfrac{1}{5} - 1\dfrac{1}{4} + 7\dfrac{4}{5}$

**(g)** $6\dfrac{1}{8} - 8\dfrac{1}{4}$  **(h)** $\dfrac{2}{3} \cdot \dfrac{7}{4} - \dfrac{2}{3} \cdot \dfrac{1}{4}$

**22. (a)** Hal owns $3\dfrac{1}{2}$ acres and just purchased an adjacent plot of $\dfrac{3}{4}$ acres. The answer is $4\dfrac{1}{4}$. What is the question?

**(b)** Janet lives $1\dfrac{3}{4}$ miles from school. On the way to school, she stopped to walk the rest of the way with Brian, who lives $\dfrac{1}{2}$ mile from school. The answer is $1\dfrac{1}{4}$. What is the question?

**(c)** A family room is $5\dfrac{1}{2}$ yards wide and 6 yards long. The answer is 33 square yards. What is the question?

**(d)** Clea made $3\dfrac{1}{2}$ gallons of ginger ale, which she intends to bottle in "fifths" (i.e., bottles that contain a fifth of a gallon). The answer is 17 full bottles and $\dfrac{1}{2}$ of another bottle. What is the question?

23. Invent interesting word problems that lead you to the given expression.

   (a) $\dfrac{3}{4} + \dfrac{1}{2}$   (b) $4\dfrac{1}{2} \div \dfrac{3}{4}$   (c) $7\dfrac{2}{3} \times \dfrac{1}{4}$

## Responding to Students

24. When asked to evaluate the sum $\dfrac{1}{3} + \dfrac{3}{5}$, a student claimed that the answer, when simplified, is $\dfrac{1}{2}$. How do you suspect the student arrived at this answer? Describe what you might do to help this student's understanding.

25. When asked to evaluate the difference $\dfrac{9}{11} - \dfrac{3}{22}$, a student gave the answer $\dfrac{165}{242}$. What would you suggest to the student?

## Thinking Critically

In 1858, the Scotsman H. A. Rhind purchased an Egyptian papyrus copied by the scribe A'h-mose (or Ahmes) in 1650 B.C. from an earlier document written in about 1850 B.C.

26. Problem 31 of the Rhind papyrus, if translated literally, reads as follows: "A quantity, its $\dfrac{2}{3}$, its $\dfrac{1}{2}$, its $\dfrac{1}{7}$, its whole, amount to 33."

   That is, in modern notation, $\dfrac{2}{3}x + \dfrac{1}{2}x + \dfrac{1}{7}x + x = 33$. What is the quantity?

27. Solve this problem from the Rhind papyrus: "Divide 100 loaves among five men in such a way that the share received shall be in arithmetic progression and that one-seventh of the sum of the largest three shares shall be equal to the sum of the smallest two." (*Suggestion:* Denote the shares as $s, s + d, s + 2d, s + 3d$, and $s + 4d$.)

28. The ancient Egyptians measured the steepness of a slope by the fraction $\dfrac{x}{y}$, where $x$ is the number of hands of horizontal "run" and $y$ is the number of cubits of vertical "rise." Seven hands form a cubit. Problem 56 of the Rhind papyrus asks for the steepness of the face of a pyramid 250 cubits high and having a square base 360 cubits on a side. The papyrus gives the answer $5\dfrac{1}{25}$. Show why this answer is correct.

29. (a) The Rhind papyrus is about 6 yards long and $\dfrac{1}{3}$ yard wide. What is its area in square yards?

   (b) The Moscow papyrus, another source of mathematics of ancient Egypt, is about the same length as the Rhind papyrus, but has $\dfrac{1}{4}$ the area. What is the width of the Moscow papyrus?

30. **The Law of the Lever.** One of Archimedes' (ca. 225 B.C.) great achievements was the law of the lever. The law can be described in terms of a condition under which weights that are

hung from a beam pivoting at 0 will be in balance. For example, the following two beams are in balance:

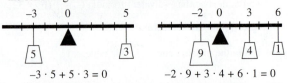

$-3 \cdot 5 + 5 \cdot 3 = 0$          $-2 \cdot 9 + 3 \cdot 4 + 6 \cdot 1 = 0$

In general, if weights $W_1, W_2, \ldots, W_n$ are hung at positions $x_1, x_2, \ldots, x_n$, then the beam is balanced if, and only if,
$$x_1 \cdot W_1 + x_2 \cdot W_2 + \cdots + x_n \cdot W_n = 0.$$

   For each diagram (not drawn to scale) that follows, find the missing weight $W$ or unknown position $x$ that will balance the beam. You can expect rational number answers.

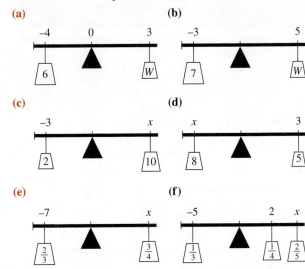

31. (a) Let $x$, $y$, and $z$ be arbitrary rational numbers. Show that the sums of the three entries in every row, column, and diagonal in the Magic Square are the same.

| $x - z$ | $x - y + z$ | $x + y$ |
|---|---|---|
| $x + y + z$ | $x$ | $x - y - z$ |
| $x - y$ | $x + y - z$ | $x + z$ |

   (b) Let $x = \dfrac{1}{2}, y = \dfrac{1}{3}$, and $z = \dfrac{1}{4}$. Find the corresponding Magic Square.

   (c) Here is a partial Magic Square that corresponds to the form shown in part (a). Find $x$, $y$, and $z$, and then fill in the remaining entries of the square.

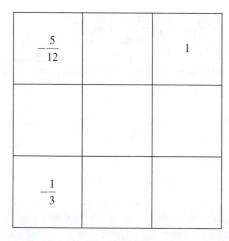

*(Hint: 2x = (x + y) + (x − y).)*

**32.** Three-quarters of the pigeons occupy two-thirds of the pigeon-holes in a pigeon house (one pigeon per hole), and the other one-quarter of the pigeons are flying around. If all the pigeons were in the pigeonholes, just five holes would be empty. How many pigeons and how many holes are there? Give an answer based on the following diagram, adding labels to the diagram and carefully describing your reasoning in words:

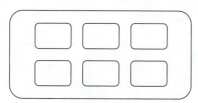

**33.** A bag contains red and blue marbles. One-sixth of the marbles are blue, and there are 20 more red marbles than blue marbles. How many red marbles and how many blue marbles are there?

   **(a)** Give an answer based on the following set diagram, adding labels and describing how to use the diagram to obtain an answer:

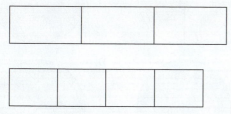

   **(b)** Give an answer based on finding and solving equations.

## Making Connections

**34.** The earth revolves around the sun once in 365 days, 5 hours, 48 minutes, and 46 seconds. Since this *solar* year is more than 365 days long, it is important to have 366-day-long *leap* years to keep the seasons in the same months of the calendar year.

   **(a)** The solar year is very nearly 365 days and 6 hours, or
   $$365\frac{6}{24} = 365\frac{1}{4} \text{ days, long. Explain why having the years}$$
   divisible by 4 as leap years is a good rule to decide when leap years should occur.

   **(b)** Show that a solar year is $365\frac{20{,}926}{24 \cdot 60 \cdot 60}$ days long.

   **(c)** Estimate the value given in part (b) with $365\frac{20{,}952}{24 \cdot 60 \cdot 60}$, and then show that this number can also be written as
   $$365\frac{1}{4} - \frac{1}{100} + \frac{1}{400}.$$

   **(d)** What rule for choosing leap years is suggested by the approximation $365\frac{1}{4} - \frac{1}{100} + \frac{1}{400}$ to the solar year?

   *(Hint: 1900 was not a leap year, but 2000 was a leap year.)*

**35.** Fractions have a prominent place in music, where the time value of a note is given as a fraction of a whole note. The note values and their corresponding fractions are shown in this table:

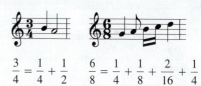

The time signature of the music can be interpreted as a fraction that gives the duration of the measure. Here are two examples:

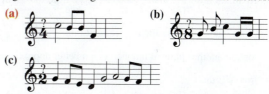

$$\frac{3}{4} = \frac{1}{4} + \frac{1}{2} \qquad \frac{6}{8} = \frac{1}{4} + \frac{1}{8} + \frac{2}{16} + \frac{1}{4}$$

In each measure shown, fill in the upper number of the time signature by adding the note values shown in the measure.

   **(a)**       **(b)**

   **(c)**

**36.** Design a stairway that connects the patio to the deck. (See Example 6.23.)

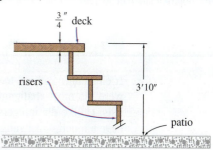

Assume that the tread of each stair is $\frac{1''}{2}$ thick.

**37.** This recipe makes six dozen cookies. Adjust the quantities to have a recipe for four dozen cookies.

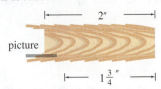

| | |
|---|---|
| 1 cup shortening | $1\frac{1}{2}$ cup sugar |
| 1 tsp baking soda | 3 eggs |
| 3 cups unsifted flour | $\frac{1}{2}$ tsp salt |
| 9 oz mincemeat | |

**38.** Anja has a box of photographic print paper. Each sheet measures 8 by 10 inches. She could easily cut a sheet into four 4-by-5-inch rectangles. However, to save money, she wants to get six prints, all the same size, from each 8-by-10-inch sheet. Describe how she can cut the paper.

**39.** Krystoff has an 8′ piece of picture frame molding, shown in cross section as follows:

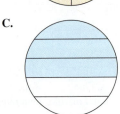

Is this 8′ piece sufficient to frame a 16″-by-20″ picture? Allow for saw cuts and some extra space to ensure that the picture fits easily into the frame.

**40.** Mathematicians from ancient times hoped to find a rational number $\frac{a}{b}$ equal to the square root of 2. A rather inaccurate choice is $\frac{3}{2}$, which is too large, since $\left(\frac{3}{2}\right)^2 = \frac{9}{4} = 2 + \frac{1}{4}$. An improved estimate is obtained by replacing the fraction $\frac{a}{b}$ with the fraction $\frac{a + 2b}{a + b}$. For example, $\frac{3}{2}$ is replaced with $\frac{3 + 2 \cdot 2}{3 + 2} = \frac{7}{5}$. Since $\left(\frac{7}{5}\right)^2 = \frac{49}{25} = 2 - \frac{1}{25}$, $\frac{7}{5}$ is a better approximation to $\sqrt{2}$ than $\frac{3}{2}$, though it is a little too small.

**(a)** Start with $\frac{7}{5}$ and use the replacement rule $\frac{a}{b} \Rightarrow \frac{a + 2b}{a + b}$ to obtain another rational number. Is it a better approximation for $\sqrt{2}$ than $\frac{7}{5}$?

**(b)** Use the replacement rule once more, starting with the rational number obtained in part (a). Do you obtain an even better approximation of $\sqrt{2}$?

**(c)** Modify the replacement rule of part (a) to become $\frac{a}{b} \Rightarrow \frac{a + 3 \cdot b}{a + b}$. Starting with $a = b = 1$, apply the rule twice to yield the rational numbers 2 and $\frac{5}{3}$, since $\frac{1}{1} \Rightarrow \frac{1 + 3 \cdot 1}{1 + 1} = \frac{4}{2} = \frac{2}{1} \Rightarrow \frac{2 + 3 \cdot 1}{1 + 2} = \frac{5}{3}$. Compute the next two numbers given by the replacement rule, always expressing the result in lowest terms.

**(d)** Square the rational numbers found in part (c), expressed as mixed numbers. For example, $\left(\frac{5}{3}\right)^2 = \frac{25}{9} = 2\frac{7}{9}$. What value seems to be estimated with increasing accuracy by the rational numbers that are obtained by the replacement rule in part (c)?

## From State Student Assessments

**41.** (Minnesota, Grade 5)
Which figure shows $\frac{3}{5}$ shaded?

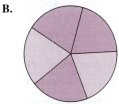

A.          B.

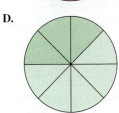

C.          D.

**42.** (Delaware, Grade 5)
John split a cake into four pieces. The pieces are *not* all the same shape. Do you believe the four pieces are the same size? Please explain.

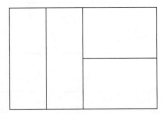

---

## The Chapter in Relation to Future Teachers

If elementary school teachers were asked to list topics in the mathematics curriculum that they felt were the most challenging, both for themselves and their students, fractions will often head their lists. Unlike the integers, which are usually associated with the familiar idea of counting, fractions have a much wider range of roles to play. Here is a list of three roles highlighted in this chapter:

- *Fractions are an extension of measurement.* The unit is subdivided, and the measurement of a quantity (distance, area, time, etc.) is given by counting both the number of whole units and the number of subdivisions of a unit.

- *Fractions represent the rational numbers.* Indeed, any given rational number can be represented by any of infinitely many equivalent fractions. Moreover, the rational numbers *are* a system of numbers. That is, like the integers, the rational numbers can be identified with a point or distance on the number line, their arithmetic operations obey certain algebraic properties, and the result of an arithmetic operation $+$, $\times$, $-$, or $\div$ is computed by an accompanying formula.

- *Fractions are operators.* That is, a fraction is an action as opposed to an object, much in the way a verb is opposed to a noun. For example, at a storewide $\frac{1}{4}$-off sale, we would determine the price of any item by multiplying its current price by $\frac{3}{4}$. Now $\frac{3}{4}$ has become an operator.

These meanings of fractions have been illustrated throughout the chapter by physical models and visualizations: paper folding, colored regions, fraction strips, fraction circles, rectangular arrays, and the like. It is important to understand how the representations and models are of value as instructional aids.

Our work with fractions and rational numbers is not yet complete. In Chapter 7, we will explore which decimal numbers represent rational numbers, see how fractions are related to ratios and proportional reasoning, and learn that a percent is a fraction with 100 as its denominator.

## Chapter 6 Summary

| Section 6.1   The Basic Concepts of Fractions and Rational Numbers | Page Reference |
|---|---|
| **CONCEPTS** | |
| • **Fraction:** A number of the form $\frac{a}{b}$ that conveys a quantity obtained by splitting a unit into $b$ equal parts, and then taking $a$ of those parts. | 275 |
| • **Colored regions, or area model:** The unit is a geometric figure such as a polygon or disc, sectioned into $b$ parts of equal area, of which $a$ parts are colored to represent the fraction $\frac{a}{b}$. | 276 |
| • **Set model:** The unit is a set of $b$ elements, so that a subset of $a$ elements represents the fraction $\frac{a}{b}$. | 277 |
| • **Fraction circle:** The unit is a circle partitioned into $b$ congruent sectors, so that shading $a$ of the sectors gives a representation of the fraction $\frac{a}{b}$. | 277 |
| • **Number line:** Each unit interval of the integer number line is partitioned into $b$ segments of the same length, so that the fraction $\frac{a}{b}$ is the length of a jump by $a$ of these segments. Moreover, the position of the point at the distance of this jump from 0 is also a representation of $\frac{a}{b}$. | 278 |
| • **Strategies for ordering fractions:** Look for a common denominator, or use a benchmark to apply the transitive or residual strategy. | 284 |
| **DEFINITIONS** | |
| • A **fraction** is an ordered pair of integers $a$ and $b$, $b \neq 0$, written $a/b$ or $\frac{a}{b}$. | 276 |
| • In the expression $\frac{a}{b}$, $a$ is **the numerator** and $b$ is the **denominator.** | 276 |
| • **Equivalent fractions** are fractions that express the same quantity. | 278 |

| | |
|---|---|
| • A fraction $\frac{a}{b}$ is in **simplest form** if $a$ and $b$ have no common divisor larger than 1 and $b$ is positive. | 280 |
| • Fractions with the same denominator are said to have a **common denominator.** | 281 |
| • The **least common denominator** is the least common multiple of two denominators. | 282 |
| • A **rational number** is any number that can be represented by a fraction or any of its equivalent fractions. | 283 |

**THEOREM**

| | |
|---|---|
| • **Cross-product property:** The fractions $\frac{a}{b}$ and $\frac{c}{d}$ are equivalent if, and only if, $ad = bc$. | 279 |

**PROPERTY**

| | |
|---|---|
| • **Fundamental law of fractions:** Let $\frac{a}{b}$ be a fraction. Then $\frac{a}{b} = \frac{an}{bn}$, for any integer $n \neq 0$. | 279 |

**NOTATION**

| | |
|---|---|
| • **Set of rational numbers, $Q$:** The set of all numbers that can be expressed as the fraction $a/b$ where $a$ and $b$ are integers and $b$ is not zero. | 283 |

| Section 6.2   Addition and Subtraction of Fractions | Page Reference |
|---|---|

**DEFINITIONS**

| | |
|---|---|
| • **Addition of fractions:** For fractions $\frac{a}{b}$ and $\frac{c}{d}$ with the common denominator $b$, let $\frac{a}{b} + \frac{c}{b} = \frac{a+c}{b}$. For fractions $\frac{a}{b}$ and $\frac{c}{d}$ with unlike denominators $b$ and $d$, use a common denominator such as $bd$ so that $\frac{a}{b} + \frac{c}{d} = \frac{ad}{bd} + \frac{bc}{bd} = \frac{ad+bc}{bd}$. | 292 |
| • **Subtraction of fractions, $\frac{a}{b} - \frac{c}{d}$:** Let $\frac{a}{b}$ and $\frac{c}{d}$ be fractions. Then $\frac{a}{b} - \frac{c}{d} = \frac{e}{f}$ if, and only if, $\frac{a}{b} = \frac{c}{d} + \frac{e}{f}$. | 297 |
| • A **mixed number** is the sum of a natural number and a positive fraction. For example, $2\frac{3}{4}$ is a mixed number. | 295 |
| • A **proper fraction** is a fraction $a/b$ for which $0 \leq |a| < b$. | 295 |

| Section 6.3   Multiplication and Division of Fractions | Page Reference |
|---|---|

**CONCEPTS**

| | |
|---|---|
| • **Multiplication:** Extending the area model of multiplication motivates the definition of multiplication of fractions: $\frac{a}{b} \cdot \frac{c}{d} = \frac{ac}{bd}$. | 301, 302, 303 |
| • **Division:** Given fractions $\frac{a}{b}$ and $\frac{c}{d} \neq 0$, the division $\frac{a}{b} \div \frac{c}{d}$ represents: | 307, 308 |
|    (a) the fractional number of times $\frac{c}{d}$ can be removed from $\frac{a}{b}$ (repeated subtraction, or grouping, model) | |

**(b)** the fractional amount per unit when the quantity $\frac{a}{b}$ is partitioned into $\frac{c}{d}$ parts (sharing, or partitive, model)

**(c)** the missing fractional factor $x = \frac{m}{n}$ for which $\frac{a}{b} = x \cdot \frac{c}{d}$ (missing factor model)

## DEFINITIONS

| | |
|---|---|
| • **Multiplication of fractions,** $\frac{a}{b} \times \frac{c}{d}$: Let $\frac{a}{b}$ and $\frac{c}{d}$ be fractions. Then their product is given by $\frac{a}{b} \cdot \frac{c}{d} = \frac{ac}{bd}$. | 305 |
| • **Division of fractions,** $\frac{a}{b} \div \frac{c}{d}$: Let $\frac{a}{b}$ and $\frac{c}{d}$ be fractions, where $\frac{c}{d}$ is not zero. Then $\frac{a}{b} \div \frac{c}{d} = \frac{m}{n}$ if and only if, $\frac{a}{b} = \frac{m}{n} \cdot \frac{c}{d}$. | 308 |
| • The **reciprocal,** or **multiplication inverse,** of a nonzero fraction $\frac{c}{d}$ is the fraction $\frac{d}{c}$, so that $\frac{c}{d} \cdot \frac{d}{c} = 1$. | 311 |

## FORMULA

| | |
|---|---|
| • **Invert-and-multiply algorithm:** The division $\frac{a}{b} \div \frac{c}{d}$ is equivalent to the product $\frac{a}{b} \cdot \frac{d}{c}$ obtained by multiplying $\frac{a}{b}$ by the reciprocal of the divisor $\frac{c}{d}$. That is, $\frac{a}{b} \div \frac{c}{d} = \frac{a}{b} \cdot \frac{d}{c}$. | 310 |

| **Section 6.4   The Rational Number System** | **Page Reference** |
|---|---|

### CONCEPT

| | |
|---|---|
| • **Rational numbers:** The system of numbers represented by fractions, so that the arithmetic operations (addition, subtraction, multiplication, division), properties, and order relations (less than and greater than) correspond to the same operations, properties, and order relations for fractions. Each rational number can be represented by any choice of the equivalent fractions corresponding to the rational numbers. | 318 |

### DEFINITION

| | |
|---|---|
| • The **negative,** or **additive inverse,** of rational number $\frac{a}{b}$ is written $-\frac{a}{b}$ and is the rational number $\frac{(-a)}{b}$. | 319 |

### THEOREMS

| | |
|---|---|
| • **Properties of addition of rational numbers:** Given three rational numbers $r$, $s$, and $t$, Then addition is closed ($r + s$ is a rational number), commutative ($rs = sr$), associative ($r + (s + t) = (r + s) + t$), 0 is the additive identity ($r + 0 = 0 + r = r$), and $-r$ is the additive inverse $\left( r + (-r) = (-r) + r = 0, \text{ where } -r = \frac{-a}{b} \text{ if } r = \frac{a}{b} \right)$. | 319 |
| • **Subtraction is equivalent to the addition of the negative:** $\frac{a}{b} - \frac{c}{d} = \frac{a}{b} + \left( -\frac{c}{d} \right) = \frac{ad - bc}{bd}$. | 320 |

- **Properties of multiplication of rational numbers:** Given three rational numbers $r$, $s$, and $t$, multiplication is closed ($r \cdot s$ is a rational number), commutative ($r \cdot s = s \cdot r$), associative ($r \cdot (s \cdot t) = (r \cdot s) \cdot t$), distributive over addition ($r \cdot (s + t) = r \cdot s + r \cdot t$), has the multiplicative identity 1 ($r \cdot 1 = 1 \cdot r = r$), and has the multiplication by 0 property ($r \cdot 0 = 0 \cdot r = 0$). Moreover, each nonzero rational number $r = \dfrac{a}{b} \neq 0$ has a the multiplicative inverse given by its reciprocal $\dfrac{b}{a}$, so that $\dfrac{a}{b} \cdot \dfrac{b}{a} = 1$.    321

- **Properties of the order relation on rational numbers:** Given three rational numbers $r$, $s$, and $t$, the order relation $<$ is transitive (if $r < s$ and $s < t$, then $r < t$), has the addition property (if $r < s$, then $r + t < s + t$), has the multiplication by a positive property (if $r < s$ and $t > 0$, then $r \cdot t < s \cdot t$), and satisfies the law of trichotomy (exactly one of the relations $r < s$, $r = s$, $r > s$ holds).    322

- **Density property:** Given two different rational numbers $r$, $s$, with $r < s$, there is a rational number $t$ between $r$ and $s$. Indeed, there are infinitely many rational numbers $t$ for which $r < t < r$.    322

## Chapter Review Exercises

### Section 6.1

1. What fraction is represented by the darker blue shading in each of the colored-region models shown? In (a) and (d), the unit is the region inside one circle. In (b) and (c), the units are the regions inside the hexagon and square, respectively.

   (a)     (b)

   (c)     (d)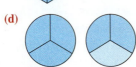

2. Label the points on the number line that correspond to these rational numbers:

   (a) $\dfrac{3}{4}$    (b) $\dfrac{12}{8}$    (c) $1$    (d) $2\dfrac{3}{8}$

3. Express each rational number by a fraction in simplest form.

   (a) $\dfrac{27}{81}$    (b) $\dfrac{100}{825}$

   (c) $\dfrac{378}{72}$    (d) $\dfrac{3^5 \cdot 7^2 \cdot 11^3}{3^2 \cdot 7^3 \cdot 11^2}$

4. Order these fractions from smallest to largest:

   $$\frac{1}{2}, \frac{13}{27}, \frac{25}{49}, \frac{13}{30}, \frac{26}{49}$$

5. Find the least common denominator of each set of fractions.

   (a) $\dfrac{4}{9}, \dfrac{5}{12}$    (b) $\dfrac{7}{18}, \dfrac{5}{6}, \dfrac{1}{3}$

### Section 6.2

6. Illustrate $\dfrac{3}{4} + \dfrac{7}{8}$ on the number line.

7. Illustrate $\dfrac{3}{4} - \dfrac{1}{3}$ with fraction strips.

8. Compute these sums and differences:

   (a) $\dfrac{3}{8} + \dfrac{1}{4}$    (b) $\dfrac{2}{9} + \dfrac{-5}{12}$

   (c) $\dfrac{4}{5} - \dfrac{2}{3}$    (d) $5\dfrac{1}{4} - 1\dfrac{5}{6}$

### Section 6.3

9. Illustrate these products by labeling and coloring appropriate rectangular regions:

   (a) $3 \times \dfrac{1}{3}$    (b) $\dfrac{2}{3} \times 4$    (c) $\dfrac{5}{6} \times \dfrac{3}{2}$

10. Gina, Hank, and Igor want to share $2\dfrac{1}{4}$ pizzas equally. Draw an appropriate diagram to show how much pizza each should be given. What conceptual model of division should you use?

11. Each quart of soup calls for $\dfrac{2}{3}$ of a cup of pinto beans. How many quarts of soup can be made with 3 cups of beans? Draw an appropriate diagram to find your answer. What conceptual model of division are you using?

12. On a map, it is $7\dfrac{1''}{8}$ from Arlington to Banks. If the scale of the map is $1\dfrac{1''}{4}$ per mile, how far is it between the two towns?

## Section 6.4

**13.** Perform these calculations, expressing your answers in simplest form:

(a) $\dfrac{-3}{4} + \dfrac{5}{8}$

(b) $\dfrac{4}{5} - \dfrac{-7}{10}$

(c) $\left(\dfrac{3}{8} \cdot \dfrac{-4}{27}\right) \div \dfrac{1}{9}$

(d) $\dfrac{2}{5} \cdot \left(\dfrac{3}{4} - \dfrac{5}{2}\right)$

**14.** Solve each equatio Give the rational number $x$ as a fraction in simplest form.

(a) $3x + 5 = 11$

(b) $x + \dfrac{2}{3} = \dfrac{1}{2}$

(c) $\dfrac{3}{5}x + \dfrac{1}{2} = \dfrac{2}{3}$

(d) $-\dfrac{4}{3}x + 1 = \dfrac{1}{4}$

**15.** Find two rational numbers between $\dfrac{5}{6}$ and $\dfrac{10}{11}$.

**16.** Do the given calculations mentally. Explain your method.

(a) $1\dfrac{1}{3} + 2\dfrac{5}{12} + \dfrac{1}{4}$

(b) $\dfrac{6}{7} \cdot \dfrac{28}{3} \cdot \dfrac{5}{8}$

(c) $\dfrac{36}{5} \div \dfrac{9}{25}$

## Chapter Test

**1.** Carefully explain why $\dfrac{a + b}{b} = \dfrac{c + d}{d}$ if, and only if,

$\dfrac{a}{b} = \dfrac{c}{d}$.

**2.** Perform these calculations:

(a) $\dfrac{1}{3} + \dfrac{5}{8} - \dfrac{5}{6}$

(b) $\left(\dfrac{2}{3} - \dfrac{5}{4}\right) \div \dfrac{3}{4}$

(c) $\dfrac{4}{7} \cdot \left(\dfrac{35}{4} + \dfrac{-42}{12}\right)$

(d) $\dfrac{123}{369} \div \dfrac{1}{3}$

**3.** Describe how the following calculations can be performed efficiently with "mental math":

(a) $\dfrac{19}{111} \cdot \left(\dfrac{2}{3} + \dfrac{-4}{6}\right)$

(b) $\dfrac{5}{6} \cdot \dfrac{36}{15}$

(c) $\dfrac{5}{8} \cdot \left(\dfrac{9}{5} - \dfrac{1}{5}\right)$

(d) $\dfrac{2}{3} \cdot \dfrac{3}{4} \cdot \dfrac{4}{5} \cdot \dfrac{5}{6}$

**4.** An acre is $\dfrac{1}{640}$ of a square mile.

(a) How many acres are in a rectangular plot of ground $\dfrac{1}{8}$ mile wide by $\dfrac{1}{2}$ mile long?

(b) A rectangular piece of property contains 80 acres and is $\dfrac{1}{2}$ mile long. What is the width of the property?

**5.** (a) What is the density property of the rational numbers?

(b) Find a rational number between $\dfrac{3}{5}$ and $\dfrac{2}{3}$.

**6.** Illustrate $\dfrac{2}{3}$

(a) on the number line,

(b) with a fraction strip,

(c) with a colored-region model, and

(d) with the set model.

**7.** What is the best approximate answer listed for each of these problems?

(a) $2\dfrac{1}{48} + 3\dfrac{1}{99} + 6\dfrac{13}{25}$ is approximately 11, $11\dfrac{1}{2}$, 12,

or $12\dfrac{1}{4}$.

(b) $8 \cdot \left(2\dfrac{1}{2} + 3\dfrac{7}{15}\right)$ is approximately 40, 44, 48, or 56.

(c) $11\dfrac{9}{10} \div \dfrac{21}{40}$ is approximately 20, 23, 26, or 30.

**8.** (a) Define *multiplicative inverse.*

(b) Find the multiplicative inverses of these rational numbers:

$\dfrac{3}{2}, \dfrac{-4}{5}$, and $-5$.

**9.** Give three different fractions, each equivalent to $-\dfrac{3}{4}$.

**10.** Solve the given equations and inequalities for all possible rational numbers $x$. Show all of your steps.

(a) $2x + 3 > 0$

(b) $\dfrac{3}{4}x + \dfrac{1}{2} = \dfrac{1}{3}$

(c) $\dfrac{5}{4}x > -\dfrac{1}{3}$

(d) $\dfrac{1}{2} < 4x + \dfrac{5}{6}$

**11.** (a) Define division in the rational number system.

(b) Justify the invert-and-multiply algorithm; that is, prove that $\dfrac{a}{b} \div \dfrac{c}{d} = \dfrac{a}{b} \cdot \dfrac{d}{c}$, where $c \neq 0$.

**12.** (a) Invent a realistic problem whose solution requires the calculation $\dfrac{4}{5} \cdot \dfrac{2}{3}$.

(b) Make up a realistic problem that leads to $\dfrac{3}{8} \div \dfrac{3}{10}$.

**13.** (a) Define *additive inverse.*

(b) Find the additive inverses of the following fractions:

$\dfrac{3}{4}, \dfrac{-7}{4}$, and $\dfrac{8}{-2}$.

**14.** Order these rational numbers from least to greatest:

$$\dfrac{16}{5}, \dfrac{2}{3}, -1\dfrac{1}{2}, 0, \dfrac{5}{8}, 3, -3$$

# Decimals, Real Numbers, and Proportional Reasoning

**7.1** Decimals and Real Numbers

**7.2** Computations with Decimals

**7.3** Proportional Reasoning

**7.4** Percent

## Hands On

### Triangles and Squares

**Materials Needed**

One 3″ × 5″ card, scissors, a sharp pencil, and one sheet of plain white paper.

**Directions**

**Step 1.** Cut a triangle with unequal sides off the corner of the card and denote the lengths of the three sides by $a$, $b$, and $c$, as shown.

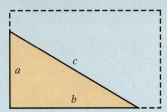

**Step 2.** With the lettering on the triangle always facing up, carefully trace around the triangle four times to form a big square with another square in the middle, as shown here:

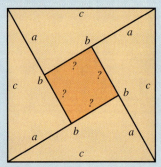

**Step 3.** Determine the length of the side of the small square in the center, and then find the area of the square. Remember that, using the distributive property of multiplication over subtraction and the commutative property, we have

$$(x - y)(x - y) = (x - y)x - (x - y)y$$
$$= x^2 - yx - xy + y^2$$
$$= x^2 - 2xy + y^2.$$

**Step 4.** The area of the large square is clearly 4 times the area of the triangle plus the area of the small inner square; it is also equal to $c^2$. Express these two ways of finding the area of the large square by an equation, and simplify it as much as possible.

**Step 5.** Relate the equation in step 4 to the diagram shown here:

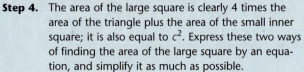

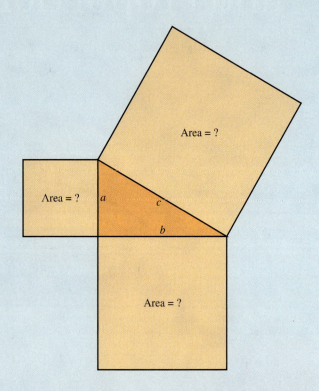

What does the equation reveal about triangles with one square corner (that is, one right angle)? Explain briefly.

**Step 6.** If $c$ is the length of the diagonal of a square one unit on a side, then the formula of step 4 gives $c^2 = 2$. Remarkably, as we will see later, this number $c$ is not a rational number.

---

**CHAPTER PREVIEW**

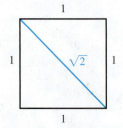

Previous chapters have introduced the natural numbers $N$, the whole numbers $W$, the integers $I$, and the rational numbers $Q$. This chapter introduces yet one more number system: the real numbers $R$. The set of real numbers is an extension of the previous number systems. We may visualize the relationship among all these systems by the Venn diagram depicted in Figure 7.1, which shows that $N \subset W \subset I \subset Q \subset R$.

In Section 1 of this chapter, the real numbers are defined as those numbers which can be represented as decimal numbers. Such a definition gives a new representation of a rational number not only as a fraction, but as a decimal number that either terminates or has an infinitely repeated string of decimal digits. What is new are those real numbers represented by a decimal number with infinitely many digits that do not have a repeating pattern. For example, $\sqrt{2} = 1.41421356\ldots$ is the irrational real number that gives the length of the diagonal of a square with sides of length 1; the list of decimal digits following the decimal point is never ending and has no repeating pattern. In Section 2, we see that we can adapt previously learned computational algorithms to perform arithmetic operations with decimal numbers. Section 3 explores proportional reasoning, which is applied in the concluding Section 4 to develop the important concept of percent.

**FIGURE 7.1**

Venn diagram for the natural numbers $N$, the whole numbers $W$, the integers $I$, the rational numbers $Q$, and the real numbers $R$, showing that $N \subset W \subset I \subset Q \subset R$.

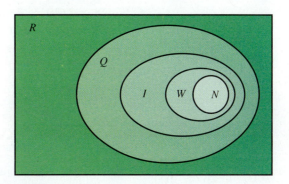

**KEY IDEAS**

- Decimal numbers, and their representations with manipulatives such as base-ten blocks and dollars–dimes–pennies
- Decimals written in expanded form
- Terminating and periodic decimals, and their conversion to a representation by a fraction, thus showing that such decimals represent rational numbers
- The order relation on decimals
- The irrationality of $\sqrt{2}$; that is, if $c^2 = 2$, then $c$ cannot be represented as a fraction $\dfrac{a}{b}$ for any natural numbers $a$ and $b$
- Computing with decimals: rounding, addition, subtraction, multiplication, and division
- Ratios, proportions, and applications of proportional reasoning
- Percent and its applications, including the solution of the three basic types of percent problems

**7.1**

# Decimals and Real Numbers

The term *decimal system* (from the Latin *decimus,* meaning "tenth") refers generally to the Indo-Arabic system of numeration in common use today. However, more colloquially, people often refer to expressions like 0.235 or 2.7142 as **decimals,** as opposed to 24, 98, 0, or 2478, which they more often speak of as whole numbers or integers. In fact, both are part of the same system of numbers represented by decimals.

The following definition provides a general description of a decimal:

**DEFINITION** *Decimal*

A **decimal** is a base-ten positional numeral, either positive or negative, in which there are finitely many digits extending to the left of a point called the **decimal point** that represent units, tens, hundreds, and so on, and a finite or infinite sequence of digits extending to the right of the decimal point that represent tenths, hundredths, thousandths, and so on.

Clearly, decimals include the integers, such as $35 = 35.0$ and $-56 = -56.0$, and fractions, such as $\dfrac{56{,}789}{1000} = 56.789$. We shall see later that every rational number can be expressed as a decimal. However, we will also discover there are decimals that represent a new type of number called an *irrational* number that is not found in the set of rational numbers.

Just as the **expanded form** of 2478 is

$$2478 = 2 \cdot 10^3 + 4 \cdot 10^2 + 7 \cdot 10^1 + 8 \cdot 10^0$$
$$= 2000 + 400 + 70 + 8,$$

the expanded form of 0.235 is

$$0.235 = 2 \cdot \frac{1}{10^1} + 3 \cdot \frac{1}{10^2} + 5 \cdot \frac{1}{10^3}$$
$$= \frac{2}{10} + \frac{3}{100} + \frac{5}{1000}.$$

Since $0.235 = \dfrac{235}{1000}$, the decimal is expressed orally as "two hundred thirty-five thousandths."

The expanded form of 23.47 is

$$23.47 = 2 \cdot 10^1 + 3 \cdot 10^0 + 4 \cdot \frac{1}{10^1} + 7 \cdot \frac{1}{10^2}$$
$$= 20 + 3 + \frac{4}{10} + \frac{7}{100}.$$

That is, $23.47 = 23 + \dfrac{47}{100}$, so we say it is "twenty-three and forty-seven hundredths." The word *and* indicates the position of the decimal point.

## Representations of Decimals

For beginning grade school students, it is helpful to introduce the study of decimals by considering concrete physical manipulative devices and pictorial representations. We discuss three such representations here.

### Unit Squares, Strips, and Small Squares   As in the introduction to the fractions in Chapter 6, if a square represents one unit, or 1, then a strip represents one-tenth, or $\dfrac{1}{10}$, and a small square represents one one-hundredth, or $\dfrac{1}{100}$, as shown in Figure 7.2.

$1$        $\dfrac{1}{10}$        $\dfrac{1}{100}$

Thus, a display of 3 unit squares, 2 strips, and 5 small squares, as shown in Figure 7.3, represents

$3 \cdot 1 + 2 \cdot \dfrac{1}{10} + 5 \cdot \dfrac{1}{100} = 3 + \dfrac{2}{10} + \dfrac{5}{100} = \dfrac{325}{100}$, which we write using the shorthand notation

3.25. Conversely, the expanded notation for 3.25 is $3 + \dfrac{2}{10} + \dfrac{5}{100}$. The decimal point is used to separate the integer part of the numeral from the fractional part.

**FIGURE 7.3**
Representation of 3.25 by
using unit squares, strips,
and small squares

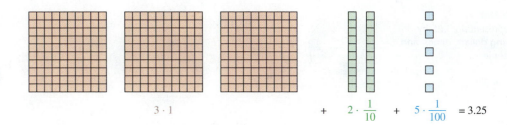

$$3 \cdot 1 \qquad\qquad + \quad 2 \cdot \frac{1}{10} \quad + \quad 5 \cdot \frac{1}{100} \quad = 3.25$$

**Base-Ten Blocks**   Consider the base-ten blocks depicted in Figure 7.4. Suppose the block is chosen as the unit. Then, since 10 flats are equivalent to a block, a flat represents $\frac{1}{10}$.

**FIGURE 7.4**
Base-ten blocks

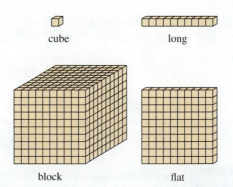

cube      long

block      flat

Similarly, 10 longs are equivalent to a flat, and $10 \cdot 10 = 100$ longs are equivalent to a block. Thus, a long represents $\frac{1}{100}$. Finally, since there are $10 \cdot 10 \cdot 10 = 1000$ cubes in a unit block, a cube represents $\frac{1}{1000}$. With all this in mind, a display of 2 blocks, 1 flat, 3 longs, and 2 cubes, as shown in Figure 7.5, represents $2 \cdot 1 + 1 \cdot \frac{1}{10} + 3 \cdot \frac{1}{100} + 2 \cdot \frac{1}{1000} = 2 + \frac{1}{10} + \frac{3}{100} + \frac{2}{1000} = \frac{2132}{1000}$, which we write using the shorthand notation 2.132. Conversely, the expanded notation for 2.132 is $2 + \frac{1}{10} + \frac{3}{100} + \frac{2}{1000}$.

**FIGURE 7.5**
Representing 2.132 using
base-ten blocks

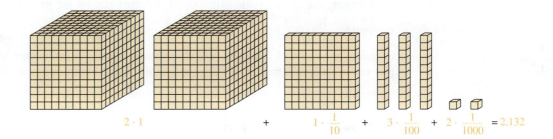

$$2 \cdot 1 \qquad\qquad + \qquad 1 \cdot \frac{1}{10} \quad + \quad 3 \cdot \frac{1}{100} \quad + \quad 2 \cdot \frac{1}{1000} \quad = 2.132$$

**Dollars, Dimes, and Pennies**   A particularly apt manipulative, already familiar to children, is money. Since 10 dimes are worth 1 dollar and 100 pennies are worth 1 dollar, a dollar represents 1, a dime represents $\frac{1}{10}$, and a penny represents $\frac{1}{100}$. Thus, 3.25 would be represented as in Figure 7.6. Such a representation is particularly useful because students are already familiar with the fact that this set of coins is worth 3 dollars and 25 cents, as well as the fact that the value of the coins is written $3.25, thus making the understanding of the expanded notation for 3.25 quite natural.

**FIGURE 7.6**
Representing 3.25 by
using dollars, dimes, and
pennies

$$3 \qquad + \qquad \frac{2}{10} \qquad + \qquad \frac{5}{100} \qquad = \qquad 3.25$$

## EXAMPLE 7.1    Using Money to Represent Decimals

How would you use money to explain the decimal 23.75 to elementary school students?

**Solution**    Use 2 ten-dollar bills, 3 dollars, 7 dimes, and 5 pennies. The students will readily see that this collection of bills and coins is worth $23.75, making it easy to explain the expanded notation

$$23.75 = 2 \cdot 10 + 3 \cdot 1 + 7 \cdot \frac{1}{10} + 5 \cdot \frac{1}{100},$$

since a dime is one-tenth of a dollar and a penny is one one-hundredth of a dollar.

---

**FROM The NCTM Principles and Standards**

When students leave grade 5, they should be able to solve problems involving whole-number computation and should recognize that each operation will help them solve many different types of problems. They should be able to solve many problems mentally, to estimate a reasonable result for a problem, to efficiently recall or derive the basic number combinations for each operation, and to compute fluently with multi-digit whole numbers. They should understand the equivalence of fractions, decimals, and percents and the information each type of representation conveys. With these understandings and skills, they should be able to develop strategies for computing with familiar fractions and decimals.

SOURCE: *Principles and Standards for School Mathematics* by NCTM, *page 149. Copyright © 2000 by the National Council of Teachers of Mathematics. Reproduced with permission of the National Council of Teachers of Mathematics via Copyright Clearance Center. NCTM does not endorse the content or validity of these alignments.*

---

By using the representations discussed, students can be led to understand that the shorthand notation for $\frac{1}{10}$ is 0.1, for $\frac{1}{100}$ is 0.01, for $\frac{1}{1000}$ is 0.001, for $\frac{2}{10}$ is 0.2, for $\frac{3}{100}$ is 0.03, and so on, and to understand that each digit of a decimal numeral contributes an amount to the number being represented that depends both on the digit and on its position in the numeral, as shown in Table 7.1.

**TABLE 7.1    POSITIONAL VALUES IN THE DECIMAL SYSTEM**

| | | | | Position Names | | | | |
|---|---|---|---|---|---|---|---|---|
| Form | . . . | Hundreds | Tens | Units | Tenths | Hundredths | Thousandths | Ten-Thousandths | . . . |
| Decimal Form | . . . | 100 | 10 | 1 | 0.1 | 0.01 | 0.001 | 0.0001 | . . . |
| Fractional Form | . . . | 100 | 10 | 1 | $\frac{1}{10}$ | $\frac{1}{100}$ | $\frac{1}{1000}$ | $\frac{1}{10,000}$ | . . . |
| Power of 10 | . . . | $10^2$ | $10^1$ | $10^0$ | $10^{-1}$ | $10^{-2}$ | $10^{-3}$ | $10^{-4}$ | . . . |

The positional values in decimal notation can also be written in exponential form by using both positive and negative powers of 10. As shown in the bottom row of Table 7.1,

$$\ldots, 10^2 = 100, 10^1 = 10, 10^0 = 1, 10^{-1} = \frac{1}{10}, 10^{-2} = \frac{1}{100}, 10^{-3} = \frac{1}{1000}, 10^{-4} = \frac{1}{10,000}, \ldots.$$

For example, in **expanded exponential form,** we have:

$$0.235 = 0 + 2 \cdot \frac{1}{10^1} + 3 \cdot \frac{1}{10^2} + 5 \cdot \frac{1}{10^3}$$
$$= 2 \cdot 10^{-1} + 3 \cdot 10^{-2} + 5 \cdot 10^{-3};$$
$$23.47 = 2 \cdot 10^1 + 3 \cdot 10^0 + 4 \cdot \frac{1}{10^1} + 7 \cdot \frac{1}{10^2}$$
$$= 2 \cdot 10^1 + 3 \cdot 10^0 + 4 \cdot 10^{-1} + 7 \cdot 10^{-2}.$$

In this form, the pattern of decreasing exponents is both clear and neat.

**EXAMPLE  7.2  Writing Decimals in Expanded Exponential Form**

Write each of these decimals in expanded exponential form:

**(a)** 234.72          **(b)** 30.0012

**Solution**

**(a)** $234.72 = 2 \cdot 10^2 + 3 \cdot 10^1 + 4 \cdot 10^0 + 7 \cdot 10^{-1} + 2 \cdot 10^{-2}$
**(b)** $30.0012 = 3 \cdot 10^1 + 0 \cdot 10^0 + 0 \cdot 10^{-1} + 0 \cdot 10^{-2} + 1 \cdot 10^{-3} + 2 \cdot 10^{-4}$

## Multiplying and Dividing Decimals by Powers of 10

There is an emphasis in elementary mathematics textbooks on what happens notationally (to the decimal point) when a number is multiplied by a power of 10. Consider the decimal

$$25.723 = 2 \cdot 10^1 + 5 \cdot 10^0 + 7 \cdot 10^{-1} + 2 \cdot 10^{-2} + 3 \cdot 10^{-3}.$$

If we multiply by $10^2$ then, using the distributive property, we obtain

$$(10^2)(25.723) = (10^2)(2 \cdot 10^1 + 5 \cdot 10^0 + 7 \cdot 10^{-1} + 2 \cdot 10^{-2} + 3 \cdot 10^{-3})$$
$$= 2 \cdot 10^{2+1} + 5 \cdot 10^{2+0} + 7 \cdot 10^{2+(-1)} + 2 \cdot 10^{2+(-2)} + 3 \cdot 10^{2+(-3)}$$
$$= 2 \cdot 10^3 + 5 \cdot 10^2 + 7 \cdot 10^1 + 2 \cdot 10^0 + 3 \cdot 10^{-1}$$
$$= 2572.3,$$

and the notational effect is to move the decimal point two places to the right. Note that 2 is both the exponent of the power of 10 by which we are multiplying and the number of zeros in 100.

$10^2 = 100$

The result is analogous if we *divide* 25.723 by $10^2$, except that the notational effect is to move the decimal point two places *to the left*. To see this, recall that we can divide by multiplying by the multiplicative inverse. Thus,

$$(25.723) \div 10^2 = (25.723) \cdot (1/10^2)$$
$$= (25.723) \cdot 10^{-2}$$
$$= (2 \cdot 10^1 + 5 \cdot 10^0 + 7 \cdot 10^{-1} + 2 \cdot 10^{-2} + 3 \cdot 10^{-3}) \cdot 10^{-2}$$
$$= 2 \cdot 10^{1+(-2)} + 5 \cdot 10^{0+(-2)} + 7 \cdot 10^{(-1)+(-2)} + 2 \cdot 10^{(-2)+(-2)}$$
$$\quad + 3 \cdot 10^{(-3)+(-2)}$$
$$= 2 \cdot 10^{-1} + 5 \cdot 10^{-2} + 7 \cdot 10^{-3} + 2 \cdot 10^{-4} + 3 \cdot 10^{-5}$$
$$= 0.25723.$$

$10^{-2} = \dfrac{1}{10^2}$

These results are typical of the general case, which we state here as a theorem:

> **THEOREM** *Multiplying and Dividing Decimals by Powers of 10*
>
> If $r$ is a positive integer, the notational effect of multiplying a decimal by $10^r$ is to move the decimal point $r$ places to the right. The notational effect of dividing a decimal by $10^r$ (that is, multiplying by $10^{-r}$) is to move the decimal point $r$ places to the left.

**EXAMPLE 7.3** **Multiplying and Dividing Decimals by Powers of 10**

Compute each of the following:

    **(a)** $(10^3)(253.26)$        **(b)** $(253.26) \div 10^3$
    **(c)** $(100)(34.764)$       **(d)** $(34.764) \div 10{,}000$

**Solution**

The preceding theorem gives the desired results:

    **(a)** $(10^3)(253.26) = 253{,}260$
    **(b)** $(253.26) \div 10^3 = 0.25326$
    **(c)** $(100)(34.764) = (10^2)(34.764) = 3476.4$
    **(d)** $(34.764) \div 10{,}000 = 34.764 \div (10^4) = 0.0034764$

## Terminating Decimals as Fractions

A decimal such as 24.357, which has a finite number of digits, is called a **terminating decimal.** Every terminating decimal represents a rational number; that is, any terminating decimal can be represented by a fraction with integers in the numerator and denominator. For example, using expanded notation, we write

$$24.357 = 20 + 4 + \frac{3}{10} + \frac{5}{100} + \frac{7}{1000}$$

$$= \frac{20{,}000}{1000} + \frac{4000}{1000} + \frac{300}{1000} + \frac{50}{1000} + \frac{7}{1000}$$

$$= \frac{24{,}357}{1000}.$$

Alternatively,

$$24.357 = 24.357 \cdot \frac{1000}{1000}$$

$$= \frac{24{,}357}{1000},$$

$$a \cdot \frac{b}{c} = \frac{ab}{c}$$

as before. In each case, the denominator is determined by the position of the rightmost digit. (In this case, the 7 is in the thousandths position.)

The preceding discussion shows how to convert a terminating decimal into a ratio of two integers—that is, a fraction. Moreover, any fraction whose denominator is a power of 10 may be represented by a terminating decimal. Indeed, the only simplified fractions that can be represented by terminating decimals are those whose denominators have prime factorizations involving only powers of 2, powers of 5, or some combination of both 2s and 5s. As an example, consider

$$\frac{17}{40} = \frac{17}{2^3 \cdot 5^1}.$$

This fraction can be written so that the denominator is a power of 10 by multiplying the numerator and denominator by $5^2$. Thus,

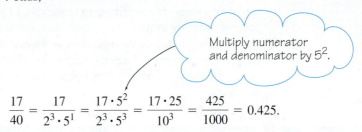

Multiply numerator and denominator by $5^2$.

$$\frac{17}{40} = \frac{17}{2^3 \cdot 5^1} = \frac{17 \cdot 5^2}{2^3 \cdot 5^3} = \frac{17 \cdot 25}{10^3} = \frac{425}{1000} = 0.425.$$

Since the numbers presented are typical of the general case, the results can be summarized as a theorem:

**THEOREM** *Rational Numbers Represented by Terminating Decimals*

If $a$ and $b$ are integers with $b \neq 0$, if $\frac{a}{b}$ is in simplest form, and if no prime other than 2 and/or 5

divides $b$, then $\frac{a}{b}$ can be represented as a terminating decimal, and conversely.

**EXAMPLE 7.4** **Writing a Terminating Decimal as a Ratio of Two Integers**

Express each of these decimals in the form $\frac{a}{b}$, where the fraction is in simplest form:

**(a)** 31.75    **(b)** 4.112    **(c)** $-0.035$

**Solution**

**(a)** $31.75 = 31.75 \cdot \frac{100}{100} = \frac{3175}{100} = \frac{127}{4}$. Note that GCD(3175, 100) = 25.

**(b)** $4.112 = 4.112 \cdot \frac{1000}{1000} = \frac{4112}{1000} = \frac{514}{125}$. Note that GCD(4112, 1000) = 8.

**(c)** $-0.035 = -0.035 \cdot \frac{1000}{1000} = \frac{-35}{1000} = \frac{-7}{200}$. Note that GCD(35, 1000) = 5.

We just saw how to write $\frac{17}{40}$ as the finite decimal 0.425 by multiplying both numerator and denominator by powers of 2 or 5. But the task can also be accomplished by division. Indeed, the standard long-division algorithm can be followed, with the difference that the digits are arranged vertically into columns that represent tens, units, tenths, hundredths, and thousandths. We have

$$
\begin{array}{r}
0.425 \\
40\overline{)17.000} \\
-16.0\phantom{00} \\
\hline
1.00\phantom{0} \\
-0.80\phantom{0} \\
\hline
0.200 \\
-0.200 \\
\hline
0
\end{array}
$$

Notice that we first removed $0.4 \cdot 40 = 16$ from 17, leaving a remainder of 1; then we removed $0.02 \cdot 40 = 0.80$ from 1.00, leaving a remainder of 0.200; and finally we removed $0.005 \cdot 40 = 0.200$, leaving a remainder of 0. The same result can also be obtained with a calculator.

**MHM** Just as we do with whole-number computations, it is important to carefully align the numerals into columns that represent place value. Perhaps the most common error children make with decimal calculation stems from their being inattentive to place value. It can be helpful for beginners to use squared paper, or to turn lined paper sideways so that the lines can be used to separate columns. It may also help to record the algorithm, at least at the beginning, in the rather detailed form shown in the previous paragraph. Later the subtraction symbols, together with many of the zeroes and decimal points, are not written explicitly; instead, their meaning is made clear by the columns in which they appear.

---

**EXAMPLE 7.5 Converting Certain Fractions to Decimals**

Convert each of the given fractions to decimals by writing each as an equivalent fraction whose denominator is a power of 10. Check by dividing with a calculator and by long division.

(a) $\dfrac{37}{40}$     (b) $-\dfrac{29}{200}$

**Solution**

(a) $\dfrac{37}{40} = \dfrac{37}{2^3 \cdot 5^1} = \dfrac{37 \cdot 5^2}{2^3 \cdot 5^3}$

$= \dfrac{37 \cdot 25}{10^3}$

$= \dfrac{925}{1000}$

$= 0.925$

$$
\begin{array}{r}
0.925 \\
40\overline{)37.0} \\
-36.0 \\
\hline
1.00 \\
-0.80 \\
\hline
0.200 \\
-0.200 \\
\hline
0
\end{array}
$$

Also, by calculator, $37 \div 40 = 0.925$.

(b) $-\dfrac{29}{200} = -\dfrac{29}{2^3 \cdot 5^2} = -\dfrac{29 \cdot 5}{2^3 \cdot 5^3}$

$= -\dfrac{145}{10^3}$

$= -\dfrac{145}{1000}$

$= -0.145$

$$
\begin{array}{r}
0.145 \\
200\overline{)29.000} \\
-20.0 \\
\hline
9.00 \\
-8.00 \\
\hline
1.00 \\
-1.00 \\
\hline
0
\end{array}
$$

Also, by calculator, $-(29 \div 200) = -0.145$.

---

## Repeating Decimals and Rational Numbers

Not all rational numbers have decimal expansions that terminate. For example,

$$\frac{1}{3} = 0.333\ldots = 0.\overline{3},$$

where the three dots indicate that the decimal continues *ad infinitum* and the bar over the 3 indicates the digit or group of digits that repeats. We can also use algebraic reasoning by setting

$$x = 0.333\ldots. *$$

$$
\begin{array}{r}
0.333\ldots \\
3\overline{)1.000\ldots} \\
-0.9 \\
\hline
0.10 \\
-0.09 \\
\hline
0.010 \\
-0.009 \\
\hline
0.0010 \\
\ldots
\end{array}
$$

---

*Actually, there is a touchy point here that we gloss over. The question is whether $0.333\ldots = \dfrac{3}{10} + \dfrac{3}{100} + \dfrac{3}{1000} + \cdots$

means anything at all, since it is the sum of an *infinite* number of numbers. That the answer is "yes" really depends on ideas from calculus!

Then, multiplying by 10, we obtain

$$10x = 3.333\ldots,$$

so that

$$10x - x = 9x = 3.$$

> $3.333\ldots$
> $-0.333\ldots$
> $3.000\ldots$

But this equation implies that

$$x = \frac{3}{9} = \frac{1}{3}.$$

Notice that the decimal expansion of $\frac{1}{3}$ is a nonterminating, but *repeating,* decimal; that is, the stream of 3s repeats without end. In general, we have the following definition:

---

**DEFINITION** *A Repeating Decimal*

A nonterminating decimal with the property that a digit or string of adjacent digits repeats *ad infinitum* from some point on is called a **periodic,** or **repeating, decimal.** The number of digits in the repeating group is called the **length of the period.**

---

For example, $0.\overline{24}$ is a repeating decimal for which the repeating part, 24, has length two. That is, $0.\overline{24} = 0.24242424\ldots$. Similarly, $3.14\overline{5} = 3.14555555\ldots$ is a repeating decimal whose repeating part, 5, has length one. The next example uses algebraic reasoning to rewrite these repeating decimals as fractions. That is, the repeating decimals represent rational numbers, and the same reasoning shows that *every* repeating decimal represents a rational number.

## EXAMPLE 7.6 Repeating Decimals as Rational Numbers

Write each of the given repeating decimals in the form $\frac{a}{b}$, where $a$ and $b$ are integers and the fraction is in simplest form. Check by dividing $a$ by $b$ with your calculator.

(a) $0.242424\ldots = 0.\overline{24}$      (b) $3.14555\ldots = 3.14\overline{5}$

**Solution**

(a) Let $x = 0.242424\ldots$.

> a decimal of period 2

Then

> Multiply by $10^2 = 100$ to move the decimal point to the right of the repeated part.

$$100x = 24.242424\ldots$$

and

$$100x - x = 99x = 24.$$

> $24.242424\ldots$
> $-0.242424\ldots$
> $24.000000\ldots$

But then

$$x = \frac{24}{99} = \frac{8}{33}.$$

Also, by calculator, $8 \div 33 \doteq 0.2424242$.

Here, the calculator answer is approximate, since only finitely many digits can appear in the calculator display.

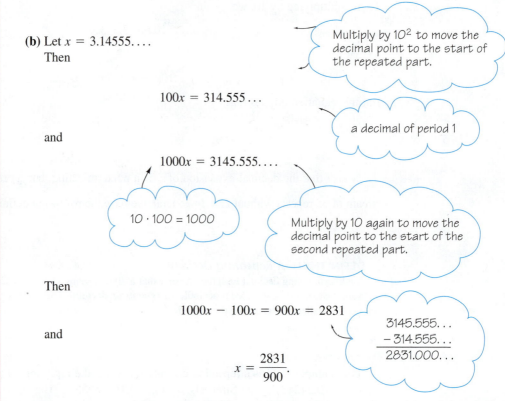

**(b)** Let $x = 3.14555\ldots$.
Then

$$100x = 314.555\ldots$$

> Multiply by $10^2$ to move the decimal point to the start of the repeated part.

> a decimal of period 1

and

$$1000x = 3145.555\ldots.$$

> $10 \cdot 100 = 1000$

> Multiply by 10 again to move the decimal point to the start of the second repeated part.

Then

$$1000x - 100x = 900x = 2831$$

> 3145.555...
> − 314.555...
> 2831.000...

and

$$x = \frac{2831}{900}.$$

Also, by calculator, $2831 \div 900 \doteq 3.1455556$. Do you see why the last digit in the calculator display is a 6?

So far, we have seen that every terminating or repeating decimal is a rational number—that is, a number that can be represented by a fraction $\frac{a}{b}$. Moreover, if a rational number is represented by a fraction in simplest form for which $b$ has no prime factor other than 2 and/or 5, then the rational number can also be written as a terminating decimal. But what about a noninteger rational number $\frac{a}{b}$ whose representation in simplest form has a denominator $b$ that is divisible by a prime other than 2 or 5? In this case, as before, the decimal representation of $\frac{a}{b}$ can be computed by carrying out the long-division algorithm to divide $b$ into $a$. We already know that the algorithm never ends, so we continue to obtain nonzero remainders at each step. Moreover, these remainders are never larger than $b$, so eventually we repeat the same sequence of steps in the algorithm, but with the digits in the quotient shifted to the right by a number of places that gives the length of the period of the repeating decimal. The next example will help your understanding. The division algorithm is written in a shortened style that suppresses unneeded zeros and decimal points, since the place value of any digit is already determined by the column in which the digit appears.

**EXAMPLE 7.7** The Decimal Expansions of $\frac{3}{7}$ and $\frac{23}{54}$

Use long division to find the decimal expansions of (a) $\frac{3}{7}$ and (b) $\frac{23}{54}$.

**Solution**

(a) Since $\frac{3}{7} = 3 \div 7$, we obtain the desired decimal expansion by dividing 3 by 7. We have

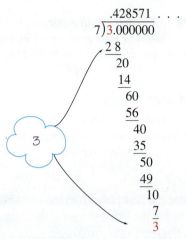

$$
\begin{array}{r}
.428571\ldots \\
7\overline{)3.000000} \\
\underline{2\ 8} \\
20 \\
\underline{14} \\
60 \\
\underline{56} \\
40 \\
\underline{35} \\
50 \\
\underline{49} \\
10 \\
\underline{7} \\
3
\end{array}
$$

and, since the remainder at this stage is 3, the number with which we began, the division will continue *ad infinitum* with that repeating pattern. Thus,

$$
\begin{array}{r}
.428571428571428571\ldots \\
3\overline{)3.0000000000000000\ldots}
\end{array}
$$

so

$$
\frac{3}{7} = 0.428571428571428571\ldots = 0.\overline{428571}.
$$

Moreover, since we are dividing by 7, and we know the decimal does not terminate, the only possible remainders at each step are 1, 2, 3, 4, 5, and 6. Thus, the length of the period can be no longer than 6.

(b) The decimal long division which follows shows that the first repeated remainder is 14, so the quotient repeats the three-digit pattern 259 without end. That is, $\frac{23}{54} = 0.4259259259259\ldots = 0.4\overline{259}$. We know in advance that the only possible remainders are between 1 and 53, so there cannot be more than 53 digits in the repeated pattern.

$$
\begin{array}{r}
.4259259259\ldots \\
54\overline{)23.0000000000\ldots} \\
\underline{216} \\
140 \\
\underline{108} \\
320 \\
\underline{270} \\
500 \\
\underline{486} \\
14
\end{array}
$$

14 is the first repeated remainder

The following theorem describes which rational numbers have a repeating decimal representation:

**THEOREM**  *Rational Numbers and Periodic Decimals*

Every repeating decimal represents a rational number $\frac{a}{b}$. If $\frac{a}{b}$ is in simplest form, and $b > 1$, then $b$ must contain a prime factor other than 2 or 5. Conversely, if $\frac{a}{b}$ is such a rational number, its decimal representation must be repeating, with a period no longer than $b$.

The last two theorems can be combined to give a decimal description of the rational numbers:

> **THEOREM** *Characterizing Rational Numbers as Decimals*
> Every rational number can be written as either a terminating or a repeating decimal. Conversely, every terminating or repeating decimal represents a rational number.

## Ordering Decimals

Elementary mathematics textbooks lay stress on ordering decimals properly. Ordering decimals is much like ordering integers. For example, to determine the larger of 247,761 and 2,326,447, write both numerals as if they had the same number of digits; that is, write

$$0{,}247{,}761 \quad \text{and} \quad 2{,}326{,}447.$$

Then determine the first place from the *left* where the digits differ. It follows from the idea of positional notation that the larger integer is the integer with the larger of these two different digits. In the present case, the first digits differ, so

$$0{,}247{,}761 < 2{,}326{,}447. \qquad \boxed{0 < 2}$$

In a similar example,

$$34{,}716 < 34{,}723 \qquad \boxed{1 < 2}$$

since the first corresponding digits that differ are the 1 and the 2, and $1 < 2$.

Now consider the decimals

$$0.2346612359 \quad \text{and} \quad 0.2348999.$$

Suppose we multiply both numbers by $10^{10}$ so that both become integers. We obtain

$$2{,}346{,}612{,}359 \quad \text{and} \quad 2{,}348{,}999{,}000.$$

We order these as integers in the manner just discussed to obtain

$$2{,}346{,}612{,}359 < 2{,}348{,}999{,}000. \qquad \boxed{6 < 8}$$

Thus,

$$(10^{10})(0.2346612359) < (10^{10})(0.2348999000).$$

But this implies that

$$0.2346612359 < 0.2348999, \qquad \boxed{\text{Divide both sides by } 10^{10}.}$$

and we are done.

These arguments could be repeated in general, with the following result: $\boxed{\text{If } ab < ac \text{ and } a > 0, \text{ then } b < c.}$

> **THEOREM** *Ordering Decimals*
> To order two positive decimals, adjoin 0s on the left if necessary so that there are the same number of digits to the left of the decimal point in both numbers and then determine the first digits from the left that differ. The decimal with the lesser of these two digits is the lesser decimal.

## EXAMPLE 7.8 Ordering Decimals

In each case, decide which of the decimals represents the lesser number.

**(a)** 2.35714 and 2.3570946     **(b)** 23.45 and 23.4$\overline{5}$     **(c)** 4.98 and 12.3

**Solution**

(a) Here, the first digits from the left that differ are 1 and 0. Since $0 < 1$, it follows that $2.3570946 < 2.35714$.

(b) Since $23.4\overline{5} = 23.4555\ldots$ and $23.45 = 23.45\overline{0}$, the first digits from the left that differ are 0 and 5. Since $0 < 5$, it follows that $23.45 < 23.4\overline{5}$.

(c) Both decimals will have the same number of digits to the left of the decimal if one 0 is adjoined to 4.98, writing it as 04.98. When we compare this decimal with 12.3, we see that the tens digit, 0, is less than the tens digit of 12.3, namely, 1. Thus, $4.98 < 12.3$.

---

**EXAMPLE 7.9   Ordering Decimals and Fractions**

Arrange these numbers in order from least to greatest:

$$\frac{11}{24}, \quad \frac{3}{8}, \quad 0.37, \quad 0.4584, \quad 0.37666\ldots, \quad 0.4583$$

**Solution**

The easiest approach is to write all the numbers as decimals. Since

$$\frac{11}{24} = 0.458333\ldots \quad \text{and} \quad \frac{3}{8} = 0.375,$$

it follows that

0.375          0.458333...

$$0.37 < \frac{3}{8} < 0.37666\ldots < 0.4583 < \frac{11}{24} < 0.4584.$$

---

## The Set of Real Numbers

Earlier, we showed that the decimal expansion of a rational number either terminates or is nonterminating and repeating. This property raises an interesting question: What kind of numbers are represented by **nonterminating, nonrepeating decimals** such as $0.101001000100001\ldots$? These numbers cannot be represented as ratios of integers and so are called **irrational numbers.** This property distinguishes them from the rational numbers considered in Chapter 6. The set consisting of all rational and irrational numbers is called the set of **real numbers.**

> **DEFINITION   *Irrational and Real Numbers***
>
> Numbers represented by **nonterminating, nonperiodic decimals** are called **irrational numbers.** The set $R$ consisting of all rational numbers and all irrational numbers is called the set of **real numbers.**

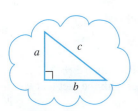

Thus, the set of real numbers is another extension of the number system. The set of real numbers contains all the earlier systems, as illustrated by the Venn diagram in Figure 7.1.

## Irrationality of $\sqrt{2}$

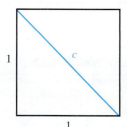

Like the set of rational numbers, the set of irrational numbers is an infinite set. To give but a single example, we show that the length of the diagonal of a square measuring 1 unit on a side is not a rational number. Recall that the equation $c^2 = a^2 + b^2$ relates the length of the long side of a triangle with one square corner to the lengths of the other two sides, as discovered in the Hands On* at the beginning of this chapter. If $c$ is the length of the diagonal of a square 1 unit on a side, it follows that

$$c^2 = 1^2 + 1^2 = 2.$$

Recall that if $c^2 = 2$, then $c$ is called the square root of 2, and we write $c = \sqrt{2}$. We now show that $\sqrt{2}$ is not a rational number.

---

*A triangle with one square corner (i.e., a corner forming a 90° angle) is called a **right** triangle. The fact that $c^2 = a^2 + b^2$ in such a triangle is called the **Pythagorean theorem.**

$c = \sqrt{2}$

**THEOREM** *Irrationality of* $\sqrt{2}$

If $c^2 = 2$, then $c$ is not a rational number.

---

**Proof (By Contradiction)**   Suppose, to the contrary, that there is a rational number $c$ for which $c^2 = 2$. Since any rational number can be expressed as a fraction in simplest form, let

$$c = \frac{u}{v},$$

where $u$ and $v$ have no common factor other than 1. But $c^2 = 2$, so

$$2 = \frac{u^2}{v^2}.$$

Thus,

$$2v^2 = u^2.$$

This equation says that 2 is a prime factor of $u^2$. Hence, by the fundamental theorem of arithmetic, 2 is a prime factor of $u$. But then $u = 2k$ for some integer $k$, and

$$2v^2 = u^2 = (2k)^2 = 4k^2.$$

This relationship implies that

$$v^2 = 2k^2,$$

so 2 is also a factor of $v^2$ and hence of $v$. But then $u$ and $v$ have a factor of 2 in common, and $\dfrac{u}{v}$ is not in simplest form. This contradicts our assumption that $\dfrac{u}{v}$ *is in simplest form.* In view of this contradiction, the assumption that $c$ is rational which started this chain of reasoning must be false. Therefore, $c$ is irrational, as was to be proved.

---

**EXAMPLE 7.10 Proving a Number Irrational**

Show that $3 + \sqrt{2}$ is irrational.

**Solution**

**Understand the Problem**

We have just seen that $\sqrt{2}$ is irrational. We must show that $3 + \sqrt{2}$ is irrational.

**Devise a Plan**

Does the assertion even make sense? Is it possible that $3 + \sqrt{2}$ is rational? If so, then $3 + \sqrt{2} = s$, where $s$ is some rational number. Perhaps we can use this equation, together with the fact that we already know that $\sqrt{2}$ is irrational, to arrive at the desired conclusion.

**Carry Out the Plan**

Since $3 + \sqrt{2} = s$, it follows that $\sqrt{2} = s - 3$. But 3 and $s$ are rational, and we know that the rational numbers are closed under subtraction. This implies that $\sqrt{2}$ is rational, and we know that that is not so. Therefore, the assumption that $3 + \sqrt{2} = s$, where $s$ is rational, must be false. Hence, $3 + \sqrt{2}$ is irrational, as was to be shown.

**Look Back**

Initially, it was not clear that the assertion stated in the problem had to be true, so we assumed briefly that it was not true. But this assumption led directly to the contradiction that $\sqrt{2}$ was rational, so the assumption that $3 + \sqrt{2}$ was rational had to be false; that is, $3 + \sqrt{2}$ had to be irrational, as we were to prove.

The preceding argument could be repeated exactly with 3 replaced by any rational number $r$. Thus, since there are infinitely many rational numbers, the preceding example shows that there are infinitely many irrational numbers. Moreover, in a very precise sense, which we will not discuss here, there are many more irrational numbers than rational numbers. Some of these irrationals may be familiar to you. For example, the number

$$\pi = 3.14159265\ldots$$

occurring in the formula $A = \pi r^2$ for the area of a circle of radius $r$ and in the formula $C = 2\pi r$ for the circumference of a circle has been shown to be irrational. Moreover, if the natural number $m$ is not a perfect square, it can be shown that $\sqrt{m}$ is also irrational. Indeed, if $m$ is not a perfect $n$th power, $\sqrt[n]{m}$, is irrational, where, by $\sqrt[n]{m}$, we mean a number $c$ such that $c^n = m$.

## Real Numbers and the Number Line

When we discussed the length of the diagonal of the square measuring 1 unit on a side and proved that $\sqrt{2}$ is irrational, we made a tacit assumption that is easily overlooked. Simply put, the assumption was that, to every possible length, there corresponds exactly one real number that names the length in question. Figure 7.7 illustrates how we can accurately plot the length $\sqrt{2}$ on the number line.

**FIGURE 7.7**
$\sqrt{2}$ on the number line

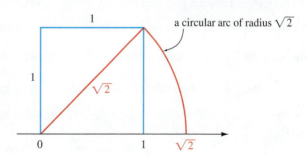

Also, the decimal expansion of $\sqrt{2}$ can be found step-by-step as follows: Using a calculator and trial and error, we find that

$$1^2 = 1 < 2 < 4 = 2^2,$$
$$1.4^2 = 1.96 < 2 < 2.25 = 1.5^2,$$
$$1.41^2 = 1.9881 < 2 < 2.0164 = 1.42^2,$$
$$1.414^2 = 1.999396 < 2 < 2.002225 = 1.415^2,$$

and so on. Thus, the decimal expansion of $\sqrt{2}$ is

$$\sqrt{2} = 1.414\ldots$$

> Note that this value is determined by the lower estimates shown.

where successive digits are found by catching $\sqrt{2}$ between successive units, between successive tenths, between successive hundredths, and so on. To show that this can be done for any real number is somewhat tricky, but the following theorem can be proved:

> **THEOREM** *Real Numbers and the Number Line*
> There is a one-to-one correspondence between the set of real numbers and the set of points on a number line. The absolute value of the number associated with any point on the line gives the point's distance from 0.

## Problem Set 7.1

Exercises numbered in red are answered in the back of the text.

### Understanding Concepts

1. Write the following decimals in expanded form and in expanded exponential form:
   **(a)** 273.412    **(b)** 0.000723    **(c)** 0.20305

2. Write the decimal of the four points shown on the number line below.

3. Match the given fractions to the nearest decimal.
   **(a)** $3\frac{3}{8}$    **(b)** $3\frac{1}{8}$    **(c)** $3\frac{1}{3}$    **(d)** $\frac{25}{7}$

   **A.** 3.1    **B.** 3.57    **C.** 3.4    **D.** 3.3

4. The unit square in the left-hand diagram is divided into 100 small squares that each represent $\frac{1}{100} = 0.01$, so that each vertical strip represents $\frac{1}{10} = 0.1$. Therefore, the right-hand diagram illustrates that $\frac{4}{5} = 0.8$ of the unit has been shaded in various colors.

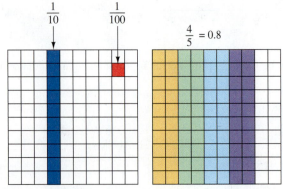

   Explain how the diagrams that follow can be used to give the decimal representation of

**(a)** $\frac{1}{4}$ and **(b)** $\frac{1}{8}$. Notice that $\frac{1}{8}$ is half of $\frac{1}{4}$. Also, half of a small $\frac{1}{100}$ square is five small strips, where a small strip represents $\frac{1}{1000} = 0.001$ (one thousandth); that is, half a small square is the decimal 0.005 (five thousandths).

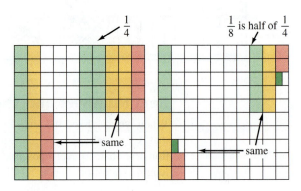

   **(c)** Describe a shading of strips, small squares, and small strips that together represent $\frac{3}{8} = \frac{1}{4} + \frac{1}{8}$.

5. Write these decimals as fractions in lowest terms, and determine, the prime factorization of the denominator in each case:
   **(a)** 0.324    **(b)** 0.028    **(c)** 4.25

6. Write these fractions as terminating decimals:
   **(a)** $\frac{7}{20}$    **(b)** $\frac{7}{16}$    **(c)** $\frac{3}{75}$    **(d)** $\frac{18}{2^2 \cdot 5^4}$

7. Represent each of these fractions as a decimal by using the long-division algorithm.
   **(a)** $\frac{7}{8}$    **(b)** $\frac{53}{40}$    **(c)** $\frac{71}{125}$

8. Represent each of these fractions as a decimal by using the long-division algorithm:
   **(a)** $\frac{5}{6}$    **(b)** $\frac{7}{12}$    **(c)** $\frac{3}{11}$
   **(d)** $\frac{2}{27}$    **(e)** $\frac{4}{7}$

**9.** Determine the fraction in lowest terms represented by each of these periodic decimals:

(a) $0.321321\ldots = 0.\overline{321}$

(b) $0.12414141\ldots = 0.12\overline{41}$

(c) $3.262626\ldots = 3.\overline{26}$

(d) $0.666\ldots = 0.\overline{6}$

(e) $0.142857142857142857\ldots = 0.\overline{142857}$

(f) $0.153846153846153846\ldots = 0.\overline{153846}$

**10.** For each of the following, determine the fraction in lowest terms represented by the repeated decimal:

(a) $0.3\overline{54}$    (b) $5.21\overline{6}$    (c) $2.3\overline{402}$    (d) $7.24\overline{86}$

**11.** (a) Give an example of a fraction whose decimal expansion is repeating and has a period of length 3.

(b) Use your calculator to check your answer to part (a). Is this check really complete? Explain.

(c) Check your answer to part (a) by some other means.

**12.** For each of these sequences of numbers, write the numbers in order of increasing size (from least to greatest):

(a) $0.017, 0.007, 0.01\overline{7}, 0.027$

(b) $25.412, 25.312, 24.999, 25.41\overline{2}$

(c) $\dfrac{9}{25}, 0.35, 0.36, \dfrac{10}{25}, 0.\overline{35}$

(d) $\dfrac{1}{4}, \dfrac{5}{24}, \dfrac{1}{3}, \dfrac{1}{6}$

**13.** Show that $\sqrt{3}$ is irrational. (*Hint:* Have you seen a similar result proved?)

**14.** (a) Show that $3 - \sqrt{2}$ is irrational.

(b) Show that $2\sqrt{2}$ is irrational.

## Teaching Concepts

**15.** Children often think that a decimal is more like a number than a a fraction. For example, 0.75 is easy to find on a ruler, but $\dfrac{3}{4}$ is the amount *of* something. How would you show youngsters that fractions and decimals are both numbers?

**16.** In Chapter 3, whole numbers were represented with counters and place-value cards. Modify this idea to represent decimal numbers. Is there a way to adjust the position of the decimals? Devise several problems and activities that teach decimal concepts with place-value cards.

## Responding to Students

**17.** Ordering decimal numbers is sometimes difficult for children. Analyze what you believe might lead to the following mistakes and how you might correct them:

(a) Jorge thinks that 0.5 is smaller than 0.06.

(b) Jenna thinks that 0.34 is smaller than 0.334.

(c) Zach thinks that 0.4567 is smaller than 0.45.

**18.** Janeshia was asked to say the number 56.127. Her response was "fifty-six tenths, one hundred twenty-seven thousandths." What error did Janeshia make with her answer?

**19.** Marita claims that since $\dfrac{1}{3} = 0.333\ldots$, it must be the case that $1 = 0.999\ldots$.

(a) How would you respond to Marita and involve the entire class in the discussion?

(b) Write the repeating decimal $0.24999\ldots$ as a fraction. Do you think your students might be surprised at the result?

(c) Could you write the finite decimal 3.23 as a repeating decimal?

## Thinking Critically

**20.** Compute the decimal expansions of each of the following numbers:

(a) $\dfrac{1}{11}$    (b) $\dfrac{1}{111}$    (c) $\dfrac{1}{1111}$

(d) Guess the decimal expansion of $1/11111$.

(e) Check your guess in part (d) by converting the decimal of your guess back into a ratio of two integers.

(f) Carefully describe the decimal expansion of $1/N_n$, where $N_n = 111\ldots 1$ with $n$ 1s in its representation.

**21.** For each of the given periodic decimals, what rational number corresponds to that decimal? (Refer to Example 7.6 if you need help.)

(a) $0.747474\ldots = 0.\overline{74}$

(b) $0.777\ldots = 0.\overline{7}$

(c) $0.235235235\ldots = 0.\overline{235}$

(d) If $a$, $b$, and $c$ are digits, what rational numbers are represented by the given periodic decimals? You should be able to guess the answers on the basis of patterns observed in parts (a), (b), and (c).

    (i) $0.aaa\ldots = 0.\overline{a}$

    (ii) $0.ababab\ldots = 0.\overline{ab}$

    (iii) $0.abcabcabc\ldots = 0.\overline{abc}$

**22.** Write the decimals representing these rational numbers without doing any calculation, or at most doing only mental calculation:

(a) $\dfrac{5}{9}$    (b) $\dfrac{22}{99}$    (c) $\dfrac{317}{999}$

(d) $\dfrac{17}{33}$    (e) $\dfrac{14}{11}$

(f) Check the answers in parts (a) through (e), using your calculator. Is this check foolproof? Explain.

**23.** (a) Give an example which shows that the sum of two irrational numbers is sometimes rational.

(b) Give an example which shows that the sum of two irrational numbers is sometimes irrational.

**24.** Give an example which shows that the product of two irrational numbers is sometimes rational.

**25.** Without resorting to the Pythagorean theorem, use the following figure to show that the diagonal $c$ of a $1 \times 1$ square satisfies the equation $c^2 = 2$:

**26.** Is $\dfrac{2}{\sqrt{2}}$ rational or irrational? Explain.

**27.** Give an example which shows that the quotient of two irrational numbers is sometimes rational.

**28.** Find a rational number between the irrational numbers $\pi$ and $2 + \sqrt{2}$.

**29.** **(a)** If $a$ is an integer, what are the possibilities for the last digit of the decimal representation of $a^2$?

| Last digit of $a$ | 0 | 1 | 2 | 3 | 4 | 5 | 6 | 7 | 8 | 9 |
|---|---|---|---|---|---|---|---|---|---|---|
| Last digit of $a^2$ | | | | | | | | | | |

**(b)** If $b$ is an integer, what are the possibilities for the last digit of the decimal representation of $2b^2$?

| Last digit of $b$ | 0 | 1 | 2 | 3 | 4 | 5 | 6 | 7 | 8 | 9 |
|---|---|---|---|---|---|---|---|---|---|---|
| Last digit of $2b^2$ | | | | | | | | | | |

**(c)** Using the results of parts (a) and (b), make a careful argument that $\sqrt{2} = \dfrac{a}{b}$, with $a$ and $b$ integers, is impossible.

**30.** In Chapter 4, you learned that if two natural numbers $a$ and $b$ have no common divisor other than 1, and if $b$ divides $a^2$, then $b$ also divides $a$. Use this fact to give a very short proof that $\sqrt{2}$ is an irrational number. [*Suggestion*: Assume that there is a fraction $\dfrac{a}{b}$ in simplest form for which $\sqrt{2} = \dfrac{a}{b}$. Next, square both sides, multiply by $b$, and carefully examine the equation you obtain.]

## Thinking Cooperatively

**31.** Cut a piece of unlined paper lengthwise into a strip about an inch wide. Mark one end of the strip with a 0 and the opposite end with an 8, as in the following diagram, so that the length of the strip is 8 units:

| 0 | 8 |
|---|---|

Discuss how to fold the strip to find good estimates of the points along the strip at these distances:

**(a)** 3.0   **(b)** 4.5   **(c)** 5.25   **(d)** 6.375

**32.** Dividing the work between members of your group, compute the decimal representations of the rational numbers shown in

parts (a) through (j) and compute the prime-power representations of their denominators:

**(a)** $\dfrac{23}{6}$   **(b)** $\dfrac{7}{24}$   **(c)** $\dfrac{11}{9}$   **(d)** $\dfrac{23}{18}$   **(e)** $\dfrac{7}{22}$

**(f)** $\dfrac{23}{22}$   **(g)** $\dfrac{13}{110}$   **(h)** $\dfrac{311}{88}$   **(i)** $\dfrac{37}{220}$   **(j)** $\dfrac{29}{5500}$

**(k)** Discuss the results of (a) through (j), and arrive at a consensus prediction about how many digits there are between the decimal point and the repeating part of the decimal expansion of a rational number $\dfrac{r}{s}$.

## Making Connections

**33.** **(a)** If it takes Suzan 1 minute to walk to her friend's house, how many minutes will it take her to walk halfway to her friend's house?

**(b)** If Suzan is halfway to her friend's house, how many minutes will it take her to walk half the remaining distance to her friend's house?

**(c)** If Suzan walks halfway to her friend's house and then half the remaining distance, how many minutes will it take her to walk half the then remaining distance?

**(d)** In order to walk to her friend's house, Suzan must first walk halfway there, then walk half the remaining distance, then half the then remaining distance, then half the still remaining distance, and so on. Will Suzan ever be able to reach her friend's house?

**(e)** What must the sum of the times in parts (a), (b), (c), and (d) be?

**(f)** What does the answer to part (e) suggest about the reasonableness of the equality $\dfrac{1}{3} = 0.333\ldots$ ?

## Using a Calculator

**34.** Use a calculator to find the decimal representations of these fractions:

**(a)** $\dfrac{1}{11}$   **(b)** $\dfrac{15}{22}$   **(c)** $\dfrac{5}{21}$   **(d)** $\dfrac{2}{13}$

**35.** **(a)** Find the decimal representation of the rational number given by the sum

$$\frac{22}{17} + \frac{37}{47} + \frac{88}{83}.$$

**(b)** Subtract your answer to part (a) from $\pi$. Is it possible that the resulting number is exactly 0? Describe what result of the subtraction is shown on your calculator.

## From State Student Assessments

**36.** (Connecticut, Grade 6)

**(a)** The shaded portion of this picture represents the number

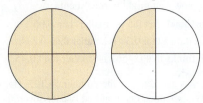

**A.** 1   **B.** 2   **C.** 1.5   **D.** 1.25

**(b)** Which of the following shows 1.63?

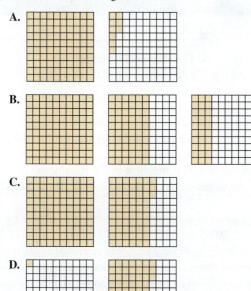

A.

B.

C.

D.

**37.** (Minnesota, Grade 5)

Use the picture below to answer the question.

Radio station **WMTH** can be found at 93.7 on your radio dial. Which letter shown represents where you would find **WMTH**?

**A.** letter A     **B.** letter B     **C.** letter C     **D.** letter D

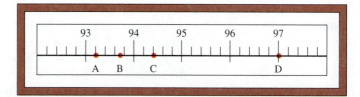

**38.** (Arizona Grade 7)

Between which two consecutive integers is the value of this irrational number? $\sqrt{117}$

**A.** 8 and 9     **B.** 10 and 11   **C.** 14 and 15   **D.** 20 and 21

**39.** (Arizona Grade 8)

Which number is irrational?

**A.** $(1.5)^2$     **B.** $\sqrt{41}$     **C.** $\sqrt{49}$     **D.** $(15)^2$

# 7.2

# Computations with Decimals

### Rounding Decimals

 It is essential that elementary school students develop a sense of *numeracy*—that is, an idea of what numbers *mean* and what makes *sense* when dealing with numbers. For example, is it useful in practice to consider a decimal such as 0.7342061? The answer, in general, is *no*. Even in scientific work, where considerable accuracy is required, a decimal correct to seven significant digits is rarely meaningful. It is much more likely that an approximation like 0.73, or 0.734, or even simply 0.7 is all that is needed. This discussion naturally leads to the question of approximation and rounding of decimals.

Consider this example: A dressmaker wants to buy material to make into a dress for her upcoming fashion show. The material comes in 40-inch widths and she needs a piece 3.75 yards long. If the material costs $15.37 per yard, how much will she have to pay? Using a calculator, we find that the price would be

$$(3.75)(\$15.37) = \$57.6375,$$

and the dressmaker would be charged $57.64, the cost rounded to the nearest cent. The process of rounding here is precisely the same as it was for integers. Thus, 2.3254071 rounded

- to the nearest integer is 2,
- to the nearest tenth is 2.3,
- to the nearest hundredth is 2.33,

and so on. As before, we are using the 5-up rule.

> **RULE**   *The 5-Up Rule for Rounding Decimals*
>
> To round a decimal to a given place, consider the digit in the next place to the right. If it is smaller than 5, replace it and all of the digits to its right with 0. If it is 5 or larger, replace it and all digits to the right by 0 and increase the digit in the given place by one. Replaced digits to the right of the decimal are then dropped to give the rounded decimal.

**EXAMPLE** **7.11** **Rounding Decimals**

Round each of these decimals to the indicated position.

(a) 23.2047 to the nearest integer    (b) 3.6147 to the nearest tenth
(c) 0.015 to the nearest hundredth    (d) 8.53972 to the nearest thousandth
(e) 3482.3 to the nearest hundred

**Solution**

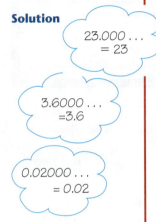

23.000 . . .
= 23

3.6000 . . .
=3.6

0.02000 . . .
= 0.02

(a) Since we are asked to round 23.2047 to the nearest integer, we consider the digit to the right of 3. Since this digit is 2 and 2 < 5, we leave the 3 unchanged and delete the digits to its right. Thus, 23.2047 rounded to the nearest integer is 23.

(b) In rounding 3.6147 to the nearest tenth, we note that the digit to the right of the 6 is 1. Since 1 < 5, we leave the 6 unchanged and delete the digits to its right. Thus, 3.6147 rounded to the nearest tenth is 3.6.

(c) Here, the digit in question is 1 and the digit to its right is 5. Thus, we increase the 1 by 1 and replace the digits to its right by 0s. Hence, 0.015 rounded to the nearest hundredth is 0.02.

(d) The digit in question is the 9, and 7 is to its right. Since $7 \geq 5$, 9 is increased to 10, requiring a regrouping. That is, 8.53972 to the nearest thousandth is 8.540. Notice that the 0 digit is retained to distinguish it from the value 8.54 obtained by rounding to the nearest hundredth.

(e) The digit in question is 4, and 8 is to its right. Since $8 \geq 5$, the 4 is replaced with 5, the 8 and 2 are replaced with 0, and the 3 to the right of the decimal point is deleted. That is, 3482.3 rounded to the nearest hundred is 3500.

## Adding and Subtracting Decimals

**FIGURE 7.8**
The sum 2.08 + 1.154 = 3.234 is illustrated with blocks (units), flats (tenths), longs (hundredths), and cubes (thousandths). Notice the regrouping, with 10 of the 13 longs replaced with a flat.

Suppose a jeweler is making a piece of jewelry that combines a large diamond weighing 2.08 carats with a smaller diamond weighing 1.154 carats. What is the combined weight of the diamonds? That is, what is the sum 2.08 + 1.154?

There are several ways to give an answer. For example, if blocks, flats, longs, and cubes are used to represent units, tenths, hundredths and thousandths, respectively (see Figure 7.4), then the answer is as shown in Figure 7.8. Note that 10 of the 13 longs were regrouped into a flat.

**2.08**

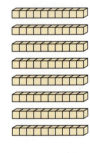

**+ 1.154**

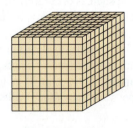

**3.234**

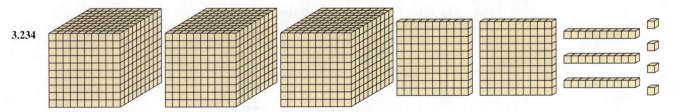

Figure 7.8 shows us that the algorithm for whole-number addition learned in Chapter 3 works just as well for decimal addition, although there are now columns representing place value to both the left and right of the vertically aligned decimal point.

Another way to add decimals is to revert to their expressions as fractions. For example,

$$2.08 + 1.154 = \frac{208}{100} + \frac{1154}{1000} = \frac{2080}{1000} + \frac{1154}{1000}$$

$$= \frac{2080 + 1154}{1000} = \frac{3234}{1000} = 3.234.$$

In performing decimal arithmetic, either by hand or with a calculator, many errors can be avoided by estimating the expected answers with mental arithmetic. In the preceding example, we are adding a number slightly more than 2 to a number slightly more than 1, so we know our answer will be a bit larger than 3.

Not surprisingly, the subtraction of decimals can also be computed with the usual algorithms of subtraction, again with attention given to careful vertical alignment of the digits columns to both the left and right of the decimal point. As an example, suppose that we want to subtract 2.71 from 37.762. The calculation is much the same as before, and we have

$$37.762 - 2.71 = \frac{37,762}{1000} - \frac{2710}{1000}$$

$$= \frac{35,052}{1000}$$

$$= 35.052.$$

$$\begin{array}{r} 37{,}762 \\ -\ 2710 \\ \hline 35{,}052 \end{array}$$

$$\begin{array}{r} 37.762 \\ -\ 2.710 \\ \hline 35.052 \end{array}$$

Notice how we write the problem in vertical style, lining up the decimal points, and then subtract essentially as we subtract integers.

If we do this operation with a calculator, we should estimate and perform mental calculation as well. Thus, we think

*approximately 38 minus approximately 3 gives approximately 35*

and thereby avoid gross calculator errors.

## EXAMPLE 7.12 Adding and Subtracting Decimals

Compute each of these by estimating, by calculator, and by hand:

**(a)** $23.47 + 7.81$      **(b)** $351.42 - 417.815$

**Solution**

**(a)** By estimating: Approximately 23 plus approximately 8 gives approximately 31.
By calculator: 23.47 $\boxed{+}$ 7.81 $\boxed{=}$ 31.28

By hand:
$$\begin{array}{r} 23.47 \\ +\ 7.81 \\ \hline 31.28 \end{array}$$

**(b)** By estimating: Approximately 350 minus approximately 400 gives approximately $-50$.
By calculator: 351.42 $\boxed{-}$ 417.815 $\boxed{=}$ $-66.395$

By hand:
$$\begin{array}{r} 4{}^{1}17.8{}^{1}15 \\ -\ 3\ 51.4\ 2 \\ \hline 66.395 \end{array} \qquad \text{or} \qquad \begin{array}{r} 417.815 \\ -\ 351.42 \\ \hline 66.395 \end{array}$$

Therefore, since $417.815 > 351.42$, the desired answer is $-66.395$.

## Multiplying Decimals

Tom Swift wanted to try out his new Ferrari on a racetrack. If he drove at 91.7 miles per hour for 15 minutes, how far did he go? Since 15 minutes equals 0.25 hour and distance traveled equals rate times elapsed time, Tom traveled $(91.7) \cdot (0.25)$ miles. For the exact answer, we need to be able to multiply decimals. Converting those decimals to fractions, we have

$$91.7 = \frac{917}{10} \quad \text{and} \quad 0.25 = \frac{25}{100}.$$

Thus,

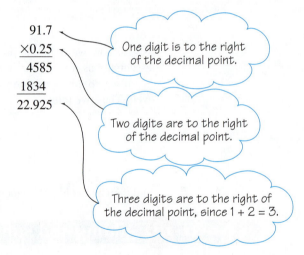

$$(91.7) \cdot (0.25) = \frac{917}{10} \cdot \frac{25}{100}$$

$$= \frac{917 \cdot 25}{10 \cdot 100}$$

$$= \frac{22{,}925}{1000}$$

$$= 22.925,$$

*Three digits are to the right of the decimal point, since we are dividing by 1000 = 10³.*

and the multiplication is performed just as is the multiplication of integers, except for the placement of the decimal point. Indeed, by hand, it is common to write the following:

$$
\begin{array}{r}
91.7 \\
\times 0.25 \\
\hline
4585 \\
1834 \phantom{0} \\
\hline
22.925
\end{array}
$$

*One digit is to the right of the decimal point.*

*Two digits are to the right of the decimal point.*

*Three digits are to the right of the decimal point, since 1 + 2 = 3.*

Since this type of calculation is typical of the general case, we summarize it as a computational algorithm.

**ALGORITHM** *Multiplying Decimals*
To multiply two decimals, do the following:

1. Multiply as with integers.
2. Count the number of digits to the right of the decimal point in each factor in the product, add these numbers, and call their sum $t$.
3. Place the decimal point in the product that is obtained so that there are $t$ digits to the right of the decimal point.

Finally, we note that since Tom's odometer gives mileage only to the nearest tenth, it actually shows that Tom traveled approximately 22.9 miles. Thus, the accuracy to three decimal places in the preceding multiplication is hardly useful to Tom. Also, Tom's estimated speed of 91.7 miles per hour, as well as his measurement of the 15-minute time interval, were almost surely not entirely accurate. Hence, the accuracy to three decimal places is surely not warranted; it is certainly much more reasonable in this case to round the answer to 22.9, or even to 23, miles.

**EXAMPLE 7.13** **Multiplying Decimals**

Compute these products by estimating, by calculator, and by hand:

**(a)** $(471.2) \cdot (2.3)$     **(b)** $(36.34) \cdot (1.02)$

**Solution**

**(a)** By estimating: Approximately 500 times approximately 2 gives approximately 1000. By calculator: $471.2 \boxed{\times} 2.3 \boxed{=} 1083.76$

By hand:
$$
\begin{array}{r}
471.2 \\
\times\ \ 2.3 \\
\hline
14136 \\
9424\ \ \\
\hline
1083.76
\end{array}
$$

> Two digits are to the right of the decimal point.   $1 + 1 = 2$

**(b)** By estimating: Approximately 36 times approximately 1 gives approximately 36.
By calculator: $36.34 \boxed{\times} 1.02 \boxed{=} 37.0668$     By hand:
$$
\begin{array}{r}
36.34 \\
\times\ \ 1.02 \\
\hline
7268 \\
36340\ \ \\
\hline
37.0668
\end{array}
$$

## Dividing Decimals

$$d = rt$$

$$r = \dfrac{d}{t}$$

Tom Swift also has his own airplane. If Tom traveled 537.6 miles in 2.56 hours in his airplane, how fast did he travel? Again, since distance traveled equals rate times elapsed time, rate equals distance traveled divided by elapsed time. Therefore, we need to compute the quotient $537.6 \div 2.56$. Converting those decimals to fractions, we have

$$
\begin{aligned}
537.6 \div 2.56 &= \frac{5376}{10} \div \frac{256}{100} \\
&= \frac{5376}{10} \cdot \frac{100}{256} \\
&= \frac{537{,}600}{2560} \\
&= \frac{53{,}760}{256} \\
&= 210.
\end{aligned}
$$

Thus, the problem is reduced to that of dividing 53,760 by 256—that is, to dividing integers. Recall that when confronted by a division like

$$2.56\overline{)537.6}$$

students are often told to move the decimal point in both the divisor and the dividend two places to the right so that the divisor becomes an integer. The preceding calculation with fractions justifies this rule, and, by hand, we have

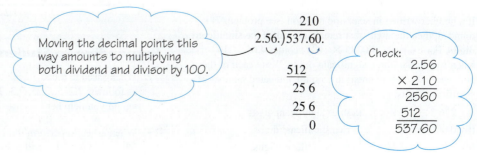

> Moving the decimal points this way amounts to multiplying both dividend and divisor by 100.

$$
\begin{array}{r}
210 \\
2.56.\overline{)537.60.} \\
\underline{512}\ \ \ \ \\
25\ 6 \\
\underline{25\ 6} \\
0
\end{array}
$$

> Check:
> $$
> \begin{array}{r}
> 2.56 \\
> \times\ 210 \\
> \hline
> 2560 \\
> 512\ \ \\
> \hline
> 537.60
> \end{array}
> $$

## Problem Set 7.2

Exercises numbered in red are answered in the back of the text.

## Understanding Concepts

1. Perform these additions and subtractions by hand:

   (a) $32.174 + 371.5$   (b) $371.5 - 32.174$
   (c) $0.057 + 1.08$   (d) $0.057 - 1.08$

2. Perform these multiplications and divisions by hand:

   (a) $(37.1) \cdot (4.7)$   (b) $(3.71) \cdot (0.47)$
   (c) $138.33 \div 5.3$   (d) $1.3833 \div 0.53$

3. Estimate the result of each of these computations mentally, and then perform the calculations with a calculator.

   (a) $4.112 + 31.3$   (b) $31.3 - 4.112$
   (c) $(4.112) \cdot (31.3)$   (d) $31.3 \div 4.112$

4. Use mental arithmetic to estimate the value of each the following decimal expressions, and then calculate the exact value by hand and by calculator:

   (a) $23.07 + 4.8 + 0.971$   (b) $41.5 - 6.48 + 13.013$

   (c) $(13.12 \times 21.3) \div 4.1$   (d) $17.8 + \left(\dfrac{3.27}{1.5}\right)$

5. (a) When the gasoline pump shut off automatically, 13.6 gallons at $\$3.19^{9/10}$ per gallon had been delivered. What is the amount that will show on the cost dial?

   (b) How many gallons of gas at $\$3.39^{9/10}$ per gallon can be purchased for $30?

6. Evaluate each of the following multiplications and divisions by correctly positioning the decimal point:

   (a) $34.796 \times 10^3$   (b) $34.796 \times 10^{-3}$
   (c) $34.796 \div 10^2$   (d) $34.796 \div 10^{-2}$

7. The number 456,123,789 can be written in **scientific notation** as the product of 4.56123789 and $10^8$. That is, $456{,}123{,}789 = 4.56123789 \times 10^8$. The decimal point always immediately follows the first nonzero digit. Determine the power of 10 needed to write these decimals in scientific notation:

   (a) $34{,}762 = 3.4762 \times 10^a$
   (b) $4{,}256{,}000 = 4.256 \times 10^b$
   (c) $0.009031 = 9.031 \times 10^c$
   (d) $0.000004320017 = 4.320017 \times 10^d$

8. If a number written in scientific notation (see problem 7) is rounded, then the digits that remain are called the **significant digits.** For example, $4.0285 \times 10^6$ becomes $4.03 \times 10^6$ when rounded to three significant digits. Write each of these numbers in scientific notation with the indicated number of significant digits:

   (a) 276,543,421   to three significant digits.
   (b) 0.000005341   to two significant digits.
   (c) 376,712.543248   to two significant digits.

9. Calculate these multiplications and divisions with a suitable calculator, and write the answer in scientific notation to three significant digits:

   (a) $0.0000127 \times 0.000008235$
   (b) $98{,}613{,}428 \times 5{,}746{,}312$
   (c) $0.0000127 \div 98{,}613{,}428$
   (d) $98{,}613{,}428 \div 0.000008234$

10. For each of these multiplications and divisions, estimate the answer, calculate the result to three significant digits on a suitable calculator, and then write the answer in scientific notation:

    (a) $(7.123 \times 10^5) \cdot (2.142 \times 10^4)$
    (b) $(7.123 \times 10^5) \div (2.142 \times 10^4)$
    (c) $(7.123 \times 10^5) \cdot (2.142 \times 10^{-9})$
    (d) $(7.123 \times 10^{-2}) \div (2.142 \times 10^8)$

## Teaching Concepts

11. One can use the rectangular area model of multiplication to help students understand multiplication of decimals, just as was done to promote their understanding of multiplication of natural numbers and rational numbers. The diagram shown illustrates the product $2.3 \times 3.2$.

    (a) Identify the colored regions in the diagram with the numbers shown in the hand calculation of the product.

    (b) How would you use the diagram to justify the exchange shown in the hand calculation?

    (c) Discuss how the diagram helps to illustrate the rule for the proper placement of the decimal point in the final answer.

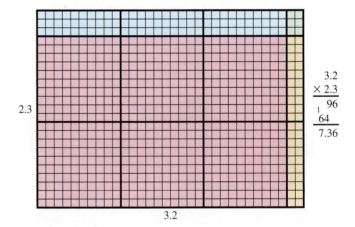

## Responding to Students

12. When asked to round 7.2447 to the nearest tenth, Toni proceeded as follows: 7.245, 7.25, 7.3. Toni seems to need help. How would you help her?

13. When asked to perform the decimal computations $47 + 3.2$, $6.9 - 5$, $3.6 \times 0.2$, and $8.36 \div 0.4$, some students submitted

the answers shown here. Respond to each student in helpful ways that provide an understanding of the error made and how it can be avoided in the future.

(a)   47
     +3.2
     ─────
      7.9

(b)  6.9
     −5
     ───
     6.4

(c)  3.6
    ×0.2
    ────
     7.2

(d)         2.9
      0.4)‾8.36‾

**14.** A student makes the following error pattern in several problems:

$$4.8 + 32 + 0.79 + 7.8 = 23.7$$

$$46.325 + 234.56 + 13.567 + 2.7964 = 111.312$$

Describe the error the student is making, and state what steps you would use to assist the student in learning how to do the problem correctly.

## Thinking Critically

**15.** Use these numbers to make a magic square (see problem 14 (a) in Problem Set 1.1):

0.123, 0.246, 0.369, 0.492, 0.615, 0.738, 0.861, 0.984, 1.107

**16.** Use the numbers in problem 15 to form a magic subtraction square. (See problem 14 (b) in Problem Set 1.1.)

**17.** Use these numbers to make a magic square:

7.02, 16.38, 11.70, 18.72, 2.34, 9.36, 4.68, 21.06, 14.04

**18.** Use the numbers in problem 17 to make a magic subtraction square.

**19.** The sum of the numbers in any two adjacent blanks is the number immediately below and between the two numbers. Complete each problem so that the same pattern holds. The first one has been completed for you.

(a)  2.107   1.3   4.26
       3.407   5.56
          8.967

(b)  21.06   3.21   ____
        ____   5.00
          ____

(c)  ____   0.041   ____
       2.415   ____
          7.723

(d)  ____   1.414   ____
       ____   ____
          3.142

(e) Can any of the problems be completed in more than one way? Explain.

**20.** Fill in the blanks so that each of these sequences is an arithmetic progression:

(a) 3.4, 4.3, 5.2, ____, ____, ____
(b) −31.56, ____, −21.10, ____, ____, ____
(c) 0.0114, ____, ____, 0.3204, ____, ____
(d) 1.07, ____, ____, ____, −9.21, ____

**21.** Fill in the blanks so that each of these sequences is a geometric progression.

(a) 2.11, 2.321, ____, ____, ____
(b) 35.1, ____, 1.404, −0.2808, ____
(c) 6.01, ____, ____, 0.75125, ____

**22.** In Chapter 3, we saw how to use positional notation to bases other than ten to represent integers. The same ideas can be used to represent rational and real numbers. Write a two- or three-page paper explaining how this would work. Be sure to include examples.

**23.** Recall that the Fibonacci numbers are the numbers 1, 1, 2, 3, 5, 8, 13, 21, 34, 55, 89, . . . .

(a) Compute the decimal expansion of $\frac{1}{89}$ correct to 10 decimal places. Note that 89 is the 11th Fibonacci number.

(b) Are you surprised at the decimal expansion of $\frac{1}{89}$, particularly in the 7th, 8th, 9th, and 10th places?

(c) Compute this sum by hand:

```
       0.0
       0.01
       0.001
       0.0002
       0.00003
       0.000005
       0.0000008
       0.00000013
       0.000000021
       0.0000000034
       0.00000000055
       0.000000000089
       0.0000000000144
       0.00000000000233
     +0.000000000000377
```

the Fibonacci numbers divided by powers of 10

(d) Make a conjecture on the basis of the result in part (c). Recall that many decimals never end and consequently are actually sums of infinitely many terms.

(e) Does it make sense to set $F_0 = 0$?

## Thinking Cooperatively

Do the next two problems with two or three other students. At each step, discuss your solution with the other members of the group and determine a consensus answer for the group.

**24.** Place numbers in the circles in these diagrams so that the numbers in the large circles are the sums of the numbers in the two adjacent smaller circles:

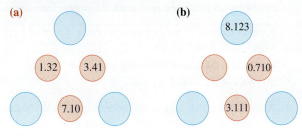

**(c)**

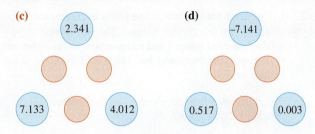

**(d)**

25. If possible, place numbers in the circles in these diagrams so that the numbers in the large circles exactly equal the sums of the numbers in the adjacent small circles:

**(a)**                              **(b)**

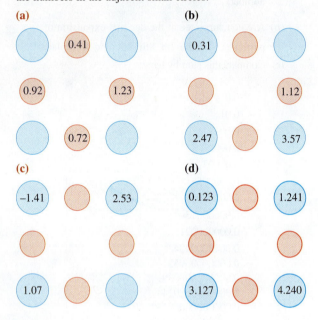

**(c)**                              **(d)**

**(e)** What must be the case for these problems to be solvable? Explain.

**(f)** Is there more than one solution to all or any of these problems?

## Making Connections

26. Kristina bought pairs of gloves as Christmas presents for three of her best friends. If the gloves cost $9.72 a pair, how much did she spend for these presents?

27. Yolanda also bought identical pairs of gloves for each of her four best friends. If her total bill was $44.92, how much did each pair of gloves cost?

28. Dante cashed a check for $74.29 and then bought an MP3 player for $42.91 and a special pair of earphones for $17.02. After paying for his purchases, how much did he have left?

29. A picture frame 2.25 inches wide surrounds a picture 17.5 inches wide by 24.75 inches high.

**(a)** What is the area of the picture frame?

**(b)** What is the area of the picture?

30. When very large or very small numbers occur, it is common to write them in scientific notation, as described in problem 7. That is, the number is written as the product of a decimal with a

single nonzero digit to the left of the decimal point and a power of 10. For example, instead of expressing the earth's mass as about 5,973,600,000,000,000,000,000,000 kilograms, it is more appropriate to write the mass as $5.9736 \times 10^{24}$, which indicates that the estimate is accurate to five **significant digits.** Similarly, it is better to write very small numbers in scientific notation. For example, the mass of an electron is $9.1093826 \times 10^{-31}$ kilograms in scientific notation with eight significant digits—a number that is simpler to read than the decimal 0.00000000000000000000000000000091093826 kilogram. Convert each of the following numbers either from or to scientific notation, and determine the number of significant digits:

**(a)** 200,000,000,000 (number of stars in the Andromeda galaxy)

**(b)** 0.000000000753 kilogram (mass of a dust particle)

**(c)** 10,300,000,000,000,000,000,000 (number of carbon atoms in a 1-carat diamond)

**(d)** $2 \times 10^{-23}$ (mass of a carbon atom in grams)

**(e)** $6.56 \times 10^9$ (current world population)

**(f)** $6.022 \times 10^{23}$ (Avogadro's number)

## Using a Calculator

31. Among the cryptic notes of the Indian mathematician Srinivasa Ramanujan is the equation

$$\pi^4 = 97.409091 \ldots .$$

This equation suggests that $\pi^4 \doteq 97.4\overline{09}$.

**(a)** Show that $97.4\overline{09} = 97\frac{1}{2} - \frac{1}{11}$.

**(b)** Use your calculator to calculate $\pi^4 - \left(97\frac{1}{2} - \frac{1}{11}\right)$ and determine just how good Ramanujan's approximation is.

32. **(a)** In Chapter 2, you were introduced to the process called Diffy. Use Diffy to complete the array shown. Remember that the first, second, and third circles in any row contain the differences (greatest minus least) of the numbers in the preceding row and that the fourth circle contains the difference of the elements in the first and fourth circles of the preceding row.

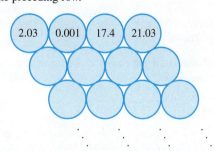

**(b)** Choose four more numbers and complete a second Diffy array.

**(c)** Can you find four numbers that cause the process to continue for at least eight steps?

**(d)** Use 17.34, 31.62, 58.14, and 107.1 to complete a Diffy process. For how many steps does the process continue?

**(e)** Do you think that the process will always terminate?

## From State Student Assessments

**33.** (Oregon, Grade 5)
Non-Calculator: Which number is between 3.7 and 3.8?

    **A.** 3.81    **B.** 3.79    **C.** 3.68    **D.** 3.5

**34.** (Georgia, Grade 4)
A weather forecaster checked and emptied a rain gauge six times one day. The measurements in inches were 0.243, 0.595, 0.903, 0.756, 0.398, and 0.112. Which is the best estimate of the total rainfall that day?

    **A.** 2.0 in.    **B.** 2.5 in.    **C.** 3.0 in.    **D.** 3.5 in.

**35.** (Georgia, Grade 5)
Your neighbor has asked you to help him build birdhouses to sell at the community craft fair. He has promised to pay you

0.01 times the amount of money that he makes selling them at the craft fair. If he sold 132 birdhouses at $12.50 each, how much money should you receive?

    **A.** $1.65    **B.** $16.50    **C.** $165.00    **D.** $1650.00

**36.** (Virginia, Grade 4)
Alyssa watched 3.5 hours of television last week. This week, she watched 4.7 hours of television. How many more hours did Alyssa watch television this week than last week?

    **A.** 0.2    **B.** 0.8    **C.** 1.2    **D.** 8.2

**37.** (Georgia, Grade 5)
Hayden paid $26.52 for 8.5 gallons of gas for his truck. What was the price for each gallon of gas?

    **A.** $2.65    **B.** $3.12    **C.** $3.32    **D.** $5.30

**38.** (Texas, Grade 4)
$2.04 - 0.96 =$

 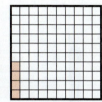 

    **A.** 1.08    **B.** 1.18    **C.** 1.92    **D.** 3.00

**39.** (Texas, Grade 4)
$1.38 + 0.62 =$

 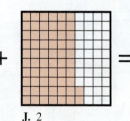

    **F.** 0.76    **G.** 1    **H.** 1.9    **J.** 2

**40.** (Connecticut, Grade 6)
Jenny bought three DVDs for $5.99 each. What was the total cost of the three DVDs before tax?

    **A.** $6.02    **B.** $8.99    **C.** $17.77    **D.** $17.97

## Examining School Book Pages

*Refer to the School Book Pages provided on page 366 to answer the following questions.*

**41.** **(a)** In Step 3 at the top of page 177 of the School Book Pages, do you feel that the determination of the placement of the decimal has been made clear?

    **(b)** Fill in the missing parenthetic notes to coordinate the rectangular area model at the top of page 176 with the following instructional multiplication notation:

$$
\begin{array}{r}
1.7 \\
\times\ 1.5 \\
\hline
0.35\ (\ 0.5 \times 0.7\ ) \\
0.5\ (\underline{\quad ?\quad }) \\
0.7\ (\underline{\quad ?\quad }) \\
\underline{1.0\ (\underline{\quad ?\quad })} \\
2.55\ (0.35 + 0.5 + 0.7 + 1.0)
\end{array}
$$

**42.** **(a)** Calculate the product $1.7 \times 2.8$, following the procedure of the example at the top of the two pages. That is, begin with rectangular area diagram, and then complete the four steps.

    **(b)** Show the product $1.7 \times 2.8$, using instructional multiplication notation. (See problem 41 at the left.)

# School Book Pages

## Multiplying Two Decimals

### Lesson 7-4

**Understand It!**
The steps for multiplying decimals by decimals are almost identical to the steps for multiplying whole numbers by whole numbers.

## Multiplying Two Decimals

**How can you multiply two decimals?**

Nancy walked 1.7 miles in 1 hour. If she walks at the same rate, how far will she walk in 1.5 hours?

**Choose an Operation**
Multiply to find $1.7 \times 1.5$.

$1 \times 1 = 1$    $1 \times 0.7 = 0.7$

$1 \times 0.5 = 0.5$    $0.7 \times 0.5 = 0.35$

**Step 1**
Estimate $1.7 \times 1.5$
$2 \times 2 = 4$

**Step 2**
Multiply as you would with whole numbers.

$$\begin{array}{r} 1.7 \\ \times\ 1.5 \\ \hline 85 \\ 170 \\ \hline 255 \end{array}$$

**Step 3**
Count decimal places in *both* factors.

Write the decimal point in the product.

$$\begin{array}{r} 1.7 \quad \text{1 decimal place}\\ \times\ 1.5 \quad \text{1 decimal place}\\ \hline 85 \\ 170 \\ \hline 2.55 \quad \text{2 places} \end{array}$$

**Step 4**
Check your answer.

Since 2.55 is close to your estimate of 4, the answer is reasonable.

In 1.5 hours, Nancy will walk 2.55 miles.

---

## Guided Practice*

**Do you know HOW?**

For **1** through **6**, estimate first. Then find each product. Check that your answer is reasonable.

**1.**
$$\begin{array}{r} 9.3 \\ \times\ 4.1 \\ \hline \end{array}$$

**2.**
$$\begin{array}{r} 3.02 \\ \times\ 0.6 \\ \hline \end{array}$$

**3.** $0.7 \times 1.9$

**4.** $12.6 \times 0.2$

**5.** $8.3 \times 10.7$

**6.** $2.04 \times 1.8$

**Do you UNDERSTAND?**

**7.** **Writing to Explain** How is multiplying two decimals different from multiplying one decimal by a whole number?

**8.** Using the example above, how many miles will Nancy walk in 2.8 hours? Show an estimate first.

## Independent Practice

For **9** through **28**, estimate first. Then find each product. Check that your answer is reasonable.

**9.**
$$\begin{array}{r} 5.2 \\ \times\ 4.6 \\ \hline \end{array}$$

**10.**
$$\begin{array}{r} 0.05 \\ \times\ 4.5 \\ \hline \end{array}$$

**11.**
$$\begin{array}{r} 19.1 \\ \times\ 8.5 \\ \hline \end{array}$$

**12.**
$$\begin{array}{r} 8.6 \\ \times\ 0.08 \\ \hline \end{array}$$

**13.** $0.6 \times 0.49$

**14.** $32.3 \times 0.7$

**15.** $3.42 \times 4.7$

**16.** $8.11 \times 0.05$

**17.** $3.5 \times 0.4$

**18.** $28.6 \times 0.17$

**19.** $0.21 \times 1.5$

**20.** $1.11 \times 6.1$

**21.** $6.8 \times 7.2$

**22.** $8.3 \times 6.4$

**23.** $9.1 \times 11.6$

**24.** $0.04 \times 15.6$

**25.** $18.1 \times 3.7$

**26.** $0.06 \times 15$

**27.** $0.28 \times 3.7$

**28.** $3.14 \times 6.2$

**26** *For another example, see Set D on page 195.*

**176**

---

### Problem Solving

**29.** The fifth-grade planning committee needs to buy items for sandwiches for its annual lunch. Fill in the chart and determine the amount of money they'll need to buy the items for sandwiches.

| Item | Amount | Price | Total |
|------|--------|-------|-------|
| | 15.5 pounds | $3.50 per pound | |
| | 10.5 pounds | $2.90 per pound | |
| | 12 packages | $2.50 per package | |

**30.** **Geometry** Karly's bedroom measures 13.2 feet long by 10.3 feet wide. Use the formula Area = length × width to determine the number of square feet for the floor of Karly's bedroom.

**31.** A bag of grass seed weighs 5.8 pounds. How many pounds would 2.5 bags weigh?

A  14.5

B  13.8

C  8.3

D  3.3

**32.** Joy drinks 4 bottles of water per day. Each bottle contains 16.5 fluid ounces. She wants to find the total number of fluid ounces she drinks per day. How many decimal places will be in the product?

A  One          C  Three

B  Two          D  Four

**33.** Mary Ann ordered 3 pens and a box of paper on the Internet. Each pen cost $1.65 and the paper cost $3.95 per box. How much did she spend?

**34.** An astronaut's Apollo space suit weighs 29.8 pounds on the moon. It weighs approximately 6.02 times as much on Earth. About how much does an Apollo space suit weigh on Earth?

**35.** **Writing to Explain** How does estimation help you place the decimal point in a product correctly?

*Lesson 7-4* **177**

---

### 7.3

# Proportional Reasoning

In grades K–4, a main focus is the development of the additive principles of arithmetic. For example, if 6 new students join a history class of 18 students, there are now 24 students in the classroom, since $18 + 6 = 24$. Even multiplication, since it is viewed as repeated addition, is initially considered within an additive conceptual framework. However, in the upper elementary and middle grades 5–8, a new goal emerges: Students should now see that multiplicative relations are essential in understanding how relative quantities can be compared and rates of changes in quantities can be measured. For example, suppose 6 new students join a PE class of 24 students, resulting in 30 students. In additive reasoning, both the history and PE class underwent the same change in number, since both classes have 6 additional students. Proportional reasoning, however, gives a different answer: Because $\frac{6}{24}$, or $\frac{1}{4}$, or "a quarter" of the students are new to history, but only $\frac{6}{30}$, or $\frac{1}{5}$, or "a fifth" of the students are new to the PE class, there is a larger *rate* of change in the history class. If 8 new students were added to the PE class, then, since $\frac{6}{24} = \frac{8}{32}$, proportional reasoning allows us to say that the history and PE classes have increased by the same *proportional* amount.

When a part is compared to another part or to a whole, the *relative* sizes of the two parts can be represented by a fraction known as a *ratio*. What is new is that the individual sizes of the parts and the whole no longer matter in the ratio. For example, if 8 new students join the PE class of 24, then the history and PE classes have the same ratio, $\frac{1}{4}$, of new students to total students, even though the classes are not the same size. In terms of the definition that will be given shortly, the two classes will be said to have grown by the same *proportion*.

In this section, we begin with ratios and proportions and then apply these concepts to solve problems by proportional reasoning. It is important to understand when and how proportional reasoning can be used as a problem-solving strategy. However, it is equally important to know when proportional reasoning is inappropriate. For example, it may be tempting to say that a "family-size" 20-inch-diameter pizza will feed twice as many people as the "small" 10-inch pizza. But we see from the formula $\pi r^2$ for the area of a circle that the respective areas of the pizzas are $\pi(10)^2 = 100\pi$ and $\pi(5)^2 = 25\pi$, so the larger pizza will feed 4 times the number of people as the smaller one. (For more examples of when proportional reasoning is not appropriate, see problems 13, 17, and 18 at the end of the section.)

## Ratio

At basketball practice, Caralee missed 18 free throws out of 45 attempts. Since she made 27 free throws, we say that the **ratio** of the number missed to the number made was 18 to 27. This ratio can be expressed by the fraction $\frac{18}{27}$ or, somewhat archaically, by the notation $18:27$. The notation 18:27 is read "18 to 27," as in the statement "The ratio of the number of free throws Caralee missed to the number she made was 18:27." We will always use the fraction notation in what follows.

Other ratios from Caralee's basketball practice are

- the ratio of the number of shots made to the number attempted, $\frac{27}{45}$;

- the ratio of the number of shots missed to the number attempted, $\frac{18}{45}$; and

- the ratio of the number of shots made to the number missed, $\frac{27}{18}$.

> **DEFINITION** *Ratio*
>
> If $a$ and $b$ are real numbers with $b \neq 0$, then the **ratio of $a$ to $b$** is the quotient $\frac{a}{b}$.

Ratios occur with great frequency in everyday life. If you use 10.4 gallons of gasoline in driving 400.4 miles, the efficiency of your car is measured in miles per gallon given by the ratio $\frac{400.4}{10.4}$, or 38.5 miles per gallon. If Lincoln Grade School has 405 students and 15 teachers, the student–teacher ratio is the quotient $\frac{405}{15}$. If José Varga got 56 hits in 181 times at bat, his batting average is the ratio $\frac{56}{181}$. The number of examples that could be cited is almost endless.

The preceding examples show that there are at least three applications of a ratio:

1. **A ratio measures the relative size of different parts**
   Here is an example from geometry:
   - Given a circle, the ratio of its circumference $C$ (distance around) to its diameter $D$ (distance across) is the same for all circles, namely, the real number universally denoted by $\pi$. That is, $\frac{C}{D} = \pi$.

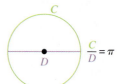

2. **A ratio measures the relative size of a part to a whole**
   Here is an example that is well known to baseball fans:
   - A player's batting average is the ratio of the number of times the player made a hit to the total number of times at bat.

3. **A ratio measures the rate of the change in one quantity with respect to a corresponding change in a second quantity**
   For example, commodities are often priced as a rate, so we may pay $\$3.15^{9/10}$ for every gallon of gas or we may pay \$8.59 for every pound of coffee. A common rate from plane coordinate geometry is the slope of a line:
   - Given a line in the coordinate $x,y$-plane, its slope (steepness) is the ratio of the change made in the vertical ($y$-axis) direction (rise) to the change made in the horizontal ($x$-axis) direction (run).

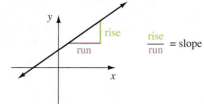

When the amount of change of a quantity is compared to a change by 1 unit of the second quantity, the rate is called a **unit rate**. For example, if a car traveled 408 miles and used 16 gallons of gasoline, then its unit rate of fuel consumption is 25.5 miles per gallon (mpg), as shown with the following calculation:

$$\frac{408 \text{ miles}}{16 \text{ gallons}} = \frac{408 \text{ miles} \div 16}{16 \text{ gallons} \div 16} = \frac{25.5 \text{ miles}}{1 \text{ gallon}} = 25.5 \text{ mpg}.$$

**EXAMPLE 7.14 Determining Ratios**

Determine these ratios:

(a) The ratio of the number of boys to the number of girls in Martin Luther King High School if there are 285 boys and 228 girls

(b) The ratio of the number of boys to the number of students in part (a)

**Solution**

(a) The desired ratio is $\frac{285}{228}$.

(b) Since the total number of students is $285 + 228$ (that is, 513), the desired ratio is $\frac{285}{513}$.

The ratio of the number of boys to the number of students in Martin Luther King High School was shown to be $\frac{285}{513}$, or 285 to 513. This is certainly correct, but it is not nearly as informative as it would be if the ratio were written in simplest form. Thus,

$$\frac{285}{513} = \frac{5}{9},$$

> $285 \div 57 = 5$
> $513 \div 57 = 9$

and this ratio says that $\frac{5}{9}$ (or a little more than $\frac{1}{2}$) of the students in Martin Luther King High School are boys. Expressing a ratio by a fraction in simplest form is often useful and informative.

---

### EXAMPLE 7.15  Expressing Ratios in Simplest Form

Express these ratios in simplest form:

    **(a)** The ratio of 385 to 440      **(b)** The ratio $\frac{432}{504}$

**Solution**    **(a)** The ratio of 385 to 440 is the quotient $\frac{385}{440}$. Expressing this quotient in simplest form, we have

$$\frac{385}{440} = \frac{7}{8}.$$

Thus, in simplest form, the ratio is 7 to 8.

**(b)** Expressing the quotient in simplest form, we have

$$\frac{432}{504} = \frac{6}{7}.$$

Thus, in simplest form, the ratio is $\frac{6}{7}$, or 6 to 7.

---

### EXAMPLE 7.16  Determining a Less Obvious Ratio

If one-seventh of the students at Garfield High are nonswimmers, what is the ratio of nonswimmers to swimmers?

**Solution**    **Understand the Problem**

The desired ratio is the number of nonswimmers attending Garfield High School divided by the number of swimmers.

**Devise a Plan**

The needed numbers are not given in the problem, and we don't even know how many students attended the school. If, for example, there were 700 students attending the school, then $\frac{1}{7} \cdot 700 = 100$ would be nonswimmers and the remaining $600 = \frac{6}{7} \cdot 700$ would be swimmers. But suppose there

> Use algebraic reasoning by introducing a variable.

are $n$ students attending Garfield. Then $\frac{1}{7} \cdot n = \frac{n}{7}$ are nonswimmers and $\frac{6}{7} n = \frac{6n}{7}$ are swimmers. Perhaps we can use these expressions to determine the desired ratio.

**Carry Out the Plan**

Letting $n$ denote the number of students attending Garfield High, we just saw that $\frac{n}{7}$ students are nonswimmers and $\frac{6n}{7}$ are swimmers. Therefore, the desired ratio is

$$\frac{\frac{n}{7}}{\frac{6n}{7}} = \frac{n}{7} \cdot \frac{7}{6n} = \frac{1}{6}.$$

**Look Back**

It turns out that we didn't need to know the actual number of students attending Garfield High, since we could use a variable and get general expressions for the numbers of swimmers and nonswimmers. Taking the quotient of these expressions, we found the desired ratio. On the one hand, using a variable in this way is often a useful strategy. On the other hand, we didn't need to use a variable: Assuming that there were 700 students attending the school, there would be 100 nonswimmers and 600 swimmers, and the desired ratio is again $\frac{100}{600} = \frac{1}{6}$. We can also solve the problem with a pictorial model, and it is often useful to create a visual model that clarifies and confirms relationships. In the figure shown next, we group the students into seven rectangles, each containing the same number of students. The brown "beach" rectangle contains the nonswimmers, and the remaining six blue "pools" contain the swimmers. The figure makes it clear that the ratio of nonswimmers to swimmers is 1 to 6, or $\frac{1}{6}$.

## Proportion

Ratios allow us to make comparisons clear when actual numbers sometimes make them more obscure. For example, at basketball practice, Caralee made 27 of 45 free throws attempted and Sonja made 24 of 40 attempts. Which player appears to be the better foul-shot shooter? For Caralee, saying that the ratio of shots made to shots tried is $\frac{27}{45}$ amounts to saying that she made $\frac{3}{5}$ of her shots. That is,

$$\frac{27}{45} = \frac{3}{5}.$$

> $\frac{27}{45}$ and $\frac{3}{5}$ are equivalent fractions.

Similarly, for Sonja, the ratio of shots made to shots attempted is

$$\frac{24}{40} = \frac{3}{5},$$

> $\frac{27}{45}, \frac{24}{40}$, and $\frac{3}{5}$ are all equivalent fractions.

and these ratios suggest that the two girls are equally skilled at shooting foul shots. Because of its importance in such comparisons, the equality of two ratios is called a **proportion.**

**DEFINITION** *Proportion*

If $\dfrac{a}{b}$ and $\dfrac{c}{d}$ are two ratios and

$$\frac{a}{b} = \frac{c}{d},$$

this equality is called a **proportion.**

From Chapter 6, we know that

$$\frac{a}{b} = \frac{c}{d}$$

for integers $a$, $b$, $c$, and $d$ if, and only if, $ad = bc$. But the same argument holds if $a$, $b$, $c$, and $d$ are real numbers. This fact leads to the next theorem.

**THEOREM** *Conditions for a Proportion*

The equality

$$\frac{a}{b} = \frac{c}{d}$$

is a proportion if, and only if, $ad = bc$.

**EXAMPLE 7.17 Determining Proportions**

In each of these equations, determine $x$ so that the equality is a proportion:

(a) $\dfrac{28}{49} = \dfrac{x}{21}$  (b) $\dfrac{2.11}{3.49} = \dfrac{1.7}{x}$

**Solution** We use the preceding theorem, which amounts to multiplying both sides of the equality by the product of the denominators, or "cross multiplying," as we often say.

(a) $\dfrac{28}{49} = \dfrac{x}{21}$  (b) $\dfrac{2.11}{3.49} = \dfrac{1.7}{x}$

$28 \cdot 21 = 49x$    $2.11x = (1.7)(3.49)$

$\dfrac{28 \cdot 21}{49} = x$    $x = \dfrac{(1.7)(3.49)}{2.11}$

$12 = x$    $x \doteq 2.81$

**EXAMPLE 7.18 Proving a Property of Proportions**

Prove that if

$$\frac{a}{b} = \frac{c}{d},$$

then

$$\frac{a+b}{b} = \frac{c+d}{d}.$$

**Solution**

**Understand the Problem**

We are given that $\dfrac{a}{b} = \dfrac{c}{d}$ is a proportion and are asked to show that $\dfrac{a+b}{b} = \dfrac{c+d}{d}$ is also a proportion.

### Devise a Plan

Since it is not immediately clear what to do, we ask what it means to say that $\dfrac{a}{b} = \dfrac{c}{d}$ and $\dfrac{a+b}{b} = \dfrac{c+d}{d}$ are proportions. Perhaps answering this question will put the problem in a form that is easier to understand and to work on. By the preceding theorem,

$$\frac{a}{b} = \frac{c}{d} \text{ if, and only if, } ad = bc$$

and

$$\frac{a+b}{b} = \frac{c+d}{d}$$

if, and only if, $(a + b)d = b(c + d)$. Perhaps we can use the first of these equations to prove the second.

### Carry Out the Plan

We want to show that $(a + b)d = b(c + d)$; that is, using the distributive property, we get

$$ad + bd = bc + bd.$$

But we know that

$$ad = bc,$$

and adding $bd$ to both sides of this equation gives

$$ad + bd = bc + bd.$$

Hence,

$$\frac{a+b}{b} = \frac{c+d}{d},$$

as was to be shown.

> Say it in a different way.

### Look Back

Here, our principal strategy was simply to ask, "What does it mean to say that $\dfrac{a}{b} = \dfrac{c}{d}$ and $\dfrac{a+b}{b} = \dfrac{c+d}{d}$ are proportions?" Answering this question allowed us to "say it in a different way"—that is, to state an equivalent problem that proved to be quite easy to solve. The strategy **say it in a different way** is often very useful.

## Applications of Proportional Reasoning

Suppose that a car is traveling at a constant unit rate of speed of 55 miles per hour. Table 7.2 gives the distances the car will travel in different periods.

**TABLE 7.2    DISTANCE TRAVELED IN $T$ HOURS AT 55 MILES PER HOUR**

| Time $t$ | 1 | 2 | 3 | 4 | 5 | 6 | 7 | 8 |
|---|---|---|---|---|---|---|---|---|
| Distance $d$ | 55 | 110 | 165 | 220 | 275 | 330 | 385 | 440 |

The ratios $\dfrac{d}{t}$ are all equal for the periods shown; that is,

$$\frac{55}{1} = \frac{110}{2} = \frac{165}{3} = \frac{220}{4} = \frac{275}{5} = \frac{330}{6},$$

and so on. Thus, each pair of ratios from the list forms a proportion. Indeed, $\dfrac{d}{t} = 55$ for every pair $d$ and $t$. This relationship is also expressed by saying that the distance traveled at a constant rate is proportional to the elapsed time. In the current example,

$$d = 55t$$

for every pair $d$ and $t$. The number 55 is called the **constant of proportionality.**

---

**DEFINITION**   *y is proportional to x*
If the variables $x$ and $y$ are related by the equation

$$y = kx,$$

$$\frac{y}{x} = k$$

then **$y$ is said to be proportional to $x$** and $k$ is called the **constant of proportionality.**

---

This situation is extremely common in everyday life. Gasoline consumed by your car is proportional to the number of miles traveled, the cost of pencils purchased is proportional to the number of pencils purchased, income from the school raffle is proportional to the number of tickets sold, and so on.

Sometimes it is said that "*y is directly proportional to x*" when $y = kx$, to distinguish that situation from "*y is inversely proportional to x,*" when the variables are related by the equation $y = \dfrac{k}{x}$ for some constant $k$. For example, if you always commute 12 miles to work, then your travel time $t$ is inversely proportional to your rate of travel $r$, since we have the equation $t = \dfrac{12}{r}$. A famous example is Newton's "inverse-square law" of gravity, which states that the force $F$ of gravity on an object is inversely proportional to the square of the distance $r$ to the earth's center. That is, there is a constant $k$ such that $F = \dfrac{k}{r^2}$.

---

**EXAMPLE 7.19  Comparing Distances**

Khalid and his brother Ahmed both left the same city at 1 P.M., but Khalid averaged 63 miles per hour in his new car and Ahmed averaged just 51 miles per hour in his older car. How much farther has Khalid traveled than Ahmed at 4:30 P.M. that afternoon?

**Solution**

One way to find the answer is to compute how far each brother traveled and then take the difference. Thus, Kahlid traveled $3.5 \times 63 = 220.5$ miles and Ahmed traveled $3.5 \times 51 = 178.5$ miles, so Khalid traveled $220.5 - 178.5 = 42$ miles farther than his brother.

A much better method is to apply proportional reasoning directly, since the distance of separation is proportional to the time of travel. Khalid travels $k = 12$ miles per hour faster than his brother, so in $t = 3.5$ hours he is $kt = 3.5 \times 12 = 42$ miles ahead of Ahmed. This calculation is so simple that it can be done with mental arithmetic.

---

**EXAMPLE 7.20  Going Nutty with Proportional Reasoning**

Marci liked the mixed nuts she made by combining 6 cups of cashews with 2 cups of pecans. She hopes to make gift boxes with the same mixture of nuts.

(a) If Marci has 5 cups of pecans, how many cups of cashews does she need?
(b) Marci has several tin gift boxes on hand of various sizes, holding 4 cups, 8 cups, 12 cups, 16 cups, and 20 cups. How many cups of each type of nut should be added to these boxes so that each box contains the same mixture of nuts?

**Solution**

(a) Since 6 cups of cashews and 2 cups of pecans make 8 cups of mixed nuts, a "half" recipe of 3 cups of cashews and 1 cup of pecans makes 4 cups of mixed nuts. Since she wants 3 times as many cashews as pecans, Marci needs to add $3 \times 5 = 15$ cups of cashews to her 5 cups of pecans. This will create 20 cups of mixed nuts.

(b) The examples in part (a) can be organized into a table in which each value in the second row is 3 times the value in the top row and each value in the bottom row is 4 times the value in row 1:

| Pecans | 1 | 2 | 3 | 4 | 5 |
|---|---|---|---|---|---|
| Cashews | 3 | 6 | 9 | 12 | 15 |
| Mixture | 4 | 8 | 12 | 16 | 20 |

Alternatively, the values in the first and second row are, respectively, $\frac{1}{4}$ and $\frac{3}{4}$ of the value in the third row.

A table with the property that the values in one row are a constant multiple of the values in another row is called a **ratio table.**

## EXAMPLE 7.21 Proportional Reasoning with Diagrams

Hannah and her brother Ethan went to the mall with an equal amount of money to buy their mother a birthday present. Hannah purchased a $26 scarf and Ethan bought his mother a jewelry box for $34. After their purchases, Ethan has $\frac{2}{3}$ of the money that Hannah has remaining. How much money do Hannah and Ethan now have, and how much did they start with before making their purchases?

**Solution**

The diagram that follows shows that, after spending $34, Ethan has $\frac{2}{3}$ of the money that Hannah has remaining after her $26 purchase. Since Hannah has $8 = \$34 - \$26$ more than Ethan, we see that Hannah has $24, Ethan has $16, and each went to the mall with $50.

## EXAMPLE 7.22 Springs and Weights

The students in Mrs. Stratton's class have created the data plot shown next. The horizontal axis shows the weight they have suspended from a spring, and the vertical axis shows how many inches the spring is stretched. They are about to measure the amount of stretch of a 5-pound weight, but Michelle thinks that she already knows how much stretch to expect. What do you think Michelle's guess is, and what reasoning did she employ to make her guess?

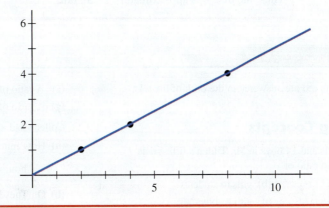

**Solution**  Michelle has noticed that the amount of stretch in inches is one-half of the weight in pounds. Therefore, a 5-pound weight can be expected to stretch the spring $\frac{5}{2}$, or $2\frac{1}{2}$, inches. Michelle has also noticed that every data point will fall on a line, as shown on the graph that follows. For example, a 10-pound weight will stretch the spring 5 inches, and the point (10, 5) will be on the line.

The graphs in Example 7.22 show that the $y$-coordinate is proportional to the $x$-coordinate. That is, we have a line with an equation of the form $y = kx$ that passes through the origin. The value of $k$ is the constant of proportionality and gives the ratio of the amount of change in $y$ that corresponds to a constant change in $x$. That is, $k$ is the *slope* of the line with equation $y = kx$. Lines and their equations will be explored in more detail in Chapter 8.

For the next example, recall that in geometry two figures are said to be similar if they are the same shape but not necessarily the same size—that is, one is a magnification of the other.

**EXAMPLE 7.23  Computing the Height of a Tree**

Ms. Gulley-Pavey's fifth-grade class had been studying the concepts of ratio and proportion. One afternoon, she took her students outside and challenged them to find the height of a tree in the school yard. After a lively discussion, the students decided to measure the length of the shadow cast by a yardstick and that cast by the tree, arguing that these should be proportional. To help convince the class that this was so, Omari drew the picture shown. If the lengths of the shadows are 4′7″ and 18′9″, respectively, complete the calculation to determine the height of the tree.

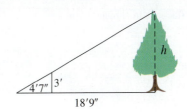

**Solution** Since the two triangles shown in the diagram are similar, the lengths of the sides are proportional. Also, $7'' = \dfrac{7}{12}$ feet and $9'' = \dfrac{9}{12}$ feet. Therefore, we have the proportion

$$\frac{h}{3} = \frac{18\frac{9}{12}}{4\frac{7}{12}}$$

> The units of both ratios must be the same.

$$= \frac{\frac{225}{12}}{\frac{55}{12}} = \frac{225}{12} \cdot \frac{12}{55} = \frac{225}{55} = \frac{45}{11},$$

and it follows that

$$h = \frac{3 \cdot 45'}{11} = \frac{135'}{11} = 12\frac{3}{11}' \approx 12\frac{3}{12}' = 12'3''.$$

Thus, the tree was approximately $12'3''$ tall.

## Problem Set 7.3

Exercises numbered in red are answered in the back of the text.

## Understanding Concepts

1. There are 10 girls and 14 boys in Mr. Tilden's fifth-grade class. What is the ratio of

   (a) boys to girls?
   (b) girls to students?
   (c) boys to students?
   (d) girls to boys?
   (e) students to girls?
   (f) students to boys?

2. Determine which of these equations are proportions:

   (a) $\dfrac{2}{3} = \dfrac{8}{12}$

   (b) $\dfrac{21}{28} = \dfrac{27}{36}$

   (c) $\dfrac{7}{28} = \dfrac{8}{31}$

   (d) $\dfrac{51}{85} = \dfrac{57}{95}$

   (e) $\dfrac{14}{49} = \dfrac{18}{60}$

   (f) $\dfrac{20}{35} = \dfrac{28}{48}$

   (g) $\dfrac{1.5}{2.1} = \dfrac{11.5}{16.1}$

   (h) $\dfrac{17.1}{6.2} = \dfrac{31.2}{9.7}$

   (i) $\dfrac{0.84}{0.96} = \dfrac{91.7}{104.8}$

3. Determine values of $r$ and $s$ so that each of these equations is a proportion.

   (a) $\dfrac{6}{14} = \dfrac{r}{21}$

   (b) $\dfrac{8}{12} = \dfrac{10}{r}$

   (c) $\dfrac{47}{3.2} = \dfrac{s}{7.8}$

4. Express each of these ratios as fractions in simplest form.

   (a) A ratio of 24 to 16
   (b) A ratio of 296 to 111
   (c) A ratio of 248 to 372
   (d) A ratio of 209 to 341
   (e) A ratio of 3.6 to 4.8

   (f) A ratio of 2.09 to 3.41
   (g) A ratio of 6.264 to 9.396

5. Collene had an after-school job at Taco Time at $5.50 per hour.

   (a) How much did she earn on Monday if she worked $3\dfrac{1}{2}$ hours?

   (b) On Tuesday she earned $27.50. How long did she work?

   (c) Show that the ratio of the time worked to the amount earned on Monday is equal to the ratio of the time worked to the amount earned on Tuesday; that is, show that these two ratios form a proportion.

   (d) Show that the ratio of the time worked on Monday to the time worked on Tuesday equals the ratio of the amount earned on Monday to the amount earned on Tuesday; that is, show that these two ratios also form a proportion.

6. David Horwitz bought four sweatshirts for $119.92. How much would it cost him to buy nine sweatshirts at the same price per sweatshirt?

7. Brand A is 43¢ per ounce and Brand B is $7.19 per pound. Compare the two unit rates to determine which brand is more expensive.

8. If $s$ is proportional to $t$ and $s = 62.5$ when $t = 7$, what is $s$ when $t = 10$?

9. The flagpole at Sunnyside Elementary School casts a shadow $9'8''$ long at the same time that Mr. Schaal's shadow is $3'2''$ long. If Mr. Schaal is $6'3''$ tall, how tall is the flagpole, to the nearest foot?

10. A kilometer is a bit more than six-tenths of a mile. If the speed limit along a stretch of highway in Canada is 90 kilometers per hour, about how fast can you travel in miles per hour and still not break the speed limit?

11. The "squareness" of a rectangle can be measured by the ratio of the lengths of the short to the long side. Consider these rectangles: 5 by 7, 8 by 10, 12 by 15, 15 by 21, and 16 by 20. A square has squareness one.

    (a) Which rectangle (or rectangles) is the most squarelike? the least squarelike?

    (b) Are there any rectangles with the same squareness?

12. The Green Cab Company charges $2.50 plus 25¢ per quarter mile traveled. The Red Taxi Company charges $1.80 plus 30¢ per quarter mile. Apparently, you should take a Red Taxi for short trips, and a Green Cab for longer trips. Use proportional reasoning to determine the break-even distance.

13. For the given $x$ and $y$ variables, decide whether $y$ is or is not proportional to $x$.

    (a) $y$ is the cost of $x$ gallons of gasoline.

    (b) $y$ is the perimeter of a square whose sides have length $x$.

    (c) $y$ is the area of a square whose sides have length $x$.

    (d) $y$ is the sales tax in Idaho of an item that costs $x$ dollars.

    (e) $y$ is the taxi fare for a ride of $x$ miles.

## Teaching Concepts

14. How could you use measurement and a diagram like the following to help your students understand proportions and the phrase "is proportional to"?

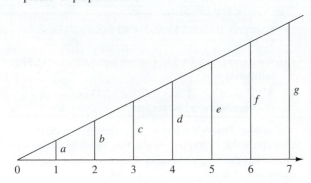

15. Some teachers use diagrams like the following, depicting $a:b = c:d$, or $a/b = c/d$, to help their students visualize proportions:

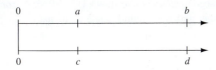

    (a) If $a = 6$ when $b = 24$, determine $c$ when $d = 72$.

    (b) If $b = 2400$ when $a = 128$, determine $d$ when $c = 512$.

    (c) If $b = 24.7$ when $a = 1.4$, determine $d$ when $c = 4.5$.

## Responding to Students

16. Jo was informed that data from the American Water Works Association show that the average person uses 20 gallons of water to take a shower. Jo was then asked to find the amount of water used by a person in a week, a month, and a year. She made the following table:

| Gallons | 20 | 140 | 4200 | 51,100 |
|---|---|---|---|---|
| Days | 1 | 7 (1 week) | 30 (1 month) | 365 (1 year) |

Give helpful advice to Jo.

17. Linda helped with her mother's 20-foot–by–20-foot garden plot. Since Linda thought it would be nice to get twice the amount of produce, she wanted a 40-foot–by–40-foot garden next year. How would you use diagrams to help Linda?

18. Allison has a 4-inch–by–6-inch digital photo. To make an enlargement, she has dragged the size handle on edges of the photo to create an 8-inch–by–10-inch photo. She thinks that the picture now looks distorted and has asked you to help with her project. How can you help make her photo?

## Thinking Critically

19. Suppose $a$ is to $b$ as $c$ is to $d$; that is,

    $$\frac{a}{b} = \frac{c}{d}.$$

    (a) Show that $b$ is to $a$ as $d$ is to $c$.

    (b) Show that $a - b$ is to $b$ as $c - d$ is to $d$.

    (c) Show that $a$ is to $a + b$ as $c$ is to $c + d$.

    (d) Show that $a + b$ is to $c + d$ as $b$ is to $d$.

20. Suppose that the variables $x$ and $y$ are related by one of the formulas (a) $y = \frac{x}{2}$, (b) $y = -\frac{x}{2}$, (c) $y = 3 + x$, and (d) $y = x^2$. Match each formula to its plot, shown here:

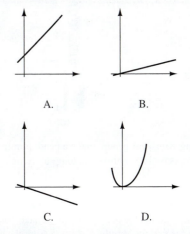

21. Pose a problem (inspired by Example 7.21) whose solution becomes evident from the figure shown. Describe how the diagram is used to answer your problem.

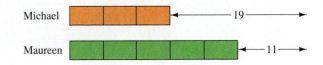

**22. (a)** If $y$ is proportional to $x^2$ and $y = 27$ when $x = 6$, determine $y$ when $x = 12$.

**(b)** Determine the ratio of the $y$-values in part (a).

**(c)** If $y$ and $x$ are related as in part (a), what happens to the value of $y$ if the value of $x$ is doubled? Explain.

**23.** Consider the sequence consisting of the odd natural numbers $1, 3, 5, 7, 9, 11, 13, 15, \ldots$.

**(a)** What is interesting about the ratio of the sum of the first $k$ odds compared with the sum of the next $k$ odds? For example, if $k = 2$, then the sum of the first two odds is $1 + 3$ and the sum of the next two odds is $5 + 7$, so the ratio of sums is $\dfrac{1 + 3}{5 + 7} = \dfrac{4}{12} = \dfrac{1}{3}$. Try other values of $k$ and make a conjecture about the ratios.

**(b)** Repeat part (a), but this time form ratios of the sum of the first $k$ odds to the sum of the next $2k$ odds.

**(c)** Investigate the ratio of the sum of the first $k$ odds to the sum of the next $nk$ odds for any given natural number $n$. Make a conjecture about these ratios.

## Thinking Cooperatively

**24.** Working with your group, hang a screen-door spring about 20 inches long from a support like a portable coat hanger and hang from the end of the spring a tin can or other container capable of holding up to a 2-pound weight. Using a meter-stick, measure as carefully as possible the *amount of stretch* of the spring if a half-pound weight is hung from the spring, a 1-pound weight is hung, and a 2-pound weight is hung. What can you conclude about the ratios of the weights to the amount of stretch? Decide on a common answer for your group.

**25.** Working with your group, make a pendulum from a long piece of string (say, 150 centimeters long) by tying three or four heavy washers onto the end of the string. Mark the string at 10-centimeter intervals starting from the center of the washers. Hold the pendulum from a suitable support and measure the time $t$ in seconds for the pendulum to make 10 complete swings for various lengths $l$ of string from the support to the center of the washers.

**(a)** Complete the following table, computing $l$ to the nearest hundredth, and arrive at a consensus conclusion for the results observed:

| $l$ | $t$ | $\sqrt{l}$ |
|-----|-----|------------|
| 10  |     |            |
| 20  |     |            |
| 30  |     |            |
| 40  |     |            |
| 50  |     |            |

**(b)** Predict how long it will take for 10 swings if the pendulum is 100 centimeters long. Then check your guess by actually timing 10 swings. Is the time obtained about what you expect?

## Making Connections

**26.** Celeste won a 100-meter race with a time of 11.6 seconds, and Michelle came in second with a time of 11.8 seconds. Given that each girl ran at a constant rate throughout the race, determine the ratio of Celeste's speed to Michelle's in simplest terms.

**27.** On a trip of 320 miles, Sunao's truck averaged 9.2 miles per gallon. At the same rate, how much gasoline would his truck use on a trip of 440 miles?

**28.** Which is the best buy in each case?

**(a)** 32 ounces of cheese for 90¢ or 40 ounces of cheese for $1.20

**(b)** A gallon of milk for $2.21 or two half-gallons at $1.11 per half-gallon

**(c)** A 16-ounce box of bran flakes at $3.85 per box or a 12-ounce box at $2.94 per box

**29.** The ratio of Dexter's salary to Claudine's is 4 to 5. If Claudine earns $3200 per month, how much of a raise will Dexter have to receive to make the ratio of his salary to Claudine's 5 to 6?

**30.** The ratio of boys to girls in Ms. Zombo's class is 3 to 2. In Mr. Stolarski's class it is 4 to 3. If there are 30 students in Ms. Zombo's class and 28 students in Mr. Stolarski's class, what is the ratio of boys to girls in the combined classes?

**31.** The accompanying table shows U.S. hat sizes from XS to XL, together with the circumference of the hat.

**(a)** Is the circumference proportional to the hat size?

**(b)** Is there a simple relationship between hat size and circumference?

(*Suggestion*: Consider subtracting 1 inch from the circumference.)

| Hat Size | $6\frac{5}{8}$ | $6\frac{3}{4}$ | $6\frac{7}{8}$ | $7$ | $7\frac{1}{8}$ | $7\frac{1}{4}$ | $7\frac{3}{8}$ | $7\frac{1}{2}$ |
|----------|----------------|----------------|----------------|-----|----------------|----------------|----------------|----------------|
| Circumference (in inches) | $20\frac{7}{8}$ | $21\frac{1}{4}$ | $21\frac{5}{8}$ | $22$ | $22\frac{3}{8}$ | $22\frac{3}{4}$ | $23\frac{1}{8}$ | $23\frac{1}{3}$ |

**32.** In the diagram that follows, use a metric ruler to *very carefully* measure the lengths $AC$, $BC$, $CD$, $BE$, and $DE$ (even trying to estimate to the nearest tenth of a millimeter—that is, to the nearest hundredth in the decimal representation of each length). Then compute the ratios

$$\frac{AC}{BC}, \frac{BC}{CD}, \frac{CD}{DE}, \frac{AD}{DC}, \text{ and } \frac{BE}{ED}.$$

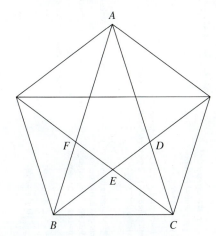

Given the difficulty in obtaining really accurate measurements, what seems to be true of all of these ratios?

**33.** If a 12″ pepperoni pizza from Ricco's costs $9.56, what should a 14″ pizza from Ricco's cost?

**34.** Suppose your car uses 8.7 gallons of gas traveling 192 miles. Determine approximately how many gallons it would use traveling a distance of 305 miles.

**35.** If it takes $1\frac{1}{3}$ cups of sugar to make a batch of cookies, how much sugar would be required to make four batches?

**36.** If three equally priced shirts cost a total of $59.97, how much would seven shirts cost at the same price per shirt?

**37.** If 12 erasers cost $8.04 and Mrs. Orton bought $14.07 worth of erasers, how many erasers did she buy?

**38.** One day Kenji took his class of sixth graders outside and challenged them to find the distance between two rocks that could easily be seen, one above the other, on the vertical face of a bluff near the school. After some discussion, the children decided to hold a rod in a vertical position at a point 100′ from the base of the cliff, as shown in the following diagram:

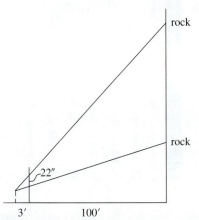

They also decided to mark the points on the rod where the lines of sight of a student standing 3′ farther from the cliff and

looking at the rocks cut the rod. If the marks on the rod were 22″ apart, what was the distance between the two rocks? (*Caution:* Convert all measurements to feet.)

**39.** *The New York Times* crossword puzzle is constructed on a 21 × 21 grid on Sundays and on a 15 × 15 grid the other days of the week. "About" a sixth of the squares must be black and must form a pattern with 180° rotational symmetry.

**(a)** Find a newspaper that publishes *The New York Times* crossword puzzle, and report on how closely the "one-sixth" rule is observed.

**(b)** Why can't the "one-sixth" rule ever be obeyed exactly? What is the number of black squares that comes closest to following the rule on a 15 × 15 grid? On a 21 × 21 grid?

**40. Bike Speeds and Gear Ratios.** A modern touring bike often has a system of three "chainrings" turned by the pedal on the front and a set of seven "cogs" on the rear wheel hub. A common setup is to have a choice of 24, 35, or 51 teeth on the chainrings, and 34, 28, 23, 19, 16, 13, or 11 teeth on the cogs. The "speed" of the bike is then proportional to the ratio of the number of teeth of the chainring engaged to that of the cog. For example, the fastest speed is expressed by the ratio $\frac{51}{11} \doteq 4.63$, for which each complete revolution of the pedals rotates the rear wheel 4.63 revolutions. For climbing hills, a rider may want to use the smallest chainring and the largest cog, giving a ratio $\frac{24}{34} \doteq 0.71$ that turns the rear wheel slowly, but with more force.

**(a)** Create a table showing the ratios of all 21 speeds.

**(b)** Does a "21-speed" bicycle truly have 21 speeds? Is there a more accurate number of speeds? Write a brief summary of your findings.

**(c)** Count the number of teeth on the chainrings and the number on cogs of your bike or that of a friend. Use your data to create a table of ratios for the bike, and report on the number of "speeds" of the bike.

**41.** The ancient Mayan astronomers were elated when they discovered how the 584-day "year" of Venus compared with the 365-day solar year. What proportion did their observations reveal?

## From State Student Assessments

**42.** (Colorado, Grade 4)

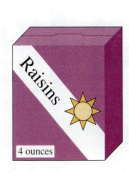

*See "Examining School Book Pages" on page 381 for questions related to the pages shown below.*

# School Book Pages

## Understanding Rates and Unit Rates

### Lesson 12-3

**Understand It!** Rates are a special type of ratio where quantities with different units of measure are being compared.

## Understanding Rates and Unit Rates

### Are there special types of ratios?

A **rate** is a special type of ratio that compares quantities with unlike units of measure, such as $\frac{150\ miles}{3\ hours}$. If the comparison is to 1 unit, the rate is called a **unit rate**, such as $\frac{50\ miles}{1\ hour}$. Find how far the car travels in 1 minute.

7 km in 4 minutes

First, write how fast the car travels as a rate.

7 km in 4 minutes

$\frac{7\ km}{4\ min}$

To find the **unit** rate, divide the first term by the second term.

Divide 7 kilometers by 4 minutes.

$$\begin{array}{r} 1.75 \\ 4\overline{)7.00} \\ -4\phantom{.00} \\ \hline 30 \\ -28 \\ \hline 20 \\ -20 \\ \hline 0 \end{array}$$

To understand why it works, remember that you can divide the terms of any ratio by the same number to find an equal ratio.

$\frac{7 \div 4}{4 \div 4} = \frac{1.75}{1}$

The unit rate is $\frac{1.75\ km}{1\ min}$.

The car can go 1.75 kilometers in 1 minute.

### Do you know HOW?

Write each as a rate and as a unit rate.

1. 60 km in 12 hours
2. 26 cm in 13 s
3. 230 miles on 10 gallons
4. $12.50 for 5 lb

### Do you UNDERSTAND?

5. What makes a unit rate different from another rate?
6. Explain the difference in meaning between these two rates: $\frac{5\ trees}{1\ chimpanzee}$ and $\frac{1\ tree}{5\ chimpanzees}$.

### Independent Practice

In **7** through **18**, write each as a rate and a unit rate.

7. 38 minutes to run 5 laps
8. 36 butterflies on 12 flowers
9. 252 days for 9 full moons
10. 18 eggs laid in 3 days
11. 56 points scored in 8 games
12. 216 apples growing on 9 trees
13. 125 giraffes on 50 hectares
14. 84 mm in 4 seconds
15. 123 miles driven in 3 hours
16. 210 miles in 7 hours
17. 250 calories in 10 crackers
18. 15 countries visited in 12 days

### Problem Solving

Use the bar graph about the top speeds that different ocean animals can swim for **19** through **21**.

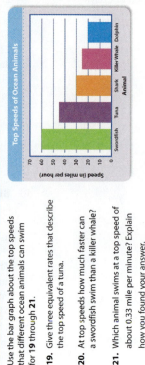

Top Speeds of Ocean Animals
Speed (in miles per hour) — 70, 60, 50, 40, 30, 20, 10, 0
Animal: Swordfish, Tuna, Shark, Killer Whale, Dolphin

19. Give three equivalent rates that describe the top speed of a tuna.
20. At top speeds how much faster can a swordfish swim than a killer whale?
21. Which animal swims at a top speed of about 0.33 mile per minute? Explain how you found your answer.
22. The *SR-71 Blackbird* is the fastest plane in the world. It can reach a maximum speed of 2,512 mph. What is its maximum rate of speed in miles per minute?
23. **Think About the Process** Mischa buys 4 tickets to a soccer game. The total cost before taxes is $90. Which equation would you use to determine the price, *p*, of each ticket?

    A $4p = 90$
    B $90p = 4$
    C $4 + p = 90$
    D $p \div 4 = 90$

24. **Writing to Explain** Make a list of three rates that describe what you do. For example, you could describe how many classes you attend in a day. For each example, explain why it is a rate.

Animated Glossary www.pearsonsuccessnet.com

306

Lesson 12-3 307

Marcus has two different-size boxes of raisins. He counts 62 raisins in the 4-ounce box.

**A.** Estimate how many raisins are in the 16-ounce box.

**B.** Explain your estimate and show your work so Marcus can see how you decided.

**43.** (Minnesota, Grade 5)
Use the drawing below to answer the question.

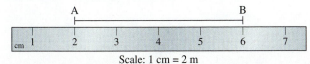

Scale: 1 cm = 2 m

The segment AB is taken from a scale drawing. What is the actual length that this segment represents?

**A.** 4 meters          **B.** 6 meters

**C.** 8 meters          **D.** 12 meters

**44.** (Connecticut, Grade 6)
20 out of every 100 high school dropouts are gifted and talented students. Which of the following also describes this situation?

**A.** $\frac{4}{25}$ of the dropouts are gifted and talented.

**B.** $\frac{1}{4}$ of the dropouts are gifted and talented.

**C.** $\frac{1}{5}$ of the dropouts are gifted and talented.

**D.** $\frac{5}{1}$ of the dropouts are gifted and talented.

**45.** (Arizona Grade 8)
Students submitted pictures for the school yearbook. Only 4/5 of the submitted pictures fit in the yearbook. There were 105 pictures that did not fit. Approximately how many total pictures were submitted for the yearbook?

**A.** 105    **B.** 210    **C.** 420    **D.** 500

**46.** (Arizona, Grade 8)
A tree is 15 feet tall and casts a shadow of 4 feet in length. A child standing next to the tree casts a shadow that is 0.25 feet in length. Which equation can be used to find the height of the child, $x$?

**A.** $\frac{15}{4} = \frac{0.25}{x}$  **B.** $\frac{15}{0.25} = \frac{4}{x}$  **C.** $\frac{15}{4} = \frac{0.25}{x}$  **D.** $\frac{15}{x} = \frac{4}{0.25}$

### Examining School Book Pages

*Refer to the School Book Pages provided on page 380 to answer the following questions.*

**47.** The *SR-71 Blackbird* set a speed record on March 6, 1990, by flying 311.4 miles from St. Louis, Missouri, to Cincinnati, Ohio, in 8 minutes and 32 seconds. Compute its unit rate of speed in miles per hour, and compare this rate with that of problem 22 on p. 307 of the School Book Pages.

**48.** Create three problems analogous to problems 19 through 21 on p. 307 of the School Book Pages, but with a bar chart that displays a different class of animals, such as birds, reptiles, or mammals.

# 7.4

# Percent

## Percent

It is essentially impossible to live in today's society and not be conversant with the notion of **percent**.

- How much will a coat regularly priced at $79.99 be when it is offered at a 30%-off sale?
- What is your new salary when you receive a 3.8% raise?
- What percent interest do you pay on the outstanding balance on your credit card?
- If you are required to make a down payment of 11% of the purchase price of $175,000 when buying a home, how much do you have to put down?
- How rapidly will your retirement grow if you make periodic payments into an account paying 5% interest compounded quarterly?

Percent (from the Latin *per centum*, meaning "per hundred") is one of the most important ratios in school mathematics. Thus, 50% is the ratio $\frac{50}{100}$, and this is quickly simplified to the fraction $\frac{1}{2}$ or written as the decimal 0.50. As another example, if I have $98 and give you 50% of what I have, I give you

$$\frac{1}{2} \cdot \$98 = \$49, \quad \text{or} \quad 0.5 \times \$98 = \$49.$$

The "of" in the preceding sentence translates into "times." Thus,

$$50\% \text{ of} \qquad \text{means} \qquad 50\% \times \text{ ,}$$

$$\frac{1}{2} \text{ of} \qquad \text{means} \qquad \frac{1}{2} \times \text{ ,}$$

and

$$0.5 \text{ of} \qquad \text{means} \qquad 0.5 \times \text{ .}$$

> **DEFINITION** *Percent*
> If $r$ is any nonnegative real number, then $r$ percent, written $r\%$, is the ratio
> $$\frac{r}{100}.$$

*(cloud note: $r\% = \frac{r}{100}$)*

Since $r\%$ is defined as the ratio $\dfrac{r}{100}$ and the notational effect of dividing a decimal by 100 is to move the decimal point two places to the left, it is easy to write a given percent as a decimal. For example, $12\% = 0.12, 25\% = 0.25, 130\% = 1.3$, and so on. Conversely, $0.125 = 12.5\%$, or $12\frac{1}{2}\%; 0.10 = 10\%; 1.50 = 150\%$; and so on.

## EXAMPLE 7.24 Expressing Decimals as Percents

Express these decimals as percents:

**(a)** 0.25      **(b)** 0.333...      **(c)** 1.255      **(d)** 0.0035      **(e)** 7

**Solution**

**(a)** $0.25 = 25\%$
**(b)** $0.33... = 33.333...\%$     *(cloud note: $= 33\frac{1}{3}\%$)*
**(c)** $1.255 = 125.5\%$
**(d)** $0.35\%$
**(e)** $700\%$

## EXAMPLE 7.25 Expressing Percents as Decimals

Express these percents as decimals:

**(a)** 40%      **(b)** 12%      **(c)** 127%      **(d)** 0.5%

**Solution**

**(a)** $40\% = 0.40$
**(b)** $12\% = 0.12$     *(cloud note: $40\% = \frac{40}{100} = 0.40$)*
**(c)** $127\% = 1.27$
**(d)** $0.005$

## EXAMPLE 7.26 Expressing Percents as Fractions

Express these percents as fractions in lowest terms:

**(a)** 60%      **(b)** $66\frac{2}{3}\%$      **(c)** 125%

**Solution**

(a) By definition, 60% means $\dfrac{60}{100}$. Therefore, $60\% = \dfrac{60}{100} = \dfrac{3}{5}$.

(b) $66\dfrac{2}{3}\% = \dfrac{66\dfrac{2}{3}}{100} = \dfrac{\dfrac{200}{3}}{100} = \dfrac{2}{3}$.

(c) $125\% = \dfrac{125}{100} = \dfrac{5}{4}$, or $1\dfrac{1}{4}$.

---

## EXAMPLE 7.27 Expressing Fractions as Percents

Express these fractions as percents:

(a) $\dfrac{1}{8}$   (b) $\dfrac{1}{3}$   (c) $\dfrac{16}{5}$

**Solution 1**

### Using Proportions

Since percents are ratios, we can use variables to determine the desired percents.

(a) Suppose $\dfrac{1}{8} = r\% = \dfrac{r}{100}$. Then

$$r = 100 \cdot \dfrac{1}{8} = 12.5$$

and

$$r\% = 12.5\%.$$

(b) If $\dfrac{1}{3} = s\% = \dfrac{s}{100}$, then

$$s = \dfrac{100}{3} = 33\dfrac{1}{3} \quad \left(= 33\tfrac{1}{3}\%\right)$$

and

$$s\% = 33\dfrac{1}{3}\%.$$

(c) If $\dfrac{16}{5} = u\% = \dfrac{u}{100}$, then

$$u = \dfrac{16}{5} \cdot 100 = 320$$

and

$$u\% = 320\%.$$

**Solution 2**

### Using Decimals

Here, we write the fractions as decimals and then as percents.

(a) By division,

$$\dfrac{1}{8} = 0.125 = 12.5\%.$$

**(b)** Here,

$$\frac{1}{3} = 0.333\ldots = 33.\overline{3}\% = 33\frac{1}{3}\%.$$

**(c)** $\dfrac{16}{5} = 3.2 = 320\%.$

## Solving the Three Basic Types of Percent Problems

A percent $p$ is a way to express a ratio of $a$ to $b$, with $\dfrac{p}{100} = \dfrac{a}{b}$. Thus, if any two of the three values $a$, $b$, or $p$ are known, then the remaining value can be determined. Each of these three cases arises naturally in realistic problems, as the next three examples illustrate. In each case, the key idea used to obtain the solution is to identify the whole that is represented by 100%. Indeed, most errors made with percent occur when the whole has not been correctly defined. The most important question to ask when working with percent is "What is the amount that corresponds to 100%?" In the three examples that follow, a useful diagram helps make it clear how the whole corresponds to 100% and how a part of the whole corresponds to $p$ percent of the whole.

MHM

**EXAMPLE 7.28** **Calculating a Percentage of a Number**

The Smetanas bought a house for \$175,000. If a 15% down payment was required, how much was the down payment?

**Solution 1** | **Using an Equation**

The down payment is 15% of the cost of the house. Thus, if $d$ is the down payment,

$$\begin{aligned}
d &= 15\% \times \$175{,}000 \\
&= 0.15 \times \$175{,}000 \\
&= \$26{,}250.
\end{aligned}$$

"Of" translates into "times."

**Solution 2** | **Using a Ratio and a Proportion**

The size of the down payment is proportional to the cost of the house; that is, $\dfrac{d}{175{,}000}$ is a ratio that is equivalent to the ratio 15%. The following diagram makes the desired proportion visually more clear:

Thus,

$$\frac{d}{\$175{,}000} = \frac{15}{100} = 0.15$$

and

$$\begin{aligned}
d &= 0.15 \times \$175{,}000 \\
&= \$26{,}250.
\end{aligned}$$

**EXAMPLE 7.29** **Calculating a Number of Which a Given Number Is a Given Percentage**

Soo Ling scored 92% on her last test. If she got 23 questions right, how many problems were on the test?

**Solution 1**    **Using a Variable**

Let $n$ denote the number of questions on the test. Since Soo Ling got 23 questions correct for a score of 92%, we know that 23 is 92% of $n$; that is,

$$23 = 92\% \times n = 0.92n.$$

Hence,

$$n = \frac{23}{0.92} = 25.$$

**Solution 2**    **Using a Ratio and a Proportion**

As seen in the diagram, the ratio of 23 to the number of questions on the test must be the same as the ratio 92%:

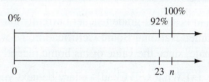

Thus,

$$\frac{23}{n} = \frac{92}{100} = 0.92.$$

Therefore,

$$23 = 0.92 \times n$$

and

$$n = 23 \div 0.92 = 25$$

as before.

**EXAMPLE 7.30** **Calculating What Percentage One Number Is of Another**

Tara got 28 out of 35 possible points on her last math test. What percentage score did the teacher record in her grade book for Tara?

**Solution 1**    **Using the Definition**

Tara got 28 out of 35 points on the test. Since

$$\frac{28}{35} = 0.80 = 80\%,$$

the teacher recorded 80% in her grade book.

**Solution 2**    **Using a Ratio and a Proportion**

Let $x$ be the desired percentage. Then, as in Examples 7.28 and 7.29, the diagram

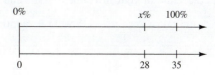

helps one visualize the proportion

$$\frac{x}{100} = \frac{28}{35}.$$

Thus,

$$x = \frac{28 \cdot 100}{35} = 80\%.$$

## Percentage Increase and Decrease

Relative gain or loss is often measured as a percent change. For example, a company may grant a 3.5% raise in salary, or a community may have experienced a loss of 15% of the value of homes in a certain year. The next example illustrates the type of questions associated with percentage increases and losses, and these questions are answered.

### EXAMPLE 7.31 Computing Percentage Increases and Decreases

Chad is a third-grade teacher currently earning $53,000 a year. However, because he was recently granted National Board Certification, he will receive a 7% increase in salary. This situation is fortunate, since the value of his home recently dropped by 15% and is now valued at $255,000.

(a) What will Chad's salary be next year?
(b) What was the value of Chad's house before the downturn in price?

**Solution**

(a) Since 7% of $53,000 is 0.07 × $53,000 = $3710, Chad's salary will be $3710 higher than it is the current year, making his total salary $53,000 + $3710 = $56,710. Notice that his new salary can be computed directly by the calculation (1 + 0.07) × $53,000 = 1.07 × $53,000 = $56,710, showing how the percentage increase is added to the current salary figure.

(b) The current value of $255,000 for Chad's house is 1 − 15% = 85% of its former valuation. Therefore, Chad's house was valued at $255,000 ÷ 0.85 = $300,000.

It's always important to keep in mind when working with percentage increases and decreases that the "whole" to which the percentage change is applied is clearly understood. For example, suppose you have a retirement portfolio of $100,000 that dropped 50% one year and rebounded by 50% the following year. Have you completely recovered the value of your investment? The answer is no, since a 50% drop applied to $100,000 reduces your portfolio to $50,000, but a 50% gain made on $50,000 brings you back to only $75,000.

## Compound Interest

If you keep money in a savings account at a bank, the bank pays you interest at a fixed rate (percentage) for the privilege of using your money. For example, suppose you invest $5000 for a year at 7% interest. How much is your investment worth at the end of the year? Since the interest earned is 7% of $5000, the interest earned is

$$7\% \times \$5000 = 0.07 \times \$5000 = \$350,$$

and the value of your investment at the end of the year is

$$\begin{aligned}
\$5000 + \$350 &= \$5000 + 0.07 \times \$5000 \\
&= \$5000 \cdot (1.07) \\
&= \$5350.
\end{aligned}$$

If you leave the total investment in the bank, its value at the end of the second year is

$$\$5350 + 0.07 \times \$5350 = \$5350 \cdot (1.07)$$
$$= \$5000 \cdot (1.07)(1.07)$$
$$= \$5000 \cdot (1.07)^2$$
$$= \$5724.50.$$

from before

Similarly, at the end of the third year, your investment would be worth

$$\$5000 \cdot (1.07)^3 \doteq \$6125.22$$

to the nearest penny. In general, it would be worth

$$\$5000 \cdot (1.07)^n$$

at the end of $n$ years. This is an example of **annual compound interest,** where the term *compound* implies that each year you earn interest on all the interest earned in preceding years as well as on the original amount invested (the **principal**).

Usually, interest is compounded more than once a year. Suppose the $5000 investment just discussed was made in a bank that pays interest at the rate of 7% compounded semiannually—that is, twice a year. Since the rate for a year is 7%, the rate for half a year is 3.5%. Thus, the value of the investment at the end of the year (that is, at the end of *two* interest periods) is

$$\$5000(1.035)^2 \doteq \$5356.13,$$

and the values at the end of two years and three years, respectively, are

$$\$5000(1.035)^4 \doteq \$5737.62$$

and

$$\$5000(1.035)^6 \doteq \$6146.28$$

Compound interest can be easily calculated with the $\wedge$ key or the built-in constant function of your calculator.

Compounding more and more frequently is to your advantage, and most banks compound monthly or even daily.

The preceding calculations are typical and are summarized in this theorem:

$\frac{r}{n}$ is the rate per interest period and $nt$ is the number of interest periods.

**THEOREM** *Calculating Compound Interest*

The value of an investment of $P$ dollars at the end of $t$ years, if interest is paid at the annual rate of $r\%$ compounded $n$ times a year, is

$$P\left(1 + \frac{r}{100n}\right)^{nt}.$$

## Into the Classroom

### Anne Lawrence Discusses Percent

To illustrate percent in a fun way, I purchase packages of M & M's® or Smarties®. I buy a package for each group of students, or, if the packages are small, one package for each student.

Initially each group (or each student) determines the total number of candies in the package. Then, working with the ratio $\frac{\text{part}}{\text{whole}}$, they determine what fraction of the total each color represents. Students compute $\frac{\text{part}}{\text{whole}}$ to obtain a decimal, and then they change the decimal to a percent. Finally I have students add to show that their percents total 100%. This activity transfers knowledge from ratio to fraction to decimals to percent. Later it can also be used with probability.

Source: Scott Foresman—Addison Wesley Middle School Math, Course 2, *p. 382D, by Randall I. Charles et al. Copyright © 2002 Pearson Education, Inc. Reprinted with permission.*

## EXAMPLE 7.32 Computing the Cost of Debt

Many credit card companies charge 18% interest compounded monthly on unpaid balances. Suppose your card was "maxed out" at your credit limit of $10,000 and that you were unable to make any payments for two years. Aside from penalties, how much debt would you owe, on the basis of compound interest alone?

**Solution**  Since the interest is computed at 18% compounded monthly, the effective rate per month is $\frac{18\%}{12} = 1.5\%$ and the number of interest periods in two years is $12 \cdot 2 = 24$. Thus, your debt, to the nearest penny, would be

$$\$10,000(1.015)^{24} \doteq \$14,295.03.$$

If the debt went unpaid for six years, you would owe

$$\$10,000(1.015)^{72} \doteq \$29,211.58.$$

This is almost triple what you originally owed! These calculations can be made by repeatedly multiplying $10,000 by 1.015, using the built-in constant feature found in most calculators. Even more easily, you can compute $\$10,000(1.015)^{24}$ directly by entering the following string into your calculator:

$$10000\ \boxed{\times}\ 1.015\ \boxed{\wedge}\ 24\ \boxed{=}.$$

### The Mathematics of Growth

Population growth occurs in exactly the same way that an investment earning compound interest grows. Suppose, for example, that the population in the Puget Sound region in northwest Washington is approximately 2.2 million and that it is growing at the rate of 5% per year. In one year, the population will be approximately

$$2.2(1.05) \doteq 2.3$$

million. If the growth continues unabated, in 14 years it will be approximately

$$2.2(1.05)^{14} \doteq 4.4$$

million, twice what it is today. Given the fact that the area has already experienced several years of water shortages, these figures are cause for concern among officials.

Like population growth, prices of commodities also rise with inflation as an investment grows by drawing compound interest.

## EXAMPLE 7.33 Pricing a Car

If the economy were to experience a steady inflation rate of 2.5% per year, what would be the price of a new car in five years if the same-quality car sells today for $18,400?

**Solution**  Using the same formula as in computing compound interest, we find that the price of the car five years from now would be approximately

$$\$18,400(1.025)^{5} \doteq \$20,818.$$

## Problem Set 7.4

Exercises numbered in red are answered in the back of the text.

### Understanding Concepts

**1.** Write each of these ratios as percents:

**(a)** $\frac{3}{16}$    **(b)** $\frac{7}{25}$    **(c)** $\frac{37}{40}$

**(d)** $\frac{5}{6}$    **(e)** $\frac{3.24}{8.91}$    **(f)** $\frac{7.801}{23.015}$

**(g)** $\frac{1.6}{7}$    **(h)** $\frac{\sqrt{2}}{\sqrt{6}}$

**2.** Write each of these numbers as percents:

**(a)** 0.19    **(b)** 0.015    **(c)** 2.15    **(d)** 3

**3.** Write each of these percents as fractions in simplest form:

   **(a)** 10%    **(b)** 25%    **(c)** 62.5%    **(d)** 137.5%

**4.** Compute each of the following percents:

   **(a)** 70% of 280       **(b)** 120% of 84

   **(c)** 38% of 751       **(d)** $7\frac{1}{2}$% of \$20,000

   **(e)** 0.02% of 27,481    **(f)** 1.05% of 845

**5.** Compute each of these percents mentally:

   **(a)** 50% of 840       **(b)** 10% of 2480

   **(c)** 12.5% of 48      **(d)** 125% of 24

   **(e)** 200% of 56      **(f)** 110% of 180

**6. (a)** Michelle's salary jumped to \$50,400 after her 5% raise. What was her former salary?

   **(b)** Jason's investment of \$12,000 is now worth \$11,160. What was his percentage loss?

**7.** Jerry and Cynthia both started with the same salary. Then Jerry received a 5% raise one year followed by a 3% raise the next year. Cynthia received a 3% raise followed by a 5% raise.

   **(a)** Who has the higher salary following the two raises?

   **(b)** Would you rather be Jerry or Cynthia? Explain carefully.

**8.** First guess the percent of each square board that is colored blue, and then determine the exact percent:

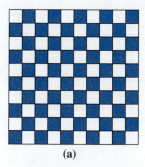
**(a)**

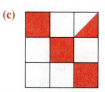
**(b)**

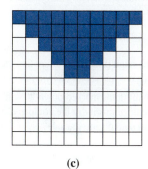
**(c)**

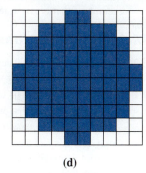
**(d)**

**9.** If the following 20-mm–by–20-mm square represents 100%, draw rectangles 20 mm wide that represent each of the given percentages.

   **(a)** 75%    **(b)** 125%    **(c)** 200%    **(d)** 20%

**10.** What percentage of each of these figures is red?

   **(a)**     **(b)**

   **(c)** 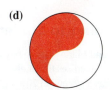    **(d)**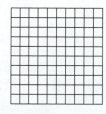

**11.** How many small squares must be shaded to represent the given percentages of the large square shown?

   **(a)** 100%    **(b)** 0%    **(c)** 25%    **(d)** 87%

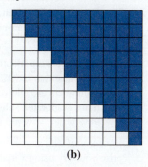

**12.** How many of the small rectangles must be shaded to represent the given percentages of the large rectangle shown?

   **(a)** 50%    **(b)** 25%    **(c)** 20%    **(d)** 37.5%

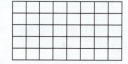

**13.** If the area of the yellow hexagon is the whole, then the remaining pattern blocks have areas that are approximately 16.67%, 19.2%, 33.3%, 38.5%, and 50%. Match the pattern block that corresponds to the given percent.

**14.** Mentally convert each of these fractions to a percent:

   **(a)** $\dfrac{7}{28}$    **(b)** $\dfrac{11}{33}$    **(c)** $\dfrac{72}{144}$    **(d)** $\dfrac{44}{66}$

**15.** Mentally estimate the numbers that should go in the blanks to make these statements *true*.

   **(a)** 27% of ____ equals 16.

   **(b)** 4 is ____% of 7.5.

   **(c)** 41% of 120 = ____.

## Teaching Concepts

**16.** There are three common types of percentage problems:

   **(i)** Find the percent: Given $a$ and $b$, what percent $p$ of $b$ is $a$?

**(ii)** Find the part: Given a percent $p$ and the whole $b$, what is $a$ if it is $p$ percent of $b$?

**(iii)** Find the whole: Given a part $a$ that is $p$ percent of the whole $b$, what is the whole $b$?

Design a classroom poster that gives a realistic problem and its solution for each of these types of percentage problems.

## Responding to Students

**17.** Tony and Maria want to buy a CD to share. Tony favors store A, which advertises that it always marks down CDs by 15% and now has a storewide 20%-off sale. Maria thinks that store B offers a better deal with its 35%-off sale? Their friend Betty says it doesn't matter. How would you respond to the three students who have come to you with their dispute?

**18.** Patrick and Heather were working on their science fair project, and they were trying to decide which plant grew the fastest. They recorded the growth of two plants. Plant A grew from 9 centimeters to 12 centimeters. Plant B grew from 13 centimeters to 16 centimeters. Patrick said that they both grew 3 centimeters, so there was no difference in the variable they were testing. Heather wasn't sure. How can you use the idea of percent to help these students?

**19.** Kelsey got all 20 words right on her spelling test and attempted 2 bonus words, which were also correct. Her friend Elizabeth graded Kelsey's test and wrote "Good Job, Kelsey, 102%!"

**(a)** What would actually be the correct percentage for 22 out of 20?

**(b)** How is Elizabeth improperly applying percents to Kelsey's grade?

**20.** Students in Mrs. Giles's class were asked which was the better deal: (1) 35% off the original price of $10 or (2) pay 65% of the original price of $10. Louis and Arnold argued that 35% off was better because the price was going "down."

**(a)** What is confusing the students (and often many shoppers)?

**(b)** How would you show the students that the answers are actually the same?

**21.** Using a regular household calculator to complete his mathematics homework on percents, Anthony had the following problem: "What percent is 20 out of 25?" He entered 20 and divided by 25, so 0.8 showed on his calculator display. He then wrote 8% as his answer.

**(a)** What is Anthony doing incorrectly?

**(b)** What would be your next step as a teacher?

**22.** Yoshi was paid $3 a day to water his neighbor's plants last year during their vacation. This year he will also look after their new dog, so he will be paid $6 a day. Since he is paid twice as much, he claims that his pay has increased by 200%, since 200% = 2. How would you respond to Yoshi?

## Thinking Critically

**23.** In a given population of men and women, 40% of the men are married and 30% of the women are married. What percentage of the adult population is married?

**24.** A garage advertised car repairs at 10% off the usual price—5% on parts and 5% on labor. The Consumer Protection Agency chided the garage for false advertising. Was the CPA correct? Explain.

**25.** A sign at the cookie store in the airport read "Increase your ecstasy by 25%—4 cookies for the price of 3." Is there anything amiss with this claim?

**26.** A customer made a purchase in a store in Washington state, where the sales tax is 8%. The customer then noticed that her 20% coupon hadn't been taken into account, so the cashier took 20% off the bill that included the sales tax.

**(a)** Should the customer insist that the 20% off coupon be applied *before* the sales tax is added?

**(b)** Should the cashier redo the calculation, first applying the 20%-off coupon and then adding the sales tax?

**27.** During the first half of a basketball game, the basketball team at Red Cloud High School made 60% of its 40 field goal attempts. During the second half, the team scored on only 25% of 44 attempts from the field. To the nearest 1%, what was Red Cloud High's field goal shooting percentage for the entire game?

**28.** During the first half of a basketball game, Skeeter Thoreson missed all 5 of her field goal attempts. During the second half, she hit 75% of her 16 attempts from the field. What was her field goal shooting percentage for the game?

**29. The Cucumber Problem.** Solve the cucumber problem, posed by the Hungarian-born American mathematician Paul Halmos (1916–2006):

Cucumbers are assumed, for present purposes, to be a substance that is 99% water by weight. If 500 pounds of cucumbers are allowed to stand overnight, and if the partially evaporated substance that remains in the morning is 98% water, how much is the morning weight?

[*Be careful!* The answer, which is not 495 pounds, will surprise you. Try using variables such as $W$ for the weight of the water in the evening and $S$ for the unchanging weight of the cucumbers that is not water.]

## Making Connections

**30.** Tabata's Furniture calculates the retail price of furniture that the company sells by marking up its cost at wholesale by a full 100%.

**(a)** If Tabata's had a sale with all items marked down 20% from the retail price, what percentage profit did the company actually make on each item sold during the sale?

**(b)** If Tabata's had a sale with all items marked down 50% from the retail price, what percentage profit did the company make on each item sold during the sale?

**31.** A merchant obtains the retail price of an item by adding 20% to the wholesale price. Later, he has a sale and marks every item down 20% from the retail price. Is the sale price the same as the wholesale price? Explain briefly. (*Hint:* Consider a specific item whose wholesale price is $100.)

**32.** Acme Electric in Boise, Idaho, purchases hot-water heaters at wholesale for $185 each and sells them after marking up the wholesale price by 45%. Since Idaho has a 5% sales tax, how much would you have to pay Acme for one of its water heaters?

**33.** There is $100 in the cash register at the start of a cashier's shift at a supermarket. At the end of the shift, the register contains $800. If the state has a 5% sales tax on all sales, how much of the $800 is for tax?

**34.** The mortgage company requires an 11% down payment on houses it finances. If the Sumis bought a house for $158,000, how much down payment did they have to make?

**35.** Mr. Swierkos invested $25,000 in a mutual fund. If his broker deducted a 6% commission before turning the rest of the money over to the mutual fund, and the value of each share increased by 18% during the year, what percentage return on his investment did Mr. Swierkos realize at the end of the first year?

**36.** Find the value of each of these investments at the end of the period specified:

    **(a)** $2500 invested at $5\frac{1}{4}$% interest compounded annually for seven years

    **(b)** $8000 invested at 7% interest compounded semiannually for ten years

**37.** The *progress bar* was invented in 1896, though it remained obscure until its rediscovery about 15 years later. Now commonplace in computing, progress bars visually show how much information has been transmitted, together with the percent copied, the transfer rate, and the size of files. In each of the following examples, first estimate $x$, the percent copied so far, to the nearest 10%, and then determine the values of $y$ and $z$.

    **(a)**

Percent copied: $x$%
Estimated time left: $z$ sec (5.0 MB of $y$ MB copied)
Transfer Rate: 2.50 MB/sec

    **(b)**

Percent copied: $x$%
Estimated time left: $z$ sec (36.0 MB of $y$ MB copied)
Transfer Rate: 2.00 MB/sec

    **(c)**

Percent copied: $x$%
Estimated time left: 3 sec ($y$ MB of 30 MB copied)
Transfer Rate: $z$ MB/sec

## Using a Calculator

**38.** How much would you have to invest at 6% interest compounded annually in order to have $16,000 at the end of five years? (*Note:* If $P$ is the amount invested, then $16,000 = P \cdot (1.06)^5$.)

**39.** Suppose you place $1000 in a bank account on January 1 of each year for nine years. If the bank pays interest on such accounts at the rate of 5.3% interest compounded annually, how much will your investment be worth on January 1 of the tenth year?

**40.** Successive powers of $1 + \frac{r}{100}$ are easily computed by using the built-in constant feature of your calculator. The value of an investment at $r$% interest compounded annually for $n$ years is $P\left(1 + \frac{r}{100}\right)^n$. Determine the least number of years for the value of an investment to double at each of these rates:

    **(a)** 5%    **(b)** 7%    **(c)** 14%    **(d)** 20%

**(e)** The "rule of 72" states that you divide 72 by the interest rate to obtain the doubling time for an initial investment. This rule is used by many bankers to give a crude approximation of the time for the value of an investment to double at a given rate. Does it seem like a reasonable rule? Explain briefly.

**41. (a)** If the population of Oregon in 1999 was 3,300,000 and it is increasing at the rate of 4% per year, what will the population be in the year 2010? Give your answer correct to the nearest one hundred thousand.

    **(b)** Under the same assumptions as in part (a), what was the population of Oregon in 1990? (*Hint:* Use the built-in constant feature of your calculator to divide repeatedly by 1.04.)

## From State Student Assessments

**42.** (Arizona Grade 8)
Melissa earned a score of 75% on her first test. She wants to earn an 85% on her second test. What is the percent increase, rounded to the nearest whole number, from 75% to 85%?

    **A.** 10%    **B.** 12%    **C.** 13%    **D.** 14%

**43.** (Oregon, Grade 5)
Richard answered 22 of the 25 questions on this week's language arts test correctly. About what percent of the total number of questions did he answer correctly?

    **A.** 22%    **B.** 40%    **C.** 80%    **D.** 90%

**44.** (Massachusetts, Grade 8)
Use the advertisement below to answer the question.

**ROXBURY BIKE SHOP**
*ONE DAY SALE – SATURDAY ONLY*
All bikes must go!!

9:00 a.m. – 10% off originally-marked price
10:00 a.m. – 10% off 9:00 price
11:00 a.m. – 10% off 10:00 price

AND SO ON UNTIL
<u>ALL</u> BIKES ARE SOLD

Mr. Howard bought a bike with an originally marked price of $400. What was the price of the bike at 12:15 P.M.?

    **A.** $262.44    **B.** $240.00
    **C.** $291.60    **D.** $280.00

**45.** (Arizona Grade 7)
A microwave oven is on sale for 20% off the regular price. The sale price is $250.00. What is the regular price of the microwave oven?

    **A.** $166.67    **B.** $200.00
    **C.** $300.00    **D.** $312.50

**46.** (Virginia, Grade 7)
A meal costs $63.00 at a restaurant. How much is a 15% tip?

    **F.** $78.00    **G.** $72.45
    **H.** $9.45    **J.** $5.00

# Finding Percent of a Whole Number

*See "Examining School Book Pages" on page 393 for questions related to the pages shown below.*

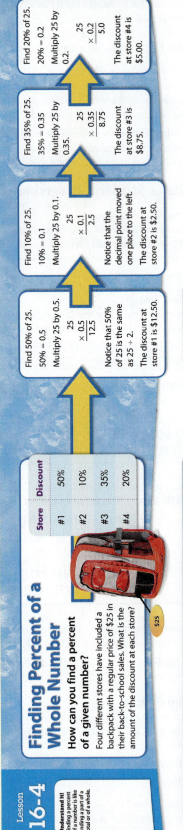

## Lesson 16-4

**Understand It!**
Finding a percent of a number is like finding a part of a total or of a whole.

## Finding Percent of a Whole Number

**How can you find a percent of a given number?**

Four different stores have included a backpack with a regular price of $25 in their back-to-school sales. What is the amount of the discount at each store?

$25

| Store | Discount |
|-------|----------|
| #1 | 50% |
| #2 | 10% |
| #3 | 35% |
| #4 | 20% |

Find 50% of 25.
50% = 0.5
Multiply 25 by 0.5.

$$\begin{array}{r} 25 \\ \times\ 0.5 \\ \hline 12.5 \end{array}$$

Notice that 50% of 25 is the same as 25 ÷ 2.

The discount at store #1 is $12.50.

Find 10% of 25.
10% = 0.1
Multiply 25 by 0.1.

$$\begin{array}{r} 25 \\ \times\ 0.1 \\ \hline 2.5 \end{array}$$

Notice that the decimal point moved one place to the left.

The discount at store #2 is $2.50.

Find 35% of 25.
35% = 0.35
Multiply 25 by 0.35.

$$\begin{array}{r} 25 \\ \times\ 0.35 \\ \hline 8.75 \end{array}$$

The discount at store #3 is $8.75.

Find 20% of 25.
20% = 0.2
Multiply 25 by 0.2.

$$\begin{array}{r} 25 \\ \times\ 0.2 \\ \hline 5.0 \end{array}$$

The discount at store #4 is $5.00.

### Guided Practice*

**Do you know HOW?**

In **1** through **4**, find the percent of each number.

1. 3% of 200
2. 25% of 48
3. 90% of 85
4. 75% of 44

**Do you UNDERSTAND?**

5. What is an easy way to find 25% of a number?

6. In the example above, what would the amount of the discount be if the backpack were discounted 40%?

### Independent Practice

In **7** through **18**, find the percent of each number.

7. 43% of 350
8. 87% of 210
9. 5% of 46
10. 100% of 37
11. 30% of 66
12. 10% of 230
13. 20% of 400
14. 15% of 90
15. 50% of 75
16. 12% of 100
17. 33% of 300
18. 77% of 10

19. Find 1% of 235. How many decimal places in 235 did the decimal point move to the left in the answer?

20. What is an easy way to find 2% of 660?

21. **Writing to Explain** What is an easy way to find 11% of a number? Use 11% of 70 to explain.

### Problem Solving

22. The total seating capacity at Fenway Park in Boston, Massachusetts, is about 36,000. About how many baseball fans would be seated if the park were filled to 85% of its capacity?

Use the information from the chart to answer **24** through **26**.

| Meat | Ounces | Cost |
|------|--------|------|
| Ham | 14 | $5.74 |
| Turkey | 11 | $4.07 |
| Pastrami | 5 | $4.85 |
| Roast Beef | 8 | $6.56 |

23. Marcia had dinner at a restaurant and wants to leave a 20% tip. Explain how she could calculate the tip using mental math.

24. What is the cost of 2 ounces of turkey?

25. Which costs more per ounce, roast beef or pastrami?

26. What is the total cost of 14 ounces of ham and 5 ounces of pastrami?

27. **Algebra** Jordan bought a $35 jacket and a $40 pair of shoes at a 25% discount. Write an equation to find the total amount of the discount on the items. Solve the equation.

28. **Reasoning** Write these numbers in order from least to greatest.
$$60\% \quad \frac{1}{4} \quad 0.75, \ 28\%, \ \frac{1}{2}, \ 0.55$$

29. The price of a computer is $1,450, and a monitor costs $350. The sales tax is 6%. What is the total amount of sales tax on both items?

30. Of the 20 tallest buildings in the world, 20% are located in the United States. How many of the world's 20 tallest buildings are in the U.S.?

31. **Critical Thinking** The price of a new bike is $90. The store is advertising a 30% discount and the sales tax is 7%. Explain how to find the cost of the bike.

*For another example, see Set D on page 409.

## Examining School Book Pages

*Refer to the School Book Pages provided on page 392 to answer the following questions.*

**47.** The example across the top of the School Book Pages gives easy ways to compute 50% and 10% of a whole number.

**(a)** Answer problem 5, which asks for an easy way to find 25% of a number.

**(b)** Describe an easy way to compute 5% of a number.

**(c)** Describe an easy way to compute 15% of a number.

## The Chapter in Relation to Future Teachers

This chapter has addressed topics of considerable importance in the development of an elementary or middle school student's number sense and quantitative reasoning skills. In particular, the idea of the decimal representation of numbers leads naturally to the real number system, which is the last number system introduced in the K–8 mathematics* curriculum. Computations with decimals highlight the importance of acquiring a good understanding of the corresponding algorithms in integer arithmetic; place value is of paramount importance. As has been shown with many real-life examples, proportional reasoning is a skill that will often play an effective role in solving problems, understanding relative comparisons of quantities, and expressing a rate of change. Percent is a specialization of proportional reasoning in which a comparison is made to the one hundred parts that make up the whole.

Table 7.3 presents a useful review of all the number systems introduced in this and the foregoing chapters. As you examine the table, think about how you would answer questions such as the following:

- How can the numbers within a system be modeled with manipulatives and visualizations?
- How can the properties of a number system be illustrated with appropriate models?
- Why do some properties hold for one number system but not another?

---

*Other systems are of value in higher mathematics. Of particular importance in advanced mathematics are the *complex numbers*. One reason for this is that every polynomial equation has a solution in the complex numbers.

**TABLE 7.3**    **NUMBER SYSTEMS AND THEIR PROPERTIES**

| Properties | Natural numbers | Whole numbers | Integers | Rational numbers | Real numbers |
|---|---|---|---|---|---|
| **Closure property for addition** | • | • | • | • | • |
| **Closure property for multiplication** | • | • | • | • | • |
| **Closure property for subtraction** | | | • | • | • |
| **Closure property for division, except for division by zero** | | | | • | • |
| **Commutative property for addition** | • | • | • | • | • |
| **Commutative property for multiplication** | • | • | • | • | • |
| **Commutative property for subtraction** | | | | | |

*(continues)*

**TABLE 7.3  NUMBER SYSTEMS AND THEIR PROPERTIES—*CONTINUED***

| Properties | Natural numbers | Whole numbers | Integers | Rational numbers | Real numbers |
|---|---|---|---|---|---|
| Commutative property for division | | | | | |
| Associative property for addition | • | • | • | • | • |
| Associative property for multiplication | • | • | • | • | • |
| Associative property for subtraction | | | | | |
| Associative property for division | | | | | |
| Distributive property for multiplication over addition | • | • | • | • | • |
| Distributive property for multiplication over subtraction | • | • | • | • | • |
| Contains the additive identity, 0 | | • | • | • | • |
| Contains the multiplicative identity, 1 | • | • | • | • | • |
| The multiplication property for 0 holds | | • | • | • | • |
| Each element possesses an additive inverse | | | • | • | • |
| Each element except 0 possesses a multiplicative inverse | | | | • | • |

## Chapter 7 Summary

| Section 7.1   Decimals and Real Numbers | Page Reference |
|---|---|
| **CONCEPTS** | |
| • **Decimal:** In general, the Indo-Arabic system of positional notation for numerals. Colloquially, nonintegers represented in positional notation to base ten. | 339 |
| • **Manipulatives to represent decimals:** Decimals can be represented with mats, strips, and units; base-ten blocks; dollars, dimes, and pennies; place-value cards; and so on. | 340 |
| • **Ordering decimals:** Write the decimals so that they have the same number of digits to the left of the decimal point (by adjoining 0s to one or the other decimal as needed). Determine the first digits from the left where the two decimals differ. The decimal having the lesser of these two digits represents the smaller number. | 350 |
| • **Real numbers:** The set of all numbers that can be represented as decimals. Alternatively, the set of all rational and irrational numbers. | 351, 353 |

**DEFINITIONS**

- A **decimal** is a base-ten position numeral, either positive or negative, in which there are finitely many digits extending to the left of the decimal point and either finitely or infinitely many digits extending to the right of the decimal point.                                         339

- **Expanded form** for integers is the written notation for the positional values such as
$$29.437 = 2 \cdot 10 + 9 + \frac{4}{10} + \frac{3}{100} + \frac{7}{1000}.$$                     340

- **Expanded exponential form** is the written notation for the positional values of decimals using both positive and negative powers of 10. For example, $2.437 = 2 \cdot 10^0 + 4 \cdot 10^{-1} + 3 \cdot 10^{-2} + 7 \cdot 10^{-3}$.                                         343

- A **terminating decimal** is a decimal that has a finite number of digits.                     344

- A **periodic decimal,** or **repeating decimal,** is a nonterminating decimal with infinitely many nonzero digits, where one digit or string of digits repeats *ad infinitum.*                     347

- **Repeating decimal:** A nonterminating decimal for which a digit or a string of adjacent digits repeats ad *infinitum.*                                         347

- A **nonterminating, nonrepeating decimal** is a decimal with infinitely many digits, no pattern of which repeats *ad infinitum.*                                         351

- **Irrational numbers** are numbers that are represented by nonterminating and nonrepeating decimals and cannot be represented as ratios of integers.                     351

- The set of all **real numbers, R,** is the set containing all rational and irrational numbers.                     351

**THEOREMS**

- **Multiplying decimals by powers of 10:** If $n$ is a natural number, multiplying a number by $10^n$ notationally moves the decimal point $n$ places to the right. Multiplying by $10^{-n}$ moves the decimal point $n$ places to the left.                                         343

- **Rational numbers represented by terminal decimals:** A rational number represented by the fraction $\frac{a}{b}$ in simplest form can be written as a terminating decimal if, and only if, the denominator $b$ has no prime divisors other than 2 and 5.                     345

- **Rational numbers represented by repeating decimals:** A rational number represented by the fraction $\frac{a}{b}$ in simplest form can be written as a periodic (or repeating) decimal if, and only if, the denominator $b$ has a prime divisor other than 2 and 5.                     349

- **$\sqrt{2}$ is irrational:** $\sqrt{2}$ and infinitely many other numbers are irrational.                     351

- **Real numbers as points on the number line:** Every real number corresponds to a unique point on the number line, and conversely.                                         354

| **Section 7.2   Computations with Decimals** | **Page Reference** |
| --- | --- |

**PROCEDURES**

- **Adding and subtracting decimals:** Align decimal points and then add or subtract the decimals as is done with integers.                                         358

- **Multiplying decimals:** Multiply as integers. Let $r$ denote the total number of digits to the right of the decimal points in the two decimals. Place the decimal point $r$ places from the right in the answer.                                         360

- **Dividing decimals:** Multiply both dividend and divisor by the appropriate power of 10 to make the divisor an integer. Using the long-division algorithm, divide as integers, placing the decimal point above the decimal point in the dividend. — 361

- **The 5-Up Rule:** To round a decimal to a given place consider the digit in the next place to the right. If it is smaller than 5, replace it and all of the digits to its right with 0. If it is 5 or larger, replace it and all digits to the right by 0 and increase the digit in the given place by one. Replaced digits to the right of the decimal are then dropped to give the rounded decimal. — 357

| Section 7.3  Proportional Reasoning | Page Reference |
|---|---|

**CONCEPTS**

- **Ratio:** A ratio is a relative comparison of two quantities. — 367

- **Applications of ratios:** A ratio measures the relative size of different parts, the relative size of a part to a whole, and a rate of change of one quantity compared to the amount of change of a second quantity. — 368

**DEFINITIONS**

- A **ratio** is a quotient written as a fraction $\frac{a}{b}$ where $a$ and $b$, $b \neq 0$, are real numbers. — 367

- The **rate of change** is a ratio that measures the change in one quantity with respect to a corresponding change in a second quantity. — 368

- A **unit rate** is a rate given by the amount of change of a quantity compared to a change by 1 unit of the second quantity. — 368

- A **proportion** is the equality of two ratios. $\frac{a}{b} = \frac{c}{d}$. — 370, 371

- If $y = kx$ for some constant $k$, then **$y$ is proportional to $x$.** — 373

- If $y = kx$ for some constant $k$, then $k$ is the **constant of proportionality.** — 373

**THEOREM**

- **Conditions for a proportion.** $\frac{a}{b} = \frac{c}{d}$ if, and only if, $ad = bc$. — 371

| Section 7.4  Percent | Page Reference |
|---|---|

**CONCEPTS**

- **Three basic percent problems:** Given a percent $p$, part $a$, or whole $b$, where $\frac{p}{100} = \frac{a}{b}$, any two of $p$, $a$, and $b$ determine the third. — 384

- **Interest:** The percentage rate paid to borrow money or earned on an investment. — 386

- **Percentage increase or decrease:** The relative change of a gain or loss, expressed as a percent. — 386

- **Compound interest:** Interest calculated so that the interest paid in any given year is paid both on the original amount and on the interest earned in previous years. — 386

**DEFINITIONS**

- A **percent** for any real number $r$, $r\% = \frac{r}{100}$. — 382

- The **percentage increase/decrease** is the relative change of a gain or loss, expressed as a percent. | 386
- **Interest** is the percentage rate paid to borrow money or earned on an investment. | 386
- **Compound interest** is the interest calculated so that the interest paid in any given year is paid both on the original amount and on the interest earned in previous years. | 387

**THEOREM**

- **Calculating compound interest:** The value of an investment of $P$ dollars at the end of $t$ years, if interest is paid at the annual rate of $r\%$ and compounded $n$ times per year, is | 387

$$P\left(1 + \frac{r}{100n}\right)^{nt}.$$

## Chapter Review Exercises

### Section 7.1

1. Write these decimals in expanded exponential form:
   (a) 273.425    (b) 0.000354

2. Write these fractions in decimal form:
   (a) $\dfrac{7}{125}$    (b) $\dfrac{6}{75}$    (c) $\dfrac{11}{80}$

3. Write these decimals as fractions in simplest form:
   (a) 0.315    (b) 1.206    (c) 0.2001

4. Arrange these numbers in order from least to greatest:
   $$\frac{4}{12}, 0.33, 0.3334, \frac{5}{13}, \frac{2}{66}.$$

5. Write these numbers as fractions in simplest form:
   (a) $10.3\overline{63}$    (b) $2.1\overline{42}$

6. Suppose $a = 0.2020020002000020000002\ldots$, continuing in this way with one more 0 between each successive pair of 2s. Is this number rational or irrational? Explain briefly.

7. Using only mental arithmetic, determine the numbers represented by these base-ten numerals as fractions in simplest form:
   (a) $0.222\ldots = 0.\overline{2}$    (b) $0.363636\ldots = 0.\overline{36}$

### Section 7.2

8. Perform these computations by hand:
   (a) $21.734 + 3.2145 + 71.24$
   (b) $23.471 - 2.89$
   (c) $35.4 \times 2.37$
   (d) $24.15 \div 3.45$

9. Compute the following, using a calculator:

   (a) $31.47 + 3.471 + 0.0027$
   (b) $31.47 - 3.471$
   (c) $31.47 \times 3.471$
   (d) $138.87 \div 23.145$

10. Write estimates of the results of these calculations, and then do the computing within the accuracy of your calculator:
    (a) $47.25 + 13.134$
    (b) $52.914 - 13.101$
    (c) $47.25 \times 13.134$
    (d) $47.25 \div 13.134$

11. Show that $3 - \sqrt{2}$ is irrational.

12. Show that the sum of two irrational numbers can be rational. (*Hint:* Consider problem 11.)

13. What can you say about the decimal expansion of an irrational number?

14. (a) A wall measures 8.25 feet by 112.5 feet. What is the area of the wall?
    (b) If it takes 1 quart of paint to cover 110 square feet, how many quarts of paint must be purchased to paint the wall in part (a)?

15. Give an example of a fraction whose decimal is repeating and has a period of length 4.

16. Use your calculator to determine the periodic decimal expansions of the given numbers. Remember that the calculator will necessarily round off decimals, so don't be misled by the last digit in the display if it seems to break a pattern.
    $$\frac{5}{18}, \frac{41}{333}, \frac{11}{36}, \frac{7}{45}, \frac{13}{80}$$
    (a) Determine where the period starts in each case.
    (b) See if you can guess a rule for determining when the period of the decimal form of a fraction $\dfrac{a}{b}$ in simplest form begins. (*Hint:* Consider the prime factorization of $b$.)

### Section 7.3

17. Maria made 11 out of 20 free-throw attempts during a basketball game. What was the ratio of her successes to failures on free throws during the game?

**18.** Determine which of these equations are proportions:

(a) $\dfrac{775}{125} = \dfrac{155}{25}$  (b) $\dfrac{31}{64} = \dfrac{15}{32}$  (c) $\dfrac{9}{24} = \dfrac{12}{32}$

**19.** If Che bought 2 pounds of candy for $3.15, how much would it cost him to buy 5 pounds of candy at the same price per pound?

**20.** It took Donnell 7.5 gallons of gas to drive 173 miles. Assuming that he gets the same mileage per gallon, how much gasoline will he need to travel 300 miles?

**21.** If $y$ is proportional to $x$ and $y = 7$ when $x = 3$, determine $y$ when $x = 5$.

**22.** If a flagpole casts a shadow 12′ long when a yardstick casts a shadow 10″ long, how tall is the flagpole?

## Section 7.4

**23.** Convert each of these numbers to percents:

(a) $\dfrac{5}{8}$  (b) 2.115  (c) 0.015

**24.** Convert each of these percents to decimals:

(a) 28%  (b) 1.05%  (c) $33\dfrac{1}{3}\%$

**25.** If the sales tax is calculated at 7.2%, how much tax is due on a $49 purchase?

**26.** If a tax of $6.75 is charged on an $84.37 purchase, what is the sales tax rate?

**27.** Refer to problem 17. What percent of free throws attempted did Maria make during the game?

**28.** (a) Alex made $48,000 last year, but has received a letter saying that his new salary is $51,000. What percent raise did Alex get?

(b) After undergoing a drop in the market by 10%, Monique's stock is now valued at $8100. What was the value of her stock before the downturn?

**29.** If you invest $3000 at 8% interest compounded every three months (quarterly), how much is your investment worth at the end of two years?

## Chapter Test

**1.** When did you invest $5000 in a bank paying $5\dfrac{3}{4}\%$ interest compounded annually if the investment is worth $6612.60 now?

**2.** Give an example of a fraction whose decimal expansion is repeating with a period of 3.

**3.** If you invest $2000 now in a bank paying 4.2% interest compounded semiannually, what is the least whole number of years you must leave your investment in the bank in order to withdraw at least $4000?

**4.** Write these fractions in decimal form:

(a) $\dfrac{84}{175}$  (b) $\dfrac{24}{99}$  (c) $\dfrac{7}{11}$

**5.** Suppose that you borrow $1000 now at 9% compounded monthly. If you make no payments in the meantime, how much will you owe at the end of two years?

**6.** Write each of these decimals as a fraction in simplest form:

(a) $0.454545\ldots = 0.\overline{45}$  (b) $31.5555\ldots = 31.\overline{5}$

(c) $0.34999\ldots = 0.34\overline{9}$

**7.** Without doing the hand or calculator calculation, determine how many digits should appear to the right of the decimal point in the product $21.432 \times 3.41$.

**8.** The Pirates won 17 of their 32 hockey games.

(a) What was the ratio of their wins to losses?

(b) What percentage of their games did they win?

**9.** Compute the product $(2.34 \times 10^{-6}) \cdot (3.12 \times 10^{5})$, using an appropriate calculator. Round your answer to the nearest thousandth.

**10.** Mr. Spence put $1425 down on a car selling for $9500. What percent of the purchase price did the dealer require as a down payment?

# Algebraic Reasoning, Graphing, and Connections with Geometry

**8.1** Algebraic Expressions, Functions, and Equations

**8.2** Graphing Points, Lines, and Elementary Functions

**8.3** Connections Between Algebra and Geometry

## Hands On

# The Equation Balance Scale

## Materials Needed

Each student needs an enlarged copy of the materials sheet shown here. Cut out the "unknowns" marked "*x*," the unit squares, and the trapezoid depicting the equation balance scale.

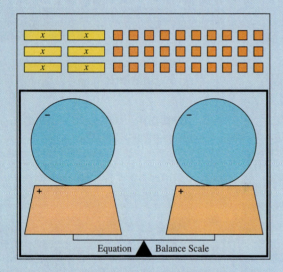

## Using the Equation Balance Scale

An algebraic equation such as $3x - 5 = x + 7$ is represented on the Equation Balance Scale by placing three "*x*" shapes in the + weight area and five unit squares in the negative "balloon" on the left side of the scale. On the right side, an "*x*" and seven unit squares are placed in the + weight area. Thinking of the scale as balanced gives the following initial representation of the equation:

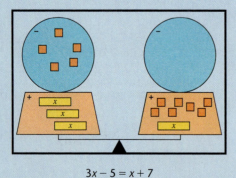

$$3x - 5 = x + 7$$

To solve the equation, we manipulate the pieces to maintain the balance and we modify the equation to reflect the manip-

ulations. We can begin by removing an "*x*" from each side of the balance:

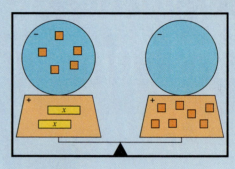

$$2x - 5 = 7$$

Next, add five unit squares to both sides:

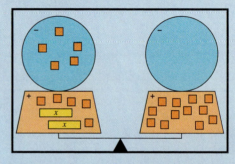

$$(2x - 5) + 5 = 7 + 5$$

On the left side of the balance, the five + weight units are matched by the five − lifting units in the balloon. Each weight-unit–lifting-unit pair with the same units is usually referred to as a "zero pair." We get the following diagram and equation:

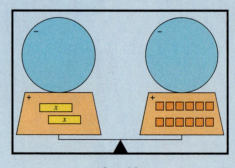

$$2x = 12$$

An equivalent manipulation would be to move the five negative units in the balloon on the left to the positive weight on the right. That is, $2x - 5 = 7$ becomes $2x = 7 + 5$, so we have $2x = 12$ as before.

Finally, we see that there are two rows of identical arrangements of an "*x*" on the left and two rows of six unit squares on the right. Therefore, we divide the number of pieces on each side of the balance by 2, and we have the following solution:

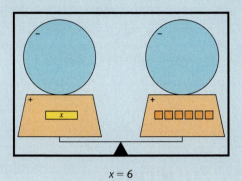

$x = 6$

## Equations to Solve with the Equation Balance Scale

Work in pairs or small groups to solve the given equations, using your Equation Balance Scale. Carefully describe each step of your solution, and show the new equation that expresses the step just completed.

**1.** $x + 4 = 9$
**2.** $x + 6 = 1$
**3.** $3x + 5 = 14$
**4.** $4x - 3 = 2x + 5$
**5.** $2x - 1 = 5 - x$
**6.** $2 - x = 10 - 3x$

---

**CHAPTER PREVIEW**

Most people are surprised that the beginnings of algebra are introduced in elementary school nowadays. The NCTM algebra standards for grades 3–5 below describe how algebra enters the life of a third grader. In this chapter, we review topics from algebra, with special attention to the concepts that are a part of grades K–8. However, the chapter is not meant to be a comprehensive discussion of coordinate geometry or algebra, as that would lead us away from the mathematics of elementary school. Instead, building on the platform of Section 1.4, we review topics such as straight lines and slopes, circles, some nonlinear functions (quadratic equations and exponentials) that can appear in elementary and middle school mathematics, and the productive way in which algebra and geometry interact. We use algebra freely in the rest of the book.

**KEY IDEAS**

■ Algebra explains patterns and solves problems (Section 1.4).
■ Algebra describes generality, conditions that lead to equations, and the relationship between quantities (formulas).
■ Algebra and the geometry of the Cartesian plane combine to form a powerful problem-solving strategy that gives surprising results from geometry.

---

**FROM The NCTM Principles and Standards**

# Algebra Standard for Grades 3-5

| Instructional programs from prekindergarten through grade 12 should enable all students to— | In grades 3–5 all students should— |
| --- | --- |
| Understand patterns, relations, and functions | • *describe, extend, and make generalizations about geometric and numeric patterns;* |
| | • *represent and analyze patterns and functions, using words, tables, and graphs.* |
| Represent and analyze mathematical situations and structures using algebraic symbols | • *identify such properties as commutativity, associativity, and distributivity and use them to compute with whole numbers;* |
| | • *represent the idea of a variable as an unknown quantity using a letter or a symbol;* |
| | • *express mathematical relationships using equations.* |
| Use mathematical models to represent and understand quantitative relationships | • *model problem situations with objects and use representations such as graphs, tables, and equations to draw conclusions.* |

Analyze change in various contexts

- *investigate how a change in one variable relates to a change in a second variable;*
- *identify and describe situations with constant or varying rates of change and compare them.*

SOURCE: *Principles and Standards for School Mathematics by NCTM, page 158. Copyright © 2000 by the National Council of Teachers of Mathematics. Reproduced with permission of the National Council of Teachers of Mathematics via Copyright Clearance Center. NCTM does not endorse the content or validity of these alignments.*

## 8.1

# Algebraic Expressions, Functions, and Equations

In this section, we review algebraic reasoning, with an emphasis on the mathematics in grades K–8. Topics include

- the meaning and uses of variables,
- how to form algebraic expressions involving variables,
- the definition and visualization of functions, and
- the solution of an equation by evaluating the unknowns, by making a graph, or through algebraic means.

We begin with the use of variables in constructing algebraic expressions.

## Variables

Mathematical expressions in elementary arithmetic involve fixed values called **constants.** For example, there are 12 in a dozen, there are four sides of a rectangle, and $2 + 5 = 7$. Constants describe static situations in which change, generality, and variability are not under consideration. Mathematical expressions in algebra still include constants, but also include quantities that are unknown, that can change, or whose value depends on how other, related values are determined or selected. Changeable quantities are referred to as **variables** and are denoted by a symbol. Usually the symbols are letters, such as the $x$ in the equation $x - 3 = 5$, but sometimes other symbols are used. For example, in elementary schools, students are asked what number must be put in the placeholder indicated by the box in the equation $\square - 3 = 5$.

Introducing quantities can give a dynamic aspect to algebraic reasoning that goes far beyond the reasoning of simple computation. Variables are used in at least four different ways in algebra.

### Variables Describe Generalized Properties    For example, the distributive property of multiplication over addition in the real numbers is succinctly stated as

$$a(b + c) = ab + ac, \quad \text{for all real numbers } a, b, \text{ and } c$$

Here, the symbols $a$, $b$, and $c$ are *generalized variables,* used to describe a general property or pattern. A generalized variable represents an arbitrary member of the set of elements for which the property or pattern holds.

How would you explain the distributive property of multiplication over addition to your students in late elementary or middle school? Of course, there are many ways to do this. One that is appealing is to lead them through the process as was sketched out in Figure 2.25 of Section 2.4. Another way is to ask them to compute the area of a swimming pool of width 4 feet and length $(6 + 3)$ feet. Follow that question with a few more which bring them to finding the area of a pool of width $a$ and length $(b + c)$, computed in two ways. Their result will be the distributive property. This mathematical habit of the mind shows how thinking with examples generates generalities.

**Variables Express Relationships**  Jolie was born on her three-year-old sister Kendra's birthday. How are their ages related? Letting $J$ and $K$ denote their respective ages, we have several choices to express the age relationship:

| | |
|---|---|
| $J = K - 3$ | ("Jolie is three years younger than Kendra.") |
| $K = J + 3$ | ("Kendra is three years older than Jolie.") |
| $K - J = 3$ | ("The difference in age between Kendra and her younger sister Jolie is three years.") |

**Variables Serve as Unknowns in Equations**  For example, in the early grades students can be asked to find the number to place in the box that makes the sentence $\square + 5 = 9$ true. In the middle grades a student can be asked to find all values of $x$ for which $(2x - 6)(x - 1) = 0$. The second example shows why it is appropriate to think of $x$ as a variable, since it can be replaced either with 3 or with 1 to make the equation true.

**Variables Express Formulas**  Variables are used in formulas, as you have seen in your earlier math courses. To give examples, several useful formulas are collected in Table 8.1.

**TABLE 8.1    SOME COMMONLY USED FORMULAS**

| Topic | Variables | Formula |
|---|---|---|
| Distance | $d$ = distance traveled<br>$r$ = rate of travel (speed)<br>$t$ = time of travel | $d = rt$ |
| Interest (compounded annually) | $A$ = current amount<br>$P$ = initial principal<br>$i$ = annual interest rate (decimal)<br>$n$ = years elapsed | $A = P(1 + i)^n$ |
| Triangular numbers | $t_n = 1 + 2 + \cdots + n$ (sum of the first $n$ integers)<br><br>$n$ = number of terms in the sum | $t_n = \dfrac{1}{2}n(n + 1)$ |
| Perimeter of a rectangle | $P$ = perimeter<br>$L$ = length<br>$W$ = width | $P = 2L + 2W$ |
| Area of a rectangle | $A$ = area<br>$L$ = length<br>$W$ = width | $A = LW$ |
| Circumference of a circle | $C$ = circumference<br>$r$ = radius | $C = 2\pi r$ |
| Area of a circle | $A$ = area<br>$r$ = radius | $A = \pi r^2$ |

The next example gives you an opportunity to check your understanding of the meaning and uses of variables. It would also be useful for you to review Figure 1.7 (Steps in Algebraic Reasoning) from Section 1.4.

**EXAMPLE 8.1  Identifying the Role of Variables**

In each part, identify the variable and the role it plays.

(a) The length of a rectangle is twice its width $w$, and the area of the rectangle is 18 square feet. What is the width $w$ of the rectangle?

(b) The associative law of addition in the set of integers states that

$$a + (b + c) = (a + b) + c, \quad \text{for all integers } a, b, \text{ and } c$$

(c) A single taxpayer with an adjusted gross income of $X$ dollars in 2003, where $X$ is between $28,400 and $68,800, owes the Internal Revenue Service $3910 + (0.25)(X - \$28,400)$.

(d) Milos is twice as tall as his little sister, Anke, so $m = 2a$, where $m$ and $a$ denote the respective heights of the siblings.

**Solution**

(a) $w$ has the role of an unknown that satisfies the equation $w(2w) = 18$, or $w^2 = 9$. Since $w$ is positive, the value of the unknown, namely, $w = 3$ feet, can be determined from the equation.

(b) $a$, $b$, and $c$ play the role of generalized variables in the set of integers.

(c) $X$ has the role of a variable in the formula used to compute the federal income tax owed.

(d) $m$ and $a$ are variables in the equation and express a relationship between the heights of the children.

## Algebraic Expressions

A **numerical expression** is any representation of a number that involves numbers and operation symbols. For example, $3 + 8$ and $22 \div 2$ are both numerical expressions for 11. An **algebraic expression** is a representation that involves variables, numbers, and operation symbols. For example, $4x + 8y$ is an algebraic expression. It might represent the cost of taking $x$ children and $y$ adults to a play, where children's tickets are $4 each and adults' tickets are $8 each.

> **DESCRIPTION**  *Algebraic Expression*
> An **algebraic expression** is a mathematical expression involving variables, numbers, and operation symbols.

In the examples that follow, you are challenged to create algebraic expressions.

## EXAMPLE 8.2  Forming Algebraic Expressions

For each situation, form an algebraic expression that represents the requested values.

(a) The cost of every item in a store is increased by 15 cents. What is the cost of an item that used to cost $c$ dollars? What is the old cost of an item that now costs $d$ dollars?

(b) There was 3% inflation each of the last two years. What is the current price of an item that cost $p$ dollars last year? If an item is $q$ dollars today, what was its price two years ago? Assume that costs exactly followed the inflation rate.

(c) There are 900 seats in the school auditorium. If $s$ seats are needed for school staff, how many tickets for seats can be given to each of $g$ graduating seniors? (*Hint:* Use the "round down" or "floor" function defined by $\lfloor x \rfloor$ = largest integer less than or equal to $x$. The floor function rounds downward to the nearest integer not larger than $x$. For example, $\lfloor 3.1416 \rfloor = 3, \lfloor 5 \rfloor = 5$, and $\lfloor 7.75 \rfloor = 7$.)

(d) The electric power company charges $5 a month plus 7¢ per kilowatt-hour of electricity used. What is the monthly cost to use $K$ kilowatt-hours?

(e) A student earned $a$ credit hours of A work, $b$ credit hours of B work, and so on. What is the student's grade point average (GPA)? Let each A contribute four points, each B three points, and so on.

**Solution**

(a) $c + 0.15, d - 0.15$ (in dollars)

(b) $1.03p, q/(1.03)^2$

(c) There are $900 - s$ tickets to be evenly distributed to the $g$ graduates, so each student can be given the largest whole number of tickets that is no larger than $\dfrac{900 - s}{g}$. That is, $\left\lfloor \dfrac{900 - s}{g} \right\rfloor$.

(d) $5 + .07K$ (in dollars)

(e) The number of grade points earned is $4a + 3b + 2c + d$. The number of credit hours is $a + b + c + d + f$. Therefore, the GPA is given by the quotient

$$\frac{4a + 3b + 2c + d}{a + b + c + d + f}.$$

The **domain of a variable** is the set of values for which the expression is meaningful. For example, if $n$ denotes the number of students in a room, the domain is the set of whole numbers. If $x$ is the width of a rectangle, the domain is the set of positive real numbers. An algebraic expression is **evaluated** by replacing each of its variables with particular values from the domain of the variables. For example, consider again the expression $4x + 8y$ that gives the cost of $x$ children and $y$ adults attending the theater. Here the domain of each of the variables $x$ and $y$ is the set of whole numbers. When evaluated at $x = 5$ and $y = 3$, the expression has the value $4 \cdot 5 + 8 \cdot 3 = 44$. We now turn our attention from expressions to equations.

## Equations and Their Solution

Two algebraic expressions with the same value form an **equation,** symbolized with the equal sign, $=$, placed between the expressions.

> **DEFINITION**  *Equation*
> An **equation** is a mathematical expression stating that two algebraic expressions have the same value. The equal sign, $=$, indicates that the expression on the left side of the symbol has the same value as the expression on the right side.

Every equation is one of two types, either an identity or a conditional equation. On the one hand, an **identity** is an equation that is true for all evaluations of the variables from their domains. For example, $(x + y)^2 = x^2 + 2xy + y^2$ is an identity in the real numbers, since the expressions on both sides of the equality sign have the same value for all real numbers $x$ and $y$. On the other hand, if only certain values of the variables give equality, then the equation is **conditional.** In this case, $x$ is referred to as the *unknown* and one hopes that all of the values of $x$ can be determined from the equation. For example, $x^2 = 9$ is a conditional equation in the unknown $x$ with the two solutions 3 and $-3$. If the domain of $x$ is more restricted—say, to the positive numbers—there would be just one solution, $x = 3$. Determining the set of values that make an equation true is an important step in algebraic reasoning.

> **DEFINITION**  *Solution Set of an Equation, Equivalent Equations*
> The **solution set** of an equation is the set of *all* values in the domain of the variables that satisfy the given equation. Two equations are **equivalent** if they have the same solution set.

Some equations, such as $x^2 + 5 = 0$ in the domain of all real numbers, do not have a solution. In this case, their solution set is the empty set.

Typically, we construct a sequence of equivalent equations to solve an equation. In doing so, we are allowed to perform the same operation on both sides of an equation if the new equation has the same solution set as the initial equation. Naturally, the hope is to obtain an equivalent equation for which the solution set is obvious. It should be clear that adding the same amount to (or subtracting it) from both sides of an equation gives an equivalent equation. (See, e.g., the Hands-On activity titled "The Equation Balance Scale" at the beginning of the chapter for a physical representation of this process.) Multiplication and division are also allowed, but *only* by nonzero values. More complex operations are allowed if care is taken that the equations are indeed equivalent. For example, consider the equation $\sqrt{2x^2 - 1} = x$. If both sides of the equation are squared, we get the new equation $2x^2 - 1 = x^2$, which is equivalent to $x^2 = 1$. The new equation therefore has two solutions, $x = 1$ and $x = -1$. Only the positive solution $x = 1$ is a solution of $\sqrt{2x^2 - 1} = x$, however. This is because it is always assumed that any square root is non-negative, so the original equation requires the $x$ also to be nonnegative. In solving equations, it is good practice to evaluate the expressions in the original equations with the values in the proposed solution set to check that equality really does hold.

Next, we discuss how the value of a variable can depend on the value of another variable or other variables. The rule that connects these variables is called a **function.** The concept of a function adds an important dynamic aspect to algebraic reasoning, providing a way to show relationships between quantities, describe change, and make predictions. Coming right after the ideas of number and operations, the concept of a function is a fundamental building block of elementary school mathematics. Functions appear frequently in state assessment exams in such forms as guessing patterns or describing a rule. More importantly, research shows that the basis for a thorough understanding of functions needs to start in elementary school in order to provide a solid foundation for the remainder of a student's mathematical education.

## Highlight from History

### Emmy Noether (1882–1935)

Emmy Noether was born in Erlangen, Germany, to a family noted for mathematical talent. Much of her life was spent at the University of Göttingen, exploring, teaching, and writing about algebra. This university—where Carl Gauss had taught a century earlier—was the first in Germany to grant a doctoral degree to a woman. Yet Noether met with frustrating discrimination there. For many years she was denied [an] appointment to the faculty; finally she was given an impressive title, "extraordinary professor"—but with no salary. Her abilities overcame the obstacles that daunted many other women in mathematics. Her work in the 1920s brought invitations to lecture throughout Europe and in Moscow. In 1933, as the Nazi party came to power in Germany, Noether met with persecution not only as a woman but as an intellectual, a Jew, a pacifist, and a political liberal. She fled to the United States, where she taught and lectured at Bryn Mawr and Princeton until her death in 1935.

*"How can it be allowed that a woman become . . . a professor . . . ? What will our soldiers think when they return to the University and find that they are expected to learn at the feet of a woman?"*
—FACULTY MEMBER AT GÖTTINGEN, IN 1918

*" . . . for two of the most significant sides of the theory of relativity, she gave at that time [1919] the genuine and universal mathematical formulation."*
—HERMANN WEYL, COLLEAGUE AT GÖTTINGEN

*"In the judgement of the most competent living mathematicians, Fräulein Noether was the most significant creative mathematical genius thus far produced since the higher education of women began. In the realm of algebra . . . she discovered methods which have proved of enormous importance. . . . "*
—ALBERT EINSTEIN, 1935

*"She was the most creative abstract algebraist in the world."*
—ERIC TEMPLE BELL IN MEN OF MATHEMATICS

SOURCE: *Biographical information is from Lynn Osen,* Women in Mathematics *(MIT Press, 1974). Quotations are cited in that source, original references including an anonymous faculty member, Constance Reid,* Hilbert *(Springer-Verlag, 1970, p. 143); Weyl,* Scripta Mathematica, *Vol. 3, 1935; Einstein,* New York Times, *May 4, 1935; Bell,* Men of Mathematics *(Simon and Schuster, 1965, p. 261). From Mathematics in Modules,* Intermediate Algebra, *A5, Teachers Edition. Reprinted by permission.*

## Defining Functions

Imagine yourself at the service station, filling your tank with gasoline priced at $2.79 per gallon. The general principle is that your bill that day at the station is a *function* of the amount of gasoline you purchase. If we let the variable $x$ (the input) represent the number of gallons of gasoline purchased and let the variable $y$ (the output) represent the final bill in dollars, then $y$ is given by the simple rule

$y = 2.79x$. Nicely enough, the pump carries out this calculation right before our eyes, and as the values of $x$ whirl by on one display of the pump, we can simultaneously watch the corresponding values of $y$ on another display.

It is easy to make a list of functions used in our lives. Here are a few examples:

- The amount of postage on a first-class letter is a function of the weight of the envelope, rounded upward to the nearest ounce.
- The recommended amount of lawn fertilizer to be applied is a function of the number of square feet of lawn area.
- The amount of federal income tax you will owe is a function of your taxable income the previous year.

These examples should help you understand the general definition of a function.

---

**DEFINITION**   *Function*

A **function** on a set $D$ is a rule that associates, with each element $x \in D$, precisely one value $y$. The set $D$ is called the **domain** of the function.

---

The definition of "function" requires that a single value $y$ be assigned to each $x$-value in the domain. This condition should seem reasonable, since it would appear strange to buy 10 gallons of gas and be given two bills, say, one for $17.99 and another for $27.90. Another method of looking at a rule to see if the assignment that it makes is a function is called the **vertical-line test.** If you draw a graph, see whether a vertical line intersects the graph. If, for any vertical line, the line doesn't intersect the graph in two or more points, then the graph is the graph of a function.

A function is frequently denoted by a letter such as $f$, and we write $y = f(x)$ to indicate that the value of the variable $y$ is determined by the value of the variable $x$ through the function $f$. Often, a function is denoted by a word or abbreviation to help remember its definition. For example, the function that computes the square root of a positive number is frequently denoted by Sqrt, so Sqrt(49) = 7.

A function can also be viewed as a set of ordered pairs: $\{(x, y) \mid x \in D \text{ and } y = f(x)\}$. Since just one $y$ value is associated with each $x$, a set of ordered pairs represents a function when, and only when, there are no two ordered pairs with the same $x$-value, but different $y$-values. This is a restatement of the "vertical-line criterion" mentioned two paragraphs ago.

If a function assigns the value $y$ to an element $x$ in the domain, then $y$ is called the **image,** or **value,** of $f$ at $x$. For example, if $f$ denotes the function that calculates our bill at the gasoline station and if gas costs $2.79 a gallon and we have purchased $x = 10$ gallons of gas, then $27.90 = f(10)$ is the value of the function at $x = 10$. We can also write $f(x) = 2.79 \cdot x$ and $D = \{x \mid x \geq 0\}$, which describes the gasoline-buying function by an algebraic equation and the domain of permissible values of $x$.

The set of all image values is called the **range** of the function.

---

**DEFINITION**   *Range of a Function*

The **range** of a function $f$ on a set $D$ is the set of images of $f$. That is,

$$\text{range } f = \{y \mid y = f(x) \text{ for some } x \in D\}.$$

---

For example, a first-class letter mailed in the United States costs $0.44 for the first ounce and $0.17 for each additional ounce. Therefore, the range of the function that gives the cost of mailing a first-class letter is $\{\$0.44, \$0.61, \$0.78, \ldots \}$.

## Highlight from History

### Two Women from Early Mathematics: Theano (ca. sixth century B.C.) and Hypatia (A.D. 370–415)

The early history of mathematics mentions few women's names. Indirect evidence, however, suggests that at least some women of ancient times had access to mathematical knowledge and likely made contributions to it. For example, the mis-named "brotherhood" of Pythagoreans, at the insistence of Pythagoras himself, included women in the order, both as teachers and as scholars. Indeed, Theano, the wife and former student of Pythagoras, assumed leadership of the school at the death of her husband. Theano wrote several treatises on mathematics, physics, medicine, and child psychology.

Hypatia was the first woman to attain lasting prominence in mathematics history. Her father, Theon, was a professor of mathematics at the Alexandrian Museum. Theon took extraordinary interest in his daughter and saw to it that she was thoroughly educated in arts, literature, science, philosophy, and, of course, mathematics. Hypatia's fame as a mathematician was secured in Athens, where she studied with Plutarch the Younger and his daughter Asclepigenia. Later she returned to the university at Alexandria, where she lectured on Diophantus's *Arithmetica* and Apollonius's *Conic Sections* and wrote several treatises of her own. The account of Hypatia's life of accomplishments in mathematics, astronomy, and teaching ends on a tragic note, for in March of 415 she was seized by a mob of religious fanatics and brutally murdered.

---

## EXAMPLE 8.3 Finding the Range of a Function

**(a)** Let $f$ be the function defined by the formula $f(x) = x(10 - x)$ on the domain $D = \{1, 2, 3, 4, 5, 6, 7, 8, 9, 10.\}$ Find the range of $f$.

**(b)** The domain of $f(x) = x^2$ is the set of all real numbers between $-2$ and $5$. What is the range of $f$?

**Solution**

**(a)** The image of $f$ at $x = 1$ is $f(1) = 1 \cdot (10 - 1) = 9$. Similarly, $f(2) = 2 \cdot 8 = 16$, $f(3) = 3 \cdot 7 = 21$, $f(4) = 4 \cdot 6 = 24$, $f(5) = 5 \cdot 5 = 25$, $f(6) = 6 \cdot 4 = 24$, $f(7) = 7 \cdot 3 = 21$, $f(8) = 8 \cdot 2 = 16$, $f(9) = 9 \cdot 1 = 9$, and $f(10) = 10 \cdot 0 = 0$. Thus, the range of $f$ is $\{0, 9, 16, 21, 24, 25\}$. Some image values, such as 9, 16, and 21, correspond to more than one $x$ in the domain, but any $x$ yields a single $y$-value in the range.

**(b)** The function $f$ squares each number. For example, at $x = -2$, $f$ gives 4, a positive number. $f(0)$ is zero and all other values are positive, with the largest value being $f(5) = 25$. Checking out a few more values, we easily see that the range is all numbers between 0 and 25 inclusive. Written in set notation, range $(f) = \{y \in R \text{ such that } 0 \le y \le 25\}$.

---

One of the most popular ways to introduce function concepts to elementary school children is to play the game "Guess My Rule."

## EXAMPLE 8.4 Guessing Erica's Rule

Erica is "it" in a game of Guess My Rule. As the children pick an input number, Erica tells what number her rule gives back, as shown in this table:

| Children's Choice, $x$ | Result of Erica's Rule, $y$ |
|:---:|:---:|
| 2 | −1 |
| 5 | 8 |
| 6 | 11 |
| 0 | −7 |
| 1 | −4 |

Can you guess Erica's rule?

**Solution**

**Understand the Problem**

The rule Erica has chosen is a function: Given a value of the input variable $x$, she uses her function to determine the value of the output variable $y$, after which she reveals that to the class. We must guess her function. We wish to express the formula for $y$ in terms of a variable $x$ or $n$ as in the preceding examples.

**Devise a Plan**

The children's choices are somewhat random. Perhaps a pattern will become more apparent if we arrange their values in order of increasing size. We anticipate that Erica's function is given by a formula.

**Carry Out the Plan**

Rearranging the children's choices in order of increasing size, we have the following table:

| Children's Choice, $x$ | Result of Erica's Rule, $y$ |
|:---:|:---:|
| 0 | $-7$ |
| 1 | $-4$ |
| 2 | $-1$ |
| 5 | 8 |
| 6 | 11 |

When $x = 0$ is the input, the formula reads $y = -7$. This suggests that $-7$ is a separate term in the formula; when $x = 0$, all the other terms are 0. Also, we observe that when $x$ increases by 1 from 0 to 1, from 1 to 2, and from 5 to 6, the output number increases by 3. This suggests that the formula also contains the term $3x$, since this quantity increases by 3 each time $x$ increases by 1. Combining these observations, we guess that Erica's function (rule), $E$, is given by the formula

$$E(x) = 3x - 7.$$

Checking, we see that $E(0) = 3 \cdot 0 - 7 = -7, E(1) = 3 \cdot 1 - 7 = -4, E(2) = -1, E(5) = 8$, and $E(6) = 11$, as in Erica's table. When challenged, Erica reveals that we have guessed correctly.

**Look Back**

Erica's rule is really a function: Given a value of $x$, her rule returns a single value for $y$. We guessed the rule by arranging the data in a more orderly way, noting that her rule associated $-7$ with 0 and that the output number increased by 3 each time the input number increased by 1. Thus, we correctly guessed Erica's function to be $E(x) = 3x - 7$.

## Describing and Visualizing Functions

There are several useful ways to describe and visualize functions:

- **Functions as formulas.** Consider, for example, a circle of radius $r$, where the variable $r$ is any positive number. The formula $area(r) = \pi r^2$ defines the function $area$ that expresses the area of the circle as a function of the radius $r$. Similarly, the formula $circum(r) = 2\pi r$ defines the function $circum$ that gives the circumference of a circle of radius $r$. Several interesting formulas were encountered in Chapter 1, each of which can be viewed as a function defined on the domain $N$, the set of natural numbers. For example, the $n$th odd number is given by the formula $h(n) = 2n - 1$, so the 50th odd number is $h(50) = 2(50) - 1 = 99$. Another example is the sum $1 + 2 + 3 + \cdots + n$ of the first $n$ natural numbers (i.e., the $n$th triangular number), which is given by Gauss's insight as $t(n) = n(n + 1)/2$. Thus, the sum of the first 100 natural numbers is $1 + 2 + 3 + \cdots + 99 + 100 = t(100) = 100(100 + 1)/2 = 5050$. Functions that are defined on the domain $N$ of the natural numbers are called **sequences,** and it is common to use the notation $f_n$ instead of $f(n)$. For example, the $n$th triangular number is given by $t_n = n(n + 1)/2$, and, in particular, $t_{100} = 5050$.

- **Functions as tables.** The following table gives the grades of three students on an essay question:

| Student | Grade |
|---------|-------|
| Raygene | 8 |
| JaiWoo | 7 |
| Leticia | 10 |

No algebraic formula connects the student to the grade. Even so, as long as the table assigns a unique grade to each student, then a function is completely described. The domain of this function is $D = \{$Raygene, JaiWoo, Leticia$\}$ and its range is $\{7, 8, 10\}$.

- **Functions as arrow diagrams.** In an arrow diagram, two loops are formed, with one loop representing the domain and the second loop representing a set that contains the values of the function and, possibly, other points as well. Every point in the domain loop must have exactly one arrow, which extends from that point to one of the points in the second loop. Figure 8.1 shows an arrow diagram in which the students Ursula, Vincent, Whitney, Yolanda, and Zach have been assigned grades on their class project. We see that Ursula and Vincent both received As and that no student received a D grade.

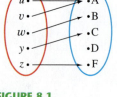

**FIGURE 8.1**

A function represented with an arrow diagram

- **Functions as machines.** Viewing a function as a machine gives students an attractive dynamic visual model. The machine has an input hopper that accepts any domain element $x$ and an output chute that gives the image $y = f(x)$. A few function machines are shown in Figure 8.2.

**FIGURE 8.2**

Three function machines

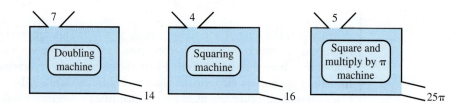

- **Functions as graphs.** A function whose domain and range are sets of numbers can be graphed on a set of $x$- and $y$-axes: If $f(x) = y$, plot the points $(x, y)$ for all $x$ in the domain. The Fibonacci sequence $F_1 = 1, F_2 = 1, F_3 = 2, F_4 = 3, \ldots$ and the doubling function $y = 2x$ are plotted in Figure 8.3. Note that these two functions have different domains.

**FIGURE 8.3**

Graphs of (a) the Fibonacci sequence and (b) the doubling function

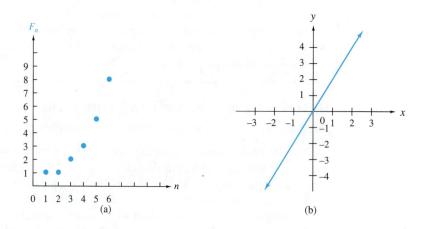

Computers and graphing calculators are very useful tools for creating graphs and investigating the properties of the function represented by a graph. However, it is still instructive to make graphs by hand, using graph paper, rulers, and colored pencils. Begin by making a table of selected values of $x$ from the domain and calculating the corresponding image values $y$. The table of values will help you to choose an appropriate range of $x$- and $y$-values to include on the axes. Next, plot the points $(x, y)$ from your table onto your graph. Finally, fill in the rest of the graph by smoothly connecting the points, as dictated by the domain.

**EXAMPLE 8.5** **Calculating the Cost of Owning and Driving a Car**

A survey of car owners shows that the monthly cost (in dollars) to own and drive an automobile is given by the function $f(x) = 0.31x + 175$. Here, $x$ represents the number of miles driven throughout the month and 175 represents the monthly cost of ownership that is independent of the miles driven (insurance, vehicle license fees, and so on).

(a) Make a table that shows the cost of having a car that is driven 0, 100, 200, . . . , 1000 miles per month.
(b) Use the table of values in part (a) to draw a graph that shows the cost of driving a car for up to 1000 miles in a month.
(c) Use your graph to estimate the corresponding limit on the number of miles driven in a month if your budget limits your car expenditures to $350.
(d) What is the exact number of miles driven throughout the month if the expenditures are $350?

**Solution**

(a)

| Miles, $x$ | 0 | 100 | 200 | 300 | 400 | 500 | 600 | 700 | 800 | 900 | 1000 |
|---|---|---|---|---|---|---|---|---|---|---|---|
| Cost, $y$ | 175 | 206 | 237 | 268 | 299 | 330 | 361 | 392 | 423 | 454 | 485 |

(b)

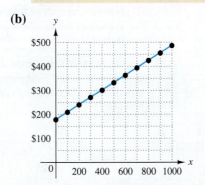

(c) The graph indicates that about 570 miles can be driven.
(d) This part requires the use of algebra. The exact value can be obtained from the equation $350 = 0.31x + 175$. Subtracting 175 from both sides and then dividing by 0.31 shows that
$$x = \frac{350 - 175}{0.31} = \frac{175}{0.31} \text{ miles (about 565 miles).}$$

The points of the graph of the function $f(x) = 0.31x + 175$ in Example 8.5 lie along a line. More generally, the graph of any function of the form $f(x) = mx + b$ is a line, where $m$ and $b$ are constants. For this reason, such functions are called **linear functions.** In the next section, additional attention is given to lines and their equations as well as two kinds of functions that appear in middle school: quadratic equations and exponentials.

## Problem Set 8.1

Exercises numbered in red are answered in the back of the text.

## Understanding Concepts

1. Classify the quantities in each part as a constant or a variable.

   (a) The number of feet in a mile
   (b) The number of hours of daylight in a day
   (c) The price of a gallon of gasoline
   (d) The speed of light in empty space
   (e) The distance from the earth's center to the moon

2. In each of the given situations, classify the role of the variables as one of the following types: generalized, expressing a relationship, expressing a formula, an unknown.

   (a) For all real numbers $x$, $y$, and $z$, $x(y + z) = xy + xz$.
   (b) Elena is 4 inches shorter than her husband, Joe, so $E = J - 4$.
   (c) To construct a circular flower bed covering 400 square feet of ground, the radius $r$ of the bed must satisfy $\pi r^2 = 400$.

**(d)** Tickets to the play are $5 for adults and $3 for children. If $A$ adults and $C$ children attend the play, the total proceeds are $5A + 3C$.

3. Alicia, Boris, Carlos, Dan, and Xavier all collect Pokémon™ cards. If $x$ denotes the number of cards in Xavier's collection, form expressions for the number of cards in the other children's collections, using the information provided. For example, Alicia has six more cards than Xavier, so Alicia has $x + 6$ cards.

**(a)** Boris is three cards short of having twice the number of cards as Xavier.

**(b)** Carlos has two more than half the number of cards owned by Xavier.

**(c)** Dan has the same number of cards as Alicia and Xavier combined.

4. Penny is $p$ years old. Form algebraic expressions with the variable $p$ that represent the ages requested.

**(a)** Penny's age in five years

**(b)** Penny's age eight years ago

**(c)** The *current* age of Penny's little brother, who will be half of Penny's age in two more years

**(d)** The *current* age of Penny's mother, who was 4 times Penny's age three years ago

5. Richie weighs $q$ pounds today, which is the last day of February. Form algebraic expressions with the variable that represent the weight requested.

**(a)** Richie's father is 10 pounds less than twice Richie's weight.

**(b)** Richie would like to lose .25 pound per day for the next week to make wrestling weight. What does he weigh at the end of the week?

**(c)** Richie would like to gain an eighth of a pound a day until the end of March. What will he weigh on April 1 if he started on March 1?

6. Five children, say, $A$, $B$, $C$, $D$, and $E$, are in a line. $A$ writes a number on a slip of paper and hands it to $B$. $B$ squares the number received and writes that value on a new slip of paper that is handed to $C$. In a similar way, $C$ adds 5 to the number obtained from $B$ and passes that number on to $D$. $D$ multiplies the number by 7 and writes it on a slip of paper that is handed to $E$.

**(a)** If $A$ writes a 3 on a slip of paper, what number will be handed to $E$?

**(b)** If child $A$ puts $x$ on the first slip of paper, what algebraic expression is handed to child $E$?

**(c)** If $E$ is given the number 35, what number did $A$ write on the initial slip of paper?

**(d)** Suppose the children line up in the order $A$, $D$, $B$, $C$, and $E$. If $A$ writes $y$ on a slip of paper, what expression is eventually handed to $E$?

7. As with problem 6, children are in a line and each is assigned one operation to perform. If the first child writes $x$ on a slip of paper and the last child is handed a slip on which the expression $(3 - 5x)^3 + 4$ appears, describe how many children are in the line and what single operation each performs.

8. Bernie weighs 90 pounds plus half his own weight. What does Bernie weigh?

9. Consider the pair of equations $y - 8x = 2$ and $y + 4 = 3x$.

**(a)** Solve each equation for $y$ as an expression in $x$.

**(b)** Equate the expressions found in part (a) to obtain an equation in the variable $x$.

**(c)** Solve the equation in part (b) for the unknown $x$.

**(d)** Solve for $y$.

10. Little Red Riding Hood rode her bike 15 miles to Grandma's house, arriving in 3 hours. When she discovered the Big Bad Wolf, she turned around and scampered home at 15 miles per hour. The *distance = rate × time* formula will be helpful to answer these questions.

**(a)** What was Little Red Riding Hood's average speed to Grandma's house?

**(b)** How long did it take to get home?

**(c)** How long was the round-trip?

**(d)** How many hours did the round-trip take?

**(e)** What is the average speed for the round-trip?

**(f)** Is the average speed for the round-trip equal to the average of the speeds to and from Grandma's house? Why is this?

11. Decide which of these arrow diagrams represent(s) a function with domain $A$. If the diagram does not define a function, explain why. If a function is defined, give the range of the function.

**(a)**

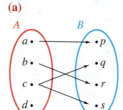

**(b)**

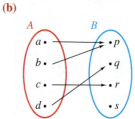

**(c)**

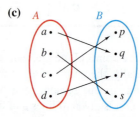

12. Draw an arrow diagram for each of the given sets of ordered pairs, where, in each diagram, the left loop represents the set $A = \{1, 2, 3, 4, 5\}$ and the right loop represents the set $B = \{1, 2, 3, 4\}$. For each set, explain why the set of ordered pairs does or does not represent a function with domain $A$.

**(a)** $\{(1, 3), (2, 3), (1, 2), (3, 2), (4, 3), (5, 4)\}$

**(b)** $\{(1, 2), (2, 1), (3, 3), (4, 2), (5, 2)\}$

**(c)** $\{(1, 4), (2, 3), (4, 1), (5, 2)\}$

13. Each pair of axes shows a plot of points. Identify those plots on the next page which represent the graph of a function $y = f(x)$. If the plot cannot be a graph of a function, explain why not. If a function graph is depicted, give both the domain and the range of the function. Use the vertical-line test.

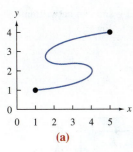

**(a)**

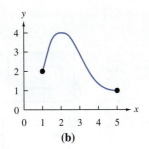

**(b)**

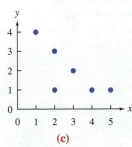

**(c)**

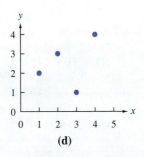

**(d)**

**14.** Let $f$ be the function given by the formula $f(x) = 8 - 2x$ on the domain $D = \{x \mid x = 2, 3, 4, 5\}$.

**(a)** Make a table of the $x$- and $y$-values.

**(b)** What is the range of $f$?

**(c)** Sketch the graph of $f$.

**15.** Let $g$ be the function given by the formula $g(x) = 2x - 2$, defined for all the real (decimal) numbers $x$ in the interval $-2 \leq x \leq 3$.

**(a)** Make a table of values of $g(x)$ for $x = -2, -1, 0, 1, 2$, and 3.

**(b)** Plot the points in your table from part (a) and then sketch the entire graph.

**(c)** What is the range of $g$?

**16.** Let $g$ be the function from $S = \{0, 1, 2, 3, 4\}$ to the whole numbers $W$ given by the formula $g(x) = 5 - 2x + x^2$.

**(a)** Find $g(0), g(1), g(2), g(3), g(4)$.

**(b)** What is the range of $g$?

**17.** Let $h$ be the function defined by $h(x) = x^2 - 1$, where the domain is the set of real numbers.

**(a)** Find $h(2)$.

**(b)** Find $h(-2)$.

**(c)** If $h(t) = 15$, what are the possible values of $t$?

**(d)** Find $h(7.32)$.

---

**18.** Karalee made a trip to the store one afternoon. Her trip is shown in the graph that follows, where her distance (in miles) from home is plotted as a function of the hours past noon. Refer to the graph to answer these questions about her trip.

**(a)** What time did she leave home?

**(b)** When did she realize that she forgot her checkbook?

**(c)** What did she do about the forgotten checkbook?

**(d)** When did Karalee park the car at the store?

**(e)** How long did she shop?

**(f)** How far away was the store?

**(g)** Did Karalee encounter slower traffic going to or coming from the store? Explain how you can determine this from the graph.

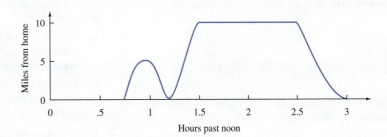

**19.** Four graphs are shown, labeled G1, G2, G3, and G4. Which of these graphs matches the function described?

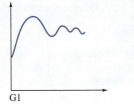

**(a)** Temperature of a pan of water placed on a hot burner

**(b)** Height of a flag being run up the flagpole

(c) Height of a weight hung from a Slinky®

(d) Length of the shadow of a flagpole throughout a sunny day in Dallas

20. Make simple approximate sketches of graphs (such as those in problem 19) that correspond to these functions of time:

(a) Temperature of a forgotten cup of hot tea

(b) Perceived pitch of a train whistle as the train passes

(c) Height of the water in a bathtub during the time someone takes a bath

(d) Hours of daylight in Chicago during a calendar year; that is, domain $= \{1, 2, \ldots, 365\}$

21. Consider the "double-square" rectangle of height $x$ and width $2x$, as shown.

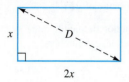

(a) Find the function $A(x)$ that gives the area of a double square of width $x$.

(b) Find the function $P(x)$ that gives the perimeter of a double square of width $x$.

(c) Use the Pythagorean theorem to obtain the function $D(x)$ for the length of the diagonal of a double square of width $x$.

22. Solve each of these Guess My Rule games:

(a)

| Guess | 4 | 7 | 2 | 0 | 10 | 1 |
|---|---|---|---|---|---|---|
| Response | 9 | 12 | 7 | 5 | 15 | 6 |

(b)

| Guess | 4 | 2 | 0 | 7 | 3 | 9 |
|---|---|---|---|---|---|---|
| Response | 10 | 6 | 2 | 16 | 8 | 20 |

(c)

| Guess | 4 | 5 | 7 | 3 | 0 | 10 |
|---|---|---|---|---|---|---|
| Response | 17 | 26 | 50 | 10 | 1 | 101 |

23. Che is "it" in a game of Guess My Rule. The students' inputs and Che's outputs are shown in the following table:

| Input Given to Che | 5 | 2 | 4 | 0 | −2 | −5 |
|---|---|---|---|---|---|---|
| Output Reported by Che | 24 | 3 | 15 | −1 | 3 | 24 |

(a) Guess Che's rule (function), $y = C(x)$.

(b) Antonio says that Che's rule is $C(x) = x^2 - 1$, but Claudette claims that it is $C(x) = (x + 1)(x - 1)$. Who is correct, Antonio or Claudette? Explain.

24. Suppose two function machines are hooked up in sequence so that the output chute of machine $g$ empties into the input hopper of machine $f$. Such a coupling of machines, which is defined if the range of $g$ is a subset of the domain of $f$, is

called the *composition* of $f$ and $g$ and can be written $F(x) = f(g(x))$ and depicted as follows:

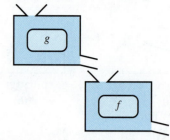

(a) Suppose $f$ is the doubling function $f(x) = 2x$ and $g$ is the "add 3" function $g(t) = t + 3$. Then $F(4) = f(g(4)) = f(4 + 3) = f(7) = 2 \times 7 = 14$. Evaluate $f(g(x))$ for $x = 0, 1, 2,$ and 3.

(b) Suppose the doubling and "add 3" function machines are coupled in reverse order to define the composition of $g$ and $f$, given by $G(x) = g(f(x))$. Then $G(4) = g(f(4)) = g(2 \times 4) = g(8) = 8 + 3 = 11$. Evaluate $g(f(x))$ for $x = 0, 1, 2,$ and 3.

## Teaching Concepts

25. A student thinks that the expressions $(a + b)^2$ and $a^2 + b^2$ are equal to one another. How would you explain to the student why this is not so?

26. A student has noticed that every squared natural number is either a multiple of 4 or 1 larger than a multiple of 4 but isn't sure if this is always true. Use algebraic reasoning to explain to the student why it is always true. (*Suggestion:* Every even natural number is of the form $2k$ for some natural number $k$, and every odd natural number has the form $2l + 1$ for some natural number $l$.)

27. Function concepts can be taught to young children by incorporating appropriate manipulatives and activities. For example, suppose a student plays the role of a function machine whose inputs are lengths of Unifix™ cubes. When handed a length of five cubes, the student returns a length of eight cubes. When given a length of two cubes, the student returns a length of five cubes.

(a) What function is the student apparently evaluating? How could it be tested? How many cubes should be put into the machine so that the output is ten cubes snapped together?

(b) Describe a function machine, again employing Unifix™ cubes, that illustrates the addition function $f(a, b) = a + b$ on the domain of pairs of natural numbers.

28. Create an activity, using commonly available manipulatives, that will illustrate a function concept. Use the Unifix™ cube activity described in problem 27 as an example, but be original.

## Responding to Students

29. Many fourth-grade students have an extremely difficult time solving the equation $7 = \frac{x}{4}$ for $x$. Oftentimes, many children won't generate an answer for $x$ at all. However, if students are given $\frac{x}{4} = 7$, more can solve the problem.

(a) What is confusing the students?

(b) What is your next step as a teacher to help students realize that this is the same problem written two different ways?

**30.** Josiah was asked to identify which of the following statements shows that $a$ is 9 less than $b$.

**A.** $9a = b$          **B.** $a + 9 = b$

**C.** $9 - a = b$          **D.** $\dfrac{a}{9} = b$

He answered C, $9 - a = b$. What is Josiah doing incorrectly?

**31.** AnnElise was asked to analyze population data for a nearby town that was growing each year. She was given the following table:

| Year | 2007 | 2008 | 2009 | 2010 |
|---|---|---|---|---|
| **Number of People** | 267 | 305 | 343 | 381 |

AnnElise was then asked to tell how many people would be living in the town in the year 2012 if the population increased at a constant rate as shown in the table. AnnElise decided that the population would be 419.

(a) What common error did she make when computing her answer?

(b) How would you guide her to use the table to find the correct answer?

**32.** Students created the following table:

| x | y |
|---|---|
| 1 | 3 |
| 2 | 5 |
| 3 | 7 |
| 4 | 9 |
| 5 | 11 |
| 10 | ? |

They decided that the rule was to add 2 more each time, and they gave the answer as 13.

(a) What pattern do most elementary school students see first?

(b) How can you help them to see the function rule for any $x$?

**33.** Tara is working to simplify the expression $4x + 2$ and gives the answer 8. She explains that 4 times 2 is 8. What is confusing her? What are some other ways to write 4 times $x$?

## Thinking Critically

**34.** Let $n$ be a two-digit whole number with this special property: If the sum of the digits is added to the product of the digits, the result is $n$. For example, $n = 29$ has the special property, since $2 + 9 + 2 \times 9 = 11 + 18 = 29$. Find all two-digit numbers with the property.

**35.** Huong spent 90 cents at the store, buying some pencils at 15 cents each and some erasers at 6 cents each. He purchased several more erasers than pencils. How many pencils and erasers did he buy? Use algebraic reasoning to find your answer.

**36.** A commuter travels to work at an average speed $u$ and returns home at an average speed $v$. Show that the average speed for the round-trip is $\dfrac{2uv}{u + v}$. Are you surprised that it is not $\dfrac{u + v}{2}$?

**37.** Suppose that $n^3$ sugar cubes are stacked to form an $n \times n \times n$ cube, as shown. The large cube is now painted yellow. Depending on where a sugar cube is positioned in the large cube, it may have one or several of its six faces painted yellow. For example, if $n = 1$, all six faces are painted. For larger $n$, there are some sugar cubes with unpainted faces.

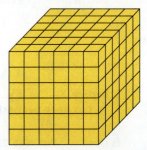

(a) Describe how the faces of the sugar cubes in a $2 \times 2 \times 2$ cube are painted.

(b) Count the number of sugar cubes in a $3 \times 3 \times 3$ cube with 0, 1, 2, or 3 painted faces. Do you account for all of the sugar cubes that form the large cube?

(c) Give expressions in the variable $n$, $n \geq 3$, for the number of sugar cubes in the $n \times n \times n$ cube with 0, 1, 2, or 3 painted faces, respectively.

(d) The four expressions obtained in part (c), when added together, should give $n^3$ for all $n$ larger than or equal to 3. Why? Use algebraic simplification to check your identity in the variable $n$.

**38.** Find the solution set in the real numbers of each of these equations.

(a) $2(3x - 6x + 1) = 3(1 - 2x) - 1$

(b) $x(x - 2) = 2(x^2 - x + 1)$

**39.** The bank robbers are 9 miles north of Dodge City and are continuing to head north at 8 miles per hour on their horses. If the posse begins the chase from Dodge City on fresher horses at 10 miles per hour, how many hours will it take for the posse to catch the thieves? Show your answer with a graph that plots both the "robber" function $9 + 8t$ and the "posse" function $10t$, each of which gives the distance north of Dodge after $t$ hours of the chase.

## Making Connections

**40.** Rug remnants can be purchased for \$3.60 per square yard, and the edges can be finished at a cost of 12¢ per foot. Let $L$ and $W$ respectively denote the length and width of a rectangular remnant, given in feet. Give an expression for the cost, in dollars, to buy and finish an $L$-by-$W$ remnant.

**41.** Zal is paid \$18 an hour for a 40-hour workweek, but is paid time and a half for overtime work. Give expressions for Zal's pay if he works $t$ hours. You'll need to distinguish between the cases where $t$ is less than or equal to 40 and $t$ is greater than 40.

## Using a Calculator

**42.** The formula for the area of a circle given implicitly in the Rhind papyrus (ca. 1650 B.C.) is $A = \left(\dfrac{16}{9}\right)^2 r^2$, where $r$ denotes the radius of the circle.

(a) How much error, in square feet, is made if this formula instead of the exact formula ($A = \pi r^2$) is used to measure the area of a circle of radius 100 feet.?

(b) Archimedes (ca. 300 B.C.) suggested that $\pi$ can be approximated by $\frac{22}{7}$. How much error is made in computing the area of a circle of radius 100 feet if the formula $A = \left(\frac{22}{7}\right)r^2$ is used instead of the exact formula?

---

**43. Tax Rate Schedules.** Federal income tax rates for a single person are given in Schedule X. Use it to find the taxes owed for Demitrius and Cyndi, both of whom are single.

| Schedule X—Use if your filing status is single. | | | | |
|---|---|---|---|---|
| **If TAXABLE INCOME** | | **The TAX Is** | | |
| | | **THEN** | | |
| **Is Over** | **But Not Over** | **This Amount** | **Plus This %** | **Of the Excess Over** |
| $0 | $7,000 | $0.00 | 10% | $0.00 |
| $7,000 | $28,400 | $700.00 | 15% | $7,000 |
| $28,400 | $68,800 | $3,910.00 | 25% | $28,400 |
| $68,800 | $143,500 | $14,010.00 | 28% | $68,800 |
| $143,500 | $311,950 | $34,926.00 | 33% | $143,500 |
| $311,950 | – | $90,514.50 | 35% | $311,950 |

(a) Demitrius had a taxable income of $41,162.

(b) Cyndi had a taxable income of $134,520.

---

## From State Student Assessments

**44.** (Oregon, Grade 5)

Tyler and Rory both collect baseball cards. Rory has eight more than twice as many as Tyler. If $T$ is the number of cards that Tyler has, which choice shows the number of cards that Rory has?

**A.** $16 - T$
**B.** $2T - 8$
**C.** $2T + 8$
**D.** $8 - 2$

**45.** (Massachusetts, Grade 4)

If ○ ○ = □, which of the following is true?

**A.** ○ ○ ○ = □
**B.** ○ ○ = □□
**C.** ○ ○ ○ ○ ○ = □□
**D.** ○ ○ ○ ○ ○ ○ = □□□

**46.** (Massachusetts, Grade 8)

The table below shows four pairs of $x$- and $y$-values.

| x | y |
|---|---|
| 1 | 0 |
| 2 | 3 |
| 3 | 8 |
| 4 | 15 |

Which of the following equations is true for all pairs of $x$- and $y$-values in the table?

**A.** $y = x + 1$
**B.** $y = x - 1$
**C.** $y = x^2 + 1$
**D.** $y = x^2 - 1$

**47.** (Massachusetts, Grade 8)

Four friends earned money by painting a house. After they divided the money equally, they each received $315. Which of the following equations could be used to determine $x$, the total amount, in dollars, that the four friends earned by painting the house?

**A.** $\frac{x}{4} = 315$

**B.** $4x = 315$

**C.** $x - 4 = 315$

**D.** $x + 4 = 315$

**48.** (Georgia, Grade 4)

The table below shows the number of milligrams of sodium in each of three different sizes of a soft drink.

| Sodium Amounts in Soft Drink Sizes | |
|---|---|
| **Drink Size (fluid ounces)** | **Sodium Amount (milligrams)** |
| 8 | 36 |
| 12 | 54 |
| 16 | 72 |

Based on the pattern in the table, what is the total number of milligrams of sodium in a 24-fluid-ounce cup of the soft drink?

**A.** 90 mg
**B.** 108 mg
**C.** 126 mg
**D.** 144 mg

**8.2**

# Graphing Points, Lines, and Elementary Functions

In this section, we explore the graphs of functions from a geometric point of view. In the next section, we add algebra to the mix through the use of the Cartesian plane. Much of the current section is a review of your previous coursework, but is included to remind you of the material, to provide a platform for the remaining chapters, and to introduce explicitly a new problem-solving strategy: using Cartesian coordinates to do geometric problems. Although your first introduction to these topics might have been in middle school (or even high school), their beginnings are included in the curriculum and standardized tests of elementary school.

In particular, we investigate how the shape of a graph reveals the properties of the corresponding function, concentrating on the functions that are part of grades K–8. Of special interest are functions of the form $f(x) = mx + b$, where $m$ and $b$ are constants (**linear functions**). We will see that the graph of a function with this form is a line whose slope is $m$. We start with the introduction of the **Cartesian plane,** also called the **coordinate** or **Cartesian coordinate plane,** in honor of the philosopher and mathematician René Descartes. (See the Highlight from History box, p. 418.)

## The Cartesian Coordinate Plane

Consider the two perpendicular number lines illustrated in Figure 8.4. Any point in the plane can be uniquely located by giving its distance to the right or left of the vertical number line and its distance above or below the horizontal number line. In the figure, the point $P$ is 5 units to the right of the vertical number line and 3 units above the horizontal number line, and there is only one such point. Thus, $P$ is identified by the ordered number pair (5, 3), and we sometimes write $P(5, 3)$ as shown. Other times we will just write (5, 3).

**FIGURE 8.4**

The Cartesian coordinate plane

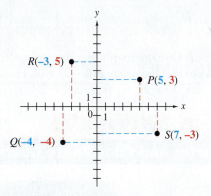

The two number lines are called **coordinate axes** or just **axes.** Typically, the horizontal number line is called the **x-axis** and the vertical number line is called the **y-axis.** The two numbers in the number pair $(a, b)$ that locate a point are called the **Cartesian coordinates** of the point. The first number in the pair is called the **x-coordinate** and gives the distance of the point to the right or left of the vertical axis—that is, in the direction of the $x$-axis. The second number in the ordered pair is called the **y-coordinate** and gives the distance of the point above or below the horizontal axis—that is, in the direction of the $y$-axis. The axes divide the plane into four regions, or **quadrants,** numbered I, II, III, and IV counterclockwise from the upper right-hand quadrant. A point

- lies in quadrant I if both its coordinates are positive,
- lies in quadrant II if the first coordinate is negative and the second coordinate is positive,
- lies in quadrant III if both coordinates are negative, and
- lies in quadrant IV if the first coordinate is positive and the second coordinate is negative.

The point (0, 0) where the axes intersect is called the **origin** of the coordinate system. All these notions are summarized in Figure 8.5. We can also write the Cartesian plane in set notation as $R^2 = \{(x, y) \mid x \in R \text{ and } y \in R\}$.

**FIGURE 8.5**
Salient features of the
Cartesian coordinate
system

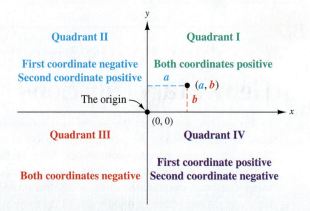

## EXAMPLE 8.6 Plotting Points

The following diagram shows the partial outline of a house:

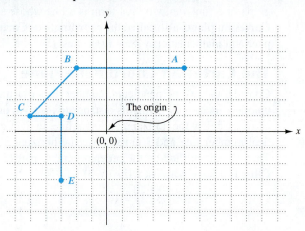

(a) Give the coordinates (i.e., the ordered pair) naming each of $A$, $B$, $C$, $D$, and $E$.
(b) Plot the points $F(8, -3)$, $G(8, 1)$, $H(10, 1)$, $I(7, 4)$, $J(6, 4)$, $K(6, 5)$, and $L(5, 5)$.
(c) Draw the segments $\overline{EF}$, $\overline{FG}$, $\overline{GH}$, $\overline{HI}$, $\overline{IJ}$, $\overline{JK}$, $\overline{KL}$, and $\overline{LA}$.

## Highlight from History

### René Descartes and Coordinate Geometry

It is often difficult to ascribe the development of any particular body of mathematics to its originator. The fact is that mathematics is the cumulative result of the efforts of numerous individuals working over hundreds or even thousands of years. The invention of coordinate geometry is customarily ascribed to René Descartes (1596–1650), one of the leading 17th-century mathematicians and philosophers, who did indeed make great strides in combining the ideas of geometry and algebra, as explained in a book titled *La géométrie*. However, Descartes never thought of an ordered pair $(a, b)$ as the coordinates of a point in the plane. Thus, the terminology "Cartesian product" and "Cartesian coordi-

nate system," ascribing these ideas to Descartes, is largely misplaced. The idea of coordinates goes back at least as far as the Greek Apollonius of Perga, in the third century B.C., and was utilized by Nicole Oresme (1323?–1382), the French Bishop of Lisieux, and by others. The idea was also known to the amateur, but inspired, Pierre de Fermat, a contemporary of Descartes, and was certainly popularized by the Dutch mathematician Frans van Schooten (1615–1700) in his *Geometria a Renato Des Cartes* (*Geometry by René Descartes*) in 1649. It is probably reasonable to say that our modern ideas of coordinate geometry were inspired by Descartes but organized and popularized by Schooten.

**Solution**

(a) $A$ is 5 units to the right of $(0, 0)$ (i.e., in the $x$-direction from the origin) and 4 units above $(0, 0)$ (i.e., in the $y$-direction from the origin). Thus, $A$ is the point $(5, 4)$. The $x$-coordinate of $A$ is 5 and the $y$-coordinate of $A$ is 4. Similarly, we determine that the coordinates of the other points are $B(-2, 4)$, $C(-5, 1)$, $D(-3, 1)$, and $E(-3, -3)$.

(b) The point $F(8, -3)$ is 8 units to the right of $(0, 0)$ and 3 units *below* $(0, 0)$. Similarly, the other points are located as shown:

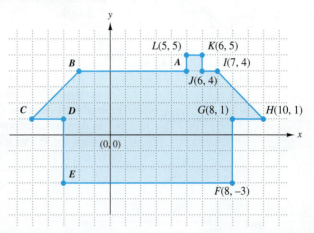

(c) After we have drawn the designated line segments, the completed figure forms the outline of a house.

## The Distance Formula

Consider the points $P(2, 5)$ and $Q(7, 8)$ shown in Figure 8.6.

**FIGURE 8.6**

The distance between points $P$ and $Q$ is found by using the Pythagorean theorem for the right triangle $PQR$

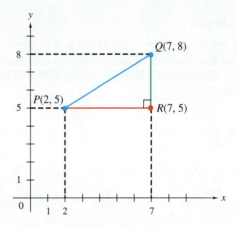

The vertical line through the upper point and the horizontal line through the lower point intersect at the point $R(7, 5)$. The two points $P(2, 5)$ and $R(7, 5)$ lie on the horizontal line of points whose $y$-coordinates are $y = 5$. The distance between $P$ and $R$, which is denoted by $PR$, is then just the absolute value of the difference in the $x$-coordinates of the points. That is, $PR = |7 - 2| = 5$. Similarly, the points $Q(7, 8)$ and $R(7, 5)$ both are on the vertical line for which $x = 7$, so the distance between $Q$ and $R$ is $QR = |8 - 5| = 3$.

To find the distance between $P$ and $Q$, we use the fact that $PQR$ is a right triangle with hypotenuse $PQ$ and legs $PR$ and $RQ$. The Pythagorean theorem then tells us that $PQ^2 = PR^2 + RQ^2$. That is,

$$PQ = \sqrt{PR^2 + RQ^2}$$
$$= \sqrt{(7 - 2)^2 + (8 - 5)^2}$$
$$= \sqrt{25 + 9} = \sqrt{34} \doteq 5.8.$$

This procedure can be followed in exactly the same way beginning with any two points $P(x_1, y_1)$ and $Q(x_2, y_2)$. This gives us the following theorem:

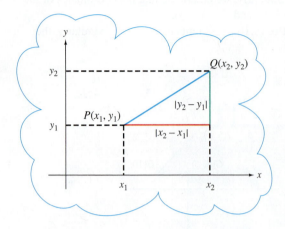

**THEOREM** *The Distance Formula*

Let $P$ and $Q$ be the points $(x_1, y_1)$ and $(x_2, y_2)$. Then the distance between $P$ and $Q$ is

$$PQ = \sqrt{(x_2 - x_1)^2 + (y_2 - y_1)^2}.$$

Conversely, if we assume the distance formula, then we can derive the Pythagorean theorem. (See Section 10.3.)

In the distance formula, it does not make any difference which point is chosen for $P$ and which is chosen for $Q$. For example, the distance between $(4, 7)$ and $(1, 3)$ is given by both

$$\sqrt{(4 - 1)^2 + (7 - 3)^2} = \sqrt{3^2 + 4^2}$$
$$= \sqrt{9 + 16} = \sqrt{25} = 5$$

and

$$\sqrt{(1 - 4)^2 + (3 - 7)^2} = \sqrt{(-3)^2 + (-4)^2}$$
$$= \sqrt{9 + 16} = \sqrt{25} = 5.$$

*$\overleftrightarrow{PQ}$ is a line, $\overline{PQ}$ is a segment, and PQ is the length of $\overline{PQ}$.*

The unique line determined by two distinct points $P$ and $Q$ in the plane is denoted by $\overleftrightarrow{PQ}$. The points on the line that are between $P$ and $Q$ form the **line segment** with endpoints $P$ and $Q$. The line segment is denoted by $\overline{PQ}$, and the length $PQ$ of the line segment is the distance between its endpoints. It is important to notice that the notation makes a distinction between the geometric object $\overline{PQ}$ (a set of points in the plane) and its length $PQ$ (a nonnegative real number).

## Slope

Consider the lines $l$, $m$, $n$, and $p$ in Figure 8.7. The properties that distinguish two lines from one another are their location on the coordinate system and their direction, or steepness. The direction, or steepness, of a line is the same as that of any segment of the line, and this fact leads to the notion of **slope.**

**FIGURE 8.7**
Lines in the plane

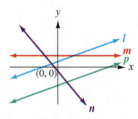

Carpenters use the ratio

$$s = \frac{h}{r},$$

**FIGURE 8.8**
Slope of a roof

where $h$ is the vertical distance a roof rises and $r$ is the horizontal distance over which the rise takes place, to compute the slope of a roof, as shown in Figure 8.8. This relationship is sometimes expressed by saying that the slope of a roof is "the rise over the run." Surveyors use the same idea to calculate the slope of a road. If a road rises 5 feet while moving forward horizontally 100 feet, the road has a slope of 0.05. In surveying, slopes are usually expressed as percents. Thus, a grade with a slope of 0.05 is said to be a 5% grade.

We also use the idea *rise over run* to determine the slope of a line segment. Consider the points $P(3, 5)$ and $Q(9, 7)$ shown in Figure 8.9. In moving from $P$ to $Q$, one moves up 2 units while moving to the right 6 units. The rise over the run gives a slope of $\frac{1}{3}$, indicated by the letter $m$. In this case,

$$m = \frac{7 - 5}{9 - 3} = \frac{2}{6} = \frac{1}{3}.$$

**FIGURE 8.9**
Slope of a segment

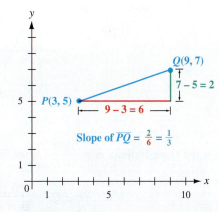

In general, the reasoning is similar and leads to this definition of slope:

**DEFINITION**  *Slope of a Line Segment or Line*
Let $P(x_1, y_1)$ and $Q(x_2, y_2)$, with $x_1 \neq x_2$, be two points. Then the **slope of the line segment $\overline{PQ}$**, or the line $\overleftrightarrow{PQ}$, is given by

$$m = \frac{y_2 - y_1}{x_2 - x_1}.$$

If $x_1 = x_2$ in the preceding definition, then $x_2 - x_1 = 0$ and $\overline{PQ}$ is vertical. Since division by 0 is undefined, we must say that *the slope of a vertical segment (or line) is undefined*. Another common usage is that a vertical segment has "no slope." It is important to realize that the last statement should *not* be confused with that of having zero slope (which means that the segment is horizontal, rather than vertical).

If $y_1 = y_2$ in the preceding definition, then $\overline{PQ}$ is horizontal and $m = 0$. Thus, saying that a line segment is horizontal is the same as saying that it has zero slope.

In computing the slope of a segment, it makes no difference which point is chosen as $P$ and which is chosen as $Q$. However, once the choice is made, one must stick with it and always subtract *in the same direction* in both numerator and denominator. For example, in computing the slope of the segment in Figure 8.9, we identified $P$ and $Q$ as $(3, 5)$ and $(9, 7)$, respectively. But this could have been reversed to obtain

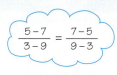

$$m = \frac{5 - 7}{3 - 9} = \frac{-2}{-6} = \frac{1}{3}$$

as before.

Finally, in Figure 8.9 the slope was positive and the segment sloped upward to the right. This is always the case for segments with positive slopes. If $y_1 = y_2$ in the definition of slope, then the slope is 0 and the segment $\overline{PQ}$ is necessarily horizontal. If the slope of a segment is negative, the segment slopes *downward to the right*. In the next example, $\overline{PS}$ has negative slope.

**EXAMPLE 8.7** **Finding the Slopes of Line Segments**

The points $P(-4, 3)$, $Q(5, 6)$, $R(5, -1)$, and $S(-1, -3)$ are the vertices of the four-sided polygon $PQRS$ shown in the given figure. Find the slope of each side of the polygon.

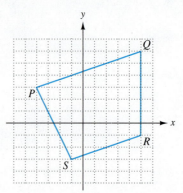

**Solution**   Using the slope formula $m = \dfrac{y_2 - y_1}{x_2 - x_1}$, we find that

$$m(\overline{PQ}) = \frac{6 - 3}{5 - (-4)} = \frac{3}{9} = \frac{1}{3},$$

$$m(\overline{RS}) = \frac{(-3) - (-1)}{(-1) - (5)} = \frac{-2}{-6} = \frac{1}{3}, \text{ and}$$

$$m(\overline{PS}) = \frac{(-3) - (3)}{(-1) - (-4)} = \frac{-6}{3} = -2.$$

The side $\overline{QR}$ is vertical, since both $R$ and $Q$ have the same $x$-coordinate, 5. Therefore, $\overline{QR}$ has undefined slope.

## Equations of Lines

With the tools of coordinate geometry, it is now possible to write equations whose graphs are lines. We begin by considering a particular example.

**EXAMPLE 8.8** **Determining the Equation of a Line through (2, 3) with Slope $\dfrac{4}{3}$**

Derive an equation of the line through point $P(2, 3)$ and having slope $\dfrac{4}{3}$.

**Solution**   **Understand the Problem**

There is one, and only one, line through the point $(2, 3)$ and having slope $\dfrac{4}{3}$. One can draw the line by plotting the point $P(2, 3)$ and then plotting the point $Q(5, 7)$ 3 units to the right and 4 units above $P$. The line segment through these points must have slope $\dfrac{4}{3}$, so the line through these points must be the desired line. Suppose $R(x, y)$ is *any* point on the line. We must find an equation involving the variables $x$ and $y$ that is satisfied by those, and only those, points that lie on the line.

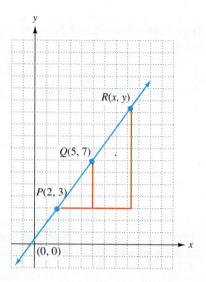

### Devise a Plan

Since the slope of a line can be determined by *any* two points on the line, $R(x, y)$ is on the line if, and only if,

$$\text{slope } \overline{PR} = \frac{4}{3}.$$

Perhaps we can use this fact to derive the desired equation.

### Carry Out the Plan

Since

$$\text{slope } \overline{PR} = \frac{y - 3}{x - 2},$$

it follows that $R$ is on the line in question if, and only if,

$$\frac{y - 3}{x - 2} = \frac{4}{3},$$

or, alternatively,

$$y - 3 = \frac{4}{3}(x - 2).$$

Hence, this must be the desired equation.

### Look Back

Since there is one, and only one, line through a given point and having a given slope, $R(x, y)$ is on the desired line if, and only if, slope $\overline{PR} = \frac{4}{3}$. By expressing slope $\overline{PR}$ in terms of $x$ and $y$, we obtained the desired equation.

The preceding example is typical, and the result can be stated as a theorem that can be proved by exactly the same argument as that of Figure 8.9.

**THEOREM**    *Point–Slope Form of the Equation of a Line*

The equation of the line through $P(x_1, y_1)$ and having slope $m$ is

$$y - y_1 = m(x - x_1).$$

This is called the **point–slope form** of the equation of a line.

As this theorem suggests, there are several forms of the equation of a line. Another particularly useful form is stated in the next theorem. First we note that if a line crosses the $y$-axis at the point $(0, b)$, $b$ is called the **$y$-intercept** of the line.

**THEOREM**    *Slope–Intercept Form of the Equation of a Line*

The **slope–intercept form** of the equation of a line is

$$y = mx + b,$$

where $m$ is the slope and $b$ is the $y$-intercept.

**PROOF**    Since $b$ is the $y$-intercept, the line passes through the point $(0, b)$. Also, the line has slope $m$. Therefore, by the point–slope form of the equation of a line, the desired equation is

$$y - b = m(x - 0),$$

or, equivalently,

$$y = mx + b,$$

as claimed.

In the theorem just proved, we started with a line in the plane, defined by its slope $m$ and its $y$-intercept, and deduced that its $y$-values are given by the function $y = f(x) = mx + b$. In the opposite direction, we see that the graph of any function of this form is a line of slope $m$ that intersects the $y$-axis at $y = b$. For example, the graph of the function $f(x) = -\dfrac{x}{2} + 3$ has slope $-\dfrac{1}{2}$ and intersects the $y$-axis at $y = 3$. It has now become clear why functions of the form $f(x) = mx + b$ are called linear functions: Their graphs are straight lines.

Linear functions have this important characterizing property: Since $y_2 - y_1 = m(x_2 - x_1)$ for a constant $m$, a change $y_2 - y_1$ in the output values of the function is proportional to a corresponding change $x_2 - x_1$ in the input values.

**EXAMPLE  8.9  Using the Slope-Intercept Form of the Equation of a Line**

Write the equations of the given lines with slope and $y$-intercept as indicated. Also, draw each line on a coordinate system.

    **(a)** $m = -3, b = 5$
    **(b)** $m = 0, b = -4$

**Solution**

    **(a)** Using the theorem about the slope–intercept form of the equation of the line, we obtain the equation $y = -3x + 5$. To draw the line, we plot the point $(0, 5)$ and the point $(1, 2)$, which is 3 units *below* and 1 unit to the right of $(0, 5)$. Then we draw the line through these two points:

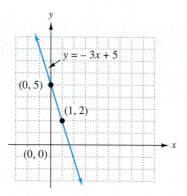

**(b)** This line goes through the point $(0, -4)$ and has slope 0. Therefore, using the slope–intercept form, we obtain the equation

$$y = 0x + (-4),$$

or just

$$y = -4.$$

This equation says that the line is horizontal and that a point is on this line if, and only if, the $y$-coordinate of the point is $-4$. The $x$-coordinates of these points are unrestricted, and the line is as shown here:

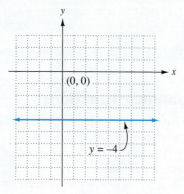

MHM    The preceding example suggests that *every* horizontal line has an equation of the form $y = b$; the slope is 0 and the $x$-values of points on the lines are left unrestricted. By analogy, *every* vertical line has an equation of the form $x = a$; there is *no* defined slope and the $y$-values of points on the lines are left unrestricted. There are many aspects of math that must be thought through carefully and that require a mathematical habit of mind.

## EXAMPLE 8.10 Determining the Equation of a Line Through Two Points

Determine the equation of the line through $P(-2, 3)$ and $Q(6, 7)$.

**Solution**    The slope of the desired line is the slope of $\overline{PQ}$:

$$\text{slope } \overline{PQ} = \frac{7 - 3}{6 - (-2)} = \frac{4}{8} = \frac{1}{2}.$$

We now employ the point–slope form of the equation of the line, using either $P$ or $Q$. With $P(-2, 3)$, we have

$$y - 3 = \frac{1}{2}(x - (-2)), \quad \text{or, equivalently,} \quad y - 3 = \frac{1}{2}(x + 2).$$

This equation can be rewritten in the form $y = \frac{1}{2}x + 1 + 3$, or $y = \frac{1}{2}x + 4$, which, from the slope–intercept form, tells us that the line intersects the $y$-axis at $y = 4$. Using the point $Q(6, 7)$, we have

$$y - 7 = \frac{1}{2}(x - 6).$$

This equation can also be rewritten in slope–intercept form, as $y = \frac{1}{2}x - 3 + 7 = \frac{1}{2}x + 4$, just as before. It makes no difference which point, $P$ or $Q$, is used.

The equation of the line through *any* two points $P(x_1, y_1)$ and $Q(x_2, y_2)$ can be found in the same way as shown in Example 8.10. Assuming that $\overline{PQ}$ is not a vertical segment, we see that it has the slope given by $m = \dfrac{y_2 - y_1}{x_2 - x_1}$. Then, using point $P(x_1, y_1)$, we find that the point–slope equation of the line is $y - y_1 = m(x - x_1)$, so we have the following theorem:

> **THEOREM** *Two–Point Form of the Equation of a Line*
> The equation of the line through $P(x_1, y_1)$ and $Q(x_2, y_2)$, where $x_1 \neq x_2$, is
>
> $$y - y_1 - m(x - x_1), \quad \text{where} \quad m = \frac{y_2 - y_1}{x_2 - x_1}.$$
>
> This is called the **two-point form** of the equation of a line with slope $m$.

## Nonlinear Functions

We have seen that it is unexpectedly easy to graph a linear function, since its graph is a straight line. For example, the linear function $f(x) = -2x + 7$ can be graphed by observing that the two points $P(0, 7)$ and $Q(1, 5)$ are on the graph of the function. The rest of the graph is obtained by drawing the line through $P$ and $Q$.

A function *not* of the form $f(x) = mx + b$ is called a **nonlinear function.** Some examples of nonlinear functions are $g(x) = x^2 - 3x + 5, h(x) = \dfrac{x}{x^2 + 2}$, and $k(x) = 2^x$. The graphs of these functions, each created with a graphing calculator, are shown in Figure 8.10.

**FIGURE 8.10**
The graphs of three nonlinear functions

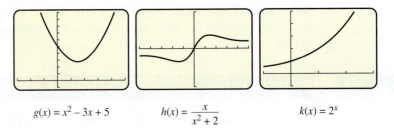

$$g(x) = x^2 - 3x + 5 \qquad h(x) = \frac{x}{x^2 + 2} \qquad k(x) = 2^x$$

As expected, none of the graphs is a straight line.

You have already studied some nonlinear functions in high school or college. However, since our emphasis is on the mathematics of K–8, we will concentrate exclusively on **quadratics** and **exponentials,** which are both a part of the middle school curriculum. Quadratic functions are polynomials of degree two, and exponentials are functions in which a fixed positive real number is raised to a variable power. Exponentials exhibit rapid growth (e.g., rabbit populations) or decay (radioactivity) and are topics that you have worked with already. In fact, $k(x)$ of Figure 8.10 is an exponential function. We will not go into detail about these two types of nonlinear functions, but will include a worked example of each. They will be in the problem set at the end of this section.

To graph nonlinear functions by hand, it is necessary to make a table of *many* points—not just two!—that are on the graph. Plotting these points will then suggest the shape of the graph that can be approximated by smoothly connecting the points with a curve. This procedure is used in Example 8.11 for a quadratic function.

**EXAMPLE 8.11  Making the Biggest Animal Pens (Quadratic)**

The third-grade class wants to make pens for its pet rabbits and guinea pigs. A parent has donated 24 feet of chain-link fencing material, which will be used to make two side-by-side rectangular pens along a wall, as shown in the figure that follows. What dimensions of $x$ and $w$ will give the pens their largest total area?

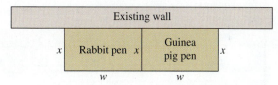

**Solution**    As seen in the figure, the pens form a rectangle $x$ feet wide and $2w$ feet long. Therefore, the total area of the pens is given by $A = 2wx$. The pens will require $3x + 2w$ feet of fencing. Since 24 feet of fencing is available, this gives the equation $3x + 2w = 24$, which can be rewritten as $2w = 24 - 3x$. Thus, the area $A$ of the pens is given by the following equation in $x$:

$$A = 2wx = (24 - 3x)x = 24x - 3x^2.$$

We can now see how the total area $A$ of the pens is given as the value of the function $f(x) = 24x - 3x^2$. Since the variable $x$ is a length of a side of the pen, we must have $x \geq 0$. Also, the three sides perpendicular to the wall, each of length $x$, must use less than the 24 feet of available fence, so $3x \leq 24$, or $x \leq 8$. Therefore, the domain of the function is $D = \{x \mid 0 \leq x \leq 8\}$.

The following table of values of the function indicates that the largest area occurs close to when $x = 4$:

| $x$ | 0 | 1 | 2 | 3 | 4 | 5 | 6 | 7 | 8 |
|---|---|---|---|---|---|---|---|---|---|
| **Area A** | 0 | 21 | 36 | 45 | 48 | 45 | 36 | 21 | 0 |

The total area of the two pens is 48 square feet and $2w = 24 - 3 \cdot 4 = 12$. Therefore, $w = 6$, so each pen is 4 feet by 6 feet.

The following graph of the function $y = 24x - 3x^2$ shows that the maximum area actually occurs when $x = 4$:

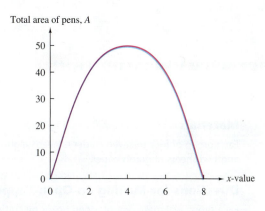

Looking back, we see that this function is a quadratic function whose maximum is the answer to our question.

The table of values of a function and its graph can be created easily with a graphing calculator.

## EXAMPLE 8.12  A Choice on a Checkerboard (Exponential)

My father put a dollar on the first square of a checkerboard. On the second square, Dad doubled to $2, on the third $4, the fourth $8, etc. Dad gives me a choice: Receive either $1 million or the money from the last square on the checkerboard. What should I do?

**Solution**   We are using the usual $8 \times 8$ checkerboard, and we have a pattern for the amount $A_n$ on the $n$th square. The last square is the 64th. The following table shows the amount of money on the first few squares:

| $n$ | 1 | 2 | 3 | 4 | 5 | 6 |
|-----|-----|-----|-----|-----|-----|-----|
| $A_n$ | $1 | $2 | $4 | $8 | $16 | $32 |

The pattern from the table gives $A_n = 2^{n-1}$, where $n \geq 1$. We answer the question posed in this example by deciding which is larger, $1 million or $A_{64}$. Using a calculator, we find that $A_{64} = 2^{63}$, which is close to $9.2234 \times 10^{18}$, or about 9 with 18 zeros after it! Certainly, as generous as Dad is, the checkerboard option is the best!

Motivated by this example, we define an exponential function, which is really about raising a fixed number, called the base to a power:

> **DEFINITION**  *Exponential Function*
> Let $a$ be a positive real number called the **base**. A function $f(k)$ is an **exponential function** if it is of the form $f(k) = Ba^k$, where $B$ is a real number.

Since $a^0 = 1$ if $a \neq 0$, an exponential function is a multiple of a power of its base and the value of the function "when time starts," which is $B$; that is, $B = f(0)$, or $B$ is the value when $k = 0$. The domain of an exponential function is usually the integers, the positive real numbers, or all real numbers. Note that if the base is less than one, the function gets smaller with time, not larger.

## Cooperative Investigation

## The Open-Topped Box Problem

### Materials

Each group of four to seven students needs eight sheets of centimeter-squared grid paper, scissors, tape, and two sheets of graph paper.

### Directions for Making an Open-Topped Box from a Rectangle

Each group will make open-topped boxes by cutting *x*–by–*x*-sized squares from the corners of a 16–by–21-centimeter rectangle cut from the centimeter-squared grid paper. Fold the rectangular sides of the box upward and tape the corners to create the box. The group should make a set of boxes corresponding to $x = 1, 2, 3, 4, 5, 6,$ and 7 centimeters.

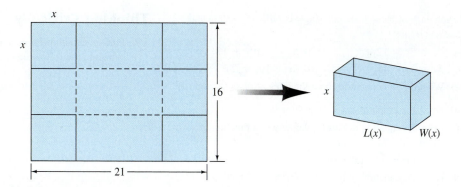

### Activities and Questions

1. Guess which box has the largest volume. Which box apparently has the smallest volume?
2. Fill in the following table, and in the last two rows compute the area $B(x)$ of the bottom of your box and the total area $S(x)$ of the sides of your box:

| x | 1 | 2 | 3 | 4 | 5 | 6 | 7 |
|---|---|---|---|---|---|---|---|
| L | | | | | | | |
| W | | | | | | | |
| V | | | | | | | |
| B | | | | | | | |
| S | | | | | | | |

3. Divide your group into two subgroups. One subgroup graphs the volume of the box as a function of $x$ for $1 \le x \le 7$ and, on the basis of its graph, decides which value of $x$ results in the open-topped box of largest volume. The other subgroup graphs the two functions $B(x)$ and $S(x)$ (on the same set of axes) and reports on the value of $x$ for which $B(x) = S(x)$. As a group, report a connection on the two reported values of $x$ from the subgroups.
4. If graphing calculators are available, express each of $V(x)$, $B(x)$, and $S(x)$ as functions of $x$. Then enter these functions on a graphing calculator to graph the functions $V(x)$, $B(x)$, and $S(x)$.

## Problem Set 8.2

Exercises numbered in red are answered in the back of the book.

## Understanding Concepts

1. Plot and label the following points on a Cartesian coordinate system drawn on a sheet of graph paper:

    (a) $P(5, 7)$     (b) $Q(5, -7)$     (c) $R(-5, 7)$

    (d) $S(-5, -7)$    (e) $T(0, 5)$      (f) $U(7, 1)$

    (g) $V(0, -5.2)$    (h) $W(-7, 1)$    (i) $X(0, 0)$

2. Plot these points and connect them in order with line segments: $(1, 1)$, $(1, 11)$, $(4, 13)$, $(5, 15)$, $(6, 13)$, $(7, 12)$, $(10, 11)$, $(9, 10)$, $(6, 9)$, $(4, 7)$, and $(1, 1)$.

3. (a) Plot the points $(5, 0)$, $(4, 3)$, $(3, 4)$, $(0, 5)$, $(-3, 4)$, $(-4, 3)$, $(-5, 0)$, $(-4, -3)$, $(-3, -4)$, $(0, -5)$, $(3, -4)$, and $(4, -3)$.

    (b) What do you observe about the points in part (a)?

4. Compute the distance between these pairs of points:

    (a) $(-2, 5)$ and $(4, 13)$      (b) $(3, -4)$ and $(8, 8)$

    (c) $(0, 7)$ and $(8, -8)$       (d) $(3, 5)$ and $(2, -4.3)$

5. Compute the slopes of the line segments determined by the given pairs of points. In each case, tell whether the segment is vertical, is horizontal, slopes upward to the right, or slopes downward to the right.

    (a) $P(1, 4)$, $Q(3, 8)$      (b) $R(-2, 5)$, $S(-2, -6)$

    (c) $U(-2, -3)$, $V(-4, -7)$    (d) $C(3, 5)$, $D(-3, 5)$

    (e) $E(1, -2)$, $F(-2, -5)$    (f) $G(-2, -2)$, $H(4, -5)$

6. Determine $b$ so that the slope of $\overline{PQ}$ is 2, where $P$ and $Q$ are the points $(b, 3)$ and $(4, 7)$, respectively.

7. Determine $d$ so that the slope of $\overline{CD}$ is undefined if $C$ and $D$ are the points $(d, 3)$ and $(-5, 5)$, respectively.

8. What is the value of $a$ if the point $(a, 3)$ is on the line $2x + 3y = 18$?

9. (a) Determine two different points on the line $3x + 5y + 15 = 0$.

    (b) Draw the graph of the line in part (a) in a coordinate system.

10. Graph each of these lines in a single coordinate system and label each line:

    (a) $3x + 5y = 12$    (b) $6x = -10y + 12$
    (c) $5y - 3x = 15$    (d) $6x + 10y = 24$

    (e) What do you conclude about the lines of parts (a) and (d)?

11. (a) Draw the graph of $3x + 2y + 6 = 0$.

    (b) Does the equation of part (a) define $y$ as a function of $x$? If so, identify the function.

    (c) Draw the graph of the equation $5x - 3y - 15 = 0$.

    (d) Does the equation of part (c) define $y$ as a function of $x$? If so, identify the function.

    (e) Does the equation of part (c) define $x$ as a function of $y$? If so, define the function.

12. (a) On a single set of axes, draw the graphs of $y = 2x + 3$, $y = 2(x - 3) + 3$ and $y = 2(x + 4) + 3$.

    (b) Compare the graphs of part (a).

13. Graph each of these functions:

    (a) $y = x^2$    (b) $y = (x - 2)^2$    (c) $y = (x + 3)^2$

    (d) Discuss the relationship between the graphs of parts (a), (b), and (c).

14. Graph each of these functions:

    **MHM** (a) $y = x^2 - 4x + 4$

    (b) $y = x^2 + 6x + 9$

    (c) $y = x^2 + 4x + 4$

    (d) Could you write each function in a different, more concise form? (*Hint:* Consider problem 13.)

15. (a) On a single set of axes, graph the equations $y = x^2$, $y = x^2 + 4$, and $y = x^2 - 3$.

    (b) Compare the graphs of part (a).

16. Use graphing techniques to find

    (a) the minimum value of the quantity $x^2 + 10x$ and the value of $x$ at which it occurs.

    (b) the maximum value of $8x - 2x^2$ and the value of $x$ at which it occurs.

    (c) the minimum value of $2x^2 - 4x + 10$ and the value of $x$ at which it occurs.

## Teaching Concepts

17. Kristi has a large detailed map showing the winding 6-mile-long trail up to the top of Pyramid Peak. She knows that she started up the trail at 8 A.M., hiked at a steady rate, and reached the summit at noon. Kristi would like to make a graph of her distance up the trail during the hike so that she can see on the map where she was at each hour and half hour along the trail. There are mileage markers on the map, but she is confused about how the graph will look because the trail was very crooked. Carefully describe how you would work with Kristi to help her accomplish her goals.

18. Children often think that all graphs are linear. Devise an activity in which measurements are made and entered into a table and graphs are made which clearly show that some data vary linearly and other, related data vary nonlinearly.

## Thinking Critically

19. Find an equation for each of the lines (a), (b), (c), and (d) shown in the following coordinate system:

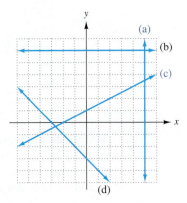

20. If $A(0, 0)$, $B(3, 5)$, $C(r, s)$, and $D(7, 0)$ are the vertices of a parallelogram, determine $r$ and $s$.

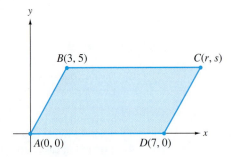

21. A square $ABCD$ in the coordinate plane has vertices at $A(2, 3)$, $B(6, 2)$, $C(r, s)$, and $D(u, v)$. Find all possible choices of $r$, $s$, $u$, and $v$.

22. Suppose the third graders in Example 8.11 want to make a third pen for baby chicks, still using the 24 feet of fence. That is, there are now to be three side-by-side pens along the wall, each measuring $x$ feet by $w$ feet. Draw a figure showing the pens along the wall, with appropriate labels, and plot a graph to show the dimensions that give the pens the largest possible area.

23. In the checkerboard example (Example 8.12), at what square would the value be more than $1 million for the first time?

24. If Dad were to put a quarter on the first square and then follow the process of Example 8.12, would you choose the checkerboard or the $1 million?

25. If Dad followed a checkerboard process as in Example 8.12, but changed the rule so that he squared the amount and put that in the next square, would you pick the checkerboard rather than the $1 million

    (a) if the first square had $2 on it?

    (b) if the first square had $1 on it?

    (c) if the first square had a quarter on it?

## ▦ Making Connections/Using a Calculator

26. (a) **ADA-Approved Ramps.** The Americans with Disabilities Act states, "The maximum slope of a ramp in new

construction shall be 1:12. The maximum rise for any run shall be 30 in." What is the minimum amount of run for a rise of 30 inches?

**(b) Highway Design.** Highway 195 into Lewiston, Idaho, undergoes a difference in elevation of 1800 feet in 7 miles. What is the average percent slope of the Lewiston grade?

**27. World Population.** The following table gives the world population (in billions) every 20 years since 1900 and an estimate of the population for 2020:

| Year | 1900 | 1920 | 1940 | 1960 | 1980 | 2000 | 2020 |
|------|------|------|------|------|------|------|------|
| Pop. | 1.6 | 1.9 | 2.3 | 3.0 | 3.7 | 6.0 | 7.6 |

**(a)** Make a graph of the world population as given in the table.

**(b)** Letting $x$ denote the number of decades (10-year periods) since 1900, plot the graph of the function $y = (1.45)1.14^x$ on the graph drawn in part (a). Does the formula mimic the population data well, in your opinion?

**(c)** If a graphing calculator is available, use it to plot the table and the function given in part (b) on the same screen and then compare the two graphs.

## Making Connections (with Linear Functions)

**28. Hooke's Law.** If a (small) weight $w$ is suspended from a spring, the length $L$ of the stretched spring is a linear function of $w$. Find $m$ and $b$ in the formula $L = mw + b$ if the unstretched spring has length $10''$ and a weight of 2 pounds stretches it to $14''$.

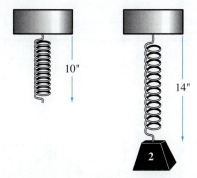

**29. Temperature Conversion.** The temperature at which water freezes is 32° Fahrenheit (0° Celsius), and the temperature at which water boils is 212° Fahrenheit (100° Celsius). Find the constants $m$ and $b$ in the formula $F = mC + b$ that expresses the Fahrenheit temperature F as a function of the Celsius temperature C.

**30. Straight-Line Depreciation.** Suppose a car originally valued at $18,500 is worth $10,400 after five years. Express the value $V$ of the car as a linear function $V = mt + b$ of the age $t$ of the car, where $t$ is measured in years. Use the formula to determine the value of the car after three years of service.

**31. The Lightning Distance Function.** The speed of sound is about 760 miles per hour. Assuming that a lightning flash takes no appreciable time to be seen and the corresponding

peal of thunder is heard after $t$ seconds, show that $d = \dfrac{t}{5}$ gives the approximate distance $d$ (in miles) to the lightning strike.

## From State Student Assessments

**32.** (Colorado, Grade 4)
This is a game board.

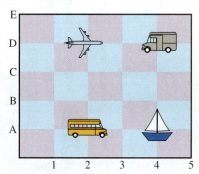

Which object is located at (2, D)?

**A.** The plane

**B.** The truck

**C.** The bus

**D.** The boat

**33.** (Colorado, Grade 4)
Look at the grid that follows. Point $X$ is identified by the ordered pair (7, 6).

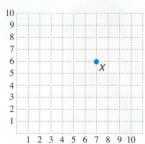

Which set of ordered pairs identifies three points that will form a straight line when connected?

**A.** (2, 1), (5, 5), and (8, 7)

**B.** (2, 7), (4, 5), and (7, 4)

**C.** (3, 2), (6, 5), and (9, 8)

**34.** (Texas, Grade 7)
Max drew a triangle on the coordinate plane shown below.

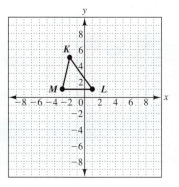

See "Examining School Book Pages" on page 433 for questions related to the pages shown below.

Algebra

# 11-10 Graphing Functions

**1. Vocabulary Review** Explain how an *expression* and an *equation* are different.

Evaluate each expression for $x = 3$.

**2.** $8 + x$   **3.** $18 \div x$

**4.** $4x$   **5.** $21 - x$

**GO for Help** Lesson 3-2

## What You'll Learn

To make a function table and to graph a function

🔊 **New Vocabulary** function

## Why Learn This?

Pretend you have a machine. You can put any number, or input, into the machine. The machine performs an operation on the number and provides a result, or output. A **function** is a rule that assigns exactly one output value to each input value.

Suppose you tell the machine to multiply by 4. A function table, such as the one at the right, shows the input and output values.

Input ➤

Function

➤ Output

| Input | Output |
|-------|--------|
| 3 | 12 |
| −7 | −28 |

### EXAMPLE   Completing a Function Table

**1** Complete the function table if the rule is Output = Input · (−2).

| Input | Output |
|-------|--------|
| −1 | 2 |
| 1 | −2 |
| 3 | −6 |

← Multiply −1 by −2. Place 2 in the Output column.
← Multiply 1 by −2. Place −2 in the Output column.
← Multiply 3 by −2. Place −6 in the Output column.

✓ **Quick Check**

**1.** Complete the function table for each rule.

**a.** Output = Input ÷ 4

| Input | Output |
|-------|--------|
| 16 | ▓ |
| −24 | ▓ |
| 36 | ▓ |

**b.** Output = Input − 8

| Input | Output |
|-------|--------|
| −6 | ▓ |
| −1 | ▓ |
| 4 | ▓ |

---

You can write the function rule in Example 1 using variables.

Output = Input · (−2)

$y = x \cdot (-2)$ or $y = -2x$

You can graph a function on the coordinate plane. Use the horizontal axis for input ($x$) and the vertical axis for output ($y$).

### EXAMPLE   Graphing a Function

**2** Make a table and graph some points of the function $y = x + 3$.

| Input (x) | Output (y) |
|-----------|------------|
| −2 | 1 |
| −1 | 2 |
| 0 | 3 |
| 1 | 4 |
| 2 | 5 |

✓ **Quick Check**

**2.** Make a table and graph some points of the function $y = x - 3$.

In Example 2, the points lie on a line. This type of function is a linear function. You can join the points with a line.

**For:** Graphing Functions Activity
**Use:** Interactive Textbook, 11-10

**Vocabulary Tip**
The graph of a *linear* function is a *line*.

### EXAMPLE   Application: Salaries

**3** Workers at a grocery store make $7 an hour. The function $m = 7h$ shows how the money $m$ they earn relates to the number of hours $h$ they work. Make a table and graph the function.

| Hours Worked | Money Earned (dollars) |
|--------------|------------------------|
| 1 | 7 |
| 2 | 14 |
| 3 | 21 |
| 4 | 28 |

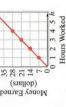

Money Earned (dollars)

Hours Worked

✓ **Quick Check**

**3.** A car is driven at a steady rate of 45 miles per hour. The function $d = 45t$ shows how time $t$ relates to distance $d$. Make a table and graph the function.

Which of the following best represents the coordinates of the vertices of $\triangle KLM$?

**A.** $(-2, 5), (1, 1), (-3, 1)$

**B.** $(-2, 5), (1, 1), (1, -3)$

**C.** $(5, -2), (1, 1), (1, -3)$

**35.** (Virginia, Grade 8)

Which of the following ordered pairs represents a point in the third quadrant of a coordinate plane?

**F.** $(-6, 4)$     **G.** $(-5, -7)$     **H.** $(3, -2)$     **J.** $(4, 2)$

**36.** (Texas, Grade 9)

The original function $y = \dfrac{2}{5}x + 4$ is graphed on the same grid as the new function $y = \dfrac{5}{2}x + 4$. Which of the following statements about these graphs is true?

**F.** The graph of the original function is steeper than the graph of the new function.

**G.** The graph of the original function is parallel to the graph of the new function.

**H.** The graphs intersect at $(4, 0)$.

**J.** The graphs intersect at $(0, 4)$.

**37.** These two School Book Pages carefully define what a function is and then give examples of functions. The first five are linear functions, as you can see, because each graph is a straight line and the equations "look like straight–line equations." This is a connection between algebra and geometry.

(a) In example 1, how much does the output $y$ increase or decrease if the input $x$ increases by one?

(b) In example 1, how much does the output $y$ increase or decrease if the input $x$ increases by a number $c$?

(c) Given the two questions posed in (a) and (b), how would you introduce your class of middle school students to the idea of slope, which is the key concept of linear functions?

## 8.3 Connections Between Algebra and Geometry

There is a tendency for students to think of mathematics as compartmentalized into algebra, geometry, probability, statistics, and other areas. In fact, in nearly all of the applications of mathematics, one uses many different subareas and, in fact, integrates them. This section is devoted to one approach to combining two or more areas to get results: the use of algebra and Cartesian coordinates in geometric problems. Our first example uses Cartesian coordinates to show that a triangle is isosceles.

**EXAMPLE 8.13  Using Cartesian Coordinates to Prove That a Triangle Is Isosceles**

Prove that the triangle with vertices $R(1, 4)$, $S(5, 0)$, and $T(7, 6)$ is isosceles (i.e., that two sides have the same length).

**Solution**  We compute the length of the three sides:

$$RS = \sqrt{(1 - 5)^2 + (4 - 0)^2} = \sqrt{16 + 16} = \sqrt{32};$$
$$RT = \sqrt{(1 - 7)^2 + (4 - 6)^2} = \sqrt{36 + 4} = \sqrt{40};$$
$$ST = \sqrt{(5 - 7)^2 + (0 - 6)^2} = \sqrt{4 + 36} = \sqrt{40}.$$

Since $RT = ST$, it follows that $\triangle RST$ is isosceles.

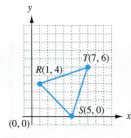

**PROBLEM-SOLVING STRATEGY**   **Use Cartesian Coordinates to Do Geometric Problems**

In solving geometric problems, it is sometimes easier and faster to place the figures in a Cartesian plane and use algebra.

We will use the preceding problem-solving strategy to show that the slope of two lines determines whether or not the lines are parallel or perpendicular. This habit is a way to think mathematically: understanding a geometric condition ("bring parallel") to be the same as an algebraic condition ("slopes are the same").

## Parallel and Perpendicular Lines

As noted earlier, the slope of a line is a measure of its steepness. Thus, it seems obvious that two different lines that are equally steep never meet. This observation gives the connection between the slopes of two lines and the notion of parallel, which we now define.

> **DEFINITION**    *Parallel Lines*
>
> The lines $l$ and $m$ in the Cartesian plane are **parallel** if they have no points in common or if they are equal. We write $l \parallel m$ if $l$ and $m$ are parallel lines and $l \nparallel m$ if $l$ and $m$ are not parallel.

There are only three alternatives for the intersection of two lines $l$ and $m$:

- $l = m$, so $l \cap m =$ a line (all points in common), or
- $l$ and $m$ are distinct lines and $l \parallel m$, so $l \cap m = \varnothing$ (no points in common), or
- $l \nparallel m$ so that $l \cap m$ is a single point (one point in common).

Given the importance of definitions, some care must be taken when one looks at the definition of parallel lines as it appears in different texts. The case in which $l = m$ is sometimes not included in the term "parallel." In addition, note that the lines which we discuss are always in the same plane. We have chosen the preceding definition (which is a standard one) so that the next theorem is easy to state. Although its proof is optional, we suggest that future middle school teachers work through it, as it is a key conceptual link and gives a good example of the relationship between algebra and geometry.

> **THEOREM**    *Condition for Parallelism*
>
> Two lines in the plane are parallel if, and only if, they both have the same slope or both are vertical lines.

---

**PROOF (OPTIONAL)**

Two vertical lines are certainly parallel. Furthermore, if $p \parallel q$ and $p$ is vertical, then $q$ must also be vertical.

Let's now explore the case where $p$ and $q$ are lines and neither is vertical. If $p = q$, then their slopes are, of course, the same. We now assume that the slope of $p$ and the slope of $q$ are equal and $p \neq q$. We let $m_1$ be the slope of $p$ (and $b_1$ its $y$-intercept) and $m_2$ the slope of $q$ (with $b_2$ its $y$-intercept). The condition that $p \parallel q$ means that there is no point $P \in p \cap q$. Assume that such a point exists and let $(c, d)$ be the coordinates of $P$. The next steps will show what this assumption means about the relationship between $m_1$ and $m_2$.

The critical condition now is that $(c, d) = P \in p \cap q$ if, and only if, $(c, d)$ satisfies the slope–intercept form of a line for *both* the line $p$ and the line $q$. The last phrase means that the real numbers $c$ and $d$ must satisfy the two equations

$$d = m_1 c + b_1 \quad \text{and} \quad d = m_2 c + b_2.$$

Subtracting the second equation from the first yields

$$0 = m_1 c - m_2 c + b_1 - b_2 \quad \text{or} \quad (m_1 - m_2)c = b_2 - b_1.$$

If $m_1 \neq m_2$, then there is a solution for $c$, which is $c = \dfrac{(b_2 - b_1)}{m_1 - m_2}$, and also one for $d$. Thus, $p$ and $q$

intersect at $P = (c, d)$ and the lines are not parallel. If $m_1 = m_2$, then the only way the two equations can both be solved is if $b_1 = b_2$. The lines $y = m_1 x + b_1$ and $y = m_2 x + b_2$ are then the same, since $m_1 = m_2$ and $b_1 = b_2$. Thus, the only time the nonvertical lines $p$ and $q$ can both have the same slope and $y$-intercept is if $p = q$, and the result is proven.

We will now make use of algebra and the condition for parallelism just completed to prove a geometric result. More precisely, we will show that the line through the midpoints of two sides of a triangle is parallel to the third side. Recall that the **midpoint** of the line segment $\overline{AB}$ is the point in $\overline{AB}$ which is the same distance from A as it is from B.

**EXAMPLE 8.14  Line Joining the Midpoints of Two Sides of a Triangle**

Using algebra, show that the line joining the midpoint of any two sides of a triangle is parallel to the third side.

**Solution**

### Understand the Problem

Let $\triangle ABC$ be given, and let $M$ be the midpoint of $\overline{AB}$ and $N$ be the midpoint of $\overline{AC}$. We must show that the lines $\overleftrightarrow{MN}$ and $\overleftrightarrow{BC}$ are parallel. The first step is to draw Figure 8.11(a), which shows the problem as originally given.

**FIGURE 8.11**
Lines joining the midpoints of two sides of a triangle

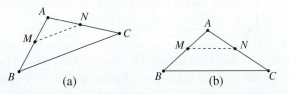

(a)          (b)

### Devise a Plan

Since rotating or moving the entire picture up, down, or sideways (translating) would not affect the relationship between $\overleftrightarrow{MN}$ and $\overleftrightarrow{BC}$, we may place $\triangle ABC$ as in Figure 8.11(b). If we put an $(x, y)$-coordinate system on the figure, we will be able to use algebra to show that $\overleftrightarrow{MN}$ is parallel to $\overleftrightarrow{BC}$. Since $\overleftrightarrow{BC}$ is not vertical, we must show that the lines have the same slope.

### Carry Out the Plan

We have placed the origin of the $(x, y)$-coordinate system at the point $B$ and located $\overleftrightarrow{BC}$ on the $x$-axis, as in Figure 8.12. Certainly, $\overleftrightarrow{BC}$ has slope zero (because the line is horizontal), so we must compute the slope of $\overleftrightarrow{MN}$ and show that it is 0 also. Since nonvertical lines are parallel exactly when they have the same slope, we will be done.

**FIGURE 8.12**
Lines joining the midpoints of two sides of a triangle placed in a Cartesian coordinate system

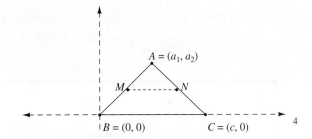

Let's name the points so that we can first compute the two midpoints. Since $B$ is the origin and $C$ is on the $x$-axis, we may write $B = (0, 0)$, $C = (c, 0)$, and $A = (a_1, a_2)$, where $c$, $a_1$, and $a_2$ are real numbers. (For simplicity, we have drawn a picture with $a_1$, $a_2$, and $c$ positive.)

What are the coordinates of $M$ in Figure 8.12? The $x$-coordinate of the midpoint must be the average of the $x$-coordinates of $A$ and $B$, and the $y$-coordinate the average of the two $y$-coordinates. Thus,

$$M = \left(\frac{a_1}{2}, \frac{a_2}{2}\right) \quad \text{and} \quad N = \left(\frac{c + a_1}{2}, \frac{a_2}{2}\right).$$

The slope of the line $\overleftrightarrow{MN}$ is certainly 0, since the points $M$ and $N$ have the same $y$-coordinate (so that the rise is 0.) Thus, both $\overleftrightarrow{MN}$ and $\overleftrightarrow{BC}$ have the same slope (0) and are parallel.

### Look Back

A little thought led us to use a coordinate system and apply algebra. We noticed that rotation and translation allowed us to move the triangle from the general one of Figure 8.11(a) to one in a simpler position with a coordinate system available (Figure 8.12). This process did not change the problem, but allowed for a much easier computation of slopes. We found that the two slopes were the same (both are 0) so that the lines $\overleftrightarrow{MN}$ and $\overleftrightarrow{BC}$ are parallel.

The technique of rigidly moving the geometric shapes is quite useful. Since rigid motions don't change geometric properties, we have come up with a new strategy. Ideas associated with rigid motions of the plane will be discussed fully in Chapter 11.

---

> **PROBLEM-SOLVING STRATEGY** Use Rigid Motions
>
> To solve a geometric problem, it may be helpful to use a rigid motion (translation, rotation, or a combination of the two) to move the geometric figure to another position in which the solution becomes easier to see.

---

There is a technical point about Example 8.14 that needs to be made. In both parts of Figure 8.11, we used the same names for the vertices of the triangle. To be rigorous, we should have used, in the second triangle, different names, such as $A'$, $B'$, and $C'$, to reflect the fact that the triangle moved (and so has different coordinates for its vertices). In the interests of clarity and because there is little ambiguity, we kept the same names for the vertices.

We now move from parallel lines to perpendicular ones. In earlier coursework, you have been taught that, provided that neither line is vertical, "Two lines are perpendicular if and only if their slopes are negative reciprocals." We shall now give a proof of that statement.

---

**DEFINITION** *Perpendicular Lines*

The lines $l_1$ and $l_2$ are **perpendicular** if they intersect at a 90° angle.

---

**THEOREM** *Condition for Perpendicularity*

Assume that $l_1$ and $l_2$ are lines that are parallel to neither the $x$-axis nor the $y$-axis. If $m_1$ is the slope of $l_1$ and $m_2$ is the slope of $l_2$ and the two lines intersect, then $l_1$ is perpendicular to $l_2$ if and only if $m_2 = -\dfrac{1}{m_1}$. (Said another way, $m_1$ and $m_2$ are negative reciprocals.)

---

**PROOF (OPTIONAL)**

Assume that $l_1$ and $l_2$ meet at a 90° angle, as shown in the accompanying figure. Then the triangle along $l_1$ with a horizontal leg of length $a$ and a vertical leg of length $b$ shows that the line $l_1$ has slope $m_1 = \dfrac{b}{a}$. Line $l_2$ is perpendicular to $l_1$ and can be viewed as the line obtained by rotating line $l_1$ about the intersection point $P$ through 90° and so rotates the triangles as pictured. What, then, is the slope of $l_2$? From the picture, the change in the $y$-coordinates is $-a$ (since the values along $l_2$ are getting smaller as $x$ gets larger) and the change in the $x$-coordinates is $b$. Thus, the slope of $l_2$ is $m_2 = \dfrac{-a}{b}$.

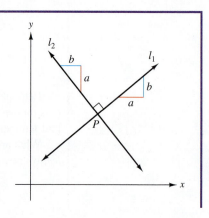

Since the slope of $l_1$ is $m_1 = \dfrac{b}{a}$, it follows that

$$m_2 = -\frac{a}{b} = -\frac{1}{\dfrac{b}{a}} = -\frac{1}{m_1},$$

and the statement before the previous definition is proved. (It can be shown that if $m_2 = -\dfrac{1}{m_1}$, then $l_1$ and $l_2$ are perpendicular, but we omit the proof here.)

We use the condition for perpendicularity, which gives a quite surprising geometric result. First, we need two definitions.

> **DEFINITION**  *Altitude of a Triangle*
> An **altitude of a triangle** is a line through a vertex of a triangle that is perpendicular to the line containing the opposite side of the triangle.

> **DEFINITION**  *Concurrent Set of Lines*
> A collection of lines is **concurrent** if the same point is on each of the lines.

## EXAMPLE 8.15  Showing That the Altitudes of a Triangle Are Concurrent

**Solution**  We will use the problem-solving strategies "Use Cartesian Coordinates to do Geometric Problems" and "Use a Rigid Motion." Our plan is to use the point–slope form of a line to find the equations for each of the three altitudes. We then show that the three have a point in common because there is a point whose coordinates lie on each of the altitudes.

Using a rigid motion, we first orient the triangle on a coordinate system with one vertex at the origin, one vertex on the positive $x$-axis, and one vertex in the upper half plane. Let $A(0, 0)$, $B(b, d)$, and $C(c, 0)$, with $c \neq b$, be these vertices. (The case in which $c = b$ is the one in which the triangle is a right triangle and can be handled separately.)

We will also use the notion of slope and the point–slope form of the equation of a line. Suppose that $\overleftrightarrow{AE}$, $\overleftrightarrow{BE}$, and $\overleftrightarrow{CD}$ are the altitudes of the triangle.

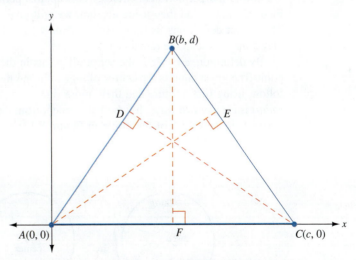

Then, because the slope of the perpendicular is the negative reciprocal of the slope of the line segment,

$$\text{slope of } \overline{BC} = \frac{d}{b - c}, \text{ so the slope of } \overline{AE} = \frac{b - c}{d}.$$

Therefore, the equation of $\overleftrightarrow{AE}$ is

$$y - 0 = -\frac{b - c}{d}(x - 0),$$

or simply,

$$dy = cx - bx.$$

Similarly,

$$\text{slope } \overline{AB} = \frac{d}{b}, \text{ so slope } \overline{DC} = -\frac{b}{d}.$$

Therefore, the equation of $\overleftrightarrow{DC}$ is

$$y - 0 = -\frac{b}{d}(x - c),$$

or, what is the same,

$$dy = -bx + bc.$$

To find where $\overleftrightarrow{AE}$ and $\overleftrightarrow{DC}$ intersect, we determine the simultaneous solution of the equations of these two lines. Subtracting the equation for $\overleftrightarrow{DC}$ from the equation for $\overleftrightarrow{AE}$, we obtain

$$0 = (cx - bx) - (-bx + bc) = cx - bc.$$

Therefore, the $x$-coordinate of the point of intersection is

$$x = \frac{bc}{c} = b.$$

Hence, without even determining the $y$-coordinate of the point of intersection of $\overleftrightarrow{AE}$ and $\overleftrightarrow{DE}$, it follows that the point of intersection lies on $\overleftrightarrow{BF}$, since $\overleftrightarrow{BF}$ is vertical, passes through the point $B(b, d)$, and so has equation $x = b$. Thus, the three altitudes are concurrent, as was to be shown. (The point that the altitudes have in common is called the **orthocenter** of the triangle.)

## Circles

We now turn to the notion of circles, a concept that permeates the mathematics of elementary school. First informally and then using algebra, we will give the definition of *circle, diameter,* and *radius.* These three definitions, as well as those of the *area* and *circumference* of a circle (Chapter 10.2), will play a major role in the remainder of the text.

By definition, a **circle** is the set of all points in the plane that are a fixed distance from a given point. The given point is the **center** of the circle and the fixed distance is the **radius.** The definitions follow, using first a figure and then, more rigorously, set notation and algebra. Note that the word *radius* is used in two ways: It is both a segment from the center to a point on the circle (segment $\overline{QC}$, where $C$ is the center of the circle in Figure 8.13) and the length of such a segment. Likewise, a *diameter* is both a segment and a length. The interior of a circle is a **disc.**

**FIGURE 8.13**

The parts of a circle

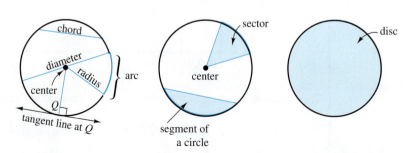

> **DEFINITION** *Circle, Center, Radius, Diameter, and Tangent Line to a Circle*
> A **circle** of **radius** $r > 0$ and **center** $C = (a, b)$ is the set
>
> $$\mathcal{C} = \{(x, y) \in R^2 \text{ such that } (x - a)^2 + (y - b)^2 = r^2\}.$$
>
> The **diameter** of $\mathcal{C}$ is twice its radius.
>      The **tangent line to the circle** $\mathcal{C}$ at the point $Q$ on $\mathcal{C}$ is the line that goes through the point $Q$ and is perpendicular to the radius.

The chord, tangent line, arc, and sector are pictured in Figure 8.13 to remind the reader of these terms, although they play little role in K–8 mathematics and will not be used much in this text (or your teaching.) Still, the tangent line is useful if you want to know how far you can see from a mountaintop as we will see Example 10.17.

We will now find a formula for the equation of a tangent line to a circle, making use of the two theorems just proven (as well as a mixture of algebra and geometry), and then, for the sake of geometric intuition, will give an example of a construction with parallel chords.

## EXAMPLE 8.16 Equation of a Tangent Line to a Circle at a Point

If $\mathcal{C}$ is a circle with center $C = (a, b)$, and if $Q = (c, d) \in \mathcal{C}$, then the equation of the tangent line to $\mathcal{C}$ at $Q$ is

$$y - d = \left(\frac{a - c}{d - b}\right)(x - c).$$

**Solution**   In order to find out the equation of the tangent line, we must know its slope and a point on it. However, from the definition of *tangent line* and the condition of perpendicularity that we just proved, the slope of the tangent line is the negative reciprocal of that of the radius $\overline{QC}$.

We first find the slope of the tangent line. Because $C = (a, b)$ and $Q = (c, d)$ are on the radius the slope of $\overline{QC}$ is $\dfrac{d - b}{c - a}$. Therefore,

$$\text{Slope of tangent line} = \frac{-1}{\text{slope of } \overline{QC}} = \frac{a - c}{d - b}.$$

We have the slope all ready for insertion into the point–slope form of a line (p. 424). We'll now use the only point we know, $Q = (c, d)$, that is on the tangent line to $\mathcal{C}$ at $Q$. The equation is then $y - d = \left(\dfrac{a - c}{d - b}\right)(x - c)$, as we were to show.

The last example of this chapter is one that is optional but gives you the advantage of experimenting with connections between different parts of a figure.

## EXAMPLE 8.17 Exploring Perpendicular Chords in a Pair of Circles

Use a compass (or trace around the bottom of a cup) to draw two congruent intersecting circles. Let $A$, $B$, $C$, and $D$ denote the respective centers and intersection points of the circles. Draw a line $m$ through $C$, and denote the intersection points of $m$ with the two circles as $R$ and $O$. Similarly, draw the line $n$ through $D$ that is perpendicular to $m$. Let $H$ and $M$ denote the points at which line $n$ intersects the circles.

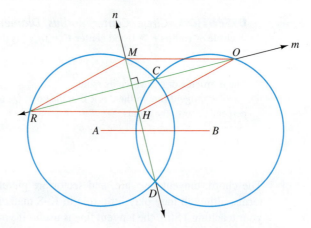

(a) Use measurement tools to describe the shape of the quadrilateral *RHOM*. What connection to the distance *AB* between the circles' centers do you discover?

(b) Use a protractor to measure ∠*RAM*, ∠*MAC*, and ∠*CBO*. What relationship do you dicover?

**Solution**

(a) *RHOM* is a rhombus whose sides have the same length as the distance *AB* between the centers of the circles.

(b) Your measurements should show that $m(\angle RAM) = m(\angle MAC) + m(\angle CBO)$.

## Problem Set 8.3

Exercises numbered in red are answered in the back of the text.

### Understanding Concepts

1. (a) Determine two points on the line $4x + 2y = 6$.

   (b) Use the points determined in part (a) to compute the slope of the line.

   (c) Solve the equation in part (a) for $y$ in terms of $x$ and thereby again determine the slope of the line, as well as the $y$-intercept. (*Hint*: Solving for $y$ in terms of $x$ gives the slope–intercept form of the equation of a line.)

   **MHM** (d) Show your answer to parts (a) and (b) to your neighbor. Although there may be a difference in the points that you two chose, what does the slope turn out to be?

2. In each case determine $k$ so that the line is parallel to the line $3x - 5y + 45 = 0$.

   (a) $7x + ky = 21$      (b) $kx - 8y - 24 = 0$

   (c) $y = kx + 5$         (d) $x = ky + 5$

3. Draw the graphs of each of these linear functions.

   (a) $y = 2x - 3$    (b) $y = 0.5x + 2$    (c) $y = -3x$

4. (a) On the same coordinate system, draw the graphs of these three linear functions: $y = 4x, y = 4x + 5$, and $y = 4x - 3$.

   (b) Briefly discuss the graphs in part (a) and find their slope.

5. (a) Prove that $R(1, 2), S(7, 10)$, and $T(5, -1)$ are the vertices of a right triangle. (*Hint*: Show that the square of one side is the sum of the squares of the other two sides.)

   (b) Draw the triangle *RST* of part (a) on graph paper.

6. In each part below, you are given an equation of a line and a point. Find the equation of the line through the given point that is perpendicular to the given line. (The slope of the perpendicular line is the negative reciprocal of the slope of the given line if the given line is neither vertical nor horizontal, as described in problem 26.)

   (a) $y = 2x, P(0, 0)$

   (b) $y = 3x + 5, Q(1, 2)$

   (c) $y = -\dfrac{2}{3}x + 7, R(4, -1)$

   (d) $2y + 6x - 5 = 0, S(0, 3)$

7. A square in the coordinate plane is shown below, with its vertices at $A(1, 0), B(1, 1), C(0, 1)$, and $D(0, 0)$. Since the squared distance between points $P(x, y)$ and $Q(a, b)$ is given by the formula $PQ^2 = (x - a)^2 + (y - b)^2$, we see that $PA^2 = (x - 1)^2 + (y - 0)^2 = x^2 - 2x + 1 + y^2$ is the squared distance between $P$ and vertex $A$ of the square.

   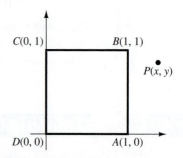

   (a) Find $PB^2, PC^2$, and $PD^2$.

   (b) Describe the set of points $P$ in the coordinate plane for which $PA^2 + PC^2 = PB^2 + PD^2$. (Yes, the answer is a surprise!)

8. Is the triangle of Example 8.13 equilateral?

9. What is the altitude through the point $S$ in the triangle of Example 8.13?

10. Let $A = (1, -2)$ and $B = (2, 4)$. What is the equation of the line through the midpoint of $\overline{AB}$ that is perpendicular to $\overline{AB}$? This line is called the **perpendicular bisector** of $\overline{AB}$.

11. (a) What is the perpendicular bisector of the segment between $C = (5, -1)$ and $D = (5, 7)$?

    (b) Did you do part (a) algebraically or geometrically?

12. (a) What is the equation of the line that is tangent to the circle of radius 3 at $(0, -3)$ and whose center is at the origin?

    (b) What is the equation of the line that is tangent to the circle of radius 3 at $(0, 3)$ and whose center is at the origin?

    (c) Is the line in part (b) the same line as that in part (a)?

13. (a) Show that the point $Q = (2, -1 + 2\sqrt{2})$ is on the circle of diameter 6 and whose center is $(1, -1)$.

    (b) What is the equation of the line that is tangent to the circle of diameter 6 at $(2, -1 + 2\sqrt{2})$ and whose center is $(1, -1)$?

14. Draw three lines $l$, $m$, and $n$ in the plane in such a way that $l$ is perpendicular to $m$ and $m$ is perpendicular to $n$. For the set of lines that you picked, what is the relationship between $l$ and $n$? Try the experiment again and see whether your answer is the same.

15. Suppose that $l$, $m$, and $n$ are lines in the plane. Show that if $l$ is perpendicular to $m$ and $m$ is perpendicular to $n$, then $l$ is parallel to $n$. (*Hint*: First draw a picture, and then use the theorem about the condition for parallelism and perpendicularity in this section.)

16. Which of the following statements are true and which are false? If the statement is true, draw a picture.

    (a) Two circles can intersect at exactly one point.

    (b) Two circles can intersect at exactly two points.

    (c) Two circles can intersect in no points.

    (d) Two circles can intersect in exactly three points.

    (e) Two circles can intersect in four or more points.

17. Draw a circle of radius 2 whose center is at the point $(2, -1)$. What does a circle of radius 3 look like when drawn on the same piece of graph paper?

18. The equation of the tangent line to the circle $\mathcal{C}$ at the point $Q$ is given in Example 8.16. Show that the point $Q$ is on this line.

19. Constructing definitions from your intuition and then making sure the definition you've given reflects your intuition is an excellent example of a mathematical habit of the mind. Let's try that approach now. Without looking at another text, give a formal definition, based on your intuition, of the following parts of a circle:

    (a) Chord

    (b) Diameter

    (c) Tangent line

    (d) Go to the library at your institution and compare your definitions to those of a high school, middle school, or elementary school text. What are the differences and similarities?

## Using Algebra in Geometry

20. Any triangle can be placed on a coordinate system so that one point is at the origin, one point is on the positive $x$-axis, and one point is in the first quadrant. Thus, without loss of generality, we can take $A = A(0, 0)$, $B = B(2a, 2b)$, and $C = C(2c, 0)$. Show that the three medians of the triangle meet at the same point whose coordinates are

$$G\left(\frac{2a + 2c}{3}, \frac{2b}{3}\right).$$

What is surprising is that all three lines go through the same point, $G$, called the **centroid** of the triangle.

21. Consider the triangle $SPQ$ inscribed in a semicircle as shown. Use coordinate methods to prove Thales's theorem; that is, show that $\overline{PQ}$ is perpendicular to $\overline{PS}$. (*Hint*: Recall that $x^2 + y^2 = r^2$ and $(x + r)(x - r) = x^2 - r^2$.)

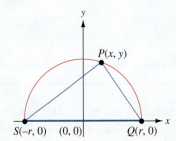

22. In "taxicab geometry," the points are the corners of a square grid of "city blocks" in a plane. In the figure shown, the shortest trip from $A$ to $B$ must cover five blocks, and so the **taxi distance** from $A$ to $B$ is 5. A "taxi segment" is the set of points on a path of shortest taxi distance from one point to another, and so $\{A, W, X, Y, Z, B\}$ is a taxi segment from $A$ to $B$.

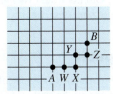

    (a) How many taxi segments join $A$ and $B$?

    (b) Find all points that are at a taxi distance of 5 from $A$. Does your "taxi circle" look like a circle drawn with a compass?

    (c) Use pencils of different colors to draw the concentric taxi circles of taxi radius 1, 2, 3, 4, 5, and 6. Describe the pattern you see.

## Thinking Critically

23. Regions can be formed in a circle by drawing chords, no three of which are concurrent. If $C$ chords are drawn and they intersect in

*l* points, determine a formula for the number of pieces *P* (that is, the regions) that are formed inside the circle.

## Thinking Cooperatively

**24.** Follow the directions given in the previous section's Cooperative Investigation activity, The Open-Topped Box Problem (p. 428), but this time start with a 12-centimeter by 12-centimeter square cut from centimeter-squared grid paper. Work in small groups to cut small *x*-by-*x* squares from the corners of the starting square to create an open-topped box *x* centimeters high.

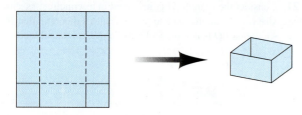

**(a)** Within your group, make boxes corresponding to *x* = 1, 2, 3, 4, and 5 centimeters. Guess which box has the largest volume.

**(b)** Derive a formula for the volume, *V*(*x*), of the box as a function of *x* and make a graph of the volume function. On the basis of your graph, what value of x will give the box of largest volume?

**(c)** Derive a formula for the area, *B*(*x*), of the bottom of the box and the total area, *S*(*x*), of the sides of the box. Plot the graphs of *B*(*x*) and *S*(*x*) on the same axes, over the domain 0 ≤ *x* ≤ 6. At what value of *x* is *B*(*x*) = *S*(*x*)?

**(d)** Do you see a connection between your answers to parts (b) and (c)? Discuss within your group and form a careful description of your observations.

## Using a Computer

**25.** Draw a circle. From a point *P* outside of your circle, draw three lines that each intersect the circle at two points. Let *A*, *B*, *C*, *A'*, *B'*, and *C'* be the intersection points, as shown. The segments $\overline{AB'}$ and $\overline{A'B}$ intersect to determine a point *Q*. Similarly, let $\overline{BC'}$ and $\overline{B'C}$, and $\overline{AC'}$ and $\overline{A'C}$, determine the respective points *R* and *S*.

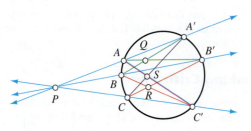

**(a)** What conjecture can you make concerning *Q*, *R*, and *S*? Drag *P* and the lines to investigate your conjecture.

**(b)** Discuss how the line $\overleftrightarrow{QR}$ can be used to construct the rays from *P* that are tangent to the circle.

## From State Student Assessments

**26.** (Michigan, Grade 6) For triangle GXU, what is the value of the following expression?

$$m\angle G + m\angle X + m\angle U$$

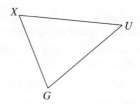

**A.** 360°
**B.** 180°
**C.** 100°
**D.** 908

**27.** (Michigan, Grade 6) What is the measure of ∠m in the right isosceles triangle shown below?

**A.** 35°
**B.** 45°
**C.** 90°
**D.** 180°

**28.** (Texas, Grade 6) Which of the following statements about angle measures is true?

**A.** An angle that measures 90° is a straight angle.
**B.** An angle that measures 25° is an obtuse angle.
**C.** An angle that measures 180° is a right angle.
**D.** An angle that measures 88° is an acute angle.

**29.** (Washington State, Grade 4) Raul is going to a friend's house. Raul remembers that his friend's house is on a street parallel to Southport. On which street does Raul's friend live?

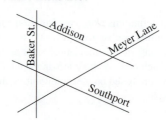

**A.** Addison    **B.** Baker Street
**C.** Meyer Lane

## The Chapter in Relation to Future Teachers

This chapter focuses on the mathematics of elementary and middle school and is not meant to be a review of the algebra you already have seen. The power of algebra and the interplay between algebra and geometry are the heart of the chapter. Two points are to be made here: (1) The introduction of algebra in elementary school ("early algebra") is important for children's future learning of mathematics (see the NCTM's *Principles and Standards for School Mathematics* for grades 3–5 that starts this chapter, p. 401), and (2) **social justice** demands that we make sure that *all* of our students have every opportunity for success in the worlds of career and education. Knowing algebra opens careers for your students, whereas not understanding or not having competence in algebra severely limits their career choices. There have been a number of examples globally of governments denying individuals or groups professional opportunities by the simple expedient of excluding them from a good education. That approach frequently translates into "no need for algebra or higher mathematics for the group" as a matter of repressive policy. In addition, unfortunately, some students self-select coursework that does not lead to higher mathematics and thereby limits their opportunities. We urge you to provide and encourage opportunities for your students to learn algebra which will then open many paths to their future success.

## Chapter 8 Summary

| Section 8.1   Algebraic Expressions, Functions, and Equations | Page Reference |
|---|---|
| **CONCEPTS** | |
| • **Algebraic reasoning:** Algebraic reasoning is used to solve problems and understand patterns by following these steps: Introduce variables, derive algebraic expressions, form equations, solve equations, and interpret the solution of the equations in the context of the original problem or pattern. | 402 |
| • **Variables:** Variables represent quantities that are unknown, that can change, or that depend on varying choices of related quantities. In particular, variables describe generalized properties, express relationships, express formulas, or serve as unknowns. | 402 |
| • **Algebraic expressions:** An algebraic expression is a mathematical expression involving variables, numbers, and operation symbols. | 404 |
| • **Equation:** Setting two algebraic expressions that represent the same quantity equal to one another creates an equation. | 405 |
| • **Solution of equations:** The values of the variables for which the equations are true are the solutions of the equations and form a set called the solution set of the equations. | 405 |
| • **Function:** A function is a rule that assigns exactly one value to each element $x$ in a set $D$. The set $D$ is the domain of the function. | 406 |
| • **Describing and visualizing functions:**. Functions can be represented by the following means: a formula, a table of values, an arrow diagram, a machine into which $x$ is input and $f(x)$ is output, and a graph. | 409 |
| • **Linear function:** A linear function is a function whose graph is a straight line. See the formal definition on next page. | 411 |

## DEFINITIONS

| | |
|---|---|
| • **Constants** are fixed values in mathematical expressions. | 402 |
| • **Variables** are quantities which vary. They are denoted by a symbol. | 402 |
| • A **numerical expression** is any representation of a number that involves numbers and operation symbols. For example, $44 \div 4$ is a numerical expression for 11. | 404 |
| • An **algebraic expression** is a mathematical expression involving variables, numbers, and operation symbols. | 404 |
| • The **domain of a variable** is the set of values for which the expression is defined. | 405 |
| • An **equation** is a mathematical expression stating that two algebraic expressions have the same value. | 405 |
| • A **conditional equation** is when only certain values of the variables give equality. | 405 |
| • The **solution set** of an equation is the set of all values in the domain of the variables that satisfy the given equation. | 405 |
| • Two equations are **equivalent** if they have the same solution set. | 405 |
| • A **function** on a set $D$ is a rule that assigns exactly one value to each element $x$ in $D$, precisely one value $y$. If the function is denoted by $f$, and if $x$ is an element of the domain $D$, then the value assigned to $x$ is denoted by $f(x)$. | 406, 407 |
| • The **domain of a function** is the set of a function $D$. | 407 |
| • The **image, or value,** of $f$ at $x$ is the value $y$ when a function assigns the $y$ to an element $x$ in the domain. | 407 |
| • The **range of a function** is the set of all values assigned by the function. | 407 |
| • A **linear function** is a function of the form $f(x) = mx + b$, where $m$ and $b$ denote constants not both zero. | 411 |

## PROCEDURES

| | |
|---|---|
| • **Evaluation of an algebraic expression:** Replace each of the variables with particular values from the domain of the variables to evaluate the expression. | 404 |
| • **Vertical-line test:** To see if the equation is a function, draw a vertical line graph and see how often it intersects the graph. If no line intersects the graph in two or more points, the graph is a function. | 407 |

| Section 8.2   Graphing Points, Lines, and Elementary Functions | Page Reference |
|---|---|

## CONCEPTS

| | |
|---|---|
| • **Cartesian coordinates:** The Cartesian coordinate system consists of two perpendicular axes, with the horizontal axis typically called the $x$-axis and the vertical axis typically called the $y$-axis. Any point $P(x, y)$ in the plane is uniquely described by its $x$- and $y$-coordinates. | 417 |
| • **Distance formula:** The distance between $P(x_1, y_1)$ and $Q(x_2, y_2)$ is given by $PQ = \sqrt{(x_2 - x_1)^2 + (y_2 - y_1)^2}.$ | 419 |
| • **Line segment:** $\overline{PQ}$ denotes the line segment with endpoints $P$ and $Q$. | 420 |
| • **Slope:** The slope of the line or line segment through the points $P(x_1, y_1)$ and $Q(x_2, y_2)$ is the ratio of the line's or line segment's "rise over run"; that is, slope $(\overline{PQ}) = \dfrac{y_2 - y_1}{x_2 - x_1}$ when $x_1 \neq x_2$. Slopes are not defined for vertical segments or lines. Lines or segments are parallel precisely when they have the same slope or are both vertical. | 420 |

| | |
|---|---|
| • **Equation of a line:** The equation of a nonvertical line can be given in point–slope, slope–intercept, and two-point forms. | 422 |
| • **Nonlinear function:** Nonlinear functions are graphed by making a table of values. The points listed in a table are plotted and then connected to approximate the graph of the function. Quadratic and exponential equations are given emphasis as they are a part of K–8 mathematics. | 426 |

## DEFINITIONS

| | |
|---|---|
| • The horizontal axis is typically called the **x-axis.** | 417 |
| • The vertical axis is typically called the **y-axis.** | 417 |
| • Any point $P(x, y)$, known as a **Cartesian coordinate** in the plane, is uniquely described by its **x-** and **y-coordinates.** The collection of the points defined by Cartesian coordinates is called the **Cartesian plane** or **coordinate plane.** | 417 |
| • The **origin** is the point $(0, 0)$. | 417 |
| • **Quadrants** are the four regions that the axes divide the plane into, as in Figure 8.5. | 417 |
| • The set of points between and including the two distinct endpoints, $P$ and $Q$, is the **line segment** $\overline{PQ}$. | 420 |
| • The **slope,** $m$, of the line or line segment through the points $P(x_1, y_1)$ and $Q(x_2, y_2)$ is the ratio of the line or line segment's "rise over run," given by $m = (y_2 - y_1)/(x_2 - x_1)$ if $x_1 \neq x_2$. If $x_1 = x_2$, then the line is vertical and its slope is undefined. | 420 |
| • **Nonlinear functions** are functions not of the form $f(x) = mx + b$. | 426 |
| • **Quadratic functions** are polynomials of degree two. | 426 |
| • **Exponential functions** are functions which are a multiple of a constent by a fixed positive real number raised to a variable power. | 428 |

## FORMULAS

| | |
|---|---|
| • Distance Formula: If $P(x_1, y_1)$, $Q(x_2, y_2)$ are points, then the distance between them is $$PQ = \sqrt{(x_2 - x_1)^2 + (y_2 - y_1)^2}.$$ | 419 |
| • Equation of Lines: If $P(x_1, y_1)$ and $Q(x_2, y_2)$ are on a line then <br> • Two-point form $$y - y_1 = m(x - x_1), \text{ where } m = \frac{y_2 - y_1}{x_2 - x_1} \text{ if } x_1 \neq x_2.$$ | 426 |
| • Point-slope form $y - y_1 = m(x - x_1)$ | 424 |
| • Slope-intercept form $y = mx + b$ where $b$ is called the $y$-intercept. | 424 |

| **Section 8.3   Connections Between Algebra and Geometry** | **Page Reference** |
|---|---|

## CONCEPTS

| | |
|---|---|
| • **Use Cartesian coordinates to solve geometric problems:** Geometric relationships can be solved by algebraic processes. | 433 |
| • **Parallel and perpendicular lines and their slopes:** The relationship between parallel lines and their slopes can be translated into statements about their slopes. The same goes for perpendicular lines and their slopes. | 434 |
| • **Rigid motions:** The use of rigid motions to solve a geometric problem is based on moving a figure to another position without changing its geometric properties but in which the solution becomes easier to see. | 436 |

| | |
|---|---|
| • **Circles:** Circles are the set of all points in the plane that are at a fixed distance from a given point and play a strong role in K–8 geometry. | 438 |

**DEFINITIONS**

| | |
|---|---|
| • **Parallel lines** are lines on a Cartesian plane that have either no points in common or are equal. | 434 |
| • The **midpoint** of a line segment is the point on the segment in which the distance from the point to each endpoint is equal. | 435 |
| • **Perpendicular lines** are lines that intersect at a 90° angle. | 436 |
| • The **altitude of a triangle** is a line through a vertex of a triangle that is perpendicular to the line containing the opposite side of the triangle. | 437 |
| • A collection of lines is **concurrent** if each of the lines contains the same point. | 437 |
| • The point at which the three altitudes of a triangle are concurrent is called the **orthocenter.** | 438 |
| • A **circle** is the set of all points in the plane that are a fixed distance from a given point. The given point is the **center** of the circle. The fixed distance is the **radius.** | 438, 439 |
| • The **diameter** of a circle is twice its radius. | 439 |
| • A **tangent line to the circle** at a point $Q$ is the line that goes through the point $Q$ and is perpendicular to the radius of the circle. | 439 |
| • **Social justice** is the concept that all students should have every opportunity for success in the worlds of career and education. | 443 |

**THEOREM**

| | |
|---|---|
| • **Condition for parallelism:** Two lines in the plane are parallel if they both have the same slope or both are vertical lines. | 434 |
| • **Condition for perpendicularity:** Two lines in the plane are perpendicular if their slopes are negative reciprocals of one another or if one is parallel to the $z$-axis and the other to the $y$-axis. | 436 |

**STRATEGIES**

| | |
|---|---|
| • **Cartesian coordinates to solve geometric problems:** Place the figures in a Cartesian plane and use algebra. | 433 |
| • **Rigid motions:** Use translation, rotation, or a combination of the two to move the geometric figure to another position in which the solution becomes easier to see. | 436 |

## Chapter Review Exercises

### Section 8.1

**1.** Let $a$, $b$, and $c$ denote the current ages of Alicia, Ben, and Cory, respectively. Write expressions in the variables $a$, $b$, and $c$ that express the given quantity.

 (a) Alicia's age in five years

 (b) The fact that Ben is younger than Cory

 (c) The difference in age between Ben and Cory

 (d) The average age of Alicia, Ben, and Cory

**2.** Let $a$, $b$, and $c$ denote the current ages of Alicia, Ben, and Cory as in problem 1. Write equations in the variables $a$, $b$, and $c$ that express the given relationship.

 (a) Alicia will be 11 years old in two more years.

**(b)** Three years ago, Ben's age was half of Cory's age last year.

**(c)** Alicia's age is the average of Ben's and Cory's ages.

**(d)** The average age of Alicia, Ben, and Cory is 10.

**3.** Solve these two Guess My Rule games, carefully describing a function that agrees with the table of values:

**(a)**

| $x$ | 4 | 2 | 0 | 5 | 1 |
|---|---|---|---|---|---|
| $y$ | 14 | 8 | 2 | 17 | 5 |

**(b)**

| $x$ | 4 | 2 | 5 | 0 | 1 |
|---|---|---|---|---|---|
| $y$ | 20 | 6 | 30 | 0 | 2 |

**4.** Let $f$ be a function defined by the formula $f(x) = 2x(x - 3)$.

**(a)** Find $f(3)$, $f(0.5)$, and $f(-2)$.

**(b)** If $f(x) = 0$, what are the possible values of $x$?

## Sections 8.2 and 8.3

**5.** **(a)** Plot the seven-sided polygon $ABCDEFG$ on graph paper, where the coordinates of the vertices (corners) of the polygon are $A(4, 2)$, $B(3, 3)$, $C(0, 3)$, $D(-2, 2)$, $E(-3, -2)$, $F(0, -2)$, and $G(4, 0)$.

**(b)** Point $A$ is in the first quadrant, and point $G$ is on the positive $x$-axis. Give similar descriptions for the other vertices of the polygon.

**(c)** The slope of side $\overline{AB}$ is $-1$, since the "rise over run" ratio is $\dfrac{-1}{1}$. Find the slopes of the other six sides of the polygon when the slope is defined. Are there any parallel sides?

**6.** Plot the hexagon $ABCDEF$ on graph paper, where the vertices of the hexagon are $A(0, 0)$, $B(7, 0)$, $C(16, 12)$, $D(7, 24)$, $E(0, 24)$, and $F(-9, 12)$.

**(a)** Find the lengths $AB$, $AC$, $AD$, $AE$, $AF$, and $CF$.

**(b)** Draw all the diagonals of the hexagon, using the symmetry of the figure, and label the lengths of all the sides and diagonals. Why do you think this figure is called an "integer hexagon"?

**7.** Find an equation of each of the lines described.

**(a)** The line through $R(3, 4)$ with slope 2

**(b)** The line through $T(6, -1)$ and $U(-2, 5)$

**(c)** The line of slope 3 that intersects the $y$-axis at $y = -4$

**8.** Find a line perpendicular to $x + 7 = 2y$ and that goes through $(7, 4)$.

**9.** What is the altitude through the point $R$ in the triangle of Example 8.13?

**10.** Suppose that $\mathcal{C}_1$ and $\mathcal{C}_2$ are circles. How many members can the set $\mathcal{C}_1 \cap \mathcal{C}_2$ have? Draw an example of each.

## Chapter Test

**1.** Consider the exponential function $y = \left(\dfrac{1}{4}\right)^x$.

**(a)** Find the values of $y$ when $x$ is 0, 1, 2, and 3, and sketch the graph of $y$.

**(b)** What is the relationship between (a) and problem 25(c) of Problem Set 8.2?

**2.** Consider the function $f(x) = 2x^2 + 4x$.

**(a)** Graph the function.

**(b)** Determine the smallest value of the function, and find the corresponding value of $x$ at which this minimum value occurs.

**3.** Classify each given equation as linear or nonlinear. If it is linear, rewrite the equation in the form $f(x) = mx + b$ of a linear function and identify the slope of the line and the point at which the line intersects the $y$-axis.

**(a)** $6x = 2y + 8$

**(b)** $y = 3x^2 + 4$

**(c)** $y - 2x = -x + 5$

**4.** Create algebraic expressions for the quantities described in each part. Be sure to first introduce and define appropriate variables.

**(a)** The cost of monthly phone service from a company that charges $5 per month plus 12¢ per minute

**(b)** The monthly cost of using a checking account from a bank that charges $8 per month and 15¢ per check

**(c)** The cost of taking a group of adults and children to the fair, where the admission fee is $4 for adults and $2.50 for children

**5.** Write the equation of each line (a), (b), and (c) shown in the following coordinate system:

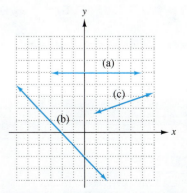

**6.** Match the graphs shown to the hike described. Each graph depicts the elevation as a function of time into the hike.

**(a)** A hike up Mount Shasta and return to base camp

**(b)** A round-trip hike into the Grand Canyon

**(c)** A hike along the wilderness beach in Olympic National Park

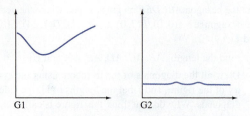

G1    G2

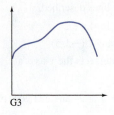

G3

**7.** What is the equation of the line that is tangent to the circle of radius 2 at (2, 0) and whose center is at the origin?

**8.** Let $P(4, 2)$, $Q(7, 6)$, $R(3, 9)$, and $S(a, b)$ be the vertices of a square.

   **(a)** What are the coordinates $a$ and $b$?

   **(b)** What is the length of each side of the square?

**9.** Let $f$ be the function given by $f(x) = x^2 - 4x + 5$ on the domain $\{1, 2, 3, 4, 5\}$. Give the range of the function.

# Geometric Figures

**9.1** Figures in the Plane

**9.2** Curves and Polygons in the Plane

**9.3** Figures in Space

**9.4** Networks

## Hands On

## Investigating Triangles via Paper Folding

### Materials Needed

Paper (thin and colorful paper similar to origami paper works well), scissors, rulers, protractors, pencils, and tape.

### Directions

Many important geometric concepts, figures, and relationships can be investigated with paper folding. In this activity, you will first practice some basic constructions using paper folding—creating perpendicular lines, angle bisectors, and perpendicular bisectors. You will then use these basic constructions to discover some properties of triangles and quadrilaterals. (A quadrilateral is a polygon with four sides.)

### The Basic Folds

Use your measuring tools to check that these constructions work as claimed:

1. **Perpendicular line.** Draw a line *l* and place a point *P* on a sheet of paper. Crease the paper so that the line is folded onto itself and the crease passes through the point *P*. Unfold your paper, and then use your protractor to check that the crease makes a 90° angle with the line *l*.

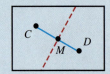

Perpendicular line

2. **Angle bisector.** Draw two rays from a point *A*, and make a crease through *A* so that one ray is folded onto the other ray. Unfold your paper, and use your protractor to show that the crease makes angles of equal size with the two rays.

Angle bisector

3. **Perpendicular bisector.** Draw a line segment joining two points *C* and *D*. Crease your paper so that point *C* is folded on top of point *D*. Unfold your paper, and label the point where the crease crosses the segment $\overline{CD}$ as point *M*. Use your measuring tools to check that *M* is the same distance from both *C* and *D* and that the crease is perpendicular to the segment.

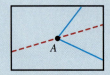

Perpendicular bisector

### Exploring Properties of Triangles

The basic folds make it simple to construct some interesting lines and line segments associated with a triangle, as shown in the following diagram:

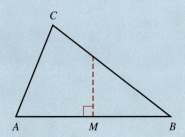

Midpoint *M* and perpendicular bisector of side $\overline{AB}$

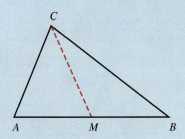

Median through vertex *C* to midpoint of side $\overline{AB}$

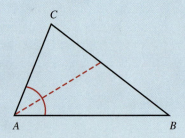

Angle bisector at vertex *A*

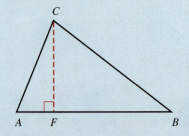

Altitude from vertex *C* perpendicular to side $\overline{AB}$

1.  **The Midpoint of a Hypotenuse of a Right Triangle.** Cut off the corner of a rectangular sheet of paper to create a right triangle *ABC*, where the 90° angle is at vertex *C*. Use folding to construct the midpoint *M* of the hypotenuse $\overline{AB}$. Now find the perpendicular bisectors of legs $\overline{AC}$ and $\overline{BC}$. What do you find interesting? How do the respective distances from *M* to *A*, *B*, and *C* compare with one another?

2.  **The Intersection of the Perpendicular Bisectors of the Sides of a Triangle.** Cut out a triangle from a sheet of paper. It may have any shape at all, but begin with a triangle with no angle larger than 90°. Next, construct the perpendicular bisectors of each of the sides of the triangle. What is interesting about how your lines intersect? Repeat your investigation with a triangle with one angle larger than 90°. Tape your unfolded triangle onto a large sheet of paper, and use a ruler to extend the crease lines. Describe what property you observe.

3.  **The Intersection of the Medians of a Triangle.** Use short creases to find the midpoints of all three sides of a paper triangle, and then make creases to construct all three medians of your triangle. What special property do you discover?

4.  **The Intersection of the Angle Bisectors of a Triangle.** Use paper folding to construct the angle bisectors of all three angles of a paper triangle. What special property do you observe?

5.  **The Intersection of the Altitudes of a Triangle.** Use paper folding to construct the altitudes through each of the vertices of a triangle. What seems special about your three lines? If your triangle has an angle larger than 90°, you will want to tape your unfolded triangle to a large sheet of paper and use a ruler to extend your crease lines.

6.  **The Angle Sum and Area of a Triangle.** Use folding to construct the altitude $\overline{CF}$ of a paper triangle *ABC*. Measure the height *h* = *CF* and the length of the base *b* = *AB* of your triangle. Next, fold all three vertices of your triangle to *F*, as shown in the right-hand diagram:

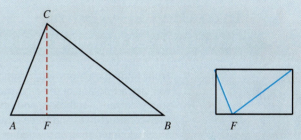

Why is the new figure a rectangle? (A rectangle is a four-sided polygon with a 90° angle at each vertex.) How do the lengths of the sides of your rectangle compare with the height and base of your triangle? How is the area of your rectangle related to the area of your triangle? What has your folding revealed about the sum of the measures of the angles of your triangle?

---

**CHAPTER PREVIEW**

This chapter is the first of four dealing with topics in geometry that are very much a part of the life of an elementary or middle school teacher or student. Our philosophy, then, in these four chapters, is to study shapes in geometry in an informal manner, but also to be careful mathematically with the material.

Before 600 B.C., geometry was both informal and practical. In the period from 600 B.C. to 300 B.C., Pythagoras, Euclid, and others organized the knowledge and experience that had been accumulated and transformed geometry into a theoretical science. Utilitarian considerations gave way to abstraction and general methods. With Euclid's *Elements,* geometry became a formal system in which geometric theorems were deduced logically from a list of statements called axioms that were accepted without proof. Many people believe that geometry is restricted to a Euclidean formalism in which exacting standards of proof and logical development must be met.

In this text, however, because our goal is to prepare K–8 teachers, we return to learning by trusting our intuition and experience. First, undefined terms are identified and careful definitions of other concepts are made from those terms. Geometric facts are then discovered by explorations of pictorial representations and physical models, with little attention given to the overall formal logical structure. This approach models the levels of learning geometry that were identified by the van Hieles' research. (See Into the Classroom on the next page.) However, there will be many opportunities to verify patterns and conjectures by examining the consequences of properties and facts that have already been accepted.

As we discussed in the previous two paragraphs, there is both a formal approach to geometry and an informal one. How, then, does one reason or give plausible arguments to show that results are true without using the rigorous formalism of Euclidean geometry? The Reasoning and Proof Standard and Representative Standard of NCTM provide some guidance, as the excerpt "Geometry in Grades Pre-K–2" on page 453 shows.

Like the objectives of geometers of ancient times, our goals are to recognize differences and similarities among shapes; to analyze the properties of a shape or class of shapes; and to model, construct, and draw shapes in a variety of ways. These goals are inseparably intertwined, but it will be seen that the discussion follows three threads of development: *classification, analysis,* and *representation* of the plane and space curves and surfaces that are presented in elementary school.

KEY IDEAS

- Understand definitions of geometric objects in the plane and what they mean.
- Recognize the similarities and differences between plane geometric objects; that is, classify them.
- Analyze the various relationships between angles in plane figures.
- Differentiate between geometric objects in space, especially polyhedra.
- Make the connection between solid and plane figures through the construction of a net from a polyhedron through representation.
- Overall, many different shapes are interesting, and as Marjorie Senechal* points out, *shape* is an indefinable term.

## Into the Classroom

## Activity-Based Learning and the van Hiele Levels

From kindergarten onward, geometry is learned best through hands-on activities. A successful teacher will take advantage of the enjoyment children experience when working with colored paper, straws, string, crayons, toothpicks, and other tangible materials. Children learn geometry by doing geometry as they construct two- and three-dimensional shapes, combine their shapes to create attractive patterns, and build interesting space figures out of plane shapes. By its nature, informal geometry provides unlimited opportunities to construct shapes, designs, and structures that all work to capture a child's interest.

According to pioneering research of the van Hieles in the late 1950s, the knowledge children construct for themselves through hands-on activities is essential to learning geometry. Dr. Pierre van Hiele and Dr. Dina van Hiele-Geldof, both former mathematics teachers in the Netherlands, theorized that learning geometry progresses through five levels, which can be described briefly as follows:

*Level 0—Recognition of shape*

Children recognize shapes holistically. Only the overall appearance of a figure is observed, with no attention given to the parts of the figure. For example, a figure with three curved sides would likely be identified as a triangle by a child at Level 0. Similarly, a square tilted point downward may not be recognized as a square.

*Level 1—Analysis of single shapes*

Children at Level 1 are cognizant of the parts of certain figures. For example, a rectangle has four straight sides that meet at "square" corners. However, at Level 1 the interrelationships between figures and properties are not understood.

*Level 2—Relationships among shapes*

At Level 2, children understand how common properties create abstract relationships among figures. For example, a square is both a rhombus and a rectangle. Also, children can make simple deductions about figures, using the analytic abilities acquired at Level 1.

*Level 3—Deductive reasoning*

The student at Level 3 views geometry as a formal mathematical system and can write deductive proofs.

*Level 4—Geometry as an axiomatic system*

This is the abstract level, reached only in high-level university courses. The focus is on the axiomatic foundations of a geometry, and no dependence is placed on concrete or pictorial models.

Ongoing research supports the thesis that students learn geometry by progressing through the van Hiele levels. This text—by means of hands-on activities and examples and problems that require constructions and drawings—promotes the spirit of the van Hiele approach. However, it is the elementary school classroom teacher who must bring geometry to life for his or her students by creating interesting activities that support each child's progression through the first three van Hiele levels.

---

*See L. A. Steen, ed., "Shape," in *On the Shoulders of Giants: New Approaches to Numeracy* (Washington, DC: National Academy Press, 1990), pp. 139–182.

## Materials for Explorations

Many examples will be presented in the form of an *exploration.* First, you will represent a shape, perhaps with a drawing or physical model, that satisfies the stated conditions. Next, you will be asked to discover, analyze, and describe the properties of the shape. Often, you will not want to read further until you have followed the directions and made some discoveries for yourself; only then should you read on to see if the patterns and relationships you have uncovered agree with those discussed in the text.

The following tools and materials will be useful in drawing, constructing, or creating the shapes you will explore:

- colored pencils
- ruler (best if marked in both inches and millimeters)
- compass (be sure it is of good quality)
- tape
- glue
- protractor
- drafting triangles ($30°-60°-90°$ and $45°-45°-90°$)
- scissors
- unlined paper
- graph paper
- dot paper in both square and triangular patterns
- patty paper (waxed meat-patty separating sheets)

Exploring shapes, figures, and their properties should start even before kindergarten. See NCTM Principles and Standards on this page.

## Geometry in Grades Pre-K-2

Children begin forming concepts of shape long before formal schooling. The primary grades are an ideal time to help them refine and extend their understandings. Students first learn to recognize a shape by its appearance as a whole or through qualities such as "pointiness." They may believe that a given figure is a rectangle because "it looks like a door."

Pre-K–2 geometry begins with describing and naming shapes. Young students begin by using their own vocabulary to describe objects, talking about how they are alike and how they are different. Teachers must help students gradually incorporate conventional terminology into their descriptions of two- and three-dimensional shapes. However, terminology itself should not be the focus of the pre-K–2 geometry program. The goal is that early experiences with geometry lay the foundation for more-formal geometry in later grades. Using terminology to focus attention and to clarify ideas during discussions can help students build that foundation.

Teachers must provide materials and structure the environment appropriately to encourage students to explore shapes and their attributes. For example, young students can compare and sort building blocks as they put them away on shelves, identifying their similarities and differences. They can use commonly available materials such as cereal boxes to explore attributes or shapes of folded paper to investigate symmetry and congruence. Students can create shapes on geoboards or dot paper and represent them in drawings, block constructions, and dramatizations.

Students need to see many examples of shapes that correspond to the same geometrical concept as well as a variety of shapes that are nonexamples of the concept. Through class discussions of such examples and nonexamples, geometric concepts are developed and refined.

Students also learn about geometric properties by combining or cutting apart shapes to form new shapes. Interactive computer programs provide a rich environment for activities in which students put together or take apart (compose and decompose) shapes. Technology can help all students understand mathematics, and interactive computer programs may give students with special instructional needs access to mathematics they might not otherwise experience.

Source: *Principles and Standards for School Mathematics by NCTM, pages 97–98. Copyright © 2000 by the National Council of Teachers of Mathematics. Reproduced with permission of the National Council of Teachers of Mathematics via Copyright Clearance Center. NCTM does not endorse the content or validity of these alignments.*

A Picture Gallery of Plane Figures

Fissures in a gelatinous preparation of tin oil

Butterfly wings

M. C. Escher's sketch of a wall mosaic in the Alhambra

A fractal, an example of a complex, beautiful image created with a computer

A snow crystal

The pattern of seeds in the head of a sunflower

A variety of manipulatives are available from commercial suppliers and are of great value in the study of geometry. Having access to such items as the following is desirable:

- geoboards
- tangrams
- pattern blocks
- geometric solids (wood or plastic)
- pentominoes
- reflective drawing tools such as a Mira®

## 9.1 Figures in the Plane

The shapes in the picture gallery of plane figures (page 454) and the picture gallery of space figures (page 491) are each highly complex when viewed as a whole, but underlying this complexity is an orderly arrangement of simpler parts. In this section, we consider the most basic shapes of geometry: points, lines, segments, rays, and angles. We will also be introduced to a large number of notations and terms that are essential for the communication of geometric concepts and relationships.

Some terms have no formal definition (*line* or *plane,* for example). Other concepts, which you have seen many times (line segment, ray, vertical angles, and so on), require careful definitions. We will define common terms in the body of a paragraph and save the displayed definitions for those concepts with which you may be less familiar.

### Points and Lines

A point on paper is represented by a dot. A point on a television monitor is represented by a small rectangle of phosphors, called a pixel, that glows when excited by a beam of electrons. Neither a dot nor a pixel is an exact representation of a geometric point. In the mind's eye, dots and pixels are decreased in size until they become ideal **points**—that is, just locations in space. On paper we still draw dots to represent points, and we label the points with uppercase letters:

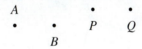

A **line,** like a point, is undefined, but its meaning is suggested by representations such as a tightly stretched thread, a laser beam, or the edge of a ruler. We assume that any two points determine one and only one line that contains the two points. Lines will often be denoted with lowercase letters such as $l$ and $m$. If $A$ and $B$ are two points, then the line through $A$ and $B$ is denoted by $\overleftrightarrow{AB}$. The following diagram shows both of these representations:

The arrows in the drawings and in the notation $\overleftrightarrow{AB}$ indicate that lines extend infinitely far in two directions. On paper, lines can be drawn with either a ruler or a **straightedge.** A straightedge is like a ruler, but without any marks on it.

Three or more points usually determine several lines, but if they lie on just one line, then we say the points are **collinear,** as shown in Figure 9.1.

**FIGURE 9.1**
Three points determine either three lines or one line

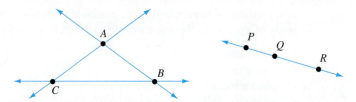

A, B, and C are noncollinear points.          P, Q, and R are collinear points.

Three noncollinear points determine a **plane,** which is yet another undefined term used to describe a set of points that idealize a flat space such as a tabletop. In this section and the next, we consider only sets of points that belong to a single plane. Subsets of a plane are called **plane figures** or **plane shapes.** In Section 9.3 we explore solid shapes, in which not all of the points belong to a single plane.

Recall from Section 8.3 that two lines in the same plane are parallel if, and only if, either they are the same line or they have no points in common. Two distinct lines $p$ and $q$ in a plane that are not parallel must have a single point in common, called their **point of intersection.** The terms that we define next show some of the different ways in which two or three lines can be arranged in the plane (Figure 9.2).

---

**DEFINITION** *Concurrent Lines*

If there is a point B that is on each of the lines $i$, $j$, and $k$, then the three lines are said to be **concurrent.**

---

**FIGURE 9.2**
The possible arrangements of two and three lines in a plane

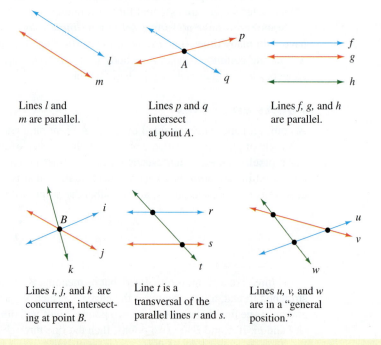

Lines $l$ and $m$ are parallel.

Lines $p$ and $q$ intersect at point $A$.

Lines $f$, $g$, and $h$ are parallel.

Lines $i$, $j$, and $k$ are concurrent, intersecting at point $B$.

Line $t$ is a transversal of the parallel lines $r$ and $s$.

Lines $u$, $v$, and $w$ are in a "general position."

---

**DEFINITION** *Transversal*

If $r$ and $s$ are distinct lines and $t$ is a line that intersects each of them, but not at the same point, then $t$ is called a **transversal** to $r$ and $s$.

---

**EXAMPLE 9.1** **Exploring Collinearity and Concurrency**

**(a)** Place three circular objects (e.g., coins and cups) of different size on a sheet of paper, and trace them to create three circles, labeled $C_1$, $C_2$, and $C_3$. Next, place a ruler tightly against one side of the objects you used to trace $C_1$ and $C_2$, and draw the line $l$ that just touches both circles. Move the ruler to the other side of your objects to draw the line $m$, as shown in the accompanying figure. The two lines you've drawn are called the external tangents to the circles $C_1$ and $C_2$. Label their point of intersection as $P$.

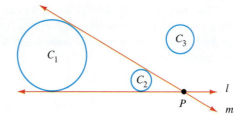

In the same way, use your ruler to draw the two lines externally tangent to $C_2$ and $C_3$, and let $Q$ be their point of intersection. Finally, draw the external tangents of $C_1$ and $C_3$, and let $R$ be their point of intersection. What conjecture do you have concerning $P$, $Q$, and $R$?

**(b)** Trace around a cup bottom (or use a compass) to draw an accurate circle. Then use a ruler to draw any three lines that are tangent to the circle at points labeled $X$, $Y$, and $Z$ and that intersect in pairs at the points labeled $A$, $B$, and $C$. Finally, draw the lines $\overleftrightarrow{AX}$, $\overleftrightarrow{BY}$, and $\overleftrightarrow{CZ}$ (in the accompanying figure). What conjecture can you make about $\overleftrightarrow{AX}$, $\overleftrightarrow{BY}$, and $\overleftrightarrow{CZ}$?

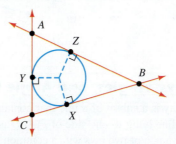

**Solution**

**(a)** $P$, $Q$, and $R$ are collinear.
**(b)** $\overleftrightarrow{AX}$, $\overleftrightarrow{BY}$, and $\overleftrightarrow{CZ}$ are concurrent.

SOURCE: B.C. Cartoon, "Vanishing Point." 9/6/90. Copyright © 1990 Creators Syndicate, Inc. Reprinted by permission.

## Line Segments and the Distance Between Points

Let $A$ and $B$ be any two points. The line $\overleftrightarrow{AB}$ can be viewed as a copy of the number line. That is, every point on $\overleftrightarrow{AB}$ corresponds to a unique real number, and every real number corresponds to a unique point on $\overleftrightarrow{AB}$. If $A$ and $B$ correspond to the real numbers $x$ and $y$, respectively, then the absolute value, $|x - y|$, gives the **distance** between $A$ and $B$. We denote this distance by $AB$:

> $AB$ with no overbar denotes the length of segment $\overline{AB}$.

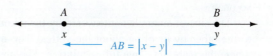

The points on the line $\overleftrightarrow{AB}$ that are between $A$ and $B$, together with $A$ and $B$ themselves, form the **line segment** $\overline{AB}$. Points $A$ and $B$ are called the **endpoints** of $\overline{AB}$, and the distance $AB$ is the **length** of $\overline{AB}$. It is important to see that the overbar used in the notation distinguishes the real number $AB$ from the line segment $\overline{AB}$.

Two segments $\overline{AB}$ and $\overline{CD}$ are said to be **congruent** if they have the same length. This relationship is symbolized by writing $\overline{AB} \cong \overline{CD}$. Thus, $\overline{AB} \cong \overline{CD}$ if, and only if, $AB = CD$. The point $M$ in $\overline{AB}$ that is the same distance from $A$ and $B$ is called the **midpoint** of $\overline{AB}$. This information is summarized in Figure 9.3.

**FIGURE 9.3**
A segment $\overline{AB}$, its length $AB$, congruent segments, and the midpoint $M$ of $\overline{AB}$

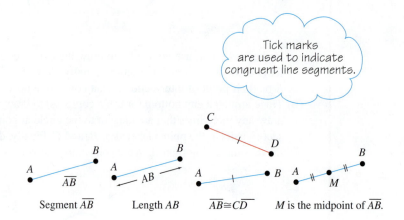

Tick marks are used to indicate congruent line segments.

Segment $\overline{AB}$          Length $AB$          $\overline{AB} \cong \overline{CD}$          $M$ is the midpoint of $\overline{AB}$.

## Rays, Angles, and Angle Measure

A **ray** is a subset of a line that contains a point $P$, called the **endpoint** of the ray, and all points on the line lying to one side of $P$. If $Q$ is any point on the ray other than $P$, then $\overrightarrow{PQ}$ denotes the ray. The union of two rays with a common endpoint is an **angle**. If the rays are $\overrightarrow{AB}$ and $\overrightarrow{AC}$, then the angle is denoted by $\angle BAC$. The common endpoint of the two rays is called the **vertex** of the angle and is the middle letter in the symbol for the angle (for example, $A$ in $\angle BAC$). The points $B$ and $C$ not at the vertex can be written in either order, so that $\angle CAB$ denotes the same angle as $\angle BAC$. The rays $\overrightarrow{AB}$ and $\overrightarrow{AC}$ are called the **sides** of the angle. (See Figure 9.4.)

**FIGURE 9.4**
A ray $\overrightarrow{PQ}$ and an angle $\angle BAC$

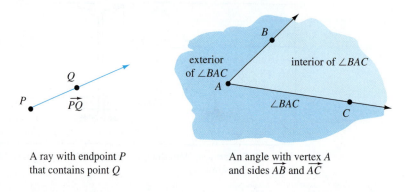

A ray with endpoint $P$ that contains point $Q$

An angle with vertex $A$ and sides $\overrightarrow{AB}$ and $\overrightarrow{AC}$

An angle whose sides are not on the same line partitions the remaining points of the plane into two parts: the **interior** and the **exterior** of the angle. The points along a line segment that joins an endpoint on side $\overrightarrow{AB}$ to an endpoint on $\overrightarrow{AC}$ are all interior points of $\angle BAC$.

If $\angle BAC$ is the only angle with its vertex at $A$, it is common to write $\angle A$ in place of $\angle BAC$. When more than one angle has a vertex at $A$, it is essential to use the full three-letter symbol. Sometimes it is useful to number the angles that appear in a drawing and refer to $\angle 1, \angle 2, \angle 3$, and so on.

The size of an angle is measured by the amount of rotation required to turn one side of the angle to the other by pivoting about the vertex. The **measure of an angle** is generally given in **degrees**, where there are $360°$ in a full revolution. The measure of $\angle A$ is denoted by $m(\angle A)$. If the rotation is imagined to pass through the interior of the angle, the measure is a number between $0°$ and $180°$. Unless stated otherwise, $m(\angle A)$ is the measure of $\angle A$ not larger than $180°$.

An angle of measure $180°$ is a **straight angle,** an angle of measure $90°$ is a **right angle,** and an angle of measure $0°$ is a **zero angle.** Angles measuring between $0°$ and $90°$ are **acute,** and angles measuring between $90°$ and $180°$ are **obtuse.**

$m(\angle A)$ denotes the measure of the angle $A$ with vertex at point $A$.

In some applications, the measure of interest corresponds to the rotation through the exterior of the angle and is therefore a number between 180° and 360°. An angle with measure greater than 180°, but less than 360°, is called a **reflex angle.**

The classification of angles according to their measure is summarized in Figure 9.5.

**FIGURE 9.5**
The classification of angles by their measure

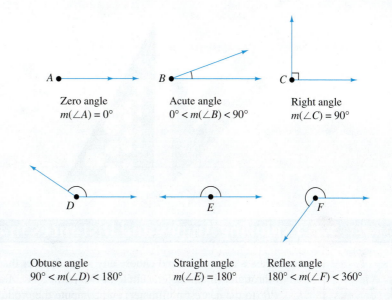

Zero angle
$m(\angle A) = 0°$

Acute angle
$0° < m(\angle B) < 90°$

Right angle
$m(\angle C) = 90°$

Obtuse angle
$90° < m(\angle D) < 180°$

Straight angle
$m(\angle E) = 180°$

Reflex angle
$180° < m(\angle F) < 360°$

Right angles in drawings are indicated by a small square placed at the vertex. A circular arc is required to indicate reflex angles.

Two lines $l$ and $m$ that intersect at right angles are called **perpendicular lines.** This relationship is indicated in writing by $l \perp m$. Similarly, two rays, two segments, or a segment and a ray are perpendicular if they are contained in perpendicular lines.

> **DEFINITION**  *Congruent Angles*
> Two angles are **congruent** if, and only if, they have the same measure.

It is important to remember that there is a significant difference between two angles being equal (meaning that the two rays defining them are the same) and being congruent (their measures being equal). There are, for example, many different angles whose measure is 30° (so they are congruent). Of course, if two angles are equal, then they are also congruent. The symbol $\cong$ is used to denote the congruence of angles. Thus,

$$\angle P \cong \angle Q \quad \text{if, and only if,} \quad m(\angle P) = m(\angle Q).$$

The **protractor** is used both to measure angles and to draw angles having a given measure. The protractor and other traditional tools useful for drawing and measuring are shown in Figure 9.6. Increasingly, these tools are being supplemented and replaced by the available geometry software for the computer.

**FIGURE 9.6**
Some useful tools for measuring and drawing geometric figures

Circle master compass

ETA/Cuisenaire® Safe Drawing Compass

**FIGURE 9.6**
(continued)

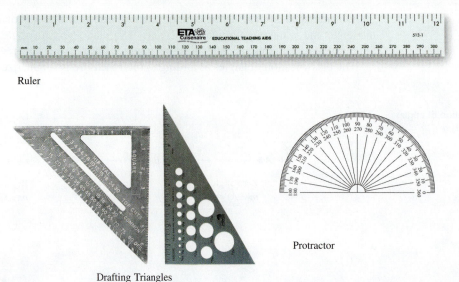

Ruler

Drafting Triangles

Protractor

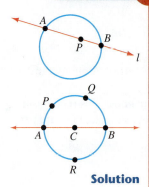

**EXAMPLE 9.2** **Exploring Angles and Distances in a Circle**

(a) Draw a large circle and choose any point $P$, other than the center, inside the circle. Any line $l$ through $P$ intersects the circle in two points, say, $A$ and $B$. Measure the distances $AP$ and $PB$ (to the nearest millimeter) and compute the product $AP \cdot PB$. Draw several other lines through $P$ and measure the distances of the two segments. Which line through $P$ makes the product of distances, $AP \cdot PB$, as large as possible?

(b) Draw a circle with center $C$. Draw a line through $C$, and let $A$ and $B$ denote its intersections with the circle. Choose any three points $P$, $Q$, and $R$ on the circle other than $A$ or $B$. Use a protractor to measure $\angle APB$, $\angle AQB$, and $\angle ARB$. Compare with other choices of points. What general result does this activity suggest?

**Solution**

(a) For every choice of $l$, the product $AP \cdot PB$ is the same. Therefore, no line through $P$ gives a larger product than any other line.

(b) Each angle is a right angle. This is one of geometry's earliest theorems, attributed to Thales of Miletus (ca. 600 B.C.).

## Pairs of Angles and the Corresponding-Angles Theorem

As shown in Figure 9.7, two angles are **complementary** if the sum of their measures is 90°. Similarly, two angles are **supplementary** if their measures sum to 180°.

**FIGURE 9.7**
Examples of complementary and supplementary angles

Adjacent angles

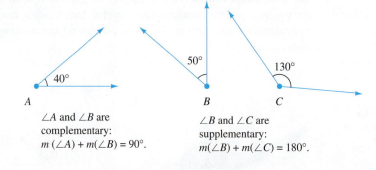

$\angle A$ and $\angle B$ are complementary:
$m(\angle A) + m(\angle B) = 90°$.

$\angle B$ and $\angle C$ are supplementary:
$m(\angle B) + m(\angle C) = 180°$.

Two angles that have a common side and nonoverlapping interiors are called **adjacent angles.** Supplementary and complementary angles frequently occur as adjacent angles, as shown in Figure 9.8.

**FIGURE 9.8**
Adjacent supplementary
and complementary
angles

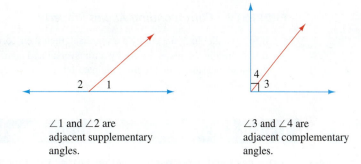

∠1 and ∠2 are
adjacent supplementary
angles.

∠3 and ∠4 are
adjacent complementary
angles.

Two nonadjacent angles formed by two intersecting lines are called **vertical angles,** as shown in Figure 9.9. Since ∠1 and ∠2 are supplementary, we know that $m(\angle 1) + m(\angle 2) = 180°$. Likewise, ∠2 and ∠3 are supplementary, so we also have $m(\angle 2) + m(\angle 3) = 180°$. Comparing these two equations shows that $m(\angle 1) = m(\angle 3)$. This proves another theorem of Thales.

**FIGURE 9.9**
Intersecting lines form two
pairs of vertical angles

∠1 and ∠3 are vertical angles.
∠2 and ∠4 are vertical angles.

**THEOREM** *Vertical-Angles Theorem*
Vertical angles have the same measure.

Now consider the angles formed when two lines *l* and *m* are intersected at two points by a transversal *t*. There are eight angles formed, in four pairs of **corresponding angles.**

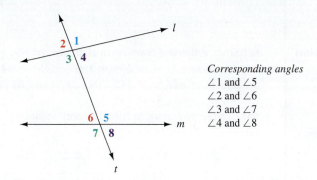

*Corresponding angles*
∠1 and ∠5
∠2 and ∠6
∠3 and ∠7
∠4 and ∠8

A case of special importance occurs when *l* and *m* are parallel lines, as shown in Figure 9.10. It would appear that each pair of corresponding angles is a pair of congruent angles. Conversely, if any one pair of corresponding angles is a congruent pair of angles, then the lines *l* and *m* appear to be parallel. We will accept the truth of these observations, giving us the **corresponding-angles property.** Many formal treatments of Euclidean geometry introduce the corresponding-angles property as an axiom.

**FIGURE 9.10**
Lines *l* and *m* are parallel
if, and only if, the angles
in some corresponding
pair have the same
measure

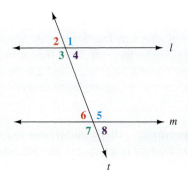

**PROPERTY**    *Corresponding-Angles Property*

- If two parallel lines are cut by a transversal, then their corresponding angles have the same measure.
- If two lines in the plane are cut by a transversal and some pair of their corresponding angles has the same measure, then the lines are parallel.

**EXAMPLE** **9.3**    **Using the Corresponding-Angles Property**

(a) Lines *l* and *m* are parallel and $m(\angle 6) = 35°$. Find the measures of the remaining seven angles.

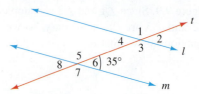

(b) Lines *t* and *j* intersect at *P* and form an angle measuring 122°. Describe how to use a protractor and straightedge to draw a line *k* through *Q* that is parallel to line *j*.

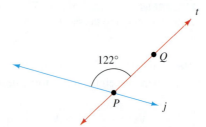

**Solution**

(a) Since $\angle 8$ and $\angle 6$ are vertical angles, $m(\angle 8) = 35°$. Also, $\angle 5$ and $\angle 7$ are supplements of $\angle 6$, so $m(\angle 5) = m(\angle 7) = 180° - 35° = 145°$. By the corresponding-angles property, $m(\angle 1) = m(\angle 5) = 145°$, $m(\angle 2) = m(\angle 6) = 35°$, $m(\angle 3) = m(\angle 7) = 145°$, and $m(\angle 4) = m(\angle 8) = 35°$.

(b) Use the protractor to form the corresponding angle measuring 122° at point *Q*.

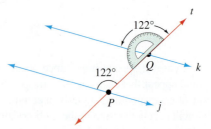

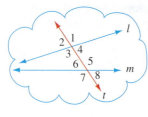

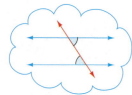

The pair of angles $\angle 4$ and $\angle 6$ between *l* and *m*, but on opposite sides of the transversal *t*, is called a pair of **alternate interior angles.** Since $\angle 2$ and $\angle 4$ are vertical angles, they are congruent by the vertical-angles theorem. Thus, the corresponding angles $\angle 2$ and $\angle 6$ are congruent if, and only if, the alternate interior angles $\angle 4$ and $\angle 6$ are congruent. This statement gives the following consequence of the corresponding-angles property:

**THEOREM**    *Alternate-Interior-Angles Theorem*

Two lines cut by a transversal are parallel if, and only if, a pair of alternate interior angles is congruent.

## The Measure of Angles in Triangles

If a triangle *ABC* is cut from paper, and its three corners are torn off, it is soon discovered that the three pieces will form a straight angle along a line *l*. (See Figure 9.11.) Thus, $m(\angle 1) + m(\angle 2) + m(\angle 3) = 180°$, and we have a physical demonstration that the sum of the measures of the angles of a triangle is 180°. Of course, an "angle of a triangle" means an *interior* angle of that triangle, as in Figure 9.11.

**FIGURE 9.11**
The torn corners of a triangle cut from paper can be placed along a line to show that $m(\angle 1) + m(\angle 2) + m(\angle 3) = 180°$

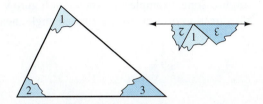

We will now see that the alternate-interior-angles theorem can be used to prove the theorem about the sum of angle measures of a triangle.

> **THEOREM**  *Sum of Angle Measures in a Triangle*
> The sum of the measures of the angles in a triangle is 180°.

**PROOF**  Consider the line *l* through point *A* that is parallel to the line $m = \overleftrightarrow{BC}$:

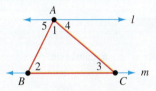

Line $\overleftrightarrow{AB}$ is a transversal to *l* and *m* for which $\angle 5$ and $\angle 2$ are alternate interior angles. Thus, $m(\angle 5) = m(\angle 2)$ by the alternate-interior-angles theorem. Similarly, $\angle 4$ and $\angle 3$ are alternate interior angles for the transversal $\overleftrightarrow{AC}$, so $m(\angle 4) = m(\angle 3)$. Since $\angle 5$, $\angle 1$, and $\angle 4$ form a straight angle at vertex *A*, we know that $m(\angle 5) + m(\angle 1) + m(\angle 4) = 180°$. Thus, by substitution, $m(\angle 2) + m(\angle 1) + m(\angle 3) = 180°$.

**EXAMPLE  9.4  Measuring an Opposite Exterior Angle of a Triangle**

In the accompanying figure, $\angle 4$ is called an **exterior angle** of triangle *PQR* and $\angle 1$ and $\angle 2$ are its **opposite interior angles.** Show that the measure of the exterior angle is equal to the sum of the measures of the opposite interior angles; that is, show that $m(\angle 4) = m(\angle 1) + m(\angle 2)$.

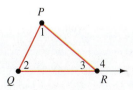

**Solution**  By the preceding theorem, we have $m(\angle 1) + m(\angle 2) + m(\angle 3) = 180°$. Also, $\angle 3$ and $\angle 4$ are supplementary, so $m(\angle 3) + m(\angle 4) = 180°$. Therefore, $m(\angle 1) + m(\angle 2) + m(\angle 3) = m(\angle 3) + m(\angle 4)$. Subtracting $m(\angle 3)$ from both sides of this equation gives $m(\angle 1) + m(\angle 2) = m(\angle 4)$.

## Directed Angles

Until now, we have measured angles without regard to their *direction*—clockwise or counterclockwise. One side rotates until it coincides with the second side. Often, it is useful to specify one side as the **initial side** and the other side as the **terminal side.** Angles are then measured by specifying the number of degrees to rotate the initial side to the terminal side. Mathematicians usually assign a positive number to counterclockwise turns, and a negative number to clockwise turns. Angles that specify an initial and final side and a direction of turn are called **directed angles.** Some examples are shown in Figure 9.12, where the arrows on the circular arcs indicate the direction of turn. Notice that an angle measure of −90° could also be assigned the measure +270°.

**FIGURE 9.12**

Directed angles, measured positively for counterclockwise turns and negatively for clockwise turns

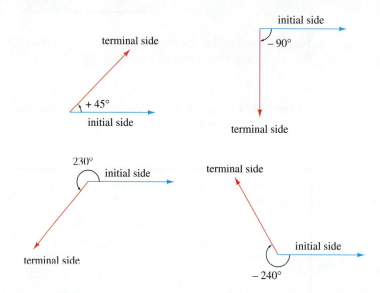

---

**EXAMPLE   9.5    Measuring Directed Angles**

Patty Pathfinder's trip through the woods to Grandmother's house started and ended in an easterly direction, but zigzagged through Wolf Woods to avoid trouble. The first two angles Patty turned through are 45° and −60°, as shown. Use a protractor to measure the three remaining turns. What is the sum of all five directed angles? Explain your surprise or lack of surprise.

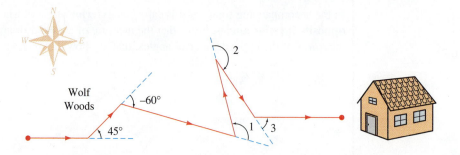

**Solution**   $m(\angle 1) = 120°, m(\angle 2) = -155°$, and $m(\angle 3) = 50°$. The sum of all five directed angles is $45° - 60° + 120° - 155° + 50° = 0°$. This is not surprising, since Patty's path started and stopped in the same direction and her path didn't make any loops.

## Problem Set 9.1

Exercises numbered in red are answered in the back of the text.

## Understanding Concepts

1. Use symbols to name each of the figures shown. If more than one symbol is possible, give all possible names.

    **(a)**

    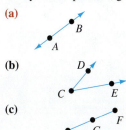

    **(b)**

    **(c)**

    **(d)**

2. The points $E$, $U$, $C$, $L$, $I$, and $D$ are as shown:

    Draw the following figures:

    **(a)** $\overleftrightarrow{EU}$      **(b)** $\overrightarrow{CL}$      **(c)** $\overline{ID}$

3. Trace the 5-by-5 square lattice shown, and draw the line segment $\overline{AB}$:

    Use colored pencils to circle all of the points $C$ of the lattice that make $\angle BAC$

    **(a)** a right angle,      **(b)** an acute angle,

    **(c)** an obtuse angle,      **(d)** a straight angle, and

    **(e)** a zero angle.

4. In the figure shown, $\angle BXD$ is a right angle and $\angle AXE$ is a straight angle:

    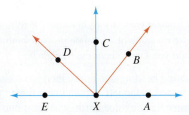

    If $m(\angle BXC) = 45°$ and $m(\angle BXE) = 140°$, explain how you can determine the measures of $\angle AXB$, $\angle CXD$, and $\angle DXE$ without using a protractor.

5. The point $P$ shown in the diagram that follows is the intersection of the two **external** tangent lines to a pair of circles. (See Example 9.1.) The point $Q$ is the intersection of the two **internal** tangent lines to two circles.

    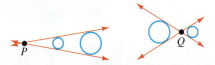

    Draw three circles $C_1$, $C_2$, and $C_3$, all of different radii and with no circle containing or intersecting either of the other circles. Let $P$ be the intersection of the external tangent lines of $C_1$ and $C_2$, and let $Q$ and $R$ be the respective intersections of the internal tangent lines of the pairs of circles $C_2$, $C_3$ and $C_1$, $C_3$. What conclusion is suggested by your drawing? Compare with others. The MHM symbol is because you are experimenting in math.

6. Two intersecting circles determine a line, as shown on the left in the accompanying diagram. Draw three circles, where each circle intersects the other two circles, as in the example shown on the right. Next, draw the three lines determined by each pair of intersecting circles. What conclusion is suggested by your drawing? The MHM symbol is because you are experimenting in math.

    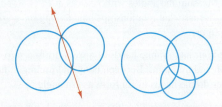

7. Use a compass (or carefully trace around a cup bottom or some other circular object) to draw three circles of the same size through point $A$. Let $B$, $K$, and $L$ be the other points of intersection of pairs of circles. Now draw a fourth circle of the same size as the other three that passes through $B$ and creates points of intersection $M$ and $N$, as shown:

    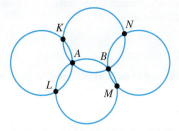

    **(a)** Draw the lines $\overleftrightarrow{KL}$ and $\overleftrightarrow{MN}$. What can you say about these two lines?

    **(b)** Draw the lines $\overleftrightarrow{LM}$ and $\overleftrightarrow{KN}$. What can you say about these two lines?

    **(c)** Draw the line $\overleftrightarrow{AB}$. What connection does it seem to have to any of the lines drawn earlier?

8. Draw a circle with center at point $A$ and a second circle of the same radius with center at point $B$, where the radius is large

enough to cause the circles to intersect at two points $C$ and $D$. Let $M$ be the point of intersection of $\overline{CD}$ and $\overline{AB}$.

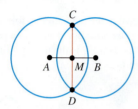

(a) Use a protractor to measure the angles at $M$. What can you say about how $\overline{CD}$ and $\overline{AB}$ intersect?

(b) Use a ruler to measure $\overline{MA}$ and $\overline{MB}$. What can you say about point $M$?

9. Draw two circles, and locate four points on each circle. Draw the segments as shown:

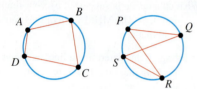

(a) Carefully measure the angles with vertices at $A$, $B$, $C$, and $D$ with a protractor. What relationships do you see on the basis of your measurements?

(b) Measure the angles with vertices at $P$, $Q$, $R$, and $S$, and discuss what relationships hold among the angles in that figure.

10. The hour and minute hands of a clock form a zero angle at noon and midnight. Between noon and midnight, how many times do the hands again form a zero angle?

11. How many degrees does the minute hand of a clock turn through

(a) in 60 minutes?     (b) in 10 minutes?

(c) in 2 minutes?

How many degrees does the hour hand of a clock turn through

(d) in 120 minutes?     (e) in 5 minutes?

12. Find the angle formed by the minute and hour hands of a clock at these times:

(a) four o'clock     (b) seven o'clock

(c) 4:30     (d) 10:20

13. The lines $l$ and $m$ are parallel. Find the measures of the numbered angles shown.

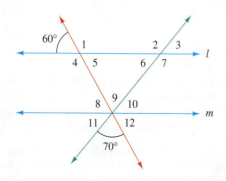

14. Determine the measure of $\angle P$ if $\overrightarrow{AB}$ and $\overrightarrow{CD}$ are parallel.

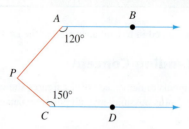

15. Find the measures of the numbered angles in the triangles shown.

(a)

(b)

(c)

(d)

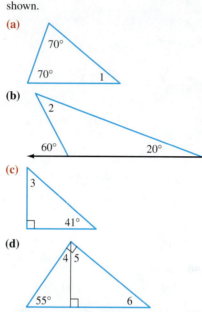

16. Find the measures of the interior angles of the following triangles:

(a)

(b)

(c)

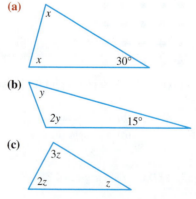

17. (a) Can a triangle have two obtuse angles? Why?

(b) Can a triangle have two right angles? Why?

(c) Suppose no angle of a triangle measures more than 60°. What do you know about the triangle?

18. A hiker started heading due north, then turned to the right 38°, then turned to the left 57°, and next turned to the right 9°. To resume heading due north, what turn must the hiker make?

19. In the figure on the next page, $\angle APC$ and $\angle BPD$ are right angles. Show that $\angle 1 \cong \angle 3$.

**(a)** What does Aja not seem to understand about naming lines (and probably rays and line segments)?

**(b)** How would you guide her in correctly naming lines, rays, and line segments?

**20.** Let $\overleftrightarrow{PQ} \parallel \overline{AB}$ and $\overleftrightarrow{RQ} \parallel \overline{AC}$. Find the measures of $\angle 1, \angle 2, \ldots, \angle 8$. Explain how you found your answers.

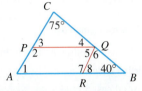

## Teaching Concepts

**21.** Youngsters (and college students, too!) often learn geometric concepts best when working with common three-dimensional objects—say, a cardboard shoebox. The corners of a box model points, and each edge of the box represents a line segment. Additional lines can be drawn on the box with a ruler. Create a lesson that investigates several of the concepts of this section, using a shoebox as a manipulative. Do you see some congruent segments? some right angles? and so on.

**22. Treasure Hunt.** Create a treasure hunt game in which groups of children are given starting points and directions in the classroom. Each group uses protractors and rulers to follow directions that, when accurately carried out, will lead them to "treasures" hidden throughout the room. For example, the directions might start, "Begin at point $A$ facing the front of the room. Turn 40° and go 8 feet to arrive at point $B$. Turn $-120°$ and go 20 feet to . . . ." In particular, show a diagram of a classroom, a starting point, and a route leading to the location $T$ of the hidden treasure. Give the corresponding directions for the route.

**23.** Children frequently have difficulty understanding the difference between two segments being equal and two segments being congruent. What problem would you give your class to show the students the difference between the two concepts?

**24.** Children have difficulty understanding the difference between two angles being equal and two angles being congruent. What problem would you give your class to show the students the difference between the two concepts?

## Responding to Students

**25.** Larisa, a second grader, is asked whether the following segments drawn on a page are parallel:

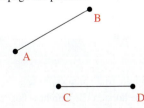

After a brief pause, she says, "Yes, they are because they don't meet." How would you respond to Larisa?

**26.** Aja's teacher asked her to name the line shown. She answered the question by naming it line ABCDEF.

**27.** Sebastian was given the following problem on his math homework last night: "Which of the following shapes does not have a right angle? Explain your answer."

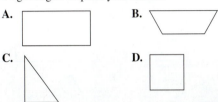

His answer was "(c) because it was not a quadrilateral."

**(a)** What incorrect statement did Sebastian make about quadrilaterals?

**(b)** How would you help guide him to the correct answer?

## Thinking Critically

**28.** Five lines are drawn in the plane.

**(a)** What is the smallest number of points of intersection of the five lines?

**(b)** What is the largest number of points of intersection?

**(c)** If $m$ is an integer between the largest and smallest number of intersection points, can you arrange the lines to have $m$ points of intersection? The MHM symbol is attached to this problem because the answer depends on $m$. You are being asked to decide which values of $m$ have such an arrangement and which don't.

**29.** Three noncollinear points determine three lines, as was shown in Figure 9.1.

**(a)** How many lines are determined by four points, no three of which are collinear?

**(b)** How many lines are determined by five points, no three of which are collinear?

**(c)** How many lines are determined by $n$ points? Assume that no three points are collinear.

**30.** The arrangement of five points shown here has two lines that each pass through three of the points:

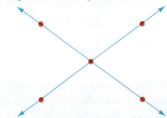

**(a)** Find an arrangement of six points that has four lines that each pass through three of your six points.

**(b)** Find an arrangement of seven points that has six lines that each pass through three of your seven points.

**31.** Suppose that a large triangle is drawn and a pencil is placed along an edge. What property of triangles is illustrated by the sequence A through H of slides and turns shown below? Explain in a carefully worded paragraph.

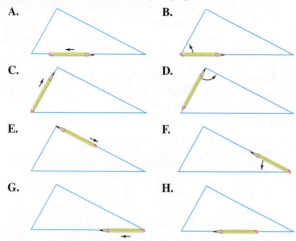

**32.** Use a ruler to draw a large four-sided polygon (a *quadrilateral*) such as the one shown here. Starting with a pencil laid along one side of the quadrilateral, slide the pencil to a corner, rotate it to the next side, slide the pencil to the next corner, and so on. (See problem 31.)

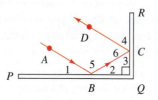

**(a)** What direction will the pencil point to when it returns to the initial side? What does this activity say about the sum of the measures of the angles at the four corners of a quadrilateral?

**(b)** Draw a diagonal across the quadrilateral to form two triangles. What does the sum of angle measures in the triangles tell you about the sum of angle measures in the quadrilateral?

**(c)** Cut the quadrilateral out with scissors and rip off the four corners. What angle can be covered with the four pieces?

**33.** The incident (incoming) and reflected (outgoing) rays of a light beam make congruent angles with a flat mirror:

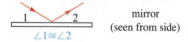

mirror
(seen from side)

Suppose two mirrors are perpendicular to one another. Show that, after the second reflection, the outgoing ray is parallel to the incoming ray. (*Hint:* Show that $\angle 5$ and $\angle 6$ are supplementary. Why does this imply that the rays are parallel?)

## Making Connections

**34.** Spirals, in two directions, create the seed pattern in the head of the sunflower shown in the picture gallery of plane figures in this section. Carefully count the number of spirals in each direction. Have you encountered these two numbers before? They belong to a famous sequence of numbers.

**35.** Why do the hands on a clock turn in the direction we call "clockwise"? It will help to think of the type of clock first used and where it originated.

**36.** An explorer made the following trip from base camp:

First leg: north 2 miles.

Second leg: southeast 5 miles.

Third leg: west 6 miles.

Fourth leg: south 1 mile.

**(a)** Make a scale drawing of the trip.

**(b)** Show the angle the explorer turned through to go from one leg of the journey to the next.

**(c)** Estimate the compass heading and approximate distance the explorer needs to follow to return most directly to base camp.

**37.** A plumb bob (a small weight on a string) suspended from the center of a protractor can be used to measure the angle of elevation of a treetop. If the string crosses the protractor's scale at the angle marked $P$, what is the measure of the angle of elevation?

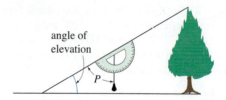

angle of elevation

**38. (a)** How many degrees does the earth turn in one hour?

**(b)** How many degrees does the earth turn in one minute?

**(c)** On a clear night with a full moon, it can be observed that the earth's rotation makes it appear that the moon moves a distance equal to its own diameter in two minutes of time. What angle does a diameter of the moon make as seen from the earth?

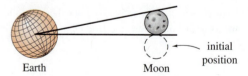

Earth                                              Moon

initial position

**39.** Suppose Polaris (the "pole star") is at an angle of elevation of 37° above the horizon. Explain how this information can be used to estimate your latitude, which is $m(\angle EOP)$ on the accompanying diagram. $N$ is the north pole, $O$ is the earth's center, $E$ is the point on the equator directly south of your position $P$, $H$ is a point on the horizon to the north, and $\overrightarrow{NS_1}$ and $\overrightarrow{PS_2}$ are parallel rays to the distant star Polaris.

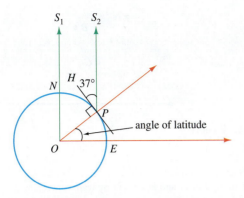

Click and drag a vertex or side of the triangle to manipulate the triangle to assume new shapes. What happens to the sum of the angles?

**(b)** Select the three sides of the triangle. (Click on the sides.) Then use Construct Menu/Point at Midpoint command to construct the midpoints $D$, $E$, and $F$ of the three sides. The preceding figure shows the segment $\overline{AD}$, called a **median** of the triangle. Construct two medians and construct the point $G$ at which your two medians intersect. Use the Measure Menu/Distance command to measure the distances $GA$ and $GD$. Then use the Measure/Calculate . . . command to compute the ratio $GA/GD$. Similarly, measure $GB$ and $GE$ and compute the ratio $GB/GE$. What conjecture can you make? Manipulate the triangle to lend support to your conjecture.

**(c)** Construct the third median of the triangle, and propose a theorem about the medians of any triangle. Manipulate the triangle to lend support to your hypothesis.

**42.** Draw two squares that share a common vertex at $A$. Label the vertices of the squares $ABCD$ and $AB'C'D'$ in counterclockwise order.

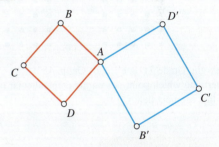

**(a)** Draw the lines $\overleftrightarrow{BB'}$ and $\overleftrightarrow{DD'}$ and let $P$ denote their intersection point. Conjecture how the lines cross.

**(b)** Draw the line $\overleftrightarrow{CC'}$. Discuss how this line crosses the two lines drawn in part (a).

**(c)** Draw the line $\overleftrightarrow{AP'}$. At what angles does it intersect the lines drawn before?

## From State Student Assessments

**43.** (Washington State, Grade 4)
Raul is going to a friend's house. Raul remembers that his friend's house is on a street parallel to Southport. On which street does Raul's friend live?

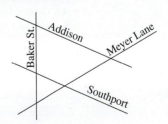

**A.** Addison  **B.** Baker Street
**C.** Meyer Lane

**44.** (Massachusetts, Grade 4)
To answer parts (a) through (d), connect dots on the dot patterns shown below. Always connect the dots to draw closed shapes with STRAIGHT SIDES.

## ▦ Using a Calculator

**40.** Machinists, engineers, astronomers, and others often require angle measurements that are accurate to a fraction of a degree. Sometimes decimal fractions are used, such as 38.24°. It is also common to follow the historic idea of first subdividing a degree into 60 equal parts called **minutes** (from the medieval Latin *pars minuta prima*, meaning "first minute [mĭ-nōōt'] part") and next subdividing a minute into 60 equal parts called **seconds** (*partes minutae secundae*, meaning "second minute part"). For example, 24°13′46″ is read "24 degrees, 13 minutes, and 46 seconds." The following computation uses the facts that

$$1' = \frac{1°}{60} \text{ and } 1'' = \frac{1°}{3600}:$$

$$24°13'46'' = 24° + \left(\frac{13}{60}\right)° + \left(\frac{46}{3600}\right)°$$
$$\doteq (24 + 0.217 + 0.013)° = 24.230°.$$

To convert to degrees–minutes–seconds from a decimal measure:

$$38.24° = 38° + (0.24)(60)' = 38° + 14.4'$$
$$= 38° + 14' + (0.4)(60)''$$
$$= 38°14'24''.$$

Use your calculator to convert the following angle measures from decimal to degrees–minutes–seconds or the reverse:

**(a)** 58° 36′ 45″   **(b)** 141° 50′ 03″
**(c)** 71.32°   **(d)** 0.913°

## 🖱 Using a Computer

**41.** Use geometry software to draw any triangle $ABC$.

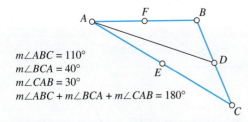

$m\angle ABC = 110°$
$m\angle BCA = 40°$
$m\angle CAB = 30°$
$m\angle ABC + m\angle BCA + m\angle CAB = 180°$

**(a)** Measure the three angles of the triangle. (Use the Measure Menu on *Geometer's Sketchpad*.) Sum the three angle measures, using the Measure Menu/Calculate . . . command.

(a) On the dot pattern labeled Part *a*, draw a shape that has EXACTLY ONE right angle. DRAW A RING around the RIGHT ANGLE.

(b) On the dot pattern labeled Part *b*, draw a shape that has NO right angles.

(c) On the dot pattern labeled Part *c*, draw a shape that has at least ONE acute angle. DRAW A RING around the ACUTE ANGLE.

(d) On the dot pattern labeled Part *d*, draw a shape that has EXACTLY TWO right angles. DRAW A RING around each RIGHT ANGLE.

**Part a** **Part b**

**Part c** **Part d**

45. (Georgia, Grade 7) (See Hands On, p. 450)
Determine which point lies on the perpendicular bisector of the line segment below.

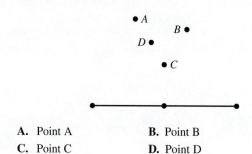

A. Point A     B. Point B
C. Point C     D. Point D

46. (Georgia, Grade 8)
Parallel lines *l* and *m* are cut by transversal *t*.

$m\angle 4 = m\angle 5$
$m\angle 6 = m\angle 7$

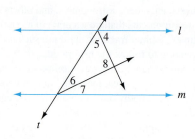

What is the measure of $\angle 8$?

A. 120°     B. 90°
C. 65°     D. 45°

## 9.2 Curves and Polygons in the Plane

### Curves and Regions

A **curve** in the plane can be described informally as a set of points that a pencil can trace without lifting until all points in the set are covered. A more precise definition is required for advanced mathematics, but this intuitive idea of curve meets our present needs. If the pencil never touches a point more than once, then the curve is **simple.** If the pencil is lifted at the same point at which it started tracing the curve, then the curve is **closed.** If the common initial and final point of a closed curve is the only point touched more than once in tracing the curve, then the curve is a **simple closed curve.** We require that a curve have both an initial and a final point, so lines, rays, and angles are *not* curves for us.

Several examples of curves are shown in Figure 9.13.

**FIGURE 9.13**
The classification of curves

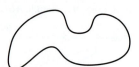

(a) Simple, not closed     (b) Simple, closed

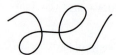

(c) Closed, not simple     (d) Not simple, not closed

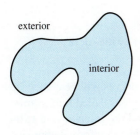

**FIGURE 9.14**

A simple closed curve and its interior and exterior

Any simple closed curve partitions the points of the plane into three disjoint pieces: the curve itself, the **interior,** and the **exterior,** as shown in Figure 9.14. This property of a simple closed curve may seem obvious, but in fact it is an important theorem of mathematics.

**THEOREM**    *Jordan Curve Theorem*

A simple closed plane curve partitions the plane into three disjoint subsets: the curve itself, the interior of the curve, and the exterior of the curve.

The French mathematician Camille Jordan (1838–1922) was the first to recognize that such an "obvious" result needed proof. To see why the theorem is difficult to prove (even Jordan's own proof was incorrect!), try to determine whether the points *G* and *H* are inside or outside the very crinkly, but still simple, closed curve shown in Figure 9.15.

**FIGURE 9.15**

Is *G* in the interior or exterior of this simple closed curve? What about *H*?

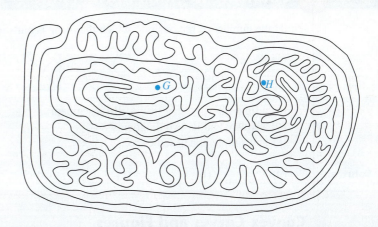

**EXAMPLE  9.6**    **Determining the Interior Points of a Simple Closed Curve in the Plane**

Devise a method to determine whether a given point is in the interior or the exterior of a given simple closed curve.

**Solution**    Think of the curve as a fence. If we jump over the fence, we go from the interior to the exterior of the curve or vice versa. Now draw any ray from the given point.

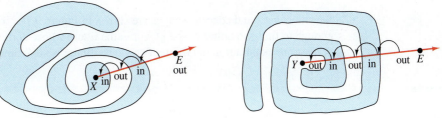

*X* is an interior point                    *Y* is an exterior point

Start at an exterior point *E* on the ray, and see how many times the fence is crossed as you move to the endpoint of the ray. If the curve is crossed an odd number of times to reach the point *X* from the exterior point *E*, then the given point *X* is an interior point. An even number of crossings from *E* to reach a point *Y* means that *Y* is an exterior point. It should now be simple to verify that *G* is exterior and *H* is interior to the curve in Figure 9.15.

We defined informally the "interior" and "exterior" of a simple closed curve. (See Figure 9.14.) We now use those terms to define the idea of **region,** as it will appear often in the chapters that follow.

**DEFINITION** *Regions Defined by a Simple Closed Curve*
The interior and exterior of a simple closed curve are called the **regions defined by the curve.**

Continuing informally, the complement of some system of lines, rays, and curves will be composed of one or more regions. For example, a line partitions the plane into two regions called **half planes.** An angle, if not zero or straight, partitions the plane into two regions called the **interior and exterior of the angle,** as in Figure 9.4 of the previous section. Since we are taking an informal approach to geometry, we will use the word **region** to mean one of the areas defined by a curve and for the area occurring in the examples of the sentences of this paragraph. While it is intuitively clear to children and adults what regions are, to define a region rigorously requires mathematics well beyond the level of this text.

**EXAMPLE 9.7** **Counting Regions in the Plane**

Count the number of regions into which the plane is partitioned by the following shapes:

**(a)** a figure 8       **(b)** a segment       **(c)** two nonintersecting circles
**(d)** a square and its two diagonals       **(e)** a pentagram
**(f)** any simple nonclosed curve

**Solution**     **(a)** 3     **(b)** 1     **(c)** 3     **(d)** 5     **(e)** 7     **(f)** 1

## Convex Curves and Figures

The interior of an angle has the property that the segment between any two interior points does not leave the interior. This means that the interior of an angle is a convex figure according to the following definition:

**DEFINITION** *Convex and Concave Figures*
A figure is **convex** if, and only if, it contains the segment $\overline{PQ}$ for each pair of points $P$ and $Q$ contained in the figure. A figure that is not convex is called **concave.**

Several convex and concave shapes are shown in Figure 9.16. To show that a figure is concave, it is enough to find two points $P$ and $Q$ within the figure whose corresponding line segment $\overline{PQ}$ contains at least one point not in the figure. A concave figure is sometimes called a **nonconvex** figure.

**FIGURE 9.16**
Convex and concave
plane figures

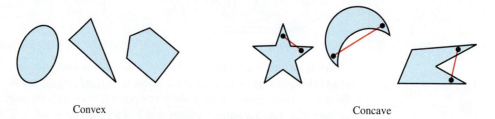

Convex                                               Concave

## Polygonal Curves and Polygons

A curve that consists of a union of finitely many line segments is called a **polygonal curve.** The endpoints of the segments are called **vertices,** and the segments themselves are the **sides** or **edges** of the polygonal curve.

**FIGURE 9.17**
The classification of polygonal curves

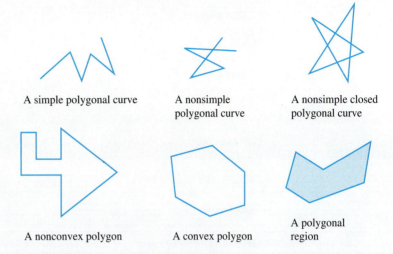

A simple polygonal curve · A nonsimple polygonal curve · A nonsimple closed polygonal curve

A nonconvex polygon · A convex polygon · A polygonal region

Polygons are named according to the number of sides or vertices they have. For example, a polygon of 17 sides is sometimes called a *heptadecagon* (*hepta* = seven, *deca* = 10). With more directness, it can also be called a 17-gon. The common names of polygons are shown in Table 9.1 on the next page.

The rays along two sides with a common vertex determine an **angle of the polygon.** For a convex polygon, the interiors of these angles include the interior of the polygon. The angles are also called **interior angles,** as shown in Figure 9.18. An angle formed by replacing one of these rays with its opposite ray is an **exterior angle** of the polygon. The two exterior angles at a vertex are congruent by the vertical-angles theorem. The interior angle and either of its adjacent exterior angles are supplementary.

**FIGURE 9.18**
Angles in a convex polygon

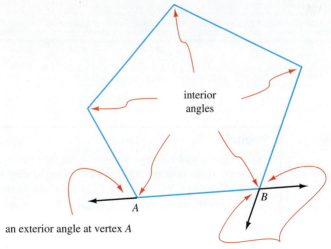

interior angles

an exterior angle at vertex *A*

the two exterior angles at vertex *B*

In the following theorem, we consider the interior angle and *one* of its supplementary exterior angles at each vertex of a convex polygon:

**TABLE 9.1    NAMES OF POLYGONS**

| Polygon | Number of Sides | Example |
|---|---|---|
| Triangle | 3 | |
| Quadrilateral | 4 | |
| Pentagon | 5 | |
| Hexagon | 6 | |
| Heptagon | 7 | |
| Octagon | 8 | |
| Nonagon (or enneagon) | 9 | |
| Decagon | 10 | |
| $n$-gon | $n$ | |

**PROOF**

(a) Imagine a walk completely around a polygon. At each vertex, we must turn through an exterior angle. At the conclusion of the walk we are heading in the same direction as we began, so our total turn is through 360°. If $\angle 1'$, $\angle 2'$, ..., $\angle n'$ denote the exterior angles, then our walk around the polygon shows that $m(\angle 1') + m(\angle 2') + \cdots + m(\angle n') = 360°$.

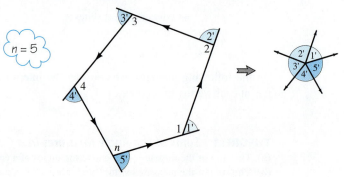

**(b)** Since an interior and exterior angle at a vertex are supplementary, we have the equations $m(\angle 1) = 180° - m(\angle 1')$, $m(\angle 2) = 180° - m(\angle 2'), \ldots, m(\angle n) = 180° - m(\angle n')$. Adding these $n$ equations gives us, by part (a),

$$m(\angle 1) + m(\angle 2) + \cdots + m(\angle n) = n \cdot 180° - [m(\angle 1') + m(\angle 2') + \cdots + m(\angle n')]$$
$$= n \cdot 180° - 360° = (n - 2) \cdot 180°,$$

where we need the result of part (a) in the second equality.

MHM    When we look at the case in which $n = 3$ in part (b) of the theorem, its statement becomes that the sum of the interior angles of a 3-gon is $(n - 2)180 = 180°$. Since a 3-gon is a triangle, the theorem generalizes the "angle sum" theorem from triangles to all convex polygons.

The idea of generalizing is an MHM. Of course, we could look at the situation in a different way. Part (b) of the theorem makes a statement about convex $n$-gons for any $n$. An example of an MHM is to ask ourselves what happens in the case that we really know: triangles ($n = 3$). The theorem is true in that case, of course, since the sum of the interior angles of a triangle is $180°$.

**EXAMPLE 9.8  Finding the Angles in a Pentagonal Arch**

Find the measures $3x$, $8x$, $y$, and $z$ of the interior and exterior angles of the pentagon *PENTA*.

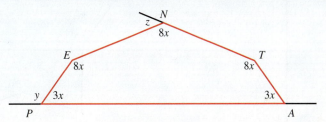

**Solution**    By the theorem just proved, we know that the sum of the measures of the five interior angles is

$$3x + 8x + 8x + 8x + 3x = (5 - 2)180°.$$

That is, $30x = 3 \cdot 180°$, so that $x = (3 \cdot 180°/30) = 18°$. Thus, the interior angles at $P$ and $A$ measure $3 \cdot 18° = 54°$ and at $E$, $N$, and $T$ measure $8 \cdot 18° = 144°$. The measures of the exterior angles are $y = 180° - 54° = 126°$ and $z = 180° - 144° = 36°$.

In a nonconvex polygon, some of the interior angles are reflex angles, with measures larger than $180°$. Nevertheless, it can be proven (see problems 34 and 35 in Problem Set 9.2) that the sum of the measures of the $n$ interior angles is still given by $(n - 2)180°$.

**THEOREM**   *Sum of Interior Angle Measures of a General Polygon*
The sum of the measures of the interior angles of any $n$-gon is $(n - 2)180°$.

An example of a nonconvex heptagon is shown in Figure 9.19.

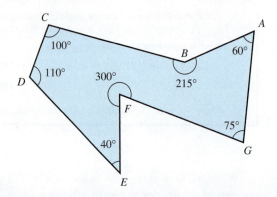

**EXAMPLE 9.9** **Measuring the Angles in a Five-Pointed Star**

The reflex angles at each of the five "inward" points of the star shown have three times the measure of the angles of the "outward" points. What is the measure of the angle at each point of the star?

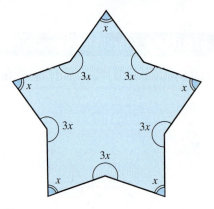

**Solution** The sum of the measures of all 10 interior angles of the star is $5x + 5 \cdot (3x)$, or $20x$. Since the star is a decagon (or 10-gon), the sum must equal $(10 - 2) \cdot 180° = 1440°$. This gives us the equation $20x = 1440°$. Solving for $x$ shows that $x = 1440° \div 20 = 72°$. Thus, each acute interior angle measures $72°$, and each of the reflex angles at the inward points measures $3x = 216°$.

A walk around any closed curve, simple or nonsimple, that returns to the starting point and to the same orientation as the walk began must have turned through some integer multiple of 360°. It is customary to measure turns to the left (counterclockwise) as positive and turns to the right (clockwise) as negative.

**THEOREM** *The Total-Turn Theorem*
The total turn around any closed curve is an integral multiple of 360°.

To help determine the total turn, draw a point $S$ at an arbitrary point along the curve and lay a pencil at that point, with the point of the pencil oriented in the direction of travel. Now trace the curve with the pencil and count the net number of rotations the pencil has made when it returns to its initial position at point $S$. For a polygonal curve, the pencil turns only when it reaches a vertex of the curve.

**EXAMPLE 9.10** **Finding Total Turns**

Find the total turn for each of the following closed curves:

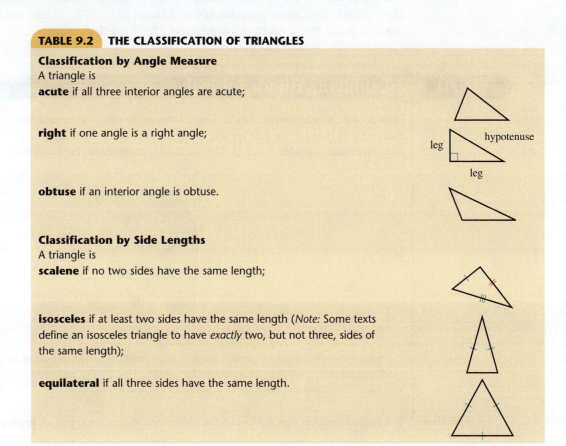

(a)

(b)

(c)

(d)

**Solution**    (a) $-360°$    (b) $0°$    (c) $720°$    (d) $720°$

## Triangles

Triangles are classified by the measures of their angles or sides, as shown in Table 9.2.

**TABLE 9.2    THE CLASSIFICATION OF TRIANGLES**

**Classification by Angle Measure**
A triangle is
**acute** if all three interior angles are acute;

**right** if one angle is a right angle;

leg    hypotenuse

leg

**obtuse** if an interior angle is obtuse.

**Classification by Side Lengths**
A triangle is
**scalene** if no two sides have the same length;

**isosceles** if at least two sides have the same length (*Note:* Some texts
define an isosceles triangle to have *exactly* two, but not three, sides of
the same length);

**equilateral** if all three sides have the same length.

---

**EXAMPLE 9.11 Classifying Triangles**

In the figure shown, there are a number of triangles with vertices at *A*, *B*, *C*, *D*, *E*, and *F*. Classify the triangles according to Table 9.2. Use the corner of an index card to check for right angles, and use a ruler or mark on the edge of an index card to check for congruent sides.

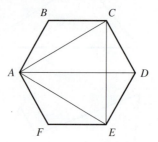

Solution | Acute: △*ACE*; Right: △*ACD* and △*AED*; Obtuse: △*ABC*, △*CDE*, and △*AFE*; Scalene: △*ACD* and △*AED*; Isosceles: △*ABC*, △*CDE*, △*AFE*, and △*ACE*; Equilateral: △*ACE*.

## Quadrilaterals

The four-sided polygons are classified as shown in Table 9.3. This classification allows a parallelogram to be described as a trapezoid; similarly, a square is a rectangle and a rectangle is a parallelogram.

The classification hierarchy is summarized by a Venn diagram. Notice that the squares are the intersection of the rhombus and rectangle loops. Arranging figures in classes that are subsets of one another can be very useful. For example, suppose we wish to show that the points *A*, *B*, *C*, and *D* are the vertices of a square. Step 1 may be to show that one pair of sides is parallel, telling us that *ABCD* is a trapezoid. Step 2 may show that the remaining pair of opposite sides is parallel, and now we know that *ABCD* is a parallelogram. If step 3 shows that *ABCD* is a kite and step 4 shows that ∠*A* is a right angle, then we correctly deduce that *ABCD* is a square.

---

**EXAMPLE 9.12 Exploring Quadrilaterals**

Draw a convex quadrilateral *ABCD*. Use a compass to erect equilateral triangles on each side, alternately pointing to the interior and exterior of the quadrilateral. Two such triangles are shown here, determining points *P* and *Q*. The equilateral triangles on the remaining sides determine points *R* and *S*.

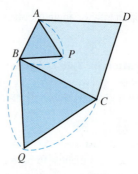

What can you say about quadrilateral *PQRS*? Support your conjecture by drawing another quadrilateral and its system of equilateral triangles. Use a ruler and protractor to measure the lengths of sides and the measure of the angles of *PQRS*.

Solution | You should discover that *PQRS* is a parallelogram; that is, each pair of opposite sides is parallel.

**TABLE 9.3**   **THE CLASSIFICATION OF QUADRILATERALS**

**a.** A **kite** is a quadrilateral with two distinct pairs of congruent adjacent sides. A kite can be either convex or concave.

**b.** A **trapezoid** is a quadrilateral with at least one pair of parallel sides. (*Note:* Some dictionaries and texts require a trapezoid to have *exactly* one pair of parallel sides.)

**c.** An **isosceles trapezoid** is a trapezoid with a pair of congruent angles along one of the parallel sides.

**d.** A **parallelogram** is a quadrilateral in which each pair of opposite sides is parallel.

**e.** A **rhombus** is a parallelogram with all of its sides the same length.

**f.** A **rectangle** is a parallelogram with a right angle.

**g.** A **square** is a rectangle with all sides of equal length.

# Regular Polygons

Polygons that are regular or that exhibit some degrees of symmetry are pleasing to the eye and have special names.

**DEFINITION**   *Equilateral, Equiangular, and Regular Polygons*

A polygon with all of its sides congruent to one another is **equilateral** (that is, "equal sided"). A convex polygon whose interior angles are all congruent is **equiangular** (that is, "equal angled"). A **regular** polygon is a convex polygon that is both equilateral and equiangular.

Some hexagonal examples are shown in Figure 9.20.

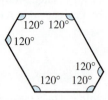

**(b)** An equiangular hexagon

**(a)** An equilateral hexagon

**(c)** A regular hexagon

**FIGURE 9.20**
Hexagons that are equilateral, equiangular, and regular

Since the six congruent interior angles in an equiangular hexagon have measures that add up to $(6 - 2) \cdot 180° = 720°$, each interior angle measures $720°/6 = 120°$. Similarly, the measures of the interior angles of an equiangular $n$-gon add up to $(n - 2) \cdot 180°$, so each of the $n$ congruent interior angles measures $(n - 2) \cdot 180°/n$.

In a regular $n$-gon, any angle with a vertex at the center of a regular polygon and sides containing adjacent vertices of the polygon is called a **central angle** of the polygon:

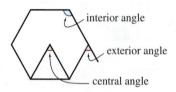

interior angle

exterior angle

central angle

The following formulas give the measures of the exterior, interior, and central angles of a regular polygon:

> **THEOREM**   *Angle Measure in a Regular n-gon*
> In a regular $n$-gon,
> * each interior angle has measure $(n - 2) \cdot 180°/n$;
> * each exterior angle has measure $360°/n$;
> * each central angle has measure $360°/n$.

It is useful to observe that an interior and an exterior angle are supplementary. Thus, the measure of an interior angle is also given by $180° - 360°/n$.

**EXAMPLE 9.13   Working with Angles in Regular $n$-Gons**

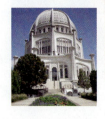

**(a)** The Baha'i House of Worship in Wilmette, Illinois, has the unusual floor plan shown in the accompanying diagram. What are the measures of $\angle ABC$ and $\angle AOB$?

**(b)** Suppose an archeologist found a broken piece of pottery such as that shown on the right. If the angle measures $160°$ and it is assumed that the plate had the form of a regular polygon, how many sides would the complete plate have had?

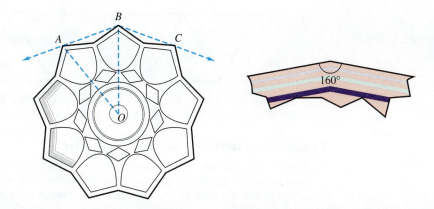

**Solution**

**(a)** $\angle ABC$ is the interior angle of a regular 9-gon and it has measure $(9 - 2) \cdot 180°/9 = 140°$. $\angle AOB$ is a central angle of a regular 9-gon, so its measure is $360°/9 = 40°$.

**(b)** The corresponding exterior angle measures $20°$. Since $20° = 360°/n$, it follows that $n = 360°/20° = 18$. Under the assumptions stated, the plate would have had 18 sides.

## Cooperative Investigation

### From Paper Discs to Polygons

#### Materials Needed

1. Two paper discs per student, each 7 to 8 inches (or 18 to 20 centimeters) in diameter. All discs used in a group should be the same size.
2. Drawing and measuring tools (pencils, protractors, rulers).

#### Directions

Work in groups of four. There are two sets of explorations, each using one paper disc per student.

#### Explorations with the First Paper Disc

1. Make a light pencil mark on the disc that you think estimates the center of the disc. To check how close you are, lightly (do not make a heavy crease) fold the disc in half. Undo your fold and lay the disc out flat. Is your mark along the diameter you have folded? Now fold the disc in half once more in a new direction, and then unfold. Is your mark at the intersection of the two diameters? Clearly mark the true center of your disc and label it *O*.
2. Fold across a chord of the disc so that the folded arc of the circle passes through the center *O*, as shown. Without unfolding the first fold, make a second fold across a chord that has the same endpoint as the first chord and again with the circular arc passing through point *O*. Finally, fold the remaining arc of the circle. Does it also pass through point *O*? What kind of a triangle seems to have been created? Check out your guess by measuring the three sides and the three angles of the triangle. Compare with others in your group.

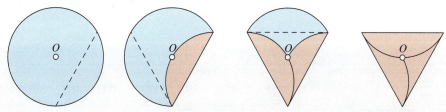

3. Find the midpoints of the sides of your triangle (how can this be done with folding?), and mark them with a pencil. Fold a vertex of your triangle to the midpoint on the opposite side. What polygon have you created? Without unfolding, fold another vertex of a triangle to the marked midpoint on the opposite side. What is the polygon now? Fold the third vertex to the midpoint marked on the opposite side. What is the name of this polygon?

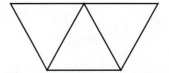 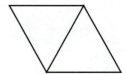 

4. Unfold your disc to return to the large equilateral triangle made in Exploration step 2. Now fold each vertex to the center point *O*. Describe the polygon you have created.

### Explorations with the Second Paper Disc

5. Mark a point well away from the center of the paper disc and label it *H*. Fold two arcs, sharing a common endpoint, so that both arcs pass through point *H*. Next, fold the remaining arc of the disc to form a triangle. Did the third arc you folded also pass through point *H*? Compare with others in your group.

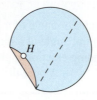   

6. Unfold your triangle, and use a ruler to draw the chord that begins at a vertex of the triangle and passes through point *H*. Similarly, draw the chords through *H* from the other two vertices of the triangle. At what angle does each chord intersect the opposite side of the triangle? Use a protractor to measure the angle, and compare your answer with those of others in your group.

## Problem Set 9.2

Exercises numbered in red are answered in the back of the text.

## Understanding Concepts

1. If the figure shown has the property listed, place a check in the table that follows.

(a)    (b)    (c) 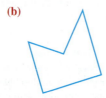   (d)

(e)    (f)    (g)    (h)

(i)    (j)    (k)    (l)

| | (a) | (b) | (c) | (d) | (e) | (f) | (g) | (h) | (i) | (j) | (k) | (l) |
|---|---|---|---|---|---|---|---|---|---|---|---|---|
| **Simple curve** | | | | | | | | | | | | |
| **Closed curve** | | | | | | | | | | | | |
| **Polygonal curve** | | | | | | | | | | | | |
| **Polygon** | | | | | | | | | | | | |

**2.** Draw figures that satisfy the given description.

   **(a)** A nonsimple closed four-sided polygonal curve

   **(b)** A concave pentagon

   **(c)** An equiangular quadrilateral

   **(d)** A convex octagon

**3.** Can a line cross a simple closed plane curve 99 times? Explain why or why not.

**4.** Classify each region as convex or concave.

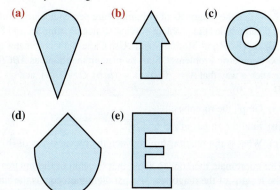

**(a)**   **(b)**   **(c)**

**(d)**   **(e)**

**5.** Imagine stretching a rubber band tightly around each figure shown. Shade the region within the band with a colored pencil. Is the shaded region always convex?

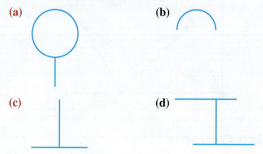

**(a)**   **(b)**

**(c)**   **(d)**

**6.** How many different regions in the plane are determined by these figures?

**(a)**   **(b)**

**(c)**   **(d)**

**7.** Determine the measures of the interior angles of this polygon.

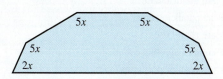

**8.** The following equilateral nonagon (9-gon) can form spiral tiling similar to the one you will see in Figure 11.26 on page 642. Find the measures of all of the interior angles.

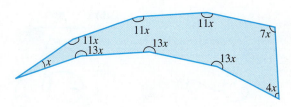

**9.** Calculate the measures of the angles in this concave polygon:

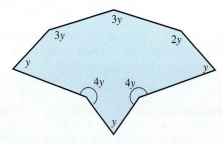

**10.** A **lattice polygon** is formed by a rubber band stretched over the nails of a geoboard. Find the sum of the measures of the interior angles of the following lattice polygons:

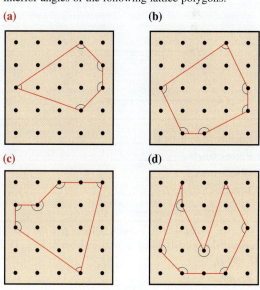

**(a)**   **(b)**

**(c)**   **(d)**

**11.** On squared dot paper, draw lattice polygons (see problem 10) whose interior angles have the given sum of their measures. Place arcs that indicate the interior angles, as in problem 9.

   **(a)** 180°   **(b)** 1080°

   **(c)** 1440°   **(d)** 1800°

**12.** The interior angles of an $n$-gon have an average measure of 175°.

   **(a)** What is $n$?

   **(b)** Suppose the polygon has flexible joints at the vertices. As the polygon is flexed to take on new shapes, what happens to the average measure of the interior angles? Explain your reasoning.

**13.** The interior angles of an $n$-gon have an average measure of 155°. How many sides can the $n$-gon have?

**14.** What is the amount of total turn for the closed curves shown? Assign a positive measure to counter-clockwise turning.

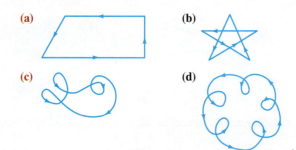

**(a)**  **(b)**

**(c)**  **(d)**

**15.** Suppose you walk north 10 paces, turn left through 24°, walk 10 paces, turn left through 24°, walk 10 paces, and so on.

**(a)** Will you return to your starting point?

**(b)** What is the shape of the path?

**16.** Fill in the missing vertices to give the type of triangle required, choosing vertices from $A, B, C, D, E, F, G$, and $H$. There may be more than one way to answer. Use a ruler and protractor to measure lengths and angles.

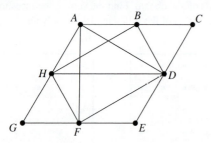

**(a)** Equilateral triangle $D$ ___ ___

**(b)** Right triangle $F$ ___ ___

**(c)** Obtuse triangle $F$ ___ ___

**(d)** Isosceles triangle $E$ ___ ___

**(e)** Acute triangle $H$ ___ ___

**17.** Refer to the figure shown in problem 16 to give the type of quadrilateral required, filling in vertices from $A, B, C, D, E, F, G$, and $H$.

**(a)** Rhombus $A$ ___ ___ ___

**(b)** Rectangle $B$ ___ ___ ___

**(c)** Isosceles trapezoid $A$ ___ ___ ___

**(d)** Nonisosceles trapezoid $G$ ___ ___ ___

**(e)** Kite $E$ ___ ___ ___

**18.** For each regular $n$-gon shown, give the measures of the interior, exterior, and central angles.

**(a)**  **(b)**

**(c)**  **(d)**

**19. (a)** A regular $n$-gon has exterior angles of measure 15°. What is $n$?

**(b)** A regular $n$-gon has interior angles each measuring $172\frac{1}{2}°$. What is $n$?

## Using Algebra in Geometry

**20.** Show that the quadrilateral whose vertices are $A = (0,0)$, $B = (1, \sqrt{3})$, $C = (3, \sqrt{3})$, and $D = (2, 0)$ is a rhombus, and graph $ABCD$.

**21.** Show that the diagonals of a rhombus are perpendicular. (*Hint:* A plan includes the problem-solving strategies from Section 8.3 called "Use Rigid Motions" and "Use Cartesian Coordinates to Do Geometric Problems." Start by placing the rhombus $ABCD$ in such a way that $A = (0,0)$, $B = (a, b)$, $C = (r, s)$, and $D = (c, 0)$.

**(a)** Graph the rhombus.

**(b)** Find the slopes of $\overline{AB}$ and $\overline{BD}$.

**(c)** What is the relationship between the two answers of (b)?

**22.** Use coordinate methods to show that the sum of the squares of the lengths of the diagonals of a parallelogram equals the sum of the squares of the lengths of the sides. (*Hint:* Any parallelogram can be placed in a coordinate system as shown. Let $P$ be the point $(a, b)$ and $R$ the point $(c, 0)$.)

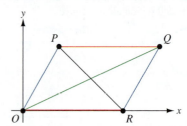

## Teaching Concepts

**23. Pattern-Block Shapes.** Pattern blocks are an especially effective manipulative to explore polygons and angles. The six shapes of pattern blocks are as follows:

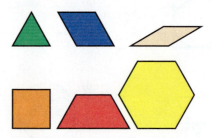

Which shapes

**(a)** are quadrilaterals?

**(b)** are parallelograms?

**(c)** are rhombuses?

**(d)** contain an obtuse angle?

**(e)** are regular polygons?

**24. Pattern-Block Angles.** The interior angles of pattern blocks (see problem 23) can be investigated by creating designs such as the ones shown here:

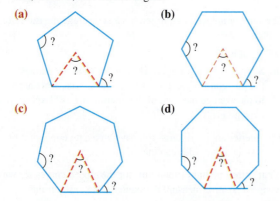

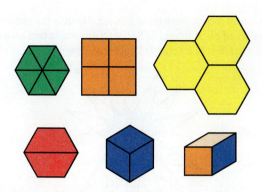

Explain how to use these designs to determine the measures of the interior angles

**(a)** of the equilateral triangle, square, and regular hexagon.

**(b)** of the red trapezoid.

**(c)** of the blue rhombus.

**(d)** of the small rhombus.

## Responding to Students

**25.** Omar has made the following statements about rectangles, squares, rhombuses, and trapezoids:

Rectangles are *always* squares.

Rhombuses are *never* squares.

Trapezoids are *sometimes* squares.

**(a)** What incorrect statements did Omar make about squares?

**(b)** How would you explain to Omar the relationships among rectangles, squares, rhombuses, and trapezoids?

**26.** JaVonte was drawing some shapes during math class. He showed his drawing to his teacher, Mr. Carter, and Mr. Carter asked him to identify the shapes. JaVonte told him that triangles (a) and (b) were right triangles and that triangle (c) was an obtuse triangle. When Mr. Carter asked how he knew that (a) and (b) were right triangles, JaVonte explained that both triangles had a right angle in them, making them right triangles. Then he said that he knew (c) was an obtuse triangle because it was bigger than the other two right triangles, so that made it obtuse.

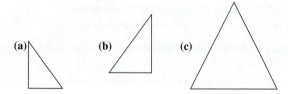

What should Mr. Carter say to JaVonte to correct his misunderstanding of obtuse triangles?

**27.** Samuel knows that each side of a quadrilateral is 1 mm in length and it has four right angles. He tells you that the figure is a rectangle. Is he right or wrong, and how would you explain to him what the figure is?

**28.** Emile, a fourth-grade student, is asked to draw a picture of a figure with four congruent sides. His picture is a square. When asked for other pictures, he changes the length of the side, but the figure is always a square. What discussion would you have with Emile?

**29.** Martine believes that if two rectangles have diagonals that are the same length, then the two rectangles are the same size (that is, have the same width and length.) Is Martine right, and how would you explain your answer to her?

## Thinking Critically

**30.** A goat is tethered at the corner of an 80-foot–by–30-foot rectangular barn. The rope is 50 feet long. Describe the region the goat can reach.

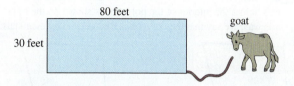

**31. (a)** A boat *B* is anchored at point *A*. Describe, in words and a sketch, the region where the boat can drift due to wind and currents.

**(b)** Suppose a second anchor at point *C* has been set, as shown in the next diagram. Describe, in words and a sketch, the region to which the boat is now confined.

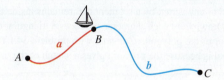

**32.** The following segment $\overline{AB}$ is to be completed to become a side of a triangle *ABC:*

Describe, in words and sketches, the set of points *C* so that

**(a)** $\triangle ABC$ is a right triangle and $\overline{AB}$ is a leg.

**(b)** $\triangle ABC$ is a right triangle and $\overline{AB}$ is a hypotenuse. (*Hint:* For (b), proceed experimentally, using the corner of a sheet of paper as a right angle.)

**(c)** $\triangle ABC$ is an acute triangle.

**(d)** $\triangle ABC$ is an obtuse triangle.

**33.** If an interior angle of a polygon has measure *m*, then $360° - m$ is called the measure of the **conjugate angle** at that vertex. Find a formula that gives the sum of the measures of the conjugate angles of an *n*-gon, and give a justification for your formula. As an example, the measures of the conjugate angles in this pentagon add up to 1260°:

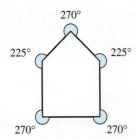

270°

225°    225°

270°    270°

**34.** The heptagonal region shown on the left has been broken into
**MHM** five triangular regions by drawing four nonintersecting diagonals across the interior of the polygon, as shown on the right. In this way, we say that the polygon is triangulated by diagonals.

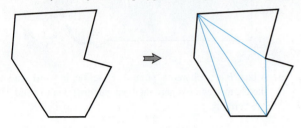

**(a)** Investigate how many diagonals are required to triangulate any *n*-gon.

**(b)** How many triangles are in any triangulation of an *n*-gon by diagonals?

**(c)** Explain how a triangulation by diagonals can give a new derivation of the formula $(n - 2) \cdot 180°$ for the sum of the measures of the interior angles of any *n*-gon.

**35.** The polygon shown contains a point *S* in its interior that can be
**MHM** joined to any vertex by a segment that remains inside the polygon. Drawing all such segments produces a triangulation of the interior of the polygon. (Compare with problem 34.) The MHM symbol is because the problem gives a sketch of the proof.

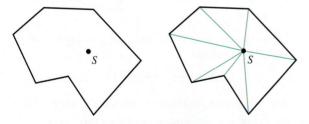

If an *n*-gon contains such a point *S*, explain how the corresponding triangulation can be used to derive the $(n - 2) \cdot 180°$ formula for the sum of interior angle measures.

**36. (a)** Find the sum of the angle measures in the five-pointed star shown on the left. Explain how the total-turn theorem can be used to obtain your answer.

**(b)** What is the measure of the angle at each point of the pentagram shown on the right?

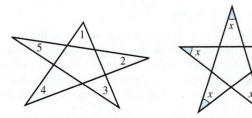

**37.** The wall mosaic from the Alhambra shown in the picture gallery of plane figures in Section 9.1 contains two nested stars, each with 16 outward points, as shown here:

**(a)** What is the measure of each angle at the points of the tan outer star?

**(b)** What is the measure of each angle at three points of the blue inner star? (*Hint:* The inner star is really two 8-pointed stars.)

**38.** What is the largest number of regions you can form with a system of 10 circles?

**39.** Regions can be formed in a circle by drawing chords, no
**MHM** three of which are concurrent. If *C* chords are drawn and they intersect in *I* points, determine a formula for the number of pieces *P* (that is, the number of regions) that are formed inside the circle. The MHM symbol is because you are forming a conjecture.

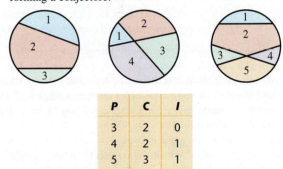

| *P* | *C* | *I* |
|-----|-----|-----|
| 3 | 2 | 0 |
| 4 | 2 | 1 |
| 5 | 3 | 1 |

**40.** Let *ABCD* be a parallelogram.

**(a)** Prove that $\angle A$ and $\angle B$ are supplementary.

**(b)** Prove that $\angle A \cong \angle C$ and $\angle B \cong \angle D$.

**41.** Let *PQRS* be a convex quadrilateral for which $\angle P \cong \angle R$ and $\angle Q \cong \angle S$.

**(a)** Prove that $\angle P$ and $\angle Q$ are supplementary.

**(b)** Prove that *PQRS* is a parallelogram.

## Thinking Cooperatively

**42.** Work in pairs, with one partner using a black pencil and the other partner a red pencil. Each partner draws a closed curve on his or her own clean sheet of paper. The papers are exchanged, and each partner draws a second closed curve. The newly drawn curve should cross the previously drawn curve several times. However, it cannot pass through an intersection of the curve first drawn, nor can it pass through a point of intersection of the previously drawn curve and itself a second time. Circle the points where the red and black curves cross one another.

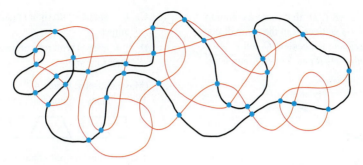

The example shows 32 points at which the red and black curves cross one another.

**(a)** Count the number of crossing points of the red and black curves that are circled. Compare your number with the number of crossing points counted by other partners, and redo the drawing and counting to gather more evidence. What kinds of numbers seem to occur? What kinds of numbers apparently never occur?

Using fresh sheets of paper, draw new closed curves. The curves will partition the plane into regions. Using the same pencil, show that each region can either be shaded or left blank to create a pattern so that regions which share a border have opposite shading. Regions that share only a point are allowed to have the same shading.

**(b)** Trade papers and draw a second closed curve of the opposite color, as done for part (a). Is your result discovered from part (a) now more obvious? Discuss and explain.

**43.** Work in pairs, with one partner using a black pencil and the other partner a red pencil. Each partner draws a *simple* closed curve on his or her own clean sheet of paper. The papers are exchanged, and a second simple closed curve is drawn. The newly drawn curve should cross the previously drawn curve several times. At each intersection point, the newly drawn curve must cross from the inside to the outside of the previously drawn curve or vice versa. (It cannot just touch and turn away.) Each partner then classifies and marks each region of the plane by its type:

✓ : Interior to both curves
× : Exterior to both curves
□ : Interior to black curve and exterior to red curve
■ : Interior to red curve and exterior to black curve

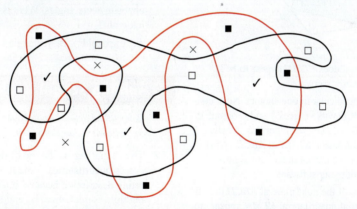

Count the number of regions of each of the four types. Compare your counts with the values obtained by other partners, and draw several fresh examples to provide additional data. What connections do you see among the numbers of regions of each type in any crossing pattern created by two simple closed curves? Make a conjecture, and create additional examples to investigate your conjecture.

---

## Making Connections

**44.** Access to underground utility cables, water pipes, and storm drains is usually provided by circular holes covered by heavy metal circular covers. What unsafe condition would be present if a square shape were used instead of the circular one?

**45.** The valve stems on fire hydrants are usually triangular or pentagonal. Fire trucks carry a special wrench with a triangular or pentagonal hole that fits over the valve stem.

**(a)** Why are squares and regular hexagons not used? (*Hint:* What is the shape of the jaws of ordinary adjustable wrenches?)

**(b)** Why are squares and regular hexagons the standard shape found in bolt heads and nuts?

## Using a Computer

Use geometry software for these problems. For example, see Appendix B.

**46.** Draw two squares *ABCD* and *AB'C'D'* that share a common vertex at *A*. The labeling of the vertices is in the same direction (say, counterclockwise) about the centers *Q* and *E*. Construct the respective midpoints *R* and *S* of $\overline{BD'}$ and $\overline{B'D}$.

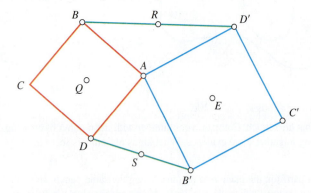

(a) What conclusion can you make about the quadrilateral *SQRE*?

(b) Does it make any difference if the squares overlap?

**47.** Construct a general quadrilateral *ABCD* and the midpoints *K*, *L*, *M*, and *N* of its sides. The quadrilateral *KLMN* is called the **medial quadrilateral** of *ABCD*.

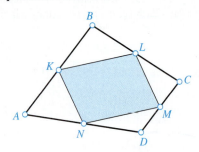

(a) What type of quadrilateral does *KLMN* appear to be? Explore with your geometry software.

(b) Construct two lines perpendicular to one another. Next, construct a quadrilateral *ABCD* with vertices *A* and *C* on one of your lines and vertices *B* and *D* on the other line. Finally, construct the medial quadrilateral *KLMN* of *ABCD*. What type of quadrilateral does the medial quadrilateral now appear to be? Explore with your software.

(c) Drag one of the vertices of the quadrilateral *ABCD* drawn in part (b) until the medial quadrilateral *KLMN* appears to be a square. What type of quadrilateral does *ABCD* appear to be? Explore with your software.

## From State Student Assessments

**48.** (Massachusetts, Grade 4)
What rule did Ray use to sort the shapes below into two groups?

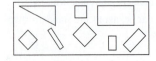    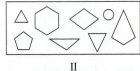

|      I      |      II      |

**A.** I = three sides, II = four sides

**B.** I = big shapes, II = small shapes

**C.** I = shapes with right angles, II = shapes without right angles

**D.** I = shapes with four or, more angles, II = shapes with less than four angles

**49.** (Massachusetts, Grade 4)
These shapes are quadrilaterals.

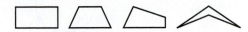

These shapes are not quadrilaterals.

(a) Write a complete definition for a quadrilateral. Be sure to tell all the important ideas about what makes a quadrilateral.

(b) This is a rhombus:

A rhombus is a special kind of quadrilateral. Explain what makes it different from other quadrilaterals.

**50.** (Georgia, Grade 4)
Which quadrilateral has exactly one pair of parallel sides?

**A.** square    **B.** rectangle    **C.** rhombus    **D.** trapezoid

**51.** (Georgia, Grade 4)
A given parallelogram has 4 congruent sides and one pair of opposite acute angles. What is the correct name for this parallelogram?

**A.** trapezoid    **B.** rectangle    **C.** rhombus    **D.** square

## Examining School Book Pages

*Refer to the School Book Pages provided on page 489 to answer the following questions.*

**52.** The banner across the top of these School Book Pages discusses quadrilaterals at the level of third graders. It is an interesting description because it allows us to look at definitions, multiple correct answers, and a curriculum issue.

(a) Compare the definitions in these School Book Pages with the definition of the same concepts in our text. (See Table 9.3.) Is any one of the five classifications from the School Book Pages different from what our text says? Can there be two contradicting definitions in mathematics?

(b) Give two examples of quadrilaterals that have more than one special name.

(c) Note that quadrilaterals are included in the third-grade curriculum. Are you surprised? When were you, as a child, first introduced to quadrilaterals or surfaces? (Curricula change over the years!)

**53.** Construct an example similar to problem 19 of the School Book Pages but with a different property of the special quadrilateral than length of opposite sides.

# Quadrilaterals

*See "Examining School Book Pages" on page 488 for questions related to the pages shown below.*

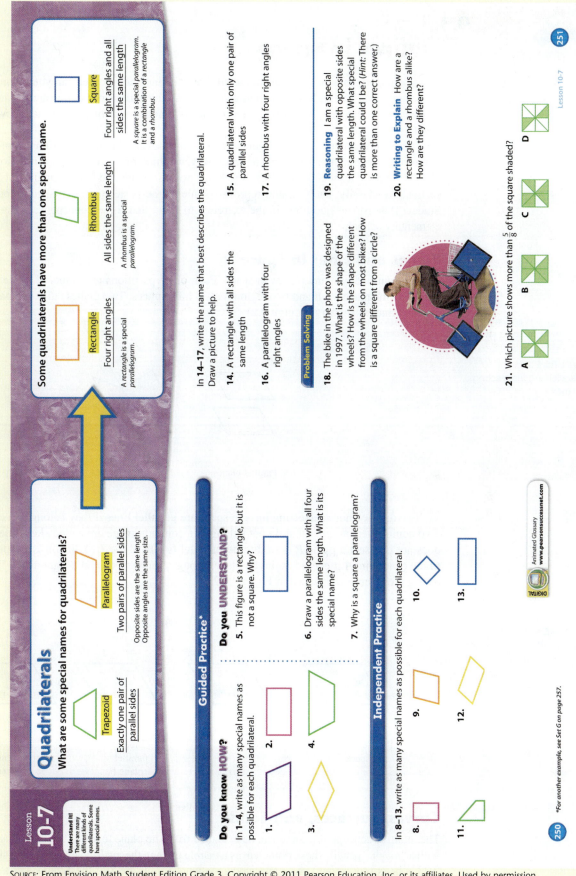

## Lesson 10-7

**Understand It!**
There are many different kinds of quadrilaterals. Some have special names.

### Quadrilaterals

**What are some special names for quadrilaterals?**

**Trapezoid**
Exactly one pair of parallel sides

**Parallelogram**
Two pairs of parallel sides
Opposite sides are the same length. Opposite angles are the same size.

Some quadrilaterals have more than one special name.

**Rectangle**
Four right angles
A *rectangle* is a special *parallelogram.*

**Rhombus**
All sides the same length
A *rhombus* is a special *parallelogram.*

**Square**
Four right angles and all sides the same length
A *square* is a special *parallelogram.* It is a combination of a *rectangle* and a *rhombus.*

### Guided Practice*

**Do you know HOW?**

In 1–4, write as many special names as possible for each quadrilateral.

1.
2.
3.
4.

**Do you UNDERSTAND?**

5. This figure is a rectangle, but it is not a square. Why?

6. Draw a parallelogram with all four sides the same length. What is its special name?

7. Why is a square a parallelogram?

### Independent Practice

In 8–13, write as many special names as possible for each quadrilateral.

8.
9.
10.
11.
12.
13.

*For another example, see Set G on page 257.

**250**

---

In 14–17, write the name that best describes the quadrilateral. Draw a picture to help.

14. A rectangle with all sides the same length

15. A quadrilateral with only one pair of parallel sides

16. A parallelogram with four right angles

17. A rhombus with four right angles

**Problem Solving**

18. The bike in the photo was designed in 1997. What is the shape of the wheels? How is the shape different from the wheels on most bikes? How is a square different from a circle?

19. **Reasoning** I am a special quadrilateral with opposite sides the same length. What special quadrilateral could I be? (*Hint:* There is more than one correct answer.)

20. **Writing to Explain** How are a rectangle and a rhombus alike? How are they different?

21. Which picture shows more than $\frac{5}{8}$ of the square shaded?

A
B
C
D

Lesson 10-7

**251**

Animated Glossary
www.pearsonsuccessnet.com
DIGITAL

---

**9.3**

# Figures in Space

As students, you may not have encountered three-dimensional geometry in your elementary or middle school days. The inclusion of solid geometry and the notions of volume and surface area in K–5 education, for example, is relatively recent and so is now a part of content math courses for future teachers.

The picture gallery of space figures below shows several interesting examples of shapes whose points do not belong to a single plane. Intuitively, we think of space as three dimensional. For example, the shape of a shoebox requires us to know not just width and length, but height as well. In this section, we classify, analyze, and represent some of the basic figures in space. Look at the State Student Assessment questions in the exercises to show that these concepts really are presented in elementary school.

## Planes and Lines in Space

There are infinitely many planes in space. Each plane partitions the points of space into three disjoint sets: the plane itself and two regions called **half-spaces.** Two planes either are **parallel** or intersect in a line, as shown in Figure 9.21.

**FIGURE 9.21**

Parallel and intersecting planes

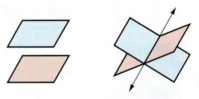

Parallel planes          Intersecting planes

Two distinct, nonintersecting lines in space are **parallel lines** if they belong to a common plane. Two nonintersecting lines that do not belong to a common plane are called **skew lines.** A line $l$ that does not intersect a plane $P$ is said to be **parallel to the plane** $P$. A line $m$ is **perpendicular to a plane** $Q$ at point $A$ if every line in the plane through $A$ intersects $m$ at a right angle. Diagrams illustrating these terms are shown in Figure 9.22.

**FIGURE 9.22**

Lines and planes in space

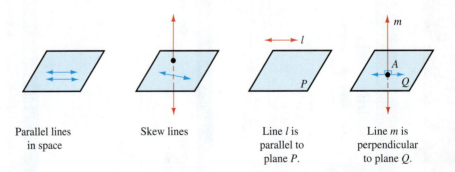

Parallel lines      Skew lines      Line $l$ is          Line $m$ is
in space                            parallel to         perpendicular
                                    plane $P$.          to plane $Q$.

## Curves, Surfaces, and Solids

The intuitive concept of a curve can be extended from the plane to space by imagining figures drawn with a "magic" pencil whose point leaves a visible trace in the air. Two examples are shown in Figure 9.23: a helix (corkscrew) and a space octagon whose sides are 8 of the 12 edges of a cube. Many of the definitions in the remainder of this section should remind you of similar figures in the plane.

**FIGURE 9.23**
Two curves in space

Helix    Space octagon (blue)

A Picture Gallery of Space Figures

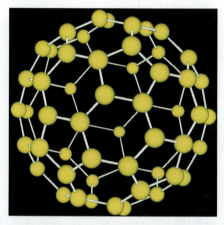

A buckyball (named for Buckminster Fuller),
the third form of pure carbon

Leonardo da Vinci's drawings of an icosahedron and a dodecahedron for
Fra Luca Pacioli's *Di Divina Proportione*

A seashell

A partial filling of space by truncated octahedra

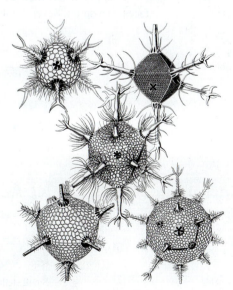

Skeletons of microscopic radiolaria

A **sphere** is the set of points in space at a constant distance from a single point called the **center.** A sphere partitions the remaining points of space into two disjoint regions, namely, the points inside the sphere and the points outside the sphere. Any surface without holes and that encloses a hollow region—its interior—is called a **simple closed surface.** An easy check to see if a figure is a simple closed surface is to imagine what shape it would take if it were made of stretchy rubber. If it can be "blown up" into a sphere, then it is a simple closed surface.

The union of all points on a simple closed surface and all points in its interior forms a space figure called a **solid.** For example, the shell of a hardboiled egg can be viewed, overlooking its thickness, as a simple closed surface; the shell, together with the white and yolk of the egg, forms a solid.

A simple closed surface is **convex** if the line segment that joins any two of its points contains no point that is in the region exterior to the surface; that is, the solid bounded by the surface is a convex set in space. The sphere, soup can, and box shown in Figure 9.24 are all convex. The potato skin surface shown in the figure is not convex, however, since it is possible to find two points on this surface for which the line segment connecting them contains points in the exterior region.

**FIGURE 9.24**
(a), (b), (c), and (d) are simple closed surfaces; (e) is a nonclosed surface; and (f) is closed, but not simple

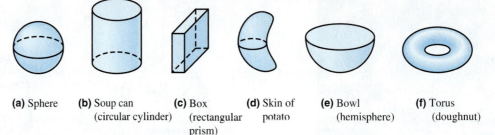

**(a)** Sphere  **(b)** Soup can (circular cylinder)  **(c)** Box (rectangular prism)  **(d)** Skin of potato  **(e)** Bowl (hemisphere)  **(f)** Torus (doughnut)

## Polyhedra

Joining plane polygonal regions from edge to edge forms a simple closed surface called a **polyhedron.** The name comes from *poly*, meaning "many," and *hedron* meaning "face." Polyhedra play the same role in three dimensions that polygons play in two dimensions.

> **DEFINITION**   *Polyhedron*
>
> A **polyhedron** is a simple closed surface formed from planar polygonal regions. Each polygonal region is called a **face** of the polyhedron. The vertices and edges of the polygonal regions are called the **vertices** and **edges,** respectively, of the polyhedron.

Polyhedra (*polyhedra* is the plural of *polyhedron*) are named according to the number of faces. For example, a **tetrahedron** has four faces, a **pentahedron** has five faces, a **hexahedron** has six faces, and so on. Several polyhedra are pictured in Figure 9.25. The word *truncated* in the name of

**FIGURE 9.25**
Examples of polyhedra

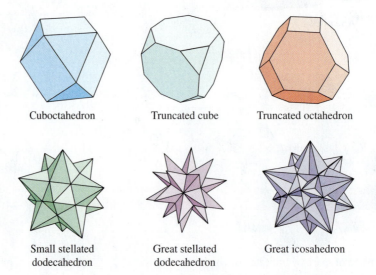

Cuboctahedron   Truncated cube   Truncated octahedron

Small stellated dodecahedron   Great stellated dodecahedron   Great icosahedron a polyhedron means that the polyhedron is formed by removing the corners of another polyhedron. For example, removing the eight corners of a cube creates a truncated cube with six hexagonal faces and eight triangular faces. The word *stellated* in the name of a polyhedron means that pyramids have been erected on the faces of another polyhedron.

The most spectacular polyhedral shapes on earth are the Egyptian and Mayan pyramids. Egyptian pyramids have a square base and four congruent triangular faces that meet at a common vertex. Mayan pyramids have a stepped form. In geometry, a **pyramid** can have any polygonal region as a base.

> **DEFINITION**  *Pyramid*
>
> A **pyramid** is a simple closed surface given by a polygon (called its **base**) and a point not in the plane of the polygon, called its **apex** or **common vertex.** The pyramid is the union of the base with all of the triangular faces that rise from the base edges to the apex.

Examples of pyramids and their names are shown in Figure 9.26.

**FIGURE 9.26**
Pyramids and their names

| Tetrahedron | Quadrilateral pyramid | Pentagonal pyramid | Hexagonal pyramid (concave) |

Another commonly occurring polyhedral shape is a prism, which can be imagined as a box with polygons as bases. More precisely, we have the following definition:

> **DEFINITION**  *Prism*
>
> A **prism** is a simple closed surface that consists of two congruent polygons which are in parallel planes (called the **bases**) and the lateral faces joining the bases, which are parallelograms.

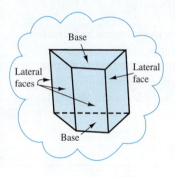

If the lateral faces of a prism are all rectangles, it is a **right prism;** otherwise, it is an **oblique prism** and the edges between the bases are not perpendicular to the plane of the base. Examples of prisms and their names are shown in Figure 9.27.

**FIGURE 9.27**
Right and oblique prisms

A right triangular prism | An oblique triangular prism | A right pentagonal prism (concave) | An oblique pentagonal prism

**EXAMPLE 9.14  Determining Angles and Planes in a Hexagonal Prism**

The bases of the right prism shown are regular hexagonal regions. How many pairs of parallel planes contain the faces of this prism?

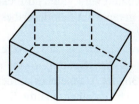

**Solution**    The opposite sides of a regular hexagon are parallel, so there are three pairs of parallel planes containing the opposite lateral faces of the prism. A fourth pair of parallel planes contains the hexagonal bases of the prism. The answer is 4.

## Regular Polyhedra

> **DEFINITION**    *Regular Polyhedron*
>
> A **regular polyhedron** is a polyhedron with these properties:
>
> - The surface is convex.
> - The faces are congruent regular polygonal regions.
> - The same number of faces meet at each vertex of the polyhedron.

The most commonly seen regular polyhedron is the cube: The six faces are congruent squares, and three squares meet at each of the eight vertices. The cube is the only regular polyhedron with square faces, since, if we were to attempt to put four squares about a single vertex, their interior angle measures would add up to 360°. That is, four edge-to-edge squares with a common vertex lie in a common plane and therefore cannot form a "corner" figure of a regular polyhedron.

Similar reasoning with equilateral triangles shows that corner figures in space can be formed with either three, four, or five congruent copies of the triangle. However, a convex corner cannot be formed with six or more equilateral triangles. Likewise, there is just one way to form a corner with congruent regular pentagons, and it is impossible to form a corner figure from regular *n*-gons for any $n \geq 6$. The possible corner figures of regular polyhedra are shown in Figure 9.28.

**FIGURE 9.28**
The five ways to form corner figures with congruent regular polygons

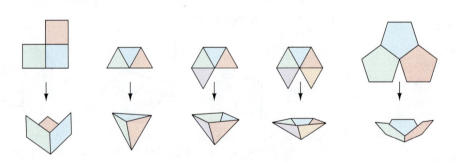

Each of the five corner figures depicted in Figure 9.28 can be completed to form a regular polyhedron. These are shown in Table 9.4 on the next page, which also shows patterns called **nets** used in elementary school. Models of the polyhedra can be made by cutting the net from heavy paper, folding, and gluing. It helps to include flaps on every other outside edge of the net; these are then coated with glue and tucked under the adjoining face, forming a sturdy model. Finding volumes, given a net that describes a solid, is a part of statewide testing. (See the Problem Set of Section 9.4.)

The five regular polyhedra were known to the ancient Greeks. These polyhedra are described in Plato's book *The Republic,* so the shapes are often referred to as the **Platonic solids.** Theaetetas (ca. 415–369 B.C.), a member of the Platonic school, is credited with the first proof that there are no regular polyhedra other than the five known to Plato.

| TABLE 9.4 | THE FIVE REGULAR POLYHEDRA | | |
| --- | --- | --- | --- |
| **Polyhedron Name** | **Face Polygons** | **Net** | **Model** |
| Cube | 6 squares | | |
| Tetrahedron | 4 equilateral triangles | | |
| Octahedron | 8 equilateral triangles | | |
| Icosahedron | 20 equilateral triangles | | |
| Dodecahedron | 12 regular pentagons | | |

## Euler's Formula for Polyhedra

The name given to a polyhedron usually indicates the number of its faces. For example, an octahedron has eight faces. A more complete description of a polyhedron includes the number of its vertices and edges. The following notation will be useful:

$$F = \text{the number of faces of a polyhedron;}$$
$$V = \text{the number of vertices of a polyhedron;}$$
$$E = \text{the number of edges of a polyhedron.}$$

For a regular octahedron, we have $F = 8$, $V = 6$, and $E = 12$.

In 1752, the great Swiss mathematician Leonhard Euler discovered that the number of faces $F$, the number of vertices $V$, and the number of edges $E$ are related to one another. Euler was unaware that he had rediscovered a formula found about 1635 by the French mathematician–philosopher René Descartes. Euler is described in a Highlight from History in the next section.

## Cooperative Investigation

### The Envelope Tetrahedron Model

Diagrams and photos of polyhedra are certainly useful, but physical models that can be seen and touched are much better. The construction of models of polyhedra is a worthwhile classroom activity; useful geometric principles are learned as students create beautiful and interesting shapes. Skeletal models are formed easily from drinking straws joined by thin string run through the straws and tied at the vertices. Paper models, in which a carefully drawn net of the polyhedron is cut, folded, and glued, can be colored in interesting ways.

Here is a quick way to construct a regular tetrahedron from an ordinary envelope:

1. Glue the flap of the envelope down.
2. Fold the envelope in half lengthwise, forming a crease $\overline{AB}$ along the centerline.
3. Fold a corner point C upward from corner D, so that C determines point E on the centerline. Once E is found, flatten out the fold.
4. Fold the envelope straight across at E and then cut the envelope off at the height of E.
5. Make sharp folds along $\overline{DE}$ and $\overline{CE}$.
6. Open up the envelope by pulling the two sides of the envelope at E apart; a regular tetrahedron should appear!

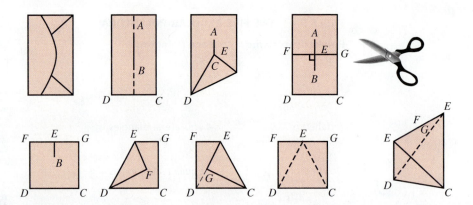

After completing your model, justify the construction procedure.

---

**EXAMPLE  9.15  Discovering Euler's Formula**

Let $V$, $F$, and $E$ denote the respective number of vertices, faces, and edges of a polyhedron. What relationship holds among $V$, $F$, and $E$?

**Solution**

**Understand the Problem**

The numbers $V$, $F$, and $E$ are not independent of one another. The goal is to uncover a formula that relates the three numbers corresponding to *any* polyhedron.

**Devise a Plan**

Formulas are often revealed by seeing a pattern in specific cases. By making a table of values of $V$, $F$, and $E$, we have a better chance to see what this pattern may be. To be confident that the pattern holds for all polyhedra, we need to examine polyhedra of varied kinds.

**Carry Out the Plan**

A pentagonal pyramid, a hexagonal prism, a "house," and a truncated icosahedron are shown. The truncated icosahedron, formed by slicing off the corners of an icosahedron to form pentagons, may look familiar; it is a common pattern on soccer balls. It is also the pattern of a buckyball, as shown in the picture gallery of space figures at the beginning of this section.

  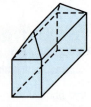 

The following table lists the number of vertices, faces, and edges for these polyhedra, as well as for some of the regular polyhedra depicted in Table 9.4:

| Polyhedron | V | F | E |
|---|---|---|---|
| Pentagonal pyramid | 6 | 6 | 10 |
| Hexagonal prism | 12 | 8 | 18 |
| "House" | 10 | 9 | 17 |
| Cube | 8 | 6 | 12 |
| Tetrahedron | 4 | 4 | 6 |
| Octahedron | 6 | 8 | 12 |
| Truncated icosahedron | 60 | 32 | 90 |

The table reveals that the sum of the number of vertices and faces is 2 more than the number of edges. That is, $V + F = E + 2$.

### Look Back

If any two values of $V$, $F$, and $E$ are known, the remaining value can be found with the use of Euler's formula $V + F = E + 2$. For example, the dodecahedron has $F = 12$ pentagonal faces. The product $5 \cdot 12$ counts *twice* the number of edges, since each edge borders two of the pentagonal faces. Thus, $E = 5 \cdot 12/2 = 30$ for the dodecahedron. Euler's formula can now be used to compute the number of vertices. Solving for $V$, we get $V = E + 2 - F = 30 + 2 - 12 = 20$, so a dodecahedron has 20 vertices.

The evidence gathered in Example 9.15 supports the next theorem. A proof of the theorem is given in Section 9.4.

### THEOREM    *Euler's Formula for Polyhedra*

Let $V$, $F$, and $E$ denote the respective number of vertices, faces, and edges of a polyhedron. Then,

$$V + F = E + 2.$$

## EXAMPLE 9.16  Searching for Polyhedra with Hexagonal Faces

The Epcot Center in Florida is the site of one of the world's largest geodesic domes. The surface of the 165-foot-diameter structure is covered with both hexagons and pentagons. Similarly, as an example from biology, the microscopic frame of the radiolarian (a unicellular planktonic organism) is covered by pentagons and hexagons. These shapes suggest the following question: *Can all the faces of a polyhedron be hexagonal?* Show that this is not possible, even if the hexagons need not all be congruent and are permitted to be irregular.

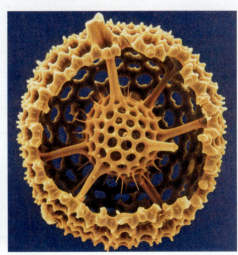

**Solution**

MHM

Suppose, to the contrary, that hexagonal faces can form a polyhedron. As usual, let $F$, $E$, and $V$ denote the number of faces, edges, and vertices. Since each face is bordered by six edges and each edge touches two faces, we obtain the formula $6F = 2E$. Thus, we have $F = \dfrac{2E}{6} = \dfrac{E}{3}$. Moreover, each of the $E$ edges has two ends, so there are $2E$ ends of edges altogether. Since at least three ends of edges meet at each of the $V$ vertices, it follows that $3V \leq 2E$, or, equivalently, $V \leq \dfrac{2E}{3}$.

Adding $V \leq \dfrac{2E}{3}$ to $F = \dfrac{E}{3}$, we get the inequality $V + F \leq \dfrac{2E}{3} + \dfrac{E}{3} = E$. But this inequality contradicts Euler's formula, which tells us that $V + F = E + 2 > E$. We conclude that there is no polyhedron whose faces are all hexagons.

Here, the MHM symbol appears because we used the tool of "proof by contradiction." Introduced in Section 1.6, proof by contradiction, also called indirect proof, is quite a subtle technique.

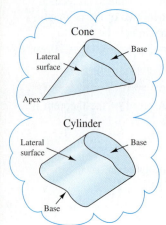

## Cones and Cylinders

Note that a pyramid or prism has a base (or bases) that is a polygon. If a surface has a base that is a region in the plane, rather than being restricted to being a polygon, it is called a **cone**. More formally, we have the following definition:

> **DEFINITION** *Cone*
>
> A **cone** is given by a simple closed curve in the plane (called its **base**) and a point, called its **apex**, which is not in the plane of the curve. A cone is a simple closed surface that is the union of its base and all line segments from the base to its apex. The **lateral surface** of the cone is generated by the line segments from the base to the apex.

A **right circular cone**, an **oblique circular cone**, and a **general cone** are shown in Figure 9.29. The line segment $\overline{AB}$ through the apex $A$ of a cone that intersects the plane of the base perpendicularly at $B$ is called the **altitude** of the cone.

**FIGURE 9.29**
A right circular cone, an oblique circular cone, and a general cone

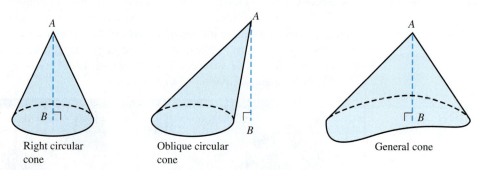

| Right circular cone | Oblique circular cone | General cone |

It will be helpful for you to look at Figure 9.30 for examples of the next concept, **cylinders**, before reading the definition. Cylinders look like cans (tilted or straight)

**FIGURE 9.30**
A right circular cylinder, an oblique circular cylinder, and a general cylinder

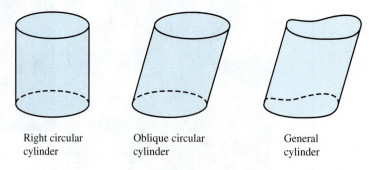

| Right circular cylinder | Oblique circular cylinder | General cylinder |

> **DEFINITION** *Cylinder*
>
> A **cylinder** is a simple closed surface generated by translating the points of a simple closed region in one plane to a parallel plane.

The points joining corresponding points on the curves bounding the bases form the **lateral surface** of the cylinder. If the line segments joining corresponding points in the two bases are perpendicular to the planes of the bases, the cylinder is a **right cylinder.** Cylinders that are not right cylinders are **oblique cylinders.**

## Problem Set 9.3

Exercises numbered in red are answered in the back of the text.

## Understanding Concepts

**1.** Which of the following figures are polyhedra?

(a)    (b)    (c)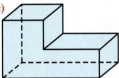

(d) 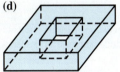   (e)    (f)

**2.** Name each of these surfaces:

(a)    (b)     (c)    (d)

(e) 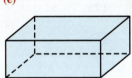   (f)    (g)

**3.** A tetrahedron is shown.

   (a) How many planes contain its faces?

   (b) Name all of the edges.

   (c) Name all of the vertices.

   (d) Name all of the faces.

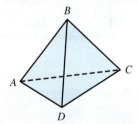

**4.** Draw freehand pictures of the figures that follow, using dashed lines to indicate hidden edges. Don't just copy—transfer the image in your mind to paper.

   (a) Cube   (b) Tetrahedron   (c) Square pyramid

   (d) Pentagonal right prism

   (e) Oblique hexagonal prism

   (f) Octahedron

   (g) Right circular cone

**5.** A cube with vertices $A$, $B$, $C$, $D$, $E$, $F$, $G$, and $H$ is shown in the accompanying figure. Vertices $D$, $E$, $G$, and $H$ are the vertices of a tetrahedron inscribed in the cube.

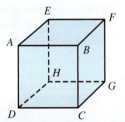

   (a) Trace the cube in one color and then draw the tetrahedron $DEGH$ in a different color.

   (b) Three of the faces of the tetrahedron $DEGH$ are subsets of the faces of the cube. Find a tetrahedron inscribed in the cube that has none of its faces in the planes of the faces of the cube. Sketch your tetrahedron and the surrounding cube.

**6.** The pattern shown on the left folds up to form the cube on the right:

Sketch the letter, *in its correct orientation,* that should appear on each blank face of each of the following cubes, where the same pattern is used:

**(a)**     **(b)**     **(c)**

**7.** The apex of the pyramid shown is at the center of the cube shown by the dashed lines. What is the dihedral angle that each lateral face of the pyramid makes

**(a)** to the square base?

**(b)** to an adjacent lateral face? (*Hint for (b):* It will help to imagine that the cube is filled with six congruent pyramids whose apexes coincide at the cube's center.)

**8.** The figure shown here is a right prism whose bases are regular pentagons.

**(a)** What is the measure of the dihedral angle between each lateral face and a base?

**(b)** What is the measure of the dihedral angle between adjacent lateral faces?

**9.** Sketch a cube. Color the eight vertices either red or blue (or mark *R* or *B* at the vertices) so that no plane through any four vertices of the cube has the same color at all four vertices.

**10.** The numbers in the 2-by-3 grid of squares correspond to the pattern of stacked cubes shown in the **isometric drawing** on the right.

| 3 | 2 | 1 |
| 1 | 1 | 0 |

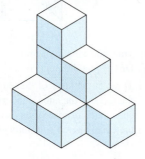

Make an isometric drawing of these patterns:

**(a)**

| 2 | 3 | 2 |
| 2 | 2 | 1 |

**(b)**

| 4 | 2 |
| 3 | 0 |
| 1 | 1 |

**11.** Are any of the regular polyhedra

**(a)** prisms?

**(b)** pyramids?

**12.** Verify Euler's formula for

**(a)** a pyramid with a hexagonal base.

**(b)** a prism with octagonal bases.

**(c)** the regular icosahedron. (*Suggestion:* Modify the counting method used for the regular dodecahedron in the Look Back step of Example 9.15.)

**13.** Use Euler's formula to complete the accompanying table. These four polyhedra are representative of a class of 13 polyhedra discovered by Archimedes.

| Polyhedron | Number of Vertices, Faces, and Edges | | |
| | V | F | E |
|---|---|---|---|
| Truncated tetrahedron | 12 | 8 | — |
| Truncated dodecahedron | — | 32 | 90 |
| Snub cube | 24 | — | 60 |
| Great rhombicosidodecahedron | 120 | 62 | — |

Truncated       Truncated
tetrahedron     dodecahedron

Snub cube           Great
              rhombicosidodecahedron

**14. A double pyramid** (or **dipyramid**) is a polyhedron with triangular faces arranged about a plane polygon and extending both upward to an upper apex and downward to a lower apex:

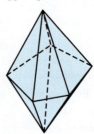

**(a)** Find the number of vertices, edges, and faces for the pentagonal double pyramid shown. Then verify that Euler's formula is satisfied.

**(b)** Repeat part (a), but for the double pyramid built from a polygon with 20 sides.

**15.** Draw nets corresponding to the following polyhedra:

**(a)** A square pyramid with equilateral triangular faces

**(b)** A truncated tetrahedron (See the figure in problem 13.)

**16.** Check whether Euler's formula holds for the figures that follow. If not, explain what assumption required for Euler's formula is not met.

**(a)**    **(b)**   **(c)**

(An octahedron with a square prism hole)

## Teaching Concepts

**17. Shape Search.** Go on a geometry walk; search for interesting three-dimensional shapes around campus, at the grocery store, in local sculptures, in nature, . . . , wherever! Photograph or make accurate drawings of three or four shapes that you find especially interesting, and then write careful descriptions that discuss the properties of your shapes. For example, if your shape is a polyhedron, count its vertices, faces, and edges and verify Euler's formula. If possible, include some shapes that can be contributed to a class collection. For example, many products at the store are packaged in ingeniously shaped boxes.

**18. Make a Shape.** Children (and college students, too) can learn important principles of geometry by constructing their own three-dimensional shapes. Often, just ordinary materials, such as toothpicks and minimarshmallows, suffice, say, to make one of the regular polyhedra or even a figure as complex as a buckyball (the truncated icosahedron). Instructions can be found readily from several interesting sites on the Internet. A well-equipped math lab might also include some commercially manufactured kits that can be used to create fun shapes, such as Polydrons™ or the Zome System. Your challenge: make an interesting shape and write a brief report about its properties and why you find it interesting.

**19. Thinking about Definitions.** Trying to define mathematical ideas by working in groups is very helpful in getting an intuitive feel for what the terms mean. A number of studies show that discussing, arguing, disagreeing, and agreeing about what the definition should mean before you have actually seen it formally helps the learner understand conceptually what the topic is. With that in mind, after looking at some polyhedrals that you bring with you,

**(a)** Ask a group of adults to try to define *vertex, edge, face, prism,* and *pyramid*. Write a short description of both what definitions were arrived at and on what the discussion centered.

**(b)** Ask a group of elementary or middle school children the same questions and write about that experience.

**20. Children's Literature.** Read a work that is accessible to elementary school children and that involves polyhedra. In a short paper, discuss what you read from both its content and its use in the classroom. One such work is *Sir Cumference and the Sword in the Cone* by Cindy Newschwander.

## Responding to Students

**21.** Frank was asked to read the following list of geometric solids:

*Cylinder, cone, and square pyramid.*

His teacher then asked him to come up with at least two ways to show that the square pyramid is different from the other two solids. His answer was the following:

- The square pyramid has no curved surfaces.
- The square pyramid has a point or vertex.

The teacher then redirected him about his second idea and asked Frank to rethink whether a cone has a vertex or not. Frank answered that it does not because it doesn't have flat faces on the side.

**(a)** What would you do next as Frank's teacher?

**(b)** What is Frank misunderstanding about solid geometric shapes?

**22.** Polina is asked to solve the following riddle:

*I have the same number of faces as vertices. What am I?*

Polina said that a triangular pyramid was the correct answer. The teacher agreed and then asked Polina to come up with a few more answers to the riddle. She told Polina to consider a square pyramid. Polina thought and then said that a square pyramid couldn't answer the riddle because it was made of four triangles and one square and, since the shapes weren't the same, it couldn't have the same number of faces as vertices.

**(a)** What is Polina misunderstanding about the definition of faces and possibly vertices in geometric shapes?

**(b)** How could you guide her to see that a square pyramid, pentagonal pyramid, hexagonal pyramid, and so on all are correct answers to the riddle?

**23.** John is shown a picture of a cube. He is asked to tell how many vertices, faces, and edges it has. His answer follows:

Faces: 3

Vertices: 7

Edges: 9

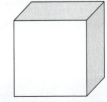

**(a)** Explain what John knows about geometric definitions and is identifying correctly.

**(b)** Identify what John is doing incorrectly.

**(c)** How would you guide him in approaching this problem in the future?

**24.** Tianna is given a set of geometric solids. She correctly identifies the various pyramids but calls all of the prisms in the set rectangular prisms. The set Tianna was given actually contains a triangular prism, a rectangular prism, a pentagonal prism, and a hexagonal prism.

**(a)** What is Tianna thinking when she improperly names the prisms?

**(b)** How would you guide her so that in the future she is able to properly identify geometric solids?

## Thinking Critically

**25.** Let $V$, $E$, and $F$ denote the number of vertices, edges, and faces, respectively, of a polyhedron.

**(a)** Explain why $2E \geq 3F$. (*Hint:* Every face has at least three sides, and every edge borders two faces.)

**(b)** Explain why $2E \geq 3V$. (*Hint:* Every vertex is the endpoint of at least three edges.)

**(c)** Show that every polyhedron has at least six edges. (*Hint:* Add the inequalities of parts (a) and (b), and use Euler's formula.)

**(d)** Use (a) and (b) to prove that no polyhedron can have seven edges. (*Hint:* Use Euler's formula.)

**(e)** Show that there are polyhedra with 6, 8, 9, 10, . . . edges.

**26.** A convex polyhedron with five faces is called a **pentahedron.** Find and sketch two different types of pentahedra. (*Hint:* One is "easy as pie.")

**27.** A polyhedron with six faces is a **hexahedron.** For example, a cube is a hexahedron.

**(a)** Draw a pyramid that is a hexahedron.

**(b)** Draw a double pyramid (see problem 14) that is a hexahedron.

**28.** Suppose a skeletal model of a convex polyhedron is made, where just the edges of the polyhedron are outlined. If the model is viewed in perspective from a position just outside the center of a face, the edges of that face form a bounding polygon inside which the remaining edges are seen. The resulting pattern of edges is called a **Schlegel diagram,** named for the German mathematician Viktor Schlegel, who invented the diagram in 1883. Schlegel diagrams for the cube and dodecahedron are as follows:

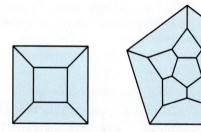

Draw Schlegel diagrams for

**(a)** the tetrahedron          **(b)** the octahedron

**(c)** the icosahedron (*Hint:* Start by drawing a large equilateral triangle, and keep in mind that each vertex must touch five edges.)

**29.** The dihedral angles of the regular polyhedra are given in the following table:

| Regular Polyhedron | Measure of Dihedral Angle (in degrees and minutes) |
| --- | --- |
| Cube | 90° |
| Tetrahedron | 70°32′ |
| Octahedron | 109°28′ |
| Dodecahedron | 116°34′ |
| Icosahedron | 138°11′ |

**(a)** How many tetrahedra can be placed around a common edge without overlap? What is the size of the gap that remains?

**(b)** Why is the cube the only regular polyhedron that will completely fill space?

## Thinking Cooperatively

**30.** Five congruent squares can be joined along their edges to form 12 distinct shapes known as **pentominoes.** Pentominoes were invented by mathematician and electrical engineer Solomon Golomb in 1953 in a talk to the Harvard Mathematics Club. They are named by the letters they somewhat resemble.

Figure for Problem 30

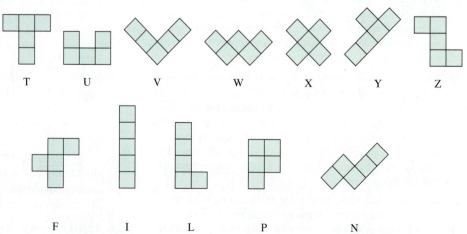

T    U    V    W    X    Y    Z

F    I    L    P    N

*SOURCE:* Golomb, Solomon; Polyominoes. © 1994 Princeton University Press. Reprinted by permission of Princeton University Press.

**(a)** Which of the 12 pentominoes shown can be folded to form a cube-shaped box with an open top?

**(b)** Copy the *T* pentomino onto paper, cut the pattern with scissors, and construct an open-topped cubical box by taping edges together. Now choose a target pentomino (not the *T*, since it's too easy!) and sketch it on the bottom of the box. Then, use scissors to cut the box apart to form the targeted pentomino shape. (*Note:* This activity was created by Marion Walter of the University of Oregon, who makes open cubical boxes from the bottoms of clean milk cartons, discarding the tops.)

**31.** A **hexomino** is formed by joining six congruent squares along their edges. There are 35 different hexominoes in all, including the 5 shown.

**(a)** Hexomino (i) is a net for a cube. Which of the other 4 hexominoes shown can be folded to form a cube?

**(b)** There are 11 hexominoes that can be folded to form a cube. Try to find all 11 shapes. Be careful not to repeat a shape; two congruent shapes may at first appear to be different when one is rotated or flipped over.

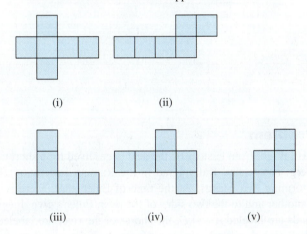

(i)                    (ii)

(iii)            (iv)              (v)

**32.** A net for a square pyramid is shown on the left. A net for a more general quadrilateral pyramid is shown on the right. The dot at *P* in each net locates the point in the plane of the base directly beneath the apex of the pyramid.

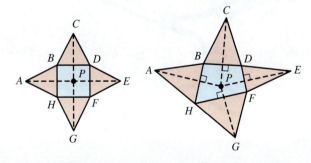

**(a)** Explain why $AB = BC, CD = DE, \ldots, GH = HA$ in the nets and why the dashed lines from *P* are perpendicular to the sides of the base polygon.

**(b)** Draw a convex polygon, a point *P* in its interior, and the rays from *P* that are perpendicular to the sides of the polygon. Choose a point *A* on one of the rays, and use a compass to draw the arc at vertex *B* that constructs point *C* as the intersection of the arc with the next ray. (See the figure.) Continue to draw circular arcs, completing your

pattern. Finally, cut, fold, and tape your pattern to construct your paper pyramid.

## Making Connections

**33.** The round door shown has a problem. What facts of space geometry create a difficulty?

What is important about the placement of door hinges?

**34.** The ancient Greeks divided physical space into five parts: the universe, earth, air, fire, and water. Each of these was associated with one of the five regular polyhedra. Investigate what correspondence was made.

**35.** Biologists and physical scientists frequently become involved with the analysis of shape and form. For example, many viruses have an icosahedral structure, and the crystalline structures of minerals are often polyhedral forms of considerable beauty. An example of a pyrite crystal is shown here:

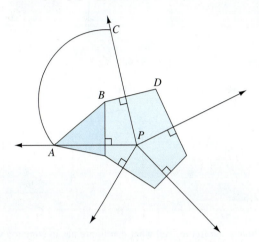

Browse through your school library, and see what three-dimensional shapes are receiving interest and attention. Report on your findings.

## From State Student Assessments

**36.** (Washington State, Grade 4)
Look at the cube below.

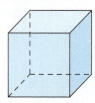

Now look at figures A, B, and C.

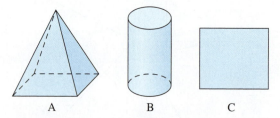

A                    B                    C

Choose one figure. Tell what that figure has in common with the cube. Explain your answer using words, numbers, or pictures. Now choose a different figure. Tell something it has in common with the cube. Explain your answer using words, numbers, or pictures.

**37.** (Illinois, Grade 5)
Angela wants to construct a cylinder from paper shapes. What shapes will she need?

**A.** 2 circles and 1 rectangle

**B.** 4 triangles and 1 square

**C.** 2 triangles and 1 rectangle

**D.** 2 hexagons and 2 rectangles

**E.** 3 circles and 3 triangles

**38.** (Massachusetts, Grade 4)
Which shape CAN be folded to form an OPEN box?

**A.**

**B.**

**C.**

**D.**

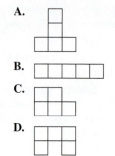

# 9.4

# Networks

## The Königsberg Bridge Problem

Leonhard Euler (1707–1783) (see the Highlight from History on the next page) lived for a short time in the East Prussian city of Königsberg, now called Kaliningrad in the Russian Federation. The Pregel River flows through the city, forming two islands. At the time of Euler, there were seven bridges connecting the islands to one another and to the two sides of the river. Euler's own drawing is reproduced in Figure 9.31. The islands are labeled *A* and *D*, the shores of the river are labeled *B* and *C*, and the bridges are labeled *a*, *b*, *c*, *d*, *e*, *f*, and *g*.

**FIGURE 9.31**
The seven bridges of Königsberg in the early 1700s

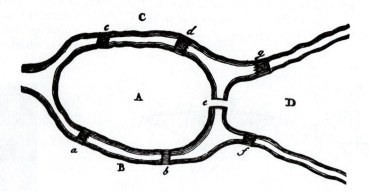

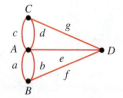

**FIGURE 9.32**
The network corresponding to the Königsberg bridge problem

It was common for Königsbergers to take Sunday walks, and people wondered whether it was possible to walk over all seven bridges without crossing any bridge more than one time. Euler solved the now famous Königsberg bridge problem to illustrate the ideas of what he called "the geometry of position" and what today is called topology. His most important step was to associate each of the four landmasses with a point—*A*, *B*, *C*, or *D*. For each bridge joining one landmass to another, he drew a curve from one point to the corresponding point. Euler's representation of the problem, shown in Figure 9.32, is a system of points and curves known as a **network.** In fact, the subject is so useful that it is in the K–8 curriculum. (See Problem 25.)

Another of the titans of mathematics was the Swiss mathematician Leonhard Euler (pronounced "Oiler"), born in Basel in 1707. Euler is the most prolific mathematician who ever lived, publishing 886 papers and books during his lifetime and posthumously for an average of approximately 800 pages of new mathematics per year. He was dubbed "Analysis Incarnate" by the French academician François Arago, who declared that Euler could produce mathematics without apparent effort "just as men breathe and eagles sustain themselves in the air." Euler went blind in 1766, to the considerable distress of his many friends

and colleagues. However, aware that the condition was coming on, Euler taught

himself to write his complicated formulas on a large slate with his eyes closed. Then with a scribe to write down the explanations of his formulas and with all the facts and formulas of the then known mathematics safely tucked away in his memory, his work continued unabated until his death.

On September 13, 1783, having earlier outlined on his slate the calculation of the orbit of the newly discovered planet Uranus, he called for his grandson to be brought in. While playing with the child he suffered a stroke and, with the words "I die," he quietly passed away.

The distances between points and the precise shapes of the curves joining points are of no importance; what is important is that there are two bridges between *A* and *B*, that there is no bridge connecting *B* and *C*, and so on. Because the network contains all of the problem's relevant information, Euler was able to phrase the Königsberg bridge problem in a new way:

*Without lifting your pencil, can you trace over **all** edges of the network exactly once?*

Euler realized that a deeper understanding of the problem would be gained if the question were asked for general networks, not just the one corresponding to the Königsberg bridges.

---

**DEFINITION** *Network*

A **network** consists of two finite sets:

- a set of **vertices,** represented by a set of points in the plane,

and

- a set of **edges** that join some of the pairs of vertices, represented by joining the corresponding points in the plane by a curve.

---

Some additional examples of networks are shown in Figure 9.33. Any edge of a network must always have its endpoints at vertices of the network, and there must be no other vertex along the edge. In particular, a point at which two edges cross one another is not a vertex of the network. For example, network (2) of Figure 9.33 has just the six vertices shown by the large dots.

**FIGURE 9.33**
Four examples of networks

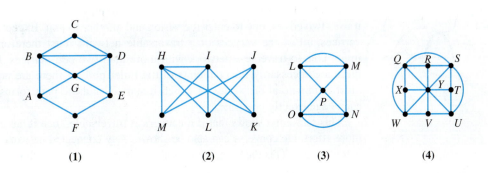

(1)    (2)    (3)    (4)

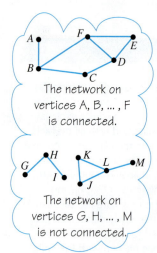

The network on vertices A, B, ... , F is connected.

The network on vertices G, H, ... , M is not connected.

A **path** in a network is a curve traced by following a sequence of edges in the network, where no edge is retraced but vertices can be revisited. If every pair of vertices of a network can be joined by some path, then we say that the network is **connected.** For example, each of the four networks in Figure 9.33 is connected. The Königsberg bridge problem is then equivalent to asking whether there is a path that covers each edge of a network once and only once.

---

**DEFINITION**    *Euler Paths and Traversable Networks*

An **Euler path** in a network is a path that traverses each edge once and only once. A network is **traversable** if, and only if, it has an Euler path.

---

In the next example, you will discover that classifying the vertices of a network as even or odd is most helpful in a search for an Euler path.

---

**DEFINITION**    *Degree, and Even and Odd Vertices*

- The **degree** of a vertex is the number of edges emanating from the vertex.
- A vertex is **odd** if it has odd degree.
- A vertex is **even** if it has even degree.

---

For example, vertices $A$ and $E$ of network (1) of Figure 9.33 are odd, since they have degree 3. Vertices $B$ and $C$ are even, with respective degrees 4 and 2.

## EXAMPLE 9.17    When Is a Network Traversable?

(a) Which of the networks in Figure 9.33 are traversable? Experiment by tracing a path on a sheet of paper laid over the network.

(b) What is the number of odd vertices in each of the networks?

(c) Do you see any connection between the traversability of a network and the number of odd vertices?

**Solution**

(a) Network (1) is traversable; one path is *ABCDEFAGBDGE.*
Network (2) is not traversable.
Network (3) is traversable; one path is *LMNOLMPNOPL.*
Network (4) is not traversable.

(b) Network (1) has 2 odd vertices: $A$ and $E$.
Network (2) has 4 odd vertices: $J$, $K$, $L$, and $M$.
Network (3) has 0 odd vertices.
Network (4) has 6 odd vertices: $Q$, $R$, $S$, $T$, $V$, and $X$.

(c) The networks with 0 or 2 odd vertices are traversable.
The networks with 4 or 6 odd vertices are not traversable.

---

It is a tribute to Euler's genius that he observed that each time a path passes through a vertex, it uses two edges: one to enter the vertex and another to exit. Except for the beginning and ending vertices, all of the vertices of a traversable network must therefore be even vertices, and it is impossible to traverse a network with more than two odd vertices. If there are two odd vertices, these are necessarily the endpoints of the Euler path. If there are no odd vertices, the Euler path must terminate at the vertex at which it started, and the path forms a closed curve passing over each edge exactly one time.

This reasoning shows that if a network is traversable, then it has zero or two odd vertices. With more effort, the converse can also be shown: Any connected network with zero or two odd vertices is traversable. This theorem, which follows, is a celebrated result of Euler.

**THEOREM**   *Euler's Traversability Theorem*
A connected network is traversable if, and only if, it has either no odd vertices or two odd vertices. If it has no odd vertices, any Euler path is a closed curve that ends at the same vertex it started from. If the network has two odd vertices, these vertices are the endpoints of any Euler path.

Since the Königsberg bridge network has four odd vertices, there is no Euler path. Königsbergers must recross some bridge on their walk.

The Königsberg bridge problem and the traversability of networks may appear to have no practical importance, but in fact there are many useful applications to real problems. Here are two examples:

*   What route can a telephone company inspection crew follow to check all of its lines without having to go over any section twice?
*   What route can a street sweeper follow to clean all of the city streets and not have to travel over any blocks that have already been cleaned?

## Counting Vertices, Edges, and Regions in Planar Networks

**DEFINITION**   *Planar Network*
A network is **planar** if it can be drawn in the plane without any intersection points of its edges other than endpoints.

For example, the network with four vertices and edges between each pair of distinct vertices is planar, as shown in Figure 9.34. There are no intersections of the edges. The network with five vertices and edges between each pair of distinct vertices is not planar, since it is impossible to arrange all of the edges so that no two of them intersect. By removing just one edge, you can arrange the remaining nine edges between five vertices to form a planar network. Try it!

**FIGURE 9.34**
A planar and a nonplanar network

Planar              Nonplanar

Any connected planar network partitions the plane into disjoint regions. It is interesting to count the number of vertices $V$, the number of edges $E$, and the number of regions $R$ that correspond to a connected network.

**EXAMPLE 9.18**   **Counting Vertices, Edges, and Regions**

The following connected network has $V = 7$ vertices and $E = 9$ edges and partitions the plane into $R = 4$ regions (the unbounded region is counted):

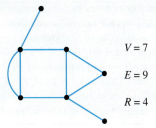

$V = 7$

$E = 9$

$R = 4$

The values 7, 4, and 9 of V, R, and E, respectively, have been entered into the table. Next, count V, R, and E for each of the following networks and enter their values into the table:

| | V | R | E |
|---|---|---|---|
| | 7 | 4 | 9 |
| **(1)** | | | |
| **(2)** | | | |
| **(3)** | | | |

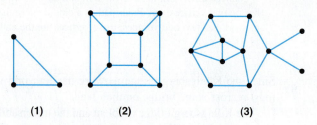

(1)          (2)          (3)

Do you see a pattern? Draw more examples to check your conjecture.

**Solution** | You should discover that the sum of the number of vertices and the number of regions is 2 more than the number of edges.

The exploration in Example 9.18 leads to the conjecture that the formula $V + R = E + 2$ holds for every connected planar network. An example is shown in Figure 9.35.

**FIGURE 9.35**
Euler's formula $V + R = E + 2$ holds for any connected planar network with V vertices, R regions, and E edges.

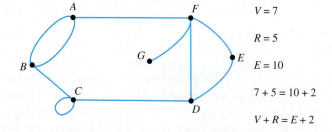

$V = 7$
$R = 5$
$E = 10$
$7 + 5 = 10 + 2$
$V + R = E + 2$

$E_0 = 0, V_0 = 1, R_0 = 1$

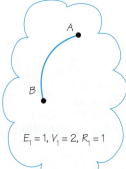

$E_1 = 1, V_1 = 2, R_1 = 1$

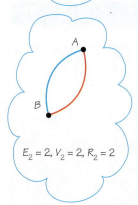

$E_2 = 2, V_2 = 2, R_2 = 2$

**THEOREM**  *Euler's Formula for Connected Planar Networks*

Let V be the number of vertices, R the number of regions, and E the number of edges of a connected planar network. Then V, R, and E satisfy **Euler's formula:**

$$V + R = E + 2.$$

**PROOF (OPTIONAL)**  An informal justification for Euler's formula rests on the idea of beginning with a single point and then appending one edge at a time until any given network is completely drawn. At each step, the new edge must maintain the connectivity of the network.

To keep the discussion concrete, consider drawing the network shown in Figure 9.35. Draw vertex A to start. This minimal network has 1 vertex ($V_0 = 1$), 1 region ($R_0 = 1$), and no edges ($E_0 = 0$). Thus, Euler's formula $V_0 + R_0 = E_0 + 2$ is satisfied, since $1 + 1 = 0 + 2$. Now add the vertex B and one edge joining A with B. The new network increases the number of vertices by $1 (V_1 = V_0 + 1)$, increases the number of edges by $1 (E_1 = E_0 + 1)$, and leaves the number of regions unchanged ($R_1 = R_0$). Adding 1 to each side of the equation $V_0 + R_0 = E_0 + 2$ gives us $(V_0 + 1) + R_0 = (E_0 + 1) + 2$. This equation can be rewritten as $V_1 + R_1 = E_1 + 2$, so Euler's formula continues to hold. Next, draw the second edge from A to B. This addition increases both the number of edges and number of regions by 1. Since adding 1 to both sides of $V_1 + R_1 = E_1 + 2$ gives $V_1 + (R_1 + 1) = (E_1 + 1) + 2$, we see that Euler's formula $V_2 + R_2 = E_2 + 2$ holds for the network consisting of the vertices A and B and the two edges joining these vertices. Continuing in this way, each new edge appended to the existing network preserves the validity of Euler's formula. In particular, the formula holds when the network is completed.

## EXAMPLE 9.19 Solving the Pizza Problem

Suppose $C$ cuts are made across a circular pizza and there are $I$ points of intersection of pairs of cuts. Assume that no two cuts intersect on the bounding circle and no three cuts intersect at the same point inside the pizza. How many pieces $P$ of pizza are there?

**Solution**

### Understand the Problem

It helps to examine a particular case, such as the one shown here. The cuts are drawn to satisfy the conditions of the problem. In the drawing, we can see that 4 cuts and 3 intersections of cuts result in 8 pieces of pizza. Our goal is to see if we can find a formula that gives us the number $P$ in terms of the variables $C$ and $I$.

$C$ = 4 cuts
$I$ = 3 intersections of cuts
$P$ = 8 pieces of pizza

### Devise a Plan

The cut-up pizza can be viewed as a connected planar network, as shown at the left. If we can determine the numbers $V$ and $E$ of vertices and edges, Euler's formula will allow us to solve for the number of regions $R$ of the network. Thus, our plan is to relate $V$ and $E$ to the numbers $C$ and $I$. In Euler's formula, $R$ includes the region labeled "9" on the adjacent figure outside the pizza, which is not a piece of pizza. Therefore, the number of pieces of pizza is given by $P = R - 1$.

### Carry Out the Plan

Each cut forms two vertices on the circle bounding the pizza, and each intersection of cuts gives one vertex of the network inside the circle. Altogether, then, $V = 2C + I$ vertices in the network. To count the number of edges in the network, let's first suppose that there are no intersecting cuts. Each cut then forms two edges on the circle and is itself an edge, giving $3C$ edges of the network. If we next suppose that some of the cuts intersect, it is seen that each intersection creates two additional edges of the network not yet counted. Altogether then, there are $E = 3C + 2I$ edges in the network. Solving for $R$ in Euler's formula $V + R = E + 2$, we get

$$R = E - V + 2 = (3C + 2I) - (2C + I) + 2 = C + I + 2.$$

Since $P = R - 1$, we arrive at the final formula:

$$P = C + I + 1.$$

### Look Back

In the example drawn at the left, there are $C = 4$ cuts intersecting in $I = 3$ points. Since $C + I + 1 = 4 + 3 + 1 = 8$, we can now see why we counted $P = 8$ pieces of pizza, and we obtain a check that our formula is correct.

## Connecting Euler's Formulas for Planar Networks and for Polyhedra

In Section 9.3, we stated without proof that the number of vertices, faces, and edges of a polyhedron are related by Euler's formula $V + F = E + 2$. It is natural to wonder whether this formula for polyhedra is related to the similar formula $V + R = E + 2$ for connected planar networks. To understand the connection, imagine that each edge of a polyhedron is replaced with a segment of a rubber band. The rubber-band skeleton of the polyhedron can then be stretched and flattened to form a connected planar network with $V$ vertices and $E$ edges. This stretching and flattening is shown in the case of a cube in Figure 9.36 on the next page.

Euler's marvelous theorem provides a connection between polyhedra and planar networks. One aspect of a mathematical habit of the mind is that it often leads to a discovery that relates two seemingly different concepts. In this case, the two topics (polyhedral and planar networks) don't even live in the same dimension!

**FIGURE 9.36**
The skeleton of edges of any polyhedron, such as the cube shown, can be stretched and flattened to form a planar network

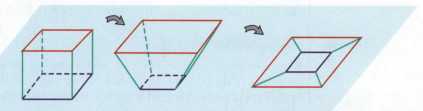

There is a one-to-one matching between the regions of the network (including the unbounded region) and the faces of the polyhedron. Thus, $R = F$, and we conclude that the two Euler formulas are equivalent to one another.

## Problem Set 9.4

Exercises numbered in red are answered in the back of the text.

### Understanding Concepts

1. Andre has met everyone but Emma, Coralee has met everyone but Bianca, and Emma has met only Coralee and Diego. Which of the networks shown represents this information? Which do not? Explain how you make your decision.

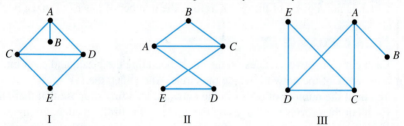

2. Decide which of the networks that follow are traversable. Give an Euler path for each traversable network.

3. For each of these networks, find an Euler path:

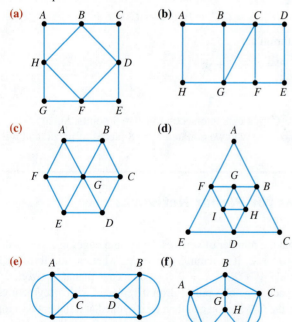

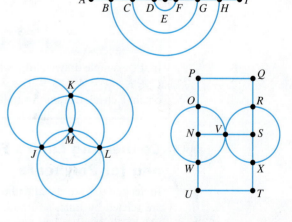

4. (a) The **total degree** $D$ of a network is the sum of the degrees of all of the vertices. For example, the network in problem 2(a) has total degree $D = 2 + 4 + 2 + 4 + 2 + 4 + 2 + 4 = 24$. This network also has $E = 12$ edges. Find $D$ and $E$ for the remaining networks shown in problem 2.

**(b)** Guess how the total degree *D* is related to the number of edges *E* in any network. Test your conjecture on several networks of your own choosing.

**5.** A connected network has the following degrees at its vertices: 2, 2, 4, 8, 3, 6, 6, and 1.

**(a)** Is the network traversable?

**(b)** How many edges does the network have? (*Hint:* See problem 4(b).)

**6.** Here are two more examples from Euler's paper on the Königsberg bridge problem:

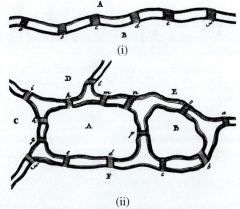

(i)

(ii)

**(a)** Draw the networks corresponding to (i) and (ii).

**(b)** Is network (i) traversable? Why?

**(c)** Is network (ii) traversable? Explain your reasoning.

**7. (a)** Draw the network that corresponds to the following system of bridges and landmasses:

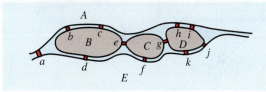

**(b)** Explain why the network is not traversable.

**(c)** What is the smallest number of new bridges required to form a traversable network? Where should the new bridge(s) be placed?

**8.** A floor plan of a house is shown. There are five rooms A, B, C, D, E and the outside O, connected by the doorways a, b, c, d, e, f, and g.

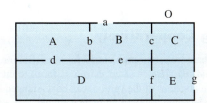

**(a)** Draw a network whose vertices are labeled *A*, *B*, *C*, *D*, *E*, and *O* and whose edges correspond to the doorways.

**(b)** Is it possible to walk through each doorway exactly once? If so, where must you begin and end your walk?

**9.** Following is a connected planar network:

**(a)** What are the numbers *V* of vertices, *R* of regions, and *E* of edges?

**(b)** Does Euler's formula hold for this network?

**10. (a)** Draw a connected planar network whose 10 edges separate the plane into 6 regions.

**(b)** Can you draw a connected planar network with 10 edges that separates the plane into 12 regions? Explain.

## Teaching Concepts

**11.** When examining a network for traversability, Karinna decided that she could overlook all vertices of degree 2. Is she justified to make this simplification? Give a careful explanation why or why not.

**12. Networks as Representations.** According to the NCTM's *Principles and Standards for School Mathematics* (pp. 295–296), "Teachers need to give students experiences in using a wide range of visual representations and introduce them to new forms of representations that are useful for solving certain types of problems. Vertex–edge graphs [that is, networks], for instance, can be used to represent abstract relationships among people or objects in many different kinds of situations." As an example, in the network shown, each vertex represents a student group at a school and an edge between two vertices indicates that at least one student belongs to both groups.

**(a)** Use the network representation to decide how many different times are needed so that five groups can meet and no student has more than one meeting at a time.

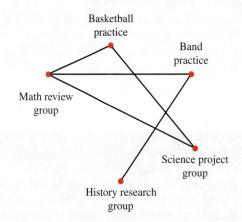

**(b)** Find another example of a situation that uses networks. Carefully describe how the vertices and edges are related to the problem, and include a specific example that would be of interest to schoolchildren.

## Thinking Critically

**13.** A connected network that does not contain a closed path of distinct edges is called a **tree.**

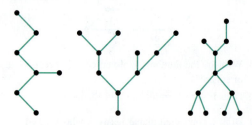

Trees

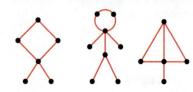

Not trees

(a) Suppose a network contains two vertices that can be joined by two different paths with no edges common to both paths. Why is it impossible for this network to be a tree?

(b) The **diameter** of a tree is the largest number of edges required to join any two vertices by a path. For example, the leftmost tree shown has diameter 5. Find the diameters of the other two trees shown.

(c) Let $V$ and $E$ denote the respective number of vertices and edges of a tree. What formula relates $V$ and $E$? Prove your result.

**14.** What trees are traversable?

**15.** Let $D$ represent the sum of the degrees of all of the vertices of a network, and let $E$ denote the number of edges in the network. ($D$ is the total degree of the network; see problem 4.) Imagine that the network is a highway map, with the vertices representing towns and the edges representing highways connecting towns. Suppose each town puts up a city-limits sign along each highway that leaves town.

(a) Show that the total number of signs is given both by $D$ and by $2E$, so that you obtain the equation $D = 2E$.

(b) Is it possible to construct a network whose total degree $D$ is 17?

**16.** In problem 4, you discovered that the total degree $D$ (the sum of the degrees of all the vertices of the network) is given by $D = 2E$, where $E$ is the number of edges. Suppose the degrees at the even vertices are $e_1, e_2, \ldots, e_m$ and the degrees at the odd vertices are $d_1, d_2, \ldots, d_n$. Thus, $2E = D = e_1 + e_2 + \cdots + e_m + d_1 + d_2 + \cdots + d_n$.

(a) Explain why $d_1 + d_2 + \cdots + d_n$ is an even integer.

(b) Since $d_1 + d_2 + \cdots + d_n$ is even, explain why $n$ is even. Since $n$ is the number of odd vertices in the network, you've proved the following result:

*The number of vertices of odd degree in a network is always even.*

**17.** Prove that the number of people at a party who have shaken hands an odd number of times is an even number. (*Hint:* See problem 16.)

**18.** The following connected network has six odd vertices, so it cannot be traced without lifting the pencil.

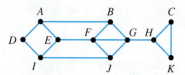

(a) Show that the network can be traced in three strokes; that is, the pencil is lifted twice and then placed at a different vertex.

(b) If a connected network has $2m$ odd vertices, with $m > 0$, explain why its edges can be traced in $m$ strokes. (*Suggestion:* Add, temporarily, $m - 1$ new edges to the network.)

**19.** Suppose that you are asked to trace a connected network, **MHM** without lifting your pencil, so that each edge is traced exactly twice. Is this always possible regardless of the number of odd vertices? Explain why or why not.

**20.** The planar network shown next on the vertices $A$, $B$, $C$, $D$, $F$, $G$, $H$, $I$, $J$, and $K$ is not connected; indeed, it is made up of $P = 3$ connected pieces.

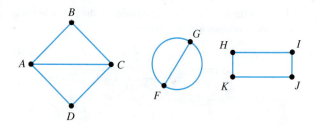

For this network, $V = 10$, $E = 12$, and $R = 6$, and we see that $V + R = 16$, but $E + 2 = 14$.

(a) Draw several more examples of disconnected planar networks. For each network, count $V$, $R$, $E$, and $P$, where $P$ is the number of connected pieces in your network. Can you guess an Euler formula that relates $V$, $R$, $E$, and $P$?

(b) Prove your conjecture stated in part (a). (*Suggestion:* Add new edges to connect the network.)

## Thinking Cooperatively

**21.** These three trees (see problem 13 for the definition of a tree) are *isomorphic* (*iso* = same, *morph* = form) to one another, since the positions of the vertices can be rearranged by bending (but not breaking) to make all three networks look exactly alike:

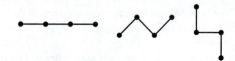

Similarly, these two trees are isomorphic:

By contrast, each tree in the first group is *non-isomorphic* to any tree in the second group. One way to see this is to note that each tree in the first group has vertices of degrees 1, 2, 2, and 1, but the trees on this page each have vertices of degrees 1, 1, 1, and 3. It is easy to check that any tree with 4 vertices must be isomorphic to one of the two types shown earlier in this problem.

Work in small groups, and compare results between groups, to carry out these investigations.

(a) Find the 3 nonisomorphic trees on 5 vertices.

(b) Find the 6 nonisomorphic trees on 6 vertices.

(c) Find the 11 nonisomorphic trees on 7 vertices.

**22.** In 1958, the American mathematician David Gale invented the two-person game **Bridg-It.** The game is played on isometric dot paper, with rows alternating between two colors of dots (say, black and red, as shown). The players take turns drawing horizontal or vertical edges between adjacent vertices of their color. The object of the game is to create a path from one side of the board to the other.

(a) If the red player started the game, who should be the winner of the game shown? What if the black player played first?

(b) Play a few games of Bridg-It.

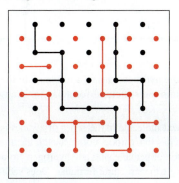

## Making Connections

**23.** An 8-pin connecting terminal is wired as shown on the left. An electrical engineer claims that 5 of the 12 connecting wires can be eliminated. On the right-hand diagram, draw 7 of the 12 original wires that provide for the same current flows as the original circuit.

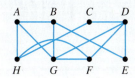 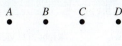

SOURCE: Reprinted with permission from the Mathematical Association of America.

**24.** Chemists frequently use a type of network called a *structural formula* to show the bonds linking the atoms of a molecule. For example, three-dimensional models of methane ($CH_4$) and ethane ($C_2H_6$), and their corresponding structural formulas are shown here:

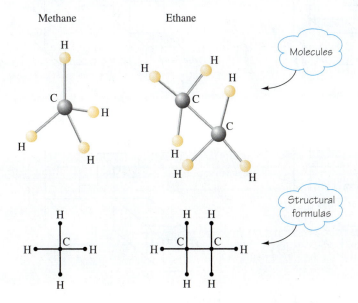

(a) What is the degree (valence) of each carbon atom? of each hydrogen atom?

(b) Sketch the structural formula of propane, $C_3H_8$.

(c) There are two forms of butane, ($C_4H_{10}$). Their "skeletons," showing the four carbon atoms and the bonds between them, are as follows:

Add the hydrogen atoms and bonds to these skeletons to obtain the structural formulas for the two forms of butane.

(d) The next molecule in the series of alkanes is pentane, which has five carbon atoms. Sketch the three forms of the skeleton of pentane, and add hydrogen atoms and bonds to complete the structural formulas. Does each form have the same number of hydrogen atoms?

(e) Make reasonable guesses for the chemical formulas of hexane, heptane, and octane, the next three hydrocarbons in the alkane series.

## From State Student Assessments

25. (New Jersey, Grade 8)
A computer network is to be set up so that

- the supervisor can communicate with every terminal, and
- each worker can communicate with the supervisor and exactly two coworkers. Which network meets these requirements?

A.

B.

C.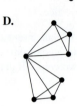

D.

---

26. (Texas, Grade 7)
The drawings below show the top, front, and right-side views of a 3-dimensional figure built using identical cubes.

  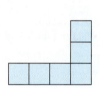

Top view          Front view          Right-side view

Which 3-dimensional figure do these views best represent?

F.

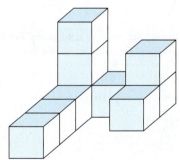

Front

H.

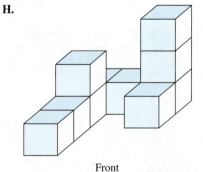

Front

G.

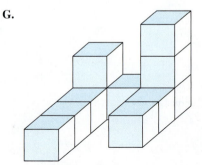

Front

J.

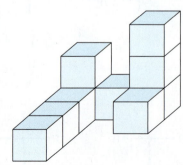

Front

## The Chapter in Relation to Future Teachers

This chapter deals with the beginning concepts of geometry in elementary and middle school. We have taken an informal approach because children learn geometry by looking at, and experimenting with, figures on the plane and in space. Their teachers therefore need to understand and use definitions (which abound in this chapter) so that they help their students comprehend what the terms mean and how they are related to each other (when they are so related). Geometry will be covered in your "methods course," but an example of a good way to start children "experimenting with math" is to have them search for and make geometric shapes. (See problems 17 and 18 of Section 9.3, for example.)

In this chapter, we have introduced many of the basic notions of geometry: point, line, plane, curve, surface, angle, distance between points, measure of an angle, region, and space. In the chapters that follow, these basic notions are developed in more depth as we encounter the ideas of measurement, transformations, tilings, symmetries, congruence, constructions, and similarity.

## Chapter 9 Summary

| Section 9.1   Figures in the Plane | Page Reference |
|---|---|
| **CONCEPTS** | |
| • **Line:** Two distinct points $A$ and $B$ uniquely determine a line $\overleftrightarrow{AB}$. | 455 |
| • **Length of a segment:** The length of the line segment $\overline{AB}$ is the distance between the points $A$ and $B$ and is written $AB$. | 457 |
| • **Corresponding-angle criterion for parallel lines:** There is an equivalence between two lines being parallel and two corresponding angles being congruent. | 461 |
| • **Angle sum in a triangle:** The sum of the measures of the three interior angles of a triangle is 180°. | 463 |
| **DEFINITIONS** | |
| • **Collinear** points are three or more points that lie on the same line. | 455 |
| • **Plane figures** are subsets of a plane. | 456 |
| • The **point of intersection** is the single point in a plane at which nonparallel lines $p$ and $q$ meet. | 456 |
| • A **transversal** is a line that intersects two distinct lines but not at the same point. | 456 |
| • **Congruent** line segments, $\overline{AB}$ and $\overline{CD}$, are line segments that have the same length. | 458, 459 |
| • A **ray**, $\overrightarrow{PQ}$, is a subset of the line $\overleftrightarrow{PQ}$ that contains the point $P$ and all points on the line to one side of $P$. | 458 |
| • An **angle**, $\angle BAC$, is the points of $\overrightarrow{AB} \cup \overrightarrow{AC}$. | 458 |
| • The **vertex of an angle** is the common endpoint of two rays. | 458 |

| | |
|---|---|
| • The **measure of an angle,** m($\angle BAC$), is the number of degrees of turn to rotate about the vertex $A$ side $\overrightarrow{AC}$ onto side $\overrightarrow{AB}$. | 458 |
| • A **straight angle** has a measure of 180°. A **right angle** has an angle measure of 90°. A **zero angle** has a measure of 0°. | 458 |
| • An **acute angle** has a measure between 0° and 90°. An **obtuse angle** has a measure between 90° and 180°. A **reflex angle** has a measure greater than 180°, but less than 360°. | 458 |
| • **Perpendicular lines,** are two lines that intersect at right angles. | 459 |
| • **Congruent angles** are two angles that have the same measure. | 459 |
| • Two angles are **complementary** if the sum of their measures is 90°. | 460 |
| • Two angles are **supplementary** if the sum of their measures is 180°. | 460 |
| • **Adjacent angles** are two angles that share a common side and nonoverlapping interiors. | 460 |
| • **Vertical angles** are two nonadjacent angles formed by two intersecting lines. | 461 |
| • **Interior** and **exterior angles of a triangle:** In triangle BAC, the angles formed by two intersecting rays (for example, $\overrightarrow{AB}$ and $\overrightarrow{AC}$) are **interior angles.** An **exterior angle** of triangle BAC is a supplementary adjacent angle. | 463 |
| • **Directed angles** are angles that specify an initial and final side and a direction of turn. | 464 |
| • The **initial side** of a directed angle is the side that is being directed to turn, and the **terminal side** is the side that indicates where the direction of turn stops. | 464 |

**THEOREMS**

| | |
|---|---|
| • **Vertical-angles theorem:** Vertical angles have the same measure (or one congruent). | 461 |
| • **Corresponding-angles property:** If two parallel lines are cut by a transversal, then their corresponding angles have the same measure. If two lines in the plane are cut by a transversal and some pair of their corresponding angles are congruent, then the lines are parallel. | 462 |
| • **Alternate-interior-angles:** Two lines cut by a transversal are parallel if, and only if, a pair of alternate interior angles is congruent. | 462 |

| **Section 9.2   Curves and Polygons in the Plane** | **Page Reference** |
|---|---|

**CONCEPTS**

| | |
|---|---|
| • **A partial classification of curves:** Curves can be simple (non–self-intersecting), closed (no endpoints), or simple closed both (simple and closed). | 470 |
| • **Polygonal curves:** A polygonal curve is a curve formed by sequentially joining points called **vertices** with line segments called **sides** of the polygonal curve. | 472, 473 |
| • **Polygon:** A polygon is a simple closed polygonal curve. A polygon with 3, 4, 5, 6, 7, 8, 9, 10, . . . , $n$ sides is called a triangle, quadrilateral, pentagon, hexagon, heptagon, septagon, octagon, nonagon (or enneagon), decagon, . . . , $n$-gon, respectively. | 472, 473 |
| • **Sum of angle measures in a polygon:** The sum of the measures of the interior angles of an $n$-gon is $(n - 2)180°$. This formula is the generalization of the statement, for $n = 3$, that "the angle sum of a triangle is 180." | 473, 475 |
| • **Regular polygon:** A polygon is regular if its sides are congruent and its interior angles are congruent. In a regular $n$-gon, the exterior and central angles each measure $360°/n$ and each interior angle measures $(n - 2)180°/n$. | 479 |

## DEFINITIONS

| | |
|---|---|
| • **Curves** are defined as **simple** (non–self-intersecting), **closed** (no endpoints), or **simple closed** (simple and closed). | 470 |
| • Regions defined by a simple closed curve are **the interior and exterior regions.** A line partitions the plane into two regions called **half planes.** An angle partitions the plane into two regions called the **interior** or **exterior of the angle.** | 471, 472 |
| • A **region** is one of the areas defined by a curve. | 472 |
| • A **convex figure** is a figure that contains the segment $\overline{PQ}$ for each pair of points $P$ and $Q$ contained in the figure. | 472 |
| • A **concave figure** (or **nonconvex figure**) is a figure that is not convex. | 472 |
| • A **polygonal curve** is a curve that consists of a union of finitely many line segments joined at the vertices. | 472 |
| • **Vertices** are the endpoints of the segments in a polygonal curve. | 472 |
| • **Sides,** or **edges,** are the segments themselves in a polygonal curve. | 472 |
| • A **polygon** is a simple closed polygonal curve. A polygon with 3, 4, 5, 6, 7, 8, 9, 10, . . . , $n$ sides is called a **triangle, quadrilateral, pentagon, hexagon, heptagon** (or **septagon**), **octagon, nonagon** (or **enneagon**), **decagon, . . . , $n$-gon,** respectively. | 473 |
| • The **polygonal region** is the interior of a polygon. | 473 |
| • A **convex polygon** is a polygon which is convex. | 473 |
| • **Interior angles** of a polygon are the angle at a vertex formed by the two sides of the polygon which intersect at the vertex and is in the polygonial region. An **exterior angle** is a supplementary adjacent angle to an interior angle. | 473 |
| • A triangle is **acute** if all three interior angles are acute, **right** if one angle is a right angle, **obtuse** if an interior angle is obtuse. | 477 |
| • A triangle is **scalene** if no two sides have the same length, **isosceles** if at least two sides have the same length, **equilateral** if all three sides have the same length. | 477 |
| • A **quadrilateral** can be a **kite** (two pairs of adjacent congruent sides), a **trapezoid** (two sides parallel), an **isosceles trapezoid** (two sides parallel and two congruent angles), a **parallelogram** (two pairs of opposite parallel sides), a **rhombus** (parallelogram with all sides of the same length), a **rectangle** (parallelogram with all right angles), or a **square** (all sides of the same length and all right angles). | 479 |
| • An **equilateral polygon** is a polygon with all of its sides congruent. | 479 |
| • An **equiangular polygon** is a convex polygon whose interior angles are all congruent. | 479 |
| • A **regular polygon** is a convex polygon that is both equilateral and equiangular. | 479 |
| • A **central angle** is an angle in a regular $n$-gon with a vertex at the center of a regular polygon and sides containing adjacent vertices of the polygon. | 480 |

## THEOREMS

| | |
|---|---|
| • **Jordan curve theorem:** A simple closed plane curve partitions the plane into three disjoint subsets: the curve itself, the interior of the curve, and the exterior of the curve. | 471 |
| • **Sums of the angle measures in a convex polygon:** The sum of the measures of the exterior angles of a convex polygon is 360°. The sum of the measures of the interior angles of a convex $n$-gon is $(n - 2)180°$. | 473 |
| • **Total-turn theorem:** The total turn made when traversing any closed curve is an integer multiple of 360°. | 476 |

| Section 9.3   **Figures in Space** | Page Reference |
|---|---|

**CONCEPTS**

- A **plane** is a flat surface that is infinite in all directions and "looks like" the Cartesian plane but is in 3-space.    490

- **Simple closed surface:** A simple closed surface is a surface without holes or boundary edges that encloses a region called its **interior.**    492

- There are only five regular polyhedra in the plane and they were known in the time of Plato.    494

- **Nets** are models of polyhedrons that depict the pattern of figures that make up the polyhedron.    494

- **Curved surfaces:** Spheres, hemispheres, cones, prisms, and so on, are examples of curved surfaces.    498

**DEFINITIONS**

- **Half-spaces** are the two regions that are separated by a plane.    490

- **Skew lines** are two lines that do not belong to a common plane.    490

- A **sphere** is the set of points in space at a constant distance from a single point called its **center.**    492

- A **solid** is a space figure that is the union of all points on a simple closed surface and all points in its interior.    492

- A **polyhedron** (*pl.* polyhedra) is a simple closed surface formed by planar polygonal regions. These polygons are called **faces,** and the sides and vertices of the faces are called the **edges** and **vertices,** respectively, of the polyhedron. There are a wide variety of polyhedra including prisms, pyramids, and the five regular polyhedra (tetrahedron, cube, octahedron, dodecahedron, and icosahedron).    492

- A **pyramid** is a simple closed surface given by a polygon and a point not in the plane of the polygon, called its apex.    493

- A **prism** is a simple closed surface that consists of two congruent polygons in parallel planes together with the lateral faces joining the bases, which are parallelograms.    493

- A **right prism** is a prism whose lateral faces are all rectangles.    493

- An **oblique prism** is a prism whose lateral faces are not perpendicular to the plan of the base.    493

- A **regular polyhedron** is a polyhedron that has a convex surface, faces that are congruent regular polygonal regions, and the same number of faces meeting at each vertex of the polyhedron.    494

- **Tetrahedron** is a three-dimensional shape with four faces.    492

- **Pentahedron** is a three-dimensional shape with five faces.    492

- **Hexadedron** is a three-dimensional shape with six faces.    492

- A **cone** is a simple closed planar curve, called the **base,** and a point, called the **apex** or the **vertex,** which is not in the plane of the curve.    498

- A **cylinder** is a simple closed surface generated by translating the points of a simple close region in one plane to a parallel plane. If the line segments joining corresponding points in the two bases are perpendicular to the planes of the bases, it is a **right cylinder.** If they are not perpendicular, the cylinder is an **oblique cylinder.**    498

**THEOREM**

- **Euler's formula:** The numbers $V$ of vertices, $F$ of faces, and $E$ of edges of a polyhedron are related by the formula $V + F = E + 2$.    495

| Section 9.4    Networks | Page Reference |
|---|---|
| **CONCEPTS** | |
| • A practical problem (Königsberg bridge problem) can start a large collection of useful and applicable mathematics. | 504 |
| • Networks have the ability to be used in a number of applications such as traversability and Euler paths. | 506 |
| • **Traversable network:** A network is traversable if there is an Euler path covering each edge of the network precisely one time. Euler showed that a connected network is traversable when the number of vertices of odd degree is either two or zero. | 506 |
| **DEFINITIONS** | |
| • A **network** is a set of vertices together with a set of edges that join some of the pairs of vertices. | 504, 505 |
| • **Degree of a vertex:** The degree of a vertex is the number of edges that have the vertex as an endpoint. A vertex is even or odd if its degree is, respectively, an even or odd number. | 506 |
| • A **connected network** is a network that has a path that can join every two vertices. | 506 |
| • **Euler's path** is a network that can be traveled by passing over each edge exactly once. | 506 |
| • A **planar network** is a network that can be drawn in the plane without any intersection points of its edges other than endpoints. | 507 |
| **THEOREMS** | |
| • **Euler's traversable theorem:** A connected network is traversable if, and only if, it has either no odd vertices or two odd vertices. If it has no odd vertices, any Euler path is a close curve that ends at the same vertex it started from. If the network has two odd vertices, these vertices are the endpoints of any Euler path. | 507 |
| • **Euler's formula for networks:** The numbers of vertices $V$, of regions $R$, and of edges $E$ of a connected planar network are related by the formula $V + R = E + 2$. | 508 |

## Chapter Review Exercises

### Section 9.1

**1.** Let $ABCD$ be the following quadrilateral:

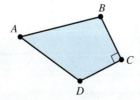

Give symbols for the following:

**(a)** The line containing the diagonal through $C$

**(b)** The diagonal containing $B$

**(c)** The length of the side containing $A$ and $D$

**(d)** The angle *not* containing $D$

**(e)** The measure of the interior angle at $C$

**(f)** The ray that has vertex $D$ and is perpendicular to a side of the quadrilateral

**2.** For the quadrilateral shown in problem 1, which angle(s) appear to be

**(a)** acute?

**(b)** right?

**(c)** obtuse?

**3.** An angle measures $37°$. What is the measure of

**(a)** its supplementary angle?

**(b)** its complementary angle?

**4.** Lines *l* and *m* are parallel. Find the measures *p*, *q*, *r*, and *s* of the angles shown.

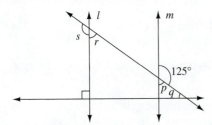

**5.** Find the measures *x*, *y*, and *z* of the angles in the following figure:

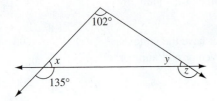

## Section 9.2

**6.** Match each curve to one of the descriptions that follow:

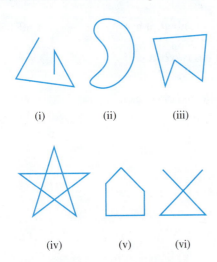

(i)       (ii)       (iii)

(iv)       (v)       (vi)

(a) Nonconvex nonsimple polygonal curve
(b) Nonclosed simple curve
(c) Nonsimple nonclosed polygonal curve
(d) Convex polygon
(e) Simple closed nonconvex nonpolygonal curve
(f) Nonconvex polygon

**7.** For each part, carefully explain your reasoning:
(a) Can a triangle have two obtuse angles?
(b) Can a convex quadrilateral have three obtuse interior angles?
(c) Is there an "acute" quadrilateral (that is, a quadrilateral whose angles are all acute)?

**8.** Find the measures of the interior angles of this polygon:

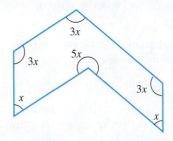

**9.** A turtle walks along the path *ABCDEFGA* in the direction of the arrows, returning to the starting point and initial direction. What total angle does the turtle turn through?

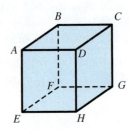

## Section 9.3

**10.** Let *ABCDEFGH* be the vertices of a cube, as follows:

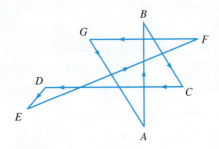

(a) How many planes are determined by the faces of the cube?
(b) Which edges of the cube are parallel to edge $\overline{AB}$?
(c) Which edges of the cube are contained in lines that are skew to the line $\overleftrightarrow{AB}$?
(d) What is the measure of the dihedral angle between the plane containing *ABCD* and the plane containing *ABGH*?

**11.** Name the following surfaces in space:

**12.** Draw the following shapes:
(a) A right circular cone
(b) A pentagonal prism
(c) A nonconvex quadrilateral pyramid

**13.** **(a)** Draw a regular octahedron.

   **(b)** Using your drawing in part (a), count the number of vertices, faces, and edges of the octahedron and then verify that Euler's formula holds for the octahedron.

**14.** A polyhedron has 14 faces and 24 edges. How many vertices does it have?

## Section 9.4

**15.** **(a)** Explain why the network shown is not traversable.

**(b)** Name two vertices that, if connected by a new edge, would make the resulting network traversable. Then list the vertices of an Euler path.

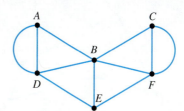

**16.** Is there a walk that crosses each of the bridges shown below exactly once? Explain your reasoning, using an appropriate network.

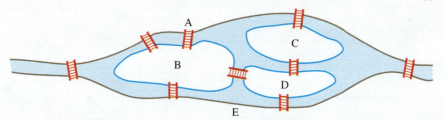

**17.** Count the number of vertices, regions, and edges in the following network, and then verify that Euler's formula holds.

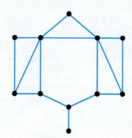

## Chapter Test

**1.** The average interior angle measure of a convex polygon is 144°. What is the number of sides of the polygon? Explain how you found your answer.

**2.** Sketch an example of each of the following types of curves:

   **(a)** a simple closed curve.

   **(b)** a convex heptagon.

   **(c)** a nonclosed simple polygonal curve.

   **(d)** a closed nonsimple polygonal curve.

**3.** A cube octahedron has eight triangular faces and six square faces.

   **(a)** What is the number of edges of a cube octahedron? Explain how you do your counting.

   **(b)** What is the number of vertices of a cube octahedron? Explain how you found your answer.

**4.** Let $P$, $Q$, $R$, $S$, and $T$ be the points shown. Draw and label the following figures:

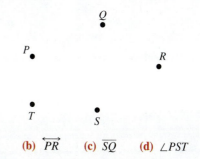

   **(a)** $\overrightarrow{PQ}$    **(b)** $\overleftrightarrow{PR}$    **(c)** $\overline{SQ}$    **(d)** $\angle PST$

**5.** **(a)** A connected planar network with 11 edges partitions the plane into 7 regions. How many vertices does this network have?

   **(b)** Draw a connected planar network with 11 edges and 7 regions.

**6.** At which vertices of the polygon does the interior angle appear to be

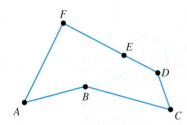

(a) acute?  (b) right?  (c) obtuse?

(d) straight?  (e) reflex?

**7.** For each of the following statements, decide whether is *true* or *false:*

(a) Every square is a rhombus.

(b) Some right triangles are obtuse.

(c) All equilateral triangles are isosceles.

(d) All squares are kites.

**8.** What is the measure of the angles in the points of symmetric eight-point star shown? Explain how you found your answer.

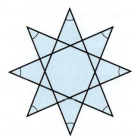

**9.** Pyramids are erected outward to both bases of a heptagonal prism.

(a) Sketch the surface that is described.

(b) Directly count the number of vertices, faces, and edges of the resulting polyhedron.

(c) Verify that Euler's formula is satisfied.

**10.** A right prism has bases bounded by regular pentagons. What is the dihedral angle at which two adjacent lateral faces meet?

**11.** Find the angle measures *r*, *s*, and *t* in the following figure, where lines *l* and *m* are parallel:

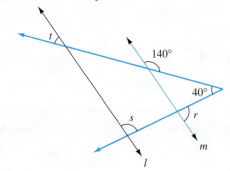

**12.** Consider the following networks:

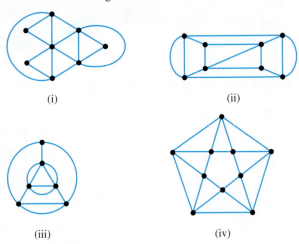

(i)                    (ii)

(iii)                   (iv)

(a) Which networks are not traversable?

(b) Which networks are traversable starting at an arbitrary vertex?

(c) Which networks are traversable starting at some, but not every, vertex?

(d) Which network becomes traversable when only one edge is added to the network? Describe the new edge.

# Measurement: Length, Area, and Volume

**10**

**10.1** The Measurement Process

**10.2** Area and Perimeter

**10.3** The Pythagorean Theorem

**10.4** Volume

**10.5** Surface Area

## Hands On

# The Metric Measurement and Estimation Tournament

## Directions

Set up the six event stations with the materials described in the forthcoming table. For each event, put a copy of the directions for that event at the event's station. Divide the class into six teams, with each team assigned to one of the event stations, and give the team the score sheet that follows the table. Each team then competes in its assigned event, records its scores on the score sheet, and rotates to its next event station. When all teams have completed all of the events, the true distances between cities are made known for the Distance Flier event and the true areas of the foot patterns are revealed for the Big Foot event. After the teams have completed filling out their score sheets, they are ranked in each event according to the lowest average error made by the team. For each event, the most accurate team is awarded 10 points, with the first and second runner-up teams given 7 and 3 points, respectively. The team with the most total points for all six events wins the tournament.

## Materials and Directions for the Events

| Event | Materials | Directions |
|---|---|---|
| **String Cut** | Ball of string, scissors, die, centimeter ruler | In turn, each team member rolls the die and cuts a piece of string whose length in centimeters is estimated to be 10 times the number on the die. Measure the actual length of the string and record the error for each team member. Then compute and record the average team error. |
| **Shot Put** | Foam ball (or wad of newspaper), 10-meter-long tape measure (if a metric tape measure is unavailable, mark meters on a tape measure that shows units in feet) | Each team member throws the ball like a shot put and estimates the distance of the throw in meters. The true distance is measured, and the error made in the estimates is recorded for each team member. Compute and record the average team error. |
| **Weight Lift** | Scale (reading in grams), collection of objects of various weights (rocks, canned goods, books, etc.) | Each team member chooses an object and estimates its weight in grams. The objects are then weighed, the errors are recorded, and the average team error is computed. |
| **Pour It On** | Bag of rice (or small dry beans), die, bowl, measuring cup marked in milliliters | In turn, each team member rolls the die to get a value $d = 1, 2, 3, 4, 5,$ or $6$. The team member then pours rice into the bowl, attempting to fill it with $d \times 100$ milliliters of rice. Finally, pour the rice in the bowl into the measuring cup to measure the actual volume of rice. Determine the individual error made and the team's average error. |

| **Distance Flier**  | Map of the United States (or a state), paper bag containing cards showing the names of about a dozen cities on the map (whose true distances apart are on an overhead transparency shown at the end of the tournament to determine the teams' errors and rankings in the event) | Each student draws two cards from the bag and estimates the distances between the cities in kilometers. The individual errors and average team error are determined when the instructor reveals the true distances between the cities. |
| **Big Foot Area**  | Centimeter-squared paper, die, collection of six foot shapes whose areas are known only to the class instructor (who reveals the areas at the end of the activity to determine the teams' errors and rankings in the event) | A die is rolled to select the team's foot pattern. The pattern is traced onto centimeter-squared paper, and the entire team estimates its area in square centimeters. The team's error is determined when the instructor reveals the true areas of the foot shapes. |

## Team Score Sheet

| Event | | Team Members | | | | | Total of errors | Average errors | Tournament points |
|---|---|---|---|---|---|---|---|---|---|
| **String Cut** | Estimate | | | | | | | | |
| | Actual | | | | | | | | |
| | Error | | | | | | | | |
| **Shot Put** | Estimate | | | | | | | | |
| | Actual | | | | | | | | |
| | Error | | | | | | | | |
| **Weight Lift** | Estimate | | | | | | | | |
| | Actual | | | | | | | | |
| | Error | | | | | | | | |
| **Pour It On** | Estimate | | | | | | | | |
| | Actual | | | | | | | | |
| | Error | | | | | | | | |
| **Distance Flier** | City A | | | | | | | | |
| | City B | | | | | | | | |
| | Est. dist. | | | | | | | | |
| | True dist. | | | | | | | | |
| **Big Foot** | # of foot measured is _____ | Estimated area of foot =          cm$^2$ | | | | | Error of measurement = | | |
| | | Actual area of foot =          cm$^2$ | | | | | | | |

**CHAPTER PREVIEW** **The Principles and Processes of Measurement**

Measurement played a limited, but important, role in Chapter 9. Only two elements were measured: line segments, measured by the distance between their endpoints; and angles, measured by the degrees of rotation needed to turn one side to the other. In this chapter, we introduce more general notions of measurement of geometric figures. The Pythagorean theorem is a key to dealing with a large number of problems. Plane regions will be measured by area and perimeter. Space figures will be measured by surface area and volume.

The process starts by asking what **attribute** of the geometric figure we want to measure. Next, we begin to discuss the general process of measurement and the concept of a unit of measurement. The two principal systems of measurement are then described: the U.S. Customary (English) System, used in the United States, but in almost no other country; and the International System (metric), used by all countries worldwide, including the United States.

**10.1**

# The Measurement Process

The geometry of the Babylonians and ancient Egyptians always had a practical purpose, and often this purpose was dependent on having knowledge of size and capacity. It was important to know the areas of fields, the volumes of granaries, and so on. Many engineering projects gave rise to geometric problems concerned with magnitudes. To be specific, suppose a canal has a given trapezoidal cross section and a known length. If we know how much volume of earth one worker can dig in one day, how many workers are needed to excavate the canal in a given amount of time?

Determining size requires that a comparison be made with a **unit.** For example, the volume of a canal could be expressed in "worker-days," where a worker-day is the volume one person can excavate in one day's labor. The worker-day is thus a unit of volume. It is analogous to the original definition of acre, which was the area of land that could be plowed in one day with one team of oxen.

In early times, units of measurement were defined more for convenience than accuracy. For example, many units of length correspond to parts of the human body, some of which are shown in Figure 10.1. The hand, span, foot, and cubit all appear in early records of Babylonia and Egypt.

**FIGURE 10.1**
Examples of traditional units of length based on the human body

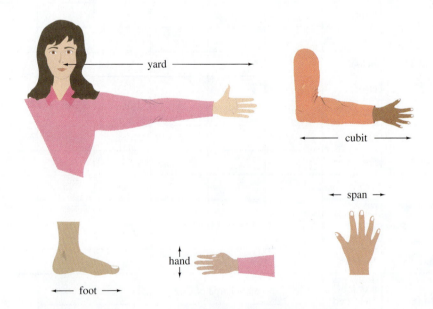

Many of these units later became standardized and persist today. For example, horses are still measured in hands, where a hand is now 4 inches. Originally, an inch was the length of 3 barleycorns placed end to end.

Learning the **measurement process** can be viewed as a sequence of steps—steps that start even before a child goes to school. Many adults think of concepts of measurement such as length, area, and volume as topics for the later grades. However, the NCTM takes the strong position that the study of measurement should start even before schooling does, and there is much research to support that assertion! (See the NCTM's *Measurable Attributes and the Processes of Measurement in Grades Pre-K–2* below.)

### The Measurement Process

(i) Choose the property, or attribute (such as length, area, volume, capacity, temperature, time, or weight), of an object or event that is to be measured.

(ii) Select an appropriate unit of measurement.

(iii) Use a measurement device to "cover," "fill," "time," or otherwise provide a comparison of the object with the unit.

(iv) Express the measurement as the number of units used.

FROM **The NCTM Principles and Standards**

## Measurable Attributes and the Processes of Measurement in Grades Pre-K–2

Children should begin to develop an understanding of attributes by looking at, touching, or directly comparing objects. They can determine who has more by looking at the size of piles of objects or identifying which of two objects is heavier by picking them up. They can compare shoes, placing them side by side, to check which is longer. Adults should help young children recognize attributes through their conversations. "That is a *deep* hole." "Let's put the toys in the *large* box." "That is a *long* piece of rope." In school, students continue to learn about attributes as they describe objects, compare them, and order them by different attributes. Seeing order relationships, such as that the soccer ball is bigger than the baseball but smaller than the beach ball, is important in developing measurement concepts.

Teachers should guide students' experiences by making the resources for measuring available, planning opportunities to measure, and encouraging students to explain the results of their actions. Discourse builds students' conceptual and procedural knowledge of measurement and gives teachers valuable information for reporting progress and planning next steps. The same conversations and questions that help students build vocabulary help teachers learn about students' understandings and misconceptions. For example, when students measure the length of a desk with rods, the teacher might ask what would happen if they used rods that were half as long. Would they need more rods or fewer rods? If students are investigating the height of a table, the teacher might ask what measuring tools would be appropriate and why.

Although a conceptual foundation for measuring many different attributes should be developed during the early years, linear measurements are the main emphasis. Measurement experiences should include direct comparisons as well as the use of nonstandard and standard units. For example, teachers might ask young students to find objects in the room that are about as long as their foot or to measure the length of a table with connecting cubes. Later, they can supply standard measurement tools, such as rulers to measure classroom plants, and use those measurements to chart the plants' growth.

In Example 10.1, a **tangram** piece is chosen to be the unit of area measurement. Tangrams originated in ancient China and continue to be a versatile manipulative that is used in the present-day classroom. The instructions that follow show how to make a set of tangram pieces by folding and cutting a square sheet of paper. A more sturdy set of tangrams can be cut from cardboard or vinyl tile, using the paper shapes as templates.

The seven tangram pieces.

Step 1: Fold the two diagonals of the square *ABCD*. Let *E* denote its center.

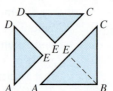

Step 2: Cut out the tangram pieces *CDE* and *ADE*, leaving triangle *ABC*.

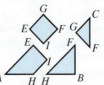

Step 3: Fold *B* and *C* to center point *E* to create folds *FG* and *FH*.

Step 4: Cut out tangram pieces *BFH*, *CFG*, and *FGEI*, leaving trapezoid *AHIE*.

Step 5: Fold *E* to *H* to create fold *IJ*.

Step 6: Cut out tangram pieces *AHIJ* and *EIJ*.

---

**EXAMPLE 10.1** **Investigating Tangram Measurements**

Label the tangram pieces I, II, . . . , VII, as shown. Use shape I, the small isosceles right triangle, as the unit of "one tangram area" (abbreviated 1 tga) to measure the following:

**(a)** the area of each of the tangram pieces,

**(b)** the area of the "fish," and

**(c)** the area of the circle that circumscribes the square. Are your measurements exact or only approximate?

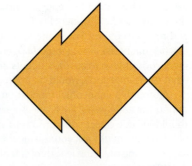

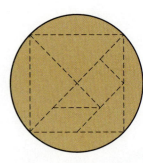

**Solution**  **(a)** Each tangram piece can be covered by copies of the unit shape I, giving the exact measurements in the table.

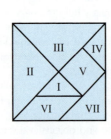

| Piece | Area |
|---|---|
| I, IV | 1 tga |
| II, III | 4 tga |
| V, VI, VII | 2 tga |

**(b)** The fish is covered by the seven tangram pieces, so its area is exactly
$$(4 + 2 + 1 + 2 + 1 + 4 + 2)\,\text{tga} = 16\,\text{tga}.$$

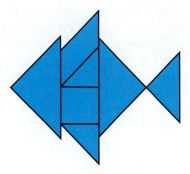

**(c)** The circle can be covered by the seven tangram pieces, together with 12 additional copies of the unit shape. This shows that the circle's area is between 16 tga and 28 tga. Thus, we might estimate the area at about 25 tga.

An important practical purpose of measurement is communication. By agreeing on common units of measurement, people are able to express and interpret information about size, quantity, capacity, and so on. Historically, as commerce developed and goods were traded over increasingly large distances, the need for a standard system of units became more and more apparent. In the seventeenth and eighteenth centuries, the rise of science and the beginning of the Industrial Revolution gave further impetus to the development of universal systems of measurement.

## The U.S. Customary, or "English," System of Measures

The English system arose from a hodgepodge of traditional informal units of measurement. Table 10.1 lists some of the units of **length** with this system. The ratios comparing one unit of length with another are clearly the result of accident, not planning. Learning the customary system requires extensive memorization, and using the system involves computations with cumbersome numerical factors.

**TABLE 10.1    UNITS OF LENGTH IN THE CUSTOMARY SYSTEM**

| Unit | Abbreviation | Equivalent Measurement in Feet |
|------|--------------|-------------------------------|
| Inch | in | $\frac{1}{12}$ ft |
| Foot | ft | 1 ft |
| Yard | yd | 3 ft |
| Rod | rd | $16\frac{1}{2}$ ft |
| Furlong* | fur | 660 ft |
| Mile | mi | 5280 ft |

*The *furlong* is a shortening of "furrow long," revealing its origin in agriculture.

**Area** is a measure of the region bounded by a closed plane curve. Any shape could be chosen as a unit, but the square is the most common. The size of the square is arbitrary, but it is natural to choose the length of a side to correspond to a unit measure of length. Areas are therefore usually measured in square inches, square feet, and so on. A moderate-sized house may have 1800 square feet of floor space, a living room carpet may cover 38 square yards, and a national forest may cover 642 square miles. An exception to this pattern is the acre: 640 acres have a total area of 1 square mile. Some common units of area are listed in Table 10.2. The superscript-2 notation shows a square unit; for example, ft$^2$ indicates square feet.

| TABLE 10.2 | UNITS OF AREA IN THE CUSTOMARY SYSTEM | |
|---|---|---|
| **Unit** | **Abbreviation** | **Equivalent Measure in Other Units** |
| Square inch | in$^2$ | $\frac{1}{144}$ ft$^2$ |
| Square foot | ft$^2$ | 144 in$^2$, or $\frac{1}{9}$ yd$^2$ |
| Square yard | yd$^2$ | 9 ft$^2$ |
| Acre | acre | $\frac{1}{640}$ mi$^2$, or 43,560 ft$^2$ |
| Square mile | mi$^2$ | 640 acres, or 27,878,400 ft$^2$ |

The ratios comparing one unit of area with another can be visualized, as shown in Figure 10.2. We see that the area of a 3-ft by 3-ft square is obtained by the multiplication 3 ft × 3 ft = 3 × 3 × ft × ft = 9 ft$^2$. *When computing with dimensioned quantities, it is essential to retain the units in all equations and expressions.* For example, it is correct to write 12 in = 1 ft; without the dimensions, this equation would be incorrect, since 12 ≠ 1. Omitting the units in expressions is a common source of errors.

**FIGURE 10.2**
Comparing units of area measure

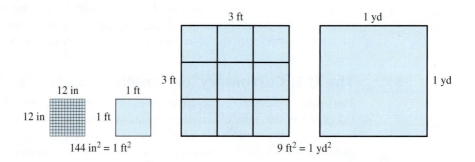

**Volume** is the measure of space taken up by a solid in three-dimensional space. The unit, as shown in Table 10.3, is the volume of a cube whose side length is one of the standard units of length.

| TABLE 10.3 | UNITS OF VOLUME IN THE CUSTOMARY SYSTEM | |
|---|---|---|
| **Unit** | **Abbreviation** | **Equivalent Measure in Other Units** |
| Cubic inch | in$^3$ | $\frac{1}{1728}$ ft$^3$ |
| Cubic foot | ft$^3$ | 1728 in$^3$, or $\frac{1}{27}$ yd$^3$ |
| Cubic yard | yd$^3$ | 27 ft$^3$ |

The ratios comparing units of volume are illustrated in Figure 10.3.

**FIGURE 10.3**
Comparing units of
volume measure

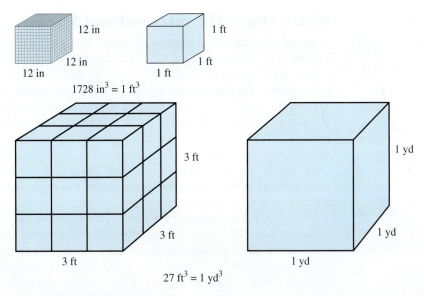

Have you ever wondered why $x^2$ is called "$x$ squared" and $x^3$ is called "$x$ cubed"? The right answer comes from thinking about the questions "What is the area of a square of side $x$?" and "What is the volume of a cube of side $x$?"

**Capacity** is the volume that can be held in a container such as a bottle, pan, basket, or tank. Capacity is often expressed in $\text{in}^3$, $\text{ft}^3$, or $\text{yd}^3$, but other units are also in common use. Some common examples are shown in Table 10.4.

| **TABLE 10.4** | **UNITS OF CAPACITY IN THE U.S. CUSTOMARY SYSTEM** | |
|---|---|---|
| **Unit** | **Abbreviation** | **Equivalent Measure in Other Units** |
| Teaspoon | tsp | $\frac{1}{3}$ tablespoon |
| Tablespoon | T or tbl | .5 fl. oz. |
| Fluid Ounce | fl. oz. | $\frac{1}{8}$ cup |
| Cup | C | 8 fl. oz., or $\frac{1}{4}$ quart |
| Quart | qt | 4 cups, or $\frac{1}{4}$ gallon |
| Gallon | gal | 4 quarts, or 231 cubic inches |
| Bushel | bu | 2150.42 cubic inches |

The bushel is a dry measure, unlike the liquid measures of the other units in Table 10.4. It has no direct relation to the gallon. In the thirteenth century, a bushel was any large amount, so a lover might shower a sweetheart with a "bushel of kisses."

## Metric Units: The International System

The metric system of measurement originated in France shortly after the revolution of 1789. The definitions of the units have been modified over succeeding years, taking advantage of scientific and technological advances. The system was codified in 1981 by the International Standardization Organization. The International System of Units, also called the **SI system,** after its French name, *Système International,* has now achieved worldwide acceptance. The metric system has been a legal standard since 1866 in the United States; indeed, the customary units were *defined* in terms of metric units in 1893. In the 1970s, a movement in the United States to replace customary units with metric units was unsuccessful. About the same time, most other English-speaking countries, including Great Britain, Canada, Australia, and New Zealand, did change to metric units. Even day-to-day measurements in those countries—speed limits, distances between cities, and amounts in recipes—were replaced with metric units.

The principal advantage of the metric system—other than its universality—is the ease of comparison of units. The ratio of one unit to another is always a power of 10, which ties the metric system conveniently to the base-ten numeration system. This relationship makes it quite simple to convert a measurement in one metric unit to the equivalent measurement in another metric unit.

Each power of 10 is given a prefix that modifies the fundamental unit. For example, the factor 1000 (that is, $10^3$) is expressed by the prefix *kilo.* Thus, a kilometer is 1000 meters. Similarly, the factor $\frac{1}{100}$ (that is, $10^{-2}$, or 0.01) is expressed by the prefix *centi.* Therefore, a centimeter is $\frac{1}{100}$ of a meter. The more commonly used prefixes and their symbols are listed in Table 10.5.

| TABLE 10.5 | THE SI DECIMAL PREFIXES | |
|---|---|---|
| **Prefix** | **Factor** | **Symbol** |
| kilo | $100 = 10^2$ | k |
| hecto | $100 = 10^2$ | h |
| deka (or deca) | $10 = 10^1$ | da |
| (none for basic unit) | $1 = 10^0$ | (none) |
| deci | $0.1 = 10^{-1}$ | d |
| centi | $0.01 = 10^{-2}$ | c |
| milli | $0.001 = 10^{-3}$ | m |
| micro | $0.000001 = 10^{-6}$ | $\mu$ (Greek *mu*) |

## Length

The fundamental unit of length in the SI system is the **meter,** abbreviated by the symbol m. The unit symbol is always written last in SI, so there can be no confusion with the prefix *milli,* which is also given the symbol m. For example, one-thousandth of a meter is a millimeter, written as 1 mm. There is no space between the first and second m, and there are no periods between or after the symbols. When typed, the symbols are always in roman font, not italic. The most commonly used metric units of length are listed in Table 10.6.

| TABLE 10.6 | METRIC UNITS OF LENGTH | |
|---|---|---|
| **Unit** | **Abbreviation** | **Multiple or Fraction of 1 Meter** |
| 1 kilometer | 1 km | 1000 m |
| 1 hectometer | 1 hm | 100 m |
| 1 dekameter | 1 dam | 10 m |
| 1 meter | 1 m | 1 m |
| 1 decimeter | 1 dm | 0.1 m |
| 1 centimeter | 1 cm | 0.01 m |
| 1 millimeter | 1 mm | 0.001 m |
| 1 micrometer (or micron) | 1 $\mu$m | 0.000001 m |

The prefix (for example, the "c" in the notation "cm") in a metric measurement can be replaced with its corresponding numerical factor. For example,

$$251 \text{ cm} = 251 \times 10^{-2} \text{ m} = 2.51 \text{ m}.$$

Similarly, a power of 10 can be replaced with the corresponding prefix, as in

$$0.179 \text{ m} = 179 \times 10^{-3} \text{ m} = 179 \text{ mm}.$$

Some metric measurements are shown in Figure 10.4. Since the items shown differ so dramatically in size, the scale for each image (except for the nickel) is greatly reduced or enlarged. The length shown as representing one micrometer is intended to make it clear that waves of red and violet light, the colon bacillus, and the smallpox virus are so tiny as to be determinable only by using sophisticated scientific equipment. Your students and you will need to estimate lengths, areas, and volumes by taking measurements in the metric system. Another important practical application in understanding what sizes look like when metric measurements are used is their appearance in Statewide Assessment exams. (See the Student State Assessment problems at the end of this section.)

**FIGURE 10.4**
Examples of metric measurements of length

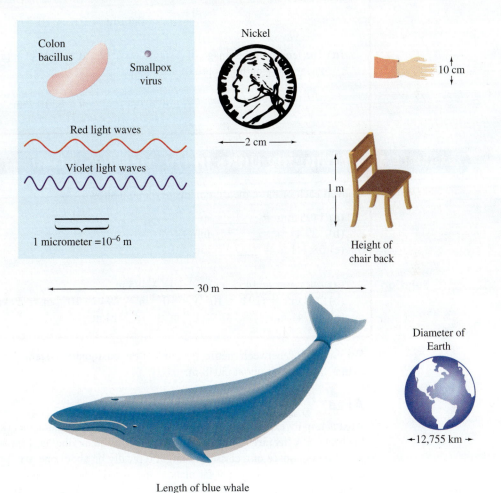

Length of blue whale

---

**EXAMPLE  10.2  Determining Tiny Lengths in Figure 10.4**

Using a metric ruler, measure the following elements from Figure 10.4 as carefully as possible and give the measurements in micrometers and meters:

   **(a)** The length of the colon bacillus
   **(b)** The diameter of the smallpox virus
   **(c)** The length of one wave of red light (i.e., the distance from one peak to the next)
   **(d)** The length of one wave of violet light

**Solution** | Recall that it is common to use both $\doteq$ and $\approx$ as symbols for "is approximately equal to."

**(a)** The length of the image of the colon bacillus is approximately 19 mm. Since the length of the unit representing one micrometer is approximately 14 mm, the length of the colon bacillus is approximately

$$\frac{19}{14}\mu m \doteq 1.4 \ \mu m = 1.4 \times 10^{-6} \, m$$

**(b)** Estimating as closely as possible, it appears that the diameter of the image of the smallpox virus is 1.5 mm. Thus, the actual length of the diameter is approximately

$$\frac{1.5}{14}\mu m \doteq 0.1 \ \mu m = 10^{-7} \, m.$$

**(c)** The length of the image of a single wave of red light is approximately 11 mm. Hence, the actual length is approximately

$$\frac{11}{14}\mu m \doteq 0.8 \ \mu m = 0.8 \times 10^{-6} \, m$$

**(d)** The length of the image of a single wave of violet light is approximately 5.5 mm. Thus, the the actual length is approximately

$$\frac{5.5}{14}\mu m \approx 0.4 \ \mu m = 0.4 \times 10^{-6} \, m$$

**EXAMPLE 10.3** **Changing Units in the Metric System**

Convert each of these measurements to the unit shown:

**(a)** 1495 mm = _____ m
**(b)** 29.4 cm = _____ mm
**(c)** 38,741 m = _____ km

**Solution**

**(a)** 1495 mm = $1495 \times 10^{-3}$ m = 1.495 m
**(b)** 29.4 cm = $(294 \times 10^{-1}) \times 10^{-2}$ m = $294 \times 10^{-3}$ m = 294 mm
**(c)** 38,741 m = $38.741 \times 10^{3}$ m = 38.741 km

For conversion between metric system and the customary system, 1 m is about 3.28 ft (a bit larger than a yard). 1 ft is about .3048 m.

## Area

Area is usually expressed in square meters ($m^2$) or square kilometers ($km^2$). Another common unit is the hectare. A **hectare** (ha) is the area of a 100-m square; that is, 1 ha = 10,000 $m^2$ (See Table 10.7.)

The floor space of a classroom might typically be about one **are** (pronounced "air"). A hectare is about 2.5 acres, so the area of farmland is measured in hectares in metric countries. The name *hectare* comes about because "hecto" is the prefix for 100 in SI (see Table 10.5) and one hectare is 100 ares.

**TABLE 10.7    METRIC UNITS OF AREA**

| Unit | Abbreviation | Multiple or Fraction of 1 Square Meter |
| --- | --- | --- |
| 1 square centimeter | 1 cm$^2$ | 0.0001 m$^2$ |
| 1 square meter | 1 m$^2$ | 1 m$^2$ |
| 1 are (1 square dekameter) | 1 a | 100 m$^2$ |
| 1 hectare (1 square hectometer) | 1 ha | 10,000 m$^2$ |
| 1 square kilometer | 1 km$^2$ | 1,000,000 m$^2$ |

## Volume and Capacity

Small volumes are typically measured in cubic centimeters (abbreviated cm$^3$). Large volumes are often measured in cubic meters (m$^3$). A convenient unit of capacity is the **liter,** which is used worldwide.

> **DEFINITION**  *Liter*
> A **liter** is the volume of a cube, each of whose sides is 10 centimeters or 1 liter is 1000 cm$^3$.

Thus, a liter holds as much liquid as a cube that is 10 cm (about the length of five fingers) on each side. (See Figure 10.5.) The liter is written as either l or L, with L preferred in the United States to avoid confusion with the numeral 1. Since 10 cm is a decimeter, a liter can also be defined as a cubic decimeter.

Since 10 cm $\times$ 10 cm $\times$ 10 cm = 1000 cm$^3$, a liter is also 1000 cubic centimeters. Recalling that *milli* is the prefix for $\dfrac{1}{1000}$, we see that a milliliter (mL or ml) is the same as one cubic centimeter:

$$1 \text{ L} = 1 \text{ liter} = 1000 \text{ cm}^3;$$
$$1 \text{ mL} = 1 \text{ milliliter} = 1 \text{ cm}^3.$$

**FIGURE 10.5**
A liter is a cubic decimeter, or, equivalently, 1000 cubic centimeters

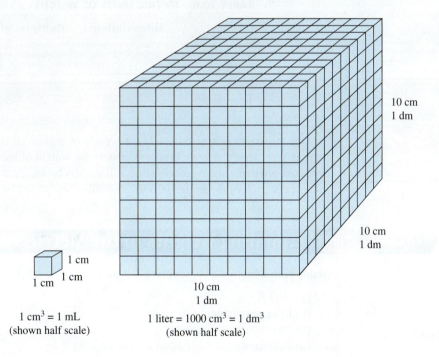

10 cm
1 dm

10 cm
1 dm

1 cm
1 cm
1 cm

10 cm
1 dm

1 cm$^3$ = 1 mL
(shown half scale)

1 liter = 1000 cm$^3$ = 1 dm$^3$
(shown half scale)

Large plastic bottles of soda usually contain 2 liters, while a typical soft drink can contains about 354 milliliters. A child's dose of cough medicine may be 3 mL. A recipe may call for 0.5 liter of water. In metric countries, gasoline is priced by the liter, and to fill a car's gas tank takes about 40 to 60 liters.

## Weight and Mass

The **weight** of an object is the force exerted on the object by gravity. For example, a brick on the surface of the earth may weigh 6 pounds, but on the surface of the moon it would weigh only about 1 pound. During the journey from earth to moon, the brick would weigh nearly nothing at all. Nevertheless, an astronaut would not care to be hit by a weightless brick, since the brick never loses its **mass.**

In science, the distinction between mass and weight is very important: Mass is the amount of matter of an object, and weight is the force of gravity on the object. But on the surface of the earth and in everyday-life situations, the weight of an object is proportional to its mass. That is, the mass of an object is accurately estimated by weighing it.

The U.S. customary unit of weight is the familiar pound. Lighter weights are often given in ounces, and very heavy weights are given in tons:

$$16 \text{ ounces (oz)} = 1 \text{ pound (lb)};$$

$$2000 \text{ pounds} = 1 \text{ ton}.$$

A base unit of weight in the metric system is the **kilogram,** which is about 2.2 pounds.

---

**DEFINITION** *Kilogram*

A **kilogram** is the weight of one liter of water.

---

Table 10.8 lists some metric units of weight. Since there are 1000 cubic centimeters in one liter and a liter of water weighs 1 kilogram, one cubic centimeter of water weighs 0.001 of a kilogram or, equivalently, 1 gram.

**TABLE 10.8   METRIC UNITS OF WEIGHT**

| Unit | Abbreviation | Multiples of Other Metric Units |
|------|-------------|--------------------------------|
| 1 milligram | 1 mg | 0.001 g |
| 1 gram | 1 g | 0.001 kg |
| 1 kilogram | 1 kg | 1000 g |
| 1 metric ton | 1 t | 1000 kg |

One milligram is approximately the weight of a grain of salt. It is a common measure of vitamins and medicines. A gram is approximately the weight of half a cube of sugar. Canned goods and dry packaged items at the grocery store will usually be weighed in grams. In metric countries, larger food items, such as meats, fruits, and vegetables, are priced by the kilogram (about 2.2 pounds).

**EXAMPLE 10.4 Estimating Weights in the Metric System**

Match each item to the approximate weight of the item taken from the list that follows:

**(a)** Nickel
**(b)** Compact automobile
**(c)** Two-liter bottle of soda
**(d)** Recommended daily allowance of vitamin B-6
**(e)** Size D battery
**(f)** Large watermelon

List of weights: 2 mg,   2 kg,   100 g,   1200 kg,   9 kg,   5 g

**Solution**   **(a)** 5 g   **(b)** 1200 kg   **(c)** 2 kg   **(d)** 2 mg   **(e)** 100 g   **(f)** 9 kg

## Temperature

There are two commonly used scales to measure temperature. According to the **Fahrenheit scale,** 32°F represents the freezing point of water and 212°F the boiling point of water. Thus, the Fahrenheit scale introduces 180 degrees of division between the freezing and boiling temperatures. The

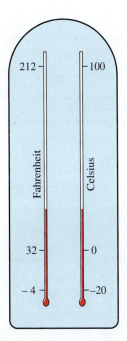

**FIGURE 10.6**
Thermometers showing Fahrenheit and Celsius scales

**Celsius scale** divides this temperature range into 100 degrees: The freezing point is 0° Celsius, and the boiling point is 100° Celsius.

The thermometers shown side by side in Figure 10.6 can be used to derive a formula that relates F degrees Fahrenheit to the equivalent temperature in C degrees Celsius. First, notice that F − 32 changes from 0 to 180 between freezing (F = 32) and boiling (F = 212), so $(F - 32)\dfrac{100}{180}$ changes from 0 to 100 between freezing and boiling. This is the same as the Celsius temperature scale, so $C = (F - 32)\dfrac{100}{180}$. The same reasoning shows that $C\left(\dfrac{180}{100}\right) + 32$ changes from 32 to 212 as the Celsius temperature C changes from freezing (C = 0) to boiling (C = 100), so this expression gives the temperature F in degrees Fahrenheit. That is, the temperature scales are related by the formulas

$$C = (F - 32)\frac{100}{180} \quad \text{and} \quad F = \frac{180}{100}C + 32.$$

## Unit Analysis

It is often of interest to express a measurement given in one unit by the equivalent measurement in a new unit. A procedure known as **unit analysis** (or **dimensional analysis**) can help arrange the calculation to make it clear if the factors comparing units are used as multipliers or divisors. The idea of unit analysis can be explained by an example. Suppose a distance has been given as 3.75 miles, and you would like the distance in yards. You recall that 1 mi = 5280 ft and 3 ft = 1 yd. These equations can also be written as $1 = \dfrac{5280 \text{ ft}}{1 \text{ mi}}$ and $1 = \dfrac{1 \text{ yd}}{3 \text{ ft}}$. Therefore,

$$3.75 \text{ mi} = 3.75 \text{ mi} \times \frac{5280 \text{ ft}}{1 \text{ mi}} \times \frac{1 \text{ yd}}{3 \text{ ft}} = \frac{3.75 \times 5280}{3} \text{ yds.}$$

Since $\dfrac{3.75 \times 5280}{3} = 6600$, it follows that 3.75 miles = 6600 yards.

Unit conversion, even using unit analysis, should always be accompanied by careful reasoning. Always ask, "Is this answer reasonable? Does this answer agree with an approximate mental estimation?" Mistakes with unit conversions have led to some unfortunate disasters. For example, in 1999 engineers mistook a measurement of force given in pounds to be given in the metric unit of newtons of force. As a result, over four times the correct amount of thrust was applied to the *Mars Climate Orbiter,* sending the $125 million space probe to an early demise in the atmosphere of the Red Planet.

---

**EXAMPLE 10.5 Computing Speed and Capacity with Unit Analysis**

(a) A cheetah can run 60 miles per hour. What is the speed in feet per second?
(b) A fish tank at the aquarium has the shape of a rectangular prism 2 m deep by 3 m wide by 3 m high. What is its capacity in liters?

**Solution** 

(a) $60\dfrac{\text{mi}}{\text{hr}} = 60\dfrac{\text{mi}}{\text{hr}} \times \dfrac{5280 \text{ ft}}{1 \text{ mi}} \times \dfrac{1 \text{ hr}}{60 \text{ min}} \times \dfrac{1 \text{ min}}{60 \text{ sec}} = \dfrac{60 \times 5280 \text{ ft}}{60 \times 60 \text{ sec}} = 88\dfrac{\text{ft}}{\text{sec}}.$

(b) Recall that a liter is a cubic decimeter, and *deci* is the prefix for one-tenth. Therefore, the volume of the tank is

$$(2 \text{ m}) \times (3 \text{ m}) \times (3 \text{ m}) = 18 \text{ m}^3 = 18 \text{ m}^3 \times \left(\frac{10 \text{ dm}}{1 \text{ m}}\right)^3 = 18 \times \text{m}^3 \times 10^3 \times \frac{\text{dm}^3}{\text{m}^3}$$

$$= 18{,}000 \text{ dm}^3 \times \frac{1 \text{ liter}}{\text{dm}^3} = 18{,}000 \text{ liters.}$$

## Problem Set 10.1

Exercises numbered in red are answered in the back of the text.

### Understanding Concepts

1. For each of the following objects, make a list of some of its measurable properties:

   (a) A bulletin board
   (b) An extension cord
   (c) A file box
   (d) A table

2. Suppose you are designing a house. Give examples of measurements you believe are important to consider. For example, the height of the house may be needed to satisfy a zoning regulation. Discuss examples of measurements of (a) length, (b) area, and (c) volume and capacity. What units are appropriate?

3. Find the area of each tangram figure shown, where a unit is the area of the small isosceles right triangle:

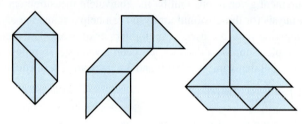

4. Let's use the term *pen* to refer to the area of a penny.

   (a) Estimate the area of a 4″ × 6″ card in pens.
   (b) Discuss why pens are a difficult unit of area to use.

5. Arrange the solids shown into a list according to volume, from smallest to largest. Are there any ties?

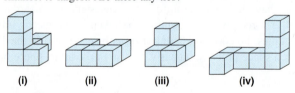

   (i)   (ii)   (iii)   (iv)

6. (a) Verify that an acre contains 43,560 square feet. Show your computation.

   (b) A square lot contains 1 acre. What is the length of each side, to the nearest foot?

7. (a) A football field is 120 yards long (including the end zones) and 160 feet wide. What is the area of a football field in acres?

   (b) A soccer field measures 110 meters by 70 meters. What is its area in ares? in hectares? (See Table 10.7).

8. A small bottle of sparkling mineral water contains 33 cL.

   (a) What is the volume in milliliters?
   (b) Will three small bottles fill a 1-liter bottle?

9. Fill in the blanks:

   (a) 58,728 g = _____ kg
   (b) 632 mg = _____ g

   (c) 0.23 kg = _____ g
   (d) A cubic meter of water weighs = _____ kg.

10. In each part, give the most reasonable answer listed.

    (a) A newborn baby weighs about: 8.3 kg,   3.5 kg,   750 g, 1625 mg.

    (b) A compact car weighs about: 5000 kg,   2000 g,   1200 kg, 50 kg.

    (c) The recommended daily allowance of vitamin C is: 250 g, 60 mg,   0.3 kg,   0.002 mg.

11. In each of the following, select the most reasonable metric measurement:

    (a) The height of a typical center in the National Basketball Association is: 6.11 m,   3 m,   95 cm,   212 cm.

    (b) The diameter of a coffee cup is about: 50 m,   50 mm, 500 mm,   5 km.

    (c) A coffee cup has a capacity of about: 8 L,   8mL,   240 mL, 500 mL.

12. Use a metric ruler to measure these items:

    (a) The size of a sheet of standard notebook paper
    (b) The length and width of the cover of this textbook
    (c) The diameter of a nickel
    (d) The perimeter of (distance around) your wrist

13. The dimensions of Noah's Ark are given in the Bible as 300 cubits long, 50 cubits wide, and 30 cubits high. Give the dimensions in (a) feet and (b) meters. Use a meterstick and ruler to measure your own cubit, as shown in Figure 10.1.

### Teaching Concepts

14. Children often enjoy word games, and this exercise can provide a fun way to learn some of the metric prefixes. For example, the prefix for $10^{-12}$ in the metric system is pico, so what are $10^{-12}$ boos? One picoboo (peekaboo), of course. Now try these:

    (a) 10 millipedes       (b) $10^{-6}$ phones
    (c) 2000 mockingbirds   (d) 10 cards
    (e) $10^{-9}$ goat

15. Most of us can visualize the length of an inch, a foot, a yard, and even a football field because we have repeatedly experienced these measurements. To develop the same feeling for metric measurements of length, use a metric ruler and meterstick or metric tape measure to determine each of the following in metric units:

    (a) The length of a new pencil
    (b) The length of your shoe
    (c) Your own height
    (d) The height and width of a door
    (e) The length of a yardstick
    (f) The length of a football field

**16.** A quart and a liter of the same brand of sparkling water are on a shelf. If they are the same price, which one should you pick?

**17.** Can you cut the board shown into just two pieces to exactly cover the 60-cm by 12-cm hole?

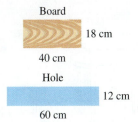

Board
18 cm
40 cm
Hole
12 cm
60 cm

## Responding to Students

**18.** Majandra was asked to decide which of the following choices would be the most reasonable length for a dining room table:

**(a)** 6 feet      **(b)** 6 miles

**(c)** 6 yards      **(d)** 6 inches

Majandra decided that the answer must be 6 yards. When her teacher asked her to explain, Majandra said that 6 inches is very small, 6 miles is very long, and 6 feet is how we would measure a person, not a table.

**(a)** What is Majandra doing incorrectly when applying measurements to objects?

**(b)** How would you guide her to understand the length of these different amounts and help her approach such problems in the future?

**19.** Brent was solving metric conversion problems in class. He was successful when converting whole-number large metric measurements such as meters and rewriting them in smaller units such as centimeters. The teacher then gave Brent the conversion

$$5 \text{ cm} = \underline{\hspace{1.5cm}} \text{ km}$$

and asked him to complete the problem. Brent answered that you cannot do this problem because you will end up with a decimal and you can't have a decimal amount when measuring.

**(a)** What is the correct answer to this metric problem?

**(b)** It is common for students who have been practicing metric conversions going from "big to small" to suddenly become very confused when switching and converting from "small to big." How can you guide Brent towards a better understanding of this conversion?

**20.** Corina thought she correctly solved the following metric problems:

18 cm = **180 mm**

4 m = **400 cm**

40 mm = **400 cm**

3000 mm = **3,000,000 m**

**(a)** Which two conversion problems did Corina solve?

**(b)** Which two conversion problems did Corina fail to solve?

**(c)** Why is Corina's mistake common and how can you guide her in the future?

## Thinking Critically

**21.** Pints, quarts, and gallons are part of a larger "doubling" system of capacity measure:

| | |
|---|---|
| 1 jigger = 2 mouthfuls | 1 pint = 2 cups |
| 1 jack = 2 jiggers | 1 quart = 2 pints |
| 1 jill = 2 jacks | 1 bottle = 2 quarts |
| 1 cup = 2 jills | 1 gallon = 2 bottles |
| | 1 pail = 2 gallons |

**(a)** How many mouthfuls are in a jill? a cup? a pint?

**(b)** Suppose one mouthful, one jigger, one jack, . . . , and one gallon are poured into an empty pail. Does the pail overflow, is it exactly filled, or is there room for more? (*Hint:* Draw an empty pail. Put one gallon in, then one bottle, and so on.)

**22.** The weight of diamonds and other precious gemstones is given in *carats,* where 1 carat = 200 mg. The largest diamond discovered thus far is the Cullinan, found in 1906 at the Premier mine in South Africa. It weighed 3106 carats. Using the conversion 1 kg = 2.2 lbs, estimate the weight of the Cullinan diamond in pounds.

## Thinking Cooperatively

**23.** Nearly 4700 years ago, the Great Pyramid of Khufu was built to astonishing accuracy with the use of a measuring unit called the cubit. (See Figure 10.1.) For further accuracy, the cubit was divided into seven *palms,* and each palm was further subdivided into four *digits* (finger widths). Longer distances were measured by the *hayt,* equal to 100 cubits.

**(a)** Use a meterstick to measure the cubit (elbow-to-fingertip distance, to the nearest centimeter) and palm (distance across four fingers, to the nearest millimeter) of 10 classmates, and make a histogram of your data. Compute the average and standard deviation of the cubit and palm measurements. Does it seem accurate that seven palms are in a cubit?

**(b)** Give reasonable ancient Egyptian measurements for the height of the ceiling in your classroom, the length of a piece of notebook paper, and the length of a football field.

## Making Connections

**24.** Metric countries rate the fuel efficiency of a car by the number of liters of gasoline required to drive 100 kilometers. If a car takes 9 liters per 100 kilometers, what is its efficiency in miles per gallon? Use the conversions 1 gal ≐ 3.7854 L and 1 mile ≐ 1.6 km

**25.** A light-year is the distance light travels in empty space in one year.

**(a)** Light travels at a speed of 186,000 miles per second. The star nearest the sun is Proxima Centauri, in the constellation Centaurus, whose distance from the earth is 4 light-years. What is the distance to Proxima Centauri in miles?

**(b)** In metric measurements, the speed of light is $3.00 \times 10^8$ meters per second. Verify that a light-year is about $10^{16}$ meters.

26. An herbicide is bottled in concentrated form. A working solution is mixed by adding 1 part concentrate to 80 parts water.

   **(a)** How many liquid ounces of concentrate should be added to 5 gallons of water?

   **(b)** How many liters of water should be added to 65 milliliters of concentrate?

27. Lumber is measured in board feet, where a board foot is the volume of a piece of lumber one foot square and one inch thick.

   **(a)** How many board feet are in a two-by-four (2″ by 4″) that is 10 feet long? (The volume of a rectangular solid is length times width times height.)

   **(b)** Lumber is priced in dollars per thousand board feet. Suppose two-by-fours 10 feet long are $690 per thousand board feet. What is the cost of 144 two-by-fours, each 10 feet long?

28. On July 23, 1983, Air Canada Flight 143 was on the ground in Montreal. The pilot had 7682 liters of fuel on board but knew the Boeing 767 would need 22,300 kilograms to reach its destination, Edmonton, Alberta. Since airliners measure fuel by weight, not volume, the pilot asked for the weight of a liter of fuel and was told it was 1.77 kilograms.

   **(a)** Calculate how many liters of fuel were added to the plane's tanks.

   **(b)** Actually, 1.77 is the number of pounds, not kilograms, of fuel per liter. There is really just 0.803 kilogram per liter. How much fuel should have been added to the plane's tanks?

   (Yes, the plane ran out of fuel, but the pilots managed to glide 22 miles to a safe landing in Winnipeg.)

## Using a Calculator

29. Verify that a hectare is about $2\frac{1}{2}$ acres. Use the approximate conversion $1.6 \text{ km} \doteq 1$ mile and show all of your steps.

30. **(a)** Use the conversion $1 \text{ In} \doteq 2.54$ cm to calculate the number of cubic inches in a liter.

   **(b)** Which volume is larger, 6.2 liters or 327 cubic inches?

31. A fortnight is 2 weeks. Convert a speed of 25 inches per minute to its equivalent in furlongs per fortnight.

32. Show that there are about 30 million seconds in a year.

## From State Student Assessments

33. (Texas, Grade 3)
   Which is the best estimate of the capacity of a baby bottle?
   
   F.  1 milliliter
   G.  cup
   H.  1 liter
   J.  1 gallon

34. (Connecticut, Grade 4)

ABOUT how many footstools would be the same height as the chair?   2   3   4   5

35. (Connecticut, Grade 4)

Use your ruler to measure the length of the wagon in this picture to the NEAREST centimeter.

5 centimeters          8 centimeters

12 centimeters         15 centimeters

36. (Washington State, Grade 4)
   Your class project is to build a bird feeder.

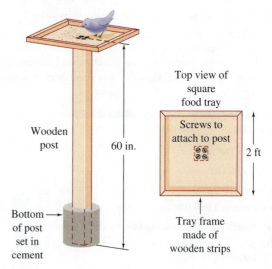

*See "Examining School Book Pages" on page 542 for questions related to the pages shown below.*

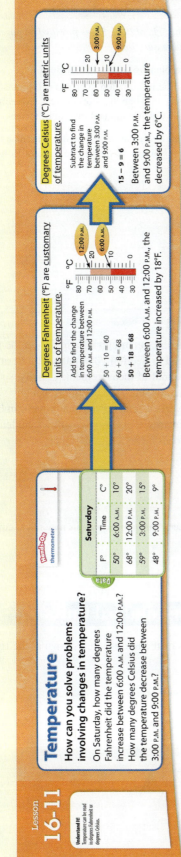

### Lesson 16-11

**Understand It!**
Temperature can be read in degrees Fahrenheit or degrees Celsius.

## Temperature

**How can you solve problems involving changes in temperature?**

On Saturday, how many degrees Fahrenheit did the temperature increase between 6:00 A.M. and 12:00 P.M.?

How many degrees Celsius did the temperature decrease between 3:00 P.M. and 9:00 P.M.?

**Hands-On** thermometer

**Data**

| Saturday | | |
|---|---|---|
| **Time** | **F°** | **C°** |
| 6:00 A.M. | 50° | 10° |
| 12:00 P.M. | 68° | 20° |
| 3:00 P.M. | 59° | 15° |
| 9:00 P.M. | 48° | 9° |

**Degrees Fahrenheit (°F) are customary units of temperature.**

12:00 A.M.   6:00 A.M.

°F  °C

Add to find the change in temperature between 6:00 A.M. and 12:00 P.M.

$50 + 10 = 60$

$60 + 8 = 68$

$\mathbf{50 + 18 = 68}$

Between 6:00 A.M. and 12:00 P.M., the temperature increased by 18°F.

**Degrees Celsius (°C) are metric units of temperature.**

3:00 P.M.   9:00 P.M.

°F  °C

Subtract to find the change in temperature between 3:00 P.M. and 9:00 P.M.

$15 - 9 = 6$

Between 3:00 P.M. and 9:00 P.M., the temperature decreased by 6°C.

---

### Guided Practice*

**Do you know HOW?**

For **1** and **2**, find each temperature change. Then tell whether each change is an increase or decrease.

**1.**
°F  °C
Start 37°F   Finish 23°F
37°F to 23°F

**2.**
°F  °C
Finish 36°C   Start 28°C
28°C to 36°C

**Do you UNDERSTAND?**

**3.** On the Celsius side of the thermometer above, there are 4 tick marks between 10°C and 20°C. What does each tick mark represent?

**4. Writing to Explain** If a temperature increases in degrees Fahrenheit, will it increase or decrease in degrees Celsius?

---

### Independent Practice

For **5** through **8**, find each change in temperature. Tell whether each change is an increase or decrease.

**5.** 24°C to 58°C

**6.** 40°F to 15°F

**7.** 44°F to 61°F

**8.** 42°C to 14°C

For **9** through **12**, read each temperature. Then tell what the temperature would be after each change described.

**9.**
°F  °C
Decrease of 14°C

**10.**
°F  °C
Increase of 17°F

**11.**
°F  °C
Increase of 35°F

**12.**
°F  °C
Decrease of 27°C

*For another example, see Set L on page 399.

---

### Problem Solving

Body temperature ranges from 86°F to 89°F.

**13.** Crocodiles are cold-blooded animals with body temperatures from 86°F to 89°F. Crocodiles control their body temperature by moving to warmer or cooler environments. What is the difference between the highest normal body temperature and the lowest normal body temperature?

**14. Reasoning** Annie, Bart, and Consuela live in three different cities. One day, the high temperature in Bart's city was 9°C less than in Annie's city. The high temperature in Consuela's city was 14°C more than in Bart's city. Which city was warmer, Consuela's city or Annie's city?

**15.** The high temperature for a day in June was 68°F. The low temperature that day was 29°F less. What was the low temperature?

A  39°F   C  39°C
B  97°F   D  97°C

**16.** As a general rule, the air temperature drops about 7°C for every 1,000 meters of elevation. If the temperature at sea level is 33°C, what is the temperature at 4,000 meters?

**17.** Heather and Irene are reading the same 439-page book. Heather read 393 pages. Irene read 121 fewer pages than Heather. How many pages does Irene have left to read?

**18.** On the Celsius scale, water boils at 100°C and freezes at 0°C. What is the temperature difference between boiling and freezing?

**19.** On the Fahrenheit scale, water boils at 212°F and freezes at 32°F. What is the temperature difference between boiling and freezing?

**DIGITAL**  Animated Glossary, eTools
www.pearsonsuccessnet.com

Lesson 16-11  **391**

---

SOURCE: From Envision Math Student Edition Grade 4. Copyright © 2011 Pearson Education, Inc. or its affiliates. Used by permission. All rights reserved.

| Item | Cost per Unit |
|------|---------------|
| wooden post | $2.50 per foot |
| wooden strips for tray frame | $1.00 per foot |
| tray bottom | $6.00 |
| tools, screws, nails, wood glue, and cement mix | loaned or donated by parents |

Explain how you could use the information given to find the total cost of materials. Use words, numbers, or pictures.

**Examining School Book Pages**

*Refer to the School Book Pages provided on page 541 to answer the following questions.*

**37. (a)** Do problem 16 of the School Book Page.

**(b)** Using the information in problem 16, translate the first sentence into one that uses degrees Fahrenheit instead of degrees Celsius and feet instead of meters.

**38.** Since water freezes at 32° F and 0° C, Frankie thinks a degree Fahrenheit is bigger than a degree Celsius. How would you respond?

## 10.2

# Area and Perimeter

### Measurements in Nonstandard Units

We now turn our attention to the notions of the **area** and **perimeter** of a region in the plane and follow the steps of the measurement process as described in Section 10.1, page 526. In order to discuss what the area of a region is, we must first specify the unit of measurement. Usually, squares are chosen to define a **unit of area,** so units such as cm$^2$, in$^2$, ft$^2$, etc., are common, but any shape that tiles the plane (that is, covers the plane without gaps or overlaps) can serve equally well. In Example 10.6, we will work with a nonstandard unit rather than squares. This practice allows students to discover important general principles of the measurement process.

> **DEFINITION    *Area of a Region in the Plane***
> Let $R$ be a region and assume that a unit of area is chosen. The number of units required to cover a region in the plane without overlap is the **area** of the region $R$.

**EXAMPLE 10.6  Making Measurements in Nonstandard Units**

Find the area of each figure $A$, $B$, $C$, and $D$ in terms of the unit of area shown at the right.

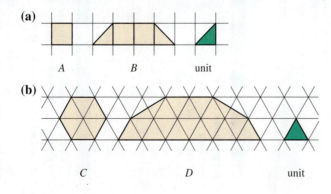

**(a)**

*A          B          unit*

**(b)**

*C          D          unit*

**Solution**

**(a)** The full square $A$ can be covered by 2 of the unit shapes, so area($A$) = 2 units. Region $B$ is covered by 6 units, so area($B$) = 6 units.

**(b)** The hexagon $C$ is covered by 6 of the triangular units, so area($C$) = 6 units. Region $D$ cannot be covered directly by the triangular units, although it is evident that the area of $D$ is between 16 and 20 units. To find the exact area, remove and then rejoin a triangular piece, as shown in the diagram that follows, to form a new shape $D'$ of the same area as $D$. That is, area($D'$) = area($D$). Since $D'$ can be covered by 18 triangular units, it follows that area($D$) = 18 units.

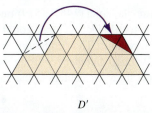

$D'$

## The Congruence and Addition Properties of Area

The solution given in Example 10.6 shows two important principles for the calculation of areas, the first of which is **congruence.** The notion of two regions being congruent will be defined carefully in the next chapter by saying that they are congruent if, using rigid motions like rotation and translation, we can superimpose either region on the other. For now, we'll use more informal language.

> **DEFINITION**  *Congruence of Two Regions in the Plane*
> If $R$ and $S$ are regions in the plane that have the same size and shape, then they are **congruent** and we write $R \cong S$.

The second principle of Example 10.6 comes from a figure being **dissected** or **partitioned**—that is, the figure is cut into a collection of nonoverlapping regions that cover the larger figure. The **congruence** and **addition properties of area** that follow will be used repeatedly throughout the rest of this chapter.

> **PROPERTIES**  *The Congruence and Addition Properties of Area*
>
> **Congruence property**
> If region $R$ is congruent to region $S$, then the two regions have the same area:
>
> $$\text{area}(R) = \text{area}(S).$$
>
> **Addition property**
> If a region $R$ is dissected into nonoverlapping subregions $A, B, \ldots, F$, then the area of $R$ is the sum of the areas of the subregions:
>
> $$\text{area}(R) = \text{area}(A) + \text{area}(B) + \cdots + \text{area}(F).$$

These properties are illustrated in Figure 10.7.

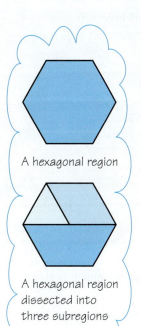

A hexagonal region

A hexagonal region dissected into three subregions

**FIGURE 10.7**
The congruence and addition properties of area

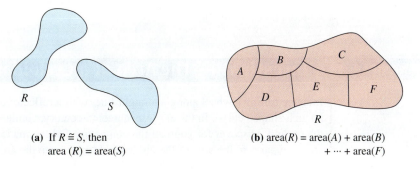

**(a)** If $R \cong S$, then
area $(R)$ = area$(S)$

**(b)** area$(R)$ = area$(A)$ + area$(B)$
        $+ \cdots +$ area$(F)$

The congruence and addition properties show that rearranging the pieces of a figure forms a new figure with the same area as the original figure.

## EXAMPLE 10.7   Solving Leonardo's Problems

Leonardo da Vinci (1452–1519) once became absorbed in showing how the areas of certain curvilinear (curved-sided) regions could be determined and compared among themselves and with rectangular regions. The pendulum and the ax are two of the examples he included in notes for his book *De Ludo Geometrico* (roughly meaning "Fun with Geometry"), which he never completed. The dots show the centers of the circular arcs that form the boundaries of the regions.

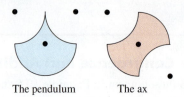

The pendulum     The ax

If the arcs forming the pendulum and the ax have radius 1, show that the areas of both figures are equal to that of a 1-by-2 rectangle.

**Solution**   After inscribing the figures in a square, we use the congruence and addition properties of area to rearrange the subregions to form a 1-by-2 rectangle:

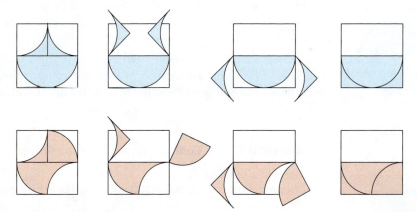

It is surprising to learn that the pendulum and ax both have an area of 2 square units. It is also a tribute to da Vinci's genius that he could see this in the fifteenth century!

*SOURCE: These examples and others are described in a booklet by Herbert Wills III,* Leonardo's Dessert, *(Reston, VA: National Council of Teachers of Mathematics, 1985.)*

Unlike Examples 10.6 and 10.7, most area measurement problems are answered by giving a reasonable *estimate* of the area. Units of square shape are easy to subdivide into smaller squares to give a more precise estimation.

## EXAMPLE 10.8   Investigating the Area of a Cycloidal Arch

Imagine rolling a wheel along a straight line, with a reflector at point *P* on the rim. Point *P* traces an arch-shaped curve. In the early seventeenth century, Galileo investigated this curve and named it the **cycloid.** Discover for yourself the conjecture Galileo made about how the area of the cycloidal arch compares to the area of the circle used to generate the arch.

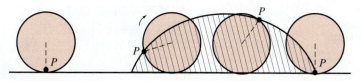

**Solution**

**Understand the Problem**

It is visually clear that the cycloidal arch has an area that is much larger than that of the circle. Our goal is to guess the ratio area(cycloid)/area(circle) that gives the comparison between the areas.

**Devise a Plan**

The areas of the arch and circle must both be measured in some unit of area. For example, we can use squares of size $U$, where the diameter of the circle is equal to the sum of four side lengths of $U$. For better accuracy, we can also use small square units of size $u$, where the side length of $u$ is half that of $U$.

**Carry Out the Plan**

The circle and arch are overlaid by a square grid, with squares of unit area $U$.

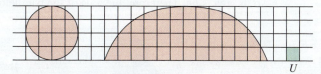

The circle is entirely within 16 squares of size $U$, but does not entirely cover about one unit of area in each of the four corners. Thus, we estimate that area(circle) $\doteq 12\,U$. Similarly, we see that area(cycloid) $\doteq 37\,U$ is a reasonable estimate.

Better accuracy is given by the grid of squares of unit area $u$. The following diagram leads us to the estimated area(circle) $\doteq 50\,u$ and area(cycloid) $\doteq 149\,u$:

Both $\dfrac{37\,U}{12\,U}$ and $\dfrac{149\,u}{50\,u}$ are nearly 3, which in fact was Galileo's conjecture. The correctness of Galileo's conjecture was proved in 1634 by Gilles Persone de Roberval.

**Look Back**

The finer grid of squares gave us additional precision in our measurements, but this required considerably more time and effort to obtain. The measurement process nearly always requires us to make a judgment about how to balance the conflicting needs of precision versus cost.

## Areas of Polygons

In this part of Section 10.2, we'll derive formulas for the areas of rectangles, parallelograms, triangles, and trapezoids based on the square as a unit. All of the formulas are very familiar to you—you will now see conceptually why they are true. This approach will help you give your students a conceptual understanding of the formulas for area.

**Rectangles**   A 3-cm–by–5-cm rectangle can be covered by 15 unit squares when the unit square is 1 cm$^2$, as shown in Figure 10.8. Similarly a 2.5-cm–by–3.5-cm rectangle can be covered by six whole units, five half-unit squares, and one quarter-unit square, giving a total area of 8.75 square centimeters. This is also the product of the width and the length, since 2.5 cm $\times$ 3.5 cm = 8.75 cm$^2$.

**FIGURE 10.8**
The area of a rectangle is
the product of its length
and width

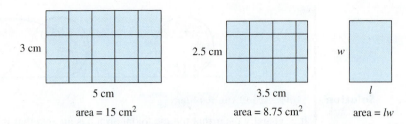

area = 15 cm²     area = 8.75 cm²     area = lw

For any rectangle, the formula for the area $A$ is as follows:

> **FORMULA**    *Area of a Rectangle*
> A rectangle of length $l$ and width $w$ has area $A$ given by the formula $A = lw$.

**Parallelograms**    Suppose a parallelogram has a pair of opposite sides $b$ units long and these sides are $h$ units apart; an example is shown in Figure 10.9. We say that $b$ is the **base** of the parallelogram and $h$ is the **altitude,** or **height.** (Unless the parallelogram is a rectangle, the altitude is *not* the same as the length of the other two sides of the parallelogram.) Removing and replacing a right triangle $T$ forms a rectangle of the same area as the parallelogram. The rectangle has length $b$ and width $h$, so its area is $bh$. Therefore, the area of the parallelogram in Figure 10.9 is also $bh$.

**FIGURE 10.9**
A parallelogram of base $b$
and altitude $h$ has the
same area as a $b$-by-$h$ rectangle. Therefore, the area
of the parallelogram is $bh$

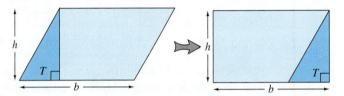

Any parallelogram with base $b$ and altitude $h$ can be dissected and rearranged to form a rectangle of length $b$ and width $h$ in a way similar to that shown in Figure 10.9. (See problem 44 in Problem Set 10.2 for a more general case.) This discussion gives the following formula:

> **FORMULA**    *Area of a Parallelogram*
> A parallelogram of base $b$ and altitude $h$ has area $A$ given by $A = bh$.
>
>

Thus, the parallelogram shown has the same area as a rectangle of width $h$ and length $b$.

**EXAMPLE  10.9  Using the Parallelogram Area Formula**

Find the area of each parallelogram and then compute the lengths $x$ and $y$.

(a)

(b)

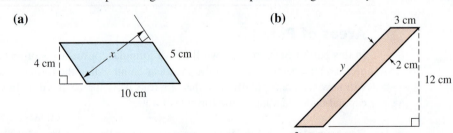

**Solution**    **(a)** The parallelogram has base 10 cm and height 4 cm, so its area is $A = (10\text{ cm})(4\text{ cm}) = 40\text{ cm}^2$. If the side of length 5 cm is considered the base, then $x$ is the corresponding height and $A = (5\text{ cm})x$. Since $A = 40\text{ cm}^2$, we find that $x = 40\text{ cm}^2/5\text{ cm} = 8\text{ cm}$.

**(b)** The procedure for (a) is followed. The area is $A = (3 \text{ cm})(12 \text{ cm}) = 36 \text{ cm}^2$. Viewing the side of length $y$ as the base with corresponding altitude 2 cm, we have $36 \text{ cm}^2 = y(2 \text{ cm})$. Therefore, $y = 36 \text{ cm}^2/2 \text{ cm} = 18 \text{ cm}$.

**Triangles** Figure 10.10 shows that a triangle of base $b$ and altitude $h$ can be dissected and rearranged to form a parallelogram of base $\frac{b}{2}$ and altitude $h$. The formula $\frac{1}{2}bh$ for the area of the triangle then follows from the area formula already derived for the parallelogram.

**FIGURE 10.10**
A triangle of base $b$ and altitude $h$ can be dissected and rearranged to form a parallelogram of base $\frac{b}{2}$ and altitude $h$

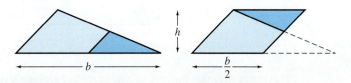

**FORMULA** *Area of a Triangle*

A triangle of base $b$ and altitude $h$ has area $A = \frac{1}{2}bh$.

Any side of a triangle can be considered as the base, so there are three pairs of bases and altitudes.

**EXAMPLE 10.10 Using the Triangle Area Formula**

Find the area of each triangle and the distances $v$ and $w$.

**(a)**

7 cm · 14 cm · $v$ · 10 cm

**(b)**

$w$ · 10 in · 12 in · 15 in

**Solution**

**(a)** The formula $A = \frac{1}{2}bh$ shows that the area of the triangle is $A = \frac{1}{2}(10 \text{ cm}) \cdot (7 \text{ cm}) = 35 \text{ cm}^2$. If the side of length 14 cm is considered the base, then the corresponding altitude is $v$. Since $A = \frac{1}{2}(14 \text{ cm}) \cdot (v)$, we have $v = A/(7 \text{ cm}) = (35 \text{ cm}^2)/(7 \text{ cm}) = 5 \text{ cm}$.

**(b)** The area of the triangle is $A = \frac{1}{2}(15 \text{ in}) \cdot (12 \text{ in}) = 90 \text{ in}^2$. Taking the side of length $w$ as the base, we find that the corresponding altitude is 10 in and $A = \frac{1}{2}w(10 \text{ in})$. Therefore, $w = (90 \text{ in}^2)/(5 \text{ in}) = 18 \text{ in}$.

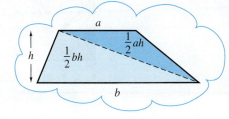

**Trapezoids** There are several ways to derive the formula for the area of a trapezoid with altitude $h$ and bases $a$ and $b$. For example, a diagonal drawn through the trapezoid dissects it into two triangles. The altitudes of both triangles are $h$, and their bases are $a$ and $b$, so the areas of the triangles are $\frac{1}{2}ah$ and $\frac{1}{2}bh$. Adding the areas gives the following formula, as is also shown in Figure 10.11:

> **FORMULA** *Area of a Trapezoid*
>
> A trapezoid with bases of length *a* and *b* and altitude *h* has area $A = \frac{1}{2}(a + b)h$.

**FIGURE 10.11**
The area of a trapezoid is
$\frac{1}{2}(a + b)h$

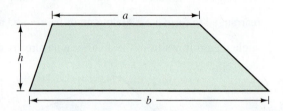

This result says that the area of a trapezoid of altitude *h* is the same as the area of a rectangle of width *h* and whose length is the *average* of the lengths of the trapezoid.

## EXAMPLE 10.11 Finding the Areas of Lattice Polygons

A polygon formed by joining points of a square array is called a **lattice polygon.** Lattice polygons are easy to draw on dot paper, or they can be formed with rubber bands on a geoboard. Find the areas of the following lattice polygons, where the unit of area is the area of a small square of the array:

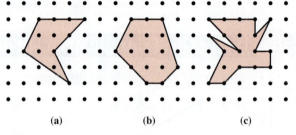

(a)    (b)    (c)

**Solution**

(a) A horizontal line dissects the polygon into a trapezoid *A* of area $\frac{1}{2}(3 + 2) \cdot (2) = 5$ and a triangle *B* of area $\frac{1}{2}(2)(2) = 2$. The area of the polygon is therefore 7.

(b) The lattice hexagon can be dissected into trapezoids *C* and *D* and triangle *E*. The total area of the hexagon is therefore

$$\frac{1}{2}(2 + 3) \cdot (2) + \frac{1}{2}(3 + 1) \cdot (2) + \frac{1}{2}(4) \cdot (1) = 11.$$

Other dissections of the hexagon can be used, but the total area will always be the same.

(c) We could solve the problem in the same way as in parts (a) and (b), but there is another useful technique: Construct a square about the polygon, and then subtract the areas of the regions *F*, *G*, *H*, *I*, and *J*. Therefore, the area of the polygon is

$$16 - \left(1 + 1\frac{1}{2} + \frac{1}{2} + 1 + 2\frac{1}{2}\right) = 9\frac{1}{2}.$$

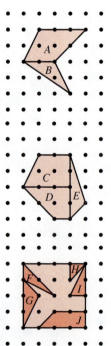

## Length of a Curve

The **length of a polygonal curve** is obtained by summing the lengths of its sides. The key to finding (and, in fact, the definition of) the **length of a nonpolygonal curve** is to measure, or at least estimate, by calculating the length of an approximating polygonal curve with vertices on the given curve. The accuracy of the estimation is improved by using an approximating polygonal curve with ever more vertices, as shown in Figure 10.12.

**FIGURE 10.12**
The length of the curve in (a) is estimated by measuring the length of a polygonal approximation, as in (b). Increasing the number of vertices gives an improved estimate carefully, as in (c)

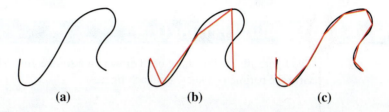

    **(a)**     **(b)**     **(c)**

The length of a curve can also be measured by first laying a string along the curve and then straightening the string along a ruler. This is the principle that makes the flexible tape measure used for sewing so useful.

**EXAMPLE 10.12** Determining the Length of a Cycloid

A circle and the cycloid it generates (see Example 10.8) are shown next. Use a marker pen and a piece of string (or thin strip of paper) to make a tape measure, where the unit of length is the diameter $d$ of the circle.

    **(a)** According to your tape measure, what is the length from point $A$ to point $B$ along the cycloid?
    **(b)** What is the approximate length of the line segment $\overline{AB}$?

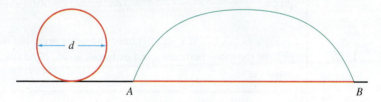

**Solution**

    **(a)** The tape measure shows that the length of the cycloid is very nearly four diameters of the circle. In 1658, Christopher Wren (1632–1723) proved that the length of a cycloid is *exactly* four diameters. Wren is perhaps best known as the architect of St. Paul's Cathedral in London.
    **(b)** The segment $\overline{AB}$ is a bit over three diameters. Because $\overline{AB}$ is covered by rolling the circle once around, $AB$ is the length around the circle; that is, $AB$ is the circumference, and "a bit over three" is the famous value now written as $\pi$.

**Perimeter**    The length of a simple closed plane curve is called the curve's **perimeter.** It is quite hard to formally define the perimeter of a region. The difficulties are in the definition of the terms *region*, *length*, and *boundary*. Because these ideas are intuitive and you will be applying them in elementary or middle school, we write the following definition of perimeter:

A loop of string forms regions with the same perimeter, but different enclosed areas.

**DEFINITION**   *Perimeter of a Region*
If a region is bounded by a simple closed curve, then the **perimeter** of the region is the length of the curve. More generally, the **perimeter** of a region is the length of its boundary.

The perimeter is a *length* measurement and is given in centimeters, inches, feet, meters, and so on. It is important not to confuse the *area* of the region enclosed by a simple closed curve with the perimeter of the figure. Area is given in cm$^2$, in$^2$, ft$^2$, m$^2$, and so on. In sum, the perimeter is the measure of the distance around a region, and the area is the measure of the size of the region within a boundary.

**EXAMPLE 10.13 Finding Perimeters**

The figures that follow have been drawn on a square grid, where each square is 1 cm on a side. Give the perimeter and area of each figure.

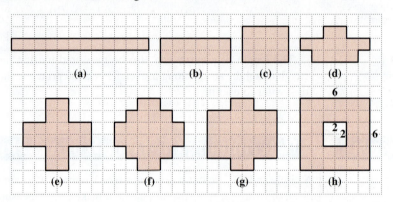

**Solution**

| Figure | (a) | (b) | (c) | (d) | (e) | (f) | (g) | (h) | |
|---|---|---|---|---|---|---|---|---|---|
| Perimeter | 26 | 16 | 14 | 18 | 24 | 24 | 24 | 32 | centimeters |
| Area | 12 | 12 | 12 | 12 | 20 | 24 | 28 | 32 | square centimeters |

Figures (a), (b), (c), and (d) have the same area, but different perimeters. Figures (e), (f), and (g) have the same perimeter, but different areas. Note that Figure (h) is not bounded by a simple closed curve.

**The Circumference of a Circle** The perimeter of a circle is called the circle's **circumference.** By using a piece of string or a tape measure, or by rolling a disc along a line (as in Example 10.12(b)), it is easy to rediscover a fact known even in ancient times: The ratio of the circumference of a circle to the circle's diameter is the same for all circles. Two examples are shown in Figure 10.13.

This ratio, which is somewhat larger than 3, is given by the symbol $\pi$, the lowercase Greek letter *pi.*

**DEFINITION** $\pi$

The ratio of the circumference $C$ to the diameter $d$ of a circle is $\pi$. Therefore,

$$\frac{C}{d} = \pi \quad \text{and} \quad C = \pi d.$$

**FIGURE 10.13**
The ratio of the circumference C to the diameter d is the same for all circles: C/d = π, or C = πd

Since the diameter $d$ is twice the radius $r$ of the circle, we also have the formula $C = 2\pi r$.

In 1761, John Lambert proved that $\pi$ is an irrational number, so it is impossible to express $\pi$ exactly by a fraction or as a terminating or repeating decimal. The values $3\frac{1}{7}$ and 3.14 are useful approximate values, but precision measurements require the use of more decimal places in the unending decimal expansion $\pi = 3.1415926\ldots$. A circle 100 feet in diameter has an *approximate* circumference of 314 feet, but the exact circumference is $100\pi$ feet. It is acceptable to use the symbol $\pi$ to express results, since this gives exact values. When an approximate numerical value is needed, an appropriate estimate of $\pi$, such as 3.1416, can be used in the calculations.

**EXAMPLE 10.14 Calculating the Equatorial Circumference of the Earth**

The equatorial diameter of the earth is 7926 miles. Calculate the distance around the earth at the equator, using the following approximations for $\pi$: **(a)** 3.14 **(b)** 3.1416.

**Solution**

**(a)** $(3.14)(7926 \text{ miles}) = 24{,}887.64 \text{ miles}$
**(b)** $(3.1416)(7926 \text{ miles}) = 24{,}900.322 \text{ miles}$

The two different approximations of $\pi$ account for the difference of about 12.7 miles in the answers.

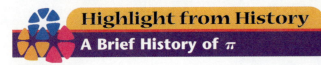

## Highlight from History

### A Brief History of $\pi$

In the third century B.C., Archimedes showed that $\pi$ is approximately $3\frac{1}{7}$. To estimate $\pi$, Archimedes inscribed a regular polygon in a circle and then calculated the ratio of the polygon's perimeter to the diameter of the circle. An inscribed hexagon shows that $\pi$ is about 3, but by using a 96-gon, Archimedes

proved that $3\frac{10}{71} < \pi < 3\frac{10}{70}$. The same idea was used by the Dutch mathematician Van Ceulen (d. 1610), who used a 32,212,254,720-gon to calculate $\pi$ to 20 decimals. A century later, the English mathematician John Machin took advantage of the invention of calculus to calculate $\pi$ to

100 decimal places. Machin's method, with some minor variations, was used well into the twentieth century. When this problem was implemented on the ENIAC, the first electronic computer, in 1949, the computer spent 70 hours calculating $\pi$ to 2037 decimal places. $\pi$ has now been calculated to more than a trillion decimal places.

## The Area of a Circle

The area of a circle of radius $r$ is given by the formula $\pi r^2$, first proved rigorously by Archimedes.

> **FORMULA**   *Area of a Circle*
> The area $A$ enclosed by a circle of radius $r$ is $A = \pi r^2$.

Since $\pi$ is defined as a ratio of lengths, it seems surprising to find that $\pi$ also occurs in the formula for the area of a circle. A convincing, but informal, derivation of the formula $A = \pi r^2$ is shown in Figure 10.14. The circle of radius $r$ and circumference $C = 2\pi r$ is dissected into congruent sectors that are rearranged to form a "parallelogram" of base $\frac{1}{2}C = \pi r$ and altitude $r$. By the formula for the area of a parallelogram, the wavy-based "parallelogram" has area $\pi r \times r = \pi r^2$. If the number of sections is made larger and larger, the sum of the areas of the thin sectors forms an increasingly exact approximation to a true parallelogram of area $\pi r^2$.

**FIGURE 10.14**
The sectors of a circle can be rearranged to approximate a parallelogram of area $\pi r^2$

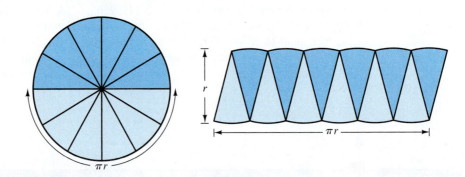

## EXAMPLE 10.15 Determining the Size of a Pizza $\pi$

A 14″ pizza has the same thickness as a 10″ pizza. How many times more ingredients are there on the larger pizza?

**Solution**    Pizzas are measured by their diameters, so the radii of the two pizzas are 7″ and 5″, respectively. Since the thicknesses are the same, the amount of ingredients used is proportional to the areas of the pizzas. The larger pizza has area $\pi(7 \text{ in})^2 = 49\pi \text{ in}^2$, and the smaller pizza has area $\pi(5 \text{ in})^2 = 25\pi \text{ in}^2$. The ratio of areas is $49\pi \text{ in}^2/25\pi \text{ in}^2 = 1.96$, showing that the 14″ pizza has about twice the ingredients of the 10″ one.

## Cooperative Investigation
### Measurements in Beanland

### Materials Needed

Dry beans (small red kidney or white navy beans); enlarged copies of the figures shown in the two activities that follow.

### Directions

In Beanland, the lengths of curves are measured in *beanlengths,* abbreviated "bl." Similarly, the areas of regions are measured in *beanareas,* abbreviated "ba." The following diagram shows that the length of the curve is about 15 bl.

The next diagram shows a region bounded by a simple closed curve. By counting the beans, we see that the region has an area of about 55 ba.

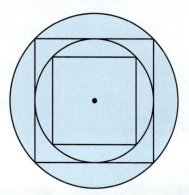

Carry out the following activities in pairs:

### Activities

1. Consider the following system of squares and circles (use an enlarged copy of this figure, with the larger circle about 14 to 16 beanlengths in diameter):

   **(a)** Measure the area of the ring-shaped region between the two circles, using your beans.
   **(b)** Measure the area of the smaller circle, and then compare this area with that of the ring.
   **(c)** Measure the area of the small square and then the area of the region between the two squares. How do these areas compare?
   **(d)** Measure the perimeter of (the distance around) the small square in beanlengths. Next measure the length of the diagonal of the large square. How do these lengths compare?
   **(e)** Measure the circumference and the diameter of the large circle. What is the ratio of the circumference to the diameter? Compare with other groups and determine the average ratio.

**2.** Consider an equilateral triangle *ABC* and its circumscribed and inscribed circles (again, use an enlargement so that the larger circle has a diameter of about 14 to 16 beanlengths):

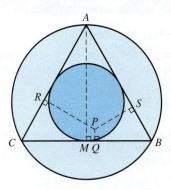

**3.** Measure the area of the small circle and the area of the ring-shaped region between the two circles. What is the ratio of the area of the ring to that of the small circle?

**4.** Choose an arbitrary point *P* inside the triangle, and measure the three distances *PQ, PR,* and *PS* to the sides of the triangle. How does the sum *PQ + PR + PS* of these three distances compare with the length *AM* of the altitude of the triangle?

## Problem Set 10.2

Exercises numbered in red are answered in the back of the text.

### Understanding Concepts

**1.** Botanists often need to measure the rate at which water is lost by transpiration through the leaves of a plant. For this measurement, it is necessary to know the leaf area of the plant. Estimate the area of the leaf shown. It has been overlaid with a grid of squares 1 cm on a side, shown at reduced scale.

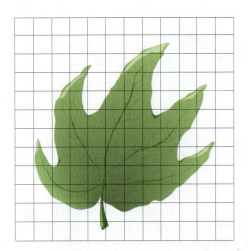

**2.** Cut a convex quadrilateral from card stock, locate the midpoints of its sides, and then cut along the segments joining successive midpoints to give four triangles $T_1, T_2, T_3,$ and $T_4$ and a parallelogram *P*.

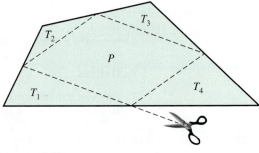

**(a)** Show that the four triangles can be arranged to cover the parallelogram.

**(b)** How does the area of the parallelogram compare with the area of the original quadrilateral?

**3.** The regular dodecagon shown next is dissected into six subregions. Carefully trace the pattern, cut out the subregions, and show how the pieces can be reassembled into a square. How are the areas of the dodecagon and square related?

**4.** The goblet shown is drawn with circular 90° arcs centered at the black dots in a grid of squares of unit area. Redraw the vase on squared paper, and then use a dissection argument similar to that in Example 10.7 to find the area of the goblet.

**5.** Measure the left-hand figure $F$ shown in each of the three nonstandard units of area **(a)**, **(b)**, and **(c)** shown to the right of $F$. Do so by tracing $F$ and then dissecting the region into subregions with the unit area shape.

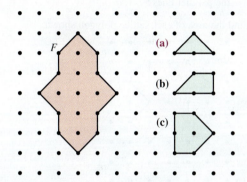

**6.** Find the area of each of these figures:

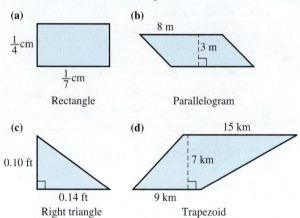

**(a)** $\frac{1}{4}$ cm   $\frac{1}{7}$ cm   Rectangle

**(b)** 8 m   3 m   Parallelogram

**(c)** 0.10 ft   0.14 ft   Right triangle

**(d)** 15 km   7 km   9 km   Trapezoid

**7.** Find the area of each of these figures:

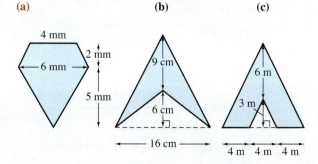

**(a)** 4 mm   2 mm   6 mm   5 mm

**(b)** 9 cm   6 cm   16 cm

**(c)** 6 m   3 m   4 m  4 m  4 m

**8.** A rectangle has a length that is twice its width.
  **(a)** If its perimeter is 14 in, what are the dimensions of the rectangle?

**(b)** If its area is 32 in², what are the dimensions of the rectangle?

**9.** Fill in the blanks.
  **(a)** $3.45\text{ m}^2 =$ —— cm²
  **(b)** $56{,}000\text{ mm}^2 =$ —— cm²
  **(c)** $56{,}700\text{ ft}^2 =$ —— yd²
  **(d)** $0.085\text{ mi}^2 =$ —— ft²
  **(e)** $47{,}000\text{ a} =$ —— ha = —— m²
  **(f)** $5{,}800{,}000\text{ m}^2 =$ —— ha = —— km²

**10. (a)** A rectangle has area 36 cm² and width 3 cm. What is the length of the rectangle?
  **(b)** A rectangle has area 60 cm² and perimeter 38 cm. Use the "guess and check" method to find the length and width of the rectangle.

**11.** Twenty-four 1-cm–by–1-cm squares are used to tile a rectangle.
  **(a)** Find the dimensions of all possible rectangles.
  **(b)** Which rectangle has the smallest perimeter?
  **(c)** Which rectangle has the largest perimeter?

**12.** Find the areas and perimeters of the parallelograms that follow. Be sure to express your answer in the appropriate units of measurement.

**(a)**

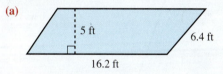

5 ft   6.4 ft   16.2 ft

**(b)**

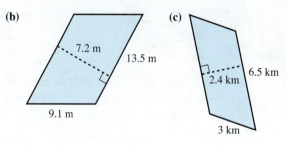

7.2 m   13.5 m   9.1 m

**(c)** 2.4 km   6.5 km   3 km

**13.** Find the areas and perimeters of these triangles:

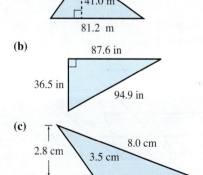

**(a)** 49.0 m   68.1 m   41.0 m   81.2 m

**(b)** 87.6 in   36.5 in   94.9 in

**(c)** 2.8 cm   8.0 cm   3.5 cm   5.4 cm

**14.** Find the areas of the figures shown. Express each area in square units.

**(a)**

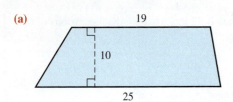

**(b)**

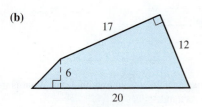

**(c)**

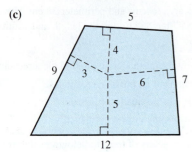

**(d)**

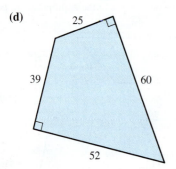

**15. (a)** Find the area and the perimeter of each of the four right triangles whose length of their legs is given in centimeters:

  **(i)** 2 cm by 2 cm

  **(ii)** 1 cm by 4 cm

  **(iii)** .5 cm by 8 cm

  **(iv)** .25 cm by 16 cm

**(b)** What is happening to the area and perimeter as you proceed from (i) to (iv), and what do the triangles look like?

**16.** Lines $k$, $l$, and $m$ are parallel to the line containing the side $\overline{AB}$ of the triangles shown here:

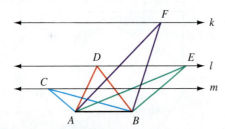

**(a)** What triangle has the smallest area? Why?

**(b)** What triangle has the largest area? Why?

**(c)** Which two triangles have the same area? Why?

**17.** Lines $k$, $l$, and $m$ are equally spaced parallel lines. Let $ABCD$ be a parallelogram of area 12 square units.

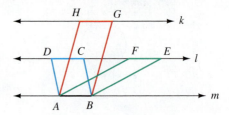

**(a)** What is the area of the parallelogram $ABEF$?

**(b)** What is the area of the parallelogram $ABGH$?

**(c)** If $AB = 3$ units of length, what is the distance between the parallel lines?

**18.** Find the area of each lattice polygon shown:

**(a)**

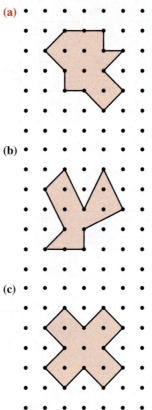

**(b)**

**(c)**

**19.** An oval track is made by erecting semicircles on each end of a 50-m-by-100-m rectangle.

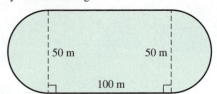

**(a)** What is the length of the track?

**(b)** What is the area of the region enclosed by the track?

**20.** A track has lanes 1 meter wide. The turn radius of the inner lane is 25 meters. To make a fair race, the starting lines in each lane must be staggered so that each competitor runs the same distance to the finish line. Find the distance between the starting line in one lane to the starting line in the next lane. Is the same distance used between the first and second lanes and between the second and third lanes?

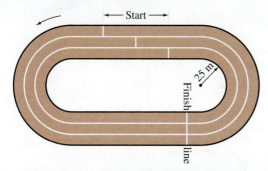

**21.** An **annulus** is the region bounded by two concentric circles.

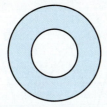

(a) If the radius of the small circle is 1 and the radius of the larger circle is 2, what is the area of the annulus?

(b) What is the perimeter of the annulus?

(c) A dartboard has four annular rings surrounding a bull's-eye.

The circles have radii 1, 2, 3, 4, and 5. Suppose a dart is equally likely to hit any point of the board. Is the dart more likely to hit in the outermost ring (shown black) or inside the region consisting of the bull's-eye and the two innermost rings?

**22.** A circle is inscribed in a square, as in the picture shown.

(a) What percentage of the area of the square is inside the circle?

(b) If the radius of the circle is 6 cm, what is the perimeter of the region formed by removing the area inside the circle from the square?

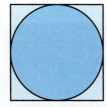

**23.** If a rectangle with length *l* and width *w* has a perimeter of 20 cm, what are the dimensions of the rectangle with the largest area and what is that area? (*Hint:* See Example 8.13 on page 433.)

**24.** This problem looks similar to the preceding one. Is it true that there is a maximum value for the perimeter of a rectangle whose area is 4 m²? More precisely, if a rectangle with length *l* and width *w* has area 4 m², then

(a) Write an equation for the perimeter of the rectangle in terms of only one of the variables.

**MHM** (b) Is your answer for part (a) a function that can become infinitely large?

**25.** Two semicircular arcs, of radius 3 m and 5 m, are centered on the diameter $\overline{AB}$ of a large semicircle as shown. Which route from *A* to *B* is shorter: along the large semicircle or along the two smaller semicircles that touch at *C*?

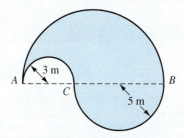

**26.** The meter was originally defined as one ten-millionth of the distance from the North Pole to the equator.

(a) Assuming that the earth is a perfect sphere, what would be the circumference of a great circle on the earth that passes through the North and South poles?

(b) The diameter of the equatorial circle of the earth is 12,755 kilometers. What is the circumference of the equator in meters?

(c) Which is longer, the polar circle or the equator? Can you account for the difference?

## Teaching Concepts

**27.** In teaching any topic, it is extremely helpful if surprising results of interest can be included. The result of Example 10.8 is such a case, as are the results of the following problems:

(a) Instead of rolling a wheel along a straight line, imagine "rolling" an equilateral triangle, as shown below. As the triangle "rolls" from left to right, the point *A* starts on the line, moves to the top in the middle position of the triangle, and again comes to rest on the line at the right end of the figure. Measure the figure shown *very carefully* with a metric ruler (estimate your measurements to the nearest millimeter), and then determine the area in square centimeters of the equilateral triangle and of the triangle *AAA* formed by the three locations of the point *A*. Then calculate the ratio of the area of triangle *AAA* to the area of the equilateral triangle.

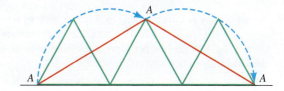

**(b)** Instead of rolling an equilateral triangle, this time "roll" a square, as shown. Again, measure this figure with a metric ruler, and then determine the area of the square and the area under the polygonal arch *AAAA*. As before, also determine the ratio of the area under the polygonal arch to the area of the square. (See Example 10.6, part (a).)

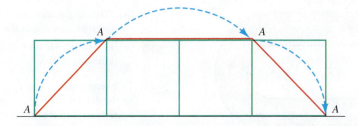

**MHM** **(c)** Repeat parts (a) and (b), but this time roll a regular pentagon, as shown.

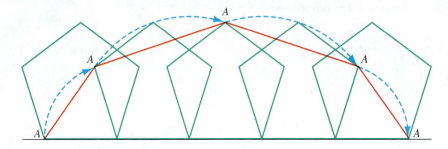

**(d)** Repeat parts (a), (b), and (c), but for a regular hexagon. (See Example 10.6, part (b).)

**(e)** Make a conjecture based on parts (a) through (d).

---

## Responding to Students

**28.** Andrew was asked to find the area of the following figure:

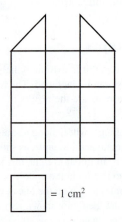

= 1 cm²

Andrew answered 11 cm².

**(a)** What does Andrew correctly understand about figuring area?

**(b)** What is Andrew doing incorrectly when figuring area, and how would you guide him in the future?

**29.** A packing box is 11 inches long by 7 inches wide by 6 inches deep. Lanisha is asked to find the perimeter of the bottom of the box. Lanisha gets out her paper, does some addition, and then writes 24 inches.

**(a)** What is the correct perimeter of the bottom of the box?

**(b)** Where did Lanisha's answer of 24 inches come from?

**(c)** How could you guide Lanisha in the future when approaching such problems?

**30.** Estelle had been practicing area and perimeter problems in math for several days. The class first learned all about perimeters and Estelle was successful. The class later learned about areas and again Estelle was successful when practicing. The teacher gave her class the following problem in which they had to calculate both the area and the perimeter for the same figure:

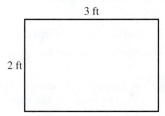

3 ft

2 ft

Here are Estelle's answers:

Perimeter: 5 feet
Area: 5 feet

**(a)** What is Estelle doing incorrectly when applying the formulas she learned for area and perimeter?

**(b)** Some students are often successful when solving area and perimeter problems in isolation but can make many mistakes when asked to complete both in the same problem. Why do you suppose this happens? What could a teacher do to remedy this confusion?

## Thinking Critically

**31.** A rectangle has length $l$ and width $w$.

**(a)** If $w$ remains the same and $l$ increases, must the area of the rectangle increase, and why?

**(b)** If the perimeter increases, does the area increase also? In this case, the conditions are that the length $l$ and width $w$ of the rectangle can vary, but if the perimeter increases, then does the area of the new rectangle always increase?

**32.** Find formulas for the perimeter and area of a regular hexagon with sides of length $b$.

**33.** Two regions $A$ and $B$ are cut from paper. Suppose the area of region $A$ is $20\,\text{cm}^2$ larger than that of region $B$. If the regions are overlapped, by how much does the area of the nonoverlapped part of region $A$ exceed the nonoverlapped part of region $B$? Explain carefully.

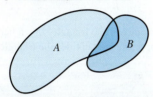

**34.** Four mutually tangent circles of diameter 10 cm with their centers at the vertices of a square are used to draw a vase, as follows:

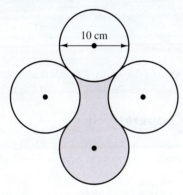

**(a)** Use dissection and rearrangement to form a square of the same area as the vase. (Show a sequence of steps similar to those in the solution to Example 10.7.)

**(b)** Show that the vase has area $100\,\text{cm}^2$.

**(c)** As an extra challenge, see if you can do part (a) by cutting the vase into just three pieces.

**35.** A square cake measures 8″ by 8″. A wedge-shaped piece is cut by two slices meeting at 90° at the cake's center. What is the area of the top of the piece? Explain your reasoning carefully.

**36.** For reasons lost in history, the two cornfields $R$ and $S$ were divided by two line segments $\overline{AB}$ and $\overline{BC}$. The friendly owners of the fields would like to divide their adjoining fields by a single straight boundary line. Carefully describe how to divide the quadrilateral into two fields $R'$ and $S'$ with a single segment so that the area of each new cornfield is the same as before.

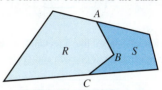

**37. (a)** The colored region shown is formed by circular arcs drawn from two opposite corners of a 1-by-1 square. What is the area of the region?

**(b)** Four semicircles are drawn with centers at the midpoints of the sides of a 1-by-1 square. What is the area of the shaded region?

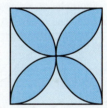

**38.** A sidewalk 8 feet wide surrounds the polygonally shaped garden of perimeter 300 feet, as shown. The sidewalk makes circular sectors of 8-foot radius at the vertices of the polygon. Explain why the area covered by the walk is $2400 + 64\pi$ square feet.

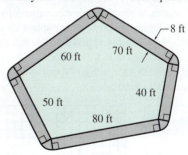

**39.** Erin walks her dog Nerd with a leash of length $L$. Nerd is very obedient and always walks directly to Erin's right at the end of his leash. Erin follows several different routes and wants to compare the length of her walk with that of Nerd. For the following routes, how much farther does Nerd walk than Erin?

**(a)** Around a circle of radius $R$

**(b)** Around a square with sides of length $S$

**(c)** Around a track shaped like a rectangle of length $A$ with half circles of radius $R$ on each end of the rectangle

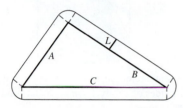

**(d)** Around a triangle with sides of length $A$, $B$, and $C$

**MHM** **(e)** Around any simple closed curve. (*Hint:* Approximate the curve by a polygon and review Section 9.2.)

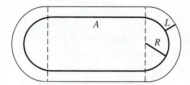

**40.** Problems 48 and 50 of the Rhind papyrus suggest that the ancient Egyptians approximated $\pi$ with $(16/9)^2$, which, to two decimal places, is the quite accurate value 3.16. Use the sequence of figures that follows to explain the reasoning which may have been used to derive this estimation. Notice that the area of the circle with diameter 9 is approximated by an octagon and that the octagon's area is then approximated by a square of side length 8.

**41.** The commentaries of the Talmud (Tosfos Pesachim 109a, Tosfos Succah 8a, Marsha Babba Bathra 27a) present a nice approach to the formula $A = \pi r^2$ for the area of a circle. Imagine that the interior of a circle is covered by concentric circles of yarn. The yarn circles are clipped along a vertical radius, and each strand is straightened to cover an isosceles triangle, as shown in the accompanying figure. Find the area of the triangle and then explain how the area formula for a circle follows.

**42.** Let $P$ be an arbitrary point in an equilateral triangle $ABC$ of altitude $h$ and side $s$, as shown. What is the sum $x + y + z$ of the distances to the sides of the triangle? (*Hint:* The areas of $\triangle ABP$, $\triangle BCP$, and $\triangle ACP$ add up to the area of $\triangle ABC$.)

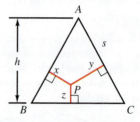

**43.** Joining each vertex of the triangle shown here to the midpoint of the opposite side divides the triangle into six small triangles:

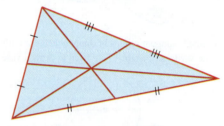

Show that all six triangles have the same area. (*Hint:* Look for pairs of triangles with the same base and height.)

## Thinking Cooperatively

For the next four problems and activities, you will need several sheets of paper (including a sheet of ruled notebook paper), scissors, and a ruler.

**44.** The derivation of the formula for the area of a parallelogram depicted in Figure 10.9 does not apply to a tall, slanted parallelogram, since more than two pieces are required to form a rectangle. Draw a parallelogram something like the one shown, where the base is, say, three vertical ruled lines long. Cut out the parallelogram and make vertical cuts along every third ruled line. Show that the pieces you obtain can be reassembled into a rectangle.

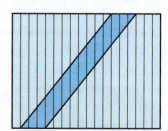

**45.** Fold a sheet of paper in half and cut out a pair of congruent triangles.

**(a)** Show that the two triangles can be arranged to form a parallelogram.

**(b)** Use the construction in part (a) to obtain a new explanation of how the formula for the area of a triangle follows from the formula for the area of a parallelogram.

**46.** Cut several triangles, as illustrated, from paper.

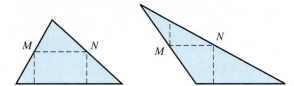

Find the midpoints $M$ and $N$ of the slanted sides (that is, the sides, not the base) by folding.

**(a)** Fold on the horizontal and vertical lines (shown dashed) to form a doubly covered (two layers of paper) rectangle.

**(b)** If the triangle has base $b$ and altitude $h$, what are the lengths of the sides of the rectangle you formed by folding? Obtain the triangle area formula $A = bh/2$.

**47.** The formula for the area of a trapezoid can be obtained in several ways with paper folding and cutting. Discuss how to obtain the formula by each of these methods:

**(a)** Fold a sheet of paper in half and cut out, simultaneously, a pair of congruent trapezoids. Show how to arrange the two trapezoids into a parallelogram, and then explain how the area formula for a trapezoid can be derived from the area formula for a parallelogram.

**(b)** Fold one of the bases of a paper trapezoid onto the other, and crease along the midline between the two bases. Now cut along the crease to create two trapezoids. Show how to arrange them into a parallelogram, and then derive the area formula for the original trapezoid from that of the parallelogram you have formed.

**48.** In groups of three people, explore the relationship between the area and perimeter of a rectangle. This question is far too imprecise in this form so we will be more specific:

**(a)** Start with a length of string that is 4 meters long, place it on the floor in the shape of a square, and calculate its area.

**(b)** Change the dimensions of the rectangle by using the string of 4 m, and still maintaining its character as a rectangle so that its area (in square meters) is less than the area (in square meters) of the rectangle of part (a).

**(c)** Now change the dimensions of the rectangle by using the string of 4 m, still maintaining its character as a rectangle so that its area (in square meters) is more than the area (in square meters) of the rectangle of part (a).

**(d)** Is it possible to shape the string into a rectangle so that its area (in square meters) is .19 $m^2$ ?

**MHM** **(e)** Suppose that $a$ is any positive real number. Is it possible to shape the string into a rectangle so that its area (in square meters) is $a$ $m^2$? (This assertion is saying that, for a fixed perimeter, you can construct a rectangle of any given area. In other words, there is no relationship between area and perimeter for rectangles!) It is important to point out that even the units don't make sense: Area is in square meters, for example, whereas perimeter is in meters. That is why we phrased things carefully.

**49.** In groups of three people, explore the relationship between the **MHM** area and perimeter of a rectangle. This question is far too imprecise so we will be specific:

**(a)** Start with a 1-m–by–1-m (paper) tile, place it on the floor, and calculate its perimeter.

**(b)** Change the dimensions of the paper tile by cutting and pasting, and still maintain its character as a rectangle of area 1 $m^2$ so that its perimeter (in meters) is less than the perimeter (in meters) of the rectangle of part (a).

**(c)** Change dimensions of the paper tile by cutting and pasting, still maintaining the character of the rectangle as a rectangle of 1 $m^2$ so that its perimeter (in meters) is more than the perimeter (in meters) of the rectangle of part (a).

**(d)** Is it possible to shape the string into a rectangle so that its perimeter (in meters) is 0.1 m? A "yes" answer implies that, for a fixed area, you can construct a rectangle of any given perimeter. In other words, there is no relationship between area and perimeter for rectangles, which is the reason for the MHM!

## Making Connections

**50.** Kelly has been hired to mow a large rectangular lawn measuring 75 feet by 125 feet. The lawn mower cuts a path 21 inches wide. Estimate how far (in feet) Kelly must walk to complete the mowing job.

**51.** Roll ends of carpet are on sale for six dollars per square yard. To finish the rough-cut edges, edging material costing 10 cents per foot is glued in place. Compute the total cost of a roll end measuring 8 feet by 10 feet.

**52.** A carpet is made by sewing a 1-inch-wide braid around and around until the final shape is an oval with semicircular ends, as shown. Estimate the length of braid required. (*Hint:* Estimate the area of the carpet.)

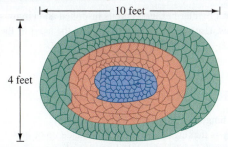

**53.** An $L$-shaped house, walkway, garage, and driveway are shown situated on a 70′ by 120′ lot. How many bags of fertilizer are needed for the lawn? Assume that the bags are each 20 pounds and 1 pound of fertilizer will treat 200 square feet of lawn.

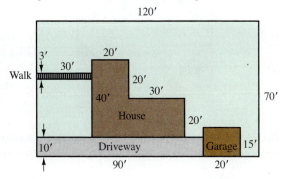

54. A 10′ by 12′ kitchen floor is to be tiled with 8″ square tiles. Estimate the number of tiles this will require.

55. **(a)** The normal-sized tires on a truck have a 14-inch radius. If oversized tires of 15-inch radius are used, how much farther does the truck travel per revolution of the wheel?

    **(b)** If the speedometer indicates that a truck is traveling at 56 miles per hour, what is the true speed when the truck is running on the oversized tires?

56. Sunaina has 600 feet of fencing. She wishes to build a corral along an existing high, straight wall. She has already decided to make the corral in the shape of an isosceles triangle, with two sides each 300 feet long. What is the measure of $\angle A$ that will give Sunaina the corral of most area? (*Hint:* Consider one of the sides of length 300 feet as a base of the triangle.)

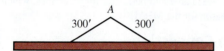

## Using a Computer

57. Use geometry software to construct any convex quadrilateral. Next, join the successive midpoints of the sides of the quadrilateral to form a parallelogram. Use the software to compute both the area of the quadrilateral and the area of the parallelogram. What relationship seems to exist between these areas?

58. Draw an equilateral triangle and its inscribed and circumscribed circles. How do the areas of the two circles compare? Investigate with your software.

59. Draw a regular hexagon and its inscribed and circumscribed circles. Use your software to compare the areas of the two circles.

## From State Student Assessments

60. (Washington State, Grade 4)
    Casey is making a quilt. Quilts are made up of quilt blocks. Each quilt block will look like the one below.

Her quilt will have 25 blocks. Casey knows how much fabric she needs to make the patterned inside squares. Tell the steps

she could take to figure out how much fabric she will need to make all of the shaded corner pieces. Explain your thinking using words, numbers, or pictures.

61. (Washington State, Grade 4)
    Which of the following is closest to the distance around the middle of an unsharpened pencil?

    **A.** 25 millimeters

    **B.** 25 centimeters

    **C.** 25 meters

62. (Illinois, Grade 5)
    The width of a rectangular rug is 4 feet. If the perimeter is 20 feet, what is the length of the rug?

    ○ 4 feet                    ○ 16 feet

    ○ 5 feet                    ○ 80 feet

    ○ 6 feet

63. (Kentucky, Grade 8).
    This is an open-response question.

### Kid City Park

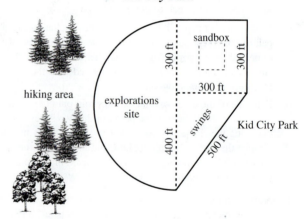

The Kid City Recreation Committee plans to put a fence around a playground area in Kid City Park. The solid line in the diagram above outlines the sections in the park that the committee wants to surround with a fence. Information about fencing prices is shown below:

| FENCE-ALL COMPANY | ACME FENCE COMPANY |
|---|---|
| Fencing = $30 per foot | Fencing = $32 per foot<br>Orders totaling $500 or more<br>will receive a 10% discount. |

    **(a)** How much fencing will the committee need to buy? Show your work.

    **(b)** Based on the information above, determine which fencing company offers the best deal for this project. Explain your reasoning and show all your work.

64. (Georgia, Grade 5)
    The original Ferris wheel introduced at the 1893 World's Fair in Chicago had a diameter of 250 feet.

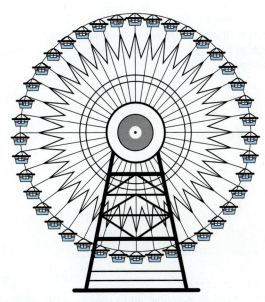

Which is closest to the distance a person who rode this wheel traveled in one complete revolution?

**A.** 393 ft  **B.** 785 ft
**C.** 1,570 ft  **D.** 49,063 ft

**65.** (Washington State, Grade 8)
Omari is making a string design for art class. Look at the design.

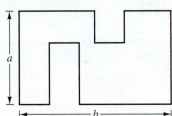

Which expression can he use to figure how much string he needs to create the design?

**A.** $a + b$  **B.** $2a + 2b$
**C.** $3a + 2b$  **D.** $4a + 2b$

**66.** (Washington, Grade 6)
Lacey's family is buying a new home. It will be her job to mow the lawn. She wants to know the size (area) of the lawn.

Map of House, Garden, and Lawn

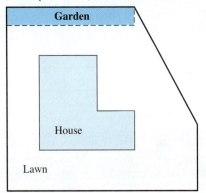

Describe at least five steps Lacey would need to take to determine the size (area) of the lawn.

**67.** (Illinois, Grade 6)
Which rectangle has an area of 24 square units and a perimeter of 20 units?

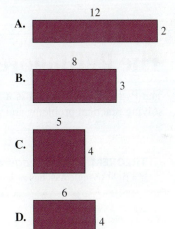

 ## Cooperative Investigation
### Discovering Pick's Formula

In 1899, the German mathematician Georg Pick discovered a remarkable formula for the area of a polygon drawn on square dot paper. Polygons of this special type are known as lattice polygons. Stretching a rubber band onto a geoboard is an easy way to form lattice polygons.

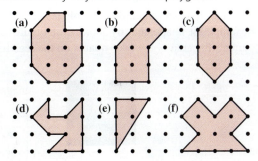

**1.** Complete the table of values for each polygon, where

$b$ = number of dots on the boundary of the polygon,
$i$ = number of dots in the interior of the polygon, and
$A$ = area of the polygon:

| Polygon | $b$ | $i$ | $A$ |
|---------|-----|-----|-----|
| (a) | 11 | 5 | $9\frac{1}{2}$ |
| (b) | | | |
| (c) | | | |
| (d) | | | |
| (e) | | | |
| (f) | | | |

The values of $b$, $i$, and $A$ for polygon (a) are given as an example.

MHM **2.** Try to guess a formula for $A$ in terms of $b$ and $i$. (If you have trouble, add a column of the values of $b/2$. You may also want to obtain more data by drawing other lattice polygons.)

## 10.3

# The Pythagorean Theorem

The Pythagorean theorem is a most remarkable result in geometry. The theorem is very useful in solving practical problems and is also aesthetically pleasing.

> **THEOREM**  *The Pythagorean Theorem*
> If a right triangle has legs of length $a$ and $b$ and its hypotenuse has length $c$, then
> $$a^2 + b^2 = c^2.$$
>

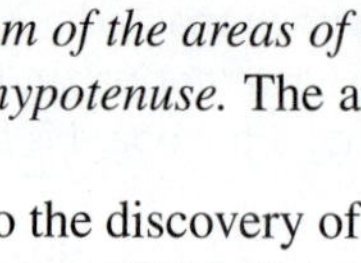

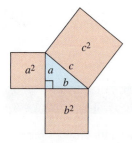

**FIGURE 10.15**
The sum of the areas of the squares on the legs of a right triangle equals the area of the square on the hypotenuse

## Proving the Pythagorean Theorem

By erecting squares on the sides of a right triangle, the Pythagorean relation $a^2 + b^2 = c^2$ can be interpreted as a result about areas: *The sum of the areas of the squares on the legs of a right triangle is equal to the area of the square on the hypotenuse.* The area interpretation of the Pythagorean theorem is shown in Figure 10.15.

The area interpretation probably led to the discovery of the theorem, at least in special cases. For example, it is apparent by looking at Figure 10.16 that the area of the square on the hypotenuse equals the area of the two squares on the legs for an isosceles right triangle.

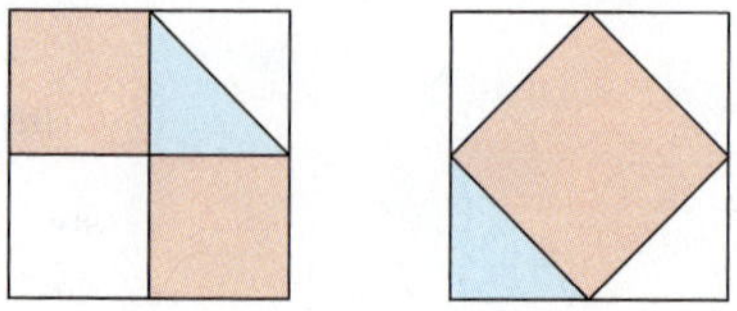

**FIGURE 10.16**
A special case of the Pythagorean theorem

(a)          (b)

The demonstration depicted in Figure 10.16 is not a general proof of the Pythagorean theorem, because the right triangle is isosceles. However, a similar idea can be followed for arbitrary right triangles, using the dissection method. In Figure 10.17(a), we begin with any right triangle, letting $a$ and $b$ denote the respective lengths of the legs and $c$ the length of the hypotenuse. Next, consider two squares with sides $a + b$, as in Figures 10.17(b) and (c). Four congruent copies of the right triangle are placed inside the squares in two different ways. In Figure 10.17(b), the four triangles leave two squares uncovered, with respective areas $a^2$ and $b^2$. In Figure 10.17(c), the four triangles leave one square of area $c^2$ uncovered. Since the four triangles must leave the same area uncovered in both arrangements, we conclude that $a^2 + b^2 = c^2$.

**FIGURE 10.17**
A dissection proof of the Pythagorean theorem

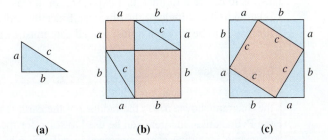

      **(a)**                  **(b)**                  **(c)**

The Hands-On exercise at the beginning of Chapter 7 showed another proof of the Pythagorean theorem, one which uses algebra rather than dissection.

No records have survived to indicate what proof, if any, Pythagoras (ca. 572–501 B.C.) may have offered. The dissection proof requires showing that the inner quadrilateral of Figure 10.17(c) is actually a square (why is it?), and Pythagoras's knowledge of angles in a right triangle was sufficient to do this. Since the time of Pythagoras, a tremendous number of proofs have been devised. In the second edition of *The Pythagorean Proposition,* E. S. Loomis catalogs 370 different proofs. An interesting dynamic proof is given in problem 26 of Problem Set 10.3.

## Applications of the Pythagorean Theorem

**EXAMPLE 10.16** **Using the Pythagorean Theorem**

Find the lengths $x$ and $y$ in the following figures:

**(a)**
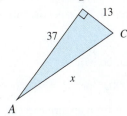

**(b)**
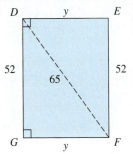

**Solution**

    **(a)** By the Pythagorean theorem, $x^2 = 13^2 + 37^2 = 169 + 1369 = 1538$. Therefore, $x = \sqrt{1538} \doteq 39.2$.

    **(b)** The diagonal $\overline{DF}$ of rectangle $DEFG$ is the hypotenuse of the right triangle $DEF$. The Pythagorean theorem, applied to $\triangle DEF$, gives $y^2 + 52^2 = 65^2$. Therefore, $y^2 = 65^2 - 52^2 = 4225 - 2704 = 1521$, and $y = \sqrt{1521} = 39$.

For many applications, it is necessary to write and solve equations based on the Pythagorean relation. Here is an example, and we'll see many more in the next section.

**EXAMPLE 10.17 Determining How Far You Can See**

Imagine yourself on top of a mountain, or perhaps in an airplane, at a known altitude given in feet. Approximately how far away, in miles, is the horizon?

**Solution**

**Understand the Problem**

Altitude is a measure of the perpendicular distance above the surface of the earth. The horizon is the circle of points where our line of sight is tangent to the sphere of the earth's surface. The problem is to derive a formula that expresses, or at least approximates, the distance to the horizon in relation to the altitude of the observer. Since the altitude is given in feet, while the distance to the horizon is to be given in miles, special care must be taken to handle the units of measure properly.

**Devise a Plan**

The earth is very nearly a sphere. A line of sight to the horizon forms a leg of a right triangle, as the diagram shows. Since the radius $r$ of the earth is about 4000 miles and the altitude $s$ is known, the Pythagorean theorem can be used to solve for the distance to the horizon. In the diagram, all distances, including $s$, are expressed in miles; if $h$ is the altitude in feet, we can use the conversion formula $h = 5280s$. (Recall that 1 mile = 5280 feet.) Note that $\overleftrightarrow{AC}$ is the line of tangency at $C$ to the circle whose center, $B$, is the center of the earth.

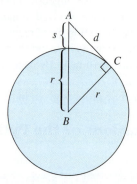

**Carry Out the Plan**

Applying the Pythagorean theorem to the right triangle $ABC$ gives $d^2 + r^2 = (s + r)^2$. The squared term on the right can be written $s^2 + 2sr + r^2$, so $d^2 + r^2 = s^2 + 2sr + r^2$. Subtracting $r^2$ from both sides shows that $d^2 = s^2 + 2sr$. Therefore, the exact distance $d$, in miles, is given by the formula

$$d = \sqrt{s^2 + 2rs}.$$

Since $r = 4000$ miles, the formula can also be written

$$d = \sqrt{s^2 + 8000s} \quad \text{or} \quad d = \sqrt{s(s + 8000)}.$$

From the top of a mountain (say, $s = 2$), or from an airplane (say, $s = 7$), or even from the International Space Station ($s = 200$ miles), it is evident that the altitude $s$ is much smaller than 8000. Therefore, little accuracy is lost if the term $(s + 8000)$ in the exact formula is replaced with simply 8000. This gives us the approximate equation

$$d \doteq \sqrt{8000s}.$$

Using the equation $s = \dfrac{h}{5280}$ gives $d \doteq \sqrt{\dfrac{8000}{5280}h}$. Finally, since $\sqrt{\dfrac{8000}{5280}} \doteq 1.2$, we obtain a simple formula for the number of miles, $d$, to the horizon as seen from an altitude of $h$ feet:

$$d \doteq 1.2\sqrt{h}.$$

For example, the distance to the horizon as seen from an airplane flying at 40,000 feet is about $1.2\sqrt{40,000} = (1.2)(200) = 240$ miles.

**Look Back**

This problem involved several steps that are typical of the way the Pythagorean theorem is used:

- Draw a figure and label all the distances.
- Identify all the right triangles in the drawing.
- Write the Pythagorean relationships for all of the right triangles.
- Solve the Pythagorean formulas to determine unknown values needed for the solution of the problem.

We also used an estimation technique while carrying out the plan.

## The Converse of the Pythagorean Theorem

The numbers 5, 12, and 13 satisfy $5^2 + 12^2 = 13^2$. Is the triangle with sides of length 5, 12, and 13 a right triangle? The answer is yes, since the Pythagorean relation $a^2 + b^2 = c^2$ holds if, *and only if*, $a$, $b$, and $c$ are the side lengths of a right triangle. That is, the converse of the Pythagorean theorem is true and is stated without proof in the following theorem:

---

**THEOREM**    *Converse of the Pythagorean Theorem*
Let a triangle have sides of length $a$, $b$, and $c$. If $a^2 + b^2 = c^2$, then the triangle is a right triangle and the angle opposite the side of length $c$ is its right angle.

---

**EXAMPLE 10.18 Checking for Right Triangles**

Determine whether the three lengths given are the lengths of the sides of a right triangle.

(a) 15, 17, 8        (b) $10, 5, 5\sqrt{3}$        (c) 231, 520, 568

**Solution**

(a) $8^2 + 15^2 = 64 + 225 = 289 = 17^2$, so 8, 15, and 17 are the lengths of the sides of a right triangle.
(b) $5^2 + (5\sqrt{3})^2 = 25 + 25 \cdot 3 = 25 + 75 = 100 = 10^2$, so 5, $5\sqrt{3}$, and 10 are the lengths of the sides of a right triangle.
(c) $231^2 + 520^2 = 53{,}361 + 270{,}400 = 323{,}761 \neq 322{,}624 = 568^2$, so 231, 520, and 568 are not the lengths of sides of a right triangle. This would be difficult to see by measuring angles with a protractor, since this triangle closely resembles the right triangle with sides of length 231, 520, and 569. Note that $569^2 = 323{,}761$.

## Problem Set 10.3

Exercises numbered in red are answered in the back of the text.

### Understanding Concepts

**1.** Find the distance $x$ in each figure.

(a)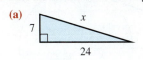

(b)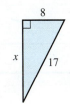

(c)

(d)

(e)

(f)

**2.** Find the distance $x$ in each figure.

**(a)**

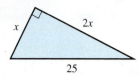

**(b)**

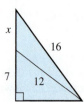

**(c)**

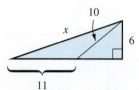

**3.** Find the area of a right triangle if

(a) Its hypotenuse is 8 in and one of its legs is 3 in.

(b) One leg is three times the other and the hypotenuse is 10 cm.

**4.** Find the distances $x$ and $y$ in the rectangular prism and the cube.

**(a)**

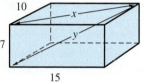

**(b)**

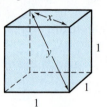

**5.** Find the distance $x$ in these space figures.

**(a)**

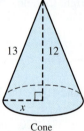

Cone

**(b)**

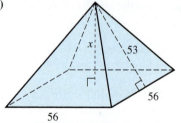

Square-based right regular pyramid, with sides 56 and slant height 53

**(c)**

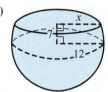

Sphere cut by plane

**6.** Find the areas of these figures:

**(a)**

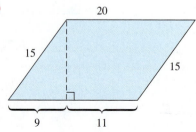

**(b)**

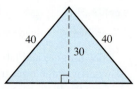

**(c)**

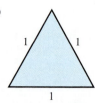

**7.** Françoise and Maurice cut diagonally across a 50-foot–by–100-foot vacant lot on their way to school. How much distance do they save by not staying on the sidewalk?

**8.** A square with sides of length 2 is inscribed in a circle and circumscribed around another circle. Which is larger, the area of the region between the circles or the area inside the smaller circle?

**9.** At noon, car $A$ left town heading due east at 50 miles per hour. At 1 P.M., car $B$ left the same town heading due north at 40 miles per hour. How far apart were the two cars at

(a) 2 P.M.?      (b) 3:30 P.M.?

**10.** Find $AG$ in this spiral of right triangles.

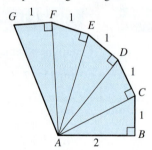

**11.** (a) What is the length of the side of a square inscribed in a circle of radius 1?

(b) What is the length of the side of a cube inscribed in a sphere of radius 1?

**12.** What is the distance between the centers of these circles?

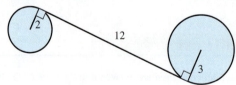

**13.** What is the radius of the following circle?

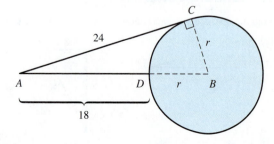

14. Which of the following can be the lengths of the sides of a right triangle?
    - (a) 21, 28, 35
    - (b) 9, 40, 41
    - (c) 12, 35, 37
    - (d) 14, 27, $\sqrt{533}$
    - (e) $7\sqrt{2}, 4\sqrt{7}, 2\sqrt{77}$
    - (f) 9.5, 16.8, 19.3

15. If $a$, $b$, and $c$ are the lengths of the sides of a right triangle, explain why $10a$, $10b$, and $10c$ are also the lengths of the sides of a right triangle.

## Teaching Concepts

16. During a lesson on the Pythagorean theorem, Sean said, "The sum of the areas of the squares on the sides of a right triangle is equal to the area of the square on the hypotenuse. Would the same thing be true of semicircles instead of squares?"
    - (a) Is the short answer to Sean's question "yes" or "no"? Justify your answer.
    - (b) How would you respond to Sean? Would you simply tell him the answer, or would you suggest that he see if he can discover the answer for himself? Or might you perhaps challenge the entire class to try to discover the answer to Sean's question?

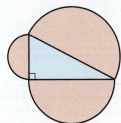

17. Repeat problem 16, but for equilateral triangles drawn on the sides of the right triangle. (*Suggestion:* Use the assertion that the altitude $h$ of an equilateral triangle of side $s$ is $h = \dfrac{\sqrt{3}}{2}s$; see part (a) of problem 22.)

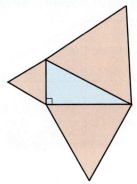

18. Do problem 19, but for equilateral triangles drawn on the sides of the original triangle. (*Suggestion:* Again use the assertion of problem 22(a).)

## Responding to Students

19. Tia says, "Suppose we draw semicircles on the sides of a triangle and compute their areas. If the sum of the areas of two of the semicircles equals the area of the third, is the triangle a right triangle?"

    - (a) Is the short answer to Tia's question "yes" or "no"? Justify your answer.
    - (b) How would you respond to Tia?

20. Sammy looks at the right triangle pictured here. He says that the area of the triangle is 10 because it is $4 \times 5$ divided by 2. How would you respond to Sammy?

21. Larisa looks at the right triangle pictured here. She writes its area as $\dfrac{1}{2}(3 \times 5)$ cm$^2$. The substitute teacher says that the correct answer is $\dfrac{1}{2}(5 \times 3)$ cm$^2$ and marks her solution as incorrect. How would you, as her teacher, respond to Larisa when she asks why it was graded as wrong?

## Thinking Critically

22. (a) Show that the altitude $h$ of an equilateral triangle with sides of length $s$ is given by $h = \dfrac{\sqrt{3}}{2}s$.
    - (b) Find a formula for the area of an equilateral triangle of side length $s$.
    - (c) Find a formula for the area of a regular hexagon of side length $s$.
    - (d) Show that the area of the inscribed circle of a regular hexagon is $\dfrac{3}{4}$ the area of the circumscribed circle.

23. Find the length of the diagonals of this isosceles trapezoid:

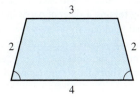

24. An ant is at corner $A$ of a shoebox that is 9 inches long, 5 inches wide, and 3 inches high. What route should the ant follow over the surface of the box to reach the opposite corner $C$ in the shortest distance? (*Suggestion:* It will help to tear along the vertical edges of the box and flatten the top.)

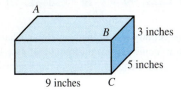

**25.** A chord of the large circle is tangent to the inner concentric circle. If the chord is 20 cm long, what is the area of the annulus (the region between the two circles)?

**26.** Justify why the light-brown regions (which are all parallelograms) in the sequence of diagrams shown have the same area. Since the same reasoning shows that the dark-brown regions also have the same area, this approach provides a striking dynamic proof of the Pythagorean theorem.

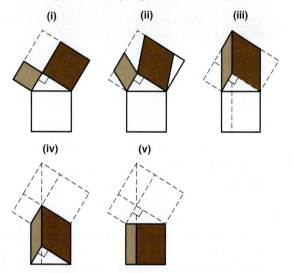

**27.** Using the Problem-Solving Strategy of Rigid Motions from Section 8.3 and the distance formula from Section 8.2, give an algebraic proof of the Pythagorean theorem.

## Thinking Cooperatively

For problems 28 through 30, you will need several sheets of paper and scissors. Begin by folding a sheet of paper in half twice and then cutting a diagonal to obtain four congruent right triangles. Next, use one of your triangles as a pattern to cut four paper squares whose sides match the sides $a$, $b$, $b - a$, and $c$ of the right triangles. Be sure to cut your pieces with care and precision.

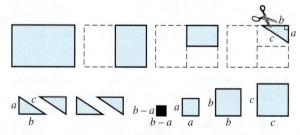

**28.** The twelfth-century Hindu mathematician Bhaskara arranged four copies of a right triangle of side lengths $a$, $b$, and $c$ into a $c$-by-$c$ square, filling in the center with the $b - a$-sided square.

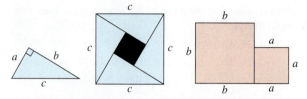

**(a)** Show how the five pieces in the $c$-by-$c$ square can be arranged to fill the "double" square region on the right.

**(b)** Explain how the Pythagorean theorem follows from part (a).

**29.** Tile the pentagon shown here in two ways:

**(a)** with two triangles and the squares of sides $a$ and $b$;

**(b)** with two triangles and the square of side $c$.

**(c)** Explain why the two tilings in parts (a) and (b) prove the Pythagorean theorem.

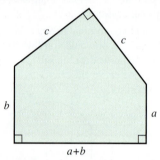

**30.** In the nineteenth century, Henry Perigal, a London stockbroker and amateur astronomer, discovered a beautiful scissors-and-paper demonstration of the Pythagorean theorem. Follow these steps to complete your own demonstration: Through the center of the larger square on the leg of the right triangle, draw one line perpendicular to the hypotenuse and a second line parallel to the hypotenuse. Cut along these two lines to divide the square into four congruent pieces and then show how to arrange the four pieces, together with the square on the shorter leg, to form a square on the hypotenuse of the right triangle.

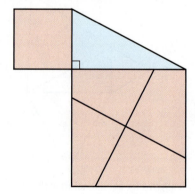

## Making Connections

**31.** A baseball diamond is actually a square 90 feet on a side. What distance must a catcher throw the ball to pick off a runner attempting to steal second base?

**32.** Approximately what height can be reached from a 24-foot ladder? What assumptions have you made to arrive at your answer?

33. The ancient Egyptians squared off fields with a rope 12 units long, with knots tied to indicate each unit. Explain how such a rope could be used to form a right angle. What theorem justifies their procedure?

34. A water lily floating in a murky pond is rooted on the bottom of the pond by a stem of unknown length.

The lily can be lifted 2 feet over the water and moved 6 feet to the side. What is the depth of the pond?

35. A stop sign is to be made by cutting off triangles from the corners of a square sheet of metal 32 inches on a side. What length $x$ will leave a regular octagon? Give your answer to the nearest eighth inch.

36. A 12-foot-wide crosswalk diagonally crosses a street whose curbs are 40 feet apart, intersecting the opposite curb with a 30-foot displacement in the direction of the street. Reflective striping tape will be applied to all four sides of the crosswalk. How many feet of striping should be ordered? (*Suggestion:* First find the length $x$ of the crosswalk. Next, find the area of the crosswalk in order to help you calculate the curb length $y$.)

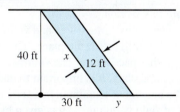

### Using a Calculator

37. Any large structure made of steel must be designed to accommodate the expansion of the metal when heated. Thus, pipelines, steel bridge decking, and train track rails have expansion joints. To understand why, consider a mile-long steel rail built without any expansion joint. Suppose the rail lengthens by 1 inch on a warm day. If its ends are firmly anchored and the track bows to one side, the amount of deflection can be estimated by considering a right triangle with one leg $\frac{1}{2}$ mile long and a hypotenuse $\frac{1}{2}$ mile $+\frac{1}{2}$ inch long. What is the deflection $x$? Convert all dimensions to feet to do your calculation.

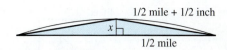

38. Use the approximate formula $d \doteq 1.2\sqrt{h}$ of Example 10.17 to answer these questions:

   (a) On a cliff top 100 feet over the ocean, what is the distance to the horizon?

   (b) The observation deck of the Sears Tower in Chicago is 1353 feet above ground level. How far can you see across Lake Michigan?

   (c) In the Dr. Seuss book *Yertle the Turtle,* Yertle stands on the backs of other turtles and can see 40 miles. How high is Yertle?

### Using a Computer

39. Use geometry software to draw any right triangle. On each side, draw outward-pointing equilateral triangles. Use your software to calculate the areas of the triangles.

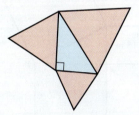

How does the sum of the areas of the triangles on the two legs compare with the area of the equilateral triangle on the hypotenuse?

40. Using geometry software, construct outward squares on each edge of a general triangle $ABC$, as shown here. Measure the areas of the squares and angle $\angle ABC$, and calculate the sum of the squares on sides $\overline{AB}$ and $\overline{BC}$. Manipulate the triangle until the sum of the areas of the squares closely agrees with the area of the square on side $\overline{AC}$. What is the measure of the angle $\angle ABC$? Write a paragraph describing your exploration.

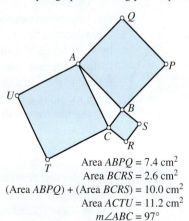

Area $ABPQ = 7.4$ cm$^2$
Area $BCRS = 2.6$ cm$^2$
(Area $ABPQ$) + (Area $BCRS$) $= 10.0$ cm$^2$
Area $ACTU = 11.2$ cm$^2$
$m\angle ABC = 97°$

### From Student State Assessments

41. (Texas, Grade 8)
Mrs. Gonzáles wants to string lights along both diagonals of a rectangular window, as shown on the next page.

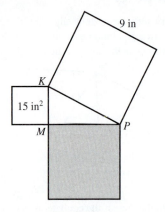

4 feet

3 feet

What is the minimum length of lights Mrs. Gonzáles will need?

**A.** 5 ft  **B.** 7 ft
**C.** 10 ft  **D.** 14 ft

**42.** (Texas, Grade 9)
Look at the drawing shown below.

9 in

K

15 in²

M  P

If $\triangle KMP$ is a right triangle formed by the placement of three squares, what is the area of the shaded square?

**A.** 135 in²  **B.** 24 in²
**C.** 66 in²  **D.** 81 in²

**43.** (Texas, Grade 9)
Mr. Carpenter built a wooden gate, as shown below.

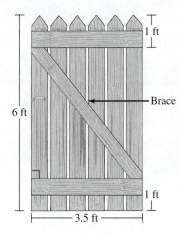

1 ft

Brace

6 ft

1 ft

3.5 ft

Which is closest to the length in feet of the diagonal board that Mr. Carpenter used to brace the wooden gate?

**A.** 4.9 ft  **B.** 5.3 ft
**C.** 1 ft  **D.** 6.9 ft

# 10.4

# Volume

*It would be useful to review Section 9.3 before starting this section.*

The two most important measures of a figure in space are its surface area and volume. These are the counterparts of the perimeter and area, respectively, of a figure in the plane. The **surface area,** often denoted by *SA*, or just *S*, measures the boundary of the space figure. The **volume,** often denoted by *V*, measures the amount of space enclosed within the boundary. It is important to understand how surface area and volume are different. For example, the amount of aluminum in a soda can is closely related to the can's surface area, whereas the amount of fluid within the can is given by the volume. Even the units are different. Surface area is given in in², cm², and so on. Volume is given in³, cm³, and the like, or possibly in a unit of capacity, such as fluid ounces, gallons, milliliters, and so on.

MHM  When we teach this material, we find that many students keep asking, as your own students will, "What is the right formula to use?" This is exactly the wrong question for someone who wants a conceptual understanding of surface or volume (or mathematics in general). Remember to apply Polya's principles and first understand the problem and devise a plan (usually, to break down the given solid into pieces, for each of which we can easily find the volume). Of course, at that point, you will need to use some formulas (which will be derived in this section) to finish your plan. However, the formulas obtained next, and indeed all of the formulas in this section, are of far less importance than the ideas used to derive them.

For example, if you were asked to find the volume of the solid in Figure 10.18, how should you go about it? The problem asks for the volume of a solid that is made of two basic solids: half of a sphere of radius 3 cm and a right circular cylinder of radius 3 cm and height 7 cm. Thus, our plan would be to partition the given solid into two: a hemisphere and a right circular cylinder.

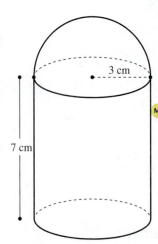

3 cm

7 cm

**FIGURE 10.18**
Right circular cylinder surmounted by a hemisphere

> **PROBLEM-SOLVING STRATEGY**  Decompose one complex problem into a number of simpler ones (with applications to volume).
>
> In this case, to find the volume of a solid, first break up the solid appropriately into a collection of solids whose volume is easy to compute, and then add those volumes.

In this section, we will derive formulas for the volume of some basic figures in space, such as right and oblique prisms and cylinders, pyramids, right circular cones, and spheres. These formulas allow us to finish problems such as the one mentioned in the previous paragraph (see problem 4 in Problem Set 10.4) by using the preceding problem-solving strategy.

## Volumes of Right Prisms and Right Cylinders

The volume of the rectangular box shown in Figure 10.19 is given by $lwh$, where $l$, $w$, and $h$ are, respectively, the length, width, and height of the box. Since $lw$ gives the area $B$ of the base of the box, the volume can also be written in the form $V = Bh$, where $B$ is the area of the base and $h$ is the height.

**FIGURE 10.19**

A rectangular box has volume $V = lwh$. Equivalently, $V = Bh$, where $B$ is the area of the base and $h$ is the height

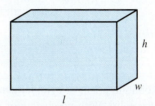

Figure 10.20(a) shows a solid composed of many (say, $n$) small right rectangular prisms, all of height $h$. If $B_1, B_2, \ldots, B_n$ are the areas of the bases, the total volume $V$ of the prisms is $B_1 h + B_2 h + \cdots + B_n h = (B_1 + B_2 + \cdots + B_n)h$. That is, the volume $V$ is given by $V = Bh$, where $B = B_1 + B_2 + \cdots + B_n$ is the total area of the base. The right cylinder depicted in Figure 10.20(b) can be approximated to arbitrary accuracy by prisms of height $h$ as shown.

**FIGURE 10.20**

Right rectangular prisms can approximate a right prism or a right cylinder

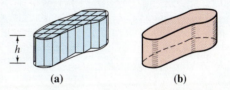

(a)　　　(b)

> **FORMULA**　*Volume of a Right Prism or a Right Cylinder*
>
> Suppose a right prism or right cylinder has height $h$ and a base of area $B$. Then its volume $V$ is given by
>
> $$V = Bh.$$
>
>
>
> $B$ = area of base

**EXAMPLE 10.19  Computing the Volume of a Right Prism and a Right Cylinder**

Find the volume of the gift box and the juice can.

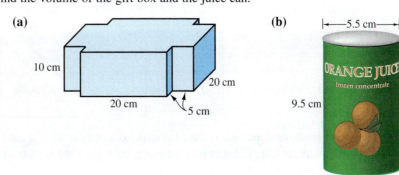

(a)

10 cm

20 cm

20 cm

5 cm

(b)

|←——5.5 cm——→|

9.5 cm

**Solution**

(a) The base area, $B$, consists of a square of length 20 cm and four 5-cm–by–20-cm rectangles, so $B = 800 \text{ cm}^2$. The height is $h = 10$ cm, so the volume is $V = Bh = 8000 \text{ cm}^3$, which can also be expressed as 8 liters.

(b) The area of the circular base of the juice can is $\pi(2.75 \text{ cm})^2 = 7.5625\pi \text{ cm}^2$. The height is $h = 9.5$ cm, so the volume $V = Bh = 71.84375\pi \text{ cm}^3$, or about 226 cm³.

## Volumes of Oblique Prisms and Cylinders

A deck of neatly stacked playing cards forms a right rectangular prism as shown in Figure 10.21. The total volume of the deck is the sum of the volumes of each card. If the cards slide easily on one another, it is easy to tilt the deck to form an oblique prism of the same base area $B$ and the same height $h$. The solid is still made up of the same cards, so the oblique prism still has volume $Bh$.

**FIGURE 10.21**
An oblique prism of base area $B$ and height $h$ has the same volume $V = Bh$ as the corresponding right prism

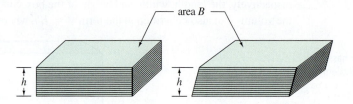

Any oblique prism or cylinder can be imagined as a stack of very thin cards, all shaped like the base of the solid. With no change of volume, the oblique stack can be straightened to form a right prism or right cylinder of the same height $h$ and base area $B$. Both the right and oblique shapes therefore have the same volume, namely, $V = Bh$. This relationship is illustrated in Figure 10.22.

**FIGURE 10.22**
Any prism or cylinder, either right or oblique, has volume $V = Bh$, where $B$ is the base area and $h$ is the height

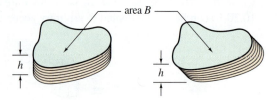

**FORMULA** *Volume of a General Prism or Cylinder*
A prism or cylinder of height $h$ and base area $B$ has volume $V = Bh$.

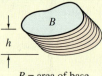

$B$ = area of base

## Volumes of Pyramids and Cones

In two-dimensional space (that is, in the plane), a diagonal dissects a square into two congruent right triangles. Thus, the area of each triangle is one-half that of the corresponding square.

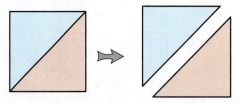

In three-dimensional space, the diagonals from one corner of a cube form the edges of three congruent pyramids that fill the cube. Therefore, each pyramid has one-third the volume of the corresponding cube, as shown in Figure 10.23.

**FIGURE 10.23**
A cube can be dissected into three congruent pyramids

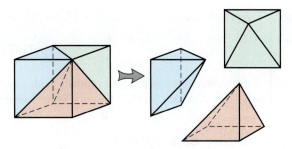

**FIGURE 10.23**
A cube can be dissected into three congruent pyramids

Instead of a cube, consider a rectangular solid and use the diagonals from one corner to decompose the solid into three pyramids. An example is shown in Figure 10.24. In general, the three pyramids are not congruent to one another. However, it can be shown that the volumes of the three pyramids are equal. Therefore, if the prism has base area $B$ and height $h$, we conclude that each pyramid has volume $\frac{1}{3}Bh$.

**FIGURE 10.24**
A rectangular prism can be dissected into three pyramids of equal volume

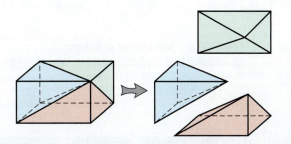

Similar reasoning shows that *all* pyramids of base $B$ and height $h$ have volume $\frac{1}{3}Bh$. The base can be any polygon, and the apex can be any point at distance $h$ to the plane of the base, as shown in Figure 10.25.

**FIGURE 10.25**
A pyramid of height $h$ and base of area $B$ has one-third the volume of a corresponding prism of base area $B$ and height $h$. Therefore, the pyramid has volume $\frac{1}{3}Bh$

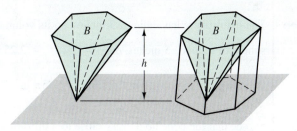

The base of a cone can be approximated to arbitrary accuracy by a polygon with sufficiently many sides, so the volume of a cone of base area $B$ and height $h$ is also given by the formula $\frac{1}{3}Bh$.

---

**FORMULA** *Volume of a Pyramid or Cone*

The volume $V$ of a pyramid or cone of height $h$ and base of area $B$ is given by

$$V = \frac{1}{3}Bh.$$

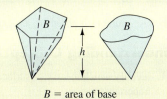

$B$ = area of base

---

**EXAMPLE 10.20 Determining the Volume of an Egyptian Pyramid**

The pyramid of Khufu is 147 m high, and its square base is 231 m on each side. What is the volume of the pyramid?

**Solution** The area of the base is $(231 \text{ m})^2 = 53{,}361 \text{ m}^2$. Therefore, the volume is

$$\frac{1}{3}(53{,}361 \text{ m}^2) \cdot (147 \text{ m}) = 2{,}614{,}689 \text{ m}^3.$$

If the stones were stacked on a football field, a rectangular prism nearly 2000 feet high would result. For comparison, the 110-story Sears Tower in Chicago reaches 1454 feet.

## Volume of a Sphere

Suppose that a solid sphere of radius $r$ is placed in a right circular cylinder of height $2r$ that just contains it. Filling the remaining space in the cylinder with water, we find that removing the sphere leaves the cylinder one-third full, as illustrated in Figure 10.26. This means that the sphere takes up two-thirds of the volume of the cylinder. Since the volume of the cylinder is $Bh = (\pi r^2)(2r) = 2\pi r^3$, the experiment suggests that the volume of a sphere of radius $r$ is given by $\frac{2}{3}(2\pi r^3) = \frac{4}{3}\pi r^3$. The first rigorous proof of this remarkable formula was given by Archimedes.

**FIGURE 10.26**
A sphere fills two-thirds of the circular cylinder containing the sphere

**FORMULA** *Volume of a Sphere*
The volume $V$ of a sphere of radius $r$ is given by the formula

$$V = \frac{4}{3}\pi r^3.$$

---

**EXAMPLE 10.21** **Using the Sphere Volume Formula**

An ice cream cone is 5 inches high and has an opening 3 inches in diameter. If filled with ice cream and given a hemispherical top, how much ice cream is there?

**Solution** The hemisphere has radius 1.5 inches, so its volume is one-half that of a sphere of radius 1.5 inches, or $\frac{2}{3}\pi(1.5 \text{ in})^3 = 2.25\pi \text{ in}^3$. The cone has

volume $\frac{1}{3}Bh = \frac{1}{3}\pi(1.5 \text{ in})^2 \cdot (5 \text{ in}) = 3.75\pi \text{ in}^3$. Thus, the total volume is

$2.25\pi \text{ in}^3 + 3.75\pi \text{ in}^3 = 6\pi \text{ in}^3$, or about $19 \text{ in}^3$. Since a gallon is $231 \text{ in}^3$, we see that the cone holds very close to a third of a quart of ice cream.

---

## Problem Set 10.4

Exercises numbered in red are answered in the back of the text.

### Understanding Concepts

1. Identify which measure—surface area or volume—is most important to know

   **(a)** about a room, to buy the correct amount of paint;

   **(b)** about a chair, to determine the amount of stuffing required to reupholster the chair;

   **(c)** about a swimming pool, to add the correct amount of chlorine;

   **(d)** about a lawn, to apply the correct amount of weed killer.

2. Find the volume of each of these prisms and cylinders.

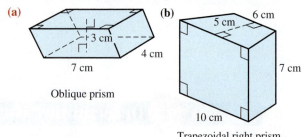

**(a)** Oblique prism

**(b)** Trapezoidal right prism

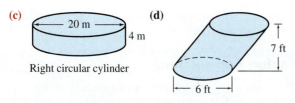

(c)                                    (d)

Right circular cylinder

Oblique circular cylinder

3. Find the volume of each of these pyramids and cones:

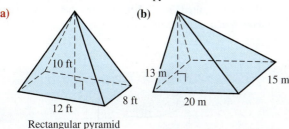

(a)                                    (b)

Rectangular pyramid

Rectangular pyramid

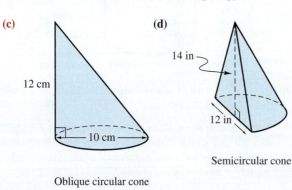

(c)                                    (d)

Oblique circular cone

Semicircular cone

4. What is the volume of the solid of Figure 10.18?

5. A circular bowl is built to hold 2 cups of mint chocolate chip ice cream. How many inches should the radius of the bowl be? (*Hint:* Use Table 10.4 of Section 10.1 to find the number of cubic inches in 2 cups.)

6. A right circular cylinder of height 7 inches has a hemisphere surmounted on top of it similar to that shown in Figure 10.18.

   (a) Show that, if we want the volume of the solid to be $\frac{23\pi}{3}$ in$^3$, then we can use a radius of 1 inch.

   **MHM** (b) Are there other possible dimensions for the solid of this problem with the same height and volume? This question asks if there are other values for the radius that give a volume of $\frac{23\pi}{3}$. If so, what are they? If not, why not? (*Hint:* Use algebra, including the quadratic formula and part (a).)

## Teaching Concepts

7. Eno is having trouble understanding that the volume of a solid nonrectangular shape (say, a pyramid, cone, or sphere) can be given in terms of a unit cube. How would you help Eno understand that this can be so?

8. Ruth Ann is having trouble believing that the volume of *any* pyramid or cone is given by the formula $V = \frac{1}{3}Bh$. What might you do to help Ruth Ann?

## Responding to Students

9. Urmi says that, since there's a third power in the volume formula and a square in the surface area formula, the volume of a sphere of radius $r$ is always greater than the surface area of the sphere.

   (a) Is Urmi's statement true?

   (b) How would you explain your answer to part (a) to Urmi, who is in fifth grade?

10. While experimenting with volume problems, Samuel, a fifth grader, computes the volume of a right circular cylinder of height 6 cm four times, using radii of 2 cm, 4 cm, 6 cm, and 8 cm, and fills in the following table:

| Radius in cm | 2 | 4 | 6 | 8 |
|---|---|---|---|---|
| Volume in cm$^3$ | | | | |

From these data, he concludes that the volume of any cylinder increases as its radius does.

   (a) Fill in Samuel's table.

   (b) Is Samuel correct?

   (c) How would you respond to him?

11. Vera was asked to calculate the volume of the following rectangular prism, which is 4 by 5 by 8 meters:

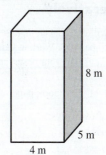

Vera's answer was 17 m$^3$.

   (a) What is the correct volume for the rectangular prism?

   (b) What did Vera do when figuring her answer?

   (c) How might you explain to Vera what she needs to do in a future problem?

12. Maurice was given the following picture of a prism, whose base has area 6 ft$^2$, and asked to calculate its volume:

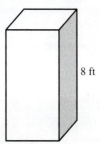

Maurice's answer was 48 ft$^2$. His teacher looked over his answer, praised it for being partly correct, and then asked him to relabel it. Maurice said that he didn't understand why he needed to change the label, because he multiplied two things and so put a little 2 behind his answer. When he multiplies three things to find out the volume, then he puts a little 3.

(a) What did Maurice do correctly?

(b) What did Maurice not understand about the figure he was given?

(c) What can his teacher do to help him calculate this problem so that Maurice understands why he is using "little numbers" behind his answer?

## Thinking Critically

**13.** A right circular cone has height $r$ and a circular base of radius $2r$. Compare the volume of the cone with that of a sphere of radius $r$. Sketch both solids, using the same scale.

**14.** The right circular cylinder and cone shown in the accompanying figure both have a base of radius $r$ and height $2r$, and the sphere has radius $r$. Show that the ratio of the volumes of the cone to the sphere to the cylinder is 1 to 2 to 3.

## Thinking Cooperatively

In these problems, you will need paper, tape, scissors, and drawing tools (ruler, compass, and pencils). Work in pairs, measuring your constructed models and verifying your observations with calculations.

**15.** A sheet of $8\frac{1}{2}''$ by $11''$ notebook paper can be rolled into a cylinder in either of two ways:

Which way encloses the largest volume? Make a prediction, and then check it.

**16.** Cut out the circular sector shown in the accompanying figure, and roll it into a right circular cone in which the two 4-inch radial segments are joined.

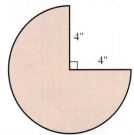

Find the following measurements, both by exact computation and by measuring your paper model:

(a) The radius of the base of the cone.

(b) The height of the cone.

(c) Use your answers to parts (a) and (b) to compute the volume of the cone.

## Making Connections

**17.** A napkin ring is being made of cast silver. It has the shape of a cylinder 1.25 inches high, with a cylindrical hole 1 inch in diameter and a thickness of $\frac{1}{16}$ inch. How many ounces of silver are required? It will help to know that silver weighs about 6 ounces per cubic inch.

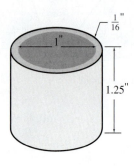

**18.** Give the dimensions of a rectangular aquarium 40 cm high that holds 48 liters of water.

**19.** A theater sells $4''$ by $5''$ by $8''$ boxes of popcorn for $1.75. It also sells cylindrical "tubs" of popcorn for $3.50, where the tub is $10''$ high and has a diameter of $6''$. Is it better to buy one tub or two boxes of popcorn?

**20.** Small grapefruits of diameter 3 inches are on sale at five for a dollar. The large, 4-inch-diameter grapefruits are three for a dollar. If you are buying $5 worth of grapefruits, should you choose small ones or large ones in order to get a better deal?

**21. World Records.** *The Guinness Book of World Records,* published annually by Facts on File, New York, contains a fascinating collection of measurements.

(a) The world's largest flawless crystal ball weighs 106.75 pounds and is 13 inches in diameter. What is the weight of a crystal ball 5 inches in diameter?

(b) The largest pyramid is the Quetzalcoatl, 63 miles southeast of Mexico City. It is 177 feet tall and covers an area of 45 acres. Estimate the volume of the pyramid. By comparison, the largest Egyptian pyramid of Khufu (called Cheops by the Greeks) has a volume of 88.2 million ft$^3$. Recall that an acre is 43,560 ft$^2$.

(c) The building with the largest volume in the world is the Boeing Company's main assembly plant in Everett, Washington. The building encloses 472 million ft$^3$ and covers 98.3 acres. What is the size of a cube of equal volume?

**22.** A water pipe with an inside diameter of $\frac{3}{4}$ inches is 50 feet long in its run from the hot-water tank to the faucet. How much hot water is wasted when the water inside the pipe cools down? Give your answer in gallons, where 1 gallon = 231 in$^3$.

See "Examining School Book Pages" on page 580 for questions related to the pages shown below.

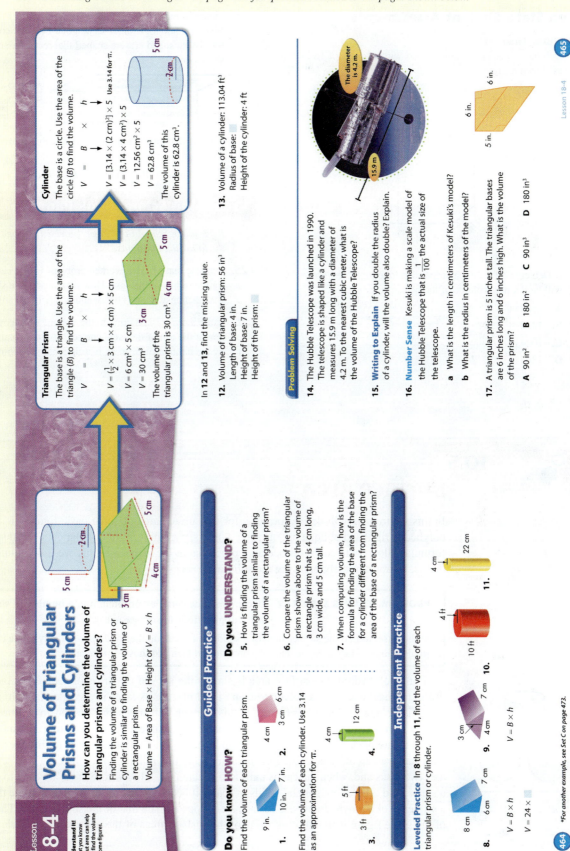

## Lesson 18-4

**Understand It!**
What you know about area can help you find the volume of some figures.

### Volume of Triangular Prisms and Cylinders

**How can you determine the volume of triangular prisms and cylinders?**

Finding the volume of a triangular prism or cylinder is similar to finding the volume of a rectangular prism.

Volume = Area of Base × Height or $V = B × h$

**Triangular Prism**
The base is a triangle. Use the area of the triangle ($B$) to find the volume.

$$V = B × h$$

$$V = [\tfrac{1}{2} × 3\text{ cm} × 4\text{ cm}] × 5\text{ cm}$$
$$V = 6\text{ cm}^2 × 5\text{ cm}$$
$$V = 30\text{ cm}^3$$

The volume of the triangular prism is 30 cm³.

**Cylinder**
The base is a circle. Use the area of the circle ($B$) to find the volume.

$$V = B × h$$

$$V = [3.14 × (2\text{ cm})^2] × 5\text{ cm}$$   Use 3.14 for π.
$$V = (3.14 × 4\text{ cm}^2) × 5$$
$$V = 12.56\text{ cm}^2 × 5$$
$$V = 62.8\text{ cm}^3$$

The volume of this cylinder is 62.8 cm³.

### Guided Practice*

**Do you know HOW?**

Find the volume of each triangular prism.

**1.** 9 in. 10 in. 7 in.

**2.** 4 cm 3 cm 6 cm

Find the volume of each cylinder. Use 3.14 as an approximation for π.

**3.** 5 ft 3 ft

**4.** 4 cm 12 cm

**Do you UNDERSTAND?**

**5.** How is finding the volume of a triangular prism similar to finding the volume of a rectangular prism?

**6.** Compare the volume of the triangular prism shown above to the volume of a rectangle prism that is 4 cm long, 3 cm wide, and 5 cm tall.

**7.** When computing volume, how is the formula for finding the area of the base for a cylinder different from finding the area of the base of a rectangular prism?

### Independent Practice

**Leveled Practice** In **8** through **11**, find the volume of each triangular prism or cylinder.

**8.** 8 cm 6 cm 7 cm

$V = B × h$
$V = 24 ×$ ☐

**9.** 3 cm 7 cm 4 cm

$V = B × h$

**10.** 10 ft 4 ft

**11.** 4 cm 22 cm

*For another example, see Set C on page 473.*

In **12** and **13**, find the missing value.

**12.** Volume of triangular prism: 56 in³
Length of base: 4 in.
Height of base: 7 in.
Height of the prism: ☐

**13.** Volume of a cylinder: 113.04 ft³
Radius of base: ☐
Height of the cylinder: 4 ft

### Problem Solving

**14.** The Hubble Telescope was launched in 1990. The telescope is shaped like a cylinder and measures 15.9 m long with a diameter of 4.2 m. To the nearest cubic meter, what is the volume of the Hubble Telescope?

The diameter is 4.2 m.

15.9 m

**15.** **Writing to Explain** If you double the radius of a cylinder, will the volume also double? Explain.

**16.** **Number Sense** Kesuki is making a scale model of the Hubble Telescope that is $\frac{1}{100}$ the actual size of the telescope.
  **a** What is the length in centimeters of Kesuki's model?
  **b** What is the radius in centimeters of the model?

**17.** A triangular prism is 5 inches tall. The triangular bases are 6 inches long and 6 inches high. What is the volume of the prism?

5 in. 6 in. 6 in.

A 90 in²   B 180 in²   C 90 in³   D 180 in³

464   465   Lesson 18-4

## From State Student Assessments

**23.** (Texas, Grade 8)
Deb has a rectangular storage box with a height of 18 inches, as shown at right.

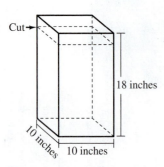

Cut

18 inches

10 inches

10 inches

If Deb cuts off a 2-inch strip around the top of the box, what will be the new volume of the box in cubic inches?

**A.** 1600 in³

**B.** 1440 in³

**C.** 1024 in³

**D.** 1800 in³

**24.** (Texas, Grade 9)
Mrs. Lee bought a small rectangular box that contains 10 tightly packaged erasers shaped like rectangular prisms, as shown below.

5.9 cm

1.3 cm

2.5 cm

What is the approximate volume in cubic centimeters of this rectangular box?

**A.** 19 cm³   **B.** 97 cm³   **C.** 192 cm³   **D.** 513 cm³

### Examining School Book Pages

*Refer to the School Book Pages provided on page 579 to answer the following questions.*

**25.** Suppose that Marilyn worked problem 13 and came up with 9 ft for the radius of the base. How do you suppose she came up with that answer and how would you help her solve it correctly?

**26.** Is the answer (62.8 cm³) to the volume of the cylinder problem at the top of the page correct? If not, explain why either by the content or from an instructional viewpoint.

## 10.5

# Surface Area

In this section, we will derive formulas for the surface area of some basic figures in space, such as polyhedra, right and oblique prisms and cylinders, pyramids, right circular cones, and spheres. These formulas allow us to solve surface area problems in the same way that we did volume problems—that is, by appropriately breaking the solid into pieces.

> **PROBLEM-SOLVING STRATEGY**  **Decompose one complex problem into a number of simpler ones (with applications to surface area).**
>
> In this case, to find the surface area of a solid, first break up the solid appropriately into a collection of solids whose surface areas are easy to compute and then add those surface areas.

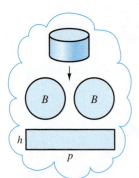

For a polyhedron, the surface area is simply the sum of the areas of each of its faces. It's often useful to imagine cutting a polyhedron apart and placing its faces in a single plane. In many cases, a plane figure or set of figures is formed in this manner, with areas that are easy to determine. For space figures with curved boundaries, it is still sometimes possible to imagine cutting and unrolling the surface to create plane figures whose areas can be easily found. For example, to find the surface area of a tin can, we can imagine cutting off both ends and down the seam of the can. This set of steps creates two discs and, when the can is unrolled, a rectangle, all of whose areas are easy to calculate. For a sphere and other more general solids in space, it becomes necessary to approximate the figure with a sequence of a polyhedra whose surface areas approximate that of the space figure. The surface area of the space figure is the limiting value of the surface areas of the approximating polyhedra.

### Surface Area of Right Prisms and Cylinders

Figure 10.27 shows how the surface of a right prism is cut into two congruent bases, with the lateral surfaces of the prism unfolded to form a rectangle. If the right prism has height *h* and the perimeter of the base is $p$, then the rectangle has area $hp$. The same reasoning applies to any right cylinder, where the lateral surface is imagined to be unrolled onto the plane to form a rectangle.

**FIGURE 10.27**
The surface of a right prism can be cut and unfolded to form two congruent bases and a rectangle

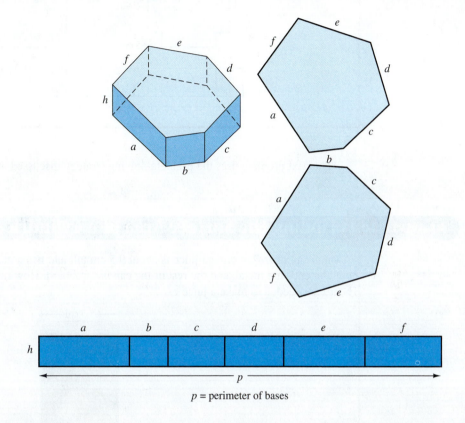

$p$ = perimeter of bases

It is helpful to understand that the total surface area of a three-dimensional solid is often the sum of the **base area** and the **lateral surface area** of the solid (recall that *lateral* means "side").

> **FORMULA** *Surface Area of a Right Prism or Right Cylinder*
> Let a right prism or cylinder have height $h$ and bases of area $B$, and let $p$ be the perimeter of each base. Then the surface area $SA$ is given by
> $$SA = 2B + ph.$$

**EXAMPLE 10.22 Finding the Surface Area of a Prism-Shaped Gift Box**

A gift box has the shape shown. The height is 10 cm, the longer edges are 20 cm long, and the short edges of the square corner cutouts are each 5 cm long. What is the surface area of the box?

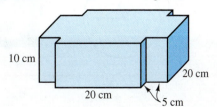

**Solution**  Each base has the area $B = 800\,\text{cm}^2$. The lateral surface area is that of a rectangle 10 cm high and 120 cm long. That is, the lateral surface area is $1200\,\text{cm}^2$. Altogether, the surface area of the box is $SA = 2 \times 800\,\text{cm}^2 + 1200\,\text{cm}^2 = 2800\,\text{cm}^2$.

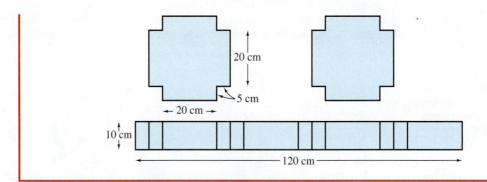

The next problem uses the problem-solving strategy discussed at the beginning of this section.

**EXAMPLE 10.23 Finding the Surface Area of a Cylindrical Juice Can**

A small can of frozen orange juice is about 9.5 cm tall and has a diameter of about 5.5 cm. The circular ends are metal, and the rest of the can is cardboard. How much metal and how much cardboard are needed to make a juice can?

**Solution**  The rectangle that follows is 9.5 cm wide and $5.5\pi$ cm long, so the area of cardboard is $(9.5) \cdot (5.5)\pi$ cm$^2$ = $52.25\pi$ cm$^2$, or about 164 cm$^2$. The circles each have a radius of 2.75 cm, so each circle has area $\pi(2.75$ cm$)^2$. Twice this is $15.125\pi$ cm$^2$, so the area of the two metal ends is about 47.5 cm$^2$.

## Surface Area of Pyramids

The surface area of a pyramid is computed by adding the area of the base to the sum of the areas of the triangles forming the lateral surface of the pyramid. Of special importance is the **right regular pyramid,** for which the base is a regular polygon and the lateral surface is formed by congruent isosceles triangles. The altitude of the triangles is called the **slant height** of the pyramid. The formula for the surface area of a right regular pyramid can be obtained from Figure 10.28. The triangles each have altitude $s$, and the sum of the lengths of the bases is the perimeter $p$ of the base polygon. The total area of the triangles is therefore $\frac{1}{2}ps$. If the base of the pyramid has area $B$, then the total surface area is $SA = B + \frac{1}{2}ps$.

**FIGURE 10.28**
A right regular pyramid has total surface area
$SA = B + \frac{1}{2}ps$

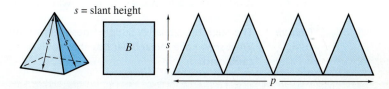

$s$ = slant height

**FORMULA**  *Surface Area of Right Regular Pyramid*
Let a right regular pyramid have slant height $s$ and a base of area $B$ and perimeter $p$. Then the surface area $SA$ of the pyramid is given by the formula

$$SA = B + \frac{1}{2}ps.$$

Once again, the reasoning that leads to the formula is much more important than the formula itself.

**EXAMPLE 10.24  Finding the Surface Area of a Right Regular Pyramid**

A pyramid has a square base that is 10 cm on a side. The edges that meet at the apex have length 13 cm. Find the slant height of the pyramid, and then calculate the total surface area (including the base) of the pyramid.

13 cm

10 cm    10 cm

**Solution**  It is clear that the base of the pyramid has area $B = 100\,\text{cm}^2$ and perimeter $p = 40\,\text{cm}$. The slant height can be calculated with the Pythagorean theorem, which shows that

$$s = \sqrt{13^2 - 5^2} = \sqrt{169 - 25} = \sqrt{144} = 12\,\text{cm}.$$

Thus, the surface area of the pyramid is $SA = 100\,\text{cm}^2 + \frac{1}{2} \cdot 40 \cdot 12\,cm^2 = 340\,\text{cm}^2$.

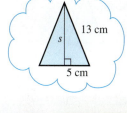

13 cm

$s$

5 cm

**Into the Classroom**

**Problem Solving with Measurement**

Each pair of students has an orange and a sheet of centimeter-squared graph paper. The following challenge is then given: *Find the area of the peel of the orange.* Students well versed in the basic principles of measurement may solve the problem in a direct, yet appropriate, way: The orange is peeled, and then the peeling is cut or torn into small pieces to tile a region of the graph paper; the region's boundary is traced; and then its area, which equals that of the orange peel, is estimated by counting the number of square centimeters covered.

Problem solving with measurement reinforces both the principles and the processes of measurement. By contrast, overemphasis on exercises that require only a routine application of a formula reduces measurement to a mechanistic level. Here are two examples illustrating the difference between a routine exercise and a problem:

*Exercise:*    A right triangle has legs of length 6" and 10". What is the area of the triangle?

*Problem:*    Two straws, of lengths 6" and 10", are joined with paper clips to form a flexible hinge. At what angle should the straws meet to form the sides of a triangle of largest possible area?

*Exercise:*    A rectangular solid has length 6 cm, width 2 cm, and height 2 cm. What is the surface area of the solid?

*Problem:*    The Math Manipulative Supply House sells wooden centimeter cubes in sets of 24 cubes. What shape of a rectangular box that holds one set of cubes requires the least amount of cardboard?

## Surface Area of Right Circular Cones

Consider a right circular cone of slant height $s$ and with a circular base of radius $r$. The formula for the surface area of the cone can be derived from the surface area formula for a pyramid. To see how, imagine that the cone is closely approximated by a right regular pyramid. An example is shown in Figure 10.29, where a cone is approximated by a pyramid with a dodecagon (12-gon) as its base.

**FIGURE 10.29**
A right circular cone has total surface area
$SA = \pi r^2 + \pi rs$

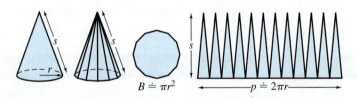

$B \doteq \pi r^2$    $p \doteq 2\pi r$

The area of the circular base of the pyramid is $B \doteq \pi r^2$, and the perimeter of the base is $p \doteq 2\pi r$. Therefore, the surface area of the pyramid is $SA = B + \frac{1}{2}ps \doteq \pi r^2 + \pi rs$. The pyramid's approximation to the cone becomes increasingly exact as the number of sides in the base polygon is increased, giving us the following formula:

> **FORMULA**    *Surface Area of a Right Circular Cone*
> Let a right circular cone have slant height $s$ and a base of radius $r$. Then the surface area $SA$ of the cone is given by the formula
>
> $$SA \doteq \pi r^2 + \pi rs.$$

## The Surface Area of a Sphere

We will now derive a formula for the surface area of a sphere of radius $r$ by making use of the formula that we already know for the volume of the sphere. This derivation is done through reasoning, rather than by formal proof, as is our approach of this chapter. The key concept will be to relate the volume of the sphere to the volume of pyramid-like solids whose base is a small piece of surface area. We first divide the sphere's surface into many (say, $n$) tiny regions of area $B_1, B_2, B_3, \ldots, B_n$. The sum $B_1 + B_2 + B_3 + \cdots + B_n$ is the surface area $S$ of the sphere. Each region can also be viewed as the base of a pyramid-like solid whose apex is the center of the sphere. Each of the pyramids has height $r$, so the pyramids have volumes $\frac{1}{3}B_1r, \frac{1}{3}B_2r, \frac{1}{3}B_3r$, and so on. An example is shown in Figure 10.30.

**FIGURE 10.30**
A solid sphere can be viewed as made up of pyramid-like pieces

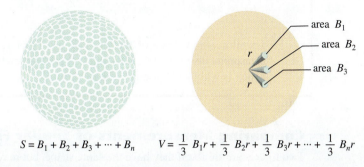

area $B_1$
area $B_2$
area $B_3$

$$S = B_1 + B_2 + B_3 + \cdots + B_n \qquad V = \frac{1}{3}B_1r + \frac{1}{3}B_2r + \frac{1}{3}B_3r + \cdots + \frac{1}{3}B_nr$$

We have the following relationships:

$$S = B_1 + B_2 + B_3 + \cdots + B_n \qquad \text{(surface area of the shere)}$$

and

$$V = \frac{1}{3}B_1r + \frac{1}{3}B_2r + \frac{1}{3}B_3r + \cdots + \frac{1}{3}B_nr. \qquad \text{(volume of the sphere)}$$

Therefore, since $\frac{r}{3}$ is a common factor,

$$V = \frac{r}{3}(B_1 + B_2 + B_3 + \cdots + B_n) = \frac{r}{3}S.$$

Since $V = \frac{4}{3}\pi r^3$, the preceding formula gives us the equation

$$\frac{4}{3}\pi r^3 = \frac{r}{3}S.$$

Multiplying both sides by 3 and dividing both sides by $r$, we can solve for the surface area $S$.

---

**FORMULA**  *Surface Area of a Sphere*
The surface area $S$ of a sphere of radius $r$ is given by the formula

$$S = 4\pi r^2.$$

---

**EXAMPLE 10.25  Comparing Earth with Jupiter**

The diameter of Jupiter is about 11 times the diameter of our planet earth. How many times greater is **(a)** the surface area of Jupiter? **(b)** the volume of Jupiter?

**Solution**

**(a)** Let $r$ denote the radius of earth and $R$ the radius of Jupiter. Therefore, $R = 11r$. Using the formula for the surface area of a sphere, we find that the ratio of the surface area of Jupiter to that of earth is

$$\frac{4\pi R^2}{4\pi r^2} = \frac{R^2}{r^2} = \left(\frac{R}{r}\right)^2 = (11)^2.$$

That is, the surface area of Jupiter is $11^2$, or 121, times the surface area of earth.

**(b)** Using the sphere volume formula, we find that the ratio of volumes is

$$\frac{\frac{4}{3}\pi R^3}{\frac{4}{3}\pi r^3} = \frac{R^3}{r^3} = \left(\frac{R}{r}\right)^3 = (11)^3.$$

Therefore, the volume of Jupiter is about $11^3$, or 1331, times the volume of earth. Precise measurements of the two not-quite-spherical planets show that the volume ratio is 1323.3, which is within 1% of our estimate of 1331.

## Comparing Measurements of Similar Figures

Two figures are similar if they have the same shape, but may be different in size. The ratio of all pairs of corresponding lengths in the two figures is a constant value called the *scale factor*, which we will denote by the letter $k$. The ratio of *any linear measurement* of the two figures—perimeter, height, diameter, slant height, and so on—is also the scale factor $k$. For example, since the diameter of Jupiter is 11 times the diameter of Earth, the scale factor is $k = 11$. We then also know that the equator of Jupiter is 11 times as long as Earth's equator.

The ratio of *areas* of similar figures is given by the *square*, $k^2$, of the scale factor $k$. The ratio of volumes is given by the *cube*, $k^3$, of the scale factor. This basic fact is evident for the cubes shown in Figure 10.31.

**FIGURE 10.31**
Area varies by the square, $k^2$, of the scale factor $k$, and volume varies by the cube, $k^3$, of the scale factor

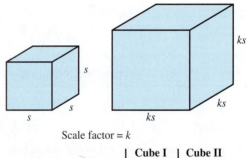

Scale factor = $k$

|  | Cube I | Cube II |
|---|---|---|
| Length of edge | $s$ | $ks$ |
| Area of each face | $s^2$ | $k^2 s^2$ |
| Volume | $s^3$ | $k^3 s^3$ |

The same comparison of areas and volumes holds for any pair of similar figures, not just the cube shown in Figure 10.31. The following theorem is an important principle for the comparison of the measurements of similar figures:

**THEOREM** *The Similarity Principle of Measurement*

Let Figures I and II be similar. Suppose some length dimension of Figure II is $k$ times the corresponding dimension of Figure I; that is, $k$ is the scale factor. Then

  **(i)** *any* length measurement—perimeter, diameter, height slant height, and so on—of Figure II is $k$ times that of the corresponding length measurement of Figure I;

 **(ii)** *any* area measurement—surface area, area of a base, lateral surface area, and so on—of Figure II is $k^2$ times that of the corresponding area measurement of Figure I; and

**(iii)** *any* volume measurement—total volume, capacity, half-fullness, and so on—of Figure II is $k^3$ times the corresponding volume measurement of Figure I.

**EXAMPLE 10.26 Using the Similarity Principle**

(a) Television sets are measured by the length of the diagonal of the rectangular screen. How many times larger is the screen area of a 40-inch model than that of a 13-inch table model?

(b) A 2″ by 4″ by 8″ rectangular brick of gold weighs about 44 pounds. What are the dimensions of a similarly shaped brick that weighs 10 pounds?

**Solution**

(a) The scale factor $k$ is $40/13 \doteq 3.08$. Since area varies by $k^2 \doteq (3.08)^2 \doteq 9.5$, the large screen has about 9.5 times the area of the similarly shaped small screen.

(b) The weight of a gold brick is proportional to its volume, and the volume of similarly shaped bricks varies by the factor $k^3$, the cube of the scale factor $k$. Therefore, $10 = k^3 44$, so $k^3 = 10/44$ and $k = (10/44)^{1/3} \doteq 0.6$. Multiplying the dimensions of the 44-pound brick by 0.6 gives the approximate dimensions of a similarly shaped 10-pound brick of gold, namely, 1.2″ by 2.4″ by 4.8″.

## Problem Set 10.5

Exercises numbered in red are answered in the back of the text.

*The Problem Set for Section 10.4 includes only volume problems. However, Problem Set 10.5 purposely has both volume and surface area problems in it because people (including the children you will be teaching) do confuse the two concepts. Reread each problem carefully before you decide whether it is a volume or a surface area problem.*

### Understanding Concepts

1. Identify which measure—surface area or volume—is most important to know

   (a) about a room, to see how much heat it will take to heat the room.

   (b) about a child's favorite stuffed animal, to determine the amount of stuffing required to mend the animal.

   (c) about a swimming pool, to purchase a pool cover.

   (d) about a lawn, to see how long it will take to mow it.

2. Find the surface areas of these prisms and cylinders:

   (a)

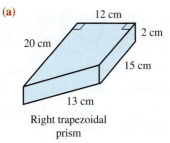

   Right trapezoidal
   prism

   (b)

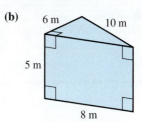

   Right triangular prism

   (c)

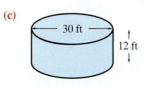

   Right circular cylinder

   (d)

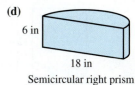

   Semicircular right prism

3. Find the surface areas of these right regular pyramids and right circular cones:

   (a)

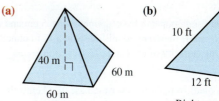

   Right square pyramid

   (b)

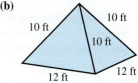

   Right square pyramid

**(c)**

Right circular cone

**(d)**

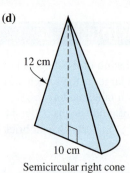

Semicircular right cone

**4.** Find the surface areas and volumes of these solids.

**(a)**

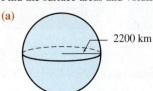

Sphere

**(b)**

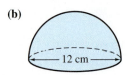

Hemisphere

**(c)**

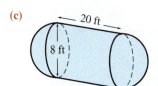

Cylindrical storage
tank with hemispherical
ends

**(d)**

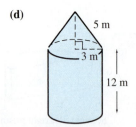

Cylindrical grain silo
with conical top

**5.** What is the surface area of the solid of Figure 10.18 (page 572)?

**6.** An aluminum soda pop can has a diameter of 6.5 cm and a height of 11 cm. If there are 30 milliliters in a fluid ounce, verify that the capacity of the can is 12 fluid ounces, as printed on the can's label.

**7.** If it takes a quart of paint to cover the base of a hemisphere, how many quarts does it take to paint the spherical part of the same hemisphere?

**8.** Archimedes showed that the volume of a sphere is two-thirds the volume of the right circular cylinder just containing the sphere. Show that the area of the sphere is also two-thirds the surface area of the cylinder. (Archimedes was so pleased with these discoveries that he requested that the figure shown be placed on his tombstone.)

**9.** A square right regular pyramid is formed by cutting, folding, and gluing the following pattern:

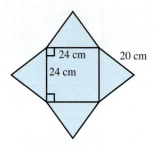

**(a)** What is the slant height of the pyramid?

**(b)** What is the lateral surface area of the pyramid?

**(c)** Use the Pythagorean theorem to find the height of the pyramid.

**(d)** What is the volume of the pyramid?

Use the similarity principle to answer problems 10 through 15. Explain carefully how the principle is used.

**10. (a)** An 8″ (diameter) pizza will feed one person. How many people will a 16″ pizza feed?

**(b)** Is it better to buy one 14″ pizza at $10 or two 10″ pizzas at $6 each? (*Hint:* $1.4^2$ is about 2.0.)

**11. (a)** Eight spherical lead fishing sinkers are melted to form a single spherical sinker. If the small sinkers each have diameter of $\frac{1}{4}$ inch, what is the diameter of the new large one?

**(b)** How many small sinkers would it take to make a sinker 1 inch in diameter?

**12.** What fraction of the area of the large circle is shaded in each figure?

**(a)**

**(b)**

(*Hint:* First compare each unshaded circle with the large circle.)

**13.** Cones I, II, and III are similar to one another. Fill in the measurements left blank in the following table:

| | **I** | **II** | **III** | |
|---|---|---|---|---|
| Height | 6 | 18 | | cm |
| Perimeter of base | | 30 | 15 | cm |
| Lateral surface area | 40 | | | cm² |
| Volume | | | 10 | cm³ |

**14.** A cylindrical can holds 100 milliliters.

 **(a)** If the radius of the base is doubled and the height halved, what is the new volume of the can?

 **(b)** If the radius of the base is halved and the height doubled, what is the new volume of the can?

**15.** A cube 10 cm on a side holds 1 liter.

 **(a)** How many liters does a cube 20 cm on a side hold?

 **(b)** What is the length of each side of a cube that holds 2 liters?

**16.** A right circular cone has a surface area of 16 cm². Its radius is the same as its slant height. What is the radius of the cone?

**17.** If the surface area of a right circular cylinder is 392 cm² and its height is three times its radius, what are the dimensions of the cylinder?

**18.** **(a)** Is there a sphere whose volume (in in³) is the same number as its surface area (in in²)?

 **(b)** Is there more than one solution to this problem? That is, are there spheres of different radii which have the property of part (a)?

## Responding to Students

**19.** A can of diameter 4 cm and height 6 cm is sitting on a table. Jerry is asked what the surface area of the can is and, after looking at the table and thinking, responds "$28\pi$ cm²." How do you think that Jerry got that answer, and how would you explain to Jerry that his answer is incorrect?

**20.** A cube whose sides are 8 cm is sitting on a table. If Annie says that the surface area of the cube is 256 cm², how would you explain her error to her?

**21.** Inez knows that the volume of a sphere involves its radius to the third power, whereas its surface area is the square of its radius. She therefore concludes that the volume is always larger than the surface area of a cube. How would you respond to her?

## Thinking Critically

**22.** The right circular cylinder and cone shown in the accompanying figure both have a base of radius $r$ and height $2r$, and the sphere has radius $r$. Show that the ratio of the surface areas of the cone to the sphere to the cylinder is $\tau$ to 2 to 3, where $\tau = (1 + \sqrt{5})/2$ is the famous golden ratio.

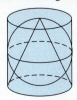

**23.** A birthday cake has been baked in a 7″ by 7″ by 2″ pan. Frosting covers the top and sides of the cake.

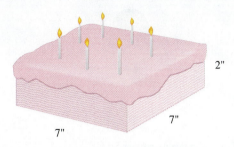

 **(a)** What is the volume of the cake?

 **(b)** What is the area covered by the frosting?

 **(c)** Describe how to cut the cake into eight pieces so that each piece is the same size (measured by volume) *and* has the same amount of frosting (measured by area covered with frosting).

 **(d)** Describe how to cut the cake into seven pieces, each of the same size and with the same amount of frosting. (*Hint:* Consider a slice made by two vertical cuts from the center that also intercepts 4 inches of the perimeter.)

**24.** The cube *ABCDEFGH* with edges of length $s$ contains the tetrahedron *ACEG*.

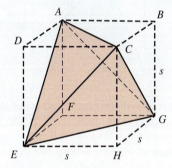

 **(a)** Explain why *ACEG* is a regular tetrahedron with edges of length $\sqrt{2}\,s$.

 **(b)** Show that the volume of tetrahedron *ACDE* is $\frac{1}{6}s^3$.

 **(c)** Show that the volume of *ACEG* is $\frac{1}{3}s^3$.

 **(d)** Use the similarity principle to explain why a regular tetrahedron with edges of length $b$ has volume $\frac{\sqrt{2}b^3}{12}$.

**25.** The ice cream soda glass on the next page is shaped like a cone of height 6 inches and has a capacity of 16 fluid ounces when filled to the rim. Use the similarity principle and the fact that the cone of liquid is similar to the cone of the entire region inside the glass to answer the following questions:

 **(a)** How high is the soda in the glass when it contains 2 fluid ounces?

 **(b)** How much soda is in the glass when it is filled to a level 1 inch below the rim?

## Thinking Cooperatively

In these problems, you will need paper, tape, scissors, and drawing tools (ruler, compass, and pencils). Work in pairs, measuring your constructed models and verifying your observations with calculations.

26. A pyramid is formed by joining a vertex of a cube of side length 8 cm to the four vertices of an opposite face.

    (a) Use your drawing tools to accurately make a pattern that, when cut and folded, will form the pyramid. What are the lengths of each edge in your pattern? Use the Pythagorean theorem to find out. Give your answer both exactly, using square roots, and as a decimal approximation.

    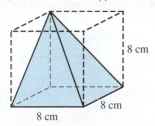

    (b) Use the lengths of the edges found in part (a) to obtain the surface area of the pyramid, giving both an exact answer, using square roots, and a decimal approximation.

    (c) Trace your pattern onto heavy paper and cut, fold, and tape three paper models of the pyramid. Show that the three congruent copies can be arranged to form a cube. What is the volume of the cube? What is the volume of each pyramid?

27. Cut out a semicircular sector, roll it up, and join the two radial segments to form a cone. Show that the diameter of the cone is equal to the slant height of the cone, both by measuring your paper model and by making a calculation.

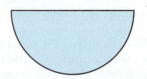 

## Making Connections

28. A rain gauge has a funnel 6 inches in diameter at the top, tapering into a Plexiglas™ collection cylinder whose inside diameter is 2 inches. How far apart should marks be placed on the cylinder to indicate the number of inches of rainfall? (*Hint:* Use the similarity principle.)

## From State Student Assessments

29. (Illinois, Grade 5)
    The scale drawing for a new clubhouse is drawn so that 1 cm = 1 meter. If the scale drawing of the clubhouse is drawn with an area of 100 square cm, what will be the area of the actual clubhouse?

    ○ 1 square meter
    ○ 10 meters
    ○ 10 square meters
    ○ 100 square meters
    ○ 100 meters

30. (Texas, Grade 8)
    Deb has a rectangular storage box with a height of 18 inches, as shown at right.

    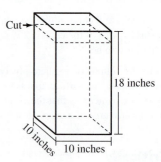

    If Deb cuts off a 2-inch strip around the top of the box, what will be the new volume of the box in cubic inches?

    A. $1600 \, \text{in}^3$
    B. $1440 \, \text{in}^3$
    C. $1024 \, \text{in}^3$
    D. $1800 \, \text{in}^3$

31. (Texas, Grade 8)
    Moffett's Candy Factory makes candy in the shape of cylinders. The net of a cylindrical piece of candy is shown on the next page.

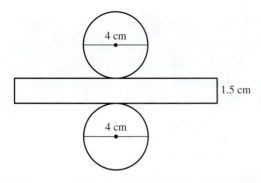

Which is closest to the total surface area of this piece of candy?

**A.** $31\text{ cm}^2$    **B.** $19\text{ cm}^2$    **C.** $44\text{ cm}^2$    **D.** $75\text{ cm}^2$

**32.** (Washington, Grade 8)
Bella Restaurant is building a curved awning for the entrance to their restaurant. They need material for only the top and the front of the awning.

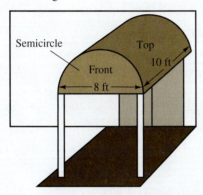

Area of a circle $= \pi r^2$
Circumference of a circle $= \pi d$

Find the surface area of the awning to determine the total amount of canvas necessary to make the awning.

Show your work using words, numbers, and or pictures.

Be sure to label your answer.

How much canvas is necessary to make the awning? _____

**33.** (Washington, Grade 6)
Gavin is building a storage shed attached to the side of his house. He needs to calculate the total surface area of the three walls of the shed to help determine how much paint he needs to purchase.

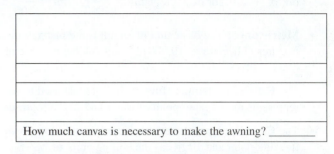

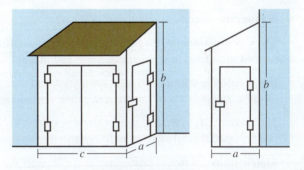

Which expression will provide a good estimate of the total surface area of all three shed walls?

**A.** $(c \times b) + 2(a \times b)$

**B.** $2(c \times b) + (a \times b)$

**C.** $2a \times 2b + c$

**D.** $a \times b \times c$

## The Chapter in Relation to Future Teachers

This chapter has introduced the basic notions of measurement, especially for length, area, and volume. Measurement is concerned with how size is determined and communicated and is generally an approximation. For some ideal shapes—triangles, prisms, pyramids, circles, and spheres, to name a few—the measurement process can be done through the use of a formula. However, these formulas must be carefully derived before they are used; they are not simply a collection of formulas. We will often need to return to the basic principles of the measurement process and apply them to complicated solids by breaking down the solids into pieces that are either easily measured or for which there is an established formula.

## Chapter 10 Summary

| Section 10.1   The Measurement Process | Page Reference |
|---|---|
| **CONCEPTS** | |
| • **Unit** is an established amount used to determine size to allow comparison. | 526 |
| • **Standardized system:** A measurement system with well-defined units used to communicate size and magnitude. The United States uses the customary system, and the entire world, including the United States, uses the metric system. | 529, 532 |

| | |
|---|---|
| • **The metric (SI) system:** A system with units related by powers of 10 described by a prefix system; for example, $milli = \dfrac{1}{1000}$, $centi = \dfrac{1}{100}$, and $kilo = 1000$. | 532 |
| • **Metric units:** The basic unit of length is the meter, with area given in square meters or hectares (1 hectare $= 10{,}000 \text{ m}^2$) and volume in cubic meters. Capacity is also given in liters (1 liter $= 1000 \text{ cm}^3$). Mass is given in grams. | 532, 534–536 |
| • The **Fahrenheit temperature scale** is a scale used to measure temperature where 32°F represents the freezing point of water and 212°F represents the boiling point of water. | 536 |
| • The **Celsius temperature scale** is a scale used to measure temperature with 0°C as the freezing point and 100°C as the boiling point of water. | 537 |

**DEFINITIONS**

| | |
|---|---|
| • A **measurable attribute** is a property of an object, such as length, area, volume, capacity, temperature, time or weight, which is to be measured. | 527 |
| • A **tangram** piece is a certain unit of measurement which originated in ancient China. | 527 |
| • The **U.S. Customary (English) system** is a standardized measurement system with well-defined units used to communicate size and magnitude. | 529 |
| • **U.S. Customary units** are: inch, foot, yard, and mile for length, $\text{in}^2$, $\text{ft}^2$, $\text{yd}^2$, acre, and $\text{mi}^2$ for area, and $\text{in}^3$, $\text{ft}^3$, $\text{yd}^3$, quart, and gallon for volume and capacity. | 527–531 |
| • The **metric (SI) system** is a measurement system used worldwide with units related by powers of 10 described by a prefix system. For example, $milli = 1/1000$ and $kilo = 1000$. | 532 |
| • **Metric units** are meter, centimeter, and kilometer for length, $\text{m}^2$, $\text{cm}^2$, $\text{km}^2$, and hectare for area, and $\text{m}^3$, $\text{cm}^3$, $\text{km}^3$, and liter for volume and capacity. | 532, 534 |
| • A **liter** is the volume of a cube, each of whose sides is 10 centimeters or, equivalently, 1 liter is $1000 \text{ cm}^3$. | 535 |
| • The **weight** of an object is the force exerted on the object by gravity. | 535 |
| • **Mass** is the amount of matter an object has. | 535 |
| • A **kilogram** is the weight of one liter of water. | 536 |

**PROCEDURES**

| | |
|---|---|
| • **The measurement process:** Step 1: Choose the property (length, area, volume, and so on) to be measured. Step 2: Select a unit of measurement. Step 3: Compare the size of the object being measured with the size of the unit by covering, filling, and so on. Step 4: Express the measurement as the number of units used. | 527 |
| • **Converting between customary system and metric system:** 1 m is about 3.28 ft and 1 ft is about .3048 m. | 537 |
| • **Unit,** or **dimension, analysis:** A process to convert a measurement given in one unit to the equivalent measurement in a new unit. | 534 |

| **Section 10.2   Area and Perimeter** | **Page Reference** |
|---|---|

**CONCEPTS**

| | |
|---|---|
| • **Area:** Area is the amount of the plane covered by a region in the plane. The unit of area is arbitrary, but usually a square one unit of length on a side is chosen. To compare the area of one region with that of another, the congruence and addition properties are often useful. | 542 |
| • The **units of area** are usually given as $\text{cm}^2$, $\text{in}^2$, $\text{ft}^2$, etc. | 542 |

- **Area formulas for common polygons:**
  Rectangle of length $l$ and width $w$: $A = lw$. | 545
  Parallelogram of base $b$ and height $h$: $A = bh$. | 546

  Triangle of base $b$ and altitude $h$: $A = \frac{1}{2}bh$. | 546

  Trapezoid with bases $a$ and $b$ and altitude $h$: $A = \frac{1}{2}(a + b)h$. | 546

- **Length:** Length is the distance along a curve. | 549

- **Perimeter:** Perimeter is the length of a simple closed curve or, more generally, the length of the boundary of a region. | 549

- **Perimeter, circumference, and area of a circle:** The perimeter of a circle is called the circumference of the circle, given by $2\pi r$, where $r$ is the radius of the circle and, by definition, $\pi$ (pi) is the ratio of the circumference to the diameter of a circle. The area of a circle is $\pi r^2$. | 550, 552

## DEFINITIONS

- Two regions in the plane are **congruent** if they have the same size and shape. | 543

- A **cycloid** is an arch-shaped curve that is created by the path a point on a circle travels when it is rolled along a flat surface. | 544

- An **altitude of a parallelogram** is the distance that separates a pair of parallel sides. | 546

- A **lattice polygon** is a polygon formed by joining points of a square array. | 548

- The **length of a polygonal curve** is obtained by summing the lengths of its sides. The **length of a nonpolygonal curve** is measured or estimated by calculating the length of an approximating polygonal curve with vertices on the original curve. | 549

- The **perimeter** of a region is the length of its boundary. | 549

## PROPERTIES

- **Congruence property of area:** If two regions are congruent then they have the same area. | 543

- **Addition property of area:** If a region $R$ is divided into nonoverlapping subregions, then the area of $R$ is the sum of the area of the subregions. | 543

## PROCEDURE

- **Dissection of a plane region into subregions:** Cut the figure into a collection of nonoverlapping regions that cover the larger figure. | 543

### Section 10.3   The Pythagorean Theorem | **Page Reference**

## CONCEPTS

- **Pythagorean theorem:** The lengths $a$, $b$, and $c$ of the sides of a right triangle with hypotenuse of length $c$ satisfies $a^2 + b^2 = c^2$. Therefore, the sum of the areas of the squares on the legs of a right triangle equals the area of the square on the hypotenuse. | 564

- **The converse of the Pythagorean theorem:** This statement as also true: If $a^2 + b^2 = c^2$, then a triangle with sides of length $a$, $b$, and $c$ is a right triangle. | 567

### Section 10.4   Volume | **Page Reference**

## CONCEPTS

- **Decomposition of solids:** Use the problem-solving strategy of breaking complicated solids into a collection of more manageable solids (decomposing one complex problem into a number of simpler ones). | 573

- **Volume formulas:**

  Prism or cylinder of base area $B$ and height $h$: $V = Bh$. | 573, 574

  Pyramid or cone of base area $B$ and height $h$: $V = \frac{1}{3}Bh$. | 575

  Sphere of radius $r$: $V = \frac{4}{3}\pi r^3$. | 576

**DEFINITION**

- The **volume, $V$,** of a solid measures the amount of space enclosed within its boundary. | 572

| Section 10.5   Surface Area | Page Reference |
|---|---|

**CONCEPTS**

- **Surface area of a polyhedron:** The surface area of a polyhedron is the sum of the areas of its plane faces. For some polyhedra, such as right prisms and right regular pyramids, it is useful to imagine that the surface is cut and unfolded into the plane. | 580

- **Surface area of a general space figure:** This quantity is found as the limiting value of the surface areas of approximating polyhedra. | 580

- **Surface area formulas:**

  Right prism or right cylinder of height $h$, bases of area $B$, and perimeter $p$: $SA = 2B + ph$. | 581

  Right regular pyramid of slant height $s$, base area $B$, and perimeter $p$: $SA = B + \frac{1}{2}ps$. | 583

  Right circular cone of slant height $s$, and base radius $r$: $SA = \pi r^2 + \pi rs$. | 584
  Surface area of a sphere of radius $r$: $S = 4\pi r^2$. | 585

- **Similarity principle of measurement:** If two space figures are similar with a scale factor $k$, then all corresponding linear measurements vary by the factor $k$, all area measurements vary by $k^2$, and all volume measurements vary by $k^3$. | 586

**DEFINITIONS**

- The **surface area of a surface in space** is the measure of its boundary. | 572

- **Lateral surface area** of a prism or cylinder is the surface area of the sides, not the base, of the solid. | 581

- A **right regular pyramid** is a pyramid whose base is a regular polygon and the lateral surface area is formed by congruent isosceles triangles. | 582

- The **slant height** of a right, regular pyramid is the distance measured along a lateral face. | 583

## Chapter Review Exercises

### Section 10.1

1. Select an appropriate metric unit of measurement for each of the following:

   (a) The length of a sheet of notebook paper

   (b) The diameter of a camera lens

   (c) The distance from Los Angeles to Mexico City

   (d) The height of the Washington Monument

   (e) The area of Central Park

   (f) The area of the state of Kentucky

   (g) The volume of a raindrop

   (h) The capacity of a punch bowl

2. Give the most likely answer.

   (a) A bottle of cider contains 30 mL, 4 L, 15 L.

   (b) Cross-country skis have length 190 cm, 190 km, 190 m.

   (c) The living area of a house is 2000 cm$^2$, 1.2 ha, 200 m$^2$.

3. An aquarium is a rectangular prism 60 cm long, 40 cm wide, and 35 cm deep. What is the capacity of the aquarium in liters?

**4.** A sailfish off the coast of Florida took out 300 feet of line in 3 seconds. Estimate the speed of the fish in miles per hour.

## Section 10.2

**5.** Let $M$ be the midpoint of side $\overline{AD}$ of the trapezoid $ABCD$. What is the ratio of the area of triangle $MBC$ to the area of the trapezoid? (*Hint:* Dissect the trapezoid by a horizontal line through $M$ and rearrange the two pieces to form a parallelogram.)

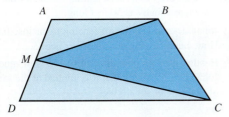

**6.** A square cake 20 inches on a side is being shared evenly among five people. Two cuts have been made to the center as shown.

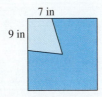

7 in

9 in

**(a)** Is the piece of cake shown a fair piece?

**(b)** Draw a figure showing where three more cuts from the edge to the center create pieces of the same size.

**7.** Find the areas of these figures:

**(a)**

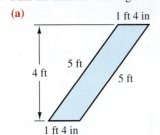

1 ft 4 in

4 ft

5 ft

5 ft

1 ft 4 in

**(b)**

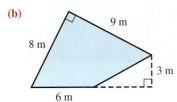

9 m

8 m

3 m

6 m

**(c)**

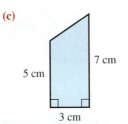

7 cm

5 cm

3 cm

**8.** Find the areas of these lattice polygons:

**(a)**

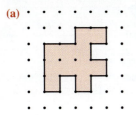

**(b)**

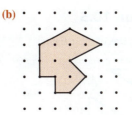

**(c)**

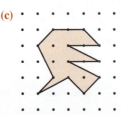

**9.** Find the areas and perimeters of these figures:

**(a)**

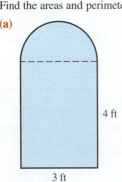

4 ft

3 ft

**(b)**

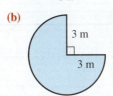

3 m

3 m

## Section 10.3

**10.** Solve for $x$ and $y$ in the figure.

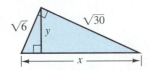

$\sqrt{6}$    $\sqrt{30}$

$y$

$x$

**11.** A right circular cone has slant height 35 cm and a base of diameter 20 cm. What is the height of the cone?

**12.** A rectangular box has sides of length 4 inches, 10 inches, and 12 inches. What are the lengths of each of the four diagonals of the box?

**13.** Find the perimeter of the following lattice polygon:

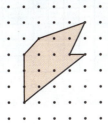

## Section 10.4 and Section 10.5

**14.** Find the volumes and surface areas of these figures:

**(a)**

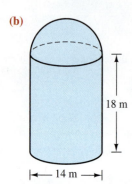

8 ft
10 ft
10 ft
10 ft
10 ft
8 ft
10 ft
30 ft
20 ft

**(b)**

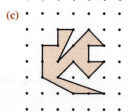

18 m

|← 14 m →|

**(c)**

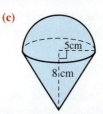

5cm
8 cm

**15.** Which has the largest volume, a sphere of radius 10 meters or four cubes with sides of length 10 meters?

**16.** Heather's garden has a shape similar to Johan's but is 75 feet long, whereas Johan's is 50 feet long.

  **(a)** Johan needed 180 feet of fencing to enclose his garden. How much fencing does Heather need?

  **(b)** Heather used 45 pounds of fertilizer. How much will Johan use, assuming that it is applied at the same number of pounds per square foot?

## Chapter Test

**1.** Find the areas of the lattice polygons. The nails are 1 cm apart.

  **(a)** 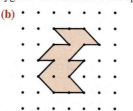     **(b)**

  **(c)**

**2.** (Washington State Student Assessment, Grade 4)

Jim says that the area of shape *A* is equal to the area of shape *B*.

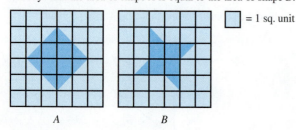

= 1 sq. unit

*A*          *B*

Explain why Jim's thinking is *wrong* using words, numbers, or pictures.

**3.** Find the surface areas and volumes of these figures:

  **(a)**

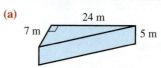

24 m
7 m
5 m

Right triangular prism

  **(b)**

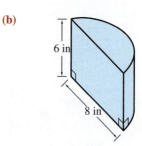

6 in

8 in

Cylinder with semicircular base

  **(c)**

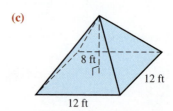

8 ft
12 ft
12 ft

Right regular square pyramid

**(d)**

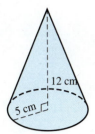

Right circular cone

**4.** Fill in the blank with the metric unit of measurement that makes the statement reasonable.

 **(a)** The haze filter on Donna's camera has a diameter of 52 _____ .

 **(b)** A gray whale has length 18 _____ .

 **(c)** In the 1968 Olympics, Bob Beaman had a long jump of 8.90 _____ .

 **(d)** The Mississippi River has a length of 1450 _____ .

 **(e)** A cup of coffee contains about 250 _____ .

 **(f)** A fill-up at the gas station took 46 _____ .

**5.** A lens is made by cutting a section from a sphere. If the lens has diameter 10 mm and height 4 mm, what is the radius of the sphere from which it was cut?

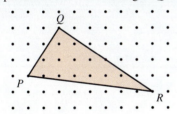

**6. (a)** Find the perimeter of the lattice triangle $PQR$.

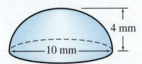

 **(b)** Is $\triangle PQR$ a right triangle?

**7.** Fill in the blanks.

 **(a)** 2161 mm = _____ cm

 **(b)** 1.682 km = _____ cm

 **(c)** 0.5 m$^2$ = _____ cm$^2$

 **(d)** 1 ha = _____ m$^2$

 **(e)** 4719 mL = _____ L

 **(f)** 3.2 L = _____ cm$^3$

**8.** What is the ratio of the area of the inscribed square to the area of the square circumscribed about the same circle?

**9.** A ladder 15 feet long rests against a vertical wall. If the bottom of the ladder is 6 feet from the base of the wall, how high does the ladder reach?

**10.** Complete the conversions of the measurements in the U.S. customary system, using your calculator when convenient.

 **(a)** 1147 in = _____ yd

 **(b)** 7942 ft = _____ mi

 **(c)** 32.4 yd$^2$ = _____ ft$^2$

 **(d)** 9402 acres = _____ mi$^2$

 **(e)** 7.6 yd$^3$ = _____ ft$^3$

 **(f)** 5961 in$^3$ = _____ ft$^3$

**11.** Papa Bear, Mama Bear, and Baby Bear have similar shapes, except that Papa Bear is 5 ft tall, Mama Bear is 4 ft tall, and Baby Bear is 2 ft tall. Fill in the values left blank in the following chart:

|  | Papa Bear | Mama Bear | Baby Bear |
|---|---|---|---|
| **Length of suspenders** |  | 40 in |  |
| **Weight** |  |  | 30 lb |
| **Number of fleas** | 6000 |  |  |

**12.** Find the area and perimeter of the following figure:

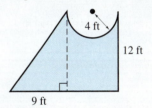

**13.** Find the areas of the figures.

 **(a)**

 **(b)**

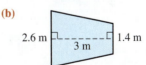

 **(c)**

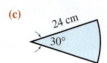

**14.** Find the area and perimeter of the following kite:

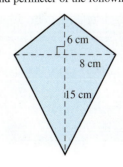

**15.** Explain how the formula for the area of a triangle can be derived from that of a parallelogram by cutting the triangle along the segment joining the midpoints of the sides opposite the base.

**16.** Find the surface areas and volumes of the figures.

**(a)**

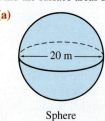

Sphere

**(b)**

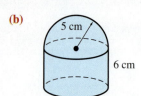

Cylindrical tank with
hemispherical top

**17.** A grapefruit has an outside diameter of 5 inches. When the grapefruit is cut open, it is discovered that the peel is $\frac{3}{4}$ inches thick. What percentage of the grapefruit's volume is peel?

# Transformations, Symmetries, and Tilings

**11.1** Rigid Motions and Similarity Transformations

**11.2** Patterns and Symmetries

**11.3** Tilings and Escher-like Designs

## Hands On

### Exploring Reflection and Rotation Symmetry

#### Materials Needed

Clear acetate sheets, overhead transparency pens, tissues to clean acetate sheets for reuse, and Mira® (if available; otherwise, small plastic or metal rectangular mirror).

#### How to Check for Reflection and Rotation Symmetry

A figure has **reflection** (or **line**) **symmetry** if there is a mirror line that reflects the figure onto itself. For example, the parafoil kite below has a vertical line of symmetry. The wheel cover at the right does not have reflection symmetry, but it does have **rotation symmetry,** since the figure turns onto itself when rotated through 72° about the center point.

Reflection symmetry can be verified by the "trace-and-flip" test. The figure and its line of symmetry are traced onto an acetate sheet. The acetate is then flipped across the proposed symmetry line, and the sheet is turned over, to check that the points of the traced figure coincide with those of the original figure. Reflection symmetry can also be investigated by placing the drawing line of a Mira on a proposed line of symmetry of a figure. Alternatively, looking in the mirror placed on the line of symmetry should make the whole figure appear.

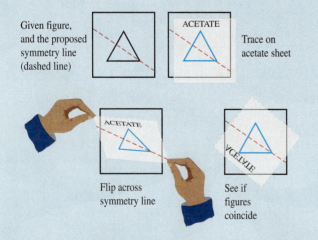

Given figure, and the proposed symmetry line (dashed line)

Trace on acetate sheet

Flip across symmetry line

See if figures coincide

Rotation symmetry can be investigated by the "trace-and-turn" test, illustrated next. The point held fixed is the **center of rotation.** Since the tracing coincides with the original figure after a 120° turn, the trace-and-turn test shows that an equilateral triangle has 120° rotation symmetry.

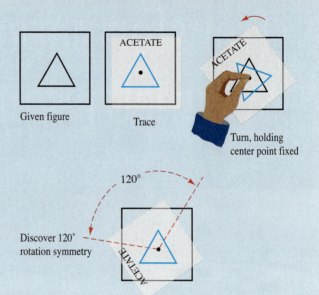

Given figure

Trace

Turn, holding center point fixed

120°

Discover 120° rotation symmetry

#### Activities

1. Use either a Mira, a mirror, or the trace-and-flip test to find all lines of symmetry of the given figures. Use dashed lines to draw the symmetry lines.

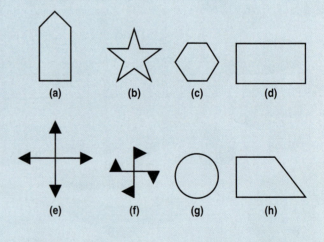

(a)  (b)  (c)  (d)

(e)  (f)  (g)  (h)

2. Use the trace-and-turn test to describe the rotation symmetries of the figures in Activity 1. Indicate the center of rotation and the angle measure of the rotation.

3. Sketch all lines of symmetry and describe all rotation symmetries for the following polygons:
   **(a)** Triangles: equilateral, isosceles, scalene
   **(b)** Quadrilaterals: square, rhombus, rectangle, parallelogram, trapezoid, isosceles trapezoid, kite

**CHAPTER PREVIEW**

This chapter investigates **transformational geometry,** a dynamic approach to geometry in which every point $P$ is moved from a starting position to a final position $P'$. Of special importance is a **rigid motion,** in which every pair of points $P$ and $Q$ move to $P'$ and $Q'$ in a way that leaves their distance unchanged; that is, $PQ = P'Q'$. Any rigid motion will be shown to be one of just four basic types: a translation, a rotation, a reflection, or a glide–reflection. In elementary school terminology, the four basic motions are more informally called, respectively, a slide, a turn, a flip, and a glide. The concept of a rigid motion then allows us, in Section 2, to investigate and classify symmetries and patterns in a precise way. In Section 3, interesting and useful patterns are created by repeatedly transforming a figure to new positions by means of rigid motions. With practice, we will even create artistic tilings that are suggestive of the graphic work pioneered by M. C. Escher.

**KEY IDEAS**

- Transformation of the plane
- Rigid motion
- The four basic rigid motions: translation (slide), rotation (turn), reflection (flip), glide reflection (glide)
- Classification theorem: Any rigid motion is one of the four basic types
- Dilations and similarity transformations
- Congruent and similar figures, as described by rigid motions and similarity transformations
- Symmetric figures
- Types of symmetry: reflection, rotation, point (half-turn)
- Border patterns and their classification
- Tilings (tessellations) of the plane, including regular and semiregular tilings
- Escher-like tilings

## 11.1

# Rigid Motions and Similarity Transformations

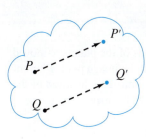

Imagine that each point $P$ of the plane is "moved" to a new position $P'$ in the same plane. Call $P'$ the **image** of $P$, and call $P$ the **preimage** of $P'$. If distinct points $P$ and $Q$ have distinct images $P'$ and $Q'$, and if every point of the plane has a unique preimage point, then the association $P \leftrightarrow P'$ defines a one-to-one correspondence of the plane onto itself. Such a correspondence is called a **transformation of the plane.**

> **DEFINITION**  *Transformation of the Plane*
> A one-to-one correspondence of the set of points in the plane onto itself is a **transformation of the plane.** If point $P$ corresponds to point $P'$, then $P'$ is called the **image** of $P$ under the transformation. Point $P$ is called the **preimage** of $P'$.

A type of transformation called a **rigid motion** is of special importance. As the name implies, a rigid motion does not allow stretching or shrinking of distances.

> **DEFINITION**  *Rigid Motion of the Plane*
> A transformation of the plane is a **rigid motion** if, and only if, the distance between any two points $P$ and $Q$ equals the distance between their image points $P'$ and $Q'$. That is, $PQ = P'Q'$ for all points $P$ and $Q$.

A rigid motion is also called an **isometry,** meaning "same measure" (*iso* = same, *metry* = measure).

A useful physical model of a rigid motion of the plane can be realized with a sheet of clear acetate and a sheet of paper containing figures with certain points labeled $A, B, C, \ldots$. The figures are traced onto the transparency, and a rigid motion is modeled by moving the transparency to a new position in the plane of the paper. An example is shown in Figure 11.1, where primed letters $A', B', C', \ldots$ indicate the points in the image figure that correspond to the respective points $A, B, C, \ldots$ in the original figure. A rigid motion actually maps *all* of the points of the plane, but usually it is enough to show how a simple figure such as a triangle is moved to describe the motion. It is allowable to turn the transparency upside down before it is returned to the plane of the paper, since the definition of rigid motion is still satisfied.

**FIGURE 11.1**
Illustrating a rigid motion of the plane

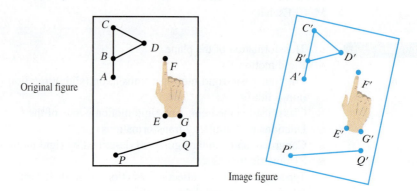

Perhaps the simplest "motion" of all is to leave the acetate sheet in place, so that $P = P'$ for all points of the plane. This is the **identity** transformation.

Note that only the initial and final positions of a transformation are of interest. The transparency could have been taken for a roller-coaster ride before reaching its final position. When the net outcomes of two motions are the same, the transformations are said to be **equivalent.**

## The Four Basic Rigid Motions

Four transformations of the plane have special importance. They are the four **basic rigid motions of the plane:** translations, rotations, reflections, and glide–reflections.

## Translations

A **translation,** also known as a **slide,** is the rigid motion in which all points of the plane are moved the same distance in the same direction. An arrow drawn from a point $P$ to its image point $P'$ completely specifies the two pieces of information required to define a translation: The direction of the slide is the direction of the arrow, and the distance moved is the length of the arrow. The arrow is called the **slide arrow** or **translation vector.**

A translation is illustrated by the "trace-and-slide" model in Figure 11.2.

**FIGURE 11.2**
A slide, or translation, moves each point of the plane through the same distance in the same direction

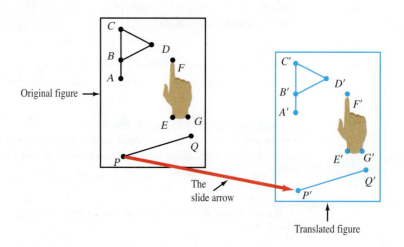

**EXAMPLE 11.1** **Finding the Image Under a Translation**

Find the image of the pentagon *ABCDE* under the slide that takes the point *C* to *C'*.

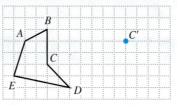

**Solution**

The slide arrow from *C* to *C'* is seven units to the right and two units up. Therefore, *A'* is found by moving seven units to the right of *A* and then two units up. The remaining points are found in the same way, always with the same slide arrow. Here is the image under the given translation:

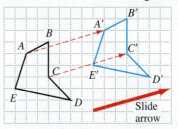

## Rotations

A **rotation,** also called a **turn,** is another basic rigid motion. One point of the plane—called the **turn center** or the **center of rotation**—is held fixed, and the remaining points are turned about the center of rotation through the same number of degrees—the **turn angle** or **angle of rotation.** A counterclockwise turn about point *O* through 120° is shown in Figure 11.3. Note that the right-hand *EFG* is taken to the right-hand *E'F'G'*.

**FIGURE 11.3**
A turn, or rotation, rotates each point of the plane about a fixed point *O*— the turn center—through the same number of degrees and in the same direction of rotation

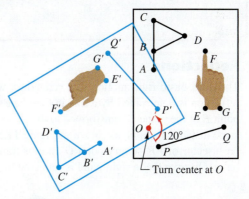

A rotation is determined by giving the turn center and the directed angle corresponding to the turn angle. This information can be pictured by a **turn arrow,** as shown in Figure 11.4. Note that the turn angle is determined by joining a point and its image to the turn center.

**FIGURE 11.4**
The rotation about center *O* by *x*° can be indicated by a turn arrow

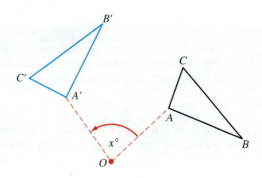

Usually, counterclockwise turn angles are assigned positive degree measures, whereas negative measures indicate that the rotation is clockwise. In this way, a $-120°$ turn is equivalent to a 240° turn about the same center. Remember that only the initial and final positions are considered, not the actual physical motion.

**EXAMPLE 11.2  Finding Images Under Rotations**

Find the image of each figure under the indicated turn.

**(a)** 90° rotation about $P$          **(b)** 180° rotation about $Q$          **(c)** $-90°$ rotation about $R$

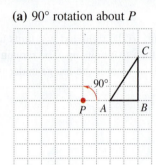   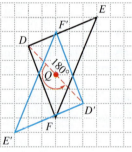   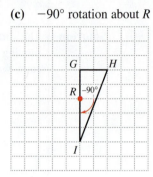

**Solution**   **(a)**                          **(b)**                          **(c)**

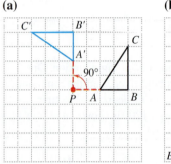   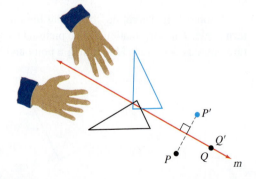   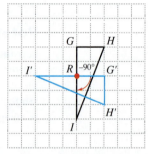

## Reflections

The third basic rigid motion is a **reflection,** which is also called a **flip** or a **mirror reflection.** A reflection is determined by a line in the plane called the **line of reflection** or the **mirror line.** Each point $P$ of the plane is transformed to the point $P'$ on the opposite side of the mirror line $m$ and at the same distance from $m$, as shown in Figure 11.5. Note that $P'$ is located so that $m$ is the perpendicular bisector of $\overline{PP'}$. Every point $Q$ on $m$ is transformed into itself; that is, $Q' = Q$ if $Q$ is any point on $m$. Observe that a right hand is reflected to a left hand, and vice versa.

**FIGURE 11.5**

A flip, or reflection, about a line $m$ transforms each point of the plane to its mirror image on the opposite side of $m$

Reflections can be performed with a trace-and-flip procedure by using an acetate transparency. First, the original figure is traced, including the line of reflection and a reference point (such as $Q$ in Figure 11.5). The transparency is then turned over to perform the flip, and the points along the line of reflection are placed over their original position. The alignment of the reference point ensures that no sliding along the reflection line occurs.

Reflections can also be carried out through paper folding, where the fold line serves as the mirror line. For example, draw a figure with ink (or drop a splotch of ink or poster paint) on one half of a piece of paper, and then, while the ink or paint is still wet, fold the other half over to cover the figure. If tracing paper (or patty paper) is available, first draw an image on the outside of one half of a folded sheet. Then turn the folded sheet upside down and trace the figure as seen through the two folded layers.

The Mira is ideally suited to draw reflections. As shown in Figure 11.6, the plastic surface of a Mira both reflects a figure in front and still allows points behind the surface to be seen. This makes it simple to draw the reflected image of a given figure, with the bottom edge of the Mira acting as the line of reflection.

**FIGURE 11.6**

The Mira on the top can be used to draw reflections, as shown on the bottom

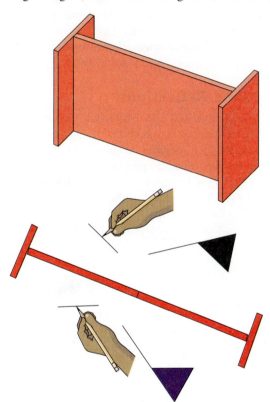

## EXAMPLE 11.3  Finding Images Under Reflections

Sketch the image of the flag under a flip across line *m*.

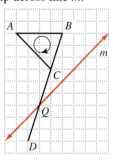

**Solution**

We can follow the trace-and-flip method if an acetate sheet or tracing paper is available, or we can use a Mira or paper folding. Alternatively, the point $A'$ that is the mirror point of $A$ across line $m$ can be plotted on the square grid. Similarly, $B'$, $C'$, and so on can be plotted, until the entire image can be sketched accurately.

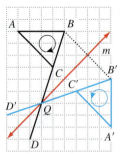

It's important to notice that a reflection reverses left-handed and right-handed orientations. For example, the left-pointing flag in Example 11.3 is transformed into a right-pointing flag, and the clockwise-pointing arrow on the circle that follows $A$, $B$, $C$ in that order becomes a counterclockwise-pointing arrow in the image as it follows $A'$, $B'$, $C'$ in order. A rigid motion that interchanges "handedness" is called **orientation reversing.** Thus, a reflection is orientation reversing. Translations and rotations, since they do not reverse handedness, are **orientation-preserving** transformations.

## Glide–Reflections

The fourth, and last, basic rigid motion is the **glide–reflection.** As the name suggests, a glide–reflection combines both a slide and a reflection. The example most easily recalled is the motion that carries a left footprint into a right footprint, as depicted in Figure 11.7. It is required that the line of reflection, called the **glide mirror,** be parallel to the direction of the slide. The slide is usually called a **glide,** and its vector is called the **glide arrow** or **glide vector.** In Figure 11.7, the slide came before the reflection, but if the reflection had preceded the slide, the net outcome would have been the same. Note that the image of the left footprint under the glide–reflection is the blue right footprint. The green footprint is only an intermediate step used in completing the transformation.

**FIGURE 11.7**
A glide–reflection combines (1) a slide and (2) a reflection, where the line of reflection is parallel to the direction of the slide

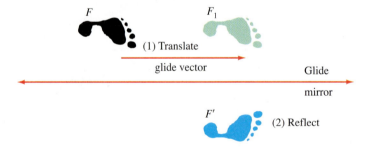

A glide–reflection changes handedness, so it is an orientation-reversing rigid motion. This property is due to the reflection part of the motion.

To determine a glide–reflection, it is useful to observe that the midpoint $M$ of the segment $\overline{PP'}$ lies on the glide mirror. (See Figure 11.8.) This information is the key to solving the problem in the next example.

**FIGURE 11.8**
If points $P$ and $P'$ correspond under a glide–reflection, then the midpoint $M$ of $PP'$ lies on the glide mirror

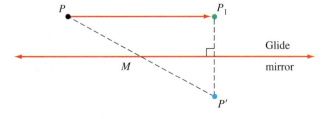

**EXAMPLE 11.4** Determining a Glide-Reflection

A glide–reflection has taken points $A$ and $B$ of triangle $ABC$ to the points $A'$ and $B'$, as shown in the accompanying grid. Find the glide mirror and the glide arrow of the glide–reflection, and then sketch the image triangle $A'B'C'$ under the glide–reflection.

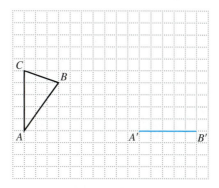

**Solution**   The square grid makes it easy to draw the respective midpoints $M$ and $N$ of the line segments $\overline{AA'}$ and $\overline{BB'}$. Since both $M$ and $N$ lie on the mirror line, $m = \overleftrightarrow{MN}$ is the glide mirror. Reflecting $A'$ across $m$ determines the point $A_1$, and the glide arrow is drawn by connecting $A$ to $A_1$. The glide arrow has components eight units to the right and four units up, which allows us to find $C_1$. Reflecting $C_1$ across the glide mirror locates $C'$; therefore, $\triangle A'B'C'$ can be completed.

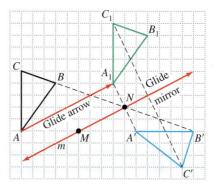

Table 11.1 on the next page summarizes useful information about the four basic rigid motions.

## The Net Outcome of Two Successive Reflections

Recall that any two rigid motions that have the same net outcome are called **equivalent.** For example, rotations of $-120°$ and $+240°$ about the same center $O$ are equivalent. Similarly, the motion consisting of two consecutive $180°$ rotations about a point $O$ is equivalent to the **identity transformation,** which is the rigid "motion" that leaves all points of the plane fixed.

Two consecutive reflections across the same line of reflection also bring each point back to its original position, so such a "double flip" is also equivalent to the identity transformation. Suppose, however, that two flips are taken in succession across two *different* lines of reflection— say, first over $m_1$ and next over $m_2$. There are two cases to consider: $m_1$ and $m_2$ are parallel, and $m_1$ and $m_2$ intersect.

| TABLE 11.1 | THE FOUR BASIC RIGID MOTIONS | | |
|---|---|---|---|
| **Name (alternate name) and Sketch** | **Information Needed** | **Description** | **Orientation Property** |
| Translation (slide) | Slide arrow, indicating distance and direction | Every point of the plane is moved the same distance in the same direction. | Orientation is preserved. |
| Rotation (turn) | Turn center and turn angle | Every point of the plane is rotated through the same directed angle about the turn center. | Orientation is preserved. |
| Reflection (flip) | Line of reflection (mirror line) | Every point of the plane not on the mirror line is moved to its mirror image on the opposite side of the line of reflection. Points on the mirror line are fixed. | Orientation is reversed. |
| Glide–reflection (glide) | Glide arrow and a glide mirror parallel to the glide direction | Every point of the plane is moved by the same translation (glide) and reflected across the same line (glide mirror) parallel to the glide direction. | Orientation is reversed. |

**EXAMPLE 11.5 Exploring Consecutive Reflections Across Parallel Lines**

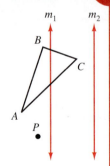

Let $m_1$ and $m_2$ be parallel lines of reflection.

(a) Sketch the images of $\triangle ABC$ and point $P$ under the reflection across $m_1$; let the images be labeled $\triangle A_1B_1C_1$ and $P_1$, respectively.

(b) Sketch the images of $\triangle A_1B_1C_1$ and $P_1$ under reflection across line $m_2$; let the images be labeled $\triangle A'B'C'$ and $P'$, respectively.

(c) Describe the net outcome of the rigid motion consisting of the two successive reflections, first across $m_1$ and next across $m_2$.

**Solution**

(a) and (b) Each reflection can be drawn with a Mira, by the trace-and-flip or paper-folding method, or, easiest of all, by using geometry software. Whatever method is used will result in the images shown on the next page.

(c) If $d$ is the directed distance from line $m_1$ to line $m_2$, then point $P$ is moved a distance $2d$ in the direction perpendicular to $m_1$ and $m_2$ and pointing from $m_1$ toward $m_2$. In fact, *all* points of the plane are moved in this direction through the same distance $2d$, so the net outcome of two successive reflections across the pair of parallel lines $m_1$ and $m_2$ is equivalent to the translation shown on the right side of the figure on the next page.

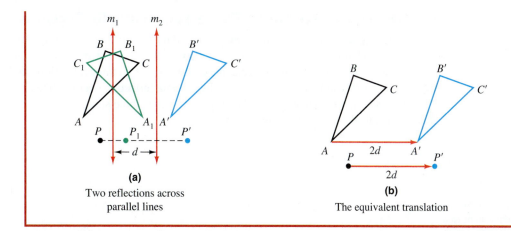

**(a)**
Two reflections across
parallel lines

**(b)**
The equivalent translation

A similar investigation can be carried out for the motion consisting of two successive reflections across lines $m_1$ and $m_2$ that intersect at a point $O$. Most people find the result very surprising: *The net outcome of the two reflections across intersecting lines is equivalent to a rotation about the point $O$ of intersection of $m_1$ and $m_2$. The angle of rotation has twice the measure of the directed angle that turns line $m_1$ onto line $m_2$.* This motion is illustrated in Figure 11.9.

**FIGURE 11.9**

Two reflections across intersecting lines are equivalent to a rotation about the point of intersection of the two lines

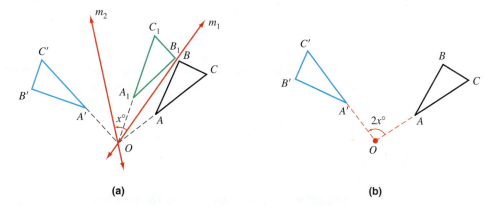

**(a)**

**(b)**

Note that when two reflections are performed, the orientation is reversed twice, so the final image has the *same* orientation as the initial image. The following theorem summarizes the two possible net outcomes of a pair of successive reflections:

**THEOREM** *The Net Outcome of Two Reflections in Distinct Lines*

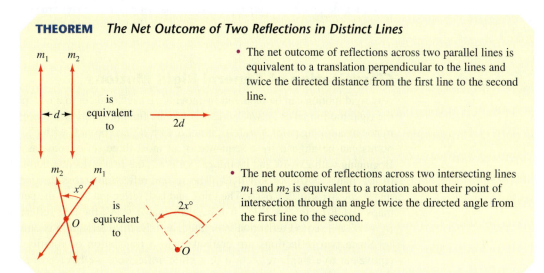

- The net outcome of reflections across two parallel lines is equivalent to a translation perpendicular to the lines and twice the directed distance from the first line to the second line.

- The net outcome of reflections across two intersecting lines $m_1$ and $m_2$ is equivalent to a rotation about their point of intersection through an angle twice the directed angle from the first line to the second.

## The Net Outcome of Three Successive Reflections

Three lines can be arranged in several ways in the plane. For example, the lines $m_1, m_2$, and $m_3$ in Figure 11.10(a) are parallel to one another. The successive images of $\triangle ABC$ across the lines are shown, with $\triangle A'B'C'$ the image at the completion of all three reflections. In Figure 11.10(b), we see that $\triangle ABC$ can be taken to $\triangle A'B'C'$ by a *single* reflection over the line $l$. Line $l$ is the image of line $m_1$ under the translation that takes $m_2$ to $m_3$. Thus, three successive reflections across parallel lines are equivalent to a single reflection.

**FIGURE 11.10**

Three reflections across parallel lines $m_1, m_2$, and $m_3$, are equivalent to a single reflection across $l$ line

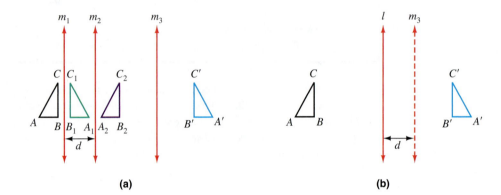

**(a)**                          **(b)**

Three reflections across concurrent lines $m_1, m_2$, and $m_3$ can also be discovered to be equivalent to a single reflection across a certain line $l$ that passes through the point $O$ of concurrence. (See problem 28 in Problem Set 11.1.) In all other cases, where the three lines are neither parallel nor concurrent, it can be shown that the net outcome of three successive reflections is equivalent to a glide–reflection. (See problem 29 in Problem Set 11.1.)

In sum, we have the following theorem:

---

**THEOREM**   *The Net Outcome of Three Reflections*

The net outcome of three successive reflections across lines $m_1, m_2$, and $m_3$ is equivalent to either

- a reflection, if $m_1, m_2$, and $m_3$ are parallel or concurrent;

or

- a glide–reflection, if $m_1, m_2$, and $m_3$ are neither parallel nor concurrent.

---

## Classification of General Rigid Motions

Any rigid motion can be modeled by moving an acetate sheet to a new position in the same plane. If the rigid motion takes $\triangle ABC$ to $\triangle A'B'C'$, the final position of the acetate sheet is uniquely determined by aligning point $A$ with $A'$, point $B$ with $B'$, and point $C$ with $C'$. Let's now see how the three points can be aligned by a sequence of at most three reflections, as illustrated in Figure 11.11. Beginning with $\triangle ABC$ and its image $\triangle A'B'C'$, the first reflection across the perpendicular bisector of $\overline{AA'}$ maps $\triangle ABC$ to $\triangle A'B_1C_1$. The second reflection across the perpendicular bisector of $\overline{B_1B'}$ maps $\triangle A'B_1C_1$ to $\triangle A'B'C_2$. The third, and last, reflection across the perpendicular bisector of $\overline{C_2C'}$ maps $\triangle A'B'C_2$ to $\triangle A'B'C'$. If it happens that $A = A'$, the first reflection is omitted. Similarly, if $B_1 = B'$, the second reflection is omitted, and the third reflection is omitted if $C_2 = C'$.

Since two reflections are equivalent to a translation or rotation, and three reflections are equivalent to a single reflection or a glide–reflection, we have proved the following remarkable theorem:

**FIGURE 11.11**
Any rigid motion is equivalent to a sequence of at most three reflections

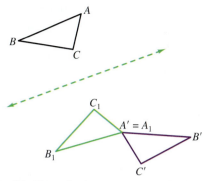

**(a)** Initial positions of the triangles

**(b)** First reflection, across perpendicular bisector of $A$ and $A'$

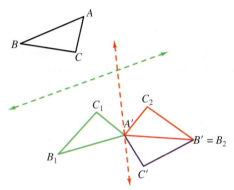

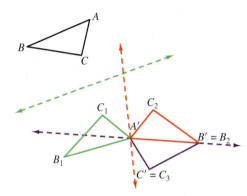

**(c)** Second reflection, across perpendicular bisector of $B_1$ and $B'$

**(d)** Third reflection, across perpendicular bisector of $C_2$ and $C'$

> **THEOREM**  *Classification of General Rigid Motions*
>
> Any rigid motion of the plane is equivalent to one of the four basic rigid motions: a translation, a rotation, a reflection, or a glide–reflection.

An important process in mathematical reasoning is the description of the significant characteristics of a given object. For example, if a rigid motion is described or shown to us, a natural question to ask is "What is the basic type of the transformation?" A good initial step in such a classification is to first observe whether the motion preserves or reverses orientation, since this characteristic is often easily determined:

- If orientation is preserved, then the transformation must be either a translation or a rotation. A translation is easy to detect, since the image figure will be parallel to and face in the same direction as its preimage. A rotation will change the direction of the figure. An image figure that is parallel to its preimage, but "upside down," is related to the original by a 180° rotation.

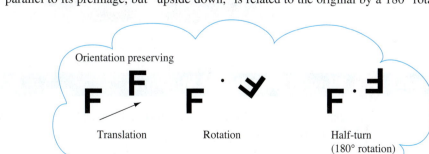

Orientation preserving

Translation          Rotation          Half-turn
                                        (180° rotation)

• If orientation is reversed, the rigid transformation is a reflection or a glide–reflection. Reflections are quickly identified since the image figure will be a mirror reflection of its preimage and the mirror line will be halfway between the image and its preimage. If the orientation-reversing transformation has no mirror line, it is necessarily a glide–reflection.

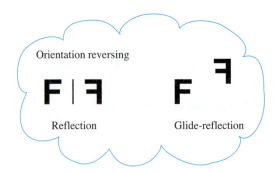

Rigid motions have many applications in geometry. For example, the informal definition of congruence to mean "same size and shape" can now be made precise:

**DEFINITION**  *Congruent Figures*
Two figures are **congruent** if, and only if, one figure is the image of the other under a rigid motion.

The periodic drawings and prints of M. C. Escher show how the plane can be tiled by congruent figures. Figure 11.12 illustrates a two-motif pattern of fish of two types.

**FIGURE 11.12**
A two-motif tiling of the plane by M. C. Escher

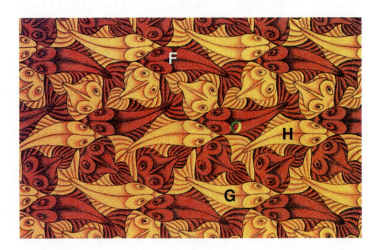

**EXAMPLE 11.6** **Classifying Rigid Motions**

Examine the tiling of M. C. Escher shown in Figure 11.12. Three congruent large fish are labeled F, G, and H.

(a) What type of rigid motion takes F onto G?
(b) What type of rigid motion takes F onto H?
(c) What type of rigid motion takes G onto H?

**Solution**

(a) Since F and G have the same orientation (both bend the tail to the left), they are related by an orientation-preserving transformation. Also, since the fish face in opposite directions, the motion is not a translation and so must be a rotation. (Can you identify the turn center and the size of the angle of rotation?)

(b) F and H have opposite orientation, so either a reflection or a glide–reflection takes F onto H. H is not a reflection of F, so the motion must be a glide–reflection. (Can you determine the glide mirror?)

(c) A glide–reflection takes G onto H. The glide vector is horizontal and points to the right.

## Did You Know?

### You Can't Listen for Congruence

In 1966, Mark Kac of Rockefeller University asked an apparently simple question: "Can you hear the shape of a drum?" A drum, for Kac, can have any shape. All that's required is that it be a two-dimensional figure having an interior (the drumhead) and a boundary (the rim). The shape of the boundary determines an infinite set of characteristic frequencies at which the interior drumhead will vibrate. Two drums of the same shape generate the same set of frequencies, but Kac wanted to know if the converse is true: If you hear the same set of frequencies from two drums, are the drums necessarily the same shape?

In 1991, Carolyn Gordon and David Webb, formerly at Washington University in St. Louis, and Scott Wolpert at the University of Maryland showed that you cannot hear the shape of a drum. They did so by finding two noncongruent shapes that, if made into drums with drumheads of the same material stretched at the same tension, would vibrate at exactly the same frequencies.

SOURCE: *Adapted from Barry Cipra, "You Can't Hear the Shape of a Drum," Science, Vol. 255: 1642, March 27, 1992.*

## Dilations and Similarity Motions

A rigid motion takes any two points $P$ and $Q$ to the image points $P'$ and $Q'$, respectively, preserving the distance between them. That is, $PQ = P'Q'$. Therefore, any figure mapped by a rigid motion is unchanged in both size and shape. Suppose, however, we wish to find transformations of the plane that preserve shape but change the size of figures. Transformations with this property are quite common: Consider making an enlargement or reduction on a photocopy machine or using the Zoom command from the View menu of a computer program.

The simplest transformation to change the size of a figure, but preserve its shape and orientation, is a **dilation** (also called a **size transformation**). A point $O$ is chosen as the center, and the points of the plane are all moved toward ($k < 1$) or away from ($k > 1$) the center $O$ by the same proportional factor $k$. More precisely, we have the following definition:

> **DEFINITION** *Dilation, or Size Transformation*
> Let $O$ be a point in the plane and $k$ a positive real number. A **dilation,** or **size transformation,** with **center $O$** and **scale factor $k$** is the transformation that takes each point $P \neq O$ of the plane to the point $P'$ on the ray $\overrightarrow{OP}$ for which $OP' = k \cdot OP$ and takes the point $O$ to itself.

Two examples of dilations are shown in Figure 11.13.

**FIGURE 11.13**
Two dilations, or size
transformations

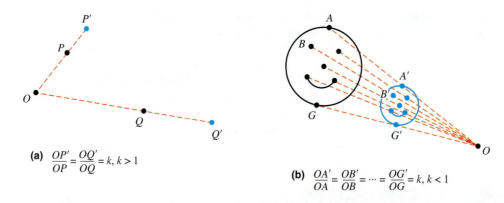

(a)  $\dfrac{OP'}{OP} = \dfrac{OQ'}{OQ} = k, k > 1$

(b)  $\dfrac{OA'}{OA} = \dfrac{OB'}{OB} = \cdots = \dfrac{OG'}{OG} = k, k < 1$

When the scale factor $k$ is larger than 1, the image of a figure is larger than the original and the dilation is an **expansion.** If $k < 1$, the dilation is a **contraction.** If $k = 1$, then all points are left unmoved—that is, $P = P'$ for all $P$—and the dilation is the identity transformation.

The most important fact about dilations is contained in the next theorem. Recall that if a point $P$ is moved to the image point $P'$, we say that $P$ is the preimage of $P'$.

> **THEOREM    *Distance Change Under a Dilation***
> Under a dilation with scale factor $k$, the distance between any two image points is $k$ times the distance between their preimages. That is, for all points $P$ and $Q$, $P'Q' = k \cdot PQ$.

**MHM**    Dilations change size but, like translations, produce images in which corresponding line segments are parallel. This property allows you to determine both the center and the scale factor of the dilation. Simply draw some lines through pairs of corresponding points in the image and preimage figures; the lines will intersect at the center $O$ of the dilation. The scale factor $k$ is then given by the ratio of distances $OP'$ to $OP$ to a pair of corresponding points $P'$ and $P$. That is, $k = \dfrac{OP'}{OP}$.

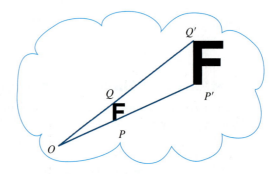

A sequence of dilations and rigid motions performed in succession is called a **similarity transformation.**

> **DEFINITION    *Similarity Transformation***
> A transformation is a **similarity transformation** if, and only if, it is a sequence of dilations and rigid motions.

We can now give a precise definition of similarity of figures.

> **DEFINITION    *Similar Figures***
> Two figures $F$ and $G$ are **similar,** written $F \sim G$, if, and only if, there is a similarity transformation that takes one figure onto the other figure.

The fish $F$ and $G$ in Figure 11.14 are similar to one another. A dilation centered at point $O$ maps $F$ to $F'$, and a reflection maps $F'$ to $G$.

**FIGURE 11.14**

A dilation centered at $O$ and followed by a reflection defines a similarity transformation taking figure $F$ onto figure $G$. Therefore, figures $F$ and $G$ are similar

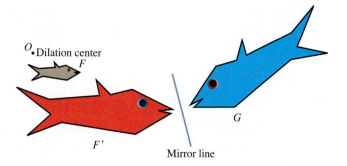

---

**EXAMPLE 11.7  Verifying Similarity**

Show that the small letter $F$ and the larger letter $F$ are similar by describing a similarity transformation that takes the smaller figure onto the larger one.

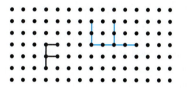

**Solution**  We need a sequence of dilations and rigid motions that rotate, stretch, and position the smaller letter onto the larger. This can be done in three steps: (a) rotate 90°, (b) dilate with scale factor $k = 2$, and (c) translate.

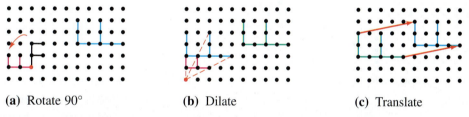

    **(a)** Rotate 90°      **(b)** Dilate      **(c)** Translate

These three steps are not unique. For example, a translation could have been taken first, then a 90° rotation, and finally a dilation with a properly chosen center. Showing that *some* similarity transformation takes one figure onto the other is all that is required.

---

## Problem Set 11.1

Exercises numbered in red are answered in the back of the text.

### Understanding Concepts

1. Which of the following "transformations" correspond to a rigid motion? Explain the reasoning you have used to give your answer.

   **(a)** A deck of cards is shuffled.

   **(b)** A completed jigsaw puzzle is taken apart and then put back together.

   **(c)** A jigsaw puzzle is taken from the box, assembled, and then placed back in its box.

   **(d)** A painting is moved to a new position on the same wall.

   **(e)** Bread dough is allowed to rise.

2. For each figure shown, find its image under the translation that takes $P$ onto $P'$.

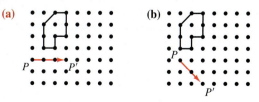

3. The translation that takes point $P$ onto $P'$ transforms triangle $ABC$ (not shown) into its image $A'B'C'$ (shown in the accompanying diagram on the next page).

   **(a)** Draw triangle $ABC$.

**(b)** Describe the rigid motion that transforms $\triangle A'B'C'$ onto $\triangle ABC$, and compare the motion with the translation that takes $\triangle ABC$ onto $\triangle A'B'C'$.

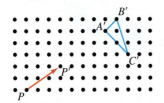

**4.** In each of the following statements, give an answer between $0°$ and $360°$:

**(a)** A clockwise rotation of $60°$ is equivalent to a counter-clockwise rotation of _____.

**(b)** A clockwise rotation of $433°$ is equivalent to a clockwise rotation of _____.

**(c)** A clockwise rotation of $3643°$ is equivalent to a clockwise rotation of _____.

**(d)** A sequence of two consecutive clockwise rotations, first of $280°$ and next of $120°$, about the same center is equivalent to a single clockwise rotation of _____.

**(e)** A rotation of $-260°$ is equivalent to a rotation of _____.

**5.** Sketch the image of $\triangle ABC$ under the given rotations.

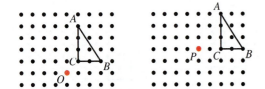

**(a)** $90°$ counterclockwise about $O$

**(b)** $180°$ about $P$

**6.** A rotation sends $A$ to $A'$ and $B$ to $B'$, as follows:

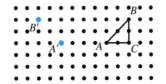

**(a)** Find the center of the rotation.

**(b)** Find the turn angle.

**(c)** Sketch the image triangle $A'B'C'$.

**7.** The equilateral triangle shown has center $O$ and is pointing upward from its horizontal base. Describe *all* nonequivalent rigid motions that move the triangle to point downward and leave point $O$ fixed.

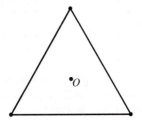

**8.** A point $P$ that is mapped onto itself by a transformation such that $P = P'$ is called a **fixed point.** What can be said about the type of rigid motion that

**(a)** has no fixed points?

**(b)** has exactly one fixed point?

**(c)** has at least two fixed points and a nonfixed point?

**(d)** has only fixed points.

**9.** Trace the given figure, which shows $\triangle ABC$ and its image under a rotation. Use any drawing tools you wish (Mira, compass, or straightedge) to construct the center of rotation. (*Hint:* Why is the center of rotation on the perpendicular bisector of $\overline{AA'}$?)

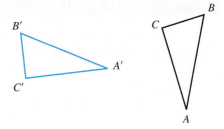

**10.** Redraw the given figure on graph paper. Then sketch the reflection of $\triangle ABC$ across the mirror line $m$.

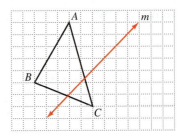

**11.** In the image that follows, a reflection sends $P$ to $P'$.

**(a)** Find the line of reflection.

**(b)** Find the image of the polygon $PQRST$ under the reflection that takes $P$ to $P'$.

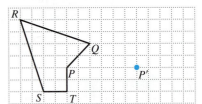

**12. (a)** A reflection across line $m$ leaves point $A$ fixed, so that $A' = A$. What can be said about $A$'s relationship to $m$?

**(b)** A reflection across line $m$ leaves two points $A$ and $B$ fixed, so that $A' = A$ and $B' = B$. What can you say about $A$, $B$, and $m$?

**(c)** A reflection takes point $C$ to point $D$. Where does the reflection take point $D$?

**13.** A glide–reflection is defined by the glide arrow and glide mirror $m$ shown. Draw the following images of the polygon $ABCDE$:

**(a)** The image $A_1B_1C_1D_1E_1$ under the slide

**(b)** The image $A'B'C'D'E'$ under the glide–reflection

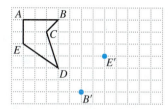

14. A glide–reflection has taken $B$ to $B'$ and $E$ to $E'$. Find

(a) the glide mirror.

(b) the glide arrow.

(c) the image $A'B'C'D'E'$ of the polygon $ABCDE$.

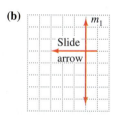

15. In each part that follows, draw a line $m_2$ so that the net outcome of successive reflections about $m_1$ and then $m_2$ is equivalent to the translation specified by the slide arrow shown.

(a)

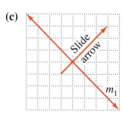

(b)

(c)

16. A reflection across line $j$ followed by a reflection across line $k$ as shown here is equivalent to the translation by four units to the right, as shown in the table that follows:

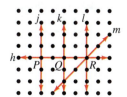

Fill in the missing entries (a) through (f) in the table.

| Reflection Lines | | |
|---|---|---|
| **First** | **Second** | **Equivalent Transformation** |
| $j$ | $k$ | Translate right four units |
| $l$ | $m$ | Rotate clockwise 90° around point $R$ |
| $j$ | $l$ | (a) |
| $k$ | (b) | Translate left four units |
| (c) | $k$ | Translate left four units |
| $h$ | $m$ | (d) |
| $m$ | (e) | Rotate 180° about point $P$ |
| $k$ | (f) | Identity transformation (all points fixed) |

17. Use dot or graph paper to copy $\triangle ABC$ and points $O$ and $P$. Then draw the image of $\triangle ABC$ for

(a) the dilation with center $O$ and scale factor 2.

(b) the dilation with center $P$ and scale factor 1/2.

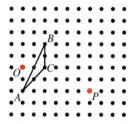

18. In the figure shown, $\triangle DEF$ is the image of $\triangle ABC$ under the dilation with center $O$ and scale factor 2.

(a) Describe the size transformation that takes $\triangle DEF$ onto $\triangle GHI$. Show the center of the transformation on a sketch and give the scale factor.

(b) Describe the dilation that takes $\triangle ABC$ onto $\triangle GHI$ by locating the center and giving the scale factor.

(c) The Pythagorean theorem shows that $AB = \sqrt{5}$, so the perimeter of $\triangle ABC$ is $3 + \sqrt{5}$. Explain how to use the scale factors determined in parts (a) and (b) to obtain the perimeters of $\triangle DEF$ and $\triangle GHI$.

(d) A dilation with scale factor 4 takes $\triangle ABC$ onto $\triangle JKL$. What is the perimeter of $\triangle JKL$?

(e) Find the areas of the three triangles shown. Explain how the areas are related to the scale factors.

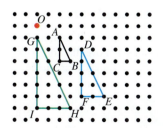

19. Sketch the image of $\triangle JKL$ under the similarity transformation composed of a dilation centered at point $P$ with scale factor 2/3 followed by a reflection across line $m$.

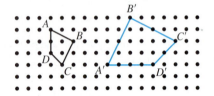

**20.** Describe a similarity transformation that takes quadrilateral $ABCD$ onto quadrilateral $A'B'C'D'$ as shown. Sketch the intermediate images of the dilation and rigid motions that compose the similarity transformation.

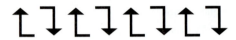

## Teaching Concepts

**21.** Create an activity that explores rigid motions by expanding on the following idea adapted from John A. Van De Walle: Each student is given, in Van De Walle's terminology, a "Motion Man," as shown at the left in the accompanying drawing. The figure, on $10 \times 10$ centimeter dot paper, can be copied onto overhead transparency sheets (several at a time, then cut). Alternatively, the figure can be copied onto both sides of a sheet of paper, so that the figures on the opposite side and front sides will match when held up to the light. Students can now be asked to carry out transformations—for example, half- and quarter-turns, and flips over the lines—and observe how the transformed figure compares against its initial upright position with the flag in the right hand. The right-hand figure in the drawing shows a flip over the lower left to upper right diagonal. To include translations and glide–reflections, have students move Motion Man around a $20 \times 20$ sheet of centimeter dot paper.

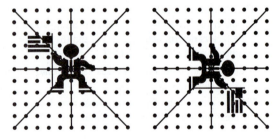

## Responding to Students

**22.** Ephraim and DeVonte were asked to reflect the pattern-block figure shown on the left over the horizontal line through the center of the square. They rearranged the blocks to form the figure on the right.

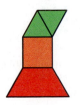   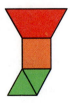

**(a)** What type of rigid motion did Ephraim and DeVonte use?

**(b)** How would you help clear up their misunderstanding?

**23.** Lisa was asked to identify the type of rigid motions used to obtain the following pattern from the single-arrow motif at the far left:

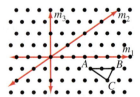

She answered, "rotation and glide–reflection."

**(a)** Is Lisa's answer correct?

**(b)** How would you help guide Lisa to the correct answer?

**24.** A student believes that all rectangles are similar, since all rectangles have four right angles and opposite sides have the same length. How would you respond to this student? In particular, how does the geometrical meaning of "similar" differ from its more common-use meaning?

## Thinking Critically

**25.** A rigid motion takes points $A$, $B$, $C$, and $P$ onto the respective image points $A'$, $B'$, $C'$, and $P'$, where $AB = 3$ cm, $AC = 4$ cm, $AP = 2$ cm, $BC = 2$ cm, $BP = 4$ cm, and $CP = 4$ cm. In each part that follows, use a compass and ruler to draw the smallest set of points that you know must contain the point $P'$ when you start with

**(a)** only point $A'$. (*Hint:* The answer is a circle.)

**(b)** points $A'$ and $B'$.

**(c)** points $A'$, $B'$, and $C'$.

**26.** Two successive $90°$ rotations are taken, first about center $O_1$ and then about center $O_2$, where $O_1O_2 = 2$ cm. Describe the basic rigid motion that is equivalent to the successive rotations. Explain carefully, using words and sketches.

**27.** Suppose that the $90°$ rotations in problem 26 are each replaced with a $120°$ rotation. What basic rigid motion is equivalent to the net outcome of the two rotations? Explain with words and sketches.

**28. (a)** Find the image $\triangle A'B'C'$ of $\triangle ABC$ under the rigid motion consisting of three consecutive reflections across the concurrent lines $m_1$, $m_2$, and $m_3$.

**(b)** Find a line $l$ so that $\triangle ABC$ is taken onto $\triangle A'B'C'$ by one reflection across $l$.

**29. (a)** Find the image $\triangle A'B'C'$ of $\triangle ABC$ under the rigid motion consisting of three consecutive reflections across lines $m_1$, $m_2$, and $m_3$.

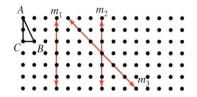

**(b)** Find the image of $\triangle ABC$ under the glide–reflection whose glide arrow extends from $P$ to $P'$ and whose glide mirror is line $l$.

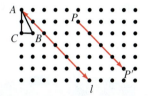

**(c)** What conclusion can you draw about the two rigid motions described in (a) and (b)?

**30.** Trace the following figure, where $\triangle ABC$ is congruent to $\triangle A'B'C'$:

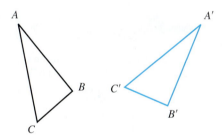

**(a)** Use a Mira (or other drawing tools) to draw the line $m_1$ across which $A$ is reflected onto $A'$. Also, draw the images of $B$ and $C$ under this reflection and label them $B_1$ and $C_1$, respectively.

**(b)** Draw the line $m_2$ across which $B_1$ reflects onto $B'$. What is the image of $C_1$ across $m_2$?

**(c)** Use the lines $m_1$ and $m_2$ to describe the basic rigid motion that takes $\triangle ABC$ to $\triangle A'B'C'$.

**31.** Trace the following figure, where $\triangle ABC$ is congruent to $\triangle A'B'C'$:

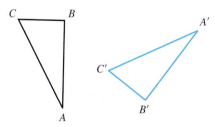

**(a)** Use a Mira (or other drawing tools) to draw three lines of reflection—$m_1, m_2,$ and $m_3$—so that

  **(i)** reflection across $m_1$ takes $A$ onto $A'$ (and $B$ and $C$ are taken to $B_1$ and $C_1$, respectively).

  **(ii)** reflection across $m_2$ takes $B_1$ onto $B'$ (and $C_1$ is taken onto $C_2$).

  **(iii)** reflection across $m_3$ takes $C_2$ onto $C'$.

**(b)** Describe the type of basic rigid motion that takes $\triangle ABC$ onto $\triangle A'B'C'$.

**32.** In each of the parts that follow, a complicated sequence of rigid motions is described. Explain how you know what type of basic rigid motion is equivalent to the net outcome of the motion described.

**(a)** Reflections are taken across 6 lines, and no point is taken back onto its original position.

**(b)** Reflections are taken across 11 lines, and there are points that are taken back onto their original positions.

**(c)** Two different glide–reflections are taken in succession, with the net outcome taking some point back onto its original location.

**33.** Let $C$ and $D$ be two circles on the same side of a mirror. Construct a tangent line to circle $C$ that, after reflection in the mirror, is also tangent to circle $D$. How many solutions can you find?

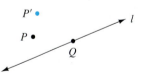

**34.** A drawing by M. C. Escher is shown.

**(a)** What rigid motion takes figure A onto figure B?

**(b)** What rigid motion takes figure A onto figure C?

**(c)** What rigid motion takes figure C onto figure D?

**35.** A size transformation centered at some point $O$ on line $l$ takes point $P$ onto $P'$. Explain how to draw (a) the center $O$ of the transformation and (b) the image $Q'$ of the point $Q$, where $Q$ lies on $l$.

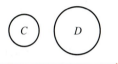

**36.** A size transformation takes $P$ onto $P'$ and $Q$ onto $Q'$, where the four points $P, P', Q,$ and $Q'$ are collinear as shown here. Redraw the figure and explain **(a)** how to draw the image $R'$ of point $R$ and **(b)** how to locate the center $O$ of the size transformation. (*Hint:* What lines through $P'$ and $R'$ must contain $R'$?)

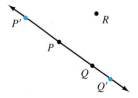

## Making Connections

**37.** A mattress should be turned periodically in order to wear evenly. The mattresses shown here have "flip marks," indicating the axis over which the mattress is flipped. The dashed marks are on the reverse side of the mattress. For example, each mattress is first flipped over the horizontal axis.

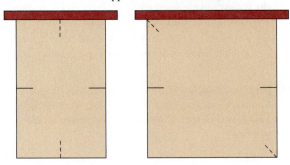

(a) Will the sequence of flips on the left-hand rectangular mattress cycle through all of the positions into which the mattress can be put on the bed? (*Suggestion:* Model the mattress with an index card, with marks on one side indicating a flip from head to foot and marks on the opposite side indicating a side-to-side flip.)

(b) Answer part (a) again, but for the square mattress shown.

**38. Fermat's Principle.** Suppose that a ray of light emanating from point $P$ is reflected from a mirror at point $R$ toward point $S$. It was known even in ancient times that the incident and reflected rays of light make congruent angles with the line $m$ of the mirror. Pierre de Fermat (1601–1665) proposed an important principle to explain why this is so: *Light follows the path of shortest distance.* According to Fermat's principle, if $Q$ is some point on the mirror other than $R$, then the distance $PQ + QS$ must exceed the distance $PR + RS$ traveled by the light.

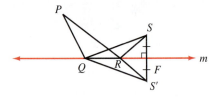

Answer the questions that follow to verify that $PQ + QS > PR + RS$. Let $S'$ be the image of $S$ under reflection across line $m$.

(a) Why are $RS' = RS$ and $QS' = QS$? (*Hint:* The reflection across $m$ is a rigid motion.)

(b) Why is $PQ + QS' > PS'$?

(c) How does the inequality of part (b) give the desired result that $PQ + QS > PR + RS$?

**39.** Let $P$ and $S$ be two points on the same side of mirror $m$. If $S'$ is the point of reflection of point $S$ across $m$, then the line drawn from $P$ to $S'$ intersects $m$ at the point $R$ of reflection. (See the figure in problem 38.) Suppose $P$ and $S$ are between *two* mirrors $m$ and $l$ as shown next.

(a) Construct a doubly reflected light path $PQRS$ that is reflected off mirror $m$ at $Q$ and then off mirror $l$ at $R$.

(b) Construct another doubly reflected path $PABS$ that reflects first off mirror $l$ at $A$ and then off mirror $m$ at $B$.

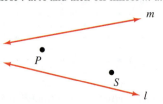

**40.** A **corner mirror** is formed by placing two mirrors together at a right angle. Explain why looking at yourself in a corner mirror is quite different from seeing yourself in an ordinary mirror. Use sketches to make your ideas clear.

**41.** A billiard ball is located at a point $P$ along an edge of a rectangular billiard table. Show that there is a billiard shot that strikes the cushions on the other three rails (sides) of the table and then returns to bounce at $P$.

(*Hint:* Suppose the table $T$ is reflected across its sides successively, forming the images $T'$, $T''$, and $T'''$.) Explain how a billiard path $PQRSP$ can be found by drawing the line segment $\overline{PP'''}$. Sketch the path $PQRSP$ on the original table $T$.

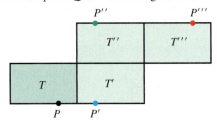

**42.** A **pantograph** is a mechanical device used to draw enlargements. The simple version pictured here can be constructed from cardboard strips that are hinged with brass fasteners: $ABCP$ forms a parallelogram. The pivot point at $O$ is held fixed as $P$ is moved over the figure. The pencil point at point $P'$ traces out an enlargement.

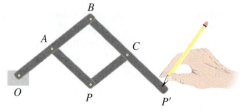

**(a)** Explain why the pantograph mechanically gives a size transformation.

**(b)** What is the scale factor of the size transformation if $A$ and $C$ are the midpoints of the two congruent strips $OB$ and $BP'$, and $ABCP$ is a rhombus?

**43. Rigid Motions with Coordinates.** Rigid motions can be usefully explored in the coordinate plane. In the figure shown here, for example, the coordinates of $\triangle PQR$ are $P = (4, 1)$, $Q = (5, 1)$, and $R = (4, 3)$. By adding 3 to the $x$-coordinates and 2 to the $y$-coordinates, the triangle is moved rigidly to $\triangle P'Q'R'$, where $P' = (7, 3)$, $Q' = (8, 3)$, and $R' = (7, 5)$. The motion is a translation, with its slide vector given by the arrow extending three units to the right and two units upward.

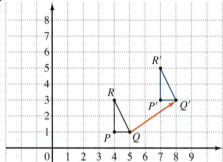

In a similar manner, use a coordinate grid to draw $\triangle PQR$ and its image $\triangle P'Q'R'$ under each of the transformations that follow, always starting with $\triangle PQR$ in its original position given in the preceding diagram. Classify each transformation as a rigid motion.

**(a)** Subtract 2 from the $x$-coordinates and add 3 to the $y$-coordinates.

**(b)** Replace each $y$-coordinate with its opposite (that is, with its negative).

**(c)** Replace each $x$-coordinate with its opposite.

**(d)** Replace both the $x$- and $y$-coordinates with their opposites.

**(e)** Exchange the $x$- and $y$-coordinates. For example, $P = (4, 1)$ is moved to $P' = (1, 4)$.

**(f)** If $P$ has the coordinates $(x, y)$, let $P'$ have the coordinates $(-y, x)$. For example, if $P = (4, 1)$ then its image is $P' = (-1, 4)$.

**(g)** If $P$ has the coordinates $(x, y)$, let $P'$ have the coordinates $(y + 3, x + 3)$. For example, if $P = (4, 1)$ then its image is $P' = (1 + 3, 4 + 3) = (4, 7)$.

**44. Size and Similarity Transformations with Coordinates.** The coordinates of $\triangle PQR$ are $P = (4, 1)$, $Q = (5, 1)$, and

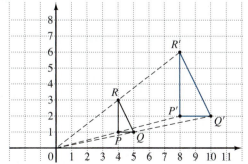

$R = (4, 3)$. By multiplying the $x$- and $y$-coordinates by 2, the triangle is moved to $\triangle P'Q'R'$, where $P' = (8, 2)$, $Q' = (10, 2)$, and $R' = (8, 6)$. This size transformation is centered at the origin $(0, 0)$ and has scale factor $k = 2$.

**(a)** On graph paper, draw the two image triangles obtained by transforming $\triangle PQR$ with size transformations centered at the origin, first with scale factor $k = 3$ and then with scale factor $k = 0.5$.

**(b)** What combination of a rigid motion and size transformation centered at the origin can map $\triangle PQR$ to the $\triangle STU$ with vertices at the points $S = (1, 2)$, $T = (3, 2)$, and $U = (1, 6)$? Carefully describe how to obtain the coordinates of $\triangle STU$, beginning with the coordinates of $\triangle PQR$.

**(c)** Why is $\triangle PQR$ similar to $\triangle ABC$, where $A = (-8, -2)$, $B = (-10, -2)$, and $C = (-8, -6)$? Use coordinates to describe the similarity motion that takes triangle $PQR$ to triangle $ABC$.

## Communicating

**45.** Explore what happens when two translations are taken in succession, and write a report on your conclusions. Give specific examples, as well as any general principles you find. In particular, include answers to the following questions:

**(a)** Why is the net outcome of two successive translations equivalent to another translation?

**(b)** If the first translation takes point $A$ onto $A_1$ and the second translation takes $A_1$ onto $A'$, why is the arrow from $A$ to $A'$ the slide arrow of the combined motion of the two translations?

**(c)** What happens to the net outcome if the order in which the two translations are applied is reversed?

## Using a Computer

**46.** Draw any convex quadrilateral $ABCD$ with geometry software, and construct the midpoint $M$ of side $\overline{AB}$. Mark point $M$ as the center of rotation, and rotate the quadrilateral $180°$ about $M$ to form the hexagon $AC'D'BCD$. Describe how to translate the hexagon to tile the plane without gaps or overlaps. Show a patch of the tiling with at least one hexagon surrounded by congruent copies of the hexagon.

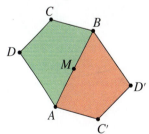

**47.** Use geometry software to draw a triangle $ABC$ and construct the outward-pointing equilateral triangles on its three sides with centers $X$, $Y$, and $Z$ as shown here:

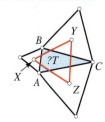

(a) Construct the triangle *XYZ*. Use your software to investigate the properties of △*XYZ*.

(b) Mark *X* as a rotation center, and rotate the entire figure shown by 120°. Similarly, rotate the figure 120° about the centers of the other equilateral triangles. What pattern is formed by the centers *X*, *Y*, and *Z* of all the equilateral triangles and their rotated images?

48. Use geometry software to construct a parallelogram *ABCD* and the outward squares on its sides with centers *X*, *Y*, *Z*, and *W*, as shown here:

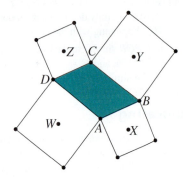

(a) Construct the quadrilateral *XYZW*. Use your software to investigate the properties of *XYZW*.

(b) Mark *X* as a rotation center and rotate the entire figure shown by 90°. Similarly, rotate the figure 90° about the centers of the other squares. What pattern is formed by the centers of all the squares and their rotated images?

## From State Student Assessments

49. (Texas, Grade 8)

Figure *STUVW* will be translated 5 units left and 7 units up to form figure *S'T'U'V'W'*. Which ordered pair best represents point *W'*?

**F.** (3, 6)  **G.** (−2, 1)  **H.** (−7, 6)  **J.** (2, −1)

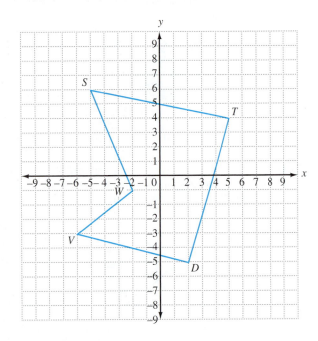

50. (Texas, Grade 8)

With the origin as the center of dilation, rectangle *PQRS* will be dilated by a scale factor of $\frac{1}{3}$ to form rectangle *P'Q'R'S'*. What will be the *y* length of $\overline{P'S'}$?

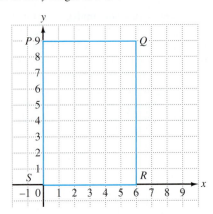

**A.** 3 units  **B.** 2 units  **C.** 27 units  **D.** 18 units

51. (Georgia, Grade 7)

If the rectangle below is rotated about the line that is shown, what three-dimensional figure will be formed?

**A.** sphere  **B.** cube  **C.** cylinder  **D.** cone

52. (Florida, Grade 5)

Carla created the figure below in her art class.

Which of these shows the figure rotated 90° clockwise?

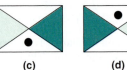

53. (Oregon, Grade 5)

Which two of these figures are congruent?

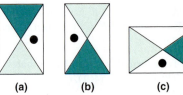

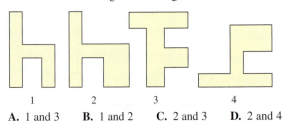

**A.** 1 and 3  **B.** 1 and 2  **C.** 2 and 3  **D.** 2 and 4

*See "Examining School Book Pages" on page 624 for questions related to the pages shown below.*

## Lesson 19-3

**Understand It!**
The size and shape of a figure do not change when it is rotated.

# Rotations

**What is one way to move a figure?**

A **rotation** moves a figure around a point.

In a computer game, you rotate a spaceship. It rotates as shown about point A.

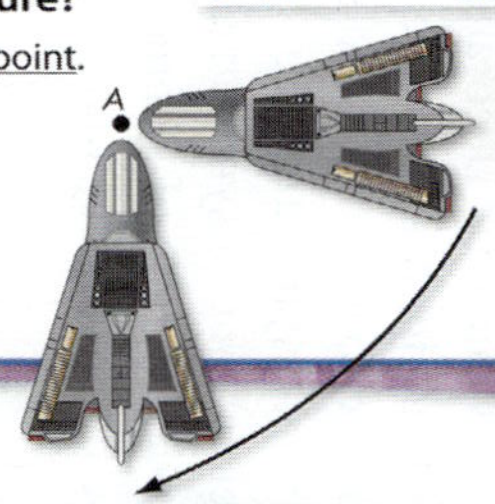

When a figure is rotated, the size and shape of the figure do not change.

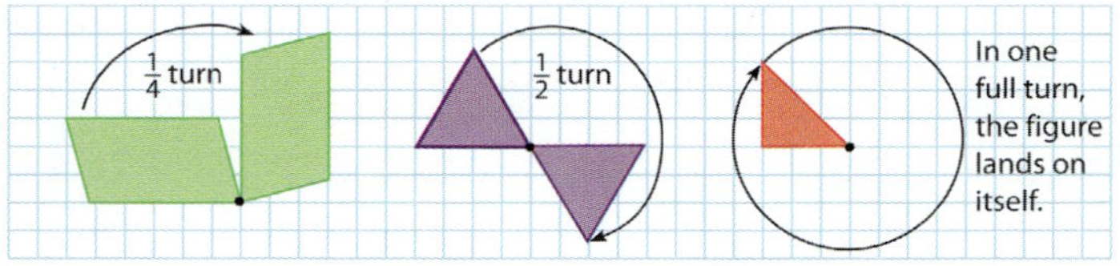

$\frac{1}{4}$ turn   $\frac{1}{2}$ turn   In one full turn, the figure lands on itself.

Hands-On
set of polygons
grid paper

## Guided Practice*

**Do you know HOW?**

For **1** through **4**, tell if the figures are related by a rotation.

1.
2.
3.
4.

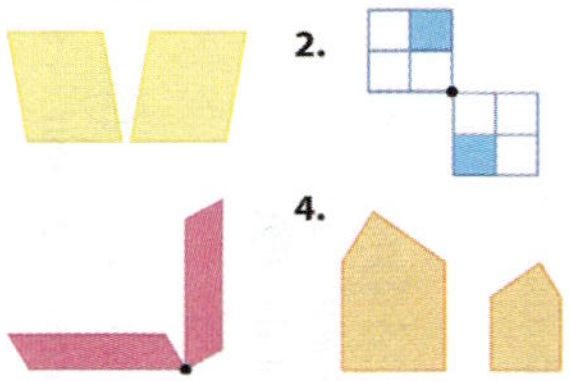

**Do you UNDERSTAND?**

5. Does a rotation change a figure's size or shape?

6. Can every figure be rotated so that it lands on top of itself?

7. If you rotate the arrow below 180 degrees about point X, in which direction will the arrow be pointing?

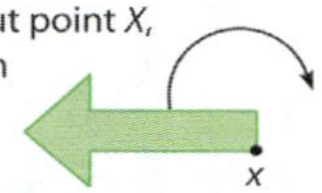

## Independent Practice

For **8** through **13**, tell if the figures are related by a rotation. You may use grid paper or pattern blocks to decide.

8.
9.
10.
11.
12.
13.

**Tip** Another name for rotation is turn.

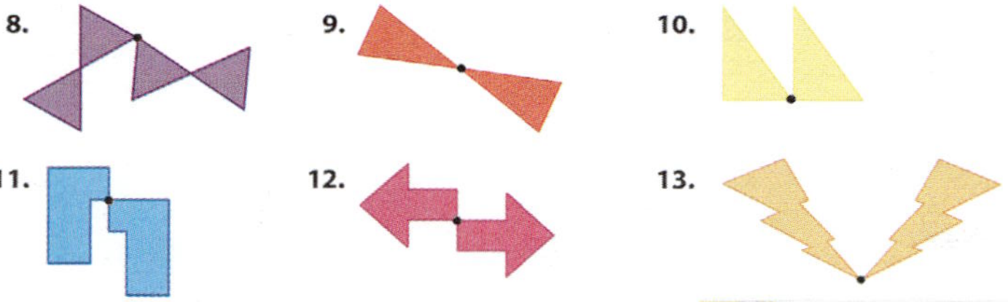

Animated Glossary, eTools
www.pearsonsuccessnet.com
DIGITAL

452   *For another example, see Set A on page 464.

For **14** through **16**, copy each figure on grid paper. Then draw a rotation of the figure $\frac{1}{4}$ turn to the right.

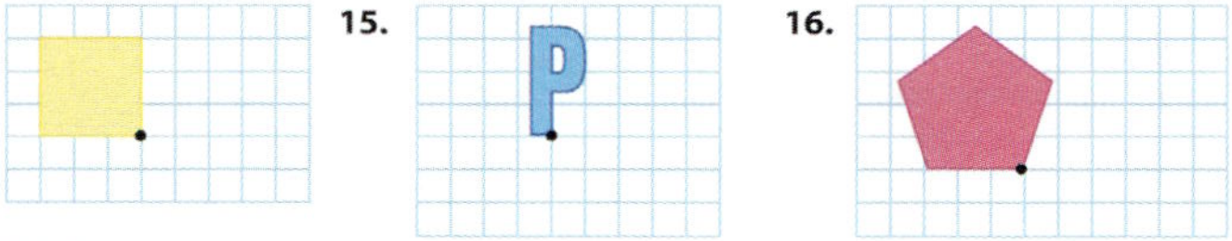

14.
15.
16.

**Problem Solving**

17. The sum of the angles of a pentagon is 540°. If every angle of the pentagon is the same measure, what is the measure of each of its angles?

18. What figure is formed when a triangle has rotated $\frac{1}{4}$ turn?
A Circle   C Rectangle
B Square   D Triangle

19. The shape to the right shows a pattern of translations, reflections and rotations. Describe each step.

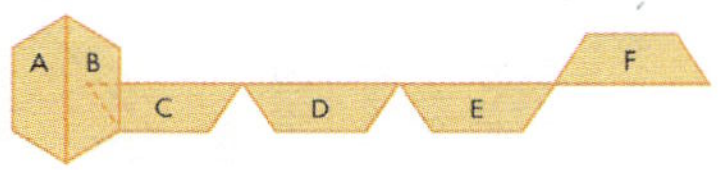

For **20** through **22**, use the table at the right.

20. How much does one Tetra cost?

21. Cal bought 2 guppies and 4 tiger barbs. How much did he pay?

22. How much would it cost to buy 1 of each fish?

| Fish | Price |
| --- | --- |
| Guppies | 5 for $1.50 |
| Tetras | 3 for $6.00 |
| Tiger Barbs | 4 for $4.00 |

453   Lesson 19-3

## Examining School Book Pages

*Refer to the School Book Pages provided on page 623 to answer the following questions.*

**54.** Jacob claims that the figures of problem 3 are related by a rotation to the right, but Loreena says the figures are related by a rotation to the left. Which student is correct?

**55.** Myron gave the answer B to problem 18, showing the following drawing to support his claim.

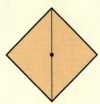

Respond to Myron.

**56.** Isabella says that the blue and green figures shown are not related by a rotation, since $AC \neq BC$. Respond to Isabella.

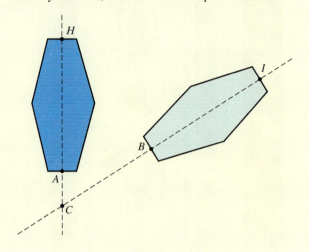

## 11.2

# Patterns and Symmetries

Symmetry is a universal principle of organization and form. The circular arc of a rainbow and the hexagonal symmetry of an ice crystal are visible expressions of the symmetry of many of the physical processes of the universe. A seashell and the fanned tail of the peacock are spectacular examples of biological symmetry.

In the human domain, all cultures of the world, even those in prehistoric times, developed a useful intuitive understanding of the basic concepts of symmetry. Decorations on pottery, walls, tools, weapons, musical instruments, and clothing are often highly symmetric. Buildings, temples, tombs, and other structures are usually designed with an eye to symmetry and balance. Music, poetry, and dance frequently incorporate symmetry into their underlying structure.

While people have long had an informal understanding of symmetry, it is only more recently that mathematics has provided a means to a deeper understanding of symmetry and how certain kinds of symmetry can be described and classified. In the classroom, symmetry can draw youngsters to the artistic and aesthetic aspects of mathematics.

### What Is Symmetry?

The concept of a rigid motion, which we defined and explored in the last section, makes it possible to give a precise definition of a symmetry of a geometric figure in the plane.

> **DEFINITION**    *A Symmetry of a Plane Figure*
> A **symmetry of a plane figure** is any rigid motion of the plane that moves all the points of the figure back to points of the figure.

Thus, all points $P$ of the figure are taken by the symmetry motion to points $P'$ that also are points of the figure. The identity motion is a symmetry of any figure, but of more interest are figures that have symmetries other than the identity. Under a nonidentity symmetry, some points in the figure move to new positions in the figure, even though the figure as a whole appears unchanged by the motion.

The classification theorem of the preceding section tells us that there are just four basic rigid motions. Therefore, any symmetry of a figure is one of these four basic types, and the symmetry properties of a figure can be fully described by listing all of the symmetries of each type.

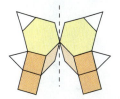
## Reflection Symmetry

A figure has **reflection symmetry** if a reflection across some line is a symmetry of the figure. The line of reflection is called a **line of symmetry,** or a **mirror line,** of the figure. Each point $P$ of the figure on one side of the line of symmetry is matched to a point $P'$ of the figure on the opposite side of the line of symmetry. Some figures and their lines of symmetry (shown dashed) are displayed in Figure 11.15. A mirror line splits the figure into two mirror-image halves.

**FIGURE 11.15**
Plane figures and their lines of symmetry

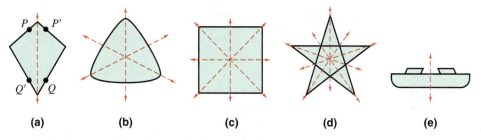

(a)　(b)　(c)　(d)　(e)

Reflection symmetry is also called **line symmetry** or **bilateral symmetry.** Like reflection symmetry, bilateral symmetry is used to describe figures in space that have a plane of symmetry. For example, ferries (as suggested in Figure 11.15(e)) are often bilaterally symmetric across midships to simplify loading and unloading of their cargo of cars and trucks. Infrequent passengers on such ferries can find it very disorienting when the bow and stern are indistinguishable.

**EXAMPLE 11.8 Identifying Lines of Symmetry**

Identify all lines of symmetry for each letter:

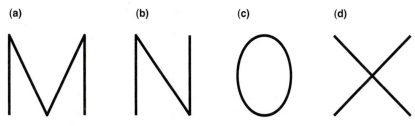

(a)　(b)　(c)　(d)

**Solution** (a) 1 vertical　(b) none　(c) 2: one vertical and one horizontal
(d) 4: one vertical, one horizontal, and the two lines given in the figure itself

## Highlight from History

### George W. Brainerd and Anna O. Shepherd, Pioneers in Mathematical Anthropology

George W. Brainerd, a North American archeologist, was the first person to use the principles of symmetry as a tool for anthropological study. His analysis of the designs on pottery of the prehistoric Anasazi of Monument Valley, Arizona, and of the Maya of the Yucatán Peninsula led him to formulate a number of principles for the use of symmetry classifications in pattern analysis. Brainerd published his ideas in the article "Symmetry in Primitive Conventional Design," which appeared in 1942 in *American Antiquity*, the leading journal of North American anthropology. Unfortunately, Brainerd's work was almost completely neglected, although it did attract the attention of Anna O. Shepherd, a geologist at the Carnegie Institution in Washington, D.C. In her monograph *The Symmetry of Abstract Design with Special Reference to Ceramic Decoration*, published

in 1948, Shepherd discusses how certain symmetries predominate within a specific culture and how changes within a culture can be identified by symmetry. Shepherd's work, like that of Brainerd, had to wait

until the mid-1970s to be fully appreciated. Today, the anthropological significance of symmetry analysis is well established. (See the book *Symmetries of Culture* described on page 631.)

## Rotation Symmetry

A figure has **rotation symmetry,** or **turn symmetry,** if the figure is superimposed on itself when it is rotated through a certain angle between 0° and 360°. The center of the turn is called the **center of symmetry.** Some examples of figures with rotation symmetry are shown in Figure 11.16.

**FIGURE 11.16**
Figures with rotation symmetry

   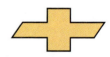

**(a)** 90° symmetry  **(b)** 72° symmetry  **(c)** 45° symmetry  **(d)** 180° symmetry

A figure with 90° rotation symmetry automatically has 180° and 270° rotation symmetry. For this reason, it is customary to give just the *smallest* positive angle measure that turns the figure onto itself. The only exception is for figures composed of concentric circles, which turn onto themselves after *any* turn about their center. Such figures have **circular symmetry.**

---

**EXAMPLE 11.9** **Finding Angles of Rotation Symmetry**

Determine the measures of the angles of rotation symmetry of these figures:

**(a)**   **(b)**  **(c)**  **(d)**

**Solution**

(a) The smallest positive angle of rotation of a regular hexagon measures 60°, so the turn angles of all of the rotation symmetries are 60°, 120°, 180°, 240°, and 300°.

(b) The only angle of rotation symmetry is 180°.

(c) The smallest amount of turn of a regular 9-gon is 360°/9 = 40°, so the turn angles are 40°, 80°, 120°, 160°, 200°, 240°, 280°, and 320°.

(d) This figure has circular symmetry.

## Point Symmetry

A figure has **point symmetry** if it has 180° rotation symmetry about some point $O$. Some familiar examples are shown in Figure 11.17. Notice that a half-turn takes the playing card back onto itself, and every point $P$ of the figure has a corresponding point $P'$ of the figure that is directly opposite the turn center $O$, with $OP = OP'$.

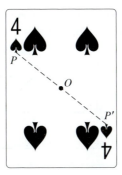
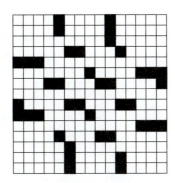

### EXAMPLE 11.10 Identifying Point Symmetry

What letters, in uppercase block form, can be drawn to have point symmetry?

**Solution**

**H, I, N, O, S, X,** and **Z.**
The letters **H, I, O,** and **X** also have two perpendicular lines of mirror symmetry. Only **N, S,** and **Z** have just point symmetry.

## Into the Classroom

### Mathematics in Motion

The words *transformation* and *symmetry* often suggest advanced topics best left for gifted middle school students or postponed to the high school curriculum. Quite the opposite is true, however, since there are activities, games, artistic constructions, and problems—all exploring "motion geometry"—that are suitable for students at every grade level. Primary school children can work with paper folding, Miras, pattern blocks, geoboards, or rubber stamps to create and investigate symmetric patterns. For example, each student can create a "half" figure with rubber bands on the upper half of a geoboard. Boards are then exchanged, and the students are challenged to complete a mirror-image figure in the lower half of the geoboard. Older children could replace the geoboard with graph paper or dot paper and investigate rotations and point symmetry, as well as reflections and line symmetry. Geometry software also offers exciting possibilities for investigations in transformation geometry.

Here are three more ideas suggesting how patterns and motions can be approached in the classroom:

- *Follow the leader.* Draw a line with a ruler down a blank sheet of paper. In pairs of students, the "leader" slowly draws a curve, and simultaneously the "follower" draws the reflected curve across the line of symmetry. The students can interchange roles of leader and follower. To explore point symmetry, a prominent dot can be drawn at the center of the sheet. Some students, with a pencil in each hand, might like to attempt a solitaire game.

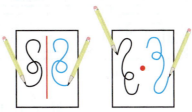

- *Punchy puzzles.* If the square shown on the far left is folded along the dashed lines, then the pattern of holes can be seen to be created with just one punch. How can a square sheet of paper be folded and punched one time only to create the other hole patterns shown?

- *Stained-glass window search.* Eight congruent isosceles right triangles, with four of each color, will form a square window. Three windows are shown here, but a reflection and rotation show that the first two windows are really the same. How many different window patterns can be made from the given outline, each with four panes of each of 2 colors? (You should be able to find 13 distinct patterns, with no 2 patterns the same, under either a rotation or a reflection.)

## Periodic Patterns: Figures with Translation Symmetries

A **periodic pattern** is a figure with translation symmetry. That is, there is at least one translation that moves the pattern so that it is superimposed on itself. To avoid considering the whole plane, or even just some set of horizontal lines, as a periodic pattern, it is assumed that there is some minimum positive distance required to translate a periodic pattern back onto itself. Thus, a periodic pattern must be an infinite figure (why?) with motifs repeated endlessly at regular intervals. Fragments of periodic patterns are common on wallpaper, decorative brick walls, printed and woven fabrics, ribbons, and friezes (ceiling or façade border decorations in older buildings). Enough of the pattern must be shown to make it clear how to extend the pattern indefinitely.

There are two types of periodic patterns in the plane, **border patterns** and **wallpaper patterns.** As their names suggest, a border pattern has a repeated motif that has been translated in just one direction to create a strip design, whereas a wallpaper pattern has a motif translated in two nonparallel directions to create an all-over planar design.

## Border Patterns and Their Classification

Seven examples of border patterns from a variety of cultures are shown in Figure 11.18.

**FIGURE 11.18**
Border patterns from around the world

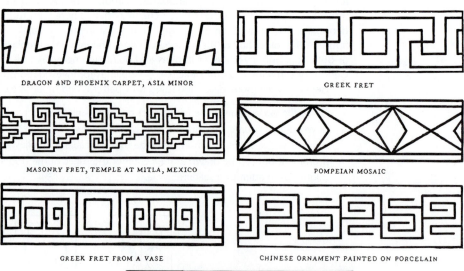

Some border patterns may have other symmetries in addition to their translation symmetries. However, the possibilities are limited, since any symmetry of a border pattern necessarily takes the infinite strip onto itself. Thus, the only possible rotation symmetry is a half-turn. A careful study has shown that every periodic border pattern has the same symmetries as one of the seven types shown in Figure 11.19 that have been created with pattern blocks.

The two-symbol name assigned by the International Crystallographic Union is shown at the left of each pattern in Figure 11.19. To find the classification symbol of any border, follow these steps:

**First Symbol:** *m*, if there is a vertical line of symmetry
       1, otherwise

**Second Symbol:** *m*, if there is a horizontal line of symmetry
       *g*, if there is glide–reflection symmetry (but no horizontal line of
        symmetry)
       2, if there is half-turn symmetry (but no horizontal line of symmetry or
        glide–reflection symmetry)
       1, otherwise

**FIGURE 11.19**

The seven symmetry types of border patterns, shown with pattern-block designs

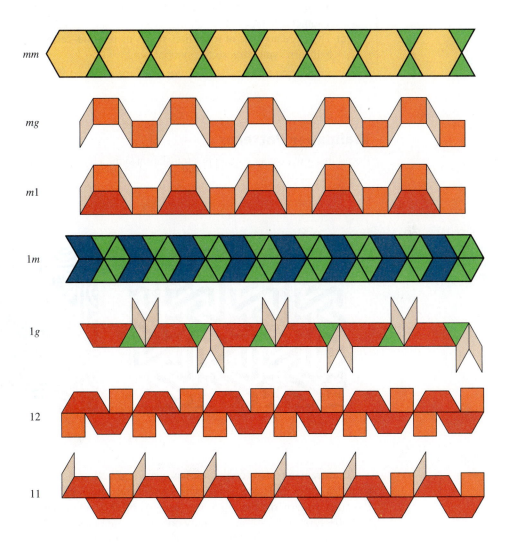

To check your understanding, cover up the two-symbol name in Figure 11.19 and then follow the preceding directions to see if you obtain the correct classification symbols. With practice, you'll be able to determine the two-symbol name for any border pattern.

**EXAMPLE 11.11 Classifying Border Patterns**

Classify the symmetry type of the following border patterns by assigning the appropriate two-symbol notation:

**(a)**

**(b)**

**(c)**

**Solution**

It is helpful to turn the patterns upside down or use a mirror or a Mira, since this will help you discover and verify what symmetries are present. A transparency copy of the pattern, if available, is an almost ideal tool to explore and classify patterns of symmetry.

**(a)** This border has both a vertical and horizontal line of reflection, so the symmetry is of type *mm*.

**(b)** There is no vertical symmetry line, so the first symbol is 1. There is no horizontal symmetry line, but there is glide–reflection symmetry, so the second symbol is *g*. Altogether, the symmetry is type 1*g*.

**(c)** There are no lines of reflection, nor is there glide–reflection symmetry. However, there is half-turn symmetry, so the symbol is 12.

## Wallpaper Patterns

Recall that a wallpaper pattern has translation symmetry in two directions. Two examples are shown in Figure 11.20.

**FIGURE 11.20**
Examples of wallpaper patterns

The Arabian pattern on the left has centers of both 60° and 120° rotational symmetry. This pattern also has a 180° rotational symmetry at the center of each of the Z-shaped black bars. The Egyptian pattern on the right has centers of 90° rotational symmetry. It can be shown that 60°, 90°, 120°, and 180° are the only possible angle measures of rotational symmetry of any wallpaper pattern, a result called the *crystallographic restriction*. This and other restrictions limit the number of symmetry types to be found in a wallpaper pattern. Indeed, it has been shown that any wallpaper pattern is one of just 17 distinct types.

In the next section, several wallpaper patterns will be created by covering the plane with tiles.

## Did You Know?

### Symmetries of Culture

In this book we demonstrate how to use the geometric principles of crystallography to develop a descriptive classification of patterned design. Just as specific chemical assays permit objective analysis and comparison of objects, so too the description of designs by their geometric symmetries makes possible systematic study of their function and meaning within cultural contexts.

This particular type of analysis classifies the underlying structure of decorated forms; that is, the way the parts (elements, motifs, design units) are arranged in the whole design by the geometrical symmetries which repeat them. The classification emphasizes the way the design elements are repeated, not the nature of the elements themselves. The symmetry classes which this method

yields, also called motion classes, can be used to describe any design whose parts are repeated in a regular fashion. On most decorated forms such repeated design, properly called pattern, is either planar or can be flattened (e.g., unrolled), so that these repeated designs can be described either as bands or strips (one-dimensional infinite) or as overall patterns (two-dimensional infinite) in a plane.

This excerpt is from the introduction to *Symmetries of Culture: Theory and Practice of Plane Pattern Analysis*. Nearly every page of *Symmetries of Culture* is graced by beautiful photographs and drawings that illustrate the principles of symmetry discovered and utilized by contemporary and historic cultures from around the world.

SOURCE: *From Symmetries of Culture: Theory and Practice of Plane Pattern Analysis, by Dorothy K. Washburn and Donald W. Crow, page ix. Copyright © 1988 by The University of Washington Press. Reprinted by permission of the University of Washington Press.*

## Problem Set 11.2

Exercises numbered in red are answered in the back of the text.

### Understanding Concepts

1. Carefully trace each figure and draw all of its lines of symmetry.

   (a)     (b)     (c)     (d)     (e)

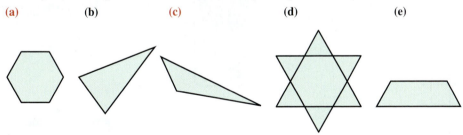

2. Carefully trace each figure and draw all of its lines of symmetry.

   (a)     (b)     (c)     (d)     (e)

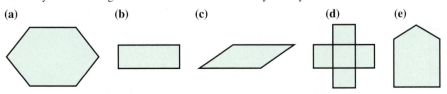

3. Draw polygons with the following symmetries, if possible:

   (a) One line of symmetry, but no rotation symmetry

   (b) Rotation symmetry, but no reflection symmetry

   (c) One line of symmetry and rotation symmetry

4. Describe the most general quadrilateral having the given symmetry property.

   (a) A line of symmetry through a pair of opposite vertices

   (b) A line of symmetry through a pair of midpoints of opposite sides

   (c) Two lines of symmetry, each through a pair of opposite vertices

   (d) Two lines of symmetry, each through a pair of midpoints of opposite sides

   (e) Exactly four lines of symmetry

   (f) A center of 180° rotational symmetry

5. Complete each figure to give it reflection symmetry about line *m*.

   (a) 　(b)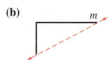

   (c) 　(d)

6. Complete each of these figures to give it point symmetry about point *O*:

   (a) 　(b)

   (c) 　(d)

7. Copy the figures shown onto graph paper. Then complete each figure to give it reflection symmetry across the dashed line.

   (a)

   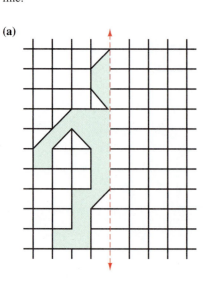

(b)

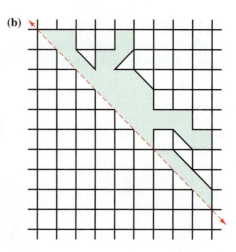

8. A symmetric valentine heart is easy to make: Cut it from a piece of construction paper folded in half once:

   (a) Suppose the paper is folded in half twice and the same cut is made. Sketch the shape you obtain when you unfold the cut pattern.

   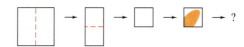

   (b) Describe how to make a sixfold symmetric snowflake by folding and cutting a sheet of paper.

9. Describe all symmetries of each of the following logos:

   (a) 　(b)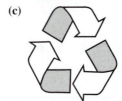

   (c) 　(d)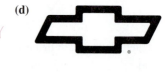

   (e)

**10.** Describe the symmetries of the wheel covers shown.

**(a)**  **(b)**

**(c)** 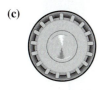 **(d)**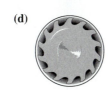

**11. (a)** Complete the figure shown to give it 90° rotation symmetry about point $O$.

$O$

**(b)** Repeat part (a), but giving the resulting figure 60° rotation symmetry.

**12.** Identify the regular $n$-gons in each part that have the given symmetries.

**(a)** There are exactly 3 lines of symmetry.

**(b)** There are exactly 4 lines of symmetry.

**(c)** There are exactly 19 lines of symmetry.

**(d)** The polygon has 10° rotation symmetry.

**(e)** The polygon has both 6° and 15° rotation symmetry.

**13.** List all the digits from the list **0, 1, 2, 3, 4, 5, 6, 7, 8,** and **9** that have

**(a)** vertical reflection symmetry.

**(b)** horizontal reflection symmetry.

**(c)** vertical and horizontal reflection symmetry.

**(d)** point symmetry.

Write the digits in the most symmetric way you can.

**14.** Repeat problem 13, but for the uppercase capital letters, A, B, . . . , Z, written as symmetrically as possible.

**15.** Repeat problem 13 for the lowercase letters, a, b, . . . , z, written as symmetrically as possible.

**16.** Describe all the symmetries of each border pattern, and classify each by the two-symbol notation used in crystallography as in Figure 11.19.

**(a)** . . . **A A A A A A** . . . .

**(b)** . . . **B B B B B B** . . . .

**(c)** . . . **N N N N N N** . . . .

**17.** Describe all the symmetries of each border pattern, and give its two-symbol classification used by crystallographers as in Figure 11.19.

**(a)** . . . **H O H O H O** . . .

**(b)** . . . **M W M W M W** . . .

**(c)** . . . **9 6 9 6 9 6** . . .

**18.** Give the two-symbol classification of each of the seven periodic border patterns shown in Figure 11.18.

**19. (a)** Give the two-symbol classification of each of the following four border patterns:

**(i)** · · · →←→←→← · · ·

**(ii)** · · · ⌃⌄⌃⌄⌃⌄ · · ·

**(iii)** · · · →→→→→ · · ·

**(iv)** · · · ⌐⌐⌐⌐⌐⌐ · · ·

**(b)** Use the arrow motif to create the three types of border patterns not shown.

## Teaching Concepts

**20. Pattern-Block Symmetries.** Children enjoy creating symmetric designs with pattern blocks. Two simple examples are shown next. This intrinsic interest can be utilized effectively to explore many of the fundamental concepts of symmetry.

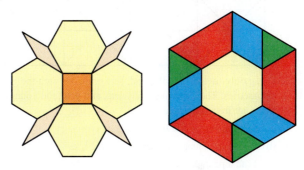

**(a)** Describe the symmetry of each of the six individual pattern-block shapes (the triangle, square, hexagon, and trapezoid, and the thick and thin rhombuses).

**(b)** Describe the symmetries of the two designs shown.

**(c)** Create a design that includes squares and has 60° rotational symmetry.

**(d)** Create a design that includes squares and has 30° rotational symmetry.

**21.** Pattern blocks are well suited to create and classify periodic border patterns. For example, all seven symmetry types are shown in Figure 11.19. Following are periodic borders of type $mg$ and 11:

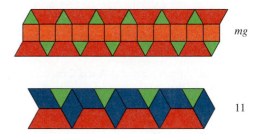

$mg$

11

**(a)** Design a lesson that asks children to create pattern-block borders and then examine them for symmetries.

**(b)** Extend your lesson from part (a) to have children in the upper elementary grades classify the types of symmetry of periodic pattern-block borders. In particular, create examples that exhibit all seven types of symmetry, where each periodic border uses at least three pattern-block shapes.

22. **Symmetry Search.** The following line grid can be made easily from graph paper:

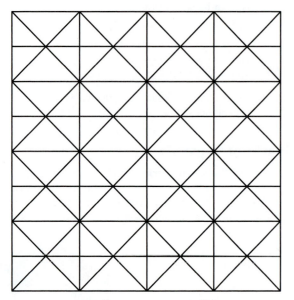

Using only segments in the grid, find polygons with the given symmetries. There are many answers, and you (and youngsters) are free to be creative.

**(a)** Find an octagon with two lines of symmetry.

**(b)** Find a quadrilateral with no symmetries.

**(c)** Find a pentagon with a line of symmetry.

**(d)** Find a heptagon with a line of symmetry that is neither horizontal nor vertical.

## Responding to Students

23. Stacey drew lines of symmetry as shown on the following shapes:

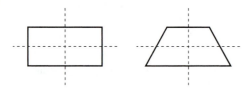

**(a)** On which shape did she draw the lines of symmetry correctly?

**(b)** How would you help explain to her why some lines on the other shape are not lines of symmetry?

24. Kahalah and Ashton agree that **A** and **C** each have a line of symmetry, but they disagree about the letter **B.** How would you help them?

## Thinking Critically

25. **The Penny Game.** Lynn and Kelly are playing a game with just a few simple rules. Each player takes turns placing a

penny on a rectangular tabletop. Each new penny must be flat on the table and cannot touch any of the pennies already on the table. The first player unable to put another penny on the table according to these rules is the loser. Lynn, who gets to make the first move, puts the first penny at the center of the table and is confident of a win. What is Lynn's strategy?

26. A **palindrome** is a word, phrase, sentence, or numeral that is read the same either forward or backward. Examples are WOW, NOON, and TOOT.

**(a)** If a word written in all capital letters has a vertical line of symmetry, why must it be a palindrome?

**(b)** DAD does not have a line of symmetry. Find another palindrome with no line of symmetry.

**(c)** What symmetry do you see in the word "pod"?

**(d)** Find a palindrome with a horizontal line of symmetry.

27. Describe what symmetries you see in these statements:

**(a)** "Sums are not set as a test on Erasmus."

**(b)** "Is it odd how asymmetrical is 'symmetry'? 'Symmetry' is asymmetrical. How odd it is."

**(c)** "Able was I ere I saw Elba." (attributed to Napoleon)

28. Carefully explain why no border pattern has the symbol *m2*. (*Hint:* If a border pattern has a vertical line of symmetry and 180° rotation symmetry, what other symmetry must it also have?)

29. The Maori, the indigenous people of New Zealand, used principles of symmetry to express their belief system. Disregarding the color scheme, classify the following Maori rafter patterns:

**(a)**

**(b)**

**(c)**

**(d)**

**30.** Classify the following Inca border patterns:

**(a)**

**(b)**

**31.** In each strip of rectangles shown, a certain rigid motion applied to the leftmost rectangle takes the figure to the next rectangle. Apply the same motion, but to the second rectangle, to draw the image of the second rectangle in the third rectangle. Continue to use the same motion to fill in the successive rectangles, and then classify the border pattern that is produced.

**(a)**  | p | p | p |   |   |   |

**(b)**  | p | q |   |   |   |   |

**(c)**  | p | d |   |   |   |   |

**(d)**  | p | b |   |   |   |   |

**32.** These drawings were made by George Pólya for his 1924 paper classifying the 17 wallpaper pattern types:

**(a)**    **(b)**

**(c)**

For each pattern, give
  **(i)** the number of directions of reflection symmetry;
  **(ii)** the number of directions of glide–reflection symmetry;
  **(iii)** the sizes of angles of rotation symmetry.

## Thinking Cooperatively

**33.** *Mu Torere.* The Maori people of New Zealand play the two-person game *mu torere* on a board whose shape is a regular eight-pointed star. The points of the star are the *kawai* and the center is the *putahi*. The two players each have four counters, say, red beans and white beans, arranged initially so that the red beans of one player are in the four upper positions and the opponent's white beans are in the lower positions. Players alternate moving one of their beans either into an empty adjacent *kawai* or into (or out of) the *putahi*. A bean can move into the *putahi* only if the bean is adjacent to an opponent's bean. If not, the move is *tapu* (taboo, not allowed). The object of the game is to move your beans to a position where the opponent is blocked: Any move of the opponent is *tapu*. Work in pairs to make, play, and investigate *mu torere*.

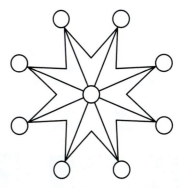

  **(a)** Describe how to make a *mu torere* board by folding and cutting a sheet of paper.
  **(b)** What is the reason a bean cannot be moved to the center unless it is adjacent to an opponent's bean?
  **(c)** Play several games of *mu torere*. Describe the formation that wins the game.
  **(d)** Make a list of games that use a symmetric board. Describe the type of symmetry found in the boards.

**34.** Cut out an interesting shape from cardboard or heavy paper. A border pattern can be drawn on a strip of paper by repeatedly tracing around the template.

  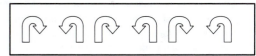

Template          Border pattern drawn on paper strip

  **(a)** Use the shape to create seven border patterns, drawing one pattern of each symmetry type on a separate strip of paper. Do not write the symmetry symbol on the strip.
  **(b)** Pair up with another student. Match each of your strips to the corresponding strip of your partner having the same symmetry type.

**35.** Young children enjoy cutting a folded strip of paper to create a border pattern. For example, the following dolls form a periodic border pattern with $m1$ symmetry:

Work as a group to determine how to cut folded strips of paper to create border patterns with different types of symmetry.

## Making Connections

**36.** Describe what symmetries, or lack of symmetry, you could see in the following forms and objects:

  **(a)** A pair of scissors
  **(b)** A T-shirt

**(c)** A dress shirt

**(d)** A golf club

**(e)** A tennis racket

**(f)** A crossword puzzle

**37.** Describe the symmetry you find in

**(a)** an addition table.

**(b)** a multiplication table.

**(c)** Pascal's triangle.

**38.** The figures shown result from a famous experiment in physics called the Chladni plate. A square metal plate is supported horizontally at its center, sprinkled with fine dry sand, and then vibrated at different frequencies. The sand migrates to the *nodal lines*, where there is no movement of the plate. In the dark regions between the nodal lines, the plate is in vertical vibrational motion.

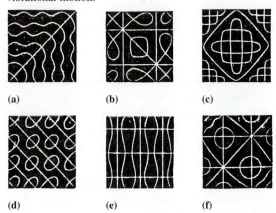

**(a)**          **(b)**          **(c)**

**(d)**          **(e)**          **(f)**

Describe the symmetries of each of the six Chladni plates shown. (These Chladni plates were published in 1834 in *Of the Connection of the Physical Sciences*, by Mary Somerville, one of the great female mathematicians of the 19th century.)

## Communicating

**39.** Write an illustrated short report entitled "Examples of Symmetry in _____," where the blank is filled in with your choice of topic. For example, you might choose "Sports," "Board Games," "Jewelry," "Musical Forms," "Native American Art," "Corporate Logos," or "Flowers." Use your imagination, and draw on your outside interests and hobbies to be creative. You should include drawings, photocopies, pictures cut from discarded magazines, and so on. Be sure to identify and classify the type of symmetry found in each example.

**40.** Go on a symmetry hunt across campus, looking for striking examples of symmetry in buildings, decorative brickwork, sculptures, gardens, or wherever you may find it. Provide photos or drawings of three or four examples that you find especially interesting. Describe and classify the types of symmetry found in your examples. Include a border pattern and a wallpaper pattern.

## Using a Computer

**41.** Use geometry software to create a bilaterally symmetric "funny face." Begin with the mirror line, which can be hidden later.

**42.** Use geometry software to create wheel-cover patterns (see problem 10) having the following required properties:

**(a)** 45° rotational symmetry only

**(b)** 60° rotational symmetry *and* bilateral symmetry

## From State Student Assessments

**43.** (Florida, Grade 5)
After studying the Aztec civilization of central Mexico, a student drew one half of an Aztec medallion as shown below. The dotted line represents a line of symmetry. Which of the following tells how you must move the drawing to make a symmetrical medallion?

**A.** Turn   **B.** Flip   **C.** Slide   **D.** Slide and turn

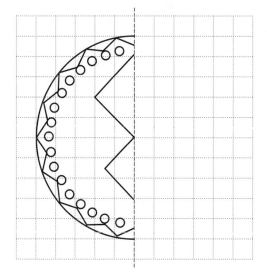

**44.** (Minnesota, Grade 5)
Ken folded a piece of paper in half and then folded it in half again. He cut out a shape and threw it away. This is how the paper looked when he unfolded it.

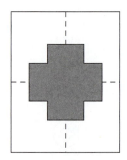

Which drawing below shows how his paper looked **before** he unfolded it?

**A.**          **B.**

**C.**          **D.**

**45.** (Arizona, Grade 8)

The shaded piece has been transformed into a frieze pattern.

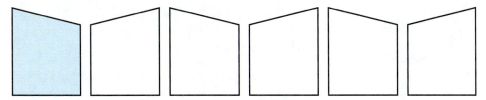

Which transformations **best** describe how the pattern was created?

**A.** reflections

**B.** translations

**C.** reflections and rotations

**D.** translations and rotations

## 11.3 Tilings and Escher-like Designs

This section explores patterns in the plane that are formed by systematically repeating shapes (or motifs). The art of tiling and decorative patterns has a history as old as civilization itself. In virtually every ancient culture, the artisan's choices of color and shape were guided as strongly by aesthetic urges as by structural or functional requirements. Imaginative and intricate patterns decorated baskets, pottery, fabrics, wall coverings, and weapons. Some examples of ornamental patterns from different cultures are shown in Figure 11.21.

In recent times, the interest in tilings and patterns has gone beyond their decorative value. For example, metallurgists and crystallographers wish to know how atoms can arrange themselves in a periodic array. Similarly, architects hope to know how simple structural components can be systematically combined to create large building complexes, and computer engineers hope to integrate simple circuit patterns into powerful processors called neural networks. The mathematical analysis of tilings and patterns is a response to these contemporary needs. At the same time, the creation and exploration of tilings provides an inherently interesting setting for geometric discovery and problem solving in the elementary and middle school classroom. In particular, children enjoy learning how to create their own periodic drawings in the style of the pioneering Dutch artist M. C. Escher (1898–1972).

### Tiles and Tilings

The precise meaning of a tile and a tiling is given in the following definition:

> **DEFINITION**  *Tiles and Tiling*
> A simple closed curve, together with its interior, is a **tile.** A set of tiles forms a **tiling** of a figure if the figure is completely covered by the tiles without overlapping any interior points of the tiles.

In a tiling of a figure (or the whole plane), since all points in the figure are covered, there can be no gaps between tiles. Tilings are also known as **tessellations,** since the small square tiles in ancient Roman mosaics were called *tesserae* (probably because each tile has four corners and four sides; Greek *tessera*, four) in Latin.

### Regular Tilings of the Plane

Each tiling shown in Figure 11.22 is a **regular tiling:** The tiles are congruent regular polygons joined edge to edge.

Any arrangement of nonoverlapping polygonal tiles surrounding a common vertex is called a **vertex figure.** Thus, four squares form each vertex figure of the regular square tiling, and three regular hexagons form each vertex figure of the hexagonal tiling. The measures of the interior

Cotton textile hanging, Chimú, Peru. 12th–15th century

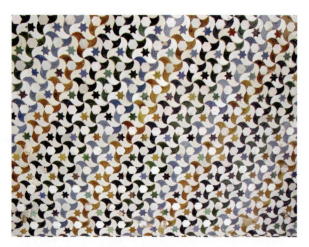

Detail of a tiled wall in the Alhambra

Potato printed fabric from Africa

Ca'd'Oro Venice Mosaic floor in courtyard

Tiling from Portugal 15th to 16th centuries

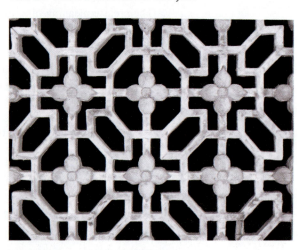

Chinese latticework, old window with geometrical and floral patterns

**FIGURE 11.21**
Patterns from various cultures

**FIGURE 11.22**
The three regular tilings of
the plane

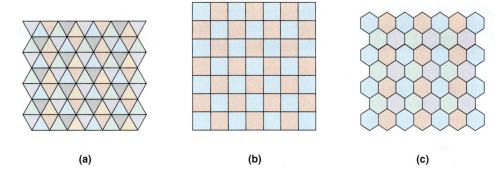

(a)                    (b)                    (c)

angles meeting at a vertex figure must add to 360°. For example, in the square tiling, $90° + 90° + 90° + 90° = 360°$.

Suppose we attempt to form a vertex figure with regular pentagons as shown in Figure 11.23. The interior angles of a regular pentagon each measure $(5 - 2) \cdot 180°/5 = 108°$, so, on the one hand, three regular pentagons fill in $3 \cdot 108° = 324°$ and leave a 36° gap. On the other hand, four regular pentagons create an overlap, since $4 \cdot 108° = 432° > 360°$. Because a vertex figure cannot be formed, no tiling of the plane by regular pentagons is possible.

**FIGURE 11.23**
Regular pentagons do not
tile the plane

Three pentagons leave a gap.     Four pentagons overlap.

Similarly, since a regular polygon of seven or more sides has an interior angle larger than 120°, three meeting at a vertex must overlap. From all these considerations, we thus have the following theorem:

> **THEOREM**  *The Regular Tilings of the Plane*
> There are exactly three regular tilings of the plane: (a) by equilateral triangles, (b) by squares, and (c) by regular hexagons.

## Semiregular Tilings of the Plane

A regular tiling uses congruent regular polygons of one type to tile the plane. What if regular polygons of several types are allowed? An edge-to-edge tiling of the plane with more than one type of regular polygon *and* with identical vertex figures is called a **semiregular tiling.** It is important to understand the restriction made about the vertex figures: *The same types of polygons must surround each vertex, and they must occur in the same order.* The two vertex figures in Figure 11.24 are not identical, since the two triangles and the two hexagons in the left-hand figure are adjacent, but on the right side the triangles and the hexagons alternate with one another.

**FIGURE 11.24**
There are two distinct
types of vertex figures
formed by two equilateral
triangles and two regular
hexagons

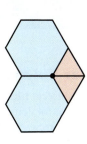    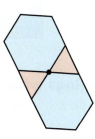

## Highlight from History

### Johannes Kepler and Tiling Patterns

The astronomer Johannes Kepler (1571–1630) is celebrated in scientific history for his identification of the elliptical shape of the orbits of the planets about the sun. Less known is Kepler's contribution to the theory of tiling. Here are some drawings from Kepler's book *Harmonice Mundi,* which he published in 1619.

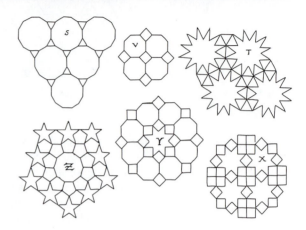

To see if the vertex figures in Figure 11.24 can be extended to form a semiregular tiling, we must check to see if the pattern can be completed to make *all* of the vertex figures match the one shown. It is soon discovered that the left-hand pattern with adjacent triangles cannot be extended. (Try it!) In contrast, the vertex figure at the right with alternating triangles and hexagons extends to a semiregular tiling. You should be able to find that tiling in Figure 11.25.

It can be shown that there are 18 ways to form a vertex figure with regular polygons of two or more types. Only 8 of them extend to a semiregular tiling; these are shown in Figure 11.25.

**FIGURE 11.25**
The 8 semiregular tilings

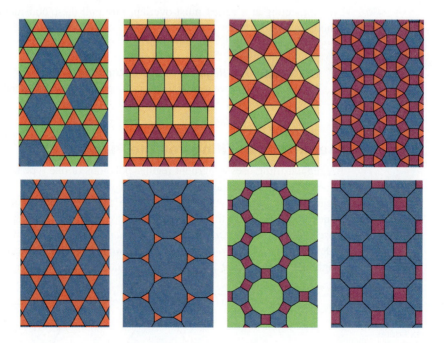

## Tilings with Irregular Polygons

In the next example, it is helpful to cut tiles from cardboard or heavy card stock. You can then trace around them to see if it is possible for congruent copies to form a tiling of the plane. Better yet, create and explore tilings with geometry software.

**EXAMPLE 11.12** **Exploring Tilings with Irregular Polygons**

Which of the following polygons tile the plane?

**(a)** Scalene triangle

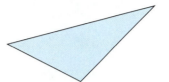

**(b)** Convex quadrilateral

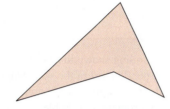

**(c)** Concave quadrilateral

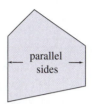

parallel sides

**(d)** Pentagon with a pair of parallel sides

**Solution**

**(a)** If the triangle is turned 180° about the midpoint of one edge, then the two triangles joined at the common edge form a parallelogram. Since it is evident that parallelograms tile the plane by translations that match opposite edges, it follows that *any triangle will tile the plane.*

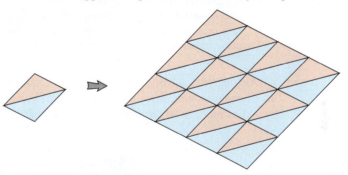

**(b)** and **(c)** As illustrated next, any quadrilateral will tile the plane. A 180° turn about the midpoint of any side rotates the quadrilateral from one position to an adjacent position and forms a convex or concave hexagon with three pairs of opposite congruent edges. Translating the hexagon while matching opposite edges produces the tiling. Notice that each vertex of the tiling is surrounded by angles congruent to the four angles of the quadrilateral, whose measures add up to 360°.

**(d)** A pentagonal tile with two parallel sides can always tile the plane in the manner shown below. If the parallel edges are congruent, the tiling will be edge to edge.

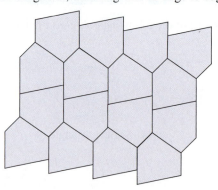

Much like the quadrilateral tiling shown in Example 11.12, a hexagon will tile the plane if it has a pair of opposite sides that are parallel and of the same length. (See problem 10 of Problem Set 11.3.) If all three pairs of opposite sides are congruent and parallel, it is not even necessary to rotate the tile from one position to any other. (See problem 9 of Problem Set 11.3.) It has been shown that no convex polygon with seven or more sides can tile the plane. The following theorem summarizes these discoveries:

> **THEOREM**   *Tiling the Plane with Congruent Polygonal Tiles*
> The plane can be tiled by
> - any triangular tile;
> - any quadrilateral tile, convex or not;
> - certain pentagonal tiles (for example, those with two parallel sides);
> - certain hexagonal tiles (for example, those with two opposite parallel sides of the same length).
>
> The plane cannot be tiled by any convex tile with seven or more sides.

Although no convex polygon of seven or more sides can tile the plane, there are many interesting examples of nonconvex polygons that do. Figure 11.26 shows a striking example of a spiral tiling by 9-gons (nonagons) created by Heinz Voderberg in 1936.

**FIGURE 11.26**
Heinz Voderberg's spiral tiling with nonagons

## Escher-like Designs

The Dutch artist Maurits Cornelius Escher (1898–1972) created a large number of artistic tilings. His designs have great appeal to the general public and have also captured the interest of professional geometers. Escher's periodic drawings are often based on modifications of known tilings by polygons. However, he also discovered new principles of formation based on symmetries that mathematicians had overlooked.

To see how Escher created his drawing of the birds on the left side of Figure 11.27, we begin by identifying the underlying grid of parallelograms shown on the right. The vertices of the parallelograms join corresponding wing tips of adjacent birds.

**FIGURE 11.27**
M. C. Escher's birds and its grid of parallelograms

The concept of a translation, discussed in Section 11.1, helps us understand how the parallelogram has been modified to become the bird-shaped motif of the tiling. First, imagine replacing the upper edge of the parallelogram with the *V*-shape separating the wings. The *V*-shape is then translated to replace the opposite edge of the parallelogram. Similarly, one of the two remaining straight edges of the parallelogram is modified to form the leading edge of the forward wing, and this curve is then translated to replace the opposite edge of the parallelogram. Finally, the outline is filled in with details such as feathers and an eye to complete the bird motif. The steps modifying the parallelogram into the bird motif are shown in Figure 11.28.

**FIGURE 11.28**
Modifying a parallelogram
with two translations

Similar procedures will transform any polygonal tiling that can be produced by translations to an Escher-like tiling. For example, sixth-grade teacher Nancy Putnam used translations to modify each of the three pairs of opposite parallel congruent sides of a hexagon. Her whale tiling, starting with hexagon *ABCDEF*, is shown in Figure 11.29.

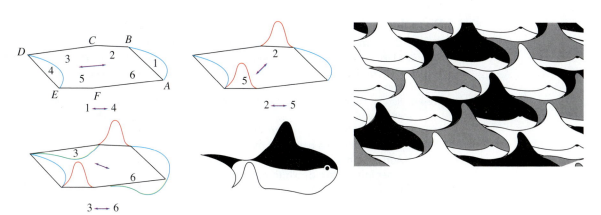

**FIGURE 11.29**
Sixth-grade teacher Nancy Putnam modified a hexagon with opposite parallel congruent sides to create an Escher-like tiling

Rotations can also be used to create **Escher-like tiles** with interesting symmetries. Figure 11.30 shows how a lizard tile can be created by modifying a regular hexagon *ABCDEF*. Side $\overline{AB}$ is first modified and then rotated about vertex *B* to modify side $\overline{BC}$. The remaining two pairs of adjacent sides are also modified by rotations, resulting in the outline of the lizard tile shown in the figure, along with its tiling.

**FIGURE 11.30**
Modifying a regular hexagon with rotations to create a lizard tiling

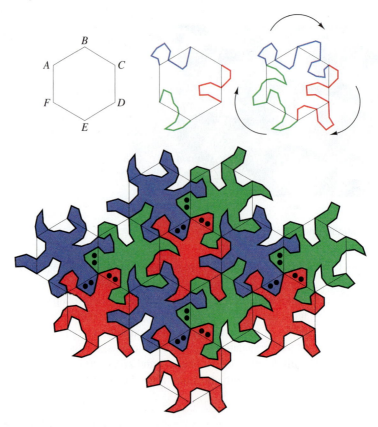

## Cooperative Investigation
### Creating an Escher-like Design

### Materials Needed
1. Note cards, 3″ × 5″ (or other card stock)
2. Scissors
2. Pencils and colored markers
4. Blank sheets of paper

### Directions

**Step 1.** Cut a small (say, $2\frac{1}{2}$″-by-3″) rectangle from a note card or card stock.

**Step 2.** Make an irregular curve joining the corners of one side of the rectangle.

**Step 3.** Cut out the curve. Translate the cutout piece to the opposite side and tape it in place.

**Step 4.** Repeat steps 2 and 3 for the remaining two parallel sides of the rectangle, as shown.

**Step 5.** Do an "inkblot" test. Is your shape a frog, a bird, a face, a _____? Brainstorm with a partner. It may help to rotate your shape or flip it over. Add eyes, mouth, nose, ears, feet, beaks, horns, clothing, scales, fur, and other imaginative details to make your tiling template recognizable and interesting.

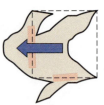

**Step 6.** Trace around the template on a blank sheet of paper. Translate and trace again, repeating to create at least three rows and three columns of your interlocking tiles to create your Escher-like tiling. Use colored markers to fill in the details, and color adjacent tiles with different colors.

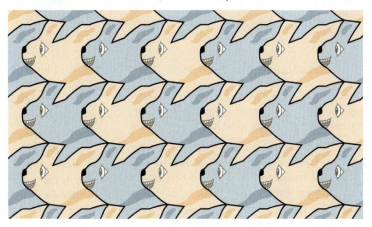

### Extensions

Instead of a rectangle, start with any parallelogram (or any hexgon with opposite sides parallel and congruent) and follow the directions just given. It is also possible to adapt this method to create templates based on other tilings of the plane. Several suggestions are described in problems 20 through 23 of Problem Set 11.3.

## Problem Set 11.3

Exercises numbered in red are answered in the back of the text.

## Understanding Concepts

**1.** On dot paper arranged in a square grid, show that the given shape will tile the plane.

**(a)**

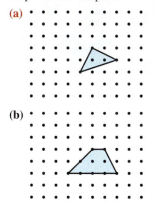

**(b)**

**2.** On "isometric" dot paper (arranged in a grid of equilateral triangles), show that the given shape will tile the plane.

**(a)**

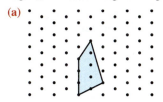

**(b)**

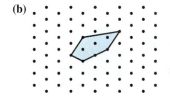

**3.** Fold a sheet of paper in half, and then use scissors to cut a pair of congruent convex quadrilaterals. Separate the quadrilaterals from one another. Cut one of the quadrilaterals along one of the diagonals, and cut the second quadrilateral along the other diagonal. Show that the four triangles can be arranged to form a parallelogram and therefore tile the plane with repeated copies of themselves.

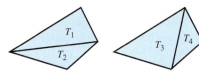

SOURCE: From Quantum Magazine, *September/October, 1992, p. 31. Reprinted with permission from Springer-Verlag. All rights reserved.*

**4.** A vertex figure of regular polygons is shown on the next page.

  **(a)** Find the angle measures of each polygon and directly verify that they add up to 360°.

  **(b)** Explain why the vertex figure does not extend to form a semiregular tiling. (*Suggestion:* Attempt to form the same vertex figure at the other two vertices of the triangle.)

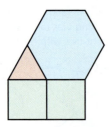

5. Consider the vertex figure formed by a square, a regular pentagon, and a regular 20-gon. Find the measures of the interior angle of each polygon and show that these three measures add up to 360°.

6. Some "letters" of the alphabet will tile the plane. For each letter shown, create an interesting tiling on square dot paper. Look for different patterns that use the same tile.

**(a)    (b)    (c)    (d)    (e)**

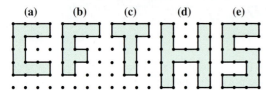

7. A tetromino is a tile formed by joining four congruent squares edge to edge, where adjacent squares must share a common edge. Two tetrominoes and two nontetrominoes are shown as follows:

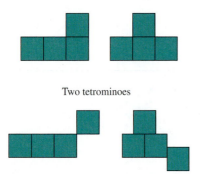

Two tetrominoes

Two nontetrominoes

(a) There are five noncongruent tetrominoes altogether. Find the other three.

(b) Which tetrominoes tile the plane, if one is allowed to use unlimited congruent copies of one tetromino?

(c) The five noncongruent tetrominoes have a total area of 20 square units. Can the five shapes tile a 4-by-5 rectangle? (*Suggestion:* Imagine that the rectangle is colored in a red-and-black checkerboard pattern of unit squares. How many red and how many black squares are covered by each tetromino?)

8. Tiles formed by joining five congruent squares edge to edge are called **pentominoes**. The 12 pentominoes are shown in problem 30 of Problem Set 9.3. Use graph paper (or dot paper) to decide which pentominoes tile the plane.

9. Fold a 3″-by-5″ note card in half, and then use scissors to cut (simultaneously) two general quadrilaterals. Rotate one quadrilateral a half-turn and tape the two quadrilaterals together along their corresponding edges to form a hexagonal tile.

Fold          Cut quadrilaterals          Rotate and tape

Show, using the paper model as a template, that the hexagon tiles the plane. Must the tile be rotated?

10. Cut a hexagon *ABCDEF* from a rectangular piece of card stock as shown, using a ruler to ensure that the opposite sides $\overline{AB}$ and $\overline{DE}$ have the same length. No restriction is placed on the position of point *C* or *F*. Use the paper template to illustrate that a hexagon with a congruent and parallel pair of opposite sides can tile the plane. (*Suggestion:* Half-turns of the template will be required.)

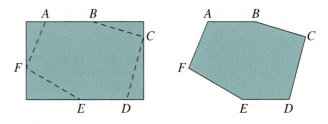

## Teaching Concepts

11. **Patterns in World Cultures.** Children's interest in patterns and symmetries can be heightened by incorporating examples from around the world. For example, the pattern shown here is a pattern on *kente* cloth, a fabric woven by the Ashanti and the Ewe in Togo, West Africa.

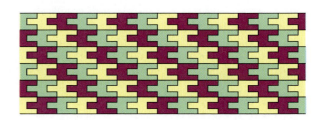

Conduct a search in your library or on the Web to discover four or five examples of wallpaper patterns from a variety of world cultures. Give a careful description of the symmetry properties of each example.

12. **Connections with Art.** The concepts of symmetry and pattern have close ties with art. For example, consider this assignment in an elementary school classroom: Each student is given a square of paper. Each student is to use three colors to decorate each square with a design having 180° symmetry. The decorated squares are then used to tile a large poster (or several posters) that is hung on the classroom wall.

(a) Carry out the design project just described in your own class.

(b) Create a similar lesson, but using a different tiling shape with different color and symmetry conditions.

## Responding to Students

**13.** Miguel claims that the following tiling is a regular tiling by squares:

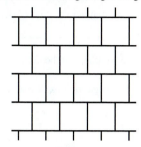

What is Miguel overlooking?

**14.** Myra cut out a regular pentagon, hexagon, and octagon, and it seems to her that they form a vertex figure such as this:

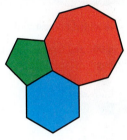

Respond to Myra.

**15.** Wailea noticed that, since two adjacent equilateral triangles, a square, and a dodecagon form a vertex figure such as that shown at *A*, there should be a semiregular tiling in which this vertex figure occurs at every vertex.

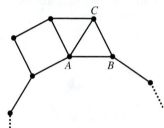

**(a)** Is Wailea correct that these four polygons create a vertex figure at *A*?

**(b)** Explain to Wailea why the vertex figure does not extend to a semiregular tiling.

**16.** Mason used computer geometry software to make the following figure:

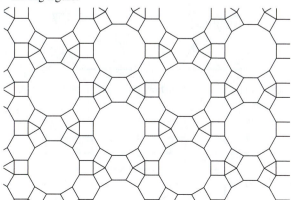

Since he used only regular polygons—equilateral triangles, squares, hexagons, and dodecagons—he believes he has found a new semiregular tiling. What has Mason overlooked?

## Thinking Critically

**17.** Branko Grünbaum and G. C. Shephard (*Tilings and Patterns,* W. H. Freeman and Co., 1987) discovered the tiling shown here in the children's coloring book *Altair Design* (E. Holiday, London: Pantheon, 1970):

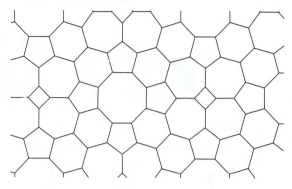

**(a)** What kinds of polygons appear?

**(b)** Grünbaum and Shephard claim that this is a "fake" tiling by regular polygons. Explain why.

**18.** Use an index card to cut out a triangle of any shape. Then, with a corner of an index card as a right angle, carefully draw and cut out the three squares whose side lengths match the respective side lengths of the triangle. Next, trace around the 3 squares and 8 copies of the triangle to create a decagon like this one at the right:

Show that the decagon can be used to tile the plane. (This construction is also interesting to investigate with geometry software on a computer.)

**19.** The **dual** of a tiling by regular polygons is obtained by joining the center of each polygon to the center of each adjacent polygon. In the following example, the dual of the tiling with black edges is the tiling with red edges:

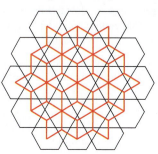

(a) What are the duals of the three regular tilings shown in Figure 11.22?

(b) Trace the semiregular tiling of Figure 11.25 whose vertex figure consists of two nonadjacent squares and three equi-

lateral triangles. Then construct the dual, which is known as the *Cairo tiling,* since the paving stones of the streets of Cairo make this pattern.

(c) What is interesting about the dual of a semiregular tiling?

---

**20.** Construct a paper hexagonal tile with each pair of opposite sides parallel and congruent. The template can be cut from a note card following the method described in problem 9. Make cutouts on three adjacent sides. Translate each cutout to the opposite side and tape along the corresponding edges to form a template. (See the instructions in the Cooperative Investigation box "Creating an Escher-like Design.")

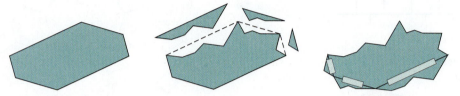

Create a design with your template, adding details such as eyes, mouths, and so forth, to give added interest to the design.

**21.** Cut an accurate square from a note card. Make cutouts on opposite sides. Rotate each cutout 90° and tape as shown. Use the paper template to create an Escher-like tiling. You will need to use 90° rotations to produce the tiling.

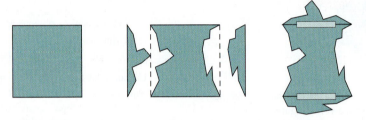

**22.** Cut an arbitrary triangle from a note card, and lightly fold (do not make a heavy crease) one vertex to another to determine the midpoint of the side between the vertices. The side can be modified by making a cutout on one side of the midpoint, rotating the cutout 180° about the midpoint, and taping it in place. The steps to modify one side of a triangle are as follows:

Midpoint of side

Modify the remaining two sides of the triangle in a similar manner and use the resulting template to create an Escher-like tiling. You will need to use 180° rotations to produce the tiling.

---

**23.** Cut a convex quadrilateral from a note card. Make midpoint modifications, as described in problem 22, to each of the four sides. Use the resulting template to create an Escher-like design.

**24.** For any integer $n$, $n \geq 3$, show that there is some $n$-gon that tiles the plane. (*Suggestion:* Consider the midpoint modification described in problems 22 and 23.)

**25.** Suppose a vertex figure of regular polygons includes a regular octagon. Show that the figure must include another octagon and a square.

**26.** An equilateral triangle and a parallelogram are each examples of "reptiles," short for "repeating tile." In each case, copies of the tile can be arranged to form a larger, similar shape.

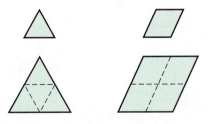

Use square dot paper to show that each of the following shapes is a "reptile":

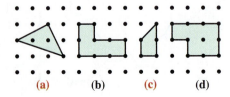

(a)          (b)          (c)          (d)

**27.** A hexiamond is formed from six congruent equilateral triangles. There are 12 different hexiamonds, including the Sphinx, Chevron, and Lobster, shown next. Find the remaining 9 hexiamonds, and see if you can match their shapes to their names: Hexagon, Crook, Crown, Hook, Snake, Yacht, Bar, Signpost, and Butterfly.

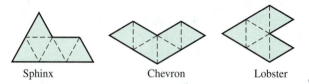

Sphinx          Chevron          Lobster

**28.** **(a)** Show that the Sphinx is a reptile. (See problems 26 and 27 for the definition of a reptile and a diagram of the Sphinx.)

   **(b)** It requires four copies of the Sphinx to form a second-generation Sphinx. How many copies of the original Sphinx are required to form a third-generation Sphinx? Explain your reasoning and provide a sketch.

   **(c)** Explain why any reptile provides a tiling of the plane.

## Thinking Cooperatively

**29.** The seven **tangram** pieces originated in ancient China. As shown here, there are five triangles, a square, and a parallelogram. A serviceable set can be cut from a square of cardboard (see Section 10.1), although plastic and wooden sets are easy to buy or make.

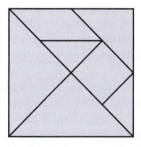

   **(a)** The most common activity with a tangram is the Chinese *tangram puzzle.* A figure is shown in outline, and the challenge is to tile the figure with *all* 7 tangram pieces. Form the following animals (inspired by the Multicultural Poster Set, National Council of Teachers of Mathematics, 1984), working in pairs:

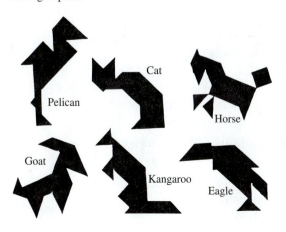

Cat

Pelican

Horse

Goat

Kangaroo

Eagle

   **(b)** Use the seven tangram pieces to form other recognizable shapes. Use a marker to draw only the outline. Then trade the tangram puzzles between groups and solve the puzzles.

**30.** Work in groups to find all of the different convex figures that can be tiled by tangrams. (See problem 29.) Be sure to use all 7 tangram pieces in each of the convex figures. There are 13 noncongruent figures in all, and most of the figures can be tiled in several ways.

## Using a Computer

**31.** The Geometer's Sketchpad geometry software includes tools that enable the user to quickly construct a variety of polygons. In particular, the regular polygons of sides 3, 4, 5, 6, and 8 are easily constructed by selecting two points to be adjacent vertices. (Details are found in the *Learning Guide* that accompanies the software; see also Appendix C.)

   **(a)** Use the software to create examples of some of the semi-regular tilings of the plane.

   **(b)** Write a brief report that shows your tiling examples and discusses what steps you discovered to make your tilings.

**32.** Use geometry software to create an Escher-like design based on the tiling of the plane by equilateral triangles, following these steps: Begin by constructing an equilateral triangle. Next, modify one side of the triangle and rotate it 60° about a vertex to modify a second side of the triangle. Alter the remaining side of the triangle by constructing the midpoint and doing a midpoint modification. (See problem 22 and the figure that follows.) Hide unwanted lines and points and add decorations to complete the tile. To make your design with the tile, first use rotations to form a six-tile arrangement as shown. Translations of the six-tile arrangement will complete your design.

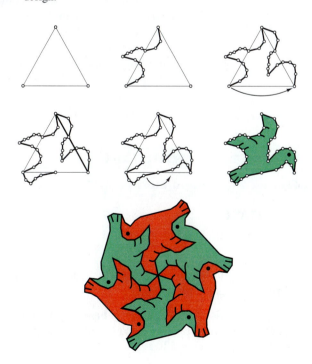

## From State Student Assessments

**33.** (New Jersey, Grade 4)
Which group of shapes was used to form the figure below? Use your colored shapes to help you.

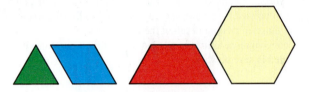

A. 2 yellow hexagons and 1 green triangle

B. 3 red trapezoids

C. 1 yellow hexagon, 1 red trapezoid, and 1 green triangle

D. 1 yellow hexagon and 3 green triangles

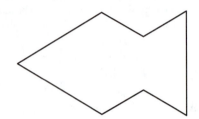

**34.** (Arizona, Grade 8)
Which shape will create a tessellation using only translations?

A. scalene triangle    B. regular hexagon

C. equilateral triangle    D. isosceles trapezoid

**35.** Provide an analysis of the following problem that was released by a state student assessment office.

Irene is making a tessellation using the shape shown below.

Which of the following tessellations can be made using only a clockwise rotation?

A.

B.

C.

D.

## The Chapter in Relation to Future Teachers

This chapter has introduced the basic concepts of transformational geometry, including the rigid and similarity motions that give precise meaning to the fundamental notions of the congruence and similarity of geometric figures. Transformations were then applied to classify patterns according to the type of symmetry they possessed. In the opposite direction, transformations were used to create patterns of interest.

While the chapter has given a thorough and at times technically detailed description of motions and symmetries, the teacher should be aware that much of this material is of appeal and interest even to very young children. For example, a preschooler typically enjoys simple picture puzzles in which a puzzle piece cut from wood must be placed into the matching hole on the puzzle board—and here the child is in fact carrying out a rigid motion and checking for congruence. Similarly, a kindergartner enjoys working with pattern blocks to create an attractive pattern—indeed, a pattern often exhibiting considerable symmetry and extendable to a tiling of the plane. Somewhat older children nearly always enjoy combining mathematics with artistic creativity—and certainly the graphic work originating with Escher has broad appeal to all ages.

## Chapter 11 Summary

| Section 11.1   Rigid Motions and Similarity Transformations | Page Reference |
|---|---|
| **DEFINITIONS** | |
| • A **transformation** of the plane is a one-to-one correspondence of the points of the plane onto itself. | 601 |
| • If point $P$ on a plane corresponds to point $P'$ under a transformation, then $P'$ is the **image** of $P$ and $P$ is the **preimage** of $P'$. | 601 |
| • A **rigid motion,** or **isometry,** is a transformation of the plane that preserves distance: $PQ = P'Q'$ for all points $P$ and $Q$ and their corresponding image points $P'$ and $Q'$. | 601 |

- The **identity transformation** is the rigid motion for which each point corresponds to itself: $P = P'$ for all points $P$ in the plane.                                                                    602

- Two transformations of the plane are **equivalent** if both transformations take each point $P$ onto the same image point $P'$.                                                                                602

- **The four basic rigid motions:** translation (or slide), rotation (or turn), reflection (or flip), and glide–reflection.                                                                                     602

- A **translation (slide)** is one of the four basic rigid motions of the plane in which all points of the plane are moved the same distance in the same direction.                                              602

- The **slide arrow,** or **translation vector,** is an arrow that characterizes a translation; the direction of the slide is the direction of the arrow and the distance of the slide is the length of the arrow.    602

- A **rotation (turn)** is one of the four basic rigid motions of the plane in which one point of the plane is held fixed and the remaining points are turned around the center of rotation through the same number of degrees.    603

- The **center of rotation** is the fixed point about which the other points rotate.                                                                                                                            603

- The **turn angle** is the number of degrees that the points rotate.                                                                                                                                           603

- The **turn arrow** is an arrow in the shape of a circular arc drawn to indicate the turn center and the directed angle corresponding to the turn center.                                                       603

- **Reflections (flips)** are one of the four basic rigid motions in which all points $P$ are transformed to the opposite side $P'$, but the same distance away, from a determined line.                          604

- The **line of reflection (mirror line)** is the line over which all the points are flipped.                                                                                                                   604

- **Glide-reflections** are one of the four basic rigid motions that combine both slides and reflections. The points reflect over a mirror line and slide a fixed distance parallel to the mirror line.          606

- The **glide arrow,** or **glide vector,** is the vector of the glide.                                                                                                                                         606

- An **orientation-reversing** motion is one that interchanges handedness, such as reflections and glide-reflections. Motions that do not reverse handedness are called **orientation-preserving,** such as translations and rotations.    606

- Two figures are **congruent** if, and only if, one figure is the image of the other under a rigid motion.                                                                                                      612

- **Dilation,** or **size transformation,** with center $O$ and scale factor $k$ takes each point $P$ other than $O$ to the point $P'$ on the ray $OP$ so that $OP = kOP$ and leaves $O$ fixed.                  613

- Scale factor $k$ is a **contraction** if $0 < k < 1$ or an **expansion** if $k > 1$.                                                                                                                          614

- A **similarity transformation** is a transformation composed of a sequence of dilations and rigid motions.                                                                                                     614

- Two figures are **similar** if, and only if, there is a similarity transformation that takes one figure onto the other.                                                                                         614

## THEOREMS

- **Equivalence properties of multiple reflections:**
  A sequence of two reflections across parallel lines is equivalent to a translation.                                                                                                                            609
  A sequence of two reflections across intersecting lines is equivalent to a rotation.                                                                                                                           609
  A sequence of three reflections across parallel or concurrent lines is equivalent to a single reflection. Otherwise, a sequence of three reflections is equivalent to a glide–reflection.                      610

- **Classification theorem for rigid motions:** Every rigid motion is equivalent to one of the four basic motions: a translation, a rotation, a reflection, or a glide–reflection. — 611

- **Distance change under a dilation:** Under a dilation with scale factor $k$, all distances change by the factor $k$: $P'Q' = kPQ$. — 614

| Section 11.2   Patterns and Symmetries | Page Reference |
|---|---|

**DEFINITIONS**

- A figure has **symmetry** if there is a rigid motion that takes every point of the figure onto an image point that is also in the figure. — 624

- A figure has **reflection symmetry** if the reflection over the mirror line, or line of symmetry, takes a figure onto itself. — 625

- A figure has **rotation symmetry,** or **turn symmetry,** if there is a rotation about some center $O$ that superimposes figure onto itself. — 626

- Figures have **circular symmetry** if they turn onto themselves for any degree of rotation about some point $O$. — 626

- A figure has **point symmetry** if it has 180° rotation symmetry about some point $O$. — 627

- A **periodic pattern** is a figure with translation symmetry. — 628

- A **periodic border pattern** is a periodic pattern with translation symmetry in one direction only. — 628

- A **wallpaper pattern** is a planar pattern with translation symmetries in more than one direction. — 628

**THEOREMS**

- **Classification of border patterns:** Every border pattern has one of seven possible symmetry types (given the symbolic descriptions $mm$, $mg$, $m1$, $1g$, $12$, or $11$) — 628, 629

- **Classification of wallpaper patterns:** Every wallpaper pattern has one of seventeen possible symmetry types. — 630

- **Crystallographic restriction:** A wallpaper pattern can have (smallest) rotation symmetries only of size 60°, 90°, 120°, or 180°. — 630

| Section 11.3   Tilings and Escher-like Designs | Page Reference |
|---|---|

**CONCEPTS**

- **Escher-like designs:** Designs resembling the work of M. C. Escher can be created by modifying the straight sides of a polygonal tile to assume more general curves, following rules that preserve some of the tiling properties of the original shape. — 642

**DEFINITIONS**

- A **tile** is a simple closed curve in the plane, together with its interior. — 637

- A **tiling,** or **tessellation,** is a covering of a figure or the whole plane with tiles, having no gaps or overlaps. — 637

- A **regular tiling of the plane** is a tiling for which the tiles are congruent regular polygons that are joined edge-to-edge. — 637

- A **vertex figure** is an arrangement of nonoverlapping polygonal tiles surrounding a common vertex. — 639

- A **semiregular tiling of the plane** is an edge-to-edge tiling of the plane with more than one type of regular polygon and with identical vertex figures.

  639

- **Tiling with irregular polygons** is tiling with shapes that are not regular polygons or shapes with sides of an equal length. The Dutch artist Escher created a large number of artistic tilings of this type.

  640

**THEOREMS**

- **Regular tilings of the plane:** There are three regular tilings of the plane, created by edge-to-edge tiles that are congruent equilateral triangles, squares, or regular hexagons.

  637

- **Semiregular tilings of the plane:** There are eight semiregular tilings of the plane.

  639

- **Tilings of the plane with a nonregular polygonal tile:** The plane can be tiled with any triangle, any quadrilateral, and certain pentagons and hexagons. No convex polygon with more than six sides can tile the plane.

  641

## Chapter Review Exercises

### Section 11.1

1. Draw the image of $ABCDE$ under the translation that takes $A$ onto $A'$.

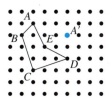

2. Determine the center and turn angle of the rotation that takes $A$ onto $A'$ and $B$ onto $B'$. Use a protractor, Mira, ruler, or whatever drawing tools you wish.

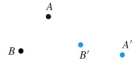

3. Describe the basic rigid motion that takes $A$, $B$, and $C$ onto $A'$, $B'$, and $C'$, respectively. Use any drawing tools you wish.

4. A glide–reflection has a horizontal line $l$ as its glide mirror and translates 4 inches to the right. Draw three lines of reflection—$m_1, m_2,$ and $m_3$—so that successive reflections across $m_1, m_2,$ and $m_3$ result in a motion equivalent to the glide–reflection.

5. Sketch the image of the square $ABCD$ under each of these transformations:

   **(a)** The dilation centered at $O$ with scale factor 2

   **(b)** The dilation centered at $A$ with scale factor 1/3.

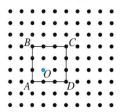

6. Describe the similarity transformation that takes the square $ABCD$ onto the square $JKLM$, where $J$, $K$, $L$, and $M$ are the midpoints of square $ABCD$ as shown.

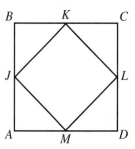

7. **(a)** Triangle ABC is equilateral with sides of length two units. Find the images of $\triangle ABC$ under successive reflections across the three lines $m_1, m_2,$ and $m_3$ that enclose $\triangle ABC$, as shown. Label the final image points $A', B',$ and $C'$.

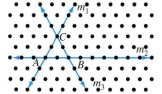

   **(b)** Describe the basic rigid motion that takes $\triangle ABC$ onto $\triangle A'B'C'$.

## Section 11.2

**8.** The geometric forms shown are from African art. Describe all lines of symmetry for each figure.

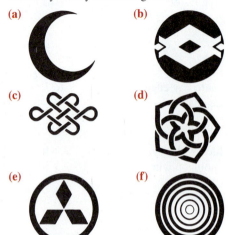

**(a)**　　　　**(b)**

**(c)**　　　　**(d)**

**(e)**　　　　**(f)**

**9.** What rule is used to separate the letters of the alphabet in the following arrangement?

ABCDE　HI K　MNO　　STUVWXYZ
　　FG　J　L　　PRQ

**10.** What is the common name for these polygons?

**(a)** A triangle with no line of symmetry

**(b)** A triangle with exactly one line of symmetry

**(c)** A triangle with three lines of symmetry

**(d)** A kite with two lines of symmetry

**(e)** A regular polygon with six lines of symmetry

**11.** Identify these polygons.

**(a)** A triangle with 120° rotational symmetry

**(b)** A quadrilateral with 180°, but not 90°, rotational symmetry

**(c)** A regular polygon with 40° as its smallest angle of rotational symmetry

**12.** For each of the figures shown in problem 8, give all of the angles of rotation symmetry.

**13.** Describe the symmetries of each of these periodic border patterns, and assign a classification symbol:

**(a)**

FRENCH RENAISSANCE ORNAMENT FROM CASKET

**(b)**

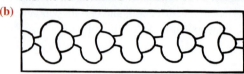

STAINED GLASS, CATHEDRAL OF BOURGES

## Section 11.3

**14.** Four regular polygons form a vertex figure in a tiling of the plane. Three of the polygons are a triangle, a square, and a hexagon. What is the fourth polygon?

**15.** Draw two different vertex figures that each incorporate three equilateral triangles and two squares.

**16.** Show that the following dart will tile the plane:

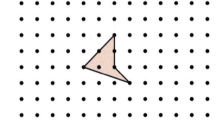

## Chapter Test

**1.** Which of the following polygons will tile the plane?

**(a)**　　　　**(b)**　　　　**(c)**

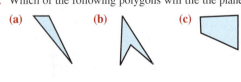

**(d)**　　　　**(e)**　　　　**(f)**

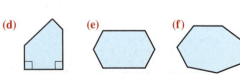

**2.** Draw two parallel lines $m_1$ and $m_2$ so that the sequence of reflections across $m_1$ and $m_2$ will map point $P$ to point $P'$.

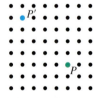

**3.** A translation takes points $A$, $B$, and $C$ onto $A'$, $B'$, and $C'$, respectively. Show the location of $C'$ and $B$.

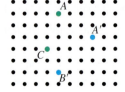

**4.** In the Escher tiling shown, what type of rigid motion

   **(a)** takes figure A onto figure B?

   **(b)** takes figure B onto figure C?

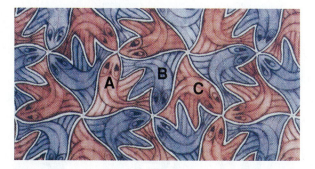

**5.** Three lines $m_1$, $m_2$, and $m_3$ are shown in each part. What type of rigid motion is equivalent to a sequence of reflections across $m_1$, $m_2$, and $m_3$?

   **(a)**

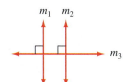

   **(b)** Parallel lines

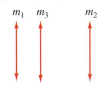

   **(c)**

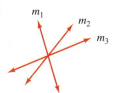

   **(d)**

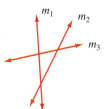

**6.** List the symmetries found in each of the border patterns shown, and assign each its classification symbol.

   **(a)**

INDIAN PAINTED LACQUER WORK

   **(b)**

MALTESE LACE

   **(c)**

ANCIENT GREEK SCROLL BORDER

   **(d)**

ITALIAN DAMASK OF THE RENAISSANCE

**7.** Describe a similarity transformation that takes the square $ABCD$ onto the square $A'B'C'D'$.

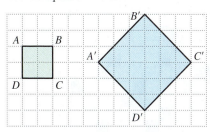

**8.** Copy the rectangle $ABCD$ and points $A'$ and $B'$ onto squared paper.

   **(a)** Show that $A'$ and $B'$ are the image of $A$ and $B$, respectively, under a rotation. Give the center of rotation and the size of the rotation angle.

   **(b)** Draw the image rectangle $A'B'C'D'$

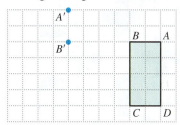

**9.** Sketch a portion of the semiregular tiling of the plane that uses square and octagonal tiles with a common side length.

**10.** Trace the drawing of $\angle A$. Suppose $A'$ is the image of $A$ under a reflection. Explain how to draw the image of $\angle A$ under the reflection.

**11.** A dilation takes $ABCDEF$ onto $AVWXYZ$ as follows, where $AV = 8$, $VB = 4$, $BC = 20$, and $AZ = 18$:

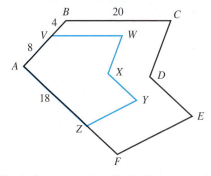

   **(a)** What is the center of the dilation?

   **(b)** What is the scale factor?

   **(c)** What is the distance $VW$?

   **(d)** What is the distance $ZF$?

**12.** Draw two lines $l_1$ and $l_2$ so that a sequence of reflections across $l_1$ and $l_2$ will rotate point $Q$ to point $Q'$ about the turn center $O$.

**13.** Two blank crossword puzzles are shown. What symmetries are found in the grid of black-and-white squares used by the puzzle maker?

**(a)**

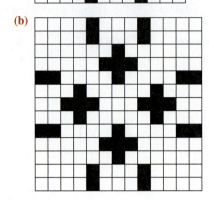

**(b)**

**14.** Find the glide arrow and glide mirror of the glide–reflection that takes rectangle *ABCD* onto *A'B'C'D'*.

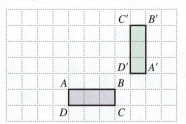

**15.** Draw all of the lines of symmetry for these figures:

**(a)**    **(b)**    **(c)**

**16.** What is the size of the smallest positive angle of rotation symmetry in each figure shown in problem 15?

# 12

# Congruence, Constructions, and Similarity

**12.1** Congruent Triangles

**12.2** Constructing Geometric Figures

**12.3** Similar Triangles

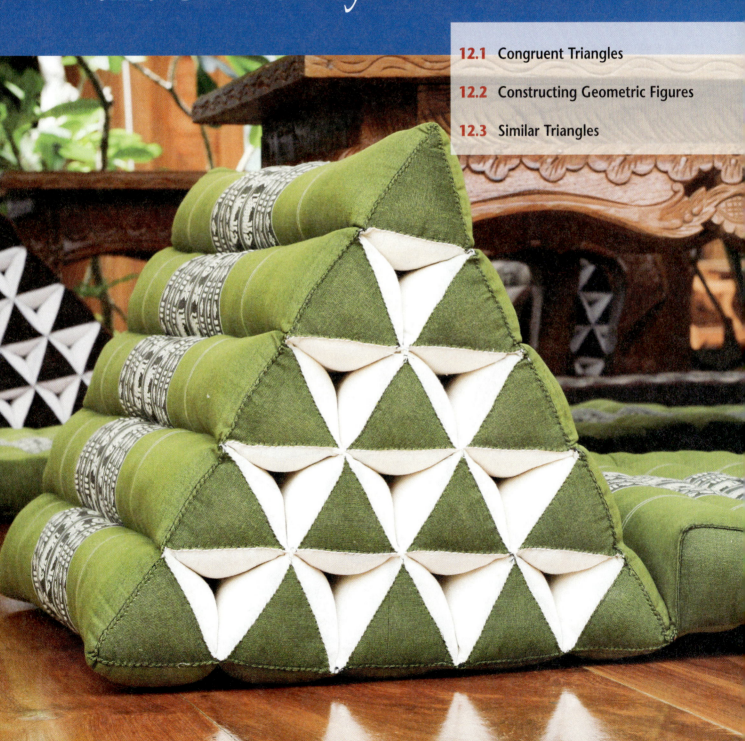

# Hands On

## Getting Rhombunctious! Folding Paper Polygons

### Materials

Rectangular sheets of paper (thin, colorful paper works best, about 4" by 6" or 5" by 7"), rulers, protractors, tape or glue sticks, scissors (optional)

### Directions

The goal of this activity is to construct rhombuses and related polygons with paper folding. Some properties of the figures will be investigated by measuring lengths and angles. Unwanted flaps that are not part of the desired final figure can be taped or glued down (or cut off with scissors). It is very important that the folds be made with considerable care. Work in small groups to answer the questions about the properties of the polygons created by your group members.

### I. A General Rhombus

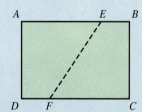

1. Fold C to A to construct segment $\overline{EF}$.

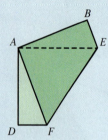

2. Fold up along $\overline{AE}$ and down along $\overline{AF}$.

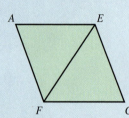

3. Unfold along $\overline{EF}$ to create the rhombus AECF (with the unneeded triangles ACE and ADF taped or glued to the back side).

### Questions

1. Use a ruler to measure the sides of AECF. Are they equal? How did the folding make this happen?

2. Measure the interior angles of AECF. How are they related?

3. Measure ∠EFC. Is $\overline{EF}$ an angle bisector?

4. Fold F on E and then unfold to create the segment $\overline{AC}$. At what angle do $\overline{AC}$ and $\overline{EF}$ intersect?

### II. A Special Rhombus

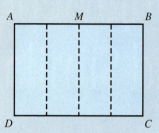

1. Fold a rectangle in half twice, and then unfold.

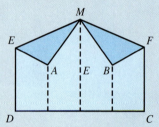

2. Fold A to the 1/4 vertical crease and B to the 3/4 crease, with both folds meeting the midpoint M of side $\overline{AB}$.

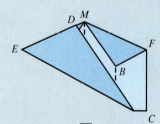

3. Fold D onto $\overline{EM}$ and glue the fold down.

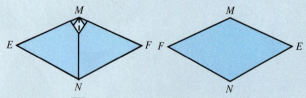

4. Fold C onto $\overline{MF}$ and glue the fold down.

5. Turn the paper over to obtain the rhombus FMEN.

### Questions

1. What special angles do you find in FMEN?

2. If FMEN is folded across $\overline{MN}$, what special triangle is formed?

3. If points F and E are both folded to the midpoint of $\overline{MN}$, what special polygon is constructed?

In the preceding chapter, rigid motions and similarity transformations allowed us to define the congruence and similarity of the most general types of geometric figures. However, as we will see in this chapter, for a simple figure such as a line segment or a triangle, congruence or similarity can be determined by knowing just a few measurements. For example, two line segments are congruent if, and only if, they have the same length. Likewise, two triangles are congruent if two side lengths and the measure of the angle included between the two sides of one triangle are equal to two side lengths and the included angle measure of the other—there is no need to measure the size of the remaining side or the other two angles, as they are guaranteed to be equal as well.

This simple measurement criterion to determine either congruence or similarity has many applications. In particular, it will be the basis upon which to construct important and useful figures that have desirable properties. For example, we can construct a midpoint of a segment, the ray that bisects a given angle, or a line either parallel or perpendicular to another line.

It will be important to distinguish the mathematical meaning of construction from the related notion of a drawing. If a figure is only to be drawn, the intent is that it look "about right" in its appearance. However, for a construction, the figure is created to have the exact properties that define the figure. For example, to construct a square, given the length of one of its sides, procedures must be followed which ensure that all sides of the figure are exactly the same length and that a right angle occurs at each vertex.

- Congruent triangles
- Properties of congruent triangles: side–side–side (SSS), side–angle–side (SAS), angle–side–angle (ASA), angle–angle–side (AAS)
- Triangle inequality
- Isosceles triangle theorem and its converse
- Thales' theorem
- Compass and straightedge constructions: congruent segment, congruent angle, parallel line, perpendicular line, midpoint and perpendicular bisector of a segment, angle bisector
- Inscribed circle and circumscribed circle of a triangle
- Construction of regular polygons
- Similar triangles
- Properties of similar triangles: angle–angle, side–side–side, side–angle–side

# 12.1

# Congruent Triangles

## Congruent Line Segments and Their Construction

Before considering triangles, it is helpful to consider line segments. Given two line segments, it is enough to know their lengths to decide whether they are congruent: Two line segments are congruent if, and only if, they have the same length. We can also take a constructive approach. Construction 1 shows how a compass and straightedge are used to construct a line segment that is congruent to a given segment.

**CONSTRUCTION 1** Construct a Line Segment Congruent to a Given Segment

On a given ray $\overrightarrow{PZ}$, construct a line segment that is congruent to a given line segment $\overline{AB}$.

**Procedure**

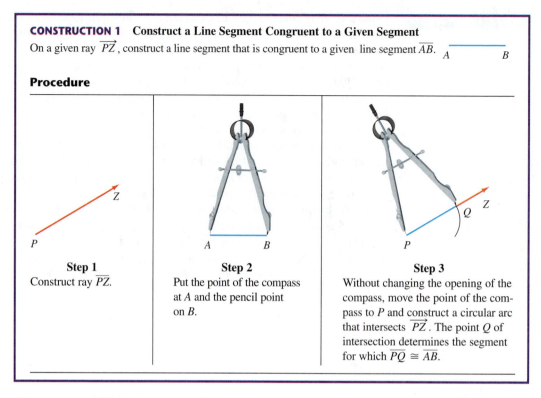

| **Step 1** | **Step 2** | **Step 3** |
|---|---|---|
| Construct ray $\overrightarrow{PZ}$. | Put the point of the compass at $A$ and the pencil point on $B$. | Without changing the opening of the compass, move the point of the compass to $P$ and construct a circular arc that intersects $\overrightarrow{PZ}$. The point $Q$ of intersection determines the segment for which $\overline{PQ} \cong \overline{AB}$. |

## Corresponding Parts and the Congruence of Triangles

The investigation of congruent triangles will consider these questions:

- What measurements of a triangle completely describe its size and shape?
- Given two triangles, what subsets of measurements are sufficient to decide whether the triangles are congruent to one another?
- Given certain measurements of a triangle $ABC$, how can a compass and straightedge be used to construct a triangle $PQR$ that is congruent to triangle $ABC$?

The size and shape of a triangle are described completely if we specify the **six parts of a triangle,** namely, the three sides $\overline{AB}, \overline{BC},$ and $\overline{CA}$ and the three angles $\angle A, \angle B,$ and $\angle C$. A second triangle $PQR$ is congruent to triangle $ABC$ if there is a matching of vertices $A \leftrightarrow P, B \leftrightarrow Q,$ and $C \leftrightarrow R$ under which *all six* parts of triangle $ABC$ are congruent to the corresponding six parts of triangle $PQR$. This situation is illustrated in Figure 12.1.

**FIGURE 12.1**
Triangles *ABC* and *PQR* are congruent under the vertex correspondence $A \leftrightarrow P, B \leftrightarrow Q,$ and $C \leftrightarrow R$ if, and only if, $\overline{AB} \cong \overline{PQ},$ $\overline{BC} \cong \overline{QR},$ and $\overline{CA} \cong \overline{RP},$ and $\angle A \cong \angle P, \angle B \cong \angle Q,$ and $\angle C \cong \angle R$

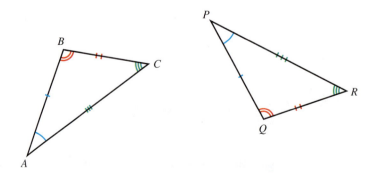

**DEFINITION** *Congruent Triangles*

Two triangles are **congruent** if, and only if, there is a correspondence of vertices of the triangles such that the corresponding sides and corresponding angles are congruent.

The notation $\triangle ABC \cong \triangle PQR$ is read "Triangle $ABC$ is congruent to triangle $PQR$." Mathematical notation and symbols must always be read with precision. This is especially true for the symbolic statement $\triangle ABC \cong \triangle PQR$, since it conveys the following information:

- The vertex correspondence is $A \leftrightarrow P$, $B \leftrightarrow Q$, and $C \leftrightarrow R$.
- The corresponding sides are congruent: $\overline{AB} \cong \overline{PQ}$, $\overline{BC} \cong \overline{QR}$, and $\overline{CA} \cong \overline{RP}$.
- The corresponding angles are congruent: $\angle A \cong \angle P$, $\angle B \cong \angle Q$, and $\angle C \cong \angle R$.

It is important to notice that the order in which the vertices are listed specifies the vertex correspondence. For the triangles depicted in Figure 12.1, we see that $\triangle ABC \ncong \triangle QRP$ ($\ncong$ is read "is not congruent to"). However, it is correct to say that $\triangle BCA \cong \triangle QRP$.

**EXAMPLE 12.1** Exploring the Congruence Relation

Use a ruler and protractor to find the two pairs of congruent triangles among the six triangles shown. State the two congruences in the symbolic form $\triangle \_\_\_ \cong \triangle \_\_\_$.

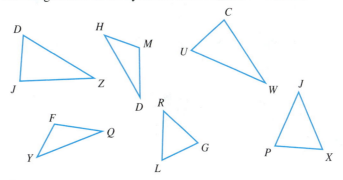

**Solution** $\triangle DJZ \cong \triangle UCW$ and $\triangle HMD \cong \triangle YFQ$. The order of the vertices may be permuted in the same way on both sides of a congruence statement. For example, it would also be correct to express the first congruence as $\triangle ZDJ \cong \triangle WUC$.

Suppose that we have only some of the measurements of a triangle $ABC$. For example, suppose that we know the lengths $AB$, $BC$, and $CA$ of the three sides, but we are not given any information about the angles. Or suppose we are given a length $AB$ and the measurements of two angles, $\angle A$ and $\angle B$. Is the information we have sufficient to construct a triangle $PQR$ that is necessarily congruent to $\triangle ABC$? These questions will be explored constructively; that is, we will attempt to use a compass and straightedge to construct a triangle $PQR$ that is congruent to $\triangle ABC$.

## The Side–Side–Side (SSS) Property

**EXAMPLE 12.2** Exploring the Side-Side-Side Property

The three sides of triangle $ABC$ are given as shown. Construct a triangle $PQR$ that has sides of the same length as $\triangle ABC$.

$$A \overset{x}{\rule{2cm}{0.4pt}} B \quad B \overset{y}{\rule{1cm}{0.4pt}} C \quad A \overset{z}{\rule{1.5cm}{0.4pt}} C$$

**Solution** **Step 1** Construct a segment $\overline{PQ}$ of length $x = AB$, using Construction 1.

**Step 2**   Set the compass to radius $y = BC$, and construct a circle of radius $y$ centered at $Q$.

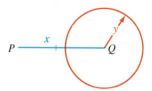

**Step 3**   Set the compass to radius $z = AC$, and construct a circular arc of radius $z$ centered at $P$. Let $R$ be either point of intersection with the circle constructed in step 2.

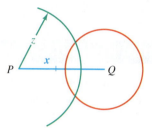

**Step 4**   Construct the segments $\overline{PR}$ and $\overline{RQ}$.

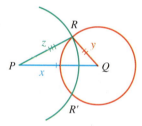

The construction in Example 12.2 shows that the three side lengths uniquely determine the size and shape of $\triangle PQR$. Even if we had chosen the second point of intersection, $R'$, $\triangle PQR'$ would still have been the same size and shape as $\triangle PQR$. Therefore, we are led to the following basic property:

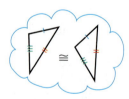

> **PROPERTY**   *Side–Side–Side (SSS)*
> If the three sides of one triangle are respectively congruent to the three sides of another triangle, then the two triangles are congruent.

In many formal treatments of Euclidean geometry, the SSS property is adopted as a postulate. That is, SSS is true by assumption, not by proof.

## EXAMPLE 12.3   Using the SSS Property

Let $ABCD$ be a quadrilateral with opposite sides of equal length: $AB = DC$ and $AD = BC$. Show that $ABCD$ is a parallelogram.

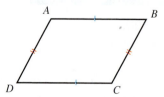

**Solution**
MHM

Many problems in geometry are solved by constructing additional lines or arcs to reveal features of the original figure that would otherwise remain hidden. In particular, it is helpful to create triangles, since the SSS property (or another congruence property) may be applicable. In this case we construct the diagonal $\overline{AC}$, creating the two triangles $ABC$ and $CDA$.

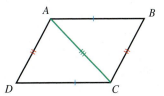

Since $\overline{AC}$ is congruent to itself, it follows that $\triangle ABC \cong \triangle CDA$ by the SSS property. Thus, the corresponding angles $\angle BAC$ and $\angle DCA$ are congruent. By the alternate-interior-angles theorem of Chapter 9, we conclude that $\overline{AB} \parallel \overline{DC}$. Similarly, the congruence $\angle BCA \cong \angle DAC$ shows that $\overline{AD} \parallel \overline{BC}$.

An important consequence of the SSS property is the following construction of an angle congruent to a given angle:

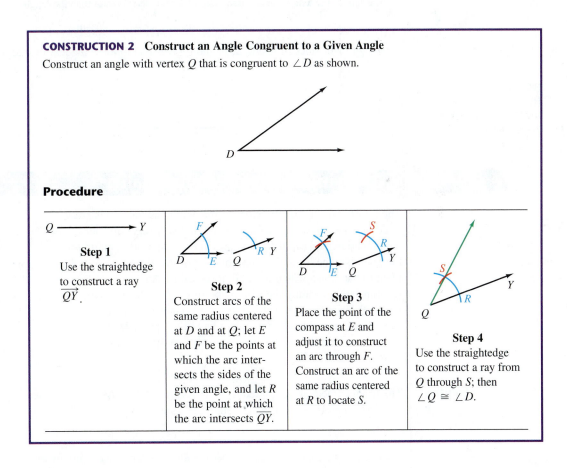

**CONSTRUCTION 2** Construct an Angle Congruent to a Given Angle
Construct an angle with vertex $Q$ that is congruent to $\angle D$ as shown.

**Procedure**

**Step 1**
Use the straightedge to construct a ray $\overrightarrow{QY}$.

**Step 2**
Construct arcs of the same radius centered at $D$ and at $Q$; let $E$ and $F$ be the points at which the arc intersects the sides of the given angle, and let $R$ be the point at which the arc intersects $\overline{QY}$.

**Step 3**
Place the point of the compass at $E$ and adjust it to construct an arc through $F$. Construct an arc of the same radius centered at $R$ to locate $S$.

**Step 4**
Use the straightedge to construct a ray from $Q$ through $S$; then $\angle Q \cong \angle D$.

The construction procedure shows that $DE = QR$, $DF = QS$, and $EF = RS$. Therefore, $\triangle DEF \cong \triangle QRS$ by the SSS property, so the corresponding angles $\angle D$ and $\angle Q$ are congruent.

## The Triangle Inequality

The SSS property guarantees that two triangles are congruent if they have corresponding sides of the same length. However, not every triple of given lengths corresponds to a triangle, as the construction in Example 12.2 shows: The two circles must intersect in order to determine the third vertex of the triangle. Thus, the length of any side must be less than the sum of the lengths of the other two sides. Figure 12.2 gives an example in which segments of length $x$, $y$, and $z$ are not the side lengths of any triangle.

**FIGURE 12.2**
If $x \geq y + z$, there is no triangle with sides of length $x$, $y$, and $z$

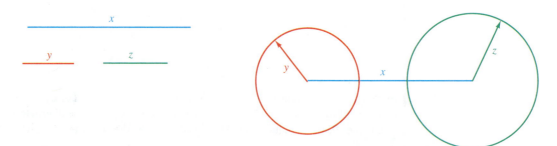

The lengths of the sides of a triangle must satisfy the following theorem:

> **THEOREM**   *Triangle Inequality*
> The sum of the lengths of any two sides of a triangle is greater than the length of the third side.

A triangle with sides of length $a$, $b$, and $c$ gives rise to three inequalities, as shown in Figure 12.3.

**FIGURE 12.3**
The lengths of the sides of any triangle satisfy the triangle inequalities

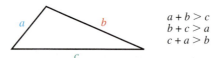

$$a + b > c$$
$$b + c > a$$
$$c + a > b$$

## EXAMPLE 12.4   Applying the Triangle Inequality

The four towns of Abbott, Brownsville, Connell, and Davis are building a new power-generating plant that will serve all four communities. To keep the costs of the power lines at a minimum, the plant is to be located so that the sum of the distances from the plant to the four towns is as small as possible. An engineer recommended locating the plant at point $E$. A mathematician, seeing that the four towns form a convex quadrilateral $ABCD$ as shown, recommended that the plant be built at point $M$, at which the diagonals of the quadrilateral intersect. Why is location $M$ better than $E$?

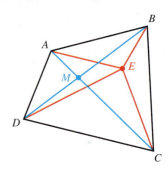

**Solution**   The triangle inequality, applied to $\triangle ACE$, gives $EA + EC > AC$. Since $M$ is on the diagonal $\overline{AC}$, it follows that $AC = MA + MC$, and therefore,

$$EA + EC > MA + MC.$$

If we apply the triangle inequality to $\triangle BDE$, the same reasoning gives us the inequality

$$EB + ED > MB + MD.$$

Adding the two inequalities gives us

$$EA + EB + EC + ED > MA + MB + MC + MD.$$

This inequality shows that the sum of the distances to the towns from point $E$ is greater than the sum of the distances to the towns from point $M$.

## Cooperative Investigation
### Exploring Toothpick Triangles

### Materials Needed

Toothpicks of equal length (about 20 per person)

### Directions

Three toothpicks, placed end to end, form a triangle in one way—an equilateral triangle. Four toothpicks do not form a triangle. Five and six toothpicks each form just one triangle. Two different (that is, noncongruent) triangles can be formed with seven toothpicks.

| Triangles | △ | △ | △ | ◁ᐳ △ |
|---|---|---|---|---|---|
| **Number of Toothpicks, _n_** | 3 | 4 | 5 | 6 | 7 |
| **Number of Triangles, _T(n)_** | 1 | 0 | 1 | 1 | 2 |

Explore how many noncongruent triangles you can form with 8, 9, 10, 11, and 12 toothpicks. Extend the table above to include your results.

### Questions for Consideration

1. How many isosceles toothpick triangles are there for which the two sides of equal length each use 4 toothpicks?
2. One side of a toothpick triangle uses 3 toothpicks, and a second side uses 5 toothpicks. What are the possible numbers of toothpicks in the third side?
3. If two sides of a toothpick triangle together use 11 toothpicks, what is the largest number of toothpicks that can be used in the third side?
4. Suppose toothpicks form a triangle with $p$, $q$, and $r$ toothpicks on its three sides. What can you say about the integer $r$ in terms of the integers $p$ and $q$?
5. In your table of the number of triangles, suppose $T(n)$ is the number of different toothpick triangles formed from $n$ toothpicks. For odd $n$, compare $T(n)$ with $T(n + 3)$. For example, compare $T(3)$ with $T(6)$, and compare $T(5)$ with $T(8)$. What pattern do you observe?

## The Side–Angle–Side (SAS) Property

The next example explores how to construct a triangle with two given sides and the angle included between the given sides.

**EXAMPLE 12.5** **Exploring the Side-Angle-Side Condition**

Two sides $\overline{AB}$ and $\overline{AC}$ and the angle $\angle A$ included between these sides are given for $\triangle ABC$ as shown. Show that a triangle $PQR$ can be constructed for which $\triangle PQR \cong \triangle ABC$.

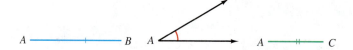

**Solution**

**Step 1** Follow the steps of Construction 2 to construct an angle congruent to ∠A; let P denote its vertex.

**Step 2** Use Construction 1 to construct segments $\overline{PQ}$ and $\overline{PR}$ along the sides of ∠P that are respectively of lengths AB and AC.

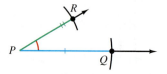

**Step 3** Construct segment $\overline{QR}$, completing △PQR. This procedure uniquely determines the size and shape of △PQR, so there is only one possible triangle whose sides and included angle are congruent to the given ones. Therefore, △PQR ≅ △ABC.

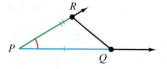

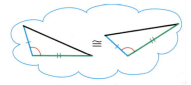

The procedure described in Example 12.5 uniquely determines the size and shape of △PQR when we are given the three parts, side–angle–side, of △ABC. The angle has to be the **included angle,** the angle between the given sides. This property is often abbreviated as **SAS (side–angle–side).**

> **PROPERTY** *Side–Angle–Side (SAS)*
> If two sides and the included angle of one triangle are congruent to two sides and the included angle of another triangle, then the two triangles are congruent.

**EXAMPLE 12.6** **Using the SAS Property**

Two line segments $\overline{AB}$ and $\overline{CD}$ intersect at their common midpoint M. Show that $\overline{AD}$ and $\overline{BC}$ are parallel and have the same length.

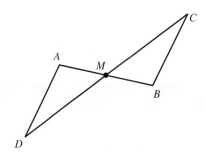

**Solution** It is a useful habit to add tick marks and arcs to your drawing to summarize the given information. In this problem, $M$ is the midpoint of $\overline{AB}$, so $AM = BM$. We indicate this equality on the drawing by putting a single tick mark on each of the segments $\overline{AM}$ and $\overline{MB}$. Similarly, $CM = DM$, and we put double tick marks on each of the segments $\overline{CM}$ and $\overline{MD}$. We also use single arcs to indicate the congruence of the vertical angles at $M$ formed by the intersecting segments.

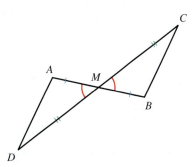

It is now apparent that the SAS property gives us the congruence $\triangle AMD \cong \triangle BMC$. It follows that the corresponding sides $\overline{AD}$ and $\overline{BC}$ are congruent, so that $AD = BC$. We also have $\angle A \cong \angle B$, so the alternate-interior-angles theorem of Chapter 9 guarantees that $\overline{AD}$ and $\overline{CB}$ are parallel.

The following theorem about isosceles triangles is an important consequence of the SAS property:

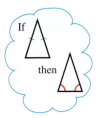

**THEOREM** *Isosceles Triangle Theorem*
The angles opposite the congruent sides of an isosceles triangle are congruent.

**PROOF** Let $\triangle ABC$ be isosceles, with $\overline{AB}$ and $\overline{AC}$ congruent. Consider the vertex correspondence $A \leftrightarrow A$, $B \leftrightarrow C$, and $C \leftrightarrow B$ (which amounts to looking at the same triangle from the back, so to speak!).

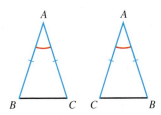

Since $\overline{AB} \cong \overline{AC}$ and $\angle A \cong \angle A$, it follows from the SAS property that $\triangle ABC \cong \triangle ACB$. But then all six corresponding parts of $\triangle ABC$ and $\triangle ACB$ are congruent, including $\angle B \cong \angle C$.

The isosceles triangle theorem has many uses. For example, it gives a simple way to prove **Thales' theorem.**

**THEOREM** *Thales' Theorem*
Any triangle $ABC$ inscribed in a semicircle with diameter $\overline{AB}$ has a right angle at point $C$.

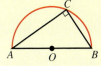

MHM

**PROOF**    Just as in Example 12.3, it is helpful to draw additional line segments to reveal relationships that would otherwise remain hidden. Draw the radius $\overline{OC}$ as in the figure shown. This divides $\triangle ABC$ into two isosceles triangles: $\triangle AOC$ and $\triangle COB$ (why?). The isosceles triangle theorem tells us that the measures $x$ of the base angles of $\triangle AOC$ are equal. Likewise, the measures $y$ of the base angles of $\triangle COB$ are equal. Since the sum of the measures of the interior angles of $\triangle ABC$ is $180°$, we have $x + y + (x + y) = 180°$. But this equation tells us that $m(\angle C) = x + y = 90°$.

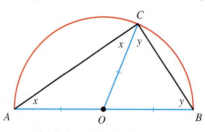

## The Angle–Side–Angle (ASA) Property

In the next example, we suppose that two angles of a triangle, and the side included between these angles, are given. Is this information sufficient to construct a congruent triangle?

**EXAMPLE 12.7    Exploring the Angle-Side-Angle Property**

Two angles and their **included side** are given for $\triangle ABC$, as shown. Construct a triangle $PQR$ that is congruent to triangle $ABC$.

**Solution**    **Step 1**    Use Construction 2 to construct $\angle P \cong \angle A$.

**Step 2**    Use Construction 1 to construct segment $\overline{PQ}$ on a side of $\angle P$ so that $PQ = AB$.

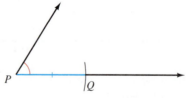

**Step 3**    Construct an angle congruent to $\angle B$ at vertex $Q$, with one side containing $P$ and the other side intersecting $\angle P$ to determine point $R$. The procedure uniquely determines the size and shape of $\triangle PQR$. Therefore, $\triangle PQR \cong \triangle ABC$.

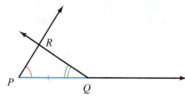

The construction just shown illustrates the **angle–side–angle property,** abbreviated as **ASA.**

> **PROPERTY**  *Angle–Side–Angle (ASA)*
> If two angles and the included side of one triangle are congruent to the two angles and the included side of another triangle, then the two triangles are congruent.

The ASA property allows us to prove that any triangle with two angles of the same measure is isosceles.

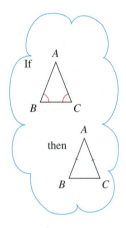

> **THEOREM**  *Converse of the Isosceles Triangle Theorem*
> If two angles of a triangle are congruent, then the sides opposite them are congruent; that is, the triangle is isosceles.

> **PROOF**  Let $\triangle ABC$ have two congruent angles, say, $\angle B \cong \angle C$. We know that $\overline{BC} \cong \overline{CB}$, since a line segment is congruent to itself. By the ASA property, it follows that $\triangle ABC \cong \triangle ACB$. This means that the corresponding sides of $\triangle ABC$ and $\triangle ACB$ are congruent, so $\overline{AB} \cong \overline{AC}$.

## The Angle–Angle–Side (AAS) Property

The side in the ASA theorem is the one included by the two angles. However, if *any* two angles of one triangle are congruent to two angles of a second triangle, then all three pairs of corresponding angles are congruent. This statement follows from the fact that the measures of the three angles of a triangle add up to 180°, so the third angle is uniquely determined by the other two angles. This gives us the **angle–angle–side property,** abbreviated as **AAS.**

> **PROPERTY**  *Angle–Angle–Side (AAS)*
> If two angles and a nonincluded side of one triangle are respectively congruent to two angles and the corresponding nonincluded side of a second triangle, then the two triangles are congruent.

## Are There SSA and AAA Congruence Properties?

There is no "SSA" congruence property, since it is possible for two noncongruent triangles to have two pairs of congruent sides and a congruent nonincluded angle. An example is shown in Figure 12.4.

**FIGURE 12.4**
Triangles *ABC* and *DEF* are not congruent, even though *AC* = *DF*, *BC* = *EF*, and $\angle A \cong \angle D$

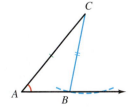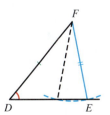

Similarly, there is no "AAA" congruence property. For example, Figure 12.5 shows two triangles with three pairs of congruent angles. These triangles are not congruent, since they are of different size. However, the shapes of the two triangles are the same, so they are similar triangles. The properties and applications of similar triangles will be discussed in Section 12.3.

**FIGURE 12.5**
The AAA condition guarantees similarity, but not congruence

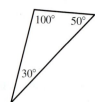

## Problem Set 12.1

Exercises numbered in red are answered in the back of the text.

## Understanding Concepts

**1.** The two triangles shown are congruent.

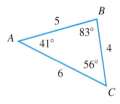

Determine the following:

**(a)** Corresponding vertices
$L \leftrightarrow$ ____, $H \leftrightarrow$ ____, $S \leftrightarrow$ ____

**(b)** Corresponding sides
$\overline{LH} \leftrightarrow$ ____, $\overline{HS} \leftrightarrow$ ____, $\overline{SL} \leftrightarrow$ ____

**(c)** Corresponding angles
$\angle L \leftrightarrow$ ____, $\angle H \leftrightarrow$ ____, $\angle S \leftrightarrow$ ____

**(d)** $\triangle LHS \cong \triangle$____.

**2.** Suppose $\triangle JKL \cong \triangle ABC$, where $\triangle ABC$ is as follows:

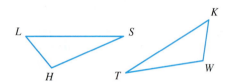

Find the following:

**(a)** $KL$    **(b)** $LJ$    **(c)** $m(\angle L)$    **(d)** $m(\angle J)$

**3.** Segments of length $x$ and $y$ are shown, with $x > y$.

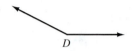

Describe procedures, using only a straightedge and a compass, to construct the following:

**(a)** a line segment $\overline{EF}$ of length $x + y$;

**(b)** a line segment $\overline{GH}$ of length $x - y$.

**4.** Use a straightedge and compass to construct a triangle $ABC$ whose sides have the lengths $x$, $y$, and $z$ shown. Carefully describe, in pictures and words, the steps in your construction.

**5.** Trace the angle $\angle D$ shown. Then use a compass and straightedge to construct an angle $\angle Q$ congruent to $\angle D$. Use a protractor to measure each angle, and report on how closely the measurements of the two angles agree.

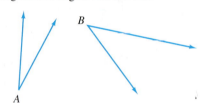

**6.** Following are two angles $\angle A$ and $\angle B$:

Describe procedures, using only a straightedge and a compass, to construct

**(a)** $\angle C$ so that $m(\angle C) = m(\angle A) + m(\angle B)$.

**(b)** $\angle D$ so that $m(\angle D) = m(\angle B) - m(\angle A)$.

**(c)** $\angle E$ so that $m(\angle E) + m(\angle A) + m(\angle B) = 180°$.

**7.** Use a ruler, protractor, and compass to construct, when possible, a triangle with the stated properties. If such a triangle cannot be drawn, explain why. Decide whether there can be two or more noncongruent triangles with the stated properties.

**(a)** An isosceles triangle with two sides of length 5 cm and an apex angle of measure 28°

**(b)** An equilateral triangle with sides of length 6 cm

**(c)** A triangle with sides of length 8 cm, 2 cm, and 5 cm

**(d)** A triangle with angles measuring 30° and 110° and a non-included side of length 5 cm

**(e)** A right triangle with legs (the sides including the right angle) of length 6 cm and 4 cm

**(f)** A triangle with sides of length 10 cm and 6 cm and a non-included angle of 45°

**(g)** A triangle with sides of length 5 cm and 3 cm and an angle of 20°

**8.** Each part that follows shows two triangles, with arcs and tick marks identifying congruent parts. If it is possible to conclude that the triangles are congruent, describe what property or theorem you used. If you cannot be sure that the triangles are congruent, state, "No conclusion possible." The first one is done for you.

**(a)**

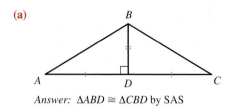

*Answer:* △ABD ≅ △CBD by SAS

**(b)**

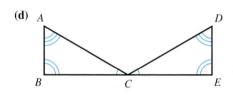

**(c)**

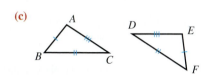

**(d)**

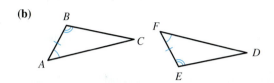

**(e)**

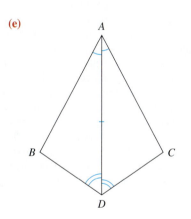

**(f)**

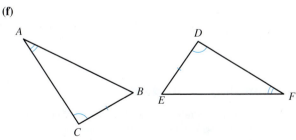

**(g)**

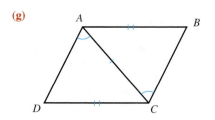

**(h)**

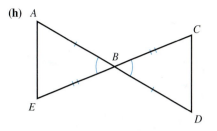

**(i)**

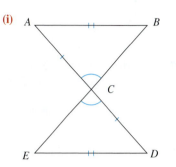

**(j)**

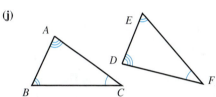

**9.** Prove that an equilateral triangle is equiangular.

**10.** Prove that an equiangular triangle is equilateral.

**11.** Draw an angle ∠BAC and use a protractor to measure the angle. Next, construct an arc centered at A to determine points D and E. Finally, draw arcs of equal radius centered at D and E, denoting their point of intersection as F.

    **(a)** Measure angles 1 and 2. How do they compare with the measure of ∠BAC?

    **(b)** Prove that △AFD is congruent to △AFE.

    **(c)** Explain why angles 1 and 2 are congruent, using the result of part (b).

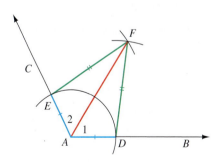

**12.** Draw a line *m* and a point *P* not on the line. Construct an arc centered at *P* that intersects the line in two points *Q* and *S*. Next, draw two arcs of equal radii centered at *Q* and *S*, labeling their intersection as point *T*. Finally, construct the segment from *P* to *T* and let *V* be its intersection with the line *m*.

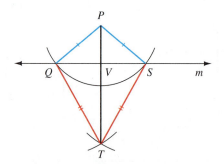

Give reasons that these relationships hold:

**(a)** $\triangle QPT \cong \triangle SPT$      **(b)** $\angle QPT \cong \angle SPT$

**(c)** $\triangle QPV \cong \triangle SPV$      **(d)** $\angle QVP$ is a right angle.

Therefore, the construction gives a line $\overleftrightarrow{PT}$ perpendicular to $m$ that passes through point $P$.

**13.** Let $ABCD$ be a parallelogram.

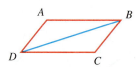

**(a)** Prove that $\triangle ABD \cong \triangle CDB$. (*Hint:* Use the ASA property.)

**(b)** Prove that opposite sides of a parallelogram have the same length.

**(c)** Prove that opposite angles of a parallelogram have the same measure.

**14.** Let the two diagonals of parallelogram $ABCD$ intersect at point $M$.

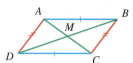

**(a)** Use the fact that $AB = CD$ (shown in problem 13(b)) to prove that $\triangle ABM \cong \triangle CDM$.

**(b)** Use part (a) to explain why $M$ is the midpoint of both diagonals of the parallelogram.

**15.** Let the two diagonals of a rhombus $ABCD$ intersect at $M$.

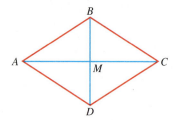

**(a)** Show that the triangles $ABM$, $CBM$, $CDM$, and $ADM$ are congruent to one another.

**(b)** Use part (a) to explain why the diagonals of a rhombus bisect the interior angles of the rhombus and intersect at a right angle at $M$.

**16.** Let $ABC$ be a right triangle with hypotenuse $\overline{AB}$ and right angle at vertex $C$. Explain why the circle centered at the midpoint $O$ of the hypotenuse and passing through point $C$ also passes through points $A$ and $B$. This gives the following:

*Converse of Thales' theorem: The hypotenuse of a right triangle inscribed in a circle is a diameter of the circle.*

(*Suggestion:* Imagine that the right triangle $ABC$ is created by constructing the diagonal $\overline{AB}$ of a rectangle $ACBD$.)

**17.** How can you locate the center of a circular plate with a piece of notebook paper and a ruler? (*Hint:* Use the converse of Thales' theorem, stated in problem 16.)

**18.** A triangle has sides of length 4 cm and 9 cm. What can you say about the length of the third side?

**19.** **(a)** A quadrilateral has sides of length 2 cm, 7 cm, and 5 cm. What inequality does the length of the fourth side satisfy?

     **(b)** Let $A$, $B$, $C$, and $D$ be any four points in the plane. Explain why $AD \leq AB + BC + CD$.

## Teaching Concepts

**20.** **Copycat Congruence Activity.** Write a detailed lesson plan that expands on the following idea:

> The class is divided into small groups. Each group constructs a triangle on a sheet of paper and uses a ruler and protractor to measure all six parts of the triangle. Next, the measures of three of the parts are written on the back of the sheet, which is taped to the chalkboard with the triangle hidden. Each group then chooses two or three measurements of triangles from other groups. The group's task is to use its measurements to construct congruent triangles cut from sheets of construction paper. Each group then places each triangle over the corresponding triangle on the reverse side of the taped sheets to test the accuracy of its constructions. Finally, each group describes, in written and oral form, how congruence properties were used, or if more than one triangle shape was possible.

Your lesson plan should clearly state the activity's goals, the standards it addresses, the materials required, the directions for carrying out the activity, your assessment of the activity, and any extensions of the activity for further investigation.

## Responding to Students

**21.** Dane has been studying quadrilaterals and wonders whether there is an SSSS congruence property for four-sided polygons. That is, if $AB$, $BC$, and $DA$ are given, then the size and shape of the quadrilateral $ABCD$ is determined. What suggestions would you offer to Dane to investigate this possibility?

**22.** Valerie believes that there is an SASAS congruence property for quadrilaterals. That is, if the lengths $AB$, $BC$, and $CD$ are given, as well as the measures of $\angle B$ and $\angle C$, then the unique size and shape of quadrilateral $ABCD$ is determined. How would you respond to Valerie?

## Thinking Critically

**23.** Following are two angles and a *nonincluded* side of △*ABC*:

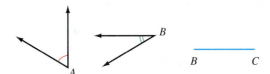

Describe and show the steps of a straightedge-and-compass construction of a triangle *PQR* that is congruent to △*ABC*.

**24.** In the following figure, *AB* = *AE* and *AC* = *AD*:

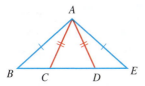

**(a)** Why is ∠*B* ≅ ∠*E*?

**(b)** Why is ∠*ACD* ≅ ∠*ADC*?

**(c)** Use the AAS property to prove that △*ABC* ≅ △*AED*.

**(d)** Prove that *BC* = *DE*.

**25.** Recall that a trapezoid with a pair of congruent angles adjacent to one of its bases is called an isosceles trapezoid.

**(a)** Prove that the sides joining the bases of an isosceles trapezoid are congruent. The following figure may help you show that $\overline{AD} \cong \overline{BC}$.

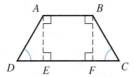

**(b)** Prove that the diagonals of an isosceles trapezoid are congruent.

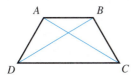

**26.** For each part that follows decide whether the given pair of conditions is sufficient to conclude that △*ABC* ≅ △*ADE*. If so, give a proof; if not, draw a figure that satisfies the information but shows that △*ABC* is not congruent to △*ADE*.

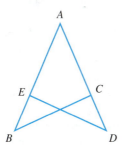

**(a)** *AB* = *AD* and *m*(∠*B*) = *m*(∠*D*)

**(b)** *AB* = *AD* and *BC* = *DE*

**(c)** *AB* = *AD* and *AE* = *AC*

**(d)** *EB* = *CD* and *BC* = *DE*

**27.** Each edge of a tetrahedron is congruent to its opposite edge. For example, $\overline{AB} \cong \overline{CD}$. Prove that the faces of the tetrahedron are congruent to one another.

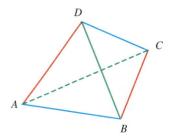

**28.** **(a)** Let *A* and *B* be two blue points and *X* and *Y* be two red points in the plane, where no three of the four points are collinear. Prove that if the blue points are joined to the red points by intersecting line segments, then the sum of their lengths is larger than the total length of the nonintersecting segments.

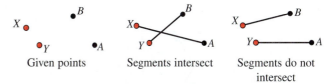

Given points    Segments intersect    Segments do not intersect

[*Suggestion*: Use the triangle inequality.]

**(b)** Let $\mathcal{B} = \{A, B, \ldots, J\}$ be a set of 10 blue points in the plane and $\mathcal{R} = \{Q, R, \ldots, Z\}$ a set of 10 red points in the plane, where no three of the 20 points are collinear. Explain why the blue points can always be joined to the red points with 10 line segments such that no two of the line segments intersect.

[*Suggestion*: Consider an arrangement with the smallest possible total sum of the lengths of the 10 connecting segments.]

**29.** **(a)** Let *T* be a point on the side $\overline{QR}$ of triangle *PQR*. Use the triangle inequality to explain why *QP* + *QR* > *TP* + *TR*.

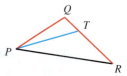

**(b)** Let *S* be a point in the interior of triangle *PQR*. Use part (a) to explain why *QP* + *QR* > *SP* + *SR*. This inequality shows that the sum of the distances from a vertex *Q* to the endpoints of the opposite side $\overline{PR}$ is larger than the sum of the distances to the same two points from a point *S* in the interior of triangle.

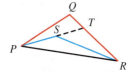

**30.** In Example 12.4, the four towns form a convex quadrilateral. Suppose instead that Davis is in the interior of the triangle formed by the other three towns, as shown in the accompanying figure. Show that the power station serving the four towns is best located at Davis, instead of an alternative point such as point $E$, by answering these questions:

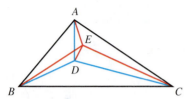

**(a)** Why is $EA + ED > DA$?

**(b)** Why is $EB + EC > DB + DC$? (*Suggestion:* Use the result of problem 29(b).)

**(c)** Why is $EA + ED + EB + EC > DA + DB + DC$?

**31.** Six towns are located at the vertices $A$, $B$, $C$, $D$, $E$, and $F$ of a regular hexagon. A power station located at $Q$ would require $QA + QB + QC + QD + QE + QF$ miles of transmission line to serve the six communities. Describe a better location $P$ for the station, and prove that it has the least possible sum of distances to $A$, $B$, $C$, $D$, $E$, and $F$.

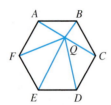

## Making Connections

**32.** A bicycle rack for a car is made from three pieces of metal box tubing. There are bolts at $A$, $B$, $C$, and $D$ that join the tubing and attach the rack to the bumper of the car.

**(a)** Why is the top of the rack likely to shift sideways?

**(b)** If a fourth piece of tubing is available, where can it be attached to make the rack rigid? Explain why this works.

**(c)** Would a rope from $A$ to $C$ make the rack rigid? How about two pieces of rope, from $A$ to $C$ and from $B$ to $D$?

**33.** Carpenters construct a wall by nailing studs to a top and bottom plate, as shown here:

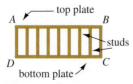

The studs are cut to the same length, and the top and bottom plates are the same length.

**(a)** If the pieces are properly cut and nailed, is $ABCD$ necessarily rectangular, or are there other shapes the framework can take?

**(b)** Carpenters frequently "square up" a stud wall by adjusting it so that it has diagonals of equal length. Prove that a parallelogram with congruent diagonals is a rectangle.

**(c)** Once the wall is "squared up," a diagonal brace is nailed across the frame. Why is this? What geometric principle is involved?

**34.** The two frameworks shown are constructed with drinking straws and pins. The triangle is a rigid framework by the SSS property, but the quadrilateral is flexible.

Decide if the straw-and-pin frameworks shown next are rigid or flexible. It may be helpful to build the frameworks to check your reasoning.

**(a)**      **(b)**      **(c)**      **(d)**      **(e)**

## Using a Computer

**35.** In the power plant location problem of Example 12.4, suppose the town at $D$ (Davis) drops out. This leaves three towns, at $A$, $B$, and $C$, that wish to jointly build a power plant at some location $P$ serving the three communities. To minimize the cost of power lines, $P$ should be situated so the total length $PA + PB + PC$ is as small as possible. Use geometry software to duplicate the figure shown here. Use the **Calculate** . . . command found under the Measure menu to compute $PA + PB + PC$. Drag point $P$ and watch the sum change to determine what seems to be the best position for point $P$.

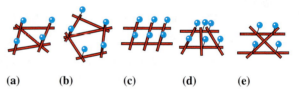

**(a)** Describe the optimal location of $P$ by considering two types of triangles:

  **(i)** At one of its vertices, $\triangle ABC$ has an angle measuring at least $120°$.

  **(ii)** No angle of $\triangle ABC$ has measure larger than $120°$. In this case, describe the location of $P$ by measuring the three angles at $P$ made by the segments joining $P$ to $A$, $B$, and $C$.

**(b)** (*For more advanced software users*) Construct an outward-pointing equilateral triangle on each of the three sides of $\triangle ABC$ considered in part a (ii). Next, construct the center of each equilateral triangle and the circle through the end-points of the corresponding side of △ABC. In the figure shown, all three equilateral triangles and two of the circles are constructed. After constructing the third circle, see if you now know how to locate the power plant serving the towns at *A*, *B*, and *C*.

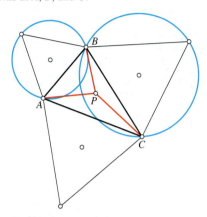

36. Construct a circle and label its center *O*. Next, construct three points *A*, *B*, and *P* on the circle, and draw two angles ∠*AOB* and ∠*APB* that both intercept the arc of the circle between *A* and *B*.

    (a) Measure ∠*AOB* and ∠*APB*. What relationship do you observe? Move *P* around the circle and investigate what happens to the measure of ∠*APB*.

    (b) Make a conjecture that relates the measures of ∠*AOB* and ∠*APB*.

    (c) Justify your conjecture. (*Hint:* Draw the diameter through *P* and then mimic the proof of Thales' theorem. There are two cases to consider, depending on whether *A* and *B* are on opposite sides of the diameter through *P* or are on the same side.)

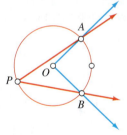

37. Draw a circle. Next, construct four points *A*, *B*, *C*, and *D* on the circle that are joined by line segments to form the inscribed quadrilateral *ABCD*.

    (a) Measure ∠*A* and ∠*C*. What relationship do you observe? Move some of the points of your quadrilateral, and see if the relationship between ∠*A* and ∠*C* is preserved.

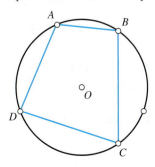

(b) Make a conjecture concerning the relationship of opposite angles of an inscribed quadrilateral.

(c) Justify your conjecture. (*Hint:* Draw the radii $\overline{OA}$, $\overline{OB}$, $\overline{OC}$, and $\overline{OD}$. This creates four isosceles triangles.)

## From State Student Assessments

38. (Massachusetts, Grade 5)
    Which of the following pairs of quadrilaterals appear to be congruent?

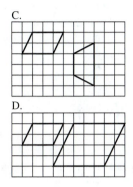

39. (Colorado, Grade 5)
    Your teacher told you in class today that the square shown is divided into eight congruent triangles. After you got home your best friend called and said he did not know what that meant. What would you say to your friend to help him out?

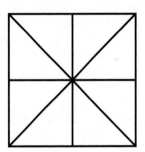

40. (Illinois, Grade 5)
    Which tangram pieces are congruent triangles?

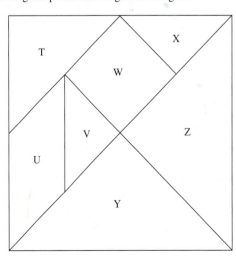

    **A.** T and W    **B.** T and Z    **C.** U and X
    **D.** V and X    **E.** X and Y

**41.** (Michigan, Grade 7)
The figures shown below are congruent.

Which is true about their corresponding sides and corresponding angles?

**A.** The corresponding angle measures are equal, but not the corresponding side lengths.

**B.** The corresponding side lengths are equal, but not the corresponding angle measures.

**C.** The corresponding angle measures and corresponding side lengths are not equal.

**D.** The corresponding angle measures and the corresponding side lengths are equal.

**42.** (Illinois, Grade 6)
Which figure does *not* appear to contain two or more congruent shapes?

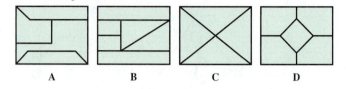

A      B      C      D

## 12.2 Constructing Geometric Figures

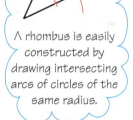

*A rhombus is easily constructed by drawing intersecting arcs of circles of the same radius.*

In the last section, two basic constructions were described:

* Construction 1      Construct a line segment congruent to a given segment.
* Construction 2      Construct an angle congruent to a given angle.

Since only the straightedge and compass were used, these are examples of Euclidean constructions. In this section, we describe a number of other Euclidean constructions and explore some related applications and theorems. In addition, we investigate constructions with the Mira and by paper folding. The constructions shown in the examples and called for in the problems can also be done with geometry software.

To be certain that a construction results in a figure that has a desired property, a proof of the validity of the construction must be given. For example, Construction 2 of a congruent angle is a consequence of the SSS property. Many constructions can be verified by appealing to the properties of a rhombus listed in Figure 12.6.

**FIGURE 12.6**
The rhombus *ABCD* has many useful properties:

* The diagonals are angle bisectors.
* The diagonals are perpendicular.
* The diagonals intersect at their common midpoint *M*.
* The sides are all congruent to one another.
* The opposite sides are parallel.

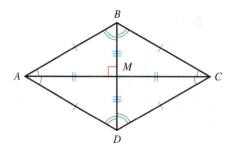

### Constructing Parallel and Perpendicular Lines

If *l* is a given line and *P* is a given point not on *l*, it is useful to know how to construct the line through *P* that is either parallel or perpendicular to *l*. There are alternative procedures that can be devised, and it is interesting to invent some of your own. The following constructions each take advantage of the properties of a rhombus:

**CONSTRUCTION 3**   **Construct a Line Parallel to a Given Line**

Given point $P$ and line $l$ as shown, construct a line through $P$ that is parallel to $l$.

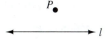

**Procedure**

| | | | |
|---|---|---|---|
| 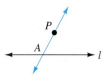 | 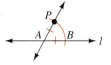 | 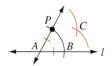 | 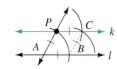 |
| **Step 1** | **Step 2** | **Step 3** | **Step 4** |
| Construct any line through $P$ that intersects $l$ at a point labeled $A$. | Construct an arc through $P$ centered at $A$, and let $B$ denote the intersection of the arc with $l$. | With the same radius $AB$, construct arcs with centers at $P$ and $B$; let $C$ be the intersection of the two arcs. | Construct the line $k = \overleftrightarrow{PC}$; since $ABCP$ is a rhombus, its opposite sides are parallel, so $k \parallel l$. |

**CONSTRUCTION 4**   **Construct a Line Perpendicular to a Given Line**
**Through a Point Not on the Given Line**

Given line $l$ and point $P$ not on $l$ as shown, construct a line through $P$ that is perpendicular to $l$.

$P_{\bullet}$

$\longleftrightarrow l$

**Procedure**

| | | |
|---|---|---|
| 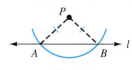 | 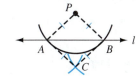 | 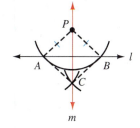 |
| **Step 1** | **Step 2** | **Step 3** |
| Construct an arc at $P$ that intersects $l$ at two points $A$ and $B$. | With the compass still at radius $AP$, construct arcs at $A$ and $B$ and let $C$ be their point of intersection. | Construct the line $\overleftrightarrow{PC}$; since $\overline{PC}$ is a diagonal of rhombus $ABPC$, it is perpendicular to $\overline{AB}$. |

The construction of perpendicular lines has several applications:

- **Nearest point $F$ on a line $l$ from a point $P$.** The line through $P$ that is perpendicular to line $l$ intersects $l$ at the point $F$ of $l$ that is closest to $P$ (Why? Use the triangle inequality). $F$ is called the **foot** of the perpendicular line from $P$, and $PF$ is called the **distance from $P$ to $l$.**
- **Point of reflection $P'$ of $P$ across mirror line $l$.** The point $P'$ on the perpendicular to $l$ through $P$ for which $PF = P'F$, where $F$ is the point of intersection of $l$ and the perpendicular through $P$, is called the **point of reflection of $P$ across $l$.**

- **Altitudes of a triangle.** The line through vertex *A* of triangle *ABC* that is perpendicular to the opposite side $\overline{BC}$ is called an **altitude** of the triangle. The distance from *A* to the line containing side $\overline{BC}$ is the **height** of the triangle when $\overline{BC}$ is considered to be the base of the triangle. Often, the word *altitude* is used to mean the height of a triangle.

These applications are illustrated in Figure 12.7.

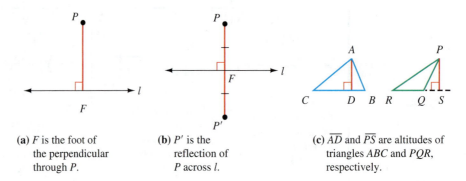

**(a)** *F* is the foot of the perpendicular through *P*.

**(b)** *P′* is the reflection of *P* across *l*.

**(c)** $\overline{AD}$ and $\overline{PS}$ are altitudes of triangles *ABC* and *PQR*, respectively.

If point *P* lies on line *l*, a small modification in the second step of the previous procedure is required to construct the line perpendicular to *l* at *P*.

---

**CONSTRUCTION 5**   **Construct the Line Perpendicular to a Given Line Through a Point on the Given Line**

Given line *l* and point *P* on *l* as shown, construct the line through *P* perpendicular to *l*.

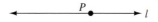

**Procedure**

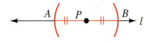

**Step 1**

Construct two arcs of equal radius centered at *P*; let *A* and *B* be their points of intersection with *l*.

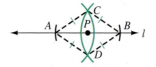

**Step 2**

Construct arcs centered at *A* and *B* with a radius *greater* than *AP*; let *C* and *D* be their points of intersection.

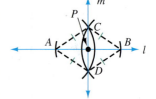

**Step 3**

Construct line $m = \overleftrightarrow{CD}$; since $\overline{CD}$ is a diagonal of the rhombus *ADBC* and *P* is the midpoint of diagonal $\overline{AB}$, *m* passes through *P* and is perpendicular to $l = \overleftrightarrow{AB}$; that is, *m* is perpendicular to *l*.

---

## Constructing the Midpoint and Perpendicular Bisector of a Line Segment

The line perpendicular to a segment at its midpoint is called the **perpendicular bisector** of the segment. The following construction is also justified by properties of the rhombus:

**CONSTRUCTION 6**    **Construct the Midpoint and Perpendicular Bisector of a Line Segment**

Construct the midpoint and perpendicular bisector of the segment $\overline{AB}$ shown.

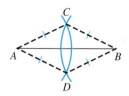

**Procedure**

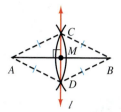

**Step 1**

Construct arcs of the same radius centered at $A$ and $B$ and intersecting in points $C$ and $D$.

**Step 2**

Construct the line $\overleftrightarrow{CD}$. Since $ADBC$ is a rhombus, $\overleftrightarrow{CD}$ intersects $\overline{AB}$ at a right angle at the midpoint $M$ of $\overline{AB}$.

The midpoint of a line segment $M$ is the same distance from $A$ and $B$. Indeed, every point $P$ of the perpendicular bisector of a segment $\overline{AB}$ is equidistant from the endpoints of the segment. That is, $PA = PB$. We state and prove this property next.

**THEOREM** *Equidistance Property of the Perpendicular Bisector*

A point lies on the perpendicular bisector of a line segment if, and only if, the point is equidistant from the endpoints of the segment.

**PROOF**    Let $l$ be the perpendicular bisector of segment $\overline{AB}$. Thus, $l$ intersects $\overline{AB}$ at right angles at the midpoint $M$, as shown on the left side of the diagram that follows. Let $P$ be any point on $l$. By the SAS property, $\triangle PMA \cong \triangle PMB$. This means that the corresponding sides $\overline{PA}$ and $\overline{PB}$ are congruent. Hence, $PA = PB$, as claimed.

The proof of the converse—that if a point $P$ is equidistant from points $A$ and $B$, then $P$ lies on the perpendicular bisector of $\overline{AB}$—is similar. (See problem 30 of Problem Set 12.2.)

**EXAMPLE 12.8** **Locating an Airport**

The Tri-Cities Airport Authority wishes to locate a new airport to serve its three cities, situated at $A$, $B$, and $C$ as shown. If possible, it would like a site $P$ that is the same distance from $A$, $B$, and $C$. How can $P$ be located?

$A$
$\bullet$

$\bullet$ $C$

$\bullet$
$B$

**Solution**   To be equidistant from *A* and *B*, *P* must be on the perpendicular bisector of the segment $\overline{AB}$. Similarly, *P* must be on the perpendicular bisector of $\overline{BC}$. Since *A*, *B*, and *C* are not collinear, the perpendicular bisectors to $\overline{AB}$ and $\overline{BC}$ are not parallel and we can choose *P* as their point of intersection. Since *PA* = *PB* and *PB* = *PC*, we have *PA* = *PC*. Therefore, *P* is also equidistant from *A* and *C*, so *P* is also on the perpendicular bisector of $\overline{AC}$. Thus, *P* is equidistant from *A*, *B*, and *C*, as desired.

Point *P* is the center of a unique circle containing *A*, *B*, and *C* as shown in Figure 12.8. The circle is called the **circumscribed circle** of △*ABC*, and *P* is called the **circumcenter** of △*ABC*. Frequently, the circumscribing circle is called the **circumcircle** of the triangle.

**FIGURE 12.8**
The perpendicular bisectors of the sides of △*ABC* are concurrent at a point *P* equidistant from *A*, *B*, and *C*. Point *P* is the center of the circumscribing circle of △*ABC*.

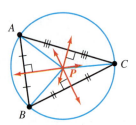

**THEOREM   *The Circumscribed Circle of a Triangle***
The perpendicular bisectors of a triangle *ABC* are concurrent at a point *P* (the *circumcenter* of the triangle) that is the center of a unique circle (the *circumscribed circle*) that passes through the three vertices *A*, *B*, and *C* of the triangle.

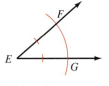

**FIGURE 12.9**
$\overrightarrow{BD}$ is the angle bisector of ∠*ABC* if ∠*ABD* ≅ ∠*DBC*

## Constructing the Angle Bisector

Given ∠*ABC* (see Figure 12.9), we wish to construct the ray $\overrightarrow{BD}$ that forms congruent angles with the sides $\overrightarrow{BA}$ and $\overrightarrow{BC}$. If ∠*ABD* ≅ ∠*CBD*, then $\overrightarrow{BD}$ is the **angle bisector** of ∠*ABC*.

Once again, the properties of a rhombus justify the following construction:

**CONSTRUCTION 7   Construct the Angle Bisector**

Construct the angle bisector of ∠*E* shown.

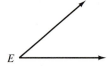

**Procedure**

| 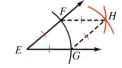 | 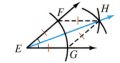 | |
|---|---|---|
| **Step 1** | **Step 2** | **Step 3** |
| Construct an arc centered at *E*; let *F* and *G* denote the points at which the arc intersects the sides of ∠*E*. | Construct arcs, centered at *F* and *G*, of radius *EF*. Let *H* be the point of intersection of the two arcs. | Construct the ray $\overrightarrow{EH}$. Since the diagonal $\overline{EH}$ forms congruent angles with the sides $\overline{EG}$ and $\overline{EF}$ of the rhombus *EGHF*, $\overrightarrow{EH}$ is the angle bisector of ∠*E*. |

The following theorem gives a condition that states exactly when points lie on the angle bisector:

**THEOREM   *Equidistance Property of the Angle Bisector***
A point lies on the bisector of an angle if, and only if, the point is equidistant from the sides of the angle.

**PROOF**   Let *P* be any point on the bisector of ∠*A* as shown. Let *F* and *F′* be the feet of the perpendiculars from *P* to the sides of ∠*A*.

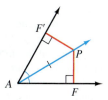

By the AAS congruence property, △*PAF* ≅ △*PAF′*. Therefore, *PF* = *PF′*. The proof of the converse is similar: It must be shown that if *P* is equidistant from the sides of ∠*A*, then $\overrightarrow{AP}$ bisects the angle. Details are left to the reader.

By mimicking the solution of the airport problem in Example 12.8, it can be shown that the bisectors of the interior angles of a triangle are concurrent at the point *I* that is equidistant from three sides of the triangle. (See Figure 12.10.) Point *I*, called the **incenter** of △*ABC*, is the center of the **inscribed circle,** or **incircle,** of △*ABC*. The inscribed circle is tangent to all three sides of △*ABC*.

**FIGURE 12.10**
The bisectors of the interior angles of a triangle are concurrent at a point *I* equidistant from the sides of the triangle. *I* is the center of the inscribed circle of the triangle, which is tangent to the sides of the triangle at points *D*, *E*, and *F*.

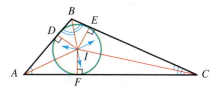

**THEOREM**   *The Inscribed Circle of a Triangle*
The angle bisectors of a triangle *ABC* are concurrent at a point *I* (the *incenter* of the triangle) that is the center of a unique circle (the *inscribed circle* or *incircle*) that is tangent to the three sides $\overline{AB}$, $\overline{BC}$, and $\overline{AC}$.

## Into the Classroom

### Constructions in Space

Constructions using a compass and a straightedge produce figures that are confined to a sheet of paper. Interest and excitement can also be generated by constructing figures in space, using sticks, brass fasteners, paper clips, string, cut paper, multilink cubes, polyhedrons, straws, or indeed whatever is available. Such figures can be held and felt, literally giving students a feel for shape. In some cases, the shapes can be bent or flexed to give a dynamic liveliness to figures that would remain of lesser interest when only drawn on a sheet of paper.

Books, pamphlets, and journals published by the National Council of Teachers of Mathematics and other publishing companies provide the teacher with a wide variety of ideas and resources for three-dimensional constructions and related activities. Every teacher will want to gather a personal collection of favorite hands-on constructions suitable for his or her classroom. Here are two suggestions for constructions to do in the classroom:

- **Hinged polygons.** Strips of card stock can be joined with brass fasteners through holes at the ends of each strip. Any triangle is rigid, demonstrating the SSS congruence property. Any quadrilateral, however, is flexible. As the quadrilateral flexes, the sum of the angle measures remains at 360°, as can be checked with a protractor.

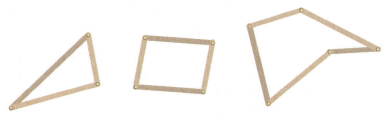

- **Space polygons and polyhedra.** Thin wooden sticks, say, from a "pick-up-sticks" game, or straws can be cut to differing lengths and joined by short pieces of rubber tubing at their endpoints. More than two sticks can meet at a single vertex by inserting a length (or several lengths) of tubing through a hole punched sideways through another section of tubing. It is easy to form quadrilaterals that flex in space, and joining the midpoints of the four sides by elastic bands shows that a parallelogram is always formed. Properties of cubes, tetrahedra, and other polyhedra can also be explored with easily constructed skeletal models.

## Constructing Regular Polygons

A square is easily constructed with compass and straightedge. For example, construct two perpendicular lines and a circle centered at the point of intersection, as shown in Figure 12.11(a).

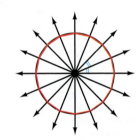

(a) Square   (b) Regular octagon   (c) Regular 16-gon

By constructing angle bisectors from the center of a square, the eight vertices of a regular octagon are constructed. Angle bisectors of the octagon's central angles can then be constructed as in Figure 12.11(b) to yield the regular 16-gon of part (c) of the figure. When the vertices of a polygon all lie on a given circle, the polygon is called an **inscribed polygon.**

A regular hexagon is particularly easy to inscribe in a given circle with a compass and straightedge: Pick any point $A$ on the circumference of the circle centered at $O$, and then successively strike arcs of radius $OA$ around the circle to locate $B$, $C$, $D$, $E$, and $F$. The hexagon $ABCDEF$ is regular, since joining the sides to the center $O$ forms six congruent equilateral triangles: $OAB$, $OBC$, . . . , and $OFA$. On the one hand, as shown in Figure 12.12, connecting every other vertex gives a construction of the inscribed equilateral triangle $ACE$. On the other hand, constructing angle bisectors of the central angles of the hexagon produces an inscribed regular dodecagon.

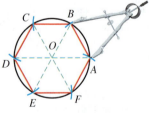
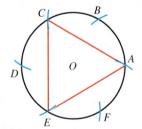
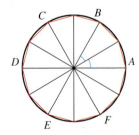

(a) Inscribed regular hexagon   (b) Inscribed equilateral triangle   (c) Inscribed regular dodecagon

A compass-and-straightedge construction of a regular pentagon requires more ingenuity. (One method is outlined in problem 21 of Problem Set 12.2 at the end of this section.)

The ancient Greek geometers knew how to construct the regular polygons shown so far. They also knew that the regular 15-gon can be constructed with compass and straightedge. (The construction is outlined in problem 33 in Problem Set 2.2.) For over 2000 years, the only regular polygons known to be constructible with compass and straightedge were the ones contained in Book IV of Euclid's *Elements*: the regular 3-, 4-, 5-, and 15-gons and, by angle bisection, the regular polygons obtained by successively doubling the number of sides.

On March 30, 1796, one month before his 19th birthday, Carl Friedrich Gauss (1777–1855) entered into a notebook his discovery that a number of other regular polygons were constructible, including the 17-gon, the 257-gon, and the 65,537-gon. The numbers 3, 5, 17, 257, and 65,537 are prime numbers of the special form $F_k = 2^{2^k} + 1$, where $k$ is a nonnegative integer. For example, $F_0 = 2^{2^0} + 1 = 2^1 + 1 = 3, F_1 = 2^{2^1} + 1 = 2^2 + 1 = 4 + 1 = 5$, and so on. Numbers of this form had been studied earlier by Pierre de Fermat (1601–1665), and prime numbers of the form $2^{2^k} + 1$ are known as **Fermat primes.**

Following is the remarkable theorem of Gauss. The proof of the "only if" part of the theorem is due to Pierre Wantzel (1814–1848).

> **THEOREM**   *The Gauss–Wantzel Constructibility Theorem*
> A regular polygon of $n$ sides is constructible with compass and straightedge if, and only if, $n$ is
>
> **1.** 4, or
> **2.** a Fermat prime, or
> **3.** a product of distinct Fermat primes, or
> **4.** a power-of-2 multiple of a number that is one of the preceding types 1, 2, or 3.

For example, the regular heptagon is not constructible, since 7 is not a prime number of the form $2^{2^k} + 1$. Nor is a regular nonagon (9-gon) constructible, since 9 has two factors of 3. However, a regular polygon of $1020 = 2^2 \cdot 3 \cdot 5 \cdot 17$ sides is constructible, since its odd prime factors are distinct Fermat primes.

Fermat believed that all numbers of the form $F_k = 2^{2^k} + 1$ were prime, but Euler proved this assertion to be false by showing that $F_5 = 2^{2^5} + 1$ is composite; in fact, $F_5 = 4,294,967,297 = (641) \cdot (6,700,417)$. Likewise, $F_6, F_7, \ldots, F_{32}$ are now known to be composite. It is generally believed, though not proved, that there are only five Fermat primes, namely, 3, 5, 17, 257, and 65,537.

## Highlight from History
## Three Impossible Construction Problems

The straightedge allows us to draw a line of indefinite length through any two given points, and the compass* allows us to draw a circle with a given point as its center and passing through any given distinct second point. It then becomes a challenge to find procedures to construct a figure with the use of only these simple tools. Many important contributions to geometry were inspired by attempts to solve the following famous problems, each of which arose in antiquity:

**1.** *The trisection of an angle:* Divide an arbitrary given angle into three congruent angles.

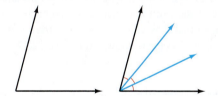

**2.** *The duplication of the cube:* Given a cube, construct a cube with twice the volume.

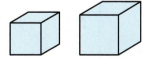

**3.** *The squaring of the circle:* Given a circle, construct a square of the same area as the circle.

Extensive efforts for over 2000 years failed to solve any of these problems. It was not until the early 1800s that it was shown that these problems were impossible to solve when only the unmarked straightedge and compass were allowed. It is interesting to note that methods of algebra were used to prove the impossibility of these geometric constructions.

*The usage "the compass" is common, but some texts and authors still prefer "compasses" or even "a pair of compasses."

## Mira™ and Paper-Folding Constructions

Figure 12.13 shows a Mira, which was used in Chapter 11 to construct images under reflection and to investigate lines of symmetry. The Mira can also be used to construct perpendicular lines, midpoints, angle bisectors, and other geometrical objects. With a little practice, constructions with a Mira are quick and yet very accurate.

**FIGURE 12.13**
The Mira and its use in
three basic constructions

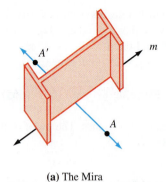

**(a)** The Mira

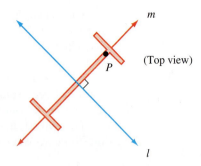

(Top view)

**(b)** Pivot the Mira about *P* until line *l*
coincides with its reflection to construct the
line *m* through *P* that is perpendicular to *l*.

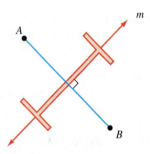

**(c)** When the reflection
of *B* coincides with *A*,
the drawing edge of the
Mira determines the
perpendicular bisector
of $\overline{AB}$.

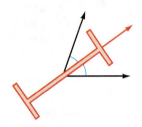

**(d)** Pivot the Mira about the
vertex until the reflection
of the near side coincides
with the far side to construct
the angle bisector.

Mira constructions can usually be converted into equivalent paper-folding procedures, in which the drawing line of the Mira is replaced by the crease line of a fold. It is helpful to draw lines and points very dark so that they can be seen from the reverse side of the paper. A folding construction of the perpendicular bisector is shown in Figure 12.14.

**FIGURE 12.14**
Folding point *A* onto point
*B* forms a crease that is the
perpendicular bisector of
$\overline{AB}$

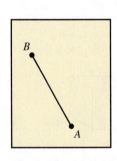
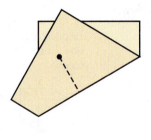
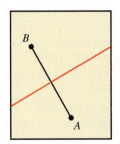

## Constructions with Geometry Software

Constructions made with tangible materials—paper, dowels, rubber bands, and so on—continue to have an important role to play in teaching and learning the principles of geometry. However, increasingly, classrooms are also taking advantage of the computer. Geometry software, as described in Appendix C, allows figures to be constructed on the screen, colored, manipulated, explored with measurement tools, and printed out for display and further investigation. The spirally tiled regular hexagon shown in Figure 12.15 is tedious to construct with compass and straightedge, but enjoyable to create with *The Geometer's Sketchpad*.

**FIGURE 12.15**
A figure constructed with geometry software

**FROM The NCTM Principles and Standards**

Students in grades 3–5 should examine the properties of two- and three-dimensional shapes and the relationships among shapes. They should be encouraged to reason about these properties by using spatial relationships. For instance, they might reason about the area of a triangle by visualizing its relationship to a corresponding rectangle or other corresponding parallelogram. In addition to studying physical models of these geometric shapes, they should also develop and use mental images. Students at this age are ready to mentally manipulate shapes, and they can benefit from experiences that challenge them and that can also be verified physically. For example, "Draw a star in the upper right-hand corner of a piece of paper. If you flip the paper horizontally and then turn it 180°, where will the star be?"

Much of the work students do with three-dimensional shapes involves visualization. By representing three-dimensional shapes in two dimensions and constructing three-dimensional shapes from two-dimensional representations, students learn about the characteristics of shapes.

Students should become experienced in using a variety of representations for three-dimensional shapes, for example, making a freehand drawing of a cylinder or cone or constructing a building out of cubes from a set of views (i.e., front, top, and side) like those shown in Figure 12.16 below.

SOURCE: *Principles and Standards for School Mathematics* by NCTM, *pages 168–169. Copyright © 2000 by the National Council of Teachers of Mathematics. Reproduced with permission of the National Council of Teachers of Mathematics via Copyright Clearance Center. NCTM does not endorse the content or validity of these alignments.*

**FIGURE 12.16**
Make a building out of 10 cubes by looking at the three pictures of it.

Front view  Top view  Right-side view

## Problem Set 12.2

Exercises numbered in red are answered in the back of the text.

### Understanding Concepts

**1.** The following sequence of steps outlines the "corresponding angles" construction to draw a line $k$ that is parallel to a line $l$ and passes through a point $P$ not on $l$:

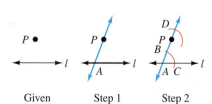

Given  Step 1  Step 2

Step 3  Step 4

**(a)** Give a written description of each of the four steps.

**(b)** Explain why the construction gives the desired line $k$.

**2. (a)** Describe, in words and drawings, a Mira construction that gives the line $k$ parallel to a line $l$ and passing through a point $P$ not on $l$.

**(b)** Answer part (a), but use paper folding instead of the Mira.

**3.** The drafting triangle and straightedge can be used to construct parallel lines as follows:

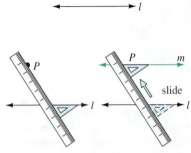

   **(a)** What geometric principle justifies this construction?

   **(b)** Describe, in words and drawings, a procedure using a straightedge and drafting triangle to construct the line *m* perpendicular to a given line *l* and passing through a given point *P*.

**4.** Practice your compass-and-straightedge skills by completing the constructions that follow. First redraw the given figure on your own sheet of paper.

   **(a)** Line perpendicular to *l* through *P*

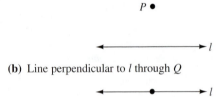

   **(b)** Line perpendicular to *l* through *Q*

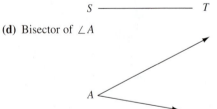

   **(c)** Perpendicular bisector of $\overline{ST}$

   S ——————— T

   **(d)** Bisector of ∠*A*

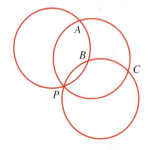

**5.** Repeat the constructions in problem 4 with a Mira (if available).

**6.** Repeat the constructions in problem 4 with paper folding.

**7.** Use a jar lid (or other handy circular object) to draw three congruent circles through a common point *P*. Let *A*, *B*, and *C* denote the three points of intersection of pairs of your circles other than *P*. Now use the jar lid to discover something amazing about the circumscribing circle of △*ABC*.

**8.** Construct an angle *ABC* and a point *T* on side $\overrightarrow{BA}$. Show, in words and drawings, how to construct a circle that is tangent to both sides of the angle, with *T* as one of the points of tangency.

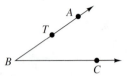

**9.** Construct the circumcenters and circumscribing circles of triangles of the three types shown. Use any tools you wish to draw the perpendicular bisectors of the sides of the triangles.

   **(a)** Acute triangle

   **(b)** Right triangle

   **(c)** Obtuse triangle

   **(d)** For each case, make a conjecture about where—inside, on, or outside the triangle—the circumcenter will be located.

**10.** Construct the incenters and inscribed circles of the three types of triangles shown in problem 9, using

   **(a)** a compass and straightedge.

   **(b)** a Mira (if available) and compass.

   **(c)** paper folding and compass (copy and cut the triangles from paper with scissors, and then fold).

**11.** Construct two circles that intersect at a point *P*, and then construct a line through *P*. Let *A* and *B* denote the points at which the line intersects the circles. Next, construct any point *C* not on the line or circles, together with the lines $\overleftrightarrow{AC}$ and $\overleftrightarrow{BC}$. Let the points at which these lines intersect the respective circles be labeled *Q* and *R* as shown below. Finally, construct the circumscribing circle of triangle *CQR*. What is interesting about the three circles in your construction?

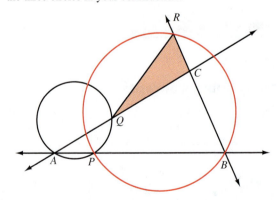

**12.** Construct a triangle *ABC* and also its incenter *I* and the points of tangency $T_1$ and $T_2$ of the incircle to sides $\overline{AC}$ and $\overline{BC}$, respectively. Next, construct the line $\overleftrightarrow{AI}$ and the perpendicular to $\overleftrightarrow{AI}$ through point *B*. What do you find unexpected in your construction?

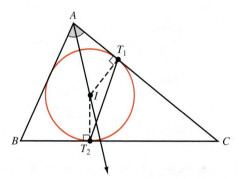

**13.** A point $P$ is exterior to a circle centered at $Q$. Use Thales' theorem to justify why drawing the circle with diameter $\overline{PQ}$ gives a construction of the two lines $\overleftrightarrow{PS}$ and $\overleftrightarrow{PT}$ that are tangent to the circle centered at $Q$.

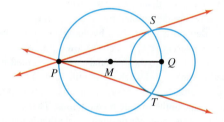

**14.** **(a)** Use any drawing tools you wish to construct the altitudes of the three types of triangles in problem 9.

 **(b)** Make a conjecture about the three altitudes of an acute triangle.

 **(c)** Make a conjecture about the three altitudes of a right triangle.

 **(d)** Make a conjecture about the three lines containing the altitudes of an obtuse triangle.

**15.** Justify the following construction of an equilateral triangle inscribed in a given circle:

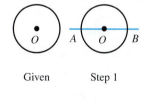

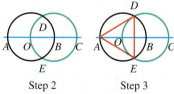

**16.** A **median** of a triangle is a line segment from a vertex to the midpoint of the opposite side. Using any drawing tools you wish, draw the three medians in each of several triangles. Give a statement that describes what you observe.

**17.** Let the lines $k$ and $l$ intersect to form two pairs of vertical angles. Prove that the lines $m$ and $n$ that bisect the vertical angles are perpendicular.

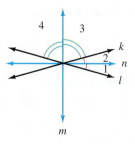

**18.** **(a)** Prove that the perpendicular bisector of any chord of a circle contains the center of the circle.

 **(b)** Trace partway around a cup or saucer to draw a circular arc. Then explain how to construct the center of the arc. (*Hint:* Use part (a) twice!)

 **(c)** The three congruent circles shown are centered at points $A$, $B$, and $C$ on the large circular arc, and the circles at centers $A$ and $C$ contain point $B$. Where do the dashed lines intersect? Explain why.

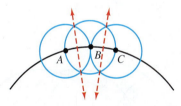

**19.** The following diagram shows Euclid's construction of an equilateral triangle $ABC$ on a given line segment $\overline{AB}$, using a compass and straightedge:

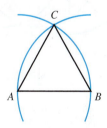

Give careful, step-by-step instructions to construct these polygons erected on a given side $\overline{AB}$:

 **(a)** A square      **(b)** A regular hexagon

**20.** Reflecting point $B$ to fall on the perpendicular bisector of $\overline{AB}$ shows how a Mira can be used to draw an equilateral triangle $ABC$ on a given side $\overline{AB}$.

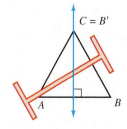

Give careful step-by-step instructions to construct these polygons on a given side with a Mira:

(a) A square  (b) A regular hexagon

21. (a) Construct a regular pentagon inscribed in a circle by following the steps outlined next.

(b) Use a ruler and protractor to check that *PENTA* is regular.

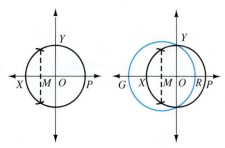

Construct perpendicular diameters to circle, and construct midpoint *M* of radius $\overline{OX}$.

Construct circle with center *M* and radius *MY*; this circle intersects $\overrightarrow{XP}$ at *G* and *R*.

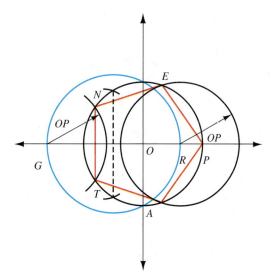

Construct circles at *G* and *R* of radius *OP* to locate the vertices of the regular pentagon *PENTA*.

22. (a) Construct a heptagon inscribed in a given circle below following the steps outlined:

Construct a radius $\overline{AB}$.

Construct an arc at *B* through *A* and then draw chord $\overline{CD}$.

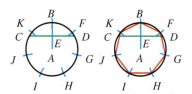

Lay off arcs of radius *DE*, starting at *B*.

Construct the heptagon *BFGHIJK*.

(b) Is it possible for *BFGHIJK* to be a regular heptagon, or is it just a close approximation?

23. List the constructible regular *n*-gons up to $n = 100$, using the Gauss–Wantzel theorem.

## Teaching Concepts

24. Design an activity that investigates which properties of a quadrilateral are determined by how their diagonals intersect. Since students often learn best by doing a constructive activity, use a constructive approach (following an idea of John Van DeWalle), where the diagonals are represented with punched strips of card stock (or manila folder) as shown. The holes are regularly spaced (say, 1″ apart), with an odd number of holes to make the middle hole obvious. Two strips are joined by a brass fastener through a hole that is the point of intersection of the two diagonals. For example, the red quadrilateral shown at the right is constructed with diagonals of different length meeting at their midpoints at a right angle.

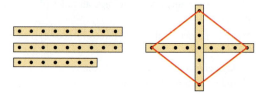

Your activity should investigate how to choose and align diagonals to construct a parallelogram, a rhombus, a square, a kite, and both types of trapezoids—isosceles and nonisosceles.

## Responding to Students

25. Waun was asked to construct a regular pentagon and drew the following figure:

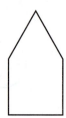

(a) What misunderstanding does Waun have of regular polygons?

(b) What advice can Waun be given about checking if a polygon is regular or not?

26. Kerry has created a new construction for the line through point *P* and perpendicular to line *k*, where *P* is not on *k*. As shown in the given figure, construct two circles through *P*

centered at two distinct points *A* and *B* on *k*. If *Q* is the second point of intersection of the circles, then $\overleftrightarrow{PQ}$ is the required perpendicular line. Write a response to Kerry. In particular, if the construction is incorrect, explain why. If it is correct, guide Kerry through a proof that justifies the construction.

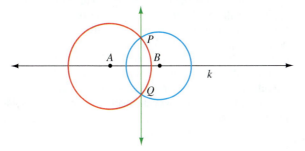

27. Someone claims that trisecting the chord $\overline{BC}$ of an arc centered at *A* gives a compass-and-straightedge trisection of ∠*A*. How would you respond to this assertion? How well does the method appear to work on an angle of measure 150°? Make a drawing and use a protractor to measure the angles.

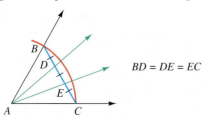

$BD = DE = EC$

28. Leanne believes that she has constructed a triangle *ABQ* with two right angles. Her construction is shown here. Draw two circles that intersect at *P* and *Q*, and then draw their two diameters $\overline{QR}$ and $\overline{QS}$. Let $\overline{RS}$ intersect the circles at *A* and *B*. Then ∠*QBR* and ∠*QAS* are both right angles by Thales' theorem. Thus, △*QAB* has two right angles. How would you respond to Leanne's assertion?

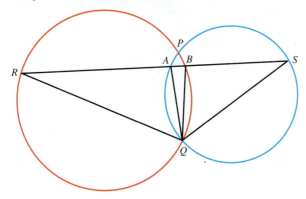

## Thinking Critically

29. Trace the following segment $\overline{AB}$ and line *l*:

(a) Construct *all* points *C* on line *l* for which triangle *ABC* is isosceles.

(b) Construct *all* points *D* on line *l* for which triangle *ABD* is a right triangle.

30. Complete the proof of the equidistance property of the perpendicular bisector. Do so by showing that if *P* is equidistant from *A* and *B*, then the line $\overleftrightarrow{PM}$ containing *P* and the midpoint *M* of $\overline{AB}$ is the perpendicular bisector of $\overline{AB}$.

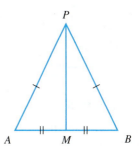

31. Prove that the angle bisectors of a triangle are concurrent, using the equidistance property of the angle bisector. The discussion in Example 12.8 can be used as a model for your proof.

32. An **altitude** of a triangle is a line through a vertex of the triangle that is perpendicular to the line containing the opposite side of the triangle. The altitude through vertex *A* has been constructed in this figure:

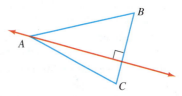

(a) Construct any triangle *ABC* and all three of its altitudes. What property do you discover about the altitudes of a triangle?

(b) Construct three congruent copies of △*ABC* on its sides to form △*PQR*, as shown. It becomes apparent that the altitudes of △*ABC* are simultaneously the perpendicular bisectors of the sides of △*PQR*. Use this fact to explain why the altitudes of any triangle are concurrent. The common point of intersection of altitudes is called the **orthocenter** of the triangle.

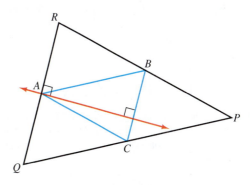

33. A regular pentagon *PENTA* and an equilateral triangle *PQR* are both inscribed in the same circle centered at *O*, with *P* a common vertex. Calculate *m*(∠*NOQ*), and explain why laying segments off of length *QN* about the circle constructs a regular inscribed 15-gon.

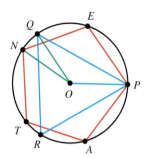

## Thinking Cooperatively

The following paper-folding constructions are enjoyable group activities. Each collaborative group needs several sheets of blank paper (origami squares or patty paper work well), scissors, ruler, protractor, and colored pencils.

**34. Folding Special Points in a Triangle.** Cut out several paper triangles with scissors. Discuss procedures to use in folding to construct the following points and segments:

**(a)** The midpoints of the sides of the triangle.

**(b)** The medians (the segments connecting a vertex to the midpoint of the opposite side). What property do you observe is satisfied by the three medians?

**(c)** The angle bisectors of a triangle. What special point of the triangle is constructed with the folds?

**(d)** The perpendicular bisectors of the sides of an acute triangle. What special point is constructed with these folds?

**(e)** The altitudes of an acute triangle. (An altitude is a line through a vertex and that is perpendicular to the opposite side.) What special point is constructed with these folds?

**35. Folding Regular Polygons.** A square can be folded from a rectangular sheet of paper by following the procedures illustrated in this sequence of steps:

Discuss procedures and give demonstrations to construct these regular polygons with paper folding:

**(a)** An equilateral triangle. Carefully describe the sequence of folds you make.

**(b)** A regular hexagon, starting with the equilateral triangle cut from your construction in part (a). (*Suggestion:* First, use folding to construct the center of the equilateral triangle.)

**(c)** A regular octagon, starting with a square. Carefully describe the folds you make.

**36.** To construct a point equidistant from the edges of a board, a carpenter will lay a ruler diagonally across the board, turning the ruler until even numbers touch opposite edges of the board. The point along the ruler with the average value of the end values is marked. For example, with the 2″ and 8″ marks aligned at the edges of the board, the point at the 5″ mark of the ruler is equidistant from the edges of the board. Use congruent triangles to show why the marked point is on the midline of the board.

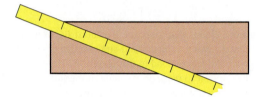

**37.** Popeye is somewhere off the coast, heading due north. At point *A*, the lighthouse at *C* is 35° off his starboard bow. After Popeye has traveled 4 miles further north, the lighthouse is 70° off the bow from point *B*. How far away is the lighthouse from point *B*? (*Hint:* What kind of a triangle *ABC* has been constructed by "doubling the angle," a common navigational technique?)

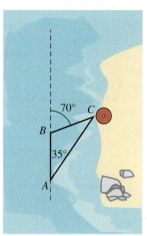

## Using a Calculator

**38.** Verify that $F_3 = 2^{2^3} + 1$ and $F_4 = 2^{2^4} + 1$ are given decimally by 257 and 65,537, respectively.

**39. (a)** Use a scientific or graphing calculator to verify that the Fermat number $F_5 = 2^{2^5} + 1$ is 4,294,967,297.

**(b)** Verify that the Fermat number $F_5 = 4,294,967,297$ is composite by computing $(641)(6,700,417)$.

## Using a Computer

**40.** Draw any triangle *ABC*. Construct the following three points: *G*, the **centroid** (intersection of the medians; see problem 16); *H*, the orthocenter (intersection of the altitudes; see problem 32); and

P, the circumcenter (intersection of the perpendicular bisectors of the sides).

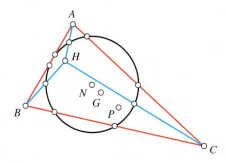

**(a)** Euler discovered an interesting fact about $G$, $H$, and $P$. What do you suppose the "Euler line" might be?

**(b)** Measure the distances $GH$ and $GP$, and then make a conjecture concerning the ratio $GH/GP$ of these distances.

**(c)** Find the midpoint $N$ of the segment $\overline{PH}$, and draw the circle centered at $N$ that passes through the midpoint of a side of your triangle. Where does the circle intersect the other sides of the triangle?

**(d)** Describe how the circle at $N$ intersects the segments $\overline{HA}$, $\overline{HB}$, and $\overline{HC}$.

**41.** Draw any triangle $ABC$. On each side, construct outward-pointing equilateral triangles $BCR$, $CAS$, and $ABT$. Also, construct the incenters $X$, $Y$, and $Z$ of the equilateral triangles.

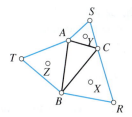

**(a)** What kind of triangle is $XYZ$? Measure lengths and angles to support your guess.

**(b)** Construct the segments $\overline{AR}$, $\overline{BS}$, and $\overline{CT}$, and show that they are concurrent at a point $F$. ($F$ is called the **Fermat point,** and in an acute triangle $ABC$ it is the point with the smallest sum $FA + FB + FC$ of distances to the vertices of $\triangle ABC$).

**(c)** At what angles do the lines drawn in part (b) intersect at $F$? Measure to verify your guess.

**(d)** Draw the segments $\overline{AX}$, $\overline{BY}$, and $\overline{CZ}$, and show that they are concurrent at a point $N$. ($N$ is called the **Napoleon point;** supposedly, it was Napoleon who discovered the theorem that you likely discovered in answering part (a).)

**(e)** Construct the circumcenter $P$ of $\triangle ABC$. What can you conjecture about the three points $F$, $N$, and $P$?

**42.** Construct three equilateral triangles that share a common vertex $A$. Let the triangles, labeled counterclockwise around their respective interiors, be $\triangle ABC$, $\triangle AB'C'$, and $\triangle AB''C''$. Draw the midpoint $T$ of $\overline{BC''}$, as shown. Similarly, draw the midpoint $R$ of $\overline{B'C}$ and the midpoint $I$ of $\overline{C'B''}$. Finally, draw the triangle $TRI$. What kind of a triangle does $TRI$ seem to be? Measure $TRI$ to check your conjecture.

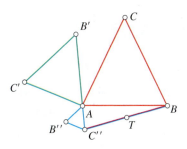

**43.** Construct a circle and the radii to four points $A$, $B$, $C$, and $D$ on the circle. Then construct perpendicular lines to the radii at $A$, $B$, $C$, and $D$. Let $Q$, $R$, $S$, and $T$ denote the points at which successive pairs of these lines intersect, giving a quadrilateral $QRST$ that is circumscribed about the circle.

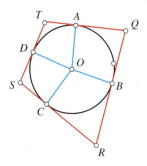

**(a)** Investigate how the sums of opposite lengths of the sides of $QRST$ compare. Make a conjecture about $QR + ST$ and $RS + TQ$.

**(b)** Use your geometry software to check that $QA = QB$, $RB = RC$, $SC = SD$, and $TD = TA$. Now prove your conjecture in part (a), using these equations.

## From State Student Assessments

**44.** (Massachusetts, Grade 4)
I have four sides. Two of my sides are parallel. My other two sides are not parallel. Draw me.

**45.** (Virginia)
Which of the following constructions is illustrated?

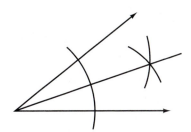

**F.** An angle congruent to a given angle

**G.** The bisector of a given angle

**H.** The bisector of a given segment

**J.** The perpendicular bisector of a given segment

### 12.3

# Similar Triangles

Two figures are **similar** if they have the same shape, but not necessarily the same size. For example, an overhead projector forms an image on the screen that is similar to the figure in the transparency. The same is true of an enlarged or reduced photocopy. Figures in space can also be similar to one another. Design engineers often build small scale models of buildings, airplanes, or ships and then make tests and measurements on the model to predict whether or not the design objectives will be met in the full–scale structure.

A map or model will indicate how its size compares with the actual size of the region mapped or object modeled by giving a **scale factor.** For example, a ship model may be scaled at $1:100$, meaning that two points at a distance $x$ on the model correspond to points on the real ship at a distance $100x$. Conversely, any length on the actual ship divided by 100 gives the corresponding length on the model.

The following definition gives an exact description of similarity for triangles:

> **DEFINITION** *Similar Triangles and the Scale Factor*
> Triangle *ABC* is **similar** to triangle *DEF*, written $\triangle ABC \sim \triangle DEF$, if, and only if, corresponding angles are congruent and the ratios of lengths of corresponding sides are all equal. That is, $\triangle ABC \sim \triangle DEF$ if, and only if, $\angle A \cong \angle D, \angle B \cong \angle E, \angle C \cong \angle F$, and
>
> $$\frac{DE}{AB} = \frac{EF}{BC} = \frac{DF}{AC}.$$
>
> The common ratio of lengths of corresponding sides is called the **scale factor** from $\triangle ABC$ to $\triangle DEF$.

This definition of similarity of triangles agrees with the definition of similarity of general figures given in Chapter 11, since, under a similarity transformation, corresponding side lengths have a common ratio and corresponding angle measures are preserved. However, the approach taken in the current section gives specific criteria for when two triangles are similar to one another. This point of view is often the more useful one for applications. For example, we will use triangle similarity to determine measurements indirectly and to derive relationships between parts of a given figure or pair of figures.

The scale factor from $\triangle DEF$ to $\triangle ABC$ is the reciprocal of the scale factor from $\triangle ABC$ to $\triangle DEF$. For example, if the sides of $\triangle DEF$ are 3 times the length of the sides of the similar triangle $ABC$, then the sides of $\triangle ABC$ are one-third the length of the sides of $\triangle DEF$.

Two examples of similar triangles and their scale factors are shown in Figure 12.17.

**FIGURE 12.17**
Two pairs of similar triangles

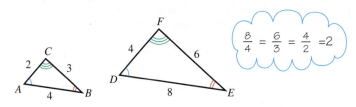

$\triangle ABC \sim \triangle DEF$
Scale factor from $\triangle ABC$ to $\triangle DEF = 2$

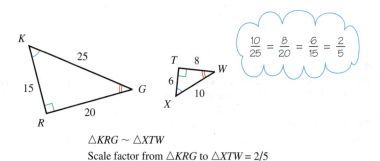

$\triangle KRG \sim \triangle XTW$
Scale factor from $\triangle KRG$ to $\triangle XTW = 2/5$

It is possible to conclude that two triangles are similar even when we have incomplete information about the sides and angles of the triangles. The most commonly used criteria for similarity are the angle–angle (AA), side–side–side (SSS), and side–angle–side (SAS) properties.*

### The Angle–Angle–Angle (AAA) and Angle–Angle (AA) Similarity Properties

In Figure 12.18, $\triangle ABC$ and $\triangle DEF$ have corresponding angles measuring 110°, 40°, and 30°. We see that $\triangle ABC \sim \triangle DEF$. The scale factor can be determined by measuring the lengths of two corresponding sides and forming their ratio. For example, the scale factor is $DE/AB$.

**FIGURE 12.18**
Two triangles with three congruent angles are similar by the *AAA* similarity property

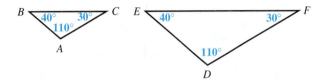

In general, two triangles with three pairs of congruent angles are similar, an observation known as the **angle–angle–angle (AAA) property** of similar triangles. However, all three angles of a triangle are determined once we know two of its angles, since the three measures of the angles add up to 180°. Therefore, the more general property is called the **angle–angle (AA) property of similarity.**

> **PROPERTY**  *The AA Similarity Property*
> If two angles of one triangle are respectively congruent to two angles of a second triangle, then the triangles are similar.
>
>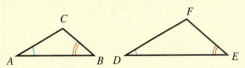

**EXAMPLE 12.9  Making an Indirect Measurement with Similarity**

A tree at point $T$ is in line with a stake at point $L$ when viewed across the river from point $N$. Use the information in the diagram to measure the width $x$ of the river.

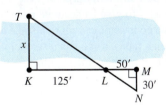

**Solution**   By the vertical-angles theorem, $\angle TLK \cong \angle NLM$. Also, $\angle K \cong \angle M$, since both are right angles. By the AA similarity property, $\triangle TLK \sim \triangle NLM$. Thus, $\dfrac{TK}{NM} = \dfrac{KL}{ML}$, since the ratios of the lengths of corresponding sides are equal. Now, $TK = x$, $NM = 30'$, $KL = 125'$, and $ML = 50'$, so we have the proportion $\dfrac{x}{30'} = \dfrac{125'}{50'}$. Therefore, $x = \dfrac{30' \cdot 125'}{50'} = 75'$. We have thus found the width $x$ of the river by an indirect measurement using similar triangles.

---

*In some books, some, or even all, of these properties are proved on the basis of other assumptions, making the properties theorems. In other texts, the properties are adopted as postulates. In this text, in keeping with an informal treatment of Euclidean geometry, we will refer to the AA, SSS, and SAS criteria for similarity as *properties*.

## The Side–Side–Side (SSS) Similarity Property

> **PROPERTY** *The SSS Similarity Property*
>
> If the three sides of one triangle are proportional to the three sides of a second triangle, then the triangles are similar. That is, if $\dfrac{DE}{AB} = \dfrac{EF}{BC} = \dfrac{DF}{AC}$, then $\triangle ABC \sim \triangle DEF$.
>
>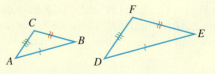

**MHM**  Wavy tick marks are helpful in identifying corresponding proportional sides of similar figures, as shown in the preceding diagram. It is always helpful to convey information in a drawing that clearly reminds you of the properties that are given or have been derived.

## EXAMPLE 12.10 Applying the SSS Similarity Property

A contractor wishes to build an *L*-shaped concrete footing for a brick wall, with a 12-foot leg of the wall meeting a 10-foot leg of the wall at a right angle. The contractor knows that a 3–by–4–by–5-foot triangle has a right angle opposite the 5-foot side. How can the contractor place stakes at points *X*, *Y*, and *Z* to form a right angle at point *Y*? The wall will be built along string lines stretched from *X* to *Y* and from *Y* to *Z*.

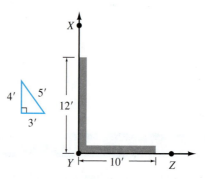

**Solution**  By the SSS similarity property, the 3–4–5-foot right triangle can be magnified by a convenient scale factor to give an accurate right triangle. A scale factor of 4 gives a 12–16–20-foot right triangle. The contractor can place a stake at *X* that is 16 feet from the corner point *Y*. By using two measuring tapes, a stake is placed at the point *Z* where the 20-foot mark on the tape from *X* crosses the 12-foot mark on the tape from *Y*.

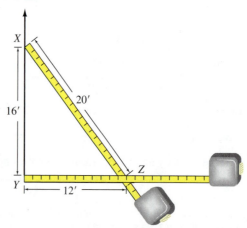

### The Side–Angle–Side (SAS) Similarity Property

> **PROPERTY**   *The SAS Similarity Property*
> If, in two triangles, the ratios of any two pairs of corresponding sides are equal and the included angles are congruent, then the two triangles are similar. That is, if $\dfrac{DE}{AB} = \dfrac{DF}{AC}$ and $\angle A \cong \angle D$, then $\triangle ABC \sim \triangle DEF$.
>
>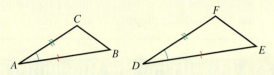

---

**EXAMPLE 12.11** **Applying the SAS Similarity Property**

The sun is about 93 million miles from the earth, and the distance from the earth to the moon is about 240,000 miles. If the diameter of the moon is 2200 miles, what is the approximate diameter of the sun? (*Hint:* From the earth, the sun and moon appear to have the same diameter.)

**Solution**   Because the moon ($M$) appears to have the same diameter as the sun ($S$) during an eclipse, they form nearly congruent angles when viewed from the earth ($E$). This illustration is far from a true scale drawing, but it does show that $\triangle EM_1M_2 \sim \triangle ES_1S_2$ by the SAS similarity property. Thus, $\dfrac{S_1S_2}{M_1M_2} = \dfrac{ES_1}{EM_1}$, so $S_1S_2 = \dfrac{ES_1}{EM_1} \cdot M_1M_2 = \dfrac{93,000,000}{240,000} \cdot 2200$ miles = 852,500 miles. This estimate compares well with the sun's actual diameter of 864,000 miles, given by more accurate methods.

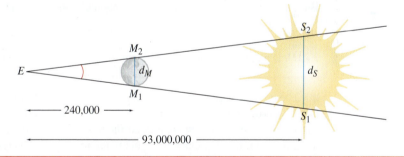

### Geometric Problem Solving with Similar Triangles

Examples 12.12 through 12.14 illustrate how similar triangles can be used to explore properties of geometric figures. These examples all explore figures constructed by joining the midpoints of sides of triangles or quadrilaterals, known as **midpoint figures.**

---

**EXAMPLE 12.12** **Exploring the Medial Triangle**

If $X$, $Y$, and $Z$ are the midpoints of the sides of $\triangle ABC$, then $\triangle XYZ$ is called the **medial triangle** of $\triangle ABC$.

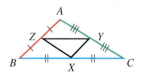

Show that $\triangle ABC \sim \triangle XYZ$, with a scale factor of $\dfrac{1}{2}$, and that each side of the medial triangle is parallel to the corresponding side of $\triangle ABC$. For example, $\overline{XY} \parallel \overline{AB}$ and $\dfrac{XY}{AB} = \dfrac{1}{2}$.

**Solution**

From the figure shown, it is seen that $\dfrac{CY}{CA} = \dfrac{CX}{CB} = \dfrac{1}{2}$. Therefore, by the SAS similarity property, $\triangle ACB \sim \triangle YCX$, with a scale factor of $\dfrac{1}{2}$. In particular, $\dfrac{XY}{BA} = \dfrac{1}{2}$. Moreover, $\angle CAB \cong \angle CYX$, so $\overline{XY} \parallel \overline{AB}$ by the corresponding-angles property. By the same reasoning, the remaining two sides of $\triangle XYZ$ are also parallel and half of the length of the corresponding sides of $\triangle ABC$. Since the sides of $\triangle XYZ$ are half the length of the corresponding sides of $\triangle ABC$, the two triangles are similar by the SSS similarity property.

---

**EXAMPLE 12.13** **Classifying the Midpoint Figure of a Quadrilateral**

Two quadrilaterals are shown. It appears that joining successive midpoints of the sides of these quadrilaterals forms a parallelogram. Prove that this is indeed the case.

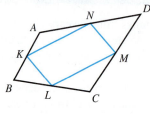
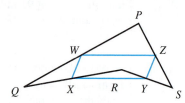

**Solution**

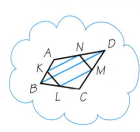

Let $KLMN$ be the midpoint figure of the quadrilateral $ABCD$. Draw the diagonal $\overline{BD}$ and consider $\triangle ABD$ and $\triangle CBD$. By Example 12.12, $\overline{KN}$ and $\overline{LM}$ are both parallel to $\overline{BD}$ and have length $\dfrac{BD}{2}$. But then $\overline{KN}$ and $\overline{LM}$ are congruent and parallel segments. The same reasoning shows that $\overline{KL}$ and $\overline{NM}$ are congruent and parallel, since both segments are parallel to $\overline{AC}$ and have length $\dfrac{AC}{2}$. By definition, $KLMN$ is a parallelogram. The same argument can be adapted to the nonconvex quadrilateral $PQRS$.

---

The proof just given is also valid for *space* quadrilaterals, for which the four vertices are not necessarily in the same plane. For example, the quadrilateral $PQRS$ shown in Example 12.13 may be easily visualized as a nonplanar quadrilateral. However, the midpoint quadrilateral $WXYZ$ is a parallelogram, so it lies in a plane. It's interesting to confirm this result with a quadrilateral made of sticks whose midpoints are joined by elastic bands to form the midpoint parallelogram.

---

**EXAMPLE 12.14** **Discovering the Centroid of a Triangle**

A **median** of a triangle is a line segment joining a vertex to the midpoint of the opposite side. Prove that the three medians of a triangle are concurrent at a point $G$ that is $\dfrac{2}{3}$ of the distance along each median from the vertex toward the midpoint. $G$ is the **centroid,** or **center of gravity,** of the triangle.

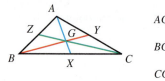

$$AG = \tfrac{2}{3}AX$$
$$BG = \tfrac{2}{3}BY$$
$$CG = \tfrac{2}{3}CZ$$

**Solution**

**Understand the Problem**

There are really *two* problems to be solved. First, there is a *distance* problem: We must show that if $G$ is the point where the two medians $\overline{BY}$ and $\overline{CZ}$ intersect, then $BG = \dfrac{2}{3}BY$, or equivalently, $BG = 2GY$. Second, there is a *concurrence* problem: We must show that if $G$ is the point of intersection of $\overline{BY}$ and $\overline{CZ}$, then the third median, $\overline{AX}$, also passes through $G$.

### Devise a Plan

Since we hope to show that $BG = 2GY$ and $CG = 2GZ$, it may be useful to consider the midpoints $M$ of $\overline{BG}$ and $N$ of $\overline{CG}$. The distance problem for medians $\overline{BY}$ and $\overline{CZ}$ will be solved if it can be shown that $M$ and $G$ trisect $\overline{BY}$ and $N$ and $G$ trisect $\overline{CZ}$. Since $Z$, $M$, $N$, and $Y$ are the successive midpoints of the quadrilateral $ABGC$, we should gain important information by constructing the midpoint figure $ZMNY$, which we know is a parallelogram by Example 12.13:

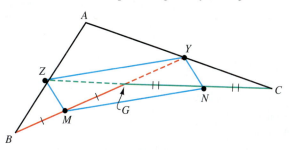

### Carry Out the Plan

Because $ZMNY$ is a parallelogram, the point $G$ at which the diagonals intersect is the midpoint of the diagonal $\overline{MY}$ of the parallelogram. Thus, $MG = GY$. But $M$ is the midpoint of $\overline{BG}$, so $BM = MG$. This shows that $G$ is $\frac{2}{3}$ of the distance from $B$ to $Y$ along the median $\overline{BY}$. The same reasoning shows that $G$ and $N$ trisect the median $\overline{CZ}$. The concurrence problem is now solved by symmetry: If $G'$ is the point of intersection of the medians $\overline{BY}$ and $\overline{AX}$, then $G'$ is $\frac{2}{3}$ of the distance from a vertex along either median; therefore, $G = G'$.

### Look Back

It is often helpful to review the problem-solving strategies that have been successful. Several strategies used in this example are likely to be helpful with other problems:

- **Divide the problem into simpler parts:** We solved a distance problem and a concurrence problem.
- **Consider a simpler problem first:** $G$ was defined as the intersection of *two* medians, and it was to be shown that $G$ was $\frac{2}{3}$ of the distances along the two medians from the vertices.
- **Use a related result:** The previous example, showing that the midpoints of the sides of any quadrilateral form a parallelogram, was a key idea in the solution.

## Problem Set 12.3

Exercises colored in red are answered in the back of the text.

## Understanding Concepts

**1.** Which of the given pairs of triangles are similar? If they are similar, explain why, express the similarity with the $\sim$ notation, and give the scale factor.

**(a)**

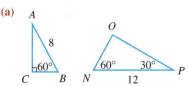

**(b)**

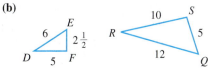

**(c)**

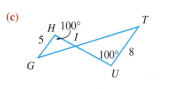

**(d)**

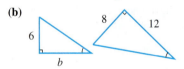

**(e)**

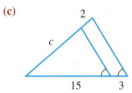

2. Are the figures described next necessarily similar? If so, explain why. If not, draw an example to show why not.

   **(a)** Any two equilateral triangles

   **(b)** Any two isosceles triangles

   **(c)** Any two right triangles having an acute angle of measure 36°

   **(d)** Any two isosceles right triangles

   **(e)** Any two congruent triangles

   **(f)** A triangle with sides of lengths 3 and 4 and an angle of 30° and a triangle with sides of lengths 6 and 8 and an angle of 30°

3. A pair of similar triangles is shown in each part. Find the measures of the segments marked with a letter *a*, *b*, *c*, or *d*.

   **(a)**

   **(b)**

   **(c)**

   **(d)**

   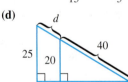

4. **(a)** A right triangle *XYZ* with legs of length 5 feet and 12 feet is similar to a triangle *ABC* of perimeter 3000 feet. Describe triangle *ABC*.

   **(b)** Triangle *XYZ* is also similar to a triangle *DEF* of area 3000 square feet. Describe triangle *DEF*.

5. Triangle *XYZ* is a right triangle with legs of length 3 and 4. Describe *all* triangles that have one side of length 60 and are similar to triangle *XYZ*.

6. **(a)** Two convex quadrilaterals *ABCD* and *EFGH* have congruent angles at their corresponding vertices: $\angle A \cong \angle E, \angle B \cong \angle F, \angle C \cong \angle G,$ and $\angle D \cong \angle H$. Can

you conclude that the two quadrilaterals are similar? Explain.

   **(b)** Two convex quadrilaterals have corresponding sides in the same ratio. Are the quadrilaterals necessarily similar? Explain.

7. Suppose $\triangle ABC \sim \triangle DEF$, where only points *D* and *E* are shown. Find all possible locations for *F* and draw the corresponding triangles *DEF*.

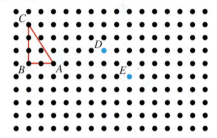

8. The diagonals of the given trapezoid *ABCD* intersect at *E*, where $\overline{AB} \parallel \overline{CD}$. Let $x = BE$ and $y = DC$.

   **(a)** Explain why $\triangle ABE \sim \triangle CDE$.

   **(b)** Determine *x* and *y*.

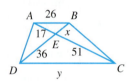

9. Let $\overline{AB}$ and $\overline{CD}$ be parallel, and let $\overline{AD}$ and $\overline{BC}$ intersect at *E*. Prove that $a \cdot y = x \cdot b$.

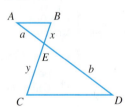

10. $\triangle ABC$ is a right triangle with altitude $\overline{CD}$, as shown.

    **(a)** Explain why $\triangle ADC \sim \triangle CDB$.

    **(b)** Find an equation for *h*, and solve it to show that $h = \sqrt{9 \cdot 25} = 3 \cdot 5 = 15$.

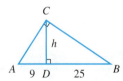

11. An isosceles triangle whose apex angle measures 36°, shown at the left, is sometimes called a **golden triangle:**

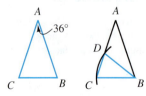

    **(a)** Draw a circular arc centered at *B* and passing through *C*. Prove that if *D* is the point at which the arc intersects $\overline{AC}$,

then △BCD is also a golden triangle. (*Hint:* What is
m(∠C)?)

**(b)** Draw an enlarged copy of △ABC, with AB at least 3″ long.
Construct three more golden triangles CDE, DEF, and EFG,
where each contains the next.

**12.** △ABC is an isosceles triangle with apex C. It has the unusual
property that the circular arc centered at A intersects the opposite side at a point D for which △ABC ~ △BCD.

**(a)** Use the preceding property to find the measures of the
base and apex angles of △ABC.

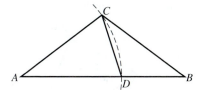

**(b)** What kind of triangle is △ACD? (*Hint:* See problem 11.)

**13.** Suppose △ABC ~ △BCA. What more can you say about
△ABC?

**14.** Lined notebook paper provides a convenient way to subdivide
a line segment into a specified number of congruent subseg-
ments. The diagram shows how swinging an arc of radius
AB subdivides the segment into five congruent parts:
$\overline{AX} \cong \overline{XY} \cong \overline{YZ} \cong \overline{ZW} \cong \overline{WB}$.

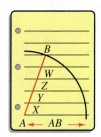

**(a)** Show how to subdivide a segment $\overline{AB}$ into seven congruent
segments.

**(b)** Carefully explain why and when the procedure you used
in (a) is valid.

## Teaching Concepts

**15. The Similarity Matching Game.** Staple manila file folders
together so that a dozen or so congruent pairs of triangles of various shapes and sizes can be cut out easily. Next, choose one of
each congruent pair and cut off a trapezoid from one of its sides,
using the side as the longer base of the trapezoid. This converts
each congruent pair into a similar pair of triangles. Next, spread
out all of the triangles on the classroom floor or perhaps on an
overhead, first turning some of the triangles upside down. Now
challenge your students to identify the pairs of similar triangles.
Have them check their guesses by aligning their chosen pairs of
triangles at a vertex to see that the uncovered part of the larger triangle is a trapezoid. Also, have them use rulers to determine the
approximate scale factor of each congruent pair of triangles.

## Responding to Students

**16.** Jackson is having trouble remembering the difference between
similar and congruent figures. He asks, "Are all congruent

triangles similar?" You think that is a wonderful question with
which to begin reflecting on how congruent and similar figures are alike and different. What could you do to help
Jackson develop this conceptual understanding?

**17.** Gloria is recording her findings about the similar triangles
shown, and she writes "△WVU ~ △YXZ" in her math journal.
She then begins to look at corresponding sides and angles.
How would you respond to Gloria?

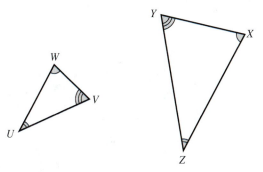

**18.** Miley thinks that a triangle with sides 5, 9, and 13 is similar
to a triangle with sides 10, 14, and 18, since each side is
increased by 5 from the one triangle to the other. Reef thinks
Miley can't expect to get a similar triangle in this way. After
all, says Reef, "If 100 is added to each side, the new triangle
would have sides of length 105, 109, and 113 and it would be
nearly equilateral, quite unlike the shape of the obtuse
5–9–13 triangle. Going in the other direction, 1 cannot be
subtracted from each side, since, by the triangle inequality, no
triangle can have sides of length 4, 8, and 12." Respond to
Miley and Reef.

**19.** After studying similar triangles, your class wonders whether
there are analogous similarity properties for quadrilaterals.
Respond to the ideas of these students:

**(a)** Megan claims that all rectangles are similar, since every
angle in a rectangle is a right angle.

**(b)** Patrick thinks that there is an SASAS quadrilateral similarity property. That is, if two quadrilaterals PQRS and WXYZ
have the relationships

$$\frac{WX}{PQ} = \frac{XY}{QR} = \frac{YZ}{RS}, \angle Q \cong \angle X, \text{ and } \angle R \cong \angle Y,$$

then PQRS is similar to WXYZ.

**(c)** Quincy thinks that there is an SSSS quadrilateral similarity property. That is, if the ratios of the lengths of
corresponding sides are all equal, then the two quadrilaterals have the same shape, though not necessarily the
same size.

## Thinking Critically

**20.** Let $\overline{CD}$ be the altitude drawn to the hypotenuse of the right
triangle ABC:

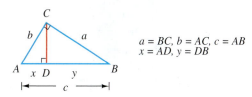

**(a)** Explain why $\triangle ABC \sim \triangle ACD$ and $\triangle ABC \sim \triangle CBD$.

**(b)** Explain why $\dfrac{x}{b} = \dfrac{b}{c}$ and $\dfrac{y}{a} = \dfrac{a}{c}$.

**(c)** Use part (b) to show that $c^2 = a^2 + b^2$. (This gives a proof of the Pythagorean theorem.)

**21.** Prove that the following square inscribed in a right triangle has sides of length $x = \dfrac{ab}{a + b}$, where $a$ and $b$ are the lengths of the legs of the triangle:

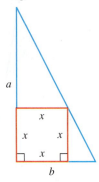

**22.** The square $ABCD$ has sides of unit length and midpoints at $J$, $K$, $L$, and $M$. The four segments that join vertices of the square to the midpoints of opposite sides form a smaller, inner square $PQRS$.

**(a)** Use the Pythagorean theorem to show that
$$DJ = \frac{1}{2}\sqrt{5}.$$

**(b)** Construct segment $\overline{ST}$ parallel to $\overline{AM}$, where $T$ is on segment $\overline{AP}$. Observe that the segment $\overline{ST}$ has length $\dfrac{1}{2}$ and creates $\triangle STP$, which is similar to $\triangle DJA$. Use this fact to compute the length $PS$.

**(c)** What is the area of the inner square?

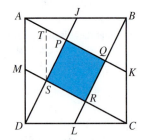

**23.** The square $ABCD$ has sides of unit length and "one-third" points at $J$, $K$, $L$, and $M$. Join the vertices of the square to successive "one-third" points to form the smaller, inner square $PQRS$. Follow the steps in problem 22 to show that the inner square formed with "one-third" points has 40% of the area of the larger square $ABCD$.

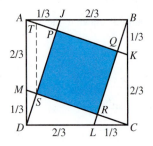

**24.** Let three arbitrary perpendiculars to the sides of $\triangle ABC$ of the diagram be drawn, meeting in pairs at the points $P$, $Q$, and $R$. Prove that $\triangle PQR \sim \triangle ABC$.

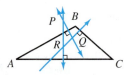

**25.** Let $PQRS$ be a space quadrilateral, and let $W$, $X$, $Y$, and $Z$ be the midpoints of successive sides. Explain why $\overline{WY}$ and $\overline{XZ}$ intersect at their common midpoint $M$.

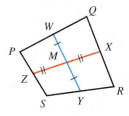

**26.** Let $ABCD$ be a trapezoid as illustrated, with bases of length $a = AB$ and $b = CD$. Let the diagonals $\overline{AC}$ and $\overline{BD}$ intersect at $P$, and suppose $\overline{EF}$ is the segment parallel to the bases that passes through $P$. Show that $EP = FP - \dfrac{ab}{a + b}$. (Thus,
$$EF = \frac{2ab}{a + b},$$
which is called the **harmonic mean** of $a$ and $b$.)

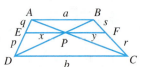

(*Hint:* Explain why $\dfrac{x}{a} = \dfrac{p}{(p + q)}$ and $\dfrac{x}{b} = \dfrac{q}{(q + p)}$. What happens when these equations are added?)

**27.** Let $M$ and $N$ be the midpoints of the sides of parallelogram $ABCD$ opposite $A$ as shown. Show that $\overline{AM}$ and $\overline{AN}$ divide the diagonal $\overline{BD}$ into three congruent segments: $BP = PQ = QD$. (*Hint:* Construct $\overline{AC}$, and see Example 12.14; alternatively, notice that $\triangle MBP \sim \triangle ADP$, with scale factor 2).

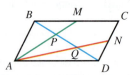

**28.** Use similarity to find the distances $AP$, $BP$, $CP$, and $DP$ in the figure shown. The smallest squares on the lattice have sides of unit length.

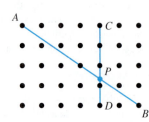

## Making Connections

**29.** Mingxi is standing 75 feet from the base of a tree. The shadow from the top of Mingxi's head coincides with the shadow from the top of the tree. If Mingxi is 5′9″ tall and his shadow is 7′ long, how tall is the tree?

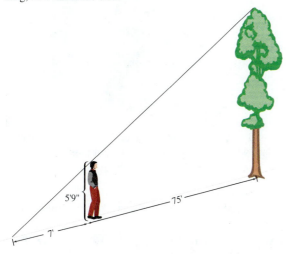

**30.** Mohini laid a mirror on the level ground 15 feet from the base of a pole, as shown. Standing 4 feet from the mirror, she can see the top of the pole reflected in the mirror. If Mohini is 5′5″ tall, how can she estimate the height of the pole? What must she allow for in her calculation?

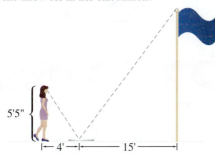

**31.** By holding a ruler 2 feet in front of her eyes as illustrated in the diagram, Ginny sees that the top and bottom points of a vertical cliff face line up with marks separated by 3.5″ on the ruler. According to the map, Ginny is about a half mile from the cliff. What is the approximate height of the cliff? Recall that a mile is 5280 feet.

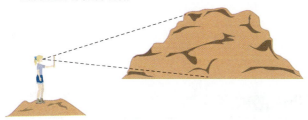

**32.** A vertical wall 18 feet high casts a shadow 6 feet wide on level ground. If Lisa is 5′3″ tall, how far away from the wall can she stand and still be entirely in the shade?

**33.** Use similar triangles to solve the following problem posed in 13th-century China: General Tsao stood 2 feet back from the edge of a vertical cliff overlooking the valley below. By holding his staff vertically 2 feet in front of him, he could see that

the far bank of the river aligned with the point 1 foot below eye level along his staff and the near bank aligned with the point 3 feet below eye level along the staff. By lowering a rope over the cliff face, he determined that his eyes were 45 feet above the level floor of the valley. How did the general determine the width of the river to know if his army could safely cross to its opposite side? (*Hint:* In the figure shown, the general's eye is at point *G*, the top of his staff is at point *A*, and *E* and *F* are points on the near and far sides of the river.)

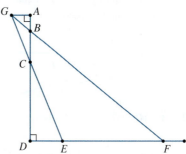

**34.** A sloping ramp is to be built with vertical supports placed at points *B*, *C*, and *D* as shown. The supports at *A* and *E* are 8 and 12 feet high, respectively. How high must the supports be at the points *B*, *C*, and *D*?

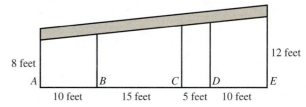

## Communicating

**35.** **(a)** In Example 12.13, it was shown that joining the successive midpoints of a quadrilateral forms a parallelogram. Explore what you find by *reversing* the construction. That is, given a parallelogram *KLMN*, can you construct a quadrilateral *ABCD* for which *KLMN* is the midpoint figure? Is *ABCD* unique?

**(b)** Write a report discussing your results in part (a).

## Using a Computer

**36.** Construct a circle and two chords $\overline{AB}$ and $\overline{CD}$ that intersect at a point *P*. Measure the angles in the triangles *BCP* and *DAP*.

**(a)** What conclusion about △*BCP* and △*DAP* is suggested by your measurements?

**(b)** Measure the lengths of $\overline{PA}$, $\overline{PB}$, $\overline{PC}$, and $\overline{PD}$, and then compare *PA* · *PB* with *PC* · *PD*. Does your answer to part (a) justify your observation about the two products?

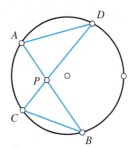

**37.** Construct a circle and a point P that is outside of the circle as shown in the accompanying diagram. Next, draw two rays from P, one of which intersects the circle at the points A and B, and the other of which intersects the circle at C and D. Measure the angles in △BCP and △DAP.

**(a)** What conclusion about △BCP and △DAP is suggested by your measurements?

**(b)** Measure the lengths of $\overline{PA}, \overline{PB}, \overline{PC},$ and $\overline{PD}$, and then compare $PA \cdot PB$ with $PC \cdot PD$. Does your answer to part (a) justify your observation about the two products?

## From State Student Assessments

**38.** (Illinois, Grade 5)
△PQR is similar to △STU. Find the length of TS.

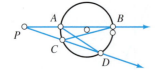

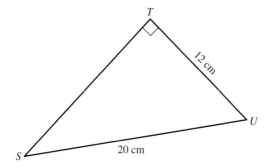

| A. 4 cm | B. 14 cm | C. 16 cm |
|---|---|---|
| D. 26 cm | E. 32 cm | |

**39.** (Massachusetts, Grade 7)
Mr. Liu wants to build a bridge across the creek that runs through his property. He made measurements and drew the map shown above.

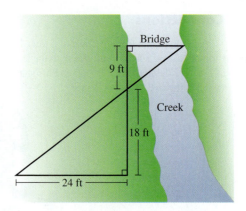

Based on this map, what is the distance across the creek at the place where Mr. Lui wants to put the bridge?

A. 9 feet    B. 12 feet    C. 18 feet    D. 24 feet

**40.** (Illinois, Grade 6)
Triangle RST is similar to triangle XYZ. $\overline{RS}$ corresponds to which side of triangle XYZ?

A. $\overline{SR}$    B. $\overline{YZ}$    C. $\overline{XZ}$    D. $\overline{XY}$

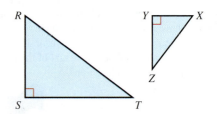

## Examining School Book Pages

*Refer to the School Book Pages provided on page 703 to answer the following questions.*

**41.** The notion of a "scale factor" has not been made explicit on the school book pages shown, even though the introductory example at the top of the pages uses the description "enlarged proportionally." Design a short follow-up lesson in which you introduce the scale factor and demonstrate how it is used to solve problems concerning similar figures.

## The Chapter in Relation to Future Teachers

This chapter concludes our study of informal geometry. Several themes, which form the basis for the geometry portion of the elementary school curriculum, have cut across these geometry chapters:

* *Congruence*
    The notion of congruence (that is, that one figure is exactly the same size and shape as another) is of great importance. General figures can be shown to be congruent with the use of rigid motions, and triangles can be shown to be congruent by means of angle and side properties.

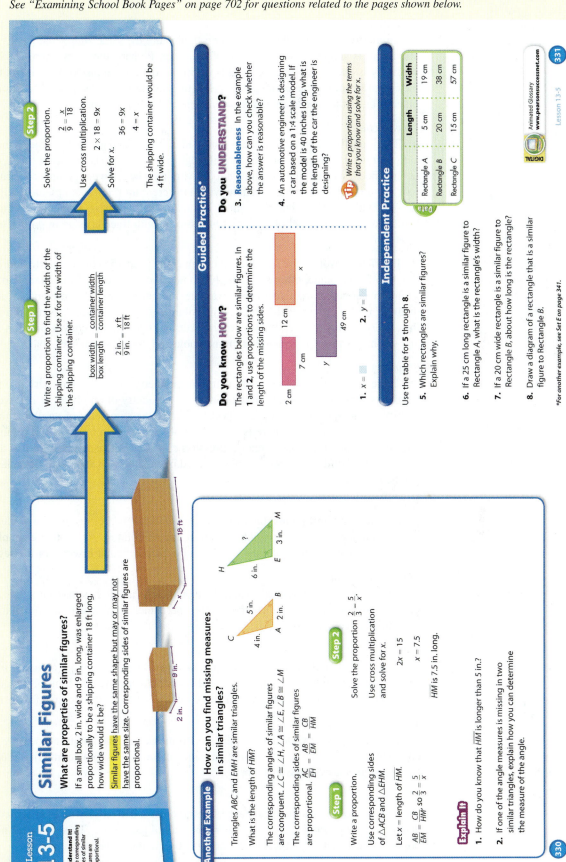

*See "Examining School Book Pages" on page 702 for questions related to the pages shown below.*

**Lesson**
# 13-5

**Understand It!**
The corresponding sides of similar figures are proportional.

## Similar Figures

### What are properties of similar figures?

If a small box, 2 in. wide and 9 in. long, was enlarged proportionally to be a shipping container 18 ft long, how wide would it be?

Similar figures have the same shape but may or may not have the same size. Corresponding sides of similar figures are proportional.

**Step 1**

Write a proportion to find the width of the shipping container. Use $x$ for the width of the shipping container.

$$\frac{\text{box width}}{\text{box length}} = \frac{\text{container width}}{\text{container length}}$$

$$\frac{2 \text{ in.}}{9 \text{ in.}} = \frac{x \text{ ft}}{18 \text{ ft}}$$

**Step 2**

Solve the proportion.

$$\frac{2}{9} = \frac{x}{18}$$

Use cross multiplication.

$$2 \times 18 = 9x$$

Solve for $x$.

$$36 = 9x$$
$$4 = x$$

The shipping container would be 4 ft wide.

---

**Another Example** How can you find missing measures in similar triangles?

Triangles *ABC* and *EMH* are similar triangles.

What is the length of $\overline{HM}$?

The corresponding angles of similar figures are congruent. $\angle C \cong \angle H$, $\angle A \cong \angle E$, $\angle B \cong \angle M$

The corresponding sides of similar figures are proportional. $\dfrac{AC}{EH} = \dfrac{AB}{EM} = \dfrac{CB}{HM}$

**Step 1**

Write a proportion.

Use corresponding sides of △*ACB* and △*EHM*.

Let $x$ = length of $\overline{HM}$.

$$\frac{AB}{EM} = \frac{CB}{HM}, \text{ so } \frac{2}{3} = \frac{5}{x}$$

**Step 2**

Solve the proportion $\dfrac{2}{3} = \dfrac{5}{x}$.

Use cross multiplication and solve for $x$.

$$2x = 15$$
$$x = 7.5$$

$\overline{HM}$ is 7.5 in. long.

**Explain It**

1. How do you know that $\overline{HM}$ is longer than 5 in.?

2. If one of the angle measures is missing in two similar triangles, explain how you can determine the measure of the angle.

---

### Guided Practice*

**Do you know HOW?**

The rectangles below are similar figures. In **1** and **2**, use proportions to determine the length of the missing sides.

1. $x =$ _____   2. $y =$ _____

**Do you UNDERSTAND?**

3. **Reasonableness** In the example above, how can you check whether the answer is reasonable?

4. An automotive engineer is designing a car based on a 1:4 scale model. If the model is 40 inches long, what is the length of the car the engineer is designing?

### Independent Practice

Use the table for **5** through **8**.

5. Which rectangles are similar figures? Explain why.

6. If a 25 cm long rectangle is a similar figure to Rectangle A, what is the rectangle's width?

7. If a 20 cm wide rectangle is a similar figure to Rectangle B, about how long is the rectangle?

8. Draw a diagram of a rectangle that is a similar figure to Rectangle B.

**Tip** *Write a proportion using the terms that you know and solve for x.*

**Data**

| | Length | Width |
|---|---|---|
| Rectangle A | 5 cm | 19 cm |
| Rectangle B | 20 cm | 38 cm |
| Rectangle C | 15 cm | 57 cm |

DIGITAL
Animated Glossary
www.pearsonsuccessnet.com

Lesson 13-5

**331**

**330**

*For another example, see Set E on page 341.*

- *Similarity*

  Similarity embodies the idea that two figures are the same *shape,* but of different size, as if one figure is simply a magnification of the other. Perhaps the most important consequence of similarity is that corresponding lengths in similar figures are proportional, with the scale factor the common ratio of the corresponding lengths. Similarity can be proved by similarity transformations or, in the case of triangles, with angle and side properties.

- *Constructions*

  Traditionally, constructions were restricted to figures and geometric objects that could be created with two Euclidean tools: the straightedge and the compass. In recent times, other construction methods, such as paper folding and the Mira may be allowed. Figures constructible with one tool may or may not be constructible with a different tool. For example, any angle can be constructed with the Mira, but not with straightedge and compass. Computer geometry programs have also enlarged the set of constructible objects, with fractals as an important example.

- *Invariance*

  Invariance involves the idea that, although many properties of geometric figures change from figure to figure, some, often surprisingly, do not. Indeed, much of the interest in, and utility of, geometry derives from this fact. For example, the ratio of the circumference of any circle to its diameter is always $\pi = 3.14159\ldots$, the volume of any cone is always one-third the volume of the corresponding cylinder, the sum of the exterior angles of any convex polygon is always $360°$, and so on. Geometry is replete with remarkable and useful invariances.

- *Symmetry*

  There are many kinds of symmetry in geometry. There is the periodic symmetry that manifests itself in tilings and tessellations; the symmetry of an object as if it were reflected in a mirror (that is, symmetry with respect to a line); the symmetry of an object through a point; and rotational symmetry. There is also a sort of symmetry in many of the formulas of geometry. For example, the Pythagorean expression $c^2 = a^2 + b^2$ is unchanged if $a$ and $b$ are interchanged, and similar symmetries are exhibited by the distance and slope formulas in coordinate geometry.

- *Loci*

  A *locus* is a set of points that satisfy certain conditions. For example, a circle is the locus of all points in a plane that are equidistant from a fixed point $O$. As another example, the locus of points equidistant from the points $A$ and $B$ is the perpendicular bisector of the segment $\overline{AB}$.

- *Maxima and minima*

  Of all triangles of fixed perimeter, the equilateral triangle has maximum area. Of all rectangles of fixed area, the square has the smallest perimeter. Such questions of maxima and minima often arise in geometry.

- *Limit*

  As an example of the notion of a limit, as $n$ gets larger and larger a regular $n$-gon more and more closely approximates a circle. Indeed, we would say that the limit of a regular $n$-gon as $n$ tends to infinity *is* a circle. This notion was used in developing the formula for the area of a circle.

- *Measurement*

  The word *geometry* means, literally, "earth measure." The ability to measure, compare, and communicate information concerning size and amount is basic to geometric thinking and applications of geometry in the real world.

- *Coordinates*

  This theme stresses the idea that geometric objects can be viewed as specified sets of points determined by ordered pairs of numbers in a coordinate plane. This powerful notion makes it possible to use methods of arithmetic and algebra to obtain geometric results.

- *Logical structure*

  As in the rest of mathematics, geometric ideas do not stand alone. Even in informal geometry, it is important to see how some results follow from others and to realize that guessing or conjecturing alone is not enough.

## Chapter 12 Summary

| Section 12.1   Congruent Triangles | Page Reference |
|---|---|
| **CONCEPTS** | |
| • **Congruent triangles:** Two triangles of the same shape and size. | 659 |
| • **Congruent line segments** are segments of the same length. | 659 |
| • **Congruent triangles** are triangles of the same shape and same size. | 660 |
| **DEFINITIONS** | |
| • Two triangles *ABC* and *DEF* are **congruent** if, and only if, corresponding angles have the same measure and corresponding sides have the same length. That is, $\triangle ABC \cong \triangle DEF$ if, and only if, $m(\angle A) = m(\angle D), m(\angle B) = m(\angle E), m(\angle C) = m(\angle F), AB = DE$, $BC = EF$, and $CA = FD$. | 659, 660 |
| • There are six **parts of a triangle** *ABC*: the three sides, *AB*, *BC*, and *CA*, and the three angles $\angle A$, $\angle B$, and $\angle C$. | 660 |
| • The **six parts** of a triangle *ABC* are its three sides $\overline{AB}$, $\overline{BC}$, and $\overline{CA}$ and its three angles $\angle A$, $\angle B$, and $\angle C$. | 660 |
| • Two triangles *ABC* and *DEF* are **congruent triangles** if, and only if, there is a correspondence of vertices $A \leftrightarrow D, B \leftrightarrow E, C \leftrightarrow F$ so that the six parts of triangle *ABC* are congruent to the corresponding six parts of triangle *DEF*. In symbols, $\triangle ABC \cong \triangle DEF$ if, and only if, $AB = DE, BC = EF, CA = FD, m(\angle A) = m(\angle D), m(\angle B) = m(\angle E)$, and $m(\angle C) = m(\angle F)$. | 660 |
| **CONSTRUCTIONS** | |
| • **Basic compass-and-straightedge constructions:** Construct a congruent copy of a line segment, construct a congruent copy of an angle. | 660, 663 |
| **PROPERTIES** | |
| • **Congruence properties of triangles:** Two triangles are congruent if they satisfy any one of the following properties: SSS (side–side–side), SAS (side–angle–side), ASA (angle–side–angle), and AAS (angle–angle–side). | 662, 666, 669 |
| **THEOREMS** | |
| • **Triangle inequality:** The length of any side of a triangle is less than the sum of the lengths of the other two sides. | 664 |
| • **Isosceles triangle theorem and converse:** A triangle has two congruent sides if, and only if, their opposite angles are congruent. | 667, 669 |
| • **Thales' theorem:** A triangle inscribed in a semicircle is a right triangle with the diameter as its hypotenuse. | 667 |
| **Section 12.2   Constructing Geometric Figures** | **Page Reference** |
| **CONCEPTS** | |
| • **Constructions and drawings:** Geometric figures can be constructed or drawn with: compass-and-straightedge, the Mira, paper folding, geometry software. | 676, 683, 684 |
| • **Construction versus drawing:** A figure is *constructed* if the defining properties of the figure have been incorporated into the construction: All lengths and angles are exact. A figure is *drawn* if the properties of the figure are only approximate to give the appearance of the desired shape of the figure. | 676, 678, 680, 681, 683, 684 |

## DEFINITIONS

- The **foot of the perpendicular** is the point on a line that is closest to a point not on the line. — 677

- The **altitude of the triangle** is the line through a vertex of a triangle that is perpendicular to the line containing the opposite side of the triangle. — 678

- The **perpendicular bisector** of a line segment is the line perpendicular to the segment at its midpoint. — 678

- **Circumscribing circle**, or **circumcircle** of a triangle, is the unique circle that passes through the three vertices $A$, $B$, and $C$ of the triangle. — 680

- The **circumcenter** of a triangle is the center of the circumscribed circle of the triangle. — 680

- An **angle bisector** is a ray that starts at the vertex of an angle and splits the angle into two congruent parts. — 680

- The **inscribed circle**, or **incircle** of a triangle, is the unique circle that is tangent to the three sides of the triangle. — 681

- The **incenter** of a triangle is the center of the inscribed circle. — 681

- The **Fermat primes** are prime numbers of the form $2^{2^k} + 1$, where $k$ is a nonnegative integer. Only five Fermat primes—3, 5, 17, 257, and 65,537—are known to exist. — 683

## CONSTRUCTIONS

- **Basic compass-and-straightedge constructions:** Construct a line parallel to a given line through a given point; construct a line perpendicular to a given line through either a point on or away from the given line; construct the midpoint of a line segment and the line perpendicular to the segment through the midpoint; construct the angle bisector of a given angle. — 677, 678, 679, 680

## THEOREMS

- **Equidistance property of the perpendicular bisector:** A point lies on the perpendicular bisector of a line segment if, and only if, the point is equidistant from the endpoints of the segment. — 679

- **Circumscribed circle:** The three perpendicular bisectors of the sides of a triangle are concurrent at a point (the *circumcenter*) that is equidistant to the three vertices of the triangle. That is, the circumcenter is the center of a circle (the *circumcircle*) that passes through the three vertices of the triangle. — 680

- **Equidistance property of the angle bisector:** A point lies on an angle bisector if, and only if, it is equidistant to the sides of the angle. — 680

- **Inscribed circle:** The three angle bisectors of a triangles are concurrent at a point (the *incenter*) that is the center of a circle (the *incircle*) that is equidistant to the three sides of the triangle. That is, the inscribed circle is tangent to all three sides of the triangle. — 681

- **Gauss-Wantzel theorem:** A regular $n$-gon has a compass-and-straightedge construction if, and only if, $n$ is power of 2 that is 4 or larger or a power-of-2 multiple of a product of distinct Fermat primes. — 683

| Section 12.3   Similar Triangles | Page Reference |
| --- | --- |

## CONCEPTS

- **Similar triangles** are triangles of the same shape but not necessarily of the same size. Corresponding angles are congruent but corresponding side lengths are magnified or reduced by a common multiplier called the *scale factor*. — 692

## DEFINITIONS

| | |
|---|---|
| • Two triangles *ABC* and *DEF* are **similar triangles** if, and only if, there is a correspondence of vertices $A \leftrightarrow D, B \leftrightarrow E, C \leftrightarrow F$ so that the corresponding angles are congruent and the corresponding side lengths are proportional. In symbols, $\triangle ABC \sim \triangle DEF$ if, and only if, $m(\angle A) = m(\angle D), m(\angle B) = m(\angle E), m(\angle C) = m(\angle F)$, $\dfrac{AB}{DE} = \dfrac{BC}{EF} = \dfrac{CA}{FD} = k$, where the constant of proportionality $k$ is the **scale factor.** | 692 |
| • The **midpoint figure** of a given polygon is the polygon whose vertices are the successive midpoints of the given polygon. | 695 |
| • The **medial triangle** is the midpoint figure of a given triangle. | 695 |
| • A **median** of a triangle is a line segment that joins a vertex to the midpoint of the opposite side of the triangle. | 696 |

## PROPERTIES

| | |
|---|---|
| • **Similarity properties of triangles:** Two triangles are similar if they have either AA (angle–angle) similarity (two pairs of congruent sides), SSS (side–side–side) similarity (three proportional sides), or SAS (side–angle–side) similarity (two proportional pairs of sides that include congruent angles). | 693, 694, 695 |

## THEOREMS

| | |
|---|---|
| • The medial triangle of a given triangle is similar to the given triangle, with a scale factor of ½. | 695 |
| • The midpoint figure of any quadrilateral is a parallelogram. | 696 |
| • The three medians of a triangle are concurrent at a point called the **centroid** of the triangle. The centroid is 2/3 of the distance from a vertex toward the opposite midpoint of the side of the triangle. | 696 |

## Chapter Review Exercises

### Section 12.1

1. Consider the following two triangles:

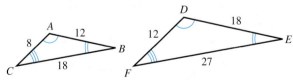

Are the assertions that follow *true* or *false*? Explain your answer.

   (a) Five parts of $\triangle ABC$ are congruent to five parts of $\triangle DEF$.

   (b) $\triangle ABC$ is congruent to $\triangle DEF$.

2. In each figure, find at least one pair of congruent triangles. Express the congruence by using the $\cong$ symbol, and state why the triangles are congruent.

(a)

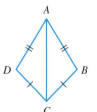

(b)

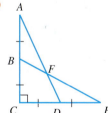

(c)

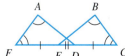

(d)

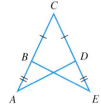

**(e)**

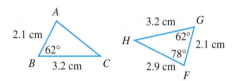

**(f)**

A    AC = BD    D

B    C

**3.** Without measuring, fill in the blanks that follow these figures:

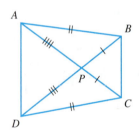

**(a)** AC = ____

**(b)** m(∠H) = ____

**(c)** m(∠A) = ____

**(d)** m(∠C) = ____

**4.** Find three pairs of congruent triangles in this figure. Justify your answers.

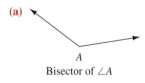

**5.** Let D be any point of the base $\overline{BC}$ of an isosceles triangle ABC. Locate E on $\overline{AC}$ and F on $\overline{AB}$ so that EC = BD and BF = DC. Draw the figure as it is described and then prove that DE = DF.

**6.** Let ABCD be any convex quadrilateral. Show that the sum of the lengths of two of the opposite sides of the quadrilateral is smaller than the sum of the lengths of the two diagonals of the quadrilateral.

## Section 12.2

**7.** Perform the constructions that follow with a compass and a straightedge. Show and describe all of your steps.

**(a)**

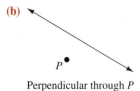

Bisector of ∠A

**(b)**

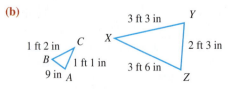

Perpendicular through P

**(c)**

Perpendicular bisector of $\overline{AB}$

**(d)**

l ∥ m

Line k equidistant to l and m

**8.** Show and describe the position of a Mira that performs each of the constructions of problem 7 in one step.

**9.** **(a)** Construct △ABC, where ∠A, $\overline{AB}$, and $\overline{BC}$ are the parts shown. Is the shape of △ABC uniquely determined?

**(b)** Is the shape of △ABC uniquely determined if ∠C is obtuse?

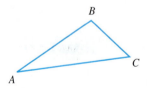

**10.** Construct a regular hexagon ABCDEF, for which diagonal AD is as follows:

A _____ D

## Section 12.3

**11.** **(a)** If only a ruler is available, is it possible to determine whether two triangles are similar?

**(b)** If only a protractor is available, is it possible to determine whether two triangles are similar?

**12.** Triangle ABC is as shown. Construct a triangle DEF for which

$$\triangle ABC \sim \triangle DEF \text{ and } DE = \left(\frac{3}{2}\right)AB,$$ using a compass and a straightedge.

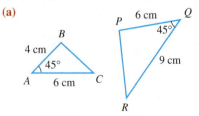

**13.** Explain why each pair of triangles is similar. State the similarity by using the ∼ symbol and give the scale factor.

**(a)**

4 cm

B

45°

A    6 cm    C

P    6 cm    Q

45°

9 cm

R

**(b)**

1 ft 2 in    C    X

B    1 ft 1 in

9 in    A

3 ft 3 in    Y

2 ft 3 in

3 ft 6 in    Z

**(c)**

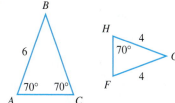

**(d)**

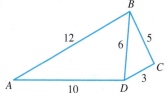

**14.** Lines $k$, $l$, and $m$ are parallel. Find the lengths $x$ and $y$, using similar triangles.

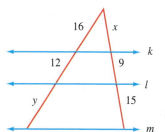

**15.** In the morning, the shadows cast by the top of a vertical stick 3 feet high and the top of a pyramid were at points $S_1$ and $P_1$, respectively, on level ground. That afternoon, because of the motion of the sun in the sky, the points were at $S_2$ and $P_2$. If $S_1S_2 = 2$ feet and $P_1P_2 = 270$ feet, what is the height of the pyramid?

## Chapter Test

**1.** A person 6 feet tall casts a shadow 7 feet long, and a tree casts a shadow 56 feet long.

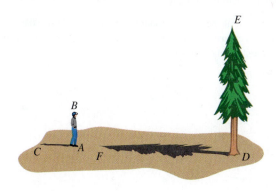

**(a)** What assumption can you make about the sun's rays?

**(b)** What other assumption can you make to conclude that $\triangle ABC \sim \triangle DEF$?

**(c)** How tall is the tree?

**2.** In $\triangle ABC$, the midpoint $M$ of side $\overline{AB}$ satisfies $MC = MA$. Prove that $\triangle ABC$ is a right triangle.

**3.** For each pair of triangles shown, explain why the triangles are similar. Express the similarity with the $\sim$ notation.

**(a)**    **(b)**

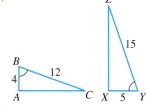

**(c)**

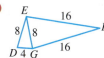

**(d)**

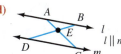

**4.** In each figure, find a pair of congruent triangles. State what congruence property justifies your conclusion, and express the congruence with the symbol $\cong$ .

**(a)**

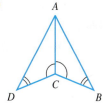

**(b)**

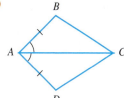

**(c)**

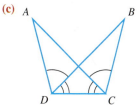

**(d)**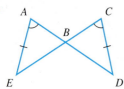

**(e)**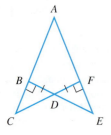

**(f)**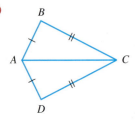

**5.** If $AB = 12$ and $AD = 2DC$, find $AE$ and $EB$.

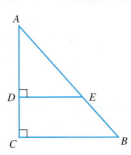

Explain how you found your answer.

**6.** Fill in the blanks that follow, where $\triangle KLM \sim \triangle UVW$.

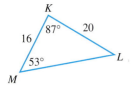

(a) $m(\angle W) = $ ____

(b) Scale factor = ____

(c) $UV = $ ____

**7.** A triangle has sides of length 10 feet and 16 feet. What is the range of lengths of the third side?

**8.** Let $ABCDE$ be a regular pentagon. Let $PQRST$ be inscribed so that $AP = BQ = CR = DS = ET$. Prove that $PQRST$ is a regular pentagon.

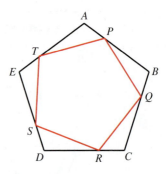

**9.** Let $\overline{PQ}$ be any segment.

(a) Use a compass and a straightedge to construct two different equilateral triangles $\triangle PQR$ and $\triangle PQS$, each with $\overline{PQ}$ as a side.

(b) Use a compass and a straightedge to construct an equilateral triangle $PTU$ for which $\overline{PQ}$ is an altitude. Describe your procedure. (*Suggestion:* First construct the line perpendicular to $PQ$ at $Q$, starting with your construction from part (a).)

**10.** Construct a triangle $DEF$ so that $\triangle DEF \cong \triangle ABC$ and $\angle A$, $\overline{AB}$, and $\angle B$ are as shown. List the steps you follow.

**11.** In $\triangle FGH$, $\angle F \cong \angle G$ and $FG = FH$. What can you conclude about the triangle?

**12.** For each of the pairs of triangles shown, decide whether they are necessarily congruent. If so, state why and give the vertex correspondence. If not, give a counterexample.

(a)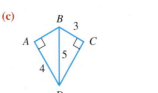

(b)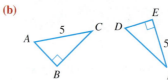

(c)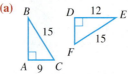

(d)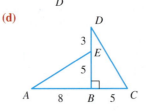

# 13

# Statistics: The Interpretation of Data

**13.1** Organizing and Representing Data

**13.2** Measuring the Center and Variation of Data

**13.3** Statistical Inference

## Hands On

### How Many Beans in the Bag?

#### Materials Needed

1. Three or four opaque bags containing about 200 beans each (this number being known only to the instructor), with the same number of beans in each bag.
2. A bright colored marker to go along with each bag.

#### Directions

1. Divide the class into groups of about ten students each and give each group a bag of beans.
2. The students in each group mark 25 beans with their colored marker and return the marked beans to their bag.
3. The beans in the bag are then thoroughly mixed.
4. Each student, without peeking, removes 5 beans from the bag (without replacement) and notes the number of marked beans obtained.
5. After all the students in a group have made their selection, the collection of all beans selected makes up the sample for the group.
6. Each group determines the fraction of marked beans in its sample (the number of marked beans in the sample divided by the total number of beans in the sample) and uses this figure to estimate the original number of beans in the bag. (Let $n$ denote the number of beans in the bag; then $\dfrac{25}{n}$ is the fraction of marked beans in the bag.)
7. The students repeat steps 2 through 6, but this time, in step 2, they mark 50 beans and return them to the bag. The students then compare the estimate obtained this time with that obtained the first time and discuss which estimate is likely to be the better one.
8. Finally, the instructor should reveal the actual number of beans in each of the bags and discuss the outcomes with the class.

---

**CHAPTER PREVIEW**

Most parents and even teachers are surprised that the various ways of picturing data and the analysis of such data are being introduced into elementary school now. In fact, the NCTM standards on data and statistics, which are quoted on page 712, emphasize the development of intuition about sets of data, how to describe them, how to get an idea of what might be called the "center" of the data, and how the data "spreads." In addition, this content is recommended in the *Curricular Focal Points for Prekindergarten Through Grade 8 Mathematics* (2007) and the well-thought-out and influential *Guidelines for Assessment and Instruction in Statistics Education (GAISE) Report: A Pre-K–12 Curriculum Framework* (2007), which advocates statistical literacy. Furthermore, statistics is very much a part of the state assessment exams throughout the United States. In fact, to show readers that statistics has a real presence in elementary school, we have included many more state assessment questions in this chapter than in others. Children need to understand basic statistics in order to build a foundation on which they can become informed citizens and to prepare them early in their development to be successful in their schooling and career.

This chapter is not a course in statistics—it couldn't be! Would you expect to be able to learn calculus, biology, or a social science by reading one chapter carefully? Of course not! Instead, the chapter introduces the tools of statistics that appear in elementary and middle school.

Statistics is a powerful and subtle science that helps citizens to become reflective and more informed. It also provides major analytical tools for such fields as medicine, social sciences, engineering, health sciences, economics, business, and many other areas. Statistics provides ways of looking at data from which careful planning and strategies for solving enormously complex problems can be formulated. To use statistics effectively requires much care and study. We hope that many of you will go on to some statistics courses to add depth to your knowledge and richness to your teaching of statistical concepts. The noted futurist and author of *War of the Worlds,* H. G. Wells, is credited with having written, in 1903, "Statistical thinking will one day be as necessary for efficient citizenship as the ability to read and write."

**KEY IDEAS**

- Statistics is a way to organize and represent data through a variety of methods.
- Statistics is a way to make sense out of data that have been gathered by computing certain numerical values that help us understand where the center of the data is and how the data set spreads out (its **variability**) from its center.

- The various numerical definitions of the center (**mean, median,** and **mode**) give different insights into which measure of the center of the data is most revealing in a given set.
- There are various ways to understand the variability of a data set, including **box and whisker plots, quartiles,** and the concept of the **standard deviation.**
- There is a difference between the population (the numerical values assigned) and a sample of the data from the population.
- An approach is given to attempt to predict the center and standard deviation of a population through collecting the standard deviation of a "reasonable" variety of samples. The normal distribution is key to this approach, which is called **statistical inference.**

> **FROM *The NCTM Principles and Standards***
>
> Prior to the middle grades, students should have had experiences collecting, organizing, and representing sets of data. They should be facile both with representational tools (such as tables, line plots, bar graphs, and line graphs) and with measures of center and spread (such as median, mode, and range). They should have had experience using some methods of analyzing information and answering questions, typically about a single population.
>
> In grades 6–8, teachers should build on this base of experience to help students answer more-complex questions, such as those concerning relationships among populations or samples and those about relationships between two variables within one population or sample. Toward this end, new representations should be added to the students' repertoire. Box plots, for example, allow students to compare two or more samples, such as the heights of students in two different classes. Scatterplots allow students to study related pairs of characteristics in one sample, such as height versus arm span among students in one class. In addition, students can use and further develop their emerging understanding of proportionality in various aspects of their study of data and statistics.
>
> SOURCE: *Principles and Standards for School Mathematics by NCTM, page 249. Copyright © 2000 by the National Council of Teachers of Mathematics. Reproduced with permission of the National Council of Teachers of Mathematics via Copyright Clearance Center. NCTM does not endorse the content or validity of these alignments.*

## 13.1

# Organizing and Representing Data

When a number of points of data are collected, we have a collection of data, or a **data set.** How can we organize the data set in a way that gives a picture of what the set actually looks like? Said a bit differently, can data be organized and represented in such a way that some properties of the data are more easily seen? In this section, various kinds of visual representations are given:

- **Dot plots:** summarizing relatively small sets of data—grades in a class, heights of students in a class, birth months of students in a class, and so on.
- **Stem-and-leaf plots:** for essentially the same purposes as dot plots; especially useful in comparing small data sets.
- **Histograms:** summarizing information from large sets of data that can be naturally grouped into intervals.
- **Line graphs:** summarizing trends over time.
- **Pie charts:** representing relative amounts of a whole.
- **Pictographs:** summarizing relative amounts, trends, and data sets; useful in comparing quantities.

We will start with dot plots and use a specific example.

## Dot Plots

In a class for prospective elementary school teachers, the final examination scores for the students were as shown in Table 13.1. This table shows the **data** simply recorded in a list.

| TABLE 13.1 | FINAL EXAMINATION SCORES IN MATHEMATICS FOR ELEMENTARY SCHOOL TEACHERS, SECTION 1 | | | | | |
|---|---|---|---|---|---|---|
| 79 | 78 | 79 | 65 | 95 | 77 | 49 |
| 91 | 63 | 58 | 78 | 96 | 74 | 68 |
| 71 | 86 | 91 | 94 | 79 | 69 | 86 |
| 62 | 78 | 77 | 88 | 67 | 78 | 84 |
| 69 | 53 | 79 | 75 | 64 | 89 | 77 |

Just scanning the data gives some idea of how the class did, but it is more revealing to organize the data by representing each score by a dot placed above a number line, as in Figure 13.1. Data depicted in this way are called a **dot plot** or sometimes a **line plot.** The dot plot makes it possible to see at a glance that the scores range from 49 through 96; that most scores are between 60 and 80, with a large group between 75 and 80; and that the "typical" score is probably about 77 or 78. It also reveals that scores like 49 and 53 are quite atypical, or **outliers.** Data organized and displayed on a dot plot are much easier to interpret than "raw," or unorganized, data.

**FIGURE 13.1**
Dot plot of the final examination scores in Mathematics for Elementary School Teachers, Section 1

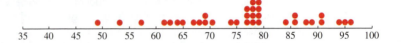

## Stem-and-Leaf Plots

**Stem-and-leaf-plots** for displaying data are quite similar to dot plots and are particularly useful for comparing two sets of data.

To draw a stem-and-leaf plot for the data that appear in Table 13.1, we let the tens digits of the scores be the stems and let the units digits be the leaves. Thus, the scores 79, 78, and 79 are represented by

$$\underbrace{7}_{stem} \mid \underbrace{8\ 9\ 9}_{leaves}$$

The completed plot appears in Figure 13.2.

**FIGURE 13.2**
Stem-and-leaf plot of the final examination scores in *Mathematics for Elementary School Teachers,* Section 1

| 4 | 9 | | | | | | | | | | | |
|---|---|---|---|---|---|---|---|---|---|---|---|---|
| 5 | 3 | 8 | | | | | | | | | | |
| 6 | 2 | 3 | 4 | 5 | 7 | 8 | 9 | 9 | | | | |
| 7 | 1 | 4 | 5 | 7 | 7 | 7 | 8 | 8 | 8 | 8 | 9 | 9 | 9 | 9 |
| 8 | 4 | 6 | 6 | 8 | 9 | | | | | | | |
| 9 | 1 | 1 | 4 | 5 | 6 | | | | | | | |

The stem-and-leaf plot gives much the same visual impression as the dot plot and allows a similar interpretation.

In comparing two sets of similar data, it is useful to construct stem-and-leaf plots on the same stem in order to develop intuition and make the (visual) comparison easier. Figure 13.3 shows such a plot for final examination scores in Sections 1 and 2 of the course *Mathematics for Elementary School Teachers.*

In this figure, it is easy to see that, although the two classes are quite comparable, Section 2 had a wider range of scores, with one lower and several higher than those in Section 1. The bottom row of Section 2 shows that three students had scores of 100 percent.

**FIGURE 13.3**
Stem-and-leaf plots of the final examination scores in *Mathematics for Elementary School Teachers,* Sections 1 and 2

| | | | | | | | | | Section 2 | | | | Section 1 | | | | | | | | | | | |
|---|---|---|---|---|---|---|---|---|---|---|---|---|---|---|---|---|---|---|---|---|---|---|---|---|
| | | | | | | | | 3 | 4 | 9 | | | | | | | | | | | | | | |
| | | | | | 9 | 8 | 7 | 5 | 5 | 3 | 8 | | | | | | | | | | | | | |
| | 8 | 8 | 5 | 5 | 5 | 5 | 3 | 1 | 6 | 2 | 3 | 4 | 5 | 7 | 8 | 9 | 9 | | | | | | | |
| | | | 5 | 5 | 4 | 4 | 3 | 0 | 7 | 1 | 4 | 5 | 7 | 7 | 7 | 8 | 8 | 8 | 8 | 9 | 9 | 9 | 9 | 9 |
| 9 | 7 | 6 | 4 | 4 | 2 | 0 | 0 | 0 | 8 | 4 | 6 | 6 | 8 | 9 | | | | | | | | | | |
| | | | | | 6 | 5 | 5 | 0 | 9 | 1 | 1 | 4 | 5 | 6 | | | | | | | | | | |
| | | | | | | 0 | 0 | 0 | 10 | | | | | | | | | | | | | | | |

## Histograms

Another common tool for organizing and summarizing data is a **histogram.** A histogram for the data in Table 13.1 is shown in Figure 13.4. In a histogram, scores are grouped into intervals and the number of scores in each interval is indicated by the height of the rectangle constructed above the interval. The number of times any particular data value occurs is called its **frequency.** Similarly, the number of data values in any interval is the **frequency of the interval.** Thus, looking at Figure 13.4, we see that there are 14 seniors whose scores are in the 70-to-79 range. A different way of saying this is that the frequency of the interval from 70 to 79 is 14. Note that the vertical axis of a histogram indicates frequency and the horizontal axis indicates data values or ranges of data values.

**FIGURE 13.4**
Histogram of the final examination scores in *Mathematics for Elementary School Teachers,* Section 1

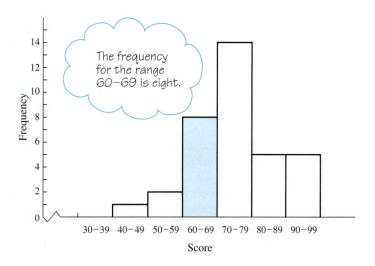

We lose some detail with the histogram. For example, the histogram in Figure 13.4 does not show how many students scored exactly 71. However, it has the advantage of giving a compact and accurate summary which is particularly useful with large collections of data that could not be conveniently represented with dot or stem-and-leaf plots.

Histograms are useful for giving visual summaries of data that either are discrete or vary continuously. For example, people's heights vary continuously. You may say that your height is 5'4" (or 64"), but that is not exactly true. Instead, it is true only *to the nearest inch.* Consider the data in Table 13.2, which gives the heights of the 80 boys at Eisenhower High School. The heights were measured to the nearest inch, so the numbers given already represent *grouped data;* that is, a measurement of 66 was recorded if a boy's height was judged to be between 65.5 and 66.5 inches. Even a height of almost exactly 66.5 inches was grouped into the 66- or 67-inch class as deemed most appropriate by the person doing the measuring. A histogram representing these data is shown in Figure 13.5. Note that in both Figure 13.4 and Figure 13.5, the sum of the heights of the rectangles gives the number of data values. The number of data values is also equal to the total area of all the rectangles.

| TABLE 13.2 | | HEIGHTS OF BOYS AT EISENHOWER HIGH SCHOOL, TO THE NEAREST INCH AND ARRANGED IN INCREASING ORDER | | | | | |
|---|---|---|---|---|---|---|---|
| 64 | 67 | 68 | 69 | 69 | 70 | 71 | 72 |
| 65 | 67 | 68 | 69 | 69 | 70 | 71 | 72 |
| 66 | 68 | 68 | 69 | 69 | 70 | 71 | 72 |
| 66 | 68 | 68 | 69 | 69 | 70 | 71 | 72 |
| 66 | 68 | 68 | 69 | 69 | 70 | 71 | 72 |
| 67 | 68 | 68 | 69 | 69 | 70 | 71 | 72 |
| 67 | 68 | 68 | 69 | 70 | 70 | 71 | 73 |
| 67 | 68 | 69 | 69 | 70 | 70 | 71 | 73 |
| 67 | 68 | 69 | 69 | 70 | 70 | 71 | 74 |
| 67 | 68 | 69 | 69 | 70 | 70 | 71 | 74 |

MHM  For those readers who have had a calculus course, the last sentence should remind you of integration of a function, as it talks about the area under a curve. Calculus is used in more advanced courses in statistics, but that level of statistics is not needed for those who will teach elementary school.

**FIGURE 13.5**

Histogram of the heights of boys at Eisenhower High School

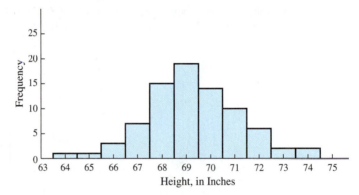

Grouping data into classes and displaying the data in a histogram is a useful visualization of the characteristics of the data set. In drawing a histogram, the scales should be chosen so that all the data can be represented. Also, the number of classes into which the data are grouped should not be so few that it hides too much information and not so numerous that one loses the visual advantage of constructing the diagram in the first place. This is an important criterion for quality and accountability of a statistical project. Comparing two different scales can greatly obscure what is really going on. (See problem 21 in Problem Set 13.1 and the pictograph of Figure 13.13.)

## Line Graphs

A **line graph** for the data in Figure 13.5 is constructed by joining the midpoints of the tops of the adjacent rectangles in the figure by line segments. (See Figure 13.6.) Without the rectangles, which would not ordinarily be drawn, the line graph appears as in Figure 13.7. Since the vertical axis

**FIGURE 13.6**

Histogram and line graph of the heights of boys at Eisenhower High School

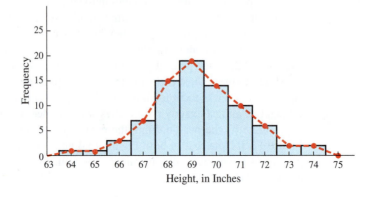

**FIGURE 13.7**
Line graph (frequency polygon) of the heights of boys at Eisenhower High School

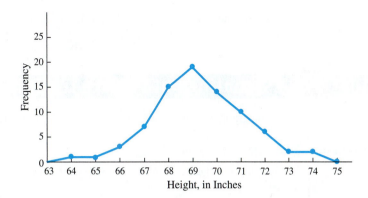

represents the frequency with which measurements occur, the line graph of a set of data like this is often called a **frequency polygon.**

A line graph, or frequency polygon, is particularly appropriate for representing data that vary continuously, since that kind of variation is strongly suggested by the sloping line segments. For those with a calculus background, this is where the derivative would come into play in a more advanced course. The rectangles in the histogram of Figure 13.5 tend to obscure the fact that the heights of boys represented, for example, by the rectangle centered at 67 range from 66.5″ to 67.5″. If, however, the data really are discrete, they are probably better represented by a histogram than a frequency polygon. Since, in constructing the frequency polygon from the histogram, we added and subtracted small triangles of equal area, the area under the frequency polygon, or line graph, still gives the number of data values, and the area under the graph and above a given interval gives the number of boys whose heights fall into that interval.

Line graphs not necessarily related to histograms are particularly effective when they are used to indicate trends over periods of years—trends in the stock market, trends in the consumption of electrical energy, and so on. For example, consider the data in Table 13.3, which gives the yearly consumer expenditure for food in the United States at five-year intervals from 1950 through 2005. These data are represented visually by the line graph in Figure 13.8. In this case, the points on the graph are determined by the year and the food expenditure for that year. The points are then connected by straight-line segments.

| TABLE 13.3 | CONSUMER EXPENDITURES FOR FOOD IN THE UNITED STATES, IN BILLIONS OF DOLLARS | | | | | | | | | | |
|---|---|---|---|---|---|---|---|---|---|---|---|
| **Year** | 1950 | 1955 | 1960 | 1965 | 1970 | 1975 | 1980 | 1985 | 1990 | 1995 | 2000 | 2005 |
| **Expenditures** | 44.0 | 53.1 | 66.9 | 81.1 | 110.6 | 167.0 | 264.4 | 345.4 | 440.6 | 499.1 | 559.4 | 622.5 |

**FIGURE 13.8**
U.S. consumer expenditures for food, in billions of dollars

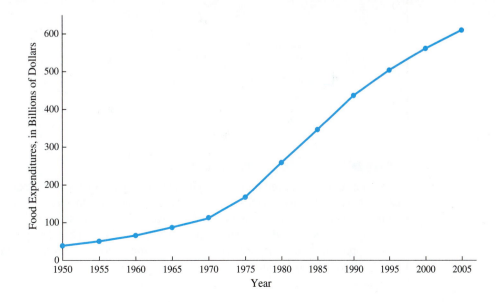

One advantage of a line graph is that it makes it possible to estimate data values not explicitly given otherwise.

## EXAMPLE 13.1 Estimating Data Values from a Line Graph

Using the graph in Figure 13.8, estimate the U.S. consumer expenditure for food in 1972.

**Solution**

### Understand the Problem

The graph gives the expenditure at five-year intervals. We are asked to estimate the expenditure for 1972.

### Devise a Plan

Having Figure 13.8 already simplifies our task. The graph suggests that the total expenditure grows steadily each year, and, while the growth is certainly not "straight-line growth" between data points as indicated by the diagram, the straight line joining the data points for 1970 and 1975 surely approximates the actual growth. If we draw a vertical line from the point representing 1972 on the horizontal axis, the height of the line segment should give us the approximate expenditure for 1972.

### Carry Out the Plan

The point on the horizontal axis representing 1972 is two-fifths of the way from 1970 to 1975. Draw a vertical line from this point to the line graph. Then draw a horizontal line from the point where the vertical line cuts the line graph to the vertical axis. This intersection determines the point on the vertical axis that gives approximately $140 billion as the value of U.S. consumer expenditure for food in 1972.

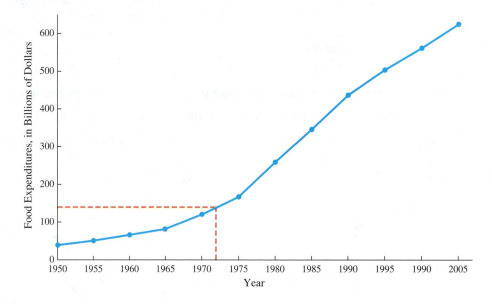

### Look Back

The solution was achieved by noting that the line graph, which gives the appropriate values of expenditures every five years, suggests that the expenditures increase steadily and that the actual values for intervening years no doubt lie relatively close to the straight-line segments joining the given data points. Indeed, it appears that a curved line through the data points might give an even better approximation somewhat less than $140 billion. However, as an estimate, $140 billion should be reasonably accurate.

| Score | Grade |
|-------|-------|
| 90–100 | A |
| 80–89 | B |
| 70–79 | C |
| 60–69 | D |
| 0–59 | F |

## Bar Graphs

**Bar graphs,** similar to histograms, are often useful in conveying information about so-called categorical data, where the horizontal scale represents some nonnumerical attribute. For example, consider the final examination scores for *Mathematics for Elementary School Teachers,* Section 1, as listed in Table 13.1. Suppose that the instructor determines grades as indicated in the accompanying table. Then members of the class were awarded 3 Fs, 8Ds, 14 Cs, 5 Bs, and 5 As. If we indicate grades on the horizontal scale and frequency on the vertical scale, we can construct the bar graph shown in Figure 13.9. In general, the rectangles in a bar graph do not abut, and the horizontal scale may be designated by any attribute—grade in class, year, country, city, and so on. As usual, however, the vertical scale will denote frequency—the number of items in the given class.

**FIGURE 13.9**
Bar graph of the final examination grades in *Mathematics for Elementary School Teachers,* Section 1

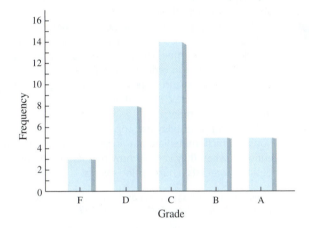

Bar graphs are useful in displaying data concerning nonnumerical items. As the next example shows, they are also useful in comparing data concerning two or more similar groups of items.

**EXAMPLE 13.2  Comparing Grades in Two Mathematics Classes by Means of a Bar Graph**

Draw a suitable bar graph to make a comparison of the grades in *Mathematics for Elementary School Teachers,* Sections 1 and 2.

**Solution**  The desired bar graph can be obtained by drawing two adjacent bars (rectangles) for each letter grade, with a suitable indication of which bars to associate with each section. If we use blue bars for Section 1 and pink bars for Section 2, a suitable graph might look like this (see Figure 13.3 on page 717 for the scores in Section 2; these scores merit 7 As, 9 Bs, 6 Cs, 8 Ds, and 5 Fs, with the same scale used as for Section 1):

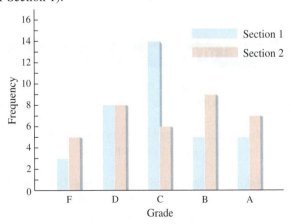

## Into the Classroom

### Clem Boyer Comments on Statistics in Elementary School

In learning statistics, graphing, and probability, students are learning about the real world. When they work with tables, charts, and graphs and use the language and notation of graphing mathematics, they are developing important real-life skills in reading, interpreting, and communicating information. Working with statistics prepares students to deal with the endless number of statistics in today's world. In using probability to predict outcomes, they are learning how to cope mathematically with the uncertainties in the real world. Students should plan and carry out the collection and organization of data to satisfy their curiosity about everyday living. They need to construct, read, and interpret simple maps, tables, charts, and graphs. In doing these things, they find out how to present information about the numerical data.

In order for students to manage statistics in this age of technology, it is important for them to learn to find measures of central tendency (mean, median, and mode) and measures of dispersion (range and deviation). Further, students need to recognize the basic uses and misuses of statistical representation and inference in order for them to be wise consumers.

All of these skills in working with data improve students' ability to interpret the data they read and hear about every day. Being able to use the terminology when displaying data will help students communicate their findings.

Learning probability has applications in the real world too. Students find out how to identify situations in which immediate past experience does not affect the likelihood of future events. Their lives are enriched when they can see how mathematics is used to make predictions regarding election results, business forecasts, and sporting events.

SOURCE: *Clem Boyer Comments on Statistics in Elementary School. From Scott Foresman Exploring Mathematics, Grades 1-7, by L. Carey Bolster, et al. © 1994 Scott Foresman and Company.*

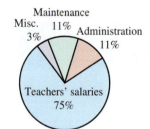

**FIGURE 13.10**
Percent of each tax dollar expended by Mile High School District, by category

## Pie Charts

Another pictorial method for conveying information is a **pie chart,** sometimes called a **circle plot.** For example, the pie chart in Figure 13.10 shows the parts of the budget that Mile High School District used for various purposes. The key to the pie chart is understanding that the number of degrees in the angular measure of each part of the chart is the appropriate fraction or percentage of 360°. Thus, the angular sector for the portion representing administration measures 11% of 360°, or

$$0.11 \times 360° = 39.6°,$$

and so on. As shown here, pie charts are most often used to show how a whole (total budget, total revenues, total sources of oil, and so on) is divided up.

---

### EXAMPLE 13.3   A Lottery Pie Chart

The 2003 volume of the *Statistical Abstract of the United States* shows that several states took in the following gross amounts of money from sales of lottery tickets during the years 1980–2002 (amounts are listed in billions of dollars for the various lottery games): Instant—18.5; Three-digit—5.3; Four-digit—2.9; Lotto—9.6; Other—5.6. Draw a pie chart showing the gross income the states received from each game.

**Solution**   Taking the sum of the gross proceeds from the various games, we find that the total gross income from all games was 41.9 billion dollars. Draw a circle, and divide it into sectors whose central angles have measures equal to the appropriate fraction of 360°. To the nearest degree, the central angles for the various games are as follows:

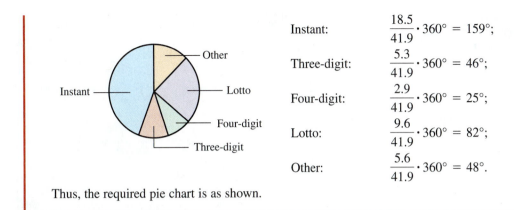

$$\text{Instant:} \quad \frac{18.5}{41.9} \cdot 360° = 159°;$$

$$\text{Three-digit:} \quad \frac{5.3}{41.9} \cdot 360° = 46°;$$

$$\text{Four-digit:} \quad \frac{2.9}{41.9} \cdot 360° = 25°;$$

$$\text{Lotto:} \quad \frac{9.6}{41.9} \cdot 360° = 82°;$$

$$\text{Other:} \quad \frac{5.6}{41.9} \cdot 360° = 48°.$$

Thus, the required pie chart is as shown.

If the pie chart is drawn in perspective, as if seen from an angle as in Figure 13.11, the central angles are no longer completely accurate. However, the pie chart still gives a good visual understanding of the apportionment of the whole being discussed. Also, in the figure, the pieces of the pie are separated slightly and are in color to produce a more pleasing visual effect.

**FIGURE 13.11**
Pie chart showing U.S. government sources of revenue for fiscal year 1991.
SOURCE: *1992 IRS Form 1040 instruction booklet*

**Where the Income Came From:**

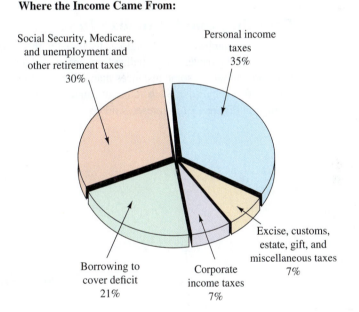

## Pictographs

A **pictograph** is a picture of a set of small figures or icons used to represent data and, often, to represent trends. Usually, the icons are suggestively related to the data being represented. Consider the pictograph presentation of past and projected growth in sheep population of the Island of Jack in Figure 13.12. The horizontal axis gives the year and the vertical axis measures sheep population. The pictograph accurately indicates that sheep population of the Island more than doubled over the 40-year period from 1950 to 1990. It also suggests that, while the rate of increase is expected to diminish, the population will almost double again in the next 60 years.

To make it possible to correctly interpret a pictograph, it is necessary to include a key that indicates the value or amount each small icon represents. For example, in Figure 13.12 each icon represents 100 sheep, and the pictograph should be read vertically. In making a pictograph, the determination of the key depends on the range of values to be represented. The key chosen must be sufficiently small that the resulting pictograph is large enough to show the desired detail, but not so small that the pictograph becomes unwieldy.

**FIGURE 13.12**
Pictograph of Island of Jack
sheep population growth:
🐑 = 100

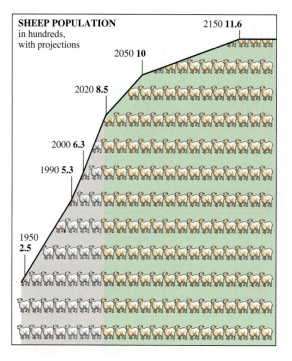

**FIGURE 13.12**
Pictograph of Island of Jack
sheep population growth:
🐑 = 100

## Choosing Good Visualizations

Each of the graphical representations discussed in this chapter is appropriate to summarize and present data so that the reader can visualize frequencies and determine trends. The various representations are more appropriate in some instances than others, and most are subject to serious distortion if the intent is to confuse the reader. Such an intent can lead to a **misleading representation.** For example, the pictograph in Figure 13.13 represents oil consumption in the United States for the years 1994 and 2004.

**FIGURE 13.13**
Oil consumption in the United States in 1994 and 2004

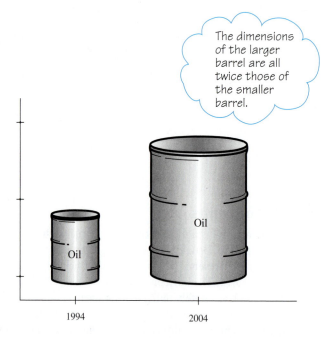

Although the vertical scale honestly indicates that approximately twice as much oil was used in 2004 as in 1994, the pictograph is misleading because the volume of the larger barrel is *8 times* the volume of the smaller barrel. The casual reader is quite likely to get a badly distorted idea of the relative amount of oil used in the two years. Of course, that may be exactly what the person who constructed the pictograph intended. Have you ever seen such distortions on television? in the newspaper? in advertisements? Be observant the next time you see this kind of a diagram.

## Problem Set 13.1

Exercises numbered in red are answered in the back of the text.

## Understanding Concepts

1. The following scores were obtained on the final examination in an introductory mathematics class of 40 students:

| 98 | 80 | 98 | 76 | 79 | 94 | 71 | 45 | 89 | 71 |
|----|----|----|----|----|----|----|----|----|----|
| 62 | 61 | 95 | 77 | 83 | 49 | 65 | 58 | 56 | 89 |
| 66 | 87 | 74 | 64 | 75 | 58 | 72 | 75 | 48 | 88 |
| 75 | 51 | 84 | 76 | 95 | 69 | 61 | 69 | 33 | 86 |

(a) After scanning the data, what do you think the "typical" or "average" score is?

(b) Make a dot plot to organize these data.

(c) After looking at the dot plot, what seems to be the "typical" score?

(d) Do you see any scores that seem to be particularly atypical of this data set? Explain.

(e) Write a two- or three-sentence description of the results of the final examination.

2. Make a stem-and-leaf plot of the data in problem 1.

3. Make a histogram for the data in problem 1, using the ranges 20–29, 30–39, . . . , 90–99 on the horizontal axis.

4. At the same time that heights of the boys at Eisenhower High School were studied, heights of the girls were also studied.

(a) Draw a histogram to summarize the data set that follows, which gives the heights, to the nearest inch, of the 75 girls at Eisenhower High School. Use intervals one unit wide centered at the whole-number values 56, 57, . . . , 74.

| 57 | 62 | 63 | 64 | 66 |
|----|----|----|----|----|
| 58 | 62 | 63 | 64 | 66 |
| 60 | 62 | 63 | 64 | 66 |
| 60 | 62 | 63 | 65 | 66 |
| 61 | 62 | 63 | 65 | 66 |
| 61 | 62 | 63 | 65 | 66 |
| 61 | 62 | 63 | 65 | 66 |
| 61 | 63 | 64 | 65 | 66 |

| 61 | 63 | 64 | 65 | 66 |
|----|----|----|----|----|
| 61 | 63 | 64 | 65 | 66 |
| 62 | 63 | 64 | 65 | 67 |
| 62 | 63 | 64 | 65 | 67 |
| 62 | 63 | 64 | 65 | 70 |
| 62 | 63 | 64 | 65 | 70 |
| 62 | 63 | 64 | 66 | 73 |

(b) Write two or three sentences describing the distribution of the heights of the girls.

5. (a) Draw a frequency polygon for the data in problem 4 by joining the midpoints of the tops of the rectangles of the histogram by straight-line segments.

(b) What does the area under the frequency polygon and between the scores 60.5 and 64.5 represent? Explain briefly.

6. The scores on the first, second, and third tests given in a class in educational statistics as the term progressed are shown in the accompanying table.

(a) Draw three separate, but parallel, dot plots for the three sets of scores.

(b) Write a three- or four-sentence analysis of your dot plots suggesting what happened during the term to account for the changing distribution of scores.

7. Ms. Smithson earned $64,000 per year, which she spent as shown in the following table:

| Taxes | $21,000 |
|-------|---------|
| Rent | $10,800 |
| Food | $5,000 |
| Clothes | $2,000 |
| Car payments | $4,800 |
| Insurance | $5,200 |
| Charity | $7,000 |
| Savings | $6,000 |
| Misc. | $2,200 |

Draw a pie chart to show how Ms. Smithson spent her yearly income.

Table for Problem 6

| **First test:** | 92, | 80, | 73, | 74, | 93, | 75, | 76, | 68, | 61, | 76, |
|-----------------|-----|-----|-----|-----|-----|-----|-----|-----|-----|-----|
| | 83, | 94, | 63, | 74, | 76, | 86, | 82, | 70, | 65, | 74, |
| | 83, | 87, | 98, | 77, | 67, | 64, | 87, | 96, | 62, | 64 |
| **Second test:** | 52, | 65, | 84, | 91, | 86, | 76, | 73, | 52, | 68, | 79, |
| | 88, | 94, | 98, | 84, | 53, | 59, | 63, | 66, | 77, | 81, |
| | 94, | 81, | 64, | 56, | 96, | 58, | 64, | 57, | 83, | 87 |
| **Third test:** | 97, | 91, | 61, | 67, | 72, | 81, | 63, | 56, | 53, | 59, |
| | 43, | 56, | 64, | 78, | 93, | 99, | 84, | 84, | 61, | 56, |
| | 73, | 77, | 57, | 46, | 93, | 87, | 93, | 78, | 46, | 87 |

8. This pie chart indicates how the city of Metropolis allocates its revenues each year:

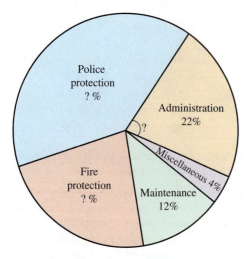

(a) What is the measurement of the central angle of the sector representing administrative expense?

(b) Using a protractor to measure the angle, determine what percent of the city budget goes for police protection.

(c) How does the city's expenditure for maintenance compare with its expenditure for police protection?

(d) How do the expenditures for administration and fire protection compare?

9. This bar graph shows the distribution of grades on the final examination in a class in English literature:

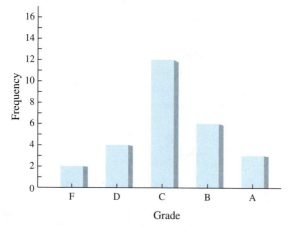

(a) From the bar graph, determine how many students in the class got Cs.

(b) How many more students got Bs than Ds?

(c) What percent of the students earned As?

10. (a) Go to a busy campus parking lot, and record the number of cars that are predominately white, black, red, gray, green, and "other."

(b) Make a bar graph to display and summarize your data.

(c) On the basis of part (a), if you were to stand on a busy street corner and watch 200 cars go by, how many would you expect to be predominately white?

(d) If you were on any street corner, how many cars would you expect to be white?

11. (a) Go to a coffee shop and, during the course of an hour, record what males and females order by hearing their preferences among (usual) coffee, decaffeinated coffee, latte, espresso, cappuccino, and others.

(b) Think about what data might be collected at a coffee shop. Go to the coffee shop and record your data in a manner similar to (a).

(c) If you came back to the coffee shop in 4 hours and again recorded males' and females' preferences among types of coffee, would you expect similar data?

(d) If you were to go to a different coffee shop, would you expect similar data?

12. (a) The data in the table on this page show the name, year, and revenue of the featured play from 2007 to 2011 at Midtown High School. Construct a bar graph for that data.

(b) From the bar graph, can you give a list, arranged from top to bottom, of the student interest in the plays?

## PLAYS AT MIDTOWN HIGH SCHOOL IN A FIVE-YEAR PERIOD

| Play | Year | Revenue |
|------|------|---------|
| 'Bye Bye Birdie' | 2007 | $4135 |
| 'Chicago' | 2008 | 4572 |
| 'Singin' in the Rain' | 2009 | 4300 |
| 'West Side Story' | 2010 | 8217 |
| 'Wicked' | 2011 | 4045 |

## Teaching Concepts

13. Collecting their own data actively engages students in the study of statistical notions, not only heightening student interest but also imparting a sense of meaning and reality to the study of statistics. Name four activities you deem particularly suitable for a class of elementary school students that would involve the collection and representation of data.

14. Buy a small package of M&M's with mixed colors. Open the package and pour out the M&M's.

(a) How many M&M's of each color are in the package?

(b) Make a bar graph of the data from part (a).

(c) Make a pictograph to display the data from part (a).

(d) Would it be reasonable to guess that most packages of M&M's contain about twice as many yellow as green candies?

**15. (a)** Roll two dice 50 times, and record the number of times (the frequency) you obtained each score.

**(b)** Draw a bar graph for the data of part (a), showing frequency on the vertical axis and score on the horizontal axis.

**16.** The accompanying figure is from page 11 of the teacher's edition of *Scott Foresman–Addison Wesley Math Grade 5*, by Randall I. Charles et al., copyright © 2002 Pearson Education, Inc. Reprinted with permission.

**(a)** The teacher's edition shows a possible correct answer. How many small icons should the plot show for the pine category if the key is such that each icon (small tree symbol) represents ten trees?

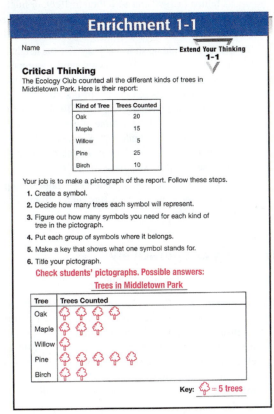

**(b)** Make your own pictograph of these data, with each icon representing two trees.

## Responding to Students

**17.** In this pictograph about books read in September, the box symbol represents two books read:

Fred

Kristen

Nancy

James

Bill

Sarita was asked the following questions about the graph:

**1.** Who read exactly four more books than James?

**2.** Who read the most books and how many did he or she read?

For the first question, Sarita studied the graph and answered that Fred read exactly four more books than James. In answering the second question, Sarita said that Fred read the most because he read five books.

**(a)** For both questions, what is Sarita misinterpreting in regard to the pictograph?

**(b)** What are the correct answers to the two questions?

**(c)** How would you guide Sarita to answer similar questions in the future?

**18.** Jeremy was shown the following graph about the number of fish caught in one week at a local lake:

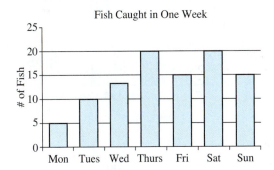

He was asked the following questions:

**1.** How many more fish were caught on the weekend (Saturday and Sunday) than on Monday?

**2.** What two days together equal the total number of fish caught on Friday?

After studying the graph,

**1.** Jeremy said that the answer to question 1 was five, because if you take the amount from Monday and put it with Saturday and Sunday, you get two full bars on the graph.

**2.** Jeremy answered that Sunday equaled the number of fish on Friday.

**(a)** How would you help Jeremy understand what was being asked in question 1? How would you guide him toward an answer?

**(b)** What is Jeremy misinterpreting in regard to question 2? How would you guide him toward an answer?

**19.** Stacy is working on a science project collecting data on the size of the circumference of her classmates' heads. She wants to represent her data graphically and is trying to decide whether to use a bar graph or a histogram. She says, "Well, aren't they the same?" Help Stacy create a graphic organizer to represent the similarities and differences between the two graphs.

## Thinking Critically

Data are often presented in a way that confuses, or even purposely misleads, the viewer.

**20. (a)** Discuss briefly why the television evening news might show histogram (A) rather than (B) in reporting stock market activity for the last seven days. Is one of these histograms misleading? Why or why not?

**(A)**

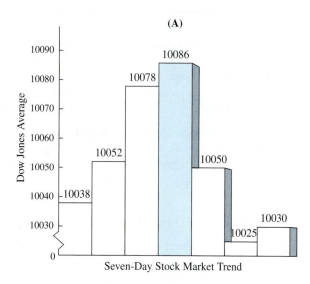

Seven-Day Stock Market Trend

**(B)**

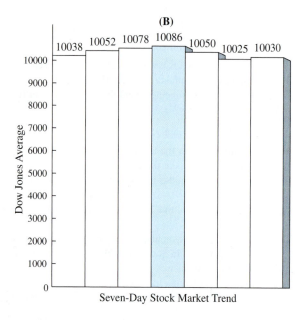

Seven-Day Stock Market Trend

**(b)** What was the percentage drop in the Dow Jones average from the fourth to the fifth day as shown in the preceding histograms? Should an investor worry very much about this 36-point drop in the market?

**(c)** Was the Dow Jones average on day 5 approximately half of what it was on day 4, as suggested by histogram (A)?

**21.** Longlife Insurance Company printed a brochure with the following pictographs showing the growth in company assets over the ten-year period 1990–1999:

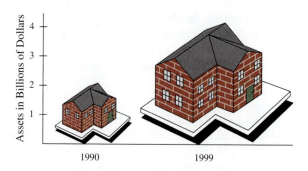

**(a)** Do the pictographs accurately indicate that the assets were $2 billion in 1990 and $4 billion in 1999, or might one assume from the pictographs that the assets were actually much greater in 1999 then in 1990? Explain briefly.

**(b)** The larger building shown is just twice the height of the smaller, and the two buildings are similar as geometrical drawings. Do these drawings accurately convey the impression that the assets of Longlife Insurance Company just doubled during the ten-year period? Explain your reasoning. What is the ratio of the volume of the large building to the volume of the small building? (*Suggestion:* Suppose both buildings were rectangular boxes, with the linear dimensions of the second just twice those of the first.)

**(c)** Would it have been more helpful (or honest) to print the actual asset value for each year on the front of each building?

## Thinking Cooperatively

This exercise is best done as a class activity.

**22.** Our measure of a "yard" was originally the length from the tip of the nose to the fingertip of the outstretched arm of an English king. Working in small groups, use a tape measure to measure this length to the nearest inch for each student in class. Record the data on the chalkboard (and for later use in Problem Set 13.2) in two sets—one set for men and one set for women. Divide the class into several small groups.

**(a)** Members of one or two small groups each make a dot plot for the data in each of the two sets.

**(b)** Members of one or two small groups each make a double stem-and-leaf plot for the data in each of the two sets.

**(c)** Members of one or two small groups each make a histogram for the data in each of the two sets.

**(d)** Members of one or two small groups each make a frequency polygon for the data in each of the two sets.

**(e)** Members of one or two small groups each make a pictograph for the data in each of the two sets.

**(f)** As a class, discuss the various representations of the data. Which ones seem most informative? What conclusions are suggested regarding the length of a "yard"? Discuss briefly.

## Making Connections

**23.** This line graph from the 2003 edition of *The Digest of Educational Statistics* shows that nearly all public schools had Internet access by 2001:

Percent of all public schools and instructional rooms
having Internet access: Fall 1994 to Fall 2001

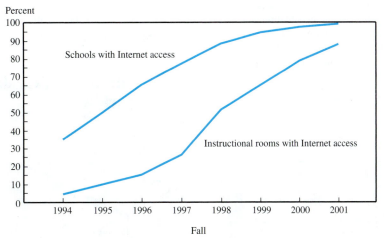

SOURCE: *U.S. Department of Education, National Center for Education Statistics, Fast Response Survey System,* Internet Access in Public Schools and Classrooms: 1994–2001.

**(a)** Determine from the graph the year that approximately 50% of all public schools had Internet access.

**(b)** In what year did approximately 90% of the schools have Internet access?

**(c)** In 2001, only approximately 90% of all classrooms had Internet access. What type of classrooms likely would not have had access? That is, what subjects would likely have been taught in the 10% of classrooms that did not have Internet access?

---

**24.** This pie chart from the *Digest of Education Statistics, 2002,* shows the percentage of persons 25 years and older in 2001 that attained various levels of education:

Highest level of education attained by persons 25 and older in March 2001

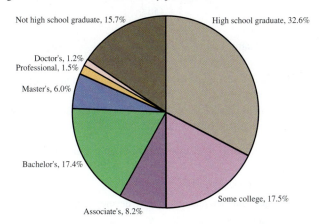

Total persons age 25 and over = 177.0 million

NOTE: Detail may not sum to totals due to rounding.

SOURCE: *U.S. Department of Commerce, Bureau of the Census, Current Population Survey, unpublished data.*

**(a)** Assuming that these figures remain relatively constant from year to year, approximately what percentage of high school graduates who go to college fail to earn a bachelor's degree? (*Hint:* Assume that people who earn master's, professional, and doctor's degrees must first earn a bachelor's degree.)

**(b)** What percentage of high school graduates earn a bachelor's degree?

**(c)** What percentage of the people who earn bachelor's degrees eventually earn a doctor's degree?

**25.** The graph below indicates Buzz Technology's (BT) net income or loss for the years 2006 through 2010 and first three months of 2011.

**(a)** Supposing that BT's income continued to come in at that rate, what would you forecast its net income for 2011 to be?

**(b)** Draw a line graph (including your estimate for 2011) for BT's income for 2006 through 2011.

**(c)** About what percentage increase in net income did BT experience in 2010 over 2008?

**(d)** If the assumption in part (a) proved to be correct, what would BT's percentage increase in net income in 2011 over 2009 be?

**BT's Net Income/Loss (in millions)**

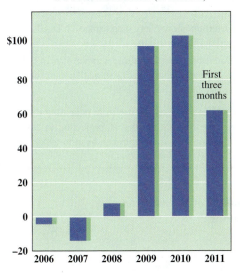

26. Mathematics has, unfortunately, been viewed traditionally as a "male" subject, which it shouldn't be. Although presently about half of the mathematics undergraduate degrees in the United States are awarded to women, the situation is quite different at the doctoral level, and there are a number of nationwide initiatives that are focused on this issue. The accompanying graphs show the number and percentage of mathematics Ph.D.s earned by women at U.S. schools.

   (a) From the graphs, determine how many times as many women earned Ph.D.s in mathematics during the 1990s as during the 1890s.

**Number of Mathematics Ph.D.s Earned by Women at U.S. Schools**

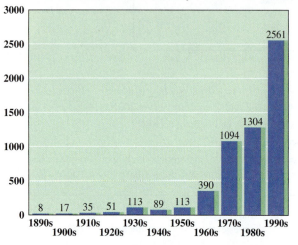

**Approximate Percentage of U.S. Mathematics Ph.D.s Earned by Women**

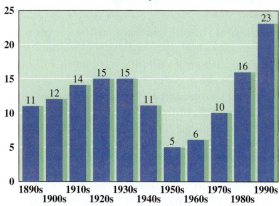

   (b) Determine how many men earned Ph.D.s during the 1890s and during the 1990s.

   (c) Determine the ratio of the number of men to the number of women earning Ph.D.s in mathematics during the 1890s and during the 1990s.

27. Line graphs are certainly useful in indicating trends over time. However, extrapolating (that is, projecting values beyond the period covered by the graph) can be quite risky. The observed trend simply may not continue.

   (a) Suppose you had guessed the number of PCs that would be shipped worldwide in 2001 on the basis of the part of the graph shown up to 2000. What might you reasonably have guessed the figure would be for 2001?

   (b) By how much would you have overestimated the number of PCs shipped in 2001, given the graph as shown?

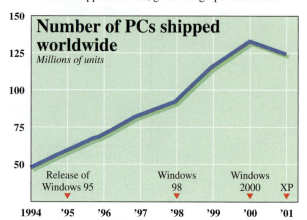

SOURCE: *Gartner Dataquest.*

28. Consider the SAT scores recorded here:

| Student | Verbal Score | Math Score |
|---------|-------------|------------|
| Dina | 502 | 444 |
| Carlos | 590 | 520 |
| Rosette | 585 | 621 |
| Broz | 487 | 493 |
| Colleen | 585 | 602 |
| Dieter | 481 | 572 |
| Darin | 605 | 599 |
| Luana | 547 | 499 |

   (a) Make a bar graph to summarize the preceding data for verbal scores.

   (b) Make a double bar graph to summarize the data, with one of each pair of bars for verbal scores and one for math scores.

29. For fiscal year 2002, federal expenditures were divided as follows:

   Social progrxams—14%

   Physical, human, and community development—14%

   Net interest on debt—14%

   Defense, veterans, and foreign affairs—24%

   Social Security, Medicare, and other retirement—32%

   Law enforcement and general government—2%

   (a) Make a pie chart that reflects these data.

   (b) Make a bar graph that reflects these data.

30. Make a line graph that graphically displays these data:

| Population of Washington, in Millions | 2.10 | 2.32 | 2.63 | 2.83 | 3.12 | 3.45 | 3.80 | 4.18 | 4.81 | 5.76 |
|---|---|---|---|---|---|---|---|---|---|---|
| Year | 1960 | 1965 | 1970 | 1975 | 1980 | 1985 | 1990 | 1995 | 2000 | 2005 |

## From State Student Assessments

*Note:* There are many SSA questions because of the variety and level of depth of these problems. (See Problem 39.)

**31.** (Illinois, Grade 3)
This graph shows the results of a classroom vote on favorite pets. How many more students voted for dogs than for cats?

**Favorite Pets**

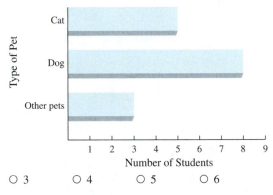

○ 3        ○ 4        ○ 5        ○ 6

**32.** (Michigan, Grade 4)
Miguel has a birdfeeder in his backyard. He made the picture graph below to show how many of each kind of bird he has seen. Miguel has seen ten purple finches.

**Number of Birds Seen**

= 4 birds

What should the picture graph show for purple finches?

**A.**

**B.**

**C.**

**D.**
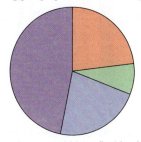

**33.** (Minnesota, Grade 5)
*Use the following pie graph to answer the question.*

Which set of numbers would best fit this pie graph?

○ **A.** 54, 8, 30, 8        ○ **B.** 47, 23, 8, 22
○ **C.** 51, 17, 15, 17      ○ **D.** 27, 26, 24, 23

**34.** (Michigan, Grade 4)
Directions: Solve the following problem. There may be more than one way to answer correctly. Show as much of your work as possible.

> Tyler read 9 books.
> Lauren read 6 books.
> Kyle read 5 books.
> Emily read 12 books.

Use the data and make a graph. Write three questions that could be answered by using the data on this graph.

**35.** (Massachusetts, Grade 4)

*Use the information in the line graph below to answer the question.*

The graph shows the weight gain of a puppy during its first week of life. Which is NOT true about the weight of the puppy?

**Weight of Puppy During First Week**

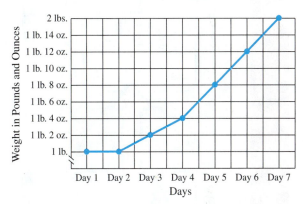

**A.** The puppy gained 2 ounces between Day 3 and Day 4.

**B.** The puppy weighed $1\frac{1}{2}$ pounds on Day 5.

**C.** The puppy's weight doubled during the first week.

**D.** The puppy's weight tripled during the first week.

**36.** (Georgia, Grade 7)
The histogram shows the heights of members of a middle school basketball team.

Use it to answer the question.

**Heights of School Basketball Team**

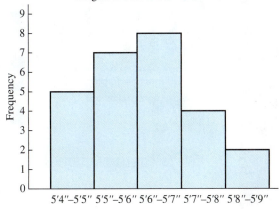

*See "Examining School Book Pages" on page 731 for questions related to the pages shown below.*

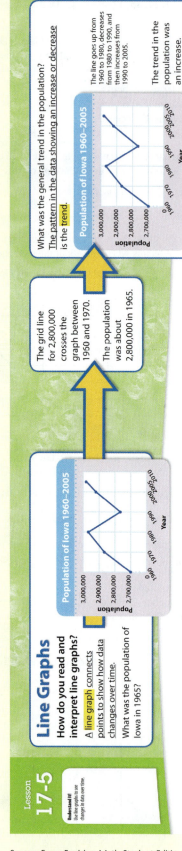

## Lesson 17-5

**Understand It!**
Use line graphs to see changes in data over time.

### Line Graphs

**How do you read and interpret line graphs?**

A line graph connects points to show how data changes over time.

What was the population of Iowa in 1965?

**Population of Iowa 1960–2005**

The grid line for 2,800,000 crosses the graph between 1950 and 1970.
The population was about 2,800,000 in 1965.

What was the general trend in the population?
The pattern in the data showing an increase or decrease is the **trend**.

The line goes up from 1960 to 1980, decreases from 1980 to 1990, and then increases from 1990 to 2005.

The trend in the population was an increase.

---

### Guided Practice*

**Do you know HOW?**

1. Use the line graph below. About how long did it take the cyclist to travel 4 miles?

**Bicycle Race**

**Do you UNDERSTAND?**

2. Did Iowa's population increase more between 1970 and 1980 or between 1990 and 2000?

3. Would you expect the population of Iowa in 2010 to be more or less than 3 million? Explain your answer.

4. How can you tell when there is an increase from the data on a graph?

### Independent Practice

For **5** through **8**, use the graph at the right.

**Distance Traveled in a Car**

5. About how far did the car travel in the first 8 hours?

6. About how long did it take the car to travel 250 miles?

7. About how far did the car travel between the 6th and 10th hours?

8. **Reasoning** What is the trend in the data?

410

*For another example, see Set E on page 427.*

---

### Problem Solving

For **9** through **11**, use the graph to the right.

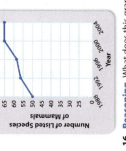

**Mary's Charity Bike Ride**

9. Between which times did Mary ride the fastest?

10. What do you think happened between 9:00 and 9:30?

11. How far did Mary ride in two hours and thirty minutes?

For **12** through **16**, use the graph to the right.

**U.S. Endangered Mammals**

12. About how many species of mammals were endangered in 1996?

13. During which four years did the number of endangered mammals increase the least?

14. **Estimation** About how many more species of endangered mammals were there in 2004 than in 1992?

15. Between which four years did the number of endangered mammals stay the same?

  A  1988–1992    C  1996–2000

  B  1992–1996    D  2000–2004

16. **Reasoning** What does this graph tell you about the number of endangered species of reptiles?

Lesson 17-5

411

DIGITAL
Animated Glossary
www.pearsonsuccessnet.com

What percent of the team is more than 5′5″ tall, but less than 5′8″ tall?

**A.** 19%     **B.** 26%     **C.** 60%     **D.** 73%

**37.** (Virginia, Grade 6)
A clerk recorded the number of pairs of jeans sold each day at a store. The data are displayed on the stem-and-leaf plot.

| Stem | Leaf |
|------|------|
| 0 | 9 |
| 1 | 2 5 5 6 8 9 |
| 2 | 0 0 1 1 1 5 5 5 5 |
| 3 | 2 5 6 |
| 4 | |
| 5 | 8 |

| Key |
|-----|
| 1\|5 = 15 |

Which of the following statements is *true* according to the data in the stem-and-leaf plot?

**F.** The number of pairs of jeans sold each day was between 0 and 8.

**G.** The stem-and-leaf plot displays 26 days of sales.

**H.** The median for the data is 25.

**J.** The mode for the data is 25.

**38.** (Illinois, Grade 6)
Carl has 16 books in his bookcase. This bar graph shows the number of each type of book.

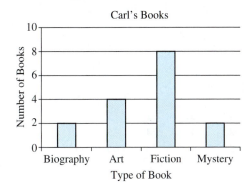

Which circle graph best shows the types of books Carl has in his bookcase?

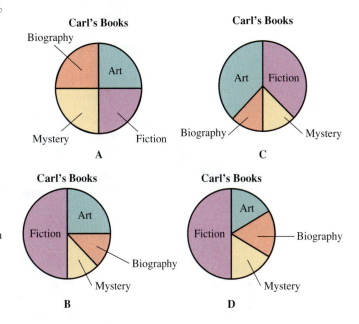

**39.** (Comparison of some State Assessment questions)
**MHM** Compare the level of mathematical depth of the State Student Assessment problems of this section. Is there a variety between states or between grade levels?

### Examining School Book Pages

*Refer to the School Book Pages provided on page 730 to answer the following questions.*

**40.** After having done problem 13 on p. 730, what do you think might have caused the least increase?

**41.** If problem 16 were about whales, rather than reptiles, how do you think your class of fourth-grade students would respond?

**13.2**

# Measuring the Center and Variation of Data

In the previous section, we saw some approaches to organizing and visualizing data. In this section, we turn to finding ways to describe numerically some properties of the data set. The two questions that will be introduced here are Where is the center? and What is the spread of the data (its **variability**)? In statistics, there are three popular ways to describe the center (**mean, median,** and **mode**), and they are usually referred to as a group as the **measures of central tendency.** We then define some measures of variability, such as **upper** and **lower quartiles, interquartile range, box plots,** and **standard deviation.** All of these terms are contained in the elementary and middle school curriculum.

## Measures of Central Tendency

We will start by looking back again to the data of Table 13.1 and the corresponding dot plot of Figure 13.1 on page 714. We will use that data set to motivate the development of the concepts of this section.

The dot plot is a considerable improvement over the disorganized raw data for assessing the performance of the class. We can see at a glance that most of the grades lie between 62 and 96, with a large cluster between 75 and 80. We also see that the lowest grade is 49 and the highest grade is 96. But even more definitive information might be desired. For example,

- What is the "typical" grade for the class?
- How did most of the students do?
- Did many of the students perform markedly differently from the bulk of the class?

There are several different possibilities for answering these questions. First, consider the following different data sets $R$, $S$, and $T$, representing grades on tests, and their corresponding dot plots:

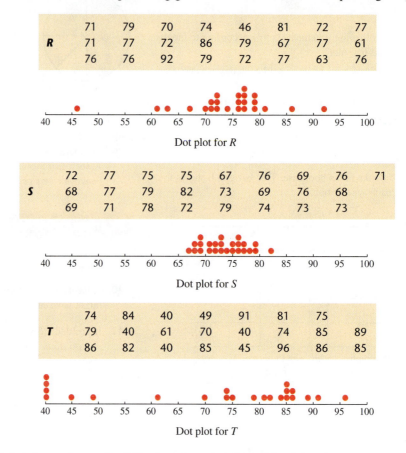

The dot plots help us observe the following characteristics of the data sets:

1. The scores in data set $R$ seem to cluster about 76, even though they range all the way from 46 to 92 and are generally rather widely spread. Apparently, some of the students did very well, while others did quite poorly. If we had to choose a single grade as typical of the entire class, it would probably be about 76.
2. The scores in data set $S$ are much less spread out than those of $R$, ranging only from 67 to 82. Thus, all the students did reasonably well, with none outstandingly good and none outstandingly poor. The grades seem to cluster about 73, and we would probably select this grade as reasonably typical of the entire class.
3. The scores in data set $T$ are very widely spread, ranging all the way from 40 to 96. Clearly, a number of students did very poorly, while a substantial number did quite well. Here, it is more difficult to select a single grade as typical. If we ignore the very poorest grades, we may want to choose 85 as typical. But there are many scores that differ widely from 85.

From these examples, two properties naturally arise when it comes to analyzing a data set:

- the typical, or central, value of the data, and
- the dispersion, or spread, of the data about the central value.

We now consider various standard approaches to identifying and quantifying these ideas. We will deal first with three ways to define a center of a data set.

## The Mean

The dot plots just considered allow one to develop an intuitive, but not very precise, notion of a typical, or central, value of a set of data. One very useful and precisely defined central value is the **mean,** frequently called the **arithmetic mean** or **average.** An effective manipulative device for introducing this notion to students that is quite independent of, and different from, the dot plots just considered is provided by a simple set of blocks. For example, consider the data 7, 5, 7, 3, 8, and 6. Arrange a number of blocks into six stacks containing 7, 5, 7, 3, 8, and 6 blocks, respectively, as follows, and ask what the typical or average height of all the stacks is:

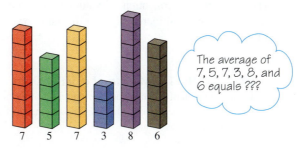

The average of 7, 5, 7, 3, 8, and 6 equals ???

If all the stacks were the same height, the answer would be obvious—it would be their common height. This suggests that a reasonable approach to answer the question might be to move blocks from taller stacks to shorter ones in an effort to even them up. Indeed, the blocks can be arranged into the following six stacks, each of height 6, and this arrangement suggests that the average height is 6:

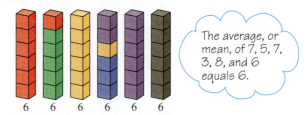

The average, or mean, of 7, 5, 7, 3, 8, and 6 equals 6.

Arithmetically, the number of blocks in the two arrangements has not changed, so

$$6 \cdot 6 = 7 + 5 + 7 + 3 + 8 + 6 \quad \text{and} \quad 6 = \frac{7 + 5 + 7 + 3 + 8 + 6}{6}.$$

Thus, the average or typical height of the original stacks is found by finding the sum of their heights and dividing by the number of stacks. This naturally leads to the following definition:

> **DEFINITION**  *The Mean of a Set of Data*
>
> The **mean,** or **average,** of a collection of values is $\bar{x} = \dfrac{S}{n}$, where $S$ is the sum of the values and $n$ is the number of values. The symbol $\bar{x}$ should be read as "$x$ bar."

For the data set $R$, we compute the mean by adding all scores and dividing by 24, the number of scores. Thus,

$$\bar{x} = (71 + 79 + 70 + 74 + 46 + 81 + 72 + 77 + 71 + 77 + 72 + 86$$
$$+ \ 79 + 67 + 77 + 61 + 76 + 76 + 92 + 79 + 72 + 77 + 63 + 76)/24$$
$$\doteq 73.8.$$

This is reasonably close to our informal feeling that 76 is reasonably representative of the scores in the data set. Actually, 73.8 is somewhat smaller than expected, which shows that the mean of a data set is sensitive to atypical data values such as 46. In this case, the mean of the data with 46 omitted is 75—very close to our informal determination.

For the data sets $S$ and $T$, we find that the means are, respectively, 73.6 and 71.2. For $S$, the mean gives a very good estimate of what we intuitively felt was the typical or central value. For $T$, the mean of 71.2 seems unduly low, and this is again a reflection of the fact that the mean can be strongly affected by the presence of extremely atypical values like 40, 40, 40, 40, 45, 49, and even 61. Without these values, the mean is a much more acceptable 82.6. At any rate, it is usually the case for most data sets that data values cluster reasonably closely about the mean. This is particularly true if we have criteria for deciding when data values are too atypical so that we may delete them from consideration. We develop such a criterion a little later, but, for now, we consider other frequently used measures of central tendency or central value.

## The Median

The **median** of a collection of values is the middle value in the collection when the values are arranged in order of increasing size, or the average of the two middle values in case the number of values is even.

> **DEFINITION**  *The Median of a Set of Data*
> Let a collection of $n$ data values be written in order of increasing size. If $n$ is odd, the **median,** denoted by $\hat{x}$, is the middle value in the list. If $n$ is even, $\hat{x}$ is the average of the two middle values. The symbol $\hat{x}$ should be read as "$x$ hat."

**EXAMPLE 13.4  Determining a Median**

Determine the median of the data in data set $R$ on page 732.

**Solution**  The scores in $R$ are arranged in order in the line plot of $R$. Since there are 24 scores, the median is the average of the twelfth and thirteenth scores. We see that $\hat{x} = 76$.

Note that the median in the preceding example not only closely approximates the mean but also agrees reasonably well with our intuitive idea of the middle value of the collection of scores.

It follows from the definition that the median is a data value if the number of data values is odd and is *not* necessarily a data value if the number of values is even. Thus, the median of the nine scores

$$24, 25, 25, 27, 29, 31, 32, 34, 37$$

is 29, the fifth score, while the median of the ten scores

$$42, 42, 43, 44, 44, 46, 47, 47, 47, 49$$

is 45, the average of the two middle scores.

## The Mode

Another value often taken as "typical" of a set of data is the value occurring most frequently. This value is called the **mode.**

> **DEFINITION**  *A Mode of a Set of Data*
> A **mode** of a collection of values is a value that occurs the most frequently. If two or more values occur equally often and more frequently than all other values, there are two or more modes.

From the definition, it should be clear that there may be more than one mode. For example, data set $S$ has three modes, namely, 69, 73, and 76, since each of those numbers appears three times and no data point occurs more than three times. The mode gives a different type of indication of the typical value of the data than either the mean or the median. Although the mode is not an important part of modern statistics, it is a part of the curriculum and is on statewide assessment tests of mathematics in grades K–8. Unlike the mean, neither the median nor the mode is affected by the existence of extremely atypical values.

---

**EXAMPLE 13.5 Determining Means, Medians, and Modes**

Determine the mean, median, and mode for each of the data sets $R$, $S$, and $T$ on page 732, and discuss which measures are most representative of the respective data sets.

**Solution**

Let $\bar{x}_R$, $\hat{x}_R$, $\bar{x}_S$, $\hat{x}_S$, $\bar{x}_T$, and $\hat{x}_T$ denote the means and medians of $R$, $S$, and $T$, respectively. We have already seen that $\bar{x}_R = 73.8$ and that $\hat{x}_R = 76$. Since the mode is the most frequently occurring score (or the several such scores if they occur equally often and more frequently than all other scores), the mode of $R$ is 77. In this case, all three measures are reasonably representative of the scores making up the data set.

Since $S$ has 25 scores,

$$\bar{x}_S = (72 + 77 + 75 + 75 + 67 + 76 + 69 + 76 + 71 + 68 + 77 + 79 + 82$$
$$+ 73 + 69 + 76 + 68 + 69 + 71 + 78 + 72 + 79 + 74 + 73 + 73)/25$$
$$\doteq 73.6.$$

Also, $\hat{x}_S$ is the middle, or thirteenth, score. Thus, counting on the line plot, we find that $\hat{x}_S = 73$. Finally, $S$ has three modes—69, 73, and 76—since each occurs three times and more often than any other score. We observe that the mean, the median, and the middle mode all seem to reasonably represent the set of scores in $S$.

Finally, since $T$ contains 23 scores,

$$\bar{x}_T = (74 + 84 + 40 + 49 + 91 + 81 + 75 + 79 + 40 + 61 + 70 + 40$$
$$+ 74 + 85 + 89 + 86 + 82 + 40 + 85 + 45 + 96 + 86 + 85)/23$$
$$\doteq 71.2,$$
$$\hat{x}_T = 79,$$

and the mode of $T$ is 40. As noted earlier, $T$ is difficult to characterize. The mean, $\bar{x}_T$, is strongly affected by the several very low scores and so does not seem to represent the data set fairly. Similarly, the mode of 40 is clearly not representative. In this case, the median seems to be the most representative value.

---

**EXAMPLE 13.6 Determining an Average**

All 12 players on the Uni Hi basketball team played in their 78-to-65 win over Lincoln. Jon Highpockets, Uni Hi's best player, scored 23 points in the game. How many points did each of the other players average?

**Solution**

**Understand the Problem**

The problem is to determine averages when we are not explicitly given the data values. What we do know is that Uni Hi scored 78 points, that Jon Highpockets scored 23 of the points, and that all 12 players on the team played in the game.

**Devise a Plan**

Since the average score for each of the 11 players other than Jon is the sum of their scores divided by 11, we must determine the sum of their scores.

**Carry Out the Plan**

Since Uni Hi scored a total of 78 points and Jon scored 23, the total for the rest of the team must have been $78 - 23 = 55$ points. Therefore, the average number of points for these players is $55 \div 11 = 5$.

**Look Back**

The solution depended on knowing the definition of average. The real question was how many points were scored by all the players on Uni Hi's team other than Jon and how many such players there were. But those figures, and hence the solution to the problem, were easily obtained by subtraction. Note that we did not need to know (and, in fact, can't figure out) what each individual player scored.

---

**EXAMPLE 13.7** **Determining a Typical Value for a Set of Data**

The owner–manager of a factory earned \$850,000 last year. The assistant manager earned \$48,000. Three secretaries earned \$18,000 each, and the other 16 employees each earned \$27,000.

(a) Prepare a dot plot of the salaries of the people deriving their income from the factory.
(b) Compute the mean, median, and mode of the salaries of the people deriving their income from the factory.
(c) Which is most typical of the salaries of those associated with the factory—the mean, median, or mode?

**Solution**

(a) The dot plot is shown here:

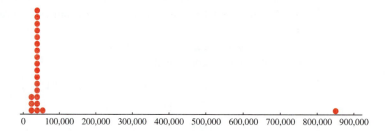

(b) The mean is

$$\bar{x} = \frac{18,000 + 18,000 + 18,000 + 27,000 + \cdots + 27,000 + 48,000 + 850,000}{21}$$

$$\doteq \$65,905.$$

The median, $\hat{x}$, is the 11th in the ordered list of salaries. Thus,

$$\hat{x} = 27,000 \text{ dollars.}$$

The mode is the most frequently occurring salary. Thus,

$$\text{mode} = 27,000 \text{ dollars.}$$

(c) The mean is clearly not typical of the salary most workers at the factory earn. The value of $\bar{x}$ is unduly affected by the huge salary earned by the owner–manager. Here, the median and mode are the same and are more typical of salaries of those deriving their income from the factory, since \$27,000 is the salary of 16 of the 21 people. Note that this last sentence is really an argument that, in this case, the most typical value is the mode. That the mode and median here are equal is incidental.

---

While the mean is the most commonly used indicator of the typical value of a data set, the preceding example makes it clear that this choice can be quite misleading. As will be seen in the problem set for this section, it is easy to construct some examples in which the median is the most typical value and other examples, like the preceding, in which the mode is most typical.

## Measures of Variability

The most useful analysis of data would reveal both the center (typical value) and the *spread,* or *variability,* of the data. We now consider how the spread of data is determined and will look at four measures of variability. The simplest measure is the **range,** the difference between the smallest and largest data values. The range certainly tells something about how the data occur, but it is often misleading, particularly if the data set contains a few extremely low or high values that are quite atypical of most of the other values. Another measure is the **midrange** (or **mid-extreme**), which is the average of the lowest and highest data points. It isn't used in statistics much, but is taught in elementary school. The midrange of the data of Table 13.1 on page 714 is $\dfrac{49 + 96}{2} = 72.5$.

A better understanding of variability is obtained by determining **quartiles** and, later in this section, the **standard deviation** of a data set. Speaking casually, quartiles divide the data set into four sections, each of which contains, in increasing order, about one-quarter of the data. More precisely, we give the following definition:

> **DEFINITION**  *Upper and Lower Quartiles*
> Consider a set of data arranged in order of increasing size. Let the number of data values, $n$, be written as $n = 2r$ when $n$ is even, or $n = 2r + 1$ when $n$ is odd, for some integer $r$. In either case, the **lower quartile,** denoted by $Q_L$, is the median of the first $r$ data values. The **upper quartile,** denoted by $Q_U$, is the median of the last $r$ data values.*

Somewhat imprecisely, the lower quartile $Q_L$ of a set of data arranged in order of increasing size and having median $\hat{x}$ is the median value of the data values *less than* $\hat{x}$. Similarly, the upper quartile $Q_U$ is the median of the data values *greater than* $\hat{x}$. The difficulty with this definition is that it can be easily misunderstood. For example, for the data set

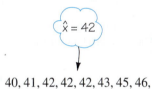

$$40, 41, 42, 42, 42, 43, 45, 46,$$

$\hat{x} = \dfrac{(42 + 42)}{2} = 42$ and lies between the two 42s, as shown. Thus, $Q_L = 41.5$ is the median of 40, 41, 42, and 42. It is *not* the median of the scores 40 and 41. Similarly, $Q_U = 44$ is the median of 42, 43, 45, and 46 and *not* the median of the scores 43, 45, and 46.

---

**EXAMPLE 13.8  Determining Quartiles**

For the four given data sets of this problem, determine $\hat{x}, Q_L$, and $Q_U$. Note that the resulting values sometimes are and sometimes are not data values.

(a) $A = \{12, 7, 14, 15, 9, 11, 10, 11, 0, 8, 17, 5\}$
(b) $B = \{27, 14, 13, 12, 26, 22, 24, 22, 23, 19, 10, 19, 22\}$
(c) $C = \{16, 22, 20, 15, 12, 14, 16, 14, 21\}$
(d) $D = \{32, 26, 29, 25, 26, 27, 29, 28, 29, 25\}$

**Solution**

(a) First, we order the values in $A$ to obtain the following list:

$$0 \quad 5 \quad 7 \quad 8 \quad 9 \quad 10 \quad 11 \quad 11 \quad 12 \quad 14 \quad 15 \quad 17$$

$$\qquad\qquad Q_L \qquad\qquad \hat{x} \qquad\qquad Q_U$$

---

*The precise definition of quartiles is not entirely standardized. For example, the lower and upper quartiles for a set of $2r + 1$ data values are often taken as the medians of the first and last $r + 1$ (rather than $r$) values, respectively, in the ordered list.

Since there are 12 data values, the median is the average of the sixth and seventh values; that is, $\hat{x} = \dfrac{10 + 11}{2} = 10.5$, as indicated earlier. Since the number of data points is even, namely, $2r = 12$, we have $r = 6$. Thus, $Q_L = \dfrac{7 + 8}{2} = 7.5$ is the median of the six data values preceding $\hat{x}$, and $Q_U = \dfrac{12 + 14}{2} = 13$ is the median of the six data values following $\hat{x}$.

**(b)** The ordered list for $B$ is as follows:

$$10 \quad 12 \quad 13 \quad 14 \quad 19 \quad 19 \quad 22 \quad 22 \quad 22 \quad 23 \quad 24 \quad 26 \quad 27$$
$$\qquad\qquad \uparrow \qquad\qquad\qquad \uparrow \qquad\qquad\qquad \uparrow$$
$$\qquad\qquad Q_L \qquad\qquad\qquad \hat{x} \qquad\qquad\qquad Q_U$$

Thus, it follows that $\hat{x} = 22$ is the middle data value. Since the number of data points is odd, namely, $2r + 1 = 13$, we have $r = 6$. Thus, $Q_L = \dfrac{13 + 14}{2} = 13.5$ is the median of the six data values preceding $\hat{x}$, and $Q_U = \dfrac{23 + 24}{2} = 23.5$ is the median of the six data values greater than $\hat{x}$.

**(c)** The ordered set for $C$ is as shown here:

$$12 \quad 14 \quad 14 \quad 15 \quad 16 \quad 16 \quad 20 \quad 21 \quad 22$$
$$\qquad \uparrow \qquad\qquad\qquad \uparrow \qquad\qquad \uparrow$$
$$\qquad Q_L \qquad\qquad\qquad \hat{x} \qquad\qquad Q_U$$

Since there are nine data values, $\hat{x} = 16$, the middle data value. Also, $2r + 1 = 9$, so $r = 4$, $Q_L = \dfrac{14 + 14}{2} = 14$ is the median of the four data values less than $\hat{x}$, and $Q_U = 20.5$ is the median of the four data values greater than $\hat{x}$.

**(d)** The ordered data set for $D$ is as follows:

$$25 \quad 25 \quad 26 \quad 26 \quad 27 \quad 28 \quad 29 \quad 29 \quad 29 \quad 32$$
$$\qquad\quad \uparrow \qquad\qquad\quad \uparrow \qquad\qquad\quad \uparrow$$
$$\qquad\quad Q_L \qquad\qquad\quad \hat{x} \qquad\qquad\quad Q_U$$

Since there are ten data points, $\hat{x}$ is the average of the fifth and sixth values so $\hat{x} = 27.5$. Also, since $2r = 10$, we have $r = 5$. Thus, $Q_L = 26$ is the third of the five data points less than $\hat{x}$, and $Q_U = 29$ is the third of the five data points greater than $\hat{x}$.

It follows from the definition that approximately 25% of the data values are less than or equal to $Q_L$, approximately 25% lie between $Q_L$ and $\hat{x}$, approximately 25% lie between $\hat{x}$ and $Q_U$, and approximately 25% are greater than or equal to $Q_U$. Thus, approximately half of the values in a data set lie between $Q_L$ and $Q_U$, so the difference between the two, called the **interquartile range,** provides a good measure of the spread of the data.

> **DEFINITION**    *Interquartile Range*
> The **interquartile range, IQR,** of a data set is the difference between the upper and lower quartile, or $\mathrm{IQR} = Q_U - Q_L$.

If a data value falls below $Q_L$ by more than $1.5 \cdot \mathrm{IQR}$ or above $Q_U$ by more than $1.5 \cdot \mathrm{IQR}$, it is called an **outlier.** Thus, *outlier* is the term applied to those values referred to earlier that seem to be atypical of the values in a data set.* The study of outliers is an active research area with questions such as whether outliers matter, how they came about, and more.

---

*As with the median, the definitions of interquartile range and outlier are not entirely standardized. The choices made here are among the most common.

> **DEFINITION**    *Outlier*
> An **outlier** in a set of data is a data value that is *less than* $Q_L - (1.5 \cdot IQR)$ or *greater than* $Q_U + (1.5 \cdot IQR)$.

**EXAMPLE 13.9    The Median, the Quartiles, the Interquartile Range, and the Outliers**

Determine the median, the quartiles, the interquartile range, and the outliers for data set $R$ on page 732.

**Solution**    The values in $R$ are ordered in the dot plot on page 732. Since $R$ contains 24 data values, the median is the average of the twelfth and thirteenth data values; that is, $\hat{x} = \dfrac{(76 + 76)}{2} = 76$.

Also, $2r = 24$, so $r = 12$ and $Q_L$ and $Q_U$ are the medians of the first and last 12 data values, respectively. Thus, $Q_L = \dfrac{(71 + 71)}{2} = 71$ and $Q_U = \dfrac{(77 + 79)}{2} = 78$. Therefore, the interquartile range is $IQR = 78 - 71 = 7$. Finally, since

$$Q_L - 1.5 \cdot IQR = 71 - (1.5 \cdot 7) = 71 - 10.5 = 60.5$$

and

$$Q_U + 1.5 \cdot IQR = 78 + (1.5 \cdot 7) = 78 + 10.5 = 88.5,$$

it follows that 46 and 92 are outliers.

Symbolically, if the 24 points shown represent the ordered data values in $R$, then $Q_L, \hat{x}, Q_U$, the interquartile range, and the outliers are as follows:

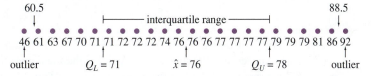

## Box Plots

The least and greatest scores, or the *extremes,* along with the lower and upper quartiles and the median, give a concise numerical summary, called the **5-number summary,** of a set of data. For instance, since the median of the data in Example 13.9 is 76 and the **extremes** are 46 and 92, the 5-number summary is 46–71–76–78–92. Graphically, the 5-number summary can be pictured as

least score–lower quartile–median–upper quartile–highest score.

A **box plot,** often called a **box-and-whisker plot,** gives a vivid graphical visulization of the 5-number summary.

> **DEFINITION**    *Box Plot, Box-and-Whisker Plot*
> A **box plot,** or **box-and-whisker plot,** consists of a central box extending from the lower to the upper quartile, with a line marking the median and with line segments, or whiskers, extending outward from the box to the extremes.

For example, the box plot for Example 13.9 is shown in Figure 13.14.

**FIGURE 13.14**
Box plot for data set $R$

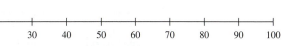

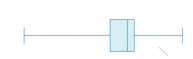

An additional advantage of box plots is that they make it possible to carry out useful comparisons between data sets containing widely differing numbers of values. This is made clear in the next example.

**EXAMPLE 13.10 Using Box Plots for Comparisons**

The data that follow are the final scores of male and female students in Calculus I. Draw box plots to compare the distribution of women's scores with the distribution of men's scores.

| **Women's scores:** | 95, | 79, | 53, | 78, | 71, | 88, | 77, | 80, | 79, | 79 | | |
|---|---|---|---|---|---|---|---|---|---|---|---|---|
| **Men's scores:** | 84, | 85, | 53, | 77, | 66, | 81, | 79, | 59, | 65, | 61, | 81, | 68, |
| | 68, | 80, | 76, | 87, | 85, | 74, | 92, | 76, | 70, | 85, | 55, | 79, |
| | 74, | 80, | 73, | 48, | 66, | 83, | 48, | 60, | 87, | 58, | 64, | 78, |
| | 82, | 69, | 76, | 83, | 94, | 86, | 73, | 85, | 75, | 69, | 49, | 52, |
| | 59, | 68, | 65, | 75, | 31, | 69, | 73, | 56, | 95 | | | |

**Solution** To make the plots, we need the 5-number summaries. First, arrange the scores in order of increasing size:

| **Women's scores:** | 53, | 71, | 77, | 78, | 79, | 79, | 79, | 80, | 88, | 95 | | |
|---|---|---|---|---|---|---|---|---|---|---|---|---|
| **Men's scores:** | 31, | 48, | 48, | 49, | 52, | 53, | 55, | 56, | 58, | 59, | 59, | 60, |
| | 61, | 64, | 65, | 65, | 66, | 66, | 68, | 68, | 68, | 69, | 69, | 69, |
| | 70, | 73, | 73, | 73, | 74, | 74, | 75, | 75, | 76, | 76, | 76, | 77, |
| | 78, | 79, | 79, | 80, | 80, | 81, | 81, | 82, | 83, | 83, | 84, | 85, |
| | 85, | 85, | 85, | 86, | 87, | 87, | 92, | 94, | 95 | | | |

For the women, the extreme scores are 53 and 95 and the median is 79, the average of the fifth and sixth scores. The lower quartile is 77, the median of the first five scores. The upper quartile is 80, the median of the last five women's scores. Thus, the 5-number summary of the women's scores is

$$53-77-79-80-95.$$

Similarly, the 5-number summary of the men's scores is

$$31-64.5-74-81.5-95.$$

These summaries give the following box plots:

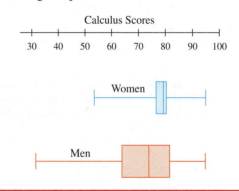

The box plots of Example 13.10 give a precise visual comparison of the performances of female and male students in calculus, even though the numbers of students are quite different. One might reasonably speculate as to why the distributions of grades differ as they do. (For example, it is almost invariably the case that larger data sets have both smaller and larger extreme values, as suggested here.)

### The Standard Deviation

We have already observed that the range is one measure of the spread of a data set. However, it is not a very precise measure, since it depends only on the extreme data values, which may differ markedly from the bulk of the data. This deficiency is largely remedied by the 5-number summary (which includes the IQR) and its visualization by a box plot. However, an even better measure of variability is the **standard deviation.** (See problems 12 and 13 in the problem set at the end of this section. These problems are answered in the answer section in the text, where we also discuss other possibilities for measuring variability, as well as a reason for choosing the standard deviation as defined here.)

> **DEFINITION**  *The Standard Deviation of a Set of Data*
>
> Let $x_1, x_2 x_3, \ldots, x_n$ be the values in a set of data and let $\bar{x}$ denote their mean. Then
> $$s = \sqrt{\frac{(\bar{x} - x_1)^2 + (\bar{x} - x_2)^2 + \cdots + (\bar{x} - x_n)^2}{n}}$$
> is the **standard deviation.**\*

**EXAMPLE 13.11  Computing a Standard Deviation**

Compute the mean and standard deviation for this set of data:

| 35 | 42 | 61 | 29 | 39 |
|----|----|----|----|----|

**Solution**

$$\bar{x} = \frac{(35 + 42 + 61 + 29 + 39)}{5} = 41.2$$

$$s^2 = \frac{[(41.2 - 35)^2 + (41.2 - 42)^2 + (41.2 - 61)^2 + (41.2 - 29)^2 + (41.2 - 39)^2}{5}$$

$$= 116.96$$

Thus,

$$s \doteq \sqrt{116.96} \doteq 10.8.$$

It turns out that there is an easier formula for calculating standard deviations that, on a calculator, requires only the $\boxed{\sqrt{\phantom{x}}}$ and $\boxed{x^2}$ keys in addition to the usual keys for arithmetic. It is only a matter of messy manipulation (which we do not reproduce here) to show that

$$s = \sqrt{\frac{x_1^2 + x_2^2 + \cdots + x_n^2}{n} - \bar{x}^2},$$

where $x_1, x_2, \ldots, x_n$ are the data values and $\bar{x}$ is their mean.

**EXAMPLE 13.12  Alternative Calculation of the Standard Deviation**

Calculate the mean and standard deviation of the data set in Example 9.11, using the alternative formula just given.

**Solution**

The mean is calculated as in Example 9.11. Then,

$$s = \sqrt{\frac{35^2 + 42^2 + 61^2 + 29^2 + 39^2}{5} - 41.2^2} \doteq 10.8.$$

---

\*For important technical reasons, professional statisticians replace the $n$ in the denominator of the fraction under the square root sign by $n - 1$. The difference is small, however, so to avoid confusion, we use the definition given here.

Scientific and business calculators frequently have built-in statistics routines that make the calculation of means and standard deviations even simpler. Alternatively, these computations can be performed automatically on a computer by means of a spreadsheet or other appropriate software. It is important to note that calculator and computer programs for computing standard deviations offer two alternatives that differentiate between the standard deviation of a population and the standard deviation of a sample of that population. The standard deviation we have discussed is the standard deviation of a population. If it is not clear which one you are obtaining when you compute a standard deviation by machine, compute both and use the smaller of the two values obtained.

Just as the mean is an indication of a typical value of a set of data, the standard deviation is a measure of the typical deviation of the values from the mean.* If the standard deviation is large, the data are more spread out; if it is small, the data are more concentrated near the mean. This relationship is immediately apparent from the dot plots of data sets $R$, $S$, and $T$ discussed earlier. In Figure 13.15, these dot plots are reproduced again, with the addition of the location of the mean as well as the spread of each data set relative to its standard deviation. A most important fact is that, for most data sets, most data values fall within 1 standard deviation of the mean and almost none lie as far as 3 standard deviations from the mean.

**FIGURE 13.15**

Dot plots for $R$, $S$, and $T$ showing the location of the mean and the spread of the data relative to the standard deviation

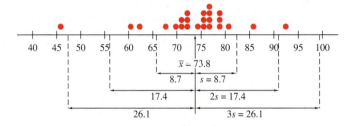

Dot plot for $R$: All but five data points lie within 1 standard deviation of the mean. Only one data point lies more than 3 standard deviations from the mean.

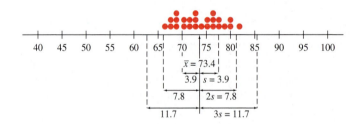

Dot plot for $S$: All but 10 data points lie within 1 standard deviation of the mean. Only one data point lies more than 2 standard deviations from the mean.

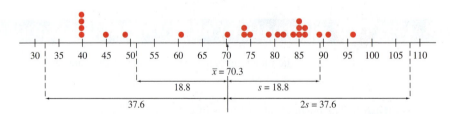

Dot plot for $T$: All but nine data points lie within 1 standard deviation of the mean. None lies beyond 2 standard deviations of the mean.

---

*The **variance**, $v = s^2$, of a set of data is also a good measure of the variability of the data. However, the more commonly used measure is the standard deviation.

**EXAMPLE 13.13** **Determining the Fraction of Data Values Near the Mean**

Compute the fraction (expressed as a percent) of the data values in Example 13.11 that falls

**(a)** within 1 standard deviation of the mean.
**(b)** within 2 standard deviations of the mean.

**Solution**

**(a)** In Example 13.11, $\bar{x} = 41.2$ and $s \doteq 10.8$. Thus, those entries within 1 standard deviation of the mean lie between 30.4 and 52.0. A count reveals that three of the entries fall into this range, and we have

$$\frac{3}{5} = .60 \ldots \doteq 60\%.$$

**(b)** Those data values within 2 standard deviations of the mean must lie between 19.6 and 62.8. This range includes all of the data values, and we have

$$\frac{5}{5} = 1 \ldots \doteq 100\%.$$

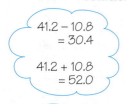

$41.2 - 10.8$
$= 30.4$

$41.2 + 10.8$
$= 52.0$

$41.2 - 2(10.8)$
$= 19.6$
$41.2 + 2(10.8)$
$= 62.8$

## Problem Set 13.2

Exercises numbered in red are answered in the back of the text.

### Understanding Concepts

**1.** Determine the mean, median, and mode for this set of data:

| 18 | 27 | 17 | 19 | 21 | 24 | 18 | 15 |
|----|----|----|----|----|----|----|----|
| 23 | 18 | 17 | 14 | 22 | 19 | 27 | 30 |

**2. (a)** Compute the mean, median, and mode for this set of data:

| 69 | 81 | 77 | 69 | 64 | 85 | 81 | 73 | 79 |
|----|----|----|----|----|----|----|----|----|
| 74 | 70 | 78 | 86 | 80 | 71 | 79 | 77 | 70 |
| 67 | 70 | 79 | 80 | 71 | 67 | 69 | 79 | 81 |

**(b)** Draw a dot plot for the data in part (a).

**(c)** Does either the mean, the median, or the mode seem typical of the data in part (a)?

**(d)** Might it be reasonable to suspect that the data in part (a) actually come from two essentially different populations (say, daily incomes from two entirely different companies)? Explain your reasoning.

**3. (a)** Compute the quartiles for the data in problem 2.

**(b)** Give the 5-number summary for the data in problem 2.

**(c)** Draw a box plot for the data in problem 2.

**(d)** Determine the interquartile range, IQR, for the data in problem 2.

**(e)** Identify any outliers in the data of problem 2.

**4. (a)** What is the midrange of problem 1?

**(b)** What is the midrange of problem 2?

**5. (a)** Draw side-by-side box plots to compare students' performances in class A and class B if the final grades are as shown here:

| **Class A:** | 91, | 63, | 65, | 73, | 65, | 86, |
|----|----|----|----|----|----|----|
| | 96, | 75, | 75, | 79, | 84, | 72, |
| | 80 | | | | | |
| **Class B:** | 87, | 72, | 95, | 89, | 69, | 79, |
| | 56, | 64, | 66, | 67, | 89, | 47 |

**(b)** Briefly compare the performances in the two classes on the basis of the box plots in part (a).

**(c)** Determine the interquartile range, IQR, for each of the classes in part (a).

**(d)** Identify any outliers in the classes of part (a).

**6.** Use the data in problem 1 to do or answer the following:

**(a)** Compute the mean.

**(b)** Compute the standard deviation.

**(c)** What percent of the data is within 1 standard deviation of the mean?

**(d)** What percent of the data is within 2 standard deviations of the mean?

**(e)** What percent of the data is within 3 standard deviations of the mean?

**7. (a)** Choose an appropriate scale, and draw a dot plot for this set of measurements of the heights, in centimeters, of 2-year-old ponderosa pine trees:

| 22.2 | 23.5 | 22.5 | 22.6 | 23.0 | 22.8 |
|------|------|------|------|------|------|
| 22.4 | 22.2 | 23.0 | 23.3 | 23.9 | 22.7 |

**(b)** Compute the mean and standard deviation for the data in (a).

**(c)** What percent of the data is within 1 standard deviation of the mean?

**(d)** What percent of the data is within 2 standard deviations of the mean?

**(e)** What percent of the data is within 3 standard deviations of the mean?

**(f)** What is the midrange of the data set?

8. **Uniform distribution.** A data set has a uniform distribution (or is a **uniform data set**) if every value has exactly the same number of data points. Here is an example: Sandy rolls a five-sided die 10 times and comes up with the data set $D_2 = \{2, 4, 3, 5, 3, 2, 1, 1, 5, 4\}$, so each integer actually occurs twice (and that's why there is a 2 in the subscript of the name of the data set.)

**(a)** What are the mean, mode, and median of $D_2$?

**(b)** Suppose that Sandy rolls the die 20 times and each of the integers comes up 4 times. (We'll call that data set $D_4$.) What are the mean, mode, and median of $D_4$?

**(c)** Suppose that Sandy rolls the die 30 times and each of the integers comes up 6 times. (We'll call that data set $D_6$.) What are the mean, mode, and median of $D_6$?

**(d)** What do you notice about the answers to the three parts of the problem? (See Problem 10.)

9. **Standard deviation of a uniform distribution.** Sandy rolls her five-sided die 5 times and comes up with $\{1, 2, 3, 4, 5\}$, which, in keeping with problem 8, we call $D_1, D_2, D_4$, and $D_6$ are as defined in that problem.

**(a)** What is the standard deviation of $D_1$ and $D_2$? Are you surprised?

**(b)** What is the standard deviation of $D_6$ and $D_4$? Are you surprised?

10. Suppose that $k$ is an integer and that Sandy rolls the five-sided die $n = 5k$ times. It turns out that the data set she comes up with has each of the integer values between 1 and 5 (inclusive) coming up exactly $k$ times. We'll call this set $D_k$. (Problem 8 contains the cases of $k = 2, 4$, and 6.) In terms of $k$ and $n$, what are the mean, mode, and median of $D_k$? Are you surprised? The MHM here is because of the use of algebra in statistics!

*(MHM)*

11. Suppose that $D$ is a data set. We construct a new data set, $E$, by doubling each element of $D$. Note that the two sets have the same number of elements. What is the relationship between

*(MHM)*

**(a)** the mode of $D$ and the mode of $E$?

**(b)** the median of $D$ and the median of $E$?

**(c)** the mean of $D$ and the mean of $E$?

Here, too, the MHM is because of the use of algebra in statistics!

## Teaching Concepts

12. Shawn asks why the sum of the differences of the data values from the mean,

*(MHM)*

$$(\bar{x} - x_1) + (\bar{x} - x_2) + \cdots + (\bar{x} - x_n),$$

isn't used as a measure of variability.

**(a)** Compute this sum for the data set in problem 7a.

**(b)** How would you respond to Shawn's question?

13. During the classroom discussion resulting from Shawn's question in problem 12, Leona suggests that the sum of the absolute values of the differences of the data values from the mean be used as a measure of variability since the terms are all positive and thus cannot cancel each other out.

**(a)** Compute the sum of the absolute values of the differences in problem 12, part (a).

**(b)** Compute the mean of the absolute values of the differences in problem 12, part (a); that is, divide the sum in part (a) of that problem by 12.

**(c)** How would you respond to Leona?

## Responding to Students

14. Ms. Chen helped her class gather data on the number of books each student read in one week. Once the data were collected, she helped her students organize the information into the tally chart shown. For homework, Ms. Chen asked her students to find the median and the mode for the data they collected. The next day, Joseph turned in his homework with the answer 4 for the median and the answer 7 for the mode of the set of data.

| Number of Books Reported | Number of Students |
|---|---|
| 1 | 8 tally marks |
| 2 | 5 tally marks |
| 3 | 6 tally marks |
| 4 | 0 tally marks |
| 5 | 2 tally marks |
| 6 | 3 tally marks |
| 7 | 2 tally marks |

**(a)** What mistake did Joseph make when finding the median and the mode for the set of data?

**(b)** How would you help guide Joseph to find the correct answer?

15. Stefanie was asked to find the mean of the numbers 14, 17, 19, and 26. She gave the answer 76.

**(a)** What error did Stefanie make when calculating the mean?

**(b)** How would you help guide Stefanie to calculate the mean of a set of numbers correctly?

16. When Yugi was asked to explain how he found the median for a set of data, he said, "I found the median by crossing off numbers until I had only one left." How would you help guide Yugi so he won't make the same mistake again?

17. Patrick is writing in his journal about the median, mean, mode, and range as measures of central tendency. Are all four of them in fact measures of central tendency?

18. Marilyn talks in class about "the mode" of a data set. Is she making a mistake and, if so, how would you rectify it?

## Thinking Critically

19. On June 1, 2009, the average age of the 33 employees at Acme Cement was 47 years. On June 1, 2010, three of the staff aged 65, 58, and 62 retired and were replaced by four employees

aged 24, 31, 26, and 28. What was the average age of the employees at Acme Cement on June 1, 2010?

**20.** **(a)** Compute the mean and standard deviation for these data:

| 28 | 34 | 41 | 19 | 17 | 23 |

**(b)** Add 5 to each of the values in part (a) to obtain 33, 39, 46, 24, 22, and 28. Compute the mean and the standard deviation for this new set of values.

**(c)** What properties of the mean and standard deviation are suggested by parts (a) and (b)?

**21.** Compute the mean and standard deviation for the data represented by the following two histograms:

**(a)**

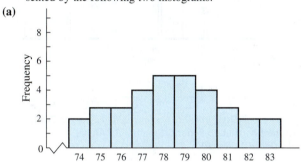

**(b)**

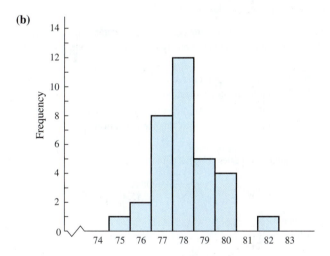

**(c)** Briefly explain why the standard deviation for the data of part (b) is less than that for the data of part (a).

**22.** Does the mean, median, or mode seem to be the most typical value for the given set of data? Explain briefly. (*Suggestion:* Draw a line plot.)

| 42 | 47 | 38 | 16 | 45 | 41 | 16 | 48 | 44 |

**23.** **(a)** Determine the mean, median, and mode of the data in the dot plot shown.

**(b)** Does the mean, median, or mode seem to be the most typical of these data? Explain briefly.

**24.** Produce sets of data that satisfy these conditions:

**(a)** mean = median < mode

**(b)** mean = mode < median

**(c)** median = mode < mean

**25.** **(a)** What can you conclude if the standard deviation of a set of data is 0? Explain.

**(b)** What can be said about the standard deviation of a set of data if the values all lie very near the mean? Explain.

**26.** Let $Q_L$, $\hat{x}$, and $Q_U$ denote the lower quartile, median, and upper quartile, respectively, of a set of data.

**(a)** Create a set of data with the property that exactly 25% of the data lies in each of these ranges:

$$x < Q_L, \quad Q_L < x < \hat{x}, \quad \hat{x} < x < Q_U, \quad Q_U < x$$

**(b)** Create a set of data for which it is not true that 25% of the data lies in the ranges specified in part (a).

**27.** A collection of data contains ten values consisting of a mix of 1s, 2s, and 3s.

**(a)** If $\bar{x} = 3$, what is the data set?

**(b)** If $\bar{x} = 2$, what are the possibilities for the data set?

**(c)** If $\bar{x} = 1$, what is the data set?

**(d)** Could $\bar{x} = 1$ and $s \neq 0$ for this data set? Explain.

**28.** Compute the means of these collections of data.

**(a)** $A = \{27, 38, 25, 29, 41\}$

**(b)** $B = \{27, 38, 25, 29, 41, 32\}$

**(c)** $C = \{27, 38, 25, 29, 41, 32, 32\}$

**(d)** $D = \{27, 38, 25, 29, 41, 32, 32, 32, 32, 32, 32\}$

**(e)** What conclusion is suggested by the calculations in parts (a) through (d)?

**(f)** Guess the mean of the following set of data, and then do the calculation to see if your guess is correct:

$$E = \{27, 38, 25, 29, 41, 60, 4, 60, 4\}$$

**(g)** What general result does the calculation in part (f) suggest?

**29.** **(a)** The mean of each of these collections of data is 45:

$$R = \{45, 35, 55, 25, 65, 20, 70\}$$
$$S = \{45, 35, 55, 25, 65, 20, 70, 45, 45\}$$
$$T = \{45, 35, 55, 25, 65, 20, 70, 80, 10\}$$

Which of $R$ and $S$ has the smaller standard deviation? No computation is needed; justify your response with a single sentence.

**(b)** Like the means of $R$ and $S$ in part (a), the mean of $T$ is 45. Is the standard deviation for this set the same as that for $S$? Note that both of these sets have the same number of entries. Explain your conclusion.

**30.** According to Garrison Keillor, all the children in Lake Wobegon are above average. Is this assertion just a joke, or is there a sense in which it could be true?

**31.** If the mean of $A = \{a_1, a_2, \ldots, a_{30}\}$ is 45 and the mean of $B = \{b_1, b_2, \ldots, b_{40}\}$ is 65, compute the mean of the combined data set. (*Hint:* The answer is not 55.)

## Thinking Cooperatively

Divide the class into groups of three or four students each. Make sure that all members of each small group agree on the answers required of their group.

**32.** As we have seen before, it often helps to understand a concept if it can be visualized using an appropriate manipulative. Work with about three other students to carry out the following activity:

**(a)** Suppose you want to demonstrate the idea of the mean of a set of data to fourth graders. Using a set of blocks, form stacks of heights 5, 1, 4, 7, 6, and 7. Now move blocks from higher stacks to lower stacks in an effort to form six stacks, all of the same height. Can this be done? If so, how many blocks are in each stack?

**(b)** Determine the mean of 5, 1, 4, 7, 6, and 7.

**(c)** Comparing the results of parts (a) and (b), what do you conclude?

**(d)** How would you elaborate on your conclusions from the first three parts of this problem to make the idea of the mean clear to your students? Explain carefully.

**(e)** How would the idea presented in this problem work with these data: 5, 1, 4, 7, 11, and 7? Discuss briefly.

**33.** Consider the data collected in problem 22 of Problem Set 13.1.

**(a)** Members of one or two small groups each determine the mode or modes, the mean, and the standard deviation of the data for men.

**(b)** Members of one or two small groups each determine the mode or modes, the mean, and the standard deviation of the data for women.

**(c)** Members of one or two small groups each determine the 5-number summaries and draw side-by-side box plots for the two sets of data.

**(d)** As a class, discuss the results obtained in (a), (b), and (c) and decide on a consensus opinion of the most appropriate length of a "yard" and on a reasonable range in which the length might lie, on the basis of the data considered. Do the results differ markedly for men and women?

**34.** In ancient times, the cubit was taken as the length of the human arm from the tip of the elbow to the tip of the middle finger (generally understood to vary from about 17 to about 21 inches). Working in groups, repeat problem 33, but for the cubit rather than the "yard."

**35.** Working in a group with about three other students, toss seven pennies 30 times and record the number of heads each time.

**(a)** Determine the mean and standard deviation of the data obtained.

**(b)** Determine what percent of the data lies within 1 standard deviation of the mean.

**(c)** What percent of the data differs from the mean by more than 2 standard deviations?

## Making Connections

**36. (a)** From the data in the bar graph shown, is it possible to determine the average median income in 2000 for men 25 years old and older with education not exceeding a master's degree? Explain briefly.

Median annual income of persons with income who are 25 years old and over, by highest level of education and sex: 2000

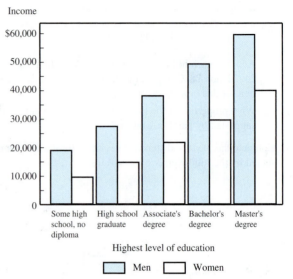

SOURCE: *U.S. Department of Commerce, Bureau of the Census, Current Population Reports, Series P-60, "Money Income in the United States: 2000."*

**(b)** What legitimate conclusions can you make on the basis of the bar graph shown?

**37. (a)** Use the data in the pie chart shown to determine the average proceeds from the various types of state-run lottery games in 1964–1995.

**(b)** Determine the percentage of the profits from lotteries that is used to finance education.

**(c)** Why do you suppose the majority of the proceeds from lottery games is used to finance education?

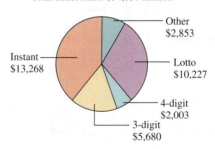

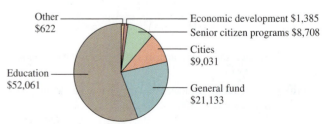

SOURCE: *Chart prepared by the U.S. Bureau of the Census. For data, see table 499. Statistical Abstract of the United States, 1997, 11th ed, Washington, D.C.: 1997.*

## From State Student Assessments

**38.** (Illinois, Grade 4)
The science class held a frog jumping contest. What is the median distance the frog jumped?

Frog Jumps

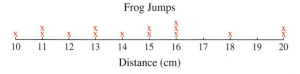

Distance (cm)

**A.** 11      **B.** 15

**C.** 16      **D.** 20

**39.** (Minnesota, Grade 5)
The members of the Spanish club sold calendars as a fundraiser. Below is a list of each person's sales.

| | |
|---|---|
| Amy | 6 |
| Chris | 9 |
| Raul | 15 |
| Ali | 9 |
| Sonya | 13 |
| Ker | 7 |
| Maya | 12 |
| Allesandro | 18 |
| Nicky | 10 |

What was the mean calendar sale for a member of the Spanish club?

○ **A.** 9

○ **B.** 10

○ **C.** 11

○ **D.** 12

**40.** (Texas, Grade 5)
Terry picked 156 tomatoes from the 12 tomato plants in his garden. On the average, how many tomatoes did each plant produce?

**A.** 11      **B.** 12

**C.** 13      **D.** 14

**E.** Not here

**41.** (Pennsylvania, Grade 5)
A total of 106,789 people attended the Rose Bowl football game. If the average ticket price was $21.52, *about* how much money did the Rose Bowl take in?

**A.** $20,000      **B.** $200,000

**C.** $2,000,000      **D.** $20,000,000

**42.** (Virginia, Grade 6)
What is missing from the box-and-whisker plot?

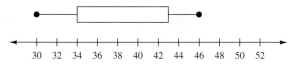

**A.** Median      **B.** Range

**C.** Upper quartile      **D.** Lower quartile

**43.** (Virginia, Grade 6)
Which statement is *false*?

**F.** A set of data always has a mode.

**G.** A set of data may have exactly one mode.

**H.** A set of data may have more than one mode.

**J.** The mode is the piece of data that occurs most frequently.

**44.** (Georgia, Grade 7)
Zack enjoys participating in the local community drama theater and was talking about it at lunch. He mentioned that the ages (in years) of the others involved in the current play were

12, 19, 14, 12, 15, 16, 16,
18, 13, 18, 15, 19, 14, 19,
16, 18, 15, 17, 17, 18.

He thinks that the mode is the most appropriate average to describe his drama group. Which answer is most reasonable?

**A.** The mode represents the average fairly.

**B.** The mode is too low to represent the average. The mean or median is a better choice.

**C.** The mode is too high to represent the average. The range is a better choice.

**D.** The mode is too high to represent the average. The mean or median is a better choice.

**45.** (Texas, Grade 9)
Millie entered her dog in a dog show. Her dog got a score of 64. Which measure of data can Millie use to determine whether her dog's score was in the top half of all scores at the show?

**A.** Median      **B.** Mode

**C.** Mean      **D.** Range

**46.** (Illinois, Grade 6)
Greg took five tests each worth 100 points.

He earned the following scores:

85, 87, 87, 89, 97

What is Greg's mean (average) score for these five tests?

**A.** 89      **B.** 88      **C.** 87      **D.** 12

## Examining School Book Pages

*Refer to the School Book Pages provided on page 748 to answer the following questions.*

**47.** In the example of Lesson 18-8, the median and the mode are equal. Do you think that it is a good idea or a bad idea to have an example whose median and mode are equal? Explain.

**48.** Find an example of a data set in which the median, mode, and range are all equal. (*Hint:* Look for a data set that has four data points, two of which are *b* and the other two of which are the same distance from, but on opposite sides of, *b*.)

*See "Examining School Book Pages" on page 747 for questions related to the pages shown below.*

## School Book Pages

# Median, Mode, and Range

### Lesson 18-8

**Understand It!**
A single number can be used to describe what is typical about a set of data.

## Median, Mode, and Range

**How can data be described by one number?**

Trey listed, in order, the playing times for the best-selling CD of each music type.

How can he describe the data with one number?

**CD Playing Times**

| Minutes | Music Type |
|---------|-----------|
| 59 | Popular |
| 61 | Country |
| 63 | Blues |
| 63 | Sound track |
| 64 | Gospel |
| 67 | Jazz |
| 72 | Classical |

**Find the median.**

List the data from least to greatest.

59, 61, 63, **63**, 64, 67, 72

Identify the **median**, or the middle data value in an odd numbered, ordered set of data.

The median of the number of minutes of playing time is 63.

**Find the mode.**

59, 61, **63, 63**, 64, 67, 72

Identify the **mode**, or the data value that occurs most often in the data set.

The mode of the number of minutes of playing time is 63.

**Find the range.**

59, 61, 63, 63, 64, 67, **72**

Identify the **range**, or the difference between the greatest and least values.

72 − 59 = 13

The range of the number of minutes of playing time is 13.

---

**Guided Practice***

**Do you know HOW?**

In **1** through **3**, identify the median, mode, and range for each set of data.

1. 5, 7, 5, 4, 6, 3, 5

2. 21, 21, 23, 32, 43

3. 13, 14, 14, 16, 17, 19

**Tip** *For an even number of values, the median is the number halfway between the two middle values.*

**Do you UNDERSTAND?**

4. What operation is used to find the range?

5. In the example at the top, how would the median and mode change if the playing time for the Blues CD changed to 61 minutes?

6. What would the range of playing times be if the 72-minute CD were removed from the list?

---

**Independent Practice**

In **7** through **9**, use the table at the right.

7. What are the median, mode, and range for the data?

8. What would happen to the range if the temperature were 82°F on Monday?

9. If the data for Friday were removed from the table, what would the median, mode, and range be?

**5-day Weather Forecast**

| Day | Temperature |
|-----|-------------|
| Monday | 80°F |
| Tuesday | 80°F |
| Wednesday | 82°F |
| Thursday | 84°F |
| Friday | 78°F |

---

**Problem Solving**

10. Ricardo kept a record of the 7 hottest days of the summer. Use the list below to find the median, mode, and range of the temperatures.

   98°F   102°F   100°F   99°F
   103°F   98°F   101°F

12. **Reasoning** For each statistical measure (mean, median, mode, and range) tell whether that number is always, sometimes, or never one of the numbers in the data set.

For **14** through **17**, use the table.

14. What was the median number of visitors to the Statue of Liberty from May to September in 2005?

15. What is the range of the data?

16. How many months had over 500,000 visitors?

17. **Writing to Explain** Why do you suppose there had been many fewer visitors in September, than in July or August?

11. **Writing to Explain** How can you tell the difference between the net for a triangular prism and the net for a triangular pyramid?

13. **Think About the Process** One side of a rectangular garden is 13 feet and the other side is 3 feet. Which expression shows how to find the perimeter?

   **A** $(2 \times 13) + (2 \times 3)$   **C** $2 \times 13 \times 3$
   **B** $13 \times 3$   **D** $3 + 13$

**Visitors to the Statue of Liberty**

| 2005 | Visitors |
|------|----------|
| May | 430,235 |
| June | 492,078 |
| July | 589,166 |
| August | 542,292 |
| September | 367,441 |

**Animated Glossary** www.pearsonsuccessnet.com

452   **For another example, see Set G on page 461.*

Lesson 18-8   453

---

## 13.3

# Statistical Inference

In this section, we give a brief introduction to one aspect of statistics—**statistical inference**—by discussing how one predicts the characteristics of a population by examining the properties of small pieces of it called *samples*. For example, we cannot interview all adults to find out for whom they will vote. On the other hand, is there a way to sample a reasonable number of adults and then predict what the outcome of the voting would most likely be? A first step to this approach is to look at a sufficiently large, unbiased number of samples of the population and use the mean and standard deviation of the samples as a way of getting an idea of what the mean and standard deviation of the population might look like. The important phrases here are "sufficiently large" and "unbiased." How many samples would it take for us to feel comfortable with our predictions, to what degree are we comfortable with those predictions, and what does it mean for the sample to be taken without bias? There are famous mistakes (such as the prediction by the Gallup poll that Thomas E. Dewey would win the 1948 election when Harry S Truman actually turned out to be the winner) that have given insights into how to make such predictions more accurate ("sampling techniques"). The questions posed in this paragraph are deep questions covered in statistics courses, not ones that can be resolved in one chapter of a book. While statistical inference is not a part of the elementary school curriculum, it is important for future teachers to see where the previous two sections (usually called *descriptive statistics*) lead.

## Populations and Samples

In statistics, a **population** is a particular set of objects about which one desires information. If the desire is to determine the average yearly income of all adults in the United States, the population is the set of *all* adults in the United States. In addition, one must be explicit as to what "adult" means. Other examples of populations are

- all boys in Eisenhower High School in Yakima, Washington,
- all lightbulbs manufactured on a given day by Acme Electric Company, and
- all employees of AT&T,

and so on. One might want to determine

- the average height of boys in Eisenhower High School,
- the average life of lightbulbs produced by Acme Electric Company, or
- the average cost of medical care for employees of AT&T.

Since it is often impractical or impossible to check each member of a population, the idea of statistics is to study a **sample,** or subset, of the population and to make inferences about the entire population on the basis of the study of the sample.

If the goal of accurate estimation of population characteristics is to be achieved, the population must first be carefully defined. The next step is to sample randomly (which will be discussed shortly). In particular, we must be sure not to favor any one outcome in designing a statistical study. Selection criteria that systematically favor certain outcomes are called **biased.**

Here are two examples of sampling, one of which is unbiased and the other biased: Suppose a study of the heights of boys at Eisenhower High School is desired. Instead of measuring each boy in the school, it is decided to study a sample of just 20 of the boys. If the sample were to be selected by choosing every fourth name out of an alphabetical listing of all 80 boys, would it likely be representative of the entire population? Probably, since there is likely little or no connection between last names and heights. However, a sample consisting of the members of the basketball team is clearly not representative, since basketball players tend to be unusually tall. It turns out that the best approach to sampling is to use a **random sample,** rather than try to find representative samples, and show that the criterion used really is representative of the population. An (unintentional) bias was one of the flaws of the Truman–Dewey election prediction mentioned earlier.

> **DEFINITION** *A Random Sample*
> A **random sample** of size *r* is a subset of *r* individuals from the population chosen in such a way that every such subset has an equal chance of being chosen.

For example, suppose an urn contains a mixture of red and white beans and you want to estimate what fraction of the beans is red by selecting a sample of 20 beans. You proceed by mixing the beans thoroughly and then, with your eyes closed, selecting 20 beans. Since each subset of 20 beans has an equal chance of being selected, the sample is indeed random. Note, however, that one must be very careful before asserting that physical mixing is sufficient to ensure randomness. (Have you ever wondered whether a deck of cards was shuffled enough?) These questions are a part of the beautiful subtlety of statistics.

Other schemes also work well. For example, suppose AT&T wishes to study the employees at one of its plants by selecting a random sample of 20 employees and asking them to respond to a questionnaire. One way to obtain a random sample would be to put the names of all the employees on tags, place the tags in a large container, mix the tags thoroughly, and then have someone close his or her eyes and select a sample of 20 tags. The employees whose tags are chosen constitute the random sample.

Another way to obtain the sample is to use a sequence of digits chosen in such a way that each digit is equally likely to be any one of the ten possibilities and the choice of each digit is independent of the choice of every other digit. Such a sequence would be a **random sequence of digits.** One way to select such a random sequence is to construct a simple spinner with ten 36° sectors numbered 0, 1, 2, 3, 4, 5, 6, 7, 8, and 9, as shown in Figure 13.16. Spinning the spinner repeatedly produces a

**FIGURE 13.16**
A simple random-digit generator

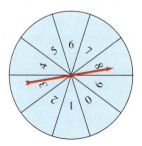

string of digits. Since the result of each spin is independent of the result of every other spin, each digit is equally likely to be selected and the digit sequence is random.

The desired sample of AT&T employees can now be obtained as follows (suppose the plant in question has 9762 employees):

1. Assign each employee a four-digit number from among $0001, 0002, \ldots, 9762$.
2. Generate a random sequence of four-digit numbers by repeatedly spinning the spinner 4 times. Since each digit is equally likely to appear on any spin, each four-digit number is equally likely to appear on any four spins. If the spinning process generates 0000, a four-digit number greater than 9762, or any number already obtained, simply ignore it and continue to generate more four-digit numbers. When 20 appropriate numbers have been generated, they can be used to identify the 20 employees to be included in the sample.

Finally, as you might expect, many calculators have built-in statistics routines that will generate **random numbers,** as do most spreadsheet programs.

## Population Means and Standard Deviations

Professional statisticians find it helpful to use different symbols for means and standard deviations of populations and of samples. For populations, the mean and standard deviation are denoted by the Greek letters $\mu$ and $\sigma$ (mu and sigma), respectively. Thus, for a population of size $N$, the population mean and population standard deviation are given by

$$\mu = \frac{x_1 + x_2 + \cdots + x_N}{N} \quad \text{and} \quad \sigma = \sqrt{\frac{(x_1 - \mu)^2 + (x_2 - \mu)^2 + \cdots + (x_N - \mu)^2}{N}},$$

where $x_1, x_2, \ldots, x_N$ are *all* the numbers in the population.

**EXAMPLE 13.14** **Computing a Population Mean and Standard Deviation**

Here is a population that consists of the scores on an exam:

| 64 | 65 | 68 | 67 | 59 | 66 | 63 | 66 | 64 | 62 | 65 | 66 | 63 | 66 | 66 | 63 |
|----|----|----|----|----|----|----|----|----|----|----|----|----|----|----|----|
| 63 | 64 | 62 | 67 | 63 | 61 | 60 | 64 | 64 | 63 | 63 | 65 | 64 | 65 | 66 | 63 |
| 65 | 62 | 63 | 65 | 61 | 64 | 63 | 64 | 62 | 69 | 65 | 65 | 64 | 64 | 63 | 64 |
| 66 | 65 | 64 | 64 | 63 | 64 | 66 | 67 | 69 | 63 | 65 | 63 | 64 | 64 | 64 | 65 |
| 67 | 68 | 64 | 62 | 66 | 62 | 64 | 61 | 65 | 62 | 65 | 62 | 65 | 62 | 66 | 63 |

Use a spreadsheet or other suitable software on your computer or the built-in statistics routine on a suitable calculator to compute $\mu$ and $\sigma$ for this population.

**Solution** Since there are 80 numbers in the population,

$$\mu = \frac{64 + 65 + \cdots + 63}{80} \doteq 64.2$$

and

$$\sigma = \sqrt{\frac{(64 - 64.2)^2 + (65 - 64.2)^2 + \cdots + (63 - 64.2)^2}{80}} \doteq 1.9.$$

## Estimating Population Means and Standard Deviations

Suppose we wish to know the mean and standard deviation of some large or inaccessible population. Since, in this case, $\mu$ and $\sigma$ may be difficult or impossible to compute, we may estimate them with the sample mean

$$\bar{x} = \frac{x_1 + x_2 + \cdots + x_n}{n}$$

and the sample standard deviation

$$s = \sqrt{\frac{(x_1 - \bar{x})^2 + (x_2 - \bar{x})^2 + \cdots + (x_n - \bar{x})^2}{n}}$$

of a suitably chosen sample $x_1, x_2, \ldots, x_n$ of size $n$.

## EXAMPLE 13.15  Estimating a Population Mean and Standard Deviation

(a) Estimate the mean and standard deviation of the population given in Example 13.14 by using a spinner, as illustrated in Figure 13.16, to select a random sample of size 10.
(b) Compare the results of part (a) with the results obtained in Example 13.14.

**Solution**

(a) Suppose your spinner generates the digit sequence 5, 5, 2, 9, 1, 0, 4, 5, 3, 1, 2, 4, 1, 9, 4, 6, 6, 9, 1, 7. Using these two at a time, we obtain the following table of two-digit numbers that will tell us which position in the table of Example 13.14 to use:

| | | | | |
|---|---|---|---|---|
| 55 | 29 | 10 | 45 | 31 |
| 24 | 19 | 46 | 69 | 17 |

Since all are different, these determine the random sample shown here:

| | | | | |
|---|---|---|---|---|
| 66 | 64 | 62 | 64 | 66 |
| 64 | 62 | 64 | 66 | 63 |

> The fifty-fifth number in the data set is 66, and so on.

Thus, the mean of the numbers in the sample is

$$\bar{x} = \frac{(66 + 64 + 62 + 64 + 66 + 64 + 62 + 64 + 66 + 63)}{10} = 64.1.$$

The variance is

$$
\begin{aligned}
v = s^2 &= [(64.1 - 66)^2 + (64.1 - 64)^2 + (64.1 - 62)^2 \\
&\quad + (64.1 - 64)^2 + (64.1 - 66)^2 + (64.1 - 64)^2 \\
&\quad + (64.1 - 62)^2 + (64.1 - 64)^2 + (64.1 - 66)^2 \\
&\quad + (64.1 - 63)^2]/10 \doteq 2.09,
\end{aligned}
$$

and the sample standard deviation is

$$s = \sqrt{v} \doteq 1.45.$$

(b) We observe that $\bar{x}$ and $s$ for the sample are reasonable approximations to $\mu$ and $\sigma$, respectively, for the population as determined in Example 13.14.

---

Suppose we were to repeat the preceding example but with a random sample of size 15. For the resulting sample, $\bar{x}$ and $s$ should be slightly better approximations to $\mu$ and $\sigma$, respectively, from Example 13.14 than the values obtained in Example 13.15. Not surprisingly, it is generally true that larger samples tend to yield better approximations to population characteristics.

## Distributions

We return now to the data of Table 13.2, in which the population consisted of all boys in Eisenhower High School. A histogram and line graph of the boys' heights to the nearest inch appear in Figures 13.6 and 13.7, respectively.

Since the heights of the columns in the histogram represent the number, or frequency, of the measurements in each range (63.5–64.5, 64.5–65.5, and so on) and the width of each column is 1, the total area of all the columns in the histogram is 80, the total number of boys in the population.

The **relative frequency** of the measurements in each range in Figure 13.5 is the fraction (expressed as a decimal) of the total number of boys represented in that range. The relative frequency is obtained by taking the frequency distribution in Table 13.5 and dividing it by 80. If the heights of the column in the histogram are determined by relative frequency, the diagram remains the same except for the designation on the vertical scale, as shown in Figure 13.17. Also, since the width of each column is 1, the *area* of each column gives the fraction of the population whose heights fall into that range. Moreover, the area of the first three columns gives the fraction of the population with heights ranging from 63.5 to 66.5 inches, and the total area of the histogram is 1.

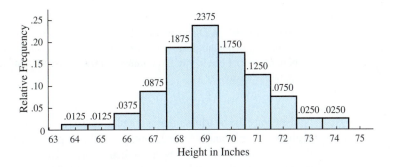

**FIGURE 13.17**

Histogram of Figure 13.5 but with the vertical scale denoting relative frequency

As noted earlier, histograms often are representations of grouped data which make it appear that all the data values in a given range are the same. However, as in the present case, this is frequently not so. The boys' heights are listed to the nearest inch, whereas people's heights actually vary continuously. A truer representation of such data is provided by a line graph, or frequency polygon, as in Figure 13.7. If the vertical scale represented relative frequency rather than frequency, the graph would appear unchanged, as shown in Figure 13.18. Also, since such a diagram can be obtained from a histogram by deleting and adding small triangles of equal area, the area under the **relative-frequency polygon** is still 1 and the area of that portion of the polygon from, say, 63.5 to 66.5 equals the fraction of the population of boys whose heights lie in this range.

**FIGURE 13.18**

Relative-frequency polygon of the heights of boys in Eisenhower High School

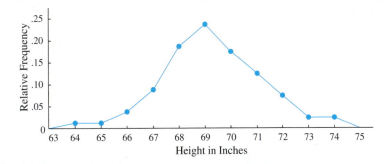

In addition, had the measurements been taken more and more closely and the range in the histogram made narrower and narrower, the tops of the columns in the histogram, as well as the corresponding relative-frequency polygon, would have more and more closely approximated a smooth bell-shaped curve called a **normal distribution,** as shown in Figure 13.19. Here also, the area under the curve and above the interval between *a* and *b* indicates the relative frequency, or fraction, of the boys measured who have heights between *a* and *b*. This fraction indicates the *likelihood,* or *probability,* that a boy chosen at random from the population will have a height in the given range.

**FIGURE 13.19**
Normal distribution of the heights of boys in Eisenhower High School

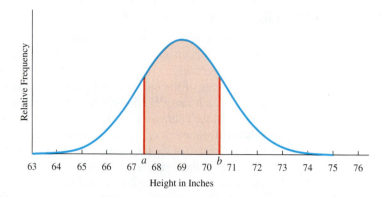

For many populations, the **distribution** of the measurements of the property being considered will be a continuous (and often normal) curve, as in Figure 13.19. However, in other cases, the observations are not continuous, are not normal, or are discrete. If the observations are discrete, the distribution "curve" is just a histogram.

**DEFINITION**    *A Distribution Curve*

A curve or histogram that shows the relative frequency of the measurements of a characteristic of a population that lies in any given range is a **distribution curve.** The area under such a curve or histogram is always 1.

Knowing the distribution of a population frequently allows one to say with some precision what the average value is and what percentage of the population lies within different ranges. In particular, the normal distribution has been studied in great detail, and it can be shown that very nearly 68% of the population lies within 1 standard deviation of the mean, very nearly 95% of the population lies within 2 standard deviations of the mean, and very nearly 99.7% (or virtually *all*) of the population lies within 3 standard deviations of the mean, as illustrated in Figure 13.20. Using the language of probability, we would say that the probability that a given data value lies within 1 standard deviation of the mean is 0.68, the probability that a given data value lies within 2 standard deviations of the mean is 0.95, and the probability that any given data value lies within 3 standard deviations of the mean is 0.997 (virtually 100%). Considerations like these are what make it possible for very carefully designed polls and other studies to claim that their results are accurate to within a given tolerance, say, 3%.

**FIGURE 13.20**
Percent of data within 1, 2, and 3 standard deviations of the mean of a normal distribution

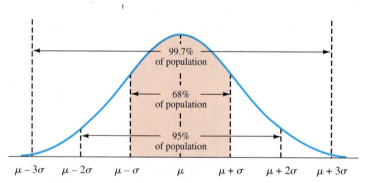

**THEOREM**    *The 68–95–99.7 Rule for Normal Distributions*

For a population that has a normal distribution, about 68% falls within 1 standard deviation of the mean, about 95% falls within 2 standard deviations of the mean, and about 99.7% falls within 3 standard deviations of the mean.

It turns out that many populations are normally distributed or approximately so. Thus, the 68–95–99.7 rule is approximately true for these populations and for samples from these populations. For samples, the approximation is increasingly accurate for increasingly larger sample sizes.

## z Scores and Percentiles

As noted previously, the normal distribution has been studied deeply and with great care. Some additional facts are as follows:

- The graph of the distribution is symmetric about a vertical line drawn through the mean; that is, if the curve were folded along this line, the two halves of the curve would exactly match each other. Thus, the area under the curve to the left of the mean equals the area under the curve to the right of the mean, and it follows that the mean of the distribution is also its median.
- The maximum height of the curve occurs at the mean, so the mean also equals the mode.
- Since the scale of the vertical axis is relative frequency, the area under the entire curve is 1. Also, the area under the curve over various intervals has been carefully tabulated, thus making such probability statements as the 68–95–99.7 rule possible.

One stratagem that makes it possible to effectively compare two different normal distributions has been the creation of the so-called **standardized** form of the distribution (also called the **z curve**). The way that the standardized form is accomplished is to start with a normal distribution with mean $\mu$ and standard deviation $\sigma$ and change to the variable $z$. This comparison is accomplished by altering the scale on the horizontal axis by the transformation

$$z = \frac{x - \mu}{\sigma}$$

while maintaining the frequency scale on the vertical axis. This transformation does not materially alter the shape of the distribution, as can be seen in Figure 13.21, which is the standard form of the distribution of Figure 13.20.

**FIGURE 13.21**
Standardized form of a normal distribution, illustrating the 68–95–99.7 rule

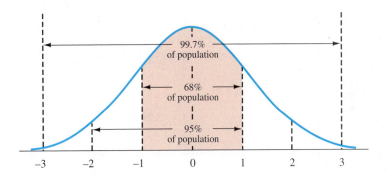

Note that *any* normal distribution in standard form will have mean 0 and standard deviation 1. To see this, set $x = \mu$; then $z = \dfrac{\mu - \mu}{\sigma} = 0$. And if we set $x = \mu + \sigma$ (that is, $x$ is 1 standard deviation above the mean), then $z = \dfrac{(\mu + \sigma) - \mu}{\sigma} = \dfrac{\sigma}{\sigma} = 1$. Thus, in standard form, 68% of the population lies between $-1$ and 1, 95% of the population lies between $-2$ and 2, and 99.7% of the population lies between $-3$ and 3, as shown in Figure 13.21.

Normal distributions in standard form may appear tall and skinny or short and fat, depending on their standard deviations (see Figure 13.22), but the foregoing statements remain valid in every case.

The preceding considerations have led to the notion of a **z score**, or **standard score.** If one wants to determine a characteristic of a population that is probably normally distributed (weights of full-term newborn babies, heights of senior boys attending Eisenhower High School, heights of senior

**FIGURE 13.22**
Three standard normal distributions with standard deviations $\sigma_1 > \sigma_2 > \sigma_3$ for (i), (ii), and (iii)

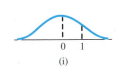

(i)

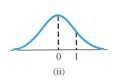

(ii)

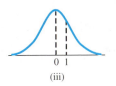

(iii)

girls attending Eisenhower High School, miles per gallon of 2010 Jeep Grand Cherokees, etc.) by a sampling procedure, it is often the case that each observation in the sample is converted to a $z$ score using the following definition:

> **DEFINITION**   *z Score*
>
> If $x$ is an observation in a set of data with mean $\bar{x}$ and standard deviation $s$, the **$z$ score** corresponding to $x$ is given by $z = \dfrac{x - \bar{x}}{s}$.

By using $z$, it is possible to tell whether an observation is only fair, quite good, or rather poor. For example, a $z$ score of 2 on a national test would be considered quite good, since it is 2 standard deviations above the mean. Indeed, we will see that the $z$ score of 2 lies in the upper 2.5% of the population.

### EXAMPLE 13.16   Calculating z Scores

Convert these data to a set of $z$ scores:

$$66 \quad 64 \quad 62 \quad 64 \quad 66 \quad 64 \quad 62 \quad 64 \quad 66 \quad 63$$

**Solution**

$$\bar{x} \doteq \frac{66 + 64 + 62 + 64 + 66 + 64 + 62 + 64 + 66 + 63}{10} = 64.1.$$

Using the alternative formula for calculating the standard deviation given on page 751, we obtain

$$s = \sqrt{\frac{66^2 + 64^2 + 62^2 + 64^2 + 66^2 + 64^2 + 62^2 + 64^2 + 66^2 + 63^2}{10} - 64.1^2}$$

$$\doteq 1.45.$$

Then the different $z$ scores are (since there are only four different data points)

$$\frac{66 - 64.1}{1.45} \doteq 1.31, \qquad \frac{64 - 64.1}{1.45} \doteq -0.07,$$

$$\frac{62 - 64.1}{1.45} \doteq -1.45, \quad \text{and} \quad \frac{63 - 64.1}{1.45} \doteq -0.76.$$

Now consider Example 13.16 further. From Table 13.4, pages 764 and 765, by indicating the area (and hence the probability) under the portion of a standard normal distribution to the left of a given point, it is possible to determine that 90.49% of the population lies to the left of (below) 1.31 and that only 7.35% of the population lies below $-1.45$. Considerations like these lead to the notion of a **percentile.**

> **DEFINITION**   *Percentile*
>
> For *any* frequency distribution, the $r$th **percentile** is the number $r$, with $0 \le r \le 100$, such that $r\%$ of the data in a data set of a population is less than or equal to $r$.

### EXAMPLE 13.17   Determining a Percentile of a Population

Use Table 13.4, pages 764 and 765, to determine the percentile corresponding to the $z$ score of $-0.76$ in a standard normal population.

**Solution**

Searching down the left column of Table 13.4 on page 764, we come to the row marked $-0.7$. Moving across this row to the column headed .06, we find .2236, the entry for $-0.76$. This entry tells us that 22.36% of the population lies to the left of $-0.76$.

## EXAMPLE 13.18   Determining a Percentile of a Sample

Determine the percentile corresponding to 63 in the data set of Example 13.16.

**Solution**   Since three of the ten scores in the data set are less than or equal to 63, and since
$\frac{3}{10} = 0.30 = 30\%$, 63 is at the 30th percentile.

Note that the score of 63 in Example 13.16 gave a $z$ score of $-0.76$. But the percentiles in Examples 13.17 and 13.18 are different. Why should this be so? The answer is that one percentile number is for a population and the other for a sample. The one for the sample should approximate the one for the population, but that does not mean they should be equal. The population mean and standard deviation were 64.2 and 1.9, respectively, while for the sample, $\bar{x}$ and $s$ were 64.1 and 1.45, respectively. Thus, the population shows more spread, and it is not surprising that the $z$ score $-0.76$ is further to the left relative to the population as a whole and that there is, therefore, relatively less of the population to its left than to the left of 63 in the sample.

## EXAMPLE 13.19   Determining the Percentage of the Population in an Interval

Use Table 13.4 on pages 764 and 765 to show that 34% of a normally distributed population lies between the $z$ scores $-0.44$ and 0.44.

**Solution**   Proceeding as in Example 13.17, we find that 33% of the population has a $z$ score that is less than or equal to $-0.44$. Similarly, we find that 67% of the population lies to the left of 0.44. Thus, by subtraction, $67\% - 33\% = 34\%$ of the population lies between $-0.44$ and 0.44, as we were to show.

## Problem Set 13.3

Exercises numbered in red are answered in the back of the text.

### Understanding Concepts

1. Describe the population that should be sampled to determine each of the following:

   (a) The percentage of freshmen in U.S. colleges and universities in 2010 who earn baccalaureate degrees within ten years

   (b) The percentage of U.S. college and university football players in 2010 who earn baccalaureate degrees within ten years

   (c) The fraction of people in the United States who feel that they have adequate police protection

   (d) The fraction of people in Los Angeles who feel that they have adequate police protection

   (e) Would you include children in the population you describe in parts (c) and (d)? people in mental institutions? known criminals?

2. Polls are often conducted by telephone. Might such a technique bias the results of the poll? Explain briefly, remembering that there are many cell phones.

3. Suppose a poll is conducted by face-to-face interviews, but the names of the interviewees are selected at random from names listed in the telephone book. Would such a poll yield valid results? Discuss briefly.

4. The registrar at State University wants to determine the percentages of students (a) who live at home, (b) who live in apartments, and (c) who live in dormitories. There are 25,000 students in the university, and the registrar proposes to select a sample of 100 students by choosing every 250th name from the list of all students arranged in alphabetical order.

   (a) What is the population?

   (b) Is the sample random? Explain.

5. In performing a study of college and university faculty attitudes in the United States, investigators first divided the population of all colleges and universities into groups according to size—25,000 or more students, 10,000 to 24,999 students, 3000 to 9999 students, and fewer than 3000 students. Using their judgment, they then chose two schools from each group and asked each school to identify a random sample of 100 of its faculty.

   (a) Was this a good way to obtain a statistically reliable (that is, random) sample of faculty? Why or why not?

   (b) What is the population? Are there four distinct populations? Discuss briefly.

**6.** The Honorable J. J. Wacaser, United States Representative, recently sent a questionnaire to his constituents to determine their opinion on several bills being considered by the House of Representatives. Discuss how representative of the voters in his district the responses to his poll are likely to be.

**7.** Discuss how Representative Wacaser (see problem 6) might actually choose a random sample of voters in his district.

**8.** To determine the average life of lightbulbs it manufactures, a company chooses a sample of the bulbs produced on a given day by selecting every 100th bulb and testing it to failure.

    **(a)** What is the population?

    **(b)** Is this a good way to select a sample? Why or why not?

    **(c)** Is the sample random? Why or why not?

**9.** Choose a representative sample of 20 students in your college or university, and ask how many hours each person in your sample watches television each week.

    **(a)** Describe how you chose your sample to ensure that it was representative of your entire student body.

    **(b)** On the basis of your sample, estimate how many hours of television most students on your campus watch each week.

    **(c)** Combine your data with those of all the other students in your class, and determine a revised estimate of the number of hours per week each student in your college or university watches television.

**10.** Describe and perform a study to determine how many of the students at your college or university have seen the movie *Gone With the Wind*.

**11.** For a population with a normal distribution with mean 24.5 and standard deviation 2.7,

    **(a)** about 68% of the population lies between what limits?

    **(b)** about 95% of the population lies between what limits?

    **(c)** about 99.7% of the population lies between what limits?

**12.** Describe two different ways in which a random sample of 100 of the 10,000 students at State University can be obtained.

**13.** Suppose that only one dentist out of ten actually prefers Whito Toothpaste over all other brands. By taking many random samples of size 10, might it be possible eventually to obtain a sample in which eight out of ten dentists in the sample preferred Whito? Explain.

**14.** Convert these data sets into sets of $z$ scores:

    **(a)** 17   22   21   19   23   19

    **(b)** 2   7   3   6   5   8

**15. (a)** Compute the sum of the $z$ scores in problem 14a.

    **(b)** Compute the sum of the $z$ scores in problem 14b.

**16. (a)** In what percentile is the data value 22 in the data set of problem 14a?

    **(b)** In what percentile is the data value 6 in the data set of problem 14b?

Use Table 13.4 on pages 764 and 765 to determine the answers to problems 17 and 18.

**17.** A population is normally distributed.

    **(a)** What percentage of the population lies to the left of the population $z$ score $-1.75$?

    **(b)** What percentage of the population lies to the left of the population $z$ score $0.26$?

**18. (a)** What percentage of the population lies between the population $z$ scores $-1.75$ and $1.75$?

    **(b)** What percentage of the population lies between the population $z$ scores $-0.67$ and $0.67$?

## Teaching Concepts

**19.** Marita claims that tossing a single die will produce a random sequence of the digits 1, 2, 3, 4, 5, and 6. How would you respond to Marita?

**20.** After the class discussion of Marita's claim (problem 19), Mark asserts that you could generate a random sequence of the numbers $2, 3, \ldots, 12$ by repeatedly tossing a pair of dice. How would you respond to Mark?

**21.** Prompted by the discussions engendered by Marita's and Mark's claims (problems 19 and 20, respectively), Rebecca claims that you could generate a random sequence of two-digit numbers by repeatedly tossing a red die and a green die and recording the result on the red die as the first digit and the result on the green die as the second digit to form a two-digit number. How would you respond to Rebecca?

## Thinking Critically

**22.** A large university was charged with sexual bias in admitting students to graduate school. Admissions were by departments, and the figures are as shown in the accompanying table.

    **(a)** Compute the percentages of men and women applicants the admitted by the school as a whole.

    **(b)** Do the figures in part (a) suggest that sexual bias affected the admission of students?

    **(c)** Compute the percentages of men and women applicants admitted by each department.

    **(d)** Do the figures in part (c) suggest that sexual bias affected admission to the various departments?

| | **MEN** | | **WOMEN** | |
|---|---|---|---|---|
| **Department** | **Number of Applicants** | **Number Admitted** | **Number of Applicants** | **Number Admitted** |
| 1 | 373 | 22 | 341 | 24 |
| 2 | 560 | 353 | 25 | 17 |
| 3 | 325 | 120 | 593 | 202 |
| 4 | 191 | 53 | 393 | 94 |
| 5 | 417 | 138 | 375 | 131 |
| 6 | 825 | 512 | 108 | 89 |
| Totals | 2691 | 1198 | 1835 | 557 |

**23.** Suppose you generate a sequence of 0s and 1s by repeatedly rolling a die and recording a 0 each time an even number comes up and a 1 each time an odd number comes up. Is this a random sequence of 0s and 1s? Explain.

**24.** A TV ad proclaims that a study shows that eight out of ten dentists surveyed prefer Whito Toothpaste. How could it possibly make such a claim if, in fact, only one dentist out of ten actually prefers Whito?

**25.** Two sociologists mailed out questionnaires to 20,000 high school biology teachers. On the basis of the 200 responses they received, they claimed that fully 72% of high school biology teachers in the United States believe the biblical account of creation. Is their claim justified by this survey? Explain.

**26.** In the shoe business, which average of foot sizes is most important—the mean, median, or mode?

**27.** Consider the data set $\{6, 11, 10, 8, 12, 8\}$, where all the data are just 11 less than those in problem 14a. It's as if the data were drawn from the same distribution moved 11 units to the left.

  **(a)** What would you expect the $z$ scores for this new set of data to be?
  **(b)** Actually compute the $z$ scores for this new set of data.

**28.** Show that the sum of the $z$ scores for any set of data is equal to 0. (*Suggestion:* Argue from a special case, say, using the data set $\{1, 2, 3\}$, but do not actually compute the $z$ scores; that is, use the strategy "Argue from a special case.")

**29.** Consider the data set $\{34, 44, 42, 38, 46, 38\}$, where all the data are just twice what they were in problem 14a.

  **(a)** What would you expect the $z$ scores of this data set to be?
  **(b)** Compute the $z$ scores for this data set.
  **(c)** How do you account for the results in part (b)?

## Thinking Cooperatively

**30.** Divide the class into groups of three or four students each and give each group eight pennies. Have each student in each group thoroughly shake and toss the pennies 5 times and record the number of heads obtained each time. Then have a member of the group record the total number of times zero heads, one head, . . . , eight heads were obtained by the group. Let the population to be studied be the combined set of data obtained by the entire class.

  **(a)** Have each group construct a relative-frequency histogram and polygon (see Figures 13.17 and 13.18, respectively) for the population. Since the polygon shows the distribution of the population, have each group determine a consensus opinion as to whether the distribution approximates a normal distribution.

  **(b)** Have each group compute the population mean and standard deviation.

  **(c)** Have each group determine whether the 68–95–99.7 rule holds for this population.

**31.** Mai Ling claims that the spinner of Figure 13.16 likely would fail to generate a truly random sequence of digits because, in order to spin it, a person would likely hold it still and start each spin with the pointer in the same (likely horizontal) position each time. But always starting with the pointer in the same position would almost surely cause the spinner to favor some digits over others. How would you respond to Mai Ling?

## Making Connections

**32.** A fish biologist is studying the effect of recent management practices on the size of the cutthroat trout population in Idaho's Lochsa River. The biologist and her helpers first catch, tag, and release 200 such trout on a given day. Two weeks later, the team catches 150 cutthroat trout and determines that only 3 of these fish were tagged two weeks earlier. Estimate the size of the cutthroat population in the Lochsa River. (*Hint:* Determine the fraction of tagged cutthroat in the river in two different ways if there are $x$ cutthroat in the river.)

## Cooperative Investigation
### Using Samples to Approximate Characteristics of Populations

The chart shown contains 100 integers (the population) displayed in such a way that they can be represented by a number pair $(a, b)$, where $a$ denotes the row and $b$ the column in which the integer appears. For example, entry $(2, 7)$ is the integer 24, and entry $(7, 3)$ is 26.

|   | 0 | 1 | 2 | 3 | 4 | 5 | 6 | 7 | 8 | 9 |
|---|---|---|---|---|---|---|---|---|---|---|
| **0** | 21 | 22 | 20 | 24 | 22 | 29 | 25 | 21 | 27 | 17 |
| **1** | 25 | 12 | 28 | 21 | 22 | 17 | 28 | 18 | 18 | 26 |
| **2** | 19 | 17 | 23 | 29 | 19 | 16 | 24 | 24 | 25 | 19 |
| **3** | 22 | 17 | 26 | 11 | 31 | 19 | 14 | 20 | 23 | 17 |
| **4** | 26 | 13 | 30 | 26 | 18 | 23 | 37 | 24 | 27 | 28 |
| **5** | 14 | 15 | 25 | 20 | 24 | 18 | 20 | 30 | 35 | 21 |
| **6** | 18 | 30 | 22 | 20 | 20 | 23 | 27 | 26 | 33 | 13 |
| **7** | 24 | 21 | 23 | 26 | 28 | 19 | 28 | 29 | 31 | 23 |
| **8** | 21 | 27 | 22 | 25 | 21 | 16 | 23 | 27 | 16 | 25 |
| **9** | 23 | 22 | 24 | 22 | 16 | 15 | 19 | 24 | 25 | 20 |

For this investigation, parts (a) through (f) should be executed by each cooperative group of two or three students. Part (g) should involve the entire class.

**(a)** Use a spinner as in Figure 13.16 to generate five number pairs $(a, b)$ to determine a sample of five numbers from the preceding table. Compute the mean and standard deviation of your five-number sample.

**(b)** Repeat part (a), but with a sample of size ten.

**(c)** On the basis of parts (a) and (b), give two estimates for each of the population mean and standard deviation.

**(d)** Record your means for parts (a) and (b) on the chalkboard.

**(e)** Determine $\bar{x}_5$, the mean of the means of the samples of size 5, and $\bar{x}_{10}$, the mean of the means of the samples of size 10, from the chalkboard. Also, compute $s_5$ and $s_{10}$, the standard deviations of the means of the samples of size 5 and size 10, respectively.

**(f)** Use the result of part (e) again to estimate the population mean and standard deviation.

**(g)** The population mean is 22.490 and the population standard deviation is 5.043. Briefly discuss the results of parts (a) through (f) in the context of these two numbers.

## The Chapter in Relation to Future Teachers

This chapter is focused on the role of statistics in elementary and middle school and is meant to prepare future teachers to introduce their students to data collection, representation, and interpretation, as well as to the notions of the center of a data set and measures of its variability. An understanding of statistics that starts in elementary school will be a platform on which your students can build as they become responsible citizens and decision makers. The power of statistics and the interplay between data and the beginning statistics that measure the data are the heart of this chapter.

## Chapter 13 Summary

| Section 13.1   Organizing and Representing Data | Page Reference |
|---|---|
| **CONCEPTS** | |
| • **Data:** A description, usually in numerical form, of a property (or properties) of a population. | 713 |
| • **Dot plot:** A representation of data that uses dots above a number line to represent data values. | 713 |
| • **Stem-and-leaf plot:** A representation of data in which the first one or more digits of each data value constitute the stem and the remaining digits constitute the leaves. | 714 |
| • **Histogram:** A representation of data in which the height of the bar at a point on the number line represents the number of data points in an interval about the point or the relative frequency of the data in the interval. | 715 |
| • **Frequency:** The number of times a data value appears in a data set. | 715 |
| • **Frequency of an interval:** The number of times a data value appears in a given interval along a number line. | 715 |
| • **Line graph:** A graph formed by joining data points. | 716 |
| • **Frequency polygon:** A line graph formed by joining the midpoints of the tops of bars of a histogram. | 717 |
| • **Bar graph:** A histogram-like representation in which the bars are drawn above points on the horizontal axis corresponding to nonnumerical categories. | 719 |
| • **Pie chart:** A circle divided into sectors whose sizes (as measured by their angle) correspond to the percentages of a whole. | 720 |

- **Pictograph:** A representation of data in which the frequency is indicated by icons chosen to bear some relationship to the data being represented. — 721

- **Misleading representations:** Ways in which representations of data can be organized to confuse. — 722

## DEFINITIONS

- A **data set** is a collection of data that can be organized and represented various ways. — 713

- **Data** is a description, usually in numerical form, of a property of a population. — 713

- The **frequency** is the number of times any particular data value occurs. — 715

- The **frequency of the interval** is the number of data values in any interval along a number line. — 715

| Section 13.2   Measuring the Center and Variation of Data | Page Reference |
|---|---|

## CONCEPTS

- **Central tendency:** Description in a number of ways (mean, median, or mode) of the center of a data set. — 732

- **Variability** is the spread of a data set, measured by the range, quartiles, or the standard deviation of the data set. — 737

- **Outlier:** A data value less than $\overline{x} - 1.5 \cdot \text{IQR}$ or greater than $\overline{x} + 1.5 \cdot \text{IQR}$. — 738

- **Box-and-whisker plot:** A representation summarized by five numbers (the least data value, $Q_L, \overline{x}, Q_U$, and the greatest data value.) — 739

- **Standard deviation:** A measure of the spread of the data in a sample. The standard formula for the standard deviation $s$ is $s = \sqrt{\dfrac{(x_1 - \overline{x})^2 + (x_2 - \overline{x})^2 + \cdots + (x_n - \overline{x})^2}{n}}$, where $x_1, x_2, \ldots, x_n$ are the $n$ data values of the data set. — 741

## DEFINITIONS

- The **mean** is the sum of the data values in a sample, divided by the number of data values. — 733

- The **median** is the middle data value for a sample with an odd number of data values, and the average of the two middle values for a sample with an even number of data values. — 734

- A **mode** is a data value in a sample which appears as least as often as every other data point. — 734

- The **range** is the difference between the greatest and least data values in a sample. — 737

- The **midrange** is the average of the highest and lowest data points in a sample. — 737

- **Quartiles, $Q_L$ and $Q_U$,** are the points such that 25% of the data set does not exceed $Q_L$ and 25% of the data is not less than $Q_U$. — 737

- The **interquartile range, $IQR$,** of a data set is the difference between the upper and lower quartile, or $IQR = Q_L - Q_U$. — 738

- An **outlier** is a data value less than $x - 1.5 \cdot IQR$ or greater than $x + 1.5 \cdot IQR$. — 739

- The **extremes** of a data set are the least and greatest scores. — 739

- The **standard deviation** is the measure of the spread of data in a sample as given by the standard formula above. — 741

- A data set has a **uniform distribution** if every value has exactly the same number of data points. — 744

| Section 13.3 Statistical Inference | Page Reference |
|---|---|

**CONCEPTS**

- **Population:** A particular set of objects about which information is desired. — 749

- **Sample:** A subset of the population. — 749

- **Random sample:** A subset chosen from a population in such a way that every such subset of the same size has an equal chance of being chosen. — 749, 750

- **Biased** data is selection criteria that systematically favor certain outcomes. — 749

- **Relative frequency:** The frequency of the occurrence of a data value in a sample, expressed as a percentage. — 753

- **Relative-frequency polygon:** A histogram in which the heights of the bars indicate relative frequency. — 753

- **Distribution:** A curve or histogram showing the relative frequency of the measurements of a characteristic of a population. — 753

- **Normal distribution:** A special bell-shaped distribution valid for many populations. — 753

- **The 68–95–99.7 rule:** In a normal distribution, 68% of the population lies within 1 standard deviation of the mean, 95% of the population lies within 2 standard deviations of the mean, and 99.7% of the population lies within 3 standard deviations of the mean. — 754

- **$z$ score:** If $x$ is a data value in a sample, the corresponding $z$ score to $x$ is $z = \dfrac{x - \bar{x}}{s}$ which standarizes normal distributions. — 755

**DEFINITIONS**

- A **random sequence of digits** is a sequence of digits chosen in such a way that, at each step, each digit has an equal chance of being chosen. — 750

- **Random numbers** are numbers formed by successively choosing the appropriate digits from a random sequence of digits. — 751

- The **relative frequency** is the frequency of the occurrence of a data value in a sample, expressed as a percentage. — 753

- The **relative-frequency polygon** is a histogram in which the heights of the bars indicate relative frequency. — 753

- The **$r$-th percentile** of a frequency distribution is the number $r$, with $0 \leq r \leq 100$, such that $r$% of the data set of the population is less than or equal to $r$. — 756

## Chapter Review Exercises

### Section 13.1

1. The following are the numbers of hours of television watched during a given week by the students in Mrs. Karnes's fourth-grade class:

| | | | | | | | | | |
|---|---|---|---|---|---|---|---|---|---|
| 17 | 8 | 17 | 13 | 16 | 13 | 8 | 9 | 17 | 7 |
| 8 | 7 | 14 | 14 | 11 | 13 | 11 | 13 | 11 | 17 |
| 12 | 15 | 11 | 10 | 12 | 13 | 9 | 21 | 19 | 12 |

(a) Make a dot plot to organize and display these data.

(b) From the dot plot, estimate the average number of hours per week the students in Mrs. Karnes's class watch television.

2. Make a stem-and-leaf plot to organize and display the data in problem 1.

3. Choosing suitable scales, draw a histogram to summarize and display the data in problem 1.

4. The following are the numbers of hours of television watched during the same week as in problem 1, but by the students in Ms. Stevens's accelerated fourth-grade class:

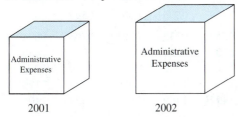

| 13 | 8  | 9  | 11 | 11 | 12 | 8  | 9  |
|----|----|----|----|----|----|----|----|
| 11 | 11 | 6  | 8  | 9  | 11 | 11 | 6  |
| 8  | 9  | 11 | 11 | 6  | 8  | 9  | 11 |

Prepare a double stem-and-leaf plot to display and compare the number of hours of television watched by Mrs. Karnes's and Ms. Stevens's classes during the given week.

5. **(a)** Draw a line graph to show the trend in the retail price index of farm `products as shown in this table:

| 1965 | 1970 | 1975 | 1980 | 1985 | 1990 | 1995 | 2000 | 2005 |
|------|------|------|------|------|------|------|------|------|
| 35   | 42   | 64   | 88   | 104  | 134  | 168  | 184  | 190  |

  **(b)** Using part (a), estimate the retail price index for farm products in 1972.

  **(c)** Using part (a), estimate what the retail price index for farm products will be in 2010.

6. Find five numbers such that four of the numbers are less than the mean of all five.

7. Draw a pie chart to accurately illustrate how the State Department of Highways spends its budget if the figures are as follows: Administration—12%; New Construction—36%; Repairs—48%; Miscellaneous—4%.

8. **(a)** Criticize this pictograph, designed to suggest that the administrative expenses for Cold Steel Metal appear to be less than double in 2002 than in 2001 even though, in fact, the administrative expenses did double:

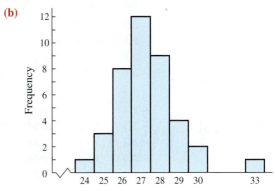

  **(b)** If the administrators are challenged by the stockholders, can they honestly defend the pictograph? (*Hint:* Measure the cubes very carefully with a metric ruler and compute their volumes.)

9. What would you need to know in order to take the following statement seriously? "A survey shows that the average medical doctor in the United States earns $185,000 annually."

## Section 13.2

10. Compute the mean, median, mode, and standard deviation for the data in problem 1.

11. **(a)** Compute the quartiles for the data in problem 1.

  **(b)** Give the 5-number summary for the data in problem 1.

  **(c)** Identify any outliers in the data of problem 1.

  **(d)** Compute the quartiles for the data in problem 4.

  **(e)** Give the 5-number summary for the data in problem 4.

  **(f)** Identify any outliers in the data of problem 4.

  **(g)** Using the same scales, draw side-by-side box plots to compare the data in problems 1 and 4.

12. Compute the mean and standard deviation for the data represented in these two histograms:

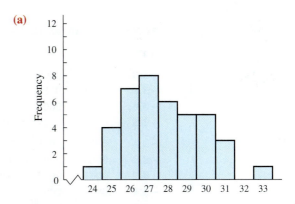

  **(c)** Briefly explain the results of your computations in parts (a) and (b).

13. Three students were absent when the remaining 21 students in the class took a test on which their average score was 77. When the 3 students took the test later on, their scores were 69, 62, and 91. Taking these grades into account, what was the new average of all the test scores?

14. Mr. Renfro's second-period Algebra I class of 27 students averaged 75 on a test, and his fourth-period class of 30 students averaged 78 on the same test. What was the average of all the second- and fourth-period test scores?

## Section 13.3

15. In a study of drug use by college students in the United States, the investigators chose a sample of 200 students from State University. Was this an appropriate choice for the study? Explain.

16. Suppose you want to use a sampling procedure to estimate the percentage of people in the United States who are unemployed. How might you describe the population that should be sampled? Should every person residing in the United States be included in the population? Discuss briefly.

17. Discuss briefly the biases that are inherent in samples obtained by voluntary responses to questionnaires like those sent out by members of Congress to their constituents.

18. Determine the $z$ scores for the data set $\{7, 9, 6, 12, 15, 7, 9\}$.

19. What percentile is 12 in problem 18?

20. Use Table 13.4 on pages 764 and 765 to determine what percentile corresponds to the population $z$ score 1.65.

21. Use Table 13.4 on pages 764 and 765 to determine what percentage of a standardized normal population lies between the population $z$ scores $-0.9$ and $0.9$.

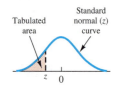

Tabulated area | Standard normal (z) curve

| TABLE 13.4 | AREAS TO THE LEFT OF z SCORES FOR A STANDARDIZED NORMAL DISTRIBUTION | | | | | | | | |
|---|---|---|---|---|---|---|---|---|---|
| z* | .00 | .01 | .02 | .03 | .04 | .05 | .06 | .07 | .08 | .09 |
| −3.8 | .0001 | .0001 | .0001 | .0001 | .0001 | .0001 | .0001 | .0001 | .0001 | .0000 |
| −3.7 | .0001 | .0001 | .0001 | .0001 | .0001 | .0001 | .0001 | .0001 | .0001 | .0001 |
| −3.6 | .0002 | .0002 | .0001 | .0001 | .0001 | .0001 | .0001 | .0001 | .0001 | .0001 |
| −3.5 | .0002 | .0002 | .0002 | .0002 | .0002 | .0002 | .0002 | .0002 | .0002 | .0002 |
| −3.4 | .0003 | .0003 | .0003 | .0003 | .0003 | .0003 | .0003 | .0003 | .0003 | .0002 |
| −3.3 | .0005 | .0005 | .0005 | .0004 | .0004 | .0004 | .0004 | .0004 | .0004 | .0003 |
| −3.2 | .0007 | .0007 | .0006 | .0006 | .0006 | .0006 | .0006 | .0005 | .0005 | .0005 |
| −3.1 | .0010 | .0009 | .0009 | .0009 | .0008 | .0008 | .0008 | .0008 | .0007 | .0007 |
| −3.0 | .0013 | .0013 | .0013 | .0012 | .0012 | .0011 | .0011 | .0011 | .0010 | .0010 |
| −2.9 | .0019 | .0018 | .0018 | .0017 | .0016 | .0016 | .0015 | .0015 | .0014 | .0014 |
| −2.8 | .0026 | .0025 | .0024 | .0023 | .0023 | .0022 | .0021 | .0021 | .0020 | .0019 |
| −2.7 | .0035 | .0034 | .0033 | .0032 | .0031 | .0030 | .0029 | .0028 | .0027 | .0026 |
| −2.6 | .0047 | .0045 | .0044 | .0043 | .0041 | .0040 | .0039 | .0038 | .0037 | .0036 |
| −2.5 | .0062 | .0060 | .0059 | .0057 | .0055 | .0054 | .0052 | .0051 | .0049 | .0048 |
| −2.4 | .0082 | .0080 | .0078 | .0075 | .0073 | .0071 | .0069 | .0068 | .0066 | .0064 |
| −2.3 | .0107 | .0104 | .0102 | .0099 | .0096 | .0094 | .0091 | .0089 | .0087 | .0084 |
| −2.2 | .0139 | .0136 | .0132 | .0129 | .0125 | .0122 | .0119 | .0116 | .0113 | .0110 |
| −2.1 | .0179 | .0174 | .0170 | .0166 | .0162 | .0158 | .0154 | .0150 | .0146 | .0143 |
| −2.0 | .0228 | .0222 | .0217 | .0212 | .0207 | .0202 | .0197 | .0192 | .0188 | .0183 |
| −1.9 | .0287 | .0281 | .0274 | .0268 | .0262 | .0256 | .0250 | .0244 | .0239 | .0233 |
| −1.8 | .0359 | .0351 | .0344 | .0336 | .0329 | .0322 | .0314 | .0307 | .0301 | .0294 |
| −1.7 | .0446 | .0436 | .0427 | .0418 | .0409 | .0401 | .0392 | .0384 | .0375 | .0367 |
| −1.6 | .0548 | .0537 | .0526 | .0516 | .0505 | .0495 | .0485 | .0475 | .0465 | .0455 |
| −1.5 | .0668 | .0655 | .0643 | .0630 | .0618 | .0606 | .0594 | .0582 | .0571 | .0559 |
| −1.4 | .0808 | .0793 | .0778 | .0764 | .0749 | .0735 | .0721 | .0708 | .0694 | .0681 |
| −1.3 | .0968 | .0951 | .0934 | .0918 | .0901 | .0885 | .0869 | .0853 | .0838 | .0823 |
| −1.2 | .1151 | .1131 | .1112 | .1093 | .1075 | .1056 | .1038 | .1020 | .1003 | .0985 |
| −1.1 | .1357 | .1355 | .1314 | .1292 | .1271 | .1251 | .1230 | .1210 | .1190 | .1170 |
| −1.0 | .1587 | .1562 | .1539 | .1515 | .1492 | .1469 | .1446 | .1423 | .1401 | .1379 |
| −0.9 | .1841 | .1814 | .1788 | .1762 | .1736 | .1711 | .1685 | .1660 | .1635 | .1611 |
| −0.8 | .2119 | .2090 | .2061 | .2033 | .2005 | .1977 | .1949 | .1922 | .1894 | .1867 |
| −0.7 | .2420 | .2389 | .2358 | .2327 | .2296 | .2266 | .2236 | .2206 | .2177 | .2148 |
| −0.6 | .2743 | .2709 | .2676 | .2643 | .2611 | .2578 | .2546 | .2514 | .2483 | .2451 |
| −0.5 | .3085 | .3050 | .3015 | .2981 | .2946 | .2912 | .2877 | .2843 | .2810 | .2776 |
| −0.4 | .3446 | .3409 | .3372 | .3336 | .3300 | .3264 | .3228 | .3192 | .3156 | .3121 |
| −0.3 | .3821 | .3783 | .3745 | .3707 | .3669 | .3632 | .3594 | .3557 | .3520 | .3483 |
| −0.2 | .4207 | .4168 | .4129 | .4090 | .4052 | .4013 | .3974 | .3936 | .3897 | .3859 |
| −0.1 | .4602 | .4562 | .4522 | .4483 | .4443 | .4404 | .4364 | .4325 | .4286 | .4247 |
| −0.0 | .5000 | .4960 | .4920 | .4880 | .4840 | .4801 | .4761 | .4721 | .4681 | .4641 |
| 0.0 | .5000 | .5040 | .5080 | .5120 | .5160 | .5199 | .5239 | .5279 | .5319 | .5359 |
| 0.1 | .5398 | .5438 | .5478 | .5517 | .5557 | .5596 | .5636 | .5675 | .5714 | .5753 |
| 0.2 | .5793 | .5832 | .5871 | .5910 | .5948 | .5987 | .6026 | .6064 | .6103 | .6141 |
| 0.3 | .6179 | .6217 | .6255 | .6293 | .6331 | .6368 | .6406 | .6443 | .6480 | .6517 |
| 0.4 | .6554 | .6591 | .6628 | .6664 | .6700 | .6736 | .6772 | .6808 | .6844 | .6879 |
| 0.5 | .6915 | .6950 | .6985 | .7019 | .7054 | .7088 | .7123 | .7157 | .7190 | .7224 |
| 0.6 | .7257 | .7291 | .7324 | .7357 | .7389 | .7422 | .7454 | .7486 | .7517 | .7549 |
| 0.7 | .7580 | .7611 | .7641 | .7673 | .7704 | .7734 | .7764 | .7794 | .7823 | .7852 |
| 0.8 | .7881 | .7910 | .7939 | .7967 | .7995 | .8023 | .8051 | .8078 | .8106 | .8133 |
| 0.9 | .8159 | .8186 | .8212 | .8238 | .8264 | .8289 | .8315 | .8340 | .8365 | .8389 |

Tabulated area
Standard normal ($z$) curve

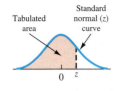

0   $z$

| **TABLE 13.4** | **CONTINUED** | | | | | | | | |
|---|---|---|---|---|---|---|---|---|---|
| **z\*** | **.00** | **.01** | **.02** | **.03** | **.04** | **.05** | **.06** | **.07** | **.08** | **.09** |
| **1.0** | .8413 | .8438 | .8461 | .8485 | .8508 | .8531 | .8554 | .8577 | .8599 | .8621 |
| **1.1** | .8643 | .8665 | .8686 | .8708 | .8729 | .8749 | .8770 | .8790 | .8810 | .8830 |
| **1.2** | .8849 | .8869 | .8888 | .8907 | .8925 | .8944 | .8962 | .8980 | .8997 | .9015 |
| **1.3** | .9032 | .9049 | .9066 | .9082 | .9099 | .9155 | .9131 | .9147 | .9162 | .9177 |
| **1.4** | .9192 | .9207 | .9222 | .9236 | .9251 | .9265 | .9279 | .9292 | .9306 | .9319 |
| **1.5** | .9332 | .9345 | .9357 | .9370 | .9382 | .9394 | .9406 | .9418 | .9429 | .9441 |
| **1.6** | .9452 | .9463 | .9474 | .9484 | .9495 | .9505 | .9515 | .9525 | .9535 | .9545 |
| **1.7** | .9554 | .9564 | .9573 | .9582 | .9591 | .9599 | .9608 | .9616 | .9625 | .9633 |
| **1.8** | .9641 | .9649 | .9656 | .9664 | .9671 | .9678 | .9686 | .9693 | .9699 | .9706 |
| **1.9** | .9713 | .9719 | .9726 | .9732 | .9738 | .9744 | .9750 | .9756 | .9761 | .9767 |
| **2.0** | .9772 | .9778 | .9783 | .9788 | .9793 | .9798 | .9803 | .9808 | .9812 | .9817 |
| **2.1** | .9821 | .9826 | .9830 | .9834 | .9838 | .9842 | .9846 | .9850 | .9854 | .9857 |
| **2.2** | .9861 | .9864 | .9868 | .9871 | .9875 | .9878 | .9881 | .9884 | .9887 | .9890 |
| **2.3** | .9893 | .9896 | .9898 | .9901 | .9904 | .9906 | .9909 | .9911 | .9913 | .9916 |
| **2.4** | .9918 | .9920 | .9922 | .9925 | .9927 | .9929 | .9931 | .9932 | .9934 | .9936 |
| **2.5** | .9938 | .9940 | .9941 | .9943 | .9945 | .9946 | .9948 | .9949 | .9951 | .9952 |
| **2.6** | .9953 | .9955 | .9956 | .9957 | .9959 | .9960 | .9961 | .9962 | .9963 | .9964 |
| **2.7** | .9965 | .9966 | .9967 | .9968 | .9969 | .9970 | .9971 | .9972 | .9973 | .9974 |
| **2.8** | .9974 | .9975 | .9976 | .9977 | .9977 | .9978 | .9979 | .9979 | .9980 | .9981 |
| **2.9** | .9981 | .9982 | .9982 | .9983 | .9984 | .9984 | .9985 | .9985 | .9986 | .9986 |
| **3.0** | .9987 | .9987 | .9987 | .9988 | .9988 | .9989 | .9989 | .9989 | .9990 | .9990 |
| **3.1** | .9990 | .9991 | .9991 | .9991 | .9992 | .9992 | .9992 | .9992 | .9993 | .9993 |
| **3.2** | .9993 | .9993 | .9994 | .9994 | .9994 | .9994 | .9994 | .9995 | .9995 | .9995 |
| **3.3** | .9995 | .9995 | .9995 | .9996 | .9996 | .9996 | .9996 | .9996 | .9996 | .9997 |
| **3.4** | .9997 | .9997 | .9997 | .9997 | .9997 | .9997 | .9997 | .9997 | .9997 | .9998 |
| **3.5** | .9998 | .9998 | .9998 | .9998 | .9998 | .9998 | .9998 | .9998 | .9998 | .9998 |
| **3.6** | .9998 | .9998 | .9999 | .9999 | .9999 | .9999 | .9999 | .9999 | .9999 | .9999 |
| **3.7** | .9999 | .9999 | .9999 | .9999 | .9999 | .9999 | .9999 | .9999 | .9999 | .9999 |
| **3.8** | .9999 | .9999 | .9999 | .9999 | .9999 | .9999 | .9999 | .9999 | .9999 | 1.0000 |

## Chapter Test

**1.** Suppose the average American spends 40% of his or her income paying taxes. If this information were to be shown with a pie chart, what should the central angle be for this portion of the chart?

**2.** Prepare a dot plot to summarize and visually display these data:

| | | | | | | | | | |
|---|---|---|---|---|---|---|---|---|---|
| 42 | 86 | 80 | 90 | 74 | 84 | 86 | 80 | 63 | 92 |
| 93 | 81 | 95 | 78 | 70 | 41 | 66 | 76 | 87 | 88 |
| 75 | 88 | 87 | 78 | 89 | 85 | 77 | 87 | 81 | 57 |

**3.** Compute the following for the data in problem 2:
   **(a)** The mean
   **(b)** The median
   **(c)** The mode
   **(d)** The standard deviation

**4.** Compute $z$ scores for 42, 86, and 80 from problem 2 as part of the entire data set.

**5.** Prepare a stem-and-leaf plot to summarize the data in problem 2.

**6.** **(a)** Sketch a box plot for the data in problem 2.
   **(b)** Would you say that these data contain any outliers? Explain.

**7.** In making inferences based on samples, why is it important to choose random samples?

**8.** What does it mean to say that a sample is a random sample? Be brief, but lucid.

**9.** What percentile is 84 in the data set of problem 2?

**10.** Suppose that Nanda obtains scores of 77%, 79%, and 72% on her first three tests in French. What total score must she earn on her last two tests in order to average at least 80% in the course?

# Probability

**14.1** Experimental Probability

**14.2** Principles of Counting

**14.3** Permutations and Combinations

**14.4** Theoretical Probability

## Hands On

## Strings and Loops

### Materials

Six pieces of string per student, all pieces the same length (about 7 inches)

### Procedure

Students work in pairs.

1. One student twists six lengths of the string into a loose bundle held with one hand. The student's partner then ties six knots, with three knots joining randomly selected pairs of the six strings at the top of the bundle and three other knots joining arbitrary pairs of strings at the bottom of the bundle. When the six knots have been tied, the bundle of string is put on a table.
2. The partners reverse roles and tie six knots in another six-string bundle.

3. The bundles are taken apart to identify what pattern of loops has been created by the six knots. There are three possible loop patterns, where any intertwining of the loops is of no importance:

*T*: three small two-string loops;
*M*: one medium four-string loop and one small two-string loop;
*L*: one large six-string loop.

### Class Project

Collect the data from all pairs of students and determine the ratios $n(T)/N$, $n(M)/N$, and $n(L)/N$, where $n(T)$, $n(M)$, and $n(L)$ are the respective numbers of timers *T*, *M*, and *L* occurred and $N = n(T) + n(M) + n(L)$ is the total number of tied bundles. Which pattern seems most likely to occur? which seems least likely? are you surprised?

**CHAPTER PREVIEW**
Probability is the branch of mathematics that quantifies uncertainty. In particular, the likelihood that an event will occur is expressed by a number called the *probability* of the event, where the probability ranges from 0 (impossibility) to 1 (certainty). For example, if we flip a coin, the probability that it will land face up is 0.5, since we expect, either on the basis of the coin's symmetry or by data gathered from past experience, that half the time we obtain heads and half the time tails.

There are two ways to determine the probability of an event: *experimental* and *theoretical.* Experimental probability is determined, or at least approximated, by observing how often the event occurs when a number of trials have been conducted or tabulating how frequently the event has occurred in the past. For example, suppose we have a bent coin that has come up heads 36 times in 100 flips. The experimental probability of a head appearing on the next flip is then 0.36. By contrast, theoretical probability is determined by counting the number of equally likely outcomes that may occur and then counting the number of these outcomes that result in the occurrence of a specified event. For example, given a number cube (that is, a die) there are six equally likely outcomes, namely, rolling a 1, 2, 3, 4, 5, or 6. If the event of interest is rolling either a 4 or a 5, then two of the six outcomes are favorable to the event, so the theoretical probability of the event is $2/6 = 1/3$. It is important to have advanced counting skills to calculate theoretical probabilities, and the sections on the principles of counting, combinations, and permutations provide the preparation needed for the concluding section on theoretical probability.

**KEY IDEAS**

- Experimental probability
- Terminology of probability: outcome, sample space, event, mutually exclusive events, independent events
- Simulation
- The addition principle of counting
- The multiplication principle of counting
- Permutation
- Combination
- Factorial
- Equally likely outcomes
- Theoretical probability
- Conditional probability
- Probability tree
- Expected value
- Geometric probability

Students in grades 3–5 should begin to learn about probability as a measurement of the likelihood of events. In previous grades, they will have begun to describe events as certain, likely, or impossible, but now they can begin to learn how to quantify likelihood. For instance, what is the likelihood of seeing a commercial when you turn on the television? To estimate probability, students could collect data about the number of minutes of commercials in an hour.

Students should also explore probability through experiments that have only a few outcomes, such as using game spinners with certain portions shaded and considering how likely it is that the spinner will land on a particular color. They should come to understand and use 0 to represent the probability of an impossible event and 1 to represent the probability of a certain event, and they should use common fractions to represent the probability of events that are neither certain nor impossible. Through these experiences, students encounter the idea that although they cannot determine an individual outcome, such as which color the spinner will land on next, they can predict the frequency of various outcomes.

SOURCE: Principles and Standards for School Mathematics by NCTM, *page 181. Copyright © 2000 by the National Council of Teachers of Mathematics. Reproduced with permission of the National Council of Teachers of Mathematics via Copyright Clearance Center. NCTM does not endorse the content or validity of these alignments.*

## 14.1

# Experimental Probability

Suppose a penny is stood on its edge on a table, and the table is given a sharp rap to topple the coin. (See problem 27 in Problem Set 14.1.) The experiment has two outcomes, since the coin will land either heads or tails up. If, in 100 experiments, the outcome heads occurs 91 times, we say that the experimental probability of obtaining a head is $\frac{91}{100}$. In symbols, this probability is written $P_e(H) = 0.91$, where $H$ denotes the event that the coin lands heads upward and the subscript $e$ indicates the probability in question is an experimental probability. More generally, we have the following definition:

> **DEFINITION**  *Experimental Probability*
> Suppose an experiment with a number of possible outcomes is performed repeatedly—say, $n$ times—and that a specific outcome $E$ occurs $r$ times. The **experimental** (or **empirical** or **experiential**) **probability,** denoted by $P_e(E)$, that $E$ will occur on any given trial of the experiment is given by
> $$P_e(E) = \frac{r}{n}.$$

If only a few experiments have been conducted, the experimental probability can vary widely and will not be a good indicator of future outcomes of the experiment. However, as the number of experiments increases, the variation decreases. This important fact, which we state without proof, is called the law of large numbers. It is also known as Bernoulli's theorem, in honor of Jakob Bernoulli (1654–1705).

> **THEOREM**  *The Law of Large Numbers*
> If an experiment is performed repeatedly, the experimental probability of a particular outcome more and more closely approximates a fixed number as the number of trials increases.

A striking example of the law of large numbers was provided by John Kerrich, an English mathematician imprisoned by the Germans during the Second World War. To while away the time, Kerrich decided to toss a coin 10,000 times and to recompute $P_e(H)$, the experimental probability of getting a head, after each toss. His first 10 tosses yielded 4 heads, so $P_e(H)$ equalled 0.4 at that point.

After 30 tosses $P_e(H)$ was 0.57, after 100 tosses it was 0.44, after 1000 tosses it was 0.49, and after that it varied up and down slightly, but stayed very close to 0.5. After 10,000 tosses, the number of heads obtained was 5067, for an empirical probability of $P_e(H) \doteq 0.51$. During the experiment, relatively long sequences of consecutive heads and of consecutive tails occurred. Nevertheless, in the long run, the law of large numbers prevailed, and the intuitive guess of 0.5 was borne out. The variation in $P_e(H)$ is effectively illustrated in Figure 14.1.

**FIGURE 14.1**

Ratio of the number of heads to the number of tosses in Kerrich's coin-tossing experiment
SOURCE: *Adaptation of Figure 2 from Statistics, Second Edition, by David Freedman, Robert Pisani, Roger Purves, and Ani Adhikari, p. 250. Copyright © 1991 by W.W. Norton & Company, Inc.; copyright © 1978 by David Freedman, Robert Pisani, Roger Purves, and Ani Adhikari.*

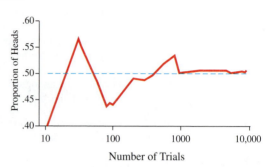

**MHM** Most people, and certainly most young students, would not have the patience shown by Kerrich. Indeed, many people, both young and older, incorrectly reason by "the law of small numbers," in which probabilities are assessed on the basis of a very limited number of trials. For example, a student may be astonished to have 8 heads appear when 10 coins are flipped. Though rare, it should be expected that a flip of 10 coins can sometimes result in 8 or even more heads. Indeed, this outcome is almost sure to happen if the experiment is repeated a large number of times. It is thus important for students to understand that, to estimate an experimental probability with confidence, a large amount of data is essential.

**EXAMPLE 14.1 Determining an Experimental Probability**

Open a book at random and note the number of the right-hand page. Do this 20 times and determine the experimental probability that the number of the right-hand page is divisible by 3.

**Solution** Since every third right-hand page is numbered with a number that is divisible by 3, we would expect that the experimental probability should be about $\frac{1}{3}$. Here are results obtained on checking 20 pages chosen at random:

| | | | | |
|---|---|---|---|---|
| 349 | 69 | 267 | 407 | 133 |
| 395 | 269 | 123 | 331 | 373 |
| 155 | 235 | 187 | 273 | 401 |
| 297 | 83 | 852 | 263 | 303 |

Since a number is divisible by 3 if, and only if, the sum of its digits is divisible by 3, we determine that seven of these page numbers are divisible by 3. Hence,

$$P_e(\text{a right-hand page number is divisible by 3}) = \frac{7}{20} = 0.35,$$

a very close approximation to $\frac{1}{3}$.

## Connections with Statistics

Most of what was said about statistics in Chapter 13 can be rephrased in terms of experimental probability. For example, saying that 28% of the items in a sample possess a certain property is the same as saying that the experimental probability that an item in the sample possesses a property $A$ is

$P_e(A) = 0.28$. Moreover, since population properties are estimated by properties of samples, one would go on to say that the experimental probability that an individual in the population possesses the property is also 0.28. Results of surveys and polls, summaries of data, and averages of all kinds also can be interpreted as experimental probabilities. Batting averages are experimental probabilities. Percentages of shots made in basketball are experimental probabilities. The life insurance industry is based on experimental probabilities derived from mortality tables.

**EXAMPLE 14.2** **Computing Experimental Probability from a Histogram**

Suppose you wanted to study the heights of high school boys in the United States and decided to take Eisenhower High School as typical. Use the following histogram (reproduced from Figure 13.17) to determine the experimental probability that the height, in inches, of a high school boy is in the range $67.5 < h < 70.5$.

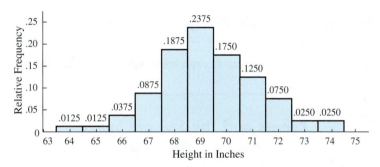

**Solution** The percentages of boys with heights in the ranges 67.5–68.5, 68.5–69.5, and 69.5–70.5 inches are, respectively, 18.75%, 23.75%, and 17.5%. Thus, the total percentage of boys with heights in the range 67.5–70.5 inches is $18.75 + 23.75 + 17.5$, or 60%. Therefore, $60\% = 0.60 = \dfrac{r}{n}$, where $r$ is the number of boys with heights in the desired range and $n$ is the number of boys in the high school. Since $P_e$ also equals $\dfrac{r}{n}$, it follows that $P_e = 0.60$.

## Additional Examples of Computing Experimental Probabilities

Experimental probabilities can be determined either from existing data or from data gathered from an experiment.

**EXAMPLE 14.3** **Computing Experimental Probability from Data**

The final examination scores of students in a precalculus class are as shown. Compute the experimental probability that a student chosen at random from the class had a score in the 70s.

| 67 | 56 | 76 | 84 | 36 | 50 | 84 |
|----|----|----|----|-----|----|----|
| 47 | 59 | 54 | 79 | 100 | 48 | 80 |
| 60 | 100 | 100 | 68 | 79 | 95 | 81 |
| 98 | 76 | 33 | 73 | 83 | 77 | 67 |

**Solution** Since 6 of the 28 students scored in the 70s, the experimental probability that a student chosen at random had a score in the 70s is $\dfrac{6}{28} = 0.21$.

**EXAMPLE 14.4** **Determining Experimental Probabilities from an Experiment**

Christine has five pennies. She is curious how often she should expect to see at most one head when all five coins are flipped onto the floor. To find an answer, she repeatedly flips the five pennies and counts the number of heads that turn up. After repeating the experiment 50 times, she obtains the following frequency table:

| Number of heads | 0 | 1 | 2 | 3 | 4 | 5 |
|---|---|---|---|---|---|---|
| Frequency | 1 | 7 | 13 | 16 | 11 | 2 |

On the basis of Christine's data, what is the experimental probability that a flip of five coins results in at most one head?

**Solution**   The data show that exactly one head appeared on seven of the trials and no heads (that is, all tails) appeared once. This means that the outcome of at most one head occurred $1 + 7 = 8$ times in the 50 trials, giving an experimental probability of $P_e(\text{at most 1 head}) = \dfrac{8}{50} = 0.16$.

## Events and the Sample Space

The following terminology will help us investigate the general properties of probability:

> **DEFINITIONS**   *The Terminology of Probability*
> **Outcome:** a result of one trial of an experiment
> **Sample space $S$:** the set of all outcomes of an experiment
> **Event $E$:** a set $E$ of some of the outcomes of an experiment (that is, a subset $E$ of the sample space $S$, so that $E \subseteq S$)
> **Mutually exclusive events $A$ and $B$:** two events $A$ and $B$ such that the occurrence of an outcome in $A$ precludes its occurrence in $B$, and vice versa (that is, $A$ and $B$ are disjoint subsets of the sample space, or $A \cap B = \varnothing$)

It is helpful to visualize the terms in the definition with a Venn diagram. The sample space $S$ is the universe represented by the outer rectangle, and events are represented by loops within the rectangle. For example, if the experiment is to roll two dice and an outcome is the total number of spots that appear on the upward faces, then the sample space is $S = \{2, 3, 4, 5, 6, 7, 8, 9, 10, 11, 12\}$. Figure 14.2 shows this sample space, together with three loops that represent the events "rolling a 7," "rolling an 11," and "rolling a 7 or an 11." The diagram makes it clear that if $A$ is "rolling a 7" and $B$ is "rolling an 11," then "rolling a 7 *or* an 11" is the event $A \cup B$.

**FIGURE 14.2**
The sample space of summing the spots on a roll of two dice. The loops show the events "rolling a 7," "rolling an 11," and "rolling a 7 or an 11"

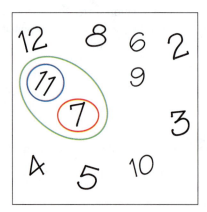

**EXAMPLE 14.5** **Computing Experimental Probability and the Word *Or***

Roll a pair of dice 50 times and compute these experimental probabilities:

**(a)** $P_e(7)$ **(b)** $P_e(11)$ **(c)** $P_e(7 \text{ or } 11)$
**(d)** Show that $P_e(7 \text{ or } 11) = P_e(7) + P_e(11)$.

**Solution**

Actually performing the experiment, we obtained these results:

| 2 | 3 | 4 | 5 | 6 | 7 | 8 | 9 | 10 | 11 | 12 |
|---|---|---|---|---|---|---|---|----|----|----|
| I | | III | IIII | HHT HHT | HHT HHT II | HHT III | IIII | IIII | II | II |

From the data, the desired experimental probabilities are as follows:

**(a)** $P_e(7) = 12/50 = 0.24$
**(b)** $P_e(11) = 2/50 = 0.04$
**(c)** $P_e(7 \text{ or } 11) = 14/50 = 0.28$
**(d)** $P_e(7 \text{ or } 11) = 0.28 = 0.24 + 0.04 = P_e(7) + P_e(11)$

The results of Example 14.5 illustrate the following very important property of mutually exclusive events (notice that $P(A \text{ or } B)$ can also be written $P(A \cup B)$):

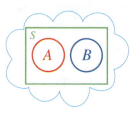

**PROPERTY** *Experimental Probability of Mutually Exclusive Events*
If $A$ and $B$ are mutually exclusive events, then $P_e(A \text{ or } B) = P_e(A) + P_e(B)$.

The next example shows how to modify the formula for non–mutually exclusive events.

**EXAMPLE 14.6** **Computing the Experimental Probability of Non-Mutually Exclusive Events**

A penny and a dime are flipped. Determine the experimental probability that the dime shows a head or both coins land with the same side up. Use the data collected in the accompanying table, which shows the outcomes of 50 flips of the pair of coins.

| | | **Dime** | |
|---|---|---|---|
| | | Head | Tail |
| **Penny** | Head | HHT HHT IIII | HHT IIII |
| | Tail | HHT HHT | HHT HHT HHT II |

**Solution**

Let $A$ denote the event "the dime shows a head," and let $B$ denote the event "both coins land with the same side up." Since the dime shows a head 24 times in the 50 trials, we see that $P_e(A) = \dfrac{24}{50} = 0.48$.

Similarly, since both coins show heads 14 times and both coins show tails 17 times, then both coins show the same side in 31 of the 50 trials and therefore $P_e(B) = \dfrac{31}{50} = 0.62$. The number of trials with the outcome $A$ or $B$ is *not* given by adding 24 and 31, since this counts twice instead of once the 14 trials in which both coins landed heads. Thus, the number of trials with an outcome in $A$ or $B$ is

$24 + 31 - 14 = 41$, so $P_e(A \cup B) = \dfrac{41}{50} = 0.82$. That is, $41 = 24 + 31 - 14$, where 14 is the

number of trials in which the events $A$ *and* $B$ occurred at the same time. All this reasoning shows us that

$$P_e(A \cup B) = P_e(A) + P_e(B) - P_e(A \cap B).$$

The formula discovered in Example 14.6 applies to any pair of events $A$ and $B$ in the sample space. Notice that $A$ *and* $B$ is the event of all outcomes that belong to both $A$ and $B$. Therefore, $P_e(A \text{ and } B)$ is the same as $P_e(A \cap B)$. Likewise, $P_e(A \text{ or } B)$ is the same as $P_e(A \cup B)$. Remember that *or* in mathematics has the inclusive meaning of *and/or*. Children need frequent reminders of this mathematical meaning of *or*, since it is different from its meaning in most nonmathematical contexts.

> **PROPERTY** *Experimental Probability of A or B for Non–Mutually Exclusive Events*
> If $A$ and $B$ are any two events, then $P_e(A \text{ or } B) = P_e(A) + P_e(B) - P_e(A \text{ and } B)$.

This formula is still correct even when $A$ and $B$ are mutually exclusive events, since in that case $P_e(A \text{ and } B) = P_e(A \cap B) = P_e(\varnothing) = 0$ and the formula simplifies to

$$P_e(A \text{ or } B) = P_e(A) + P_e(B).$$

## Independent Events

Often, an experiment can be viewed as a combination of two (or more) other experiments. For example, if we roll a pair of dice—say, one red and one green die—then we are combining two experiments: rolling the red die and rolling the green die. When experiments are conducted by combining two or more other experiments, the outcomes are known as **compound events.** Example 14.7 explores the probability of a compound event of tossing two distinct coins.

### EXAMPLE 14.7 Computing Experimental Probability and the Word *And*

Determine the experimental probability of obtaining two heads on a single toss of two coins—that is, the probability of obtaining a head on the first coin **and** a head on the second coin. Does the probability turn out to be about what you would expect? So that you can tell the coins apart, use a penny and a dime.

**Solution**  It is instructive to generate your own data, filling in a frequency table similar to the one shown here, which reproduces the data in Example 14.6. As before, let $A$ denote the event that a head appears on the dime. This time, let $B$ denote the event that a head appears on the penny. Using the data in the table, we find that $P_e(A) = \dfrac{24}{50} = 0.48$, $P_e(B) = \dfrac{23}{50} = 0.46$, and

$P_e(A \text{ and } B) = \dfrac{14}{50} = 0.28$. Since $(0.48) \cdot (0.46) \doteq 0.22 \approx 0.28$, we have the approximate equation

$$P_e(A \text{ and } B) \approx P_e(A) \cdot P_e(B).$$

|        |      | **Dime** | |
|--------|------|------|------|
|        |      | Head | Tail |
| **Penny** | Head | 14 | 9 |
|        | Tail | 10 | 17 |

In Example 14.7, it was important to understand that the outcome of one coin had no influence on the other. Events with this property are called **independent events** according to the following definition:

> **DEFINITION** *Independent Events*
> Events $A$ and $B$ are **independent events** if the occurrence or nonoccurrence of event $A$ does not affect the occurrence or nonoccurrence of event $B$, and vice versa.

For an example of *dependent* events, you might imagine flipping a dime and penny that are glued tail to tail. If $A$ and $B$ are the respective events that the dime and penny land with head facing upward, it is clear that the occurrence of $A$ affects the occurrence of $B$.

The property of independent events that was illustrated in Example 14.7 can be stated this way:

> **PROPERTY**  *Experimental Probability of Independent Events* **A** *and* **B**
> If $A$ and $B$ are independent events, then $P_e(A \text{ and } B) \approx P_e(A) \cdot P_e(B)$.

### Experimental Probability and Geometry

There are many interesting connections between geometry and probability. These connections can be explored through a variety of activities using readily available manipulatives or materials. The next example uses an easily constructed spinner; the "arrow" can be a partially unbent paper clip that pivots about the tip of a pencil held down at the center of the spinner.

---

**EXAMPLE 14.8  Determining Experimental Probability Geometrically**

**(a)** What do you intuitively feel the probability is that the arrow will fall into region A?

**(b)** Spin the spinner 20 times, and record the number of times the arrow falls into each region. Then compute $P_e(A)$, $P_e(B)$, and $P_e(C)$, the experimental probabilities that the arrow falls into regions A, B, and C, respectively.

**Solution**

**(a)** Since the arc length associated with regions B and C is one-quarter of the circumference of the spinner and that of region A is one-half the circumference, it is reasonable to guess that
$$P_e(A) \doteq \frac{1}{2} \text{ and } P_e(B) \doteq P_e(C) \doteq \frac{1}{4}.$$

**(b)** Actually spinning the arrow, denote the number of times the arrow falls into A, B, and C, respectively, by $n(A)$, $n(B)$, and $n(C)$. Then,

$$P_e(A) = \frac{n(A)}{20}, \qquad P_e(B) = \frac{n(B)}{20}, \qquad \text{and} \qquad P_e(C) = \frac{n(C)}{20}.$$

As guessed in part (a), these ratios should approximate $\frac{1}{2}, \frac{1}{4},$ and $\frac{1}{4}$, or 0.5, 0.25, and 0.25, respectively.

---

### Simulation

**Simulation** is a method for determining answers to real problems by conducting experiments whose outcomes are analogous to the outcomes of the real problems. Often, computer simulations are conducted, since a very large number of trials can be made quickly at a low cost.

Consider, for example, a couple interested in understanding how many boys or girls they might anticipate if they decide to have children. In this case, we assume

• that the birth of either a boy or a girl is equally likely and
• that the sex of one child is completely independent of the sex of any other child.

These assumptions suggest tossing a coin, since the occurrence of a head or a tail is equally likely and what happens on one toss of the coin is completely independent of what happens on any other toss.

---

**EXAMPLE 14.9  Using Simulation to Determine Experimental Probability**

Use simulation to determine the experimental probability that a family with three children contains at least one boy and at least one girl.

**Solution** | Using the preceding assumptions, we can simulate the real problem by repeatedly tossing three coins. Here are the results of such an experiment:

| | | | | |
|---|---|---|---|---|
| TTH | TTH | HHT | HHT | TTH |
| TTT | HTT | HTT | HHT | HHT |
| HHH | HHT | HHT | HHT | HHH |
| TTT | HHH | HTT | HHT | HHT |
| HHT | TTH | TTH | HHT | TTH |

The experimental probability based on these results is

$$P_e = \frac{20}{25} = 0.80.$$

## Problem Set 14.1

Exercises numbered in red are answered in the back of the text.

### Understanding Concepts

1. The heights of the students in a class are (in inches) 69, 62, 59, 63, 66, 67, 63, 67, 64, 70, 68, 64, 65, 67, 64, 62, 63, 64, 62, and 63. What is the probability that a randomly chosen student

   (a) is less than 5 feet tall?

   (b) is 5 feet, 4 inches, tall?

   (c) is more than 5 feet tall?

2. Prepare a $3'' \times 5''$ card by writing the numbers 1, 2, 3, and 4 on it as shown. Show the card to 20 college or university students and ask them to choose a number and tell you their choice. Record the results on the back of the card and then compute $P_e(3)$, the experimental probability that a person chooses 3. Are you surprised at the result? Explain briefly.

   | 1 2 3 4 |
   |---|

3. (a) On a $3'' \times 5''$ card, write the digits 1, 2, 3, 4, and 5 as shown. Show the card to 20 different students and ask them to select a digit on the card and tell you which digit they selected. Record the results on the back of the card and compute the probabilities $P_e(1), P_e(2), P_e(3), P_e(4)$, and $P_e(5)$.

   | 1 2 3 4 5 |
   |---|

   (b) Compute $P_e(1) + P_e(2) + P_e(3) + P_e(4) + P_e(5)$.

   (c) Did you need to perform the actual calculations in part (b) to be sure what the answer would be? Explain briefly.

   (d) If you were to repeat part (a) with 100 different students, how many do you think would select the digit 4?

4. (a) Toss three coins 20 times and determine the experimental probability of obtaining three heads.

   (b) Using the data from part (a), determine the empirical probability of *not* obtaining three heads.

   (c) Using the data from part (a), determine the empirical probability of obtaining two heads and a tail.

   (d) Could part (b) of this question be easily determined from your answer to part (a)? Explain.

5. (a) Make an orderly list of all possible outcomes resulting from tossing three coins. (*Hint:* Think of tossing a penny, a nickel, and a dime.)

   (b) Does your listing in part (a) give you reason to believe that the result of problem 4(a) is about as expected? Explain briefly.

6. Describe the sample space for each of these experiments:

   (a) A coin is tossed and a single die is rolled.

   (b) A paper cup is tossed into the air and lands on the floor.

   (c) A card is drawn from an ordinary deck of 52 playing cards.

7. A red and a green die are rolled, with the outcome the pair of numbers on the two dice. For example, (3, 1) is the outcome that the red die shows 3 spots and the green die shows 1 spot.

   (a) Draw a Venn diagram of the sample space, where each outcome is an ordered pair showing the number of spots on the red and the green die in that order.

   (b) Draw loops in the sample space diagram that show each of these events:

   $A$ = there is a total of 5 spots on the two dice,
   $B$ = there is a total of 9 or more spots on the two dice,
   $C$ = the green die shows a 5.

   (c) Which pairs of events—$A$ and $B$, $B$ and $C$, or $A$ and $C$—are mutually exclusive? For each pair, explain why or why not.

8. A computer is programmed to simulate experiments and to compute experimental probabilities. Match at least one of the computed probabilities with each of the descriptive sentences listed.

   (a) $P_e(A) = 0$              (b) $P_e(B) = 0.5$

   (c) $P_e(C) = -0.5$           (d) $P_e(D) = 1$

   (e) $P_e(E) = 1.7$            (f) $P_e(F) = 0.9$

**(i)** This event occurred every time.

**(ii)** There was a bug in the program.

**(iii)** This event occurred often, but not every time.

**(iv)** This event never occurred.

**(v)** This event occurred half the time.

9. **(a)** Drop five thumbtacks on your desktop, and determine the empirical probability that a tack dropped on a desktop will land point up.

   **(b)** Repeat part (a) but with 20 thumbtacks.

   **(c)** Give your best estimate of the number of thumbtacks that would land point up if 100 tacks were dropped on the desktop.

10. Construct a spinner with three regions A, B, and C as in Example 14.8, but such that you would expect $P_e(A) = \frac{1}{2}$, $P_e(B) = \frac{1}{3}$, and $P_e(C) = \frac{1}{6}$ on, say, 18 spins. Of what sizes are the angles that determine the regions A, B, and C?

11. Construct a spinner as in Example 14.8 but with the circle marked as shown here:

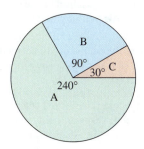

   **(a)** Spin the spinner 20 times and compute $P_e(A)$, $P_e(B)$, and $P_e(C)$.

   **(b)** Are the results of part (a) about as you expected? Explain briefly.

12. A die is rolled repeatedly until a 6 is obtained. Perform the experiment 10 times, and determine the experimental probability that 6 first appears on the second roll.

13. **(a)** A die is rolled repeatedly until a 6 is obtained. Repeat this experiment 10 times and record the results. Estimate how many rolls it should take to obtain a 6.

   **(b)** Might it take 10 rolls to obtain a 6? Explain briefly.

   **(c)** Might it take 100 rolls to obtain a 6? Why or why not?

14. From the data in problem 13, part (a), compute the experimental probability that a 6 first appears on the fourth roll of the die.

15. Consider a spinner similar to the one shown. The head of the spinner arrow falls into the outer ring, and the tail of the arrow falls into the inner ring. Let A be the event that the head of the arrow lands in a red sector, and let B denote the event that the tail of the arrow lands in a yellow sector.

   **(a)** Assuming that you were to conduct a large number of spins, give estimates for each of the experimental probabilities $P_e(A)$, $P_e(B)$, $P_e(A \text{ or } B)$, and $P_e(A \text{ and } B)$.

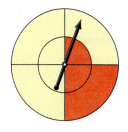

   **(b)** What formula can be used to check your answers to part (a)?

   **(c)** Are the events A and B mutually exclusive? Explain why or why not.

   **(d)** Are the events A and B independent? Explain why or why not.

## Teaching Concepts

16. **(a)** Write up, with careful instructions, graphics, and so on, the following activity:

   *Work in pairs, with each person first making a paper number cube with blank faces. Each person, unseen by the other, writes a number from 1 through 6 on each face with a pencil, with repetitions and omissions allowed. Each person then rolls his or her cube, keeping it hidden but announcing the outcome of each successive roll. The person continues to roll the cubes until one person announces "stop" and guesses what is written on the faces of the hidden cube. If the guess is correct, that person wins, but if it is incorrect, the opponent is the winner.*

   **(b)** Play the game with a partner, and write a report on the game and what principles of probability can be learned and taught.

17. It is often interesting to examine real data to see how experimental probabilities are used in today's society. Use the following table to discuss whether travel is safer by car or by air:

|     | Deaths per billion journeys | Deaths per billion kilometers |
|-----|-----|-----|
| Car | 40 | 3.1 |
| Air | 117 | 0.05 |

## Responding to Students

18. Robbie heard on last night's weather forecast that there was a 30% chance of rain. However, it has rained all day long, and Robbie thought it would rain only 30% of the day. How would you help Robbie better understand the meaning of "a 30% chance of rain"?

19. A spinner has three 120° equally sized sectors colored red, green, and yellow, respectively. Maria is certain that her third spin will be yellow, since her first two spins were red and green and she knows that the probability of yellow is $\frac{1}{3}$. What probability concept is Maria overlooking? Help her with a well-written paragraph.

20. Jessie claims that skydiving is safer than getting out of bed, since there were just 22 skydiving deaths in 2003 in the United States compared with 594 deaths from falling out of bed. Is Jessie's assessment correct?

## Thinking Critically

**21.** Suppose that an experiment is conducted 100 times.

  (a) If event $A$ never occurs, what is $P_e(A)$? Explain briefly.

  (b) If event $A$ occurs every time, what is $P_e(A)$? Explain briefly.

  (c) What range of values is possible for $P_e(A)$? Explain briefly.

**22.** Roll a pair of dice 20 times and count the number of times you get a 7 and the number of times you get an 8.

  (a) Compute $P_e(7)$.

  (b) Compute $P_e(8)$.

  (c) Compute $P_e(7 \text{ or } 8)$.

  (d) Compute $P_e(7) + P_e(8)$.

  (e) Explain why the results of parts (c) and (d) are as they are.

**23.** Consider the experiment of shuffling a deck of playing cards and selecting a card at random. Repeat this experiment 20 times and note the result each time. Let $P_e(R)$ denote the experimental probability that a card is red, let $P_e(F)$ denote the experimental probability that a card is a face card, let $P_e(R \text{ or } F)$ denote the experimental probability that a card is red or is a face card, and let $P_e(R \text{ and } F)$ denote the experimental probability that a card is red and is a face card. Compute these probabilities:

  (a) $P_e(R)$       (b) $P_e(F)$

  (c) $P_e(R \text{ or } F)$       (d) $P_e(R \text{ and } F)$

  (e) $P_e(R) + P_e(F) - P_e(R \text{ and } F)$

  (f) Compare the results of parts (c) and (e). Do these results suggest a general property? Explain.

**24.** Consider an experiment of simultaneously tossing a single coin and rolling a single die. Repeat the experiment 20 times and compute these experimental probabilities:

  (a) $P_e(H)$, the experimental probability that a head occurs

  (b) $P_e(5)$, the experimental probability that a 5 occurs

  (c) $P_e(H \text{ and } 5)$, the experimental probability that a head and a 5 occur simultaneously

  (d) $P_e(H) \cdot P_e(5)$

  (e) Should the results of parts (c) and (d) be about the same? Explain briefly.

**25.** Make up a three-card deck consisting of two aces and a queen. An experiment consists of shuffling the cards and inspecting the card on top and the card on the bottom. Let $A$ denote the event that the top card is an ace, and let $B$ denote the event that the bottom card is an ace. Repeat the experiment 30 times, keeping notes on the occurrence of the events $A$ and $B$.

  (a) Use your data to compute the experimental probabilities $P_e(A)$, $P_e(B)$, $P_e(A) \cdot P_e(B)$, and $P_e(A \text{ and } B)$.

  (b) Do you expect that $P_e(A \text{ and } B)$ should be approximately equal to $P_e(A) \cdot P_e(B)$? Explain why or why not.

**26.** You are shown three cards: one black on both sides, one white on both sides, and one black on one side and white on the other. One card is selected and shown to be black on one side, with the opposite side hidden.

  (a) Considering the possibilities, what do you think is the likelihood or probability that the selected card is black on the other side as well?

  (b) Conduct the experiment just described by selecting at random one of the three cards and looking at *one side only* of the card selected. If it is white, ignore it. If it is black, record it and record the color of the other side of the card. Repeat the experiment 10 times, carefully shuffling the cards between experiments. Compute the empirical probability that the second side of the card is black given that the first side is black. Does your experiment tend to confirm or refute your guess in part (a)?

## Thinking Cooperatively

**27.** Between 1959 and 2008, the reverse side of the Lincoln penny depicted the Lincoln Memorial in Washington, DC. In small groups, stand 25 of these pennies on edge on a flat tabletop. (It is helpful to use newer, unworn pennies.) Next, gently rap on the table until all of the pennies have fallen.

  (a) On the basis of your group's experiment, what is the experimental probability that a penny falls heads upward? What is the probability determined by the combined data of all of the groups? Are you surprised?

  (b) In 2010, the reverse side of the penny was given a union shield design. Repeat the experiment with the current style of penny to see if you detect any differences from your results in part (a).

**28.** Work in a room whose floor is tiled with squares. Each student is given a thin wooden skewer (used to barbecue), cut to the length of the side of a tile. An experiment consists of throwing the skewer onto the floor and seeing whether or not the skewer crosses one of the parallel lines separating rows of floor tile. The lines separating columns of floor tiles will not be considered. Each student repeats the experiment 20 times and computes the experimental probability $P_e(C)$ that a throw crosses one of the lines. According to a calculation of Comte de Buffon (1707–1788), $P_e(C)$ is approximately $\dfrac{2}{\pi}$, or about 0.64.

  (a) Do you expect any one student to have an empirical probability close to $\dfrac{2}{\pi}$?

  (b) Combine the data of individual students and compute a class value of $P_e(C)$. Do you expect to get better agreement with $\dfrac{2}{\pi}$?

**29.** Cover a large corkboard or bulletin board with a rectangular pattern of tangent circles, as shown. An experiment consists of throwing a dart and recording whether the dart lands within a circle or not. Use circles about 1 inch in diameter so that, although it can be certain that the dart lands on the board, it is uncertain whether the dart lands inside any circle. If darts are inconvenient, throw small pins onto the horizontal board and determine whether the point of the pin lies in the interior of a circle or not.

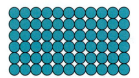

(a) Repeat the experiment numerous times, and compute the experimental probability of hitting within one of the circles on the board.

(b) Does your experimental probability seem to be a good approximation of the ratio of the area of a circle to the area of the square that just contains the circle?

## Making Connections

30. The four blood types are O, A, B, and AB. These occur with the empirical probabilities $P_e(O) = 0.45$, $P_e(A) = 0.41$, $P_e(B) = 0.10$, and $P_e(AB) = 0.04$. What is the probability that, for a married couple,

   (a) both spouses are type O?

   (b) both spouses are type AB?

   (c) one spouse is type O and the other type B? (Be careful; the answer is *not* 0.045.)

31. The following abbreviated mortality table shows, for example, that, of every 10,000 people living at birth, 9806 live to see their 10th birthday:

| Age | Living at Beginning of Year | Age | Living at Beginning of Year |
|---|---|---|---|
| 0 | 10,000 | 50 | 8762 |
| 10 | 9806 | 60 | 7699 |
| 20 | 9666 | 70 | 5592 |
| 30 | 9480 | 80 | 2626 |
| 40 | 9241 | 90 | 468 |

Use the table to compute the empirical probability that

   (a) a newborn lives to be 10 years old.

   (b) a newborn lives to be 90 years old.

   (c) a person now 20 lives to be 50.

   (d) a person now 30 will die before reaching age 70.

## Using a Computer

*The next two problems can be investigated with a spreadsheet. For example, the cell with the formula "= If (Rand( ) > 0.5, 1, 0)" returns a 1 (head) if the value Rand( ) is between 0.5 and 1.0, and returns a 0 (tail) if the value of Rand( ) is between 0 and 0.5.*

32. Flip four coins to simulate the birth of four children in a family. Use 100 repetitions to determine the experimental probability there that are two boys and two girls.

33. Consider the experiment of flipping 10 coins $n$ times. Draw line graphs showing the number of heads that appear for the given values of $n$.

   [*Suggestion*: Copy the formula "= If (Rand( ) > 0.5, 1, 0)" into columns A1:J1 and the formula "= Sum(A1:J1)" into cell K1, so that the value of cell K1 is the number of heads in the 10 simulated flips shown in cells A1:J1. Select A1:K1, copy

into rows 1 through 10 for part (a), and use the histogram function found under the Data/Data Analysis tab.]

   (a) $n = 10$     (b) $n = 50$     (c) $n = 100$

   (d) If 100 coins were flipped one million times, sketch the general shape you would anticipate that the histogram would take. (Don't attempt to simulate this experiment, since the computation time would be too large.)

## From State Student Assessments

34. (Texas, Grade 5)
   Susan, Dorothy, and Allison play on the same softball team. They keep a record of how many times each girl goes to bat and how many hits she gets. The chart shows how each girl did last week.

| Softball Hits Record | | |
|---|---|---|
| **Name** | **Number of Times at Bat** | **Number of Hits** |
| Dorothy | 8 | 2 |
| Susan | 10 | 4 |
| Allison | 14 | 9 |

   What is the probability that Susan will get a hit the next time she goes to bat?

   **A.** $\dfrac{1}{8}$     **B.** $\dfrac{4}{11}$     **C.** $\dfrac{2}{5}$     **D.** $\dfrac{2}{3}$

35. (Illinois, Grade 5)
   A table shows the result of 100 spins. The spinner has six equal sections. Which drawing probably shows the way the spinner was drawn?

| Color | Number of Times This Color Was Spun |
|---|---|
| Orange | 32 |
| White | 16 |
| Gray | 34 |
| Tan | 18 |

## 14.2

# Principles of Counting

Experimental probability, as its name reminds us, is an event's estimated probability determined from historical data or repeated trials. For example, an automobile insurance company compiles extensive records of traffic accidents to help set its price schedule properly. Since teens have a higher probability of an accident than adult drivers, higher premiums are assessed to teenage drivers. Notice that the probability of an auto accident cannot be determined theoretically, but only on the basis of statistical data.

By contrast, there is no need to rely on data when we roll a die *if we assume that the die is fair.* Each of the six outcomes in the sample space $S = \{1, 2, 3, 4, 5, 6\}$ is assumed to be equally likely, so the theoretical probability of each outcome is $\frac{1}{6}$. If we want to know the probability of rolling a prime number, we see that there are three primes in the sample space and conclude that the probability of rolling a prime number is $\frac{3}{6}$, or 0.5. That is, $P(E) = 0.5$ for the event $E = \{2, 3, 5\}$. This simple example suggests how to determine the probability of an event $E \subseteq S$ in any sample space $S$ of equally likely outcomes: First, count the total number $n(S)$ of all possible outcomes and the number $n(E)$ of outcomes of the event. Then, $P(E) = \dfrac{n(E)}{n(S)}$ is the theoretical probability of the event $E$.

Therefore, the calculation of theoretical probability is a matter of counting.

In this section, we investigate the general principles of counting. These principles are applied in Section 14.3 to count the number of ways selections can be made from a set of distinct objects. If the order of the selection matters, we obtain a permutation; if the order in which objects are selected does not matter, then we have a combination. Both sections on counting are of interest in their own right, but our main goal is to apply counting techniques to the calculation of theoretical probabilities, as taken up in Section 14.4.

## Counting and the Word *Or*

Consider the question "How many diamonds or face cards are in an ordinary deck of playing cards?" Of course, we can simply count the 13 diamonds and then proceed to count the other 9 face cards (kings, queens, and jacks) that are not diamonds. Thus, the answer, 22, is easily found. But there is another way to determine this sum. It seems more involved but reveals an important pattern that greatly facilitates solving more complex problems. Let $D$ denote the set of diamonds in the deck of cards, and let $F$ denote the set of face cards. The two sets are shown in a Venn diagram in Figure 14.3; we see that there are $n(D) = 13$ diamonds, $n(F) = 12$ face cards, and $n(D \cap F) = 3$ cards that are both diamonds and face cards. The 22 cards that are diamonds or face cards are not given by $n(D) + n(F) = 13 + 12 = 25$, since the 3 cards in the intersection of the sets will be counted twice. To compensate, the number of cards in the intersection can be subtracted, so $n(D) + n(F) - n(D \cap F) = 13 + 12 - 3 = 22$ gives the correct count, $n(D \cup F) = 22$. Thus, we have the formula $n(D$ or $F) = n(D) + n(F) - n(D \cap F)$, where the word *or* is used to indicate the union of the sets.

**FIGURE 14.3**
$n(D \cup F) = n(D) + n(F) - n(D \cap F)$

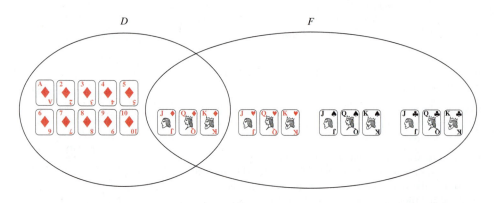

*Sidebar:* 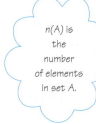 $n(A)$ is the number of elements in set A.

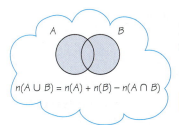

$n(A \cup B) = n(A) + n(B) - n(A \cap B)$

The same argument applies more generally to any two sets $A$ and $B$ and proves the next theorem. In the terminology introduced in the preceding section, the formula allows us to count events that may not be mutually exclusive.

**THEOREM**    *The Addition Principle of Counting*

If $A$ and $B$ are events, then $n(A \text{ or } B) = n(A) + n(B) - n(A \cap B)$.

## EXAMPLE 14.10  Counting and the Word *Or*

In how many ways can you select a red card or an ace from an ordinary deck of playing cards?

**Solution 1**

There are 26 red cards in a deck (including two red aces) as well as two black aces. Thus, the desired answer is 28.

**Solution 2**

Let $R$ denote the set of red cards and let $A$ denote the set of aces. Then $n(R) = 26$, $n(A) = 4$, $n(R \cap A) = 2$, and

$$
\begin{aligned}
n(R \text{ or } A) &= n(R) + n(A) - n(R \cap A) \\
&= 26 + 4 - 2 \\
&= 28,
\end{aligned}
$$

as before.

A very important special case of the addition principle of counting is illustrated by Example 14.11, which follows, recall from Section 14.1 that two events $A$ and $B$ are **mutually exclusive** if no outcome belongs (or "is favorable") to both $A$ and $B$. That is, $A \cap B = \varnothing$.

## EXAMPLE 14.11  Counting and *Or* When Events Are Mutually Exclusive

Determine the number of ways of obtaining a score of 7 or 11 on a single roll of two dice.

**Solution 1**

One way to solve this problem is simply to list all possible outcomes obtained upon rolling two dice and then to count those which are favorable. Thinking of rolling a red die and a green die makes it clear that there are 36 possible outcomes, as shown in the accompanying array, and that 8 (see circled pairs) are favorable—6 outcomes yield a score of 7 and 2 yield a score of 11. Thus,

$$n(7 \text{ or } 11) = 8 = 6 + 2 = n(7) + n(11).$$

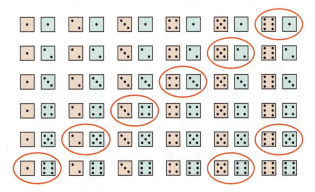

**Solution 2**

Let $F$ be the set of favorable outcomes obtained upon rolling the dice, let $D$ be the set of outcomes yielding 7, and let $E$ be the set of outcomes yielding 11.

Since $F = D \cup E$, we may use the addition principle of counting to obtain

$$n(F) = n(D \cup E)$$
$$= n(D \text{ or } E)$$
$$= n(D) + n(E) - n(D \cap E).$$

But $n(D \cap E) = 0$, since $D \cap E = \varnothing$ and $n(\varnothing) = 0$. Thus,

$$n(F) = n(D) + n(E) = 6 + 2 = 8,$$

as before.

The preceding solution illustrates that

$$n(D \text{ or } F) = n(D \cup F) = n(D) + n(F)$$

when $D$ and $F$ are mutually exclusive events—that is, when $D \cap F = \varnothing$ and therefore $n(D \cap F) = 0$. This result is general and can be formalized as follows:

> **THEOREM** **_The Addition Principle of Counting for Mutually Exclusive Events_**
> If $A$ and $B$ are mutually exclusive events, then $n(A \text{ or } B) = n(A) + n(B)$.

**EXAMPLE 14.12 Choosing a Chocolate**

A box of 40 chocolates contains 14 cremes, 16 caramels, and 10 chocolate-covered nuts. In how many ways can you select a creme or a caramel from the box?

**Solution** Let $C$ denote the set of cremes and let $C^*$ denote the set of caramels. Then $C \cap C^* = \varnothing$, so, by the addition principle for the mutually exclusive events $C$ and $C^*$,

$$n(C \text{ or } C^*) = 14 + 16 = 30.$$

Thus, the number of ways of choosing a creme or a caramel is 30.

**EXAMPLE 14.13 Determining How Many Are on an Airplane**

On an airplane from Frankfurt to Paris, all the people speak French or German. If 71 speak French, 85 speak German, and 29 speak both French and German, how many people are on the plane?

**Solution 1** Let $F$ denote the set of French speakers on the plane and let $G$ denote the set of German speakers. Of course, a person who speaks both French and German belongs to *both* sets $F$ and $G$. Since all people on the plane speak French or German, it follows that the number of persons on the plane is $n(F \cup G)$. But, by the addition principle of counting,

$$n(F \cup G) = n(F) + n(G) - n(F \cap G)$$
$$= 71 + 85 - 29 = 127.$$

$n(F \cup G) = n(F \text{ or } G)$

Thus, 127 people are on the plane.

**Solution 2** Let $F$ and $G$ be as before, and consider the Venn diagram shown. Starting with the innermost region of the diagram, one fills in the appropriate numbers. Since 29 people fall into the set $F \cap G$, the common region of the two circles, and 71 are in the $F$ circle, then $71 - 29 = 42$ people must fall inside the $F$ circle but outside the common region, as shown. Similarly, $85 - 29 = 56$ people must fall inside the $G$ circle but outside the common region. Thus, finally,

$$n(F \cup G) = 42 + 29 + 56 = 127,$$

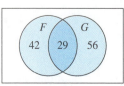

as before.

**FIGURE 14.4**
A marble bag holds three red marbles and one green marble

## Counting and the Word *And*

A bag of marbles contains three red marbles and one green marble, as shown in Figure 14.4. Consider the following **two-stage experiment:**

**Stage 1.** Draw a marble from the bag and place it in your left hand.
**Stage 2.** Keeping the first marble in your left hand, draw a second marble from the three remaining in the bag, and place it in your right hand.

If we denote the three red marbles as $r_1$, $r_2$, and $r_3$, respectively, and the green marble as $g$, one possible outcome of the two-stage experiment is $r_1 r_3$, meaning that the red marble $r_1$ is placed in the left hand and the red marble $r_3$ is placed in the right hand. Of course, several other outcomes are also possible, so we ask the following question: In how many ways can this two-stage experiment be analyzed?

One strategy is to **make an orderly list:**

| | | | | | |
|---|---|---|---|---|---|
| $r_1 r_2$ | $r_1 r_3$ | $r_2 r_3$ | $r_2 r_1$ | $r_3 r_1$ | $r_3 r_2$ |
| $r_1 g$ | $r_2 g$ | $r_3 g$ | $g r_1$ | $g r_2$ | $g r_3$ |

The list shows that there are 12 outcomes. Note that outcome $r_1 r_2$ is not the same as outcome $r_2 r_1$; that is, order makes a difference.

A second strategy is to make a **possibility tree,** as shown in Figure 14.5. (Curiously, trees are most often drawn sideways or upside down.) Following each "limb" from its "root" to its "leaf" corresponds to one of the 12 possible outcomes of the two-stage experiment.

**FIGURE 14.5**
A possibility tree for drawing two marbles without replacement

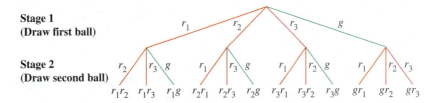

Let's next ask a somewhat different question: In how many ways will both the left hand *and* the right hand hold a red marble? In symbols, if $A$ denotes the set of first-stage outcomes in which a red marble is put into the left hand and $B$ denotes the set of second-stage outcomes in which a red marble is put into the right hand, then we want to count $n(A$ and $B)$. From the list of possibilities, we see that the first row of outcomes corresponds to a red marble in each hand, so $n(A$ and $B) = 6$. There is, however, a second way to obtain the answer by carefully examining the possibility tree in Figure 14.5. First, there are three ways to perform Stage 1 in which a red marble is placed in the left hand. That is, $n(A) = 3$. Next, *given* that one of the red marbles has been placed in your left hand, there are two ways to put a second red marble in your right hand. This number is symbolized by $n(B \mid A) = 2$ and is read as "the number of ways $B$ can occur given that $A$ has already occurred is 2." Observing that $n(A$ and $B) = 6 = 3 \cdot 2 = n(A)n(B \mid A)$, we have illustrated the following general counting principle:

---

**THEOREM**   *The Multiplication Principle of Counting*
Let $A$ be a set of outcomes of Stage 1 and $B$ a set of outcomes of Stage 2. Then the number of ways, $n(A$ and $B)$, that $A$ and $B$ can occur in a two-stage experiment is given by

$$n(A \text{ and } B) = n(A)n(B \mid A),$$

where $n(B \mid A)$ denotes the number of ways that $B$ can occur given that $A$ has already occurred.

---

In a useful modification of the possibility tree shown in Figure 14.5, the number of ways an event can occur is used to label edges, replacing the need for a separate edge for each outcome of the event. For example, since there are 3 ways a red ball can be drawn in Stage 1, the corresponding edge of the tree leading to event $A$ in which a red ball is drawn is labeled with $3 = n(A)$, as shown in Figure 14.6. The other edge corresponds to the event $\overline{A}$, the 1 way in which a red ball is not drawn. At Stage 2, the counts are conditioned according to the outcome of Stage 1, so, for example, the red edge at the left in Figure 14.6 is given the label $2 = n(B \mid A)$, since there are 2 ways to select a red ball on the second draw given that a red ball was already withdrawn at Stage 1. This type of possibility is simpler to create, especially when there are a large number of outcomes of a multistage experiment.

**FIGURE 14.6**
The multiplicative possibility tree for drawing two marbles without replacement from a bag containing three red and one green marble. Event $A$ occurs if the first marble drawn is red, and event $B$ occurs if the second marble drawn is also red. $\overline{A}$ denotes the complementary event in which the first marble drawn is not red, and $\overline{B}$ denotes the event in which the second marble drawn is not red

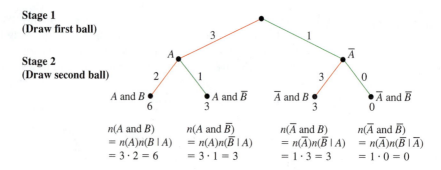

It is important to notice that $n(B) = 9$. (See Figures 14.5 and 14.6.) That is, of the 12 outcomes of the two-stage experiment, there are 9 cases where the right-hand marble is red. In 3 of these cases, the left-hand marble drawn first was green. Since $n(B) \neq n(B \mid A)$, we see that $A$ and $B$ are dependent events.

In other two-stage experiments, the number of outcomes of the event $B$ does not depend on whether or not event $A$ has occurred. That is, $A$ and $B$ are **independent events** by the definition given in Section 14.1. In symbols, $n(B) = n(B \mid A)$ for independent events. This formula gives us a special case of the multiplication principle:

> **THEOREM**   *The Multiplication Principle of Counting for Independent Events*
>
> Let $A$ be a set of outcomes of Stage 1 and $B$ a set of outcomes of Stage 2. If $A$ and $B$ are independent events, then the number of ways, $n(A \text{ and } B)$, that $A$ and $B$ can occur in a two-stage experiment is given by
>
> $$n(A \text{ and } B) = n(A)n(B).$$

The next two examples give practice in using the multiplication principle of counting.

## EXAMPLE 14.14   Counting the Number of Ways to Draw Two Aces

How many ways can two aces be drawn in succession from an ordinary deck of 52 cards if

**(a)** the first card drawn is replaced in the deck, the cards are reshuffled, and then the second card is drawn?

**(b)** the first card is drawn, but not replaced in the deck, and then the second card is drawn?

**Solution**

### Understand the Problem

In both parts of the problem, we are asked in how many ways we can draw two aces from an ordinary deck of 52 playing cards. There is a difference, however: In part (a), after the first card is drawn, it is replaced and the deck is reshuffled before the second card is drawn; in part (b), the first card is *not* replaced before the second card is drawn.

### Devise a Strategy

Let $A$ be the event of choosing an ace on the first draw, and let $B$ be the event of choosing an ace on the second draw. Because of the replacement and reshuffling in part (a), it is clear that the choice of the first card cannot affect the choice of the second card. Thus, the two events are clearly independent. However, this is not the case in part (b). If, for example, the ace of clubs is chosen on the first draw, there remain only three possible favorable choices for the second draw, instead of four. Thus, in part (b), $A$ and $B$ are *dependent* events. For part (a), we can use the formula $n(A \text{ and } B) = n(A) \cdot n(B)$, but for part (b), we must use the formula $n(A \text{ and } B) = n(A) \cdot n(B \mid A)$.

### Carry Out the Plan

For part (a), $n(A \text{ and } B) = n(A) \cdot n(B) = 4 \cdot 4 = 16$, since there are four ways to choose an ace on each draw. For part (b), however, $n(A \text{ and } B) = n(A) \cdot n(B \mid A) = 4 \cdot 3 = 12$, since, if an ace is chosen on the first draw, there remain only three favorable choices for the second draw.

### Look Back

We can also find our answers with possibility trees, shown as follows:

**(a)** With replacement of first card drawn

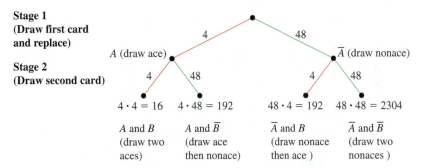

**(b)** Without replacement of first card drawn

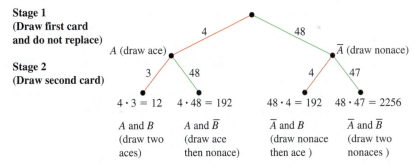

The tree diagrams contain extra information. For example, we see that, either with or without replacement of the first card, there are $2 \cdot 192 = 384$ ways to draw the two cards so that exactly one of the cards is an ace.

## EXAMPLE 14.15  Determining the Number of Slates of Officers

The Math Club has four women members and two men. In how many ways can the president, secretary, and treasurer be chosen, where not all of the officers are women?

**Solution**    **Understand the Problem**

We could attempt to list all of the slates of officers that meet the condition that not all three officers are women, but this is likely to be a large list and it would be difficult to know whether we have overlooked a possible slate or perhaps have listed the same one more than once. We need to find a better method of counting, one that could just as easily solve the problem for *any* number of men and women in the club.

**Devise a Plan**

Suppose we envisage a three-stage process in which the president, then the secretary, and finally the treasurer is selected. The associated events are knowing whether a man or a woman is chosen for the post. Accordingly, let *WP, MP, WS, MS, WT,* and *MT* denote the event that a woman president, man president, woman secretary, and so on, has been selected. We can then construct the possibility tree for the three-stage selection process.

**Carry Out the Plan**

The tree is easily created as follows, where we need to account for how earlier choices affect the number of ways that subsequent choices can be made:

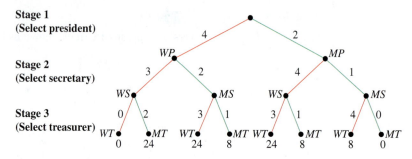

Altogether, we see that there are $0 + 24 + 24 + 8 + 24 + 8 + 8 + 0 = 96$ different slates of officers. Of course, the possibility tree reveals even more detailed information. For example, the three 8s in the sum represent the 24 ways that both men are appointed to offices.

**Look Back**

It's often instructive to look for alternative solutions. Alternatives provide a check of other solutions and enlarge our repertoire of problem-solving techniques. For this problem, first consider the event *M* in which exactly one of the offices is held by a man. We can choose which of the men holds some office in 2 ways, choose which office he fills in 3 ways, choose the woman that holds one of the unfilled offices in 4 ways, and finally choose the second woman that holds office in 3 ways. We see, then, that there are $n(M) = 2 \cdot 3 \cdot 4 \cdot 3 = 72$ slates of officers filled by one man and two women. Next, consider the event *N* in which both men hold office. There are 3 choices of office for the first man and 2 choices of office for the other man, with 4 choices among the women to fill the remaining office. This means that there are $n(N) = 3 \cdot 2 \cdot 4 = 24$ ways to fill the slate of officers with both men and one woman, in agreement with our observation made on the basis of the possibility tree. Since *M* and *N* are mutually exclusive events, we again find there are $n(M \text{ or } N) = n(N) + n(M) = 72 + 24 = 96$ slates of officers.

The previous examples illustrate an important "habit of the mind" when counting: Devise a sequence of stages that yield all possible outcomes. If you count the number of ways to perform each stage, then the total number of outcomes is obtained by multiplying together all the ways to perform each stage. It is also helpful to divide the work into mutually exclusive events. If each event can be counted, their sum is the desired answer.

## Complementary Events and Counting

Often there are many ways for an event *E* to occur, making it difficult to determine $n(E)$. However, it may be quite simple to count the number of ways that *E* does *not* occur. This is the **complementary event,** denoted by $\overline{E}$. Since $S = E \cup \overline{E}$, and since *E* and $\overline{E}$ are mutually exclusive, we see that $n(S) = n(E \cup \overline{E}) = n(E) + n(\overline{E})$. Thus, we have the following result:

**THEOREM**  *Counting with Complements*

Let $\overline{E}$ denote the complement of event $E \subseteq S$. Then $n(E) = n(S) - n(\overline{E})$.

The next example shows that counting the complementary event is especially effective for counting where an "at least" condition must be satisfied.

**EXAMPLE 14.16** **Using Complements to Solve an "At Least" Problem**

A fair coin is tossed 10 times. In how many ways will at least two heads appear?

**Solution**    Since the tosses are independent events and each toss can happen in two ways, there are $2 \times 2 \times \cdots \times 2 = 2^{10} = 1024$ ways in which the tosses occur. There are many ways in which two or more heads occur. However, the complementary event is when either no head or only one head occurs. There is just one way to get no head, namely, if all 10 tosses are tails. There are 10 ways to get one head and 9 tails, so altogether there are 11 ways in which at most one head occurs. Thus, there are $1024 - 11 = 1013$ ways in which at least two heads appear in the 10 tosses.

## Problem Set 14.2

Exercises numbered in red are answered in the back of the text.

### Understanding Concepts

1. Two dice are thrown. Determine the number of ways a score of 4 or 6 can be obtained. For example, $4 = 3 + 1 = 1 + 3 = 2 + 2$, and so on.

2. Two dice are thrown. Determine the number of ways to obtain a score of at least 4. (*Hint:* In how many ways can you fail to obtain a score of at least 4? How many outcomes are possible, all told?)

3. A coin is tossed and a die is rolled.

   (a) In how many ways can the outcome consist of a head and an even number?

   (b) In how many ways can the outcome consist of a head or an even number?

4. There are 26 students in Mrs. Pietz's fifth-grade class at the International School of Tokyo. All of the students speak either English or Japanese, and some speak both languages. If 18 of the students can speak English and 14 can speak Japanese,

   (a) how many speak both English and Japanese?

   (b) how many speak English, but not Japanese? (*Hint:* Draw a Venn diagram.)

5. All of the 24 students in Mr. Walcott's fourth-grade class at the International School of Tokyo speak either English or Japanese. If 11 of the students speak only English and 9 of the students speak only Japanese, how many speak both languages?

6. In how many ways can you draw a club or a face card from an ordinary deck of playing cards?

7. In how many ways can you select a red face card or a black ace from an ordinary deck of playing cards?

8. (a) How many four-digit natural numbers can be named with each of the digits 1, 2, 3, 4, 5, and 6 used at most once?

   (b) How many of the numbers in part (a) begin with an odd digit? (*Hint:* Choose the first digit first.)

   (c) How many of the numbers in part (b) end with an odd digit? (*Hint:* Choose the first digit first and the last digit second.)

9. (a) If repetition of digits is not allowed, how many three-digit numbers can be formed from the digits 1, 2, 3, 4, and 5?

   (b) How many of the numbers in part (a) begin with either the digit 2 or the digit 3?

   (c) How many of the numbers in part (a) are even?

10. Construct a possibility tree to determine all three-letter code words using only the letters $a$, $b$, and $c$ without repetition. For example, $bac$ and $cba$ are two of the code words.

11. Construct a possibility tree to determine in how many ways one can obtain two heads and two tails when four coins are tossed.

12. A bag contains three red marbles, $r_1$, $r_2$, and $r_3$, and two green marbles, $g_1$ and $g_2$. Two marbles are drawn in succession without replacing the marble drawn first.

    (a) Construct a detailed possibility tree (as in Figure 14.5) for this two-stage experiment.

    (b) Let $A$ be the first-stage event that the marble drawn first is green, and let $B$ be the second-stage event that the marble drawn second is red. List the outcomes of the two-stage experiment that are in the compound event $A$ and $B$.

    (c) Verify that $n(A \text{ and } B) = n(A)n(B \mid A)$.

13. How many 4-letter "words" can be formed from a standard 26-letter alphabet

    (a) if repetition is allowed?    (b) if repetition is not allowed?

14. How many five-digit numbers can be formed with the first three digits odd and the last two digits even

    (a) if repetition of digits is allowed?

    (b) if repetition of digits is not allowed?

15. (a) If a pair of dice is rolled, in how many ways are the two numbers different?

    (b) If three dice are rolled, in how many ways are at least two of the dice the same?

16. (a) Draw the possibility tree for a three-game series between teams A and B where the series ends when a team has two wins.

**(b)** Draw the possibility tree for a five-game series between teams A and B where the series ends when a team has three wins.

**(c)** In how many five-game series does the winning team lose the first two games?

**(d)** In how many five-game series does the winning team lose the first game?

**17.** The Chess Club has 5 freshmen, 2 juniors, and 3 seniors.

**(a)** Make a possibility tree (see Example 14.15) to determine how many slates of officers can fill the two offices of president and treasurer, where the two officers cannot be from the same class?

**(b)** Answer the problem of part (a) a new way, by considering the three cases where the two offices are filled by a freshman and a junior, a freshman and a senior, and a junior and a senior.

**18.** Use possibility trees to determine how many ways two face cards can be drawn, where the first card drawn

**(a)** is replaced in the deck of 52 cards or

**(b)** is not replaced.

## Teaching Concepts

**19.** Children often want to relate classroom concepts to their own lives. For each of the following situations from everyday life, create a minilesson and accompanying problems to illustrate the multiplication principle of counting:

**(a)** How many ways can you order an ice cream cone? You will need to describe the number of choices of type of cone, flavor, number of scoops, toppings, and so on.

**(b)** How many ways can you drive from town A to town C, always passing through town B? Note how many roads connect the towns.

**(c)** How many ways can you and your friends line up at the drinking fountain?

**(d)** Choose a situation from your own life. Be creative!

## Responding to Students

**20.** Alejandro knows that, of the first thousand positive integers, 250 are divisible by 4 and 200 are divisible by 5. He then asserts that 450 are divisible by either 4 or 5. Help Alejandro see where his analysis went astray.

**21.** Tamara has mix-and-match outfits that include four skirts and six blouses. She claims that she has ten different outfits. How can you help Tamara understand the error in her reasoning?

## Thinking Critically

**22.** Two dice are thrown.

**(a)** In how many ways can the score obtained be even?

**(b)** In how many ways can the score be a multiple of 5?

**(c)** In how many ways can the score be a multiple of 3? (*Hint:* All possibilities when two dice are rolled are shown in Example 14.11.)

**23.** How many ways can 2 successive cards be drawn from a standard 52-card deck (without replacement) such that

**(a)** the first card is a king and the second card is not a face card?

**(b)** the first card is a king and the second card is a heart? (Watch out for the king of hearts!)

**24.** A straight is a sequence of 5 cards, in order, from a 52-card deck, but with no regard to the suit of the cards. The ace can be the lowest card in a "five-high straight," or it can be the highest card in a ten–jack–queen–king–ace "ace-high" straight.

**(a)** How many straights exist in a deck?

**(b)** If all 5 cards in a straight are from the same suit, it is a straight flush. How many straight flushes are there?

**25.** Marc's collection of sports cards includes ten baseball, seven basketball, and nine football cards. He wants to give away two cards from different sports to his friend for a birthday present. How many ways can he choose the two cards?

**26.** A multiple-choice quiz has ten questions, with four choices per question.

**(a)** How many ways can the quiz be answered?

**(b)** How many of these ways give an A grade of 90 percent or higher?

**27.** Art, Bev, Carly, and Dave are at a party.

**(a)** In how many ways can the months in which they celebrate their birthday occur?

**(b)** In how many ways can their birthdays all be in different months?

**(c)** In how many ways will at least two of them have a birthday in the same month?

**28.** Lucy stuffed invitations into three preaddressed envelopes, forgetting that each invitation was individualized with the recipient's name.

**(a)** In how many ways can the invitations be placed in the envelopes?

**(b)** In how many ways will no one receive the correct invitation?

**29. (a)** How many five-digit numbers are there? (The first digit cannot be 0.)

**(b)** How many five-digit numbers are even?

**(c)** How many five-digit numbers have exactly one 0?

**(d)** How many five-digit numbers have exactly one 7?

**30.** How many of the first 10,000 positive integers contain exactly one digit 3 and one digit 5?

**31. (a)** How many ways can a red checker and a black checker be placed on an $8 \times 8$ checkerboard?

**(b)** How many ways can two identical black checkers be placed on an $8 \times 8$ board?

**(c)** How many ways can a red checker and a black checker be placed on an $8 \times 8$ board so that both are in the same row or the same column?

## Thinking Cooperatively

**32.** Working first in pairs, play the following two-person game with three $3 \times 5$ note cards: On one card, write an X on both sides of the card; on another, write O on both sides; and on the third card, write an X on one side and an O on the other side. Player A shuffles the deck, perhaps turning it over as well, and places the deck on the table. Player B can choose "same" or "different" and wins if the hidden side of the top card of the deck has the same or a different symbol, respectively, from one that is visible.

**(a)** Trading roles between players A and B, play a number of games, keeping a record of whether "same" or "different" won the game.

**(b)** After completing part (a), work in foursomes to analyze the game.

**(c)** Is the game a toss-up, or is there a strategy to help you win? In particular, discuss the validity of this reasoning: If I see an X, the top card is either the XX or the XO card. Therefore, the opposite side is the same or different equally often and there is no preferred strategy to guess either "same" or "different."

## Making Connections

**33.** An electrician must connect a red, a white, and a black wire to a yellow, a blue, and a green wire in some order. How many different connections are possible?

**34.** In the state of Washington, each automobile license plate shows three letters followed by three digits, or three digits followed by three letters. How many different license plates can be made

  **(a)** if repetition of digits and letters is allowed?

  **(b)** if repetition of digits and letters is not allowed?

**35.** A four-bit code word is any sequence of four digits, where each digit is either a 0 or a 1. For example, 0100 and 1011 are four-bit code words.

  **(a)** How many different four-bit code words are there?

  **(b)** How many different six-bit code words, such as 001011, are there?

  **(c)** If a vocabulary of 1000 code words is required, how long must the words be?

## ▦ Using a Calculator

**36.** The illegal chain letter scam works this way: You receive a letter with a list of (say) 5 names and addresses. You are instructed to send something—say, a dollar—to the person at the top of the list, then remove that name and add your own to the bottom of the list, and send the letter to 10 people not on the list. Your name will be at the bottom of 10 letters but then rises to fourth position on 100 letters, and so on. Eventually, your name is at the top of 100,000 letters, and for a $1 investment plus small postage and copying costs, you receive $100,000.

  **(a)** Suppose everyone obeys the instructions, sending their 10 letters within a week. In one week, 10 people have been sent letters, and in two weeks $10 + 100$ people have been sent letters. How many people have been sent letters in eight weeks?

  **(b)** Assuming that no one gets a second letter, in how many weeks will all 7 billion people on earth have a letter?

**37. (a)** Could every person in the United States be given a distinct 6-letter identification code using a 26-letter alphabet? A person's code might be YWAWHK.

  **(b)** Would a 5-letter code work if both upper- and lowercase letters were used?

  **(c)** If 7 billion people are to be given identification codes using only strings of capital letters, what is the smallest length of the string required?

## From State Student Assessments

**38.** (Texas, Grade 5)
Ricky is trying to decide which outfit to wear to a party. His choices are shown in the diagram.

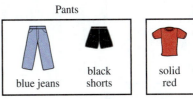

Pants       Shirts
blue jeans   black shorts    solid red   striped yellow   plaid green

Shoes
tennis shoes   sandals

How many possible different outfits can Ricky create if he chooses one pair of pants, one shirt, and one pair of shoes?

**F.** 7    **G.** 8    **H.** 10    **I.** 12

**39.** (Kentucky, Grade 5)
David put these cards into a box.

| 4 | 8 | 7 | 4 | 3 | 2 | 8 |

If he draws one card out of the box without looking, the number on the card will MOST LIKELY be

**A.** an even number.     **B.** an odd number.

**C.** a number greater than 4.     **D.** a number less than 4.

**40.** (Oregon, Grade 7)
Bicycles come in 3 colors: black, red, and blue. They can have 2 different types of seats, and 2 different types of tires. How many different bicycles can be made?

**A.** 1 bicycle   **B.** 7 bicycles   **C.** 10 bicycles   **D.** 12 bicycles

## Examining School Book Pages

*Refer to the School Book Pages provided on page 790 to answer the following questions.*

**41.** The "tree diagram" shown at the top of p. 470 is not in fact a tree. (The mathematical definition is given in problem 13 in Problem Set 9.4.) Indeed, it is a diagram with *two trees* that is called, quite naturally, a forest.

  **(a)** Redraw the figure to create a possibility tree that is truly a tree and not a forest. (See Figure 14.5 of this section.)

  **(b)** Why is the answer given in "Another Way" at the top of the page made clearer with the tree diagram you drew in part (a)?

**42.** Students may be expected to answer Problem 12 in various ways. Discuss why each of these answers might be proposed:

  **(a)** $2 \times 2 \times 1 = 4$        **(b)** $6 \times 2 \times 2 \times 1 = 24$

  **(c)** $5 \times 5 \times 5 = 125$      **(d)** $5 \times 4 \times 3 = 60$

**43.** Students may respond to Problem 13 in various ways. Discuss why a student might provide a list with the given number of outcomes.

  **(a)** $3 \times 2 = 6$          **(b)** $3 \times 3 = 9$

  **(c)** $12 \times 11 = 132$     **(d)** $12 \times 12 = 144$

*See "Examining School Book Pages" on page 789 for questions related to the pages shown below.*

## Lesson 20-2

**Understand It!**
Make a tree diagram or multiply to find the number of possible outcomes.

## Outcomes and Tree Diagrams

### What are the possible results?

Each possible result is an **outcome**. How many outcomes are possible when you spin Spinner 1 and Spinner 2?

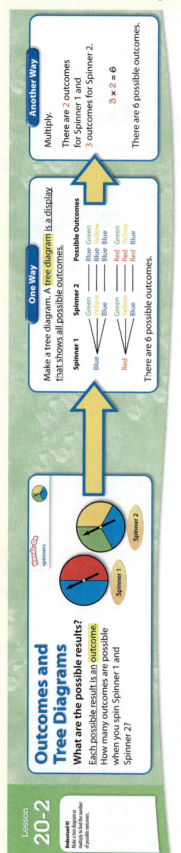

Hands-On spinners

Spinner 1

Spinner 2

### One Way

Make a tree diagram. A **tree diagram** is a display that shows all possible outcomes.

| Spinner 1 | Spinner 2 | Possible Outcomes |
|---|---|---|
| Blue | Green | Blue Green |
| | Yellow | Blue Yellow |
| | Blue | Blue Blue |
| Red | Green | Red Green |
| | Yellow | Red Yellow |
| | Blue | Red Blue |

There are 6 possible outcomes.

### Another Way

Multiply.

There are 2 outcomes for Spinner 1 and 3 outcomes for Spinner 2.

$$3 \times 2 = 6$$

There are 6 possible outcomes.

## Guided Practice*

### Do you know HOW?

For **1** and **2**, use the diagrams below.

Bag 1 Bag 2

1. List all the possible outcomes for picking one card from Bag 2.

2. Make a tree diagram to show all the possible outcomes for picking one card from Bag 1 followed by one card from Bag 2.

### Do you UNDERSTAND?

3. What number sentence can you use to find the number of possible outcomes in Exercise 2?

4. **Writing to Explain** In the example at the top, why is Blue Blue an outcome but Red Red is not?

5. A board game uses Spinner 1 shown above. On each turn, Spinner 1 is spun twice. How many outcomes are possible for each turn?

## Independent Practice

For **6** through **8**, make a tree diagram to list all the possible outcomes for each situation.

**TIP** When you make a tree diagram, you can list the outcomes in any order you like.

6. Spin Spinner 3 once and toss the number cube once.

7. Pick one card from Bag 3 and toss the number cube once.

8. Pick one card from Bag 3 and spin Spinner 3 once.

Bag 3

X Y Z

Number Cube

Spinner 3

DIGITAL
Animated Glossary, eTools
www.pearsonsuccessnet.com

For **9** and **10**, multiply to find the number of possible outcomes.

9. Flip a coin and toss a number cube that is numbered 1 through 6.

10. Pick one card from each of two piles. One pile has the cards labeled F, I, T, P, N, C, and O. The other has the cards labeled A, R, S, and Q.

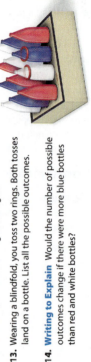

Dodecahedron: 12 sides

Octahedron: 8 sides

## Problem Solving

For **11**, use the number cubes at the right.

11. How many outcomes are there for one toss of the octahedron and one toss of the dodecahedron?

12. Candy Cummings is credited with pitching the first curveball in a baseball game in 1867. Some pitchers know how to throw 2 types of curveballs, 2 types of fastballs, and 1 knuckleball. If a pitcher strikes out a batter on three pitches, how many different combinations of pitches can be thrown?

For **13** and **14**, use the drawing at the right.

13. Wearing a blindfold, you toss two rings. Both tosses land on a bottle. List all the possible outcomes.

14. **Writing to Explain** Would the number of possible outcomes change if there were more blue bottles than red and white bottles?

## 14.3 Permutations and Combinations

Two types of counting situations are encountered so often that they deserve special attention: permutations and combinations. A **permutation** is an *arrangement* of a given number of objects from a specified set into an *ordered list*. A **combination** is a *selection* of a given number of objects from a set to form an *unordered subset* of the objects.

Thus, if we wish to count how many choices can be made, it is very important to ask these questions so that permutations and combinations are not confused:

MHM
• *Are the selected objects arranged into an order?*

If so, then we are considering a permutation.

• *Do we need to know only which objects are selected, with the order of the objects making no difference?*

In this situation, we are considering a combination.

Here is a short example to help distinguish the two concepts: Suppose that we have four different textbooks—an algebra book, a biology book, a chemistry book, and a drama book. If we wish to arrange two of the books on a shelf, then order does matter, since there is a book on the left and a different book on the right. That is, each arrangement is a permutation. In fact, in accordance with the multiplication principle, there are four choices for the left-hand book and three choices for the right-hand book. Altogether, there are $3 \times 4 = 12$ permutations of the two objects chosen from the set of four objects. This equation will be written as $P(4, 2) = 4 \times 3 = 12$.

Now suppose that, instead of arranging two books on a shelf, we want to put any two of the four books on the top of our desk. This time it only matters which two books are selected, since the two books are not arranged into a sequence. Each unordered selection of two of the books is therefore a combination. To count the number of combinations, we observe that each combination of two books can be placed on a bookshelf in two ways, depending on which book is placed to the left. Therefore, there are twice as many permutations as there are combinations, and we conclude that there are $12 \div 2 = 6$ combinations. This equation will be written as $C(4, 2) = 6$, where $C(4, 2)$ denotes the number of combinations of two objects selected from four different objects.

The general definition should now be meaningful.

---

**DEFINITION** *Permutations and Combinations*

Let $U$ be a set of distinct objects.
• An *ordered* sequence of the objects in $U$ is called a **permutation** of the objects of $U$. If $r$ objects are in the permutation, the sequence is called an ***r-permutation.***
• An *unordered* selection, or subset, of $U$ is called a **combination** of the objects of $U$. If $r$ objects are in the combination, the selection is called an ***r-combination.***

---

**EXAMPLE 14.17** **Choosing a Social Committee and Officers for the Math Club**

There are five members of the Math Club.

**(a)** In how many ways can the slate of two officers—a president and a treasurer—be chosen?
**(b)** In how many ways can the two-person Social Committee be chosen?

**Solution**  For convenience, suppose the five members of the Math Club form the set $U = \{a, b, c, d, e\}$.

**(a)** Choosing the officers is the same as choosing a sequence of two members of $U$, first the president and then the treasurer. That is, we wish to know the number of permutations of five objects taken two at a time. By the multiplication principle of counting, there are five choices for the president, and once the president is chosen, there are four remaining members from which to choose the treasurer. Thus, the number of ways to choose the two officers is 20. As a check, we can make a list of the 20 possible slates of officers, where the first person in each pair is president and the second person is treasurer:

| ab | ac | ad | ae | bc | bd | be | cd | ce | de |
|----|----|----|----|----|----|----|----|----|----|
| ba | ca | da | ea | cb | db | eb | dc | ec | ed |

**(b)** Unlike the officers, the members of the Social Committee form an unordered subset of two elements. For example, a committee consisting of *a* and *b* is the same committee whether *b* is chosen first and then *a* or *a* is chosen first and then *b*. Thus, the number of two-person committees is the number of combinations of five objects taken two at a time. Hence, there are ten committees, as shown in the following list:

$$\{a, b\} \ \{a, c\} \ \{a, d\} \ \{a, e\} \ \{b, c\} \ \{b, d\} \ \{b, e\} \ \{c, d\} \ \{c, e\} \ \{d, e\}$$

In most problems, it is not important to list all of the permutations or all of the combinations. What is of interest is the number of *r*-permutations or the number of *r*-combinations there are when *r* objects are taken from a set of *n* different objects. That is, the important questions are these:

- How many permutations of *n* things taken *r* at a time are there?
- How many combinations of *n* things taken *r* at a time are there?

The following notation will be helpful:

> **NOTATION** *P(n, r) and C(n, r)*
> $P(n, r)$ denotes the number of *r*-permutations from a set of *n* different objects.
> $C(n, r)$ denotes the number of *r*-combinations from a set of *n* different objects.

Alternative notations are sometimes used. In particular, nPr may denote $P(n, r)$ and nCr may denote $C(n, r)$. This is the notation most often used by graphing calculators. Sometimes $C(n, r)$ is written $\binom{n}{r}$ and is read as "*n* choose *r*," since it gives the number of ways to choose a subset of *r* objects from a set of *n* objects.

## Factorials

Often, all of the objects in a set are arranged into an ordered sequence. For example, suppose that we have seven different books and we wish to arrange all of them from left to right on a shelf. There are seven choices for the leftmost book, six choices for the second book from the left, five choices for the next book, and so on, until we are left with just one choice for the rightmost book. Therefore, the number of 7-permutations of seven books is $7 \cdot 6 \cdot 5 \cdot 4 \cdot 3 \cdot 2 \cdot 1 = 5040$. Since products of this type arise frequently, they are written with the notation 7!, which is read as "seven factorial."

In general, we define *n*! for every integer $n \geq 0$ as follows:

> **DEFINITION** *The Factorial, n!*
> Let *n* be a whole number. Then *n* **factorial**, or *n*!, is defined by
> $$n! = n(n - 1)(n - 2) \cdots 1 \quad \text{for } n \geq 1$$
> and
> $$0! = 1.$$

That 0! is defined to be 1 may seem strange, but we justify this part of the definition shortly.

**EXAMPLE 14.18** **Manipulating Factorials**

Compute each of these expressions:

(a) $1!, 2!, 3!, 4!$      (b) $4 \cdot 3!$      (c) $(4 \cdot 3)!$

(d) $4! + 3!$      (e) $4! - 3!$      (f) $\dfrac{8!}{5!}$

(g) $\dfrac{8!}{7!}$      (h) $\dfrac{8!}{8!}$      (i) $\dfrac{8!}{0!}$

**Solution**

(a) $1! = 1, 2! = 2 \cdot 1 = 2, 3! = 3 \cdot 2 \cdot 1 = 6, 4! = 4 \cdot 3 \cdot 2 \cdot 1 = 24$

(b) $4 \cdot 3! = 4 \cdot (3 \cdot 2 \cdot 1) = 4! = 24$

(c) $(4 \cdot 3)! = 12! = 479,001,600$, using a calculator

(d) $4! + 3! = 4 \cdot 3! + 3! = 5 \cdot 3! = 30$

(e) $4! - 3! = 4 \cdot 3! - 3! = 3 \cdot 3! = 18$

(f) $\dfrac{8!}{5!} = \dfrac{8 \cdot 7 \cdot 6 \cdot 5 \cdot 4 \cdot 3 \cdot 2 \cdot 1}{5 \cdot 4 \cdot 3 \cdot 2 \cdot 1} = 8 \cdot 7 \cdot 6 = 336$

(g) $\dfrac{8!}{7!} = \dfrac{8 \cdot 7 \cdot 6 \cdot 5 \cdot 4 \cdot 3 \cdot 2 \cdot 1}{7 \cdot 6 \cdot 5 \cdot 4 \cdot 3 \cdot 2 \cdot 1} = 8$

(h) $\dfrac{8!}{8!} = 1$

(i) $\dfrac{8!}{0!} = \dfrac{8!}{1} = 8 \cdot 7 \cdot 6 \cdot 5 \cdot 4 \cdot 3 \cdot 2 \cdot 1 = 40,320$

## Formulas for Permutations and Combinations

To derive formulas for $P(n, r)$, $P(n, n)$, and $C(n, r)$, let's consider counting how many "code words" can be formed, where a code word is a sequence of 5 different letters from the 26-letter alphabet. For example, WORDS and VWXZY are legitimate code words, but LEGAL is not allowed, since the L is repeated. Since the order in which letters appear in a code word certainly matters, this is precisely the problem of determining the number $P(26, 5)$. Since there are 26 choices for the first letter, 25 choices for the second letter, and so on, the answer is

$$P(26, 5) = 26 \cdot 25 \cdot 24 \cdot 23 \cdot 22.$$

*five factors, since we must choose five letters*

By the same reasoning, the number of "words" of length $r$ using distinct letters from an alphabet of $n$ letters is given by

$$P(n, r) = n(n - 1)(n - 2) \cdots (n - r + 1).$$

*Here, there are r factors, since we are choosing r letters.*

Note also that

$$P(n, r) = \frac{n(n - 1) \cdots (n - r + 1)(n - r) \cdots 1}{(n - r)(n - r - 1) \cdots 1}$$

$$= \frac{n!}{(n - r)!}.$$

Setting $r = n$ in the preceding two formulas, we obtain

$$P(n, n) = n! \quad \text{and} \quad P(n, n) = \frac{n!}{(n - n)!} = \frac{n!}{0!}.$$

Since these must be the same, it follows that we should define $0!$ to be 1, as we did earlier.

Suppose we wanted 26-letter code words without repetition; that is, suppose we wanted to compute $P(26, 26)$. Repeating the foregoing argument, we have the following sequence of statements:

- The first letter can be chosen in 26 ways.
- The second letter can be chosen in 25 ways.
- The third letter can be chosen in 24 ways.
  $\vdots$
- The last letter can be chosen in 1 way.

Since the product of these numbers gives the desired result, the number of permutations of 26 things taken all at a time is

$$P(26, 26) = 26 \cdot 25 \cdot 24 \, \cdots \, 1 = 26!.$$

Repeating the argument for a general $n$, we have

$$P(n, n) = n!.$$

Lastly, consider again the problem of determining the number of permutations of 26 things taken 5 at a time. One way to determine such a permutation is to view it as a two-stage process:

**Stage 1**  Choose, without regard to order, the 5 letters to appear in the permutation, *and*
**Stage 2**  determine the order in which the 5 chosen letters are to appear.

We can choose the 5 letters in $C(26, 5)$ ways, and the 5 chosen objects can be put in order in 5! ways. Thus, by the multiplication principle of counting,

$$P(26, 5) = C(26, 5) \cdot 5!.$$

Dividing both sides of the equation by 5!, we obtain

$$C(26, 5) = \frac{P(26, 5)}{5!}$$
$$= \frac{26 \cdot 25 \cdot 24 \cdot 23 \cdot 22}{5!}.$$

> five factors in both numerator and denominator, since $5! = 5 \cdot 4 \cdot 3 \cdot 2 \cdot 1$

This argument could be repeated in general to give

$$C(n, r) = \frac{n(n - 1) \, \cdots \, (n - r + 1)}{r!}.$$

> $r$ factors in both numerator and denominator

Since $P(n, r) = \dfrac{n!}{(n - r)!}$ and $C(n, r) = \dfrac{P(n, r)}{r!}$, we also have the formula $C(n, r) = \dfrac{n!}{r!(n - r)!}$.

The formulas we have discovered can be collected to give the following important theorem:

**THEOREM**  *Formulas for P(n, r) and C(n, r)*
Let $n$ and $r$ be natural numbers with $0 < r \le n$. Then

$$P(n, r) = n(n - 1)(n - 2) \, \cdots \, (n - r + 1),$$
$$P(n, n) = n!,$$

and

$$C(n, r) = \frac{n(n - 1)(n - 2) \cdots (n - r + 1)}{r!} = \frac{n!}{r!(n - r)!}.$$

A useful observation from these formulas is that $C(n, r) = C(n, n - r)$, for example, $C(10, 7) = C(10, 3)$.

**EXAMPLE 14.19** **Computing $P(n, r)$ and $C(n, r)$**

Compute each of the following:

    **(a)** $P(7, 2)$      **(b)** $P(8, 8)$      **(c)** $P(13, 8)$
    **(d)** $C(7, 2)$      **(e)** $C(8, 8)$      **(f)** $C(13, 8)$

**Solution**

    **(a)** $P(7, 2) = 7 \cdot 6 = 42$
    **(b)** $P(8, 8) = 8! = 40{,}320$
    **(c)** $P(13, 8) = 13 \cdot 12 \cdot 11 \cdot 10 \cdot 9 \cdot 8 \cdot 7 \cdot 6 = 51{,}891{,}840$
    **(d)** $C(7, 2) = \dfrac{7 \cdot 6}{2!} = 21$
    **(e)** $C(8, 8) = \dfrac{8!}{8!} = 1$
    **(f)** $C(13, 8) = \dfrac{13!}{8!5!} = \dfrac{13 \cdot 12 \cdot 11 \cdot 10 \cdot 9 \cdot 8 \cdot 7 \cdot 6}{8 \cdot 7 \cdot 6 \cdot 5 \cdot 4 \cdot 3 \cdot 2 \cdot 1} = 1287$ or $C(13, 8) = C(13, 5) =$
    $\dfrac{13 \cdot 12 \cdot 11 \cdot 10 \cdot 9 \cdot 8}{5 \cdot 4 \cdot 3 \cdot 2 \cdot 1} = 1287$

## Problem Solving with Combinations and Permutations

Many counting problems ask for the number of ways objects can be selected, arranged, or distributed. Usually there are several conditions that must be observed, and it is helpful to answer these questions:

**MHM**

- *Are the objects being considered distinct, or are they essentially identical?*
  For example, the people on a baseball team are distinct, but the balls used by the team are usually considered to be identical.
- *Are repetitions allowed, or must the choices all be different?*
  For example, if we are buying ice cream cones for the team, we can certainly order several chocolate cones, but if we are selecting members of the cleanup crew, then repetition is not allowed.
- *Does the order matter, or is there no difference in which order the objects are selected?*
  For example, order matters when we are creating a batting rotation for a baseball team, but order is of no concern when we count the number of ways to choose two cocaptains of the team.

The solutions of such problems require a good conceptual understanding of permutations and combinations, together with the ability to work algebraically and numerically with the formulas that give the number of permutations and combinations. The next three examples apply this type of combinatorial reasoning.

**EXAMPLE 14.20** **Forming Committees**

The stamp club has nine members, including its president, Alicia. A four-person refreshment committee is to be formed.

    **(a)** How many committees include Alicia?
    **(b)** How many committees do not include Alicia?
    **(c)** How many committees are there altogether? Answer in two ways.

**Solution**

    **(a)** If Alicia is on the committee, then three more members must be selected from the other eight club members. Since order doesn't matter, this can be done in $C(8, 3) = \dfrac{8 \cdot 7 \cdot 6}{3!} = 56$ ways.

**(b)** If Alicia is not on the committee, then the four committee members can be selected in

$$C(8, 4) = \frac{8 \cdot 7 \cdot 6 \cdot 5}{4!} = 70 \text{ ways.}$$

**(c)** There are $56 + 70 = 126$ ways to choose a four-person committee, since parts (a) and (b) can be combined by the additive principle of counting. The answer can also be found directly: It is the numbers of combinations of nine objects taken four at a time, namely, $C(9, 4)$. Since both methods give the same answer, it follows that $C(8, 3) + C(8, 4) = C(9, 4)$.

The reasoning used in Example 14.20 applies more generally to forming a committee of $r$ members from a club of $n$ members, proving the identity

$$C(n, r - 1) + C(n, r) = C(n + 1, r).$$

This result is known as **Pascal's Identity** and explains why the combinations $C(n, r)$ are the numbers found in Pascal's triangle. (See problem 26 in Problem Set 14.3.)

---

**EXAMPLE 14.21 Permutations of Four Red Flags, Three Blue Flags, and Two Green Flags**

How many ways can you run four red flags, three blue flags, and two green flags up a pole if the flags are indistinguishable except for color?

**Solution**

**Understand the Problem**

We must put four red flags, three blue flags, and two green flags in order. Since the flags are indistinguishable except for color, interchanging flags of the same color will not make any difference; that is, the arrangement

$$\text{R R B G B G R B R}$$

will not change if we interchange red flags among themselves, or blue flags among themselves, or green flags among themselves. Apparently, the only way to obtain a different arrangement is to choose different locations in which to place the red, blue, and green flags.

**Devise a Plan**

How can we determine in how many ways we can choose the four places for red flags, the three places for blue flags, and the two places for green flags? This is just the number of ways we can choose four of the nine places to receive red flags *and* three of the remaining five places to receive blue flags *and* two of the remaining two places to receive green flags. The words *and* in the preceding sentence are the key. They suggest that we use the multiplication principle of counting.

**Carry Out the Plan**

1. The number of ways we can choose four of the nine places to receive red flags is $C(9, 4)$, the number of combinations of nine things (spaces) taken four at a time.
2. Having chosen the four places to receive red flags, we must now choose three of the remaining five places to receive blue flags, and this can be done in $C(5, 3)$ ways.
3. This leaves two places from which we must choose the places to receive the two green flags, and that can be done in $C(2, 2)$ ways.

But we have to do step 1 *and* step 2 *and* step 3, so, by the multiplication principle of counting, the desired answer is just the product of the number of ways we can complete each step:

$$C(9, 4) \cdot C(5, 3) \cdot C(2, 2) = \frac{9 \cdot 8 \cdot 7 \cdot 6}{4!} \cdot \frac{5 \cdot 4 \cdot 3}{3!} \cdot \frac{2 \cdot 1}{2!} = \frac{9!}{4! \, 3! \, 2!}.$$

Some arithmetic shows that this value is 1260.

MHM

### Look Back

The solution just derived is unexpectedly simple. When this happens, it is always useful to see if there is an alternative way to obtain the solution by more direct reasoning. The factorials suggest that permutations should be considered. Suppose, temporarily, that the flags are all made different by adding numbered tags. That is, the four red flags are now distinct flags $R_1$, $R_2$, $R_3$, and $R_4$, and the blue and green flags are similarly labeled. Then any permutation of the nine *distinct* flags $R_1$, $R_2$, $R_3$, $R_4$, $B_1$, $B_2$, $B_3$, $G_1$, and $G_2$ describes an arrangement of the colored flags on the flagpole. There are 9! permutations of the nine distinct flags, including, for example,

$$R_2\, R_1\, B_3\, G_2\, B_1\, G_1\, R_4\, B_2\, R_3.$$

If we stand back so far that the numbers can no longer be read, this permutation looks the same for all 4! permutations of the four red flags. Similarly, the 3! permutations of the three blue flags have the same color arrangement, and finally the 2! permutations of the two green flags make no change in the color arrangement of the flags. Altogether, the 9! permutations of the distinctly labeled flags give the same color arrangement of the flags 4! 3! 2! times, so the number of different color arrangements is $\dfrac{9!}{4!3!2!}$.

The alternative solution given in Example 14.21 provides a way to count permutations in which repetition is allowed. For example, to know how many ways the 15 letters of PANAMABANANAMAN can be arranged into a list, we notice there are one P, seven As, four Ns, two Ms, and one B. Therefore, the 15 letters can be arranged into $\dfrac{15!}{1!7!4!2!1!}$ different lists.

### EXAMPLE 14.22 Determining the Number of Zip Code Groups

The bar code commonly seen under the address on pieces of mail is the zip code in machine-readable form. When the code is broken down, it turns out that each code group consists of two long bars and three short bars—for example, ılıl represents the digit 2. How many different code groups can be formed in this way?

**Solution**

We seek the number of ways one can choose the positions of the two long bars from the five positions available. The result is

$$C(5, 2) = \frac{5 \cdot 4}{2 \cdot 1} = 10.$$

The result is opportune, since the ten code groups are just adequate to represent the ten digits —0, 1, 2, . . . , 9—needed to express a zip code. Here are the 10 arrangements of the 5-symbol code groups—two long and three short bars—and the associated digit coded by the group:

| ıılll | ıllıl | ılllı | ılııl | ıllıl |
|:---:|:---:|:---:|:---:|:---:|
| 1 | 2 | 3 | 4 | 5 |
| ıllıı | lıııl | lılıı | lılıı | llııı |
| 6 | 7 | 8 | 9 | 0 |

### Problem Set 14.3

Exercises numbered in red are answered in the back of the text.

### Understanding Concepts

**1.** For each situation described, first decide whether it is a permutation or a combination and then answer the question.

**(a)** A coin is flipped ten times. In how many ways can heads and tails appear equally often?

**(b)** If Olivia has ten dolls, in how many ways can four of them be displayed in a row on a shelf?

(c) Morrie coaches 12 players on the tennis team. How many ways can he choose 5 players for a match, where the players must be ranked?

(d) How many different hands of 3 cards can be drawn from a deck of 15 cards numbered 1 through 15?

(e) How many ways can a hand of five cards be played one at a time?

2. How many ways can a group of 12, including 4 boys and 8 girls, be formed into two 6-person volleyball teams

(a) with no restrictions?

(b) so that each team has two of the boys?

(c) so that all of the boys are on the same team?

3. How many ways can a group of seven people go from Allentown to Bovill if one person rides a unicycle, two ride a tandem bike, and the rest walk? (*Careful:* How many ways can two people ride a tandem bike?)

4. The Chess Club has six members. In how many ways

(a) can all six members line up for a picture?

(b) can the club choose a president and a secretary?

(c) can the club choose three members to attend the regional tournament, with no regard to order?

5. There are 14 members of the debate team, including 8 girls and 6 boys.

(a) How many ways can the club members line up for a year-book photo?

(b) How many ways can they take the yearbook photo with the girls in the front row and the boys in the back row?

(c) How many ways can they randomly choose a slate of three officers, including a president, a secretary, and a treasurer?

(d) How many ways can they form a social committee of four members, including two boys and two girls?

6. In how many ways can a two-scoop cone be purchased at Raskin-Bobbins Thirty-One Flavors Ice Cream Shoppe? Vary the conditions that affect your answer. For example, is a vanilla + chocolate cone different from a chocolate + vanilla cone? Can both scoops be the same flavor?

7. Evaluate each of these expressions:

(a) $7!$        (b) $9! - 7!$

(c) $9! \div 7!$     (d) $9! + 7!$

(e) $7 \cdot 7!$       (f) $0!$

8. Evaluate each of the following:

(a) $P(13, 8)$

(b) $P(15, 15)$

(c) $P(15, 2)$

(d) $C(13, 8)$

(e) $C(15, 15)$

(f) $C(15, 2)$

9. In Example 14.20, combinatorial reasoning proved that $C(8, 3) + C(8, 4) = C(9, 4)$. Now use algebraic reasoning to verify the formula, by showing that $\dfrac{8!}{3!5!} + \dfrac{8!}{4!4!}$ is equal to $\dfrac{9!}{4!5!}$. (*Suggestion:* Remember that $5! = 5 \cdot 4!$.)

10. A bag contains 10 blue balls $b_1, b_2, \ldots, b_{10}$ and 15 red balls $r_1, r_2, \ldots, r_{15}$.

(a) Explain why there are $C(10 + 15, 2)$ ways to select 2 balls from the bag. (Order doesn't matter.)

(b) Explain why there are $C(10, 2) + C(15, 2) + 10 \cdot 15$ ways to choose two balls from the bag. [*Suggestion*: Take cases depending on the colors of the chosen balls.]

(c) Parts (a) and (b) show that $C(10 + 15, 2) = C(10, 2) + C(15, 2) + 10 \cdot 15$. Use an argument about a bag with colored balls to show that $C(m + n, 2) = C(m, 2) + C(n, 2) + m \cdot n$ for any natural numbers $m$ and $n$.

11. Show that $C(m + n, 3) = C(m, 3) + C(n, 3) + mC(n, 2) + nC(m, 2)$ for all natural numbers $m$ and $n$ by giving two answers to the following question:

*How many ways can 3 balls be selected from a bag containing m blue and n red distinct balls?*

[*Suggestion*: Modify the combinatorial method of reasoning used in problem 10.]

12. How many different signals can be sent up on a flagpole if each signal requires three blue and three yellow flags and the flags are identical except for color?

13. (a) How many different arrangements are there of the letters in TOOT?

(b) How many different arrangements are there of the letters in TESTERS?

## Teaching Concepts

14. Younger children especially want to check that the counting formulas give correct results by comparing those results with an answer given by direct counting. Design two activities in which groups of four verify that the number of permutations and combinations are indeed given by the respective formulas

$$P(n, r) = n(n - 1)\cdots(n - r + 1) \quad \text{and} \quad C(n, r) = P(n, r)/r!.$$

(a) **Permutation Activity.** Have each group of four make "photos" of all of the ways in which there are (i) one person, (ii) two persons side by side, and (iii) three persons in a line in the photo. The photo can be an actual digital photo or just a written record of who was in the photo and in what order. After the photos are taken, check that the number of photos in the three cases is matched by the number of permutations given by the formula $P(4, r)$ for $r = 1, 2$, and 3.

(b) **Combination Activity.** Modify part (a) by placing a loop of string on the floor and having groups of one, two, three, or four stand within the loop. Again, keep a record of all possible ways, and verify that the number of ways is correctly given by the formula for $C(4, r)$ for $r = 1, 2, 3,$ and 4. Comment on why $C(4, 0) = 1$ seems to be reasonable.

## Responding to Students

15. Dillon was playing with three cards numbered 4, 5, and 6. He decided to see how many different two-digit numbers could be created with two of the cards. He came up with the numbers 44, 45, 46, 55, 54, 56, 66, 64, and 65. As Dillon's teacher, how would you assess Dillon's answer?

16. Mr. Brown was introducing counting strategies to his fourth grade students, preparing them for a unit on probability. He challenged his class to count how many pizzas can be ordered, given a choice of either thick or thin crust and one of four toppings: green peppers, mushrooms, sausage, or pepperoni. How should Mr. Brown respond to the following claims of Ernie and Donna?

   (a) Ernie claims that there are six types of pizza that can be ordered.

   (b) When Mr. Brown informed the class that there was no pepperoni, Donna claimed that there were now only three types of pizza available.

17. The Math Club has four seniors and seven juniors. They wish to form a steering committee of four members, including at least two of the seniors. Being curious, they wondered how many ways the committee could be formed, and three club members presented answers:

   • Shelley argued that this could be done by picking two seniors in $C(4, 2)$ ways and then filling out the committee by picking two more people from the ten remaining club members in $C(10, 2)$ ways. Therefore, the committee can be selected in $C(4, 2)C(10, 2)$ ways.

   • Murial claimed that there was one committee with all four seniors, $4 \cdot 7$ ways with one junior, and $C(4, 2)C(7, 2)$ ways with an equal number of juniors and seniors. Therefore, there are $1 + 28 + C(4, 2)C(7,2)$ possible committees.

   • Jisoo claims that since there are $C(7, 4)$ committees with all juniors and $4C(7, 3)$ committees with just one senior, then $C(11, 4) - C(7, 4) - 4C(7, 3)$ gives the number of committees with two or more seniors.

   Determine which, if any, of the students are correct, and explain what mistakes were made in any incorrect answer.

18. Bai knows that there are two equivalent formulas for $C(n, r)$, namely, $C(n, r) = \dfrac{n(n - 1) \cdots (n - r + 1)}{r!}$ and $C(n, r) = \dfrac{n!}{r!(n - r)!}$. Choosing $r = n$, he finds that $C(n, n) = \dfrac{n!}{n!} = 1$ and $C(n, n) = \dfrac{n!}{n!0!}$. For this to make sense, he observes that we are again led to define $0! = 1$. How do you respond to Bai?

## Thinking Critically

19. Two cards are dealt from a shuffled deck. In how many ways

   (a) do the two cards form a pair?

   (b) do the cards not form a pair?

20. In how many ways can you arrange the nine letters $a, a, a, a, b, b, b, c,$ and $c$ in a row?

21. How many of the arrangements in problem 20 start with $a$ and end with $b$?

22. (a) In how many of the 120 arrangements of $a, b, c, d,$ and $e$ does $b$ immediately follow $a$? (*Hint:* Think of $ab$ as a single symbol.)

   (b) In how many of the 120 possible arrangements of $a, b, c, d,$ and $e$ are $a$ and $b$ adjacent?

   (c) In how many arrangements of $a, b, c, d,$ and $e$ does $a$ precede $e$?

23. Sets of six cards are selected without replacement from an ordinary deck of playing cards.

   (a) In how many ways can you choose a set of six hearts?

   (b) In how many ways can you select a set of three hearts and three spades?

   (c) In how many ways can you select a set of six hearts or six spades?

24. How many different sequences of ten flips of a coin result in five heads and five tails?

25. The Debate Team has six girls and five boys. In how many ways can a four-person team be selected if there are to be two boys and two girls on the team?

26. Use the formula $C(n, r) = \dfrac{n!}{r!(n - r)!}$ to evaluate the entries in this table.

   | | | | | |
   |---|---|---|---|---|
   | | | $C(0, 0)$ | | |
   | | $C(1, 0)$ | | $C(1, 1)$ | |
   | $C(2, 0)$ | | $C(2, 1)$ | | $C(2, 2)$ |
   | $C(3, 0)$ | $C(3, 1)$ | $C(3, 2)$ | $C(3, 3)$ | |
   | $C(4, 0)$ | $C(4, 1)$ | $C(4, 2)$ | $C(4, 3)$ | $C(4, 4)$ |

   Do you need the formula for $C(n, r)$ to extend the table two more rows? Explain.

27. (a) The first few rows of Pascal's triangle are shown, together with a hexagon that has the values 1, 1, 5, 10, 6, and 3 in its six corners. Notice that the product of the numbers in the odd corners is $1 \cdot 5 \cdot 6 = 30$ and the product of the numbers in the even corners is $1 \cdot 10 \cdot 3 = 30$. Extend Pascal's triangle several more rows, and move the hexagon to different positions. Report on the pattern that you observe.

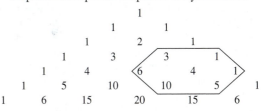

   (b) Prove that $C(n - 1, r - 1)C(n, r + 1)C(n + 1, r) = C(n - 1, r)C(n, r - 1)C(n + 1, r + 1)$ by writing each factor in terms of factorials. For example, the first factor is $C(n - 1, r - 1) = \dfrac{(n - 1)!}{(r - 1)!(n - r)!}$.

28. A bag contains eight marbles of assorted colors, of which just one marble is red. Use the symbol $C(n, r)$ to answer these questions:

**(a)** In how many ways can a subset of any five marbles be chosen?

**(b)** In how many ways can a subset of five nonred marbles be chosen?

**(c)** In how many ways can a subset of five marbles be chosen, including the red marble?

**(d)** What formula expresses the fact that your answer to part (a) is the sum of your answers to parts (b) and (c)?

**(e)** Create a "marble story" to derive the formula $C(10, 4) = C(9, 4) + C(9, 3)$.

**29.** There are 11 members of the choir. Six members are to be selected to perform a sextet, and 1 of these 6 is to be chosen for the solo part. Assuming that every choir member is equally capable, suppose we wish to know how many sextets with soloist can be selected.

**(a)** Why is $C(11, 6) \cdot 6$ a correct answer?

**(b)** Why is $11 \cdot C(10, 5)$ also a correct answer?

**(c)** Numerically check that $6 \cdot C(11, 6) = 11 \cdot C(10, 5)$.

**(d)** Invent a "choir story" that shows why $8 \cdot C(14, 8) = 14 \cdot C(13, 7)$.

**30.** The 15 members of the Chess Club can send 8 members to the state meet, including 2 of the 8 named as cocaptains. In how many ways can the 8-person delegation, with the cocaptains, be named?

**(a)** Why is one correct answer $C(15, 8) \cdot C(8, 2)$?

**(b)** Why is another correct answer $C(15, 2) \cdot C(13, 6)$?

**(c)** Algebraically check that $C(15, 8) \cdot C(8, 2) = C(15, 2) \cdot C(13, 6)$.

**(d)** Invent a "Chess Club" story that shows why $C(19, 7) \cdot C(7, 3) = C(19, 3) \cdot C(16, 4)$.

**31. Combinations with Repetition.** Jen & Berry's ice cream store offers four flavors: strawberry (*S*), vanilla (*V*), chocolate (*C*), and peppermint (*P*). A group can order several cones by putting check marks on the order card. For example, the following card indicates an order of 3 strawberry, 0 vanilla, 2 chocolate, and 5 peppermint ice cream cones, for a total of 10 cones ordered:

| S | V | C | P |
|---|---|---|---|
| ✓✓✓ | | ✓✓ | ✓✓✓✓✓ |

This order card suggests how an ice cream order is compactly represented as the list ✓ ✓ ✓ | | ✓ ✓ | ✓ ✓ ✓ ✓ ✓ of 10 checks and 3 bars, where the bars separate the 4 flavors from one another. As another example, the list | ✓ | ✓ ✓ ✓ | ✓ ✓ represents an order of 0 strawberry, 1 vanilla, 3 chocolate, and 2 peppermint ice cream cones, for a total of 6 cones ordered. The question "How many ways can 10 cones be ordered from 4 flavors?" can now be rephrased as "How many ways can 10 checks and 3 bars be arranged?" This question is easy to answer: There are $10 + 4 - 1$ positions, and we can choose the 10 positions for the checks in $C(10 + 4 - 1, 10) = C(13, 10) =$
$$C(13, 3) = \frac{13 \cdot 12 \cdot 11}{3 \cdot 2 \cdot 1} = 286 \text{ ways.}$$

**(a)** Show that 6 cones can be ordered from Jen & Berry's in 84 ways.

**(b)** Jen & Berry's just introduced two new flavors, making 6 flavors in all. Verify that there are now 1287 ways to place an order for 8 cones.

**(c)** To meet and beat the competition, Jen & Berry now have 32 flavors of ice cream. How many ways can 4 cones be ordered now?

**(d)** Carefully explain why there are $C(n + k - 1, n)$ ways to select a total of *n* objects from *k* types where repetition is allowed. (That is, there can be any number of objects of each type selected.)

**32. (a)** Each "half" of a domino from a "double-six" set of dominoes has anywhere from no spots to six spots. Show that there are 28 dominoes in a double-six set.

**(b)** How many dominoes constitute a "double-twelve" set?

## Thinking Cooperatively

**33. Making Rod Trains.** In small cooperative groups, investigate making trains with Cuisenaire® rods, as described in the Hands On activity in Chapter 2. In particular, use the rods to form all possible trains of length five. For example, four ways to form a train of length five are shown. Notice that these trains contain varying numbers of cars (that is, rods), from one car to four cars.

**(a)** In how many total ways can trains of length five be formed?

**(b)** How many length-five trains contain one car? two cars? three cars? four cars? five cars?

**(c)** In the following figure, each dashed segment can either be left as is or made solid:

Use the figure to explain why there are $2 \times 2 \times 2 \times 2$, or $2^4$, trains of length five.

**(d)** To make a three-car train of length five, two of the four dashed lines must be made solid to show a separation between adjacent cars. Discuss why this requirement means that there are $C(4, 2)$, or six, trains of length five, each of which has three cars.

**(e)** Carefully explain how to find a formula giving the number of trains of length *n*.

**(f)** Carefully explain how to find a formula, in terms of $C(m, t)$ for appropriate choices of *m* and *t*, giving the number of trains of length *n* that have *c* cars.

**34.** It is not always obvious when events are dependent or independent. Answer the following open-ended problem, taking taste and culture into consideration:

*A restaurant serves chicken, steak, tofu, beef, mashed potatoes, French fries, baked potatoes, and green beans. How many different ways are there to select two items for the meal?*

## Making Connections

**35. (a)** Ms. Ruiz has 13 boys and 11 girls in her class. In how many ways can she select a committee to organize a class party if the committee must contain 3 boys and 3 girls?

(b) Lourdes, a girl, and Andy, a boy, always fight. How many ways can Mrs. Ruiz select the committee of part (a) if she does not want both Lourdes and Andy on the committee? Note that Lourdes can be on the committee and Andy not on the committee, or vice versa.

**36.** (a) How many ways can four tennis players divide up to play a set of doubles?

(b) How many ways can five players play doubles with one player sitting out?

(c) How many ways can six basketball players divide up to play three against three?

(d) How many ways can seven basketball players divide up to play three against three with one player sitting out?

**37.** It is well known that the candidate listed first on a ballot has an advantage in an election. To be equally fair to all candidates, many states require that the ballots be printed in all possible orders with an equal number of ballots in each order. Suppose there are three candidates for governor, four candidates for senate, and five for representative. How many different forms of ballots must be prepared, where all ballots list the races for governor, senator, and representative in that order?

**38.** Joe is at the corner of Second Avenue and B Street. He intends to walk to the corner of Eighth Avenue and K Street.

(a) If the city blocks form a square grid, how many blocks long is Joe's walk? Assume that he takes an efficient route.

(b) How many shortest-distance routes can Joe take to his destination?

(c) How many of these routes allow him to drop by the mailbox at the corner of Fourth Avenue and E Street?

### Using a Calculator

Scientific and graphing calculators have built-in functions to compute factorials $n!$, permutations $P(n, r)$, and combinations $C(n, r)$. For example, there may be a key labeled ! or $n!$ on a scientific calculator. A graphing calculator will have functions !, nPr, and nCr under the Math and Probability menus. For example, 5! ENTER will give 120, 5 nPr 3 ENTER will yield 60, and 5 nCr 3 ENTER will yield 10.

**39.** Use a calculator to evaluate the following expressions:

(a) $9!$  (b) $11!$  (c) $P(7, 5)$

(d) $P(8, 6)$  (e) $C(7, 4)$  (f) $C(9, 5)$

**40.** Use a calculator to evaluate the number of ways

(a) ten people can get in a single line for a photograph.

(b) to place six books on a shelf, choosing from a set of ten books.

(c) to choose a set of eight hearts from a deck of cards.

(d) to choose your six "lucky numbers" in a lottery, choosing from the numbers 1 through 44.

## 14.4 Theoretical Probability

We now turn our attention to the study of **theoretical probability,** which we refer to simply as **probability.** The terminology of Section 14.1 for experimental probability—outcome, sample space, event, mutually exclusive events, dependent events, and independent events—will continue to be important in describing the key concepts.

Unlike experimental probability, theoretical probability assumes that the probability of each outcome $s_j$ in the sample space $S = \{s_1, s_2, \ldots, s_m\}$ is a known value, $p_i$. The probability of an event is then simply the sum of the probabilities of the outcomes in the event. For example, suppose that a "loaded die" has the probabilities $p_1 = p_2 = p_5 = p_6 = 0.1, p_3 = p_4 = 0.3$, where $p_i$ is the probability of rolling an $i$. Then the event of rolling a 3 or a 4 is $0.3 + 0.3 = 0.6$.

For many random events, there is good reason to believe that each outcome of the sample space has the same probability of occurrence. When this is the case, we say that the outcomes are **equally likely.** For example, a die is said to be fair if each face has the same probability of landing upward. Since there are six faces, each outcome has the same probability, namely, $\frac{1}{6}$. The probability of rolling a 3 or a 4 with a fair die is, therefore, $\frac{1}{6} + \frac{1}{6} = \frac{1}{3} = 0.\overline{3}$, a far less likely event than would be the case for the loaded die mentioned in the previous paragraph. It is important that the assumption of equal likelihood be checked carefully. For example, if a fair coin is flipped twice, it might mistakenly be assumed that there are three equally likely outcomes: two heads, two tails, a head and a tail. But more careful thought shows there are *four* equally likely outcomes: two heads, two tails, a head followed by a tail, and a tail followed by a head. The four equally likely outcomes are often abbreviated succinctly as HH, TT, HT, TH. The probability that a head and a tail occur in either order of the flips is thus a half, not a third. That is, $P(\text{HT or TH}) = 0.5$.

When the sample space $S$ has equally likely outcomes, the probability of an event $E \subseteq S$ is determined by the following definition:

> **DEFINITION** *Theoretical Probability of an Event*
>
> Let $S$, the **sample space**, denote the set of **equally likely outcomes** of an experiment, and let $E$, an **event,** denote a subset of outcomes of the experiment. Let $n(S)$ and $n(E)$ denote the number of outcomes in $S$ and $E$, respectively. Then the **probability** of $E$, denoted by $P(E)$, is given by
>
> $$P(E) = \frac{n(E)}{n(S)}.$$

It is clear that $0 \leq P(E) \leq 1$, where $P(E) = 0$ means that $E = \emptyset$ (the event is impossible) and $P(E) = 1$ means that $E = S$ (the event is certain). Moreover, the probability of each outcome is $\frac{1}{n}$ if there are $n$ equally likely outcomes in $S$.

The phrase *equally likely* is of critical importance in the preceding definition. If the outcomes in the sample space are not equally likely, the definition of probability simply doesn't make sense. For example, suppose the experiment consists of rolling two dice. It would not do to think of the sample space as the 11 outcomes $\{2, 3, 4, \ldots, 12\}$, since these outcomes are not equally likely. The difficulty is that there is only one way to obtain a 2, two ways to obtain a 3, three ways to obtain a 4, $\ldots$, six ways to obtain a 7, $\ldots$, and only one way to obtain a 12. Thus, the event of obtaining a 3 is twice as likely as the event of obtaining a 2, and so on. If we mistakenly thought of the sample space as the set with each of 2, 3, 4, $\ldots$, 11, and 12 equally likely, we would obtain

$$P(2) = P(3) = \cdots = P(12) = \frac{1}{11},$$

a manifest absurdity. In fact, as we have seen before, there are 36 equally likely ways two dice can come up, so

$$P(2) = \frac{1}{36}, P(3) = \frac{2}{36}, \ldots, P(7) = \frac{6}{36}, \ldots, P(12) = \frac{1}{36}.$$

Moreover, these probabilities are closely approximated by the corresponding experimental probabilities.

The definition of probability assumes that we can count the number of outcomes, both in the event and in the sample space. This implies that the sample space is finite. Thus, our discussion of theoretical probability will be largely restricted to the finite case. It is possible to treat the infinite case as well, as with geometric probability, but the general theory is beyond the scope of this text.

The needed techniques of counting are perhaps best understood by considering several examples.

**EXAMPLE 14.23 Determining the Probability of Rolling a Score of 11 with Two Dice**

Compute the probability of obtaining a score of 11 on a single roll of two fair dice.

**Solution** Here, the sample space $S$ is the set of all 36 equally likely outcomes illustrated in Example 14.11. Let $E$ denote the event of rolling a score of 11. Since exactly two of the outcomes in the sample space result in 11,

$$P(11) = \frac{n(E)}{n(S)} = \frac{2}{36} = \frac{1}{18}.$$

**EXAMPLE 14.24 Computing the Probability of Rolling a Sum of 5 or 8 with Two Dice**

Determine the probability of rolling a sum of 5 *or* 8 on a single roll of two fair dice.

**Solution 1**   As we have just seen, the sample space $S$ is the set of all 36 ways two dice can come up. The favorable outcomes are as shown here, where $F$ is the event of rolling a 5 and $E$ is the event of rolling an 8:

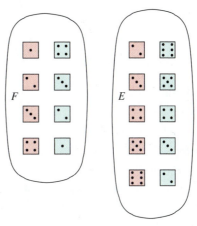

It follows that

$$P(5 \text{ or } 8) = \frac{4 + 5}{36} = \frac{1}{4}.$$

**Solution 2**   Note that if 5 is rolled, then 8 is not, and vice versa. Thus, rolling 5 and rolling 8 are mutually exclusive events, and the *or* in the statement of the problem reminds us that we can use the addition principle of counting mutually exclusive events. Thus,

$$P(5 \text{ or } 8) = \frac{n(5 \text{ or } 8)}{n(S)}$$

$$= \frac{n(5) + n(8)}{n(S)}$$

$$= \frac{4 + 5}{36}$$

$$= \frac{1}{4},$$

as before. Notice that

$$P(5 \text{ or } 8) = \frac{4}{36} + \frac{5}{36} = P(5) + P(8).$$

The second solution in Example 14.24 illustrates a general principle: If $A$ and $B$ are mutually exclusive events, so that $A \cap B = \varnothing$, then $P(A \text{ or } B) = P(A) + P(B)$.

**EXAMPLE 14.25 Computing the Probability of Obtaining a Face Card or a Diamond**

Determine the probability of obtaining a face card *or* a diamond if a card is drawn at random from an ordinary deck of playing cards.

**Solution 1** | The sample space $S$ is the set of all 52 cards in the deck. Let $D$ denote the event of selecting a diamond, and let $F$ denote the event of selecting a face card. Since there are 13 diamonds (including face cards) and 9 nondiamond face cards,

$$P(D \text{ or } F) = \frac{13 + 9}{52} = \frac{22}{52} = \frac{11}{26}.$$

**Solution 2** | Using the addition principle of counting, we obtain

$$P(D \text{ or } F) = \frac{n(D \text{ or } F)}{n(S)}$$

$$= \frac{n(D) + n(F) - n(D \cap F)}{n(S)}$$

$$= \frac{13 + 12 - 3}{52}$$

$$= \frac{22}{52} = \frac{11}{26},$$

*Three face cards are diamonds.*

as before.

The formula revealed in solution 2 of Example 14.25 is quite useful: For any two events $E$ and $F$,

$$P(E \text{ or } F) = P(E) + P(F) - P(E \text{ and } F).$$

## Conditional Probability

**EXAMPLE 14.26 Determining Probabilities with Restrictive Conditions**

All 24 students in Mr. Henry's preschool are either 3 or 4 years old, as shown in the accompanying table. A student is selected at random.

|  | Age Three | Age Four |
|---|---|---|
| **Boys** | 8 | 3 |
| **Girls** | 6 | 7 |

**(a)** What is the probability that the student is 3 years old?
**(b)** What is the probability that the student is 3 years old given that a boy was selected?

**Solution** | Let $B$ denote the set of boys, $T$ the set of 3-year-olds and $S$ the set of all students in the class.

**(a)** $P(T) = \dfrac{n(T)}{n(S)} = \dfrac{14}{24} = \dfrac{7}{12}.$

**(b)** Since a boy was selected, the sample space is not the set $S$ of all students, but the set $B$ of all of the boys in class. Similarly, the event is not the set $T$ of all the 3-year-olds, but the set $T \cap B$ of students that are both 3 years old and a boy. The desired probability is, then,

$$\frac{P(T \cap B)}{P(B)} = \frac{8}{11}.$$

In Example 14.26(b), we were asked to compute a probability based on an extra condition, namely, that the student not only is 3 years old but also is a boy. This is an example of **conditional probability.**

**DEFINITION** *Conditional Probability*
Let $A$ and $B$ be events in a probability space. The probability that event $B$ occurs given that event $A$ has occurred is the **conditional probability** of event $B$ given event $A$ and is denoted by $P(B \mid A)$.

Conditional probability can be computed with the formula displayed in the following theorem:

> **THEOREM** *Formula for Conditional Probability*
>
> $$P(B \mid A) = \frac{P(A \cap B)}{P(A)}$$

**PROOF** A Venn diagram makes it clear that if we assume that event $A$ has happened, then event $B$ can occur only if it also belongs to $A$. That is, the event $B \mid A$ is equivalent to the event $A \cap B$ considered as a subset of $A$. Therefore,

$$P(B \mid A) = \frac{n(A \cap B)}{n(A)} = \frac{\dfrac{n(A \cap B)}{n(S)}}{\dfrac{n(A)}{n(S)}} = \frac{P(A \cap B)}{P(A)}.$$

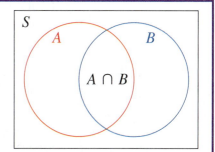

The formula in the foregoing theorem can also be written in the form $P(A \cap B) = P(A) \cdot P(B \mid A)$, which is useful for computing the probability of the compound event "$A$ and $B$" when $A$ and $B$ are **dependent events** (that is, the probability of $B$ depends on knowing that event $A$ has occurred). In many problems, the probability of event $B$ is unchanged whether or not $B$ has occurred. That is, $P(B \mid A) = P(B)$. In this case, we say that $A$ and $B$ are **independent events** and we have $P(A \cap B) = P(A) \cdot P(B)$.

In computing the probability of the compound event "$A$ and $B$," it is important to ask "Are $A$ and $B$ independent events?" If $A$ and $B$ are dependent, you'll want to use the conditional probability formula $P(A \cap B) = P(A) \cdot P(B \mid A)$. If $A$ and $B$ are independent events, you will use the formula $P(A \cap B) = P(A) \cdot P(B)$.

**EXAMPLE 14.27  Using the Multiplication Principle of Counting for Independent Events**

A red die and a green die are rolled. What is the probability of obtaining an even number on the red die *and* a multiple of 3 on the green die?

**Solution** The sets of favorable outcomes on the red and green die, respectively, are $R = \{2, 4, 6\}$ and $G = \{3, 6\}$; therefore, $P(R) = \frac{3}{6}$ and $P(G) = \frac{2}{6}$. Since $R$ and $G$ are independent events, the desired probability is

$$P(R \text{ and } G) = P(R) \cdot P(G) = \frac{3}{6} \cdot \frac{2}{6} = \frac{6}{36} = \frac{1}{6}.$$

**EXAMPLE 14.28  Selecting Balls Without Replacement**

An urn contains three identical red and two identical white balls. Two balls are drawn one after the other without replacement.

    **(a)** What is the probability that the first ball is red?
    **(b)** What is the probability that the second ball is red given that the first ball is red?
    **(c)** What is the probability that both balls are red?

**Solution**

**(a)** Since there are initially five balls and three are red, $P(\text{1st ball is red}) = \frac{3}{5}$.

**(b)** Since a red ball has already been selected on the first draw, the count changes for the selection of the second ball. For the second selection, there remain four balls of which two are red. Thus,

$$P(\text{2nd ball is red} \mid \text{1st ball is red}) = \frac{2}{4} = \frac{1}{2}.$$

*read as "given that"*

**(c)** If $A$ is the event that the first ball drawn is red and $B$ is the event that the second ball drawn is red, we have, from part (a),

$$P(A) = P(\text{1st ball drawn is red}) = \frac{3}{5}$$

and, from part (b),

$$P(B \mid A) = P(\text{2nd ball drawn is red} \mid \text{1st ball is red}) = \frac{2}{4}.$$

Thus,

$$P(\text{both balls red}) = P(A \cap B) = P(A) \cdot P(B \mid A)$$

$$= P(\text{1st ball is red}) \cdot P(\text{2nd ball is red} \mid \text{1st ball is red}) = \frac{3}{5} \cdot \frac{2}{4} = \frac{6}{20}.$$

## Probability Trees

Conditional probabilities can often be calculated easily with the construction of a **probability tree.** A probability tree is similar in appearance to a possibility tree, such as that shown in Figure 14.6, but its branches are labeled with the probabilities of the corresponding outcomes. The probability of a compound experiment is obtained by multiplying the probabilities along each branch that leads to the outcome in question.

As an example, the probability tree shown in Figure 14.7 reexamines Example 14.28, in which two balls are drawn without replacement from an urn containing three identical red and two identical white balls. The results calculated in Example 14.28 appear once more, together with additional information. For example, the probability that both balls are white is $\frac{2}{20}$.

**FIGURE 14.7**

The probability tree for drawing two balls without replacement from an urn containing three red and two white balls

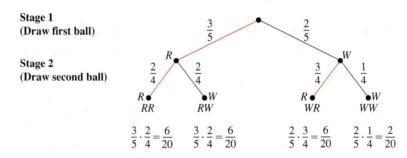

Here is another example of solving a probability problem with a probability tree.

**EXAMPLE 14.29** **Using a Probability Tree**

Ronnie likes blue jellybeans and green jellybeans, but hates red ones. His bag initially contains 5 blue, 4 red, and 3 green jellybeans. He draws out two jellybeans in succession and either eats a jellybean if it's blue or green or returns it to the bag if it's red. What is the probability that Ronnie gets to eat (a) two jellybeans? (b) just one jellybean? (c) no jellybean at all?

**Solution** | The following probability tree satisfies the conditions of the problem:

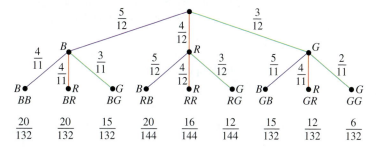

We can now easily compute the needed probabilities:

**(a)** $P(\text{two eaten}) = P(BB \cup BG \cup GB \cup GG)$
$= P(BB) + P(BG) + P(GB) + P(GG)$
$= \dfrac{20}{132} + \dfrac{15}{132} + \dfrac{15}{132} + \dfrac{6}{132} = \dfrac{56}{132} = 0.\overline{42}$

**(b)** $P(\text{one eaten}) = P(BR \cup RB \cup RG \cup GR)$
$= P(BR) + P(RB) + P(RG) + P(GR)$
$= \dfrac{20}{132} + \dfrac{20}{144} + \dfrac{12}{144} + \dfrac{12}{132} = 0.\overline{46}$

**(c)** $P(\text{none eaten}) = P(RR) = \dfrac{16}{144} = \dfrac{1}{9} = 0.\overline{1}$

As a check, it is interesting to notice that $0.\overline{42} + 0.\overline{46} + 0.\overline{1} = 0.\overline{9} = 1$.

## Computing Probability by Using Permutations and Combinations

To compute the probability $P(E) = \dfrac{n(E)}{n(S)}$ of an event $E$ in a sample space $S$ of equally likely outcomes, we must count the number $n(S)$ of outcomes in $S$ and the number $n(E)$ of outcomes in event $E$. Often, the outcomes in $S$ and $E$ are permutations or combinations, so we can apply the counting formulas derived in the previous section.

**EXAMPLE 14.30  Computing Probabilities with Permutations and Combinations**

Suppose there are 6 boys and 8 girls, all of different heights, on the Pep Squad.

**(a)** If four members are randomly chosen to line up for a photo, what is the probability that no two boys and no two girls stand side by side?

**(b)** If a committee of three is chosen by a random drawing of names, what is the probability that all three committee members are boys?

**(c)** If a committee of four is chosen at random, what is the probability that the committee has two boys and two girls?

**(d)** If a committee of five is chosen at random, what is the probability there is at most one girl on the committee?

**Solution** | For each problem, we must describe the sample space $S$ and the event $E$, then count the number of equally likely outcomes in both $S$ and $E$, and finally take the ratio of the two counts to give the probability.

**(a)** The sample space is the number of 4-permutations of the 14 members, so $n(S) = P(14, 4) = 14 \cdot 13 \cdot 12 \cdot 11 = 24{,}024$. There are $P(6, 2) = 6 \cdot 5 = 30$ ways to line up two of the six boys and $P(8, 2) = 8 \cdot 7 = 56$ ways to line up the two girls. There are also two allowable arrangements of two boys and two girls with no two boys and no two girls standing side by side: boy–girl–boy–girl and girl–boy–girl–boy. By the multiplication principle, this gives $2 \cdot 30 \cdot 56 = 3360$ boy–girl–boy–girl arrangements. Therefore, the probability is $\dfrac{3360}{24{,}024} \doteq 0.14$.

**(b)** The sample space consists of all 3-combinations of the 14 members, so $n(S) = C(14, 3) = \dfrac{14 \cdot 13 \cdot 12}{3 \cdot 2 \cdot 1} = 364$. Similarly, there are $n(E) = C(6, 3) = \dfrac{6 \cdot 5 \cdot 4}{3 \cdot 2 \cdot 1} = 20$ ways to choose three of the six boys for the committee. Therefore, the probability is $\dfrac{20}{364} \doteq 0.055$.

**(c)** There are $n(S) = C(14, 4) = \dfrac{14 \cdot 13 \cdot 12 \cdot 11}{4 \cdot 3 \cdot 2 \cdot 1} = 1001$ ways to select 4 of the 14 squad members to be on the committee. Since there are $C(6, 2) = \dfrac{6 \cdot 5}{2 \cdot 1} = 15$ ways to choose 2 of the 6 boys and $C(8, 2) = \dfrac{8 \cdot 7}{2 \cdot 1} = 28$ ways to choose 2 of the 8 girls, there are $15 \cdot 28 = 420$ committee choices with 2 boys and 2 girls. Therefore, the probability that two boys and two girls are on the randomly selected committee is $\dfrac{420}{1001} \doteq 0.42$.

**(d)** There are $n(S) = C(14, 5) = \dfrac{14 \cdot 13 \cdot 12 \cdot 11 \cdot 10}{5 \cdot 4 \cdot 3 \cdot 2 \cdot 1} = 2002$ ways to select a five-member committee. Of these ways, $C(6, 5) = 6$ committees have all boys. Since there are 8 ways to select one girl and $C(6, 4) = C(6, 2) = \dfrac{6 \cdot 5}{2 \cdot 1} = 15$ ways to select 4 of the 6 boys, there are also $8 \cdot 15 = 120$ committees with 1 girl and 4 boys. Altogether, there are $6 + 120 = 126$ committees with at most one girl, so the probability that this occurs with a random choice of the committee is $\dfrac{126}{2002} \doteq 0.06$.

## Complementary Events

Suppose a card is drawn from a deck and $A$ is the event "draw a face card." Then the set of outcomes *not* in $A$ is called the *complementary event*, denoted by $\overline{A}$. Since there are 12 face cards in the 52-card deck, we have

$$n(A) = 12, \qquad n(\overline{A}) = 40, \qquad P(A) = \frac{12}{52}, \qquad \text{and} \qquad P(\overline{A}) = \frac{40}{52}.$$

More generally, if $A$ and $\overline{A}$ are events such that $A \cup \overline{A} = S$ and $A \cap \overline{A} = \varnothing$, then $A$ and $\overline{A}$ are called **complementary events.** Moreover, $n(A) + n(\overline{A}) = n(S)$, and this equation implies that

$$P(A) + P(\overline{A}) = 1.$$

$$\frac{n(A)}{n(S)} + \frac{n(\overline{A})}{n(S)} = \frac{n(S)}{n(S)}$$
$$P(A) + P(\overline{A}) = 1$$

Alternatively,

$$P(A) = 1 - P(\overline{A}).$$

In ordinary language, suppose obtaining $A$ is considered success. Then obtaining $\overline{A}$ is failure, and we have

$$P(\text{success}) = 1 - P(\text{failure}).$$

> **THEOREM** *Probability of Complementary Events*
>
> Let $A$ and $\overline{A}$ be complementary events; that is, $A \cup \overline{A} = S$ and $A \cap \overline{A} = \varnothing$. Then,
>
> $$P(A) = 1 - P(\overline{A}).$$
>
> Equivalently, the probability of success in an experiment is 1 minus the probability of failure.

The preceding theorem is often useful, as the next example shows.

## EXAMPLE 14.31  Using Complementary Probability

Compute the probability of obtaining a score of at least 4 on a single roll of two dice.

**Solution**  Here, success is obtaining a 4 or a 5 or a 6 or . . . or a 12. The probability of doing this is the sum of all the individual probabilities, and determining these requires considerable computation. However, failure occurs if we obtain a sum of either 2 or 3, and the probability of doing this is much easier to compute. Since $S$ contains 36 equally likely outcomes and we fail by rolling two 1s, a 1 and a 2, or a 2 and a 1, the probability of failure is $\frac{3}{36} = \frac{1}{12}$. Thus, the desired probability is $1 - \frac{1}{12} = \frac{11}{12}$.

## EXAMPLE 14.32  Combining Concepts: Combinations, Mutually Exclusive Events, and Complementary Events

A hand of 5 cards is drawn from a standard 52-card deck. What is the probability that both colors—red and black—are represented in the hand? The cards are red if they are hearts or diamonds and are black if they are clubs or spades.

**Solution**  Let $E$ be the event of all 5-card hands containing at least 1 red and 1 black card. The complementary event is, then, $\overline{E} = R \cup B$, where $R$ is the event of all hands with 5 red cards and $B$ is the event of all hands with 5 black cards. Since $R$ and $B$ are mutually exclusive events, $P(\overline{E}) = P(R \cup B) = P(R) + P(B)$. There are $\binom{26}{5}$ combinations of 5 cards taken from the set of 26 red cards. Also, there are $\binom{52}{5}$ 5-card hands altogether. Together, they give the probability

$$P(R) = \frac{\binom{26}{5}}{\binom{52}{5}} = \frac{26 \cdot 25 \cdot 24 \cdot 23 \cdot 22}{52 \cdot 51 \cdot 50 \cdot 49 \cdot 48}.$$ Since there are also 26 black cards, it follows that $P(B) = P(R)$

and $P(\overline{E}) = 2 \cdot \frac{26 \cdot 25 \cdot 24 \cdot 23 \cdot 22}{52 \cdot 51 \cdot 50 \cdot 49 \cdot 48} = 0.05. \ . \ . \ .$ Thus, $P(E) = 1 - P(\overline{E}) \doteq 1 - 0.05 = 0.95.$

That is, there is about a 95% probability that a hand of 5 cards contains both colors.

## Properties of Probability

The preceding examples revealed a number of important properties of probability, which can be collected in the following theorem:

> **THEOREM**  *Properties of Probability\**
> 1. $P(A) = 0$ if, and only if, $A$ cannot occur.
> 2. $P(A) = 1$ if, and only if, $A$ always occurs.
> 3. For any event $A$, $0 \leq P(A) \leq 1$.

*(continues)*

---

\*It is worth remembering that, in discussing probability in this chapter, we are limiting our discussions to situations where the sample space is finite. The infinite case can be successfully treated, and all the properties remain true except for properties 1 and 2. In the infinite case, it is possible that $P(A) = 0$ and yet event $A$ can still occur. Similarly, it is possible that $P(A) = 1$ and yet event $A$ never occurs. These anomalies, however, need not concern us here.

4. For any events $A$ and $B$,

$$P(A \text{ or } B) = P(A) + P(B) - P(A \text{ and } B).$$

5. If $A$ and $B$ are mutually exclusive events, then

$$P(A \text{ or } B) = P(A) + P(B).$$

6. For any events $A$ and $B$,

$$P(A \text{ and } B) = P(A)P(B \mid A).$$

7. If $A$ and $B$ are independent events, then

$$P(A \text{ and } B) = P(A)P(B).$$

8. If $E$ and $\overline{E}$ are complementary events, then $P(E) + P(\overline{E}) = 1$.

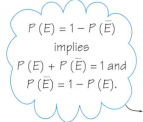

$P(E) = 1 - P(\overline{E})$
implies
$P(E) + P(\overline{E}) = 1$ and
$P(\overline{E}) = 1 - P(E)$.

---

**PROOF**

Let $S$ be the sample space.

1. Event $A$ cannot occur if, and only if, $n(A) = 0$. Therefore, $P(A) = \dfrac{n(A)}{n(S)} = 0$ if, and only if, $A$ cannot occur.

2. $A$ always occurs if, and only if, $n(A) = n(S)$. Therefore, $P(A) = \dfrac{n(A)}{n(S)} = \dfrac{n(S)}{n(S)} = 1$ if, and only if, $A$ always occurs.

3. An event $A$ never occurs, sometimes occurs, or always occurs. Therefore, $0 \leq n(A) \leq n(S)$, and, dividing by $n(S)$, we obtain

$$0 \leq P(A) \leq 1.$$

4–7. These are general results from earlier representative examples.

8. Since $E \cup \overline{E} = S$ and $E \cap \overline{E} = \varnothing$, it follows that $n(S) = n(E) + n(\overline{E})$ and hence that $1 = P(E) + P(\overline{E})$.

Divide
through
by $n(S)$.

---

The next example uses several of the properties of probability to reexamine the Strings and Loops Hands On activity that opened the chapter. This time, our point of view is theoretical, rather than experimental, probability.

**EXAMPLE 14.33  Determining the Theoretical Probabilities of the Strings and Loops Activity**

Six pieces of string of equal length are held in a bundle in one person's hand. A second person ties three knots at each end of the bundle of strings, where each knot joins a randomly selected pair of strings. After the six knots are tied, the bundle is examined to see what pattern of loops has been formed. There are three possibilities:

$T$: three small two-string loops
$M$: one medium four-string loop and one small two-string loop
$L$: one large six-string loop

What are the probabilities (**a**) $P(T)$, (**b**) $P(L)$, and (**c**) $P(M)$ of these events?

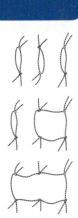

**Solution**

We might as well suppose that the first three knots are tied on the same end of the bundle, so that we begin with the pattern

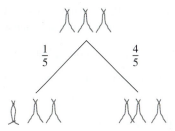

We now consider the compound event in which the next three knots are tied, drawing the probability tree as we proceed.

### The Fourth Knot

There are $C(6, 2) = 6 \cdot 5/2 = 15$ ways to choose a pair of loose ends to tie, including 3 pairs that form a small two-string loop. Thus, the probability of forming a small loop with the fourth knot is $\frac{3}{15} = \frac{1}{5}$. (Another way to see this is to grab any loose end and see that there are five other loose ends, with just one of the five forming a small loop.) By complementary probabilities, the probability that no loop is created is $\frac{4}{5}$. We now see that our probability tree begins this way:

### The Fifth Knot

After the fourth knot is tied, there are four loose ends remaining. The next pair to be tied can be selected in $C(4, 2) = 6$ ways. If the left branch of the preceding tree is followed, two of these pairs create a small two-string loop, so there is a probability of $\frac{2}{6} = \frac{1}{3}$ that the fifth knot creates a second small loop. By complementary probability, there is a probability of $\frac{2}{3}$ that no loop is formed. Following the right branch of the tree, we see that there is one pair of loose ends that makes a small two-string loop and one pair that makes a medium four-string loop; evidently, the other four pairs do not make a loop. The respective probabilities to complete the next part of the probability tree are therefore $\frac{1}{6}, \frac{1}{6}$, and $\frac{4}{6} = \frac{2}{3}$. We can now extend the probability tree to account for the fifth knot:

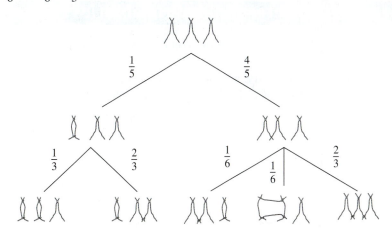

**The Sixth Knot**

Since only one pair of loose ends remains, the outcome has already been determined once five knots are tied. Thus, we have the following results:

$$\frac{1}{5} \cdot \frac{1}{3} = \frac{1}{15} \qquad \frac{1}{5} \cdot \frac{2}{3} = \frac{2}{15} \qquad \frac{4}{5} \cdot \frac{1}{6} = \frac{2}{15} \qquad \frac{4}{5} \cdot \frac{1}{6} = \frac{2}{15} \qquad \frac{4}{5} \cdot \frac{2}{3} = \frac{8}{15}$$

We see that $P(T) = \dfrac{1}{15}$, $P(M) = \dfrac{2}{15} + \dfrac{2}{15} + \dfrac{2}{15} = \dfrac{6}{15}$, and $P(L) = \dfrac{8}{15}$. Most people are surprised to learn that obtaining three small loops is quite rare and that a single large loop occurs a little more than half the time.

## Odds

When someone speaks of the **odds** in favor of an event $E$, they are comparing the likelihood that the event will happen with the likelihood that it will not happen. Consider an urn containing 4 blue balls and 1 yellow ball. If a ball is chosen at random, what are the odds that the ball is blue? Since a blue ball is 4 times as likely to be selected as a yellow ball, it is typical to say that the odds are 4 to 1. The odds are actually the ratio $\dfrac{4}{1}$, but when quoting odds, one usually writes $4 : 1$, which is read "four to one." The latter formulation is the basis for the following definition:

> **DEFINITION** *Odds*
>
> Let $A$ be an event and let $\overline{A}$ be the complementary event. Then the **odds in favor** of $A$ are $n(A)$ to $n(\overline{A})$, and the **odds against** $A$ are $n(\overline{A})$ to $n(A)$.

**EXAMPLE 14.34** **Determining the Odds in Favor of Rolling a 7 or an 11**

In the game of craps, one wins on the first roll of the pair of dice if a 7 or an 11 is thrown. What are the odds of winning on the first roll?

**Solution** Let $W$ be the set of outcomes that result in 7 or 11. Since $W = \{(1, 6), (2, 5), (3, 4), (4, 3), (5, 2), (6, 1),$ $(5, 6), (6, 5)\}$ and there are 36 ways two dice can come up, $n(W) = 8$, and $n(\overline{W}) = 36 - 8 = 28$. Thus, the odds in favor of $W$ are 8 to 28 or, more simply, 2 to 7.

$$\frac{8}{28} = \frac{2}{7}$$

**EXAMPLE 14.35** **Determining Probabilities from Odds**

If the odds in favor of event $E$ are 5 to 4, compute $P(E)$ and $P(\overline{E})$.

**Solution** Since $E$ and $\overline{E}$ are complementary, $n(S) = n(E) + n(\overline{E})$. Also, since the odds in favor of $E$ are 5 to 4, $n(E) = 5k$ and $n(\overline{E}) = 4k$ for some integer $k$. Therefore,

$$P(E) = \frac{n(E)}{n(S)} = \frac{n(E)}{n(E) + n(\overline{E})} = \frac{5k}{5k + 4k} = \frac{5}{9}$$

and

$$P(\overline{E}) = \frac{n(\overline{E})}{n(S)} = \frac{n(\overline{E})}{n(E) + n(\overline{E})} = \frac{4k}{5k + 4k} = \frac{4}{9}.$$

In lowest terms, $\dfrac{n(E)}{n(\overline{E})}$ is $\dfrac{5}{4}$.

$A \cup \overline{A} = S$
$A \cap \overline{A} = \varnothing$

**EXAMPLE 14.36** **Odds from Probabilities**

Given $P(E)$, determine the odds in favor of $E$ and the odds against $E$.

**Solution**

The odds in favor of $E$ are

$$\frac{n(E)}{n(\bar{E})} = \frac{n(E)/n(S)}{n(\bar{E})/n(S)}$$

$$= \frac{P(E)}{P(\bar{E})} \qquad \left( P(\bar{E}) = 1 - P(E) \right)$$

$$= \frac{P(E)}{1 - P(E)}.$$

This last ratio would be expressed as a ratio of integers $\frac{a}{b}$ in lowest terms, and the odds quoted would be stated as $a$ to $b$.

The odds against $E$ are given by the reciprocal of the ratio giving the odds in favor of $E$. Thus, the odds against $E$ are

$$\frac{1 - P(E)}{P(E)} = \frac{b}{a} \qquad \left( = \frac{P(\bar{E})}{P(E)} \right)$$

and are quoted as $b$ to $a$.

## Expected Value

At a carnival, for a \$4 fee you are offered the chance to play a game that consists of rolling a single die just once. If you play, you win the amount in dollars shown on the die. If you play the game several times, how much would you expect to win? Of course, you may be lucky and win \$6 on each of a series of rolls. However, because of the law of large numbers, you would *expect* to roll a 6 only about $\frac{1}{6}$ of the time. Since this is so for each of the numbers on the die, you should expect to win, on average, approximately

$$\frac{1}{6} \cdot 1 + \frac{1}{6} \cdot 2 + \frac{1}{6} \cdot 3 + \frac{1}{6} \cdot 4 + \frac{1}{6} \cdot 5 + \frac{1}{6} \cdot 6$$

$$= \frac{1}{6} \cdot (1 + 2 + 3 + 4 + 5 + 6)$$

$$= \frac{1}{6} \cdot 21 = \$3.50$$

per roll. But since it costs you \$4 to play the game, the carnival confidently expects players to *lose* 50¢ per game, on average. Thus, the carnival stands to make a handsome profit if a large number of patrons play the game each night.

The preceding discussion introduces the notion of **expected value.**

**DEFINITION** *Expected Value of an Experiment*

Let the outcomes of an experiment be a sequence of real numbers (values) $v_1, v_2, \ldots, v_n$, and suppose the outcomes occur with respective probabilities $p_1, p_2, \ldots, p_n$. Then the **expected value** of the experiment is

$$e = v_1 p_1 + v_2 p_2 + \cdots + v_n p_n.$$

## EXAMPLE 14.37 Winning at Roulette

An American roulette wheel has 38 compartments around its rim. Two of these are colored green and are numbered 0 and 00. The remaining compartments are numbered from 1 to 36 and are alternately colored black and red. When the wheel is spun in one direction, a small ivory ball is rolled in the opposite direction around the rim. When the wheel and the ball slow down, the ball eventually falls into any one of the compartments with equal likelihood if the wheel is fair. One way to play is to bet on whether the ball will fall into a red slot or a black slot. If, for example, you bet on red, you win the amount of the bet if the ball lands in a red slot; otherwise, you lose. What is the expected win if you consistently bet $5 on red?

**Solution**  Since the probability of winning on any given try is $\frac{18}{38}$ and the probability of losing is $\frac{20}{38}$, your expected win is

$$\frac{18}{38} \cdot 5 + \frac{20}{38} \cdot (-5) = \frac{90 - 100}{38}$$
$$\doteq -0.26.$$

On average, you should expect to lose 26¢ per play. Is it any wonder that casinos consistently make a handsome profit?

In the preceding example, it was pretty clear that you should expect to lose slightly more often than win. This next example is less clear.

## EXAMPLE 14.38 Determining the Expected Value of an Unusual Game

Suppose you are offered the opportunity to play a game that consists of a single toss of three coins. It costs you $21 to play the game, and you win $100 if you toss three heads, $20 if you toss two heads and a tail, and nothing if you toss more than one tail. Would you play the game?

**Solution**  Many people would play the game hoping to "get lucky" and roll HHH frequently. But is this reasonable? What is your expected return? The expected value of the game is

$$\frac{1}{8} \cdot 100 + \frac{3}{8} \cdot 20 + \frac{3}{8} \cdot 0 + \frac{1}{8} \cdot 0 = \frac{160}{8} = \$20.$$

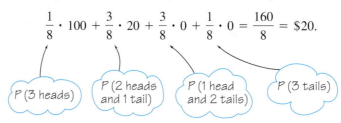

Thus, on average, you should expect to win $1 less than it costs you to play the game each time. Unless the excitement is worth at least $1, you should not play the game.

## Geometric Probability

In Section 14.1, we considered the experimental probability of a spinner marked like that in Figure 14.8 stopping at any particular place. Here, $P_e(A)$, $P_e(B)$, and $P_e(C)$ all turn out to be approximately equal to $\frac{1}{3} = 0.\overline{3}$. This is not surprising, since the three arcs bordering regions A, B, and C are equally long. More generally, we would define the theoretical **geometric probability** of a region on the spinner to be the ratio of the region's corresponding arc length to the circumference of the circle. Equivalently, the probability of stopping a spinner on a sector is the ratio of the measure of the central angle of the sector to 360°.

**FIGURE 14.8**
A spinner with equally
likely outcomes

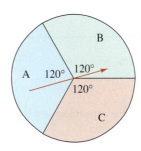

Similarly, consider the diagram of Figure 14.9. The probability that a point chosen at random in the square (say, by using a sequence of random numbers) will belong to region A should be $\frac{1}{4}$, since one-fourth of the *area* of the region lies in A.

**FIGURE 14.9**
Geometric probability as a
ratio of areas

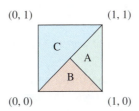

**EXAMPLE 14.39  Determining the Geometric Probability of a Carnival Game**

At a carnival, a "double your money" game is played by tossing a quarter onto a large table that has been ruled into a grid of squares of the same size. If your quarter lands entirely within any square, you win back two quarters, but if the coin overlaps a grid line, you lose the quarter you tossed. If a quarter is 2.5 centimeters in diameter and the squares have sides 6 centimeters long, should you play the game?

**Solution**

The sample space $S$ can be considered as the points in a 6–by–6-centimeter square. To win, the center of the quarter must land at least 1.25 centimeters from each side of the large square. That is, the winning region $W$ is a 3.5-centimeter square centered in the larger square, as shown in the diagram at the right. The probability of a win is

$$P(W) = \frac{\text{area of small square}}{\text{area of large square}} = \frac{3.5^2}{6^2} = \frac{12.25}{36} = \frac{49}{144} \doteq 0.34.$$

3.5 cm

6.0 cm

We can now compute the expected value of the game, remembering that a win gives us a net gain of $0.25 (we must subtract the cost of playing from the $0.50 won) and a loss is −$0.25.

$$\text{expected value} = \frac{49}{144} \cdot \$0.25 + \frac{95}{144} \cdot (-\$0.25) \doteq -\$0.08.$$

We expect to lose, and the operator to win, about 8¢ per play.

## Problem Set 14.4

Exercises numbered in red are answered in the back of the text.

### Understanding Concepts

1. **(a)** List explicitly all the outcomes for the experiment of tossing a penny, a nickel, a dime, and a quarter.

   **(b)** Determine the probability $P$(HHTT) of obtaining a head on each of the penny and nickel and a tail on each of the dime and quarter in the experiment of part (a).

   **(c)** Determine the probability of obtaining two heads and two tails in the experiment of part (a).

   **(d)** Determine the probability of obtaining at least one head in the experiment of part (a). (*Hint:* Note that the complementary event consists of obtaining four tails.)

2. Determine the probability of obtaining a total score of 3 or 4 on a single throw of two dice.

3. A family has two children, including at least one boy. What is the probability that the other child is a girl? (*Note:* The answer is *not* one-half.)

4. Acme Auto Rental has three red Fords, four white Fords, and two black Fords. Acme also has six red Hondas, two white Hondas, and five black Hondas. If a car is selected at random for rental to a customer,

   **(a)** what is the probability that it is a white Ford?

   **(b)** what is the probability that it is a Ford?

   **(c)** what is the probability that it is white?

   **(d)** what is the probability that it is white given that the customer demands a Ford?

5. Five black balls numbered 1, 2, 3, 4, and 5 and seven white balls numbered 1, 2, 3, 4, 5, 6, and 7 are placed in an urn. If one is chosen at random,

   **(a)** what is the probability it is numbered 1 or 2?

   **(b)** what is the probability that it is numbered 5 or that it is white?

   **(c)** what is the probability that it is numbered 5 given that it is white?

6. Mrs. Ricco has seven brown-eyed and two blue-eyed brunettes in her fifth grade class. She also has eight blue-eyed and three brown-eyed blondes. A child is selected at random.

   **(a)** What is the probability that the child is a brown-eyed brunette?

   **(b)** What is the probability that the child has brown eyes or is a brunette?

   **(c)** What is the probability that the child has brown eyes given that he or she is a brunette?

7. Suppose that you randomly select a two-digit number (that is, one of 00, 01, 02, . . . , 99) from a sequence of random numbers obtained by repeatedly spinning a spinner. What is the probability that the number selected

   **(a)** is greater than 80?

   **(b)** is less than 10?

   **(c)** is a multiple of 3?

   **(d)** is even or is less than 50?

   **(e)** is even and is less than 50?

   **(f)** is even given that it is less than 50?

8. In a certain card game, you are dealt two cards face up. You then bet on whether a third card dealt is between the other two cards. (For example, a 10 is between a 9 and a queen, and so on.) What is the probability of winning your bet if you are dealt

   **(a)** a 5 and a 7?

   **(b)** a jack and a queen?

   **(c)** a pair of 9s?

   **(d)** a 5 and a queen?

9. In playing draw poker, a flush is a hand with five cards, all in one suit. You are dealt five cards and can throw away any of these and be dealt more cards to replace them. If you are dealt four hearts and a spade, what is the probability that you can discard the spade and be dealt a heart to fill out your flush?

10. A bag contains 3 white and 5 black balls. Two balls are drawn without replacement. Construct a probability tree to determine the following probabilities:

   **(a)** Both balls are white.

   **(b)** One ball of each color is drawn.

   **(c)** At least one white ball is drawn.

11. Two dice are "loaded" in such a way that both the 3 and the 4 appear with probability 0.3 and each of the other faces appears with probability 0.1. What is the probability of a 7 being rolled with these unfair dice?

12. A bent coin lands heads up with probability 0.7.

   **(a)** Construct a probability tree for three flips of the unfair coin.

   Now use the probability tree to determine these probabilities:

   **(b)** $P$(HHH)

   **(c)** $P$(two heads and a tail in any order)

   **(d)** $P$(at least one head appears in the three flips)

   **(e)** $P$(a head and a tail appear among the three flips)

13. Determine the probabilities $u$, $v$, $w$, $x$, $y$, and $z$ in the following probability tree:

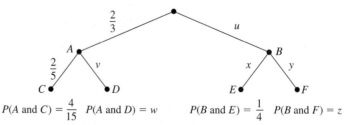

14. You are dealt three cards at random from an ordinary deck of playing cards. What is the probability that all three cards are hearts? (*Hint:* How many ways can you select three cards at random from the deck? How many ways can you select three cards at random from among the hearts?)

**15.** Consider a spinner marked and shaded as indicated here:

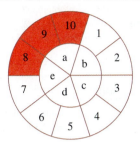

(a) What is the probability that the spinner lands on the shaded area?

(b) What is the probability that the spinner lands on region 1 or region 2?

(c) What is the probability that the spinner lands on region 10 or region 6?

(d) What is the probability that the spinner lands on region e?

(e) What is the probability that the spinner lands on region 8 given that it lands on the shaded area?

(f) What is the probability that the spinner lands on a region marked by a vowel given that it lands on an odd-numbered region?

(g) What is the probability that the spinner lands on a region marked by a vowel or an odd number?

**16.** A dartboard is marked as shown:

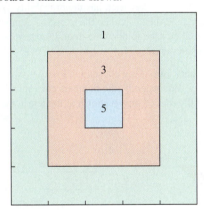

Josie is good enough that she always hits the dartboard with her darts, but, beyond that, the darts hit in random locations. If a single dart is thrown, compute these probabilities:

(a) $P(1)$

(b) $P(3)$

(c) $P(5)$

(d) If Josie wins the number of dollars indicated by the number of the region into which her dart falls, how much is her expected win (the expected value)?

(e) Suppose it costs Josie $2 each time she throws a dart. Should she play darts as in part (d)? Explain.

**17.** A dartboard is marked like the spinner in problem 15. The radius of the inner circle is 1, and that of the outer circle is 2. What is the probability that a dart hitting the board at random

(a) hits in region b?

(b) misses region b given that it hits the inner circle?

(c) hits in region b given that it hits in a, b, or c?

(d) hits in region 1 given that it hits in a, 1, or 2?

**18.** Two dice are thrown.

(a) What are the odds in favor of getting a score of 6?

(b) What are the odds against getting a 6?

(c) What is the probability of getting a 6?

**19.** If $P(A) = \dfrac{2}{5}$, compute the odds in favor of $A$ resulting from a single trial of an experiment.

**20.** If $P(A) = \dfrac{1}{2}, P(B) = \dfrac{1}{3}, P(C) = \dfrac{1}{6}$, and $A, B,$ and $C$ are mutually exclusive, compute the odds in favor of $A$ or $C$ resulting from a single trial of an experiment.

$$A \cup B \cup C = S$$
$$A \cap B = \varnothing$$
$$A \cap C = \varnothing$$
$$B \cap C = \varnothing$$

**21.** Compute the expected value of the score obtained by rolling two dice.

**22.** A game consists of rolling a pair of dice. You win the amounts shown for rolling the score shown in the following table:

| Roll | 2 | 3 | 4 | 5 | 6 | 7 | 8 | 9 | 10 | 11 | 12 |
|---|---|---|---|---|---|---|---|---|---|---|---|
| $ Won | 4 | 6 | 8 | 10 | 20 | 40 | 20 | 10 | 8 | 6 | 4 |

Compute the expected value of the game.

## Teaching Concepts

Students are often interested in first performing an experiment to calculate an experimental probability and then comparing the result obtained with the theoretical probability of the event. For the experiment outlined in each of the problems which follow, create a lesson plan that describes the materials needed and how to carry out the experiment, either as a class or with small groups. Be sure to give a careful derivation of the mathematical probabilities.

**23.** Ten note cards are numbered 1 through 10 and placed in a sack. In succession without replacement, two students each draw a card from the sack. Which, if either, of the following is the more likely outcome: The sum of the numbers on the cards is even or the sum is odd?

**24.** On a two-student team, one student puts either a black or a white marble into a sack without the second student looking. The second student puts a white marble in the sack, shakes the sack, and then draws out one marble. Is the preceding information helpful in guessing the color of the marble initially placed in the sack? (This is a problem proposed by Lewis Carroll of *Alice in Wonderland* fame in his book *Pillow Problems*.)

**25.** In a two-player game, player A rolls two ordinary dice, with the faces of each die marked 1 through 6. Player B, however, uses number cubes, with the faces of a red cube marked 1, 3, 4, 5, 6, 8 and the faces of a green cube marked 1, 2, 2, 3, 3, 4. If the player rolling the higher total wins, would you prefer to be player A or player B, or does it matter?

## Responding to Students

**26.** A fifth grader tells you she is certain it will rain sometime over the weekend. It seems that she heard on the weather forecast that there is a 50% chance of rain both Saturday and Sunday, and, of course, 50% + 50% = 100%, a certainty. Write an imagined dialogue with the student to convince her that it may not rain after all.

**27.** José reads the following problem in his math homework: "Bill and Susan are playing a game with a pair of 1–6 number cubes. They decide that Bill will earn a point if he rolls a multiple of 4 and Susan will earn a point if she rolls an odd number. Are these rules fair or unfair?" After some thought, José answers: fair, because Susan probably won't roll an odd number.

**(a)** Is José's answer correct?

**(b)** How would you help correct José's misconceptions of the rules?

**28.** Mischa and Jorge are playing a game with three sticks as shown here:

The sticks are put into a paper sack, and then one is drawn halfway out. Jorge sees that the stick has a red spot, so he knows that it is not the stick with two black spots. Since two sticks have a red spot, he claims that the probability that the hidden spot on the stick is black is $\frac{1}{2}$. Mischa doesn't think Jorge is right. Respond to Jorge and Mischa.

## Thinking Critically

**29.** Two balls are drawn at random from an urn containing six white and eight red balls.

**(a)** Use combinations to compute the probability that both balls are white. Recall that

$$C(n, r) = \frac{n(n - 1)(n - 2) \cdots (n - r + 1)}{r!}.$$

**(b)** Compute the probability that both balls are red.

**30.** An urn contains eight red, five white, and six green balls. Four balls are drawn at random.

**(a)** Compute $P$(all four are red).

**(b)** Compute $P$(exactly two are red and exactly two are green).

**(c)** Compute $P$(exactly two are red or exactly two are green).

**31.** Consider the set of all five-letter code words without repetition of letters. Recall that

$$P(n, r) = n(n - 1)(n - 2) \cdots (n - r + 1).$$

**(a)** What is the probability that a code word begins with the letter $a$?

**(b)** What is the probability that, in a code word, $c$ is immediately followed by $d$?

**(c)** What is the probability that a code word starts with a vowel and ends with a consonant?

**(d)** In how many of the original set of five-letter code words are $c$ and $d$ adjacent?

**32.** Six dice are rolled. What is the probability that all six numbers—1, 2, 3, 4, 5, and 6—are obtained? (*Hint:* This can happen in more than one way. For example, 1, 2, 3, 4, 5, 6, and 6, 5, 1, 2, 3, 4 are just two of the possibilities.)

**33.** What is the probability that the six volumes of Churchill's *Second World War* appear in the correct order if they are randomly placed on a shelf?

**34.** What is the probability that a randomly dealt five-card hand from an ordinary deck of playing cards will contain

**(a)** exactly two aces?

**(b)** at least two aces?

**35.** If seven dice are tossed, what is the probability that every number will appear? (*Hint:* In how many ways can the number that appears twice be chosen?)

**36.** Rudy has 9 loose keys in his pocket, all nearly alike, but only one will open his door. He randomly chooses a key and tries it, but if it is an incorrect key, he randomly draws another key, not replacing any of the keys already tried.

**(a)** Let $p_1, p_2, \ldots, p_9$ be the probabilities that the 1st, 2nd, . . . , 9th key that Rudy tries is the correct one. Show that the 9 probabilities are all the same.

**(b)** What is the expected number of keys Rudy will need to open the door?

**(c)** Generalize parts (a) and (b) by assuming that Rudy has $n$ keys in his pocket, with just one being the correct key. Show that each key tried has the probability $1/n$ of being correct, and then calculate the expected number of keys that will be tried to open the door. [*Suggestion:* Look for triangular numbers!]

**37.** Two numbers $x$ and $y$ are chosen randomly between 0 and 1, with $x < y$. Equivalently, the numbers correspond to a point $P(x, y)$ in the shaded region shown at the left in the following diagram:

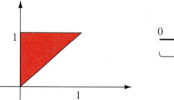 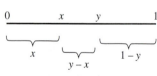

Points $x$ and $y$ divide the unit segment into three segments of length $x$, $y - x$, and $1 - y$. Carry out the following steps to determine the probability that the three segments form a triangle:

**(a)** Use the triangle inequalities (for example, $x < (y - x) + (1 - y)$, to show that a triangle can be formed if, and only if, $P$ is to the left of the vertical line $x = \frac{1}{2}$, above the horizontal line $y = \frac{1}{2}$, and below the 45° slanted line with equation $y = x + \frac{1}{2}$.

**(b)** Graph the region described in part (a) to show that it is a triangle of area $\frac{1}{8}$.

(c) Use parts (a) and (b) to show by geometric probability that the probability that the points $x$ and $y$ in the unit interval form segments from a triangle is $\frac{1}{4}$.

## Thinking Cooperatively

**38.** Modify the Strings and Loops experiment described in Example 14.33 by using eight lengths of string instead of six.

   **(a)** How many patterns of loops can be formed by tying eight knots, four at each end, of the eight-string bundle?

   **(b)** Perform the experiment and combine the data from the class. Use the data to estimate the experimental probabilities that four small loops are formed and one large loop is formed.

   **(c)** Determine the theoretical probability of obtaining four small loops. It may be helpful to construct a probability tree.

   **(d)** Determine the theoretical probability of obtaining one large loop.

**39.** On a TV game show, there are three doors. Behind one door is a valuable prize, but the other doors hide trivial prizes. The contestant is asked to pick one of three doors, but before the door is opened, one of the other doors is opened to reveal a trivial prize. The contestant can then either stay with the door initially chosen or switch to the other unopened door. In small groups, discuss which strategy, "switch" or "don't switch," offers the best probability of winning.

## Using a Calculator

**40.** There are $7 \times 7 = 7^2$ ways in which two people's birthdays can fall on the days of the week. They will have birthdays on different days in $7 \cdot 6$ ways, so the probability that two people have birthdays on different days of the week is $P(W_2) = \dfrac{7 \cdot 6}{7 \cdot 7} = \dfrac{6}{7}$. By complementary probabilities, the probability that two people were born on the same day of the week is (not surprisingly) $P(\overline{W}_2) = 1 - P(W_2) = 1 - \dfrac{6}{7} = \dfrac{1}{7}$.

   **(a)** Find the probability $P(W_3)$ that three people's birthdays are on different days. Then find the probability $P(\overline{W}_3)$ that, in a group of three people, at least two share a birthday on the same day of the week.

   **(b)** Find the probabilities requested in part (a), but for four people.

## Making Connections

**41.** In one unfortunate shipment, 10% of the MP3 players manufactured by Imperfect Electronics had defective switches, 5% had defective batteries, and 2% had both defects. If you purchased an MP3 player from this shipment, what is the probability that your player

   **(a)** has a defective switch or a defective battery?

   **(b)** has a good switch but a defective battery?

   **(c)** has both a good switch and a good battery?

**42.** California originally operated a 6/49 lottery, meaning that the grand prize went to a player (or players) who picked the same six numbers that were later drawn at random from the set of numbers 1 through 49. In 1990, California went to a 6/53 lottery, but later the state went to a 6/51 lottery.

   **(a)** Find the probability of winning a 6/49 lottery.

   **(b)** Find the probability of winning a 6/53 lottery.

   **(c)** Find the probability of winning a 6/51 lottery.

   **(d)** Why do you think California changed to a 6/53 lottery?

   **(e)** Why do you think the state went to a 6/51 lottery?

**43.** In the casino game Keno, the player purchases a ticket and marks eight of the "spots" numbered 1 through 80. Every 20 minutes or so, the casino randomly draws 20 balls from a drum of 80 numbered balls. If sufficiently many of the player's spots are among the 20 numbers, the player wins. Usually the player must have five winning spots to receive a prize, and a larger prize is awarded if six, seven, or all eight winning spots are marked.

   **(a)** What is the probability of marking exactly five winning spots?

   **(b)** What is the probability of marking exactly six winning spots?

   **(c)** What is the probability of marking exactly seven winning spots?

   **(d)** What is the probability of marking exactly eight winning spots?

## From State Student Assessments

**44.** (Washington State, Grade 4)
Special cakes are baked for May Day in France. A small toy is dropped into the batter for each cake before baking. Whoever gets the piece of cake with the toy in it is "king" or "queen" for the day.

Which cake below would give you the best chance of finding the toy in your piece?

**A.**   **B.**

**C.**   **D.**

**45.** (Illinois, Grade 5)
A supply box has only three markers left: blue, purple, and green. If, without looking, two markers are pulled together, how likely is it that they will be blue and green?

   ○ 2/5   ○ 2/2   ○ 3/5   ○ 1/2   ○ 1/3

**46.** (Kentucky, Grade 8)
Tasha and Kelly are watching television, each in her own home. Tasha can get five cable channels—A, B, C, D, E—but Kelly can get only four—A, B, F, G.

   **(a)** List all possible combinations of channels that can be watched by the two girls.

   **(b)** What is the theoretical probability that Tasha and Kelly are watching the same channel? Explain your reasoning.

   **(c)** What is the theoretical probability that they are watching different channels? Explain your reasoning.

**47.** (Texas, Grade 8)

Fiona has a bag containing six red, eight blue, five green, nine yellow, and two white marbles that are all the same size and shape. What is the probability of randomly choosing a white marble on the first pick, replacing it, and then randomly choosing a green marble on the second pick?

**A.** $\dfrac{1}{6}$   **B.** $\dfrac{1}{15}$   **C.** $\dfrac{1}{87}$   **D.** $\dfrac{1}{90}$

**48.** (Washington, Grade 8)

Darin played a game with two spinners. The game is played by spinning each spinner and then adding the two resulting numbers. The goal is to spin two numbers that add up to eleven.

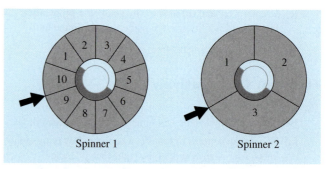

Spinner 1     Spinner 2

What is the probability that Darin will spin two numbers that add up to eleven?

**A.** $\dfrac{1}{3}$   **B.** $\dfrac{1}{10}$   **C.** $\dfrac{3}{5}$   **D.** $\dfrac{3}{10}$

## The Chapter in Relation to Future Teachers

This chapter has explored both experimental and theoretical probability. In the lower elementary grades, simple experiments can be performed, with the collected data displayed and analyzed with the strategies of the previous chapter. At the same time, it will be appropriate to introduce some of the terms—*outcome, event, probability*—associated with quantifying the likelihood of a future experiment. These earlier concrete experiences are essential for the continued progress of students in the upper elementary and middle school grades, where counting techniques become increasingly important in the determination of theoretical probabilities.

## Chapter 14 Summary

| Section 14.1  Experimental Probability | Page Reference |
|---|---|
| **CONCEPTS** | |
| • **Probability:** The branch of mathematics that quantifies the likelihood of events. | 768 |
| • **Experimental probability:** An estimation of probability obtained by conducting repeated trials or by tabulating historical data. | 768 |
| • **Theoretical probability:** A determination of probability made by assuming the probability of each outcome. | 768 |
| • **Simulation:** A method of determining answers to real problems by conducting experiments with outcomes analogous to those of the real problems. | 775 |
| **DEFINITIONS** | |
| • An **outcome** is the result of a single trial of an experiment. | 772 |
| • **Experimental probability, $P_e(E)$,** is the fraction of the number of times an event occurs over a large number of trials. | 769 |
| • The **sample space, $S$,** is the set of all possible outcomes of an experiment. | 772 |
| • An **event, $E$,** is a subset of the sample space. | 772 |
| • A **mutually exclusive event** is an event in which events $A$ and $B$ are disjoint subsets of the sample space. That is, $A \cap B = \varnothing$. | 772 |

| | |
|---|---|
| • A **compound event** is an event consisting of a combination of two or more events. | 774 |
| • **Independent events** are events in which the outcome of one event does not affect the probability of the outcome of the other event. | 774 |

**PROPERTIES**
| | |
|---|---|
| • **Experimental probability of mutually exclusive events:** If $A \cap B = \varnothing$, then $P_e(A \cup B) = P_e(A) + P_e(B)$. | 773 |
| • **Experimental probability of non-mutually exclusive events:** For any two events, $P_e(A \cup B) = P_e(A) + P_e(B) - P_e(A \cap B)$. | 774 |
| • **Experimental probability of independent events:** $P_e(A \text{ and } B) = P_e(A \cap B) \approx P_e(A) \cdot P_e(B)$ | 775 |

**THEOREM**
| | |
|---|---|
| • **Law of large numbers:** The experimental probability of an event approximates a fixed number more and more closely as the number of trials increases. | 769 |

| **Section 14.2   Principles of Counting** | **Page Reference** |
|---|---|

**NOTATIONS**
| | |
|---|---|
| • $n(E)$: the number of ways event $E$ can happen | 780 |
| • $n(B \mid A)$: the number of ways $B$ can occur given that $A$ has already occurred. | 783 |

**CONCEPTS**
| | |
|---|---|
| • **Addition principle of counting:** For any events $A$ and $B$, $n(A \text{ or } B) = n(A) + n(B) - n(A \text{ and } B)$. If $A \cap B = \varnothing$, then $n(A \text{ or } B) = n(A) + n(B)$. | 780, 781 |
| • **Possibility tree:** A visualization of an experiment in which each outcome corresponds to a branch of a tree. Alternatively, each branch is labeled with the number of ways an outcome can occur. | 783 |
| • **Multiplication principle of counting:** For any events $A$ and $B$, $n(A \text{ and } B) = n(A) \cdot n(B \mid A)$. For independent events $A$ and $B$, $n(A \text{ and } B) = n(A) \cdot n(B)$. | 783, 784 |
| • **Complementary event:** $\overline{E}$ is the set of outcomes for which event $E$ does not occur. Thus, $n(E) = n(S) - n(\overline{E})$. | 786 |

**DEFINITIONS**
| | |
|---|---|
| • The word **"or,"** $\cup$, is used to indicate the union of sets. | 780 |
| • The word **"and,"** $\cap$, is used to indicate the intersection of sets. | 783 |
| • **Independent events** are events in which the outcome of one event does not affect the outcome of the other, $A$ and $B$ if $P(B \mid A) = P(B)$. Then $P(A \text{ and } B) = P(A) \cdot (B)$. | 784 |
| • A **complementary event,** $\overline{E}$, is the event counting the number of ways that event $E$ does not occur, so that $P(E) + P(\overline{E}) = 1$. | 786 |

| **Section 14.3   Permutations and Combinations** | **Page Reference** |
|---|---|

**CONCEPTS**
| | |
|---|---|
| • **Combination:** An unordered selection of objects that form a subset. | 791 |
| • **Permutation:** An ordered arrangement of objects. | 791 |

## DEFINITIONS

- An *r*-combination is a subset of *r* things taken from set of *n* distinct things. 791

- An *r*-permutation is an ordered arrangement of *r* things taken from a set of *n* distinct things. 791

## NOTATION

- *n* factorial: $n! = n(n - 1)\cdots 1; 0! = 1$ 792

## THEOREM

- **Pascal's identity:** $C(n, r - 1) + C(n, r) = C(n + 1, r)$ 796

## FORMULAS

- **Number of *r*-permutations from a set of *n* different objects:** 793, 794
  $P(n, r) = n(n - 1)\cdots(n - r + 1) = n!/(n - r)!$

- **Number of *r*-combinations from a set of *n* different objects:** 794
  $C(n, r) = \binom{n}{r} = n(n - 1)\cdots(n - r + 1)r! = n!/[r!(n - r)!]$

## Section 14.4 Theoretical Probability | Page Reference

### CONCEPTS

- **Theoretical probability:** If each outcome $s_i$ of a sample space $S$ has an assumed probability $p_i$, then the theoretical probability of an event $E$ is the sum of probabilities of the outcomes that belong to $E$. 801

- **Probability of complementary events:** For complementary events $E$ and $\overline{E}$, $P(E) + P(\overline{E}) = 1$. 812

### DEFINITIONS

- The **sample space, *S*,** is the set of all possible outcomes of an experiment. 802

- **Theoretical probability with equally likely outcomes:** The theoretical probability of an event $E \subseteq S$ is the ratio of the number of outcomes in $E$ to the total number of equally likely outcomes in $S$; that is, $P(E) = \dfrac{n(E)}{n(S)}$. 802

- **Equally likely outcomes** occur if the $n$ possible outcomes in a sample space $S$ each have the same probability, $1/n$, of occurring. 802

- **Conditional probability** is the probability, $P(B \mid A)$, of event $B$ occurring, given that event $A$ has already occurred. 804

- **Independent events:** Events $A$ and $B$ are independent if $P(B \mid A) = P(B)$—that is, if the probability of $B$ is not dependent on whether or not event $A$ occurs. 805

- A **complementary event,** $\overline{E}$, is the event $E$ does not occur, so $\overline{E} = S - E$. 808

- **Odds** are the ratio of the number of times the event can occur to the number of times the event does not occur. 812

- The **expected value** is the average value that can be anticipated if the numerical outcomes of an experiment are $u_1, u_2, \ldots, u_s$ and they occur with respective probabilities $p_1, p_2, \ldots, p_s$. The expected value of the experiment is $e = p_1u_1 + p_2u_2 + \cdots p_su_s$. 813

- **Geometric probability** is the probability depending on the geometry of an experiment. 814

## PROPERTIES

| | |
|---|---|
| • **Range of probabilities:** Since $\varnothing \subseteq E \subseteq S$, the probability of the event $E$ satisfies $0 \le P(E) \le 1$, where $P(E) = 0$ means that the event is impossible and $P(E) = 1$ means that the event is certain to occur. | 802 |
| • **Probability of mutually exclusive events:** If $A$ and $B$ are mutually exclusive events, so that $A \cap B = \varnothing$, then $P(A \text{ or } B) = P(A \cup B) = P(A) + P(B)$. | 803, 810 |
| • **Probability of two non-mutually exclusive events:** If $A$ and $B$ are any two events, then $P(A \text{ or } B) = P(A \cup B) = P(A) + P(B) - P(A \cap B)$. | 804, 810 |
| • **Conditional probability:** The conditional probability that event $B$ occurs, given that event $A$ has occurred, is $P(B \mid A) = \dfrac{P(A \cap B)}{P(A)}$. | 804 |
| • **Probability of compound events:** If $A$ and $B$ are any two events, then $P(A \text{ and } B) = P(A \cap B) = P(A)P(B \mid A)$. | 805, 810 |
| • **Probability of independent events:** If $A$ and $B$ are independent events, then $P(A \text{ and } B) = P(A \cap B) = P(A)P(B)$. | 805, 810 |
| • **Probability of a complementary event:** The probability of the event $\overline{E} = S - E$ complementary to event $E$ is given by $P(\overline{E}) = 1 - P(E)$. | 808, 810 |

## STRATEGIES

| | |
|---|---|
| • **Probability tree:** At each stage of an experiment, label each branch of a tree with the probability that the corresponding outcome occurs. | 806 |

## Chapter Review Exercises

### Section 14.1

1. Toss four coins 20 times, and determine the experimental probability of obtaining three heads and one tail.

2. (a) Roll three dice 20 times, and determine the experimental probability of obtaining a total score of 3 or 4.

   (b) From the data in part (a), determine the experimental probability of obtaining a score of at least 5.

3. From the data of problem 2, determine

$$P_e(5 \text{ or } 6 \text{ or } 7 \mid 5 \text{ or } 6 \text{ or } 7 \text{ or } 8 \text{ or } 9).$$

4. Conduct a survey of 20 randomly chosen college students at your college or university, and determine the experimental probability that chocolate is the favorite flavor of ice cream.

5. (a) Drop five thumbtacks on a tabletop 20 times, and determine the experimental probability that precisely three of the tacks land point up.

   (b) From the data of part (a), determine the experimental probability that two or three of the five tacks in part (a) land point up.

6. (a) A die is rolled repeatedly until a 5 or a 6 appears. Perform this experiment 10 times and estimate the number of rolls required.

   (b) From the data in part (a), compute the experimental probability that it takes precisely five rolls to obtain a 5 or 6 for the first time.

7. Shuffle a deck of cards and select a card at random. Return the card to the deck, shuffle, and draw again for a total of 20 trials.

   (a) Compute $P_e(\text{ace or heart})$.

   (b) Compute $P_e(\text{ace and heart})$.

   (c) Compute $P_e(\text{ace} \mid \text{heart})$.

8. Number a set of 3″ by 5″ note cards from 1 to 10. Shuffle the deck thoroughly and deal the cards face up on a table while at the same time counting the number of cards dealt. If the number of the card is the same as the number of cards dealt, say you have a match. For example, if the sixth card dealt is the card with a 6 on it, you have a match. Perform the experiment 25 times, and compute the experimental probability that a match occurs.

### Section 14.2

9. (a) Three coins are tossed. Make an orderly list of all possible outcomes.

   (b) In how many ways can you obtain two heads and one tail?

**10. (a)** All of the 90 students in Ferry Hall speak at least one of French, English, or German. If 38 speak English, 24 speak French and English, 27 speak German and English, and 17 speak German, French, and English, how many speak German or French?

**(b)** How many of the students in part (a) speak French and English, but not German?

**11. (a)** How many five-letter code words can be made if repetition of letters is not allowed?

**(b)** How many of the five-letter code words in part (a) start and end with vowels?

**(c)** How many of the code words in part (a) contain the three-letter sequence *aef*?

**12.** In Morse code, each letter is coded by a sequence of symbols, where each symbol is either a dot or a dash. For example, a single dot · represents the letter *e*, and the letter *o* is three dashes – – –. The distress signal SOS is transmitted as ··· – – – ···.

**(a)** How many letters can be formed if at most three symbols are allowed?

**(b)** Can all 26 letters be coded if up to four symbols are used?

**13.** A bicycle lock has a sequence of four cylinders on an axle, where each cylinder has the digits 0 through 9. If a thief can dial a new 4-digit combination each second, how long, at most, will it take to steal the bicycle?

**14.** A 5-digit ZIP code number is "detour prone" if it appears to be a valid but different ZIP number when read upside down. For example, **98601** becomes **10986** when read upside down.

**(a)** How many 5-digit numbers look like 5-digit numbers when read upside down?

**(b)** How many 5-digit numbers are detour prone? Be careful, since a number like **99166** is unchanged when read upside down.

**15.** An urn contains 4 red, 5 blue, and 2 green balls. Construct the possibility tree in which two balls are drawn randomly from the urn, with the first ball not replaced. Use the tree to find the number of ways, *x*, that both balls have the same color, and the number of ways, *y*, that at least one green ball was drawn.

## Section 14.3

**16. (a)** How many ways can you select 9 players for a baseball team from among 15 players if any player can play any position?

**(b)** How many ways can you select the team in part (a) if only 2 players can pitch and only 3 others can catch? Note that these 5 players can also play all other positions.

**17. (a)** How many ways can you select two clubs from an ordinary deck of playing cards?

**(b)** How many ways can you select two face cards from an ordinary deck of playing cards?

**(c)** How many ways can you select two clubs or two face cards from an ordinary deck of playing cards?

**18. (a)** In how many ways can the letters in STREETS be placed in recognizably different orders?

**(b)** In how many of the orderings of part (a) are the two *E*s adjacent?

**(c)** How many of the orderings in part (a) begin with a *T*?

**19.** A family has three girls and two boys. In how many ways can the children line up for a photo

**(a)** with no restriction?

**(b)** so that the two boys are side by side?

**(c)** so that no two girls are side by side?

**20.** If two circles are drawn, they can intersect in as many as two points.

**(a)** Show that three circles can intersect in 6 points.

**(b)** Show that four circles can intersect in 12 points.

**(c)** In how many points can *n* circles intesect? (*Suggestion:* Notice how many points of intersection are created by any two circles.)

**21.** Place *n* points randomly on a circle and then draw all of the chords between the pairs of points. Assume that no more than two chords intersect at the same point. When *n* = 4 there is 1 point of intersection, and when *n* = 5 there are 5 points of intersection, as shown in the following figure:

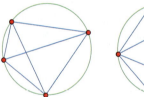

**(a)** How many points of intersection are created with *n* = 6 points?

**(b)** How many points on the circle are needed to determine any point of intersection of two of the chords?

**(c)** What combination number *C*(*n*, *r*) gives the number of points of intersection of the chords drawn between the *n* points of the circle?

## Section 14.4

**22. (a)** List explicitly all elements in the sample space if two coins and a die are tossed.

**(b)** Compute *P*(T, T, 5), the probability of getting two tails on the coins and a 5 on the die in part (a).

**23.** Compute *P*(5 | T, T), the probability of obtaining a 5 on the die given that both coins came up tails in problem 22.

**24.** Compute the probability of obtaining a sum of at most 11 on a single roll of two dice.

**25.** An urn contains five white, six red, and four black balls. Two balls are chosen at random without replacement.

**(a)** What is the probability that they are the same color?

**(b)** What is the probability that both are white?

**(c)** What is the probability that both are white given that they are the same color?

**(d)** Verify your answers with a probability tree.

**26.** Consider a spinner made as shown in Example 14.8 but marked as indicated here:

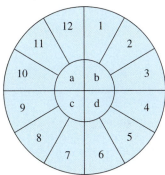

Compute these probabilities:

**(a)** $P(\text{b and } 8)$

**(b)** $P(\text{b or } 8)$

**(c)** $P(\text{b} \mid 8)$

**(d)** $P(\text{b and } 2)$

**(e)** $P(\text{b or } 2)$

**(f)** $P(2 \mid \text{b})$

**27.** Three coins are tossed.

**(a)** What are the odds in favor of getting two heads and one tail?

**(b)** What are the odds in favor of getting three heads?

**28.** **(a)** If $P(A) = 0.85$, what are the odds in favor of $A$ occurring on any given trial?

**(b)** If the odds in favor of $A$ are 17 to 8, determine $P(A)$.

**29.** You play a game where you win the amount shown with the probability shown:

$$P(\$5) = 0.50 \qquad P(\$10) = 0.25 \qquad P(\$20) = 0.10$$

**(a)** What is the expected value of the game?

**(b)** If it costs you $10 to play the game of part (a), is it wise to play? Explain.

**30.** A census taker was told by a neighbor that a family of five lived in the next house—two parents and three children. When the census taker visited the house, he was greeted by a girl. What is the probability that the other two children were both boys? Explain briefly.

## Chapter Test

**1.** Calculate each of the following:

**(a)** $7!$

**(b)** $\dfrac{9!}{6!}$

**(c)** $\dfrac{8!}{(8-8)!}$

**(d)** $7 \cdot 6!$

**(e)** $P(8, 5)$

**(f)** $P(8, 8)$

**(g)** $C(9, 3)$

**(h)** $C(9, 9)$

**2.** An urn contains five yellow, four blue, and eight green marbles.

**(a)** In how many ways can one select five green marbles?

**(b)** In how many ways can one select five yellow and five green marbles?

**(c)** In how many ways can one select five yellow or five green marbles?

**3.** If you select five marbles from the urn in problem 2, what is the probability that two are yellow given that three are green?

**4.** We claim that the probability is about 0.6 that a person shown a card with the numbers 1, 2, 3, and 4 printed on it will, when asked, choose the number 3. How can such a probability be calculated? Explain briefly.

$$\boxed{1 \; 2 \; 3 \; 4}$$

**5.** If $P(E) = 0.35$, what are the odds of obtaining $E$ on a single trial of an experiment?

**6.** How many four-letter code words can be made from the letters $a, b, c, d, e, f,$ and $g$

**(a)** with repetition allowed?

**(b)** with repetition not allowed?

**7.** How many of the code words in problem 6, part (b),

**(a)** begin with a vowel?

**(b)** have $c$ and $d$ adjacent?

**8.** What kind of probability is used when an assertion such as "The probability that penicillin will cure a case of strep throat is 0.9" is made? Explain briefly.

**9.** In Ms. Spangler's calculus class, all of the students are also studying one or more foreign languages. If

27 students study French,
29 students study German,
17 students study Chinese,
12 students study German and French,
3 students study German and Chinese,
2 students study French and Chinese, and
1 student studies French, German, and Chinese,

**(a)** how many students are in Ms. Spangler's class?

**(b)** how many students in the class study Chinese only?

**(c)** how many students study French and German, but not Chinese?

**10.** What are the odds in favor of selecting a yellow marble if a single marble is drawn from the urn described in problem 2?

**11.** The faces of a red cube are each marked with one A, two Bs, and 3 Cs. A second, blue cube has faces marked with three As, one B, and two Cs. Construct a probability tree to determine

**(a)** the probability of rolling a double (both cubes the same).

**(b)** the probability of rolling an A on at least one of the cubes.

# Appendix A

# Manipulatives in the Mathematics Classroom

## What Are Manipulatives?

More and more, we are hearing calls for a greater use of manipulatives in elementary mathematics teaching. Manipulatives are concrete materials that are used for modeling or representing mathematical operations or concepts. In much the same way that children make models of airplanes or clipper ships so that they can study and learn about them, your students can make and learn from models of two-digit numbers or division. The difference between the two situations is that while the airplane and boat models are smaller versions of actual concrete things, the number models and division models are concrete models of abstract concepts.

When children use bundles of Popsicle™ sticks and single sticks to represent 10s and 1s, or stretch rubber bands around nails on a geoboard to show squares and triangles, they are using manipulatives to model mathematical ideas. Technically, even when young children count on their fingers, they are concretely modeling numbers!

It is important to note that some frequently used "manipulative" materials fail to fit this definition of manipulatives. Flash cards, for instance, even though they are certainly manipulated, are never used to model mathematical ideas. Other objects, such as checkers in a checker game, also are manipulated, but are not used to directly represent mathematical ideas.

## What Kinds of Things Can Be Used as Manipulatives?

Good teachers use a great variety of things as manipulatives. Popsicle™ sticks, dried beans, smooth stones, egg cartons, and poker chips are all inexpensive and effective materials. Some teachers even like to use the students in their classes themselves as models for sets and numbers.

There are also, however, commercial materials that serve more specific modeling purposes. Some of these are base-ten blocks, geoboards, fraction strips or pieces, and algebra tiles. What's important about the materials you select is not their cost, but that they accurately represent the concept or operation that your students are ready to learn about.

## What Does Research Say About Using Manipulatives?

For the last 20 years, research support for using manipulatives in elementary math teaching has been growing. Suydam and Higgins (1977) were able to identify and review 23 research studies that addressed the question of the effectiveness of manipulative materials for instruction. They concluded that instruction using manipulative materials had a higher probability of producing greater mathematics achievement than nonmanipulative instruction.

Twelve years later, Sowell had 60 studies to work with in a similar review. These studies were conducted at all educational levels, from kindergarten to college, and focused on many different mathematical topics. After using a sophisticated statistical procedure called meta-analysis, Sowell was able to offer a much stronger conclusion than Suydam and Higgins: that manipulative materials do, indeed, have a significant positive effect on achievement, especially when they are used over a long time (Sowell, 1989). In addition, Sowell found that the use of concrete materials for instruction was effective in improving students' attitudes toward mathematics.

## What Do the Professional Organizations Say?

Because of growing research support, professional organizations and leading educators have been urging the increased use of concrete materials in teaching. Manipulatives play a prominent role in the National Council of Teachers of Mathematics *Principles and Standards for School Mathematics*. Even though there is no single standard which says that manipulatives should be used more frequently, their use is supported for many different topics at all levels, from kindergarten through twelfth grade. In the area of numbers and operations, for example, the *Standards* suggest the following:

> *Representing numbers with physical materials should be a major part of mathematics instruction in the elementary grades.* (Standards, *p. 33*)

The *Standards* also make the following assertion:

> *Students' understanding and ability to reason will grow as they represent fractions and decimals with physical materials and on number lines as they learn to generate equivalent representations of fractions and decimals.* (Standards, *p. 33*)

Representations that include concrete materials are discussed in the *Standards* for grades 6–8, which describes their applicability and desirability in the upper grades as well as in the lower elementary school grades:

> *Representations—such as physical objects, drawings, charts, graphs, and symbols—also help students communicate their thinking. Representations are ubiquitous in the middle grades mathematics curriculum proposed here.* (Standards, *p. 280*)

## How Does Concrete Modeling Help Children Learn Mathematics?

The mechanism by which concrete modeling promotes the learning process is still somewhat of a mystery to us, but the fact that it does is becoming more certain all the time. Most research shows that the best instructional sequence to follow for the presentation of elementary mathematical material is concrete–pictorial–symbolic. Activities with concrete materials should precede those which show pictured relationships, and the latter type of activity should, in turn, precede formal operations with symbols. Ultimately, students need to reach that final level of symbolic proficiency with many of the mathematical skills that they master, but the meanings of those symbols and abstract operations must be firmly rooted in experiences with real objects. Otherwise, their performance of the symbolic operations will simply be rote repetitions of meaningless, memorized procedures.

Concrete and pictorial models are, at best, imperfect representations of abstract mathematical ideas and concepts. Not every characteristic of the concrete model is important mathematically. For example, many teachers use a yellow wooden rod to represent the number 5, but "yellow-ness" certainly has nothing to do with "fiveness." To prevent the child from abstracting inappropriate characteristics of the model as characteristics of the mathematical idea, multiple models should be used for important concepts. Multiple models of the same idea that are perceptually very different from each other direct the student to abstract from them only what they have in common—the mathematical concept. This abstraction is what leads to meaningful mathematics learning.

# When Should Manipulatives Be Used?

Manipulatives and concrete models can be used almost anywhere in the elementary mathematics curriculum and should be used with all students. The most frequent occurrence of modeling in the curriculum will probably be at the point of introduction of new topics. The use of concrete materials while introducing a new topic allows students to gain that necessary foundational experience before trying to demonstrate their understandings symbolically. But the intelligent use of manipulatives can also provide the most effective form of remediation. Engaging students in concrete activities related to the mathematics that they are struggling with will frequently help them to identify exactly which part of the process is causing the confusion and then to work through it.

The use of manipulatives is important not only for younger children: Older children can benefit just as much from appropriate concrete activity. The skills and concepts that they are asked to deal with are increasingly complex, and concrete introductions can frequently pave the way toward true understanding. Good concrete and pictorial models are available to help students deal with percents, ratios, geometric formulas, integers, and even the solution of algebraic equations.

# Manipulative *Do's* and *Don'ts*

Elementary mathematics teachers who have been using manipulatives for many years have learned some rules that make their use in classrooms more effective. Don't use the materials exclusively for demonstrations and teacher explanations. The most effective way to use manipulatives is to have the children work directly with the materials. It is through touching and moving that learning takes place. Watching the teacher do the manipulation is much less successful.

Discuss appropriate behavior before distributing the materials, and allow plenty of free exploration time after. Children need to have time to do what *they* want with the materials before they will do what *you* want them to. This exploration time is also learning time: The more familiar they become with the materials, the more effective their later use of them will be.

Have children work with the materials in small groups and explain their thinking to each other as they do so. Asking children to verbalize their thoughts for others gives them the opportunity to clarify their own thinking. By listening to the discussions, you can make judgments about how well they understand the concepts.

# How Can I Get More Information About Using Manipulatives?

The list of references that follows is a good place to start. The first two citations will be helpful for the practitioner, while the second two are the research reviews mentioned earlier.

National Council of Teachers of Mathematics. *Principles and Standards for School Mathematics.* Reston, VA: NCTM, 2000.

Reys, Robert E., Marilyn N. Suydam, and Mary Montgomery Lindquist. *Helping Children Learn Mathematics,* 2d ed. Englewood Cliffs, NJ: Prentice Hall, 1989.

Sowell, Evelyn J. "Effects of Manipulative Materials in Mathematics Instruction." *Journal for Research in Mathematics Education,* Vol. 20, No. 5, November 1989, pp. 498–505.

Suydam, Marilyn N., and Jon L. Higgins. *Activity-Based Learning in Elementary School Mathematics: Recommendations from Research.* Columbus, OH: ERIC Center for Science, Mathematics, and Environmental Education, 1977.

Van de Walle, John. *Elementary and Middle School Mathematics.* Boston: Allyn & Bacon, 2007.

# Appendix B

# Getting the Most Out of Your Calculator

Nearly everyone who reads these words is the owner of at least one calculator and knows how to add, subtract, multiply, and divide with a calculator. However, most calculators have useful features that are often not well understood and are not employed by some users. In this appendix, we discuss some of these special features.

Several types of calculators are commonly found in the elementary and middle school classroom. The most basic is the calculator based on arithmetic (pronounced *ar ith met'ic*) logic. The priorities of the operations vary considerably from machine to machine, and it is often difficult to understand which rules are followed in a calculation. In view of these shortcomings, we recommend that students, even in the earlier grades, become familiar with a calculator based on algebraic logic. The priorities of the operations on an algebraic calculator not only are uniform, but also can be controlled by the placement of parentheses. Indeed, it is the presence of parenthesis keys, $($ and $)$, which makes it readily clear that the machine is algebraic.

In this appendix, we assume that we are working with a calculator with algebraic logic. We also assume that the calculator has a single memory into which values can be stored and recalled for convenience. Most calculators also have additional function keys, such as a squaring key, $x^2$, a square root key, $\sqrt{\phantom{x}}$, and a power key, $\wedge$. It is becoming more common for classroom calculators to have an integer divide key, $\text{Int} \div$, which yields a quotient and remainder instead of a decimal.

Many interesting calculations, and even algorithms, can be carried out with such an inexpensive calculator. Of course, there are still limitations, and we hope you are inspired to develop additional advanced skills—say, by learning to create tables, graphs, and programs with a graphing calculator such as the TI-73 or TI-83/84.

classrooms envisioned in *Principles and Standards,* every student has access to technology to facilitate his or her mathematics learning under the guidance of a skillful teacher.

SOURCE: *Principles and Standards for School Mathematics by NCTM, pages 24–25. Copyright 2000 by the National Council of Teachers of Mathematics. Reproduced with permission of the National Council of Teachers of Mathematics via Copyright Clearance Center. NCTM does not endorse the content or validity of these alignments.*

## Priority of Operations

Suppose you enter

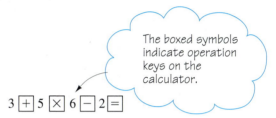

The boxed symbols indicate operation keys on the calculator.

$$3 \boxed{+} 5 \boxed{\times} 6 \boxed{-} 2 \boxed{=}$$

into your calculator. A calculator with arithmetic logic would perform each operation in exactly the order entered and would give the answer 46; that is,

$$3 + 5 = 8$$
$$8 \times 6 = 48$$
$$48 - 2 = 46.$$

In contrast, a calculator with algebraic logic multiplies and divides *before* adding and subtracting. Also, if there are pending operations of equal priority, these calculators execute them from left to right. Since the priorities on such a calculator are those generally accepted in mathematics, algebraic machines correspond well to the standard rules and properties of arithmetic. Thus, the preceding sequence of entries in an algebraic calculator gives the answer 31, obtained as follows:

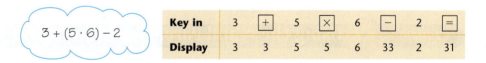

$3 + (5 \cdot 6) - 2$

| Key in | 3 | $\boxed{+}$ | 5 | $\boxed{\times}$ | 6 | $\boxed{-}$ | 2 | $\boxed{=}$ |
|---|---|---|---|---|---|---|---|---|
| Display | 3 | 3 | 5 | 5 | 6 | 33 | 2 | 31 |

When $\boxed{-}$ was pressed, the calculator *first* multiplied $5 \times 6$ to get 30 and *then* completed the pending addition to 3, giving 33. When 2 and $\boxed{=}$ were pressed, it then subtracted the 2 to give 31.

Although we have not yet discussed the use of all of these keys, the priority of operations for machines with algebraic logic is shown in Table B.1.

| TABLE B.1 | PRIORITY OF OPERATIONS ON CALCULATORS WITH ALGEBRAIC LOGIC | |
|---|---|---|
| **Priority** | **Keys** | **Explanation** |
| 1 | $\boxed{(}$ $\boxed{)}$ | Operations in parentheses are performed before other operations. |
| 2 | $\boxed{x^2}$ $\boxed{\sqrt{\phantom{x}}}$ | Operations performed on a single number. |
| 3 | $\boxed{\wedge}$ | Exponentiation. |
| 4 | $\boxed{\times}$ $\boxed{\div}$ | Multiplications and divisions are completed before additions and subtractions. |
| 5 | $\boxed{+}$ $\boxed{-}$ | Additions and subtractions are completed last. |
| 6 | $\boxed{=}$ | Performs all pending operations |

**EXAMPLE B.1 Understanding the Order of Calculator Operations**

(a) Indicate what should be entered into a calculator with algebraic notation to compute

$$27 \div 3 + 24 \cdot 4.$$

(b) Actually key the sequence in part (a) into your calculator and complete the computation.

**Solution**

(a) Because of the priority of operations, it is necessary to key in only the following:

$$27 \boxed{\div} 3 \boxed{+} 24 \boxed{\times} 4 \boxed{=} .$$

(b) On a machine with algebraic logic, the calculator makes the following sequence of calculations:

$$27 \div 3 = 9, 24 \cdot 4 = 96, 9 + 96 = 105.$$

## Using the Parentheses Keys $\boxed{(}$ and $\boxed{)}$

It is possible to override the priority of operations built into the calculator by use of the parentheses keys. Suppose you want to compute

$$(789 + 364) \cdot (863 + 939).$$

This computation is accomplished by keying the sequence

$$\boxed{(} \, 789 \, \boxed{+} \, 364 \, \boxed{)} \, \boxed{\times} \, \boxed{(} \, 863 \, \boxed{+} \, 939 \, \boxed{)} \, \boxed{=}$$

into the calculator. The desired answer is 2,077,706. If we keyed in

$$789 \, \boxed{+} \, 364 \, \boxed{\times} \, 863 \, \boxed{+} \, 939 \, \boxed{=}$$

(the same entries, but omitting the parentheses), the calculator would show 315,860, determined by computing the product of 364 and 863 and then adding 789 and 939 in that order.

**EXAMPLE B.2 Using the $\boxed{=}$ and Parentheses Keys**

Perform this computation on your calculator:

$$216 \div (3 + 24) \cdot 4.$$

**Solution**

Key in $216 \, \boxed{\div} \, \boxed{(} \, 3 \, \boxed{+} \, 24 \, \boxed{)} \, \boxed{\times} \, 4 \, \boxed{=}$ to obtain 32. Remember that division and multiplication are operations of the same priority. Thus, working left to right, the calculator first computes the sum in parentheses, divides 216 by that sum, and multiplies the result by 4. In clearer notation, what the calculator is computing is

$$(216 \div (3 + 24)) \cdot 4,$$

but the built-in priority of operations makes it unnecessary to key the expression into the calculator this way.

Before proceeding, several observations should be made:

1. It is always a good idea to begin each calculation by pressing the $\boxed{\text{ON}}$ key. This key turns the calculator on. Equally importantly, it clears all preceding data from all parts of the calculator so that present work will not be rendered incorrect by the presence of unexpected and unwanted information from a preceding calculation.

**2.** Pressing the $\boxed{=}$ key causes the calculator to complete all entered calculations up to that point. This key can be used on occasion to simplify calculation. For example, to compute $(29 + 37) \div 11$, one could use parentheses or, alternatively, enter

$$29 \boxed{+} 37 \boxed{=} \boxed{\div} 11 \boxed{=}$$

to obtain the correct answer of 6. As a check, key in

$$\boxed{(}\, 29 \boxed{+} 37 \boxed{)} \boxed{\div} 11 \boxed{=}$$

to see that you obtain the same answer.

**3.** Parentheses must always be entered in pairs; that is, for each left parenthesis entered, a right parenthesis must be entered later. Otherwise, when $\boxed{=}$ is entered, an error message will appear in the display to inform you of an error in entering parentheses.

If, in the midst of a calculation, you obtain an error message of any kind, you must press the $\boxed{\text{ON}}$ key to clear the machine. Then repeat the calculation, being careful to restructure your procedure to avoid the previous error.

It may be useful to consider one more example concerning the priority of operations.

**EXAMPLE  B.3  Prioritizing Operations**

Compute $\dfrac{323 - 4 \cdot 38}{19}$.

**Solution**   If you enter

$$323 \boxed{-} 4 \boxed{\times} 38 \boxed{\div} 19 \boxed{=}$$

into the calculator, you obtain the incorrect answer 315. Because of the priority of operations, this sequence of commands computes $4 \cdot 38 \div 19$ and subtracts the result from 323. However, the problem requires that the entire quantity $323 - 4 \cdot 38$ be divided by 19. This can be accomplished in several ways, but perhaps the following two are easiest: Using parentheses, enter

$$\boxed{(}\, 323 \boxed{-} 4 \boxed{\times} 38 \boxed{)} \boxed{\div} 19 \boxed{=}.$$

Using $\boxed{=}$ twice, enter

$$323 \boxed{-} 4 \boxed{\times} 38 \boxed{=} \boxed{\div} 19 \boxed{=}.$$

Key in each of these sequences and note that each gives the correct answer of 9.

## Using the $\boxed{x^2}$ and $\boxed{\sqrt{\phantom{x}}}$ keys

Each of these keys causes the calculator to perform an operation on a single number. To compute

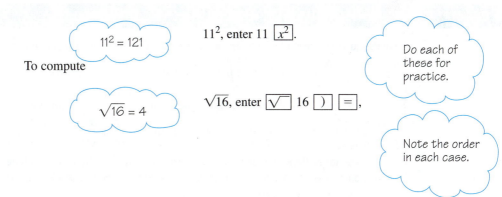

$11^2$, enter $11 \boxed{x^2}$.

$11^2 = 121$

To compute

$\sqrt{16} = 4$

$\sqrt{16}$, enter $\boxed{\sqrt{\phantom{x}}}\, 16 \boxed{)} \boxed{=}$,

Do each of these for practice.

Note the order in each case.

since, when the $\boxed{\sqrt{\phantom{x}}}$ button is pressed, the display actually shows $\sqrt{\phantom{x}}$ ( , and this requires depressing the right parenthesis key and the equals key to complete the calculation. On some calculators, to compute $\sqrt{16}$, you must enter $\boxed{\sqrt{\phantom{x}}}$ $\boxed{(}$ 16 $\boxed{)}$ $\boxed{=}$, and on others, you simply enter 16 $\boxed{\sqrt{\phantom{x}}}$. In what follows, we will use the first notation discussed, but you should consult the instruction booklet for your calculator to see which you should use. Alternatively, just trying each possibility on your calculator should make your choice clear.

In each case, the operation is carried out immediately; it is not necessary to use the $\boxed{=}$ key to complete the computation.

## Using the $\boxed{\wedge}$ Key

To compute $5^3$, we use the $\boxed{\wedge}$ key. Here, we have to tell the calculator what number we want to raise to a power and what power to raise it to. For $5^3$, we enter 5 $\boxed{\wedge}$ 3 $\boxed{=}$ to obtain 125. Check to see that the entry strings

$$2 \boxed{\wedge} 5 \boxed{=}$$

and

$$2 \boxed{\times} 2 \boxed{\times} 2 \boxed{\times} 2 \boxed{\times} 2 \boxed{=}$$

both give 32 as the value of $2^5$.

Note that, on some calculators, exponentiation is accomplished by use of a $\boxed{y^x}$ key. On these calculators, $2^5$ would be calculated by entering 2 $\boxed{y^x}$ 5.

## Using the Memory Keys— $\boxed{M}$, $\boxed{M+}$, $\boxed{M-}$, $\boxed{MR}$, and $\boxed{R}$

Most calculators with algebraic logic have a memory accessed with keys like $\boxed{M}$, $\boxed{M+}$, and $\boxed{M-}$. $\boxed{M}$ places the number in the display in the memory while still keeping it in the display. The $\boxed{M+}$ and $\boxed{M-}$ keys respectively add the number in the calculator display to, or subtract the number in the calculator display from, the number in the memory while maintaining the number shown in the display. If nothing has been placed in the memory, it is assumed to contain a 0. Also, when a number has been placed in the memory, the display shows a small "m" to remind you that the memory is not empty. Keys like $\boxed{MR}$, $\boxed{RM}$, and $\boxed{R}$, recall what is in the memory and show it in the display. These capabilities are useful in elementary ways but, with a little imagination, serve more surprising and powerful purposes. In the text that follows, we will use the notations $\boxed{M+}$, $\boxed{M-}$, and $\boxed{MR}$, even though your calculator may use other designations and may not have all the possible capabilities of the $\boxed{M+}$ and $\boxed{M-}$ keys.

---

**EXAMPLE   B.4**   **Using the $\boxed{M+}$ and $\boxed{MR}$ Keys**

By the quadratic formula from algebra, the positive solution of the equation $x^2 - x - 1 = 0$ is given by $\tau = \dfrac{1 + \sqrt{5}}{2}$. (Here $\tau$ denotes the Greek letter tau.)

**(a)** Use your calculator to compute the decimal value for $\tau$ and store it to the memory.

**(b)** Compute the decimal values of the numbers $\dfrac{\tau}{\sqrt{5}}, \dfrac{\tau^2}{\sqrt{5}}, \dfrac{\tau^3}{\sqrt{5}}, \dfrac{\tau^4}{\sqrt{5}}, \dfrac{\tau^5}{\sqrt{5}}, \dfrac{\tau^6}{\sqrt{5}}, \ldots$ Use mental arithmetic to round the values you obtain to the nearest integer, recording your answer on a piece of paper. What is interesting about this sequence of integers?

**Solution**

(a) The sum in the numerator must be calculated first, so we use parentheses and then divide by 2 to calculate $\tau$:

The display now shows that $\tau$ has the decimal value 1.618034. In the last step, the memory key, $\boxed{M+}$, has placed $\tau$ into the calculator's memory, anticipating that we will want to use $\tau$ again for part (b).

(b) Since $\tau$ is in the display from part (a), the additional keystrokes $\boxed{\div}$ 5 $\boxed{\sqrt{\phantom{x}}}$ $\boxed{=}$ show that $\dfrac{\tau}{1\,5}$ is 0.77236068, which rounds off to the nearest integer, 1. To multiply $\dfrac{\tau}{1\,5}$ by $\tau$, we press the keys $\boxed{\times}\,\boxed{MR}\,\boxed{=}$ and see that $\dfrac{\tau^2}{2\,5}$ is 1.1708204, which also rounds to 1. Similarly, pressing the keys $\boxed{\times}\,\boxed{MR}\,\boxed{=}$ shows that $\dfrac{\tau^3}{2\,5}$ is 1.8944272, which rounds to 2. We now see that the pattern can be continued easily for as many steps as we like:

$$\boxed{\div}\,5\,\boxed{\sqrt{\phantom{x}}}\,\boxed{=}\,\boxed{\times}\,\boxed{MR}\,\boxed{=}\,\boxed{\times}\,\boxed{MR}\,\boxed{=}\,\boxed{\times}\,\boxed{MR}\,\boxed{=}\,\boxed{\times}\,\boxed{MR}\,\boxed{=}\,\boxed{\times}\,\boxed{MR}\,\boxed{=}\,\boxed{\times}\,\boxed{MR}\,\boxed{=}\,\ldots$$

$$0.77\ldots \quad 1.17\ldots \quad 1.89\ldots \quad 3.06\ldots \quad 4.95\ldots \quad 8.02\ldots \quad 12.98\ldots$$

When these decimals are rounded to the nearest integers, we get 1, 1, 2, 3, 5, 8, 13, .... That is, $\dfrac{\tau^n}{2\,5}$ rounds to the $n$th Fibonacci number.

---

**EXAMPLE B.5**  **Using the $\boxed{M+}$ and $\boxed{MR}$ Keys to Compute the Mean and the Standard Deviation**

Given the data $x_1, x_2, \ldots, x_n$, the mean and the standard deviation are given, respectively, by the formulas

$$\bar{x} = \frac{x_1 + x_2 + \cdots + x_n}{n}$$

and

$$s = \frac{1}{n}2\,\overline{n(x_1^2 + x_2^2 + \cdots + x_n^2)^2 - (x_1 + x_2 + \cdots + x_n)^2}.$$

Use the $\boxed{M+}$ key to compute the mean and the standard deviation of the data 35, 42, 61, 29, 39, where each datum is entered just once in your calculator. [*Note:* The data are the same as those seen in Example 13.11.]

**Solution**

The formulas show that we need both a sum of the data and a sum of the squared data. This can be accomplished by summing each new datum $x_i$ into the memory before its value is squared. Consider the following keystrokes:

$$\boxed{On}\,5\,\boxed{\times}\,\boxed{(}\,35\,\boxed{M+}\,\boxed{x^2}\,\boxed{+}\,42\,\boxed{M+}\,\boxed{x^2}\,\boxed{+}\,61\,\boxed{M+}\,\boxed{x^2}\,\boxed{+}\,29\,\boxed{M+}\,\boxed{x^2}\,\boxed{+}\,39\,\boxed{M+}\,\boxed{x^2}\,\boxed{)}\,\boxed{=}$$

So far, $n(x_1^2 + x_2^2 + \cdots + x_n^2)^2 = 45{,}360$ appears in the display and $x_1 + x_2 + \cdots + x_n = 206$ is stored in the memory. The following additional keystrokes compute the standard deviation:

$$\boxed{-}\,\boxed{MR}\,\boxed{x^2}\,\boxed{=}\,\boxed{\sqrt{\phantom{x}}}\,\boxed{\div}\,5\,\boxed{=}$$

The standard deviation $s$ of about 10.8 is now displayed. To find the mean, we again recall the value of $x_1 + x_2 + \cdots + x_n = 206$ from the memory and divide it by 5, using these keystrokes:

$$\boxed{\text{MR}}\ \boxed{\div}\ 5\ \boxed{=}$$

The mean $\bar{x} \doteq 41.2$ now appears in the display.

## Using the $\boxed{\text{INT}\div}$ Key to Compute Integer Division with Remainders

For calculators designed for use in elementary school classrooms, it was thought appropriate to provide the capability of dividing one natural number by another and displaying both the quotient and the remainder as integers. Because of limited space in the display, there is a limitation on the size of the numbers that can be used. If either the quotient or the remainder is too large, an error message will appear in the calculator display, and the problem will have to be completed by some other method.

### EXAMPLE B.6  Using the $\boxed{\text{INT}\div}$ Key

(a) Using the $\boxed{\text{INT}\div}$ key, compute the quotient and the remainder when 89,765 is divided by 78.

(b) Using the $\boxed{\text{INT}\div}$ key, compute the quotient and the remainder when 897,654 is divided by 81.

**Solution**

(a) Entering 89765 $\boxed{\text{INT}\div}$ 78 $\boxed{=}$ into your calculator, you see the quotient, 1150, and the remainder, 65, in the display. Use your calculator to check this result by showing that

$$1150 \cdot 78 + 65 = 89765.$$

(b) When you enter 897654 $\boxed{\text{INT}\div}$ 81 $\boxed{=}$ into your calculator, the display may give an error message, since the quotient is a five-digit number. Since 897654 $\boxed{\div}$ 81 gives the decimal 11082.148, the quotient is 11,082. Subtracting this from 11082.148 leaves the fractional part 0.148148. Multiplying the fractional part by 81 gives a decimal approximation of 11.999988 to the remainder. Thus $897654 \div 81 = 11082$ R 12.

## Using the Built-in Constant Function

Consider the arithmetic progression

$$3, 7, 11, 15, 19, \ldots, 67.$$

It is easy to use your calculator to compute all the terms in this progression. Simply enter 3 $\boxed{+}$ 4 and then repeatedly press the key $\boxed{=}$ to repeatedly add 4. This sequence utilizes the **built-in constant function** of most calculators with algebraic logic. Note that, on some calculators, you may need to enter 4 $\boxed{+}$ 3 and then repeatedly press $\boxed{=}$.

### EXAMPLE B.7  Finding the Sum of an Arithmetic Progression

Compute the sum $3 + 7 + 11 + \cdots + 67$ of the first 17 terms in the preceding arithmetic progression.

**Solution**

1. If we remember young Gauss's insight on page 30, then we have

$$S = 3 + 7 + 11 + \cdots + 67,$$

$$S = 67 + 63 + 59 + \cdots + 3, \text{ and}$$

$$2S = 70 + 70 + 70 + \cdots + 70 = 17 \cdot 70.$$

So

$$S = \frac{17 \cdot 70}{2} = 595.$$

2. An alternative approach to this problem is to use the $\boxed{M+}$ and the built-in constant function of your calculator. Thus, we enter

$$3 \boxed{M+} \boxed{+} 4 \boxed{=} \boxed{M+} \boxed{=} \boxed{M+} \boxed{=} \ldots,$$

repeating the $\boxed{M+}$ $\boxed{=}$ sequence until the display shows 67. We then press $\boxed{M+}$ once more and $\boxed{MR}$ to again obtain 595 as the answer.

## EXAMPLE B.8   Finding the Sum of a Geometric Progression

Find the sum of the first 15 terms of the geometric progression whose first four terms are 4, 12, 36, 108.

**Solution**

The consecutive terms of the progression can be found on your calculator by entering $4 \boxed{\times} 3 \boxed{=}$ and then pressing $\boxed{=}$ repeatedly.

As with the arithmetic progression, this problem can also be solved on algebraic-notation machines with a built-in constant function. Thus, if we enter

$$4 \boxed{M+} \boxed{\times} 3 \boxed{=} \boxed{M+} \boxed{=} \boxed{M+} \boxed{=} \cdots \boxed{=} \boxed{M+} \boxed{MR},$$

where we use the $\boxed{=}$ key 14 times (to add 15 terms), we obtain the desired answer of 28,697,812. Check this on your calculator.

## EXAMPLE B.9   Repeatedly Adding the Same Number to Different Numbers

Compute these sums: $3 + 17$, $7 + 17$, $9 + 17$, and $24 + 17$.

**Solution**

The built-in constant function capability of many calculators is useful in ways other than those shown in Examples B.7 and B.8. In the present case, we can proceed as follows: Entering $3 \boxed{+} 17$ $\boxed{=}$ yields the desired sum of 20. Now, instead of entering $7 \boxed{+} 17 \boxed{=}$, just enter $7 \boxed{=}$ to obtain 24, $9 \boxed{=}$ to obtain 26, and $24 \boxed{=}$ to obtain 41. In any case, if you have to add the same number to a large number of other numbers, this approach greatly simplifies the chore. Note that the same approach also works for subtraction.

## EXAMPLE B.10   Repeatedly Multiplying Several Different Numbers by the Same Number

Compute these products: $5 \times 7$, $8 \times 7$, $20 \times 7$, and $30 \times 7$.

**Solution**

As in the preceding example, we simply enter $5 \boxed{\times} 7 \boxed{=}$, $8 \boxed{=}$, $20 \boxed{=}$, and $30 \boxed{=}$ to obtain the desired products—35, 56, 140, and 210, respectively. Also, the same idea works for division.

### Algorithmic Thinking

An approach to doing mathematics that is particularly important in working with calculators and computers is **algorithmic thinking:** the doing of mathematical tasks by means of a sequential, and often repetitive, set of steps. The methodology was illustrated modestly in the preceding examples explaining the repeated use of the $\boxed{=}$ and $\boxed{M+}$ keys. But much more can be done with your calculator to illustrate this approach to problem solving. To clarify the idea, consider the following example.

---

**EXAMPLE B.11  Generating the Fibonacci Sequence Algorithmically**

Develop an efficient algorithm for generating successive terms of the Fibonacci sequence 1, 1, 2, 3, 5, . . ., using the special capabilities of your calculator.

**Solution**

The Fibonacci numbers can be computed with the straightforward use of the $\boxed{+}$ and $\boxed{=}$ keys on your calculator. But this approach requires repeatedly entering the proper numbers. More efficient algorithmic approaches can be devised that require entering only one or two numbers initially and then, repetitively, using the special keys on your calculator to complete the task. (*Note:* Since not all calculators operate exactly the same, great care must be exercised in devising an algorithm suitable for your machine.)

The following algorithm generates the Fibonacci numbers by making particularly effective use of the $\boxed{MR}$ and $\boxed{M+}$ keys found on most calculators. The following table gives the entry (a number or a keystroke), the value $x$ seen in the display, and the value $M$ contained in the memory:

| Entry | 1 | M+ | + | M+ | MR | + | M+ | MR | + | M+ | MR | + | ... |
|---|---|---|---|---|---|---|---|---|---|---|---|---|---|
| **x** | 1 | 1 | 1 | 1 | 2 | 3 | 3 | 5 | 8 | 8 | 13 | 21 | ... |
| **M** | 0 | 1 | 1 | 2 | 2 | 2 | 5 | 5 | 5 | 13 | 13 | 13 | ... |

The Fibonacci numbers generated by the algorithm are shown in red. Each repetition of the three-keystroke pattern $\boxed{M+}$ $\boxed{MR}$ $\boxed{+}$ first repeats the last number displayed and then generates the next two numbers of the Fibonacci sequence. Since two of each three successive keystrokes generate a new Fibonacci number, the algorithm is highly efficient.

---

## Problem Set B.1

Exercises numbered in red are answered in the back of the text.

### Understanding Concepts

**1.** Use your calculator to compute each of the following:
- **(a)** 284 + 357
- **(b)** 357 − 284
- **(c)** 284 · 357
- **(d)** 284 ÷ 71
- **(e)** 781 − 35 + 24
- **(f)** 781 − (35 + 24)
- **(g)** 781 − (35 − 24)
- **(h)** 861 − 423 − 201
- **(i)** 861 − (423 + 201)

**2.** Compute the following, using your calculator:
- **(a)** 271 · 365
- **(b)** 18,147 ÷ 23
- **(c)** 1024 ÷ 16 ÷ 2
- **(d)** 1024 ÷ (16 ÷ 2)

**3.** Use your calculator to calculate each of these division problems:
- **(a)** $\dfrac{420 + 315}{15}$
- **(b)** 423 + 315 ÷ 15
- **(c)** $\dfrac{4441 + 2332}{220 + 301}$
- **(d)** $\dfrac{1567 - 5 \cdot 161}{5 \cdot 127 + 127}$

**4.** Evaluate the following, using your calculator:
- **(a)** $29^2$
- **(b)** $\sqrt{1849}$
- **(c)** $\sqrt{2569 - 1480}$
- **(d)** $\sqrt{1444} - \sqrt{784}$

**5.** Write out an entry string to compute
$$\frac{\sqrt{784} - 91 \div 13}{8 \cdot 49 - 11 \cdot 35},$$

(a) using parentheses.

(b) without using parentheses, but using the memory.

6. Use the $\boxed{M+}$, $\boxed{M-}$, and $\boxed{MR}$ keys to compute

$$\frac{4041 + 1237}{91} + \frac{3381 + 2331}{84} - \frac{2113 + 2993}{46}.$$

(*Note:* You should be able to do this entirely with your calculator. Nothing need be (should be) written down but the answer.)

7. (a) Write out the expression you are evaluating if you enter 1831 $\boxed{-}$ 17 $\boxed{\times}$ 28 $\boxed{+}$ 34 $\boxed{=}$ into a calculator with algebraic logic.

(b) Write the numerical answer to part (a).

8. (a) Write out the expression you are evaluating if you enter

42 $\boxed{\times}$ 34 $\boxed{-}$ 14 $\boxed{\times}$ 6 $\boxed{=}$ $\boxed{\div}$ 28 $\boxed{=}$

into your calculator.

(b) What expression does the following string evaluate?

42 $\boxed{\times}$ 34 $\boxed{-}$ 14 $\boxed{\times}$ 6 $\boxed{x^2}$ $\boxed{=}$ $\boxed{\div}$ 28 $\boxed{=}$

9. (a) Make your calculator count by 2s by entering

0 $\boxed{+}$ 2 $\boxed{=}$ $\boxed{=}$ $\boxed{=}$ $\cdots$ .

(b) Make your calculator generate the odd numbers by entering

1 $\boxed{+}$ 2 $\boxed{=}$ $\boxed{=}$ $\boxed{=}$ $\cdots$ .

10. (a) Make your calculator count by 17s by entering

0 $\boxed{+}$ 17 $\boxed{=}$ $\boxed{=}$ $\boxed{=}$ $\cdots$ .

(b) If you count by 17s, do you ever get to 323? If so, when?

11. Use the built-in constant function to generate the first ten terms of the arithmetic progression whose first four terms are 2, 6, 10, and 14; that is, use the $\boxed{=}$ key repeatedly.

12. Use the built-in constant function to generate the first ten terms of the geometric progression whose first four terms are 3, 15, 75, and 375.

13. (a) Use the $\boxed{=}$ and $\boxed{M+}$ keys to compute the sum

$$S = 5 + 8 + 11 + \cdots + 47$$

of the arithmetic progression 5, 8, 11, . . . , 47.

(b) Compute the sum in part (a) by using Gauss's insight. That is, notice that

$$S = 47 + 44 + \cdots + 8 + 5.$$

14. (a) Use the $\boxed{=}$ and $\boxed{M+}$ keys to compute the sum

$$S = 3 + 15 + 75 + \cdots + 234{,}375.$$

of the geometric progression 3, 15, 75, . . . , 234,375.

(b) Let $S$ denote the sum required in part (a). Using this sum, write out the sum for $5S$. (Note that the common ratio for the geometric progression is 5.) Then $4S = 5S - S$ and $S = 4S \div 4$. Compute $S$ by hand in this way.

(c) The hand calculation in part (b) is rather neat and should be taught to students. How would you use the calculator calculation of part (a) to help your students to better understand the hand calculation of part (b)?

15. Use the procedure demonstrated in Example B.5 to compute the mean and the standard deviation of the data 6.59, 13.04, 4.89, and 7.48, where each datum is entered just once into your calculator.

16. (a) The Lucas numbers are 1, 3, 4, 7, 11, 18, . . . , where we start with 1 and 3 and, as with the Fibonacci numbers, and then add any two consecutive terms to obtain the next term. Notationally, we will set $L_1 = 1$, $L_2 = 3$, $L_3 = 4, \ldots$, $L_n$ = the $n$th Lucas number, and so on, In Example B.11, we developed an algorithm for successively generating the Fibonacci numbers. Modify the algorithm to obtain an algorithm that generates the Lucas numbers. (*Suggestion:* Try inserting a 3 after the first $\boxed{M+}$ in the algorithm of Example B.11.)

(b) Use the algorithm of part (a) to compute the first ten Lucas numbers.

17. The number $\tau = \dfrac{1 + 2\overline{5}}{2} = 1.61033989\ldots$ is a fascinating number called the **golden ratio.** In Example B.4, it was discovered that $\{\tau^n\}$ is the $n$th Fibonacci number, where $\{x\}$ denotes that "round to the nearest integer" function. First, compute $\tau$ and store it in your calculator's memory. Then perform these tasks:

(a) Verify that $(2\tau - 1)^2 = 5$.

(b) Verify that $\tau^2 - \tau = 1$, $\tau^3 - 2\tau = 1$, $\tau^4 - 3\tau = 2$, $\tau^5 - 5\tau = 3$, and $\tau^6 - 8\tau = 5$.

(c) First guess, and then verify, the next three equations in the pattern of part (b).

(d) Verify that $\{\tau^2\} = 3$, $\{\tau^3\} = 4$, $\{\tau^4\} = 7$, $\{\tau^5\} = 11$, and $\{\tau^6\} = 18$.

(e) First guess, and then verify, the next three equations in the pattern of part (d). [*Suggestion:* See problem 16.]

# Appendix

# A Brief Guide to
# *The Geometer's Sketchpad*

Exciting new possibilities for exploring geometric concepts on the computer are available with geometry software. This software allows the user to construct geometric figures and graphs with both speed and precision. The software will also give the measures of angles, lengths of segments, and areas of regions. Once a figure is constructed, it can be manipulated to a continuum of new shapes that preserve the geometric relationships used to construct the original figure. In this way, the geometric properties of the configuration can be explored in a dynamic environment that is not possible with traditional paper-and-pencil sketches.

A large number of geometry programs are currently available, including the following:

*Cabri Geometry*™ (CABRILOG SAS)
*The Geometry Inventor* (PCI Educational Publishing)
*The Geometer's Sketchpad* (Key Curriculum Press, Inc.)

This appendix provides a short introduction to *The Geometer's Sketchpad* (*GSP*), *Version 5*. More advanced features of Sketchpad are described in the written manuals and online help that accompany the software. Users of other programs will need to refer to the support documents their own software. Even so, there is much common ground, and it should not be difficult to modify the procedures in the examples that follow to accommodate the software being used.

## The Sketch Window

The Sketch Window (Windows platform) is shown in Figure C.1.

**FIGURE C.1**
The Sketch Window (*Windows* platform) in *The Geometer's Sketchpad*, showing a caption; a labeled sketch; measurements of lengths *a*, *b*, and *c*; and calculations that illustrate the Pythagorean theorem

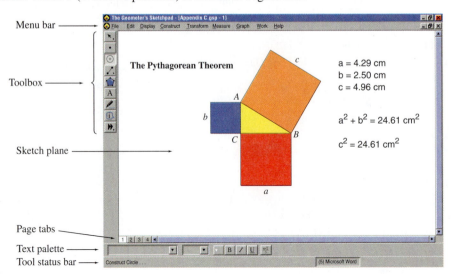

- **Menu bar**     Dragging downward accesses a list of commands available to create and investigate figures.
- **Toolbox**     Clicking the icon activates the corresponding tool.
- **Sketch plane**     The area where figures and graphs appear.
- **Page tabs**     Click to go to a different page.
- **Text palette**     Add captions and labels.
- **Tool status bar**     Shows which tool is active.

## Using the Toolbox

The Toolbox, shown in Figure C.2, is located along the left side of the Sketch Window. It contains tools for selecting; dragging; creating basic objects such as points, circles, lines, and polygons; labeling objects and writing captions; and accessing a menu to use or create custom tools. Clicking on a tool icon activates the corresponding tool.

**FIGURE C.2**
The Toolbox

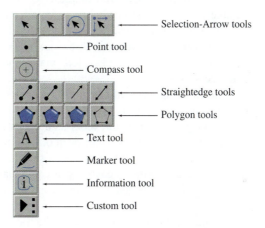

When the Selection Arrow is the active tool, clicking on an object in the sketch plane will cause the object to be outlined in pink, indicating that the object is selected. For example, if you select a line segment, you can then open the Display Menu to choose the line style (hairline, thin, medium, thick) and color. Clicking on a sequence of objects will create a group of selected objects. For example, if you select two points, you can open the Construct Menu and use the **Circle by Center + Point** command to construct the circle that is centered at the first selected point and passes through the second selected point. Notice that the order in which objects are selected may be quite important. An easy way to select multiple objects is to use the Selection Arrow to click and drag a box, since this action will select all of the objects within the box. If an unwanted object is inadvertently selected, it can be deselected by clicking on it, which will also cause its pink outline to be removed. To deselect all objects, click on any blank space in the sketch plane.

The **Selection Arrow tools** are accessed by clicking and dragging the arrow icon to the right. Any of the three tools can be used to select an object or group of objects in the figure. The **Translate tool** is used to translate the selected objects to other positions in the Sketch Window. The **Rotate tool** is used to rotate the selected object around a point previously marked as the rotation center. Similarly, the **Dilate tool** changes the size of the selected objects by performing a size transformation about the marked center. The center point of a rotation or dilation is chosen by selecting the point and executing the **Mark Center** command under the Transform Menu. Alternatively, double-clicking a point will mark it as the center.

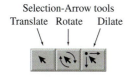

The **Point tool** creates points. Each click constructs a point at the cursor position in the sketch plane.

The **Compass tool** creates a circle by clicking to create the center point and then dragging the cursor to a second point in the sketch plane. The point at which the mouse button is released is a point on the circle.

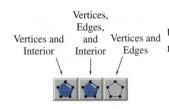

Straightedge tools
Segment   Ray   Line

There are three **Straightedge tools,** activated by clicking and dragging the straightedge tool icon to the right. The **Segment, Ray,** and **Line tools** create, respectively, a segment, ray, and line by clicking on a point and dragging the cursor to a second point in the sketch plane.

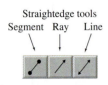

Vertices,
Edges,
Vertices and    and    Vertices and
Interior    Interior    Edges

The **Polygon tool** constructs a polygon of any number of vertices. Each click creates an additional vertex, and a double-click determines the last vertex. There is a choice of constructing the interior, the edges, or both the interior and the edges of the polygon.

The **Text tool** allows you to add labels to the objects in the sketch plane or to hide the labels. Double-clicking opens an edit box to let you change the label. Dragging the cursor creates a box into which text can be inserted.

The **Marker tool** lets you insert tick marks and angle marks with ease. It is also a free marker tool, letting you place "handwritten" marks and notes to add emphases  or and explanations to your constructions.

The **Information tool** provides descriptions of objects' mathematical definitions and the relationships between objects in a sketch.

Clicking on the **Custom tools** icon opens a menu that gives you access to custom tools found either in the custom tools folder or in other active documents. You can also create a new tool which will reproduce an object that has been selected in the sketch plane. For example, if you have constructed a square with its center, you can create a custom tool that will construct a square and its center by just clicking and dragging from one vertex to another; there is no need to repeat all of the construction steps again.

Figure C.3 has been created with the toolbox, beginning with a circle constructed with the circle tool. Next, the polygon tool has been used to construct an inscribed quadrilateral, showing the edges and interior of the polygon. The text tool has been used to label the points $O$ at the circle's center, the point $P$ on the circle, the circle label $c_1$, and the vertices of the quadrilateral $ABCD$. The marker tool has been used to place angle and tick marks on the polygon, as well as drawing the red arrows. The information tool was clicked on the circle, opening the balloon containing information about the circle.

**FIGURE C.3**
A figure constructed with toolbox commands

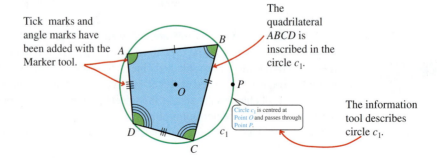

Tick marks and angle marks have been added with the Marker tool.

The quadrilateral *ABCD* is inscribed in the circle $c_1$.

Circle $c_1$ is centred at Point $O$ and passes through Point $P$.

The information tool describes circle $c_1$.

**EXAMPLE C.1**  **Constructing a Triangle with the Toolbox**

Construct a triangle, and investigate how it can be labeled and manipulated.

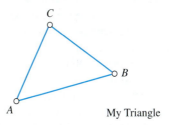

My Triangle

**Solution**  Begin with a clear sketch plane. (*Note:* The **New Sketch** command in the File Menu will create a new sketch window with a blank sketch plane.) Activate the Segment tool, and move the cursor back to the sketch plane. Now click and drag from point to point to draw a triangle. Next, return to the toolbox and activate the Text tool. Clicking the pointer when it turns black provides a label of the vertex or side of your triangle. A second click on the labeled object will hide the label. Double-clicking a label allows you to edit the label. With the Text tool still active, click and drag at an empty place in the sketch plane to create a box in which text can be typed. Similarly, explore other tools in the toolbox to discover their functions.

The use of the toolbox can be explored in "free play" experimentation. You will quickly discover how to construct circles, rays, line segments, and polygons. However, for more sophisticated constructions, you will want to use commands from the Construct and Transform menus.

| Construct |
| --- |
| Point On Object |
| Midpoint |
| Intersection |
| Segment |
| Ray |
| Line |
| Parallel Line |
| Perpendicular Line |
| Angle Bisector |
| Circle By Center + Point |
| Circle By Center + Radius |
| Arc On Circle |
| Arc Through 3 Points |
| Interior |
| Locus |

# Using the Menus

## The Construct Menu

An alternative method for creating a line segment is to select the desired endpoints of the segment in the sketch plane. The **Segment** command will construct the segment between the selected points. Rays and lines are constructed similarly; the first point selected is the endpoint of the ray. Each command in the Construct Menu requires certain objects in your sketch to be selected in advance. When the command appears in a light gray color in the menu, you do not have the proper objects selected to execute that command.

**EXAMPLE C.2**  **Constructing an Equilateral Triangle, the Medians, and the Centroid with the Construct Menu**

Construct any two points $A$ and $B$. Then construct an equilateral triangle $ABC$, and construct the midpoints of the sides. Construct each segment from the vertex of the triangle to the midpoint of the opposite side. These three segments, the medians, are concurrent at the centroid $G$ of the triangle.

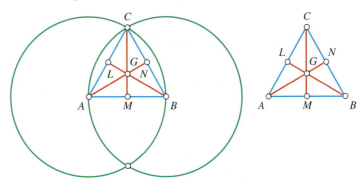

**Solution** | Activate the Point tool from the toolbox, and place two points *A* and *B* in the sketch plane. Choose the Select tool from the toolbox, and select *A* and then *B*. Use the **Circle By Center + Point** command to construct the circle centered at *A* that passes through *B*. In the same way, select point *B* and then point *A*, and construct the circle centered at *B* that passes through point *A*. Next, select the two circles and use the **Intersection** command. The two points at which the circles intersect will be constructed. Use the Text tool to label one of these point *C*. Now select *A*, *B*, and *C*, and execute the **Segment** command from the Construct Menu. This will construct the sides of the desired equilateral triangle *ABC*. The three sides just drawn are automatically selected, so the **Midpoint** command will construct the midpoints of the sides of the triangle. Label them *L*, *M*, and *N* with the Text tool. The centroid *G* of the triangle is now easy to construct: Construct $\overline{AN}$ and $\overline{BL}$, and then construct their intersection and label it *G*. Finally, construct the segment $\overline{CM}$. To check that $\overline{CM}$ passes through *G*, you can construct the intersection of $\overline{CM}$ and $\overline{AN}$ and see that it is the same point *G*. Selecting the circles and executing the **Hide** command from the Display Menu will hide the circles from view.

## The Difference Between a Construction and a Drawing

The triangle constructed in Example C.1 has no special property other than being a triangle. By dragging any vertex or side, the triangle can be manipulated to assume any triangular shape (including the degenerate case in which the three vertices lie on the same line). It is possible to drag point *C* so that △*ABC* appears to be an equilateral triangle. In this way, you will have *drawn* an "equilateral" triangle. However, dragging a vertex quickly changes the triangle to become nonequilateral, so you can easily check that you have not *constructed* a true equilateral triangle. By contrast, the triangle created in Example C.2 is equilateral by *construction*. Once points *A* and *B* were given, the point *C* was *constructed* to make △*ABC* equilateral, since *AB* and *AC* are radii of the same circle and *AB* and *BC* are radii of the same circle. You can still drag either point *A* or point *B*, but point *C*, the intersection of the circles, will always move so that △*ABC* remains equilateral. It is often best to use commands from the Construct Menu to construct a figure, since figures created with the toolbox are frequently just drawings.

> **IMPORTANT TIP:** *Construct Your Figure, Don't Just Draw It*
> Determine whether you have made a construction or a drawing by dragging several different test points in your figure and checking angle and length measurements.
>
> - **The Drag Test.** If the correct geometric relationships are retained in the figure throughout the manipulation, you likely have constructed the figure.
> - **The Measurement Test.** If incorrect geometric relationships become apparent (for example, a "right angle" changes size), you know that you have made a drawing, not a construction.

| Transform |
| --- |
| **Mark Center** |
| **Mark Mirror** |
| **Mark Angle** |
| **Mark Ratio** |
| **Mark Vector** |
| **Mark Distance** |
| Translate . . . |
| Rotate . . . |
| Dilate . . . |
| Reflect |
| Iterate . . . |
| Define Custom Transform . . . |
| Edit Custom Transforms . . . |

## The Transform Menu

The Transform Menu allows objects to be translated, rotated, dilated, and reflected. For example, to perform a reflection, select the desired line of reflection and execute the **Mark Mirror** command. Next, back in the sketch plane, select all of the objects that you wish to reflect. Now execute the **Reflect** command. This will construct the reflection of the selected objects across the mirror line. Translations, rotations, and dilations are performed in a similar way, and again some experimentation will quickly make it clear how the commands in the Transform Menu are used in constructions and investigations.

**EXAMPLE C.3** **Creating a Hexagonal Tiling with the Transform Menu**

Construct a hexagon *ABCDEF* with a pair of opposite sides $\overline{AB}$ and $\overline{DE}$ that are parallel and congruent. Construct the midpoint *M* of $\overline{BC}$, and rotate the hexagon by 180° about the midpoint to create a 10-sided polygonal tile. Then show that translations of the decagon will tile the plane.

**Solution**   Use the Segment tool to construct three adjacent sides $\overline{AB}$, $\overline{BC}$, and $\overline{CD}$. Select points *B* and *D*, in that order, and execute the **Mark Vector** command in the Transform Menu. Next, select point *A* and segment $\overline{AB}$, and then execute the **Translate . . . By Marked Vector** command in the Transform Menu. This will extend *ABCD* to become *ABCDE*, where $\overline{DE}$ is parallel to, and the same length as, $\overline{AB}$. Now complete the hexagon by constructing any point *F* and segments $\overline{EF}$ and $\overline{FA}$. Construct the midpoint *M* of $\overline{BC}$ by selecting $\overline{BC}$ and executing the **Midpoint** command from the Construct Menu. Now select *M*, and execute the **Mark Center** command to choose *M* as the center of rotation. Next, select the hexagon (all six sides and all six vertices) and execute the **Rotate . . . By Fixed Angle** (namely, by 180°) command. This creates the desired ten-sided double-hexagon tile. Selecting the tile and repeatedly executing the **Translate . . . By Marked Vector** command will quickly produce a row of repeated double hexagons. To extend the tiling in a downward direction, select the initial point and terminal point of the dashed arrow and execute **Mark Vector.** Then select the whole row of tiles and execute **Translate . . . By Marked Vector.**

**Measure**

Length
Distance
Perimeter
Circumference
Angle
Area
Arc Angle
Arc Length
Radius
Ratio
Value of Point

Coordinates
Abscissa (x )
Ordinate (y )
Coordinate Distance
Slope
Equation

**Number**

New Parameter . . .

Calculate . . .

Tabulate
Add Table Data . . .
Remove Table Data . . .

New Function . . .

Define Derivative Function
Define Function from
    Drawing

# The Measure and Number Menus

Distances, lengths, areas, perimeters, angles, and so forth can be measured by executing commands in the Measure Menu. For example, selecting three points *A*, *B*, and *C* (in that order) and executing the **Angle** command will display the measure of $\angle ABC$ in the sketch plane. The measurement caption can be dragged to any convenient position in the sketch plane.

The **Value of Point** command (new in Version 5) gives the proportional distance of a point confined to a path. For example, if *P* is a point on a line $\overline{AB}$, the value of *P* is its proportional distance $t, 0 \leq t \leq 1$, from *A* toward *B*. In particular, *P* has the value 0.5 at the midpoint of $\overline{AB}$. If *A* is a point on the graph of a function, the value of *A* is the value of the independent variable in the domain of the function.

The **Number** menu, though new to version 5, collects commands that are in most cases available in either the Measure or Graph menus in earlier versions of GSP. In particular, the **Calculate . . .** command allows you to explore the numerical relationships and properties of measurements of figures and graphs, the **Tabulate** commands allow you to record particular instances of numerical relationships in a tabular form, and the command **Define Function from Drawing,** new to Version 5, defines a function that was drawn with the Marker tool.

EXAMPLE **C.4** # Exploring the Converse of the Pythagorean Theorem with the Measure Menu

Draw any triangle, and use the Text tool to label the three vertices $A$, $B$, and $C$ and the three respective opposite sides $a$, $b$, and $c$. Measure the lengths $a$, $b$, and $c$ of the three sides and measure $\angle ACB$. Use the **Calculate . . .** command to display $a^2 + b^2 - c^2$, and make a table that records values of $a^2 + b^2 - c^2$ and $m\angle ACB$. Drag point $C$ to new positions, and add new data to the table for new positions of $C$. What kind of a triangle is $ABC$ when $a^2 + b^2 - c^2$ is zero? positive? negative?

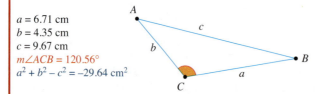

$a = 6.71$ cm
$b = 4.35$ cm
$c = 9.67$ cm
$m\angle ACB = 120.56°$
$a^2 + b^2 - c^2 = -29.64$ cm$^2$

| $a^2 + b^2 - c^2$ | $m\angle ACB$ |
|---|---|
| 66.05 cm$^2$ | 32.33° |
| 39.45 cm$^2$ | 50.84° |
| 15.76 cm$^2$ | 72.82° |
| 0.00 cm$^2$ | 90.00° |
| −10.97 cm$^2$ | 102.39° |
| −29.64 cm$^2$ | 120.56° |
| −29.64 cm$^2$ | 120.56° |

**Solution**   We have already described how a triangle can be drawn. Manipulating the triangle should reveal that $\angle ACB$ is a right angle precisely when the expression $a^2 + b^2 - c^2$ is 0. If $a^2 + b^2 - c^2 > 0$, the angle measure at vertex $C$ is less than 90°. On the other hand, if $a^2 + b^2 - c^2 < 0$, then the angle measure at vertex $C$ is greater than 90°.

---

**Graph**

Define Coordinate System
Mark Coordinate System
Grid Form

Show Grid
Dotted Grid
Snap Points

Plot Value on Axis . . .
Plot Points . . .
Plot Table Data . . .

Plot New Function . . .
Plot Parametric Curve . . .

# The Graph Menu

The **Define Coordinate System** command turns the sketch plane into a coordinate plane showing the coordinate $x$- and $y$-axes and points at the origin $(0, 0)$ and at $(1, 0)$. Dragging these points allows you to reposition the origin and vary the scale of the coordinate system. The **Grid Form** command permits you to choose among three grid forms. In the square grid form, the $x$- and $y$-axes have the same scale. In the rectangular form, the two axes can be scaled independently of one another. In the polar grid form, the grid lines are circles and rays from the origin, and points are plotted by their distance $r$ from the origin and their counterclockwise angle $\theta$ from the positive $x$-axis.

The **Plot Points . . .** command opens a dialog box in which you enter the coordinates of the points you wish to plot in the coordinate plane.

EXAMPLE **C.5** # Plotting Points and Finding Equations

Plot the points $C$, $D$, $E$, and $F$, as $(3, 4)$, $(9, 1)$, $(-1, 1)$, and $(2, 7)$, respectively, and then construct the lines $\overleftrightarrow{CD}$ and $\overleftrightarrow{EF}$ and the point $G$ where the lines intersect. Find the equations and slopes of the two lines, and show that the product of the slopes is $-1$. Next, plot the point $H$ as $(4, 1)$, and construct the circle centered at $H$ that passes through $G$. Find the equation of the circle to verify that the radius is 5, and check that the circle also passes through $D$ and $E$.

Slope $\overleftrightarrow{CD} = -0.5$
Slope $\overleftrightarrow{EF} = 2.0$
(Slope $\overleftrightarrow{CD}$) · (Slope $\overleftrightarrow{EF}$) = $-1.0$
$\overleftrightarrow{CD}: y = -0.5x + 5.5$
$\overleftrightarrow{EF}: y = 2.0x + 3.0$
$\odot HG: (x - 4.0)^2 + (y - 1.0)^2 = 5.0^2$

**Solution**

The points can be plotted by opening the **Plot Points . . .** dialog box. Alternatively, the points can be plotted directly by selecting the Point tool and clicking on the appropriate intersections of the grid lines. Use the Text tool from the toolbox to label all the points in your sketch, starting with $A$ as $(0, 0)$ and $B$ as $(1, 0)$. The two lines, $\overleftrightarrow{CD}$ and $\overleftrightarrow{EF}$, can be constructed with the Straightedge tool. With both lines selected, use the **Slope** and **Calculate** commands from the Measure Menu to display the slopes of the lines and compute their product. Clicking on the intersection of the two lines with the Selection-Arrow tool will construct their point of intersection, which is then labeled $G$. Next, use the Compass tool to construct the circle centered at $H$ that passes through $G$. With the two lines and the circle selected, use the **Equation** command in the Measure Menu to obtain their equations. In particular, the radius of the circle is seen to be 5. Since both $D$ and $E$ are five units from $H$, $\overline{DE}$ is a diameter of the circle.

Graphs of functions can also be plotted on coordinate axes in the sketch plane. The **New Function . . .** command opens an entry box into which a function expression is typed. To graph the function, select the function expression in the sketch window and execute the **Plot Function** command. To examine the values of the function, select the plot and execute the **Point on Function Plot** command in the Construct Menu. With that point selected, the $x$- and $y$-values along the plot can be displayed by using the **Coordinates** command, or the **Abscissa (x)** and **Ordinate (y)** commands, under the Measure Menu. The function values can be displayed in a table in Sketchpad: Select the measures and use the **Tabulate** command in the Graph Menu.

**EXAMPLE  C.6  Finding the Rectangle of Largest Area in a Semicircle**

Find the rectangle of largest area that can be inscribed in a semicircle, with one side of the rectangle along the diameter.

**Solution**

We may as well assume that the radius of the semicircle is 1. The following diagram shows an inscribed rectangle whose side along the diameter has length $2x$:

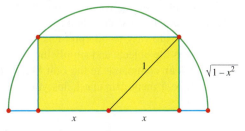

By the Pythagorean theorem, the vertical side has length $\sqrt{1-x^2}$. The area of the rectangle is therefore given by the function $f(x) = 2x\sqrt{1-x^2}$, where $0 < x < 1$. The following figure shows the graph of this function, as plotted with *The Geometer's Sketchpad*:

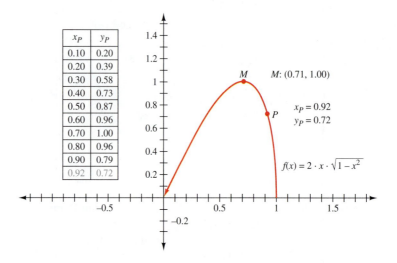

| $x_P$ | $y_P$ |
|------|------|
| 0.10 | 0.20 |
| 0.20 | 0.39 |
| 0.30 | 0.58 |
| 0.40 | 0.73 |
| 0.50 | 0.87 |
| 0.60 | 0.96 |
| 0.70 | 1.00 |
| 0.80 | 0.96 |
| 0.90 | 0.79 |
| 0.92 | 0.72 |

$M$: (0.71, 1.00)

$x_P = 0.92$
$y_P = 0.72$

$f(x) = 2 \cdot x \cdot \sqrt{1-x^2}$

The coordinates of point $P$ have been tabulated at several sample locations along the plot. The largest ordinate is $y = 1.0$, occurring when $x$ is about 0.71. A more detailed analysis would show that the exact maximum area is indeed 1, occurring when the rectangle has width $2x = \sqrt{2}$ and height $\sqrt{1 - (1/\sqrt{2})^2} = \sqrt{1 - 1/2} = \sqrt{1/2} = 1/\sqrt{2}$. That is, the rectangle of largest area is the one shaped like a domino (a double-square), with its length twice that of its width.

# The File, Edit, and Display Menus

The File Menu allows you to create a new sketch window or open a saved sketch. Newly created sketches and modified sketches can be saved for future use. New pages can be added to a sketch by using the **Document Options . . . /Add Page** command. This command is particularly useful when you wish to create a sequence of related sketches.

The Edit Menu permits you to undo and redo steps in your constructions, as well as perform the usual cuts, copies, and pastes. Deleting or clearing an object will also remove those objects in the sketch which depend on the deleted object, so these functions must be used with care. Sketchpad is a powerful drawing tool, and copied graphics can be inserted into other documents. To find out how a point, a line, or another object is related to the rest of your sketch, select the object of interest and use the **Properties . . .** command. Even more easily, select the Information Tool and click the question mark cursor on the object of interest.

The Display Menu gives you choices of line styles, colors, and text styles. It also allows you to hide selected parts of your sketch from view, a feature which is often useful for making uncluttered sketches that are easy to interpret and understand. The **Hide Objects** command, as the name suggests, retains the objects and simply hides them from view. In this way, it is very different from the **Cut** and **Clear** commands in the Edit Menu. The **Show/Hide Text Palette** command allows you to show or hide a menu bar that helps you format captions and labels. The Text palette is shown in Figure C.1.

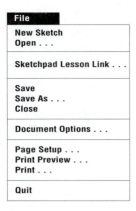

# Advanced Features

The construction methods described and illustrated in the preceding examples will enable the user of *The Geometer's Sketchpad* to create a wide variety of interesting figures to investigate. However, Sketchpad has other features that more experienced users will find valuable. For example, Sketchpad can add an exciting dynamic dimension to a sketch by incorporating animation, movement, hide/show buttons, and so on. The user's manuals and online help for the software describe these features and how they are employed.

## Problem Set C

Exercises numbered in red are answered in the back of the text.

1. **Drawing Figures.** Construct a general quadrilateral and perform the following manipulations:

   (a) Drag the vertices of the quadrilateral until your quadrilateral appears to be a rhombus. See how close you've come by measuring the lengths of the four sides. Why is the rhombus a drawing and not a construction?

   (b) Drag the vertices of the quadrilateral until your quadrilateral appears to be a rectangle. What measurements can be made to see how close your drawing comes to a true rectangle?

2. **Constructing Figures.** Construct each figure listed, using commands from the Construct Menu. In words, describe the construction steps that you followed. Hide any midpoints, perpendicular bisectors, parallel lines, circles, and so on that you used to construct your figure. Check that your figure is a construction by dragging various points and observing whether the figure retains all of the necessary properties which define that type of figure. Look for alternative constructions of the figures.

   (a) Isosceles triangle (given base $\overline{AB}$)

   (b) Kite *KITE* (given *K* and *T*)

   (c) Isosceles trapezoid *ABCD* (given base $\overline{AB}$)

   (d) Parallelogram *ABCD* (given *A*, *B*, and *C*)

   (e) Rhombus *ABCD* (given *A* and *C*)

   (f) Square *ABCD* (given *A* and *B*)

3. **A Hexagonal Tiling.** Construct any convex quadrilateral and construct the midpoint of one of its sides. Mark the midpoint as a rotation center. (Alternatively, just double-click the desired rotation center.) Select the entire quadrilateral, and, from the Transform Menu, use **Rotate . . .** (by 180° about the marked center) to create a six-sided polygonal tile. Finally, translate the hexagonal tile repeatedly to create a tiling of the plane. Does your quadrilateral still tile the plane if you drag one of its vertices to form a concave quadrilateral?

4. **Measuring and Calculating.** Construct a general quadrilateral *ABCD*. Then construct the midpoints *J*, *K*, *L*, and *M* of the sides and join them with line segments to construct the inscribed quadrilateral *JKLM* as shown here:

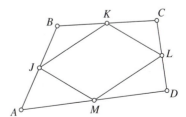

   (a) What is the sum of the measures of the interior angles of *ABCD*?

   (b) What relationships hold for the measures of the interior angles of the quadrilateral *JKLM*?

(c) What relation exists between the lengths of the sides of *JKLM* and the diagonal distances *AC* and *BD* across the quadrilateral?

(d) Select (in order) the vertices of *ABCD* and use **Polygon Interior** from the Construct Menu to construct the interior of the quadrilateral. Similarly, construct the interior of *JKLM*. Select the interiors of both *ABCD* and *JKLM*, and measure their respective areas with **Measure/Area.** What relationship do you observe between the areas?

5. **Constructing Figures with Coordinates.** To keep the points visible in the plots requested in this exercise, select cm (centimeter) as the unit of distance measure under **Preferences . . .** in the Edit Menu. Also, select **Show Grid** and **Snap Points** under the Graph Menu.

(a) Plot the points $(0, 6)$, $(-3, 0)$, and $(9, -6)$, and show that they are the vertices of a right triangle.

(b) Show that $(6, 3)$, $(-3, 0)$, $(-5, -4)$, and $(4, -1)$ are the vertices of a parallelogram.

(c) Show that $(13, 1)$, $(-3, 9)$, and $(0, -12)$ are the vertices of a triangle inscribed in a circle centered at $(2, -1)$.

6. **Creating Graphs of Functions.**

(a) Plot the graph of the function $f(x) = x + \dfrac{2}{\sqrt{x}}$, and estimate the coordinates of the point $M$ corresponding to the minimum value of the function.

(b) On the same axes used in part (a), plot the graph of the function $g(x) = \dfrac{x^2}{2} - 1$ and estimate the coordinates of the point $I$ at which the two graphs intersect.

# Resources

The organizations, materials sources, journals, and Web sites listed in this appendix are of value to both preservice and in-service teachers. They represent, however, only a small sample of what is available. We recommend that you create and maintain your own personal list of resources.

## Organizations

National Council of Teachers of Mathematics (NCTM)
    1906 Association Drive, Reston, VA 20191
    www.nctm.org
Local affiliates of the NCTM
    (see listing at www.nctm.org/aboutaffiliates/)

## Conferences

Annual meeting of the NCTM, April
    Regional and affiliate conferences
      (see www.nctm.org/conferences/)

## NCTM *Principles and Standards for School Mathematics* and *Curriculum Focal Points*

Standards
    Print form: ISBN 0–87353–480–8
    Electronic form: www.nctm.org/standards/
Focal Points
    Print form: ISBN 0-87353-595-2
    Electronic form: www.nctm.org/standards/content

## Journals

*Journal of Computers in Mathematics and Science Teaching*
*Journal of Research in Mathematics Education*
*The Mathematics Teacher*
*Mathematics Teaching in the Middle School*

*School Science and Mathematics*
*Teaching Children Mathematics*
*Teaching K–8*

# Technology

The Geometer's Sketchpad: Key Curriculum Press (www.keymath.com)
Texas Instruments (http://education.ti.com/)

# Internet Sites: General

Math Archives (http://archives.math.utk.edu/)
Math Central (http://mathcentral.uregina.ca/)
Mathematics Education and Outreach Resources (Carl Lee home page)
    (http://www.ms.uky.edu/~lee/outreach.html)
Math Forum (http://mathforum.org/)
MathWorld (http://mathworld.wolfram.com/)
Suzanne's Math Lessons (http://mathforum.org/alejandre/)

# Internet Sites by Topic

Border and Wallpaper Patterns
    Kali Java Applet (http://www.geom.uiuc.edu/java/Kali/program.html)
    Steffen Weber's Page (http://jcrystal.com/steffenweber/)
Fibonacci Numbers
    Fibonacci Association Official Web Site (http://www.mscs.dal.ca/Fibonacci/)
    http://www.maths.surrcy.ac.uk/hostcd-sitcs/R.Knott/Fibonacci/fib.html
Fractions
    Visual Fractions (http://www.visualfractions.com/)
    The Rational Number Project (http://www.cehd.umn.edu/rationalnumberproject/rnp2.html)
Geometry
    Geometry Games (http://www.gamequarium.com/geometry.html)
    The Geometry Center (www.geom.uiuc.edu/)
History
    The MacTutor History of Mathematics Archive (http://turnbull.dcs.st-and.ac.uk/~history/)
    Biographies of Women Mathematicians (http://www.agnesscott.edu/lriddle/women/women.htm)
Integer Sequences
    Encyclopedia of Integer Sequences (http://www.research.att.com/~njas/sequences/)
Measurement
    Powers of Ten (http://www.powersof10.com/)
Prime Numbers
    The Prime Pages (http://www.utm.edu/research/primes/)
Tilings, Tessellations, Escher-like designs, and Geometric Dissections
    Totally Tessellated (http://library.thinkquest.org/16661)
    Tesellations.org (http://www.tessellations.org/)
    Geometric dissections on the web
    (http://www.cs.purdue.edu/homes/gnf/book/webdiss.html)
Virtual Manipulatives
    Computing Technology for Math Excellence
    (http://www.ct4me.net/math_manipulatives.htm#Manipulatives)
    Shodor Interactivate (http://www.shodor.org/interactivate/activities/)

# Answers to Problems

# Chapter 1

## Problem Set 1.1 (page 6)

**1. (a)** 21 bikes, 6 trikes.
**4. (a)**

**5.** 3 dimes, 3 nickels, 3 pennies (Make an orderly list.)
**6.** 12 (Work backward from 52.)
**9. (a)**

```
      6                        1
   1     2        or        6     5
  5   3   4                2   4   3
```

**11. (a)**

```
 7   15   8        (b)  7   12   5

  11    20              10     21

 4   16   12        3   19   16
```

**(c)**

```
 1   7   6        (d) There is no solution.

    9                16

 8   18   10
```

**12. (a)** 1, 2, 3, 5, 8, 13, 21 **(c)** 3, 5, 8, 13, 21, 34, 55
**(e)** 2, 1, 3, 4, 7, 11 **14. (b)** Each result is 5.

## Problem Set 1.2 (page 16)

**1.** No. When 10 is multiplied by 5 and 13 is added, the result is
63, not 48. **2.** 3
**4. (a)** Yes. Yes. The rules are really the same.
**5. (a)**

```
      8
    7   1
 11   4   5
```

**(b)**

```
      19
    8   11
 9   1   12
```

**(c)**

```
      7
   2.5   4.5
 11   8.5   13
```

**(d)**

```
      -2
   -3   1
 7   10   11
```

**7.** 49

**11.** Assuming that the bags are identical, the possibilities are as shown:

| Bag 1 | Bag 2 | Bag 3 |
|-------|-------|-------|
| 23 | 1 | 1 |
| 21 | 3 | 1 |
| 19 | 5 | 1 |
| 19 | 3 | 3 |
| 17 | 7 | 1 |
| 17 | 3 | 5 |
| 15 | 9 | 1 |
| 15 | 7 | 3 |
| 15 | 5 | 5 |
| 13 | 11 | 1 |
| 13 | 9 | 3 |
| 13 | 7 | 5 |
| 11 | 11 | 3 |
| 11 | 9 | 5 |
| 11 | 7 | 7 |
| 9 | 9 | 7 |

**13.** 4 and 24, 6 and 16, 8 and 12
**15.** 9 minutes **18.** Dawkins, Chalmers, Ertl, Albright, Badgett

## Problem Set 1.3 (page 26)

**1. (a)** 14, 17, 20 **(c)** 10, 15, 15 **(e)** 162, 486, 1458 **3. (a)** 16
**4. (a)** Yes, the difference of consecutive terms is the constant $-3$.
**(b)** The difference between the last and the first is $-52 - 8 = -60$.
Thus, the number of terms is one more than $-60/(-3) = 20$. There
are 21 terms.
**5. (a)** $1 + 2 + 3 + 4 + 5 + 4 + 3 + 2 + 1 = 25$
$1 + 2 + 3 + 4 + 5 + 6 + 5 + 4 +$
$3 + 2 + 1 = 36$
**8. (a)** 86 **(d)** 42
**10. (a)** $1 - 4 + 9 - 16 + 25 = 15$
$1 - 4 + 9 - 16 + 25 - 36 = -21$
**(b)** $1 - 4 + 9 - 16 + 25 - 36 + 49 = 28$
$1 - 4 + 9 - 16 + 25 - 36 + 49 - 64 = -36$
**(c)** For even $n$, $1 - 4 + 9 - \cdots - n^2 = -\dfrac{n(n + 1)}{2}$.

For odd $n$, $1 - 4 + 9 - \cdots + n^2 = \dfrac{n(n + 1)}{2}$.
**15. (a)** 6 **(c)** 4950 **19. (a)** 30; 2100; 29,400

## Problem Set 1.4 (page 36)

**1. (a)** Each pattern has one more column of dots than the previous
one. The next three patterns are shown:

**(d)** The $n$th even number    **2.** Let $n$ be Toni's number. Toni is doubling it to get $2n$ and then adding 11 (ending with $2n + 11$). Thus, $2n + 11 = 39$, or $2n = 28$, so $n = 14$.    **6. (a)** Each additional table increases the number of seats by 4. Thus, the number seated at $n$ tables has the form $a + 4n$, for some $a$. Since 6 are seated at the first table (when $n = 1$), it follows that $a = 2$. Thus, $2 + 4n$ people can be seated at $n$ tables.    **(b)** To seat 24 people, $n$ must be the smallest integer for which $2 + 4n$ is at least 24. This occurs at $n = 6$ and leaves two empty places.

**7. (a)** Person A shakes with person B and C. Since B and C have already shaken hands with A, only one shake remains: B with C. Total is $2 + 1 = 3$.    **(c)** The logic is the same as (b). The first person shakes hands with the other 199, the second with 198, the third with 197, etc., until we get to the penultimate person, who has only one new hand to shake. Total $= 199 + 198 + 197 + 196 + \cdots + 2 + 1 = (200)(199)/2 = 19{,}900$, where we have used Gauss insight.    **13. (a)** In each figure, dots are added to the upper left, upper right, and lower right sides to complete the next larger pentagon:

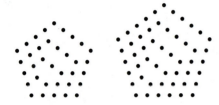

**(b)** $1, 5, 12, 22, 35, 51, \ldots$
**(c)** $1 + 4 + 7 + 10 + 13 = 35$
$1 + 4 + 7 + 10 + 13 + 16 = 51$
**(d)** 10th term $= 1 + 3(9) = 28$
**(e)** Use Gauss insight:

$$
\begin{aligned}
s &= 1 + 4 + 7 + \cdots + 28 \\
s &= 28 + 25 + 22 + \cdots + 1 \\
2s &= 29 + 29 + 29 + \cdots + 29 \\
\text{Sum} &= \frac{(10)(29)}{2} = 145.
\end{aligned}
$$

**(f)** $n$th term $= 1 + 3(n - 1) = 3n - 2$
**(g)** Using Gauss insight, we see that there are $n$ terms of $(3n - 1)$. The sum is $\dfrac{n(3n - 1)}{2}$. Therefore, $p_n = \dfrac{n(3n - 1)}{2}$.

**16. (a)** The entries in the second row are $x + 8$ and 9, so $(x + 8) + 9 = 23$, or equivalently, $x + 17 = 23$. Subtracting 17 from both sides gives $x = 6$. The entries in the second row are then 14 and 9, respectively.

**17.** Suppose that $x$ denotes the value in the lower small circle. Then the entries in the other small circles are $17 - x$ and $26 - x$, giving the equation $(17 - x) + (26 - x) = 11$. This equation simplifies to $43 - 2x = 11$, or $2x = 43 - 11 = 32$. Therefore, $x = 16$, and the entries in the other two circles are $17 - 16 = 1$ and $26 - 16 = 10$. Alternatively, one can work clockwise to see that the upper-left small circle is $17 - x$ and therefore the remaining small circle value is $11 - (17 - x) = x - 6$. Then $(x - 6) + x = 26$, or $2x - 6 = 26$. As before, $x = 16$.

**18.** Let $x$ be the unknown value in the lowermost circle. Working clockwise, we find that the entries in the other small circles are $13 - x, 13 + x, 18 - x$, and $x - 1$. Thus, $x + (x - 1) = 23$, or equivalently, $2x = 24$ and $x = 12$. In clockwise order from the bottom, the entries are then 12, 1, 25, 6, and 11.

**19. (b)** Let $x, y, z, w$ be integers in the circles.

(diagram: circles labeled $x$, 13, $y$ on top row; 10 and 8 in middle; $z$, 6, $w$ on bottom row)

The conditions of the problem are $x + y = 13$, $x + z = 10$, $y + w = 8$, and $w + z = 6$. Subtracting the first two yields $y - z = 3$. Subtracting the last two yields $y - z = 2$, which is impossible. Thus, there are no solutions.

**20. (a)**

| $n$ | 1 | 2 | 3 | 4 | 5 | 6 |
|---|---|---|---|---|---|---|
| $n^2$ | 1 | 4 | 9 | 16 | 25 | 36 |
| $(n + 1)^2$ | 4 | 9 | 16 | 25 | 36 | 49 |
| difference | 3 | 5 | 7 | 9 | 11 | 13 |

**24.** Let $L$ and $W$ denote the length and width, respectively, of the rectangle and $S$ denote the length of the sides of the square. Since the rectangle is 3 times as long as it is wide, $L = 3W$. Therefore, the perimeter of the rectangle is $2L + 2W = 6W + 2W = 8W$, and its area is $LW = 3W^2$. The perimeter of the square is $4S$, and its area is $S^2$. We know that the rectangle and the square have the same perimeter, so $8W = 4S$, or $2W = S$. Also, the area of the square is 4 square feet more than the area of the rectangle, so $S^2 = 3W^2 + 4$. By substitution, $(2W)^2 = 3W^2 + 4$, or $4W^2 = 3W^2 + 4$. Therefore, $W^2 = 4$, and the positive width of the rectangle is $W = 2$. Its length is $L = 3W = 6$. The square has sides of length $S = 2W = 4$.

## Problem Set 1.5   (page 44)

**1.** Yes. The second player can add enough tallies to make a multiple of 5 at each step, forcing the first player to be the one to exceed 30.
**3. (a)** $28
**6.** Moe was wearing Hiram's coat and Joe's hat. Hiram was wearing Joe's coat and Moe's hat.
**7. (a)** 25. Not all of the information was needed.
**8.**

| | Choc. Malt | Straw. Shake | Banana Split | Walnut cone |
|---|---|---|---|---|
| Aaron | X | X | X | O |
| Boyd | X | X | O | X |
| Carol | O | X | X | X |
| Donna | X | O | X | X |

Aaron had the walnut cone. Boyd had the banana split. Carol had the chocolate malt. Donna had the strawberry shake.
**12. (a)** 3    **14.** Since there are only 10 digits $(0, 1, 2, \ldots, 9)$ in any collection of 11 natural numbers, there must be two that have the same units digit. The difference of these two numbers must have a 0 as its units digit and is thus divisible by 10.
**16.** If five points are chosen in a square with diagonal of length $1\sqrt{2}$, then, by the Pigeonhole Principle, at least two of the points must be in or on the boundary of one of the four smaller squares

shown. The farthest these two points can be from each other is $\sqrt{2}/2$ units, if they are on opposite corners of the small square.

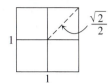

**18.** If the cups of marbles are arranged as described, each cup will be part of three different groups of three adjacent cups. The sum of all marbles in all groups of three adjacent cups is $3 \cdot (10 \cdot 11/2) = 165$, since each cup of marbles is counted three times. With the marble count of 165 and 10 possible groups of three adjacent cups, by the pigeonhole principle at least one group of three adjacent cups must have 17 or more marbles, since $165 \div 10 = 16.5 > 16$.
**20. (i)** Since there are 20 people at the party, if each person has at least one friend at the party, each must have either 1 or 2 or so on, up to 19, friends at the party. Since $20 > 19$, it follows from the Pigeonhole Principle that at least 2 of the 20 people must have the same number of friends at the party. **(ii)** In this case, 19 people have from 1 to 18 friends at the party. Thus, again by the Pigeonhole Principle, at least 2 people must have the same number of friends at the party. **(iii)** In this case, since at least 2 people have no friends at the party, they have the same number of friends at the party.

## Problem Set 1.6   (page 55)

**1. (a)** $81, 711, 6111, 51111$
**3. (a)** $9, 98, 987$   **6. (a)** The values at each given point are 0.
**10. (a)** There are $F_5 = 5$ arrangements of five logs, supporting the generalization:

However, there are nine arrangements of six logs, instead of eight as suggested by the Fibonacci pattern:

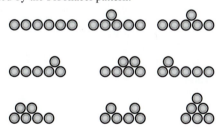

**12. (a)** Two pennies must be moved.   **13. (a)** The 1 is represented by the dot in the middle of the bottom row, the 4 by the 4 adjacent dots, the 7 by the next layer of dots, and so on.

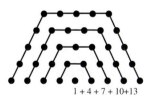

$1 + 4 + 7 + 10 + 13$

**15. (a)** The starting position and the 15 moves to interchange the frogs are shown in a table:

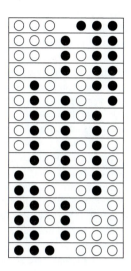

**16. (a)** Additional examples, support the conclusion that all such numbers are divisible by 30.

## Chapter 1 Review Exercises   (page 62)

**1.** 28
**2. (a)** Answers will vary. One solution is as follows:

$$\begin{array}{r} 179 \\ 368 \\ +452 \\ \hline 999 \end{array}$$

**(b)** Yes. The digits in any column can be arranged in any order.
**(c)** No. The hundreds-column digits must add up to 8 to allow for a carry from the tens column. If the digit 1 is not in the hundreds column, the smallest this sum can be is $2 + 3 + 4 = 9$. Thus, the digit 1 must be in the hundreds column.  **3.** 9  **4.** 60  **5.** 88 square feet  **6.** 9  **7. (a)** Multiply by 5 and then subtract 2.
**(b)** Answers will vary. A good strategy is to give Chanty consecutive integers starting with 0.  **8. (a)** 24, 48, 96  **(b)** 8, 32, 64, 128
**(c)** 6, 36, 1296, 7776  **(d)** 10, 50, 250, 6250  **(e)** 7, 7, 7, 7
**9.** Kimberly is the lawyer and the painter; Terry is the engineer and the doctor; Otis is the teacher and the writer.
**10. (a)** $14 + 16 + 18 + 20 = 4^3 + 4$
$22 + 24 + 26 + 28 + 30 = 5^3 + 5$
$32 + 34 + 36 + 38 + 40 + 42 = 6^3 + 6$
**(b)** $92 + 94 + 96 + 98 + 100 + 102 + 104 + 106 + 108 + 110 = 10^3 + 10$
**11. (a)** 25  **(b)** 1075  **12. (a)** 11th  **(b)** 6141
**(c)** Duly observed.
**(d)** $(6 + 12 + \cdots + 3072 + 6144) - (3 + 6 + \cdots + 3072) = 6144 - 3 = 6141$

**Table for Problem 16**

| $n$ | 1 | 2 | 3 | 4 | 5 | 6 | 7 | 8 | 9 | 10 |
|---|---|---|---|---|---|---|---|---|---|---|
| $(n\char`^5 - n)$ | 0 | 30 | 240 | 1020 | 3120 | 7770 | 16800 | 32760 | 59040 | 99990 |
| $(n\char`^5 - n)/30$ | 0 | 1 | 8 | 34 | 104 | 259 | 560 | 1092 | 1968 | 3333 |

**13.** 442,865   **14.** **(a)** $\frac{n(n+1)}{2}+1$   **(b)** $\frac{n(n-1)}{2}$   **(c)** $n^2$

**15.** The product of the squared entries equals the product of the circled entries.   **16.** **(a)** 3   **(b)** 9   **(c)** 27

**(d)** $P_0 + P_1 \cdot 2^1 + P_2 \cdot 2^2 + \cdots + P_n \cdot 2^n = 3^n$, where $P_k$ is the $k$th element of the $n$th row of Pascal's triangle.   **(e)** 4, 16, 64

**(f)** $P_0 + P_1 \cdot r^1 + P_2 \cdot r^2 + \cdots + P_n r^n = (r + 1)^n$

**17.** Let $x$ be Bernie's weight. Bernie weighs $90 + x/2$. The condition of the problem is, then, that $x = 90 + x/2$, which yields $2x = 180 + x$, or $x = 180$ pounds.   **18.** **(a)** A one-car train uses 6 toothpicks to form the hexagon. Adding a square + hexagon combination requires an additional 8 toothpicks, so the trains with $1, 3, 5, 7, \ldots$, cars use $6, 6 + 8, 6 + 8 + 8$, $6 + 8 + 8 + 8, \ldots$ toothpicks. In general, a train with $2m + 1$ cars will require $6 + 8m$ toothpicks, where $m = 0, 1, 2, 3, \ldots$. A two-car train uses 9 toothpicks, so trains with $2, 4, 6, 8, \ldots$ cars use $9, 9 + 8, 9 + 8 + 8, 9 + 8 + 8 + 8, \ldots$ toothpicks. In general, a train with $2m + 2$ cars uses $9 + 8m$ toothpicks for $m = 0, 1, 2, 3, \ldots$

**(b)** Since $9 + 8m$ is always an odd number, a train with 102 toothpicks has an odd number of cars, say, $2m + 1$. Then $6 + 8m = 102$, or $8m = 96$. Therefore, $m = 12$, and there are $2(12) + 1 = 25$ cars in the train.   **19.** **(a)** Guessing will come up with 8 for one of the values, and the other is $-1$.   **(b)** Let $x$ and $y$ be the numbers. Then $x + y = 7$ and $x - y = 9$. Adding gives $2x = 16$, so that $x = 8$. Substitution into either equation gives $y = -1$ and the solution checks.   **20.** **(a)** 5   **(b)** 9   **(c)** 50   **21.** 17   **22.** **(a)** 4489, 444,889, 44,448,889   **(b)** 44,444,448,888,889 No, as noted earlier patterns can break down.   **23.** **(a)** 142,857; 285,714; 428,571; 571,428; 714,285   **(b)** All of the answers shown are obtained by starting at an appropriate place in the following circle:

**(c)** The answer to $7 \times 142,857$ is not clear. In fact, $7 \times 142,857 = 999,999$.   **(d)** Apparent patterns may be misleading. **24.** One possibility is shown. In fact, $P$, $Q$, and $R$ are collinear for every placement of $\triangle ABC$ and $\triangle A'B'C'$.

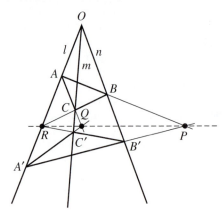

**25.** Since one of any two consecutive integers must be even, $\dfrac{s(s+1)}{2}$ must be an integer, say, $q$. Thus, $n^2 = 8q + 1$, as was to be shown.   **26.** No, 12 is a multiple of 6, but the sum of its digits is 3, which is not divisible by 6.

## Chapter 1 Test   (page 65)

**1.** 3   **2.** 21,111,111; 12,111,111; 11,211,111; 11,121,111; 11,112,111; 11,111,211; 11,111,121; 11,111,112

**3.** **(a)** $2 \times 100 - 1 = 199$   **(b)** 10,000

**4.** **(a)** $2 + 5 + 8 + 11 + 8 + 5 + 2 = 41 = 3^2 + 2 \cdot 4^2$
$2 + 5 + 8 + 11 + 14 + 11 + 8 + 5 + 2 = 66 = 4^2 + 2 \cdot 5^2$

**(b)** $2 + 5 + 8 + \cdots + 26 + 29 + 26 + \cdots + 8 + 5 + 2 = 281 = 9^2 + 2 \cdot 10^2$   **5.** 10 days   **6.** The sum of the elements of the $n$th row of Pascal's triangle is $2^n$.
$S = 1 + 2 + 4 + 8 + 16 + 32 + 64 + 128 + 256 + 512 = 1023$   **7.** 36   **8.** **(a)** $17 + 18 + 19 + 20 + 21 + 22 + 23 + 24 + 25 = 64 + 125 = 225 - 36$;
$26 + 27 + 28 + 29 + 30 + 31 + 32 + 33 + 34 + 35 + 36 = 125 + 216 = 441 - 100$   **(b)** $82 + 83 + 84 + \cdots + 98 + 99 + 100 = 729 + 1000 - 3025 - 1296$

**(c)** $[(n-1)^2 + 1] + [(n-1)^2 + 2] + \cdots + n^2 =$
$$(n-1)^3 + n^3 = \left(\frac{n(n+1)}{2}\right)^2 - \left(\frac{(n-1)(n-2)}{2}\right)^2$$

**9.** **(a)**

| 57 | 2 | 37 |
|---|---|---|
| 12 | 32 | 52 |
| 27 | 62 | 7 |

**(b)**

| 7 | 2 | 27 |
|---|---|---|
| 12 | 32 | 52 |
| 37 | 62 | 57 |

**10.** It appears that the sum always equals the quotient of the two numbers in the denominator of the last fraction being added on. Thus, we would guess that

$$S_n = \frac{1}{n(n+1)} + \frac{n-1}{n}$$
$$= \frac{1}{n(n+1)} + \frac{(n-1)(n+1)}{n(n+1)}$$
$$= \frac{1 + n^2 - n + n - 1}{n(n+1)}$$
$$= \frac{n^2}{n(n+1)}$$
$$= \frac{n}{n+1},$$

as expected. Thus,

$$\frac{1}{1 \cdot 2} + \frac{1}{2 \cdot 3} + \cdots + \frac{1}{n(n+1)} = \frac{n}{n+1}.$$

## Chapter 2

### Problem Set 2.1   (page 76)

**1.** **(a)** {Arizona, California, Idaho, Oregon, Utah}

**2.** **(a)** {l, i, s, t, h, e, m, n, a, o, y, c}

**3.** **(a)** $\{7, 8, 9, 10, 11, 12, 13\}$   **(c)** $\{4, 8, 12, 16, 20\}$

**4.** **(a)** $\{x \in U | 11 \le x \le 14\}$ or $\{x \in U | 10 < x < 15\}$

**(c)** $\{x \in U | x = 4n \text{ and } 1 \le n \le 5\}$

**5.** **(a)** $\{x \in N | x \text{ is even and } x > 12\}$ or $\{x \in N | x = 2n \text{ for } n \in N \text{ and } n > 6\}$

**7.**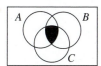

**(a)** $B \cup C = \{a, b, c, h\}$

**(c)** $B \cap C = \{a, b\}$  **(e)** $\overline{A} = \{f, g, h\}$

**8. (a)** $M = \{45, 90, 135, 180, 225, 270, 315, \ldots\}$
**(b)** $L \cap M = \{90, 180, 270, \ldots\}$ = the set of simultaneous multiples of 6 and 45 = the set of multiples of 90  **(c)** 90

**10. (a)**   **(c)**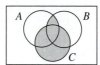

**(e)**

**11. (a)**

**12.** No, it is possible that there are elements of $A$ that are also elements of $B$ but not $C$ or elements of $C$ but not $B$. For example, let $A = \{1, 2\}$, $B = \{2, 3\}$, and $C = \{3\}$.
**13. (a)** $\overline{A \cap B} = \{1, 2, 3, 4, 5, 7, 8, 9, 10, 11, 13, 14, 15, 16, 17, 19, 20\}$
$\overline{A} \cup \overline{B} = \{1, 2, 3, 4, 5, 7, 8, 9, 10, 11, 13, 14, 15, 16, 17, 19, 20\}$
$\overline{A \cup B} = \{1, 5, 7, 11, 13, 17, 19\}$
$\overline{A} \cap \overline{B} = \{1, 5, 7, 11, 13, 17, 19\}$

**14. (a)**

red circles

**(c)**

triangles and hexagons

**(e)**

blue figures not circles

**15. (a)** $L \cap T$  **(c)** $S \cup T$
**16. (a)** Answers will vary. One possibility is $B$ = set of students taking piano lessons, $C$ = set of students learning a musical instrument.
**19. (a)** 8 regions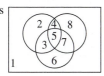

**(c)** $\overline{A} \cap B \cap C \cap \overline{D}$
**20. (a)**

**21. (a)** $6 \times 2 \times 2 = 24$

**23. (a)** There are eight subsets: $\varnothing$, $\{P\}$, $\{N\}$, $\{D\}$, $\{P, N\}$, $\{P, D\}$, $\{N, D\}$, $\{P, N, D\}$.
**24.**

**26.** Answers will vary. Consult a thesaurus.

# Problem Set 2.2  (page 85)

**1. (a)** 13: ordinal first: ordinal
**2. (a)** Equivalent, since there are five letters in the set $\{A, B, M, N, P\}$  **4. (a)** $n(A) = 7$ because $A = \{21, 22, 23, 24, 25, 26, 27\}$.
**(c)** $n(C) = 2$, since $C$ is $\{1, 9\}$ because 1 and 9 are the only solutions.
**6. (a)** The correspondence $0 \leftrightarrow 1, 1 \leftrightarrow 2, 2 \leftrightarrow 3, \ldots$, $w \leftrightarrow w + 1, \ldots$ shows that $W \sim N$.  **7. (a)** Finite
**8. (a)** Answers will vary. For example, $Q_1 \leftrightarrow Q_2$, $Q_3 \leftrightarrow Q_4$, and so on.

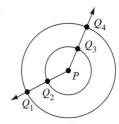

**(c)** Answers will vary. For example $Q_1 \leftrightarrow Q_2$, and so on.

**9. (a)** True  **(c)** True  **10. (a)** $n(A \cap B) \leq n(A)$. The set $A \cap B$ contains only the elements of $A$ that are also elements of $B$. Thus, $A \cap B$ cannot have more elements than $A$.
**12. (a)** $1000 \div 6 = 166.666\ldots$, so the largest element of $S$ is $166 \cdot 6 = 996$. Therefore, $n(S) = 166$.
**13.**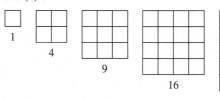

**15. (a)**

|   |   |   |   |   |
|---|---|---|---|---|
| 1 | 4 | 9 | 16 | 25 |

**16. (a)** 31  **(b)** 45  **(c)** 3
**23. (a)** Six ways: yrg, rgy, gyr, ygr, gry, ryg
**24. (a)** Row 0:     1
Row 1:     1 1
Row 2:     1 2 1
Row 3:     1 3 3 1
Row 4:     1 4 6 4 1

**25.** Since we are given that $k < l$ and $l < m$, we can choose sets $K$, $L$, and $M$ satisfying $K \subset L \subset M$ and $n(K) = k$, $n(L) = l$, and $n(M) = m$. By the transitive property of set inclusion (see Section 2.1, or just look at a Venn diagram), we have $K \subset M$, so $k < m$.

**29. (a)** Using a Venn diagram and guess and check, we discover that 4 students have visited all three countries.   **(b)** 14 students have been only to Canada.

**30. (a)** All three will meet every $3 \times 4 \times 5 = 60$th day, so there will be 6 days when all three meet.

## Problem Set 2.3   (page 96)

**1. (a)** (i) 5 (ii) 5 (iii) 4   **(b)** (ii) and (iii)

**2. (a)** 4, 5, 6, 7, or 8   **(b)** 4

**3. (a)**

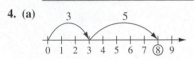

**4. (a)**

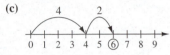

**(c)**

**(e)**

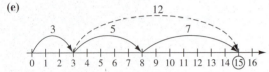

**7. (a)** Closed   **(c)** Closed   **(f)** Closed

**8. (a)** Commutative property of addition
**(c)** Additive-identity property of zero

**9. (a)** 210   **(b)** Associative and commutative properties

**10. (a)**                          **(c)**

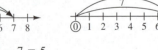

**11. (a)** $5 + 7 = 12$     $12 - 7 = 5$
        $7 + 5 = 12$     $12 - 5 = 7$
   **(b)** $4 + 8 = 12$     $12 - 8 = 4$
        $8 + 4 = 12$     $12 - 4 = 8$

**12. (a)**

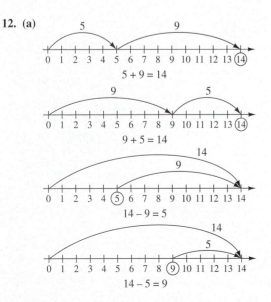

$5 + 9 = 14$

$9 + 5 = 14$

$14 - 9 = 5$

$14 - 5 = 9$

**15.** $257 - 240 = 17$ pages   **16. (a)** $(8 - 5) - (2 - 1) = 2$
**(c)** $((8 - 5) - 2) - 1 = 0$

**17. (a)**

| 5 | 2 | ⑦ |
|---|---|---|
| 1 | 2 | ③ |

⑥ ④ ⑦

**18. (a)**

1
6  ⑩  4
3 ——— 5
   2

**28.**

$A \cup B$      $A$     $B$      $A \cap B$

$n(A \cup B)$ = $n(A)$ + $n(B)$ $-n(A \cap B)$

**32.** $\{0\}$

**34. (a)**

| $n$ | 1 | 2 | 3 | 4 | 5 | 6 | 7 | 8 |
|---|---|---|---|---|---|---|---|---|
| $t_n$ | 1 | 3 | 6 | 10 | 15 | 21 | 28 | 36 |
|  | 9 | 10 | 11 | 12 | 13 | 14 | 15 |  |
|  | 45 | 55 | 66 | 78 | 91 | 105 | 120 |  |

**(b)** $11 = 10 + 1, 12 = 6 + 6, 13 = 10 + 3,$
$14 = 10 + 3 + 1, 15 = 15, 16 = 15 + 1,$
$17 = 15 + 1 + 1, 18 = 15 + 3, 19 = 10 + 6 + 3,$
$20 = 10 + 10, 21 = 21, 22 = 21 + 1, 23 = 10 + 10 + 3,$
$24 = 21 + 3, 25 = 15 + 10$

**36.**

| + | 5 | 4 | 1 | 6 | 9 | 2 | 0 | 8 | 7 | 3 |
|---|---|---|---|---|---|---|---|---|---|---|
| 3 | 8 | 7 | 4 | 9 | 12 | 5 | 3 | 11 | 10 | 6 |
| 9 | 14 | 13 | 10 | 15 | 18 | 11 | 9 | 17 | 16 | 12 |
| 6 | 11 | 10 | 7 | 12 | 15 | 8 | 6 | 14 | 13 | 9 |
| 4 | 9 | 8 | 5 | 10 | 13 | 6 | 4 | 12 | 11 | 7 |
| 0 | 5 | 4 | 1 | 6 | 9 | 2 | 0 | 8 | 7 | 3 |
| 7 | 12 | 11 | 8 | 13 | 16 | 9 | 7 | 15 | 14 | 10 |
| 5 | 10 | 9 | 6 | 11 | 14 | 7 | 5 | 13 | 12 | 8 |
| 2 | 7 | 6 | 3 | 8 | 11 | 4 | 2 | 10 | 9 | 5 |
| 1 | 6 | 5 | 2 | 7 | 10 | 3 | 1 | 9 | 8 | 4 |
| 8 | 13 | 12 | 9 | 14 | 17 | 10 | 8 | 16 | 15 | 11 |

**38. (a)** $0 = 5 - (1 + 4), 1 = 5 - 4, 2 = (1 + 5) - 4,$
$3 = 4 - 1, 4 = 5 - 1, 5 = 1 + 4, 6 = 1 + 5$

**42.** Statement B.

## Problem Set 2.4   (page 112)

**1. (a)** $3 \times 5 = 15$, repeated addition
**(d)** $3 \times 6 = 18$, number-line model

**2. (a)** 55 dominoes, array model   **(c)** 50 miles, number-line model

**4. (a)** Each of the $a$ lines coming from set $A$ intersects each of the $b$ lines coming from set $B$.

**(b)** $\{\square, \triangle\} \times \{♥, ♦, ♣, ♠\}$

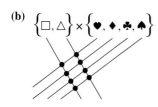

**5. (a)** Not closed. $2 \times 2 = 4$, and 4 is not in the set.   **(c)** Not closed. $2 \times 4 = 8$, and 8 is not in the set.   **(e)** Closed. The product of any two odd whole numbers is always another odd whole number.   **(g)** Closed. $2^m \times 2^n = 2^{m+n}$ for any whole numbers $m$ and $n$.   **7. (a)** Commutative property of multiplication   **(c)** Multiplication-by-0 property   **(e)** Associative property of multiplication   **8. (a)** Commutative property: $5 \times 3 = 3 \times 5$
**9. (a)**

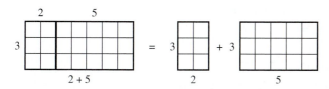

**13. (a)** Distributive property   **14. (a)** $18 \div 6 = 3$
**15. (a)** $4 \times 8 = 32, 8 \times 4 = 32, 32 \div 8 = 4, 32 \div 4 = 8$
**16 (a)** Repeated subtraction   **17. (a)** $19 - 5 = 14$, which is greater than 5, so we must subtract by 5 again. $14 - 5 = 9$, which is still larger than 5. Doing it again, yields $9 - 5 = 4$, which is less than 5, so we are finished. Since we subtracted 5 three times, the quotient is 3. The remainder is 4, which is circled. In terms of the arrows, $a = 19 \xrightarrow{-5} 19 - 5 = 14 \xrightarrow{-5} 14 - 5 = 9 \xrightarrow{-5} 9 - 5 = 4$, finished.   **(d)** $14 - 7 = 7$. Since $7 \leq 7$, we subtract another 7 to get $7 - 7 = 0$. Thus, there is a remainder of 0. We subtracted twice, so the quotient is 2.   **19. (a)** 6   **(c)** 6 R 12   **20. (a)** 29
**21. (a)** $3^{35}$   **(e)** $(yz)^3$   **22. (a)** $2^3$   **(c)** $2^{10}$   **23. (a)** 4   **(b)** 10
**24.** Asnwers will vary   **25.** Asnwers will vary   **29.** Answers vary, but you could first ask for her solution. She presumably says that since the total cost of one nut and one bolt together is $1.00, and she is buying 18 of them, the total cost is $18. This is a wonderful opportunity for the Mathematical Habit of the Mind, because you could then ask her to justify her response ($18 \cdot 86 + 18 \cdot 14 = 18 \cdot (86 + 14) = 18 \cdot 100 = 1800$ cents, or $18). You could then ask her a question that would lead to her saying that it is the distributive law.   **33. (a)** The magic multiplication constant is $4096 = 2^{12}$.
**(b)** The exponents form a magic addition square with the magic addition constant 12. It is now clear how the multiplication square has been formed. For example, the product of the upper row is $2^3 \times 2^8 \times 2^1 = 2^{3+8+1} = 2^{12}$. That is, the product is always $2^{12}$.
**(c)**

| $27 = 3^3$ | $6561 = 3^8$ | $3 = 3^1$ |
|---|---|---|
| $9 = 3^2$ | $81 = 3^4$ | $729 = 3^6$ |
| $2187 = 3^7$ | $1 = 3^0$ | $243 = 3^5$ |

**34. (a)** "How many tickets must still be sold?"
**38. (a)** Note that $T_{n+1} = T_n + t_{n+1}$ for $n \geq 1$. The pattern continues to hold.   **(b)** $T_{100} = \frac{100 \cdot 101 \cdot 102}{6} = 171{,}700$

# Chapter 2 Review Exercises   (page 122)

**1. (a)**   $S = \{4, 9, 16, 25\}$
$P = \{2, 3, 5, 7, 11, 13, 17, 19, 23\}$
$T = \{2, 4, 8, 16\}$

**(b)**   $\overline{P} = \{4, 6, 8, 9, 10, 12, 14, 15, 16, 18, 20, 21, 22, 24, 25\}$
$S \cap T = \{4, 16\}$
$S \cup T = \{2, 4, 8, 9, 16, 25\}$
$S \cap \overline{T} = \{9, 25\}$
**2.**

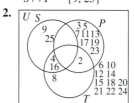

**3. (a)** $\subseteq$   **(b)** $\subset$   **(c)** $\cap$   **(d)** $\cup$
**4.** $n(S) = 3, n(T) = 6, n(S \cup T) = 7, n(S \cap T) = 2,$
$n(S \cap \overline{T}) = 1, n(T \cap \overline{S}) = 4$
**5.**

| 1 | 4 | 9 | 16 | 25 | 36 | 49 | 64 | 81 | 100 |
|---|---|---|---|---|---|---|---|---|---|
| ↕ | ↕ | ↕ | ↕ | ↕ | ↕ | ↕ | ↕ | ↕ | ↕ |
| a | b | c | d | e | f | g | h | i | j |

**6.** There is a one-to-one correspondence between the set of cubes and the natural numbers. For example,

| 1 | 8 | 27 | 64 | 125 | ... | $k^3$ | ... |
|---|---|---|---|---|---|---|---|
| ↕ | ↕ | ↕ | ↕ | ↕ | | ↕ | |
| 1 | 2 | 3 | 4 | 5 | ... | $k$ | ... |

**7.**

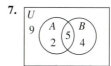

**8. (a)** Suppose $A = \{a, b, c, d, e\}$ and $B = \{\blacksquare, \star\}$. Then $n(A) = 5, n(B) = 2, A \cap B = \varnothing$, and $n(A \cup B) = 5 + 2 = 7$.
**(b)**

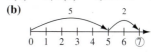

**9. (a)** Commutative property of addition: $7 + 3 = 3 + 7$
**(b)** Additive-identity property of 0: $7 + 0 = 7$
**10. (a)**                                    **(b)**

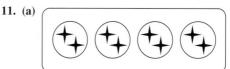

**11. (a)**

**(b)**                                          **(c)**

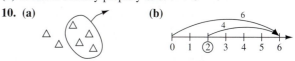

**(d)**                                          **(e)**

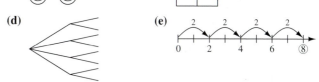

**12. (a)** $A \times B = \{(p, x), (p, y), (q, x), (q, y), (r, x),$
$(r, y), (s, x), (s, y)\}$   **(b)** $4 \times 2 = 8$
**13.** $6'' \times 6'' \times 8''$   **14.** Eight rows, with seven full rows and eight soldiers in the back row

**15. (a)**

**(b)**

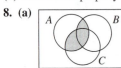

**(c)**

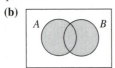

## Chapter 2 Test   (page 123)

**1. (a)** $4 \times 2 = 8$   **(b)** $12 \div 3 = 4$
**(c)** $5 \cdot (9 + 2) = 5 \cdot 9 + 5 \cdot 2$   **(d)** $10 - 4 = 6$
**2.** 15th—ordinal; 1040—nominal; $253—cardinal
**3. (a)** Yes   **(b)** No
**4.** Answers can vary. For example, let $A = \{a, b, c, d, e\}$ and
$B = \{a, b, c, d, e, f, g, h\}$ . Then $A \subset B$, so $n(A) < n(B)$. That is,
$5 < 8$.   **5. (a)** $W$ is closed under &, since $a + b + ab$ is an element of $W$ for any two whole numbers $a$ and $b$.   **(b)** From the
properties of whole-number arithmetic, it follows $a \& b = a + b + ab$
$= b + a + ba = b \& a$ for all whole numbers $a$ and $b$, so & is
commutative.   **(c)** From the properties of whole-number arithmetic, it follows that $a \&(b \& c) = a + (b \& c) + a(b \& c) =$
$a + b + c + bc + a(b + c + bc) = a + b + c +$
$ab + bc + ac + abc$. A similar calculation shows that $(a \& b) \&$
$c$ has the same expanded form, so & is associative.
**(d)** $0 \& a = 0 + a + 0(a) = a$ and $a \& 0 = a + 0 + (a)0 = a$
for all whole numbers $a$, showing that 0 is an identity for &.
**6. (a)** Number line   **(b)** Comparison   **(c)** Missing addend
**7. (a)** Associative property of addition   **(b)** Distributive property
of multiplication over addition   **(c)** Additive-identity property of 0
**(d)** Associative property of multiplication
**8. (a)**

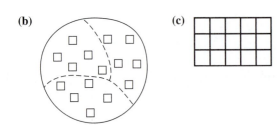

**(b)**

**(c)**

**9. (a)**

**(b)**

**10.** 1, 3, 7, and 21   **11. (a)** 10   **(b)** 4   **(c)** 2   **(d)** 20
**12.** $n(A \cap B) = 5, n(\overline{A \cap B}) = 21$   **13.** $A \cap \overline{B} = \varnothing$
**14. (a)** 64 bottles   **(b)** Grouping

# Chapter 3

## Problem Set 3.1 (page 136)

**1. (a)** 2137   **(c)** 120,310   **(e)** 697   **(g)** 60   **(i)** 7242   **(k)** 16,920

**2. (a)** ∩ |   **3. (a)** IX   **4. (a)** ▼▼▼▼❮▼   **5. (a)** ⸚

**9. (a)** MMII, MMIII, MMIV
**10. (a)** 3795   **(c)** 6048
**11. (a)** ꓿ 𐦀 ⊥ |||   **(c)** 𐦀 ||||
**12. (a)** ⊤ ☰ |||| $374 + 281 = 655$
**(c)** ☰ |||| ☰ || $6224 - 732 = 5492$
**13.**

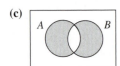

**17.** First trade 10 of your units for a strip to get 3 mats, 25 strips,
and 3 units. Then trade 20 strips for 2 mats to get 5 mats, 5 strips,
and 3 units.

## Problem Set 3.2 (page 140)

**1.**

| |
| --- |
| 0 |
| 1 |
| 2 |
| 3 |
| 4 |
| 10 |
| 11 |
| 12 |
| 13 |
| 14 |
| 20 |
| 21 |
| 22 |
| 23 |
| 24 |
| 30 |
| 31 |
| 32 |
| 33 |
| 34 |
| 40 |
| 41 |
| 42 |
| 43 |
| 44 |
| 100 |

**5. (a)** 108   **(c)** 5   **(e)** 125   **6. (a)** 14
**(e)** 217   **9. (a)** 153   **(c)** 6   **(e)** 216
**10. (a)** 591   **(c)** 12   **(e)** 1728
**11. (a)** $2422_{\text{five}}$   **(c)** $10_{\text{five}}$
**12. (a)** $1330_{\text{six}}$   **(c)** $10_{\text{six}}$
**13. (a)** $1707_{\text{twelve}}$   **(c)** $100_{\text{twelve}}$

**14. (a)**

| One Thousand Twenty-Fours | Five Hundred Twelves | Two Hundred Fifty-Sixes |
| --- | --- | --- |
| 1024 | 512 | 256 |
| $2^{10}$ | $2^9$ | $2^8$ |

| One Hundred Twenty-Eights | Sixty-Fours | Thirty-Twos |
|---|---|---|
| 128 | 64 | 32 |
| $2^7$ | $2^6$ | $2^5$ |

| Sixteens | Eights | Fours | Twos | Units |
|---|---|---|---|---|
| 16 | 8 | 4 | 2 | 1 |
| $2^4$ | $2^3$ | $2^2$ | $2^1$ | $2^0$ |

**(c) (i)** $11,000_{two}$ **(ii)** $10,010_{two}$ **(iii)** $10_{two}$ **(iv)** $1000_{two}$
**19. (a)** $100,000,000_{two}$ **20. (a)** $7_{ten} = 111_{two}$, $2^3 = 8$ odd entries
**21. (a)** 000, 100, 010, 110, 001, 101, 011, 111. Append a 0 onto
the end of the 4 two-digit sequences; then append a 1 onto the end
of the 4 two-digit sequences. **22. (a)** 0, 1, 2, 3, 4, 5, 6, 7
**(c)** The whole numbers from 0 to $2^n - 1$. There are $2^n$ of these
whole numbers, each with a different $n$-digit base-two representation
corresponding to one of the $n$-digit sequences of 0s and 1s.

## Problem Set 3.3 (page 153)

**1. (a)**

$$36 + 75 = 111$$

**2. (a)**
```
    23
  + 44
     7
    60
    67
```

**3. (b)**

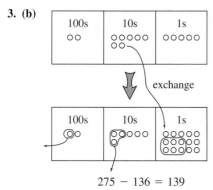

$$275 - 136 = 139$$

**4. (a)**
```
   78
 − 35
   43
```

**7.** In these problems, we must exchange 60 seconds for 1 minute
and 60 minutes for 1 hour, or vice versa.
**(a)**
```
      3 hours, 24 minutes, 54 seconds
   +  2 hours, 47 minutes, 38 seconds
      5 hours, 71 minutes, 92 seconds
   =  5 hours, 72 minutes, 32 seconds
   =  6 hours, 12 minutes, 32 seconds
```
**(c)**
```
      5 hours, 24 minutes, 54 seconds
   −  2 hours, 47 minutes, 38 seconds
      4 hours, 84 minutes, 54 seconds
   −  2 hours, 47 minutes, 38 seconds
      2 hours, 37 minutes, 16 seconds
```

**9. (a)**
```
0
1
2
3
10
11
12
13
20
21
22
23
30
31
32
33
```

**11. (a)** 1012 four **(c)** 2120 four
**(e)** 111 four **(g)** 113 four
**19.** Even though it would be quite simple
to line up the numbers and add, students
are trying to do this problem mentally.
While mental math is obviously encouraged, these kinds of errors do occur. In (a),
Drew went to the millions place and simply "added one" in the millions, resulting
in the number 10 being written out instead
of carrying the one to the 10 million digit.
In (b), Alonzo went to the ten millions
spot and just "added one," resulting in the
number 3 in the ten millions digit.

**20. (a)**
```
   6763
 + 5519
  12,282
```
**(c)**
```
   881
 + 362
  1243
```
**(e)**
```
   4002
 − 1843
   2159
```

**21. (a)**
```
    2437
     281
 +  3476
    6194
```
**(c)**
```
    3891
    2493
 +  5125
   11,509
```

**22. (a)**
```
    835
 −  241
    594
```
**(c)**
```
   7342
 − 6534
    808
```

**23. (a)** Five **(c)** Seven or greater **(e)** Seven **(g)** Twelve
**29. (a)**
```
      3'    8"
      4'    2"
      6'   10"
  +   5'   11"
     18'   31"
  =  20'    7"
```

## Problem Set 3.4 (page 164)
**1. (a)**

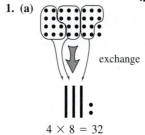

$$4 \times 8 = 32$$

**3. (a)** The number of hundreds in $30 \times 70 + 100$; i.e., 200
**(b)** Twenty 10s are being exchanged for two 100s.
**5. (a)** Distributive property of multiplication over addition
**(c)** Associative property of addition **9. (a)** $27 = 4 \cdot 6 + 3$
**10. (a)**
```
          21
           1
          20
  351)7425
       7020
        405
        351
         54
```

**11. (a)**
```
   1 7 4 R 3
 5)8³7²3
```

**14. (a)**  $23_{\text{five}}$  **(d)**  13
   $\times\, 3_{\text{five}}$    $\times\, 3$
   $\overline{124_{\text{five}}}$    $\overline{39}$

   117
   $\times\, 21$
   $\overline{117}$
   234
   $\overline{2457}$
   258
   $\times\, 13$
   $\overline{774}$
   258
   $\overline{3354}$

**15. (a)**   $\dfrac{31\,\text{R}\,2}{}$
   $4\overline{)231}$
   $\underline{22}$
   11
   $\underline{\phantom{0}4}$
   2

**18. (a)** Yes  **(b)**     285
   $\times$    362
   $\overline{855}$
   1710
   570
   $\overline{103{,}170}$

**24. (a)** $34 \cdot 54 = (17 \cdot 2) \cdot 54 = 17 \cdot (2 \cdot 54) = 17 \cdot 108$, since 2 evenly divides 34.

**25. (a)**    7531
   $\times\,\phantom{00}9$
   $\overline{67{,}779}$

**33. (a)** Without clearing the calculator and reentering the numbers after the equals signs, we obtain the following results: $276{,}523 \boxed{\div} 511 \boxed{=} 541.1409 \boxed{-} 541 \boxed{=} 0.14909002 \boxed{\times} 511 \boxed{=} 71.999997$. Therefore, $q = 541$ and $r = 72$. To check, note that $541 \cdot 511 + 72 = 276{,}523$.

## Problem Set 3.5 (page 176)

**1. (c)** 92  **(e)** 240  **2. (c)** 138  **(e)** 576  **3. (a)** 787  **(e)** 1026
**5. (a)** Round down because there is a 1 in the thousands place. 630,000  **6. (a)** 900  **(c)** 27,000,000  **8. (a)** 52,000  **(c)** 49,000  **(e)** 13,000  **9. (a)** 90,000  **10. (a)** 750
**15.** Sally recognized that the hundreds digit was a 4 and knew that it meant that the number 4 would be "rounded down." She should, however, have been looking at the tens digit to make the rounding decision for the nearest hundred. She looked at the 4 as a low number and rounded the number to the nearest thousands place instead of rounding it to the nearest hundred and getting 8500 (using the 5 in the tens digit.)  **20. (a) (i)** 3  **(ii)** 17.5  **(iii)** 400
**21. (a)** 27,451, since the last digit should be 1.

## Chapter 3 Review Exercises (page 182)

**1. (a)** 2353  **(b)** 58,331  **(c)** 1998
**2.**

**3.** Exchange 30 units for 3 strips, and then exchange all 30 strips for 3 mats. The result is 8 mats, 0 strips, and 2 units.
**4. (a)** $45_{\text{ten}}$  **(b)** $181_{\text{ten}}$  **(c)** $417_{\text{ten}}$  **5. (a)** $2122_{\text{five}}$
**(b)** $100{,}011{,}111_{\text{two}}$  **(c)** $560_{\text{seven}}$
**6.**

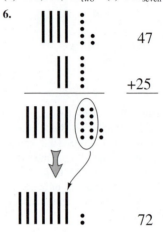

47
+25

72

**7. (a)**     42  **(b)**     47  **(c)**     59
   $+\,54$    $+\,35$    $+\,63$
   $\overline{\phantom{0}6}$    $\overline{12}$    $\overline{12}$
   90    70    110
   $\overline{96}$    $\overline{82}$    $\overline{122}$

**8. (a)**

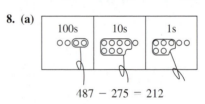

$487 - 275 = 212$

**(b)**

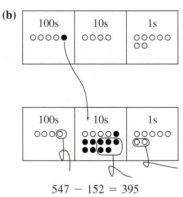

$547 - 152 = 395$

**9. (a)**    2433  **(b)**    2433  **(c)**     243
   $+\,141$    $-\,141$    $\times\,42$
   $\overline{3124}$    $\overline{2242}$    $\overline{1041}$
      $\underline{21320}$
      22,411

**10. (a)**   357  **(b)**     642
   $\times\,4$    $\times\,27$
   $\overline{28}$    $\overline{14}$
   200    280
   1200    4200
   $\overline{1428}$    40
      800
      12000
      $\overline{17{,}334}$

**11. (a)**

$$\begin{array}{r} 127 \\ 7 \\ 20 \\ 100 \\ 7\overline{)895} \\ 700 \\ \overline{195} \\ 140 \\ \overline{55} \\ 49 \\ \overline{6} \end{array}$$

**(b)**

$$\begin{array}{r} 79 \\ 9 \\ 70 \\ 347\overline{)27483} \\ 24290 \\ \overline{3193} \\ 3123 \\ \overline{70} \end{array}$$

**12. (a)**

$$\begin{array}{r} 5487\,\text{R}\,1 \\ 5\overline{)27436} \end{array}$$

**(b)**

$$\begin{array}{r} 4948\,\text{R}\,0 \\ 8\overline{)39584} \end{array}$$

**13. (a)** $2121_{\text{five}}$  **(b)** $2{,}023{,}221_{\text{five}}$

**14.**

$$\begin{array}{ll} \cancel{42} & \cancel{35} \\ 21 & 70 \\ \cancel{10} & \cancel{140} \\ 5 & 280 \\ \cancel{2} & \cancel{560} \\ 1 & 1120 \\ \hline & 1470 \end{array}$$

**15. (a)** 30,000  **(b)** 270,000  **(c)** 275,000

**16.** 657 rounds to 700, 439 rounds to 400, 1657 rounds to 2000, and 23 rounds to 20. Thus,  **(a)** $657 + 439$ is approximately $700 + 400 = 1100$. The actual sum is 1096.  **(b)** $657 - 439$ is approximately $700 - 400 = 300$. The actual answer is 218.  **(c)** $657 \cdot 439$ is approximately $700 \cdot 400 = 280{,}000$. The actual answer is 288,423.  **(d)** $1657 \div 23$ is approximately $2000 \div 20 = 100$. The actual answer, to the nearest hundredth, is 72.04.

## Chapter 3 Test (page 183)

**1.**

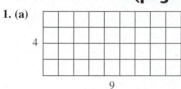

74
+48
122

**2. (a)** 3,000,000  **(b)** 3,400,000  **(c)** 3,380,000  **(d)** 3,377,000

**3.**

$$\begin{array}{r} 751 \\ \times\ 93 \\ \hline 69{,}843 \end{array}$$

**4. (a)** 1, 2, 5, 12  **(b)** 29, 70  **(c)** $f_n = 2f_{n-1} + f_{n-2}$ for $n \geq 3$.

**5. (a)** $197_{\text{ten}}$  **(b)** $207_{\text{ten}}$  **(c)** $558_{\text{ten}}$

**6.**

$$\begin{array}{r} 2837 \\ +\ 7224 \\ \hline 10{,}061 \end{array}$$

**7.**

$$\begin{array}{r} 8236 \\ -\ 3542 \\ \hline 4694 \end{array}$$

**8.** 4800

**9. (a)** 1 and 1
9 and 9
36 and 36
100 and 100

**(b)** 1, 3, 6, 10  **(c)** $\left(\dfrac{n(n+1)}{2}\right)^2$

**10.** 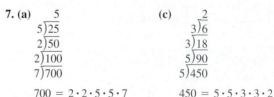  **11.** 1575  **12.**

$$\begin{array}{r} 468 \\ \times\ 20 \\ \hline 9360 \end{array}$$

**13.** Answers may vary. One possibility is as follows: 2 $\boxed{\text{M+}}$ 5 $\boxed{+}$ $\boxed{\text{M+}}$ $\boxed{\text{MR}}$ $\boxed{+}$ $\boxed{\text{M+}}$ $\boxed{\text{MR}}$ $\boxed{+}$ ..., with the repeating sequence $\boxed{\text{M+}}$ $\boxed{\text{MR}}$ $\boxed{+}$.  **14. (a)** 340  **(b)** 144  **(c)** 23,111  **15.** 1,464,843
**16. (a)** $2111_{\text{five}}$  **(b)** $100{,}011{,}001_{\text{two}}$  **(c)** $1E5_{\text{twelve}}$

# Chapter 4

## Problem Set 4.1 (page 195)

**1. (a)**

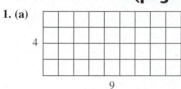

$36 = 4 \cdot 9$
4 divides 36.

**3. (a)** 8, 16, 24, 32, 40, 48, 56, 64, 64, 72, 80

**6. (a)**

```
      72
     / \
    8   9
   /\  /\
  2 4 3 3
   /\
  2 2
```

**(c)**

```
       264
      /  \
     8    33
    /\   /\
   2 4  3 11
    /\
   2 2
```

**7. (a)**

$$\begin{array}{r} 5 \\ 5\overline{)25} \\ 2\overline{)50} \\ 2\overline{)100} \\ 7\overline{)700} \end{array}$$

$700 = 2 \cdot 2 \cdot 5 \cdot 5 \cdot 7$

**(c)**

$$\begin{array}{r} 2 \\ 3\overline{)6} \\ 3\overline{)18} \\ 5\overline{)90} \\ 5\overline{)450} \end{array}$$

$450 = 5 \cdot 5 \cdot 3 \cdot 3 \cdot 2$

**8. (a)** 1, 2, 3, 4, 5, 6, 8, 12, 16, 24, 48

**9. (a)** $136 = 2^3 \cdot 17^1$, $102 = 2^1 \cdot 3^1 \cdot 17^1$
**(b)** The divisors of 136 are
$2^0 \cdot 17^0 = 1, 2^1 \cdot 17^0 = 2, 2^2 \cdot 17^0 = 4,$
$2^3 \cdot 17^0 = 8, 2^0 \cdot 17^1 = 17, 2^1 \cdot 17^1 = 34,$ and
$2^2 \cdot 17^1 = 68, 2^3 \cdot 17^1 = 136.$

**10. (a)** $48 = 2^4 \cdot 3^1$  **(c)** $2250 = 2^1 \cdot 3^2 \cdot 5^3$  **11. (a)** Yes, because $28 = 2^2 \cdot 7^1$, so all the prime factors of 28 appear in $a$ and to at least as high a power.  **(c)** $2^1 \cdot 7^2$  **15. (a)** No. For example, $10 = 2 \cdot 5$, with 2 and 5 both primes. Yet $5 > 3.162\ldots = \sqrt{10}$.

**17. (a)** True. $n \cdot 0 = 0$ for every natural number $n$.  **(c)** True. $1 \cdot n = n$ for every natural number $n$.  **(e)** False. $0 \div 0 = q$ if, and only if, $0 \cdot q = 0$ for a *unique* integer $q$. However, this is true for *every* integer $q$.  **23. (a)** $1, 3, 3^2 = 9$  **24. (a)** $496 = 2^4 \cdot 31^1$  **(b)** $1 + 2 + 4 + 8 + 16 + 31 + 62 + 124 + 248 = 496$
**25. (a)** Deficient  **(b)** Abundant  **28.** Yes. If $p \mid bc$, then $p$ must appear in the prime factorization of the product $bc$ and hence in the prime factorization of $b$ or $c$. But then $p \mid b$ or $p \mid c$, as claimed.

**32. (a)** If the prime $p$ divides $n$, then $n = pk$ for some natural number $k$. But then $n + 1 = pk + 1$, which shows that $p$ does not divide $n + 1$, since it leaves a remainder of 1.  **(b)** If the prime $p$ divides $n$, then, by part (a), $p$ cannot divide $n + 1$. Therefore, if $q$ is

any prime divisor of $n + 1$, then $p$ and $q$ are distinct divisors of $n(n + 1)$.   **(c)** By part (b), since 2 and 3 divide 6, then neither can divide $6 + 1 = 7$. Thus, any prime divisor of 7 (which is 7, of course) must be different from both 2 and 3, meaning that $6 \cdot 7 = 42$ has three different prime divisors: 2, 3, and 7.
**33. (a)** Since the sum is odd, one of the two numbers is even and the other is odd. But the only even prime is 2, so the other number is 311. Since $\sqrt{311} \doteq 17.6$ and no prime 2, 3, 5, 7, 11, 13, or 17 is a divisor of 311, we see that 311 is prime and conclude that the only pair of primes that sum to 313 is the pair 2 and 311.
**38. (a)** $2^2 \cdot 137^1$   **(c)** $2^1 \cdot 137^1$   **(e)** $(2^1 \cdot 137^1)$ divides $(2^2 \cdot 137^1)$, and $(2^3 \cdot 3^2 \cdot 13^1)$ divides $(2^3 \cdot 3^2 \cdot 7^2 \cdot 13^1)$.
**39. (a)** $2^2 \cdot 3^3 \cdot 7^2 \cdot 13^2$   **(c)** $3^4 \cdot 5^6$   **(e)** The exponents in the prime-power representation are even.

## Problem Set 4.2 (page 207)

**1. (a)** Divisible by 2 and 3   **(c)** Divisible by 5   **2. (a)** 1554
**(c)** None   **4. (a)** Divisible by 7 and 13   **(c)** Divisible by 7
**5. (a)** None   **(c)** None   **10. (a)** For any palindrome with an even number of digits, the digits in the odd positions are the same as the digits in the even positions, but with the order reversed. Thus, the difference of the sums of the digits in the even and odd positions is 0, which is divisible by 11.
**16. (a)** Since 2 is a divisor of both 11! and 2, it is also a divisor of the sum $11! + 2$, by the divisibility-of-sums theorem. The same reasoning shows that 3 divides the sum $11! + 3$, and so on.
**17. (a)** $686 \leftrightarrow 68 - 12 = 56 = 7 \cdot 8$, so 686 is divisible by 7.
**18. (a)** $10m = 10q - 20r = 7k - r - 20r = 7k - 21r = 7(k - 3r)$, so $10m$ is divisible by 7. Since the prime factors of 10 are 2 and 5, $m$ must have 7 as a prime factor. That is, $m$ is divisible by 7.   **19.** In testing for divisibility by 7, 11, and 13, the digits of the number are broken up into three-digit groups. If a number has the form $abc, abc$, then the difference between the sums of the three-digit numbers in odd positions and even positions will be 0, which is divisible by each of 7, 11, and 13.   **23.** No. He or she could have made other kinds of errors that by chance resulted in the record being out of balance by an amount that is a multiple of 9.

## Problem Set 4.3 (page 216)

**1. (a)** 3   **2. (a)** 216
**3. (a)** $GCD(24, 27) \cdot LCM(24, 27) = 3 \cdot 216 = 648 = 24 \cdot 27$
**4. (a)** $GCD(r, s) = 2^1 \cdot 3^1 \cdot 5^2 = 150$; $LCM(r, s) = 2^2 \cdot 3^3 \cdot 5^3 = 13{,}500$   **8. (a)** The 1-, 3-, and 9-rods   **(d)** Any rods or trains with length 1, 2, 3, 6, 9, or 18.   **9. (a)** 12   **(b)** 12
**16. (a)** Since $60 = 2^2 \times 3 \times 5$ and $105 = 3 \times 5 \times 7$, it follows that $GCD(60, 105) = 3 \times 5 = 15$. Thus, the largest square tile possible is 15″ by 15″.   **(b)** Since $60 \div 15 = 4$ and $105 \div 15 = 7$, there will be 4 rows of 7 tiles each. Thus, $4 \times 7 = 28$ tiles are required.   **(c)** Since $GCD(48, 216) = GCD(2^4 \times 3, 2^3 \times 3^3) = 2^3 \times 3 = 24$, the hallway can be tiled with 24″-by-24″ square tiles. Since $48 \div 24 = 2$ and $216 \div 24 = 9, 2 \times 9 = 18$ tiles are required.   **(d)** The largest square tile is $GCD(m, n)$ on each side. By the theorem $mn = GCD(m, n) \cdot LCM(m, n)$, the number of tiles required is

$$\frac{m}{GCD(m, n)} \times \frac{n}{GCD(m, n)} = \frac{LCM(m, n)}{GCD(m, n)}.$$

**18. (a)** $GCD(a, b, c) = 2^0 \cdot 3^1 \cdot 5^1 \cdot 7^0 = 15$; $LCM(a, b, c) = 2^2 \cdot 3^3 \cdot 5^3 \cdot 7^1 = 94{,}500$

**19. (a)** $D_{18} = \{1, 2, 3, 6, 9, 18\}$
$D_{24} = \{1, 2, 3, 4, 6, 8, 12, 24\}$
$D_{12} = \{1, 2, 3, 4, 6, 12\}$
$GCD(18, 24, 12) = 6$
$M_{18} = \{18, 36, 54, 72, 90, \ldots\}$
$M_{24} = \{24, 48, 72, 96, \ldots\}$
$M_{12} = \{12, 24, 36, 48, 60, 72, 84, \ldots\}$
$LCM(18, 24, 12) = 72$

**21. (a)** $2^4 \cdot 3^1 \cdot 5^2 \cdot 7^1$   **23. (a)** 18; 76; 1364   **(c)** No, $F_{19} = 4181 = 37 \cdot 113$.   **(h)** If $GCD(F_{16}, F_{20}) = 4$, then the conjecture must be false.   **26. (a)** 1224 seconds, $1224 = LCM(72, 68)$
**29. (a)** The following keystrokes give the remainder 21 of the division of 117 by 48 (the quotient is the integer part of the result of the decimal division):

| Key In | Display | Memory |
|--------|---------|--------|
| 117    | 117     | 0      |
| ÷      | 117     | 0      |
| 48     | 48      | 0      |
| M+     | 48      | 48     |
| =      | 2.4375  | 48     |
| −      | 2.4375  | 48     |
| 2      | 2       | 48     |
| =      | 0.4375  | 48     |
| ×      | 0.4375  | 48     |
| MR     | 48      | 48     |
| =      | 21      | 48     |

**(b)** Since 3 is the last nonzero remainder, $3 = GCD(117, 48)$ by the Euclidean algorithm.   **30. (a)** $10{,}500 \div 6600 = 1$ R 3900, $6600 \div 3900 = 1$ R 2700, $3900 \div 2700 = 1$ R 1200, $2700 \div 1200 = 2$ R 300, $1200 \div 300 = 4$ R 0. Therefore, $GCD(6600, 10{,}500) = 300$.   **(b)** $LCM(6600, 10{,}500) = 6600 \cdot 10{,}500/300 = 22 \cdot 10{,}500 = 231{,}000$.

## Chapter 4 Review Exercises (page 224)

**1.**

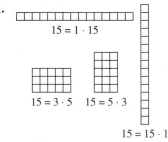

$15 = 1 \cdot 15$
$15 = 3 \cdot 5$   $15 = 5 \cdot 3$
$15 = 15 \cdot 1$

**2.**
```
        96
       /  \
      8    12
     /\    /\
    2 4   3 4
      /\    /\
     2 2   2 2
```

**3. (a)** $D_{60} = \{1, 2, 3, 4, 5, 6, 10, 12, 15, 20, 30, 60\}$
**(b)** $D_{72} = \{1, 2, 3, 4, 6, 8, 9, 12, 18, 24, 36, 72\}$
**(c)** $D_{60} \cap D_{72} = \{1, 2, 3, 4, 6, 12\}$, so $GCD(60, 72) = 12$.
**4. (a)** $1200 = 2^4 \cdot 3^1 \cdot 5^2$   **(b)** $2940 = 2^2 \cdot 3^1 \cdot 5^1 \cdot 7^2$
**(c)** $GCD(1200, 2940) = 2^2 \cdot 3^1 \cdot 5^1 \cdot 7^0 = 60$;
$LCM(1200, 2940) = 2^4 \cdot 3^1 \cdot 5^2 \cdot 7^2 = 58{,}800$

**5.** Composite; $847 = 11 \times 77$   **6. (a)** Answers will vary; for example, $15 = 3 \cdot 5; 5 > \sqrt{15}$.   **(b)** Yes, $3 \le \sqrt{15}$   **7.** Answers will vary. For example, 8 divides 16 and 4 divides 16, but 32 does not divide 16.   **8.** Since $n = 2536$, the prime 2 divides $3 \cdot 5 \cdot 7 + 11 \cdot 13 \cdot 17$.   **9. (a)** Divisible by 2 and 5   **(b)** Divisible by 3 and 11   **(c)** Divisible by 5   **(d)** Divisible by 5 and 11
**10. (a)** Divisible by 11   **(b)** Divisible by 7 and 13   **(c)** Divisible by 11 and 13 **11. (a)** False   **(b)** True   **(c)** False   **(d)** True
**12. (a)** $(1 + 4)(1 + 2) = 15$   **(b)** 1, 3, 7, 9, 21, 27, 49, 63, 81, 147, 189, 441, 567, 1323, 3969   **13.** $d = 5$
**14. (a)** $2^3 \cdot 3^5 \cdot 7^3 \cdot 11^3 \cdot 13^1 = 11{,}537{,}501{,}976$
**(b)** $2^2 \cdot 3^5 \cdot 7^2 \cdot 11 = 523{,}908$   **15. (a)** $D_{63} = \{1, 3, 7, 9, 21, 63\}$, $D_{91} = \{1, 7, 13, 91\}$, and $D_{63} \cap D_{91} = \{1, 7\}$, so $\text{GCD}(91, 63) = 7$.   **(b)** $M_{63} = \{63, 126, 189, 252, 315, 378, 441, 504, 567, 630, 693, 756, 819, 882, 945, 1008. \ldots\}$ $M_{91} = \{91, 182, 273, 364, 455, 546, 637, 728, 819, 910, \ldots\}$, and $M_{63} \cap M_{91} = \{819, 1638, \ldots\}$,   so $\text{LCM}(63, 91) = 819$.
**15. (c)** $7 \cdot 819 = 5733 = 63 \cdot 91$   **16. (a)** $2 \cdot 11^2 = 242$
**(b)** $2^3 \cdot 3^2 \cdot 5^2 \cdot 7^1 \cdot 11^3 = 16{,}770{,}600$

**17. (a)**
$$12{,}100 \overline{)119{,}790} \quad 9 \text{ R } 10{,}890$$

$$10{,}890 \overline{)12{,}100} \quad 1 \text{ R } 1210 \qquad 1210 \overline{)10{,}890} \quad 9 \text{ R}$$

Thus, $\text{GCD}(119{,}790, 12{,}100) = 1210$.
**(b)** $\text{LCM}(119{,}790, 12{,}100) = 119{,}790 \cdot 12{,}100/1210 = 1{,}197{,}900$
**18.** 2192

## Chapter 4 Test (page 225)

**1. (a)** Divisible by 2 and 3   **(b)** Divisible by 3
**2. (a)** No. The prime-power representation of $r$ contains two 7s, but the prime-power representation of $m$ contains only one 7, so $r$ does not divide $m$.   **(b)** $(3 + 1)(2 + 1)(1 + 1)(4 + 1) = 120$
**(c)** $2^2 \cdot 5^0 \cdot 7^1 \cdot 11^3 = 37{,}268$   **(d)** $2^3 \cdot 5^2 \cdot 7^2 \cdot 11^4 = 143{,}481{,}800$
**3. (a)** $2^5 = 32$   **4. (a)** 90   **(c)** 3,402,000   **5. (a)** $2^3 \cdot 5^2 \cdot 7^1$
**6. (a)** F   **(b)** T   **(c)** T   **(d)** F   **7.** Since $\sqrt{281} \doteq 16.7$, we must check for divisibility by 2, 3, 5, 7, 11, and 13. Standard divisibility tests immediately rule out divisibility by 2, 3, and 5. Also, $281 = 40 \cdot 7 + 1, 281 = 11 \cdot 25 + 6$, and $281 = 13 \cdot 21 + 8$. Therefore, 281 is a prime.   **8.** Since $553 = 3 \cdot 154 + 91$, $154 = 1 \cdot 91 + 63, 91 = 1 \cdot 63 + 28, 63 = 2 \cdot 28 + 7$, and $28 = 4 \cdot 7$, it follows that $\text{GCD}(154, 553) = 7$ and $\text{LCM}(154, 553) = (154 \times 553) \div 7 = 12{,}166$.

**9. (a)**
$$13{,}534 \overline{)997{,}476} \quad 73 \text{ R } 9494 \qquad 9494 \overline{)13{,}534} \quad 1 \text{ R } 4040$$

$$4040 \overline{)9494} \quad 2 \text{ R } 1414 \qquad 1414 \overline{)4040} \quad 2 \text{ R } 1212$$

$$1212 \overline{)1414} \quad 1 \text{ R } 202 \qquad 202 \overline{)1212} \quad 6 \text{ R } 0$$

$\text{GCD}(997{,}476, 13{,}534) = 202$
**(b)** $\text{LCM}(997{,}476, 13{,}534) = 997{,}476 \cdot 13{,}534/202 = 66{,}830{,}892$

**10. (a)**
```
        8532
       /    \
      12     711
     /\      /\
    3  4    9  79
      /\   /\
     2 2  3 3
```
**(b)** $8532 = 2^2 \cdot 3^3 \cdot 79^1$   **(c)** 4266   **(d)** 17,064

# Chapter 5

## Problem Set 5.1 (page 236)

**1. (a)**
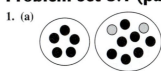
**(c)**
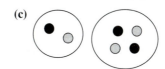

**2. (a)**

**(c)** No counters

**3. (a)** At mail time, you are delivered a check for $14.
**(6) (a)** $-15$.
**7. (a)**
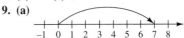
**8. (a)** 4   **(c)** 6
**9. (a)**

**(c)**

**10. (a) (i)** 34   **(iii)** 76   **11. (a)** 13, $-13$
**14.** Remind them that the absolute value of a number is the number's distance on the number line from 0 and that $-n$ is $n$ units from 0.
**17. (a)** Four red counters
**18. (a)** $-12, -10, -8, -6, -4, -2, 0, 2, 4, 6, 8, 10, 12$
**20. (a)** $\{n \mid n \text{ is an integer and } -12 \le n \le 12\}$
**23. (a)** 100 black, 110 red

## Problem Set 5.2 (page 252)

**1. (a)**

$8 + (-3) = 5$
**(c)**
$-8 - (-3) = -5$
**(e)**
$9 + 4 = 13$
**(g)**
$(-9) + 4 = -5$

**2. (a)**   At mail time, you receive a bill for $27 and a bill for $13; $(-27) + (-13) = -40$.   **(c)** The mail carrier brings you a check for $27 and a check for $13; $27 + 13 = 40$.   **(e)** At mail time, you receive a bill for $41 and a check for $13; $(-41) + 13 = -28$.
**(g)** At mail time, you receive a bill for $13 and a check for $41; $(-13) + 41 = 28$.
**3. (a)**
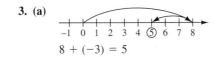
$8 + (-3) = 5$

**(c)**

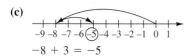

$-8 + 3 = -5$

**(e)**

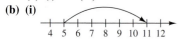

$4 + (-7) = -3$

**(g)**

$(-4) + 7 = 3$

**4. (a)** $13 + (-7)$ **(c)** $(-13) + (-7)$ **(e)** $3 + (-8)$
**(g)** $(-8) + (-13)$ **5. (a)** $40$ **(c)** $-27$ **(e)** $-135$ **(g)** $-135$
**10. (a)** More, by $106 **12. (a)** $-117 < -24$
**20. (a)** True **(c)** True **22.** Not necessarily; If $a \geq b$, then it is
possible that $a = b$, so $a > b$ is false.
**24.** $-6, -5, -4, -3, -2, -1, 0, 1, 2, 3, 4, 5, 6$
**26. (a) (i)** $6$ **(iii)** $15$
**(b) (i)**

Distance is 6.
**(iii)**

Distance is 15.
**27. (a) (i)** $|7 + 2| = 9, |7| + |2| = 9$
**(iii)** $|7 + (-6)| = 1, |7| + |-6| = 13$
**28. (a)**

| $-1$ | $4$ | $-3$ |
|------|-----|------|
| $-2$ | $0$ | $2$ |
| $3$ | $-4$ | $1$ |

**29. (a)**

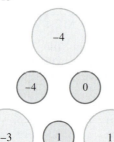

**30. (a) (i)** $7 - (-3) = 10, (-3) - 7 = -10$
**(ii)** $(-2) - (-5) = 3, (-5) - (-2) = -3$
**34. (a)** The sums of the oddly indexed Fibonacci numbers are 1, 3,
8, 21, 55, ..., which are the values of the next evenly indexed
Fibonacci number. That is, $F_1 + F_3 + F_5 + \cdots + F_{2n-1} = F_{2n}$.
**35. (a)** The alternating sums of the first $n$ oddly indexed
Fibonacci numbers are 1, −1, 4, −9, 25, ..., which are the
alternating signed squares of the Fibonacci numbers. That is,
$F_1 - F_3 + F_5 - \cdots + 500(-1)^{n+1}F_{2n-1} = (-1)^{n+1}(F_n)^2$.
**36. (a)** $101 + 3 = 104$
**39. (a)**

| $t$ | $h$ |
|-----|-----|
| 0 | 0 |
| 1 | 80 |
| 2 | 128 |
| 3 | 144 |
| 4 | 128 |
| 5 | 80 |
| 6 | 0 |
| 7 | $-112$ |

**41. (a)** $50$ **42. (a)** $1575$ **(c)** $-5909$ **(e)** $2053$

## Problem Set 5.3 (page 264)

**1. (a)** $77$ **(c)** $-77$ **(e)** $108$ **(g)** $-108$ **(i)** $0$
**2. (a)** $4$ **(c)** $-4$ **(e)** $-13$ **(g)** $16$ **(i)** $36$
**3.** $(-25, 753) \cdot (-11) = 283, 283; 283, 283 \div (-11) =$
$-25, 753; 283, 283 \div (-25, 753) = -11$
**5. (a)** Richer by $78; $6 \cdot 13 = 78$ **6. (a)** $6 \cdot 3 = 18$
**8. (a)**

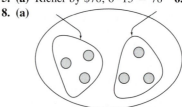

$2 \times (-3)$

**(b)**

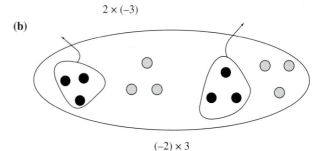

$(-2) \times 3$

**9. (a)** $-15 \div 4 = -4 \, \text{R} \, 1$
**11. (a)** $-21 \times 18 \approx -20 \times 20 = -400$
**13. (i)** Multiplicative property of 0. **17. (a)** Can't tell
**20. (a)** False. $-1 < 0$, but $(-1)^2 > 0$.
**22. (b)** not unique

**27. (a)**

| $+_{12}$ | 0 | 1 | 2 | 3 | 4 | 5 | 6 | 7 | 8 | 9 | 10 | 11 |
|------|---|---|---|---|---|---|---|---|---|---|----|----|
| 0 | 0 | 1 | 2 | 3 | 4 | 5 | 6 | 7 | 8 | 9 | 10 | 11 |
| 1 | 1 | 2 | 3 | 4 | 5 | 6 | 7 | 8 | 9 | 10 | 11 | 0 |
| 2 | 2 | 3 | 4 | 5 | 6 | 7 | 8 | 9 | 10 | 11 | 0 | 1 |
| 3 | 3 | 4 | 5 | 6 | 7 | 8 | 9 | 10 | 11 | 0 | 1 | 2 |
| 4 | 4 | 5 | 6 | 7 | 8 | 9 | 10 | 11 | 0 | 1 | 2 | 3 |
| 5 | 5 | 6 | 7 | 8 | 9 | 10 | 11 | 0 | 1 | 2 | 3 | 4 |
| 6 | 6 | 7 | 8 | 9 | 10 | 11 | 0 | 1 | 2 | 3 | 4 | 5 |
| 7 | 7 | 8 | 9 | 10 | 11 | 0 | 1 | 2 | 3 | 4 | 5 | 6 |
| 8 | 8 | 9 | 10 | 11 | 0 | 1 | 2 | 3 | 4 | 5 | 6 | 7 |
| 9 | 9 | 10 | 11 | 0 | 1 | 2 | 3 | 4 | 5 | 6 | 7 | 8 |
| 10 | 10 | 11 | 0 | 1 | 2 | 3 | 4 | 5 | 6 | 7 | 8 | 9 |
| 11 | 11 | 0 | 1 | 2 | 3 | 4 | 5 | 6 | 7 | 8 | 9 | 10 |

**29. (a)** $7 **(b)** $(-105) \div 15 = -7$. A loss of $105 shared among
15 people results in each person losing $7.
**33. (a)** $(e, e, e, e)$ is all even from the start.
$(d, e, e, e) \rightarrow (d, e, e, d) \rightarrow (d, e, d, d) \rightarrow (d, d, d, d) \rightarrow (e, e, e, e)$
$(d, d, e, e) \rightarrow (e, d, e, d) \rightarrow (d, d, d, d) \rightarrow (e, e, e, e)$
$(d, e, d, e) \rightarrow (d, d, d, d) \rightarrow (e, e, e, e)$
$(d, d, d, e) \rightarrow (e, e, d, d) \rightarrow (e, d, e, d) \rightarrow (d, d, d, d) \rightarrow (e, e, e, e)$
$(d, d, d, d) \rightarrow (e, e, e, e)$
**(b)** After four steps, a two can be factored from each number
of the 4-tuple. After four more steps played on the 4-tuple of quotients, again all even numbers are obtained. In view of the 2 already

factored out, the numbers in the 4-tuple after 8 steps are each divisible by 4. Similarly, after 12 steps the resulting 4-tuple contains numbers each divisible by 8, and after 16 steps the numbers in the 4-tuple are each divisible by 16. Starting with (81, 149, 274, 504), four steps later we have the 4-tuple of even numbers (40, 74, 136, 250), then four more steps gives the 4-tuple (20, 36, 68, 124) of numbers, each divisible by 4. After 12 and 16 steps, the corresponding 4-tuples are (16, 16, 32, 64) and (0, 32, 0, 32), which respectively contain numbers, each divisible by 8 and 16.
**(c)** After 4, 8, 12, 16, 20, . . . steps, the corresponding 4-tuples contain only numbers divisible by 2, 4, 8, 16, 32, . . . . At the same time, the numbers in the 4-tuples are nonnegative integers that are not increasing in size. The only integer divisible by all of the numbers 2, 4, 8, 16, 32, . . . is 0, so, after sufficiently many steps, the 4-tuple (0, 0, 0, 0) must be reached. (*Note:* It can be shown that there is no bound on the number of steps that may be required to reach (0, 0, 0, 0). For example, start with a 4-tuple of successive "tribonacci" numbers from the sequence 0, 1, 1, 2, 4, 7, 13, 24, 44, 81, 149, 274, 504, . . . in which each new term is the sum of the preceding three terms.)
**(d)** The "Three Number Game" need not terminate with (0, 0, 0). Instead, it may reach a cycle such as this:

$$:(0, 0, 1) \rightarrow (0, 1, 1) \rightarrow (1, 0, 1) \rightarrow (1, 1, 0)$$

It can be shown that an "*n* Number Game" necessarily terminates with all zeros when, and only when, *n* is a power of 2, namely, 1, 2, 4, 8, 16, 32, . . . . **34. (b)** 59

## Chapter 5 Review Exercises (page 271)

**1. (a)** $-1$, **(b)** 5 **(c)** $-15, -13, -11, . . . , 11, 13, 15$
**2. (a)** Richer by \$12; 12 **(b)** Poorer by \$37; $-37$
**3. (a)** 12 **(b)** $-24$
**4. (a)** Answers will vary. Any loop that shows five more red counters than black counters represents the integer $-5$.
**(b)** Any loop that shows six more black counters than red counters represents the integer 6. **5.** Answers will vary. **(a)** At mail time, you receive a bill for \$114 and a check for \$29. **(b)** The mail carrier brings you a bill for \$19 and a check for \$66.
**6. (a)** $-44$ **(b)** 61 **7.** $2 + (-4) = -2$ **8.** $(-1) - (-3) = 2$
**9. (a)** $45 + (-68) = -23$, poorer **(b)** $45 - (-68) = 113$, richer
**10. (a)** $6 + 3 = 9$ **(b)** $8 + (-4) = 4$ **(c)** $7 - 5 = 2$
**(d)** $3 - 9 = -6$ **(e)** $(-3) + (-4) = -7$ **(f)** $(-3) - (-7) = 4$
**(g)** $(-5) - 6 = -11$ **11. (a)** $-2$ **(b)** $-22$ **(c)** $-32$ **(d)** 12
**(e)** 20 **(f)** $-4$ **12. (a)** 27° below 0 **(b)** $(-15) - 12 = -27$
**13. (a)** \$25 **(b)** $(-12) + 37 = 25$
**14. (a)**

| $-9$ | | $-5$ | | $-2$ | 0 | 2 | | | 7 | |

**(b)** $-9, -5, -2, 0, 2, 7$ **(c)** $-9 + 4 = -5, -5 + 3 =$
$-2, -2 + 2 = 0, 0 + 2 = 2, 2 + 5 = 7$ **15. (a)** $3 \cdot 4 = 12$
**(b)** $3 \cdot (-4) = -12$ **(c)** $(-3) \cdot 4 = -12$ **(d)** $(-3) \cdot (-4) = 12$
**16. (a)**

| $3 \cdot 0 = 0$ | multiplicative property of 0 |
| $3 \cdot [5 + (-5)] = 0$ | definition of negative |
| $3 \cdot 5 + 3 \cdot (-5) = 0$ | distributive property |

**(b)** $3 \cdot (-5) = -(3 \cdot 5)$    definition of negative
**(c)**

| $0 \cdot (-5) = 0$ | multiplicative property of 0 |
| $[3 + (-3)] \cdot (-5) = 0$ | definition of negative |
| $3 \cdot (-5) + (-3) \cdot (-5) = 0$ | distributive property |
| $-(3 \cdot 5) + (-3) \cdot (-5) = 0$ | by part (b) |

**(d)** $(-3) \cdot (-5) = -(-(3 \cdot 5)) = 3 \cdot 5$, definition of negative and theorem on page 242 **17. (a)** 56 **(b)** $-56$ **(c)** $-56$ **(d)** $-7$
**(e)** $-12$ **(f)** 12 **18. (a)** At mail time, you receive 7 checks, each for \$12. **(b)** The mail carrier takes away 7 checks, each for \$13. **(c)** The mail carrier takes away 7 bills, each for \$13.
**19.** If $d$ divides $n$, there is an integer $c$ such that $dc = n$. But then $d \cdot (-c) = -n, (-d) \cdot (-c) = dc = n$, and $(-d) \cdot c = -dc = -n$. Thus, $d$ divides $-n, -d$ divides $n$, and $-d$ divides $-n$.
**20. (a)** 3 **(b)** 11
**21.** By the division algorithm, $n$ must be of one of these forms: $6q$, $6q + 1, 6q + 2, 6q + 3, 6q + 4$, and $6q + 5$. If $n$ is not divisible by 2, however, then $n$ cannot be of any of the forms $6q, 6q + 2$, or $6q + 4$. Likewise, if $n$ is not divisible by 3, $n$ cannot be of the form $6q + 3$ either. Thus, there must be an integer $q$ such that either $n = 6q + 1$ or $n = 6q + 5$.
*Case 1*    $n = 6q + 1$
$$n^2 - 1 = (6q + 1)^2 - 1$$
$$= (36q^2 + 12q + 1) - 1$$
$$= 36q^2 + 12q$$
$$= 12q(3q + 1)$$
If $q$ is even, then 24 divides $12q$ and $n^2 - 1$ is divisible by 24. If $q$ is odd, then $3q + 1$ is even, so again 24 divides $12q(3q + 1)$, and hence $n^2 - 1$ is divisible by 24.
*Case 2*    $n = 6q + 5$
$$n^2 - 1 = (6q + 5)^2 - 1$$
$$= (36q^2 + 60q + 25) - 1$$
$$= 36q^2 + 60q + 24$$
$$= 12(3q^2 + 5q + 2)$$
$$= 12(3q + 2)(q + 1)$$
If $q$ is even, $3q + 2$ is even. If $q$ is odd, $q + 1$ is even. In either case, it follows that $n^2 - 1$ is divisible by 24.

## Chapter 5 Test (page 272)

**1.** \$381; $129 + 341 - 13 - 47 - 29 = 381$
**2.** Richer by \$135; $(-5) \cdot (-27) = 135$
**3. (a)**
$$1 = 1$$
$$1 - 4 = -3$$
$$1 - 4 + 9 = 6$$
$$1 - 4 + 9 - 16 = -10$$
$$1 - 4 + 9 - 16 + 25 = 15$$
**(b)** $1 - 4 + \cdots + n^2 = \dfrac{n(n + 1)}{2} = t_n$ if $n$ is odd.
$$1 - 4 + \cdots - n^2 = -\dfrac{n(n + 1)}{2} = -t_n \text{ if } n \text{ is even.}$$
**4. (a)** $-18, -17, -16, . . . , -3, -2, -1, 0, 1, 2, 3, . . . , 16, 17, 18.$
**(b)** Yes **5. (a)** $-26$ **(b)** 12 **(c)** 26 **(d)** $-12$ **(e)** $-361$
**(f)** $-408$ **(g)** $-864$ **(h)** 105 **(i)** 0 **6. (a)** $a = 3$ or $-7$
**(b)** $m = -5$ **(c)** $n = -19$ **(d)** $t = 0, 2,$ or $-2$ **7.** At mail time, the mail carrier delivers a check for \$7 and takes away a bill for \$4. You are \$11 richer. **8. (a)** $-5, -3, -8, -11, -19, -30$
**(b)** $7, -5, 2, -3, -1, -4$ **(c)** $6, -8, -2, -10, -12, -22$
**9.** Poorer by \$9; $(-27) \div 3 = -9$
**10. (a)** $(-7) + 10 = 3$

| $-8$ $-7$ $-6$ $-5$ $-4$ $-3$ $-2$ $-1$ 0 1 2 ③ | |

**(b)** $10 - (-7) = 17$

| 0 2 4 6 8 10 12 14 ⑰ | |

**(c)** $7 \cdot (-5) = -35$

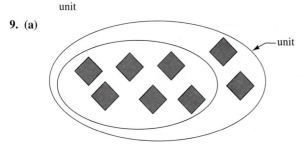

$\underset{-35}{\longleftarrow} \; -30 \; -25 \; -20 \; -15 \; -10 \; -5 \quad 0$

**11.** 2160, the same as LCM(240, 54)

# Chapter 6

## Problem Set 6.1 (page 286)

**1. (a)** $\dfrac{1}{6}$ **(c)** $\dfrac{0}{1}$ **(e)** $\dfrac{2}{6}$

**2. (a)** 　　　　　　**(c)**

$\dfrac{1}{8}$ 　　　　　　　$\dfrac{3}{4}$

**5. (a)** $A: \dfrac{1}{4}, B: \dfrac{3}{4}, C: \dfrac{3}{2}$ or $\dfrac{6}{4}$ **(c)** $D: \dfrac{1}{3}, E: \dfrac{5}{3}, F: \dfrac{9}{3}$ or $\dfrac{3}{1}$

**6. (a)** $\dfrac{-5}{3}, \dfrac{2}{3}, \dfrac{5}{3}$

**8. (a)**

unit

unit

**9. (a)**

unit

**10. (a)** 　　　　　**11. (a)** $\dfrac{1}{3}$ **(c)** $\dfrac{5}{7}$ **(e)** $\dfrac{1}{4}$ **(g)** $\dfrac{2}{3}$

**13. (a)** $\dfrac{3}{6} = \dfrac{1}{2}$ **15. (a)**

**16. (a)** 24 **(c)** $-140$ **17. (a)** Equivalent **(c)** Not equivalent
**18. (a)** Equivalent **19. (a)** Yes **(c)** Yes
**20. (a)** $\dfrac{7}{12}$ **(c)** $\dfrac{-31}{43}$ **21. (a)** $\dfrac{96}{288} = \dfrac{2^5 \cdot 3^1}{2^5 \cdot 3^2} = \dfrac{1}{3}$
**22. (a)** $\dfrac{15}{55}$ and $\dfrac{22}{55}$ **(c)** $\dfrac{32}{24}, \dfrac{15}{24}$, and $\dfrac{4}{24}$
**23. (a)** $\dfrac{9}{24}$ and $\dfrac{20}{24}$ **(c)** $\dfrac{136}{96}$ and $\dfrac{21}{96}$

**25. (a)** $\dfrac{7}{12}, \dfrac{2}{3}$ **(c)** $\dfrac{29}{36}, \dfrac{5}{6}$
**27. (a)** True. Given two fractions, two equivalent fractions with a common denominator may be found by finding a common multiple of the two original denominators. Once these fractions, say, $\dfrac{a}{c}$ and $\dfrac{b}{c}$, are found, infinitely many more pairs of equivalent fractions can be found, namely, $\dfrac{a \cdot n}{c \cdot n}$ and $\dfrac{b \cdot n}{c \cdot n}$ for any integer $n$ other than 0.
**(c)** False. Given any positive fraction, a smaller positive fraction may be found by multiplying the denominator by 2. So there cannot be a least positive fraction.

**35. (a)** 　　　　　$\dfrac{4}{8}$ 　　　**(d)** $\overset{72°}{\curvearrowleft}$ $\dfrac{1}{5}$

**36.** The four triangles can be reattached to form a figure with 5 squares, each congruent to the shaded inner square. Therefore, $\dfrac{1}{5}$ of the large square is covered by the shaded inner square.

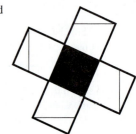

**39. (a)** Add tick marks to show that the rope was originally 60 feet long.

| 10 ft | 10 ft | 10 ft | 10 ft | 10 ft | 10 ft |
|---|---|---|---|---|---|

Used for painter 　　　Used for  20 feet unused, so
　　　　　　　　　　　　carpet 　each part is 10
　　　　　　　　　　　　　　　　　feet long.

**42. (a)** $\dfrac{1}{2}, \dfrac{1}{6}, \dfrac{1}{3}$ **45. (a)** 18 gal. **46. (a)** $\dfrac{3}{5}$ **(c)** $\dfrac{1}{4}$

## Problem Set 6.2 (page 298)

**1. (a)** $\dfrac{1}{3} + \dfrac{1}{2} = \dfrac{5}{6}$

**2. (a)**

$\dfrac{2}{5}$ 　+　 $\dfrac{6}{5}$ 　=　 $\dfrac{8}{5}$

**4. (a)**

$\dfrac{1}{8}$ 　 $\dfrac{3}{8}$

$0 \; \dfrac{1}{8} \; \dfrac{2}{8} \; \dfrac{3}{8} \; \dfrac{4}{8} \; \dfrac{5}{8} \; \dfrac{6}{8} \; \dfrac{7}{8} \; \dfrac{8}{8}$

**5. (a)**

$0 \; \dfrac{1}{4} \; \dfrac{2}{4} \; \dfrac{3}{4} \; \dfrac{4}{4}$ 　　$\dfrac{3}{4} + \dfrac{-2}{4} = \dfrac{1}{4}$

**6. (a)** $\dfrac{5}{7}$ **(c)** $\dfrac{5}{6}$ **(e)** $\dfrac{19}{15}$ **(g)** $\dfrac{73}{100}$ **7. (a)** $2\dfrac{1}{4}$ **(c)** $4\dfrac{19}{23}$
**8. (a)** $\dfrac{19}{8}$ **(c)** $\dfrac{557}{5}$ **9. (a)** $\dfrac{5}{6} - \dfrac{1}{4} = \dfrac{7}{12}$ **10. (a)** $\dfrac{3}{4} - \dfrac{1}{6} = \dfrac{7}{12}$
**11. (a)** $\dfrac{3}{4} - \dfrac{1}{3} = \dfrac{9}{12} - \dfrac{4}{12} = \dfrac{5}{12}$

**12. (a)** $\dfrac{3}{8}$   **(c)** $1\dfrac{1}{3}$   **(e)** $\dfrac{1}{3}$   **(g)** $\dfrac{625}{642}$

**14. (a)** $\dfrac{3}{4} - \dfrac{2}{3} = \dfrac{9}{12} - \dfrac{8}{12} = \dfrac{1}{12} > 0$

**22. (a)**

| $\dfrac{1}{2}$ | $\dfrac{1}{12}$ | $\dfrac{5}{12}$ |
|---|---|---|
| $\dfrac{1}{4}$ | $\dfrac{1}{3}$ | $\dfrac{5}{12}$ |
| $\dfrac{1}{4}$ | $\dfrac{7}{12}$ | $\dfrac{1}{6}$ |

**24. (a)** Simply add

**25. (a)** $\dfrac{1}{5} + \dfrac{1}{45} = \dfrac{9}{45} + \dfrac{1}{45} = \dfrac{10}{45} = \dfrac{5 \cdot 2}{5 \cdot 9} = \dfrac{2}{9}$

**26. (a)** It terminates.

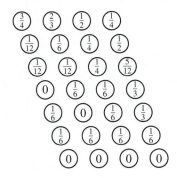

**29. (a)** $1\dfrac{1}{4} - \dfrac{5}{8} + \dfrac{1}{16} = \dfrac{5}{4} - \dfrac{10}{16} + \dfrac{1}{16} = \dfrac{20}{16} - \dfrac{9}{16} = \dfrac{11}{16}$

# Problem Set 6.3 (page 313)

**1. (a)** $4 \times \dfrac{2}{5} = \dfrac{8}{5}$

**2. (a)** $4 \cdot \dfrac{3}{8} = \dfrac{12}{8}$

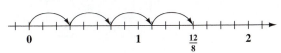

**3. (a)** $\dfrac{5}{6} \times 4 = \dfrac{20}{6} = 3\dfrac{2}{6}$

**4. (a)** $3 \times \dfrac{5}{2} = \dfrac{15}{2}$

**5. (a)**

$2 \times \dfrac{3}{5} = \dfrac{6}{5}$

**7. (a)** $\dfrac{8}{3}$   **(c)** $\dfrac{4}{9}$   **(e)** $\dfrac{1}{5}$   **9. (a)** $\dfrac{5}{3}$   **(b)** $\dfrac{11}{8}$

**10. (a)** $\dfrac{8}{15}$   **(c)** $\dfrac{10}{11}$   **(e)** $\dfrac{4}{7}$   **11. (a)** 1

**12. (a)** $2\dfrac{1}{2} \times 3\dfrac{3}{4} = \dfrac{5}{2} \times \dfrac{15}{4} = \dfrac{75}{8} = 9\dfrac{3}{8}$ miles

**13. (a)** $\dfrac{2}{5}x - \dfrac{3}{4} = \dfrac{1}{2}$. Add $\dfrac{3}{4}$ to each side:

$\dfrac{2}{5}x = \dfrac{1}{2} + \dfrac{3}{4} = \dfrac{2}{4} + \dfrac{3}{4} = \dfrac{5}{4}$. Multiply both sides by $\dfrac{5}{2}$:

$x = \dfrac{5}{2} \cdot \dfrac{2}{5}x = \dfrac{5}{2} \cdot \dfrac{5}{4} = \dfrac{25}{8} = 3\dfrac{1}{8}$

**26. (a)** $3\dfrac{1}{2} + 1\dfrac{2}{5} = \dfrac{7}{2} + \dfrac{7}{5} = \dfrac{35}{10} + \dfrac{14}{10} = \dfrac{49}{10}$ and

$3\dfrac{1}{2} \times 1\dfrac{2}{5} = \dfrac{7}{2} \times \dfrac{7}{5} = \dfrac{49}{10}$

**31. (a)**

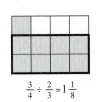

**32.** 3, 3, 4, 5, 6, 6   **35.** 23 bows   **37.** $42

**45.** Start with a unit area rectangle that is shaded to represent $\dfrac{3}{4}$.

Next, draw a rectangle that encloses an area of $\dfrac{2}{3}$. Redistribute the shaded area to show that the number of regions of area $\dfrac{2}{3}$ covered by $\dfrac{3}{4}$ is $1\dfrac{1}{8}$.

$$\dfrac{3}{4} \qquad \dfrac{2}{3} \qquad \dfrac{3}{4} \div \dfrac{2}{3} = 1\dfrac{1}{8}$$

# Problem Set 6.4 (page 326)

**1.** Commutative and associative properties of addition:

$(3 + 2 + 8) + \left(\dfrac{1}{5} + \dfrac{2}{5} + \dfrac{1}{5}\right)$

**3. (a)** $\dfrac{-4}{5}$

**(c)** $\dfrac{8}{3}$

**4. (a)** $\dfrac{-1}{2}$   **(c)** $\dfrac{11}{8}$   **5. (a)** $\dfrac{-7}{20}$   **(c)** $\dfrac{7}{24}$   **(e)** $-3\dfrac{5}{12}$

**6. (a)** $\dfrac{7}{8}$   **(c)** $\dfrac{1}{2}$   **(e)** 8

**7. (a)** $\dfrac{2}{3}$

(c) $\frac{-11}{-4}$ or $\frac{11}{4}$

(e) $-\frac{1}{2}$

8. (a) $\frac{2}{3}$  (c) 0   9. (a) Addition of rational numbers—definition

10. $\frac{7}{6}$, since $\frac{a}{b} = \frac{2}{3} \div \frac{4}{7} = \frac{2}{3} \cdot \frac{7}{4} = \frac{14}{12} = \frac{7}{6}$.

11. (a) $x = \frac{-3}{4}$   (c) $x = \frac{-6}{5}$

12. (a) Closure property for subtraction and the existence of a multiplicative inverse

13. (a) $-\frac{1}{5}, \frac{2}{5}, \frac{4}{5}$

(c) $\frac{3}{8}, \frac{1}{2}, \frac{3}{4}$

14. (a) $-4 \cdot 4 = -16 < -15 = 5 \cdot (-3)$

15. (a) $x + \frac{2}{3} > -\frac{1}{3}$    (c) $\frac{3}{4}x < -\frac{1}{2}$

$x > -\frac{1}{3} - \frac{2}{3} = -1$    $x < -\frac{1}{2} \div \frac{3}{4}$

$x < -\frac{1}{2} \cdot \frac{4}{3}$

$x < -\frac{2}{3}$

16. (a) Answers will vary. One answer is $\frac{1}{2}$, since $\frac{4}{9} < \frac{1}{2} < \frac{6}{11}$.

(c) Answers will vary. Since $\frac{7}{12} = \frac{14}{24} = \frac{28}{48}$ and $\frac{14}{23} = \frac{28}{46}$, one answer is $\frac{28}{47}$.   19. (a) $\frac{1}{4}$  (c) $-1$  20. (a) 9  21. (a) $\frac{3}{2}$

(c) $\frac{3}{5}$  (e) 40  (g) $-2\frac{1}{8}$   22. (a) What is his new total acreage?

23. Answers will vary. Possible answers include the following:

(a) Two pizzas were ordered. $\frac{3}{4}$ of one pizza and $\frac{1}{2}$ of another were eaten. How much pizza was eaten in all?   28. $\frac{1260}{250} = 5\frac{1}{25}$

29. (a) 2 square yards   30. (a) 8  (c) $\frac{3}{5}$  (e) $\frac{56}{9}$

35. (a) 4, since $\frac{1}{2} + \frac{2}{8} + \frac{1}{4} = \frac{2}{4} + \frac{1}{4} + \frac{1}{4} = \frac{4}{4}$

38. Cut the 8-inch side in half and the 10-inch side in thirds to get six $3\frac{1}{3}$-by-4-inch rectangles.

40. (a) The replacement rule gives $\frac{7 + 2 \cdot 5}{7 + 5} = \frac{17}{12}$. This is a good approximation of $\sqrt{2}$, since $\left(\frac{17}{12}\right)^2 = \frac{289}{144} = 2 + \frac{1}{144}$.

(c) The next two rational numbers are $\frac{7}{4}$ and $\frac{19}{11}$, since $\frac{5}{3} \Rightarrow \frac{5 + 3 \cdot 3}{5 + 3} = \frac{14}{8} = \frac{7}{4} \Rightarrow \frac{7 + 3 \cdot 4}{7 + 4} = \frac{19}{11}$.

## Chapter 6 Review Exercises (page 334)

1. (a) $\frac{2}{4}$  (b) $\frac{6}{6}$  (c) $\frac{0}{4}$  (d) $\frac{5}{3}$

2.

3. (a) $\frac{1}{3}$  (b) $\frac{4}{33}$  (c) $\frac{21}{4}$  (d) $\frac{297}{7}$   4. $\frac{13}{30}, \frac{13}{27}, \frac{1}{2}, \frac{25}{49}, \frac{26}{49}$

5. (a) 36  (b) 18

6.

7.

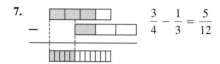

$\frac{3}{4} - \frac{1}{3} = \frac{5}{12}$

8. (a) $\frac{5}{8}$  (b) $\frac{-7}{36}$  (c) $\frac{2}{15}$  (d) $\frac{41}{12}$, or $3\frac{5}{12}$

9. (a)

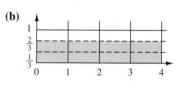

(b)

$3 \times \frac{1}{3} = 1$    (c)

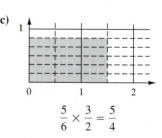

$\frac{5}{6} \times \frac{3}{2} = \frac{5}{4}$

10. $\frac{3}{4}$; this problem corresponds to the sharing (partitive) model of division.   11. $4\frac{1}{2}$; this problem corresponds to the grouping (measurement) model of division.   12. $\frac{57}{10}$ miles $= 5\frac{7}{10}$ miles

13. (a) $\frac{-1}{8}$  (b) $\frac{3}{2}$  (c) $\frac{-1}{2}$  (d) $\frac{-7}{10}$

14. (a) $x = 2$  (b) $x = \frac{-1}{6}$  (c) $x = \frac{5}{18}$  (d) $x = \frac{9}{16}$

15. Write $\frac{5}{6} = \frac{55}{66}$ and $\frac{10}{11} = \frac{60}{66}$. Then $\frac{56}{66}$ and $\frac{57}{66}$ are between $\frac{5}{6}$ and $\frac{10}{11}$. Other answers may be given.   16. (a) 4  (b) 5  (c) 20

# Chapter 6 Test (page 335)

**1.** $\dfrac{a + b}{b} = \dfrac{c + d}{d}$ if, and only if, $(a + b)d = b(c + d)$—that is, if, and only if, $ad + bd = bc + bd$. But this is so if, and only if, $ad = bc$. And this is so if, and only if, $\dfrac{a}{b} = \dfrac{c}{d}$.   **2. (a)** $\dfrac{1}{8}$

**(b)** $\dfrac{-7}{9}$   **(c)** 3   **(d)** 1   **3. (a)** 0, since $\dfrac{2}{3} + \dfrac{-4}{6} = 0$

**(b)** 2, since $\dfrac{5}{6} \cdot \dfrac{36}{15} = \dfrac{5}{15} \cdot \dfrac{36}{6} = \dfrac{1}{3} \cdot 6 = 2$   **(c)** 1, since

$\dfrac{9}{5} - \dfrac{1}{5} = \dfrac{8}{5}$ is the reciprocal of $\dfrac{5}{8}$   **(d)** $\dfrac{1}{3}$, since

$\dfrac{2}{3} \cdot \dfrac{3}{4} \cdot \dfrac{4}{5} \cdot \dfrac{5}{6} = \dfrac{2}{6} = \dfrac{1}{3}$   **4. (a)** 40 acres   **(b)** $\dfrac{1}{4}$ mile   **5. (a)** If $\dfrac{a}{b}$ and $\dfrac{c}{d}$ are two rational numbers with $\dfrac{a}{b} < \dfrac{c}{d}$, then there is a rational number $\dfrac{e}{f}$ such that $\dfrac{a}{b} < \dfrac{e}{f} < \dfrac{c}{d}$.   **(b)** Write $\dfrac{3}{5} = \dfrac{18}{30}$ and $\dfrac{2}{3} = \dfrac{20}{30}$ to see that $\dfrac{19}{30}$ is between $\dfrac{3}{5}$ and $\dfrac{2}{3}$.

**6. (a)** $\dfrac{2}{3}$   **(b)**

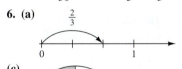

**(c)**
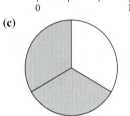
**(d)**
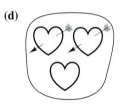

**7. (a)** $11\dfrac{1}{2}$   **(b)** 48   **(c)** 23   **8. (a)** If $\dfrac{a}{b}$ is a rational number with $a \neq 0$, then its multiplicative inverse is the rational number $\dfrac{b}{a}$.

**(b)** $\dfrac{2}{3}, -\dfrac{5}{4}, \dfrac{-1}{5}$   **9.** Answers will vary. Possibilities include $\dfrac{-6}{8}, \dfrac{-9}{12}$, and $\dfrac{-12}{16}$.   **10. (a)** $x > \dfrac{-3}{2}$   **(b)** $x = \dfrac{-2}{9}$

**(c)** $x > \dfrac{-4}{15}$   **(d)** $x > \dfrac{-1}{12}$

**11. (a)** If $\dfrac{a}{b}$ and $\dfrac{c}{d}$ are rational numbers with $\dfrac{c}{d} \neq 0$, then $\dfrac{a}{b} \div \dfrac{c}{d} = \dfrac{e}{f}$ if, and only if, $\dfrac{a}{b} = \dfrac{c}{d} \cdot \dfrac{e}{f}$.

**(b)** If $\dfrac{a}{b} \div \dfrac{c}{d} = \dfrac{e}{f}$, then $\dfrac{a}{b} = \dfrac{c}{d} \cdot \dfrac{e}{f} = \dfrac{e}{f} \cdot \dfrac{c}{d}$.

So $\dfrac{a}{b} \cdot \dfrac{d}{c} = \dfrac{e}{f} \cdot \dfrac{c}{d} \cdot \dfrac{d}{c} = \dfrac{e}{f}$. Thus, $\dfrac{a}{b} \div \dfrac{c}{d} = \dfrac{a}{b} \cdot \dfrac{d}{c}$.

**12. (a)** Answers will vary.   **(b)** Answers will vary.

**13. (a)** If $\dfrac{a}{b}$ is a rational number, then its additive inverse is the rational number $\dfrac{-a}{b}$.   **(b)** $\dfrac{-3}{4}, \dfrac{7}{4}, \dfrac{8}{2}$

**14.** $-3, -1\dfrac{1}{2}, 0, \dfrac{5}{8}, \dfrac{2}{3}, 3, \dfrac{16}{5}$

# Chapter 7

## Problem Set 7.1 (page 354)

**1. (a)** $273.412 = 200 + 70 + 3 + \dfrac{4}{10} + \dfrac{1}{100} + \dfrac{2}{1000}$;

$273.412 = 2 \cdot 10^2 + 7 \cdot 10^1 + 3 \cdot 10^0 + 4 \cdot 10^{-1} + 1 \cdot 10^{-2} + 2 \cdot 10^{-3}$   **2. (a)** 0.21

**4. (a)** $\dfrac{1}{4} = 0.25$ (2 strips and 5 small squares, or 25 small squares)

**5. (a)** $\dfrac{81}{250}$; $250 = 2 \cdot 5^3$   **6. (a)** 0.35   **(c)** 0.04

**7.** Solution.

**(a)**
$$\begin{array}{r} 0.875 \\ 8\overline{)7.000} \\ -6.4 \phantom{00} \\ \hline 0.60 \phantom{0} \\ -0.56 \phantom{0} \\ \hline 0.040 \\ -0.040 \\ \hline 0 \end{array}$$

**8. (a)** $\dfrac{5}{6} = 0.8\overline{3}$   **9. (a)** $\dfrac{107}{333}$   **(e)** $\dfrac{1}{7}$

**10. (a)** $\dfrac{39}{110}$   $x = 0.3\overline{54}$,   $10x = 3.\overline{54}$,   $1000x = 354.\overline{54}$,

$990x = 354.\overline{54} - 3.\overline{54}, = 351,$   $x = \dfrac{351}{990} = \dfrac{39}{110}$

**(c)** $\dfrac{7793}{3330}$   $x = 2.3\overline{402}$,   $10x = 23.\overline{402}$,   $10000x = 23402.\overline{402}$,

$9990x = 23402.\overline{402} - 23.\overline{402} = 23379,$   $x = \dfrac{23379}{9990} = \dfrac{7793}{3330}$

**11. (a)** $\dfrac{358}{999} = 0.\overline{358}$   **12. (a)** $0.007, 0.017, 0.01\overline{7}, 0.027$

**14. (a)** Assume $3 - \sqrt{2}$ is rational; then $3 - \sqrt{2} = q$, where $q$ is rational. This implies that $\sqrt{2} = 3 - q$. But $3 - q$ is rational, since the rational numbers are closed under subtraction. This can't be true, since we know that $\sqrt{2}$ is irrational. Thus, the assumption that $3 - \sqrt{2}$ is rational must be false. So $3 - \sqrt{2}$ is irrational.

**20. (a)** $0.\overline{09}$   **(e)** $0.\overline{0009}$   **21. (a)** $\dfrac{74}{99}$   **22. (a)** $0.\overline{5}$   **(d)** $0.5\overline{1}$

**23.** Answers will vary.   **(a)** One example is $\sqrt{2} + (3 - \sqrt{2}) = 3$. $\sqrt{2}$ and $(3 - \sqrt{2})$ are both irrational. (See the answer to problem 14.)   **(b)** One example is $\sqrt{3} + \sqrt{3} = 2\sqrt{3}$. $\sqrt{3}$ and $2\sqrt{3}$ are both irrational.   **27.** Answers will vary. For example, $\dfrac{\sqrt{2}}{2\sqrt{2}} = \dfrac{1}{2}$, and $\dfrac{1}{2}$ is rational.

## Problem Set 7.2 (page 362)

**1. (a)** 403.674   **(c)** 1.137   **2. (a)** 174.37   **(c)** 26.1
**3. (a)** 35, 35.412   **(c)** 124, 128.7056
**6. (a)** 34,796   **(c)** 0.34796
**7. (a)** $a = 4$   **(c)** $c = -3$   **8. (a)** $2.77 \times 10^8$
**9. (a)** $1.05 \times 10^{-10}$   **(c)** $1.29 \times 10^{-13}$
**10. (a)** $1.53 \times 10^{10}$

**15.**

| 0.492 | 1.107 | 0.246 |
|-------|-------|-------|
| 0.369 | 0.615 | 0.861 |
| 0.984 | 0.123 | 0.738 |

**19. (c)** $\underline{\begin{array}{r} 2.374 \\ \underline{0.041} \\ 2.415 \end{array}}$ $\underline{\begin{array}{r} 5.267 \\ \underline{5.308} \end{array}}$
$\underline{\begin{array}{r} 7.723 \end{array}}$

**20. (a)** 3.4, 4.3, 5.2, 6.1, 7.0, 7.9
**(c)** 0.0114, 0.1144, 0.2174, 0.3204, 0.4234, 0.5264
**21.** 2.11, 2.321, 2.5531, 2.80841, 3.089251

**24. (a)**

```
          (4.73)
     (1.32)    (3.41)
 (8.42) (7.10)  (10.51)
```

**(c)**

```
          (2.341)
     (2.731)  (−0.39)
 (7.133) (4.402) (4.012)
```

**25. (a)**

| (1.33) | (0.41) | (1.64) |
| (0.92) | | (1.23) |
| (1.64) | (0.72) | (1.95) |

**(c)** Answers will vary. However, all possible solutions have 5.01 in the lower right corner.  **26.** $29.16  **29. (a)** 210.375 in$^2$
**30. (a)** $2 \times 10^{11}$, one sig. digit  **(b)** $7.53 \times 10^{-10}$, 3 sig. digits
**32. (a)**

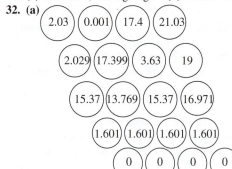

```
 (2.03) (0.001) (17.4) (21.03)
   (2.029) (17.399) (3.63) (19)
  (15.37) (13.769) (15.37) (16.971)
     (1.601) (1.601) (1.601) (1.601)
        (0)   (0)   (0)   (0)
```

**(c)** 5, 9, 17, and 31

## Problem Set 7.3 (page 376)

**1. (a)** $\frac{7}{5}$  **(c)** $\frac{7}{12}$  **(e)** $\frac{12}{5}$  **2. (a)** Yes  **(c)** No  **(e)** No

**(g)** Yes  **3. (a)** $r = 9$  **4. (a)** $\frac{3}{2}$  **(c)** $\frac{2}{3}$  **5. (a)** $19.25

**(c)** $\frac{3.5}{19.25} = 0.\overline{18}$, $\frac{5}{27.5} = 0.\overline{18}$  **9. (a)** 19 ft

**13. (a)** proportional: $y = kx$, where $k$ is the price per gallon of gasoline  **(c)** not proportional: $y = x^2$

**19. (a)** $\dfrac{a}{b} = \dfrac{c}{d}$
$ad = bc$
$da = cb$
$\dfrac{d}{c} = \dfrac{b}{a}$

**(c)** $\dfrac{a}{b} = \dfrac{c}{d}$
$ad = bc$
$ac + ad = ac + bc$
$a(c + d) = (a + b)c$
$\dfrac{a}{a + b} = \dfrac{c}{c + d}$

**22.** $y = 108$  **26.** 59 to 58  **28. (a)** 32 ounces for 90¢
**31. (a)** The table is not quite a ratio table. For example,
$21\frac{1}{4} \div 6\frac{3}{4} = \frac{85}{27} \approx 3.15$ but $23\frac{1}{2} \div 7\frac{1}{2} = \frac{47}{15} \approx 3.13$.
**33.** $13.01  **36.** $139.93
**40. (a)**

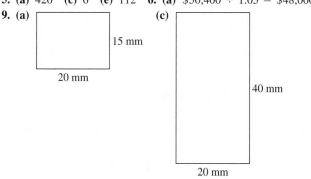

|  |  | Cog | | | | | |
|---------|----|------|------|------|------|------|------|------|
|  |  | 34 | 28 | 23 | 19 | 16 | 13 | 11 |
| Chainring | 24 | 0.71 | 0.86 | 1.04 | 1.26 | 1.50 | 1.85 | 2.18 |
|  | 35 | 1.03 | 1.25 | 1.52 | 1.84 | 2.19 | 2.69 | 3.18 |
|  | 51 | 1.50 | 1.82 | 2.22 | 2.68 | 3.19 | 3.92 | 4.64 |

## Problem Set 7.4 (page 388)

**1. (a)** 18.75%  **(c)** 92.5%  **(e)** $36.\overline{36}$%  **(g)** 22.86%

**2. (a)** 19%  **(c)** 215%  **3. (a)** $\frac{1}{10}$  **(c)** $\frac{5}{8}$

**4. (a)** 196  **(c)** 285.38  **(e)** 5.4962
**5. (a)** 420  **(c)** 6  **(e)** 112  **6. (a)** $50,400 \div 1.05 = $48,000
**9. (a)**

```
    ┌──────────┐
    │          │
    │          │ 15 mm
    │          │
    └──────────┘
      20 mm
```

**(c)**

```
  ┌──────┐
  │      │
  │      │
  │      │ 40 mm
  │      │
  │      │
  └──────┘
   20 mm
```

**10. (a)** $\frac{1}{8} = 0.125 = 12.5\%$  **(c)** $\frac{7}{8} = 0.3888\ldots = 39\%$

**11. (a)** 100  **(c)** 25  **12. (a)** 20  **(c)** 8  **14. (a)** 25%
**(c)** 50%  **23.** 34.29%  **27.** 42%  **30. (a)** 60%  **34.** $17,380
**36. (a)** $3576.80  **37. (a)** $x = 10, y = 50, z = 18$
**38.** $11,956.13  **40. (a)** 15  **(c)** 6  **41. (a)** 5,100,000

## Chapter 7 Review Exercises (page 397)

**1. (a)** $2 \cdot 10^2 + 7 \cdot 10^1 + 3 \cdot 10^0 + 4 \cdot 10^{-1} + 2 \cdot 10^{-2} + 5 \cdot 10^{-3}$
**(b)** $3 \cdot 10^{-4} + 5 \cdot 10^{-5} + 4 \cdot 10^{-6}$

**2. (a)** 0.056  **(b)** 0.08  **(c)** 0.1375  **3. (b)** $\frac{603}{500}$  **(c)** $\frac{2001}{10,000}$

**4.** $\frac{2}{66}, 0.33, \frac{4}{12}, 0.3334, \frac{5}{13}$  **5. (a)** $\frac{3451}{333}$  **(b)** $\frac{707}{330}$

**6.** Irrational. The decimal expansion of $a$ does not have a repeating sequence of digits, and it does not terminate.

**7. (a)** $\frac{2}{9}$  **(b)** $\frac{4}{11}$  **8. (a)** 96.1885  **(b)** 20.581  **(c)** 83.898

**(d)** 7.0  **9. (a)** 34.9437  **(b)** 27.999  **(c)** 109.23237  **(d)** 6.0

**10.** **(a)** About 60, 60.384   **(b)** About 40, 39.813
**(c)** About 500, 620.5815   **(d)** About 3, 3.5975
**11.** Suppose $3 - \sqrt{2} = r$, where $r$ is rational. Then $3 - r = \sqrt{2}$.
But this implies that $\sqrt{2}$ is rational, since the rationals are closed
under subtraction. This is a contradiction, since $\sqrt{2}$ is irrational.
Therefore, by contradiction, $3 - \sqrt{2}$ is irrational.
**12.** $(3 - \sqrt{2}) + \sqrt{2} = 3$   **13.** The decimal expansion of an
irrational number has no repeating sequence of digits and is
nonterminating.   **14.** **(a)** $928.125 \text{ ft}^2$   **(b)** 8.4375 qts, rounded
to 9 qts   **15.** Answers will vary. For example, $\dfrac{4123}{9999}$ is such a
fraction.   **16.** **(a)** $\dfrac{5}{18} = 0.2\overline{7}$; the period starts in the second decimal
place. $\dfrac{41}{333} = 0.\overline{123}$; the period starts right after the decimal point.
$\dfrac{11}{36} = 0.30\overline{5}$; the period starts in the third decimal place. $\dfrac{7}{45} = 0.1\overline{5}$;
the period starts in the second decimal place. $\dfrac{13}{80} = 0.1625$; this
decimal is terminating.   **(b)** Consider the prime-factor representation
of the denominator in each of the given fractions. If the highest
power of 2 and/or 5 appearing in this prime-factor representation is
$r$, the period begins in the $(r + 1)$st decimal place.   **17.** **(a)** 11 to 9
**18.** **(a)** Yes   **(b)** No   **(c)** Yes   **19.** $7.88   **20.** 13 gal   **21.** $y = \dfrac{35}{3}$
**22.** 43.2 ft   **23.** **(a)** 62.5%   **(b)** 211.5%   **(c)** 1.5%   **24.** **(a)** 0.28
**(b)** 0.0105   **(c)** $0.\overline{3}$   **25.** $3.53   **26.** 8%   **27.** 55%   **29.** $3514.98

## Chapter 7 Test (page 398)

**1.** 5 years ago   **2.** Answers will vary. A suitable choice is $\dfrac{125}{999}$.
**3.** 17 yrs   **4.** **(a)** 0.48   **(b)** $0.\overline{24}$   **(c)** $0.\overline{63}$
**5.** $1196.41   **6.** **(a)** $\dfrac{5}{11}$   **(b)** $\dfrac{284}{9}$   **(c)** $\dfrac{7}{20}$
**7.** 5   **8.** **(a)** 17 to 15   **(b)** 53.125%
**9.** $(2.34 \times 10^{-6})(3.12 \times 10^5) = 0.73008 \approx 0.730$   **10.** 15%

# Chapter 8

## Problem Set 8.1 (page 411)

**1.** **(a)** Constant   **(b)** Variable   **4.** **(a)** $p + 5$   **(c)** $\dfrac{1}{2}(p + 2) - 2$
**6.** **(a)** 98   **(b)** $(x^2 + 5) \cdot 7$   **9.** **(a)** $y = 8x + 2$ and $y = 3x - 4$
**10.** **(a)** Using distance $=$ rate $\times$ time ($d = rt$) we find that the
average speed is distance divided by time. Therefore, her
average speed was $15 \text{ mi} \div 3 \text{ hr} = 5 \text{ mph}$.
**(b)** Since $t = \dfrac{d}{r}$, it took $15 \text{ mi} \div 15 \text{ mph} = 1 \text{ hr}$ to get home.
**(f)** The average of 5 mph and 15 mph is 10 mph, which is not
equal to the average speed of $7\dfrac{1}{2}$ mph for the round-trip.
This is because Little Red Riding Hood spent much more time
riding at 5 mph than riding at 15 mph.
**11.** **(a)** Not a function, since element $c$ is associated with more
than one element of set $B$ and element $d$ is not associated with any
elements of set $B$.   **(b)** A function, with range $\{p, q, r\} \subset B$

**12.** **(a)** Not a function, a point is assigned two points.

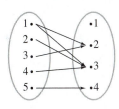

**13.** **(a)** Not the graph of a function: for example, there are three
$y$-values associated with the value $x = 3$.   **(c)** Not the graph of a
function, since the two $y$-values 1 and 3 correspond to $x = 2$
**16.** **(a)** $g(0) = 5, g(1) = 4, g(2) = 5, g(3) = 8, g(4) = 13$
**(b)** $\{4, 5, 8, 13\}$   **18.** **(a)** 12:45   **(b)** 1:00   **19.** **(a)** G3
**20.** **(a)**

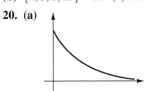

**21.** **(a)** $A = 2x^2$   **(b)** $P = 6x$   **(c)** $D = \sqrt{5}\,x$
**22.** **(a)** Add 5: $y = x + 5$.   **24.** **(a)** 6, 8, 10, 12
**31.** **(a)** AnnElise correctly figured out that the town is growing
by 38 people each year. However, she extended her data only one
year, not two.   **34.** Let $t$ and $u$ respectively denote the tens and
units digits of $n$. Then $n = 10t + u$. The sum of the digits is
$t + u$ and the product of the digits is $tu$, so we get the condition
$10t + u = t + u + tu$. If $t$ and $u$ are subtracted from each side of
the equation, we get $9t = tu$. Since $t$ is not 0, the equation can be
divided by $t$ to get $9 = u$. We conclude that *every* two-digit
number ending in 9 has the property. That is, the solution set is
$\{19, 29, 39, 49, 59, 69, 79, 89, 99\}$.
**36.** We assume that the commuter travels the same distance $d$ in
both directions. From the $d = rt$ formula of Table 8.1, the time
taken to go to work is therefore given by the expression $\dfrac{d}{u}$.
Similarly, the time taken to return home is given by $\dfrac{d}{v}$. The
round-trip distance $2d$ is traveled in the total time of $\dfrac{d}{u} + \dfrac{d}{v}$, so the
average speed of the round-trip is given by $\dfrac{2d}{\dfrac{d}{u} + \dfrac{d}{v}} = \dfrac{2uv}{v + u}$.
It was MHM because it wasn't necessary to know the value of the
variable $d$ to solve the problem. The very common error is to
answer the problem by just taking the average of the two speeds
without thinking about the answer conceptually.
**40.** Since there are 9 square feet in a square yard, the cost of a
remnant is $\dfrac{\$3.60}{9} = \$0.40$ per square foot. An $L$-by-$W$ remnant
will therefore cost $(\$0.40)LW$. The perimeter of the remnant is
$2L + 2W$, so the cost to finish the edges is $(\$0.12)(2L + 2W)$.
This gives a total cost of $(\$0.40)LW + (\$0.12)(2L + 2W)$.
**42.** **(a)** The approximate formula gives that area as $\left(\dfrac{16}{9}\right)^2 100^2 =$
$31,604.9\ldots$. The area as calculated with the more exact value of $\pi$
used by a calculator is $\pi\,100^2 = 31415.9\ldots$. The error is about
189 square feet.

# Problem Set 8.2 (page 429)

**1.** (a), (c), (e), (g), (i)

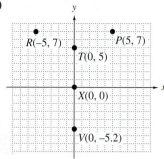

**4.** (a) $\sqrt{(4-(-2))^2 + (13-5)^2} = \sqrt{36+64} = \sqrt{100} = 10$
(c) $\sqrt{(8-0)^2 + (-8-7)^2} = \sqrt{64+225} = \sqrt{289} = 17$
**5.** (a) 2; upward   (c) 2; upward   (e) 1; upward   **6.** 2

**8.** (a) $a = \dfrac{9}{2}$

**10.** (a), (c)

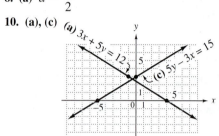

**11.** (a)

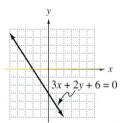

**(b)** Yes. The function is $y = -\dfrac{3}{2}x - 3$.

**(d)** Yes. The function is $y = \dfrac{5}{3}x - 5$.

**13.** (a)

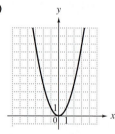

**14.** (a)

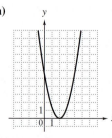

**16.** (a) The minimum value of $x^2 + 10x$ is $-25$. It occurs when $x = -5$.

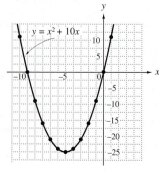

**19.** (a) $x = 5$   (c) $y = \dfrac{1}{2}x + 1$   **20.** $r = 10, s = 5$

**26.** (a) 30 ft   (b) about 5%   **28.** $m = 2, b = 10$

**29.** $m = \dfrac{9}{5}$ and $b = 32$

# Problem Set 8.3 (page 440)

**2.** (a) $-\dfrac{35}{3}$   (c) $\dfrac{3}{5}$

**3.** (a)

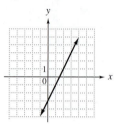

**5.** (a) $(RS)^2 = (\sqrt{(7-1)^2 + (10-2)^2})^2 =$
$(\sqrt{36+64})^2 = (\sqrt{100})^2 = 100$
$(RT)^2 = (\sqrt{(5-1)^2 + (-1-2)^2})^2 = (\sqrt{16+9})^2 =$
$(\sqrt{25})^2 = 25$  $(ST)^2 = (\sqrt{(5-7)^2 + (-1-10)^2})^2 =$
$(\sqrt{4+121})^2 = (\sqrt{125})^2 = 125$. Since $(RS)^2 + (RT)^2 =$
$100 + 25 = 125 = (ST)^2$, by the Pythagorean theorem, $\triangle RST$ is a right triangle.
**7.** (a) $PB^2 = (x-1)^2 + (y-1)^2 = x^2 - 2x + 1 + y^2$
$- 2y + 1 = x^2 + y^2 - 2x - 2y + 2$
$PC^2 = (x-0)^2 + (y-1)^2 = x^2 + y^2 - 2y + 1 =$
$x^2 + y^2 - 2y + 1$  $PD^2 = (x-0)^2 + (y-0)^2 = x^2 + y^2$
**(b)** $PA^2 + PC^2 = (x^2 + y^2 - 2x + 1) + (x^2 + y^2$
$- 2y + 1) = 2x^2 + 2y^2 - 2x - 2y + 2$
$PB^2 + PD^2 = (x^2 + y^2 - 2x - 2y + 2)$
$+ (x^2 + y^2) = 2x^2 + 2y^2 - 2x - 2y + 2$
These equations show that $PA^2 + PC^2 = PB^2 + PD^2$ for all $x$
and $y$. That is, all points $P(x, y)$ in the plane satisfy the condition.
The point is that the equation holds no matter what point $P$ was
picked. That is surprising and a part of what MHM is.
**9.** The slope of $\overline{RT}$ is $(6-4)/(7-1) = 1/3$. The slope of the
altitude is $-3$, and the altitude must run through $S = (5, 0)$. The
answer is the line, $y = -3x + 15$.

**10.** The midpoint of $\overline{AB}$ is $\left(\dfrac{3}{2}, 1\right)$. The slope of $\overline{AB}$ is 6, so the

perpendicular of $\overline{AB}$ has slope $-1/6$ and goes through $\left(\dfrac{3}{2}, 1\right)$. Using

the point–slope form gives $y - 1 = -\dfrac{1}{6}\left(x - \dfrac{3}{2}\right)$

for the perpendicular bisector.   **12.** (a) By sketching the circle, is it
clear that the answers are (a) $y = -3$   **14.** Responses vary, but the
conclusion is that $l$ is parallel to $n$.   **16.** All are true except (d). (e)
is true because the two circles can be the same.   **22.** (a) By trial
and error, 10 taxi segments. Alternatively, this is the number of
sequences of 3 E(east) and 2 N(north) segments, and there are 10
ways to form such sequences: NNEEE, NENEE, . . . , EEENN.

# Chapter 8 Review Exercises (page 446)

**1.** (a) $a + 5$   (b) $b < c$   (c) $c - b$   (d) $\dfrac{(a+b+c)}{3}$

**2.** (a) $a + 2 = 11$   (b) $b - 3 = \dfrac{1}{2}(c - 1)$   (c) $a = \dfrac{(b+c)}{2}$

**(d)** $\dfrac{(a + b + c)}{3} = 10$   **3. (a)** $y = 3x + 2$

**(b)** $y = x(x + 1)$, or $y = x^2 + x$

**4. (a)** $f(3) = 0, f(0.5) = -2.5, f(-2) = 20$   **(b)** $x = 0$ or $x = 3$

**5. (a)**

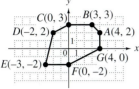

**(b)** $B$ is in the first quadrant, $C$ is on the positive $y$-axis, $D$ is in the second quadrant, $E$ is in the third quadrant, and $F$ is on the negative $y$-axis.   **(c)** slope $\overline{BC} = \dfrac{0}{3} = 0$, slope $\overline{CD} = \dfrac{1}{2}$, slope $\overline{DE} = \dfrac{4}{1} = 4$, slope $\overline{EF} = \dfrac{0}{3} = 0$, slope $\overline{FG} = \dfrac{2}{4} = \dfrac{1}{2}$, slope $\overline{GA}$ is undefined, $\overline{BC}$ is parallel to $\overline{EF}$, and $\overline{CD}$ is parallel to $\overline{FG}$.

**6.**

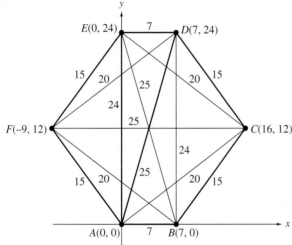

**(a)** $AB = 7, AC = \sqrt{16^2 + 12^2} = \sqrt{400} = 20$,
$AD = \sqrt{7^2 + 24^2} = \sqrt{625} = 25, AE = 24$,
$AF = \sqrt{(-9)^2 + 12^2} = \sqrt{225} = 15, CF = 16 + 9 = 25$
**(b)** The lengths of all the sides and diagonals of the hexagon are positive integers.   **7. (a)** $y = 4 + 2(x - 3)$, using the point–slope form of the equation of a line. In slope–intercept form, the equivalent equation is $y = 4 + 2(x - 3) = 2x - 2$.

**(b)** $y = -1 + \dfrac{5 - (-1)}{(-2) - 6}(x - 6) = -1 - \dfrac{3}{4}(x - 6)$, using the two-point form. In slope–intercept form, the equivalent equation is $y = -\dfrac{3}{4}x + \dfrac{7}{2}$.   **(c)** $y = 3x - 4$, using the slope–intercept form of the equation of a line.

## Chapter 8 Test (page 447)

**2. (a)**

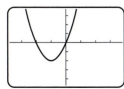

**(b)** The minimum function value is $y = -2$, the value of the function at $x = -1$.   **3. (a)** Linear, equivalent to $y = 3x - 4$;

slope is 3, $(0, -4)$   **(b)** Nonlinear, since $x^2$ appears in the equation
**(c)** Linear, equivalent to $y = x + 5$. Slope is $+1$, intercept is $(0, 5)$.
**4. (a)** Let $t$ denote the charged time, in total minutes for the month. Then $5 + 0.12t$ is the phone bill (in dollars) for that month.
**(b)** Let $n =$ number of checks. Then the cost of checking is $8 + 0.15n$.   **(c)** Let $a$ and $c$ denote the number of adults and children, respectively. Then the admission fee is $4a + 2.50c$, in dollars.   **5. (a)** $y = 5$   **(b)** $y = -x - 2$, since the slope is $-1$ and the line intersects the $y$-axis at $-2$   **(c)** The line has slope $\dfrac{1}{3}$ and passes through $P(2, 2)$, so its equation in point–slope form is $y - 2 = \dfrac{1}{3}(x - 2)$.   **6. (a)** G3   **(b)** G1   **(c)** G2

**8. (a)** $a = 0$ and $b = 5$, since each side has either a horizontal run of 3 and a rise of 4 or a horizontal run of 4 and a fall of 3.
**(b)** $\sqrt{4^2 + 3^2} = \sqrt{25} = 5$   **9.** $\{1, 2, 5, 10\}$

# Chapter 9

## Problem Set 9.1 (page 465)

**1. (a)** $\overleftrightarrow{AB}$ or $\overleftrightarrow{BA}$   **2. (a)**

$\xleftarrow{\hspace{2cm}} \underset{E}{\bullet} \hspace{1cm} \underset{U}{\bullet} \xrightarrow{\hspace{2cm}}$

**3. (a)**

**4.** $m(\angle AXB) = m(\angle AXE) - m(\angle BXE) = 180° - 140° = 40°$
$m(\angle CXD) = m(\angle BXD) - m(\angle BXC) = 90° - 45° = 45°$
$m(\angle DXE) = m(\angle BXE) - m(\angle BXD) = 140° - 90° = 50°$
**6.** The three lines are concurrent.   **9. (a)** Opposite angles are supplementary: $m(\angle A) + m(\angle C) = 180°$ and $m(\angle B) + m(\angle D) = 180°$.   **10.** Ten times: once between 1 and 2, once between 2 and 3, . . . , and once between 10 and 11.   **11 (a)** $360°$
**(d)** $60°$   **12. (a)** The minute hand is on the 12 and the hour hand is on the 4, so the hands form an angle of $120°$.   **(c)** The minute hand is on the 6 and the hour hand is halfway between the 4 and the 5. The angle between two consecutive numbers is $\dfrac{1}{12}$ of a revolution, or $30°$. So the angle is $(1.5)(30°) = 45°$.
**14.** Draw a horizontal ray $\overleftrightarrow{PQ}$ at $P$, in the opposite direction of $\overleftrightarrow{AB}$ and $\overleftrightarrow{CD}$. The opposite-interior-angles theorem then gives $m(\angle APQ) = 120°$ and $m(\angle CPQ) = 150°$. Thus, $m(\angle P) = 360° - 120° - 150° = 90°$.   **15. (a)** $40°$, since the measures of the interior angles of a triangle add up to $180°$   **(c)** $49°$; since the interior angles of a triangle add up to $180°$ and a right angle has measure $90°$, we have $m(\angle 3) = 180° - (41° + 90°) = 49°$.
**16. (a)** $x + x + 30° = 180°$, so $x = 75°$. The interior angles measure $75°, 75°$, and $30°$.   **17. (a)** No, because an obtuse angle has measure greater than $90°$ and adding two such measures would exceed $180°$, which is the sum of all three interior angle measures for any triangle   **28. (a)** Zero intersection points if the five lines are parallel to each other.   **29. (a)** 6 lines   **31.** The pencil turns through each interior angle of the triangle. Since the pencil faces the opposite direction when it returns to the starting side, it has turned a total of $180°$. This demonstrates that the sum of measures of the interior angles of a triangle is $180°$.   **35.** The earliest clocks were sundials used in the northern hemisphere. The shadow cast by the gnomon follows an arc in the direction we call clockwise.

**38. (a)** A full revolution takes 24 hours. In 1 hour, the earth turns $\frac{1}{24}$ of a revolution, or 15°. **39.** The angle of latitude is equal to the angle of elevation to Polaris.

**40. (a)** $58° 36' 45'' = 58° + \left(\frac{36}{60}\right)° + \left(\frac{45}{3600}\right)° = 56.6125°$
**(c)** $71.32° = 71° + (0.32)(60)' = 71° + 19.2' = 71° + 19' + (0.2)(60)'' = 71° 19' 12''$ **42. (a)** The lines $\overleftrightarrow{BB'}$ and $\overleftrightarrow{DD'}$ intersect at a right angle at $P$.

## Problem Set 9.2 (page 482)

**1.**

|  | (a) (b) (c) (d) |
|---|---|
| **Simple Curve** | ✓ |
| **Closed Curve** | ✓ ✓ ✓ |
| **Polygonal Curve** | ✓ ✓ |
| **Polygon** | ✓ |

**2.** An example of each figure is given.
**(a)**  **(c)**

**4. (a)** Convex **(b)** Concave

**5. (a)**  **(c)**

**6. (a)** 6 **(c)** 8 **7.** $2x + 5x + 5x + 5x + 5x + 2x = (6 - 2)(180°)$, or $24x = 720°$, so $x = 30°$. The angles measure 60°, 150°, 150°, 150°, 150°, and 60°.
**10. (a)** $(5 - 2)(180)° = 540°$ **(c)** $(6 - 2)(180)° = 720°$
**11.** Pictures will vary. **(a)** Triangle **(c)** Decagon
**14. (a)** 360° **(c)** 0° **16. (a)** $DAF$ and $DBC$
**18.**

| $n$ | Interior Angle | Exterior Angle | Central Angle |
|---|---|---|---|
| 5 | 108° | 72° | 72° |
| 7 | $128\frac{4}{7}°$ | $51\frac{3}{7}°$ | $51\frac{3}{7}°$ |

**19. (a)** $\frac{360°}{n} = 15°$, so $n = 24$.

**31. (a)** The boat can drift to any position inside the circle centered at $A$, where the radius of the circle is the length of the anchor rope.
**32. (a)**  $C$ could be any point (other than $A$ or $B$) on either of the two lines drawn through $A$ and through $B$ and that are perpendicular to $\overline{AB}$.

**(b)**  $C$ could be any point (other than $A$ or $B$) on the circle with $\overline{AB}$ as its diameter.

**33.** At a vertex, the interior angle and the conjugate angle add up to 360°. For an $n$-gon, the sum of all interior and all conjugate angles is $n \cdot 360°$. All the interior angles add up to $(n - 2) \cdot 180°$, so all the conjugate angles add up to $360°n - (n - 2) 180° = 360°n - 180°n + 360° = 180°n + 360° = (n + 2) \cdot 180°$.
**35.** Such a point $S$ allows for $n$ triangles to be formed, all with the vertex $S$. The sum of all the interior angles of these $n$ triangles is $n \cdot 180°$, which is equal to the sum of all the interior angles of the $n$-gon plus 360° for the angles that surround the point $S$. Thus, the sum of the interior angles of the $n$-gon is $n \cdot 180° - 360° = (n - 2) \cdot 180°$. **37. (a)** The total turn made when tracing the star is $2 \times 360°$, so the turn made at each point of the star is $7 \times 360°/16 = 157.5°$. Therefore, the angle at each point measures $180° - 157.5° = 22.5°$. **38.** Each new circle creates a new region each time it intersects a previously drawn circle. Since the new circle intersects each of the old circles in two points, this creates the following pattern:

| NUMBER OF | | NUMBER OF | |
|---|---|---|---|
| **Circles** | **Regions** | **Circles** | **Regions** |
| 1 | 2     = 2 | 6 | $22 + 2 \cdot 5 = 32$ |
| 2 | $2 + 2 \cdot 1 = 4$ | 7 | $32 + 2 \cdot 6 = 44$ |
| 3 | $4 + 2 \cdot 2 = 8$ | 8 | $44 + 2 \cdot 7 = 58$ |
| 4 | $8 + 2 \cdot 3 = 14$ | 9 | $58 + 2 \cdot 8 = 74$ |
| 5 | $14 + 2 \cdot 4 = 22$ | 10 | $74 + 2 \cdot 9 = 92$ |

**41. (a)** The sum of the interior angles is $360° = m(\angle P) + m(\angle Q) + m(\angle R) + m(\angle S)$. We also know that $m(\angle P) = m(\angle R)$ and $m(\angle Q) = m(\angle S)$, so $360° = m(\angle P) + m(\angle Q) + m(\angle P) + m(\angle Q)$, giving us $180° = m(\angle P) + m(\angle Q)$.
**(b)** $m(\angle Q) + m(\angle q) = 180° = m(\angle P) + m(\angle Q) = 180°$, so $m(\angle q) = m(\angle P)$. $\angle q$ and $\angle P$ are corresponding angles, so segments $\overline{PS}$ and $\overline{QR}$ are parallel. $m(\angle q) = m(\angle P)$ and $m(\angle P) = m(\angle R)$, so $m(\angle q) = m(\angle R)$. $\angle q$ and $\angle R$ are alternate interior angles, so their congruence gives $\overline{PQ}$ parallel to $\overline{SR}$. Hence, the figure is a parallelogram.

$$P \qquad\qquad Q$$
$$\begin{array}{|c c|} \angle P & \angle Q \\ \angle S & \angle R \end{array} \angle q$$
$$S \qquad\qquad R$$

**42. (a)** Drawings will vary. **(b)** Suppose the black curve has been drawn. It will be seen that it is easy to shade some of the regions in such a way that exactly one of any two regions sharing a common boundary is shaded and the other region is left unshaded. Now imagine adding the red closed curve. Each time the red curve crosses the black curve, it alternates between shaded and unshaded regions. Since the red curve is closed, the red curve closes upon itself in a region of the same type as its starting point. Thus, the number of color alternations must be even. That is, the number of intersection points of the red and black curves is necessarily even.
**43.** The number of regions interior to both simple curves is always equal to the number of regions exterior to both curves. The number of regions inside the red curves and outside the black curves is always equal to the number of regions inside the black curves and outside the red curves. There is no connection between the two pairs of equal numbers.

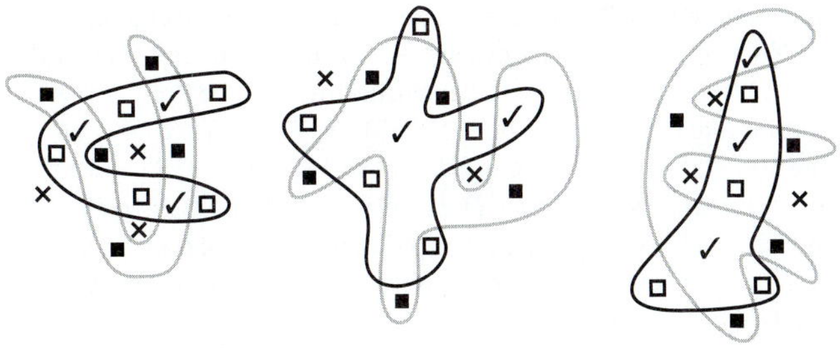

**46.** **(a)** *SQRE* is square. **(b)** No

## Problem Set 9.3 (page 499)

**1.** **(a)** Polyhedron **(c)** Polyhedron **(e)** Not a polyhedron
**2.** **(a)** Pentagonal prism **(c)** Oblique circular cone
**(e)** Right rectangular prism **3.** **(a)** 4 **(c)** $A, B, C, D$
**5.** **(a)**

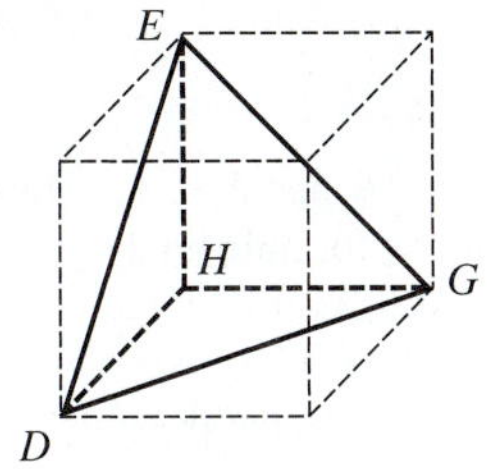


**6.** **(a)**

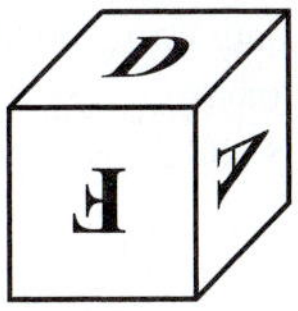


**7.** **(a)** 45°, since the dihedral angle between the adjacent sides of the cube is 90° and another pyramid would fit into the gap between the original pyramid and a vertical side of the cube **(b)** Filling the cube with six such pyramids, one sees that three pyramids surround the edge between the cube's center and any corner. Thus, three copies of the dihedral angle give a full revolution of 360° around this edge, so the dihedral angle measures 120°.
**14.** **(a)** $F = 10, V = 7$, and $E = 15$, so $V + F = E + 2$, since $7 + 10 = 15 + 2$.
**15.** **(a)**

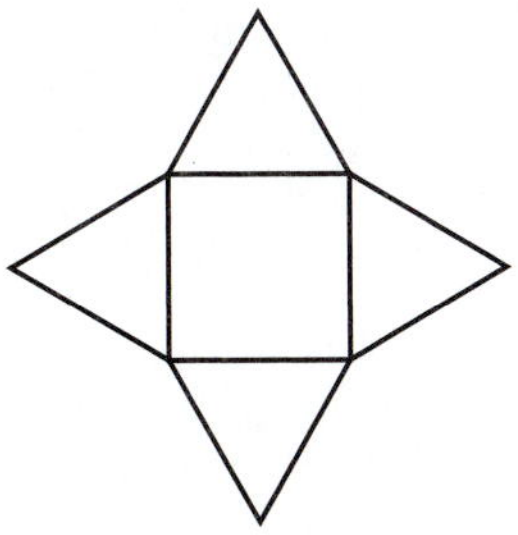

**16.** The MHM symbol is used because the student will see that relaxing one of the hypotheses of a statement may result in the conclusion being wrong. **(a)** $V = 10, F = 12$, and $E = 20$. $V + F = 22 = E + 2$, so Euler's formula holds.
**25.** The MHM symbol is used because the student needs to convert an equality into an inequality for the first three parts. **(a)** Suppose the faces of a polyhedron consist of a $p$-gon, a $q$-gon, an $r$-gon, and so on. Since each edge of the polyhedron borders two faces, the sum $p + q + r + \cdots$ is twice the number of edges. That is, $p + q + r + \cdots = 2E$. Since there are $F$ faces and $p, q, r, \ldots$ are all 3 or greater, we get $2E \geq 3 + 3 + \cdots = 3F$. **(b)** Each of the $V$ vertices of a polyhedron is the endpoint of three or more edges that meet at the vertex. Thus, $3V$ is less than or equal to the total number of ends of the edges. But each of the $E$ edges has two ends, so there are $2E$ ends of edges. We see that $3V \leq 2E$. **(c)** Adding $3V \leq 2E$ and $3F \leq 2E$ shows that $3V + 3F \leq 4E$. But $V + F = E + 2$ (Euler's formula), so $3V + 3F = 3E + 6$. Comparing this result with the inequality, we see that $3E + 6 \leq 4E$. Subtracting $3E$ from both sides shows that $6 \leq E$. **(d)** Suppose $E = 7$. Since $3F \leq 2E = 14$, we see that $F$ is no larger than 4. ($F \geq 5$ would give $3F \geq 15$.) Similarly, $3V \leq 2E = 14$ means that $V \leq 4$. Since both $V \leq 4$ and $F \leq 4$, $V + F \leq 8$. But $V + F = E + 2$ (Euler's formula), and $E = 7$, so $V + F = 9$. This contradicts $V + F \leq 8$, so our assumption, $E = 7$, is not possible. **(e)** A pyramid with a base of $3, 4, 5, \ldots, n, \ldots$ sides has $6, 8, 10 \ldots, 2n, \ldots$ edges, respectively. Slicing off a tiny corner at one vertex somewhere on the base of the pyramid adds three new edges, giving us polyhedra with $9, 11, 13, \ldots, 2n + 3, \ldots$ edges. Altogether, the pyramids and pyramids with a truncated base corner give us polyhedra with $6, 8, 9, 10, 11, \ldots$ edges.
**27.** **(a)** The base is a pentagon.

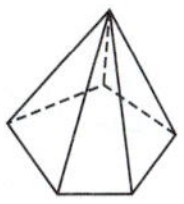

**(b)** The center polygon is a triangle.

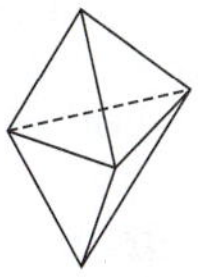

**28.** **(a)**

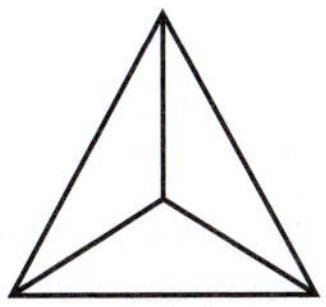

Tetrahedron

**(b)**

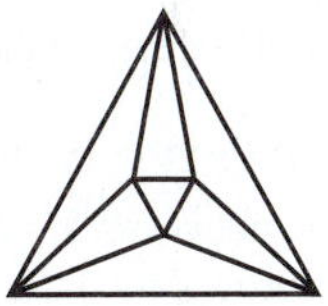

Octahedron

**(c)**

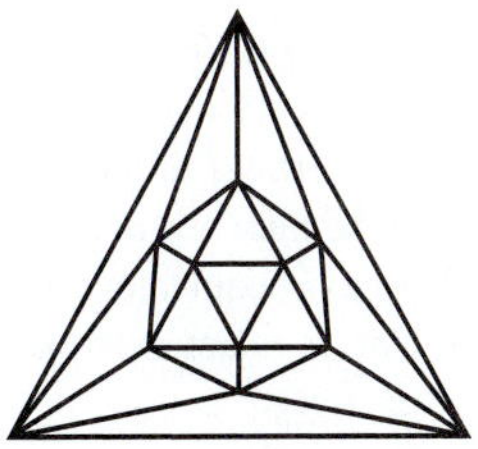

Icosahedron

**32.** **(a)** When folded, these edges coincide and so must be the same length in the net. The dashed segment $\overline{AP}$ is perpendicular to edge $\overline{BH}$ because folding along $\overline{BH}$ moves point $A$ along a circle that is in a plane perpendicular to the axis $\overline{BH}$ of the fold.
**33.** The axis of all the hinges on a door must be along the intersection of the planes of the wall and the plane of the opened door. Since planes meet in a line, the axes of the hinges must be along a single line.
**37.** A, C (if the cylinder can be triangular), or D (if the cylinder can be hexagonal).

# Problem Set 9.4 (page 510)

**1.** The networks I and III each represent the information correctly, since there is an edge between vertices when, and only when, the individuals have met. Network II does not represent the information given; for example, it incorrectly indicates that Coralee has met Bianca.    **2. (a)** Yes. *AHGFEDCBHFDBA* is one Euler path. **(c)** No    **(e)** Yes. *CEAEFBFDBACD* is one Euler path
**4. (a)** $D = 24, E = 12$ for (a); $D = 22, E = 11$ for (b); $D = 24, E = 12$ for (c); $D = 30, E = 15$ for (d); $D = 22, E = 11$ for (e); $D = 30, E = 15$ for (f)
**5. (a)** Yes, since exactly two vertices are odd
**(b)** $D = 2 + 2 + 4 + 8 + 3 + 6 + 6 - 1 = 32$, so $E = 16$.
**7. (a)**

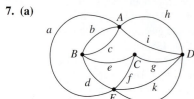

**8. (a)**

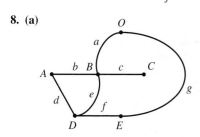

**9. (a)** $V = 6, R = 7$, and $E = 11$    **12. (a)** The triangle in the network shows that at least three different times must be scheduled, say, science at 2:00, math at 3:00, and basketball at 4:00. Then the band can meet at 2:00 and history can meet at 3:00, with no student having a conflict.    **13. (a)** Combining these two paths gives a closed path with distinct edges.
**14.** The traversable trees are those of the form

**17.** Consider a network with a vertex for each person and an edge between two vertices for each time the corresponding persons have shaken hands. By the result stated in problem 15, there are an even number of people with odd numbers of handshakes.
**18. (a)** One possibility is *AB, JFBGJIDAEI, EFGHCKH.*
**(b)** Temporarily add $m - 1$ edges between $m - 1$ distinct pairs of the odd vertices. The new edges make these vertices into even vertices. Only two odd vertices remain, so the network is traversable. Following one of the added edges is equivalent to lifting the pencil. The $m - 1$ lifts mean that there are $m$ strokes.
**21. (a)**

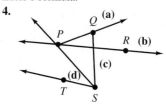

**23.** One collection of edges is *HA, AB, BG, GF, FD, DC,* and *DE.*

# Chapter 9 Review Exercises (page 519)

**1. (a)** $\overleftrightarrow{AC}$    **(b)** $\overline{BD}$    **(c)** $\overrightarrow{AD}$    **(d)** $\angle ABC$ or $\angle CBA$
**(e)** $m(\angle BCD)$, or $90°$    **(f)** $\overrightarrow{DC}$    **2. (a)** $\angle BAD$    **(b)** $\angle BCD$
**(c)** $\angle ABC, \angle ADC$    **3. (a)** $143°$    **(b)** $53°$
**4.** $p = 55°, r = 55°, s = 125°, q = 35°$    **5.** $x = 45°$,
$y = 33°, z = 147°$    **6. (a)** (iv) **(b)** (i)    **(c)** (vi)    **(d)** (v)
**(e)** (ii)    **(f)** (iii)    **7. (a)** No, because obtuse angles have a measure greater than $90°$ and the sum of the three interior angles of a

triangle is $180°$    **(b)** Yes; try angles of $100°, 100°, 100°$, and $60°$. **(c)** No, because acute angles have a measure less than $90°$ and the sum of the interior angles of a quadrilateral must be $360°$    **8.** The interior angles add up to $(6 - 2)(180)° = 720°$, so $16x = 720°$ and $x = 45°$. The angles are $135°, 135°, 135°, 45°, 225°$, and $45°$.
**9.** $360°$    **10. (a)** 6    **(b)** $\overline{CD}, \overline{EF}, \overline{GH}$    **(c)** $\overline{DH}, \overline{GC}, \overline{EH}, \overline{FG}$
**(d)** $45°$    **11.** Square right prism; triangular pyramid, or tetrahedron; oblique circular cylinder; sphere; hexagonal right prism
**12. (a)**    **(b)**

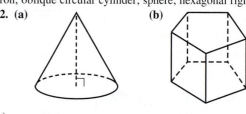

**(c)**

**13. (a)** See Table 9.4.    **(b)** $V = 6, F = 8$, and $E = 12$. Thus, $V + F = 14$ and $E + 2 = 14$, so Euler's formula holds.
**14.** By Euler's formula, $V + 14 = 24 + 2$, so $V = 12$.
**15. (a)** It has four odd vertices.    **(b)** An edge between any two of the vertices A, B, C, and E. Many Euler paths are possible.
**16.** Construct a network with vertices $A, B, C, D$, and $E$ and edges corresponding to bridges. Since just two vertices, $A$ and $D$, have odd degree, there is an Euler path. The Euler path corresponds to a walking path that crosses each bridge exactly once.
**17.** $V = 11, R = 7$, and $E = 16$. $V + R = 18$ and $E + 2 = 18$, so $V + R = E + 2$ holds.

# Chapter 9 Test (page 521)

**1.** The average interior angle measure for an *n*-gon is $\dfrac{(n - 2)(180°)}{n}$. We want this value to be $144°$, so $\dfrac{180(n - 2)}{n} = 144$. This gives $n = 10$.    **2.** Many examples of each are possible.

**(a)**    **(b)**    **(c)**    **(d)**

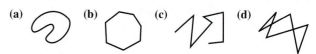

**3. (a)** 24. Each edge borders a square face and a triangular face. So just count the edges of all the square faces (or all the edges of the triangular faces).    **(b)** 12. Either count in the diagram or use Euler's formula.
**4.**

**5. (a)** By Euler's formula, $V + 7 = 11 + 2$; so $V = 6$.
**(b)** Many such networks can be drawn.    **6. (a)** $C, A$    **(b)** $F$
**(c)** $D$    **(d)** $E$    **(e)** $B$    **7. (a)** True    **(b)** False    **(c)** True
**(d)** True    **8.** The total-turn angle is $1080°$, so the turn at each of the seven vertices is $1080°/8 = 135°$. This means that the interior angle at each point is $180° - 135° = 45°$.

**9. (a)** Diagrams will vary.   **(b)** $V = 16, F = 21, E = 35$
**(c)** $V + F = 37$ and $E + 2 = 37$, so Euler's formula holds.
**10.** The same as an interior angle of a regular pentagon, which is
$\dfrac{3 \cdot 180°}{5} = 108°$   **11.** $t = 40°, r = 80°, s = 100°$

**12. (a)** (iii)   **(b)** (iv)   **(c)** (i), (ii)   **(d)** (iii); add an edge
between any two of the four odd vertices.

# Chapter 10

## Problem Set 10.1 (page 538)

**1. (a)** Height, length, thickness, area, diagonal, weight
**(c)** Height, length, depth   **4. (a)** Answers will vary anywhere
from 40 to 54.   **(b)** The circular portions of area don't fit well
together, but leave gaps between them.

**6. (a)** 1 acre $= \dfrac{1}{640}$ mi$^2$ $= \left(\dfrac{1}{640}\text{mi}^2\right)\left(\dfrac{5280 \text{ ft}}{1 \text{ mi}}\right)^2 = 43{,}560$ ft$^2$

**8. (a)** 33 cL $= 33 \times 10^{-2}$ L $= 330 \times 10^{-3}$ L $= 330$ mL
**(b)** Not quite; 1 L $= 1000$ mL and $3 \times 33$ cL $= 990$ mL
**9. (a)** 58.728 kg   **(c)** 230 g   **10. (a)** 3.5 kg   **12. (a)** About
28 cm by 22 cm   **(c)** About 2 cm   **14. (a)** one centipede
**(b)** one microphone   **(c)** two kilo mockingbirds (*To Kill a
Mockingbird*)   **(d)** one decacards (*deck of cards*)
**(e)** Since $10^{-9}$ is nano, the answer is "nanogoat."
**19. (a)** The correct answer is 0.00005 km.
**(b)** Answers may vary, but Brent needs to be shown why getting
a decimal is a possible correct answer. He needs to see what 5 cm
looks like and then compare 5 cm with 1 decimeter. Next, he
should be shown that 5 cm $= 0.5$ dm and why. His teacher can
then show him 5 cm compared with meters and show that
5 cm $= 0.05$ m and why. Seeing this comparison may help Brent
realize why there can be a decimal when converting. It is important
to really discuss the reasons why the number looks so different
when converting from cm to km.   **21. (a)** 8, 16, 32

**24.** $\left(\dfrac{100 \text{ km}}{9 \text{ L}}\right)\left(\dfrac{3.7854 \text{ L}}{1 \text{ gal}}\right)\left(\dfrac{1 \text{ mi}}{1.6 \text{ km}}\right) \doteq 26.3$ mi/gal

**26. (a)** $(5 \text{ gal})\left(\dfrac{4 \text{ qt}}{1 \text{ gal}}\right)\left(\dfrac{32 \text{ oz}}{1 \text{ qt}}\right) = 640$ oz.

Since $\dfrac{640}{80} = 8$, add 8 liquid ounces of concentrate.

**(b)** Add $80 \times 65$ mL $= 5200$ mL $= 5.2$ L of water.
**28. (a)** 4917 liters were added

**29.** 1 ha $\doteq (10{,}000 \text{ m}^2)\left(\dfrac{1 \text{ km}}{1000 \text{ m}}\right)^2\left(\dfrac{1 \text{ mi}}{1.6 \text{ km}}\right)^2$
$\left(\dfrac{640 \text{ acres}}{1 \text{ mi}^2}\right) = 2.5$ acres

**31.** $\left(\dfrac{25 \text{ in}}{1 \text{ min}}\right)\left(\dfrac{60 \text{ min}}{1 \text{ hr}}\right)\left(\dfrac{24 \text{ hr}}{1 \text{ day}}\right)\left(\dfrac{14 \text{ day}}{1 \text{ fortnight}}\right)$
$\left(\dfrac{1 \text{ ft}}{12 \text{ in}}\right)\left(\dfrac{1 \text{ furlong}}{660 \text{ ft}}\right) \doteq 63.6$ furlong/fortnight

## Problem Set 10.2 (page 554)

**3.** The dodecagon and square have the same area, equal to the sum
of the areas of the same subregions in their dissections.

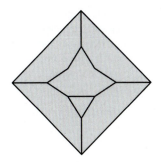

**5. (a)** 12 units

**7. (a)** $\dfrac{1}{2} \times (4 \text{ mm} + 6 \text{ mm}) \times 2 \text{ mm} + \dfrac{1}{2} \times$
6 mm $\times$ 5 mm $= 25$ mm$^2$   **10. (a)** 12 cm
**11. (a)** 1 cm by 24 cm; 2 cm by 12 cm; 3 cm by 8 cm; 4 cm
by 6 cm. The dimensions can also be given in opposite order.
**12. (a)** 81 ft$^2$, 45.2 ft   **13. (a)** 1664.6 m$^2$, 198.3 m
**14. (a)** 220 square units   **16. (a)** $\triangle ABC$; all triangles have the
same base and $\triangle ABC$ has the smallest height.   **(b)** $\triangle ABF$; it
has the largest height.   **(c)** $\triangle ABD$ and $\triangle ABE$; they have equal
heights and the same base.   **18. (a)** 9 square units
**19. (a)** 100 m $+$ 100 m $+ 2\pi \cdot 25$ m $= (200 + 50\pi)$m $\doteq 357$ m
**(b)** $(50 \text{ m})(100 \text{ m}) + \pi(25 \text{ m})^2 = (5000 + 625\pi)\text{m}^2 \doteq 6963$ m$^2$
**21. (a)** $\pi(2)^2 - \pi(1)^2 = 3\pi$ square units $\doteq 9.4$ square units
**24. (b)** Yes, the perimeter will get infinitely large as either $w$ gets
closer to zero or $w$ gets very large itself. This MHM is that long,
skinny rectangles can all have the same area (of 4 cm$^2$), which is a
different type of result than the previous problem.

**25.** Along the large semicircle: $\dfrac{1}{2}(2 \cdot \pi \cdot 8 \text{ m}) = 8\pi$ m; along the

two smaller semicircles $\dfrac{1}{2}(2 \cdot \pi \cdot 3 \text{ m}) + \dfrac{1}{2}(2 \cdot \pi \cdot 5 \text{ m}) = 8\pi$ m.

The distances are the same.   **26. (a)** 40,000,000 m
**(b)** $12{,}755\pi$ km $\doteq 40{,}071{,}000$ m   **(c)** The equator is larger, since
the earth bulges slightly at the equator and is slightly flattened at
the poles.   **33.** 20 cm$^2$. The common overlap reduces the area of
both regions by the same amount, so the difference in area is
unchanged.

**37. (a)**

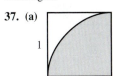

The unshaded region at the
left has area
$1^2 - \dfrac{1}{4}\pi(1^2) = 1 - \dfrac{\pi}{4}$

The shaded region at the
left has area
$1 - \left(1 - \dfrac{\pi}{4}\right) - \left(1 - \dfrac{\pi}{4}\right) = \left(\dfrac{\pi}{2}\right) - 1$

**38.** The areas of the rectangular portions of the sidewalk total 2400 ft². The pieces formed with circular areas have a total turning of 360°, so, when placed together, they form a circle with radius 8 ft and area $\pi(8 \text{ ft})^2 = 64\pi$ ft². Total area is $(2400 + 64\pi)$ ft².
**39. (a)** Erin walks $2\pi R$ and Nerd walks $2\pi(R + L)$, so Nerd walks $2\pi L$ farther than Erin. **42.** Draw $\overline{AP}, \overline{BP},$ and $\overline{CP}$. Then

area $(\triangle ABC) = \dfrac{1}{2} sh =$ area $(\triangle ABP) +$ area $(\triangle BPC) +$

area $(\triangle CPA) = \dfrac{1}{2} sx + \dfrac{1}{2} sz + \dfrac{1}{2} sy = \dfrac{1}{2} s(x + y + z).$ Therefore,

$\dfrac{1}{2} sh = \dfrac{1}{2} s(x + y + z),$ and $h = x + y + z.$ *Alternative, visual proof:*

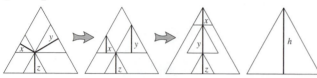

**50.** The lawn has an area 75 ft × 125 ft = 9375 ft².
Since 21 in $= \dfrac{7}{4}$ ft, the lawn area is equivalent to a rectangle 21 in

wide and $9375 \div \dfrac{7}{4} = 5357.14\ldots$ That is, Kelly will walk about

5357 feet, a bit over a mile (1 mile = 5280 ft). **52.** Consider the carpet as a 6-ft–by–4-ft rectangle with semicircular ends of radius 2. Then the carpet's area is $(6 \text{ ft})(4 \text{ ft}) + \pi(2 \text{ ft})^2 = 36.57$ ft² $\doteq 5266$ in². The carpet contains about 5266 inches of

braid, or about 439 ft. **54.** Since each tile measures $\dfrac{8}{12} = \dfrac{2}{3}$ feet

on a side, the dimensions of the kitchen, in tiles, are

$10 \div \dfrac{2}{3} = 15$ and $12 \div \dfrac{2}{3} = 18.$ Therefore, the numbers of tiles

needed is 15 × 18 = 270. **56.** 90°, since if we view one side of length 300' as the base, the altitude of the triangle is greatest if the angle is 90° **58.** The circumscribed circle has four times the area of the inscribed circle.

# Problem Set 10.3 (page 567)

**1. (a)** $x^2 = 7^2 + 24^2 = 49 + 576 = 625,$ so $x = \sqrt{625} = 25.$
**(c)** $x^2 + 5^2 = 22^2,$ so $x = \sqrt{459}.$
**(e)** $x^2 = 1^2 + 1^2 = 1 + 1 = 2,$ so $x = \sqrt{2}.$
**2. (a)** $x^2 + (2x)^2 = (25)^2, 5x^2 = 625, x = \sqrt{125} = 5\sqrt{5}$
**4. (a)** $x^2 = 10^2 + 15^2 = 325,$ so $x = \sqrt{325};$
$y^2 = x^2 + 7^2 = 325 + 49 = 374,$ so $y = \sqrt{374}.$
**5. (a)** $x = \sqrt{13^2 - 12^2} = 5$
**6. (a)** Height $= \sqrt{15^2 - 9^2},$ so area $= (20)(12) = 240$ square units.
**8.** The areas are equal. The small circle of radius 1 has area $\pi,$ and the large circle of radius $\sqrt{2}$ has area $\pi(\sqrt{2})^2 = 2\pi,$ so the area between the circles is $2\pi - \pi = \pi.$ **10.** $AG = 3,$ since $AC = \sqrt{5}, AD = \sqrt{6}, AE = \sqrt{7}, AF = \sqrt{8},$ and $AG = \sqrt{9} = 3.$
**12.**

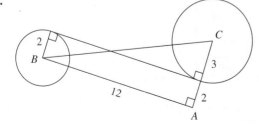

The distance between centers $B$ and $C$ is $\sqrt{12^2 + 5^2} = 13.$
**14. (a)** $(21)^2 + (28)^2 = 1225 = (35)^2;$ yes.
**(c)** $(12)^2 + (35)^2 = 1369 = (37)^2;$ yes.
**(e)** $(7\sqrt{2})^2 + (4\sqrt{7})^2 = 210 \neq 308 = (2\sqrt{77})^2;$ no.
**16. (a)** Yes
**22.**

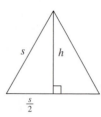

**(a)** $\left(\dfrac{s}{2}\right)^2 + (h)^2 = s^2,$ by the Pythagorean theorem. Therefore,

$h = \dfrac{\sqrt{3}}{2} s.$ **24.** Flattening the top of the box as suggested
gives the diagram shown. By the Pythagorean theorem,
$AC' = \sqrt{12^2 + 5^2} = \sqrt{169} = 13$ and $AC'' = \sqrt{9^2 + 8^2} = \sqrt{145} = 12.04.$ The shortest distance is therefore about 12 inches, crossing over the 9-inch edge.

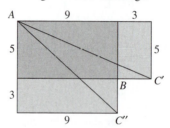

**28. (a)**

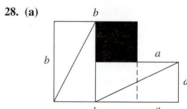

**(b)** Since the square and double-square are covered by the same five shapes, their areas are equal. The respective areas are $c^2$ and $a^2 + b^2,$ so $c^2 = a^2 + b^2.$

**30.**

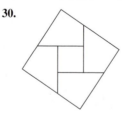

**32.** Answers will vary, but your ladder cannot be vertical, so the height is less than 24 feet. If the base is 7 feet from the wall, the top of the ladder is still nearly 23 feet off the ground.
**34.** Let $d$ be the depth of the pond. The stem length is $d + 2$ (in feet). With the stem held to the side, a right triangle is formed with legs of length 6 and $d$ and hypotenuse of length $(d + 2).$ Then $6^2 + d^2 = (d + 2)^2,$ so $d = 8.$
**38. (a)** $d \doteq 1.2\sqrt{100} = 1.2(10) = 12$ miles
**(b)** $d \doteq 1.2\sqrt{1353} = 1.2(36.78) = 44.1$ miles **(c)** Yertle is approximately 1111 feet high. **39.** The sum of the areas of the equilateral triangles on the legs equals the area of the equilateral triangle on the hypotenuse.

## Problem Set 10.4 (page 576)

**2. (a)** $V = Bh = (7\,\text{cm})(4\,\text{cm})(3\,\text{cm}) = 84\,\text{cm}^3$
**(c)** $\pi \times (10\,\text{m})^2 \times 4\,\text{m} = 400\pi\,\text{m}^3 \doteq 1257\,\text{m}^3$

**3. (a)** $\dfrac{1}{3}(12\,\text{ft})(8\,\text{ft})(10\,\text{ft}) = 320\,\text{ft}^3$

**(c)** $\dfrac{1}{3} \times \pi(5\,\text{cm})^2 \times (12\,\text{cm}) = 100\pi\,\text{cm}^3 \doteq 314\,\text{cm}^3$

**4.** The volume of the solid is the sum of the volume of the right circular cylinder of radius 3 cm and height 7 cm and the volume of the hemisphere of radius 3 cm. Thus, the answer is $(3^2\pi)7 + (2\pi3^3)/3 = 81\pi$. **6.** The volume, in cubic inches, of the solid with radius $r$ is $2\pi r^3/3 + \pi r^2 7$, since the height is 7 inches. **(a)** If $r = 1$, the formula yields $2\pi/3 + \pi7 = (2\pi + 21\pi)/3 = 23\pi/3\,\text{in}^3$. **7.** Have Eno carefully fill an oddly shaped container with an open top completely and exactly full of rice. Then have him pour the rice into a suitable rectangular box and measure the volume.
**16. (a)** The circumference of the cone is $\dfrac{3}{4} \cdot 2 \cdot \pi(4\,\text{in}) = 6\pi\,\text{in}$, so

the radius is 3 in. **19.** $V(\text{box}) = 160\,\text{in}^3$ and $V(\text{tub}) = \pi(3\,\text{in})^2(10\,\text{in}) \doteq 283\,\text{in}^3$. Two boxes is a better buy.

**21. (a)** $\left(\dfrac{5}{13}\right)^3(106.75) \doteq 6.07$ pounds

## Problem Set 10.5 (page 587)

**2. (a)** $SA = 2 \cdot \dfrac{1}{2}(20\,\text{cm} + 15\,\text{cm})(12\,\text{cm}) +$

$(2\,\text{cm})(60\,\text{cm}) = 540\,\text{cm}^2$ **(c)** $SA = 2 \cdot \pi(15\,\text{ft})^2 +$
$2\pi(15\,\text{ft})(12\,\text{ft}) = 810\pi\,\text{ft}^2 \doteq 2545\,\text{ft}^2$ **3. (a)** Slant height $=$

$\sqrt{(40\,\text{m})^2 + (30\,\text{m})^2} = 50\,\text{m}; SA = (60\,\text{m})^2 +$

$4 \cdot \dfrac{1}{2}(60\,\text{m})(50\,\text{m}) = 9600\,\text{m}^2$ **(c)** $SA = \pi(6\,\text{in})^2 +$

$\pi(6\,\text{in})(15\,\text{in}) = 126\pi\,\text{in}^2 \doteq 396\,\text{in}^2$
**4. (a)** $S = 4\pi(2200\,\text{km})^2 = 19{,}360{,}000\pi\,\text{km}^2 \doteq 6.08 \times$

$10^7\,\text{km}^2; V = \dfrac{4}{3}\pi(2200\,\text{km})^3 \doteq 4.46 \times 10^{10}\,\text{km}^3$

**(c)** $SA = 4\pi(4\,\text{ft})^2 + (20\,\text{ft})(2\pi)(4\,\text{ft}) = 224\pi\,\text{ft}^2 \doteq$

$704\,\text{ft}^2; V = \dfrac{4}{3}\pi(4\,\text{ft})^3 + \pi(4\,\text{ft})^2(20\,\text{ft}) \doteq 1273\,\text{ft}^3$

**5.** By similar reasoning, the surface area is the sum of $2\,\pi9, 9\pi$, and $7(6\pi) = 69\pi$. **8.** Area (sphere) $= 4\pi r^2$ square units. Area (cylinder) $= 2 \cdot \pi \cdot r^2 + 2\pi r \cdot (2r) = 6\pi r^2$ square units. Thus, $4\pi r^2/6\pi r^2 = \dfrac{2}{3}$. **9. (a)** 16 cm **10. (a)** 4, considering area
**(b)** One 14" pizza is nearly the same amount of pizza, but will save \$2.

**12. (a)** $1 - \dfrac{1}{4} - \dfrac{1}{4} = \dfrac{1}{2}$ (each small circle has $\dfrac{1}{2}$ the diameter, so

$\dfrac{1}{4}$ the area) **14. (a)** 200 mL (doubling the radius increases the

volume by a factor of 4; halving the height halves the volume)
**15. (a)** 8 liters (doubling the sides increases the volume by a factor of 8) **16.** If $r$ is the radius and the slant height is equal to the radius, the surface area is $\pi r^2 + \pi r^2$.

Since $2\pi r^2 = 16, r = \sqrt{\dfrac{8}{\pi}}\,\text{cm}$. **25. (a)** 3", since $\dfrac{2}{16} = \dfrac{1}{8} = \left(\dfrac{1}{2}\right)^3$

and $\dfrac{1}{2} \cdot 6" = 3"$

**26. (a)**

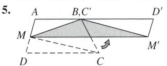

**27.** Let $s$ be the radius of the semicircle. Then the slant height of

the cone is $s$. Let $d$ be the diameter of the cone. Then $\pi d = \dfrac{1}{2}2\pi s$,

so $d = s$. **28.** The circular cross sections are related by a scale factor of 3, so 9 inches of water in the cylinder corresponds to 1 inch of rainfall.

## Chapter 10 Review Exercises (page 594)

**1. (a)** Centimeters **(b)** Millimeters **(c)** Kilometers **(d)** Meters
**(e)** Hectares **(f)** Square kilometers **(g)** Milliliters **(h)** Liters
**2. (a)** 4 L **(b)** 190 cm **(c)** 200 m2 **3.** 84 L

**4.** $\dfrac{300\,\text{ft}}{3\,\text{sec}} \cdot \dfrac{1\,\text{mile}}{5280\,\text{ft}} \cdot \dfrac{60\,\text{sec}}{1\,\text{min}} \cdot \dfrac{60\,\text{min}}{1\,\text{hr}} \doteq 68$ miles per hour

**5.**

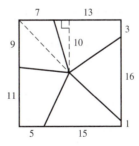

The triangle has half the area of the parallelogram $AD'M'M$, so it also has half the area of the trapezoid $ABCD$.
**6. (a)** A line from the center to the corner dissects the piece into two triangles of altitude 10, one with base 9 inches and the other with base 7 inches. The area of the piece is

$$\dfrac{1}{2} \cdot 7 \cdot 10 + \dfrac{1}{2} \cdot 9 \cdot 10 = \dfrac{1}{2} \cdot 16 \cdot 10 = 80\,\text{in}^2,$$

which is one-fifth of the total area, $20^2\,\text{in}^2 = 400\,\text{in}^2$, of the cake.
**(b)** The reasoning shown in part (a) demonstrates that any piece with 16 inches along the perimeter has area 80 in². Therefore, the cuts are arranged as shown in the figure.

**7. (a)** $768\,\text{in}^2 = 5\dfrac{1}{3}\,\text{ft}^2$ **(b)** $\dfrac{1}{2}(8\,\text{m})(9\,\text{m})\dfrac{1}{2}(3\,\text{m}) \cdot (6\,\text{m}) = 45\,\text{m}^2$

**(c)** $\dfrac{1}{2}(5\,\text{cm} + 7\,\text{cm})(3\,\text{cm}) = 18\,\text{cm}^2$

**8. (a)** 11 square units **(b)** 9 square units **(c)** $9\dfrac{1}{2}$ square units

**9. (a)** $A = (3\,\text{ft})(4\,\text{ft}) + \dfrac{1}{2}\pi(1.5\,\text{ft})^2 \doteq 15.5\,\text{ft}^2, P =$

$11\,\text{ft} + \pi(1.5\,\text{ft}) \doteq 15.7\,\text{ft}$ **(b)** $A = \dfrac{3}{4}\pi(3\,\text{m})^2 \doteq 21.2\,\text{m}^2,$

$P = \dfrac{3}{4} \cdot 2\pi(3\,\text{m}) + 6\,\text{m} = 20.1\,\text{m}$

**10.** $x = 6, y = \sqrt{5}$ **11.** $\sqrt{1125}$ cm $\doteq 33.5$ cm

**12.** $\sqrt{116}$ in, $\sqrt{160}$ in, $\sqrt{244}$ in, $\sqrt{260}$ in

**13.** $9 + \sqrt{2} + \sqrt{10} + \sqrt{5} \doteq 15.8$ units

**14. (a)** $V = [(10 \text{ ft})(20 \text{ ft}) + \frac{1}{2}(8 \text{ ft} + 20 \text{ ft})(8 \text{ ft})](30 \text{ ft})$

$= 9360 \text{ ft}^3$; $SA = 2 \cdot \frac{1}{2}(8 \text{ ft} + 20 \text{ ft})(8 \text{ ft}) + 2 \cdot (10 \text{ ft})(20 \text{ ft}) + 2 \cdot$

$(10 \text{ ft})(30 \text{ ft}) + 2 \cdot (10 \text{ ft})(30 \text{ ft}) + (8 \text{ ft})(30 \text{ ft}) + (20 \text{ ft})(30 \text{ ft}) =$

$2664 \text{ ft}^2$ **(b)** $V = \pi(7 \text{ m})^2(18 \text{ m}) + \frac{1}{2} \cdot \frac{4}{3}\pi(7 \text{ m})^3 \doteq 3489 \text{ m}^3$;

$SA = \frac{1}{2} \cdot 4\pi(7 \text{ m})^2 + 2\pi(7 \text{ m})(18 \text{ m}) + \pi(7 \text{ m})^2 \doteq 1253 \text{ m}^2$

**(c)** $V = \frac{1}{3}\pi(5 \text{ cm})^2 \cdot (8 \text{ cm}) + \frac{1}{2} \cdot \frac{4}{3}\pi(5 \text{ cm})^3 \doteq 471 \text{ cm}^3$;

$SA = \frac{1}{2} \cdot 4\pi(5 \text{ cm})^2 + \pi(5 \text{ cm})(\sqrt{25 + 64} \text{ cm}) = 50\pi +$

$\pi(5 \text{ cm})(\sqrt{25 + 64} \text{ cm}) = (50 + 5\sqrt{89}) \pi \text{ cm}^2 \doteq 305 \text{ cm}^2$

**15.** $V(\text{sphere}) = \frac{4}{3}\pi(10 \text{ m})^3$ and $V(\text{four cubes}) = 4(10 \text{ m})^3$. Since

$\pi > 3, \frac{4}{3}\pi > 4$, showing that the sphere has the larger volume.

**16. (a)** $(180 \text{ ft})(1.5) = 270 \text{ ft}$, since $k = 1.5$ is the scale factor.

**(b)** $\dfrac{45 \text{ pounds}}{(1.5)^2} = 20$ pounds, since Johan's garden area is $(1/1.5)^2$

times that of Heather's.

## Chapter 10 Test (page 596)

**1. (a)** $8 \text{ cm}^2$ **(b)** $8 \text{ cm}^2$ **(c)** $8.5 \text{ cm}^2$

**2.** Each figure contains four full units of area. Figure A contains an additional eight half-units of area, and figure B contains an additional four half-units of area. Jim should conclude that Figure A is four half-units, or two units, of area larger than B.

**3. (a)** $SA = 2 \cdot \frac{1}{2}(7 \text{ m})(24 \text{ m}) + (7 \text{ m} + 24 \text{ m} + 25 \text{ m}) \cdot (5 \text{ m}) =$

$448 \text{ m}^2$, since the diagonal is 25 m; $V = \frac{1}{2}(7 \text{ m})(24 \text{ m})(5 \text{ m}) =$

$420 \text{ m}^3$ **(b)** $SA = 2 \cdot \frac{1}{2}\pi(4'')^2 + \frac{1}{2} \cdot 2\pi(4'')(6'') +$

$(6'')(8'') \doteq 173.7 \text{ in}^2$; $V = \frac{1}{2}\pi(4'')^2(6'') \doteq 150.8 \text{ in}^3$ **(c)** Slant

height is 10 ft. $SA = 4 \cdot \frac{1}{2}(12 \text{ ft})(10 \text{ ft}) + (144 \text{ ft})^2 = 384 \text{ ft}^2$;

$V = \frac{1}{3}(12 \text{ ft})^2(8 \text{ ft}) = 384 \text{ ft}^3$. **(d)** Slant height is 13 cm.

$SA = \pi(5 \text{ cm})^2 + \pi(5 \text{ cm})(13 \text{ cm}) = 90\pi \text{ cm}^2 \doteq 283 \text{ cm}^2$;

$V = \frac{1}{3}\pi(5 \text{ cm})^2(12 \text{ cm}) = 100\pi \text{ cm}^3 \doteq 314 \text{ cm}^3$.

**4. (a)** mm **(b)** m **(c)** m **(d)** km **(e)** mL **(f)** liters

**5.** Cross-sectional view:

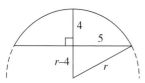

$(r - 4)^2 + (5)^2 = r^2$, or $r^2 - 8r + 16 + 25 = r^2$. Then

$r = (16 + 25)/8 \text{ mm} = 5.125 \text{ mm}$.

**6. (a)** $P = \sqrt{52} + \sqrt{13} + \sqrt{65} \doteq 18.9$ units

**(b)** Yes, $(\sqrt{52})^2 + (\sqrt{13})^2 = 65 = (\sqrt{65})^2$

**7. (a)** 216.1 cm **(b)** 168,200 cm **(c)** 5000 cm$^2$ **(d)** 10,000 m$^2$

**(e)** 4.719 L **(f)** 3200 cm$^3$ **8.** Let the radius of the circle be $r$.

Then the circumscribed square has sides of length $2r$ and the inscribed square has sides of length $\sqrt{2}\, r$. Thus,

$$\frac{\text{area (inscribed)}}{\text{area (circumscribed)}} = \frac{(\sqrt{2}r)^2}{(2r)^2} = \frac{2r^2}{4r^2} = \frac{1}{2}.$$

*Alternative solution:* The scale factor of the large to the small square is $1/\sqrt{2}$, so the small square has $(1/\sqrt{2})^2 = 1/2$ the area of the large square.

**9.** $\sqrt{189}$ ft $\doteq 13.7$ ft, by the Pythagorean theorem

**10. (a)** Approximately 31.86 yd **(b)** Approximately 1.5 mi

**(c)** 291.6 ft$^2$ **(d)** Approximately 14.69 mi$^2$ **(e)** 205.2 ft$^3$

**(f)** Approximately 3.45 ft$^3$

**11.**

| | Papa | Mama | Baby |
|---|---|---|---|
| Length of Suspenders | 50 | 40 | 20 |
| Weight | 468.75 | 240 | 30 |
| Number of Fleas | 6000 | 3840 | 960 |

| Scale Factors | |
|---|---|
| PB to MB | 4/5 |
| MB to BB | 1/2 |

**12.** $A = \frac{1}{2}(9 \text{ ft})(12 \text{ ft}) + (8 \text{ ft})(12 \text{ ft}) - \frac{1}{2}\pi(4 \text{ ft})^2 \doteq 125 \text{ ft}^2$;

$P = 15 \text{ ft} + 9 \text{ ft} + 8 \text{ ft} + 12 \text{ ft} + \frac{1}{2} \cdot 2\pi(4 \text{ ft}) \doteq 56.6 \text{ ft}$

**13. (a)** $\frac{2}{3}\pi(5 \text{ in})^2 \doteq 52.4 \text{ in}^2$

**(b)** $\frac{1}{2}(2.6 \text{ m} + 1.4 \text{ m})(3 \text{ m}) = 6.0 \text{ m}^2$

**(c)** $\frac{1}{12} \cdot \pi(24 \text{ cm})^2 \doteq 151 \text{ cm}^2$

**14.** $A = \frac{1}{2} \cdot (6 \text{ cm}) \cdot (16 \text{ cm}) + \frac{1}{2}(15 \text{ cm})(16 \text{ cm}) = 168 \text{ cm}^2$.

Sides are 10 cm and 17 cm by the Pythagorean theorem, so $P = 54$ cm.

**15.**

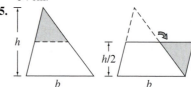

area (triangle) = area (parallelogram) = $(b)(h/2) = \frac{1}{2}bh$

**16. (a)** $SA = 4\pi(10 \text{ m})^2 = 400\pi \text{ m}^2 \doteq 1257 \text{ m}^2$;

$V = \frac{4}{3}\pi(10 \text{ m})^3 \doteq 4189 \text{ m}^3$ **(b)** $SA = \pi(5 \text{ cm})^2 +$

$2\pi(5 \text{ cm})(6 \text{ cm}) + \frac{1}{2} \cdot 4\pi(5 \text{ cm})^2 = 135\pi \text{ cm}^2 \doteq 424 \text{ cm}^2$;

$V = \pi(5 \text{ cm})^2(6 \text{ m}) + \frac{1}{2} \cdot \frac{4}{3}\pi(5 \text{ cm})^3 \doteq 733 \text{ cm}^3$

**17.** $V(\text{peel}) = \frac{4}{3}\pi(2.5 \text{ in})^3 - \frac{4}{3}\pi(1.75 \text{ in})^3 \doteq 43.0 \text{ in}^3$, and

$V(\text{grapefruit}) = \frac{4}{3}\pi(2.5 \text{ in})^3 \doteq 65.4 \text{ in}^3$. About 66 percent is peel.

*Alternative solution:* The scale factor is $\left(2\frac{1}{2} - \frac{3}{4}\right)\Big/ 2\frac{1}{2} = 0.7$. Since $(0.7)^3 = 0.343$, it follows that 34.3 percent of the grapefruit is not peel and 65.7 percent is peel.

# Chapter 11

## Problem Set 11.1 (page 615)

**1. (a)** Not a rigid motion; distances between particular cards will change.    **(c)** No, distances between particular pieces almost certainly will have changed.

**2. (a)**

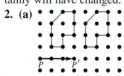

**4. (a)** 300°   **(c)** 43°

**5. (a)**

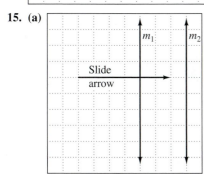

**6. (a)** Center O is the intersection of $\overleftrightarrow{AB}$ and $\overleftrightarrow{A'B'}$.

**7.** Rotations about $O$ through 60°, 180°, or 300°, or a reflection across one of the three mirror lines through $O$ and parallel to one of the sides of the triangle.

**11. (a)** Draw a vertical line through the midpoint of $\overline{PP'}$.

**13. (a), (b)**

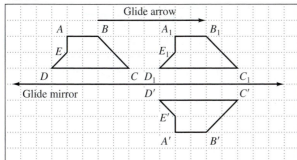

**15. (a)**

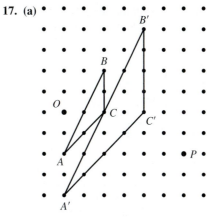

**17. (a)**

**(b)**

**18. (a)** Center $P$, scale factor $\frac{3}{2}$

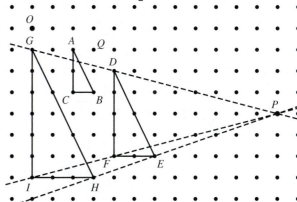

**20.** Rotate 90° counterclockwise about $B$. Then perform a size transformation centered at $P$ with scale factor 2. (Other sequences will also work.) See illustration below.

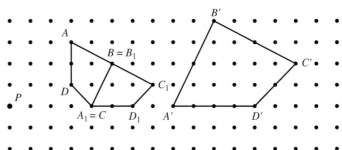

**25. (a)** $P'$ is some point yet to be determined on the circle of radius 2 cm centered at $A'$.

**26.** On a 1-cm-square grid, the two 90° rotations take $O_1$ to $O'_1$ and $O_2$ to $O'_2$. This motion is equivalent to a 180° rotation about the point $O$.

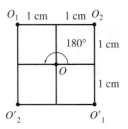

**28.** (a), (b)

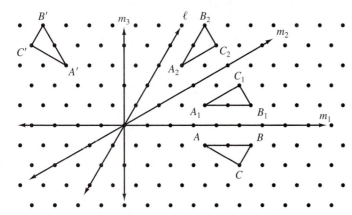

**30.** (a), (b)

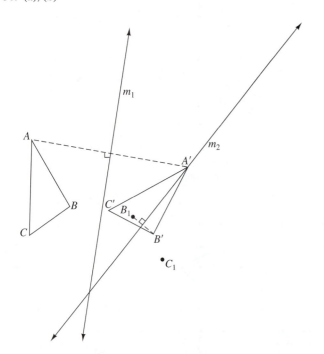

(c) A reflection first across line $m_1$ and then across line $m_2$ is equivalent to a rotation about the point $P$ of intersection of $m_1$ and $m_2$, through an angle twice the measure $x$ of the directed angle from line $m_1$ toward line $m_2$. **32.** (a) A translation: Six reflections give an orientation-preserving rigid motion, so it is either a rotation or a

translation. Since a rotation has a fixed point (namely, the rotation center), the motion is a translation. **34.** (a) A glide–reflection **35.** The line $PP'$ passes through $O$, so constructing this line determines point $O$. $\overline{PQ}$ and $\overline{P'Q'}$ are parallel, so the line through $P'$ that is parallel to $\overline{PQ}$ will determine $Q'$.

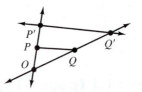

**38.** (a) $\overline{RS'}$ is the reflection of $\overline{RS}$ across $m$, so $RS' = RS$, since a reflection preserves all distances. Similarly, $QS' = QS$.
**40.** A single mirror reverses orientation, so the double reflection seen in a corner mirror preserves orientation. The corner-mirror reflection of your right hand will appear as a right hand.
**47.** (a) Measurements show that triangle XYZ is an equilateral triangle. (b) The centers of the rotated equilateral triangles form an equilateral triangular grid.

# Problem Set 11.2 (page 631)

**1.** (a)      (c)

None

**3.** (a) Many figures are possible.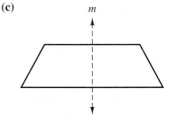

**4.** (a) A kite (b) An isosceles trapezoid

**5.** (a)    $m$      (c)    $m$

**8.** (a)

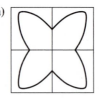

**9.** (a) One line of symmetry
**10.** (a) Five lines of symmetry and 72° rotation symmetry
(b) 72° rotation symmetry
**11.** (a)

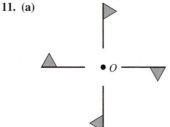

**12. (a)** Equilateral triangle **(b)** Square **13. (a)** $0, 8$ **(b)** $0, 3, 8$
**(c)** $0, 8$ **(d)** $0, 8$ **16. (a)** $m1$ **17. (a)** There are vertical lines of
symmetry through the center of each letter, and there is a horizontal
line of symmetry. The symbol type is *mm*. **26. (a)** No letter or digit
reflects vertically onto a different letter or digit, so it must reflect onto
itself. **28. (a)** The pattern must have a horizontal line of symmetry, so it would be an *mm* pattern. **29. (a)** $1g$ **(c)** *mg*
**31. (a)** 11

| p | p | p | p | p | p |
|---|---|---|---|---|---|

**(c)** 12

| p | d | p | d | p | d |
|---|---|---|---|---|---|

**32. (a)** Three directions of reflection symmetry; three directions of
glide symmetry; 120° rotation symmetry **36. (a)** As left-handed
people know well, not all scissors are symmetric.
**(c)** A man's dress shirt is not quite symmetric, since it buttons
right handed. **(e)** Tennis rackets have two planes of bilateral
symmetry. **37. (a)** Across the line of diagonal entries

## Problem Set 11.3 (page 645)

**1.** Many different tilings can be formed, including the following:
**(a)**
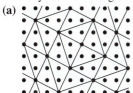

**2.** Yes, tilings are possible, among which are the following:
**(a)**
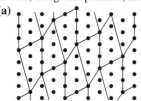

**17. (a)** Squares, pentagons, hexagons, heptagons, octagons
**(b)** Many vertex figures that appear in the tiling cannot
correspond to regular polygons. For example, regular 5-, 6-, and
8-gons have interior angles of measure 108°, 120°, and 135°.
These add up to $108° + 120° + 135° = 363° \neq 360°$.
**24.** Here's one way to make a tiling 12-gon by modifying a square tile:

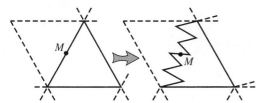

Similarly, modifying an equilateral triangle by a midpoint modification with opposite parallel congruent sides will form an 11-gon that
tiles as follows:

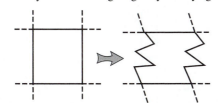

The same idea applies to any $n \geq 6$, using a modified square for
even $n$ and a modified equilateral triangle for odd $n$.
**26. (a)** 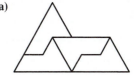 **(c)**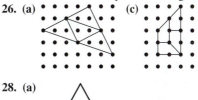

**28. (a)**
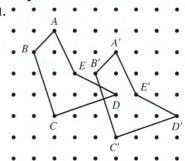

## Chapter 11 Review Exercises (page 653)

**1.**
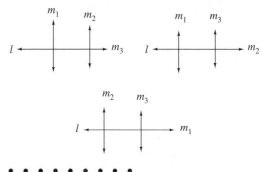

**2.** Find the perpendicular bisectors of segments $\overline{AA'}$ and $\overline{BB'}$.
Their intersection is the turn center $O$, and the measure of $\angle AOA'$
is the turn angle. **3.** Reflection across line $l$, the perpendicular
bisector common to all three segments $AA'$, $BB'$, and $CC'$:

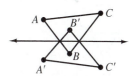

**4.** Draw any two vertical lines 2 inches apart. There are then three
ways to choose the successive lines of reflection:

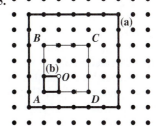

**5.**

**6.** Rotate $ABCD$ $45°$ about the center $P$ of the square. Then do a dilation about $P$ with scale factor $\dfrac{\sqrt{2}}{2}$.

**7. (a)**

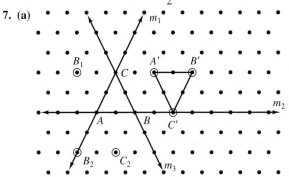

**(b)** Glide–reflection, three units to the right and reflecting across the line $l$ parallel to $\overline{AB}$ and midway between $C$ and $A$.   **8. (a)** 1
**(b)** 2   **(c)** 0   **(d)** 0   **(e)** 3   **(f)** All lines through the center point, since the figure has circular symmetry   **9.** The letters in the upper row have either rotational or mirror symmetry, unlike those in the second row.   **10. (a)** Scalene triangle   **(b)** Isosceles, but not equilateral, triangle   **(c)** Equilateral triangle.   **(d)** Rhombus
**(e)** Regular hexagon   **11. (a)** Equilateral triangle
**(b)** Parallelogram   **(c)** A regular 9-gon (enneagon, or nonagon)
**12. (a)** None   **(b)** $180°$   **(c)** $180°$   **(d)** $72°, 144°, 216°, 288°$
**(e)** $120°, 240°$   **(f)** Any angle   **13. (a)** There is a vertical line of symmetry. The classification symbol is $m1$.   **(b)** There is no vertical line of symmetry, but there is a horizontal line of symmetry. The classification symbol is $1m$.   **14.** The angles are $60°$ for the triangle, $90°$ for the square, and $120°$ for the hexagon. The angles of the four polygons must add up to $360°$, so the fourth angle is $90°$, and therefore the fourth polygon is a square.

**15.**

**16.** Use $180°$ rotations of the tile about the midpoints of the sides.

## Chapter 11 Test (page 654)

**1.** (a), (b), (c), (d), and (e) tile the plane
**2.** Various pairs of lines are possible. The distance between the lines must be half the distance between $P$ and $P'$.

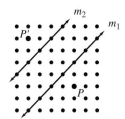

**3.** $C'$ is two units right of $B'$; $B$ is two units left of $C$
**4. (a)** Rotation   **(b)** Rotation   **5. (a)** Glide–reflection
**(b)** Reflection   **(c)** Reflection   **(d)** Glide–reflection
**6. (a)** Glide–reflection (1g)   **(b)** Vertical and horizontal lines of symmetry (mm), and glide and half-turn symmetries   **(c)** Half-turn symmetry (12)   **(d)** Half-turn symmetry, vertical line of symmetry, glide–reflection (mg)

**7.** Many transformations are possible. Here is one sequence: Translate the square so that $A$ is taken to $A'$; rotate about $A'$ by $45°$; and perform a dilation about $A'$ with scale factor $3\sqrt{2}/2$ (since $A'B' = 3\sqrt{2}$ and $AB = 2$).
**8. (a)** Center $P$ and rotation angle $90°$.
**(b)**

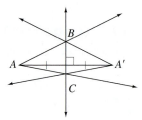

**9.** A vertex figure uses two octagons and one square.
**10.** Construct the perpendicular bisector of $\overline{AA'}$, and suppose it intersects the sides of $\angle A$ at points labeled $B$ and $C$. Then $\angle BA'C$ is the desired angle.

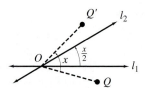

**11. (a)** A   **(b)** $\dfrac{2}{3}$   **(c)** $\dfrac{40}{3}$   **(d)** 9

**12.** Many pairs of lines are possible. The two lines need to intersect at point $O$, and the directed angle between the lines should be half the measure of $\angle QOQ'$.

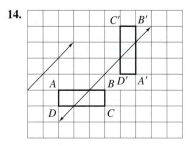

**13. (a)** Point ($180°$ rotation) symmetry, and two diagonal lines of symmetry   **(b)** Four lines of symmetry, and $90°$ rotation symmetry

**14.**

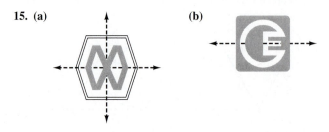

**15. (a)**                                   **(b)**

**(c)**

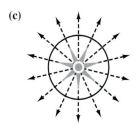

**16. (a)** 180°   **(b)** None   **(c)** 360°/7

# Chapter 12

## Problem Set 12.1 (page 670)

**1. (a)** $L \leftrightarrow K, H \leftrightarrow W, S \leftrightarrow T$   **(b)** $\overline{KW}, \overline{WT}, \overline{TK}$
**(c)** $\angle K, \angle W, \angle T$   **(d)** $\triangle KWT$   **3. (a)** Draw a line $l$ and mark any point as $E$. Set your compass to $AB$, and determine a point $G$ on your line segment with an arc centered at $E$. Set your compass to distance $CD$, and draw an arc centered at $G$ to determine $F$ on $l$, away from $E$.   **(b)** Begin as in (a). Set your compass to $CD$, and draw an arc centered at $G$ to determine $F$ on $l$, back toward $E$.
**7. (a)** One such triangle   **(c)** Impossible by the triangle inequality, since $2 + 5 < 8$   **(e)** One such triangle
**8. (a)** $\triangle ABD \cong \triangle CBD$ by SAS   **(c)** $\triangle ABC \cong \triangle EFD$ by SSS
**(e)** $\triangle ABD \cong \triangle ACD$ by ASA   **(g)** No conclusion possible
**(i)** No conclusion possible   **9.** Let $\triangle ABC$ be equilateral. Since $AB = BC$, it follows from the isosceles triangle theorem that $\angle A \cong \angle C$. In the same way, since $BC = CA$, it follows that $\angle B \cong \angle A$. Thus, all three angles are congruent.
**12. (a)** $\triangle QPT \cong \triangle SPT$ by the SSS congruence property.
**13. (a)** $\angle ABD \cong \angle CDB$, as alternate interior angles between parallel lines. Likewise, $\angle ADB \cong \angle CBD$, and $DB = BD$. By ASA, $\triangle ABD \cong \triangle CDB$.   **17.** Place a corner $C$ of the sheet of paper at the edge of the plate, and lay the ruler across the plate to meet the points $A$ and $B$ on the edge of the plate crossed by the perpendicular sides of the sheet of paper, as shown in the following figure:

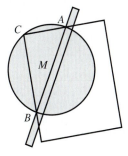

By the converse of Thales' theorem, $\overline{AB}$ is a diameter of the plate. Repeating the procedure at a second point $C'$ will allow you to construct a second diameter $\overline{A'B'}$. The center of the circle is where the two diameters intersect.

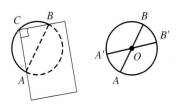

**18.** It is longer than 5 cm and shorter than 13 cm. (Remember the triangle inequality.)   **19. (a)** $0 < s < 14$ cm, where $s$ is the length of the fourth side   **24. (a)** $\triangle ABE$ is isosceles, with $AB = AE$, so the base angles are congruent by the isosceles triangle theorem.   **(b)** $\triangle ACD$ is isosceles, so its base angles are congruent.   **(c)** $\angle ACB$ and $\angle ACD$ are supplementary, as are $\angle ADC$ and $\angle ADE$. Since $\angle ACD \cong \angle ADC$, we have $\angle ACB \cong \angle ADE$. By using $\angle B \cong \angle E$ and $AC = AD$, the AAS property gives $\triangle ABC \cong \triangle AED$.   **(d)** From part (c), $\overline{BC} \cong \overline{ED}$   **26. (a)** Yes, using ASA   **(c)** Yes, using SAS   **27.** If $AB = CD = a$, $BC = AD = b$, and $AC = BD = c$, then each face of the tetrahedron is a triangle with sides of length $a$, $b$, and $c$. By the SSS property, the faces of the tetrahedron are congruent to one another.
**29. (a)** By the triangle inequality, $QP + QT > TP$. Therefore, $QP + QT + TR > TP + TR$. But $QT + TR = QR$, so $QP + QR > TP + TR$.   **30. (a)** $EA + ED > DA$ by the triangle inequality.   **32. (a)** The angles at the vertices of a quadrilateral can change even though the lengths of the sides are fixed. (There is no "SSSS congruence property" for a quadrilateral.)   **33. (a)** The framework forms a parallelogram, but not necessarily a rectangle.
**36. (a), (b)** The measure of $\angle APB$ is always a constant satisfying the equation $m(\angle AOB) = 2 \cdot m(\angle APB)$.   **(c)** Draw the diameter $\overline{PQ}$. There are two cases to consider.
*Case 1:*

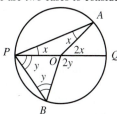

*A and B lie on opposite sides of* $\overline{PQ}$. We see that $\triangle POA$ is isosceles, so the base angles are congruent. That is, $m(\angle APO) = m(\angle OAP) = x$. Therefore, $m(\angle AOQ) = 2x = 2m(\angle APO)$. By the same reasoning, $m(\angle BOQ) = 2y = 2m(\angle BPO)$. Thus, $m(\angle AOB) = 2x + 2y = 2m(\angle APB)$.
*Case 2:*

*A and B are on the same side of* $\overline{PQ}$. Nearly the same analysis holds, but now $m(\angle AOB) = 2x - 2y = 2m(\angle APB)$.

## Problem Set 12.2 (page 685)

**1. (a)** Step 1:  Draw a line through $P$ that intersects $l$. Label the intersection point $A$.
Step 2:  Draw arcs of equal radius centered at $A$ and $P$. Label as $B$ the intersection point of the arc at $A$ with $\overleftrightarrow{AP}$. Label as $C$ the intersection point of the arc at $A$ with $l$. Label as $D$ the intersection point of the arc at $P$ with $\overrightarrow{AP}$.
Step 3:  Set the compass to radius $BC$ and draw the arc centered at $D$. Label as $E$ the intersection with the arc drawn at $P$.
Step 4:  Construct the line $k$ through $P$ and $E$.

**(b)** The construction gives the congruence of the corresponding angles, $\angle PAC \cong \angle DPE$. Therefore, $k \parallel l$ by the corresponding-angles property. **3. (a)** The corresponding-angles property guarantees that $m$ is parallel to $l$. **(b)** Align the ruler with the line; slide the drafting triangle, with one leg of the right triangle on the ruler, until the second leg of the triangle meets point $P$. **7.** The jar lid will also give the circle through $A$, $B$, and $C$. When it is drawn, each of the four points $A$, $B$, $C$, and $P$ is the intersection of three of the circles. **8.** Construct the perpendicular to side $\overrightarrow{BA}$ at $T$ and the angle bisector. Let $O$ be their point of intersection. The circle centered at $O$ and passing through $T$ is the desired circle.

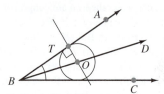

**9. (a)** The circumcenter will be inside the acute triangle. **(b)** The circumcenter will be at the midpoint of the hypotenuse of a right triangle. **(c)** The circumcenter will be outside an obtuse triangle. **11.** The three circles intersect at a single point. **13.** Since $\triangle PQS$ is inscribed in the circle with diameter $\overline{PQ}$, it has a right angle at $S$ by Thales' theorem. Thus, $\overline{PS} \perp \overline{SQ}$. Similarly, $\overline{PT} \perp \overline{TQ}$. **15.** By Thales' theorem, $\angle ADB$ is a right angle. We also see that $\triangle ODB$ is an equilateral triangle, since all sides have the length of the radius. Moreover, $ODBE$ is a rhombus, so the side $\overline{DE}$ is a bisector of the $60°$ angle $\angle ODB$. Thus, $m(\angle ADE) = m(\angle ADB) - m(\angle EDB) = 90° - 30° = 60°$. Similarly, $m(\angle AED) = 60°$. Therefore, all angles of $\triangle ADE$ have measure $60°$, so $\triangle ADE$ is equilateral. **17.** Since $m(\angle 1) + m(\angle 2) + m(\angle 3) + m(\angle 4) = 180°$, $m(\angle 1) = m(\angle 2)$, and $m(\angle 3) = m(\angle 4)$, it follows that $m(\angle 2) + m(\angle 3) = 180°/2 = 90°$. **18. (a)** Suppose the perpendicular bisector of chord $\overline{AB}$ intersects the circle at a point $C$. Then the circle is the circumscribing circle of $\triangle ABC$. The center of the circumscribing circle is the point of concurrence of the perpendicular bisectors of all three sides of $\triangle ABC$. In particular, the perpendicular bisector of side $\overline{AB}$ contains the center of the circle. **19. (a)** Extend $\overline{AB}$ and construct the line at $A$ that is perpendicular to $\overline{AB}$. Set the compass to radius $AB$, and mark off this distance on the perpendicular line to determine a point $C$ for which $AC = AB$. Similarly, construct a perpendicular line at $B$ to $\overline{AB}$, and determine a point $D$ (on the same side of $\overline{AB}$ as $C$) on this perpendicular so that $BD = AB$. $ABDC$ is a square with given side $\overline{AB}$. (Other constructions also work.) **20. (a)** Extend $\overline{AB}$ to a longer segment. Erect perpendicular rays to $\overline{AB}$ at both $A$ and $B$ to the same side of $\overline{AB}$. Bisect the right angle at $A$, and let its intersection with the ray at $B$ determine point $C$. Erect the perpendicular at $C$ to $\overline{BC}$, and let $D$ be the intersection with the ray constructed at $A$. Then $ABCD$ is a square erected on the given side $\overline{AB}$. **(b)** Construct the equilateral triangle $\triangle ABO$ with the given side $\overline{AB}$. The reflection of $A$ across $\overline{OB}$ determines the point $C$. Repeat reflections to determine the remaining vertices $D$, $E$, and $F$ to construct the regular hexagon $ABCDEF$. **23.** Constructible: 3, 4, 5, 6, 8, 10, 12, 15, 16, 17, 20, 24, 30, 32, 34, 40, 48, 51, 60, 64, 68, 80, 85, 96 **29. (a)** There are five points $C$ on line $l$ for which triangle $ABC$ is isosceles. As shown in the accompanying diagram, they are constructed by the circle at $A$ through $B$, the circle at $B$ through $A$, and the perpendicular bisector of $\overline{AB}$.

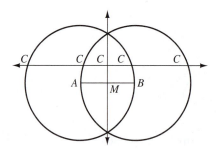

**32. (a)** The three altitudes of a triangle are concurrent (pass through a single point). **(b)** The perpendicular bisectors of $\triangle PQR$ are concurrent, since they intersect at the center of the circle that circumscribes $\triangle PQR$. Since the perpendicular bisectors of $\triangle PQR$ are also the altitudes of $\triangle ABC$, the three altitudes are concurrent. **33.** $m(\angle NOQ) = m(\angle PON) - m(\angle POQ) = 144° - 120° = 24°$, since a central angle of a regular pentagon is $72°$ and a central angle of an equilateral triangle is $120°$. A regular 15-gon has central angle $\dfrac{360°}{15} = 24°$, so laying off segments of length $QN$ would give 15 equally spaced points around the circle. **39. (a)** $F_5 = 2^{2^5} + 1 = 2^{32} + 1 = 4{,}294{,}967{,}296 + 1 = 4{,}294{,}967{,}297$ **40. (a)** $G$, $H$, and $P$ are collinear. The Euler line passes through $G$, $H$, and $P$. **(b)** $\dfrac{GH}{GP} = 2$. Thus, $G$ is one-third of the distance from $P$ to $H$ along the Euler line. **(c)** The circle intersects all sides of $\triangle ABC$ at their midpoints. **(d)** The circle bisects each of the segments $\overline{AH}$, $\overline{BH}$, and $\overline{CH}$. **42.** $\triangle TRI$ is equilateral.

## Problem Set 12.3 (page 697)

**1. (a)** First notice that $m(\angle O) = 180° - 60° - 30° = 90°$. Therefore, by the AA similarity property, $\triangle ABC \sim \triangle PNO$. The scale factor from $\triangle ABC$ to $\triangle PNO$ is $\dfrac{12}{8} = \dfrac{3}{2}$.
**(c)** By the AA similarity property, $\triangle GHI \sim \triangle TUI$, with scale factor $\dfrac{8}{5}$. **2. (a)** Yes, by AA; all angles are the same, $60°$.
**(c)** Yes, by the AA similarity property **(e)** Yes, by the SSS similarity property, or AA or SAS **3. (a)** $\dfrac{12}{15} = \dfrac{8}{a}$, so $a = 10$
**(c)** $\dfrac{c}{15} = \dfrac{c+2}{18}$; $18c = 15c + 30$; $c = 10$
**4. (a)** By the Pythagorean theorem, the hypotenuse of triangle $XYZ$ is $\sqrt{5^2 + 12^2} = \sqrt{169} = 13$, so its perimeter is $5 + 12 + 13 = 30$. Since the perimeter of triangle $ABC$ is 3000 feet, the scale factor is 100. Thus, triangle $ABC$ is a right triangle with legs of lengths 500 and 1200 and a hypotenuse of length 1300. **6. (a)** No. A square and a nonsquare rectangle are convex quadrilaterals with congruent angles, yet are not similar. **8. (a)** $\overline{AB}$ is parallel to $\overline{CD}$, so, by alternate interior angles, $\angle BAE \cong \angle DCE$. Also, $\angle AEB \cong \angle CED$, and they are vertical angles, so the AA similarity property gives $\triangle ABE \sim \triangle CDE$.
**(b)** By similarity, $\dfrac{x}{36} = \dfrac{17}{51}$, so $x = 12$. Also, $\dfrac{26}{y} = \dfrac{17}{51}$, so $y = 78$. **10. (a)** $\angle CAD \cong \angle BAC$, since they are the same angle and $m(\angle ADC) = m(\angle ACB) = 90°$. By the AA similarity property, $\triangle ADC \sim \triangle ACB$. Likewise, $\triangle CDB \sim \triangle ACB$. Thus, $\triangle ADC \sim \triangle CDB$. **14. (a)** Draw an arc of large enough radius so that point $B$ is on the seventh line above the line with point $A$.

**20. (a)** Use the AA similarity property.

**(b)** Using $\triangle ACD \sim \triangle ABC$, we get $\dfrac{AD}{AC} = \dfrac{AC}{AB}$, or $\dfrac{x}{b} = \dfrac{b}{c}$.

Similarly, $\triangle CBD \sim \triangle ABC$ gives $\dfrac{BD}{BC} = \dfrac{CB}{AB}$, or $\dfrac{y}{a} = \dfrac{a}{c}$.

**(c)** $x = \dfrac{b^2}{c}$ and $y = \dfrac{a^2}{c}$. Also, $x + y = c$, so $c = \dfrac{b^2}{c} + \dfrac{a^2}{c}$, or

$c^2 = a^2 + b^2$. **22. (a)** $DJ = \sqrt{1^2 + \left(\dfrac{1}{2}\right)^2} = \sqrt{\dfrac{5}{4}} = \dfrac{1}{2}\sqrt{5}$

**(b)** $PS = \dfrac{PS}{AD} = \dfrac{ST}{DJ} = \dfrac{1/2}{\sqrt{5}/2} = \dfrac{1}{\sqrt{5}}$ **(c)** Area$(PQRS) =$

$(PS)^2 = \dfrac{1}{5}$ **25.** The midpoints $W$, $X$, $Y$, and $Z$ are the vertices of a

parallelogram, and we know that the diagonals of any parallelogram intersect at their common midpoints. **27.** Let $L$ denote the midpoint of $\overline{AC}$, which is also the midpoint of $\overline{BD}$. By Example 12.14,

$P$ is the centroid of $\triangle ABC$ and $BP = \dfrac{2}{3} BL$. Since $BL = \dfrac{1}{2} BD$,

$BP = \dfrac{2}{3} \cdot \dfrac{1}{2} BD = \dfrac{1}{3} BD$. By the same reasoning, $Q$ is the centroid

of $\triangle ADC$ and $QD = \dfrac{1}{3} BD$. Finally, $PQ = BD - BP - QD =$

$\left(1 - \dfrac{1}{3} - \dfrac{1}{3}\right) BD = \dfrac{1}{3} BD$. **28.** The right triangles $\triangle ACP$ and

$\triangle BDP$ have congruent vertical angles at $P$. Thus, $\triangle ACP \sim \triangle BDP$

by AA similarity. Since $\dfrac{AC}{BD} = \dfrac{4}{2}$, the scale factor is 2. Therefore,

$CP = 2DP$. Since $CD = 4$ and $CD = CP + DP$, it follows that

$CP = \dfrac{2}{3}(4) = \dfrac{8}{3}$ and $DP = \dfrac{1}{3}(4) = \dfrac{4}{3}$. By the Pythagorean

theorem, $AP = \sqrt{4^2 + (8/3)^2} = \left(\dfrac{4}{3}\right)\sqrt{13}$, so $BP = \left(\dfrac{2}{3}\right)\sqrt{13}$.

**30.** Mohini's eyes and the tree's top are corresponding vertices of similar right triangles, since the angles at the vertex at the mirror are congruent. Assuming that Mohini's eyes are 5″ beneath the

top of her head gives the proportion $\dfrac{h}{5'} = \dfrac{15'}{4'}$, making the height

of the pole $h = (5')\left(\dfrac{15'}{4'}\right) = 18'9''$. **32.** By similar triangles,

$\dfrac{6' - x}{6'} = \dfrac{5.25'}{18'}$. Therefore, $x = 6'\left(1 - \dfrac{5.25'}{18'}\right) = 4.25' = 4'3''$.

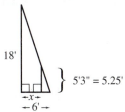

**36. (a)** $\triangle BCP \sim \triangle DAP$ **(b)** $\dfrac{PA}{PC} = \dfrac{PD}{PB}$, so $PA \cdot PB = PC \cdot PD$.

## Chapter 12 Review Exercises (page 707)

**1. (a)** True. Three pairs of angles and two pairs of sides are congruent. **(b)** False. After pairing up congruent angles, we see that the sides with equal lengths are not corresponding sides in the triangles, so the two triangles are not congruent.

**2. (a)** $\triangle ACD \cong \triangle ACB$ by SSS **(b)** $\triangle ACD \cong \triangle ECB$ by SAS
**(c)** $\triangle ADF \cong \triangle BEC$ by AAS **(d)** $\triangle ACD \cong \triangle ECB$ by SAS
**(e)** $\angle B \cong \angle E$, since $\triangle ABE$ is isosceles. Therefore,
$\triangle ABC \cong \triangle AED$ by ASA, and $\triangle ABD \cong \triangle AEC$ by ASA.
**(f)** $\triangle ABC \cong \triangle DCB$ by SSS
**3. (a)** 2.9 cm **(b)** 40° **(c)** 78° **(d)** 40°
**4.** $\triangle APB \cong \triangle DPC$; $\triangle ABC \cong \triangle DCB$; $\triangle ABD \cong \triangle DCA$
**5.** $\angle B \cong \angle C$, since $\triangle ABC$ is isosceles. By construction,
$BF = DC$ and $BD = EC$. Therefore, $\triangle BDF \cong \triangle CED$
by SAS, so $DE = DF$. **6.** Let the diagonals intersect at $P$.
By the triangle inequality applied to $\triangle APB$ and $\triangle CPD$,
we have $AB < AP + BP$ and $CD < PC + PD$.
Adding the inequalities shows that $AB + CD < AP + PC + BP + PD = AC + BD$. Similarly, $BC + DA < BD + CA$.
**7. (a), (b), (c)** Standard constructions as in Section 12.2.
**(d)** Draw a circle at any point $A$ on line $m$, and let it intersect line $l$ at $B$ and $C$. Construct $\overline{AB}$ and $\overline{AC}$. Draw circles of the same radius at $B$ and $C$ to determine the respective midpoints $M$ and $N$ of $\overline{AB}$ and $\overline{AC}$. Then $k = \overleftrightarrow{MN}$ is the desired line. Alternatively, construct a line perpendicular to $l$ at a point on $l$. This determines a perpendicular segment between $l$ and $m$. The perpendicular bisector of the segment is the desired line $k$.

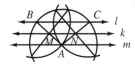

**8. (a)**

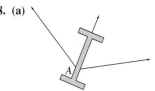

Reflect one side of $\angle A$
onto the other.

**(b)**

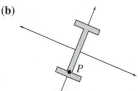

Pivot the Mira about $P$ until
the line reflects onto itself.

**(c)**

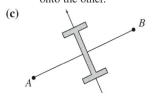

Reflect $A$ onto $B$.

**(d)**

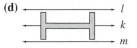

Reflect line $m$ onto line $l$.

**9. (a)** Construct $\angle A$, lay off length $AB$, and draw a circle at $B$ of radius $BC$. The circle intersects the other ray from $A$ at two points $C_1$ and $C_2$, giving two triangles $\triangle ABC_1$ and $\triangle ABC_2$.

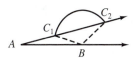

**(b)** Only $\triangle ABC_1$ has $\angle C = \angle C_1$ obtuse.
**10.** Find the midpoint $M$ of $\overline{AD}$. Then draw circles of radius $AM$ centered at $A$, $D$, and $M$.

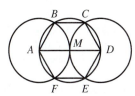

**11. (a)** Yes, by using the SSS similarity property **(b)** Yes, by using the AA similarity property **12.** Bisect sides $\overline{AB}$ and $\overline{AC}$ to determine their respective midpoints $M$ and $N$. Extend $\overline{AB}$ beyond $B$, and draw the circle at $B$ through $M$. Let $E$ be the intersection with the extension. Similarly, extend $\overline{AC}$ beyond $C$, draw the circle at $C$ through $N$, and let $F$ be the intersection of this circle with the extension. By choosing $D = A$, the SAS similarity property guarantees that $\triangle ABC \sim \triangle DEF$. **13. (a)** $\triangle BAC \sim \triangle PQR$ by SAS similarity. The scale factor is $\dfrac{6 \text{ cm}}{4 \text{ cm}} = \dfrac{3}{2}$. **(b)** $\triangle ABC \sim \triangle YZX$ by SSS similarity. The scale factor is $\dfrac{42''}{14''} = 3$. **(c)** $\triangle ABC \sim \triangle HGF$ by AA similarity. The scale factor is $\dfrac{4}{6} = \dfrac{2}{3}$. **(d)** $\triangle ADB \sim \triangle BCD$ by SSS similarity. The scale factor is $\dfrac{5}{10} = \dfrac{1}{2}$.

**14.** Draw additional line segments parallel to the given transversals. This creates similar triangles, from which it follows that $\dfrac{x}{9} = \dfrac{16}{12}$, so $x = 9\left(\dfrac{16}{12}\right) = 12$ and $\dfrac{y}{12} = \dfrac{15}{9}$. Therefore, $y = 12 \cdot \left(\dfrac{15}{9}\right) = 20$.

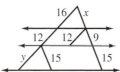

**15.** Let $K$ be the top of the stick and $Y$ the top of the pyramid. Then $\triangle KS_1S_2 \sim \triangle YP_1P_2$, with scale factor $\dfrac{P_1P_2}{S_1S_2} = \dfrac{270}{2} = 135$. Therefore, the height of the pyramid is $135 \times 3$ feet $= 405$ feet.

## Chapter 12 Test (page 709)

**1. (a)** That they form the same angle relative to the ground, namely, the angle of elevation, since the distant sun's rays are parallel **(b)** That the person and the tree stand at the same angle with the ground; for example, both vertical. Then $\triangle ABC \sim \triangle DEF$ by the AA similarity property. **(c)** $\dfrac{DE}{6'} = \dfrac{56'}{7'}$, so $DE = 48'$.

**2.** Draw the circle with radius $MC$ centered at $M$. The circle passes through $A$, $B$, and $C$. Thus, by Thales' theorem, $\triangle ACB$ is a right triangle because it is inscribed in a semicircle of diameter $\overline{AB}$. **3. (a)** $\triangle ADE \sim \triangle ACB$ by the AA similarity property, since both triangles contain $\angle A$ and a right angle. **(b)** $\triangle ABC \sim \triangle XYZ$ by the SAS similarity property, since $\dfrac{5}{4} = \dfrac{15}{12}$. **(c)** $\triangle DEG \sim \triangle EFG$ by the SSS similarity property, since $\dfrac{16}{8} = \dfrac{16}{8} = \dfrac{8}{4}$. **(d)** $\triangle AEB \sim \triangle CED$ by the AA similarity property, with $\angle AEB \cong \angle CED$ being vertical angles and $\angle EBA \cong \angle EDC$ being alternate interior angles between parallel lines. **4. (a)** $\triangle ADC \cong \triangle ABC$ by AAS **(b)** $\triangle ABC \cong \triangle ADC$ by SAS **(c)** $\triangle ADC \cong \triangle BCD$ by ASA **(d)** $\triangle ABE \cong \triangle CBD$ by AAS **(e)** $\triangle BDC \cong \triangle FDE$ by ASA and $\triangle ABE \cong \triangle AFC$ by ASA **(f)** $\triangle ABC \cong \triangle ADC$ by SSS **5.** $\triangle ADE \sim \triangle ACB$ by the AA similarity property, since both triangles contain $\angle A$ and a right angle. Thus, $\dfrac{AE}{AB} = \dfrac{AD}{AC} = \dfrac{AD}{(AD + DC)} = \dfrac{2DC}{(2DC + DC)} = \dfrac{2}{3}$.

Then $AE = \dfrac{2}{3}(AB) = \dfrac{2}{3}(12) = 8$ and $EB = AB - AE = 12 - 8 = 4$. **6. (a)** $m(\angle W) = m\angle M = 53°$ **(b)** $\dfrac{20}{16} = \dfrac{5}{4}$ **(c)** $UV = \dfrac{5}{4}KL = \dfrac{5}{4}(20) = 25$

**7.** The third side is greater than 6 feet and less than 26 feet by the triangle inequality. **8.** The small triangles are congruent to one another by the SAS congruence property, so $PQRST$ is equilateral. Let $x$ and $y$ be the measures of the acute angles in $\triangle APT$. Then each interior angle of $PQRST$ has measure $180° - x - y$, so $PQRST$ is equiangular. Altogether, $PQRST$ is regular. **9. (a)** Draw circles of radius $PQ$, one centered at $P$ and one centered at $Q$. The circles intersect at points $R$ and $S$ for which $\triangle PQR$ and $\triangle PQS$ are equilateral. **(b)** Construct the line $l$ that is perpendicular to $\overline{PQ}$ at point $Q$. Then, construct the angle bisectors of both $\angle QPR$ and $\angle QPS$ and denote their intersections with line $l$ as $T$ and $U$. Since both $\angle QPR$ and $\angle QPS$ measure $60°$, it follows that $\angle TPQ$ and $\angle UPQ$ each measure $30°$. Thus, $\angle PTQ$, $\angle PUQ$, and $\angle TPU$ each measure $60°$. Since $\triangle PTU$ has now been shown to be equiangular, it is also equilateral.

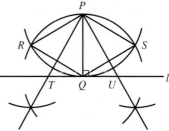

**10.** Construct a segment $\overline{DE}$ that is congruent to $\overline{AB}$. Construct rays at $D$ and $E$ to form angles that are respectively congruent to $\angle A$ and $\angle B$. Let $F$ be a point of intersection of the rays. Then $\triangle DEF \cong \triangle ABC$. **11.** $\triangle FGH$ is equilateral. **12. (a)** The Pythagorean theorem shows that $AB = 12$ and $DF = 9$. Therefore, $\triangle ABC \cong \triangle DEF$ by SSS or SAS. **(b)** Not congruent. The hypotenuse of $\triangle ABC$ is 5. Since $EF = 5$, the hypotenuse of $\triangle DEF$ is larger than 5, so the hypotenuses cannot correspond. **(c)** The Pythagorean theorem shows that $AB = 3$ and $CD = 4$. Therefore, $\triangle ABD \cong \triangle CBD$ by SSS or SAS. **(d)** $\triangle ABE \cong \triangle DBC$ by SAS

# Chapter 13

## Problem Set 13.1 (page 723)

**3.**

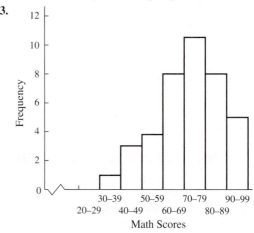

**4. (a)**

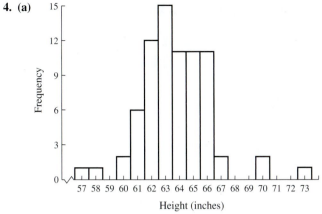

**7.**

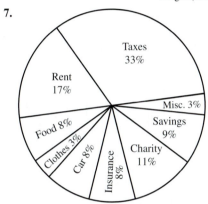

**9. (a)** 12  **20. (a)** Histogram (A) emphasizes the changes in the daily Dow Jones average by its choice of vertical scale. The changes appear to be large in histogram (A), thus exaggerating the report of stock activity on the evening news. Histogram (B) makes it clear that the changes are minimal.  **(b)** $\left(\dfrac{36}{10086}\right) \cdot 100\% \doteq 0.36\%$, which an investor probably would not worry about.
**21. (a)** The pictographs are misleading. One would guess the assets had more than doubled.  **24. (a)** 49.6%
**28. (a)**

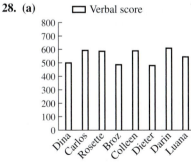

**29. (a)**

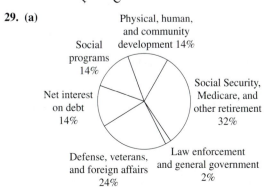

**30.**

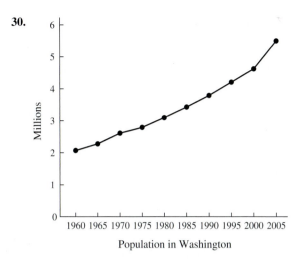

Population in Washington

## Problem Set 13.2 (page 743)

**1.** $\bar{x} \doteq 20.6, \hat{x} = 19$, mode $= 18$  **3. (a)** $Q_L = 70, Q_U = 80$
**(b)** $64-70-77-80-86$  **6. (a)** 20.56  **(b)** 4.44  **(c)** 69%
**(d)** 94%  **(e)** 100%  **12. (a)** Except possibly for round-off error, the sum of the deviations equals 0 for every data set.  **(b)** Compute the sum in part (a), and point out that the negative terms just balance out the positive terms so that the sum is 0.  **13. (a)** 4.9  **(b)** 0,41
**(c)** Compliment Leona on a good idea that avoids the canceling out of the effects of the various terms.  **14. (a)** Instead of finding the median for the number of students, Joseph found the median for the number of books reported. When calculating the mode, Joseph looked at the most number of books possible to report, not the most number of books students had read, which was eight. The mode is 1 and median 3.  **(b)** Ms. Chen could explain the difference between the label (number of books reported) and the outcome (number of students who read that many books).  **20. (a)** $\bar{x} = 27, s \doteq 8.4$
**(b)** $\bar{x} = 32, s \doteq 8.4$  **23. (a)** $\bar{x} \doteq 36,900, \hat{x} \doteq 30,000$,
mode $= 22,000$  **24. (a)** 5, 7, 10, 14, 14  **25. (a)** If $s = 0$, then all the data values are equal.  **27. (a)** All 3s  **28. (a)** 32  **(b)** 32
**31.** The total of data values in $A$ is $30 \cdot 45 = 1350$. The total of data values in $B$ is $40 \cdot 65 = 2600$. For the combined data,
$$\bar{x} = \frac{1350 + 2600}{30 + 40} \doteq 56.4.$$  **36. (a)** No, since the number of individuals in each category is unknown.

## Problem Set 13.3 (page 757)

**1. (a)** All freshmen in U.S. colleges and universities in 2010
**(c)** All people in the United States  **2.** Yes. Many poorer people cannot afford telephones and some people have only cell phones. Also, many people are irritated by telephone surveys and sales pitches, and so on. These factors could certainly bias a sample.
**5. (a)** This is surely a poor sampling procedure. The sample is clearly not random. The selection of the colleges or universities could easily reflect biases of the investigators. The choices of the faculty to be included in the study almost surely also reflect the bias of the administrators of the chosen schools.
**(b)** Presumably, the population is all college and university faculty. But the opinions of faculty at large research universities are surely vastly different from those of their colleagues at small liberal arts colleges. Indeed, there are almost surely four distinct populations here.  **11. (a)** Between 21.8 and 27.2  **14. (a)** $\bar{x} \doteq 20.2, s \doteq 2$.
The $z$ scores corresponding to the data, in the order listed, are $-1.6$,

0.9, 0.4, −0.6, 1.4, and −0.6.   **15. (a)** −0.1   **16. (a)** $83\frac{1}{3}$

percentile   **17. (a)** $0.04 = 4\%$ to the nearest hundredth
**18. (a)** $0.96 - 0.04 = 0.92 = 92\%$ to the nearest hundredth
**23.** Yes, since all sides of the die are equally likely to come up, all sequences of 0s and 1s are equally likely to appear.   **27. (a)** Since the $z$ scores indicate the location of data points in a data set, in this case they are likely to be the same as in problem 14a.
**(b)** −1.6, 0.9, 0.4, −0.6, 1.4, −0.6   **28.** Consider the data set
$\{1, 2, 3\}$. Then, $\bar{x} = \dfrac{1 + 2 + 3}{3}$ and the $z$ scores are $\dfrac{1 - \bar{x}}{s}, \dfrac{2 - \bar{x}}{s},$
and $\dfrac{3 - \bar{x}}{s}$. Therefore, their sum is

$$
\frac{1 - \bar{x}}{s} + \frac{2 - \bar{x}}{s} + \frac{3 - \bar{x}}{s}
$$
$$
= \frac{1 + 2 + 3 - 3\left(\frac{1 + 2 + 3}{3}\right)}{s}
$$
$$
= \frac{\frac{3(1 + 2 + 3)}{3} - 3\left(\frac{1 + 2 + 3}{3}\right)}{s}
$$
$$
= 0,
$$

and the same computation would be true for $x_1, x_2, \ldots, x_n$.
**29. (b)** −1.6, 0.9, 0.4, −0.6, 1.4, −0.6

# Chapter 13 Review Exercises (page 762)

**1. (a)**

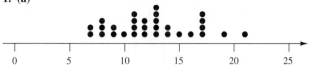

**(b)** About 13

**2.**

```
0 | 7 7 8 8 8 9 9
1 | 0 1 1 1 1 2 2 2 3 3 3 3 3 4
  | 4 5 6 7 7 7 7 9
2 | 1
```

**3.**

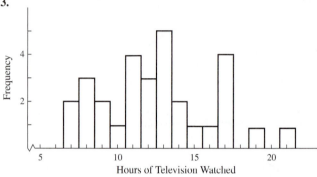

**4.** Put Mrs. Karnes's class on the left of the stems and Ms. Stevens's class on the right of the stems.

| Mrs. Karnes | | Ms. Stevens |
|---|---|---|
| 9 9 8 8 8 7 7 | 0 | 6 6 6 8 8 8 8 8 9 9 9 9 9 |
| 9 7 7 7 7 6 5 4 4 3 3 3 3 3 2 2 2 1 1 1 1 0 | 1 | 1 1 1 1 1 1 1 1 1 2 3 |
| 1 | 2 | |

**5. (a)**

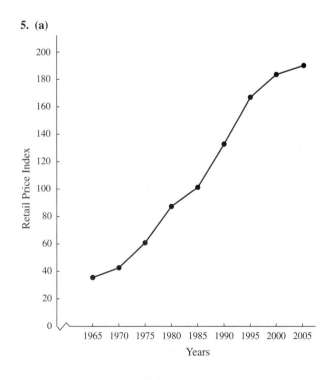

**b)** About 48   **(c)** About 200   **6.** Many examples exist. One example is 1, 2, 3, 4, 90, with a mean of 20.
**7.**

New Construction 36%
Administration 12%
Misc. 4%
Repairs 48%

**8. (a)** The volume of the larger box is about double that of the smaller box. But the length of a side of the larger box is less than double the length of a side of the smaller box, suggesting that the change was less than doubling.   **(b)** The volume of the larger is about twice that of the smaller, which defends the pictograph.
**9.** How is "medical doctor" defined? Does the term include all specialists? osteopaths? naturopaths? chiropractors? acupuncturists? How was the sampling done to determine the stated average?
**10.** $\bar{x} = 12.6, \hat{x} = 12.5, \text{mode} = 13, s = 3.6$
**11. (a)** $Q_L = 10, Q_U = 15$   **(b)** 7−10−12.5−15−21
**(c)** There are no outliers.   **(d)** $\bar{x} = 9, Q_L = 8, Q_U = 11$

**(e)** $6-8-9-11-13$    **(f)** There are no outliers.

**(g)**
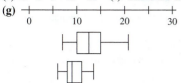

**12. (a)** $\bar{x} \doteq 27.8, s \doteq 2.0$    **(b)** $\bar{x} = 27.3, s \doteq 1.6$
**(c)** The means are about the same for the two sets of data, but the standard deviation is smaller for the second histogram, since the data are less spread out from the mean.    **13.** There are $21 \cdot 77 = 1617$ points for the 21 students. So there are 1839 points for all 24 students. Thus, the average is $1839 \div 24 \doteq 76.6$.    **14.** There are $27 \cdot 75 = 2025$ points for the second-period students and $30 \cdot 78 = 2340$ points for the fourth-period students. Thus, the average for all students is $\dfrac{2340 + 2025}{57} \doteq 76.6$.

**15.** No. The sample represents only the population of students at State University, not university students nationwide.
**16.** You might want to limit your sample to persons 20 years old and older who want to work. Alternatively, you might want to define several populations and determine figures for each: persons 20 years old and older who want to work, teenagers who want full-time employment, teenagers who want part-time employment, adults 20 years old and older who want part-time employment, and so on.    **17.** Voluntary responses to mailed questionnaires tend to come primarily from those who feel strongly (either positively or negatively) about an issue or who represent narrow special-interest groups. They are rarely representative of the population as a whole.    **18.** $\bar{x} \doteq 9.3$ and $s \doteq 3$. The $z$ scores, in order, are $-0.8, -0.1, -1.1, 0.9, 1.9, -0.8, -0.1$.    **19.** Since 12 is the sixth-largest number in the data set, and $\dfrac{6}{7} = 0.8571$ to the nearest ten-thousandth, 12 is the 85.71th percentile, to the nearest hundredth.    **20.** From Table 13.4, we see that 0.9505 corresponds to 1.65. Therefore, 1.65 is essentially at the 95th percentile.
**21.** From Table 13.4, the entry for $-0.9$ is 0.1841 and the entry for 0.9 is 0.8159. Therefore, the desired percentage is $81.59\% - 18.41\% = 63.18\%$.

## Chapter 13 Test (page 765)

**1.** $(0.40) \cdot (360°) = 144°$
**2.**

**3. (a)** $\bar{x} \doteq 78.5$    **(b)** $\hat{x} = 81$    **(c)** mode $= 87$    **(d)** $s \doteq 13.2$
**4.** To the nearest tenth, the $z$ scores for 42, 86, and 80 are $-2.8$, 0.6, and 0.1, respectively. With a normal distribution, 68% of the data will be within 1 standard deviation of the mean, 95% of the data will be within 2 standard deviations of the mean, and 99.7% of the data will be within 3 standard deviations of the mean.

**5.**

| 4 | 1 2 |
|---|---|
| 5 | 7 |
| 6 | 3 6 |
| 7 | 0 4 5 6 7 8 8 |
| 8 | 0 0 1 1 4 5 6 6 7 7 7 8 8 9 |
| 9 | 0 2 3 5 |

**6. (a)** $41 - 75 - 81 - 87 - 95$    **(b)** 41 and 42 are outliers, since they are less than $Q_L - 1.5 \cdot \text{IQR} = 57$.

**7.** If the sample is not chosen at random, it is quite likely to reflect bias—bias of the sampler, bias reflecting the group from which the sample was actually chosen (for example, views of teamsters or AARP members), and so on.    **8.** A random sample is a sample chosen in such a way that every subset of the population has an equal chance of being included.    **9.** $\dfrac{17}{30} = 0.5\overline{6}$, so, to the nearest hundredth, 17 is the 57th percentile.    **10.** To average 80% on all five tests, she must score at least 400. Thus, the total score for her last two tests should be $400 - (77 + 79 + 72) = 172$.

# Chapter 14

## Problem Set 14.1 (page 776)

**1. (a)** $\dfrac{1}{20}$, or 0.05, or 5%    **3. (b)** 1

**6. (a)** $S = \{H1, H2, H3, H4, H5, H6, T1, T2, T3, T4, T5, T6\}$
**8. (a)** iv    **(c)** ii    **(e)** ii

**11. (a)** Answers will vary. One solution is $P_e(A) = \dfrac{12}{60} = 0.6$, $P_e(B) = \dfrac{6}{20} = 0.3$, and $P_e(C) = \dfrac{2}{20} = 0.1$.    **(b)** About right, since there are 360° in a complete revolution and $\dfrac{240}{360} = 0.\overline{6}$, $\dfrac{90}{360} = 0.25$, and $\dfrac{30}{360} = 0.08\overline{3}$    **14.** Answers will vary. Using the answer to 13(a), we obtain $P_e$ (first 6 on fourth roll) $= 0.2$.
**23.** Answers will vary. When we did the experiment, we obtained four hearts, including one face card; seven diamonds, including three face cards; five spades, including two face cards; and four clubs with no face cards. This yielded the following results:

**(a)** $P_e(R) = \dfrac{11}{20} = 0.55$    **(b)** $P_e(F) = \dfrac{6}{20} = 0.3$

**(c)** $P_e(R \text{ or } F) = \dfrac{13}{20} = 0.65$    **(d)** $P_e(R \text{ and } F) = \dfrac{4}{20} = 0.2$
**(e)** $P_e(R) + P_e(F) - P_e(R \text{ and } F) = 0.55 + 0.3 - 0.2 = 0.65$
**(f)** This suggests that $P_e(R \text{ or } F) = P_e(R) + P_e(F) - P_e(R \text{ and } F)$, unlike the result suggested by problem 22.    **24.** Answers will vary. When we did the experiment, H occurred alone 12 times, 5 occurred alone 3 times, and 5 and H occurred together 2 times. This yielded the following results:    **(a)** $P_e(H) = \dfrac{12}{20} = 0.6$

**(b)** $P_e(5) = \dfrac{3}{20} = 0.15$    **(c)** $P_e(H \text{ and } 5) = \dfrac{2}{20} = 0.1$
**(d)** $P_e(H) \cdot P_e(5) = (0.6)(0.15) = 0.09$    **(e)** Yes. Since the events H and 5 are independent, the number of simultaneous occurrences of H and 5 should be about $P_e(H) \cdot$ (the number of occurrences of 5). But then

$$P_e(H \text{ and } 5) \doteq \frac{P_e(H) \cdot (\text{the number of occurrences of 5})}{20}$$

$$= P_e(H) \cdot P_e(5).$$

**30. (a)** $(0.45) \times (0.45) = 0.2025$, or about 20% of all couples
**31. (a)** $\dfrac{9806}{10,000} = 0.9806$ **33.** Answer for (a) will vary. following line graph is representative (the point with coordinate $(x, y)$ shows that $x$ heads occurred $y$ times for $x = 0, 1, 2, \ldots, 10$):
**(a)** $n = 10$

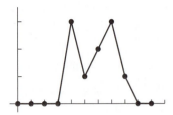

## Problem Set 14.2 (page 787)

**1.** $4 = 1 + 3 = 2 + 2 = 3 + 1; 6 = 1 + 5 = 2 + 4 = 3 + 3 = 4 + 2 = 5 + 1$. There are eight ways to roll a 4 or 6.
**3. (a)** 3 ways: H and 2, H and 4, H and 6 **5.** The Venn diagram shows that 4 students speak both English and Japanese.

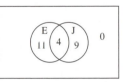

**7.** Let $R$ be the set of red face cards and let $A$ be the set of black aces. Since $R \cap A = \varnothing$, the addition principle of counting for mutually exclusive events applies, and $n(R \text{ or } A) = n(R) + n(A) = 6 + 2 = 8$.
**8. (a)** $6 \cdot 5 \cdot 4 \cdot 3 - 360$
**(b)** $3 \cdot 5 \cdot 4 \cdot 3 = 180$
**(c)** $3 \cdot 2 \cdot 4 \cdot 3 = 72$
**10.**

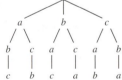

The code words are $abc, acb, bac, bca, cab,$ and $cba$.
**14. (a)** $5 \cdot 5 \cdot 5 \cdot 5 \cdot 5 = 3125$
**16. (a)**

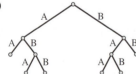

**22. (a)** To obtain an even sum, two odd faces or two even faces must come up. This can happen in $3 \cdot 3 + 3 \cdot 3 = 18$ ways.
**23. (a)** 160, since there are 4 kings and 40 nonface cards and $4 \cdot 40 = 160$ **24. (a)** 10,240. There are ten types of straights, namely, 5 high, 6 high, . . . , king high, and ace high. Each type can be filled in $4^5 = 1024$ ways, since there are four choices for each of the five cards. Then, $10 \cdot 1024 = 10,240$ is the number of straights. **27. (a)** 20,736, since $12^4 = 20,736$ and each of the four persons' birthdays can be in one of 12 months.
**29. (a)** 90,000, since $9 \cdot 10 \cdot 10 \cdot 10 \cdot 10 = 90,000$ **31. (a)** 4032, since there are 64 choices for the red checker and then 63 for the black, and $64 \cdot 63 = 4032$. **35 (a)** $2^4$, or 16, words

## Problem Set 14.3 (page 797)

**1. (a)** Combination, $C(10, 5) = 252$ ways **(b)** Permutation, $P(10, 4) = 5040$ ways **4. (a)** $P(6, 6) = 6! = 720$
**5. (a)** 14!, around 90 billion **7. (a)** 5040 **(c)** 72 **(e)** 35,280
**8. (a)** $13 \cdot 12 \cdot 11 \cdot 10 \cdot 9 \cdot 8 \cdot 7 \cdot 6 = 51,891,840$
**(c)** $15 \cdot 14 = 210$ **(e)** $\dfrac{15!}{15!} = 1$ **10. (a)** Since order doesn't matter, the answer is the number of 2-combinations chosen from the $10 + 15$ balls in the bag, so there are $C(10 + 15, 2)$ ways to choose 2 of the 25 balls. **(b)** There are three mutually exclusive cases, depending on whether both balls are red, both are blue, or there is one of each color. There are $C(10, 2)$ ways to choose 2 of the 10 red balls, and there are $C(15, 2)$ ways to choose 2 of the 15 blue balls. Finally, there are $10 \cdot 15$ ways to choose a red ball and a blue ball. Altogether, this gives $C(10 + 25, 2) = C(10, 2) + C(15, 2) + 10 \cdot 15$ ways to choose 2 of the balls. **(c)** Consider a bag with $m$ red and $n$ blue balls, and ask how many ways can 2 of the $m + n$ balls be selected. One answer is $C(m + n, 2)$, but considering the cases where both balls are red, both are blue, or one is red and the other is blue gives the answer $C(m, 2) + C(n, 2) + m \cdot n$. Equating the two answers proves the formula. **13. (a)** $\dfrac{4!}{2!2!} = 6$
**22. (a)** If we think of $ab$ as a single entity, then there are four things to put in order. This can be done in $4! = 24$ ways.
**(b)** There are 24 with $b$ immediately following $a$ and, by the same reasoning as in part (a), 24 with $a$ immediately following $b$. Therefore, there are 48 with $a$ and $b$ adjacent. **(c)** By symmetry, in half the possible arrangements $a$ would precede $e$ and in half $e$ would precede $a$. Therefore, $a$ precedes $e$ in $\dfrac{5!}{2} = 60$ arrangements. Alternatively, if $a$ is first, $a$ precedes $e$ in $4! = 24$ arrangements. If $a$ is second, $a$ precedes $e$ in $3 \cdot 3! = 18$ arrangements. If $a$ is third, $a$ precedes $e$ in $2 \cdot 3! = 12$ arrangements, and if $a$ is fourth, $a$ precedes $e$ in $3! = 6$ arrangements. Adding, we again obtain 60 as before. **27. (a)** The products of the terms in odd corners and in even corners is the same wherever the hexagon is positioned.
**(b)** $C(n - 1, r - 1)C(n, r + 1)C(n + 1, r)$
$$= \frac{(n - 1)!}{(r - 1)!(n - r)!} \frac{n!}{(r + 1)!(n - r - 1)!} \frac{(n + 1)!}{r!(n + 1 - r)!}$$
$$= \frac{(n - 1)!}{r!(n - r - 1)!} \frac{n!}{(r - 1)!(n + 1 - r)!} \frac{(n + 1)!}{(r + 1)!(n - r)!}$$
$$= C(n - 1, r)C(n, r - 1)C(n + 1, r + 1)$$
**28. (a)** $C(8, 5)$ **(b)** $C(7, 5)$, since there are seven nonred marbles from which to choose 5. **29. (a)** First choose the members of the sextet in $C(11, 6)$ ways, and then choose the soloist from among the six already chosen. **30. (a)** Pick the 8 of the 15 members in $C(15, 8) = 6435$ ways, and pick the two cocaptains from the 8 delegates in $C(8, 2) = 28$ ways. Thus, there are $6435 \cdot 28 = 180,180$ ways altogether. **31. (a)** $C(6 + 4 - 1, 6) = C(9, 6) = C(9, 3) = \dfrac{9 \cdot 8 \cdot 7}{3 \cdot 2 \cdot 1} = 84$ **(d)** The number of combinations with repetition is equivalent to the number of ways $n$ ice cream cones can be ordered from $k$ flavors. That is, it is the number of lists of $n$ check marks and $k - 1$ bars that separate one flavor from the next. Therefore, $n$ objects can be chosen from $k$ types, with repetition allowed, in $C(n + k - 1, n)$ ways. **32. (a)** First notice that there are 7 choices for the number of spots for each half-domino. Thus, there are $C(7, 2) = 7 \cdot 6/2 = 21$ dominoes with a different number

of spots on each half and 7 more dominoes with the same number of spots on each half, giving 21 + 7 = 28 in all. Alternatively, this problem can be viewed as consisting of a combination with repetition (see problem 31) in which 2 objects are selected from 7 types (number of spots), with the possibility of selecting the same type twice. By the formula of problem 31(d), there are $C(2 + 7 - 1, 2) = C(8, 2) = 8 \cdot 7/2 = 28$ in a double-six set.
**33. (a)** There are 16 trains of length 5.
**(b)** There are 1 one-car, 4 two-car, 6 three-car, 4 four-car, and 1 five-car trains of length 5.
**36. (a)** 3. There are several ways to reason this problem out. If the players are A, B, C, and D, there are three partners for player A, with the remaining two players forming the opposing team. Alternatively, choose two of the four players in $C(4, 2) = 6$ ways and divide by 2, since it doesn't matter which team is chosen first.
**(b)** 15. For example, choose the player sitting out in 5 ways and divide up the remaining four players in 3 ways as described in part (a). Alternatively, choose a team of two of the five players in $C(5, 2) = 10$ ways, and choose one player from the remaining three players to sit out in 3 ways. This gives $10 \cdot \dfrac{3}{2} = 15$ ways to set up the doubles match, where the division by 2 accounts for the fact that it doesn't matter which team is chosen first.
**38. (a)** 15 blocks. From Second to Eighth Avenue requires six blocks of walking along avenues, and getting from B to K Street requires 9 more blocks walking along streets.   **(b)** 5005. Each block walked is along either an avenue or a street, where 6 avenue blocks and 9 street blocks must be walked. Each walk can be described as a permutation of 6 As and 9 Ss. For example, the sequence SSAAASSSASASSAS indicates that Joe walks along a street, then a street, then an avenue, and so on. He can choose any 6 of the 16 blocks as avenues, with the remaining 9 blocks walked along streets. Thus, Joe can reach his destination in $C(15, 6) = 5005$ ways.
**39. (a)** 362,880   **(c)** 2520
**(d)** 20,160   **(e)** 35
**40. (a)** $10! = 3,628,800$
**(c)** $C(13, 8) = 1287$

## Problem Set 14.4 (page 816)

**1. (a)** Outcomes listed in order of penny, nickel, dime, and quarter are as follows:

HHHH  THHH  HTHT  TTTH  TTTT
HTHH  HHTT  TTHT
HHTH  TTHH  THTT
HHHT  THTH  HTTT
      THHT
      HTTH

**(c)** $P(2 \text{ heads and 2 tails}) = \dfrac{6}{16} = 0.375$

**4. (a)** $\dfrac{4}{22} \doteq 0.18$   **(c)** $\dfrac{6}{22} \doteq 0.27$

**5. (a)** $\dfrac{4}{12} \doteq 0.33$

**6. (a)** $\dfrac{7}{20} = 0.35$  **7. (a)** 0.19   **(c)** 0.33   **(e)** 0.25

**8. (a)** $\dfrac{4}{50} = 0.08$   **(c)** $\dfrac{0}{50} = 0$   **10. (a)** $\dfrac{3}{8} \cdot \dfrac{2}{7} = \dfrac{6}{56}$

**12. (a)**

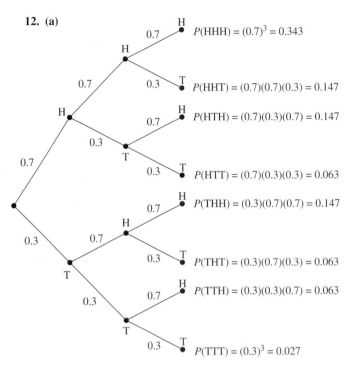

**14.** $P(3H) = \dfrac{C(13, 3)}{C(52, 3)} = \dfrac{13 \cdot 12 \cdot 11}{52 \cdot 51 \cdot 50} \doteq 0.013$   **15.** These answers are determined by ratios of angular measures of appropriate regions.

**(a)** $P(\text{shaded area}) = \dfrac{3}{10} = 0.3$

**(c)** $P(\text{region 10 or region 6}) = \dfrac{2}{10} = 0.2$

**(e)** $P(8 \mid \text{shaded area}) = \dfrac{1}{3}$

**(g)** $P(\text{a vowel or odd-numbered region}) = \dfrac{7}{10} = 0.7$

**16.** The following probabilities are ratios of regional areas:

**(a)** $P(1) = \dfrac{16}{25} = 0.64$   **(c)** $P(5) = \dfrac{1}{25} = 0.04$

**17. (a)** $P(b) = \dfrac{1}{20}$   **(b)** $P(\text{a or c or d or e} \mid \text{a or b or c or d or e}) = \dfrac{4}{5}$

**18. (a)** 5:31 or, equivalently, $\dfrac{5}{31}$

**20.** $P(A \text{ or } C) = P(A) + P(C) = \dfrac{1}{2} + \dfrac{1}{6} = \dfrac{4}{6} = \dfrac{2}{3}$. Thus, the odds in favor of $A$ or $C$ are $\dfrac{\frac{2}{3}}{1 - \frac{2}{3}} = \dfrac{2}{1}$, or 2 : 1.

**22.** $E = \$4 \cdot \dfrac{1}{36} + \$6 \cdot \dfrac{2}{36} + \$8 \cdot \dfrac{3}{36} + \$10 \cdot \dfrac{4}{36} + \$20 \cdot \dfrac{5}{36} +$
$\$40 \cdot \dfrac{6}{36} + \$20 \cdot \dfrac{5}{36} + \$10 \cdot \dfrac{4}{36} + \$8 \cdot \dfrac{3}{36} + \$6 \cdot \dfrac{2}{36} + \$4 \cdot \dfrac{1}{36} =$
$\dfrac{\$600}{36} = \$16.67$ to the nearest penny

**28.** Mischa is justifiably suspicious of Jorge's reasoning. There are three equally likely red spots that can be seen, and in just one of the cases is the hidden spot black. The correct probability is $\dfrac{1}{3}$.

**29. (a)** $P(2 \text{ white}) = \dfrac{C(6, 2)}{C(14, 2)} = \dfrac{\frac{6 \cdot 5}{2 \cdot 1}}{\frac{14 \cdot 13}{2 \cdot 1}} \doteq 0.16$

**30. (a)** $P(\text{all 4 red}) = \dfrac{C(8, 4)}{C(19, 4)} = \dfrac{\frac{8 \cdot 7 \cdot 6 \cdot 5}{4 \cdot 3 \cdot 2 \cdot 1}}{\frac{19 \cdot 18 \cdot 17 \cdot 16}{4 \cdot 3 \cdot 2 \cdot 1}} \doteq 0.02$

**31. (a)** $P(\text{a code word begins with } a) =$
$\dfrac{25 \cdot 24 \cdot 23 \cdot 22}{26 \cdot 25 \cdot 24 \cdot 23 \cdot 22} \doteq 0.04$   **34. (a)** $P$ (a five-card hand contains

exactly two aces) $= \dfrac{C(4, 2) \cdot C(48, 3)}{C(52, 5)} = \dfrac{\frac{4 \cdot 3}{2 \cdot 1} \cdot \frac{48 \cdot 47 \cdot 46}{3 \cdot 2 \cdot 1}}{\frac{52 \cdot 51 \cdot 50 \cdot 49 \cdot 48}{5 \cdot 4 \cdot 3 \cdot 2 \cdot 1}} \doteq 0.04$

**35.** The seven numbers with two alike in a fixed order appear with

probability $\left(\dfrac{1}{6}\right)^7$. To compute the number of ways in which seven

such numbers can appear, note that we can choose the number to

appear twice in six ways *and* each of the other numbers in only one

way, *and* we can then order these numbers in $\left(\dfrac{7!}{2!}\right)$. ways. Thus,

the desired probability is $6 \cdot \dfrac{7!}{2!} \cdot \left(\dfrac{1}{6}\right)^7 \doteq 0.05$.   **36. (a)** Since one

of the 9 keys is the correct one, $p_1 = \dfrac{1}{9}$. The first key tried is therefore

incorrect with probability $\dfrac{8}{9}$, and the probability that second key is

correct is $\dfrac{1}{8}$, so, by conditional probabilities $p_2 = \dfrac{8}{9} \cdot \dfrac{1}{8} = \dfrac{1}{9}$.

Similarly, $p_3 = \dfrac{8}{9} \cdot \dfrac{7}{8} \cdot \dfrac{1}{7} = \dfrac{1}{9}$, and so on.

**(b)** The expected number of keys to be tried is

$e_9 = 1 \cdot \dfrac{1}{9} + 2 \cdot \dfrac{1}{9} + \cdots + 9 \cdot \dfrac{1}{9} = \dfrac{1}{9}(1 + 2 + \cdots + 9)$

$= \dfrac{1}{9} \cdot \dfrac{9 \cdot 10}{2} = 5$, where the formula for the triangular numbers

$1 + 2 + \cdots + n = \dfrac{n(n + 1)}{2}$ is used in the case $n = 9$.

**37. (a)** A triangle with side lengths $x$, $y - x$, and $1 - y$ must
satisfy the inequalities $x < y - x + 1 - y = 1 - x$, $1 - y <$
$x + y - x = y$, and $y - x < x + 1 - y$, which algebraically

simplify to the inequalities $x < \dfrac{1}{2}$, $y > \dfrac{1}{2}$, and $y < x + \dfrac{1}{2}$.

**(b)**

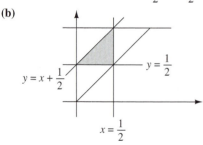

**(c)** The shaded triangle of part (b) is a right triangle with each leg

of length $\dfrac{1}{2}$, so its area is $\dfrac{1}{8}$. The sample space is a triangle of area

$\dfrac{1}{2}$, so the ratio of areas is $\dfrac{1}{8} \div \dfrac{1}{2} = \dfrac{1}{4}$. By geometric probability,

this is the probability of forming a triangle by a random choice of
the points along the given segment.   **38. (a)** There are five patterns: four 2-loops (that is, the small loops formed by two strings),

two 2-loops and a 4-loop, one 2-loop and a 6-loop, two 4-loops,

and one 8-loop.   **(c)** There are $C(8, 2) = \dfrac{8 \cdot 7}{2} = 28$

**40. (a)** $P(W_3) = \dfrac{7 \cdot 6 \cdot 5}{7 \cdot 7 \cdot 7} = \dfrac{30}{49}$,

$P(\overline{W}_3) = 1 - P(W_3) = 1 - \dfrac{30}{49} = \dfrac{19}{49}$

**42. (a)** $\dfrac{1}{C(49, 6)} = \dfrac{1}{13,983,816}$, or about 1 in nearly 14 million

**43. (a)** $\dfrac{C(8, 5) \cdot C(72, 15)}{C(80, 20)} \doteq 0.0183$   **44. B**

# Chapter 14 Review Exercises (page 823)

**1.** Answers will vary. When we did the experiment, three heads

and a tail occurred 5 times, so $P_e = \dfrac{5}{20} = 0.25$.

**2.** Answers will vary. When we did the experiment, we obtained
the following:

| 2 | 3 | 4 | 5 | 6 | 7 | 8 | 9 | 10 | 11 | 12 |
|---|---|---|---|---|---|---|---|----|----|----|
| I | I | II | II | III | III | IIII | I | II | I |

Using these data, we obtain the following:   **(a)** $P_e(3 \text{ or } 4) -$

$\dfrac{3}{20} = 0.15$   **(b)** $P_e(\text{score at least } 5) = \dfrac{16}{20} = 0.80$   **3.** Answers

will vary. Using the data from problem 2, we obtained

$P_e(5 \text{ or } 6 \text{ or } 7 \mid 5 \text{ or } 6 \text{ or } 7 \text{ or } 8 \text{ or } 9) = \dfrac{8}{13} \doteq 0.6$.   **4.** Answers will

vary. In our study, 7 our of 20 chose chocolate, so $P_e = \dfrac{7}{20} = 0.35$.

**5.** Answers will vary. When we did the experiment, we obtained
the following data:

| Point Up | 5 | 4 | 3 | 5 | 2 | 4 | 3 | 2 | 2 | 3 | 2 | 3 |
|----------|---|---|---|---|---|---|---|---|---|---|---|---|
| Head Up | 0 | 1 | 2 | 0 | 3 | 1 | 2 | 3 | 3 | 2 | 3 | 2 |

| Point Up | 3 | 1 | 2 | 0 | 4 | 4 | 3 | 2 |
|----------|---|---|---|---|---|---|---|---|
| Head Up | 2 | 4 | 3 | 5 | 1 | 1 | 2 | 3 |

Using these data, we obtain the following:

**(a)** $P_e(3 \text{ tacks land point up}) = \dfrac{6}{20} = 0.30$.

**(b)** $P_e(2 \text{ or } 3 \text{ tacks land point up}) = \dfrac{12}{20} = 0.60$.   **6.** Answers will

vary. Doing the experiment, we obtained the following data, with
the results indicated in (a) and (b):

| Number of Trials to Get a 5 or 6 | 1 | 2 | 3 | 4 | 5 | 6 | 7 |
|----------------------------------|---|---|---|---|---|---|---|
| | | II | IIII | III | | | I |

**(a)** Average number of rolls required is
$\dfrac{3 + 3 + 4 + 4 + 4 + 4 + 5 + 5 + 5 + 7}{10} = 4.4$.

We guess that it should take four or five rolls to get a 5 or 6.

**(b)** $P_e(\text{it takes precisely five rolls to obtain 5 or 6}) = \dfrac{3}{10} = 0.30$.

**7.** Answers will vary. Doing the experiment, we obtained the following data, yielding the results in (a), (b), and (c):

**(a)** $P_e(\text{ace or heart}) = \dfrac{11}{20} = 0.55$.

**(b)** $P_e(\text{ace and heart}) = \dfrac{1}{20} = 0.05$.

**(c)** $P_e(\text{ace} \mid \text{heart}) = \dfrac{1}{9} \doteq 0.11$.    **8.** A match will occur with a probability of about 0.63. Thus, you will usually get around 15 or 16 matches in 25 trials.

**9. (a)** HHH  HTT    **(b)** 3
HHT  THT
HTH  TTH
THH  TTT

**10.** Fill in the Venn diagram from the inside out.

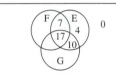

**(a)** $90 - 4 = 86$  **(b)** 7  **11. (a)** $26 \cdot 25 \cdot 24 \cdot 23 \cdot 22 =$ 7,893,600  **(b)** $5 \cdot 4 \cdot 24 \cdot 23 \cdot 22 = 242,880$
**(c)** $3 \cdot 23 \cdot 22 = 1518$  **12. (a)** $2 + 4 + 8 = 14$  **(b)** Since $2 + 4 + 8 + 16 = 30$, four symbols are sufficient to code each letter.
**13.** The $10^4 = 10,000$ combinations can all be tried in $10,000 \div 60 = 166.666 \ldots$ minutes, which is a bit under 2 hours and 47 minutes.  **14. (a)** 3125. There are 5 digits that still look like digits when upside down: 0, 1, 6, 8, and 9. Therefore, there are $5^5 = 3125$ ZIP numbers that still appear to be ZIP numbers when read upside down.  **(b)** 3050. The middle digit must by unchanged when read upside down, so it is a 0, 1, or 8. Therefore, there are $5 \cdot 5 \cdot 3 = 75$ ZIP numbers that are unchanged when read upside down. This means that $3125 - 75 = 3050$ ZIP numbers are detour prone.

**15.**

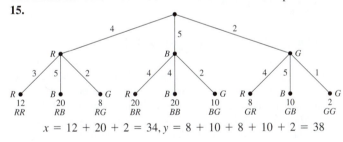

$x = 12 + 20 + 2 = 34, y = 8 + 10 + 8 + 10 + 2 = 38$

**16. (a)** $C(15, 9) = \dfrac{15 \cdot 14 \cdot 13 \cdot 12 \cdot 11 \cdot 10 \cdot 9 \cdot 8 \cdot 7}{9 \cdot 8 \cdot 7 \cdot 6 \cdot 5 \cdot 4 \cdot 3 \cdot 2 \cdot 1} = 5005$

**(b)** $C(2, 1) \cdot C(3, 1) \cdot C(13 \cdot 7) = \dfrac{2}{1} \cdot \dfrac{3}{1} \cdot \dfrac{13 \cdot 12 \cdot 11 \cdot 10 \cdot 9 \cdot 8 \cdot 7}{7 \cdot 6 \cdot 5 \cdot 4 \cdot 3 \cdot 2 \cdot 1} =$

10,296  **17. (a)** $C(13, 2) = \dfrac{13 \cdot 12}{2 \cdot 1} = 78$

**(b)** $C(12, 2) = \dfrac{12 \cdot 11}{2 \cdot 1} = 66$

**(c)** $C(13, 2) + C(12, 2) - C(3, 2) = 78 + 66 - 3 = 141$

**18. (a)** $\dfrac{7!}{2!2!2!1!} = 630$  **(b)** $\dfrac{6!}{2!2!1!1!} = 180$  **(c)** $\dfrac{6!}{2!2!1!1!} = 180$

**19. (a)** $5! = 120$  **(b)** $2 \cdot 4! = 48$  **(c)** $3! \cdot 2! = 12$

**20. (b)** Easily seen in figures  **(c)** There are $C(n, 2) = \dfrac{n(n-1)}{2}$ ways to choose a pair of circles, and each pair creates up to two points of intersection. Altogether, the $n$ circles can intersect in up to $n(n-1)$ points.  **21. (a)** 15  **(b)** The four endpoints of the intersecting chords determine the point of intersection.

**(c)** There are $C(n, 4)$ ways to choose a set of four of the $n$ points, and each choice gives one point of intersection. Therefore, the number of points of intersection is $C(n, 4)$.

**22. (a)** HH1, HH2, HH3, HH4, HH5, HH6
HT1, HT2, HT3, HT4, HT5, HT6
TH1, TH2, TH3, TH4, TH5, TH6
TT1, TT2, TT3, TT4, TT5, TT6

**(b)** $P(TT5) = \dfrac{1}{24} \doteq 0.04$  **23.** $P(5 \mid TT) = \dfrac{1}{6} \doteq 0.17$

**24.** $P(\text{sum at most } 11) = 1 - P(\text{sum is } 12) = 1 - \dfrac{1}{36} \doteq 0.97$

**25. (a)** $[C(5, 2) + C(6, 2) + C(4, 2)]/C(15,2) =$
$\left(\dfrac{5 \cdot 4}{2 \cdot 1} + \dfrac{6 \cdot 5}{2 \cdot 1} + \dfrac{4 \cdot 3}{2 \cdot 1}\right) \bigg/ \dfrac{15 \cdot 14}{2 \cdot 1} \doteq 0.30$

**(b)** $P(\text{both white}) = \dfrac{C(5, 2)}{C(15, 2)} = \dfrac{\dfrac{5 \cdot 4}{2 \cdot 1}}{\dfrac{15 \cdot 14}{2 \cdot 1}} \doteq 0.10$

**(c)** $P(\text{both white} \mid \text{both the same}) =$
$\dfrac{C(5, 2)}{C(5, 2) + C(6, 2) + C(4, 2)} = \dfrac{10}{10 + 15 + 6} \doteq 0.32$

**(d)**

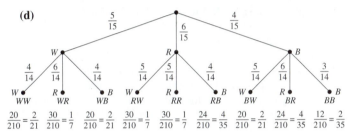

$\dfrac{20}{210} = \dfrac{2}{21}$  $\dfrac{30}{210} = \dfrac{1}{7}$  $\dfrac{20}{210} = \dfrac{2}{21}$  $\dfrac{30}{210} = \dfrac{1}{7}$  $\dfrac{30}{210} = \dfrac{1}{7}$  $\dfrac{24}{210} = \dfrac{4}{35}$  $\dfrac{20}{210} = \dfrac{2}{21}$  $\dfrac{24}{210} = \dfrac{4}{35}$  $\dfrac{12}{210} = \dfrac{2}{35}$

$P(\text{same color}) = \dfrac{2}{21} + \dfrac{1}{7} + \dfrac{2}{35} = \dfrac{10 + 15 + 6}{105} = \dfrac{31}{105}$

$P(\text{WW}) = \dfrac{2}{21}$

$P(\text{WW} \mid \text{same color}) = \dfrac{P(\text{WW \& same color})}{P(\text{same color})} =$

$\dfrac{P(\text{WW \& same color})}{P(\text{same color})} = \dfrac{\dfrac{2}{21}}{\dfrac{31}{105}} = \dfrac{10}{31}$

**26. (a)** $P(\text{b and } 8) = 0$

**(b)** $P(\text{b or } 8) = P(\text{b}) + P(8) = \dfrac{90}{360} + \dfrac{30}{360} = \dfrac{1}{3} \doteq 0.33$

**(c)** $P(\text{b} \mid 8) = 0$  **(d)** $P(\text{b and } 2) = \dfrac{30}{360} \doteq 0.08$

**(e)** $P(\text{b or } 2) = P(\text{b}) + P(2) - P(\text{b and } 2)$
$= \dfrac{90}{360} + \dfrac{30}{360} - \dfrac{30}{360} = 0.25$

**(f)** $P(2 \mid \text{b}) = 30/90 \doteq 0.33$  **27. (a)** 3:5, or $\dfrac{3}{5}$  **(b)** 1:7, or $\dfrac{1}{7}$

**28. (a)** $P(A)/[1 - P(A)]$; that is,
$\dfrac{0.85}{1 - 0.85} = \dfrac{0.85}{0.15} = \dfrac{17}{3}$, or 17:3

**(b)** $P(A) = 17/25 = 0.68$

**29. (a)** $E = \$5 \cdot (.50) + \$10 \cdot (.25) + \$20 \cdot (.10) = \$7$
**(b)** No. On average, you expect to lose \$3 per game.

**30.** There are 8 equally likely possibilities for the 3 children, BBB, BBG, BGB, BGG, GBB, GBG, GGB, and GGG. However, the family has at least one girl, so there are 7 remaining equally likely possibilities. Out of those 7, only 3 have 2 boys, so the probability that the other 2 children are both boys is $\frac{3}{7}$.

## Chapter 14 Test (page 825)

**1. (a)** 5040   **(b)** 504   **(c)** 40,320   **(d)** 5040   **(e)** 6720
**(f)** 40,320   **(g)** 84   **(h)** 1

**2. (a)** $C(8, 5) = \dfrac{8 \cdot 7 \cdot 6 \cdot 5 \cdot 4}{5 \cdot 4 \cdot 3 \cdot 2 \cdot 1} = 56$

**(b)** $C(5, 5) \cdot C(8, 5) = \dfrac{5 \cdot 4 \cdot 3 \cdot 2 \cdot 1}{5 \cdot 4 \cdot 3 \cdot 2 \cdot 1} \cdot \dfrac{8 \cdot 7 \cdot 6 \cdot 5 \cdot 4}{5 \cdot 4 \cdot 3 \cdot 2 \cdot 1} = 56$

**(c)** $C(5, 5) + C(8, 5) = \dfrac{5 \cdot 4 \cdot 3 \cdot 2 \cdot 1}{5 \cdot 4 \cdot 3 \cdot 2 \cdot 1} + \dfrac{8 \cdot 7 \cdot 6 \cdot 5 \cdot 4}{5 \cdot 4 \cdot 3 \cdot 2 \cdot 1} = 57$

**3.** $P(2 \text{ yellow balls} \mid 3 \text{ green balls}) = \dfrac{C(5, 2)}{C(14, 2)} \doteq 0.11$

**4.** Prepare a card as shown and ask a number of people to choose a number. Calculate the experimental probability of choosing 3 as the number of times 3 is chosen divided by the number of people questioned.   **5.** 7 to 13   **6. (a)** $7^4 = 2401$
**(b)** $7 \cdot 6 \cdot 5 \cdot 4 = 840$   **7. (a)** $2 \cdot 6 \cdot 5 \cdot 4 = 240$   **(b)** Choose $cd$ as a single unit in 1 way, choose two more letters in $C(5, 2) = 10$ ways, and arrange these three items in order in $3! = 6$ ways. Proceed similarly for $dc$. Therefore, the desired number is $2 \cdot 1 \cdot 10 \cdot 6 = 120$.   **8.** This would be an experimental probability obtained by keeping records for a large number of trials of treating strep throat with pencillin.   **9. (a)** Fill in the regions in the Venn diagram, starting with the innermost region.

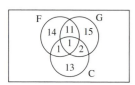

Adding all the counts, we find that there are 57 students in all.
**(b)** 13 students   **(c)** 11 students   **10.** 5 to 12
**11.** Probability tree

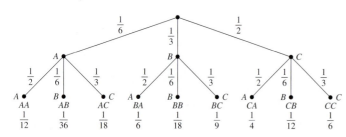

**(a)** $P(AA \cup BB \cup CC) = P(AA) + P(BB) + P(CC) =$
$\dfrac{1}{12} + \dfrac{1}{18} + \dfrac{1}{6} + \dfrac{11}{36}$
**(b)** $P(AA \cup AB \cup AC \cup BA \cup CA)$
$= P(AA) + P(AB) + P(AC) + P(BA) + P(CA)$
$= \dfrac{1}{12} + \dfrac{1}{36} + \dfrac{1}{18} + \dfrac{1}{6} + \dfrac{1}{4} = \dfrac{3 + 1 + 2 + 6 + 9}{36} = \dfrac{21}{36} = \dfrac{7}{12}$

or
$P(A \text{ on red cube} \cup A \text{ on blue cube}) = P(A \text{ on red cube}) +$
$P(A \text{ on blue cube}) - P(A \text{ on red cube and } A \text{ on blue cube})$
$= \dfrac{1}{6} + \dfrac{1}{2} - \dfrac{1}{12} = \dfrac{21}{36} = \dfrac{7}{12}$

# Appendix B

## Problem Set B (page 830)

**1. (a)** 641   **(c)** 101,388   **(e)** 770   **(g)** 770   **(i)** 237
**2. (a)** 98,915   **(c)** 32   **3. (a)** 49   **(c)** 13
**4. (a)** 841   **(c)** 33

**5. (a)** $\boxed{(}\;\boxed{\sqrt{\phantom{x}}}\;784\;\boxed{)}\;\boxed{-}\;91\;\boxed{\div}\;13\;\boxed{)}\;\boxed{\div}\;\boxed{(}\;8\;\boxed{\times}\;49\;\boxed{-}\;11\;\boxed{\times}$
$35\;\boxed{)}\;\boxed{=}$   **7. (a)** $1831 - (17 \times 28) + 34$

**13. (a)** The $\boxed{=}$ key needs to be pressed 14 times. $5\;\boxed{M+}\;\boxed{+}\;3\;\boxed{=}$
$\boxed{M+}\;\boxed{=}\;\boxed{M+}\;\boxed{=}\;...\;\boxed{=}\;\boxed{M+}\;\boxed{MR}$, 390
**15.** $s = 3.055...,\ \bar{x} = 8$
**16. (a)** The algorithm that follows generates the Lucas numbers. We show, at each step, the entry, the value of $x$ in the display, and the value $M$ in the memory. The Lucas numbers are printed in bold.
**17. (c)** The coefficients are the successive Fibonacci numbers $\tau^7 - 13\tau = 8$, $\tau^8 - 21\tau = 13$, $\tau^9 - 34\tau = 21$. In general, we expect that $\tau^n - F_n\tau = F_{n-1}$   **(e)** It seems that $\{\tau^n\} = L_n, n \geq 2$, where $L_n$ is the $n$th Lucas number, since $\{\tau^7\} = 29, \{\tau^8\} = 47, \{\tau^9\} = 76$.

# Appendix C

## Problem Set C (page 840)

**1. (a)** The sides are only approximately, not exactly, all the same length.   **2. (a)** Construct the midpoint $M$ of the segment $\overline{AB}$. Construct the perpendicular bisector to the segment through $M$. Construct any point $C \neq M$ on the perpendicular bisector. The triangle $ABC$ is isosceles.   **(c)** Construct any point $M$ on the perpendicular bisector of segment $\overline{AB}$. Construct a line parallel to $\overline{AB}$ through point $M$, and construct any circle centered at $M$. If the circle intersects the parallel line at points $C$ and $D$, then $ABCD$ is an isosceles trapezoid.   **(e)** Construct the segment $\overline{AC}$ and the perpendicular bisector of the segment. Construct a point $B$ on the perpendicular bisector. Construct a circle centered at $A$ through $B$. If the circle intersects the perpendicular bisector at $D$, then $ABCD$ is a rhombus with opposite vertices at $A$ and $C$.   **4. (a)** The angle measures sum to $360°$.   **5. (a)** Let the respective points be $C$, $D$, and $E$. There are several methods to show that triangle $CDE$ is a right triangle with the right angle at vertex $D$. *Method One:* Use **Length** to measure the lengths $CD$, $DE$, and $CE$, and use **Calculate** ... to show that $CD^2 + DE^2 = CE^2$. Triangle $CDE$ is a right triangle by the converse of the Pythagorean theorem. *Method Two:* Measure the slopes of $\overline{CD}$ and $\overline{DE}$, and show that the product of the slopes is $-1$. This shows that the segments are perpendicular to one another. *Method Three:* Measure $\angle CDE$ and see that it is $90°$.   **6. (a)** The point $M$ is $(1, 3)$.

# Credits

## Chapter 1

Page 1, 3 kids with shapes on a table, Gage/Stone/Getty Images.
Page 9, George Pólya, AP Images. Page 31, Carl Frederick Gauss, The Image Works.

## Chapter 2

Page 67, collection of Racing Cars (toys), Bruno Monteny/iStockphoto. Page 69, Rhind papyrus, Bridgeman Art Library. Page 69, Inca quipu (counting cords), The Granger Collection. Page 74, Visual of Shapes in Sets, Olga Langerova/Shutterstock. Page 82, Cubes—rectangle, prism, and pyramid, Photos of MathLink® Cubes courtesy of ETA/Cuisenaire®. Copyright © 2010 ETA/Cuisenaire.

## Chapter 3

Page 125, Maya Numbers Monument in Plaza Central, Playa del Carmen, Quintana Roo State, Mexico, North America, Jan Csernoch/Alamy. Page 130, Mayan artifact, Courtesy of Duane De Temple. Page 134, Mary Cavanaugh, Courtesy of Mary Cavanaugh. Calvin and Hobbes comic strip date of publication: 11.26.1990, *Calvin and Hobbes* copyright © 1990 and 2010 by Bill Watterson/Distributed by Universal Uclick.

## Chapter 4

Page 185, candy shop, Barcelona, Spain, Lillis Photography/iStockphoto. Page 190, Sophie Germain, The Image Works. Page 215, round Mayan calendar, Courtesy of Duane De Temple.

## Chapter 5

Page 227, girl counting candles on birthday cake, Comstock/Thinkstock. Page 244, Nancy Rolson, Courtesy of Nancy Rolson. Pages 250 and 263, hot air balloon, Shutterstock. Page 250, cliff, Shutterstock.

## Chapter 6

Page 273, pizzas on table, David H. Lewis/iStockphoto. Page 298, Charlotte Jenkins, Courtesy of Charlotte Jenkins. Page 276, Hagar The Horrible cartoon, "At the count of ten, we'll charge the enemy!", HAGAR © 1995 KING FEATURES SYNDICATE.

## Chapter 7

Page 337, girl counting change near piggy bank, Brand X Pictures/Thinkstock. Page 387, Anne Lawrence, Courtesy of Anne Lawrence. Page 353, Foxtrot cartoon by Bill Amend: "Do you get the sense our playing football is irrational?" 11/13/03. © 2003 Universal Press Syndicate., FoxTrot © 2003. Bill Amend. Used by permission of Universal Uclick. All rights reserved.

## Chapter 8

Page 399, Indian girls making rangoli design in rural village, Tim Gainey/Alamy. Page 406, Emmy Noether, Alamy. Page 418, Rene Descartes, Library of Congress Prints and Photographs Division [LC-USZ62-61365].

## Chapter 9

Page 449, origami decoration of a Japanese festival, Keiichi Hiki/iStockphoto. Page 452, kids at chalkboard, The Image Works. Page 454, fissures in tin foil, Manfred P. Kage/Peter Arnold, Inc. Page 454, butterfly wings, John Bove/Photo Researchers. Page 454, Escher's "Wall Mosaic in the Alhambra" 1922, *Wall Mosaic in the Alhambra*, M.C. Escher. Copyright © 2004 The M.C. Escher Company, Holland. All Rights Reserved. Page 454, snow crystal, Science Source/Photo Researchers. Page 454, fractal image created with computer, "Tail of the Seahorse," courtesy of author's colleague: Tyre Newton. Page 454, seed pattern in sunflower head, Ray E. Ellis/Photo Researchers. Page 459, circle master compass, Beth Anderson. Page 459, Safe Drawing Compass, Photos of tools for measuring and drawing geometric figures courtesy of ETA/ Cuisenaire®. Copyright © 2010 ETA/Cuisenaire. Page 460, ruler, Beth Anderson. Page 460, drafting triangles—larger, SuperStock. Page 460, drafting triangles—smaller, Alamy. Page 460, protractor, Shutterstock. Page 480, National Baha'I Headquarters in Wilmette IL, white-windmill.co.uk/Alamy. Page 491, buckyball, S. Camazine/ Photo Researchers. Page 491, seashell, Scott Sanders/Shutterstock. Page 491, Leonardo Da Vinci's icosahedron, The Image Works. Page 491, Leonardo Da Vinci's dodecahedron, SSPL/Science Museum Library/The Image Works. Page 491, drawing truncated octahedra, drawn by Duane De Temple. Page 491, drawing radiolaria skeletons, From *Report on the Scientific Results of the Voyage of the H. M. S. Challenger*, Vol. 18, by E. H. Haeckel (London, 1887). Page 497, Epcot center geodesic dome, Imac/Alamy. Page 497, radiolarian protozoan, Juergen Berger/Photo Researchers, Inc. Page 503, pyrite crystal, H. Chaumeton/Photo Researchers. Page 505, Leonhard Euler (1707–1783), Alamy.

## Chapter 10

Page 523, boy with chemistry experiment, Index Stock/Alamy. Page 551, Earth from space, NASA. Babylonian tablet, The Trustees of the British Museum/Art Resource, NY.

## Chapter 11

Page 599, topview of the palace garden at the Palace "Het Loo" in Apeldoorn, The Netherlands, Sjoerd van der Wal/iStockphoto. Page 612, M. C. Escher's two-motif tilling of plane, yellow and red fish, Copyright © 2004 The M.C. Escher Company, Holland. All rights reserved. Page 613, Carolyn Gordon and David Webb, University Archives, Department of Special Collections, Washington University Libraries. Page 619, M.C. Escher's pink lizards, Copyright © 2004 The M.C. Escher Company, Holland. All rights reserved. Page 620, Cornered Mirror Girl holding hand up, Beth Anderson/Pearson. Page 631, Pfembe maternity statue, Royal Museum for Central Africa, Tervuren, Belgium. Page 634, Maori rafter patterns, From *Maori Art* (1896) by Augustus Hamilton. Page 638, Cotton textile hanging, 82 × 63-7/8 in. Chimú, Peru. 12th–15th century, The Michael C. Rockefeller Memorial Collection, Bequest of Nelson A. Rockefeller, 1979 [1979.206.601]. Image copyright © The Metropolitan Museum of Art/Art Resource,

NY. Page 638, detail of tiled wall in the Alhambra, Vladimir Korostyshevskiy/Shutterstock. Page 638, potato printed fabric from Africa, Courtesy of Duane De Temple. Page 638, Ca'd'Oro Venice Mosaic floor in courtyard, Sarah Quill/Alamy. Page 638, tilings from Portugal, 15th to 16th centuries, Portuguese and Sevillian 15th–16th century glazed tiles; detail of decoration in the Crown Room, Palacio Nacional da Pena Sintra Portugal. The Art Gallery Collection/Alamy. Page 638, Chinese latticework, old window with geometrical and floral patterns, Shi Yali/Shutterstock. Page 643, M. C. Escher's birds and its grid of parallelograms, Copyright © 2004 The M.C. Escher Company, Holland. All rights reserved. Page 643, Escher-like tiling by Nancy Putnam, Drawing by Nancy Putnam/ Courtesy of the author. Page 655, M.C. Escher red and blue fish, Copyright © 2004 The M.C. Escher Company, Holland. All rights reserved.

## Chapter 12

Page 657, close-up of Thai pillows, Gina Smith/Shutterstock.

## Chapter 13

Page 711, middle-school student making a bar graph with colored pencils, Mark Scheuern/Alamy. Page 720, Clem Boyer, Courtesy of Clem Boyer. Page 750, Sidney Harris cartoon, "Bizarre Sequence of Computer-Generated Random Numbers." Copyright © 2007 by Sidney Harris, Reprinted with permission from Sidney Harris. ScienceCartoonsPlus.com.

## Chapter 14

Page 767, view from fictious boardgame, complete set with pawns, dices, cards, and plastic houses, Baris Simsek/iStockphoto. Page 814, roulette wheel, Shutterstock.

# Mathematical Lexicon

Many of the words, prefixes, and suffixes forming the vocabulary of mathematics are derived from words and word roots from Latin, Greek, and other languages. Some of the most common terms are listed below, to serve as an aid to learning and understanding the terminology of mathematics.

**acute**   from Latin *acus* ("needle") by way of *acutus* ("pointed, sharp")

**algorithm**   distortion of Arabic name *al-Khowarazmi* ("the man from Khwarazm"), whose book on the use of Indo-Arabic numeration was translated into Latin as *Liber Algorismi,* meaning "Book of al-Khowarazmi"

**angle**   from Latin *angulus* ("corner, angle")

**apex**   from Latin word meaning "tip, peak"

**area**   Latin *area* ("vacant piece of ground, plot of ground, open court")

**associative**   from Latin *ad* ("to") and *socius* ("partner, companion")

**axis**   from Latin word meaning "axle, pivot"

**bi-**   from Latin prefix derived from *dui-* ("two"); *bi*nary, *bi*nomial, *bi*sect

**calculate**   from Latin *calc* ("chalk, limestone") and diminutive suffix -*ulus* (a *calculus* was a small pebble; *calculare* meant "to use pebbles" = to do arithmetic)

**cent-**   from Latin *centum* ("hundred"); *cent*imeter, per*cent*

**circum-**   from Latin *circum* ("around"); *circum*ference, *circum*scribe

**co-, col-, com-, con-**   from Old Latin *com* ("together with, beside, near"); *com*mutative, *col*linear, *com*plement, *con*gruent

**commutative**   from Latin *co-* ("together with") and *mutare* ("to move")

**concurrent**   from Latin *co-* ("together with") and *currere* ("to run")

**conjecture**   from Latin *co-* ("together with") and *iactus* ("to throw") [conjecture = throw (ideas) together]

**cylinder**   from Greek *kulindros* ("a roller")

**de-**   Latin preposition *de* ("from, down from, away from, out of"); *de*nominator, *de*duction

**deca-, deka-**   from Greek *deka-* ("ten"); *deca*gon, dode*ca*hedron, *deka*meter

**deci-**   from Latin *decimus* ("tenth"); *deci*mal, *deci*meter

**diagonal**   from Greek *dia-* ("through, across") and *gon-* ("angle")

**diameter**   from Greek *dia-* ("through, across") and *metron* ("measure")

**digit**   from Latin *digitus* ("a finger")

**distribute**   from Latin prefix *dis-* ("apart, away") and Latin *tribu* ["a tribe (of Romans)"]

**empirical**   from Latin *empiricus* ("a physician whose art is founded solely on practice")

**equal**   from Latin *æquus* ("even, level")

**equilateral**   from Latin *æquus* ("even, level") and *latus* ("side")

**equivalent**   from Latin *æquus* ("even, level") and *valere* ("to have value")

**exponent**   from Latin *ex* ("away") and *ponent-* = present participial stem of *ponere* ("to put")

**figure**   from Latin *figura* ("shape, form, figure")

**fraction**   from Latin *fractus,* past participle of *frangere* ("to break")

**geometry**   from Greek *geo-* ("earth") and *metron* ("measure")

**-gon**   from Greek *gonia* ("angle, corner"); poly*gon*, penta*gon*

**-hedron**   from Greek *hedra* ("base, seat"); poly*hedron*, tetra*hedron*

**hept-, sept-**   Greek *hept*, from prehistoric Greek *sept*, meaning "seven"; *hept*agon

**heuristic**   from Greek *heuriskein* ("to find, discover")

**hex-**   from Greek *hex*, from prehistoric Greek *sex*, meaning "six"; *hex*agon, *hex*omino

**icosahedron**   from Greek *eikosi* ("twenty") and *hedra* ("bases, seat")

**inch**   from Latin *uncia*, a unit of weight equal to one twelfth of the *libra*, or Roman pound

**inscribe**   from Latin *in* ("in") and *scribere* ("to scratch"); hence, "to write"

**integer**   from Latin *in-* ("not") and Indo-European root *tag-* ("to touch") (an integer is untouched, hence "whole")

**inverse**   from Latin *in* ("in") and *versus*, past participle of *vertere* ("to turn")

**isosceles**   from Greek *isos* ("equal") and *skelos* ("leg")

**kilo-**   from Greek *khiloi* ("thousand"); *kilo*gram, *kilo*meter

**lateral**   from Latin *latus* ("side")

**lb.**   abbreviation for pound, from *libra*, the Roman unit of weight

**line**   from Latin *linum* ("flax") (The Romans made *linea*, linen thread, from flax.)

**median**   from Latin *medius* ("in the middle")

**meter**   from Greek *metron* ("measure, length")

**milli-**   from Latin *mille* ("one thousand")

**multiply**   from Latin *multi* ("many") and Indo-European *pel* ("to fold")

**nonagon**   from Latin *nonus* ("ninth") and Greek *gon* ("angle")

**number**   from Latin *numerus* ("number")

**obtuse**   from Latin *ob* ("against, near, at") and *tusus* ("to strike, to beat") (*obtusus* = beaten down to the point of being dull)

**oct-**   from Greek *octo* ("eight"); *oct*agon, *oct*ahedron

**parallel**   from Greek *para* ("alongside") and *allenon* ("one another")

**pent-**   Greek *pent* ("five"); *pent*agon, *pent*agram, *pent*omino

**percent**   from Latin *per* ("for") and *centum* ("hundred") [percent = for (each) hundred]

**peri-**   from Greek *peri* ("around"); *peri*meter

**plane**   from Latin *planus* ("flat")

**poly-**   from Greek *polus* ("many"); *poly*gon, *poly*hedra, *poly*omino

**prism**   from Greek *prisma* ("something that has been sawed")

**quadr-**   Latin *quadr-* ("four"); *quadr*ant, *quadr*ilateral

**rectangle**   from Latin *rectangulus* ("right-angled")

**-sect**   from Latin *sectus,* past participle of *secui* ("to cut"); bi*sect*, inter*sect*

**surface**   from Latin *super* ("over") and *facies* ("form, shape")

**symmetric**   from Greek *sun-* ("together with") and *metron* ("measure")

**tetra-**   Greek *tetra-* ("four"); *tetra*hedron, *tetr*omino

**trans-**   Latin *trans* ("across"); *trans*itive, *trans*lation, *trans*versal

**tri-**   from Latin *tri* ("three"); *tri*angle, *tri*sect

**vertex**   from Latin verb *vertere* ("to turn")

**zero**   from Arabic *çifr* ("empty")

# Index

**A**

Abacus, classroom, 133–134
Absolute values
    determining with number-line model, 236
    of integers, 230
Activity-based learning, 452
Acute angles, 458, 459
Acute triangles, 477
Addends, 89
Addition
    addends, 89
    additive-identity property of, 91
    algorithms for, 143–156
    associative property of, 91
    in base five, 151–152
    closure property of, 91
    cumulative property of, 91
    of decimals, 358–359
    defined, 89
    with exchanging, 147–148
    fraction, 292–296
    front-end, 174
    of integers, 240–244
    measurement (number-line) model of, 90–91
    properties of, 91–92
    properties to learn addition facts, 93
    of rational numbers, 318–319
    set model of, 89–90
    summands, 89
    whole-number, 89–92
Addition algorithm, 143, 144–148
    defined, 144
    developing, 145–147
Addition principle of counting
    defined, 781
    for mutually exclusive events, 781–782
Addition property
    of area, 543
    for rational numbers, 322
Addition-by-0 property, 233
Additive identity
    defined, 229
    rational number, 319
Additive inverses
    defined, 228, 229, 319
    integer, 228, 229
    rational number, 319
Additive-identity property
    of integer addition, 242
    of whole-number addition, 91
Adjacent angles, 460, 461
Adjustment, 171–172
Algebra
    equations, 33–34, 405–406
    functions, 406–411
    geometry connections, 433–442
    as great explainer, 29, 35
    NCTM Principles and Standards, 401–402
    as problem-solving strategy, 29–39

rate problem, solving, 34
    steps in reasoning, 32
    variables, 29–39, 402–404
Algebraic expressions, 404–405
    checking, 33
    defined, 404
    evaluation of, 33, 405
    formation, 33
    forming, 404–405
Algorithms
    addition, 143, 144–148
    base five, 150–153
    decimal multiplication, 360
    defined, 126, 211
    division, 162–169
    Euclidean, 211–212
    final, 146
    fraction division, 309–310
    instructional, 146, 148, 159
    multiplication, 156–161
    NCTM Principles and Standards, 158
    partial-difference, 148
    partial-products, 159
    partial-sum, 146
    scaffold, 162, 163
    subtraction, 143, 148–150
Alternate-interior angles, 462
Altitude
    of cones, 498
    of parallelograms, 546
Altitude of triangles, 437–438
    defined, 437, 678, 689
    intersection of, 451
Amanda's telephone number trick, 35–36
*And*
    counting and, 783–786
    operation, 51
Angle bisectors
    constructing, 680–682
    equidistance property of, 680
    intersection of, 451
    paper folding and, 450
Angle sum, of triangle, 451
Angle-angle (AA) property, 693
Angle-angle-angle (AAA) property, 693
Angle-angle-side (AAS) property, 669
Angles
    acute, 458, 459
    adjacent, 460, 461
    alternate interior, 462
    central, 480
    in circles, 460
    complementary, 460, 461
    congruent, 459
    conjugate, 485
    corresponding, 461
    defined, 458
    degrees of, 458
    determining in hexagonal prism, 493–494
    directed, 464

exterior of, 458
    finding in pentagonal arch, 475
    included, 666
    initial side, 464
    interior of, 458, 462
    measure of, 458, 459, 463
    obtuse, 458, 459
    pattern-block, 484–485
    of polygons, 473
    protractors and, 459, 460
    reflex, 459
    in regular *n*-gons, 480–481
    right, 458, 459
    of rotation, 603
    of rotation symmetry, 626
    sides of, 458
    straight, 458, 459
    supplementary, 460, 461
    terminal side, 464
    turn, 603
    vertical, 461
    zero, 458, 459
Angle-side-angle (ASA) property,
        668–669
    congruent triangles, 668–669
    defined, 669
    exploring, 668
Annual compound interest, 387
Apex
    cone, 498
    pyramid, 493
Approximating by rounding, 175–176
Are, metric unit, 534
Area
    addition property of, 543
    of circles, 403, 552
    congruence property of, 543
    of cycloidal arch, 544–545
    defined, 530
    of lattice polygons, 548
    measurement of, 542–564
    of parallelograms, 546–547
    of polygons, 545–548
    of rectangles, 403, 545–546
    of region in the plane, 542
    surface, 572, 580–591
    of trapezoids, 547–548
    of triangles, 69, 451, 547
    units of, 530, 542
Arguing from a special case, 26
Arithmetic
    fundamental theorem of, 191
    mental, 169–172
Arithmetic mean, 733
Arithmetic progressions, 26
Array model for multiplication, 101
Arrows
    diagrams, functions as, 410
    glide, 606
    in integer representation, 235–236

Arrows (*continued*)
  slide, 602
  turn, 603
Associative property
  with Cuisenaire rods, 91
  defined, 74
  of fraction addition, 294
  of integer addition, 242
  of integer multiplication, 259
  of intersections, 74
  with number strips, 91
  of rational number addition, 319
  of rational number multiplication, 321
  of unions, 74
  of whole-number addition, 91
  of whole-number multiplication, 104, 105
Average. *See also* Mean
  defined, 733
  determining, 735–736
Axes, 417

**B**

Babylonian system, 129–130
Backwards problem-solving strategy, 39–40
Balloon rides
  addition and subtraction, 250
  multiplication and division, 263
Bar graphs, 719
Base-10 blocks
  as decimal representation, 341
  defined, 135
  illustrated, 135
Base
  area, 581
  defined, 111, 493
  prism, 493
  pyramid, 493
Base five
  adding in, 151–152
  algorithms, 150–153
  converting from base-ten notation
    to, 139–140
  converting to base-ten notation, 139
  digits and positional values, 139
  notation, 138
  subtracting in, 152–153
  symbols, 151
Base six
  digits and positional values, 139
  multiplication in, 161–162
Base ten
  converting from base-five notation
    to, 139
  converting to base-five notation, 139–140
  positional values in, 133
  system definition, 126
Base twelve, 139
Base-three trick, 142–143
Biased selection criteria, 749
Bilateral symmetry, 625
Border patterns. *See also* Patterns
  classifying, 630
  defined, 628
  illustrated, 628
  symmetry types of, 629
Box and whisker plots. *See* Box plots

Box plots
  advantages, 740
  defined, 713, 739
  illustrated, 739
  as measure of variability, 731
  using for comparisons, 740
Braces, in set definitions, 70
Brainerd, George W., 626
Bridg-It game, 513

**C**

Calculators
  integer addition with, 252
  integer subtraction with, 252
  NCTM Principles and Standards, 144
  statistics routines, 742
Capacity
  defined, 531
  units of, 531, 535
Caps, 72
Cardinal numbers, 79
Cardinality, 79
Cartesian coordinate plane, 417–419
  axes, 417
  defined, 417
  features illustration, 418
  for geometry problems strategy, 433
  illustrated, 417
  origin, 417
  points, plotting, 418–419
  quadrants, 417
Cartesian coordinates
  defined, 417
  in proving triangles as isosceles, 433
Cartesian product, 103
Celsius scale, 537
Center
  of circle, 438, 439
  of dilation, 613
  of gravity, 696
  measuring, 731–748
  numerical definitions, 713, 731
  of rotation, 600
  of symmetry, 626
  variability from, 712
Central angles, 480
Centroid, triangle
  defined, 441, 690
  discovering, 696–697
Checking algebraic expressions, 33
Children's literature, 501
Cicadas, 219
Circle plots. *See* Pie charts
Circles, 438–440
  angles in, 460
  area of, 403, 552
  center of, 438, 439
  circumference of, 403, 550–551
  circumscribed, 680
  defined, 438
  diameter of, 438, 439
  disc, 438
  distances in, 460
  inscribed, 682
  parts of, 438
  perpendicular chords in, 439–440

  radius of, 438, 439
  tangent line to, 439
Circular symmetry, 626
Circumcenter, 680
Circumference of a circle, 550–551
  defined, 550
  Earth calculation, 551
  formula, 403
  $\pi$ (p), 550, 552
Circumscribed circles, 680
Classification problem, solving, 84
Classroom abacus, 133–134
Closed curves, 470
Closure property
  of integer addition, 242
  of integer multiplication, 259
  of integer subtraction, 249
  of rational number addition, 319
  of rational number multiplication, 321
  of whole-number addition, 91
  of whole-number multiplication,
    104, 105
Collinear points. *See also* Points
  defined, 455
  example, 456–457
  illustrated, 456
Colored counters
  addition-by-0 property with, 233
  integer addition with, 240–242
  integer multiplication with, 257–258
  integer subtraction with, 246–248
  interpreting sets of, 232
  negatives with, 233–234
  representing integers with, 231–232
Colored region models, 276–277
Combinations, 791–801
  activity, 798–799
  computing, 795
  computing probability using, 807–808
  defined, 791
  formulas for, 793–795
  mutually exclusive/complementary events
    and, 809
  notation, 792
  problem solving with, 795–797
  *r*-combination, 791
  with repetition, 800
Combining divisibility tests, 205
Common denominators. *See also* Denominators;
  Fractions
  defined, 281
  division by finding, 310
  finding, 282–283
  least, 282
  in rational number addition, 319
Common multiples, 221
Common vertex, 493
Commutative property
  of integer addition, 242
  of intersections, 74
  of rational number addition, 319
  of rational number multiplication, 321
  of unions, 74
  of whole-number addition, 91
  of whole-number multiplication,
    104, 105
Comparison model, 94

Comparisons
  box plots for, 740
  rational number, 285
Complement of a set *A,* 71
Complementary angles, 460, 461
Complementary events, 786–787
  mutually exclusive events/combinations
      and, 809
  probability of, 808–809
Composite numbers
  defined, 189
  via rectangular arrays, 186
Compound interest
  annual, 387
  calculating, 387
  defined, 386–387
  principal and, 387
Computational estimation. *See* Estimation
Concave figures, 472
Conclusions, 53
Concurrent lines
  defined, 456
  example, 456–457
  set of, 437
Conditional equations, 405
Conditional probability
  defined, 804
  determining, 804
  formula for, 805
Conditional statements, 52–53
Cones
  altitude of, 498
  defined, 498
  general, 499
  lateral surface of, 498
  oblique circular, 498
  right circular, 498, 584
  surface area of, 584
  volume of, 574–575
Congruence, 702
  copycat activity, 672
  measurement criterion to determine, 659
  property of area, 543
  relation, 661
Congruent angles
  defined, 459
  to given angle, 663
Congruent figures, 612
Congruent line segments
  constructing, 659–660
  defined, 458, 659
Congruent triangles, 659–676
  angle-angle-side (AAS) property, 669
  angle-side-angle (ASA) property, 668–669
  corresponding parts and, 660–661
  defined, 660
  line segments, 659–660
  side-angle-side (SAS) property, 665–668
  side-side-side (SSS) property, 663
  triangle inequality, 663–665
Conjecture, 49
Conjugate angles, 485
Constant of proportionality, 373
Constants, 402
Constructions, 676–691, 704
  of angle bisectors, 680–682
  with geometry software, 684–685

of midpoints, 679
Mira, 683–684
paper-folding, 683–684
of parallel lines, 676–677
of perpendicular bisectors, 678–679
of perpendicular lines, 677–678
of regular polygons, 682–683
in space, 681
Contraction, 614
Contradiction, proof of, 54
Convex curves, 472
Convex figures, 472
Convex polygons, 473
Coordinate axes, 417
Coordinate geometry, 418
Coordinates, 704
  Cartesian, 417, 433
  rigid motions with, 621
  similarity transformation with, 621
  size transformation with, 621
  *x,* 417
  *y,* 417
Copycat congruence activity, 672
Corner mirrors, 620
Corresponding angles, 461
Corresponding angles property, 461–462
Cost of debt, computing, 388
Counterexamples, 47, 75
Counting
  addition principle, 781
  addition principle for mutually exclusive
      events, 782
  complementary events and, 786–787
  Hands On, 68
  multiplication principle, 783
  multiplication principle for independent
      events, 784
  principles of, 780–790
  word *and* and, 783–786
  word *or* and, 780–782
Cubes, 495
  dissection of, 575
  for whole number representation, 82
Cuisenaire rods, 82, 91
Cups, 73
*Curricular Focal Points for Prekindergarten
    Through Grade 8 Mathematics,* 712
Curves
  classification of, 470
  convex, 472
  distribution, 754
  Jordan curve theorem, 471
  length of, 549–551
  perimeter, 549–550
  polygonal, 472
  simple, 470
  simple closed, 470, 470–471
  in space, 490–491
Customary system. *See also* Measurement
  units of area, 530
  units of capacity, 531
  units of length, 529
  units of volume, 530–531
Cycloids
  area of arch, 544–545
  defined, 544
  length of, 549

Cylinders
  defined, 498
  lateral surface of, 498
  oblique, 498
  right, 498
  surface area of, 580–581, 582
  volume of, 574, 579

**D**

da Vinci, Leonardo, 544
Data
  grouping into classes, 716
  organizing and representing, 713–731
  variation of, 731–748
Data sets
  characteristics observed by dot plots, 732
  defined, 713
  mean of, 733
  median of, 734
  mode of, 734
  standard deviation of, 741
  typical value, determining, 736
  uniform, 744
Debit/Credit Game (Hands On), 228
Decagons, 474
Decimal point, 339
Decimal system, 126, 127, 132, 339. *See also*
    Indo-Arabic system
Decimals
  adding, 358–359
  base-ten blocks representation, 341
  characterizing rational numbers as, 350
  computations with, 357–366
  converting fractions to, 346
  defined, 339
  dividing, 361
  dividing by powers of 10, 343–344
  dollars, dimes and pennies representation,
      341–342
  expanded exponential form, 343
  expanded form, 340
  expansions, 348–349
  manipulatives for, 340–343
  multiplying, 360–361
  multiplying by powers of 10, 343–344
  nonterminating, nonrepeating, 351
  ordering, 350–351
  as percents, 382
  percents as, 382
  positional values, 342
  repeating, 346–350
  representations of, 340–343
  rounding, 357–358
  small squares representation, 340–341
  strips representation, 340–341
  subtracting, 358–359
  terminating, 344–346
  unit squares representation, 340–341
Decomposing problems strategy, 573, 580
Deductive reasoning. *See also* Reasoning
  conclusion, 53
  defined, 53
  examples, 53
  premises (hypotheses), 53
  as problem-solving strategy, 55
  rule of direct reasoning, 53–54

Deductive reasoning (*continued*)
    rule of indirect reasoning, 54
    using, 54–55
Definitions, 501
Degree, vertex, 506
Degrees, angle
    defined, 458
    minutes, 469
    seconds, 469
Denominators. *See also* Fractions
    common, 281–283
    defined, 276
    negative integer or zero, 276
Density property of rational numbers, 322–323
Dependent events, 774, 805
Descartes, René, 103, 418
Descriptive statistics, 749
Diagram problem-solving strategy, 14–16
    defined, 14
    using, 15–16
Diagrams
    colored-counter, 240–241
    fraction-circle, 302
    functions as, 410
    number-line, 244, 245–246, 251
    place-value, 146
    proportional reasoning with, 374
    tree, 790
    Venn, 71, 72–73, 75, 84
Diameter
    of circles, 438, 439
    of trees, 512
Differences, divisibility of, 201–202
Diffy, 95–96
    defined, 95
    with fractions, 300
Digits, 133
    random sequence of, 750
    significant, 364
Dilations
    center of, 613, 615
    contraction, 614
    defined, 613
    distance change under, 614
    expansion, 614
    illustrated, 615
    scale factor, 613
Dimensional analysis, 537
Dimes, as decimal representation, 341–342
Direct reasoning, rule of, 53–54
Directed angles, 464
Discs
    defined, 438
    paper, 481–482
Disjoint sets, 72
Distance formula, 403, 419–420
Distances
    between points, 457–458
    change under dilation, 614
    in circles, 460
    viewing, 566–567
Distribution curve, 754
Distributions, 753–757
    nonuniform, 744
    normal, 753–754
    standardized form, 755
    uniform, 744

Distributive property
    of integer multiplication, 259
    of intersections, 74
    of rational number multiplication, 321
    of unions, 74
    of whole-number multiplication, 104, 105
Dividends, 107
Divides, 188
Divisibility
    by 2, 202
    by 3, 203–204
    by 4, 202–203
    by 5, 202
    by 7, 206
    by 8, 202–203
    by 9, 203–204
    by 10, 202
    by 11, 204–205, 206
    by 13, 206
    combining tests for, 205
    defined, 188
    of natural numbers, 187–201
    by products, 205
    summary of tests, 207
    of sums and differences, 201–202
    tests for, 201–209
    unified test for, 206
Division
    balloon rides and, 263
    decimals, 361
    decimals by powers of 10, 343–344
    defined, 106
    dividends, 107
    divisors, 107
    of exponentials, 110–112
    fraction, 301, 302, 307–313
    by grouping, 106
    integer, 260–263
    measurement, 106
    NCTM Principles and Standards, 110
    partition model of, 106
    partitive, 106
    quotients, 107
    of rational numbers, 321–322
    with remainders, 108–109
    repeated-subtraction model, 106
    by sharing, 106
    of whole numbers, 105–112
    by zero, 108
Division algorithms
    defined, 109
    in integers, 262–263
    long-division, 162–163
    in problem solving, 109–110
    short-division, 164
    theorem, 162
Divisors
    defined, 107, 188
    greatest common, 187, 209
    of natural numbers, 192
    prime, 193
    proper, 188
Dodecahedra, 495
Dollars, as decimal representation, 341–342
Dot plots
    data set characteristics, 732
    defined, 713, 714

    illustrated, 714
    outliers, 714
    standard deviation, 742
Dot representations, 50–51
Dot symbol (*), 101
Double pyramids (dipyramids), 500
Drafting triangles, 460
Drawing lines, 455
Dual, tiling, 647

**E**

Earth
    circumference calculation, 551
    comparing with Jupiter, 585–586
Easier, similar problem strategy, 23
Easy combinations. *See also* Mental arithmetic
    defined, 169
    using, 171
Edges
    counting, 507–508
    polygonal curve, 472
    polyhedra, 492
Egyptian numeration system, 127–128
Elements. *See also* Sets
    defined, 69
    order of, 70
Eliminate possibilities strategy, 41–42
Empty sets
    defined, 72
    properties of, 74
Endpoints
    line segments, 457
    rays, 458
English system. *See* Customary system
Envelope tetrahedron model, 495–496
Equal sets, 72
Equal sign ($=$), 405
Equally likely outcomes, 801, 802
Equation Balance Scale (Hands On), 400–401
Equations. *See also* Algebra
    conditional, 405
    defined, 405
    equal sign ($=$), 405
    equivalent, 405
    identity, 405
    of lines, 422–426
    setting up and solving, 33–34
    solution set, 405
    tangent line to circle at a point, 439
    variables as unknowns in, 403
Equiangular hexagons, 480
Equiangular polygons, 479
Equidistance property
    of angle bisector, 680
    of perpendicular bisector, 679
Equilateral hexagons, 480
Equilateral polygons, 479
Equilateral triangles, 477
Equivalent equations, 405
Equivalent fractions
    cross-product property of, 279
    defined, 278
    equality symbol, 278
    fraction-strip model for, 278
    fundamental law of fractions and, 279
    using, 279–280

Equivalent rigid motions, 607
Equivalent sets, 80–81
Equivalent transformations, 602
Escher, Maurits Cornelius, 642
Escher-like tilings, 642–645
    creating, 644–645
    illustrated, 643, 644, 645
Estimation
    defined, 173
    fraction, 323–324
    front-end, 174
    goal of, 174
    methods for, 126
    NCTM Principles and Standards, 174
    population means and standard deviation,
        751–752
    rounding, 175–176
Euclidean algorithm
    defined, 212
    greatest common divisor from, 211–212
    least common multiple by, 215
    theorem, 212
    using, 212
Euler, Leonhard, 504, 505
Euler paths, 506
Euler's formula for polyhedra
    defined, 495
    discovering, 496–497
    notation, 495
    theorem, 497
Euler's traversability theorem, 507
Evaluation of algebraic expressions, 33, 405
Even numbers, 188
Even vertex, 506
Events
    complementary, 786–787, 808–809
    defined, 772
    dependent, 774, 805
    independent, 774–775, 784, 805
    mutually exclusive, 772, 773–774
    non-mutually exclusive, 773–774
    theoretical probability of, 802
Exchanges
    addition with, 147–148
    creating with units, strips, and mats, 144–145
    defined, 126
Exchanging
    multiplication with, 160
    use of, 126
Existence
    of additive inverses, 319
    of multiplicative inverse, 321
    of negatives of integer addition, 242
Expanded form
    decimals, 340
    exponential, 343
Expanded notation, 133, 159
Expansion, 614
Expected value, 813–814
Experimental probability, 769–779. See also
        Probability
    computing examples, 771–772
    computing from data, 771
    computing from experiments, 772
    computing from histogram, 771
    connections with statistics, 770–771
    defined, 769

    determining, 768, 770
    determining geometrically, 775
    determining with simulation, 775–776
    of independent events, 775
    of mutually exclusive events, 773
    of non-mutually exclusive events, 773–774
Experiments
    determining experimental probabilities
        from, 772
    expected value of, 813
    two-stage, 783
Exploring Reflection and Rotation Symmetry
        (Hands On), 600
Exponential expressions, 111
Exponential functions, 426, 428
Exponents
    division rules for, 112
    multiplication rules of, 111
    working with, 111
    zero as, 112
Exterior
    of angles, 458
    angles of polygons, 473
    of simple closed curves, 471

F

Faces of polyhedra, 492, 497–498
Fact families, 107
Factor trees, 189–190
Factorials, 792–793
Factors. See also Divisors
    defined, 101, 188
    finding, 190
    greatest common, 209
    prime, 1, 195
Fahrenheit scale, 536
Fermat point, 691
Fermat primes, 683
Fermat's principle, 620
Fibonacci (Leonardo of Pisa), 19
Fibonacci numbers, 19
Fibonacci sequence, 19
Figures, 449–522
    concave, 472
    congruent, 612
    constructing, 676–685
    convex, 472
    geometric, 449–522
    midpoint, 695, 696
    plane, 455–470
    reflection symmetry, 600
    rotation symmetry, 600
    similar, 614, 692, 703
    similar, comparing measurements of, 586–587
    in space, 490–504
    with translation symmetries, 628
    vertex, 637
Final algorithm, 146
Finite sets, 81
5-up rule
    for rounding, 175
    for rounding decimals, 357
Five-pointed star, 476
Fixed points, 616
Flips, 604
Folded Fractions (Hands On), 274

Formulas
    area of a circle, 403, 552
    area of a parallelogram, 546
    area of a rectangle, 403, 546
    area of a trapezoid, 548
    area of a triangle, 547
    circumference of a circle, 403
    for combinations, 793–795
    commonly used, 403
    for conditional probability, 805
    distance, 403, 419–420
    for division of fractions, 310
    Euler's, 495, 496–497
    expressing with variables, 403
    functions as, 409
    interest, 403
    perimeter of a rectangle, 403
    for permutations, 793–795
    Pick's, 563–564
    for subtraction of rational numbers, 320
    surface area of right circular cone, 584
    surface area of right regular pyramid, 583
    surface area of sphere, 585
    triangular numbers, 403
    variables for determining, 30–32
    volume of a sphere, 576
    volume of general prism and cylinder, 574
    volume of pyramid or cone, 575
    volume of right prism or right cylinder, 573
Fraction addition. See also Fractions
    associative property, 294
    defined, 292
    fraction-circle model for, 292, 293
    fraction-strip model for, 293
    introducing, 298
    number-line model for, 292, 293
    performing, 293–294
    with unlike denominators, 293
Fraction circles, 277
    in fraction addition, 292, 293
    in fraction multiplication, 302
Fraction division. See also Fractions
    computation, 301
    defined, 308
    by finding common denominators, 310
    by finding common numerators, 309
    formulas for, 310
    by grouping, 308–309
    by "invert and multiply" rule, 310
    missing-factor interpretation, 308
    with missing-factor model, 312–313
    performing, 310
    questions for, 302
    with rectangular area model, 316
    as repeated subtraction, 307
    by sharing, 308–309
Fraction multiplication. See also Fractions
    computation, 301
    example, 306–307
    by fraction, 304–305
    by integers, 302–303
    on number line, 307
    products, 305–306
    questions for, 302
Fraction strips
    defined, 277
    for equivalent fractions, 278

Fraction strips (*continued*)
in fraction addition, 293
illustrated, 277
in ordering fractions, 284–285
Fraction subtraction. *See also* Fractions
defined, 297
introducing, 298
models, 296
performing, 297
Fraction tiles, 286
Fractions
basic concepts, 275–292
colored-region models, 276–277
common denominators, 281–283
converting to decimals, 346
defined, 276
denominator, 276
Diffy with, 300
division, 307–313
equivalent, 278–280
estimating, 323–324
as extension of measurement, 330
fraction multiplication by, 304–305
in lowest terms, 280
in measurement problems, 275–276
mental arithmetic, 324–325
models for, 276
NCTM Principles and Standards, 284
number-line model, 278
numerator, 276
as operators, 331
ordering, 284–285
as percents, 383–384
percents as, 382–383
proper, 295
as rational number representation, 331
rational numbers, 284–285
reciprocals, 310–312
residual strategy, 284
rounding, 323–324
set model, 277
in simplest form, 280–281
simplifying, 281
terminating decimals as, 344–345
transitive strategy, 284
Frequency
defined, 715
of the interval, 715
polygons, 717
relative, 753
Front-end estimation, 174
Functions. *See also* Algebra
as arrow diagrams, 410
defined, 406, 407
defining, 406–409
denoted by letters, 407
describing and visualizing, 409–411
examples, 407
exponential, 426, 428
as formulas, 409
graphing, 417–429
as graphs, 410
image values, 407
linear, 411, 417
as machines, 410
nonlinear, 426–429
quadratic, 426–427

range of, 407, 408
as sequences, 409
as tables, 410
vertical-line test, 407
Fundamental theorem of arithmetic, 191

**G**

Gauss, Carl, 30, 31
Gauss-Wantzel constructibility theorem, 683
GCD. *See* Greatest common divisor
General cones, 498
Generalized variables, 402
Geometric figures. *See* Figures
Geometric probability
defined, 814
determining, 815
Geometric progressions, 63
Geometry
algebra connections between, 433–442
manipulatives, 455
materials for explorations, 453
NCTM Principles and Standards, 453
software, 684–685
taxicab, 441
transformational, 601
Germain, Sophie, 190
Germain primes, 197, 220–222
Getting Rhombunctious! Folding Paper Polygons
(Hands On), 658
Glide arrows, 606
Glide mirror, 606
Glide vectors, 606
Glide-reflections. *See also* Rigid motions
defined, 606
determining, 607
illustrated, 608
Glides, 606
Gold Coin Game
Hands On, 2
working backwards strategy, 39–40
Goldbach conjecture, 222
Golden triangles, 698
Graphing functions, 417–429
Cartesian coordinate plane, 417–419
distance formula, 419–420
equations of lines, 422–426
exponentials, 426
nonlinear, 426–429
quadratics, 426
slope, 420–422
Graphs
bar, 719
functions as, 410
line, 716–718, 730
points of, 411
Greater than, 245
Greater than or equal to, 245
Greatest common divisors
defined, 187, 209
from Euclidean algorithm, 211–212
by intersection of sets, 210
from prime factorization, 210–211
technology for finding, 216
Grouping, division of fractions
by, 308–309
Growth, mathematics of, 388

Guess and check strategy
defined, 4
examples, 5–6, 11–13
Pólya's principles and, 10–13
Guess My Rule game, 16
*Guidelines for Assessment and Instruction in
Statistics Education (GAISE) Report*, 712

**H**

Hands On. *See also* Manipulatives
Counting Cars and Trains, 68
Debit/Credit Game, 228
Equation Balance Scale, 400–401
Exploring Reflection and Rotation
Symmetry, 600
Folded Fractions, 274
Gold Coin Game, 2
How Many Beans in the Bag?, 712
Metric Measurement and Estimation
Tournament, 524–525
Numbers from Rectangles, 126
Primes and Composites via Rectangular
Arrays, 186
Strings and Loops, 768
Triangles and Squares, 338
Triangles via Paper Folding, 450–451
Hectare, metric unit, 534
Heptadecagon, 473
Heptagons, 474
Hexagons
defined, 474
illustrated, 474
types of, 480
Hexominos, 503
Hieroglyphics, 127
Hinged polygons, 681
Histograms
computing experimental probability from, 771
defined, 713, 715
frequency, 715
frequency of the interval, 715
illustrated, 715, 716
Hooke's law, 431
How Many Beans in the Bag? (Hands
On), 712
Hypatia, 408
Hypotenuse, midpoint of, 451
Hypotheses, 53

**I**

Icosahedra, 495
Identification, 79
Identity equations, 405
Identity transformation, 602, 607
"If…then" statements
defined, 52
proving, 52–53
Images
defined, 407, 601
finding under reflections, 605–606
finding under rotations, 604
finding under translation, 603
Incenter, 681
Incircles, 681
Included angles, 666

Inclusion, transitivity of, 74
Incorrect, 44
Independent events, 774–775
 defined, 784, 805
 multiplication principle of counting
  for, 784, 805
Indirect reasoning, rule of, 54
Indo-Arabic system
 defined, 132
 digits, 133
 expanded notation, 133
 positional values, 133
 power of, 127
 symbols, 132
Inductive reasoning. *See also* Reasoning
 counterexamples, 47
 defined, 47
 as problem-solving strategy, 49
 with pyramidal sums, 50
 using, 47–49
Infinite sets, 81
Initial side, angles, 464
Inscribed circles of triangles, 682
Inscribed polygons, 682
Instructional algorithms, 146, 148, 159
 adding with, 148
 base five and, 151, 152
 subtracting with, 149, 150
Integer addition, 240–244. *See also*
  Addition
 balloon rides and, 250
 with calculator, 252
 with colored-counter sets, 240–241
 defined, 241
 with mail-time stories, 242–243, 249
 with number line, 243–244
 properties of, 242
 using, 241–242
Integer division, 260–264. *See also* Division
 defined, 261
 performing, 261, 262
 with remainders, 262
 rule of signs, 261
 zero and, 261
Integer multiplication, 257–260. *See also*
  Multiplication
 balloon rides and, 263
 with colored counters, 257–258
 fractions, 303–304
 with mail-time stories, 259
 with number line, 259–260
 by positive integers, 257
 properties, 259
 rule of signs, 258
 using, 258
Integer representation, 229–233
 addition-by-0 with colored counters, 233
 arrows in, 235–236
 colored counter sets, 240, 246
 colored counters, 231–232, 257–258
 criteria for, 230–231
 mail-time, 234
 negatives with colored counters,
  233–234
 nonzero number, 230
 number-line, 234–236
 zero, 231

Integer subtraction, 246–256. *See also* Subtraction
 by adding the opposite, 248–249
 balloon rides and, 250
 with calculator, 252
 closure property, 249
 with colored-counter sets, 246–248
 defined, 248
 diagrams for, 247
 with number line, 250–252
Integers, 227–272
 absolute value of, 230
 additive inverse, 228
 defined, 228
 mail-time situations for, 234
 multiplication of fractions by, 302–303
 NCTM Principles and Standards, 229
 negative, 228
 opposite, 228, 229, 231
 pairs, ordering, 245
 positive, 228
 sets, ordering, 244–246
 understanding, 239
Interest
 compound, 386–387
 formula, 403
Interior
 of angles, 458
 angles of polygons, 473
 of simple closed curves, 471
Interquartile range
 defined, 738
 determining, 739
 as measure of variability, 731
Intersections
 of altitudes of triangle, 451
 of angle bisectors, 451
 associative property of, 74
 commutative property of, 74
 distributive property of, 74
 greatest common divisors by, 210
 least common multiple by, 213
 of lines, 434
 of medians of triangle, 451
 of perpendicular bisectors, 451
 planes, 490
 of sets, 72, 210, 213
Invariance, 704
Invert-and-multiply rule, 310
 consequence of, 310–311
 formula, 310
IQR. *See* Interquartile range
Irrational numbers
 defined, 340, 351
 proving, 352–353
Irrationality of √2, 351–352
Irregular polygons, 640–642
Isometric drawings, 500
Isometry. *See* Rigid motions
Isorhythmic patterns, 212
Isosceles trapezoids, 479
Isosceles triangles, 477
 converse theorem, 669
 theorem, 667

**J**

Jordan curve theorem, 471

**K**

Kepler, Johannes, 640
Kilogram, metric unit, 536
Kites, 479
Königsberg bridge problem, 504–507

**L**

Lateral surface
 area, 581
 of cones, 498
 of cylinders, 498
Lattice polygons, 483
Law of large numbers, 769
Law of trichotomy, 245
Least common denominators, 282
Least common multiples, 212–216, 221
 application of, 215
 defined, 187, 213
 by Euclidean algorithm, 215
 by intersection of sets, 213
 from prime factorizations, 213–214
 technology for finding, 216
Length
 of curves, 549–551
 of cycloids, 549
 of line segments, 457
 metric units of, 532–533
 of nonpolygonal curves, 549
 of the period, 347
 of polygonal curves, 549
 units of, 529
Less than
 defined, 245
 in order relation on rational numbers, 285
Less than or equal to, 245
Lightening distance function, 431
Limits, 704
Line equations, 422–426
 determining, 422–423
 point-slope form, 424
 slope-intercept form, 424–425
 through two points, 425–426
 two-point form, 425–426
Line graphs, 716–718, 730
 defined, 713, 716
 estimating data values from, 718
 frequency polygon, 717
 illustrated, 717
Line plots. *See* Dot plots
Line segments
 congruent, 458, 659–660
 defined, 420, 457
 endpoints, 457
 length of, 457
 midpoint of, 435, 458, 678–680
 perpendicular bisector of, 678–680
 slope of, 421
Line symmetry. *See* Reflection symmetry
Linear functions, 417
 characterizing property, 424
 defined, 411
Lines
 arrangements in a plane, 456
 concurrent, 456
 concurrent set of, 437

Lines (*continued*)
  defined, 455
  drawing, 455
  intersection of, 434
  parallel, 434–436, 490
  perpendicular, 436–438, 459
  of reflection, 604
  skew, 490
  slope of, 375, 421
  in space, 490
  of symmetry, 625
  traversal, 456
Liter, metric unit, 535
Loci, 704
Logical structures, 704
Long-division algorithm. *See also* Division
    algorithms
  defined, 162
  scaffold, 163
  using, 163
Look back principle, 10
Lower quartiles, 731, 737
Lowest terms, fractions in, 280

**M**

Machines, functions as, 410
Mail-time representations of integers, 234
Mail-time stories
  integer addition with, 242–243
  integer multiplication with, 259
  integer subtraction with, 249
Manipulatives
  abacuses, 133–134
  addition algorithm with, 144
  base-10 blocks, 135
  computing quotients with, 107
  for decimal representation, 340–343
  geometry, 455
  sticks and bundles, 134–135
  units, strips, and mats, 135
  use of, 134
Mass, 535–536
Matching sets, 80
Mathematical habit of the mind (MHM),
    25, 68
Mathematical statements, 51–53
Mathematics
  early origins of, 69
  of growth, 388
  in motion, 627–628
  problem solving in, 58
Mats
  defined, 135
  exchanges with, 144–145
Maxima, 704
Mayan numeration system
  defined, 130
  numerals, 131
  position values, 131
  using, 132
  vertical style, 131
Means
  arithmetic, 733
  as center description, 713, 731
  defined, 733
  determining, 735

estimating, 751–752
finding, 733–734
fraction of data values near, 743
population, 751–752
Measure of angles. *See also* Angles
  defined, 458
  degrees, 458
  directed angles, 464
  in five-pointed star, 476
  in regular *n*-gon, 480
  sums in convex polygon, 473
  tools for, 459, 460
  in triangles, 463
Measurement, 704
  area, 542–564
  attributes, 526
  comparison, 586–587
  customary system, 529–531
  fractions as extension of, 330
  length of curves, 549–551
  metric system, 532–537
  NCTM Principles and Standards, 527
  in nonstandard units, 542–543
  perimeter, 542–564
  practical purpose of, 529
  principles and processes, 526
  problem solving with, 583–584
  problems, fractions in, 275–276
  process, 526–537
  process steps, 527
  similarity principle of, 586–587
  tangram, 527–529
  units, 526
Measurement division, 106
Measurement model
  illustrating properties via, 92
  in subtraction of fractions, 296
  of whole-number addition, 90–91
Measures of central tendency, 731
Measures of variability, 737–739
  examples of, 731
  midrange, 737
  range, 737
Medial triangles, 695–696
Medians, 748
  as center definition, 713, 731
  of data set, 734
  defined, 469, 687, 734
  determining, 735, 739
  intersection of, 451
Members. *See* Elements
Mental arithmetic
  adjustment, 171–172
  easy combinations, 169–171
  fractions, 324–325
  one-digit facts, 169
  working from left to right, 172–173
Meter, metric unit, 532
Metric Measurement and Estimation Tournament
    (Hands On), 524–525
Metric system, 532–537
  are, 534
  Celsius scale, 537
  defined, 532
  hectare, 534
  kilogram, 536
  liter, 535

meter, 532
prefixes, 532
SI system and, 532
units, changing, 534
units of area, 534
units of capacity, 535
units of length, 532–533
units of mass, 535–536
units of temperature, 536–537
units of volume, 535
units of weight, 535–536
MHM (mathematical habit of the
    mind), 25
Midpoints
  constructing, 678–680
  defined, 458
  figures, 695, 696
  of hypotenuse, 451
  line segment, 435
  of two sides of triangle, 435–436
Midrange, 737
Minima, 704
Minuend, 93
Minutes, 469
Mira, 605, 683–684
Mirror lines, 604, 625
Mirrors
  corner, 620
  glide, 606
Misleading representations, 722
Missing-addend model, 94, 296
Missing-factor model, 312–313
Mixed numbers
  defined, 295
  visualization, 295
  working with, 295–296
Modes, 748
  as center definition, 713, 731
  defined, 734
  determining, 735
Multilink Cubes, 82
Multiples, 188, 221
Multiplication
  array model, 101
  associative property of, 104, 105
  base six, 161–162
  of binomial expressions, 105
  Cartesian product model, 102–103
  closed under, 104, 105
  commutative property of, 104
  of decimals, 360–361
  of decimals by powers of 10, 343–344
  distributive property of, 104, 105
  dot symbol, 101
  with exchanging, 160
  of exponentials, 111
  factors, 101
  fraction, 301, 302–307
  integer, 257–260
  multidigit numbers, 160
  multiplicative identity property, 104, 105
  NCTM Principles and Standards, 110
  properties of, 104–105
  of rational numbers, 320–321
  rectangular area model, 101–102
  as repeated addition, 100–101
  skip counting, 101

skip-count model, 102
tree model, 102
of whole numbers, 100–105
Multiplication algorithm, 156–161
defined, 157
developing, 158
partial-products, 159
Multiplication by zero, 321
Multiplication principle of counting
defined, 783
for independent events, 784, 805
Multiplicative inverses
defined, 311
rational numbers, 320, 321
reciprocals as, 310–312
solving equations with, 321
Multiplicative property
of integer multiplication, 259
of rational numbers, 322
Multiplicative-identity property
of integer multiplication, 259
of rational numbers, 321
Mutually exclusive events
addition principle of counting for, 782
complementary events/combinations
and, 809
counting and *or* and, 781–782
defined, 772
experimental probability of, 773

**N**

Napoleon point, 691
National Council of Teachers of Mathematics
(NCTM), 2
Natural numbers
composite, 189–191
defined, 70
divisibility of, 187–201
divisors of, 192
prime, 189–191
NCTM Principles and Standards
algebra, 401–402
algorithms, 158
calculators, 144
estimation, 174
fractions, 284
fractions, decimals, percents equivalence, 342
geometry, 453
integers, 229
measurement, 527
multiplication and division operations, 110
numbers, 187
place-value concepts, 144
probability, 769
problem solving, 3, 9
proof, 48
reasoning, 47, 48
representations, 49, 50
statistics, 713
symmetry, 625
three-dimensional shapes, 685
Negative integers
with colored counters, 233–234
defined, 228, 229
denominator, 276
numerator, 276

Negatives
with colored counters, 233–234
defined, 319
determining, 233
existence, integer addition property, 242
integer, 228
rational number, 319
Networks, 504–510
defined, 504, 505
illustrated examples, 505
Königsberg bridge problem, 504–507
paths, 506
planar, 507, 508, 509–510
as representations, 511
total degree, 510
traversable, 506
*n*-gons, 474
Noether, Emmy, 406
Nominal numbers, 79
Non uniform distribution, 744
Nonagons, 474
Nondecimal positional systems, 138–143
Nonlinear functions, 426–429
defined, 426
exponential, 426, 428
graphing, 427
quadratic, 426–427
Non-mutually exclusive events, 773–774
Nonstandard units, 542–543
Nonterminating, nonrepeating decimals, 351
Normal distribution. *See also* Distributions
areas to left of *z* scores for, 764–765
defined, 753
illustrated, 754
68-95-99.7 rule for, 754
Number lines
fraction multiplication on, 307
for given sum, 244
integer addition with, 243–244
integer multiplication with, 259–260
integer subtraction with, 250–252
real numbers and, 353–354
representation of integers, 234–236
subtraction model, 94–95
for whole number representation, 83,
90–91
Number strips
associative property with, 91
for whole number representation, 82
Number systems
properties of, 393–394
rational, 318–325
Number theory, 185–225
Number-line diagrams
for given sum, 244
for integer subtraction, 251
properties of inequalities with, 245–246
Number-line models
determining absolute values with, 236
for fraction addition, 292, 293
fractions, 278
Numbers
cardinal, 79
composite, 186, 189–191
even, 188
expression of, 79
irrational, 340, 351

large, law of, 769
least common multiple, 187
mixed, 295–296
natural. *See* Natural numbers
NCTM Principles and Standards, 187
nominal, 79
odd, 188
odd perfect, 222
ordinal, 79
perfect, 197
prime, 186, 189–191
random, 751
rational. *See* Rational numbers
real, 351
from rectangles, 126
symbols for writing, 126
triangular, 403
whole. *See* Whole numbers
Numbers from Rectangles (Hands On), 126
Numerals, 126
Numeration systems
Babylonian, 129–130
defined, 126
Egyptian, 127–128
history of, 127
Indo-Arabic, 127, 132–133
Mayan, 130–132
Roman, 128–129
Numerators. *See also* Fractions
common, division by finding, 309–310
defined, 276
negative integer or zero, 276
Numerical sequences, looking for patterns in,
18–20

**O**

Objects, 69
Oblique circular cones, 498
Oblique cylinders, 498
Oblique prisms, 493
Obtuse angles, 458, 459
Obtuse triangles, 477
Octagons, 474
Octahedra, 495
Odd numbers
defined, 188
perfect, 222
representing, 188
Odd vertex, 506
Odds
defined, 812
from probabilities, 813
probabilities from, 812
One-digit facts, 169
One-to-one correspondence, 80
Open-Topped Box problem, 428–429
Operations
and/or, 51
power, 110
on sets, 68, 71–73
Operators
fractions as, 331
multiplication of integers by fractions, 303
Opposite
defined, 228, 229, 231
of the opposite of an integer, 233

Opposite (*continued*)
  rational number, 319
  subtraction by addition, 248–249
Or
  counting and, 780–782
  mutually exclusive events and, 781–782
  operation, 51
Order relation
  properties on rational numbers, 322
  on rational numbers, 285
Ordered pairs, 102
Ordering
  decimals, 350–351
  fractions, 284–285
  integer sets, 244–246
  whole numbers, 83–84
Orderly list strategy
  in counting, 783
  defined, 13
  Pólya's principles and, 13–14
Ordinal numbers, 79
Orientation-preserving transformations, 606
Orientation-reversing transformations, 606
Origin, Cartesian coordinate plane, 417
Orthocenter, of triangles, 689
Outcomes, 772
  equally likely, 801, 802
  tree diagrams and, 790
Outliers
  defined, 714, 738, 739
  determining, 739

P

Palindromes, 634
Pantographs, 620
Paper discs, 481–482
Paper-folding constructions, 683–684
Parallel lines
  condition for, 434
  constructing, 676–678
  defined, 434
  example, 435–436
  proof, 434
  in space, 490
Parallel planes, 490
Parallelograms
  altitude, 546
  area of, 546–547
  base, 546
  defined, 479
  height, 546
  illustrated, 479
  modifying with translations, 643
Partial-difference algorithm, 148
Partial-products algorithm, 159
Partial-sum algorithm, 146
Partition model of division, 106
Partitive division, 106
Pascal, Blaise, 24
Pascal's identity, 796
Pascal's triangle, 22–26
  defined, 22, 23
  finding patterns in, 25–26
  illustrated, 24
  numbered rows and diagonals, 24
Paths, 506

Pattern-block angles, 484–485
Pattern-block shapes, 484
Pattern-block symmetries, 633
Patterns
  border, 628–630
  dot representations in discovering, 50–51
  periodic, 628
  problem-solving strategy, 18–20
  in row sums of Pascal's triangle, 25–26
  wallpaper, 628, 630
  in world cultures, 638, 646
Pennies, as decimal representation, 341–342
Pentagonal arch, 475
Pentagons, 474
Pentominoes, 646
Percentiles
  defined, 756
  of population in an interval, 757
  of populations, 756
  of samples, 757
Percents, 381–393
  compound interest, 386–387
  cost of debt, computing, 388
  as decimals, 382
  decimals as, 382
  decreases, computing, 386
  defined, 381, 382
  examples of, 381
  finding, of whole number, 392
  as fractions, 382–383
  fractions as, 383–384
  given number, calculating, 385
  illustrating in fun way, 387
  increases, computing, 386
  number, calculating, 384
  one number of another, calculating,
    385–386
  problems, solving, 384–386
Perfect numbers
  defined, 197
  odd, 222
Perimeters
  of circle (circumference), 403, 550–551
  of curve, 549–550
  as length measurement, 550
  measurement of, 542–564
  of rectangle, 403
  of region, 549
Periodic decimals. *See* Repeating decimals
Periodic patterns, 628
Permutations, 791–801
  activity, 798
  computing, 795
  computing probability using, 807–808
  defined, 791
  formulas for, 793–795
  notation, 792
  problem solving with, 795–797
  *r*-permutation, 791
Perpendicular bisectors
  constructing, 678–680
  defined, 441, 678
  equidistance property, 679
  intersection of, 451
  paper folds and, 450
Perpendicular chords, in pair of circles,
  439–440

Perpendicular lines
  applications, 677–678
  condition for, 436
  constructing, 676–678
  defined, 436, 459
  example, 437–438
  paper folding and, 450
  proof, 436–437
Pi ($\pi$), 550, 552
Pick, Georg, 563
Pick's formula, 563–564
Pictographs
  defined, 713, 721
  illustrated, 722
  interpretation, 721
Pie charts
  defined, 713
  illustrated, 721
  in perspective, 721
  using, 720–721
Pigeonhole principle, 42–44
  defined, 42–43
  using, 43–44
Place value
  in Babylonian system, 129
  defined, 129, 143
  Indo-Arabic system, 133
  in Mayan system, 131
  NCTM Principles and Standards, 144
Place-value cards
  adding with, 148
  base five and, 151, 152
  defined, 146
  multiplying with, 160
  subtracting with, 149, 150
Place-value diagrams
  adding with, 148
  base five and, 151, 152
  defined, 146
  subtracting with, 149, 150
Planar networks. *See also* Networks
  connecting Euler's formula for, 509–510
  defined, 507
  Euler's formula for, 508
Planes
  angles, 458–464
  area of region in, 542
  convex curves/figures, 472
  curves, 470–472
  determining in hexagonal prism,
    493–494
  figure illustrations, 454
  figure symmetry, 624
  figures, 455–470, 472
  intersecting, 490
  line segments, 457–458
  lines, 455–457
  parallel, 490
  parallel to, 490
  perpendicular to, 490
  points, 455–457
  polygonal curves, 472–478
  polygons, 472–478
  quadrilaterals, 478–479
  rays, 458–460
  regions, 470–472
  regular polygons, 479–481

regular tilings of, 637–639
rigid motions of, 601
semiregular tilings of, 639–640
in space, 490
transformation of, 601
Platonic solids, 494
Point symmetry, 627
Points
    collinear, 455, 456
    defined, 455
    distance between, 457–458
    equation of a line through, 425–426
    Fermat, 691
    fixed, 616
    locus, 704
    Napoleon, 691
    noncollinear, 456
    plotting, 418–419
    of reflection, 677
Point-slope form, equation of a line, 424
Pólya, George, 9
Pólya's problem-solving principles, 8–18
    carry out the plan, 10
    devise a plan, 9
    diagram strategy and, 14–16
    guess and check strategy and, 10–13
    look back, 10
    orderly list strategy and, 13–14
    understand the problem, 8–9
Polygonal curves
    classifications of, 473
    defined, 472
    sides/edges, 472
    vertices, 472
Polygonal regions, 473
Polygons. *See also specific polygons*
    angle of, 473
    area of, 545–548
    convex, 473
    defined, 473
    equiangular, 479
    equilateral, 479
    exterior angles of, 473
    folding paper, 658
    frequency, 717
    hinged, 681
    inscribed, 682
    interior angles of, 473
    irregular, 640–642
    lattice, 483, 548
    names of, 474
    paper discs and, 481–482
    regular, 479–481, 682–683
    relative-frequency, 753
    space, 681
Polyhedra, 492–498
    connecting Euler's formulas for, 509–510
    defined, 492
    edges, 492
    Euler's formula for, 495, 496–497
    faces of, 492, 497–498
    prism, 493
    pyramid, 493
    regular, 494–495
    space, 681
    types of, 492
    vertices, 492

Populations
    approximating characteristics with samples, 759–760
    defined, 713, 749
    distribution, 754
    mean, 751–752
    percentile of, 756, 757
    standard deviation, 751–752
Positional notation. *See* Place value
Positional systems
    Babylonian, 129–130
    base-10 blocks, 135
    base-five notation, 138–140
    classroom abacus, 133–134
    Indo-Arabic, 132–133
    Mayan, 130–132
    nondecimal, 138–143
    physical models for, 133–135
    sticks in bundles, 134–135
    Unifix cubes, 135
    units, strips, and mats, 135
Positional values, in decimal system, 342
Positive integers
    defined, 228, 229
    multiplication by, 257
    representing, 231
Possibility elimination strategy, 41–42
Possibility trees, 783
Power, 111
Power operation, 110
Powers of 10
    dividing decimals by, 343–344
    Egyptian symbols for, 127
    multiplying decimals by, 343–344
Preimages, 601
Premises, 53
Primality, 193–194
Prime divisors, 193
Prime factorizations
    determining, 195
    greatest common divisor from, 210–211
    least common multiples from, 213–214
Prime numbers
    defined, 189
    Fermat, 683
    Germain, 197, 220–222
    largest known, 195
    as natural numbers building blocks, 189
    number of, 193
    questions about, 193
    via rectangular arrays, 186
Prime-power representations, 191
Principal, 387
*Principles and Standards for School Mathematics. See* NCTM Principles and Standards
Prisms, 493
    dissection of, 575
    illustrated, 493
    oblique, 493, 574
    right, 493, 573–574
    triangular, 579
Probability, 767–825
    of complementary events, 808–809
    computing using permutations and combinations, 807–808
    conditional, 804–806

    defined, 768
    event *E,* 772
    expected value, 813–814
    experimental, 768, 769–779
    geometric, 814–815
    methods to determine, 768
    mutually exclusive events, 772
    NCTM Principles and Standards, 769
    odds, 812–813
    outcome, 772
    permutations/combinations and, 791–801
    principles of counting and, 780–790
    properties of, 809–812
    sample space, 772
    terminology of, 772
    theoretical, 768, 801–820
    trees, 806–807
Problem solving
    algebra as strategy, 29–39
    carry out the plan principle, 10
    Cartesian coordinates for geometric problems strategy, 433
    with combinations, 795–797
    decompose complex problem strategy, 573, 580
    deductive reasoning strategy, 55
    defined, 58
    devise a plan principle, 9–10
    diagram strategy, 14–16
    division algorithm in, 109–110
    easier, similar strategy, 23
    eliminate possibilities strategy, 41–42
    guess and check strategy, 4, 5–6, 10–13
    incorrect responses and, 44
    inductive reasoning strategy, 49
    introduction to, 3–8
    look back principle, 10
    in mathematics, 58
    with measurement, 583–584
    NCTM Principles and Standards, 3, 9
    orderly list strategy, 13–14
    with Pascal's triangle, 22–26
    pattern strategy, 18–20
    percents, 384–386
    with permutations, 795–797
    pigeonhole principle, 42–44
    Pólya's principles, 8–18
    rate problems, 34
    reasoning in, 47–58
    rigid motions strategy, 436
    as school mathematics cornerstone, 3
    sets for, 73–75
    with similar triangles, 695–697
    special cases strategy, 22
    table strategy, 20–22
    two variables strategy, 34–36
    understand the problem principle, 8–9
    variables and, 22
    with Venn diagrams, 84
    with whole numbers, 84
    working backwards strategy, 39–40
Problems
    classification, 84
    experimenting with, 23
    rate, 34
    understand principle, 8–9

Products
Cartesian, 103
defined, 305
divisibility by, 205
fraction and integer, 304
of fractions, calculating, 305–306
Proofs
conjecture and, 49
of contradiction, 54
converse of isosceles triangle theorem, 669
Euler's formula for planar networks, 508
formula for conditional probability, 805
integer addition, 242
irrational number, 352–353
isosceles triangle theorem, 667
NCTM Principles and Standards, 48
parallelism, 434
properties of probability, 810
Pythagorean theorem, 564–565
sum of angle measures, 474–475
Thales' theorem, 668
Proper divisors, 188
Proper fractions, 295
Proper subsets, 72
Properties. *See also specific properties*
of addition, 91–92
of addition of integers, 242
of addition of rational numbers, 319
of division of rational numbers, 321–322
of empty sets, 74
generalized variables for describing, 402
of inequalities, 245–246
of multiplication, 91–92
of multiplication of integers, 259
of multiplication of rational numbers,
320–321
of number systems, 393–394
of order relation of rational numbers, 320
of probabilities, 809–812
of subtraction of rational numbers, 320
of triangles, 450
Venn diagrams and, 75
Proportional reasoning, 367–381
applications of, 372–376
constant of proportionality, 373
defined, 367
with diagrams, 374
proportions, 370–372
ratio, 367–370
Proportions, 367, 370–372
conditions for, 371
defined, 370, 371
determining, 371
inverse, 373
property of, proving, 371–372
*y* to *x*, 373
Protractors, 459, 460
Pyramid algorithm, 163
Pyramidal sums, 50
Pyramids
defined, 493
double, 500
illustrated, 493
right regular, 582–583
slant height, 583
surface area of, 582–583
volume of, 574–576

Pythagorean theorem, 564–572
applications of, 565–567
converse of, 567
defined, 351, 564
proving, 564–565
Pythagorean triples, 220

**Q**

Quadrants, 417–418
Quadratics, 426–427
Quadrilaterals, 478–479, 489
classification of, 479
defined, 474
exploring, 478
illustrated, 474
midpoint figure of, 696
Quartiles, 713
determining, 737–738, 739
lower, 731, 737
as measure of variability, 731
upper, 731, 737
Quipus, 69
Quotients
computing with manipulatives, 107
defined, 107
in division algorithm, 162
with remainder, 109
special, 170

**R**

Radius, 438, 439
Ramanujan, Srinivasa, 206
Random numbers, 751
Random samples, 749, 750
Random sequence of digits, 750
Range, 748
defined, 737
of functions, 407–408
interquartile, 731, 738, 739
Rates
problems, 34
understanding, 380
unit, 368
Ratio tables, 374
Rational numbers. *See also* Fractions
addition properties, 318–319
additive inverses, 319
basic concepts, 275–292
characterizing as decimals, 350
comparing, 285
computational strategies for arithmetic, 324
computations with, 323
defined, 283
density property of, 322–323
division properties, 321–322
finding, between two rational numbers, 323
fractions, 284–285
invert-and-multiply rule and, 310–311
mental arithmetic, 324–325
multiplication properties, 320–321
negatives, 319
opposite, 319
order relation on, 285, 322
reciprocals as multiplicative inverses in,
310–312

repeating decimals and, 346–350
representing, 283
representing by terminating decimals, 345
sets of, 283
subtraction properties, 320
system of, 318–325
Ratios. *See also* Proportional reasoning
applications of, 368
defined, 367, 368
determining, 368–369
examples, 369–370
fraction notation, 367
in simplest form, 369
Rays
defined, 458
endpoint, 458
union of, 458
vertex, 458
*r*-combinations, 791
Real numbers
defined, 351
number line and, 353–354
set of, 351
Reasoning, 47–58
algebraic, 399–448
deductive, 53–55
direct, rule of, 53–54
indirect, rule of, 54
inductive, 47–49
NCTM Principles and Standards, 47, 48
proportional, 367–381
representational, 49–51
Reciprocals. *See also* Fractions
defined, 311
as multiplicative inverses, 310–312
using, 311–312
Rectangles
area of, 403, 545–546
defined, 479
illustrated, 479
numbers from, 126
perimeter of, 403
Rectangular area model
for fraction division, 316
illustrated, 102
for multiplication, 101–102
Rectangular arrays, primes and composites
via, 186
Reflection symmetry, 600
Reflections. *See also* Rigid motions
consecutive, across parallel lines, 608–609
defined, 604
finding images under, 605–606
illustrated, 608
lines of, 604
mirror, 604
points of, 677
three successive, 610
two, in distinct lines, 609
two successive, 607
Reflex angles, 459
Regions
area in the plane, 542
congruence in the plane, 543
counting, 472, 507–508
defined, 472
defined by simple closed curve, 472

perimeter of, 549
polygonal, 473
Regular polygons, 479–481
central angle, 480
constructing, 682–683
defined, 479
folding, 690
hexagon, 480
*n*-gon, 480–481
Regular polyhedra, 494–495
Regular tilings. *See also* Tilings
defined, 637
illustrated, 639
theorem, 639
Relationships, expressing with variables, 403
Relative frequency, 753
Relative-frequency polygons, 753
Remainders. *See also* Division
defined, 108
in division algorithm, 162
division with, 108–109
integer division with, 262
quotient with, 108, 109
Repeated-subtraction model, 106
Repeating decimals, 346–350
defined, 347
length of the period, 347
as rational numbers, 347–348
Repetition, combinations with, 800
Representational reasoning, 49–51
Representations
colored-counter, 231, 233, 246
data, 713–731
of decimals, 340–343
defined, 49
dot, 50–51
even numbers, 188
integer, 229–239
misleading, 722
NCTM Principles and Standards, 49, 50
number line, 235
odd numbers, 188
positive integer, 231
prime number, 191
rational number, 283
whole number, 82, 83, 90–91
Residual strategy, in ordering fractions, 284
Rhind papyrus, 69
Rhombus, 479
Right angles, 458, 459
Right circular cones, 498, 584
Right cylinders, 498, 573–574
Right prisms, 493
surface area of, 580–582
volume of, 573–574
Right regular pyramids, 582–583
Right triangles, 477, 567
Rigid motions
classification of, 610–613
with coordinates, 621
defined, 601
equivalent, 607
glide-reflection, 606–607
orientation reversing, 606
orientation-preserving, 606
of plane, 601
problem-solving strategy, 436

reflection, 604–606
rotation, 603–604
summary, 608
translation, 602–603
Roman numerals, 128
Roman system of numeration, 128–129
Rotation symmetry
angles of, 626
defined, 600, 626
Rotations, 623. *See also* Rigid motions
angle of, 603
center of, 600, 603
defined, 603
finding images under, 604
illustrated, 608
Rounding
approximating by, 175–176
decimals, 357–358
defined, 175
with 5-up rule, 175
fractions, 323–324
*r*-permutations, 791
Rules
of direct reasoning, 53–54
for exponents, 111, 112
5-up, 175, 357
of indirect reasoning, 54
invert-and-multiply, 310–311
of signs, 258, 261

**S**

Sample space, 772
Samples, 713
for approximating characteristics of
populations, 759–760
defined, 749
percentile of, 757
random, 749–750
Say it in a different way strategy, 372
Scaffold algorithm, 162, 163
Scale factor, 692
Scalene triangles, 477
Scratch method, 143
Search
shape, 501
symmetry, 634
Seconds, 469
Semiregular tilings, 639–640
Sequences
defined, 409
Fibonacci, 19
functions as, 409
looking for patterns in, 18–20
random, 750
Set models
of addition, 89–90
of fractions, 277
Set-builder notation, 70
Sets
Cartesian product of, 103
colored counters, 232, 240–241, 246–248
complements of, 71
concurrent, of lines, 437
defined, 68
definition methods, 70
denoting, 70

describing, 70
disjoint, 72
education for elementary school children, 74
elements (members), 69, 70
empty, 72
equal, 72
equivalent, 80–81
finite, 81
infinite, 81
integer, ordering, 244–246
intersection of, 72
listing in braces, 70
membership, 70
one-to-one correspondence, 80
operations on, 68, 71–73
for problem solving, 73–75
rational number, 283
set-builder notation, 70
subsets, 71–72
union of, 72–73
Venn diagrams, 71
well defined, 69
word description, 70
Shapes
making, 501
pattern-block, 484
search, 501
three-dimensional, 685
Sharing model, of division of fractions, 309
Shepherd, Anna O., 626
Short division. *See also* Division
algorithm, 164
stacked, 190
SI system, 532
Side-angle-side (SAS) property
congruent triangles, 665–668
defined, 665, 666
exploring, 665–666
included angle, 666
isosceles triangle theorem, 667
similar triangles, 695
Thales' theorem, 667
using, 666–667
Sides of angles, 458, 464
Side-side-side (SSS) property
angle congruent to given angle, 663
congruent triangles, 661–663
defined, 662
exploring, 661–662
similar triangles, 694
using, 662–663
Sieve of Eratosthenes, 194
Significant digits, 364
Similar triangles, 692–697
angle-angle (AA) property, 693
angle-angle-angle (AAA) property, 693
defined, 692
geometric problem solving with, 695–697
illustrated, 692
scale factor and, 692
side-angle-side (SAS) property, 695
side-side-side (SSS) property, 694
Similarity, 704
of figures, 614, 692, 703
indirect measurement with, 693
matching game, 699
measurement criteria to determine, 659

Similarity (*continued*)
    principle, 586–587
    transformation, 614, 621
    verifying, 615
Simple closed curves, 470–471
    defined, 470
    determining interior points of, 471
    exterior, 471
    illustrated, 470
    interior, 471
    regions defined by, 471–472
Simple closed surfaces, 492
Simple curves, 470
Simple-product form of fundamental theorem of
        arithmetic, 191
Simplest form
    fractions in, 280–281
    rational number as fraction, 352
    ratios in, 369
Simplifying fractions, 281
Simulation
    defined, 775
    determining experimental probability with,
        775–776
Size transformations. *See also* Dilations
    with coordinates, 621
    defined, 613
    illustrated, 614
Skew lines, 490
Skip counting, 101
Skip-count model, 102
Slant height, pyramid, 583
Slide arrows, 602
Slides, 602
Slope
    defined, 420
    finding, 422
    line, 375
    line segment, 421
    roof, 420
Slope-intercept form, equation of a line, 424–425
Small squares, as decimal representation,
        340–341
Social justice, 443
Solids
    defined, 492
    platonic, 494
Space
    constructions in, 681
    curves in, 490–491
    figures in, 490–504
    lines in, 490
    planes in, 490
    sample, 772
    surfaces in, 492
Special cases
    arguing from, 26
    problem-solving strategy, 22
Spheres
    defined, 492
    surface area of, 584–586
    volume of, 576
Squares, 479
Stacked short division, 190
Standard deviation, 713, 741–743
    alternative calculation of, 741
    computing, 741

    defined, 741
    as deviation measure, 742
    dot plots showing, 742
    estimating, 751–752
    as measure of variability, 731
    of nonuniform distribution, 744
    population, 751–752
Statements
    conditional, 52–53
    defined, 51
    mathematical, 51–53
    and operation in, 51
    or operation in, 51
Statistical inference, 749–760
Statistics, 711–765
    biased selection criteria, 749
    calculator routines, 742
    defined, 712
    descriptive, 749
    distributions, 753–754
    experimental probability connection with,
        770–771
    NCTM Principles and Standards, 713
    percentiles, 756–757
    populations, 749–751
    samples, 749–751
    statistical inference, 749–760
    terminology, 712–713
    *z* score, 755–756
Stem-and-leaf plots
    defined, 713, 714
    illustrated, 714, 715
Sticks in bundles, 134–135
Straight angles, 458, 459
Straightedges, 455
Straight-line depreciation, 431
Strings and Loops activity
    Hands On, 768
    theoretical possibility, 810–812
Strips
    as decimal representation, 340–341
    defined, 135
    exchanges with, 144–145
Subsets. *See also* Sets
    defined, 71
    proper, 72
    Venn diagram, 72
Subtraction
    in base five, 152–153
    with colored counters, 247
    comparison model, 94
    of decimals, 358–359
    defined, 92
    with exchanging, 149–150
    without exchanging, 149
    fraction, 296–297
    front-end, 174
    integer, 246–256
    minuend, 93
    missing addend model, 94
    models, identifying, 95
    number line model, 94–95
    of rational number, 320
    subtrahend, 93
    take-away model, 93, 94
    of whole numbers, 92–96
Subtraction algorithm, 143, 148–150

Subtrahend, 93
Summands, 89
Sums
    in convex polygons, 473
    defined, 89
    divisibility of, 201–202
    in general polygons, 475–476
    pyramidal, 50
Supplementary angles, 460, 461
Surface area, 580–591
    base, 581
    of cylinders, 580–581, 582
    defined, 572
    lateral, 498, 581
    problem-solving strategy, 580
    of pyramids, 582–583
    of right circular cones, 584
    of right prisms, 580–582
    of spheres, 584–586
    volume versus, 572
Surfaces
    lateral, 498, 581
    simple closed, 492
    in space, 492
Symmetries, 704
    bilateral, 625
    center of, 626
    circular, 626
    of culture, 631
    defined, 624
    lines of, 625
    NCTM Principles and Standards, 625
    pattern-block, 633
    of plane figure, 624
    point, 627
    reflection, 600, 625
    rotation, 600, 626
    search for, 634
    translation, 628

T

Table problem-solving strategy, 20–22
    applying, 20–22
    defined, 20
Tables
    functions as, 410
    ratio, 374
Take-away model, 93
    example, 94
    in subtraction of fractions, 296
Tangent line to circle
    defined, 439
    equation, 439
    illustrated, 438
Tangram puzzle, 649
Tangrams
    defined, 527
    measurements with, 527–529
Tax rate schedules, 416
Taxicab geometry, 441
Temperature, 541
    Celsius scale, 537
    conversion, 431
    Fahrenheit scale, 536
    measure, 536–537
Terminal side, angles, 464

Terminating decimals
    defined, 344
    as fractions, 344–346
    as ratio of two integers, 345
    rational numbers represented by, 345
Tessellations, 637
Tests
    for divisibility, 201–209
    for primality, 193
    vertical-line, 407
Tetrahedra
    defined, 495
    envelope model, 495–496
    illustrated, 495
Thales' theorem, 667
Theano, 408
Theorems
    addition principle for mutually exclusive
        events, 782
    addition principle of counting, 781
    alternate-interior angles, 462
    angle measure in regular *n*-gon, 480
    calculating compound interest, 387
    characterizing rational numbers as
        decimals, 350
    circumscribed circle of, 680
    classification of general rigid motions, 611
    closure property for subtraction of integers, 249
    condition for parallelism, 434
    conditions for proportions, 371
    converse of isosceles triangle theorem, 669
    converse of Pythagorean theorem, 567
    defined, 49
    density property of rational numbers, 323
    distance change under a dilation, 614
    distance formula, 420
    divisibility by products, 205
    divisibility of sums and differences, 202
    division algorithm, 162
    division algorithm in integers, 262–263
    equidistance property of perpendicular
        bisector, 679
    Euclidean algorithm, 212
    Euler's formula for connected planar
        networks, 508
    Euler's formula for polyhedra, 497
    Euler's traversability, 507
    formula for conditional probability, 805
    formulas for division of fractions, 310
    formulas for *P(n, r)* and *C(n, r)*, 794
    formulas for subtraction of rational
        numbers, 320
    fundamental, of arithmetic, 191
    Gauss-Wantzel constructibility, 683
    GCD and division algorithm, 211
    greatest common divisor from prime
        factorizations, 211
    "if...then" form, 52
    irrationality of $\sqrt{2}$, 351–352
    isosceles triangle, 667
    Jordan curve, 471
    law of large numbers, 769
    law of trichotomy, 245
    least common multiple from prime-power
        factorizations, 214
    $mn = \text{GCD}(m, n) * \text{LCM}(m, n)$, 214
    multiplication properties of integers, 259

net outcome of three reflections, 610
opposite of the opposite of an integer, 233
ordering decimals, 350
point-slope form of equation of a line, 424
prime divisors of *n*, 193
properties of addition of rational numbers, 319
properties of integer addition, 242
properties of multiplication of rational
    numbers, 321
properties of order relation on rational
    numbers, 322
properties of probability, 809
Pythagorean, 351, 564–572
rational numbers and periodic decimals, 349
rational numbers represented by terminating
    decimals, 345
real numbers and number line, 354
regular tilings of the plane, 639
rule of signs for division of integers, 261
rule of signs for multiplication of integers, 258
similarity principle of measurement, 586
68-95-99.7 rule for, 754
slope-intercept form of equation of line, 424
subtracting by adding the opposite, 249
sum of interior angle measure of general
    polygon, 475–476
sums of angle measures in convex polygon, 473
test for divisibility for 11, 204
tests for divisibility by 2, 5, and 10, 202
tests for divisibility by 4 and 8, 203
tests for divisibility of 3 and 9, 204
Thales,' 667
tiling the plane with congruent polygonal
    tiles, 642
total-turn, 476–477
triangle inequality, 664
two-point form of equation of a line, 426
vertical-angles, 461
Theoretical probability, 801–820. *See also*
    Probability
    of complementary events, 808–809
    computing using permutations and
        combinations, 807–808
    conditional, 804–806
    counting and, 780
    defined, 801
    determining, 768
    equally likely outcomes, 801, 802
    of events, 802
    expected value, 813–814
    geometric, 814–815
    odds, 812–813
    probability trees, 806–807
    properties of, 809–812
    of strings and loops activity, 810–812
Tiles
    defined, 637
    for whole number representation, 82
Tilings, 637–650
    defined, 637
    dual of, 647
    Escher-like, 642–645
    with irregular polygons, 640–642
    Kepler and, 640
    regular, 637–639
    semiregular, 639–640
Toothpick inequality, 665

Total degree of network, 510
Total-turn theorem, 476–477
Transformational geometry, 601
Transformations
    dilation, 613–614
    equivalent, 602, 607
    glide-reflection, 606–608
    identity, 602, 607
    orientation-preserving, 606
    orientation-reversing, 606
    of plane, 601
    reflection, 604–606, 608–610
    rotation, 603–604, 608
    similarity, 614–615
    translation, 602–603, 608
Transitive property
    in ordering fractions, 284
    for rational numbers, 322
Transitivity of inclusion, 74
Translations. *See also* Rigid motions
    defined, 602
    finding images under, 603
    illustrated, 608
    modifying parallelograms with, 643
    vector, 602
Trapezoids
    area of, 547–548
    defined/illustrated, 479
    isosceles, 479
Traversable networks, 506
Traversal, 456
Trees
    factor, 189–190
    possibility, 783
    probability, 806–807
Triangle inequality, 663–665
    applying, 664–665
    theorem, 664
Triangles, 477–478
    acute, 477
    altitude of, 437–438, 678, 689
    angle sum of, 451
    area of, 69, 451, 547
    centroid of, 441, 690
    circumscribed circle of, 680
    classification of, 477–478
    congruent, 659–676
    equilateral, 477
    folding special points in, 690
    golden, 698
    hypotenuse, 451
    illustrated, 474
    inscribed circle of, 682
    isosceles, 477
    medial, 695–696
    medians of, 451, 469, 687
    obtuse, 477
    orthocenter of, 689
    paper folding and, 450–451
    properties of, 450
    right, 477, 567
    scalene, 477
    similar, 692–697
    six parts of, 660
    toothpick, 665
Triangles and Squares (Hands On), 338
Triangular numbers formula, 403

Triangular prisms, 493, 579
Trichotomy property for order relations, 322
Turn angle, 603
Turn arrows, 603
Turn center, 603
Turn symmetry, 626
Turns, 603
Twin-prime conjecture, 220
Two variables
    in problem solving, 34–36
    using, 35–36
Two-point form, equation of a line, 425–426
Two-stage experiments, 783

**U**

Unifix cubes, 135
Uniform distribution, 744
Unions
    associative property of, 74
    commutative property of, 74
    distributive property of, 74
    of rays, 458
    of sets, 72–73
Unit analysis, 537
Unit rates, 368, 380
Unit squares, as decimal representation, 340–341
U.S. customary system. *See* Customary system
Units
    of area, 530, 534, 542
    of capacity, 531, 535
    changing, 534
    customary system, 529–531
    defined, 135, 189
    examples of, 275
    exchanges with, 144–145
    of length, 529, 532–533
    measurement, 526
    metric system, 532–537
    nonstandard, 542–543
    parts of, 275
    subdivision of, 275, 276
    of temperature, 536–537
    of volume, 530–531, 535
    of weight and mass, 535–536
Universe of objects, 69
Upper quartiles, 731, 737

**V**

Values
    defined, 407
    expected, 813–814
    image, 407
    positional, 342
van Hiele levels, 452
Variability, 712
    defined, 731
    measures of, 731, 737–739
    understanding, 713

Variables. *See also* Algebra
    defined, 30, 402
    in describing generalized properties, 402
    in expressing formulas, 403
    in expressing relationships, 403
    Gauss' strategy, 30
    for general formula determination, 30–32
    generalized, 402
    identifying role of, 403–404
    as problem-solving strategy, 22, 29–39
    two, 34–36
    as unknowns in equations, 403
    use of, 29–34, 402
Vectors
    glide, 606
    translation, 602
Venn diagrams
    defined, 71
    disjoint sets, 72
    illustrated, 71
    intersection of sets, 72
    problem solving with, 84
    properties and, 75
    subsets, 72
    union of sets, 72–73
Vertex figures, 637
Vertical angles theorem, 461
Vertical-line test, 407
Vertices
    common, 493
    counting, 507–508
    degree, 506
    even, 506
    odd, 506
    polygonal curves, 472
    polyhedra, 492
    ray, 458
Visualizations. *See also* Representations
    choosing, 722
    statistical, 713–731
Voderberg, Heinz, 642
Volume, 572–580
    capacity, 531
    of cones, 574–575
    of cylinders, 574, 579
    defined, 530, 572
    of Egyptian pyramid, 575–576
    of oblique prisms, 574
    of pyramids, 574–576
    of right cylinders, 573–574
    of right prisms, 573–574
    of spheres, 576
    surface area versus, 572
    of triangular prisms, 579
    units of, 530–531

**W**

Wallpaper patterns. *See also* Patterns
    defined, 628

    examples of, 630
Weight
    defined, 535
    estimating in metric system, 536
    metric units, 535–536
Whole numbers, 81
    addition of, 89–92
    algorithms for, 143–169
    cubes and, 82
    defined, 68, 81
    determining, 81
    division of, 105–112
    even, 188
    finding percents of, 392
    multiplication of, 100–105
    number lines and, 83
    number strips/rods and, 82
    number theory, 185–225
    odd, 188
    ordering, 83–84
    power operation for, 110
    problem solving with, 84
    representations for, 82–83
    subtraction of, 92–96
    tiles and, 82
Word description, in defining sets, 70
Work backwards problem-solving strategy, 39–40
Working from left to right. *See also* Mental
        arithmetic
    defined, 172
    positional notation and, 173
    using, 173

**X**

*x*-coordinate, 417

**Y**

*y*-coordinate, 417

**Z**

*z* scores
    areas to left, for standardized normal
        distribution, 764–765
    calculating, 756
    defined, 755, 756
Zero
    addition-by property, 233
    denominator, 276
    as exponent, 112
    integer division and, 261
    integer representation, 231
    multiplication by, 321
    numerator, 276
Zero angles, 458, 459